15th Edition

2006 North American
Coins & Prices

A GUIDE TO U.S., CANADIAN AND MEXICAN COINS

Last Ag 10⊄ 1964 .9000
25⊄
50⊄ 1964
1965-70 .4000
1⊄

Edited by David C. Harper, editor of Numismatic News,
World Coin News and Bank Note Reporter

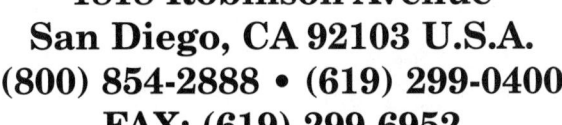

Contents

Preface

Providing coin collectors with accurate, independently produced pricing information on collectible coins has become a trademark of F+W Publications' numismatic division in its 50 years of publishing. Visit our Web site at www.collect.com for more information about us. We employ a full-time staff of market analysts who monitor auction results, trading on the Internet and trading at major shows.

This information is compiled by our analysts and they determine what price most accurately reflects the trading that has occurred for each date and mintmark in each grade listed in *North American Coins & Prices*. By studying this information and referring back to it repeatedly, a collector can arm himself with the necessary knowledge to go out in the market and make wise purchasing decisions. It must be remembered that these prices are intended solely as a guide. They are neither offers to buy or sell. Because prices do fluctuate, those that appear in this book may be in some cases obsolete by the time of publication. By checking the more than 40 price charts in the U.S. section, you can get a feel as to how price swings have occurred since 1972.

U.S. coins are the most popularly collected issues in the world. This is attributable in part to the popularity of coin collecting in the United States, but collectors in many other countries also covet collectible U.S. coins. After collecting U.S. coins for a while, many collectors in the United States branch out into issues of Canada and Mexico. These coins also enjoy a popular following in their countries of origin.

Thus, *North American Coins & Prices* brings together pricing information on all three of these countries. But this book also takes the price-guide concept a step further by providing information on the nuts and bolts of collecting coins: acquiring coins, grading them, organizing them into a collection, storing them properly and much more. Novice collectors can gain the necessary knowledge to collect coins enjoyably; veterans can pick up some pointers to add to their knowledge.

1

'A small beginning'
The U.S. Mint grew from a modest start

By Robert R. Van Ryzin

It was a "small beginning" but a significant one. In July 1792, a site for the new U.S. Mint not yet having been secured, 1,500 silver half dismes were struck on a small screw press nestled in the cellar of a Philadelphia building owned by sawmaker John Harper. Though some have since categorized these early emissions of the fledgling U.S. Mint as patterns, it is clear that first President George Washington – who is said to have deposited the silver from which the coins were struck – considered this small batch of half dismes the first official U.S. coins.

It is true that this limited coinage, the first since passage of the act establishing the Mint on April 2, 1792, pales by comparison to modern U.S. Mint presses. Today's machines can churn out up to 750 coins a minute, striking as many as four coins at a time and boasting yearly mintages in the billions. But it is also true that these first small pieces – struck from silver and stamped with a plump Liberty on the obverse and a scrawny eagle in flight on the reverse – have tremendous historical importance.

For within what Washington would declare in his 1792 address to Congress as a "small beginning" were the seeds of a monetary system that has lasted more than 200 years and has become the study and admiration of many.

Before the U.S. Mint

Collectors today can trace much of the nation's development and learn of its struggles and growth through its coinage: from a cumbersome system first proposed by Robert Morris, a Revolutionary War financier and first superintendent of finance, to the refinements tendered by Thomas Jefferson and Alexander Hamilton, which firmly placed the nation on an easily understood decimal system of coinage.

At first there was little coinage in circulation, except for foreign coins that arrived through trade or in the purses of the first settlers. Despite a dire need for coinage in the Colonies, Great Britain considered it a royal right and granted franchises sparingly. Much of the Colonial economy, therefore, revolved around barter, with food staples, crops, and goods serving as currency. Indian waupum or bead money also was used, first in the fur trade and later as a form of money for Colonial use.

Copper pieces were produced around 1616 for the Sommer Islands (now Bermuda), but coinage within the American Colonies apparently didn't begin until 1652, when John Hull struck silver threepence, sixpence and shillings under authority of the General Court of Massachusetts. This coinage continued, with design changes (willow, oak and pine trees), through 1682. Most of the coins were dated 1652, apparently to avoid problems with England.

In 1658 Cecil Calvert, second Lord Baltimore, commissioned coins to be struck in England for use in Maryland. Other authorized and unauthorized coinages – including those of Mark Newby, John Holt, William Wood, and Dr. Samuel Higley – all became part of the landscape of circulating coins. In the 1780s this hodgepodge of coinage was augmented by influxes of counterfeit British halfpenny coins and various state coinages.

In terms of the latter, the Articles of Confederation had granted individual states the right to produce copper coins. Many states found this to be appealing, and merchants in the mid-1780s traded copper coins of Vermont, Connecticut, Massachusetts, New Jersey, and New York. Not all were legal issues; various entrepreneurs used this as an invitation to strike imitation state coppers and British halfpence. Mutilated and worn foreign coins also circulated in abundance. Included among these were coins of Portugal, Great Britain and France, with the large majority of the silver arriving from Spain.

The accounting system used by the states was derived from the British system of pounds, shillings and pence. Each state was allowed to set its own rates at which foreign gold and silver coins would trade in relation to the British pound.

In 1782 Robert Morris, newly named superintendent of finance, was appointed to head a committee to determine the values and weights of the gold and silver coins in circulation. Asked simply to draw up a table of values, Morris took the opportunity to propose the establishment of a federal mint. In his Jan. 15, 1782, report (largely prepared by his assistant, Gouverneur Morris), Morris noted that the exchange rates between the states were complicated.

He observed that a farmer in New Hampshire would be hard-pressed if asked to determine the value of a bushel of wheat in South Carolina. Morris recorded that an amount of wheat worth four shillings in his home state of New Hampshire would be worth 21 shillings and eightpence under the accounting system used in South Carolina.

Morris claimed these difficulties plagued not only farmers, but that "they are perplexing to most Men and troublesome to all." Morris further pressed for the adoption of an American coin to solve the problems of the need for small change and debased foreign coinages in circulation.

In essence, what he was advocating was a monometallic system based on silver. He said that gold and silver had fluctuated throughout history. Because these fluctuations resulted in the more valuable metal leaving the country, any nation that adopted a bimetallic coinage was doomed to have its gold or silver coins disappear from circulation.

Robert Morris devised a complicated plan for a national coinage based on a common denominator of 1,440.

Gouverneur Morris calculated the rate at which the Spanish dollar traded to the British pound in the various states. Leaving out South Carolina, because it threw off his calculations, Gouverneur Morris arrived at a common denominator of 1,440. Robert Morris, therefore, recommended a unit of value of 1/1,440, equivalent to a quarter grain of silver. He suggested the striking of a silver 100-unit coin, or cent; a silver 500-unit coin, or quint; a silver 1,000-unit coin, or mark; and two copper coins, one of eight units and the other of five units.

On Feb. 21, 1782, the Grand Committee of Congress approved the proposal and directed Morris to press forward and report with a plan to establish a mint. Morris had already done so. Apparently feeling confident that Congress would like his coinage ideas, Morris (as shown by his diary) began efforts at the physical establishment prior to his January 1782 report. He had already engaged Benjamin Dudley to acquire necessary equipment for the mint and hoped to have sample coins available to submit with his original report to Congress.

Things went awry, however.

By Dec. 12, 1782, 10 months after Congress had approved his plan, Morris still could not show any samples of his coins. He was forced, ironically, to suggest that Congress draw up a table of rates for foreign coins to be used until his report was ready. It was not until April 2, 1783, that Morris was able to note in his diary that the first of his pattern coins were being struck.

"I sent for Mr. Dudley who delivered me a piece of Silver Coin," he wrote, "being the first that has been struck as an American Coin."

He also recorded that he had urged Dudley to go ahead with production of the silver patterns.

It wasn't until April 23, 1783, that Morris was able to send his Nova Constellatio patterns to Congress and suggest that he was ready to report on establishing a mint. Apparently nothing came of Morris' efforts. Several committees looked into the matter, but nothing was accomplished. Dudley was eventually discharged as Morris' hopes dimmed.

Thomas Jefferson was the next to offer a major plan. Jefferson liked the idea of a decimal system of coinage, but disliked Morris' basic unit of value. As chairman of the Currency Committee, Jefferson reviewed Morris' plan and formulated his own ideas.

To test public reaction, Jefferson gave his "Notes on Coinage" to *The Providence Gazette*, and *Country Journal,* which published his plan in its July 24, 1784, issue. Jefferson disagreed with Morris' suggestion for a 1/1,440 unit of value and instead proposed a decimal coinage based on the dollar, with the lowest unit of account being the mil, or 1/1,000.

"The most easy ratio of multiplication and division is that by ten," Jefferson wrote. "Every one knows the facility of Decimal Arithmetic."

Jefferson argued that although Morris' unit would have eliminated the unwanted fraction that occurred when merchants converted British farthings to dollars, this was of little significance. After all, the original idea of establishing a mint was to get rid of foreign currencies.

Morris' unit, Jefferson said, was too cumbersome for use in normal business transactions. According to Jefferson, under Morris' plan a horse valued at 80 Spanish dollars would require a notation of six figures and would be shown as 115,200 units.

Jefferson' coinage plan suggested the striking of a dollar, or unit; half dollar, or five-tenths; a double tenth, or fifth of a dollar, equivalent to a pistereen; a tenth, equivalent to a Spanish bit; and a one-fifth copper coin, relating to the British farthing. He also wanted a gold coin of $10, corresponding to the British double guinea; and a copper one-hundredth coin, relating to the British halfpence.

In reference to his coinage denominations, Jefferson said, it was important that the coins "coincide in value with some of the known coins so nearly, that the people may by quick reference in the mind, estimate their value."

More than a year, however, passed without any further action on his plan or that proposed by Morris. In a letter to William Grayson, a member of the Continental Congress, Washington expressed concern for the establishment of a national coinage system, terming it "indispensably necessary." Washington also complained of the coinage in circulation: "A man must travel with a pair of scales in his pocket, or run the risk of receiving gold at one-fourth less than it counts."

A plan at last

On May 13, 1785, the 13-member Grand Committee, to whom Jefferson's plan had been submitted, filed its report, generally favoring Jefferson's coinage system. The committee did, however, make slight alterations, including the elimination of the gold $10 coin, the addition of a gold $5 coin, and the dropping of Jefferson's double

Thomas Jefferson proposed that the United States adopt a decimal system of coinage.

tenth, which it replaced with a quarter dollar. The committee also added a coin equal to 1/200th of a dollar (half cent). On July 6, 1785, Congress unanimously approved the Grand Committee's plan. It failed, however, to set a standard weight for the silver dollar or to order plans drawn up for a mint. These two factors led to new proposals.

On April 8, 1786, the Board of Treasury, which had been reinstated after Morris' resignation as superintendent of finance two years prior, tendered three distinct coinage proposals based on varying weights and bimetallic ratios for the silver dollar. The first of these three plans (the one passed by Congress on Aug. 8, 1786) required the silver dollar to contain 375.64 grains of pure silver. The board's proposal varied from earlier coinage plans in that it advocated a higher bimetallic ratio of 15.256-to-1 and differing charges to depositors for coining of gold and silver. It called for minting of gold $5 and $10 coins, and silver denominations of the dime, double dime, half dollar, and dollar. In copper were a cent and half cent. The proposal came during the peak of state coinages and influxes of debased coppers, which, as the board reported, were being "Imported into or manufactured in the Several States."

Concerned over the need to control state coinages and foreign coppers, the board suggested that, within nine months of passage of its proposal, the legal-tender status of all foreign coppers be repealed and that values be set at which the state coppers would circulate. The board obviously expected immediate action and ordered a supply of copper that was being stored in Boston to be brought to New York in the hope that it might soon be coined. Their hopes, however, rested on the positive and quick action of Congress, something that hadn't occurred with the other proposals and would not occur this time.

Opposition to the mint was beginning to surface. Several members of Congress expressed their belief that the supply of foreign gold and silver coins in circulation was sufficient to preclude any need for a mint. They also argued that the problem with debased coppers could be solved by contracting with private individuals to strike the nation's cents and half cents.

Several proposals were offered for a contract coinage. On April 21, 1787, the board accepted a proposal by James Jarvis to strike 300 tons of copper coin at the federal standard. Jarvis, however, delivered slightly less than 9,000 pounds of his contract. The contract was voided the following year for his failure to meet scheduled delivery times, but helped to delay further action on a mint. Concerted action on a coinage system and a mint would wait until the formation of the new government.

Alexander Hamilton, named in September 1789 to head the new Treasury, offered three different methods by which the new nation could achieve economic stability, including the funding of the national debt, establishment of the Bank of North America, and the founding of the U.S. Mint. On Jan. 21, 1791, Hamilton submitted to Congress a "Report on the Establishment of a Mint." It was compiled through his study of European economic theories and the earlier works of Morris and Jefferson, along with the 1786 report of the Board of Treasury.

Hamilton agreed with Jefferson that the dollar seemed to be best suited to serve as the basic unit, but believed it necessary to establish a proper weight and fineness for the new coin. To do so, Hamilton had several Spanish coins assayed to determine the fine weight of the Spanish dollar. He also watched the rate at which Spanish dollars traded for fine gold (24 3/4 grains per dollar) on the world market.

From his assays and observations he determined that the Spanish dollar contained 371 grains of silver. He then multiplied 24 3/4 by 15 (the gold value of silver times his suggested bimetallic ratio) and arrived at 371 1/4 as the proper fine silver weight for the new silver dollar.

In regard to his findings, Hamilton admitted that Morris had made similar assays and had arrived at a weight of 373 grains for the Spanish dollar. Hamilton attributed the discrepancy to the differing equipment used in making the assays. He failed, however, to observe that silver coins were traded in the world market at actual weight rather than the weight at time of issue. The Spanish dollar contained 376 grains of pure silver when new, 4 3/4 grains more than Hamilton's proposed silver dollar.

Hamilton also wanted a bimetallic ratio of 15-to-1, in contrast to the Board of Treasury's 15.6-to-1 ratio. Hamilton said his ratio was closer to Great Britain's, which would be important for trade, and Holland's, which would be important for repaying loans from that country.

His report suggested the striking of a gold $10; gold dollar; silver dollar; silver tenth, or disme; and copper one-hundredth and half-hundredth. Hamilton felt the last of these, the half cent, was necessary because it would enable merchants to lower their prices, which would help the poor.

Congress passed the act establishing the U.S. Mint in April 1792. It reinstated several coin denominations left out by Hamilton and dropped his gold dollar. In gold, the act authorized at $10 coin, or "eagle"; a $5 coin, or "half eagle"; and a $2.50 coin, or "quarter eagle." In silver were to be a dollar, half dollar, quarter dollar, disme, and half disme, and in copper a cent and half cent.

Though it established a sound system of U.S. coinage, the act failed to address the problem of foreign coins in circulation. It was amended in February 1793 to cancel their legal-tender status within three years of the Mint's opening.

Coinage begins

Coinage totals at the first mint were understandably low. Skilled coiners, assayers and others who could handle the mint's daily operations were in short supply in the United States. Also in want were adequate equipment and supplies of metal for coinage. Much of the former had to be built or imported. Much of the latter was also imported or salvaged from various domestic sources, including previously struck tokens and coins, and scrap metal.

Coinage began in earnest in 1793 with the striking of half cents and cents at the new mint located at Seventh Street between Market and Arch streets in Philadelphia. Silver coinage followed in 1794, with half dimes, half dollars and dollars. Gold coinage did not begin until 1795 with the minting of the first $5 and $10 coins. Silver dimes and quarters and gold $2.50 coins did not appear until 1796.

Under the bimetallic system of coinage by which gold and silver served as equal representations of the unit of value, much of the success and failure of the nation's coinage to enter and remain in circulation revolved around the supply and valuation of precious metals. One need only to gain a cursory knowledge of such movements to understand what role precious metals played in development of U.S. coinage. That role, to a large extent, determined why some coins today are rare and why some passed down from generation to generation are still plentiful and of lower value to collectors.

From the Mint's beginning, slight miscalculations in the proper weight for the silver dollar and a proper bimetallic ratio led gold and silver to disappear from circulation. The U.S. silver dollar traded at par with Spanish and Mexican dollars, but because the U.S. coin was lighter, it was doomed to export.

A depositor at the first mint could make a profit at the mint's expense by sending the coins to the West Indies. There they could be traded at par for the heavier Spanish or Mexican eight reales, which were then shipped back to the United States for recoinage. As a result, few early silver dollars entered domestic circulation; most failed to escape the melting pots.

Gold fared no better. Calculations of the bimetallic ratio by which silver traded for gold on the world market were also askew at first and were always subject to fluctuations. Gold coins either disappeared quickly after minting or never entered circulation, languishing in bank vaults. These problems led President Jefferson to halt coinage of the gold $10 and silver dollar.

Production at the first U.S. mint, in Philadelphia, was minuscule by today's standards.

The gold $10 reappeared in 1838 at a new, lower-weight standard. The silver dollar, not coined for circulation since 1803, returned in 1836 with a limited mintage. Full-scale coinage waited until 1840.

Nor was the coinage of copper an easy matter for the first mint. Severe shortages of the metal led the Mint to explore various avenues of obtaining sufficient supplies for striking cents and half cents.

Witness, for example, the half-cent issues of 1795 and 1797 struck over privately issued tokens of the New York firm of Talbot, Allum & Lee because of a shortage of copper for the federal issue. Rising copper prices and continued shortages forced the Mint to lower the cent's weight from 208 grains to 168 grains in 1795.

By that same year Congress had begun to investigate the Mint. Complaints about high costs and low production had been raised. Suggestions that a contract coinage might be more suitable for the new nation surfaced again, despite bad experiences with previous attempts.

The Mint survived this and another investigation, but the problems of fluctuating metal supplies continued to plague the nation. In 1798, because of the coinage shortage, the legal-tender status of foreign coins was restored. Several more extensions were given during the 1800s, ending with the withdrawal of legal-tender status for Spanish coins in 1857.

In the 1830s great influxes of silver from foreign mints raised the value of gold in relation to silver, which made it necessary for the Mint to lower the standard weight of all gold coins in 1834. It also led to the melting of great numbers of gold coins of the old specifications.

By the 1850s discovery of gold in California had again made silver the dearer metal. All silver quickly disappeared from circulation. Congress reacted in 1853 by lowering the weight of the silver half dime, dime, quarter, and half dollar, hoping to keep silver in circulation. A new gold coin of $20 value was introduced to absorb a great amount of the gold from Western mines.

Not long after, silver was discovered in Nevada. By the mid-1870s the various mines that made up what was known as the Comstock Lode (after its colorful early proprietor, Henry P. Comstock) had hit the mother lode. Large supplies of silver from the Comstock, combined with European demonetization, caused a severe drop in its value, which continued through the close of the 19th century.

It was believed that the introduction of a heavier, 420-grain silver dollar in 1873, known as the Trade dollar, would create a market for much of the Comstock silver, bolster its price, and at the same time wrest control from Great Britain of lucrative trade with the Orient. It didn't. Large numbers of Trade dollars eventually flooded back into the United States, where they were, ironically, accepted only at a discount to the lesser-weight Morgan dollars.

The latter had been introduced in 1878 as a panacea to the severe economic problems following the Civil War. Those who proudly carried the banner of free silver contended that by taking the rich output of the Comstock mines and turning it into silver dollars, a cheaper, more plentiful form of money would become available. In its wake, they believed, would be a much needed economic recovery.

The Free Silver Movement gained its greatest support during the late 19th century when William Jennings Bryan attempted to gain the White House on a plank largely based on restoration of the free and unlimited coinage of the standard 412.5-grain silver dollar. He failed. Silver failed. Shortly thereafter the United States officially adopted a gold standard.

Silver continued to be a primary coinage metal until 1964, when rising prices led the Mint to remove it from the dime and quarter. Mintage of the silver dollar had ended in 1935. The half dollar continued to be coined through 1970 with a 40-percent-silver composition. It, too, was then debased.

Gold coinage ended in 1933 and exists today only in commemorative issues and American Eagle bullion coins with fictive face values. A clad composition of copper and nickel is now the primary coinage metal. Even the cent is no longer all copper; a copper-coated zinc composition has been used since 1982.

Precious-metal supplies were also linked to the opening of additional mints, which served the parent facility in Philadelphia. The impact of gold discoveries in the 1820s in the southern Appalachian Mountains was directly tied to the construction of branch mints in Dahlonega, Ga., and Charlotte, N.C., in 1838. These new mints struck only gold coins. New Orleans also became the site of a branch mint in the same year as Dahlonega and Charlotte. It took in some of the outflow of gold from Southern mines, but also struck silver coins.

Discovery of gold in California in the late 1840s created a gold rush, and from it sprang a great western migration. Private issues of gold coinage, often of debased quality, were prevalent, and the cost of shipping the metal eastward for coinage at Philadelphia was high. A call for an official branch mint was soon heard and heeded in 1852 with the authorization of the San Francisco Mint, which began taking deposits in 1854.

The discovery of silver in the Comstock Lode led to yet another mint. Located only a short distance via Virginia & Truckee Railroad from the fabulous Comstock Lode, the Carson City mint began receiving bullion in early 1870. It struck only silver coins during its tenure.

Denver, also located in a mineral-rich region, became the site of an assay office in 1863 when the government purchased the Clark, Gruber & Co. private mint. It became a U.S. branch mint in 1906. In addition to the Denver and Philadelphia mints, San Francisco and a facility in West Point, N.Y., continue to serve as U.S. mints, but the others have left behind a rich legacy.

The collector taking a more extended journey into the history of U.S. coinage can find plenty of interesting tales – some as tall as the day is long and others factually based – all of which are part of the rich and ever-changing panoply of U.S. coinage history. There are stories of denominations that failed, great discoveries, great rarities, great collectors, and, for those with an artistic bent, a rich field of pattern coins to be explored and a wealth of much-heralded designs by famous sculptors such as Augustus Saint-Gaudens, Adolph Weinman, James Earle Fraser, and others.

For those who are drawn to the hobby by the allure of age-old relics of days gone by, or by coins handed down through the family, or even by dreams of great wealth, coin collecting has much to offer. The history of the U.S. Mint, with its small but ever so important beginning, is the starting point.

2

Making money
How coins are manufactured

By Alan Herbert

Just as printing is the process by which paper money is made, so is minting the method of manufacturing coins. The two are often confused by the public, but they are completely different.

The history of minting goes back several centuries before the birth of Christ. The Lydians are credited with making the first crude coins in the Middle East about 700 B.C., although the Chinese and Koreans trace their coinage back even further.

Some early coins were cast. That process continued in China into the 1900s, but only for low-value pieces. Here again the average person often assumes that all coins are cast, but as you will see, only a tiny fraction of a percent are – or were – actually made that way.

The methods developed by the Greeks and Romans centered on making dies that could be hammered by hand into the surface of a lump of metal, flattening it and impressing a design. Hammered coinage continued until after the end of the Middle Ages, about 1500. After that the first machines that could strike coins were invented. Today their successors can pound out 750 or more coins a minute.

From the early days when the fixed die was driven into a stump or a hole drilled in a rock, through fixing it in an anvil (the fixed die is still called the anvil die), to today's modern coin presses, the process is much the same. Force is applied to devices that impress or apply a design to a piece of material, which is transformed into a coin.

Early dies were made of wood. Then came copper, bronze, and finally iron as technology advanced. Today dies are made from exotic steels with special qualities that make them ideal for striking coins.

The history of coinage is fascinating. Interwoven into it are several familiar names: Leonardo da Vinci is credited with inventing one of the first coin presses. James Watt, English inventor of the steam engine, was the first to incorporate steam power to drive the coin presses that earlier had depended on horses or human arms.

Whether the power comes from a hand holding a hammer or a mechanical ram, and whether it comes from above, below, or the side, the process is called "striking" a coin. Modern coin presses use a variety of methods in applying brute force to a piece of metal to turn it into a coin.

Another fable that traces to casting coins is the common belief that coins are made from liquid metal or at the least are red hot when they are struck. Neither is true. A coin's design is formed by the pressure that causes the metal to cold-flow into the pattern that you see on the coins in your pocket.

There are three basic parts of the minting process: (1) the making of the planchet, which is divided into the selection and processing of the metal and the preparation of the planchets, (2) the making of the dies, and (3) the use of the dies to strike the planchets. To help you remember these three parts, think of "P," "D" and "S" for planchet, die and striking.

Choosing a metal

Many different metals have and are being used for coins. The most popular coinage metals are those commonly found and relatively cheap, so they can be used for striking low-value coins. Precious metals – like silver, gold and platinum – are still used for commemorative coins.

A good coinage metal requires certain properties. The metal must be soft enough to be easily worked yet hard enough to withstand the wear and tear of a thousand pockets, a hundred thousand transactions. Few metals have all the right properties, so coin metals usually are an alloy, or mixture of two or more metals.

Copper is a favorite coin metal, either by itself or in an alloy. Zinc, nickel, iron, and aluminum are also found in coins struck by the United States and other countries. Silver and gold have to be alloyed with some metal, usually copper, to be hard enough to withstand commercial life. The so-called "pure" coins of silver or gold are known as "bullion coins," bought and sold primarily for their precious-metal content.

The metals chosen for a coin are melted and mixed together, and either poured into ingots or blocks, or extruded from furnaces that continuously cast a long strip of the metal. The ingots are passed several times between the big rolls in a rolling mill to reduce the ingot to the thickness of the blanks needed.

Once the strip is rolled to the correct thickness, it is sent to a blanking press. A gang of blunt-end punches are driven through the sheet, producing a dozen or more blanks with each stroke. The rough blanks are then ready to be processed.

Making the 'blanks'

The piece of metal (occasionally some other material, so it isn't always metal) that becomes a coin is known as a "blank." This is a usually round, flat piece that usually has been punched or cut from a sheet or strip of coin metal.

Strips of coin metal stand ready to be cut into "blanks."

A binful of blanks are ready for the coin press.

Before a blank can become a coin it has to be processed, cleaned, softened, and given what is known as an "upset edge" – a raised ridge or rim around both sides. The blank then becomes a "planchet" and is ready to be struck into a coin by the dies.

First they go through what looks like a monstrous cement mixer. A huge cylinder revolves slowly as the planchets are fed in at one end and spiral their way through. This is an annealing oven, which heats the planchets to soften them. When they come out the end, they fall into a bath where they are cleaned with a diluted acid or soap solution.

As the final step, they go through the upsetting mill, the machine that puts the raised rim on the blank and turns it into a planchet, ready to be struck. In a different department the process of making the dies used to strike the coins has already begun.

Preparing the dies

For those who haven't studied metallurgy, the concept of hard metal flowing about is pretty hard to swallow, but this is actually what happens. It is basically the same process as the one used in an auto plant to turn a flat sheet of steel into a fender with multiple curves and sharp bends. The cold metal is moved about by the pressure applied.

To make the metal move into the desired design, there has to be a die. Actually there has to be two dies, because one of the laws of physics is that for every action there has to be an equal and opposite reaction. You cannot hold a piece of metal in midair and strike one side of it. Instead you make two dies, fix one, and drive the other one against it – with a piece of metal in between to accept the design from each die.

A die is a piece of hard metal, like steel, with a design on its face that helps to form a mirror image on the struck coin. Early dies were made by hand. Engravers used hand tools to laboriously cut each letter, each digit, and each owl or eagle or whatever design was being used into the face of the die. Notice that this is "into" the surface of the die. Each part of the die design is a hole or cavity of varying shape and depth.

This is because we want a mirror image on the coin, but we want it raised, or in "relief." To make a relief image on a coin, the image on the die has to be into the face of the die, or "incuse." Of course, if we want an incuse image on the coin, such as the gold $2.50 and $5 coins of 1908-1929, the design on the die face would have to be in relief.

To fully understand this, take a coin from your pocket and a piece of aluminum foil. Press the foil down over the coin design and rub it with an eraser. When you take the foil off and look at the side that was in contact with the coin, you have a perfect copy of a die. Everywhere there is a relief design on the coin there is an incuse design on your foil "die."

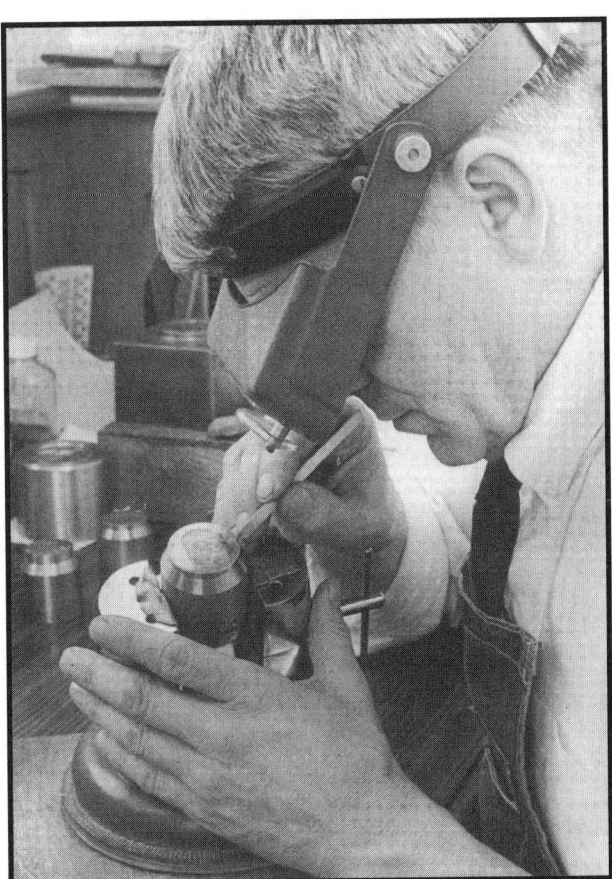

An engraver at the
U.S. Mint puts the
finishing touches on
a die.

A galvano goes on the
reducing lathe.

From sketchbook to coin

The design process begins with an artist's sketch. This is translated into a three-dimensional relief design that is hand-carved from plaster or, in recent years, from a form of plastic.

The plaster or plastic design is then transformed into a "galvano," which is an exact copy of the design that has been plated with a thin layer of copper. This is used as a template or pattern in a reducing lathe, which cuts the design into a die blank.

This die becomes the master die, from which all of the following steps descend. The process can be reversed so that the designs will be cut in relief, forming a tool called a "hub," which is simply a piece of steel with the design in relief, exactly the same as the relief design on the intended coin.

To make working dies, pieces of special steel are prepared, with one end shaped with a slight cone. The die blank is softened by heating it. Then the hub is forced into the face of the die, forming the incuse, mirror-image design in the face of the die.

The process usually has to be repeated because the die metal will harden from the pressure. The die is removed, softened, and returned to the hubbing press for a second impression from the hub. As you can imagine, it takes several hundred tons per square inch to force the hub into the die. Logically, this process is called "hubbing" a die.

The advantage of hubbing a die is that thousands of working dies can be made from a single hub, each one for all practical purposes as identical as the proverbial peas in a pod. This enables, for example, U.S. mints to strike billions of one-cent coins each year, each with the identical design.

Die making has come a long way from the early days when it took a skilled engraver a full day to carve a single letter into a die. The use of punches with the digits, letters or even parts of the design on the end reduced the amount of time required for the process. Today, thanks to the use of hubs, a complete die can be finished in a matter of hours.

Striking the coin

Yesterday's die might strike only a few hundred coins. Today it is not unusual for a die to strike well over a million coins.

The coin press used to strike modern coins is a complicated piece of equipment that consists basically of a feed system to place the planchets in position for the stroke of the hammer die to form a coin. This process takes only a fraction of a second, so the press has to operate precisely to spew out the hundreds of coins that are struck every minute.

The end of the early hammered coinage came with the introduction of the collar, which often is called the "third" die. The collar is nothing more than a steel plate with a hole in it. This hole is the exact diameter of the intended coin and often is lined with carbide to prolong its life. It surrounds the lower, or fixed, die. Its sole

Rows of modern coin presses at the Philadelphia Mint turn out billions of coins a year.

A hopper is full of shiny new one-cent coins ready for shipment.

purpose is to contain the coin metal to keep it from spreading sideways under the force of the strike.

If the intended coin has serrations, or "reeds," on the edge, then the collar has the matching design. The strike forces the coin metal against the serrations in the collar, forming the reeded edge at the same time that the two dies form the front and back, or obverse and reverse, of the coin.

Lettered-edge coins are produced usually by running the planchets through an edge-lettering die, or by using a segmented collar that is forced against the edge of the planchet during the strike by hydraulic pressure.

Several hundred tons were required to drive a hub into a die. Not as much but still significant amounts of force are needed to strike coins. A cent, for example, requires about 30 tons per square inch. One of the silver dollars took 150 tons. The other denominations fall in between.

Modern coin presses apply pressure in a variety of ways. A ram, carrying the moving or "hammer" die, is forced against the planchet. Most commonly this is with the mechanical advantage of a "knuckle" or connected pieces to which pressure is applied from the side. When the joint straightens – like straightening your finger – the ram at the end of the piece is driven into the planchet.

Once the strike is complete, at the final impact of the die pair, the coin has been produced. It is officially a coin now, and it's complete and ready to be spent.

The making of proof coins

While the high-speed coining presses are turning out billions of coins for commerce, there are other presses working at much slower speeds to produce collector coins, such as "proof" coins.

Proof coins started out as special presentation pieces. They were and still are struck on specially prepared planchets with specially prepared dies. Today the definition of a proof coin also requires that it be struck two or more times.

To make a proof coin, the planchets go through much the same process, but with some special care and some extra steps. Currently all proof versions of circulating U.S. coins are struck at the San Francisco Mint, but some of the proof commemorative coins have been struck at the other mints, including West Point.

After the proof blanks are punched from the strip, they go through the annealing oven, but on a conveyor belt rather than being tumbled in the revolving drum. After cleaning and upsetting they go into a huge vibrating machine where they are mixed with steel pellets that look like tiny footballs. The movement of the steel pellets against the planchets burnishes, or smooths, the surface so any scratches and gouges the planchets pick up during processing are smoothed over.

Proof dies get an extra polishing before the hubbing process. Like all other dies, they are made at Philadelphia and shipped to the branch mints.

When the proof dies arrive at San Francisco, they are worked on by a team of specialists who use diamond dust and other polishing agents to turn the fields of the proof dies into mirrorlike surfaces. The incuse design is sandblasted to make the surface rough, producing what is known as a "frosted" design.

Because collectors like the frosted proofs, the design is periodically swabbed with acid to keep the surface rough and increase the number of frosted proofs from each die. This is a relatively recent improvement, so frosted examples of earlier proofs are considerably scarcer.

The presses that strike proof coins usually are hand-operated rather than automatic. Some of the newer presses use equipment such as vacuum suction devices to pick up the planchets, place them in the coining chamber, and then remove the struck coins. This avoids handling the pieces any more than necessary.

On a hand-operated press, the operator takes a freshly washed and dried planchet and, using tongs, places it in the collar. The ram with the die descends two or more times before the finished coin is removed from the collar and carefully stored in a box for transport to storage or the packaging line. After each strike the operator wipes the dies to make sure that lint or other particles don't stick to the dies and damage the coins as they are struck.

Proof dies are used for only a short time before being discarded. Maximum die life is usually less than 10,000 coins, varying with the size of the coin and the alloy being struck.

Keeping up with demand

The minting process has come a long way from the first metal pellets that are barely recognizable as coins. Companies that manufacture equipment used in the world's mints are constantly researching to develop new methods of producing coins.

The purpose is to strike coins at as low a cost as possible and still retain the desired beauty in the design. Modern machines and new methods help the mints keep up with demand for coins.

The important point to remember is that the coins in your pocket are made no differently from the coins in the pocket of an English schoolchild or a Spanish police officer or an Italian opera singer. Mints around the world use the same methods, same equipment, and same common coin metals, with few if any variations from the basic methods. The minting process was shrouded in secrecy for centuries, but now has become common knowledge.

For the collector, knowing exactly how coins are minted can be some of the most valuable knowledge that can be learned. It often will make the difference between accepting a coin as a valuable addition to a collection or spotting it as a fake, counterfeit, or altered coin.

Because of the improvements in the making of coins, collecting the rare misstrikes and defective coins that escape quality control has become an important segment of the numismatic hobby. For a detailed description of over 400 categories of minting varieties, see the "U.S. Minting Varieties and Errors" section in this book.

3

The thrill of the hunt

How to acquire coins for your collection

By Al Doyle

Among the many pleasures coin collecting offers is the satisfaction of acquiring that long-sought piece that fills an important hole in a set or completes a collection. Many collectors say half the fun of pursuing the hobby is the thrill of the hunt — trying to find that needed coin in the condition desired and for a good price. Following are the main sources from which collectors acquire coins.

Circulation finds

Once the most popular method of building a collection, hunting through pocket change has declined substantially since 1965, when silver dimes and quarters were replaced by clad (base-metal) coinage.

Most collectors from 1935 into the 1960s got started in numismatics by searching through circulating coinage. It was worth the effort, as scarce and interesting coins such as the 1909-S VDB and 1914-D Lincoln cents, Liberty and Buffalo nickels, 1916-D and 1921 Mercury dimes, and Barber and Standing Liberty quarters were often found. Hobbyists who searched bank rolls and bags obtained at face value had no downside risk, and entire date collections of Lincoln cents were obtained in this manner.

Other denominations were also pursued in the treasure hunt. One Midwestern dealer found dozens of 1939-D Jefferson nickels (worth $1 to $30 each at the time, depending on condition) by searching through change obtained from parking meters of a nearby city. Another well-known numismatist put together a complete date and mintmark set of Walking Liberty half dollars in one afternoon by searching through coins obtained at his bank. Needless to say, those days are gone forever.

What is available to pocket-change searchers today? Even the pre-1959 cents, with the Wheat-Ears reverse, are rare sights, but some interesting coins remain undiscovered.

It's still possible to find collectible coins by searching large quantities of change, such as rolls.

Jefferson nickels can provide plenty of collecting enjoyment for virtually no financial commitment. A recent sampling of five rolls (200 coins, or $10) turned up 58 different date and mintmark combinations. Some of the highlights were a 1938-S (mintage 4.1 million) in grade fine, a 1947 in very fine, and a 1953-S. Looking through Jeffersons on a regular basis should lead to building the better part of a date and mintmark set.

Washington quarters experienced a circulation finds rebirth of sorts when the 50-state commemorative program began in 1999. Millions of Americans who had never collected coins before joined the hunt to acquire each of the new state designs as they were released at the rate of five per year.

Half dollars in your area may be another relatively untapped area in modern coinage. The 40-percent-silver pieces of 1965 to 1969 can sometimes be found in bank rolls. Half dollars seldom circulate, which means that older coins may be gathering dust in your local bank vault at this very moment.

Collecting Lincoln cents with the Memorial reverse, from 1959 to date, makes an excellent starter set. Many of the dates can be found in circulation.

What else might turn up in pocket change? Modern proofs enter circulation from time to time, and foreign coins are found occasionally. Canadian and U.S. coins frequently cross their respective borders.

Collectors of error coins sometimes find unusual pieces in circulation. What may be scorned as a reject by the average person is a valuable item to the error and variety specialist.

Start examining your pocket change. It's an inexpensive and pleasant way to get involved in the coin hobby.

Coin shops

Most medium-sized or larger cities and suburbs have at least one coin shop within driving distance, and a surprising number of small towns also boast of having a store that caters to local numismatists. Living in or near a metropolitan area is an advantage for the coin-shop enthusiast. For example, more than 15 dealers live in or near

Cincinnati, and southern California and the New York area are home to hundreds of numismatic firms.

In some ways, a coin shop is similar to a small museum. All kinds of items from early coppers to gold coinage and other collectibles such as paper currency, stock certificates, and historic curiosities can be seen. A visit to a well-stocked shop is a visual treat.

It is likely that some of those coins in the display cases will appeal to you, and that means some comparison shopping and determining the value of your favorite coin are desirable. Prices do fluctuate, although collector-oriented coins tend to maintain steadier values than coins sought by investors.

If you are a casual collector, consider a subscription to *Coins* magazine. A monthly publication, *Coins* offers articles on a wide range of topics as well as a Coin Value Guide of retail prices for U.S. coins in most grades.

Serious collectors and others who want more frequent information will find *Numismatic News* to be a timely source of knowledge. Published weekly, the *News* includes coverage of recent market trends and reports from major coin conventions. *World Coin News* is published monthly and covers non-U.S. issues. All three publications also carry display advertisements from dozens of coin dealers.

Prices are determined by supply and demand as well as the grade, or state of preservation. Grading is often described as a subjective art rather than an exact science, and it does take some study and experience to become a competent grader (see Chapter 4).

Numismatic education is a never-ending process. Getting to know an experienced dealer who is enthusiastic about his product will certainly increase your knowledge of coins. Most shops carry a wide assortment of items, but dealers (like anyone else) have their personal favorites. If you find a dealer who is especially knowledgeable about a certain series, it could be to your advantage to do business with him or her if that also happens to be your favorite area too.

Strangely enough, doing business with a dealer who does not share your particular interest could work in your favor. Learning about collectible coins is a massive undertaking, and no one knows everything. Collectors of large cents and Bust half dollars are willing to pay substantial premiums for coins that have minor differences from other specimens struck during the same year, and specialists in those areas frequently "cherrypick" rare varieties that are offered at common-date prices.

Never be embarrassed to ask questions about coins or the dealer's experience in the hobby. As the old saying goes, "There is no such thing as a dumb question." A question asked at the right time could save you plenty of grief and money.

Mail order

This is one area that generates a fair amount of emotion among collectors. Many hobbyists swear by the convenience of shopping at home; others swear at mail-order firms that send overgraded and overpriced coins. Common sense and the same guidelines that apply to shopping for any other item should be used in selecting a mail-order coin dealer.

Look for someone who has a fair amount of experience in coins as well as enthu-

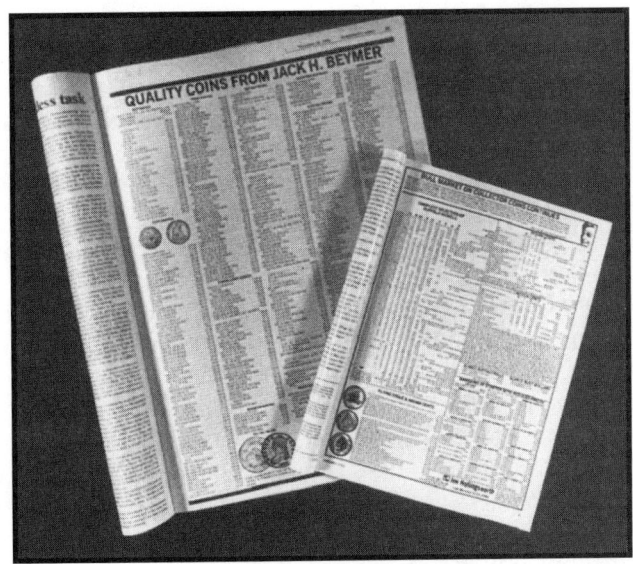

Advertisements in numismatic publications provide the convenience of shopping at home.

siasm for the hobby. Reputable dealers are willing to answer questions about their numismatic backgrounds and business practices. Word of mouth is often said to be one of the most effective forms of advertising, and it pays to ask other collectors about their favorite mail-order companies.

If several people agree that a firm provides accurately graded coins at fair prices, chances are excellent that you will also be a satisfied customer. How do you avoid being cheated? Collectors can be their own worst enemies and are often victimized by their own greed.

Take a coin that has a retail value in the $100 range in a particular grade. If that same coin is advertised at the same grade for $49.95, the savvy collector should immediately become suspicious. When a coin is offered at a price far under the going rate, remember these two sayings: "If it sounds too good to be true, it usually is," and "there is no Santa Claus in numismatics."

A dealer will generally pay $70 to $80 to acquire a popular coin with a retail value of $100. With that in mind, how can someone offer the same coin in the same grade at far less than wholesale cost? Wouldn't it be much easier to sell those coins to other dealers at a higher price and save on advertising expenses?

Obviously, the "underpriced" coins are not the same quality as their properly graded counterparts. It pays to keep up with current prices and grading standards. It is possible to find good deals at less than full retail cost, but don't expect to purchase decent coins for half price.

Does that mean all coins sold at real market prices are properly graded? Don't get complacent; overgraded coins are sometimes sold at full retail. But not everyone who sells an overgraded coin is intentionally fraudulent.

Grading standards are not carved in stone, which means that one person's MS-63 can be someone else's MS-64. Even though most dealers are extremely knowledge-able about coins, they can be fooled at times. The altered coin that a dealer bought as problem-free may be passed on to a collector in good faith, with no intention of deceit.

There is one important means of protection for consumers who buy through the mail: the return policy. Reputable firms allow buyers to return any unsatisfactory item for a full refund. The time allowed for returns varies widely from three working days to a month, but seven to ten days seems to be the most popular policy among mail-order dealers.

Look for "terms of sale" in dealer ads. Always read them before placing your order.

If you don't like coins received through the mail for any reason, send them back within the alloted time for a full refund. Companies might extend the deadline by a day or two if you call and ask for extra time.

What happens if you don't receive a refund or cannot satisfactorily resolve a problem with a mail-order dealer? There are several options:

The first step is to file a written complaint with the advertising department of any publication in which the dealer advertises. Include copies of invoices and other documentation. The publication cannot act on verbal complaints.

Written complaints can also be filed with a local or state chapter of the Better Business Bureau as well as any hobby-related organizations (the American Numismatic Association, Professional Numismatists Guild, and so on) in which the dealer holds membership. If you do business with a reputable dealer, it is unlikely that you will ever have to endure such a drawn-out complaint process, but be ready to take the proper steps if necessary.

For those who live in rural areas or prefer to shop at home, buying coins through the mail can be a rewarding experience and a convenient way to build a collection.

Coin shows

Dozens of shows are held every weekend across the nation. These events range from simple one-day shows with 10 to 20 tables to nationally known events such as the annual American Numismatic Association convention, Florida United Numismatists convention, the three-times-a-year shows held in Long Beach, Calif., and the Central States Numismatic Society convention.

Admission to club-sponsored shows is usually free. Commercially sponsored shows oftentimes charge a small admission fee.

Somewhere between the show at the local VFW hall and Long Beach are state and regional conventions. Often sponsored by a club, these shows will have 40 to 150 dealer tables as compared to the 400 to 600 tables at a major convention. Tables at local and some regional conventions are often manned by part-time, or "vest pocket," dealers. Smaller shows tend to feature less expensive items; the larger shows will have a greater variety of scarce and expensive coins in addition to the more affordable pieces.

Major conventions will have a stunning array of merchandise ranging from coins of ancient Greece to major U.S. rarities. Even if you can't afford the expensive items, it doesn't cost anything to stroll the aisles and see some historic coins.

**Shows big and small
are held across the
nation every weekend.**

The big-ticket items are just part of the action at regional and major shows. A large assortment of affordable coins are available, and prices are often lower than at coin shops.

Dealers buy and sell thousands of coins among themselves at shows, and new purchases can often be had for a small markup. Good buys can sometimes be found later in the show when dealers are preparing to return home. A reasonable offer will often result in a new addition to your collection.

Speaking of offers, negotiating and dickering are as much a part of coin shows as silver dollars, but be reasonable. Tossing out an offer of $50 on a $200 coin is not shrewd; it's insulting.

If you make an offer on a coin and it is accepted, the coin is yours. Backing out of a deal is considered bad form. The coin business tends to be informal, and verbal offers carry serious weight. Your word is your bond on the bourse floor.

Purchases at a coin show do not carry a return policy. Unlike a mail-order transaction, you have ample opportunity to carefully examine the coin firsthand before making a financial commitment.

Why attend a show when you can acquire coins through the mail or from a local shop? There are many reasons to give the show circuit a try:

Conventions are an educational experience. Touring the bourse floor and talking to dealers and other collectors will increase your knowledge of numismatics, but there are other learning opportunities as well.

Many shows offer educational forums featuring speakers and presentations on various topics. These seminars cover everything from little-known specialties to advice on obtaining the best buys in a particular area of numismatics.

Exhibits will also add to your knowledge. Most medium-sized and major shows reserve a section of the bourse for collectors to display some of their holdings and compete for awards based on the educational value of their exhibit. The exhibit section offers an excellent opportunity to view something new and different.

You might be motivated to put together an exhibit yourself after a visit to a show. Keep in mind that it does not require a major collection to create a decent exhibit. Some of the most interesting displays incorporate low-priced coins and other collectibles.

Shows are excellent places to search for key-date coins and other material that may not be in stock at your local shop. Dealers do much of their shopping at shows, which should tell you something about the opportunities at a good-sized convention.

Want to introduce a friend or relative to coin collecting? Take them to a show and let them look around. Chances are excellent that the newcomer will become a fellow collector.

Looking for something different to collect? Paper money, world coins, tokens, medals, and medieval coins are often found at shows. You could find a new area of interest, and shows provide collectors with a chance to meet dealers and well-known hobbyists from across the country.

Have a game plan when you attend a show. Decide beforehand what you want to buy and how much money you plan to spend. Buying whatever looks nice will soon deplete your funds.

Coin shows offer something for everyone, so consider bringing the family. Jewelry (usually for much less than jewelry-store prices), baseball cards, antiques, and arts and crafts are also sometimes found at bourse tables.

One final note on coin-show etiquette: If you don't agree with a dealer's prices or grading, do not tell him that you can buy the same coin for less at another table or call him a crook. Just move on to the next table, and enjoy the rest of the show.

Information on upcoming shows in your area can be found in *Coins* and *Numismatic News*. Shows that feature a significant number of world coins are also listed in *World Coin News*. Coin-show advertising sometimes appears in local newspapers during the week prior to a show or in the paper's free listings of community events.

Auctions

Public auctions play an important role in the coin business. Prices realized at major auctions can indicate where the coin market is headed, as price fluctuations are a fact of life in numismatics. Important collections with major rarities are usually

It's OK to bargain with a dealer at a show or shop, but collectors should be reasonable with their offers.

sold at a public auction. These sales are often held in conjunction with major shows.

However, affordable coins are often sold along with the rarities. A typical sale for a major auction firm will contain 1,000 to 6,000 lots, and most of those coins are not of the headline-grabbing variety. The larger the sale, the greater the likelihood that it will be broken into sessions conducted over a number of days.

The vast number of coins offered at a typical coin auction can work in favor of the collector who has a limited budget. Typical low- to medium-priced coins are often overlooked, as dealers and collectors focus on the trophy items. That may allow you to pick up some coins at reasonable prices. Internet auctions are another venue for lower priced items (See Chapter 13 for Web addresses and information.)

How can you participate in a public auction that is being held thousands of miles from your home? Catalogs are produced by auction companies for each sale, and mail, telephone and Internet bids are encouraged.

A typical auction catalog is illustrated with black and white as well as color photos of hundreds of coins. Descriptions of each lot give you an idea of the appearance of any coins that might be of interest. Many major firms post their catalogs on their Internet Web site.

If you are located near an auction site, it pays to examine your potential purchases

A collector doesn't have to actually attend an auction to participate in it.

at the pre-auction viewing session. The process is simple: Just visit the auction location (usually a major hotel or convention center) prior to the sale. The auction company sets up a room where the lots can be viewed. Long rows of tables with good lighting are provided. All you have to do is tell one of the attendants the lot numbers of the coins you want to view.

You can place written bids before you leave the premises, but it might pay to hang around for the auction and bid on coins in person. The action can be fast and furious at a major auction. Bidding increments of thousands of dollars are the rule when an expensive coin is being sold. It's an unforgettable sight to watch five or six serious competitors run up the price on a truly rare coin.

Keep several things in mind before you get involved in buying through auctions:

■ You are legally responsible to honor all winning bids placed, so plan accordingly. It is unlikely that you will win every coin on which you bid, but placing too many bids could be hazardous to your financial health.

■ Return policies vary among the major firms. Generally, floor bidders (those who personally attend the sale) do not have return privileges, as it is assumed that an adequate opportunity was provided to examine coins during the pre-auction viewing session.

One auction house does not allow any returns by mail bidders on certified coins, which are independently graded and encapsulated in a protective holder by an outside grading service. However, return privileges are the rule for all coins graded by the auction company's staff.

■ Winning bids are generally subject to a 15 percent premium, or buyer's fee. If you successfully bid $300 on a coin, your final cost will be $345 plus postage and handling. Consider the buyer's fee when deciding on bids.

Getting started in buying through auctions requires a catalog of an upcoming sale. Typically priced at $10 to $25, auction catalogs can be excellent buys even if you don't participate in the sale, as they provide a wealth of numismatic information.

Following are six major U.S. auction houses:

■ American Numismatic Rarities, LLC, P.O. Box 1804, Wolfeboro, NH 03894.

■ Bowers and Merena Galleries, 18022 Cowan, Suite 200D. Irvine, CA 92614.

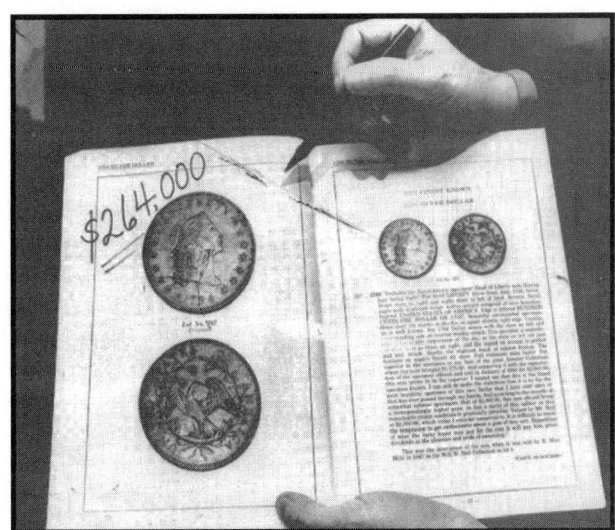

An auction catalog describes each lot offered.

■ Ira and Larry Goldberg Coins and Collectibles, Inc., 350 S. Beverly Drive, Suite 350, Beverly Hills, CA 90212.

■ Heritage Numismatic Auctions, 3500 Maple Ave., 17th Floor, Dallas, TX 75219-3941.

■ Stack's, 123 W. 57th St., New York, NY 10019.

■ Superior Galleries, 9478 W Olympic Blvd., Beverly Hills, CA 90212-4246.

Smaller auctions will allow you to test the bidding process before you compete at a major sale. Local firms concentrate on less expensive coins, and a typical sale for these companies ranges from 250 to 1,000 lots. Catalogs are less elaborate, but they are also inexpensive. Prices range from free to $3, and mail bids are accepted.

Among the dozens of local companies that conduct coin auctions are the following:

■ Michael Aron, P.O. Box 4388, San Clemente, CA 92674.

■ Sonny Henry's Auction Service, 1510 Illinois Ave., Mendota, IL 61342.

Where to write for more information

Coins Magazine: 700 E. State St, Iola, WI 54990.

Numismatic News: 700 E. State St., Iola, WI 54990.

World Coin News: 700 E. State St., Iola, WI 54990.

American Numismatic Association: 818 N. Cascade Ave., Colorado Springs, CO 80903-3279. Web address is http://www.money.org

Visit the Krause Publications Web site
http://www.collect.com

4

The grading factor
How to classify a coin's condition

By Arlyn G. Sieber

Grading is one of the most important factors in buying and selling coins as collectibles. Unfortunately, it's also one of the most controversial. Since the early days of coin collecting in the United States, buying through the mail has been a convenient way for collectors to acquire coins. As a result, there has always been a need in numismatics for a concise way to classify the amount of wear on a coin and its condition in general.

A look back

In September 1888, Dr. George Heath, a physician in Monroe, Mich., published a four-page pamphlet titled *The American Numismatist*. Publication of subsequent issues led to the founding of the American Numismatic Association, and *The Numismatist*, as it's known today, is the association's official journal. Heath's first issues were largely devoted to selling world coins from his collection. There were no formal grades listed with the coins and their prices, but the following statement by Heath indicates that condition was a consideration for early collectors:

"The coins are in above average condition," Heath wrote, "and so confident am I that they will give satisfaction, that I agree to refund the money in any unsatisfactory sales on the return of the coins."

As coin collecting became more popular and *The Numismatist* started accepting paid advertising from others, grading became more formal. The February 1892 issue listed seven "classes" for the condition of coins (from worst to best): mutilated, poor, fair, good, fine, uncirculated, and proof. Through the years, the hobby has struggled with developing a grading system that would be accepted by all and could apply to all coins. The hobby's growth was accompanied by a desire for more grades, or classifications, to more precisely define a coin's condition. The desire for more precision, however, was at odds with the basic concept of grading: to provide a concise method for classifying a coin's condition.

For example, even the conservatively few classifications of 1892 included fudge factors.

"To give flexibility to this classification," *The Numismatist* said, "such modification of fine, good and fair, as 'extremely,' 'very,' 'almost,' etc., are used to express slight variations from the general condition."

The debate over grading continued for decades in *The Numismatist*. A number of articles and letters prodded the ANA to write grading guidelines and endorse them as the association's official standards. Some submitted specific suggestions for terminology and accompanying standards for each grade. But grading remained a process of "instinct" gained through years of collecting or dealing experience.

A formal grading guide in book form finally appeared in 1958, but it was the work of two individuals rather than the ANA, *A Guide to the Grading of United States Coins* by Martin R. Brown and John W. Dunn was a break-through in the great grading debate. Now collectors had a reference that gave them specific guidelines for specific coins and could be studied and restudied at home.

The first editions of Brown and Dunn carried text only, no illustrations. For the fourth edition, in 1964, publication was assumed by Whitman Publishing Co. of Racine, Wis., and line drawings were added to illustrate the text.

The fourth edition listed six principal categories for circulated coins (from worst to best): good, very good, fine, very fine, extremely fine, and about uncirculated. But again, the desire for more precise categories were evidenced. In the book's introduction, Brown and Dunn wrote, "Dealers will sometimes advertise coins that are graded G-VG, VG-F, F-VF, VF-XF. Or the description may be ABT. G. or VG plus, etc. This means that the coin in question more than meets minimum standards for the lower grade but is not quite good enough for the higher grade."

When the fifth edition appeared, in 1969, the "New B & D Grading System" was introduced. The six principal categories for circulated coins were still intact, but variances within those categories were now designated by up to four letters: "A," "B," "C" or "D." For example, an EF-A coin was "almost about uncirculated." An EF-B was "normal extra fine" within the B & D standards. EF-C had a "normal extra fine" obverse, but the reverse was "obviously not as nice as obverse due to poor strike or excessive wear." EF-D had a "normal extra fine" reverse but a problem obverse.

But that wasn't the end. Brown and Dunn further listed 29 problem points that could appear on a coin – from No. 1 for an "edge bump" to No. 29 for "attempted re-engraving outside of the Mint." The number could be followed by the letter "O" or "R" to designate whether the problem appeared on the obverse or reverse and a Roman numeral corresponding to a clock face to designate where the problem appears on the obverse or reverse. For example, a coin described as "VG-B-9-O-X" would grade "VG-B"; the "9" designated a "single rim nick"; the "O" indicated the nick was on the obverse; and the "X" indicated it appeared at the 10 o'clock position, or upper left, of the obverse.

The author's goal was noble – to create the perfect grading system. They again, however, fell victim to the age-old grading-system problem: Precision comes at the expense of brevity. Dealer Kurt Krueger wrote in the January 1976 issue of *The Numismatist*, "Under the new B & D system, the numismatist must contend with a minimum of 43,152 different grading combinations! Accuracy is apparent, but simplicity has been lost." As a result, the "New B & D Grading System" never caught on in the marketplace.

The 1970s saw two important grading guides make their debut. The first was *Photograde* by James F. Ruddy. As the title implies, Ruddy uses photographs instead of line drawings to show how coins look in the various circulated grades. Simplicity is also a virtue of Ruddy's book. Only seven circulated grades are listed (about good, good, very good, fine, very fine, extremely fine, and about uncirculated), and the designations stop there.

In 1977 the longtime call for the ANA to issue grading standards was met with the release of *Official A.N.A. Grading Standards for United States Coins*. Like Brown and Dunn, the first edition of the ANA guide used line drawings to illustrate coins in various states of wear. But instead of using adjectival descriptions, the ANA guide adopted a numerical system for designating grades.

The numerical designations were based on a system used by Dr. William H. Sheldon in his book *Early American Cents*, first published in 1949. He used a scale of 1 to 70 to designate the grades of large cents.

"On this scale," Sheldon wrote, "1 means that the coin is identifiable and not mutilated – no more than that. A 70-coin is one in flawless Mint State, exactly as it left the dies, with perfect mint color and without a blemish or nick."

(Sheldon's scale also had its pragmatic side. At the time, a No. 2 large cent was worth about twice a No. 1 coin; a No. 4 was worth about twice a No. 2, and so on up the scale.)

With the first edition of its grading guide, the ANA adopted the 70-point scale for grading all U.S. coins. It designated 10 categories of circulated grades: AG-3, G-4, VG-8, F-12, VF-20, VF-30, EF-40, EF-45, AU-50, and AU-55. The third edition, released in 1987, replaced the line drawings with photographs, and another circulated grade was added: AU-58. A fourth edition was released in 1991.

Grading circulated U.S. coins

Dealers today generally use either the ANA guide or Photograde when grading circulated coins for their inventories. (Brown and Dunn is now out of print.) Many local coin shops sell both books. Advertisers in *Numismatic News*, *Coins* Magazine, and *Coin Prices* must indicate which standards they are using in grading their coins. If the standards are not listed, they must conform to ANA standards.

Following are some general guidelines, accompanied by photos, for grading circulated U.S. coins. Grading even circulated pieces can be subjective, particularly when attempting to draw the fine line between, for example, AU-55 and AU-58. Two longtime collectors or dealers can disagree in such a case.

But by studying some combination of the following guidelines, the ANA guide, and *Photograde*, and by looking at a lot of coins at shops and shows, collectors can gain enough grading knowledge to buy circulated coins confidently from dealers and other collectors. The more you study, the more knowledge and confidence you will gain. When you decide which series of coins you want to collect, focus on the guidelines for that particular series. Read them, reread them, and then refer back to them again and again.

AU-50

Indian cent   Lincoln cent

Buffalo nickel   Jefferson nickel

Mercury dime

Standing Liberty quarter

Washington quarter

Walking Liberty half dollar

Morgan dollar

Barber coins

AU-50 (about uncirculated): Just a slight trace of wear, result of brief exposure to circulation or light rubbing from mishandling, may be evident on elevated design areas. These imperfections may appear as scratches or dull spots, along with bag marks or edge nicks. At least half of the original mint luster generally is still evident.

XF-40

Indian cent

Lincoln cent

Buffalo nickel

Jefferson nickel

Mercury dime

Standing Liberty quarter

Washington quarter

Walking Liberty half dollar

Morgan dollar

Barber coins

XF-40 (extremely fine): The coin must show only slight evidence of wear on the highest points of the design, particularly in the hair lines of the portrait on the obverse. The same may be said for the eagle's feathers and wreath leaves on the reverse of most U.S. coins. A trace of mint luster may still show in protected areas of the coin's surface.

VF-20

Indian cent

Lincoln cent

Buffalo nickel

Jefferson nickel

Mercury dime

Standing Liberty quarter

Washington quarter

Walking Liberty half dollar

Morgan dollar

Barber coins

VF-20 (very fine): The coin will show light wear at the fine points in the design, though they may remain sharp overall. Although the details may be slightly smoothed, all lettering and major features must remain sharp.

Indian cent: All letters in "Liberty" are complete but worn. Headdress shows considerable flatness, with flat spots on the tips of the feathers.

Lincoln cent: Hair, cheek, jaw, and bow-tie details will be worn but clearly separated, and wheat stalks on the reverse will be full with no weak spots.

Buffalo nickel: High spots on hair braid and cheek will be flat but show some detail, and a full horn will remain on the buffalo.

Jefferson nickel: Well over half of the major hair detail will remain, and the pillars on Monticello will remain well defined, with the triangular roof partially visible.

Mercury dime: Hair braid will show some detail, and three-quarters of the detail will remain in the feathers. The two diagonal bands on the fasces will show completely but will be worn smooth at the middle, with the vertical lines sharp.

Standing Liberty quarter: Rounded contour of Liberty's right leg will be flattened, as will the high point of the shield.

Washington quarter: There will be considerable wear on the hair curls, with feathers on the right and left of the eagle's breast showing clearly.

Walking Liberty half dollar: All lines of the skirt will show but will be worn on the high points. Over half the feathers on the eagle will show.

Morgan dollar: Two-thirds of the hair lines from the forehead to the ear must show. Ear should be well defined. Feathers on the eagle's breast may be worn smooth.

Barber coins: All seven letters of "Liberty" on the headband must stand out sharply. Head wreath will be well outlined from top to bottom.

F-12

Indian cent

Lincoln cent

Buffalo nickel

Jefferson nickel

Mercury dime

Standing Liberty quarter

Washington quarter

Walking Liberty half dollar

Morgan dollar

Barber coins

F-12 (fine): Coins show evidence of moderate to considerable but generally even wear on all high points, though all elements of the design and lettering remain bold. Where the word "Liberty" appears in a headband, it must be fully visible. On 20th century coins, the rim must be fully raised and sharp.

VG-8

Indian cent

Lincoln cent

Buffalo nickel

Jefferson nickel

Mercury dime

Standing Liberty quarter

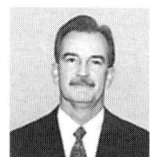

G-4

Indian cent

Lincoln cent

Buffalo nickel

Jefferson nickel

Mercury dime

Standing Liberty quarter

Washington quarter   **Walking Liberty half dollar**

Morgan dollar   **Barber coins**

G-4 (good): Only the basic design remains distinguishable in outline form, will all points of detail worn smooth. The word "Liberty" has disappeared, and the rims are almost merging with the lettering.

About good or fair: The coin will be identifiable by date and mint but otherwise badly worn, with only parts of the lettering showing. Such coins are of value only as fillers in a collection until a better example of the date and mintmark can be obtained. The only exceptions would be rare coins

Grading uncirculated U.S. coins

The subjectivity of grading and the trend toward more classifications becomes more acute when venturing into uncirculated, or mint-state, coins. A minute differ-

Collectors have a variety of grading services to choose from. This set of Arkansas half dollars that appeared in an Early American History Auctions sale used two of the services.

ence between one or two grade points can mean a difference in value of hundreds or even thousands of dollars. In addition, the standards are more difficult to articulate in writing and illustrate through drawings or photographs. Thus, the possibilities for differences of opinion on one or two grade points increase in uncirculated coins.

Back in Dr. George Heath's day and continuing through the 1960s, a coin was either uncirculated or it wasn't. Little distinction was made between uncirculated coins of varying condition, largely because there was little if any difference in value. When *Numismatic News* introduced its value guide in 1962 (the forerunner of today's Coin Market section in the *News*), it listed only one grade of uncirculated for Morgan dollars.

But as collectible coins increased in value and buyers of uncirculated coins became more picky, distinctions within uncirculated grade started to surface. In 1975 *Numismatic News* still listed only one uncirculated grade in Coin Market, but added this note: "Uncirculated and proof specimens in especially choice condition will also command proportionately higher premiums than these listed."

The first edition of the ANA guide listed two grades of uncirculated, MS-60 and MS-65, in addition to the theoretical but non-existent MS-70 (a flawless coin). MS-60 was described as "typical uncirculated" and MS-65 as "choice uncirculated." *Numismatic News* adopted both designations for Coin Market. In 1981, when the second edition of the ANA grading guide was released, MS-67 and MS-63 were added. In 1985 *Numismatic News* started listing six grades of uncirculated for Morgan dollars: MS-60, MS-63, MS-65, MS-65+, and MS-63 prooflike.

Then in 1986, a new entity appeared that changed the nature of grading and trading uncirculated coins ever since. A group of dealers led by David Hall of Newport Beach, Calif., formed the Professional Coin Grading Service. For a fee, collectors could submit a coin through an authorized PCGS dealer and receive back a professional opinion of its grade.

The concept was not new; the ANA had operated an authentication service since 1972 and a grading service since 1979. A collector or dealer could submit a coin directly to the service and receive a certificate giving the service's opinion on authenticity and grade. The grading service was the source of near constant debate among dealers and ANA officials. Dealers charged that ANA graders were too young and inexperienced, and that their grading was inconsistent.

Grading stability was a problem throughout the coin business in the early 1980s, not just with the ANA service. Standards among uncirculated grades would tighten during a bear market and loosen during a bull market. As a result, a coin graded MS-65 in a bull market may have commanded only MS-63 during a bear market.

PCGS created several innovations in the grading business in response to these problems:

1. Coins could be submitted through PCGS-authorized dealers only.

2. Each coin would be graded by at least three members of a panel of "top graders," all prominent dealers in the business. (Since then, however, PCGS does not allow its graders to also deal in coins.)

3. After grading, the coin would be encapsulated in an inert, hard-plastic holder with a serial number and the grade indicated on the holder.

4. PCGS-member dealers pledged to make a market in PCGS-graded coins and honor the grades assigned.

5. In one of the most far-reaching moves, PCGS said it would use all 11 increments of uncirculated on the 70-point numerical scale: MS-60, MS-61, MS-62, MS-63, MS-64, MS-65, MS-66, MS-67, MS-68, MS-69, and MS-70.

The evolution of more uncirculated grades had reached another milestone.

Purists bemoaned the entombment of classic coins in the plastic holders and denounced the 11 uncirculated grades as implausible. Nevertheless, PCGS was an immediate commercial success. The plastic holders were nicknamed "slabs," and dealers couldn't get coins through the system fast enough.

In subsequent years, a number of similar services have appeared. Among them, one of the original PCGS "top graders," John Albanese, left PCGS to found the Numismatic Guaranty Corp. The ANA grading service succumbed to "slab mania" and introduced its own encapsulated product.

There now are numerous other reputable private third-party grading services. PCGS and NGC are the oldest and remain the leaders. In 1990 the ANA sold its grading service to a private company. It operates under the ANACS acronym.

How should a collector approach the buying and grading of uncirculated coins? Collecting uncirculated coins worth thousands of dollars implies a higher level of numismatic expertise by the buyer. Those buyers without that level of expertise should cut their teeth on more inexpensive coins, just as today's experienced collectors did. Inexperienced collectors can start toward that level by studying the guidelines for mint-state coins in the ANA grading guide and looking at lots of coins at shows and shops.

Study the condition and eye appeal of a coin and compare it to other coins of the same series. Then compare prices. Do the more expensive coins look better? If so, why? Start to make your own judgments concerning relationships between condition and value.

According to numismatic legend, a collector walked up to a crusty old dealer at a show one time and asked the dealer to grade a coin the collector had with him. The dealer looked at the coin and said, "I grade it a hundred dollars." Such is the bottom line to coin grading.

Grading U.S. proof coins

Because proof coins are struck by a special process using polished blanks, they receive their own grading designation. A coin does not start out being a proof and then become mint state if it becomes worn. Once a proof coin, always a proof coin.

In the ANA system, proof grades use the same numbers as circulated and uncirculated grades, and the amount of wear on the coin corresponds to those grades. But the number is preceded by the word "proof." For example, Proof-65, Proof-55, Proof-45, and so on. In addition, the ANA says a proof coin with many marks, scratches or other defects should be called an "impaired proof."

Grading world coins

The state of grading non-U.S. issues is similar to U.S. coin grading before Brown and Dunn. There is no detailed, illustrated guide that covers the enormous scope and variety of world coins; collectors and dealers rely on their experience in the field and knowledge of the marketplace.

The *Standard Catalog of World Coins* gives the following guidelines for grading world coins, which apply to the Canadian and Mexican value listings in this book:

In grading world coins, there are two elements to look for: (1) overall wear and (2) loss of design details, such as strands of hair, feathers on eagles, designs on coats of arms, and so on. Grade each coin by the weaker of the two sides. Age, rarity or type of coin should not be considered in grading.

Grade by the amount of overall wear and loss of detail evident in the main design on each side. On coins with a moderately small design element that is prone to early wear, grade by that design alone.

In the marketplace, adjectival grades are still used for Mexican coins. The numerical system for Canadian coins is now commonplace:

Uncirculated, MS-60: No visible signs of wear or handling, even under a 30X microscope. Bag marks may be present.

Almost uncirculated, AU-50: All detail will be visible. There will be wear on only the highest points of the coin. There will often be half or more of the original mint luster present.

Extremely fine, XF-40: About 95 percent of the original detail will be visible. Or, on a coin with a design that has no inner detail to wear down, there will be light wear over nearly the entire coin. If a small design is used as the grading area, about 90 percent of the original detail will be visible. This latter rule stems from the logic that a smaller amount of detail needs to be present because a small area is being used to grade the whole coin.

Very fine, VF-20: About 75 percent of the original detail will be visible. Or, on a coin with no inner detail, there will be moderate wear over the entire coin. Corners of letters and numbers may be weak. A small grading area will have about 60 percent of the original detail.

Fine, F-12: About 50 percent of the original detail will be visible. Or, on a coin with no inner detail, there will be fairly heavy wear over the entire coin. Sides of letters will be weak. A typically uncleaned coin will often appear dirty or dull. A small grading area will have just under 50 percent of the original detail.

Very good, VG-8: About 25 percent of the original detail will be visible. There will be heavy wear on the entire coin.

Good, G-4: Design will be clearly outlined but with substantial wear. Some of the larger detail may be visible. The rim may have a few weak spots of wear.

About good, AG-3: Typically only a silhouette of a large design will be visible. The rim will be worn down into the letters, if any.

Where to write for more information

American Numismatic Association: 818 N. Cascade Ave., Colorado Springs, CO 80903-3279.

Independent Coin Grading Co.: 7901 E. Belleview Ave., Suite 50, Englewood, CO 80111.

Numismatic Guaranty Corp: P.O. Box 4776, Sarasota, FL 34230.

NTC (Numistrust Corp.): 2500 N. Military Trail, Suite 210, Boca Raton, FL 33431.

PCI, Inc.: P.O. Box 486, Rossville, GA 30741.

Professional Coin Grading Service: P.O. Box 9458, Newport Beach, CA 92658.

Sovereign Entities Grading Service: 401 Chestnut St., Suite 103, Chattanooga, TN 37402-4924.

Visit the Krause Publications Web site
http://www.collect.com

5

Get a map
How to organize a collection

By David C. Harper

Do you have a jar full of old coins? Did a favorite relative give you a few silver dollars over the years? Or did you just come across something unusual that you set aside?

All three circumstances make good beginnings for collecting coins. It may surprise you, but this is how just about everybody starts in the hobby. It is a rare collector who decides to start down the hobby road without first having come into a few coins one way or another.

What these random groupings lack is organization. It is organization that makes a collection. But think about it another way: Organization is the map that tells you where you can go in coin collecting and how you can get there.

Have you ever been at a large fair or a huge office building and seen the maps that say "you are here"? Did you ever consider that, over time, thousands of other people have stood on the same spot? This is true in numismatics also. Figuratively, you are standing on the same spot on which the writers of this book stood at some point in their lives.

At a fair, the map helps you consider various ways of seeing all the sights. In coin collecting, too, there are different ways to organize a collection. The method you choose helps you see the hobby sights you want to see.

It should be something that suits you. Remember, do what you want to do. See what you want to see. But don't be afraid to make a mistake; there aren't any. Just as one can easily retrace steps at a fair, one can turn around and head in another direction in the coin-collecting hobby. Besides, when you start off for any given point, often you see something along the way that was unplanned but more interesting. That's numismatics.

There are two major ways to organize a collection: by type, and by date and mint-mark. These approaches work in basically the same fashion for coins of the United States, Canada and Mexico. Naturally, there are differences. But to establish the concepts, let's focus first on U.S. coins.

United States

Let's take collecting by type first. Look at your jar of coins, or take the change out of your pocket. You find Abraham Lincoln and the Lincoln Memorial on current cents. You find Thomas Jefferson and his home, Monticello, on the nickel. Franklin D. Roosevelt and a torch share the dime. George Washington and an eagle (or since 1999, designs honoring states) appear on the quarter. John F. Kennedy and the presidential seal are featured on the half dollar. Sacagawea and an eagle are on the dollar.

Each design is called a "type." If you took one of each and put the five coins in a holder, you would have a type set of the coins that are currently being produced for circulation by the U.S. Mint.

With just these six coins, you can study various metallic compositions. You can evaluate their states of preservation and assign a grade to each. You can learn about the artists who designed the coins, and you can learn of the times in which these designs were created.

As you might have guessed, many different coin types have been used in the United States over the years. You may remember seeing some of them circulating. These designs reflect the hopes and aspirations of people over time. Putting all of them together forms a wonderful numismatic mosaic of American history.

George Washington did not mandate that his image appear on the quarter. Quite the contrary. He would have been horrified. When he was president, he headed off those individuals in Congress who thought the leader of the country should have his image on its coins. Washington said it smacked of monarchy and would have nothing of it.

Almost a century and a half later, during the bicentennial of Washington's birth in 1932, a nation searching for its roots during troubled economic times decided that it needed his portrait on its coins as a reminder of his great accomplishments and as reassurance that this nation was the same place it had been in more prosperous days.

In its broadest definition, collecting coins by type requires that you obtain an example of every design that was struck by the U.S. Mint since it was founded in 1792. That's a tall order. You would be looking for denominations like the half cent, two-cent piece, three-cent piece, and 20-cent piece, which have not been produced in over a century. You would be looking for gold coins ranging in face value from $1 to $50.

But even more important than odd-sounding denominations or high face values is the question of rarity. Some of the pieces in this multi-century type set are rare and expensive. That's why type collectors often divide the challenge into more digestible units.

Type collecting can be divided into 18th, 19th, 20th and 21st century units. Obviously, a 21st century set is a short one. Just pull the change out of your pocket and ask the local bank for the half and dollar. Starting type collectors can focus on 20th century coin designs, which are easily obtainable. The fun and satisfaction of putting the 20th century set together then creates the momentum to continue backward in time.

In the process of putting a 20th century type set together, one is also learning how to grade, learning hobby jargon, and discovering how to obtain coins from dealers, the U.S. Mint, and other collectors. All of this knowledge is then refined as the collector increases the challenge to himself.

This book is designed to help. How many dollar types were struck in the 20th century? Turn to the U.S. price-guide section and check it out. We see the Morgan dollar, Peace dollar, Eisenhower dollar, and Anthony dollar. Hobbyists could also add the Ike dollar with the Bicentennial design of 1976 and the silver American Eagle bullion coin struck since 1986. One can also find out their approximate retail prices from the listings.

The beauty of type collecting is that one can choose the most inexpensive example of each type. There is no need to select a 1903-O Morgan when the 1921 will do just as well. With the 20th century type set, hobbyists can dodge some truly big-league prices.

As a collector's hobby confidence grows, he can tailor goals to fit his desires. He can take the road less traveled if that is what suits him. Type sets can be divided by denomination. You can choose over two centuries of one-cent coins. You can take just obsolete denominations or copper, silver or gold denominations.

You can even collect by size. Perhaps you would like to collect all coin types larger than 30 millimeters or all coins smaller than 20 millimeters. Many find this freedom of choice stimulating.

Type collecting has proven itself to be enduringly popular over the years. It provides a maximum amount of design variety while allowing collectors to set their own level of challenge.

The second popular method of collecting is by date and mintmark. What this means, quite simply, is that a collector picks a given type – Jefferson nickels, for example – and then goes after an example of every year, every mintmark, and every type of manufacture that was used with the Jefferson design.

Looking at this method of collecting brings up the subject of mintmarks. The "U.S. Mint" is about as specific as most non-collectors get in describing the government agency that provides everyday coins. Behind that label are the various production facilities that actually do the work.

In the more than two centuries of U.S. coinage, there have been eight such facilities. Four are still in operation. Those eight in alphabetical order are Carson City, Nev., which used a "CC" mintmark to identify its work; Charlotte, N.C. ("C"); Dahlonega, Ga. ("D"); Denver (also uses a "D," but it opened long after the Dahlonega Mint closed, so there was never any confusion); New Orleans ("O"); Philadelphia (because it was the primary mint, it used no mintmark for much of its history, but currently uses a "P"); San Francisco ("S"); and West Point, N.Y. ("W").

A person contemplating the collecting of Jefferson nickels by date and mintmark will find that three mints produced them: San Francisco, Denver and Philadelphia. Because of first two are branch mints serving smaller populations, their output has tended over time to be smaller than that of Philadelphia. This fact, repeated in other series, has helped give mintmarks quite an allure to collectors. It provides one of the major attractions in collecting coins by date and mintmark.

The key date for Jeffersons is the 1950-D when using mintages as a guide. In that year, production was just 2.6 million pieces. Because collectors of the time were aware of the coin's low mintage, many examples were saved. As a result, prices are

A basic type set of 20th century dollar coins would consist of (from top) a Morgan type, Peace type, Eisenhower type and Anthony type.

reasonable.

The Depression-era 1939-D comes in as the most valuable regular-issue Jefferson nickel despite a mintage of 3.5 million – almost 1 million more than the 1950-D. The reason: Fewer were saved for later generations of coin collectors.

Date and mintmark collecting teaches hobbyists to use mintage figures as a guide but to take them with a grain of salt. Rarity, after all, is determined by the number of surviving coins, not the number initially created.

The Jefferson series is a good one to collect by date and mintmark, because the mintmarks have moved around, grown in size, and expanded in number.

When the series was first introduced, the Jefferson nickel was produced at the three mints previously mentioned. In 1942, because of a diversion of certain metals to wartime use, the coin's alloy of 75 percent copper and 25 percent nickel was

Jefferson nickels have been produced at the (from top) Philadephia, Denver and San Francisco Mints. Note the Denver and San Francisco mintmarks to the right of Monticello.

The wartime nickels of 1942-1945 marked the first time a "P" mintmark, for Philadelphia, was used.

changed. The new alloy was 35 percent silver, 56 percent copper, and 9 percent manganese.

To denote the change, the mintmarks were moved and greatly enlarged. The pre-1942 mintmarks were small and located to the right of Monticello; the wartime mintmarks were enlarged and placed over the dome. What's more, for the first time in American history, the Philadelphia Mint used a mintmark ("P").

The war's end restored the alloy and mintmarks to their previous status. The "P" disappeared. This lasted until the 1960s, when a national coin shortage saw all mintmarks removed for three years (1965-1967) and then returned, but in a different location. Mintmarks were placed on the obverse, to the right of Jefferson's portrait near the date in 1968. In 1980 the "P" came back in a smaller form and is still used.

Another consideration arises with date and mintmark collecting: Should the hobbyist include proof coins in the set? This can be argued both ways. Suffice to say that anyone who has the desire to add proof coins to the set will have a larger one. It is not necessary nor is it discouraged.

Some of the first proof coins to carry mintmarks were Jefferson nickels. When proof coins were made in 1968 after lapsing from 1965 to 1967, production occurred at San Francisco instead of Philadelphia. The "S" mintmark was placed on the proof coins of that year, including the Jefferson nickel, to denote the change. Since that time, mintmarks used on proof examples of various denominations have included the "P", "D", "S", and "W".

For all of the mintmark history that is embodied in the Jefferson series, prices are reasonable. For a first attempt at collecting coins by date and mintmark, it provides excellent background for going on to the more expensive and difficult types. After all, if you are ever going to get used to the proper handling of a coin, it is far better to experiment on a low-cost coin than a high-value rarity.

As one progresses in date and mintmark collecting and type collecting, it is important to remember that all of the coins should be of similar states of preservation. Sets look slapdash if one coin is VG and another is MS-65 and still another is VF. Take a look at the prices of all the coins in the series before you get too far, figure out what you can afford, and then stick to that grade or range of grades.

Sure, there is a time-honored practice of filling a spot with any old example until a better one comes along. That is how we got the term "filler." But if you get a few placeholders, don't stop there. By assembling a set of uniform quality, you end up

In 1968 the mintmarks reappeared on U.S. coins and production of proof coins resumed, this time at the San Francisco Mint. On the nickels, the mintmark moved from the reverse to the obverse below the date.

with a more aesthetically pleasing collection.

The date and mintmark method used to be the overwhelmingly dominant form of collecting. It still has many adherents. Give it a try if you think it sounds right for you.

Before we leave the discussion of collecting U.S. coins, it should be pointed out that the two major methods of organizing a collection are simply guidelines. They are not hard-and-fast rules that must be followed without questions. Collecting should be satisfying to the hobbyist. It should never be just one more item in the daily grind. Take the elements of these collecting approaches that you like or invent your own.

It should also be pointed out that U.S. coinage history does not start with 1792 nor do all of the coins struck since that time conform precisely to the two major organizational approaches. But these two areas are good places to start.

There are coins and tokens from the American Colonial period (1607-1776) that are just as fascinating and collectible as regular U.S. Mint issues. There are federal issues struck before the Mint was actually established. See the Colonial price-guide section in this book.

There are special coins called commemoratives, which have been struck by the U.S. Mint since 1892 to celebrate some aspect of American history or a contemporary event. They are not intended for circulation. There was a long interruption between 1954 and 1982, but currently annual commemoratives are being offered for sale directly to collectors by the Mint.

Collecting commemoratives has always been considered something separate from collecting regular U.S. coinage. It is, however, organized the same way. Commemoratives can be collected by date and mintmark or by type.

Current commemoratives can be purchased from the U.S. Mint. To get on its mailing list, write U.S. Mint, Customer Care Center, 801 Ninth St., N.W., Washington, D.C. 20220. Check the U.S. Mint Web site at www.usmint.gov. Once on the list, hobbyists will get the various solicitations for not only commemoratives, but regular proof sets and mint sets and proof American Eagle bullion coins. Hobbyists who order from the U.S. Mint's Web site receive notices of product availability by e-mail.

Buying coins from the Mint can be considered a hobby pursuit in its own right. Some collectors let the Mint organize their holdings for them. They buy complete sets and put them away. They never buy anything from anywhere else.

Admittedly, this is a passive form of collecting, but there are individuals around the world who enjoy collecting at this level without ever really going any deeper. They like acquiring every new issue as it comes off the Mint's presses.

Once done, there is a certain knowledge that one has all the examples of the current year. Obviously, too, collectors by date and mintmark of the current types would have to buy the new coins each year, but, of course, they do not stop there.

Varieties and errors make up another area. Under this heading come the coins the Mint did not intend to make. There are all kinds of errors. Many of them are inexpensive. Check out the U.S. Minting Varieties and Errors section in the price guide. If you want to pursue it further, there are specialty books that deal with the topic in more detail.

Canada

Starting point for the national coinage of Canada is popularly fixed at 1858. In that year a large cent was first produced for use in Upper and Lower Canada (Ontario and Quebec). These prices were intended to supplant local copper coinage, which in turn had been attempts to give various regions a medium of exchange.

What was circulating in Canada at the time was a hodgepodge of world issues. The large cent predates a unified national government by nine years, but it is considered the beginning of national issues nevertheless.

There are many similarities between the United States and Canada and their respective monetary systems. Both continent-sized nations thought in terms of taming the frontier, new settlements, and growth. Both came to use the dollar as the unit of account because of the pervasiveness of the Spanish milled dollar in trade. For each, the dollar divides into 100 cents.

However, Canada had a far longer colonial history. Many of its residents resisted the tide that carried the United States to independence and worked to preserve their loyalties to the British crown. As a result, Canada was firmly a part of the British Empire. So even today with its constitution (the British North America Act transferred from Westminster to Ottawa in 1982), parliamentary democracy, and a national consciousness perhaps best symbolized by the maple leaf, Canada retains a loyalty to the crown in the person of Queen Elizabeth II of the United Kingdom. Canada is a member of the British Commonwealth of Nations.

The effect of this on coins is obvious. Current issues carry the queen's effigy. How Canada got its coins in the past was also influenced. The fledgling U.S. government set about creating its own mint as one of its earliest goals, despite that better-quality pieces could be purchased abroad at lower cost. Canada found that ties to mints located in England were logical and comfortable.

The Royal Canadian Mint was not established until 1908, when it was called the Ottawa branch of the British Royal Mint, and it was not given its present name until 1931. Both events are within living memory. Canadian coins, therefore, have a unique mixture of qualities. They are tantalizingly familiar to U.S. citizens yet distinctly different.

The coinage of a monarchy brings its own logic to the organization of a collec-

Canadian coins have depicted (from top) Queen Victoria, King Edward VII, King George V, King George VI and Queen Elizabeth II.

tion. Type collecting is delineated by the monarch. United Canada has had six. The first was Queen Victoria, whose image appeared on those large cents of 1858. Her reign began in 1837 and lasted until 1901.

She was followed by Edward VII, 1901-1910; George V, 1910-1936; Edward VII, 1936; George VI, 1936-1952; and Queen Elizabeth II, 1952-present. All but Edward VIII had coins struck for circulation in Canada. The collectible monarchs, therefore, number five, but the longer reigns inspired changes of portraits over time to show the aging process at work. Legends also changed. When George VI ceased being emperor of India, Canada's coins were modified to recognize the change.

Like U.S. coins, sizes and alloys were altered to meet new demands placed on the coinage. However, the separateness of each nation might best be summed up this way: Though the United States abolished its large cent in 1857, Canada's was just getting under way in 1858. The United States put an end to the silver dollar in 1935, the very year Canada finally got its series going.

And Canada, the nickel-mining giant, used a small-sized silver five-cent coin until 1921, almost 50 years after the half dime was abolished in the United States. But whereas the Civil War was the major cause of the emergence of modern U.S. coinage as specified by the Coinage Act of 1873, World War I influenced the alterations that made Canada's coins what they are today.

It might be assumed that change in the monarch also signaled a change in the reverse designs of the various denominations. A check of the Canadian price guide section shows this is not necessarily the case. Current designs paired with Queen Elizabeth II basically date back to the beginning of her father's reign. The familiar maple-leaf cent, beaver five-cent piece, schooner 10-cent, caribou 25-cent, and coat-of-arms 50-cent have been running for over 50 years. Significant changes were made to the 50-cent coin in 1959, but the reverse design remains the coat of arms.

So where does that leave type collectors? It puts them in a situation similar to categorizing the various eagles on U.S. coins. They can be universalists and accept the broadest definitions of type, or they can narrow the bands to whatever degree suits them best.

By checking the price-guide section, date and mintmark collectors will quickly note that their method of organization more or less turns into collecting by date. Though currently there are three mints in Canada – Hull, Quebec; Ottawa, Ontario; and Winnipeg, Manitoba – they don't use mintmarks. Historically, few mintmarks were employed.

Ottawa used a "C" on gold sovereigns of 1908-1919 and on some exported colonial issues. The private Heaton Mint in Birmingham, England, used an "H" on coins it supplied to Canada from 1871 to 1907.

But the coins supplied to Canada by the British Royal Mint and later by its Ottawa branch did not carry any identifying mark. Collectors who confine their activities to the more recent issues need never think about a mintmark.

It would be easy to slant a presentation on Canadian issues to stress similarities or differences to U.S. issues. One should remember that the monetary structures of each evolved independently, but each was always having an impact on the other.

Common events, such as World War II, had a similar impact. For example, the Canadian five-cent coin changed in much the same way as the U.S. nickel. In

Canada, nickel was removed and replaced first by a tombac (brass) alloy and then by chromium-plated steel. Peace brought with it a return to the prewar composition.

To see an example of differences between the United States and Canada, take the Canadian approach to the worldwide trend of removing silver from coinage. Canada made its move in 1968, three years after the United States. Instead of choosing a copper-nickel alloy as a substitute for silver, Canada looked to its own vast natural resources and employed pure nickel.

Canada also seems more comfortable with its coinage than the United States. Whereas the United States often feared confusion and counterfeiting from making the least little changes in its coins, Canada has long embraced coinage to communicate national events, celebrations and culture. Its silver-dollar series actually began as a celebration of George V's 25 years on the throne.

Succeeding years saw additional commemorative $1 designs interspersed with the regular Voyageur design. When the centennial of national confederation was observed in 1967, all of the denominations were altered for one year. The United States only reluctantly tried out the idea on three of its denominations for the nation's Bicentennial.

Ultimately, Canada began an annual commemorative dollar series in 1971. It issued coins for the 1976 Montreal Olympic Games and again in 1988 for the Calgary Olympic Games. Bullion coins were created to market its gold, silver and platinum output. A commemorative series of gold $100 coins was also undertaken. Canada, too, issues special proof, prooflike and specimen sets, similar to the United States.

Hobbyists who would like to be informed of new issues should write Royal Canadian Mint, P.O. Box 457, Station A, Ontario K1A 8V5, Canada. The mint also maintains special toll-free lines. In the United States, hobbyists may telephone the Royal Canadian Mint at 1-800-268-6468. In Canada, the number is 1-800-267-1871. You can get on the mailing list by using these numbers and you can buy currently available coins. (See Chapter 6 for Web information.)

When collecting Canada, another thing to remember is the importance varieties play in the nation's various series. Certainly, a type collector has no need to dwell on this information, but the date and mintmark collector may puzzle over the many extra identifying abbreviations in the price guide for certain coins. These varieties should not be confused with the U.S. variety-and-error category.

Here the varieties are not mistakes; they are deliberately created and issued variations of the standard design. We see Voyageur dollars on which the number of water lines changes. Other dollars count the number of beads.

These differences are minor. Though they were deliberately done to meet varying mint needs, they were not intended to be set apart in the public mind. The hobby, however, likes to look at things under a microscope.

Some varieties were indeed intended to be deliberately and noticeably different. An example of this occurs with 1947-dated issues. A maple leaf was placed on the 1947-dated cent through 50-cent issues. This indicated the coin was struck after George VI lost his title of emperor of India, as proclaimed in the Latin legend, but that the design had not yet been altered to reflect this. All of these varieties are considered integral parts of the Canadian series, and they are listed as such.

Like the U.S. Mint, the Royal Canadian Mint offers sets of coins in a variety of finishes to the collector market.

Do not construe any of this to mean there is no collecting of varieties and errors of the type common in the United States. There is. Collecting Royal Canadian Mint mistakes is just as active, just as interesting, and just as rewarding. After all, mint errors are universal. The methods of manufacture are the same. So the mistakes can be classified in the same manner.

Canada's numismatic listings also include items from various provinces issued before they were part of the confederation. The largest portion of this section is devoted to Newfoundland, because it retained a separate status far longer than the other provinces – until 1949 in fact.

Advice given to collectors of U.S. coins also applies to collectors of Canadian coins: Do what interests you. Do what you can afford. Create sets of uniform grade.

The rules of rarity transcend national boundaries. The only thing to keep in mind is the relative size of the collecting population. Because Canada has only a tenth of the U.S. population, it stands to reason that the number of collectors in that nation is but a fraction of the U.S. number. A mintage that seems to indicate scarcity for U.S. coin, therefore, could indicate something quite common in Canada. Don't forget that mintage is just a guide. The same factors that caused loss of available specimens or preserved unusually large quantities were at work in Canada, too.

Mexico

Coinage produced in Mexico dates to the establishment of a mint in Mexico City in 1536, over 250 years before a federal mint was set up in the United States and more than 300 years before Canada circulated its own coins. The output of those extra centuries alone would make organizing a Mexican coin collection more challenging than a collection of U.S. or Canadian coins. But there are numerous other factors involved.

You say you like the kings and queens on Canada's coins? Mexico has kings, too

– nearly 300 years' worth, plus a couple of emperors. You say the ideals of liberty embodied by the great men and women on U.S. coins is more your cup of tea? Mexico's coins also feature men and women committed to liberty.

In addition, Mexico is the crossroads of civilizations and empires. The great pyramid-building society of southern Mexico and Central America met its end at the hands of the Spanish conquistadors led initially by Hernando Cortez. The great Aztec empire was looted and overturned in 1519-1521 in the name of Spain.

The great natural resources of the area then supported successive Spanish kings in their grand dreams of dominating Europe. Through the doors of the Mexico City Mint and later facilities scattered about the country passed legendary quantities of silver. Even today the country ranks at the top of the list of silver producers.

But while Spain could dominate Mexico for a long time, the basic ideals of liberty and human dignity eventually motivated the people to throw off the foreign yoke. Unfortunately, victory was often neither complete nor wisely led. And in more recent years, the scourge of inflation had exacted a high toll on the currency itself. The numismatic consequences of a long history punctuated by periods of turmoil are an abundance of denominations, metals and types.

It is tempting for a would-be collector of Mexican coins to forget about anything that happened in the country prior to its monetary reform of 1905. By starting at that point, a hobbyist can happily overlook anything other than a decimal monetary system in which 100 centavos equal 1 peso. That system is as modern as any. The coins' striking quality is high. Legends are easy to read and understand, and the variety of issues is wide but not overwhelming.

There always is a certain logic to begin the collecting of any country with recent issues. The costs of learning are minimized, and as one becomes comfortable, a level of confidence can be built up sufficient to prompt diving further into the past.

The issues of 1905 to date also more easily fit into the mold of type collecting and collecting by date and mintmark. To take type collecting, for example, let's look at the peso. In 1905 it was a silver-dollar-sized coin with a silver-dollar-sized quantity of bullion in it, 0.786 ounces. In 1918 it was reduced to 0.4663 ounces; in 1920, 0.3856 ounces; in 1947, 0.2250 ounces; 1950, 0.1285 ounces; 1957, 0.0514 ounces; and in 1970 silver was eliminated completely in favor of a copper-nickel alloy.

At almost every one of those steps, the design changed, too. After sinking to 3,300 to the U.S. dollar, monetary reform dropped three zeroes in 1993. The new peso, equal to 1,000 old ones, is now 10 to the U.S. dollar.

By beginning with 1905, a date and mintmark collector misses out on issues of the various branch mints that were located around the country. Regular issues were all struck in Mexico City. Yearly output was reasonably regular for the various denominations, so date sets are extensive.

There have been rumblings since the early 1980s that Mexico would abandon the peso because of its greatly reduced value. The government, however, has been working hard to retain it since the monetary reform. So far it has succeeded.

One thing the government cannot do, however, is turn the clock back to a time when the fractional denominations of 1, 2, 5, 10, 20, 25, and 50 centavos were relatively high face values. However, it is stimulating to assemble sets because they offer a range of rarities. They are neither so expensive that it would prevent a collector

One thousand of these equaled one new peso as 1993 began.

from acquiring them at some point, but neither are they so common that you can walk into a shop, write a check, and come away with all of the 20th century sets complete. Check out the price guide section and see.

Gold in the post-1905 era is basically so much bullion. There are some scarcer pieces and some strikingly beautiful designs, such as the Centenario, a gold 50-peso coin containing 1.2 ounces of bullion. It was first struck in 1921 to mark 100 years of independence. Because Mexico actively restruck its gold coins, however, it is virtually impossible to tell an original issue from the newer version.

The result is a retail price structure based on metallic content. Gold, however, does not conjure up the images that silver does. Silver is the magic word for Mexico. That, of course, means the peso.

The modern Mexico City Mint also strikes commemoratives and collector sets from time to time. These are generally marketed to collectors through private firms, details of which are published in hobby newspapers like *World Coin News*. Mexico, like the United States and Canada, also issues gold and silver bullion coins.

These also are marketed through arrangements with private firms. Interestingly, Mexico's many gold-coin restrikes were the bullion coins of their day. They had the advantage of ready identification, and they were legally tradable according to gold-coin regulations that existed in the United States from 1933 through 1974.

It is appropriate that we conclude discussion of the modern period on the concept of bullion, because bullion is at the root of Mexico's numismatic history. That is a period to which we now turn.

When Cortez toppled the Aztec Empire, for a time the wealth returning to Spain was merely that taken by the victors from the vanquished. But the business of permanently administering a vast area in the name of the Spanish king, exploiting its natural resources, and funneling the proceeds to Spain quite soon involved the establishment of a mint in Mexico City. This was undertaken in 1536, just 15 years after the end of Aztec dominion.

At first, the authorized coins were low denominations: silver quarter, half, 1, 2, 3, and 4 reales, and copper 2 and 4 maravedis. To understand their face values and how they related to each other, let's take the common reference point of a silver dollar. The silver dollar is 8 reales, and you might recognize the nickname for the denomination of "piece of eight" from pirate lore. The eighth part, the silver real, was divided into 34 copper maravedis. That means the 8 reales was worth 272 copper maravedis.

Mexico also strikes commemorative coins for the collector market. They are available through private firms in the United States.

The copper coinage was hated and soon abolished, not to reappear until 1814. The silver coins were fine as far as they went. When the mines of Mexico began producing undreamed of quantities of metal, however, it was the 8 reales that took center stage. This occurred after 1572. The piece of eight became the standard form for shipping silver back to Spain.

Mexico City's output was prodigious. Minting standards were crude. All denominations produced are called "cobs," because they are basically little more than irregular-looking lumps of metal on which bits and pieces of design can be seen. The only constant was weight, fineness, and the appearance of assayer's initials (which guaranteed the weight and fineness). Not showing those initials was cause for severe punishment.

Designs showed the arms of the monarch on one side, a cross on the other, appropriate legends, and an indication of denomination. The period of cob issues lasted until 1732. Rulers of the period start with Charles and Johanna, 1516-1556; Philip II, 1556-1598; Philip III, 1598-1621; Philip IV, 1621-1665; Charles II, 1665-1700; Philip V, 1700-1724 and 1724-1746; and Luis I, 1724.

Modern mint machinery began turning out coins in 1732. Quality was similar to today. The arms design was continued. It was not until 1772 that the monarch's portrait began appearing. The honor of this numismatic debut belongs to Charles III. Kings of this period are Ferdinand VI, 1746-1759; Charles III, 1760-1788; Charles IV, 1788-1808; and Ferdinand VII, 1808-1821. *The Standard Catalog of Mexican Coins* by Colin R. Bruce II and Dr. George W. Vogt is recommended to those who want to study this period in greater depth.

The revolutionary period begins in 1810, when a parish priest, Miguel Hidalgo y Costilla, issued the call for independence. The first attempts to achieve this were violently suppressed. Hidalgo was executed, but independence did come in 1821.

With revolt against central authority came a dispersal of the right to strike coins. Mexico City continued as the major facility, but other operations began. The list of these over the next century is lengthy. Mintmarks and assayer initials proliferated.

The old colonial coinage standard survived the period. The 8 reales and its parts carried on. A slight reduction in bullion content had been ordered by the king in 1760, but otherwise things continued as they were. Gold was coined during the colonial period beginning in 1679 based on an 8-escudo piece, which divided into eighths just like the 8 reales. Gold, however, was not as important as silver.

Mexico's first emperor came shortly after independence. He was a leader in the struggle that set Mexico free from Spain. Augustin de Iturbide, originally an officer in the service of Spain, was proclaimed emperor in 1822. He abdicated in 1823 and was executed in 1824.

The second emperor had a reign almost as short as the first. Maximilian I, emperor only because he had a French army to secure the throne, reigned from 1863 to 1867. He was shot by a firing squad when the French left.

He is remembered numismatically because he decided to decimalize the coinage. The centavo and peso were born. Soon afterward, the republic was re-established. Further monetary changes were minor thereafter until 1905.

Collectors focusing on Mexico can devote much time to the study of the quasi-official issues of rebels during the periods of instability. They can look at hacienda tokens, which were issued by large farms or ranches that employed hundreds or thousands of people. Or they can pick whichever period in Mexico's history that fascinates them most. Whatever collectors of Mexico eventually settle on, they will find it rewarding.

Where to write for more information

World Coin News: 700 E. State St., Iola, WI 54990.

Better than map

Three mints have Web sites

By David C. Kranz

Here's a handy electronic means of finding North American coinage.

The U.S. Mint's Web site, www.usmint.gov, has been most active, making several limited, exclusively online offers. These have involved small bags of the nation's 50 states quarter issues as well as numismatic-philatelic covers and Sacagawea dollars. The U.S. Mint also sells its traditional annual products such as mint sets and proof sets on the Web, along with commemorative coins and other Mint sales catalog items.

Online orders can be more convenient for many hobbyists. Shipping charges are currently the same between sets ordered online or by mail.

Canadian gold and silver, annual sets and commemoratives are available for purchase on the Royal Canadian Mint's site, www.mint.ca. Both French and English language versions of the RCM site are available. The site is set up for online orders (placed from Canada and the United States only), and the mint accepts Visa, Mastercard and American Express.

At the site of the Mexican Mint, www.cmonedam.com.mx/cmm, you can learn that it was the first mint in America, and that it has served without interruption since its inception by Spanish decree. The Mexican Mint site has Spanish and English language versions, with coinage history, current news, sales and promotions Web pages as well as technical information about the circulating coinage of Mexico. Telephone, fax, mail and e-mail information is provided for placing orders.

The fourth component of the North American continent, Greenland, has no mint within its borders and uses coins of Denmark in commerce. For more on these coins, see the *Standard Catalog of World Coins*, published by F+W Publications (www.collect.com).

For a quick introduction to these countries' latest coinage, their Web sites can't be beat.

7

Caring for coins
How to store and preserve your collection

By Alan Herbert

From the day you acquire your first collectible coin, you have to consider where and how to store your collection. Often a shoebox or a small cardboard or plastic box of some kind will be the principal storage point as you start to gather coins, even before they can be considered a collection. Sooner or later you will outgrow that first box and need to think seriously about what to do with your coins to protect and preserve them.

All too often security takes precedence over preservation. We're more worried that the kids will dip into the coins for candy or ice cream or that burglars will somehow learn about your "valuable" collection and pay a visit. It often isn't until years later when you suddenly notice that your once beautiful coins are now dingy and dull, with spots and fingerprints all over them, that preservation becomes a primary consideration.

Learning good storage habits should be one of the first things to do right along with acquiring those first coins. There are a multitude of storage products on the market that are intended for more or less specific situations, so learning which to use and how to use them is vital to the health of your collection. Most if not all of the products mentioned here should be available at your nearest coin shop or hobby store.

Safe storage methods

The common impulse is to use what's available around the house; never allow that impulse to control your collecting. Plastic wrap, aluminum foil, cardboard, stationery envelopes, and other common household products are not designed for coin storage and never should be used for your collection. The same goes for soaps and cleansers found around the home.

There are specific products that have been designed, tested and found safe to use for coins. These are the media your collection deserves. The slight added expense

Two-by-two cardboard holders are a common form of short-term, inexpensive coin storage.

Many dealers sell coins in 2-by-2 plastic "flips," but these should not be used for long-term storage.

will pay a thousand dividends years from now when you sell you collection or pass it on to your heirs.

The most common storage media are 2-inch by 2-inch cardboard holders with Mylar windows, 2-by-2 plastic "flips," coin tubes, hard-plastic holders, coin boards, and coin albums.

The 2-by-2 cardboard holders are the cheapest and most commonly used storage method. They are usually folded and stapled around the coin. They are intended for short-term general storage. They are not airtight or watertight, and staples driven too close to the coin can ruin it.

The 2-by-2 plastic flips come in good and bad varieties. The old, usually soft flips are made of plastics that contain polyvinyl chloride, a chemical found in many plastics. Over time it breaks down into substances that put a green slime on your coins, which attacks the surface and ruins them.

The good flips are made of Mylar, but they are brittle and prone to splitting. So they should not be used to mail coins or when the coins are moved about frequently. Mylar flips, too, are for short-term general storage.

Often you will find coins in PVC holders when you buy them from a dealer. Remove them immediately and put them in some better storage medium.

Coin tubes come in clear and cloudy, or translucent, plastic. These are made of an inert plastic that will not harm your coins. Tubes are intended for bulk, medium- to long-term storage, with one caution: Use care when inserting the coins. Merely

Coin tubes are often used for bulk storage, but there is a proper technique to placing the coins in the tube.

dropping one coin onto another in a tube can damage both coins. The best technique is to make a stack or pile of the coins, then slide the pile carefully into the tube while holding it at an angle.

Hard-plastic holders are the elite items for storing your collection. There are a number of varieties, some of which come in three parts that are screwed together. Some come in two pieces that fit together. Some of these are airtight and watertight. They are more expensive, but they deserve to be used for any really valuable coins in your collection.

Coins processed by the third-party grading services come in hard-plastic holders, most of which are at least semi-airtight. The hard-plastic holders used by the U.S. Mint for proof sets since 1968 are not airtight, so coins should be watched carefully for signs of problems. In recent years these holders have been improved, but you should check your proof sets periodically.

Any stored coins should be checked regularly, at least twice a year. Check coins for signs of spotting or discoloration. Check the storage media for any signs of deterioration, rust, mildew, or other problems.

The older mint sets and proof sets – issued from 1955 to 1964 – come in soft-plastic envelopes that are not intended for long-term storage. Coins in these envelopes should be put in better storage media for the long term. In recent years the Mint has switched to an inert, stiffer plastic for the mint sets. This plastic is safe.

A coin folder is frequently the first piece of equipment the beginning collector buys. It is simply a piece of cardboard with holes to hold the coins. The holder folds up for storage. It is intended for inexpensive circulated coins only.

They give no protection from contamination or fingerprints. Worn coins will often fall out of the holes, which leads some novice collectors to tape the coins in the

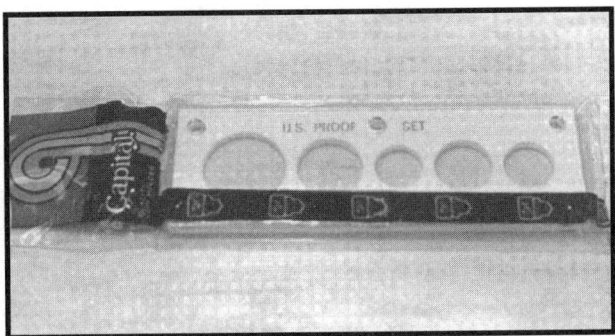

Hard-plastic holders are the top of the line in coin storage.

Coin folders are a low-cost and attractive way to store inexpensive circulated coins.

album. This is another example of misuse of a household product; tape can permanently damage a coin's surface.

Pride of ownership and the desire to show off a collection are the moving forces behind the sale of thousands of coin albums. They should also be used for inexpensive circulated coins only, with a couple of exceptions.

Some albums are merely coin boards mounted between covers. Others have pages with sliding plastic strips on both sides of the page so both sides of the coin can be seen.

The open-face albums are subject to fingerprints and contamination. Sneezing on your coins can do as much damage as gouging them with a knife. The slides will rub

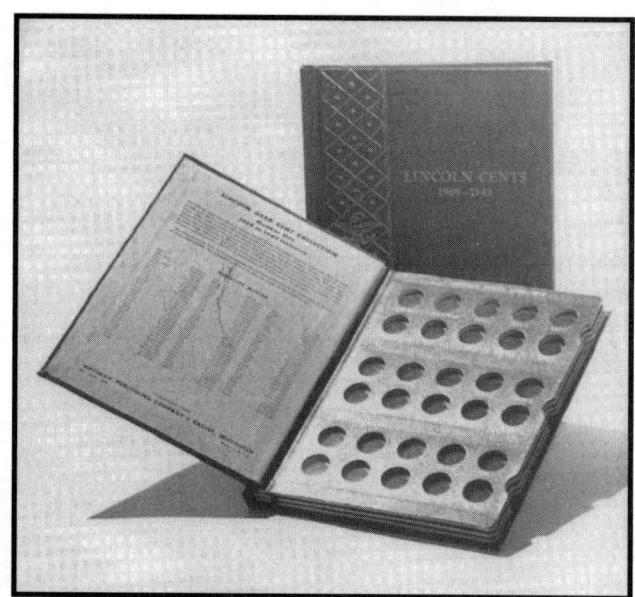

Coin albums also provide attractive storage for inexpensive circulated coins.

on your coins, damaging the high points of the design over time. These two types of albums should never be used for expensive uncirculated or proof coins, although they are fine for circulated coins that you want to display.

Fairly new on the market are albums designed for coins in inert, airtight holders. This allows you to display your coins and still keep them safe from handling and contact with the atmosphere.

One more storage medium that deserves mention is the clear-plastic notebook page that has pockets for 2-by-2 holders or flips. Here again there are good and bad. Most old pocket sheets contain PVC, so they cannot be used to hold coins in non-airtight holders because the gases will migrate into the holders and damage the coins. The newer Mylar pages are brittle but will not generate damaging gases or liquids.

When buying storage media, make sure the dealer guarantees that his products are safe for coins. Many of the old albums, flips and pocket pages are still around, especially at flea markets. If you are in doubt, don't buy.

There are also thin, two-piece, inert plastic holders that many collectors use to protect coins put in flips or 2-by-2 cardboard holders, especially to protect them from moving about against the holder and getting scratched. They are virtually airtight, so they do offer some protection.

Coins need to be protected from burglars. A box under the bed or in the closet offers no protection. If you must keep coins at home, a good, fireproof safe is a must. Otherwise, rent a safe-deposit box at a bank, but read the fine print on your box contract to make sure a coin collection is covered.

Most homeowner's insurance policies will not cover a coin collection or will cover only a fraction of its value. Special riders are expensive, but if you keep most of your coins at the bank, this will cut costs. For details, consult your insurance agent. The American Numismatic Association also offers collection insurance.

Where to store coins is often a problem. The commonest solution is to put them in the attic or basement. Those are the two worst places for your collection. Attics are notoriously hot. Heat can damage almost any storage media, and if there is the slightest hint of PVC, you've got trouble.

Basements are equally bad. They can flood, and humidity is high. Mildew can attack holders and other material stored with your coins.

So what's left? Ideally coins should be treated like a family member. They should be stored in some part of the house where temperature and humidity are relatively constant year round. If it's comfortable for you, it's probably much more comfortable for your coins than the basement or attic.

Protecting coins from humidity is always a good idea, even in areas where it is not a major health problem. For your coins, too much dampness can become a serious problem, often before you realize it. A good solution is to get several good-sized packets of silica gel and store them with your coins in your safe or a container of some kind that will isolate them from the general climate in the home.

To clean or not to clean

Before you store your coins, you should be aware that coins are like dishes: They should never be put away dirty. Ah, but you've probably already heard or read that you should never clean a coin. If you haven't, I'll say it now: Never clean a coin.

OK, so there are exceptions, but be careful of those exceptions and for good reason. Ignoring the exception can be excruciatingly and embarrassingly expensive.

Coins get dirty, just like anything else. The impulse is to shine them up – polish them to a brilliance that will dazzle the viewer. If you've already succumbed to the temptation to clean even a single coin, stand up, kick yourself, then sit back down and read on. The one exception is loose dirt, grease, oil, or something similar, and there are even exceptions to that rule.

Use a neutral solvent to dissolve the grease and oils that usually coat uncirculated coins as they come from the mint. Follow the instructions on the container exactly, and if the directions say to use the product outdoors, they mean it.

For circulated coins, lighter fluid will often dissolve the accumulated "gunk" that sticks to them, but I don't recommend it for uncirculated coins, especially copper alloy coins. Air dry the coins; don't rub or wipe them. Even the softest cloth or paper towel can pick up sharp-edged particles that will ruin a coin's surface. Proof coins are clean when they are packaged, so this should not be necessary and should be done only as a last resort if they have somehow picked up oil in handling.

Using dips, household cleansers, metal polish, and even soap can permanently damage a coin. Avoid acid-based cleaners at all costs. They work by eating away the coin's surface to remove the embedded dirt or discoloration. Cleaning a coin with any of these products will sharply reduce its collectible value. To put it simply, collectors do not want cleaned coins, so they are heavily discounted.

One of the reasons for this is that once a coin has been cleaned, it will discolor much more quickly, requiring fresh cleaning. Each time it is cleaned, the surface is further dulled, reducing the coin's appeal and reducing its value.

Obviously this advice applies especially to uncirculated and proof coins, but it applies to any coin that is or has the potential to become valuable. But if you clean it, its career ends right there.

There are products specifically designed for removing the green PVC slime from coins. They do not contain acid, so they are safe. They will stop but cannot reverse the damage that the PVC has already done to the coin. Read the label, and use exactly as directed.

I frequently am asked about ultrasonic cleaners. They fall under the same heading as the various cleaning products I've described. In other words, the apparatus should not be used for uncirculated, proof, or other valuable coins. If you do use one, do one coin at a time so there is no chance for the vibration to rub two coins together. Change or filter the cleaning solution frequently to keep abrasive particles from coming in contact with the vibrating coin.

Like anything else, cleaning can be carried to an extreme, so I'll give you one horror story and just such a mistake: Years ago I had a collector fly several hundred miles to bring his collection for me to sell for him. When he laid out the coins on the table, I was shocked to discover that the hundreds of coins had all been harshly cleaned.

When I questioned him he calmly recounted that he had decided that the coins needed cleaning, so he dumped them all into a rock tumbler and left it on for several hours. It ruined all his coins, reducing them to face value. With his passion for cleanliness he had destroyed several thousand dollars worth of collectible value, plus air fare, a rental car, and a motel bill.

The key to a long-term collection that might appreciate in value is to learn what not to do to your coins and what care they need to survive years of waiting in the wings. Learning to protect your coins with the best available storage methods and media is a key first step toward enjoying your collection for years to come.

A private firm, Numismatic Conservation Services, LLC, will clean coins that need it for a fee. The firm's Web site address is www.ncscoin.com.

Where to write for more information

American Numismatic Association: 818 N. Cascade Ave., Colorado Springs, CO 80903-3279. Web address is http://www.money.org.

8

Join the club
Coin collecting has lots of organizations

By David C. Harper

More than 160 years ago, Alexis de Tocqueville noted in his *Democracy in America* the penchant of people in the United States to create and voluntarily join public groups for a multitude of purposes. This urge to join carries over into coin collecting.

Whether it be a national organization or local coin club, groups have been organized in the United States, Canada and Mexico to help collectors enhance their hobby knowledge and enjoyment. They serve as clearinghouses for new information, maintain libraries, and bring collectors together in meetings to share their hobby experiences with each other. Clubs are so well defined that collectors can find one to serve any activity level and any degree of personal interaction with other collectors.

At the extreme, you can join a national organization by mail, spend a hobby lifetime utilizing its services, and yet never leave the privacy and comfort of home. At the other end, some areas offer such a multitude of clubs that you can find a meeting to attend on many nights of the week.

There are many ways to find a club. Some hobbyists inquire at the local coin shop to identify the organization nearest them. *Numismatic News* publishes news about clubs. Also, watch your local newspaper for listings of community events.

How does a collector match his needs with an appropriate club? The closest thing to a one-stop shopping place for an answer is the American Numismatic Association.

It is the United States' national coin-collecting organization and was granted a perpetual charter by Congress with a mission of education. It can be reached at 818 N. Cascade Ave., Colorado Springs, CO 80903-3279. Its Web address is www.money.org. It offers a wide array of personal hobby services, and its benefits cross national boundaries. In fact, when it was founded in 1891, it was expected that Canadians and Mexicans would be just as likely to join as U.S. citizens.

The most obvious benefit to an ANA member is a subscription to *The Numismatist*, the association's monthly magazine. In it you find news, historical features, membership information, and advertisements placed by dealers who are ready to fill every collector's want list.

More than 30,000 titles are available in the ANA library, and you don't have to walk into the ANA building to check them out. Any member anywhere can do that by mail. The ANA has called upon renowned numismatic authorities to create a correspondence course, which distills into 29 separate readings information that has taken many people a lifetime to learn. There are ANA educational seminars held in Colorado Springs and other sites across the United States.

The ANA sponsors two conventions annually. The early spring convention is usually held in March at locations across the country, selected and announced well in advance. The summer convention, which is so huge that it's billed as the "World's Fair of Money," is a tradition that dates back almost to the organization's founding.

Members also are offered a variety of optional services, ranging from coin-collection insurance to credit cards and car rental discounts. And if you do go to Colorado Springs, the ANA maintains its Money Museum at its headquarters. In it are some of the rarest and most famous coins in history.

Joining the ANA is easy. The membership fee is $39 the first year and $33 thereafter. Members over 65 years old get a $4 discount, and junior members (those under 18) are charged $15.

Beyond simply belonging to the ANA, though, are the doors that open to members. If you want to find a regional, state or local club, you can get help from the ANA. The important thing to remember is that you set your own level of involvement. If your profession is so hectic that you don't need another meeting to go to, the ANA is the place for you. If your hours are so regular that joining in the fun and camaraderie of a local club is just what you are looking for, the ANA can help you find that, too.

And just because the American Numismatic Association has "American" in its name, it doesn't mean that members are focused only on U.S. coins. Far from it. It is more accurate to say that if a coin was struck at any time anywhere in the world in the last 2,600 years, there are ANA members who collect it.

The ANA, if it connotes any exclusivity at all, is basically a regional designation based on where its members live. The farther one gets from the United States, the longer correspondence takes and the greater the possibility of a language barrier between the ANA staff and a potential member. It is therefore not surprising to find that 29,000 members are predominantly located in the United States.

The Canadian Numismatic Association dates to 1950. It publishes *The Canadian Numismatic Journal*, published 11 times a year, and it also sponsors an annual convention. Membership is considerably smaller than the ANA's, in line with the population difference between the United States and Canada. Membership fee is $33 a year. The mailing address is Executive Secretary, Canadian Numismatic Association, P.O. Box 226, Barrie, Ontario L4M 4T2, Canada.

The Sociedad Numismatica de Mexico A.C. was established in 1952. Basically, it oversees an annual convention in Mexico City. It may be contacted through its U.S. representative, Don Bailey, at PMB #139, 250 "D" South Lyon Ave., Hemet, CA 92543. A related group at the same address is the U.S. Mexican Numismatic Society.

That covers the national hobby umbrella groups. There are many more organizations of a national character that have somewhat narrower poses. Among these is the American Numismatic Society in New York City. It is older than the ANA, having been established in 1858. It also maintains a superb museum of U.S. and world coins, and a world-class library. Emphasis in the ANS is on scholarly research.

Numismatics would be nothing if it were not for its research pioneers. If that is what appeals to you, you can write the ANS at Broadway and 155th St., New York, NY 10032, for information regarding its structure and various classes of membership.

Other national organizations focus on specific collectible areas, such as Seated Liberty coinage or tokens and medals. These are popular and active. Many are member organizations of the ANA and hold meetings in conjunction with the ANA's conventions.

Coin dealers have organizations of their own. The Professional Numismatists Guild Inc. maintains high standards of membership qualification and conduct. Members are a who's who of the commercial sector of the hobby. All are ready to serve you in furthering your collecting goals. For a membership roster, contact Robert Brueggeman, Executive Director, 3950 Concordia Lane, Fallbrook, CA 92028.

This brief review merely puts you on the threshold of the organized numismatic world. It is up to you to open that door or walk away. Over the years, many collectors have found membership to be the most rewarding aspect of the hobby. They have benefited from working with others with a common interest to further their own knowledge and advance their collecting goals in an environment of mutual support and friendship.

9

Rarity records
$1 million ain't what it used to be

By David C. Harper

Are you old enough to remember 1967? If you are and you had had a spare $46,000 then, you could have purchased a 1913 Liberty Head nickel and tucked it away for retirement. A collector with $1 million then could have had the pick of anything he wanted. No more. Nowadays, $1 million may not get you in the door as more and more coins soar far beyond it.

Taking the 1913 Liberty Head nickel out again in 2006, you would find yourself sittin' pretty. How pretty? Well, in May of 2005, a private transaction occurred that priced one of the five known 1913 Liberty Head nickels at $4.15 million. The price appreciation for this classic American numismatic rarity is way ahead of the inflation rate since 1967. Remember, $46,000 in 1967 wasn't pocket change. You could have purchased two average three-bedroom tract homes in most suburbs in America for that sum of money. Had this sum simply kept up with the inflation of the last 39 years, it would be approximately $268,000 today. Obviously, buying the coin was a way better deal. What's going on?

Real estate isn't the only thing going up in price in 21st century America. Prices for classic U.S. rarities are skyrocketing far beyond the rate of inflation. Buyers recognize coins for the rarities they are and they seem bent on chasing them to the

Top 10 auction prices for U.S. coins

Rank	Coin	Auction house	Year sold	Price
1.	1933 gold $20	Sotheby's	2002	$7,590,020
2.	1804 silver $1	Bowers	1999	$4,140,000
3.	1787 Brasher doubloon, unique punch on breast	Heritage	2005	$2,990,000
4.	1787 Brasher doubloon, punch on wing	Heritage	2005	$2,415,000
5.	1804 silver $1	Stack's	2002	$1,840,000
6.	1913 Liberty Head nickel	Superior	2001	$1,840,000
7.	1804 silver $1	Bowers	1997	$1,815,000
8.	1913 Liberty Head nickel	Bowers	1996	$1,485,000
9.	1796 No Stars gold $2.50	American Numis. Rarities	2005	$1,380,000
10.	1894-S Barber dime	DLRC	2005	$1,322,500

The reigning champion U.S. coin as determined by auction price is the 1933 $20 gold piece at right. However, with private transaction prices of over $4 million for 1913 Liberty Head nickels, left, how long will it be before the current top price is surpassed?

moon. More and more of them have passed the $1 million mark. The prices for most coins are going up. But it is the classic rarities that are getting the headlines for leading the way.

The top 10 list of rarities compiled by Robert R. Van Ryzin, editor of *Coins* Magazine, for coins sold at public auction show all of them well over $1 million. Now there is nothing wrong with coins sold in private transactions, but the numbers reported can be a little bit "soft" sometimes. Consider an event in 1980. Then the $500,000 mark was mind-boggling. One of 15 known 1804 dollars was sold in a private transaction. The new owner said he had paid almost half a million dollars for it. Years later, it was revealed that the actual price was $425,000, which was $25,000 over the prior auction result. An additional $25,000 wasn't exactly small change then, but the real price certainly was closer to $400,000 than to the $500,000 used in the public relations buzz. Prices from public auctions are much easier to verify. So with apologies to the latest buyer of the 1913 Liberty Head nickel, only rarities sold at public auction are on the list.

Right now the all-time champion U.S. record coin price is $7,590,020 paid to buy

the one legally available example of a 1933 $20 gold piece. This occurred at a Sotheby's/Stack's auction in New York City in 2002. It was a major event. Hundreds of hobby luminaries packed the Sotheby's gallery to watch history being made. TV cameras recorded the event. It was a one-item auction and it took 20 minutes for the auctioneer to gavel the coin into the history books.

How long this record will stand is anyone's guess, but if the frisky market trends of the past year are any guide, the record may fall sooner rather than later. Any one of the coins on the list on the prior page is a contender for setting a new record. It is a fair bet that one of them will push its way past the current record before many more years have passed.

There are just 15 known 1804 dollars. It has been called the "King of American Coins" for many years. Can the coin remain the king if it doesn't wear the top price crown?

One thing is certain. Current owners of great rarities that haven't been on the market in many years must be sorely tempted to sell while buyers are so eager to pay record prices. Most rare coin owners are astute. They hang on to their collections when prices are weak. They decide to cash out when prices are strong. It is apparent that we are in a period of strong prices. What might be attracted to this market?

There are a number of other great rarities. There is but one known example of the 1870-S $3 gold piece. It last sold for $687,500 in a 1982 auction. What might it bring should its owners ever decide to sell? Then there are near misses from the Top 10 list. An 1885 Trade dollar, one of only five known, sold for $1,006,250 in November of 2004. A 1794 silver dollar offered the same night as the No. 9 record 1796 No Stars gold $2.50 was sold for $1.15 million, making it a very close miss to get on the Top 10 list. What is particularly interesting is that it was a big deal that the coin was graded MS-64 by the Numismatic Guaranty Corp. grading service. It is the fourth finest known 1794. Speculation has already started that when the finest known 1794 dollar is next sold at auction, its price will definitely be in the Top 10. Most collectors would be pleased to own any 1794 dollar, but even now, picky buyers are making price distinctions among the great American rarities depending on very small variations in condition. Accurate grading is always important, but as the prices paid for rarities leap ever higher, it is essential.

Here is No. 9 on the Top 10 list.

10

Up and coming quarters
U.S. Mint program hitting home stretch

By Todd Haefer

A bold experiment by the U.S. Mint has reinvigorated the field of coin collecting and shows no signs of slowing down.

The 50 States Quarters Program welcomed California and Kansas into its fold in 2005 as of this writing, with Minnesota, Oregon and West Virginia scheduled to complete the year. That brings the number of different quarter designs so far to 35, with 15 more coins left in the program.

The U.S. Mint estimates that more than 140 million Americans are collecting the new quarters and perhaps branching out into other areas as well.

The coins are being released in the order the states joined the Union, so Delaware, which became the first state on Dec. 7, 1787, had the honor of being the first coin released in 1999. Virginia holds the distinction of the highest mintage at 1,594,616,000; Maine is the lowest so far with 448,800,000. (See table on Page 87)

After posting some impressive production numbers

California and Minnesota were the first two coins released in 2005 as part of the 50 States Quarters Program.

from 1999-2001, state quarter production began slowing down, with 2003 seeing the lowest overall numbers. Numbers began climbing slightly in 2004 and the first two quarters of 2005 have higher mintages than the release of the first two quarters of 2004.

Collectors have a choice of collecting each type, which would eventually result in a 50-coin collection, or they can collect one each from both the Denver and Philadelphia mints, which would double the number. Add proofs and silver proofs and you get another 100 pieces for the complete set.

The biggest news the past year regarding the quarter program was the discovery of not just one, but two minting varieties of the Wisconsin quarter. (See Chapter 11 for photographs.)

The varieties showed up on D-mintmark coins as an extra leaf on an ear of corn. They are referred to as the Extra Leaf High and Extra Leaf Low varieties. It is estimated that as many as 5,000 of the varieties may exist in circulation. These discoveries have led to prices for the coins reaching up up to $1,500 for three-piece sets (the two errors plus a regular Wisconsin quarter). Prices for the three-piece set retreated to $450 just before this book went to press.

They aren't the only state quarters selling for a pretty penny – all state quarters are receiving sometimes more than $100 if graded by a grading service as being in upper proof grades (Proof-67 to Proof-70).

Some of the special sets featuring state quarters might increase in value, also. For instance, the Formation of the Union Set of 2001 sold out its mintage of 50,000. The five-quarter silver proof set of 2004 sold out its 600,000 units in only 10 weeks, but current price is $14.95.

The quarter schedule for coming years is:

2006: Nevada, Nebraska, Colorado, North Dakota and South Dakota.

2007: Montana, Washington, Idaho, Wyoming and Utah.

2008: Oklahoma, New Mexico, Arizona, Alaska

Oregon, Kansas and West Virginia are scheduled for release to finish the 2005 production of state quarters.

The Wisconsin quarter caused a sensation in the hobby when two varieties were found in 2005.

and Hawaii.

The program may not end in 2008, however. There is a bill in Congress that would extend the program to include U.S. territories, such as the District of Columbia, Commonwealth of Puerto Rico, Guam, American Samoa, United States Virgin Islands and Commonwealth of the Northern Mariana Islands. If passed, these coins would be released in 2009.

If you have been missing all the fun, current state quarters are sold by the U.S. Mint in various sets, in rolls and in bags. The 2005 U.S. Silver Proof Set contains all the 2005 state quarters, as

State Quarter Production

States	Philadelphia	Denver
Delaware (1999)	373,400,000	401,424,000
Pennsylvania	349,000,000	358,332,000
New Jersey	363,200,000	299,028,000
Georgia	451,188,000	488,744,000
Connecticut	688,744,000	657,880,000
Massachusetts (2000)	628,600,000	535,184,000
Maryland	678,200,000	556,532,000
South Carolina	742,576,000	566,208,000
New Hampshire	673,040,000	495,976,000
Virginia	943,000,000	651,616,000
New York (2001)	655,400,000	619,640,000
North Carolina	627,600,000	427,876,000
Rhode Island	423,000,000	447,100,000
Vermont	423,400,000	459,404,000
Kentucky	353,000,000	370,564,000
Tennessee (2002)	361,600,000	286,468,000
Ohio	217,200,000	414,832,000
Louisiana	362,000,000	402,204,000
Indiana	362,600,000	327,200,000
Mississippi	290,000,000	289,600,000
Illinois (2003)	225,800,000	237,400,000
Alabama	225,000,000	232,400,000
Maine	217,400,000	231,400,000
Missouri	225,000,000	228,200,000
Arkansas	228,000,000	229,800,000
Michigan (2004)	233,800,000	225,800,000
Florida	240,200,000	241,600,000
Texas	278,800,000	263,000,000
Iowa	213,800,000	251,800,000
Wisconsin	226,400,000	226,800,000
California (2005)	257,200,000	263,200,000
Minnesota	239,600,000	248,400,000
Oregon	NA	NA
Kansas	NA	NA
West Virginia	NA	NA

well as the Sacagawea dollar, Roosevelt dime, Kennedy half dollar, Lincoln cent and the two new Westward Journey nickels. All of the coins except the dollar, nickels and cent are 90-percent silver. The 2005 U.S. Mint Uncirculated Coin Set features twice the coins in standard base metal alloys, but two of each – one from the Philadelphia and one from Denver in uncirculated condition. Sets for 2006 should be similar.

To order products from the Mint, call (800) 872-6468 from 8 a.m. to midnight, seven days a week; or visit its Web site at www.usmint.gov.

You can always collect the quarters from circulation. It is not unusual to find as many as five different state quarters in your pocket after a day of shopping. Why not try it?

11

Wisconsin quarter craze
Error variety touches off a buying frenzy

By Peter Lindblad

It's still a mystery how it happened and there's no consensus among error experts as to what it really is. But a debate in early 2005 raged on about the 2004-D Wisconsin quarters with the so-called "extra leaves." Collectors didn't wait for an answer.

They bought them up as fast as people found them. Some cashed in on the novelty of the find; others probably absorbed a loss.

No matter what aspect of the story piques your interest, be it financial or otherwise, the tale of the Wisconsin quarter leaf variety continues to fascinate hobbyists.

It all started in December of 2004. That's when Bob Ford, a collector from Tucson, Ariz., made the discovery. For the past 15 years, Ford has scoured through coins in circulation looking for varieties and errors. On Dec. 11, he found one that made all that work worthwhile. He brought the first pieces to Rob Weiss at Old Pueblo Coin in Tucson.

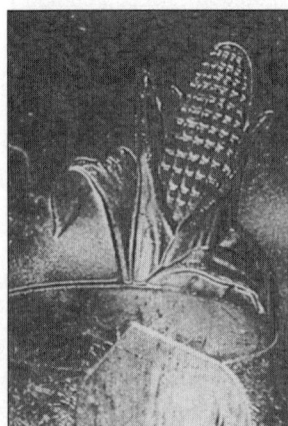  

From left to right, normal Wisconsin quarter, in the middle is the error with Extra Leaf High and at right the error with Extra Leaf Low.

After the initial discovery, more started showing up and it turned out, there were two varieties – one with a low leaf, called Extra Leaf Low, and one with a high leaf, called Extra Leaf High, which is considered the rarer of the two. Not many were found. Estimates place the total at around 5,500 and it seems the findings were limited to Tucson and a few surrounding communities, as well as in Texas around San Antonio, most notably in Kerryville, Texas.

Almost immediately, the coins started showing up on eBay and it wasn't long before three Tucson coin dealers, including Weiss and Eagle Eye Rare Coins, made initial public offerings of three-piece sets featuring the varieties and they sold out quickly. On the Internet, sets went for more than $1,000 initially, and individual coins fetched between $360, for the low-leaf variety, and as much as $800 for the high-leaf variety. That was in February. Prices had dropped

Rick Snow of Eagle Eye Rare Coins in Tucson, Ariz., shows the Wisconsin extra leaf variety quarters set sold by his firm and two other Tucson dealers.

40 to 50 percent by late March. Flash forward to July and a listing on eBay shows how much prices vary. One set of 2004-D Wisconsin leaf variety quarters, graded MS-67 by Numismatic Guaranty Corp., according to the listing, brought in $1,625. Another with the same grade was bought for $1,595. Most sets, however, were in the $300 to $350 range. A recent retail offering from Ken Pines' Coast to Coast Coins was selling sets for $450.

Individual coins were going for less than $100, in at least one instance, $455 was paid for a high-leaf variety graded MS-66 by NGC.

At this point, how the extra leaf, or whatever it is, got on the coins is a matter of conjecture. Some error experts, like Ken Potter and Jose Cortez, think it's the result of a damaged die. Potter has stated he believes they are nothing more than die gouges and posted a statement on his Web site that detailed why he thought so. His contention is that it was caused by a random metal displacement, that something was either punched into the die or scraped across it.

Cortez said in an article in *Numismatic News* that he thought there was some play in a plate. A die chip could have fallen into a die below, that caused the leaf to appear. In fact, he stated the leaves are caused by fragments that fell from a die.

Others aren't so sure. Though he had come around to the idea that it was caused by something that happened in the die department at Denver, Alan Herbert says it may be an intentional design element. In the same *Numismatic News* article, Herbert opined that the leaf, actually a corn husk, looks too much like the real thing to be an accidental die gouge. As evidence, he pointed to a rib or vein that he says is in perfect position.

So far, the U.S. Mint has been mum on what happened. The last statement from the Mint was issued Feb. 8, 2005 and said little more than the Mint was aware of the extra leaf varieties and was looking into the matter. Since then, the Mint has been silent. Whether or not the coin becomes a collectible remains to be seen. But it did capture the imagination of the hobby and for that, many say it was a blessing.

12

What's hot for 2006?

Everything!

By David C. Kranz

If I had a crystal ball, it would tell me that 2006 will be a great year for coin collectors, and for the coin market.

Circulating commemoratives are starting to pay off for the coin hobby. The public's awareness is rising, some newcomers are moving beyond pulling state quarters from pocket change and are seeking deeper collecting pursuits. This group of people is making itself felt in the marketplace.

Initially, the prices of state quarters themselves, then older Washington quarters, were the beneficiaries, and now interest is spreading. Quarters all the way back to the beginning have gone up in price in recent years. Nickels have appreciated thanks to the 2004-2005 Westward Journey nickel series. Watch for the new 2006 nickel design of Jefferson and Monticello. Cents have started to tick upward as we approach the 2009 centennial of the Lincoln cent. The wave of interest should buoy traditionally popular type coins in general.

Creeping fears of inflation that have brought U.S. interest rates up from lowest-ever levels have also reminded people of gold's traditional role as a store of value. With the price of oil on a dramatic upward run, could gold fail to follow?

Combining the allure of gold with fresh interest that's likely to boost type coins leads me to suggest that Saint-Gaudens $20s will be hot in 2006. The design is widely regarded as one of the best of all U.S. coins, something that even the newest newcomer appreciates, and each example contains just shy of an ounce of gold.

Rather than looking at the most common Saint, consider the 1910 and 1910-D, each with mintage under 500,000. In MS-63 either one is priced at $700, in MS-60, $600. As this is written, an ounce of gold is trading around $425, meaning the double eagle contains about $410 worth of gold (of course, as the market price of gold goes up and down, this value fluctuates as well). Is $600 worth it? Let me add that the prices for these dates had not changed from a year prior when gold traded around $380 an ounce – today you're getting about $40 more gold value for the same coin price. At some point a price adjustment will occur.

The 1913-S gold $20 has a mintage of 34,000.

Want to get more serious? Look at the 1913-S double eagle, mintage 34,000. In MS-60, this coin costs $1,350, in MS-65 $3,650. That MS-60 price is amazing – the mintage is 14 times lower than the 1910 or 1910-D, yet the 1913-S price is only a little more than double their MS-60 listing. Now, survival rates play an important role and you should do your research, but even if all 34,000 of the 1913-S remain available to this day, only a percentage of them will grade MS-60 or higher. At a price of $1,350, you get a beautiful, low-mintage American coin, struck at the San Francisco Mint to boot, containing nearly an ounce of gold.

Some of us are not of a mind to collect gold and want to focus more tightly than a type collection. Barber halves might suit. You can pick the grade level of the set you want to complete based on how much you want to spend over the course of the series. With about 73 dates, depending on what you choose to include, you could pursue examples in very fine and pay an average of $185 per coin at today's prices. In extremely fine you'd pay about $300 a coin, and on upward into the uncirculated grades. The highest mintage is 5.4 million while most are under half that and branch mint strikes from New Orleans, Denver and San Francisco appear over the course of the series.

I like Barber dimes, too, but half dollars are more appropriate for 2006 because two Benjamin Franklin silver dollar non-circulating commemorative coins are coming this year. A by-product of their release should be an increase in interest in Franklin halves.

Even more deserving of collector interest, however, are Kennedy halves. Prices for low-mintage dates 2002 and later have reached $10 in MS-65 and higher in ultra-grades. Compare this with Franklin halves, where issues of 50 years ago in MS-65 with full bell lines and mintages 10 times higher cost around $75 and up. There are plenty of Kennedy dates from the early 1980s and late 1990s with mintages similar to some of the Franklins, and the Kennedy halves don't command near the prices some of the Franklins do. There is room for Kennedy half dollar price appreciation in business strikes as well as proofs.

A rising tide lifts all boats. Prices for many coins have been going up, possibly due to growing numbers of hobby participants putting greater demand on supplies. As new collectors grow more knowledgeable, watch for further demand increases.

13

Internet now standard
Collectors take online use to new heights

By Ray Sidman

Everywhere you look, everything you read, the Internet has permeated our culture. Whether promoting a business or a personal Web site, "www" has become a common word at all levels of our culture, and "dot-com" – no longer vast enough to cover it all – has been joined by "dot-net," "dot-org" and many other extensions.

Coin collectors congregate online in chatrooms, dealers operate solely from their online sites. Libraries and other public facilities and even private enterprises offer Internet access services for individuals who don't have a home computer.

Week by week the level of person-to-person interaction and business growth increases with this technology. Don't be left in the cold. See what's available to you.

Grading Services
ANACS
www.anacs.com
Currency Grading & Certification
www.currencygradingcertification.com
Digital Coin Grading Service
www.digitalcoingrading.com
Global Certification Services
www.globalcertified.com
Independent Coin Grading Company
www.icgcoin.com
Numismatic Guaranty Corporation of
   America
www.ngccoin.com
Numistrust
www.numistrust.com
PCI Coin Grading Services
www.chattanooga.net/pci
Professional Coin Grading Service
www.pcgs.com

Sovereign Entities Grading Service
www.segsgrading.com

Auction Firms
America West Archives
www.americawestarchives.com
American Numismatic Rarities
www.anrcoins.com
Best Collectors
www.bestcollectors.com
BidXS.com
www.bidxs.com
Bowers & Merena Galleries
www.bowersandmerena.com
Centennial Auctions
www.centennialauctions.com
Certified Coin Auction
www.cce-auction.com
Collector Online
www.collectoronline.com

Currency Auctions of America
www.currencyauction.com
Gary Duskie Rare Coins
www.coinmall.com/duskie
eBay
www.ebay.com
E-Bid
www.ebid.com.au
Early American History Auctions
www.earlyamerican.com
El Mundo de la Moneda
www.elmundodelamoneda.com
Jean Elsen s.a.
www.elsen.be
eWanted
www.ewanted.com
Ira & Larry Goldberg Coins &
    Collectibles
www.goldbergcoins.com
Heritage Numismatic Auctions
www.heritagecoin.com
Jeffrey Hoare Auctions
www.jeffreyhoare.on.ca
Fred Holabird Americana
www.holabird.org
Jackson's
www.jacksonsauction.com
Lyn Knight Currency Auctions
www.lynknight.com
Lone Star Auctioneers
www.lonestarauctioneers.com

Please Note

Web sites often incorporate capital letters as part or all of their addresses. This is not always necessary. Please note that capital letters found in the addresses shown in this directory are ones necessary in order to arrive at the correct Web site.

Also, the prefix "www." is not always needed, and often it is necessary to leave it off. Please note that when a Web address listed here does not start with "www." that address will only work without this prefix.

Malter Galleries
www.maltergalleries.com
Greg Manning Auctions
www.gregmanning.com
MastroNet
www.mastronet.com
Ponterio & Associates
www.ponterio.com
Roxbury's Auction House
www.roxburys.com
Smythe
www.smytheonline.com
Sotheby's
www.sothebys.com
Spink & Son Ltd
www.spink-online.com
Stack's
www.stacks.com
Superior Galleries
www.superiorgalleries.com
Surpluzz.com
www.surpluzz.com
Tangible Asset Galleries
www.tagz.com
Teletrade Auctions
www.teletrade.com
Whyte's
www.whytes.ie

Numismatic Dealers
A-Mark Precious Metals
www.amark.com
Abbott's Corporation
www.abbottscorp.com
Alaska Mint
www.akmint.com
Albanese Rare Coins
www.coinace.com
All American Coin Company
www.aacoinco.com
American Gold Exchange
www.amergold.com
American Heritage Mint
www.mtnhighcoin.com
American Rare Coin Supply
www.rarecoinsupply.com
American Rarities
www.americanrarities.com
Amphora Coins
www.amphoracoins.com
Joel Anderson
www.joelscoins.com

Antique Carta
www.antiquecarta.com
Aspen Coins
www.aspencoins.com
Aspen Park Rare Coins
www.aprci.com
ATSnotes.com
www.atsnotes.com
Austin Rare Coins & Bullion
www.austincoins.com
Lois & Don Bailey Numismatic
    Services
www.donbailey-mexico.com
Bank Note Reporter
www.banknotereporter.com
BankNote1 Currency
www.banknote1.com
Ken Barr Numismatics
www.kenbarr.com
Alexander Basok
www.rustypennies.com
Harlan J. Berk, Ltd.
www.harlanjberk.com
Allen G. Berman
www.bermania.com
Blanchard and Company
www.blanchardonline.com
Bob's Coins & Collectibles
www.bobscoins.com

Bob's Coins, Collectibles and More
biblecom.tripod.com/aa-index.html
Bonavita Ltd.
www.eligi.ca/bonavita
Brooklyn Gallery Coins & Stamps
www.brooklyngallery.com
Byers Numismatic Corporation
www.byersnc.com
C & D Gale
www.cdgale.com/default.htm
Calgary Coin & Antique
www.calgarycoin.com
California Numismatic Investments
www.golddealer.com
Camco
www.camcocoin.com
Cameo CC
www.cameocc.com
Canadian Coinoisseur
www.coinoisseur.com
Cape Mint
www.exinet.co.za/pagliari/index.htm
Capital Collectors Plastics
www.capitalplastics.com/nnn
Carat-Coin-Collectibles
www.caratcoin.com
Carolina Gold & Silver
www.carolinacoin.com
CDA Bullion Precious Metals
www.cdabullion.com
Tom Cederlind Numismatics &
    Antiquities
www.tomcederlind.com
Centerville Coin & Jewelry
www.centercoin.com
CH Coins
www.chcoins.com
Robert Charles Coin Company
www.robertcharlescoins.com
Cheap Slab Store
www.cheapslabs.com
Chicago Coin Company
www.chicagocoin.com
David F. Cieniewicz
www.banknotestore.com
Civil War Tokens
www.civilwartokens.com
Cline's Rare Coins
www.slqs.com
Coast to Coast Coins
www.coastcoin.com

Cochran's Coins
www.cochran14k.com
The Coin and Currency Institute
www.coin-currency.com
Coincraft
www.coincraft.com
CoinCrazy.com
www.coincrazy.com
Coin Dealer Newsletter
www.greysheet.com
CoinFacts.com
www.coinfacts.com
Coin Gallery Online
www.coin-gallery.com
TheCoinGuy.com
www.thecoinguy.com
CoinIndex.com
www.coinindex.com
Coin Prices
www.coinpricesmagazine.net
Coin Restoration Service
www.crs-stockton.com
CoinScape
www.coinscape.com
Coin Shop
www.coin-shop.com
Coins International
www.coinsinternational.com
Coins Magazine
www.coinsmagazine.net
CoinsOfTheUSA.com
www.coinsoftheusa.com
Coin Webstore
www.coinwebstore.com
Coinwire.com
www.coinwire.com
Collectors Universe
www.collectors.com
Colonial Acres Coins
www.colonialacres.com
Compu-Quote
www.compu-quote.net
Continental Coin Investors
www.internet4coins.com
Corrosion Free Coin Supply, LLC
www.coinshield.com
Cybercoins
www.cybercoins.net
D & M Coins
www.dmcoins.com
Chuck D'Ambra Coins
www.telesphere.com/ts/coins

Dallas Gold & Silver Exchange
www.dgse.com
David Hall Rare Coins
www.davidhall.com
Denly's of Boston
www.denlys.com
Distinctive Coins
www.distinctivecoins.com
DistinctiveGiftware.com
www.distinctivegiftware.com
Michael Dixon Rare Coins
www.michaeldixonrarecoins.com
Dolphin Coins and Medals Ltd.
www.dolphincoins.com
Downies Ltd.
www.downies.com
Eagle Coin Supplies
www.eaglecoinholders.com
Eagle Eye Rare Coins
www.indiancent.com
Eagle Numismatics
www.coinmaven.com
Eureka Trading System
www.eurekatrading.com
Educational Coin Company
www.educationalcoin.com
Eligi Consultants
www.eligi.ca
Ellesmere Numismatics
www.ellesmerecoin.com
Elusive Spondulix
www.rarecoin.com
Estate Wholesalers
www.estatewholesaler.com
Steve Estes, P.N.
www.steveestes.com
Euro Collections International
www.eurocollections.com
Steve Eyer
www.eyersworld.com
Florida Coin & Jewelry
www.floridacoin.com
The Franklin Mint
www.franklinmint.com
Gaithersburg Coin Exchange
www.gaithersburgcoin.com
Gallery Mint Museum
www.gallerymint.com
Gatewest Coin Ltd.
www.gatewestcoin.com
Ronald J. Gillio
www.gillio.com

Goldline International
www.goldline.com
Gold Rarities Gallery
www.goldrarities.com
Graded Currency
www.gradedcurrency.com
Orville J. Grady
www.gradybooks.com
Great Lakes Coin Company
www.greatlakescoin.com
Hallenbeck Coin Gallery
www.hallenbeck-coins.com
Hancock & Harwell
www.raregold.com
H.E. Harris & Co.
www.heharris.com
Hans W. Hercher Munzen GmbH
www.herchercoins.com
Wayne Herndon Rare Coins
www.wayneherndon.com
Hobby Coin Exchange
www.hobbycoinexchange.com
Hoffman Mint
www.hoffmanmint.com
Richard Hokanson Rare
    Coin Investments
www.hokanson-coins.com
Randall P. Holder Rare Coins
www.rpholdercoins.bigstep.com
Horwedel's Currency
www.horwedelscurrency.com
House of Coins
www.houseofcoins.com
Hudson Rare Coins
www.hudsonrarecoins.com
International Coins & Currency
www.iccoin.com
J & J Coins
www.jjcoins.com
J & M Coin
www.jandm.com
Eric Jackson
www.ericjackson.com
Jake's Marketplace
www.jakesmp.net
Jamestown Stamp Company
www.jamestownstamp.com
Jefferson Coin & Bullion
www.jeffinc.com

Jencius Coins
www.vaticancoins.com
J.G.M. Numismatics
www.jgmnumismatics.com
Jim's Stamp & Coin Shop
www.thepilot.com/busdir/jimsstamp
Glen Johnson Rare U.S. Currency
www.uspapermoney.com
Kagin's
www.kagins.com
The Kanawha Coin Shop
www.kanawhacoin.com
Kelgory Coin and Currency Supply
www.kelgory.com
Don C. Kelly
www.donckelly.com
Jonathan K. Kern Company
www.jkerncoins.com
Keshequa Coins
www.keshequacoins.com
Jeff Kierstead Rare Coins
www.jkrarecoin.com
King of Carson City
www.carsoncityking.com
Kitco
www.kitco.com
Knight Coin
www.knightcoin.com
George Frederick Kolbe
www.numislit.com
Bill Kracov
www.choiceworldbanknotes.com
Krause Publications
www.collect.com
www.krause.com
www.coincollecting.net
Tim Kyzivat
www.kyzivatcurrency.com
George H. LaBarre Galleries
www.glabarre.com
Harry Laibstain Rare Coins
www.hlrc.com
David Lawrence Rare Coins
www.davidlawrence.com
Legend Numismatics
www.legendcoin.com
Julian M. Leidman
www.juliancoin.com
Bret Leifer Numismatics
www.coinguy.com

Liberty Coin Service
www.libertycoinservice.com
Libnick's Coins and Currency
www.libnick.com
Limited Editions
www.limitededitionsinc.org
Littleton Coin Company
www.littletoncoin.com
Lone Star Coins & Collectibles
www.lonestarcoins.com
Lone Star Mint
www.lsmint.com
Louisiana Gold & Gems
www.louisianagold.com
Luck 'E' Penny
www.wcmassey.com/lep/index.htm
Marc One Numismatics
www.marconenumismatics.com
Mark Johnson Coins & Supplies
www.mjcoins.com
Mayer Mint GmbH Germany
www.mayermint.com
McKinn's Coins
www.mckinn.com
McQueeney Coins
www.mcqueeneycoins.com
Mexican Coin Company
www.mexicancoincompany.com
Midwest Estate Buyers
www.midwest-estate-buyers.com
Mietens & Partner
www.mietens.de
Miller's Mint Ltd.
www.millersmint.com
Minneapolis Gold, Silver and
  Numismatic Services
www.coindeals.com
Mintmark Numismatics
www.mintmark.com
Money-Changers
www.home.earthlink.net/
  ~moneychanger/index.html
Mountain High Coins & Collectibles
www.mtnhighcoin.com
Mount Vernon Coin Company
www.mtvcoins.com
The Naples Bank Note Company
www.banknotables.com
Colin Narbeth & Son
www.colin-narbeth.com
National Collectors Mint
www.ncmint.com

National Gold Exchange
www.ngegold.com
New World Rarities Ltd.
www.nwrarities.com
North American Certified Trading
www.natcoin.com
Northeast Numismatics
www.northeastcoin.com
www.foreigncoin.com
Nostomania
www.nostomania.com
NumisAd
www.numisgroup.com
Numismatic Assets
www.numismaticassets.com
Numismatic News
www.numismaticnews.net
NumisMedia
www.numismedia.com
Numis-Phil Pte. Ltd.
www.worldcurrency.com
Old Coin Shop
www.oldcoinshop.com
Olde Towne Coin Company
www.oldetownecoin.com
Old Pueblo Coin
www.oldpueblocoin.com
Original Weather Coin Company
www.weathercoin.com
Pacific Atlantic Coin Company
www.pacoin.com
PandaAmerica
www.pandaamerica.com
PaperMoneyFacts.com
www.papermoneyfacts.com
Paradise Coin & Gift
www.paradisecoin.com
Park Avenue Numismatics
www.parkavenumis.com
Jay Parrino's The Mint LLC
www.jp-themint.com
Penny Farmer
www.pennyfarmer.com
Perth Numismatics
www.perthmoney.com
Pinnacle Rarities
www.pinnaclerarities.com
Tony Pisciotta
www.banknotesoftheworld.com
Ken Potter
koinpro.tripod.com

Premier Precious Metals
www.premierpreciousmetals.com
Tim Prusmack
www.money-art.com
Puro's Coins and Jewelry
www.vtcoins.com
R & I Coins
www.ricoins.com
Rare Coin Company of America
www.coinsthatmatter.com
RareCurrency.com
www.rarecurrency.com
Hans & Beate Rauch
www.apcpapercollect.com
Richard J. Reed World Paper Money
www.misterbanknote.com
James J. Reeves
www.jamesjreeves.com
Regency Coins
www.rgncycoin.com
Bob Reis' Anything Anywhere
www.anythinganywhere.com
Joel D. Rettew
www.fastcoin.com
Roy Reynolds Coins
*www.geocities.com/rodeodrive/7533/
    royhomepage.html*
River City Coins & Jewelry
www.rivercitycoins.com
Frank S. Robinson
www.albany.net/~fr/index.html
RR Rare Coins and Currency
www.rrcoins.net
Sahara Coins LLC
www.saharacoins.com
San Joaquin Valley Rare Coins
goldcoin.dds-tech.net
Wayne G. Sayles
www.ancientcoins.ac
Jim Sazama
www.jimsazama.com
Rich Schemmer
www.richerrors.com
Reinhard Schimmer GmbH
www.schimmer.de
Scotsman Coin and Currency
www.scoins.com
Daniel Frank Sedwick
www.sedwickcoins.com
David Seelye
www.thempcman.net

Shawnee Coin Company
www.shawneecoin.com
Showcase Coins
www.showcasecoins.com
Showgard
www.showgard.com
Sigma Ancient Coins
www.sigmacoins.com
Silver State Coin & Bullion
www.silverstatecoin.com
SilverTowne
www.silvertowne.com
Slater Numismatics
www.slatercoins.com
Sam Sloat Coins
sloat.coinnet.com
Southern Coin Investments
www.southerncoin.com
Southern Coins and Precious Metals
www.scpm.com
Spectrum Numismatics
www.spectrumnumismatics.com
Stanton Books & Supplies
www.stantonbooks.com
Steinberg's
www.steinbergs.com
Sunshine Rarities
www.sunshinerarities.com
Anthony J. Swiatek Numismatics
www.anthonyjswiatek.com
Swiss America Trading Corporation
www.swissamerica.com
M. Louis Teller Numismatic Company
www.tellercoins.com
G.R. Tiso Numismatics
www.grtiso.com
Tiitus Syngraphics
www.syngraphics.net/imbl
Token Publishing
www.medal-news.com
Scott Travers Rare Coin Galleries
www.inch.com/~travers/travers3.htm
Trove Software
www.trovesoftware.com
The Tulving Company
www.tulving.com
UBS Gold & Numismatics
*www.ubs.com/e/pb/solutions/
    numismatics.html*

USA Rare
www.usarare.com
USCents.com
www.uscents.com
U.S. Currency Online
www.uscurrencyonline.com
USMintQuarters.com
www.usmintquarters.com
U.S. State Quarters.com
www.usstatequarters.com
Valley View Coins & Collectibles
www.valleyviewcoins.com
Edward J. Waddell, Ltd.
www.coin.com
Washington Mint
www.washingtonmint.com
Washington Square Coin Exchange
www.wscoin.com
Fred Weinberg & Co.
www.fredweinberg.com
West Bay Trading Company
www.westbaytrading.com
Pam West British Bank Notes
www.west-banknotes.co.uk
Scott J. Winslow Associates
www.scottwinslow.com
Douglas Winter Numismatics
www.raregoldcoins.com
Charles W. Woodruff Rare
    Coins & Currency
www.cwwoodruff.com
The Working Man's Rare Coins
www.workingmancoins.com
World Coin News
www.worldcoinnews.net
World Exonumia
www.exonumia.com
WorldWide Coins
www.wwc.coins.ru
WVW Classics
www.wvwclassics.com
William Youngerman
www.williamyoungerman.com
Jeffrey S. Zarit
www.klippes.com

Numismatic Organizations

Albuquerque Coin Club
www.albuquerquecoinclub.org
Alexandria Coin Club
*www.members.cox.net/
    alexandriacoinclub*

American Israel
    Numismatic Association
www.amerisrael.com
American Medallic
    Sculpture Association
www.amsamedals.org
American Numismatic Association
www.money.org
American Numismatic Society
www.amnumsoc.org
www.numismatics.org
American Play Money Society
*www.members.tripod.com/
    playmoneytoo/apms/home.html*
American Society of Check Collectors
members.aol.com/asccinfo
Americans for Common Cents
www.pennies.org
APL Coin Club
www.money.org/clubs/apl_index.html
Atlantic Provinces
    Numismatic Association
www.nunetcan.net/apna.htm
Baltimore Coin Club
www.money.org/club_bcc.html
Bexley Coin Club
www.bexleycoinclub.org.uk
Big Island Coin Club
www.collectibleshawaii.com
Blue Ridge Numismatic Association
www.brna.org
British Association of
    Numismatic Societies
www.coinclubs.freeserve.co.uk
Calgary Numismatic Society
www.ucalgary.ca/~cns
California State
    Numismatic Association
www.coinmall.com/CSNA
Canadian Association of
    Numismatic Dealers
www.nunetcan.net/cand.htm
Canadian Association of Token
    Collectors
www.nunetcan.net/catc.htm
Canadian Association of Wooden
    Money Collectors
www.nunetcan.net/cawmc.htm
Canadian Numismatic Association
www.canadian-numismatic.org

Canadian Numismatic
  Research Society
www.nunetcan.net/cnrs.htm
Canadian Paper Money Society
www.nunetcan.net/cpms.htm
Casino Chips and Gaming Tokens
  Collectors Club
www.ccgtcc.com
Central Florida Coin Club
www.centralfloridacoinclub.org
Central States Numismatic Society
www.centralstates.info
Chicago Coin Club
www.chicagocoinclub.org
Chippewa Valley Coin Club
www.54701.com/clubs/cvcc/index.htm
Civil War Token Society
www.cwtsociety.com
Classical & Medieval
  Numismatic Society
www.nunetcan.net/cmns.htm
Clements High School Coin Club
*www.fortbendisd.com/campuses/chs/
  ActivityDetail.cfm?activityIndex=
  10067*
Coin Master's Online Coin Club
www.coinmasters.org
Columbus Numismatic Society/
  Central Ohio International
  Numismatic Society
www.cnscoins.com
Combined Organization of Numis-
  matic Error Collectors of America
www.conecaonline.org
CopperCoins.com
www.coppercoins.com
Crescent City Coin Club
www.money.org/clubs/cccc_index.html
Croatian Philatelic Society
www.croatianmall.com/cps/index.htm
CSA Collectors Page
www.csacurrency.com
Denver Coin Club
www.telesphere.com/ts/dcc
Early American Coppers
www.eacs.org
Edmonton Numismatic Society
www.edmontoncoinclub.com
Elgin Coin Club
www.prairienet.com/coins/ecc
The Elongated Collectors
www.tecnews.org

Florida United Numismatists
www.funtopics.com
Fox Valley Coin Club
www.prairienet.com/coins/fvcc
Fractional Currency Collectors Board
www.fractionalcurrency.org
Full Horn Buffalo Nickel Club
*www.geocities.com/
  RodeoDrive/4044/fullhorn.html*
Garden State Numismatic Association
www.gsna.org
Glendale Coin Club
www.glencoin.com
Greater Houston Coin Club
www.money.org/sum-ross.html
Greater Jacksonville Coin Club
www.angelfire.com/fl/gjccweb
Hawaii State Numismatic Association
www.hawaiicollectibles.org
Illinois Numismatic Association
www.ilnaclub.org
International Association of
  Professional Numismatists
www.iapn.ch/iapn
International Bank Note Society
www.ibns.it
International Bond & Share Society
www.scripophily.org
International Numismatic
  Commission
www.amnumsoc.org/inc
Islamic Coins Group
www.islamiccoinsgroup.50g.com
John Reich Collectors Society
www.jrcs.org
Johnson County Numismatic Society
www.money.org/club_jcns.html
Liberty Seated Collectors Club
www.numismalink.com/lscc.html
Lincoln Coin Club
*www.geocities.com/jb91437/
  LincolnCoinClub.html*
Lower Cape Fear Coin Club
www.money.org/clubs/lcfcc.html
Marion Coin Club
*www.members.tripod.com/
  marioncoinclub*
Maryland State Numismatic
  Association
www.money.org/club_msna.html

Maryland Token and Medal Society
www.money.org/clubs/mdtams/mdtams
.html
Metropolitan Coin Club of Atlanta
www.mccatl.org
Model City Coin Club
home.tricon.net/alanphil/mccc.html
Montgomery County Coin Club
www.money.org/club_mccc.html
Mount Vernon Numismatic Society
www.money.org/clubs/mvns_main.htm
National Collectors Association of
    Die Doubling
www.geocities.com/Research Triangle/
    Facility/4968/NCADD.html
National Token Collectors Association
home.pacbell.net/tokenbob
North Carolina Numismatic
    Association
www.ncnaonline.org
Numismatic Association of
    Southern California
www.nasc.net
Numismatic Bibliomania Society
www.coinbooks.org
Numismatic Literary Guild
www.numismaticliteraryguild.org
Numismatic Network Canada
www.nunetcan.net
Oak Park Coin Club
www.oakparkcoinclub.com
Ontario Numismatic Society
www.nunetcan.net/ona.htm
Oriental Numismatic Society
www.onsnumis.org
Original Hobo Nickel Society
www.hobonickels.org
Oslo Numismatic Society
www.mynter.org/onf
Pacific Coast Numismatic Society
www.pcns.org
Pacific County Friends of
    Lewis and Clark
www.lewisandclarkingot.com
Pacific Northwest Numismatic
    Association
www.pnna.org
Peninsula Coin Club
www.stanford.edu/~clint/pcc
Pennsylvania Association of
    Numismatists
www.money.org/club_pan.html

Pensacola Numismatic Association
coinclub.freeyellow.com
Prince Edward Island Numismatic
    Association
www.angelfire.com/art/peina
Professional Numismatists Guild
www.pngdealers.com
Raleigh Coin Club
www.raleighcoinclub.org
Rockford Area Coin Club
www.exonumia.com/racc.htm
Roxbury Coin Club
www.ledgewood.net/rcc
Royal Numismatic Society
www.rns.dircon.co.uk
Royal Numismatic Society of
    New Zealand
www.geocities.com/rnsnz
San Jose Coin Club
www.sanjosecoinclub.org
Society for U.S.
    Commemorative Coins
www.money.org/clubs/suscc.html
Society of Paper Money Collectors
www.spmc.org
Society of Philatelists and
    Numismatists
span.atsecure.net
Society of U.S. Pattern Collectors
www.uspatterns.com
Stanislaus County Coin Club
www.stancocoinclub.com
Swedish Numismatic Society
www.users.wineasy.se/snf
Tasmanian Numismatic Society
www.vision.net.au/~pwood/tns.html
Tennessee State Numismatic Society
www.tsns.org
Texas Numismatic Association
www.tna.org
Token and Medal Society
www.money.org/clubs/tams/index.html
U.S. Mexican Numismatic Association
www.grasshoppernet.com/walrafen/us
    mexna.html
Victoria Numismatic Society
www.victoria.tc.ca/Recreation/VNS
Washington Historical Autograph and
    Certificate Organization
www.whaco.com

Washington Numismatic Society
*www.money.org/clubs/wns/wns_index.
    html*
Waterloo Coin Society
www.angelfire.com/tx/wcshomepage
Willamette Coin Club
www.pdxcoinclub.org
Wilmington Coin Club
www.money.org/clubs/wcc.html
Women In Numismatics
www.money.org/sum-baber.html
Wooden Nickel Collector's
    Organization
www.wooden-nickel.org
Worldwide Bi-Metallic Collectors
    Club
www.wbcc-online.com
Young Numismatists of America
www.ynaclub.org

Miscellaneous Related Sites
American Bankers Association
www.abacoins.com
Art in the Hand Gallery
www.artinthehand.com
Asset Strategies International
www.assetstrategies.com
Bank for International Settlements –
    Central Bank Web sites
www.bis.org/cbanks1.htm
The Harry Bass Research Foundation
www.hbrf.org
Bick International
www.bick.net
The British Museum
www.thebritishmuseum.ac.uk
Bureau of Engraving and Printing
www.moneyfactory.com
www.bep.treas.gov
California Gold Marketing Group
www.sscentralamerica.com
Canadian Coin Reference Site
www.canadiancoin.com
Canadian Numismatic
    Bibliography Project
www.julaine.ca/canbiblio
Carlisle Development Corporation
www.carlisledevelopment.com
CCE and FACTS
www.certifiedcoinexchange.com
www.cce-auction.com

CNN Financial Network
cnnfn.cnn.com
CoinClubs.com
www.coinclubs.com
Coin Coalition
www.coincoalition.org
CoinGrading.com
www.coingrading.com
CoinLink
www.coinlink.com
Coin Optics
www.coinoptics.com
CoinResource.com
www.coinresource.com
Coinsheet Numismatic Directory
www.coinsheetlinks.com
Coinstar
www.coinstar.com
Coin Today
www.goldstockcenter.com/index2.htm
Collectify
www.collectify.com
Collectorama Show
*www.hometown.aol.com/
    collectoramashow/index.html*
Collectors Software
www.vpackrat.com
U.S. Commission of Fine Arts
www.cfa.gov
Congressional Medal of Honor
    Society
www.cmohs.org
Enroute.ca
www.enroute.ca
Federal Reserve Bank of Richmond
    Money Museum
*www.rich.frb.org/econed/museum/
    index.html*
Forrest's Token Page
*users.pullman.com/fjstevens/tokens/
    index.html*
GFMS Ltd.
www.gfms.co.uk
Gold Institute
www.goldinstitute.org
Gold Rush Gallery
www.goldrushgallery.com
Goldsheet Numismatic Web Page
www.goldsheetlinks.com/index.htm
Industry Council for Tangible Assets
www.ictaonline.org

International Collectible Expo
www.collectibleshow.com
Jewish-American Hall of Fame
www.amuseum.org/jahf
Johnson Matthey
www.johnsonmatthey.com
Krause Publications
www.collect.com
www.krause.com
www.coincollecting.net
Londoh.com
www.londoh.com
London Banknote and Monetary
 Research Centre Ltd.
www.lbmrc.co.uk
Long Beach Coin, Stamp &
 Collectibles Expo
www.longbeachshow.com
MonsterCoin.com
www.monstercoin.com
Museum of American Financial
 History
www.financialhistory.org
National Numismatic Collection
www.americanhistory.si.edu/csr/
 cadnnc.htm
National Trust for Historic
 Preservation
www.nationaltrust.org
Norfed
www.norfed.org
Numismatica
www.limunltd.com/numismatica
Numismaticards
www.cointradingcards.com
Platinum Guild International
www.platinumguild.org
Saint-Gaudens National Historic Site
www.sgnhs.org
Santa Clara Coin, Stamp &
 Collectibles Expo
www.santaclarashow.com
Silver Institute
www.silverinstitute.org
Smithsonian Institute
www.si.edu
Southeast Asian Treasury
www.seasiantreasury.com
Stonewalls Civil War Currency
www.home.earthlink.net/~icepick119

Trade Token Tales
members.fortunecity.com/tokenguy/
 tokentales
U.S. Secret Service
www.treas.gov/usss
U.S. Treasury
www.ustreas.gov
U.S. Treasury – Office of the
 Inspector General
www.ustreas.gov/oig
Universal Currency Converter
www.xe.net/ucc
University of Notre Dame – Coin and
 Currency Collections
www.coins.nd.edu
Vendio
www.vendio.com
Where's George?
www.wheresgeorge.com
Where's Willy?
www.whereswilly.com
World Gold Council
www.gold.org

World Mint Sites

Austrian Mint
www.austrian-mint.com
 Austria's North American rep.
  www.eurocollections.com
Bermuda Monetary Authority
www.bma.bm
British Royal Mint
www.royalmint.com
Czech Mint
www.bcm.cz
The French Mint
www.monnaiedeparis.com
Israel Government Coins and
 Medals Corp. Ltd.
www.coins.co.il
Mexican Mint
www.cmonedam.com.mx
The Mint Bureau (Japan)
www.mint.go.jp
Mint of Finland
www.mint.fi
Perth Mint
www.perthmint.com.au
Pobjoy Mint Ltd.
www.pobjoy.com

Polish State Mint
www.mennica.com.pl
Royal Australian Mint
www.ramint.gov.au
Royal Canadian Mint
www.mint.ca
www.monnaie.ca
Royal Norwegian Mint
www.dkm.no
San Marino Mint
www.aasfn.sm
Singapore Mint
www.singaporemint.com.sg
South African Mint
www.samint.co.za
Spanish Mint
www.fnmt.es
Turkish State Mint
www.mint.gov.tr/english.htm
U.S. Mint
www.usmint.gov

U.S. Federal Reserve Banks

Atlanta, Ga.
www.atl.frb.org
Board of Governors of the Federal
    Reserve System
www.federalreserve.gov
Boston, Mass.
www.bos.frb.org
Chicago, Ill.
www.chicagofed.org
Cleveland, Ohio
www.clevelandfed.org

Dallas, Texas
www.dallasfed.org
Kansas City, Kan.
www.kc.frb.org
Minneapolis, Minn.
www.minneapolisfed.org
New York, N.Y.
www.ny.frb.org
Philadelphia, Pa.
www.phil.frb.org
Richmond, Va.
www.rich.frb.org
San Francisco, Calif.
www.sf.frb.org
St. Louis, Mo.
www.stls.frb.org

Theft Reporting Sites

CoinFacts.com
*www.coinfacts.com/Administrative/
    stolen_coin_reports.htm*
World Exonumia
www.exonumia.com/stolen.htm

Euro Sites

Euro Bill Tracker
www.eurobilltracker.com
Euro Issues
home.hetnet.nl/~asliesem
European Union
www.europa.eu.int/euro
Euro-sceptic Web Resource
www.euro-sceptic.org
Microsoft Windows – Euro Support
www.microsoft.com/windows/euro.asp

Newsgroups

For those who wish to communicate with other collectors more directly, there are newsgroups.

search.mailgate.org/rec/rec.colle cting.coins
search.mailgate.org/rec/rec.colle cting.paper-money
groups.google.com

Missing?

If your group or organization's Internet address has never appeared in our Web directory, let us know and we'll put it in a future edition.

Just contact us by writing to *North American Coins & Prices*, F+W Publications, 700 E. State St., Iola, WI 54990 or send e-mail to David.Harper@FWPubs.com.

Glossary of coin terms

Adjustment marks: Marks made by use of a file to correct the weight of over-weight coinage planchets prior to striking. Adjusting the weight of planchets was a common practice at the first U.S. Mint in Philadelphia and was often carried out by women hired to weigh planchets and do any necessary filing of the metal.

Altered coin: A coin that has been changed after it left the mint. Such changes are often to the date or mintmark of a common coin in an attempt to increase its value by passing to an unsuspecting buyer as a rare date or mint.

Alloy: A metal or mixture of metals added to the primary metal in the coinage composition, often as a means of facilitating hardness during striking. For example, most U.S. silver coins contain an alloy of 10 percent copper.

Anneal: To heat in order to soften. In the minting process planchets are annealed prior to striking.

Authentication: The act of determining whether a coin, medal, token or other related item is a genuine product of the issuing authority.

Bag marks: Scrapes and impairments to a coin's surface obtained after minting by contact with other coins. The term originates from the storage of coins in bags, but such marks can occur as coins leave the presses and enter hoppers. A larger coin is more susceptible to marks, which affect its grade and, therefore, its value.

Base metal: A metal with low intrinsic value.

Beading: A form of design around the edge of a coin. Beading once served a functional purpose of deterring clipping or shaving parts of the metal by those looking to make a profit and then return the debased coin to circulation.

Blank: Often used in reference to the coinage planchet or disc of metal from which the actual coin is struck. Planchets or blanks are punched out of a sheet of metal by what is known as a blanking press.

Business strike: A coin produced for circulation.

Beading ➜

Cast copy: A copy of a coin or medal made by a casting process in which molds are used to produce the finished product. Casting imparts a different surface texture to the finished product than striking and often leaves traces of a seam where the molds came together.

Center dot: A raised dot at the center of a coin caused by use of a compass to aid the engraver in the circular positioning of die devices, such as stars, letters, and dates. Center dots are prevalent on early U.S. coinage.

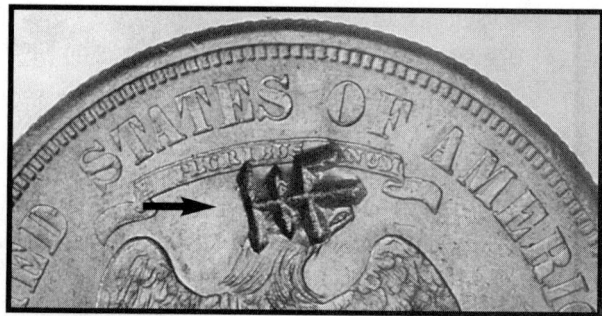

Chop mark ➜

Chop mark: A mark used by Oriental merchants as a means of guaranteeing the silver content of coins paid out. The merchants' chop marks, or stamped insignia, often obliterated the original design of the host coin. U.S. Trade dollars, struck from 1873 through 1878 and intended for use in trade with China, are sometimes found bearing multiple marks.

Clash marks: Marks impressed in the coinage dies when they come together without a planchet between them. Such marks will affect coins struck subsequently by causing portions of the obverse design to appear in raised form on the reverse, and vice versa.

Clipping: The practice of shaving or cutting small pieces of metal from a coin in circulation. Clipping was prevalent in Colonial times as a means of surreptitiously extracting precious metal from a coin before placing it back into circulation. The introduction of beading and a raised border helped to alleviate the problem.

Coin alignment: U.S. coins are normally struck with an alignment by which, when a coin is held by the top and bottom edge and rotated from side-to-side, the reverse will appear upside down.

Collar: A ring-shaped die between which the obverse and reverse coinage dies are held during striking. The collar contains the outward flow during striking and can be used to produce edge reeding.

Commemorative: A coin issued to honor a special event or person. United States commemorative coins have historically been produced for sale to collectors and not placed in circulation, though the 50-states quarters are circulating commemoratives.

Copy: A replica of an original issue. Copies often vary in quality and metallic composition from the original. Since passage of the Hobby Protection Act (Public Law 93-167) of Nov. 29, 1973, it has been illegal to produce or import copies of coins or other numismatic items that are not clearly and permanently marked with the word "Copy."

Counterfeit: A coin or medal or other numismatic item made fraudulently, either for entry into circulation or sale to collectors.

Denticles: The toothlike pattern found around a coin's obverse or reverse border.

Die: A cylindrical piece of metal containing an incuse image that imparts a raised image when stamped into a planchet.

Die crack: A crack that develops in a coinage die after extensive usage, or if the die is defective or is used to strike harder metals. Die cracks, which often run through border lettering, appear as raised lines on the finished coin.

Device: The principal design element.

Double eagle: Name adopted by the Act of March 3, 1849, for the gold coin valued at 20 units or $20.

Rim

Field

Mintmark

Exergue

Obverse

Legend

Reverse

Eagle: Name adopted by the Coinage Act of 1792 for a gold coin valued at 10 units or $10. Also a name used to refer to gold, silver, and platinum coins of the American Eagle bullion coinage program begun in 1986.

Edge: The cylindrical surface of a coin between the two sides. The edge can be plain, reeded, ornamented, or lettered.

Electrotype: A copy of a coin, medal, or token made by electroplating.

Exergue: The lower segment of a coin, below the main design, generally separated by a line and often containing the date, designer initials, and mintmark.

Face value: The nominal legal-tender value assigned to a given coin by the governing authority.

Fasces: A Roman symbol of authority consisting of a bound bundle of rods and an axe.

Field: The flat area of a coin's obverse or reverse, devoid of devices or inscriptions.

Galvano: A reproduction of a proposed design from an artist's original model produced in plaster or other substance and then electroplated with metal. The galvano is then used in a reducing lathe to make a die or hub.

Glory: A heraldic term for stars, rays or other devices placed as if in the sky or luminous.

Grading: The largely subjective practice of providing a numerical or adjectival ranking of the condition of a coin, token, or medal. The grade is often a major determinant of value.

Gresham's law: The name for the observation made by Sir Thomas Gresham, 16th century English financier, that when two coins with the same face value but different intrinsic values are in circulation at the same time, the one with the lesser intrinsic value will remain in circulation while the other is hoarded.

Half eagle: Name adopted by the Coinage Act of 1792 for a gold coin valued at five units or $5.

Hub: A piece of die steel showing the coinage devices in relief. The hub is used to produce a die that, in contrast, has the relief details incuse. The die is then used to produce the final coin, which looks much the same as the hub. Hubs may be reused to make new dies.

These Canadian Olympic commemoratives have lettered edges.

Legend: A coin's principal lettering, generally shown along its outer perimeter.

Lettered edge: Incuse or raised lettering on a coin's edge.

Matte proof: A proof coin on which the surface is granular or dull. On U.S. coins this type of surface was used on proofs of the early 20th century. The process has since been abandoned.

Magician's coin: A term sometimes used to describe a coin with two heads or two tails. Such a coin is considered impossible in normal production due to physical differences in obverse and reverse die mountings, though as of 2001 two have been certified as genuine by professional coin authenticators. The vast majority are products made outside the Mint as novelty pieces.

Medal: Made to commemorate an event or person. Medals differ from coins in that a medal is not legal tender and, in general, is not produced with the intent of circulating as money.

A medal usually commemorates an event but has no monetary value. It can be issued by a private entity or a government.

Medal alignment: Medals are generally struck with the coinage dies facing the same direction during striking. When held by the top and bottom edge and rotated from side-to-side, a piece struck in this manner will show both the obverse and reverse right side up.

Mintage: The total number of coins struck during a given time frame, generally one year.

Mintmark: A letter or other marking on a coin's surface to identify the mint at which the coin was struck.

Mule: The combination of two coinage dies not intended for use together.

Numismatics: The science, study or collecting of coins, tokens, medals, paper money, and related items.

Obverse: The front or "heads" side of a coin, medal, or token.

Overdate: Variety produced when one or more digits of the date are repunched over an old date on a die at the Mint, generally to save on dies or correct an error. Portions of the old date can still be seen under the new one.

Overmintmark: Variety created at the Mint when a different mintmark is punched over an already existing mintmark, generally done to make a coinage die already punched for one mint usable at another. Portions of the old mintmark can still be seen under the new one.

Overstrike: A coin, token or medal struck over another coin, token, or medal.

Pattern: A trial strike of a proposed coin design, issued by the Mint or authorized agent of a governing authority. Patterns can be in a variety of metals, thicknesses, and sizes.

This U.S. Trade dollar has a reeded edge.

Phrygian cap: A close-fitting, egg-shell-shaped hat placed on the head of a freed slave when Rome was in its ascendancy. Hung from a pole, it was a popular symbol of freedom during the French Revolution and in 18th century United States.

Planchet: A disc of metal or other material on which the image of the dies are impressed, resulting in a finished coin. Also sometimes called a blank.

Proof: A coin struck twice or more from specially polished dies and polished planchets. Modern proofs are prepared with a mirror finish. Early 20th century proofs were prepared with a matte surface.

Prooflike: A prooflike coin exhibits some of the characteristics of a proof despite having been struck by regular production processes. Many Morgan dollars are found with prooflike surfaces. The field will have a mirror background similar to that of a proof, and design details are frosted like some proofs.

Quarter eagle: Name adopted by the Coinage Act of 1792 for a gold coin valued at 2.5 units or $2.50.

Reeding: Serrated (toothlike) ornamentation applied to the coin's edge during striking.

Relief: The portion of a design raised above the surface of a coin, medal, or token.

A token is issued by a private entity and can be redeemed for its face value in trade or service.

Restrike: A coin, medal or token produced from original dies at a later date, often with the purpose of sale to collectors.

Reverse: The backside or "tails" side of a coin, medal or token, opposite from the principal figure of the design or obverse.

Rim: The raised area bordering the edge and surrounding the field.

Series: The complete group of coins of the same denomination and design and representing all issuing mints.

Token: A privately issued piece, generally in metal, with a represented value in trade or offer of service. Tokens are also produced for advertising purposes.

Type coin: A coin from a given series representing the basic design. A type coin is collected as an example of a particular design rather than for its date and mint-mark.

Variety: Any coin noticeably different in dies from another of the same design, date and mint. Overdate and overmintmarks are examples of varieties.

Wire edge: Created when coinage metal flows between the coinage die and collar, producing a thin flange of coin metal at the outside edge or edges of a coin.

Introduction to pricing

The following value guide is divided into six sections:
1. U.S. minting varieties and errors.
2. Colonial coins, issued prior to the establishment of the United States
3. U.S. issues of 1792.
4. U.S. issues of 1793-present.
5. Canadian coins.
6. Mexican coins.

Value listings

Values listed in the following price guide are average retail prices. These are the approximate prices collectors can expect to pay when purchasing coins from dealers. They are not offers to buy or sell. The pricing section should be considered a guide only; actual selling prices will vary.

The values were compiled by Krause Publications' independent staff of market analysts. They derived the values listed by monitoring auction results, business on electronic dealer trading networks, and business at major shows, and in consultation with a panel of dealers. For rare coins, when only a few specimens of a particular date and mintmark are known, a confirmed transaction may occur only once every several years. In those instances, the most recent auction result is listed.

Grading

Values are listed for coins in various states of preservation, or grades. Standards used in determining grades for U.S. coins are those set by the American Numismatic Association. See Chapter 4 for more on grading.

Dates and mintmarks

The dates listed are the individual dates that appear on each coin. The letter that follows the date is the mintmark and indicates where the coin was struck: "C" — Charlotte, N.C. (1838-1861); "CC" — Carson City, Nev. (1870-1893); "D" — Dahlonega, Ga. (1838-1861), and Denver (1906-present); "O" New Orleans (1838-1909); "P" — Philadelphia (1793-present); "S" San Francisco (1854-present); and "W" — West Point, N.Y. (1984-present). Coins without mintmarks were struck at Philadelphia.

A slash mark in a date indicates an overdate. This means a new date was engraved on a die over an old date. For example, if the date is listed as "1899/8," an 1898 die had a 9 engraved over the last 8 in the date. Portions of the old numeral are still visible on the coin.

A slash mark in a mintmark listing indicates an overmintmark (example: "1922-P/D"). The same process as above occurred, but this time a new mintmark was engraved over an old.

See the "U.S. Minting Varieties and Errors" section for more information on overdates and overmintmarks.

Price charts

Pricing data for the selected charts in the U.S. section were taken from the January issues of "Coin Prices" for the years indicated.

Mexican coin mintages

Quantities minted of each date are indicated when that information is available, generally stated in millions and rounded off to the nearest 10,000 pieces. The following mintage conversion formulas are used:

10,000,000 — 10.000.
1,000,000 — 1,000.
100,000 — 100.
10,000 — .010.
9,999 — 9,999.
1,000 — 1,000.
842 — 842 pcs. (pieces).
27 — 27 pcs.

Precious-metal content

Throughout this book precious-metal content is indicated in troy ounces. One troy ounce equals 480 grains, or 31.103 grams.

Abbreviations

AGW. Actual gold weight.

APW. Actual platinum weight.

ASW. Actual silver weight.

BV. Bullion value. This indicates the coin's current value is based on the amount of its precious-metal content and the current price for that metal.

Est. Indicates the exact mintage is not known and the figure listed is an estimate.

G. Grams.

Inc. Abv. Indicates the mintage for the date and mintmark listed is included in the previous listing.

KM#. In the Canadian and Mexican price sections, indicates "Krause-Mishler number." This sequential cataloging numbering system originated with the *Standard Catalog of World Coins* by Chester L. Krause and Clifford Mishler, and provides collectors with a means for identifying world issues.

Leg. Legend.

Mkt value. Market value.

MM. Millimeters.

Obv. Obverse.

P/L. Indicates "prooflike," a type of finish used on some Canadian coins.

Rev. Reverse.

Spec. Indicates "specimen," a type of finish used on some Canadian coins.

PRICING
SECTION

U.S. Minting Varieties and Errors

Introduction

By Alan Herbert

The P.D.S. cataloging system used here to list minting varieties was originally compiled by Alan Herbert in 1971. PDS stands for the three main divisions of the minting process, "planchet," "die" and "striking." Two more divisions cover collectible modifications after the strike, as well as non-collectible alterations, counterfeits and damaged coins.

This listing includes 445 classes, each a distinct part of the minting process or from a specific non-mint change in the coin. Classes from like causes are grouped together. The PDS system applies to coins of the world, but is based on U.S. coinage with added classes for certain foreign minting practices.

Price ranges are based on a U.S. coin in MS-60 grade (uncirculated.) The ranges may be applied in general to foreign coins of similar size or value although collector values are not usually as high as for U.S. coins. Prices are only a guide as the ultimate price is determined by a willing buyer and seller.

To define minting varieties, "A coin which exhibits a variation of any kind from the normal, as a result of any portion of the minting process, whether at the planchet stage, as a result of a change or modification of the die, or during the striking process. It includes those classes considered to be intentional changes, as well as those caused by normal wear and tear on the dies or other minting equipment and classes deemed to be "errors."

The three causes are represented as follows:
1. (I) = Intentional Changes
2. (W) = Wear and Tear
3. (E) = Errors
Note: A class may show more than one cause and could be listed as (IWE).

Rarity level

The rarity ratings are based on the following scale:
1 - Very Common. Ranges from every coin struck down to 1,000,000.
2 - Common. From 1,000,000 down to 100,000.
3 - Scarce. From 100,000 down to 10,000.

4 - Very Scarce. From 10,000 down to 1,000.

5 - Rare. From 1,000 down to 100.

6 - Very Rare. From 100 down to 10.

7 - Extremely Rare. From 10 down to 1.

Unknown: If there is no confirmed report of a piece fitting a particular class, it is listed as Unknown. Reports of finds by readers would be appreciated in order to update future presentations.

An Unknown does not mean that your piece automatically is very valuable. Even a Rarity 7 piece, extremely rare, even unique, may have a very low collector value because of a lack of demand or interest in that particular class.

Classes, definitions and price ranges are based on material previously offered in Alan Herbert's book, *The Official Price Guide to Minting Varieties and Errors* and in *Coin Prices* Magazine.

Pricing information has also been provided by John A. Wexler and Ken Potter, with special pricing and technical advice from Del Romines.

Also recommended is the *Cherrypicker's Guide to Rare Die Varieties* by Bill Fivaz and J.T. Stanton. Check your favorite coin shop, numismatic library or book seller for availability of the latest edition.

For help with your coin questions, to report significant new finds and for authentication of your minting varieties, include a loose first class stamp and write to Alan Herbert, 700 E. State St., Iola, WI 54990-0001. Don't include any numismatic material until you have received specific mailing instructions from me.

Quick check index

If you have a coin and are not sure where to look for the possible variety:

If your coin shows doubling, first check V-B-I.

Then try II-A, II-B, II-C, II-I (4 & 5), III-J, III-L, or IV-C.

If part of the coin is missing, check III-B, III-C, or III-D.

If there is a raised line of coin metal, check II-D, II-G.

If there is a raised area of coin metal, check II-E, II-F, or III-F.

If the coin is out of round, and too thin, check III-G.

If coin appears to be the wrong metal, check III-A, III-E, III-F-3 and III-G.

If the die appears to have been damaged, check II-E, II-G. (Damage to the coin itself usually is not a minting variety.)

If the coin shows incomplete or missing design, check II-A, II-E, III-B-3, III-B-5 or III-D.

If only part of the planchet was struck, check III-M.

If something was struck into the coin, check III-J and III-K.

If something has happened to the edge of the coin, check II-D-6, II-E-10, III-I, III-M and III-O.

If your coin shows other than the normal design, check II-A or II-C.

If a layer of the coin metal is missing, or a clad layer is missing, check III-B and III-D.

If you have an unstruck blank, or planchet, check I-G.

If your coin may be a restrike, check IV-C.

If your coin has a counterstamp, countermark, additional engraving or apparent official modifications, check IV-B and V-A-8.

Do not depend on the naked eye to examine your coins. Use a magnifying lens whenever possible, as circulation damage, wear and alterations frequently can be mistaken for legitimate minting varieties.

Division I: planchet varieties

The first division of the PDS System includes those minting varieties that occur in the manufacture of the planchet upon which the coins will ultimately be struck and includes classes resulting from faulty metallurgy, mechanical damage, faulty processing, or equipment or human malfunction prior to the actual coin striking.

Planchet alloy mix (I-A)

This section includes those classes pertaining to mixing and processing the various metals which will be used to make a coin alloy.

I-A-1 Improper Alloy Mix (WE), Rarity Level: 3-4, Values: $5 to $10.

I-A-2 Slag Inclusion Planchet (WE), Rarity Level: 5-6, Values: $25 up.

Damaged and defective planchets (I-B)

To be a class in this section the blank, or planchet, must for some reason not meet the normal standards or must have been damaged in processing. The classes cover the areas of defects in the melting, rolling, punching and processing of the planchets up to the point where they are sent to the coin presses to be struck.

I-B-1 Defective Planchet (WE), Rarity Level: 6, Values: $25 up.

I-B-2 Mechanically Damaged Planchet (WE), Rarity Level: –, Values: No Value. (See values for the coin struck on a mechanically damaged planchet.)

I-B-3 Rolled Thin Planchet (WE), Rarity Level: 6 - (Less rare on half cents of 1795, 1797 and restrikes of 1831-52.) Values: $10 up.

I-B-4 Rolled Thick Planchet (WE), Rarity Level: 7 - (Less rare in Colonial copper coins. Notable examples occur on the restrike half cents of 1840-52.) Values: $125 up.

I-B-5 Tapered Planchet (WE), Rarity Level: 7, Values: $25 up.

I-B-6 Partially Unplated Planchet (WE), Rarity Level: 6, Values: $15 up.

I-B-7 Unplated Planchet (WE), Rarity Level: 6-7, Values: $50 up.

I-B-8 Bubbled Plating Planchet (WE), Rarity Level: 1, Values: No Value.

I-B-9 Included Gas Bubble Planchet (WE), Rarity Level: 6-7, Values: $50 up.

I-B-10 Partially Unclad Planchet (WE), Rarity Level: 6, Values: $20 up.

I-B-11 Unclad Planchet (WE), Rarity Level: 6-7, Values: $50 up.

I-B-12 Undersize Planchet (WE), Rarity Level: 7, Values: $250 up.

I-B-13 Oversize Planchet (WE), Rarity Level: 7, Values: $250 up.

I-B-14 Improperly Prepared Proof Planchet (WE), Rarity Level: 7, Values: $100 up.

I-B-15 Improperly Annealed Planchet (WE), Rarity Level: - , Values: No Value.

I-B-16 Faulty Upset Edge Planchet (WE), Rarity Level: 5-6, Values: $10 up.

I-B-17 Rolled-In Metal Planchet (WE), Rarity Level: 6-7, Values: $50 up.

I-B-18 Weld Area Planchet (WE), Rarity Level: Unknown, Values: No Value Established. (See values for the coins struck on weld area planchets.)

I-B-19 Strike Clip Planchet (WE), Rarity Level: 7, Values: $150 up.

I-B-20 Unpunched Center-Hole Planchet (WE), Rarity Level: 5-7, Values: $5 and up.

I-B-21 Incompletely Punched Center-Hole Planchet (WE), Rarity Level: 6-7, Values: $15 up.

I-B-22 Uncentered Center-Hole Planchet (WE), Rarity Level: 6-7, Values: $10 up.

I-B-23 Multiple Punched Center-Hole Planchet (WE), Rarity Level: 7, Values: $35 up.

I-B-24 Unintended Center-Hole Planchet (WE), Rarity Level: Unknown, Values: -.

I-B-25 Wrong Size or Shape Center-Hole Planchet (IWE), Rarity Level: 5-7, Values: $10 up.

Clipped planchets (I-C)

Clipped blanks, or planchets, occur when the strip of coin metal fails to move forward between successive strokes of the gang punch to clear the previously punched holes, in the same manner as a cookie cutter overlapping a previously cut hole in the dough. The size of the clip is a function of the amount of overlap of the next punch.

The overlapping round punches produce a missing arc with curve matching the outside circumference of the blanking punch. Straight clips occur when the punch overlaps the beginning or end of a strip which has had the end sheared or sawed off. Ragged clips occur in the same manner when the ends of the strip have been left as they were rolled out.

The term "clip" as used here should not be confused with the practice of clipping or shaving small pieces of metal from a bullion coin after it is in circulation.

I-C-1 Disc Clip Planchet (WE), Rarity Level: 3-5, Values: $5 up.

I-C-2 Curved Clip Planchet - (To 5%) (WE), Rarity Level: 5-6, Values: $5 up.

I-C-3 Curved Clip Planchet - (6 to 10%) (WE), Rarity Level: 6, Values: $10 up.

I-C-4 Curved Clip Planchet - (11 to 25%) (WE), Rarity Level: 5-6, Values: $15 up.

I-C-5 Curved Clip Planchet - (26 to 60%) (WE), Rarity Level: 6-7, Values: $25 up.

I-C-6 Double Curved Clip Planchet (WE), Rarity Level: 6, Values: $10 up.

I-C-7 Triple Curved Clip Planchet (WE), Rarity Level: 5-6, Values: $25 up.

I-C-8 Multiple Curved Clip Planchet (WE), Rarity Level: 6-7, Values: $35 up.

I-C-9 Overlapping Curved Clipped Planchet (WE), Rarity Level: 6-7, Values: $50 up.

I-C-10 Incompletely Punched Curved Clip Planchet (WE), Rarity Level: 6, Values: $35 up.

I-C-11 Oval Curved Clip Planchet (WE), Rarity Level: 6-7, Values: $50 up.

I-C-12 Crescent Clip Planchet - (61% or more) (WE), Rarity Level: 7, Values: $200 up.

I-C-13 Straight Clip Planchet (WE), Rarity Level: 6, Values: $30 up.

I-C-14 Incompletely Sheared Straight Clip Planchet (WE), Rarity Level: 6, Values: $50 up.

I-C-15 Ragged Clip Planchet (WE), Rarity Level: 6-7, Values: $35 up.

I-C-16 Outside Corner Clip Planchet (E), Rarity Level: -, Values: No Value.

I-C-17 Inside Corner Clip Planchet (E), Rarity Level: -, Values: No Value.

I-C-18 Irregularly Clipped Planchet (E) Rarity Level: -, Values: Value not established.

I-C-19 Incompletely Punched Scalloped or Multi-Sided Planchet (E), Rarity Level: 7, Values: $25 up.

Laminated, split, or broken planchet (I-D)

For a variety of reasons the coin metal may split into thin layers (delaminate) and either split completely off the coin, or be retained. Common causes are included gas or alloy mix problems. Lamination cracks usually enter the surface of the planchet at a very shallow angle or are at right angles to the edge. The resulting layers differ from slag in that they appear as normal metal.

Lamination cracks and missing metal of any size below a split planchet are too common in the 35 percent silver 1942-1945 nickels to be collectible or have any significant value.

I-D-1 Small Lamination Crack Planchet (W), Rarity Level: 4-5, Values: $1 up.

I-D-2 Large Lamination Crack Planchet (W), Rarity Level: 3-4, Values: $5 up.

I-D-3 Split Planchet (W), Rarity Level: 5-6, Values: $15 up.

I-D-4 Hinged Split Planchet (W), Rarity Level: 6-7, Values: $75 up.

I-D-5 Clad Planchet With a Clad Layer Missing (W), Rarity Level: 5-6, Values: $35 up.

I-D-6 Clad Planchet With Both Clad Layers Missing (W), Rarity Level: 6-7, Values: $75 up.

I-D-7 Separated Clad Layer (W), Rarity Level: 5, Values: $25 up.

I-D-8 Broken Planchet (WE), Rarity Level: 3-4, Values: $5 up.

Wrong stock planchet (I-E)

The following classes cover those cases where the wrong coin metal stock was run through the blanking press, making blanks of the correct diameter, but of the wrong thickness, alloy or metal or a combination of the wrong thickness and the wrong metal.

I-E-1 Half Cent Stock Planchet (IE), Rarity Level: Unknown, Values: No Value Established.

I-E-2 Cent Stock Planchet (IE), Rarity Level: Unknown, Values: No Value Established.

I-E-3 Two Cent Stock Planchet (E), Rarity Level: Unknown, Values: No Value Established.

I-E-4 Three Cent Silver Stock Planchet (E), Rarity Level: Unknown, Values: No Value Established.

I-E-5 Three Cent Nickel Stock Planchet (E), Rarity Level: Unknown, Values: No Value Established.

I-E-6 Half Dime Stock Planchet (E), Rarity Level: Unknown, Values: No Value Established.

I-E-7 Dime Stock Planchet (E), Rarity Level: 7, Values: $200 up.

I-E-8 Twenty Cent Stock Planchet (E), Rarity Level: Unknown, Values: No Value Established.

I-E-9 Quarter Stock Planchet (E), Rarity Level: Unknown, Values: No Value Established.

I-E-10 Half Dollar Stock Planchet (E), Rarity Level: Unknown, Values: No Value Established.

I-E-11 Dollar Stock Planchet (E), Rarity Level: 7, Values: $300 up.

I-E-12 Token or Medal Stock Planchet (E), Rarity Level: Unknown, Values: No Value Established.

I-E-13 Wrong Thickness Spoiled Planchet (IWE), Rarity Level: Unknown, Values: No Value Established.

I-E-14 Correct Thickness Spoiled Planchet (IWE), Rarity Level: Unknown, Values: No Value Established.

I-E-15 Cut Down Struck Token Planchet (IWE), Rarity Level: Unknown, Values: No Value Established.

I-E-16 Experimental or Pattern Stock Planchet (IE), Rarity Level: Unknown, Values: No Value Established.

I-E-17 Proof Stock Planchet (IE), Rarity Level: Unknown, Values: No Value Established.

I-E-18 Adjusted Specification Stock Planchet (IE), Rarity Level: 7, Values: $25 up.

I-E-19 Trial Strike Stock Planchet (IE), Rarity Level: Unknown, Values: No Value Established.

I-E-20 U.S. Punched Foreign Stock Planchet (E), Rarity Level: 7, Values: $75 up.

I-E-21 Foreign Punched Foreign Stock Planchet (E), Rarity Level: 7, Values: $75 up.

I-E-22 Non-Standard Coin Alloy Planchet (IE), Rarity Level: 7, Values: Unknown.

Extra metal on a blank, or planchet (I-F)

True extra metal is only added to the blank during the blanking operation. This occurs as metal is scraped off the sides of the blanks as they are driven down through the thimble, or lower die in the blanking press. The metal is eventually picked up by a blank passing through, welded to it by the heat of friction.

A second form of extra metal has been moved to this section, the sintered coating planchet, the metal deposited on the planchet in the form of dust during the annealing operation.

I-F-1 Extra Metal on a Type 1 Blank (W), Rarity Level: 7, Values: $50 up.

I-F-2 Extra Metal on a Type 2 Planchet (W), Rarity Level: 6-7, Values: $75 up.

I-F-3 Sintered Coating Planchet (W), Rarity Level: 7, Values: $75 up.

Normal or abnormal planchets (I-G)

This section consists of the two principal forms – the blank as it comes from the blanking press – and in the form of a planchet after it has passed through the upsetting mill. It also includes a class for purchased planchets and one for planchets produced by the mint.

I-G-1 Type I Blank (IWE), Rarity Level: 3-5, Values: $2 up.

I-G-2 Type II Planchet (IWE), Rarity Level: 3-4, Values: 50 up.

I-G-3 Purchased Planchet (I), Rarity Level: 1, Values: No Value.

I-G-4 Mint Made Planchet (I), Rarity Level: 1, Values: No Value.

I-G-5 Adjustment-Marked Planchet (I), Rarity Level: Unknown, Values: No Value.

I-G-6 Hardness Test-Marked Planchet (I), Rarity Level: -, Values: No Value Established.

Note: There are no classes between I-G-6 and I-G-23

I-G-23 Proof Planchet (IE), Rarity Level: 6-7, Values: $1 up.

Coin metal strip (I-H)

When the coin metal strip passes through the blanking press it goes directly to a chopper. This cuts the remaining web into small pieces to be sent back to the melting furnace. Pieces of the web or the chopped up web may escape into the hands of collectors.

I-H-1 Punched Coin Metal Strip (IWE), Rarity Level: 4-6, Values: $5 up, depending on size, denomination and number of holes showing.

I-H-2 Chopped Coin Metal Strip (IE), Rarity Level: 3-5, Values: $5 up.

The die varieties
Division II

Die varieties may be unique to a given die, but will repeat for the full life of the die unless a further change occurs. Anything that happens to the die will affect the appearance of the struck coin. This includes all the steps of the die making:

● Cutting a die blank from a tool steel bar.
● Making the design.
● Transferring it to a model.
● Transferring it to the master die or hub.
● The hubbing process of making the die.
● Punching in the mintmark.
● Heat treating of the die.

The completed dies are also subject to damage in numerous forms, plus wear and tear during the striking process and repair work done with abrasives. All of these factors can affect how the struck coin looks.

Engraving varieties (II-A)

In all cases in this section where a master die, or master hub is affected by the class, the class will affect all the working hubs and all working dies descending from it.

Identification as being on a master die or hub depends on it being traced to two or more of the working hubs descended from the same master tools.

II-A-1 Overdate (IE), Rarity Level: 1-7, Values: $1 up.

II-A-2 Doubled Date (IE), Rarity Level: 1-7, Values: $1 up.

II-A-3 Small Date (IE), Rarity Level: 2-5, Values: $1 up.

II-A-4 Large Date (IE), Rarity Level: 2-5, Values: $1 up.

II-A-5 Small Over Large Date (IE), Rarity Level: 4-6, Values: $15 up.

II-A-6 Large Over Small Date (IE), Rarity Level: 3-5, Values: $10 up.

II-A-7 Blundered Date (E), Rarity Level: 6-7, Values: $50 up.

II-A-8 Corrected Blundered Date (IE), Rarity Level: 3-5, Values: $5 up.

II-A-9 Wrong Font Date Digit (IE), Rarity Level: 5-6, Values: Minimal.

II-A-10 Worn, Broken or Damaged Punch (IWE), Rarity Level: 5-6, Values: $5 up.

II-A-11 Expedient Punch (IWE), Rarity Level: 5-6, Values: $10 up.

II-A-12 Blundered Digit (E), Rarity Level: 4-5, Values: $50 up.

II-A-13 Corrected Blundered Digit (IE), Rarity Level: 3-6, Values: $10 up.

II-A-14 Doubled Digit (IWE), Rarity Level: 2-6, Values: $2 up.

II-A-15 Wrong Style or Font Letter or Digit (IE), Rarity Level: 3-5, Values: Minimal.

II-A-16 One Style or Font Over Another (IE), Rarity Level: 4-6, Values: $10 up.

II-A-17 Letter Over Digit (E), Rarity Level: 6-7, Values: $25 up.

II-A-18 Digit Over Letter (E), Rarity Level: 6-7, Values: $25 up.

II-A-19 Omitted Letter or Digit (IWE), Rarity Level: 4-6, Values: $5 up.

II-A-20 Blundered Letter (E), Rarity Level: 6-7, Values: $50 up.

II-A-21 Corrected Blundered Letter (IE), Rarity Level: 1-3, Values: $10 up.

II-A-22 Doubled Letter (IWE), Rarity Level: 2-6, Values: $2 up.

II-A-23 Blundered Design Element (IE), Rarity Level: 6-7, Values: $50 up.

II-A-24 Corrected Blundered Design Element (IE), Rarity Level: 3-5, Values: $10 up.

II-A-25 Large Over Small Design Element (IE), Rarity Level: 4-6, Values: $2 up.

II-A-26 Omitted Design Element (IWE), Rarity Level: 5-7, Values: $10 up.

II-A-27 Doubled Design Element (IWE), Rarity Level: 2-6, Values: $2 up.

II-A-28 One Design Element Over Another (IE), Rarity Level: 3-6, Values: $5 up.

II-A-29 Reducing Lathe Doubling (WE), Rarity Level: 6-7, Values: $50 up.

II-A-30 Extra Design Element (IE), Rarity Level: 3-5, Values: $10 up.

II-A-31 Modified Design (IWE), Rarity Level: 1-5, Values: No Value up.

II-A-32 Normal Design (I), Rarity Level: 1, Values: No Extra Value.

II-A-33 Design Mistake (IE), Rarity Level: 2-6, Values: $1 up.

II-A-34 Defective Die Design (IWE), Rarity Level: 1, Values: No Value.

II-A-35 Pattern (I), Rarity Level: 6-7, Values: $100 up.

II-A-36 Trial Design (I), Rarity Level: 5-7, Values: $100 up.

II-A-37 Omitted Designer's Initial (IWE), Rarity Level: 3-7, Values: $1 up.

II-A-38 Layout Mark (IE), Rarity Level: 5-7, Values: Minimal.

II-A-39 Abnormal Reeding (IWE), Rarity Level: 2-5, Values: $1 up.

II-A-40 Modified Die or Hub (IWE), Rarity Level: 1-5, Values: No Value up.

II-A-41 Numbered Die (I), Rarity Level: 3-5, Values: $5 up.

II-A-42 Plugged Die (IW), Rarity Level: 5-6, Values: Minimal.

II-A-43 Cancelled Die (IE), Rarity Level: 3-6, Values: No Value up.

II-A-44 Hardness Test Marked Die (IE), Rarity Level: 7, Values: $100 up.

II-A-45 Coin Simulation (IE), Rarity Level: 6-7, Values: $100 up, but may be illegal to own.

II-A-46 Punching Mistake (IE), Rarity Level: 2-6, Values: $1 up.

II-A-47 Small Over Large Design (IE), Rarity Level: 4-6, Values: $5 up.

II-A-48 Doubled Punch (IE), Rarity Level: 5-7, Values: $5 up.

II-A-49 Mint Display Sample (I) Rarity Level: 7, Values not established.

II-A-50 Center Dot, Stud or Circle (IE) Rarity Level: 7, much more common on early cents, Values not established

Hub doubling varieties (II-B)

Rotated hub doubling

Hub break

This section includes eight classes of hub doubling. Each class is from a different cause, described by the title of the class. At the latest count over 2,500 doubled dies have been reported in the U.S. coinage, the most famous being examples of the 1955, 1969-S and 1972 cent dies.

II-B-I Rotated Hub Doubling (WE), Rarity Level: 3-6, Values: $1 up

II-B-II Distorted Hub Doubling (WE), Rarity Level: 3-6, Values: $1 up.

II-B-III Design Hub Doubling (IWE), Rarity Level: 3-6, Values: $1 up to five figure amounts.

II-B-IV Offset Hub Doubling (WE), Rarity Level: 4-6, Values: $15 up.
II-B-V Pivoted Hub Doubling (WE), Rarity Level: 3-6, Values: $10 up.
II-B-VI Distended Hub Doubling (WE), Rarity Level: 2-5, Values: $1 up.
II-B-VII Modified Hub Doubling (IWE), Rarity Level: 2-5, Values: $1 up.
II-B-VIII Tilted Hub Doubling (WE), Rarity Level: 4-6, Values: $5 up.

Mintmark varieties (II-C)

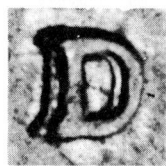 

Double   **Triple**

Mintmarks are punched into U.S. coin dies by hand (Up to 1985 for proof coins, to 1990 for cents and nickels and 1991 for other denominations). Variations resulting from mistakes in the punching are listed in this section. Unless exceptionally mispunched, values are usually estimated at 150 percent of numismatic value. Slightly tilted or displaced mintmarks have no value.

II-C-1 Doubled Mintmark (IE), Rarity Level: 2-6, Values: 50 cents up.
II-C-2 Separated Doubled Mintmark (IE), Rarity Level: 5-6, Values: $15 up.
II-C-3 Over Mintmark (IE), Rarity Level: 3-6, Values: $2 up.
II-C-4 Tripled Mintmark (IE), Rarity Level: 3-5, Values: 50 up.
II-C-5 Quadrupled Mintmark (IE), Rarity Level: 4-6, Values: $1 up.
II-C-6 Small Mintmark (IE), Rarity Level: 2-5, Values: No Extra Value up.
II-C-7 Large Mintmark (IE), Rarity Level: 2-5, Values: No Extra Value up.
II-C-8 Large Over Small Mintmark (IE), Rarity Level: 2-5, Values: $2 up.
II-C-9 Small Over Large Mintmark (IE), Rarity Level: 3-6, Values: $5 up.
II-C-10 Broken Mintmark Punch (W), Rarity Level: 5-6, Values: $5 up.
II-C-11 Omitted Mintmark (IWE), Rarity Level: 4-7, Values: $125 up.
II-C-12 Tilted Mintmark (IE), Rarity Level: 5-7, Values: $5 up.
II-C-13 Blundered Mintmark (E), Rarity Level: 4-6, Values: $5 up.
II-C-14 Corrected Horizontal Mintmark (IE), Rarity Level: 4-6, Values: $5 up.
II-C-15 Corrected Upside Down Mintmark (IE), Rarity Level: 4-6, Values: $5 up.
II-C-16 Displaced Mintmark (IE), Rarity Level: 4-6, Values: $5 to $10.
II-C-17 Modified Mintmark (IWE), Rarity Level: 1-4, Values: No Extra Value up.
II-C-18 Normal Mintmark (I), Rarity Level: 1, Values: No Extra Value.
II-C-19 Doubled Mintmark Punch (I), Rarity Level: 6-7, Values: No Extra Value up.
II-C-20 Upside Down Mintmark (E) Rarity Level 6-7, Values: $5 up.
II-C-21 Horizontal Mintmark (E) Rarity Level 6-7, Values: $5 up.
II-C-22 Wrong Mintmark (E) Rarity Level 6-7, Values $15 up. (Example has a D mintmark in the date, but was used at Philadelphia.)

Die, collar and hub cracks (II-D)

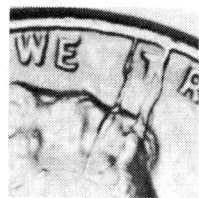

Die cracks

Cracks in the surface of the die allow coin metal to be forced into the crack during the strike, resulting in raised irregular lines of coin metal above the normal surface of the coin. These are one of the commonest forms of die damage and wear, making them easily collectible.

Collar cracks and hub cracks are added to this section because the causes and effects are similar or closely associated.

Die cracks, collar cracks and hub cracks are the result of wear and tear on the tools, with intentional use assumed for all classes.

II-D-1 Die Crack (W), Rarity Level: 1-3, Values: 10 to $1, $25 up on a proof coin with a rarity level of 6-7.

II-D-2 Multiple Die Cracks (W), Rarity Level: 1-3, Values: 25 cents to $2.

II-D-3 Head-To-Rim Die Crack (Lincoln Cent) (W), Rarity Level: 2-6, Values: 25 to $10 for multiple die cracks.

II-D-4 Split Die (W), Rarity Level: 5-6, Values: $10 up.

II-D-5 Rim-To-Rim Die Crack (W), Rarity Level: 2-5, Values: $1 up.

II-D-6 Collar Crack (W), Rarity Level: 4-6, Values: $10 up.

II-D-7 Hub Crack (W), Rarity Level: 3-5, Values: $1-$2.

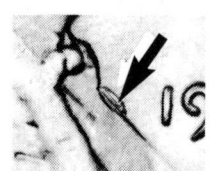

Small die break II-E-2

Clogged letter II-E-1

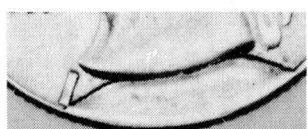

Major die break, date missing, II-E-5

Rim die break II-E-4

Die breaks (II-E)

Breaks in the surface of the die allow coin metal to squeeze into the resulting holes, causing raised irregular areas above the normal surface of the coin. Die chips and small die breaks are nearly as common as the die cracks, but major die breaks, which extend in from the edge of the coin, are quite rare on the larger coins.

If the broken piece of the die is retained, the resulting design will be above or below the level of the rest of the surface.

II-E-1 Die Chip (W), Rarity Level: 1-2, Values: 10 to $1.

II-E-2 Small Die Break (W), Rarity Level: 1-3, Values: 10 to $2.

II-E-3 Large Die Break (W), Rarity Level: 3-5, Values: $1 to $50 and up.

II-E-4 Rim Die Break (W), Rarity Level: 2-3, Values: 25 cents to $5.

II-E-5 Major Die Break (WE), Rarity Level: 3-6, Values: $5 to $100 and up.

II-E-6 Retained Broken Die (W), Rarity Level: 3-5, Values: $1 to $10 and up.

II-E-7 Retained Broken Center of the Die (W), Rarity Level: 6-7, Values: $100 up.

II-E-8 Laminated Die (W), Rarity Level: 3-5, Values: 10 cents to $5.

II-E-9 Chipped Chrome Plating (W), Rarity Level: 4-5, Values: $10 to $25 on proofs.

II-E-10 Collar Break (W), Rarity Level: 4-6, Values: $5 to $25 and up.

II-E-11 Broken Letter or Digit on an Edge Die (W), Rarity Level: 4-6, Values: Minimal.

II-E-12 "Bar" Die Break (W), Rarity Level: 3-5, Values: 25 to $20.

II-E-13 Hub Break (W), Rarity Level: 4-6, Values: 50 to $10 and up.

"BIE" varieties (II-F)

A series of small die breaks or die chips in the letters of "LIBERTY" mostly on the wheat-reverse Lincoln cent are actively collected. The name results from the resemblance to an "I" between the "B" and "E" on many of the dies, but they are found between all of the letters in different cases. Well over 1,500 dies are known and cataloged. Numerous more recent examples are known.

II-F-1 ILI Die Variety (W), Rarity Level: 4-5, Values: 25 cents to $10.

II-F-2 LII Die Variety (W), Rarity Level: 3-5, Values: 50 cents to $15.

II-F-3 IIB Die Variety (W), Rarity Level: 3-5, Values: 50 cents to $15.

BIE variety II-F-4

II-F-4 BIE Die Variety (W), Rarity Level: 3-5, Values: $1 to $20.
II-F-5 EIR Die Variety (W), Rarity Level: 3-5, Values: 50 to $15.
II-F-6 RIT Die Variety (W), Rarity Level: 4-5, Values: $2 to $25.
II-F-7 TIY Die Variety (W), Rarity Level: 4-5, Values: $5 to $30.
II-F-8 TYI Die Variety (W), Rarity Level: 4-5, Values: $2 to $25.

Worn and damaged dies, collars and hubs (II-G)

Die clashes and design transfer

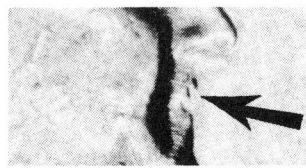

Many dies are continued deliberately in service after they have been damaged, dented, clashed or show design transfer, since none of these classes actually affect anything but the appearance ofthe coin. The root cause is wear, but intent or mistakes may enter the picture.

II-G-1 Dented Die, Collar or Hub (IWE), Rarity Level: 3-5, Values: 25 to $5.

II-G-2 Damaged Die, Collar or Hub (IWE), Rarity Level: 3-5, Values: 25 to $5.

II-G-3 Worn Die, Collar or Hub (IWE), Rarity Level: 2-3, Values: No Extra Value to Minimal Value.

II-G-4 Pitted or Rusted Die, Collar or Hub (IWE), Rarity Level: 3-4, Values:No Extra Value, marker only.

II-G-5 Heavy Die Clash (IWE), Rarity Level: 4-5, Values: $1 to $10 and up.

II-G-6 Heavy Collar Clash (IWE), Rarity Level: 3-4, Values: $1 to $5 and up.

II-G-7 Heavy Design Transfer (IWE), Rarity Level: 3-4, Values: 10 cents to $1.

Die progressions (II-H)

The progression section consists of three classes. These are useful as cataloging tools for many different die varieties, but especially the die cracks and die breaks which may enlarge, lengthen or increase in number.

II-H-1 Progression (W), Rarity Level: 3-5, Values: $1 up.

II-H-2 Die Substitution (IW), Rarity Level: 2-4, Values: No Extra Value to Minimal Value.

II-H-3 Die Repeat (I), Rarity Level: 2-4, Values: No Extra Value to Minimal Value.

Die scratches, polished and abraded dies (II-I)

Die scratches II-I-1

This section consists of those classes having to do with the use of an abrasive in some form to intentionally polish proof dies, or repair the circulating die surface. Several classes which previously were referred to as "polished" now are listed as "abraded."

II-I-1 Die Scratch (IW), Rarity Level: 1-2, Values: No Extra Value to 10 cents to 25 cents, as a marker.

II-I-2 Polished (proof) Die (IW), Rarity Level: 1, Values: No Extra Value.

II-I-3 Abraded (Circulation) Die (IW), Rarity Level: 1-2, Values: No Extra Value up to $10.

II-I-4 Inside Abraded Die Doubling (IW), Rarity Level: 1-3, Values: No Extra Value to $1.
II-I-5 Outside Abraded Die Doubling (IW), Rarity Level: 1-3, Values: No Extra Value to $1.
II-I-6 Lathe Marks (IW), Rarity Level: 5-7, Values: No Extra Value, marker only.

Striking varieties
Division III

Once the dies are made and the planchets have been prepared, they are struck by a pair of dies and become a coin. In this division, we list the misstrikes resulting from human or mechanical malfunction in the striking process. These are one-of-a-kind varieties, but there may be many similar coins that fall in a given class.

Multiples and combinations of classes must be considered on a case by case basis. The first several sections match the planchet sections indicated in the title.

Struck on defective alloy mix planchets (III-A)

This section includes those classes of coins struck on planchets that were made from a defective alloy.
III-A-1 Struck on an Improper Alloy Mix Planchet (IE), Rarity Level: 2-3, Values: 10 cents to $2.
III-A-2 Struck on a Planchet With Slag Inclusions(IE), Rarity Level: 5-6, Values: $10 up.

Struck on damaged, defective or abnormal planchet (III-B)

Struck on a defective planchet III-B-1   **Struck on a tapered planchet III-B-5**

Coins get struck on many strange objects. The more common of course are planchets which have been damaged in some way in the production process. In most of the classes in this section intent is at least presumed, if not specifically listed as a cause.

III-B-1 Struck on a Defective Planchet (IWE), Rarity Level: 4-6, Values: $5 to $10 and up.
III-B-2 Struck on a Mechanically Damaged Planchet (IWE), Rarity Level: 5-6, Values: $10 to $20 and up.
III-B-3 Struck on a Rolled Thin Planchet (IWE), Rarity Level: 5-6, Values: $2 to $5 and up.
III-B-4 Struck on a Rolled Thick Planchet (IWE), Rarity Level: 5-6, Values: $35 to $50 and up.
III-B-5 Struck on a Tapered Planchet (WE), Rarity Level: 4-6, Values: $2 to $5 and up.
III-B-6 Struck on a Partially Unplated Planchet (WE), Rarity Level: 5, Values: $10 up.
III-B-7 Struck on an Unplated Planchet (WE), Rarity Level: 6-7, Values: $100 up.
III-B-8 Struck on a Bubbled Plating Planchet (IWE), Rarity Level: 1, Values: No Value.
III-B-9 Struck on an Included Gas Bubble Planchet (WE), Rarity Level: 5-6, Values: $5 up.
III-B-10 Struck on a Partially Unclad Planchet (WE), Rarity Level: 5-6, Values: $5 up.
III-B-11 Struck on an Unclad Planchet (WE), Rarity Level: 4-5, Values: $5 and up.
III-B-12 Struck on an Undersize Planchet (WE), Rarity Level: 4-6, Values: Minimal.
III-B-13 Struck on an Oversize Planchet (WE), Rarity Level: 6-7, Values: Minimal.
III-B-14 Struck on an Improperly Prepared Proof Planchet (IWE), Rarity Level: 3-5, Values: $5 up.
III-B-15 Struck on an Improperly Annealed Planchet (IWE), Rarity Level: 4-5, Values: $5 up.
III-B-16 Struck on a Faulty Upset Edge Planchet (IWE), Rarity Level: 4-5, Values: $1 to $2.
III-B-17 Struck on a Rolled In Metal Planchet (WE), Rarity Level: 4-6, Values: $2 up.
III-B-18 Struck on a Weld Area Planchet (WE), Rarity Level: 6, Values: $25 to $50.
III-B-19 Struck on a Strike Clip Planchet (W), Rarity Level: 6-7, Values: $25 up.
III-B-20 Struck on an Unpunched Center Hole Planchet (WE), Rarity Level: 4-6, Values: $1 and up.
III-B-21 Struck on an Incompletely Punched Center Hole Planchet (WE), Rarity Level: 6-7, Values: $5 up.

III-B-22 Struck on an Uncentered Center Hole Planchet (WE), Rarity Level: 6-7, Values: $10 up.

III-B-23 Struck on a Multiple Punched Center Hole Planchet (WE), Rarity Level: 7, Values: $25 up.

III-B-24 Struck on an Unintended Center Hole Planchet (WE), Rarity Level: 6-7, Values: $25 and up.

III-B-25 Struck on a Wrong Size or Shape Center Hole Planchet (WE), Rarity Level: 5-7, Values: $5 up.

III-B-26 Struck on Scrap Coin Metal (E), Rarity Level: 4-6, Values: $10 up.

III-B-27 Struck on Junk Non Coin Metal (E), Rarity Level: 4-6, Values: $15 up.

III-B-28 Struck on a False Planchet (E), Rarity Level: 3-5, Values: $35 up.

III-B-29 Struck on Bonded Planchets (E), Rarity Level: 6-7, Values: $50 up.

Struck on a clipped planchet (III-C)

Ragged edge clip III-C-15

Multiple clip III-C-8   **Incomplete curved clip III-C-10**

Coins struck on clipped blanks, or planchets, exhibit the same missing areas as they did before striking, modified by the metal flow from the strike which rounds the edges and tends to move metal into the missing areas. Values for blanks will run higher than planchets with similar clips.

III-C-1 Struck on a Disc Clip Planchet (WE), Rarity Level: 4-5, Values: $1 on regular coins, $20 and up for clad coins.

III-C-2 Struck on a Curved Clip Planchet - to 5% (WE), Rarity Level: 3-5, Values: 50 cents up.

III-C-3 Struck on a Curved Clip Planchet - (6 to 10%) (WE), Rarity Level: 4-5, Values: $1 up.

III-C-4 Struck on a Curved Clip Planchet - (11 to 25%) (WE), Rarity Level: 4-5, Values: $2 up.

III-C-5 Struck on a Curved Clip Planchet - (26 to 60%) (WE), Rarity Level: 4-6, Values: $10 up.

III-C-6 Struck on a Double Curved Clip Planchet (WE), Rarity Level: 3-4, Values: $2 up.

III-C-7 Struck on a Triple Curved Clip Planchet (WE), Rarity Level: 4-5, Values: $5 up.

III-C-8 Struck on a Multiple Curved Clip Planchet (WE), Rarity Level: 4-6, Values: $5 up.

III-C-9 Struck on an Overlapping Curved Clipped Planchet (WE), Rarity Level: 5-6, Values: $15 up.

III-C-10 Struck on an Incomplete Curved Clip Planchet (WE), Rarity Level: 4-5, Values: $10 up.

III-C-11 Struck on an Oval Clip Planchet (WE), Rarity Level: 5-6, Values: $20 up.

III-C-12 Struck on a Crescent Clip Planchet - (61% or more) (WE), Rarity Level: 6-7, Values: $100 up.

III-C-13 Struck on a Straight Clip Planchet (E), Rarity Level: 4-6, Values: $10 up.

III-C-14 Struck on an Incomplete Straight Clip Planchet (WE), Rarity Level: 5-6, Values: $20 up.

III-C-15 Struck on a Ragged Clip Planchet (E), Rarity Level: 4-6, Values: $15 up.

III-C-16 Struck on an Outside Corner Clip Planchet (E), Rarity Level: 7, Values: $100 up.

III-C-17 Struck on an Inside Corner Clip Planchet (E), Rarity Level: Unknown outside mint., Values: -.

III-C-18 Struck on an Irregularly Clipped Planchet (E), Rarity Level: 6-7, Values: $20 up.

III-C-19 Struck on an Incompletely Punched Scalloped or Multi-Sided Planchet (E), Rarity Level: 7, Values: $20 up.

Struck on a laminated, split or broken planchet (III-D)

This section has to do with the splitting, cracking or breaking of a coin parallel to the faces of the coin, or at least very nearly parallel, or breaks at right angles to the faces of the coin.

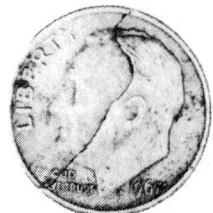

Lamination crack III-D-1   **Layer peeled off III-D-2**   **Split planchet III-D-3**

Lamination cracks and missing metal of any size below a split planchet are too common in the 35-percent silver 1942-1945 nickels to be collectible or have any significant value.

III-D-1 Struck on a Small Lamination Crack Planchet (W), Rarity Level: 3-4, Values: 10 up.

III-D-2 Struck on a Large Lamination Crack Planchet (W), Rarity Level: 3-6, Values: $1 up.

III-D-3 Struck on a Split Planchet (W), Rarity Level: 4-6, Values: $5 up.

III-D-4 Struck on a Hinged Split Planchet (W), Rarity Level: 5-6, Values: $35 up.

III-D-5 Struck on a Planchet With a Clad Layer Missing (W), Rarity Level: 4-5, Values: $15 up.

III-D-6 Struck on a Planchet With Both Clad Layers Missing (W), Rarity Level: 4-5, Values: $25 up.

III-D-7 Struck on a Separated Clad Layer or Lamination (W), Rarity Level: 6-7, Values: $75 up.

III-D-8 Struck on a Broken Planchet Before the Strike (W), Rarity Level: 3-5, Values: $10 up.

III-D-9 Broken Coin During or After the Strike (W), Rarity Level: 4-6, Values: $20 up.

III-D-10 Struck Coin Fragment Split or Broken During or After the Strike (W), Rarity Level: 3-5, Values: $5 up.

III-D-11 Reedless Coin Broken During or After the Strike (W), Rarity Level: Unknown, Values: -.

Struck on wrong stock planchets (III-E)

Quarter on dime stock
III-E-7 (lower coin edge)

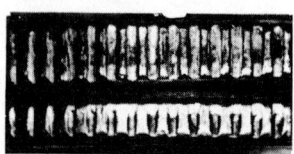

These classes cover those cases where the wrong stock was run through the blanking press, making planchets of the correct diameter, but of the wrong thickness, alloy or metal or a combination of incorrect thickness and metal.

III-E-1 Struck on a Half Cent-Stock Planchet (IE), Rarity Level: Unknown, Values: No Value Established.

III-E-2 Struck on a Cent-Stock Planchet (IE), Rarity Level: Unknown, Values: No Value Established.

III-E-3 Struck on a Two-Cent-Stock Planchet (E), Rarity Level: Unknown, Values: -.

III-E-4 Struck on a Three-Cent-Silver Stock Planchet (E), Rarity Level: Unknown, Values: -.

III-E-5 Struck on a Three-Cent-Nickel Stock Planchet (E), Rarity Level: Unknown, Values: -.

III-E-6 Struck on a Half Dime-Stock Planchet (E), Rarity Level: Unknown, Values: -.

III-E-7 Struck on a Dime-Stock Planchet (E), Rarity Level: 5-6, Values: $20 up.

III-E-8 Struck on a Twenty-Cent-Stock Planchet (E), Rarity Level: Unknown, Values: -.

III-E-9 Struck on a Quarter-Stock Planchet (E), Rarity Level: 6, Values: $50 up.

III-E-10 Struck on a Half Dollar-Stock Planchet (E), Rarity Level: 6-7, Values: $100 up.

III-E-11 Struck on a Dollar-Stock Planchet (E), Rarity Level: 6-7, Values: $300 up.

III-E-12 Struck on a Token/Medal-Stock Planchet (E), Rarity Level: 7, Values: No Value Established.

III-E-13 Struck on a Wrong Thickness Spoiled Planchet (IWE), Rarity Level: 7, Values: $50 up.

III-E-14 Struck on a Correct Thickness Spoiled Planchet (IWE), Rarity Level: Unknown, Values: No Value Established.

III-E-15 Struck on a Cut Down Struck Token (IWE), Rarity Level: 6-7, Values: $50 up.

III-E-16 Struck on an Experimental or Pattern-Stock Planchet (IE), Rarity Level: 7, Values: $50 up.

III-E-17 Struck on a Proof-Stock Planchet (IE), Rarity Level: 7, Values: $100 up.

III-E-18 Struck on an Adjusted Specification-Stock Planchet (IE), Rarity Level: 3-7, Values: No Value to $5 and up.

III-E-19 Struck on a Trial Strike-Stock Planchet (IE), Rarity Level: Unknown, Values: No Value Established.

III-E-20 U.S. Coin Struck on a Foreign-Stock Planchet. (E), Rarity Level: 5, Values: $35 up.

III-E-21 Foreign Coin Struck on a Foreign-Stock Planchet (E), Rarity Level: 5-6, Values: $25 up.

III-E-22 Struck on a Non-Standard Coin Alloy (IE), Rarity Level: 4-7, Values: $20 up.

Extra metal (III-F)

Extra metal on a struck coin (III-F-2)

Sintered coating III-F-3

The term "extra metal" for the purpose of this section includes both extra metal added to the blank during the blanking operation and metal powder added to the planchet during the annealing operation.

III-F-1 Struck on a Type 1 Blank With Extra Metal (W), Rarity Level: Unknown, Values: -.

III-F-2 Struck on a Type 2 Planchet With Extra Metal (W), Rarity Level: 4-5, Values: $10 up.

III-F-3 Struck on a Sintered Coating Planchet (W), Rarity Level: 6-7, Values: $35 up.

Struck on normal or abnormal blanks, or planchets (III-G)

Cent on dime planchet III-G-10

Half on dime planchet III-G-10

Half on quarter planchet III-G-11

This section includes coins struck on either a blank, as it comes from the blanking press, or as a planchet that has passed through the upsetting mill. Added to this section are those planchets which are normal until they are struck by the wrong dies. These differ from the wrong stock planchets because the wrong stock planchets are already a variety before they are struck.

III-G-1 Struck on a Type 1 Blank (IWE), Rarity Level: 4-6, Values: $10 up.

III-G-2 Struck on a Type 2 Planchet (I), Rarity Level: 1, Values: No Extra Value.

III-G-3 Struck on a Purchased Planchet (I), Rarity Level: 1, Values: No Extra Value.

III-G-4 Struck on a Mint-Made Planchet (I), Rarity Level: 1, Values: No Extra Value.

III-G-5 Struck on an Adjustment-Marked Planchet (I), Rarity Level: 4-7, Values: Minimal, and may reduce value of coin in some cases.

III-G-6 Struck on a Hardness Test-Marked Planchet (I), Rarity Level: 6-7, Values: $10 up.

III-G-7 Wrong Planchet or Metal on a Half Cent Planchet (IE), Rarity Level: 5-7, Values: $100 up.

III-G-8 Wrong Planchet or Metal on a Cent Planchet (IE), Rarity Level: 3-6, Values: $25 up.

III-G-9 Wrong Planchet or Metal on a Nickel Planchet (E), Rarity Level: 4-6, Values: $35 up

III-G-10 Wrong Planchet or Metal on a Dime Planchet (E), Rarity Level: 4-6, Values: $50 up.

III-G-11 Wrong Planchet or Metal on a Quarter Planchet (E), Rarity Level: 4-6. Values: $100 up.

III-G-12 Wrong Planchet or Metal on a Half Dollar Planchet (E), Rarity Level: 6-7, Values: $500 up.

III-G-13 Wrong Planchet or Metal on a Dollar Planchet (E), Rarity Level: 7, Values: $500 up.

III-G-14 Wrong Planchet or Metal on a Gold Planchet (E), Rarity Level: 7, Values: $1000 up.

III-G-15 Struck on a Wrong Series Planchet (IE), Rarity Level: 6-7, Values: $1500 up.

III-G-16 U.S. Coin Struck on a Foreign Planchet (E), Rarity Level: 5-7, Values: $35 up.

III-G-17 Foreign Coin Struck on a U.S. Planchet (E), Rarity Level: 6-7, Values: $50 up.

III-G-18 Foreign Coin Struck on a Wrong Foreign Planchet (E), Rarity Level: 6-7, Values: $50 up.

III-G-19 Struck on a Medal Planchet (E), Rarity Level: 6-7, Values: $100 up.

III-G-20 Medal Struck on a Coin Planchet (IE), Rarity Level: 3-5, Values: $10 up.

III-G-21 Struck on an Official Sample Planchet (IE), Rarity Level: Unknown, Values: No Value Established.

III-G-22 Struck Intentionally on a Wrong Planchet (I), Rarity Level: 6-7, Values: Mainly struck as Presentation Pieces, full numismatic value.

III-G-23 Non-Proof Struck on a Proof Planchet (IE), Rarity Level: 6-7, Values: $500 up.

Struck on coin metal strip (III-H)

Pieces of the coin metal strip do manage at times to escape into the coin press.

III-H-1 (See I-H-1 Punched Coin Metal Strip), Rarity Level: Impossible, Values: -.

III-H-2 Struck on Chopped Coin Metal Strip (E), Rarity Level: 6-7, Values: $25 up.

Die adjustment strikes (III-I)

As the dies are set up and adjusted in the coin press, variations in the strike occur until the dies are properly set. Test strikes are normally scrapped, but on occasion reach circulation.

III-I-1 Die Adjustment Strike (IE), Rarity Level: 5-6, Values: $35 up.

III-I-2 Edge Strike (E), Rarity Level: 5-6, Values: $10 to $20 and up.

III-I-3 Weak Strike (W), Rarity Level: 1, Values: No Extra Value.

III-I-4 Strong Strike (IWE), Rarity Level: 1, Values: No value except for the premium that might be paid for a well struck coin.

III-I-5 Jam Strike (IE), Rarity Level: 7, Values: $50 up.

III-I-6 Trial Piece Strike (I), Rarity Level: 6-7, Values: $100 up.

III-I-7 Edge-Die Adjustment Strike (I), Rarity Level: 5-7, Values: $5 up.

III-I-8 Uniface Strike (I), Rarity Level 7, Values: $50 up.

Indented, brockage and counter-brockage strikes (III-J)

Indented strike III-J-1   **Counter-brockage strike III-J-11**   **Capped die strike III-J-15**

Indented and uniface strikes involve an extra unstruck planchet between one of the dies and the planchet being struck. Brockage strikes involve a struck coin between one of the dies and the planchet and a counter-brockage requires a brockage coin between one of the dies and the planchet.

A cap, or capped die strike results when a coin sticks to the die and is squeezed around it in the shape of a bottle cap.

III-J-1 Indented Strike (W), Rarity Level: 3-6, Values: $5 up.

III-J-2 Uniface Strike (W), Rarity Level: 3-5, Values: $15 up.

III-J-3 Indented Strike By a Smaller Planchet (WE), Rarity Level: 5-7, Values: $100 up.

III-J-4 Indented Second Strike (W), Rarity Level: 3-5, Values: $10 up, about the same as a regular double strike of comparable size.

III-J-5 Partial Brockage Strike (W), Rarity Level: 3-6, Values: $15 up.

III-J-6 Full Brockage Strike (W), Rarity Level: 3-6, Values: $5 up.

III-J-7 Brockage Strike of a Smaller Coin (WE), Rarity Level: 6-7, Values: $200 up.

III-J-8 Brockage Strike of a Struck Coin Fragment (WE), Rarity Level: 4-6, Values: $5 up.

III-J-9 Brockage Second Strike (WE), Rarity Level: 3-5, Values: $5 up.

III-J-10 Partial Counter-Brockage Strike (WE), Rarity Level: 3-5, Values: $10 up.

III-J-11 Full Counter-Brockage Strike (WE), Rarity Level: 5-7, Values: $100 up.

III-J-12 Counter-Brockage Second Strike (WE), Rarity Level: 4-6, Values: $10 up.

III-J-13 Full Brockage-Counter-Brockage Strike (WE), Rarity Level: 6-7, Values: $150 up.

III-J-14 Multiple Brockage or Counter-Brockage Strike (WE), Rarity Level: 5-7, Values: $100 up.

III-J-15 Capped Die Strike (WE), Rarity Level: 6-7, Values: $500 up.

III-J-16 Reversed Capped Die Strike (WE), Rarity Level: 7, Values: $1,000 up.

Struck through abnormal objects (III-K)

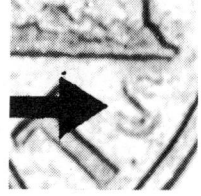

Struck through cloth III-K-1   **Struck through a filled die III-K-4**   **Struck through a dropped filling III-K-5**

This section covers most of the objects or materials which might come between the planchet and the die and be struck into the surface of the coin. Unless noted, the materials - even the soft ones - are driven into the surface of the coin.

III-K-1 Struck Through Cloth (IWE), Rarity Level: 3-6, Values: $35 up.

III-K-2 Struck Through Wire (IWE), Rarity Level: 3-6, Values: $5 up.

III-K-3 Struck Through Thread (IWE), Rarity Level: 3-6, Values: $5 up.

III-K-4 Struck Through Dirt-and-Grease-Filled Die (IWE), Rarity Level: 1-4, Values: 10 cents to 25 cents up, but no value on a worn or circulated coin.

III-K-5 Struck Through a Dropped Filling (IWE), Rarity Level: 5-6, Values: $10 up.

III-K-6 Struck Through Wrong Metal Fragments (IWE), Rarity Level: 4-6, Values: $1 up.

III-K-7 Struck Through an Unstruck Planchet Fragment (IWE), Rarity Level: 3-5, Values: $1 up.

III-K-8 Struck Through a Rim Burr (IWE), Rarity Level: 3-5, Values: $1 to $2 and up.

III-K-9 Struck Through plit-Off Reeding (IWE), Rarity Level: 5-6, Values: $25 up.

III-K-10 Struck Through a Feed Finger (IWE), Rarity Level: 5-7, Values: $25 to $50 and up.

III-K-11 Struck Through Miscellaneous Objects (IWE), Rarity Level: 4-6, Values: $1 up.

III-K-12 Struck Through Progression (IWE), Rarity Level: 4-6, Values: $1 up.

Note: Some 1987 through 1994 quarters are found without mintmarks, classed as III-K-4, a Filled Die. Values depend on market conditions. Filled dies have value ONLY on current, uncirculated grade coins.

Double strikes (III-L)

Only coins which receive two or more strikes by the die pair fall in this section and are identified by the fact that both sides of the coin are affected. Unless some object interferes, an equal area of both sides of the coin will be equally doubled.

The exception is the second strike with a loose die, which will double only one side of a coin, but is a rare form usually occurring only on proofs. A similar effect is flat field doubling from die chatter.

III-L-1 Close Centered Double Strike (WE), Rarity Level: 4-6, Values: $15 up.

III-L-2 Rotated Second Strike Over a Centered First Strike (WE), Rarity Level: 4-6, Values: $15 up.

III-L-3 Off-Center Second Strike Over a Centered First Strike (WE), Rarity Level: 4-6, Values: $15 up.

III-L-4 Off-Center Second Strike Over an Off-Center First Strike (WE), Rarity Level: 4-6, Values: $10 up.

III-L-5 Off-Center Second Strike Over a Broadstrike (WE), Rarity Level: 5-6, Values: $20 up.

III-L-6 Centered Second Strike Over an Off-Center First Strike (WE), Rarity Level: 5-6, Values: $50 up.

III-L-7 Obverse Struck Over Reverse (WE), Rarity Level: 5-6, Values: $25 up.

III-L-8 Nonoverlapping Double Strike (WE), Rarity Level: 5-6 Values: $20 up.

III-L-9 Struck Over a Different Denomination or Series (WE), Rarity Level: 6, Values: $300 and up.

III-L-10 Chain Strike (WE), Rarity Level: 6, Values: $300 up for the pair of coins that were struck together.

**Off-center second strike over
centered first strike III-L-3**

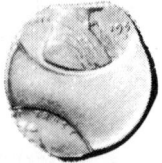

**Non-overlapping
double strike III-L-8**

Multiple strike III-L-16

Chain strike III-L-10

III-L-11 Second-Strike Doubling From a Loose Die (W), Rarity Level: 6-7, Values: $200 up.

III-L-12 Second-Strike Doubling From a Loose Screw Press Die (W), Rarity Level: 5-6, Values: $100 up.

III-L-13 Second Strike on an Edge Strike (WE), Rarity Level: 5-6, Values: $20 up.

III-L-14 Folded Planchet Strike (WE), Rarity Level: 5-7, Values: $100 up.

III-L-15 Triple Strike (WE), Rarity Level: 6-7, Values: $100 up.

III-L-16 Multiple Strike (WE), Rarity Level: 6-7, Values: $200 up.

III-L-17 U.S. Coin Struck Over a Struck Foreign Coin (WE), Rarity Level: 6-7, Values: $300 up.

III-L-18 Foreign Coin Struck Over a Struck U.S. Coin (WE), Rarity Level: 6-7, Values: $400 up.

III-L-19 Foreign Coin Struck Over a Struck Foreign Coin (WE), Rarity Level: 7, Values: $500 up.

III-L-20 Double Strike on Scrap or Junk (E), Rarity Level: 6, Values: $50 up.

III-L-21 Struck on a Struck Token or Medal (E), Rarity Level: 5-6, Values: $100 up.

III-L-22 Double-Struck Edge Motto or Design (E), Rarity Level: 6-7, Values: $200 up.

III-L-23 One Edge Motto or Design Struck Over Another (E), Rarity Level: 7, Values: $300 up.

III-L-24 Flat Field Doubling (W), Rarity Level: 2-3, Values: $1 to $5.

III-L-25 Territorial Struck over Struck U.S. Coin: (I) Rarity Level: 6-7, Values: $200 up.

III-L-26 Pattern Struck over Struck U.S. Coin: (I) Rarity Level: 6-7, Values: $200 up.

III-L-27 Pattern Struck over Struck Pattern:(I) Rarity Level 6-7, Values: $200 up.

III-L-28 Pattern Struck Over Foreign Coin:(I) Rarity Level 6-7, Values - $200 up.

Collar striking varieties (III-M)

The collar is often referred to as the "Third Die," and is involved in a number of forms of misstrikes. The collar normally rises around the planchet, preventing it from squeezing sideways between the dies and at the same time forming the reeding on reeded coins.

If the collar is out of position or tilted, a partial collar strike results; if completely missing, it causes a broadstrike; if the planchet is not entirely between the dies, an off-center strike.

III-M-1 Flanged Partial Collar Strike (WE), Rarity Level: 5-6, Values: $20 up.

III-M-2 Reversed Flanged Partial Collar Strike (WE), Rarity Level: 6-7, Values: $35 up.

III-M-3 Tilted Partial Collar Strike (WE), Rarity Level: 5-6, Values: $20 up.

III-M-4 Centered Broadstrike (WE), Rarity Level: 5-6, Values: $5 up.

III-M-5 Uncentered Broadstrike (WE), Rarity Level: 5, Values: $3 up.

III-M-6 Reversed Broadstrike (WE), Rarity Level: 6, Values: $10 up.

III-M-7 Struck Off-Center 10-30% (W), Rarity Level: 3-6, Values: $3 up.

Flanged partial collar III-M-1

**Struck off center
10 to 30 percent III-M-7**

**Struck off center
31 to 70 percent III-M-8**

**Struck off center
71 percent or more
III-M-9**

III-M-8 Struck Off-Center 31-70% (W), Rarity Level: 4-6, Values: $5 up.
III-M-9 Struck Off-Center 71% or More (W), Rarity Level: 3-5, Values: $2 up.
III-M-10 Rotated Multi-sided Planchet Strike (W), Rarity Level: 5-6, Values: $10 up.
III-M-11 Wire Edge Strike (IWE), Rarity Level: 1-2, Values: No Extra Value.
III-M-12 Struck With the Collar Too High (WE), Rarity Level: 6-7, Values: $20 up.
III-M-13 Off-Center Slide Strike (W), Rarity Level:3-6 $4 up.

Misaligned and rotated (die) strike varieties (III-N)

Misaligned die III-N-1

Normal rotation   **90 degrees**   **180 degrees**

One (rarely both) of the dies may be Offset Misaligned, off to one side, or may be tilted (Vertically Misaligned). One die may either have been installed so that it is turned in relation to the other die, or may turn in the holder, or the shank may break allowing the die face to rotate in relation to the opposing die.

Vertical misaligned dies are rarely found, and like rotated dies, find only limited collector interest. Ninety and 180 degree rotations are the most popular. Rotations of 14 degrees or less have no value. The 1989-D Congress dollar is found with a nearly 180 degree rotated reverse, currently retailing for around $2,000. Only about 30 have been reported to date.

III-N-1 Offset Die Misalignment Strike (WE), Rarity Level: 3-5, Values: $2 up.
III-N-2 Vertical Die Misalignment Strike (WE), Rarity Level: 4-6, Values: $1 up.
III-N-3 Rotated Die Strike - 15 to 45 Degrees (IWE), Rarity Level: 4-6, Values: $2 up.
III-N-4 Rotated Die Strike - 46 to 135 Degrees (IWE), Rarity Level: 5-6, Values: $10 up.
III-N-5 Rotated Die Strike - 136 to 180 Degrees (IWE), Rarity Level: 5-6, Values: $25 up.

Lettered and design edge strike varieties (III-O)

Early U.S. coins and a number of foreign coins have either lettered edges, or designs on the edge of the coin. Malfunctions of the application of the motto or design to the edge fall in this section.

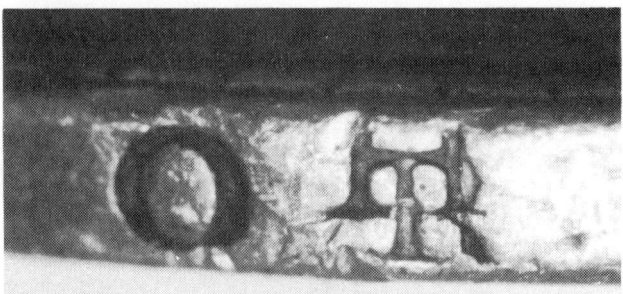

Overlapping edge letters III-O-1

III-O-1 Overlapping Edge Motto or Design (WE), Rarity Level: 3-4, Values: $5 to $10 and up.
III-O-2 Wrong Edge Motto or Design (WE), Rarity Level: 5-6-7, Values: $50 up.
III-O-3 Missing Edge Motto, Design or Security Edge (IWE), Rarity Level: 5-6-7, Values: $50 up.
III-O-4 Jammed Edge Die Strike (W), Rarity Level: 6, Values: $10 up.
III-O-5 Misplaced Segment of an Edge Die (E), Rarity Level: 4-7, Values: $25 up.
III-O-6 Reeded Edge Struck Over a Lettered Edge (IE), Rarity Level: 3-6, Values: No Extra Value up.

Defective strikes and mismatched dies (III-P)

The final section of the Striking Division covers coins which are not properly struck for reasons other than those in previous classes, such as coins struck with mismatched (muled) dies. The mismatched die varieties must be taken on a case by case basis, while the otherclasses presently have little collector demand or premium.

III-P-1 Defective Strike (WE), Rarity Level: 1, Values: No Extra Value.
III-P-2 Mismatched Die Strike (E), Rarity Level: 4-7, Values: $25 up.
III-P-3 Single-Strike Proof (WE), Rarity Level: 4-5, Values: Minimal.
III-P-4 Single Die-Proof Strike (IE), Rarity Level: 5-6, Values: $100 up.
III-P-5 Reversed Die Strike (I), Rarity Level: 4-5, Values: No Extra Value to Minimal.

Official Mint modifications
Division IV

Several mint produced varieties occur after the coin has been struck, resulting in the addition of the fourth division to my PDS System. Since most of these coins are either unique or are special varieties, each one must be taken on a case by case basis. All classes listed here are by definition intentional.

I have not listed values as the coins falling in these classes which are sold through regular numismatic channels, are cataloged with the regular issues or are covered in specialized catalogs in their particular area.

Matte proofs (IV-A)

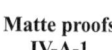

Matte proofs
IV-A-1

Matte proofs as a section include several of the forms of proof coins which have the striking characteristics of a mirror proof but have been treated AFTER striking to give them a grainy, non-reflective surface.

IV-A-1 Matte Proof (I), Rarity Level: 3-5, Values: Normal Numismatic Value.
IV-A-2 Matte Proof on One Side (I), Rarity Level: 7, Values: Normal Numismatic Value.
IV-A-3 Sandblast Proof (I), Rarity Level: 4-6, Values: Normal Numismatic Value.

Additional engraving (IV-B)

Counterstamp IV-B-3

This section includes any added markings which are placed on the struck coin and struck coins which later were cut into pieces for various purposes. The warning is repeated: Anything done to a coin after the strike is extremely difficult to authenticate and is much easier to fake than a die struck coin.

IV-B-1 Counterstamp and Countermark (I), Rarity Level: 3-6, Values: Normal Numismatic Value.
IV-B-2 Perforated and Cut Coins (I), Rarity Level: 4-6, Values: Normal Numismatic Value.

Restrikes (IV-C)

Restrike with new dies IV-C-7

Restrikes cover a complicated mixture of official use of dies from a variety of sources. Whether or not some were officially sanctioned is always a problem for the collector.

IV-C-1) Restrike on the Same Denomination Planchet (I), Rarity Level: 4-6, Values: Normal Numismatic Value.
IV-C-2 Restrike on a Different Denomination or Series Planchet (I), Rarity Level: 4-6, Values: Normal Numismatic Value.
IV-C-3 Restrike on a Foreign Coin (I), Rarity Level: 6-7, Values: Normal Numismatic Value.
IV-C-4 Restrike on a Token or Medal (I), Rarity Level: 5-6, Values: Normal Numismatic Value.
IV-C-5 Restruck With the Original Dies (I), Rarity Level: 4-6, Values: Normal Numismatic Value.
IV-C-6 Restruck With Mismatched Dies (I), Rarity Level: 4-6, Values: Normal Numismatic Value.
IV-C-7 Copy Strike With New Dies (I), Rarity Level: 3-5, Values: Normal Numismatic Value.
IV-C-8 Fantasy Strike (I), Rarity Level: 4-6, Values: Normal Numismatic Value.

After strike modifications
Division V

This division includes both modifications that have value to collectors – and those that don't. I needed a couple of divisions to cover other things that happen to coins to aid in cataloging them. This avoids the false conclusion that an unlisted coin is quite rare, when the exact opposite is more likely to be the case.

Collectible modifications after strike (V-A)

Mint modification V-A-8

This section includes those classes having to do with deliberate modifications of the coin done with a specific purpose or intent which makes them of some value to collectors. Quite often these pieces were made specifically to sell to collectors, or at least to the public under the guise of being collectible.

V-A-1 Screw Thaler, Rarity Level: 5-6, Values: Normal Numismatic Value.
V-A-2 Love Token, Rarity Level: 3-6, Values: $10 up.
V-A-3 Satirical or Primitive Engraving, Rarity Level: 6-7, Values: $5 up.
V-A-4 Elongated Coin, Rarity Level: 2-7, Values: 50 cents to $1 and up.
V-A-5 Coin Jewelry, Rarity Level: 2-5, Values: $1 up.
V-A-6 Novelty Coin, Rarity Level: 1-3, Values: No Value up to $5 to $10.
V-A-7 Toning, Rarity Level: 3-6, Values: No value up, depending on coloration. Easily faked.
V-A-8 Mint Modification, Rarity Level: 4-7, Values: $5 up. Easily faked.
V-A-9 Mint Packaging Mistake, Rarity Level: 5-7, Values: Nominal $1. Very easily faked.

Alterations and damage after the strike (V-B)

Machine doubling damage V-B-1

This section includes those changes in a coin which have no collector value. In most cases their effect on the coin is to reduce or entirely eliminate any collector value - and in the case of counterfeits they are actually illegal to even own.

V-B-1 Machine Doubling Damage: NOTE: Machine doubling damage is defined as: "Damage to a coin after the strike, due to die bounce or chatter or die displacement, showing on the struck coin as scrapes on the sides of the design elements, with portions of the coin metal in the relief elements either displaced sideways or downward, depending on the direction of movement of the loose die." Machine doubling damage, or MDD, is by far the most common form of doubling found on almost any coin in the world. Rarity Level: 0, Values: Reduces the coin's value.

V-B-2 Accidental or Deliberate Damage, Rarity Level: 0, Values: Reduces the coin's value.

V-B-3 Test Cut or Mark, Rarity Level: 0, Values: Reduces value of coin to face or bullion value.

V-B-4 Alteration, Rarity Level: 0, Values: Reduces value to face or bullion value.

V-B-5 Whizzing, Rarity Level: 0, Values: Reduces value sharply and may reduce it to face or bullion value.

V-B-6 Counterfeit, Copy, Facsimile, Forgery or Fake, Rarity Level: 0, Values: No Value and may be illegal to own.

V-B-7 Planchet Deterioration. Very common on copper-plated zinc cents. Rarity level: 0, Values: No Value.

COLONIAL AMERICA
COLONIAL COINAGE
MARYLAND
Lord Baltimore

PENNY (DENARIUM)

KM# 1 • Copper •

Date	AG	Good	VG	Fine	VF	XF	Unc
(1659) 4 known	—	—	—	—	—	—	—

4 PENCE (GROAT)

KM# 2 • Silver • Obv: Large bust **Rev:** Large shield

Date	AG	Good	VG	Fine	VF	XF	Unc
(1659)	750	1,250	2,500	4,500	8,500	15,000	—

KM# 3 • Silver • Obv: Small bust **Rev:** Small shield

Date	AG	Good	VG	Fine	VF	XF	Unc
(1659) unique	—	—	—	—	—	—	—

Note: Norweb $26,400

6 PENCE

KM# 4 • Silver • Obv: Small bust **Note:** Known in two other rare small-bust varieties and two rare large-bust varieties.

Date	AG	Good	VG	Fine	VF	XF	Unc
(1659)	450	950	1,750	3,500	6,750	12,500	—

SHILLING

KM# 6 • Silver • Note: Varieties exist; one is very rare.

Date	AG	Good	VG	Fine	VF	XF	Unc
(1659)	500	1,000	2,000	4,000	8,000	14,500	—

MASSACHUSETTS
New England

3 PENCE

KM# 1 • Silver • Obv: NE Rev: III

Date	AG	Good	VG	Fine	VF	XF	Unc
(1652) 2 known	—	—	—	—	—	—	—

6 PENCE

KM# 2 • Silver • Obv: NE Rev: VI

Date	AG	Good	VG	Fine	VF	XF	Unc
(1652) 8 known	—	—	—	—	—	—	—

Note: Garrett $75,000

SHILLING

KM# 3 • Silver • Obv: NE Rev: XII

Date	AG	Good	VG	Fine	VF	XF	Unc
(1652)	2,000	4,500	7,500	15,000	35,000	—	—

Oak Tree

2 PENCE

KM# 7 • Silver •

Date	AG	Good	VG	Fine	VF	XF	Unc
1662	150	300	550	850	2,150	—	—

3 PENCE

KM# 8 • Silver • Note: Two types of legends.

Date	AG	Good	VG	Fine	VF	XF	Unc
1652	200	400	650	1,000	2,600	—	—

6 PENCE

KM# 9 • Silver • Note: Three types of legends.

Date	AG	Good	VG	Fine	VF	XF	Unc
1652	250	450	750	1,250	3,000	—	—

SHILLING

KM# 10 • Silver • Note: Two types of legends.

Date	AG	Good	VG	Fine	VF	XF	Unc
1652	175	300	650	1,150	2,850	—	—

Pine Tree

3 PENCE

KM# 11 • Silver • Obv: Tree without berries

Date	AG	Good	VG	Fine	VF	XF	Unc
1652	150	300	450	750	1,600	—	—

KM# 12 • Silver • Obv: Tree with berries

Date	AG	Good	VG	Fine	VF	XF	Unc
1652	165	325	500	850	1,850	—	—

6 PENCE

KM# 13 • Silver • Obv: Tree without berries; "spiney tree"

Date	AG	Good	VG	Fine	VF	XF	Unc
1652	525	950	1,650	2,000	3,000	—	—

KM# 14 • Silver • Obv: Tree with berries

Date	AG	Good	VG	Fine	VF	XF	Unc
1652	150	300	575	1,150	2,100	—	—

KM# 15 • Silver • Note: Large planchet. Many varieties exist; some are very rare.

Date	AG	Good	VG	Fine	VF	XF	Unc
1652	200	425	775	1,350	2,650	—	—

KM# 16 • Silver • Note: Small planchet; large dies. All examples are thought to be contemporary fabrications.

Date	AG	Good	VG	Fine	VF	XF	Unc
1652	—	—	—	—	—	—	—

KM# 17 • Silver • Note: Small planchet; small dies. Many varieties exist; some are very rare.

Date	AG	Good	VG	Fine	VF	XF	Unc
1652	150	300	575	1,250	2,300	—	—

Willow Tree

3 PENCE

KM# 4 • Silver •

Date	AG	Good	VG	Fine	VF	XF	Unc
1652 3 known	—	—	—	—	—	—	—

6 PENCE

KM# 5 • Silver •

Date	AG	Good	VG	Fine	VF	XF	Unc
1652	3,500	7,500	10,000	18,000	35,000	—	—

SHILLING

KM# 6 • Silver •

Date	AG	Good	VG	Fine	VF	XF	Unc
1652	4,000	10,000	12,500	20,000	36,500	—	—

NEW JERSEY
St. Patrick or Mark Newby

FARTHING

KM# 1 • Copper •

Date	AG	Good	VG	Fine	VF	XF	Unc
(1682)	20.00	40.00	80.00	200	425	—	—

KM# 1a • Silver •

Date	AG	Good	VG	Fine	VF	XF	Unc
(1682)	350	550	1,150	1,650	2,750	—	—

HALFPENNY

KM# 2 • Copper •

Date	AG	Good	VG	Fine	VF	XF	Unc
(1682)	50.00	100.00	200	400	900	—	—

EARLY AMERICAN TOKENS
American Plantations

1/24 REAL

KM# Tn5.1 • Tin • Obv. Legend: ET HIB REX

Date	AG	Good	VG	Fine	VF	XF	Unc
(1688)	65.00	125	165	210	285	450	—

KM# Tn5.3 • Tin • Rev: Horizontal 4

Date	AG	Good	VG	Fine	VF	XF	Unc
(1688)	175	300	400	500	650	1,350	—

KM# Tn5.4 • Tin • Obv. Legend: ET HIB REX

Date	AG	Good	VG	Fine	VF	XF	Unc
(1688)	—	—	—	—	—	—	6,000

KM# Tn6 • Tin • Rev: Arms of Scotland left, Ireland right

Date	AG	Good	VG	Fine	VF	XF	Unc
(1688)	450	750	1,250	2,000	2,500	—	—

KM# Tn5.2 • Tin • Obv: Rider's head left of "B" in legend **Note:** Restrikes made in 1828 from two obverse dies.

Date	AG	Good	VG	Fine	VF	XF	Unc
(1828)	35.00	65.00	100.00	150	225	325	—

Elephant

KM# Tn1.1 • Copper • Note: Thick planchet.

Date	AG	Good	VG	Fine	VF	XF	Unc
(1664)	60.00	100.00	150	250	450	850	—

KM# Tn1.2 • Copper • Note: Thin planchet.

Date	AG	Good	VG	Fine	VF	XF	Unc
(1664)	80.00	150	200	350	600	1,250	—

KM# Tn2 • Copper • Rev: Diagonals tie shield

Date	AG	Good	VG	Fine	VF	XF	Unc
(1664)	120	185	225	400	700	1,450	—

KM# Tn3 • Copper • Rev: Sword right side of shield.

Date	AG	Good	VG	Fine	VF	XF	Unc
(1664) 3 known	—	—	—	—	—	—	—

Note: Norweb $1,320

KM# Tn4 • Copper • Rev. Legend: LON DON.

Date	AG	Good	VG	Fine	VF	XF	Unc
(1684)	175	300	500	1,000	1,850	3,750	—

KM# Tn7 • Copper • Rev. Legend: NEW ENGLAND.

Date	AG	Good	VG	Fine	VF	XF	Unc
(1694) 2 known	—	—	—	—	—	—	—

Note: Norweb $25,300

KM# Tn8.1 • Copper • Rev. Legend: CAROLINA (PROPRIETORS).

Date	AG	Good	VG	Fine	VF	XF	Unc
(1694) 5 known	—	—	—	—	—	—	—

Note: Norweb $35,200

KM# Tn8.2 • Copper • Rev. Legend: CAROLINA (PROPRIETORS, O over E).

Date	AG	Good	VG	Fine	VF	XF	Unc
1694	700	1,100	1,700	2,750	5,750	11,000	—

Note: Norweb $17,600

Gloucester

KM# Tn15 • Copper •

Date	AG	Good	VG	Fine	VF	XF	Unc
(1714) 2 known	—	—	—	—	—	—	—

Note: Garrett $36,000

Hibernia-Voce Populi

FARTHING

KM# Tn21.1 • Copper • Note: Large letters

Date	AG	Good	VG	Fine	VF	XF	Unc
1760	90.00	150	275	450	750	1,550	—

KM# Tn21.2 • Copper • Note: Small letters

Date	AG	Good	VG	Fine	VF	XF	Unc
1760 extremely rare	—	—	—	—	—	—	—

Note: Norweb $5,940.

HALFPENNY

KM# Tn22 • Copper •

Date	AG	Good	VG	Fine	VF	XF	Unc
1700 date is error, extremely rare	—	—	—	—	—	—	—

Note: ex-Roper $575. Norweb $577.50. Stack's Americana, VF, $2,900

1760 varieties	10.00	30.00	50.00	100.00	185	350	—
1760 legend VOOE POPULI	20.00	35.00	60.00	110	200	400	—

Higley or Granby

KM# Tn16 • **Copper** • **Obv. Legend:** CONNECTICVT. **Note:** THE VALVE OF THREE PENCE.

Date	AG	Good	VG	Fine	VF	XF	Unc
1737	—	—	—	—	—	—	—

Note: Garrett $16,000

KM# Tn17 • **Copper** • **Obv. Legend:** THE VALVE OF THREE PENCE. **Rev. Legend:** I AM GOOD COPPER.

Date	AG	Good	VG	Fine	VF	XF	Unc
1737 2 known	—	—	—	—	—	—	—

Note: ex-Norweb $6,875

KM# Tn18.1 • **Copper** • **Obv. Legend:** VALUE ME AS YOU PLEASE. **Rev. Legend:** I AM GOOD COPPER.

Date	AG	Good	VG	Fine	VF	XF	Unc
1737	6,500	8,500	10,500	14,500	25,000	—	—

KM# Tn18.2 • **Copper** • **Obv. Legend:** VALVE ME AS YOU PLEASE. **Rev. Legend:** I AM GOOD COPPER.

Date	AG	Good	VG	Fine	VF	XF	Unc
1737 2 known	—	—	—	—	—	—	—

KM# Tn19 • **Copper** • **Rev:** Broad axe.

Date	AG	Good	VG	Fine	VF	XF	Unc
(1737)	—	—	—	—	—	—	—

Note: Garrett $45,000

Date	AG	Good	VG	Fine	VF	XF	Unc
1739 5 known	—	—	—	—	—	—	—

Note: Eliasberg $12,650. Oechsner $9,900. Steinberg (holed) $4,400.

Date	AG	Good	VG	Fine	VF	XF	Unc
1739 5 known	—	—	—	—	—	—	—

Note: Eliasberg $12,650. Oechsner $9,900. Steinberg (holed) $4,400.

KM# Tn20 • **Copper** • **Obv. Legend:** THE WHEELE GOES ROUND. **Rev:** J CUT MY WAY THROUGH.

Date	AG	Good	VG	Fine	VF	XF	Unc
(1737) unique	—	—	—	—	—	—	—

Note: Roper $60,500

New Yorke

KM# Tn9 • Brass • Note: The 1700 date is circa.

Date	AG	Good	VG	Fine	VF	XF	Unc
1700	650	1,250	2,850	4,500	7,500	—	—

KM# Tn9a • White Metal •

Date	AG	Good	VG	Fine	VF	XF	Unc
1700 4 known	—	—	—	—	—	—	—

Pitt

FARTHING

KM# Tn23 • Copper •

Date	AG	Good	VG	Fine	VF	XF	Unc
1766	—	—	—	1,350	2,850	6,000	—

HALFPENNY

KM# Tn24 • Copper •

Date	AG	Good	VG	Fine	VF	XF	Unc
1766	45.00	85.00	175	350	700	1,500	—

ROYAL PATENT COINAGE
Hibernia

FARTHING

KM# 20 • Copper • Note: Pattern.

Date	AG	Good	VG	Fine	VF	XF	Unc
1722	25.00	50.00	125	220	325	700	—

KM# 24 • Copper • Obv: 1722 obverse **Obv. Legend:** ...D:G:REX.

Date	AG	Good	VG	Fine	VF	XF	Unc
1723	20.00	40.00	60.00	90.00	150	350	—

KM# 25 • Copper • Obv. Legend: DEI • GRATIA • REX •

Date	AG	Good	VG	Fine	VF	XF	Unc
1723	10.00	20.00	40.00	65.00	90.00	200	—

KM# 25a • Silver •

Date	Good	VG	Fine	VF	XF	Unc	Proof
1723	—	—	—	800	1,600	—	2,700
1724	45.00	75.00	125	250	485	—	—

HALFPENNY

KM# 21 • Copper • Rev: Harp left, head right

Date	AG	Good	VG	Fine	VF	XF	Unc
1722	—	15.00	35.00	65.00	135	350	—

KM# 22 • Copper • Obv: Harp left, head right **Note:** Pattern.

Date	AG	Good	VG	Fine	VF	XF	Unc
1722	7.00	—	—	1,150	1,750	3,000	—

KM# 23.1 • Copper • Rev: Harp right

Date	AG	Good	VG	Fine	VF	XF	Unc
1722	2.00	15.00	35.00	60.00	125	250	—
1723	7.00	15.00	25.00	40.00	80.00	175	—
1723/22	10.00	20.00	45.00	90.00	185	375	—
1724	7.00	15.00	35.00	60.00	125	265	—

KM# 23.2 • Copper • Obv: DEII error in legend

Date	AG	Good	VG	Fine	VF	XF	Unc
1722	40.00	90.00	180	300	500	750	—

KM# 26 • Copper • Rev: Large head **Note:** Rare. Generally mint state only. Probably a pattern.

Date	AG	Good	VG	Fine	VF	XF	Unc
1723	—	—	—	—	—	—	—

KM# 27 • **Copper** • **Rev:** Continuous legend over head

Date	AG	Good	VG	Fine	VF	XF	Unc
1724	30.00	65.00	150	300	475	750	—

Rosa Americana

HALFPENNY

KM# 1 • **Copper** • **Obv. Legend:** D • G • REX •

Date	AG	Good	VG	Fine	VF	XF	Unc
1722	20.00	40.00	60.00	100.00	220	475	—

KM# 2 • **Copper** • **Obv:** Uncrowned rose **Obv. Legend:** DEI GRATIA REX. **Note:** Several varieties exist.

Date	AG	Good	VG	Fine	VF	XF	Unc
1722	18.00	35.00	55.00	100.00	200	475	—
1723	285	525	750	1,350	2,250	—	—

KM# 3 • **Copper** • **Rev. Legend:** VTILE DVLCI

Date	AG	Good	VG	Fine	VF	XF	Unc
1722	250	450	650	1,100	—	—	—

KM# 9 • **Copper** • **Rev:** Crowned rose

Date	AG	Good	VG	Fine	VF	XF	Unc
1723	18.00	35.00	55.00	100.00	200	450	—

PENNY

KM# 4 • **Copper** • **Rev. Legend:** UTILE DULCI **Note:** Several varieties exist.

Date	AG	Good	VG	Fine	VF	XF	Unc
1722	18.00	35.00	55.00	100.00	175	385	—

KM# 5 • Copper • Note: Several varieties exist. Also known in two rare pattern types with long hair ribbons, one with V's for U's on the obverse.

Date	AG	Good	VG	Fine	VF	XF	Unc
1722	18.00	35.00	55.00	100.00	220	475	—

KM# 10 • Copper • Note: Several varieties exist.

Date	AG	Good	VG	Fine	VF	XF	Unc
1723	18.00	35.00	55.00	100.00	200	420	—

KM# 12 • Copper • Note: Pattern.

Date	AG	Good	VG	Fine	VF	XF	Unc
1724 2 known	—	—	—	—	—	—	—

KM# 13 • Copper •

Date	AG	Good	VG	Fine	VF	XF	Unc
(1724) 5 known	—	—	—	—	—	—	—

Note: Norweb $2,035

KM# 14 • Copper • Obv: George II **Note:** Pattern.

Date	AG	Good	VG	Fine	VF	XF	Unc
1727 2 known	—	—	—	—	—	—	—

2 PENCE

KM# 6 • Copper • Rev: Motto with scroll

Date	AG	Good	VG	Fine	VF	XF	Unc
(1722)	35.00	60.00	110	200	350	700	—

KM# 7 • Copper • Rev: Motto without scroll

Date	AG	Good	VG	Fine	VF	XF	Unc
(1722) 3 known	—	—	—	—	—	—	—

KM# 8.1 • Copper • Obv: Period after REX **Rev:** Dated

Date	AG	Good	VG	Fine	VF	XF	Unc
1722	25.00	40.00	70.00	125	265	500	—

KM# 8.2 • Copper • Obv: Without period after REX

Date	AG	Good	VG	Fine	VF	XF	Unc
1722	22.00	40.00	70.00	125	275	525	—

KM# 11 • Copper • Note: Several varieties exist.

Date	AG	Good	VG	Fine	VF	XF	Unc
1723	25.00	45.00	75.00	140	285	550	—

KM# 15 • Copper • Note: Pattern. Two varieties exist; both extremely rare.

Date	AG	Good	VG	Fine	VF	XF	Unc
1724	—	—	—	—	—	—	—

Note: ex-Garrett $5,775. Stack's Americana, XF, $10,925

KM# 16 • Copper • Note: Pattern.

Date	AG	Good	VG	Fine	VF	XF	Unc
1733 4 known	—	—	—	—	—	—	—

Note: Norweb $19,800

Virginia Halfpenny

KM# Tn25.1 • Copper • Rev: Small 7s in date. **Note:** Struck on Irish halfpenny planchets.

Date	Good	VG	Fine	VF	XF	Unc	Proof
1773	—	—	—	—	—	—	3,500

KM# Tn25.2 • Copper • Obv: Period after GEORGIVS. **Rev:** Varieties with 7 or 8 strings in harp.

Date	AG	Good	VG	Fine	VF	XF	Unc
1773	6.00	12.00	25.00	50.00	100.00	250	465

KM# Tn25.3 • Copper • Obv: Without period after GEORGIVS. **Rev:** Varieties with 6, 7 or 8 strings in harp.

Date	AG	Good	VG	Fine	VF	XF	Unc
1773	7.00	15.00	30.00	60.00	135	275	525

KM# Tn25.4 • Copper • Obv: Without period after GEORGIVS. **Rev:** 8 harp strings, dot on cross.

Date	AG	Good	VG	Fine	VF	XF	Unc
1773	—	—	—	—	—	—	—

Note: ex-Steinberg $2,600

KM# Tn26 • Silver • Note: So-called "shilling" silver proofs.

Date	AG	Good	VG	Fine	VF	XF	Unc
1774 6 known	—	—	—	—	—	—	—

Note: Garrett $23,000

UNITED STATES

REVOLUTIONARY COINAGE
Continental "Dollar"

KM# EA1 • Pewter • Obv. Legend: CURRENCY.

Date	AG	Good	VG	Fine	VF	XF	Unc
1776	—	—	1,850	3,000	4,750	8,750	18,500

KM# EA2 • Pewter • Obv. Legend: CURRENCY, EG FECIT.

Date	AG	Good	VG	Fine	VF	XF	Unc
1776	—	—	1,750	2,850	4,250	7,750	16,000

KM# EA2a • Silver • Obv. Legend: CURRENCY, EG FECIT.

Date	AG	Good	VG	Fine	VF	XF	Unc
1776 2 known	—	—	—	—	—	—	—

KM# EA3 • Pewter • Obv. Legend: CURRENCY.

Date	AG	Good	VG	Fine	VF	XF	Unc
1776 extremely rare	—	—	—	—	—	—	—

KM# EA4 • Pewter • Obv. Legend: CURRENCY. **Rev:** Floral cross.

Date	AG	Good	VG	Fine	VF	XF	Unc
1776 3 recorded	—	—	—	—	—	—	—

Note: Norweb $50,600. Johnson $25,300

KM# EA5 • Pewter • Obv. Legend: CURENCY.

Date	AG	Good	VG	Fine	VF	XF	Unc
1776	—	—	1,650	2,750	4,000	8,000	16,000

KM# EA5a • Brass • Obv. Legend: CURENCY. **Note:** Two varieties exist.

Date	AG	Good	VG	Fine	VF	XF	Unc
1776	—	—	—	—	13,500	17,500	—

KM# EA5b • Silver • Obv. Legend: CURENCY.

Date	AG	Good	VG	Fine	VF	XF	Unc
1776 unique	—	—	—	—	—	—	—

Note: Romano $99,000

STATE COINAGE
CONNECTICUT

KM# 1 • **Copper** • **Obv:** Bust facing right.

Date	AG	Good	VG	Fine	VF	XF	Unc
1785	20.00	30.00	50.00	85.00	190	450	—

KM# 2 • **Copper** • **Obv:** "African head."

Date	AG	Good	VG	Fine	VF	XF	Unc
1785	25.00	45.00	85.00	200	450	1,500	—

KM# 3.1 • **Copper** • **Obv:** Bust facing left.

Date	AG	Good	VG	Fine	VF	XF	Unc
1785	60.00	100.00	150	275	400	750	—
1786	20.00	30.00	50.00	90.00	185	465	—
1787	22.00	35.00	60.00	110	125	350	—
1788	20.00	30.00	50.00	100.00	220	500	—

KM# 3.3 • **Copper** • **Obv:** Perfect date. **Rev. Legend:** IN DE ET.

Date	AG	Good	VG	Fine	VF	XF	Unc
1787	35.00	65.00	85.00	135	250	600	—

KM# 3.4 • **Copper** • **Obv. Legend:** CONNLC.

Date	AG	Good	VG	Fine	VF	XF	Unc
1788	15.00	25.00	40.00	80.00	175	400	—

KM# 4 • **Copper** • **Obv:** Small mailed bust facing left. **Rev. Legend:** ETLIB INDE.

Date	AG	Good	VG	Fine	VF	XF	Unc
1786	22.00	35.00	55.00	85.00	165	400	—

KM# 5 • **Copper** • **Obv:** Small mailed bust facing right. **Rev. Legend:** INDE ET LIB.

Date	AG	Good	VG	Fine	VF	XF	Unc
1786	30.00	55.00	75.00	115	225	475	—

KM# 6 • Copper • Obv: Large mailed bust facing right.

Date	AG	Good	VG	Fine	VF	XF	Unc
1786	30.00	50.00	90.00	165	350	850	—

KM# 7 • Copper • Obv: "Hercules head."

Date	AG	Good	VG	Fine	VF	XF	Unc
1786	25.00	40.00	75.00	135	300	700	—

KM# 8.1 • Copper • Obv: Draped bust.

Date	AG	Good	VG	Fine	VF	XF	Unc
1786	22.00	35.00	65.00	120	275	600	—

KM# 8.2 • Copper • Obv: Draped bust. **Note:** Many varieties.

Date	AG	Good	VG	Fine	VF	XF	Unc
1787	12.00	20.00	40.00	80.00	135	275	—

KM# 8.3 • Copper • Obv. Legend: AUCIORI.

Date	AG	Good	VG	Fine	VF	XF	Unc
1787	15.00	25.00	50.00	110	250	600	—

KM# 8.4 • Copper • Obv. Legend: AUCTOPI.

Date	AG	Good	VG	Fine	VF	XF	Unc
1787	20.00	30.00	60.00	125	265	650	—

KM# 8.5 • Copper • Obv. Legend: AUCTOBI.

Date	AG	Good	VG	Fine	VF	XF	Unc
1787	15.00	25.00	50.00	110	225	550	—

KM# 8.6 • Copper • Obv. Legend: CONNFC.

Date	AG	Good	VG	Fine	VF	XF	Unc
1787	12.00	20.00	40.00	85.00	200	525	—

KM# 8.7 • Copper • Obv. Legend: CONNLC.

Date	AG	Good	VG	Fine	VF	XF	Unc
1787	—	30.00	60.00	125	265	650	—

KM# 8.8 • Copper • Rev. Legend: FNDE.

Date	AG	Good	VG	Fine	VF	XF	Unc
1787	15.00	25.00	45.00	90.00	210	535	—

KM# 8.9 • Copper • Rev. Legend: ETLIR.

Date	AG	Good	VG	Fine	VF	XF	Unc
1787	15.00	25.00	45.00	90.00	210	535	—

KM# 8.10 • Copper • Rev. Legend: ETIIB.

Date	AG	Good	VG	Fine	VF	XF	Unc
1787	20.00	30.00	50.00	100.00	225	550	—

KM# 9 • Copper • Obv: Small head. **Rev. Legend:** ETLIB INDE.

Date	AG	Good	VG	Fine	VF	XF	Unc
1787	25.00	40.00	90.00	150	350	800	—

KM# 10 • Copper • Obv: Small head. **Rev. Legend:** INDE ET LIB.

Date	AG	Good	VG	Fine	VF	XF	Unc
1787	75.00	135	175	275	450	950	—

KM# 11 • Copper • Obv: Medium bust. **Note:** Two reverse legend types exist.

Date	AG	Good	VG	Fine	VF	XF	Unc
1787	50.00	80.00	140	200	325	625	—

KM# 12 • Copper • Obv: "Muttonhead" variety. **Note:** Extremely rare with legend INDE ET LIB.

Date	AG	Good	VG	Fine	VF	XF	Unc
1787	30.00	50.00	120	250	650	1,500	—

KM# 13 • Copper • Obv: "Laughing head."

Date	AG	Good	VG	Fine	VF	XF	Unc
1787	22.00	35.00	60.00	110	250	700	—

KM# 14 • Copper • Obv: "Horned head."

Date	AG	Good	VG	Fine	VF	XF	Unc
1787	15.00	25.00	40.00	70.00	175	475	—

KM# 15 • Copper • Rev. Legend: IND ET LIB.

Date	AG	Good	VG	Fine	VF	XF	Unc
1787/8	25.00	40.00	75.00	130	250	650	—
1787/1887	20.00	30.00	50.00	90.00	200	520	—

KM# 16 • Copper • Obv. Legend: CONNECT. **Rev. Legend:** INDE ET LIB. **Note:** Two additional scarce reverse legend types exist.

Date	AG	Good	VG	Fine	VF	XF	Unc
1787	22.00	37.50	60.00	115	220	550	—

KM# 20 • Copper • Obv: Mailed bust facing right.

Date	AG	Good	VG	Fine	VF	XF	Unc
1788	15.00	25.00	45.00	90.00	200	425	—

KM# 21 • Copper • Obv: Small mailed bust facing right.

Date	AG	Good	VG	Fine	VF	XF	Unc
1788	75.00	150	285	550	1,100	2,500	—

KM# 22.1 • Copper • Obv: Draped bust facing left. **Rev. Legend:** INDE ET LIB.

Date	AG	Good	VG	Fine	VF	XF	Unc
1788	12.00	20.00	35.00	55.00	135	375	—

KM# 22.2 • Copper • Rev. Legend: INDLET LIB.

Date	AG	Good	VG	Fine	VF	XF	Unc
1788	20.00	30.00	55.00	90.00	185	400	—

KM# 22.3 • Copper • Obv. Legend: CONNEC. **Rev. Legend:** INDE ET LIB.

Date	AG	Good	VG	Fine	VF	XF	Unc
1788	22.00	35.00	60.00	100.00	200	425	—

KM# 22.4 • Copper • Obv. Legend: CONNEC. **Rev. Legend:** INDL ET LIB.

Date	AG	Good	VG	Fine	VF	XF	Unc
1788	22.00	35.00	60.00	100.00	200	425	—

MASSACHUSETTS

HALFPENNY

KM# 17 • Copper •

Date	AG	Good	VG	Fine	VF	XF	Unc
1776 unique	—	—	—	—	—	—	—

Note: Garrett $40,000

PENNY

KM# 18 • Copper •

Date	AG	Good	VG	Fine	VF	XF	Unc
1776 unique	—	—	—	—	—	—	—

HALF CENT

KM# 19 • Copper • Note: Varieties exist; some are rare.

Date	AG	Good	VG	Fine	VF	XF	Unc
1787	30.00	50.00	90.00	175	350	800	—
1788	35.00	55.00	100.00	185	375	850	—

CENT

KM# 20.1 • Copper • Rev: Arrows in right talon

Date	AG	Good	VG	Fine	VF	XF	Unc
1787 7 known	—	—	—	—	—	—	—

Note: Ex-Bushnell-Brand $8,800. Garrett $5,500

KM# 20.2 • Copper • Rev: Arrows in left talon

Date	AG	Good	VG	Fine	VF	XF	Unc
1787	25.00	40.00	65.00	120	285	785	—

KM# 20.3 • Copper • Rev: "Horned eagle" die break

Date	AG	Good	VG	Fine	VF	XF	Unc
1787	28.00	45.00	70.00	130	300	785	—

KM# 20.4 • Copper • Rev: Without period after Massachusetts

Date	AG	Good	VG	Fine	VF	XF	Unc
1788	28.00	45.00	70.00	135	320	850	—

KM# 20.5 • Copper • Rev: Period after Massachusetts, normal S's

Date	AG	Good	VG	Fine	VF	XF	Unc
1788	28.00	45.00	70.00	120	275	775	—

KM# 20.6 • **Copper** • **Rev:** Period after Massachusetts, S's like 8's

Date	AG	Good	VG	Fine	VF	XF	Unc
1788	22.00	35.00	60.00	120	275	775	—

NEW HAMPSHIRE

KM# 1 • **Copper** •

Date	AG	Good	VG	Fine	VF	XF	Unc
1776 extremely rare	—	—	—	—	—	—	—

Note: Garrett $13,000

NEW JERSEY

KM# 8 • **Copper** • **Obv:** Date below draw bar.

Date	AG	Good	VG	Fine	VF	XF	Unc
1786 extremely rare	—	—	—	—	—	—	—

Note: Garrett $52,000

KM# 9 • **Copper** • **Obv:** Large horse head, date below plow, no coulter on plow.

Date	AG	Good	VG	Fine	VF	XF	Unc
1786	75.00	150	285	550	1,450	5,500	—

KM# 10 • Copper • Rev: Narrow shield, straight beam.

Date	AG	Good	VG	Fine	VF	XF	Unc
1786	25.00	40.00	65.00	150	350	975	—

KM# 11.1 • Copper • Rev: Wide shield, curved beam. **Note:** Varieties exist.

Date	AG	Good	VG	Fine	VF	XF	Unc
1786	28.00	45.00	85.00	180	425	1,000	—

KM# 11.2 • Copper • Obv: Bridle variety (die break). **Note:** Reverse varieties exist.

Date	AG	Good	VG	Fine	VF	XF	Unc
1786	30.00	50.00	90.00	185	425	1,000	—

KM# 12.1 • Copper • Rev: Plain shield. **Note:** Small planchet. Varieties exist.

Date	AG	Good	VG	Fine	VF	XF	Unc
1787	20.00	30.00	60.00	100.00	200	675	—

KM# 12.2 • Copper • Rev: Shield heavily outlined. **Note:** Small planchet.

Date	AG	Good	VG	Fine	VF	XF	Unc
1787	22.00	35.00	75.00	125	285	800	—

KM# 13 • Copper • Obv: "Serpent head."

Date	AG	Good	VG	Fine	VF	XF	Unc
1787	40.00	60.00	120	285	700	1,275	—

KM# 14 • Copper • Rev: Plain shield. **Note:** Large planchet. Varieties exist.

Date	AG	Good	VG	Fine	VF	XF	Unc
1787	22.00	35.00	75.00	135	300	850	—

KM# 15 • Copper • Rev. Legend: PLURIBS.

Date	AG	Good	VG	Fine	VF	XF	Unc
1787	30.00	50.00	100.00	225	600	1,100	—

KM# 16 • Copper • Obv: Horse's head facing right. **Note:** Varieties exist.

Date	AG	Good	VG	Fine	VF	XF	Unc
1788	20.00	30.00	65.00	125	375	750	—

KM# 17 • Copper • Rev: Fox before legend. **Note:** Varieties exist.

Date	AG	Good	VG	Fine	VF	XF	Unc
1788	—	55.00	110	275	725	1,550	—

KM# 18 • Copper • Obv: Horse's head facing left. **Note:** Varieties exist.

Date	AG	Good	VG	Fine	VF	XF	Unc
1788	65.00	125	285	575	1,150	3,000	—

NEW YORK

KM# 1 • Copper • Obv. Legend: NON VI VIRTUTE VICI.

Date	AG	Good	VG	Fine	VF	XF	Unc
1786	1,200	2,200	3,750	6,000	11,500	—	—

KM# 2 • Copper • Obv: Eagle on globe facing right.

Date	AG	Good	VG	Fine	VF	XF	Unc
1787	175	750	1,250	3,500	6,500	12,750	—

KM# 3 • Copper • Obv: Eagle on globe facing left.

Date	AG	Good	VG	Fine	VF	XF	Unc
1787	350	700	1,200	3,250	6,000	12,000	—

KM# 4 • Copper • Rev: Large eagle, arrows in right talon.

Date	AG	Good	VG	Fine	VF	XF	Unc
1787 2 known	—	—	—	—	—	—	—

Note: Norweb $18,700

KM# 5 • Copper • Obv: George Clinton.

Date	AG	Good	VG	Fine	VF	XF	Unc
1787	2,250	4,000	5,500	9,500	20,000	—	—

KM# 6 • Copper • Obv: Indian. **Rev:** New York arms.

Date	AG	Good	VG	Fine	VF	XF	Unc
1787	1,000	2,000	4,000	6,500	10,500	25,000	—

KM# 7 • Copper • Obv: Indian. **Rev:** Eagle on globe.

Date	AG	Good	VG	Fine	VF	XF	Unc
1787	1,650	3,000	6,500	11,500	23,500	35,000	—

KM# 8 • Copper • Obv: Indian. **Rev:** George III.

Date	AG	Good	VG	Fine	VF	XF	Unc
1787	125	200	350	650	1,350	4,200	—

Nova Eboracs

KM# 9 • Copper • Obv. Legend: NOVA EBORAC. **Rev:** Figure seated right.

Date	AG	Good	VG	Fine	VF	XF	Unc
1787	40.00	75.00	125	260	525	1,100	—

KM# 10 • Copper • Rev: Figure seated left.

Date	AG	Good	VG	Fine	VF	XF	Unc
1787	35.00	55.00	110	225	500	1,000	—

KM# 11 • Copper • Obv: Small head, star above. **Obv. Legend:** NOVA EBORAC.

Date	AG	Good	VG	Fine	VF	XF	Unc
1787	300	600	1,750	3,000	4,500	6,500	—

KM# 12 • **Copper** • **Obv:** Large head, two quatrefoils left. **Obv. Legend:** NOVA EBORAC.

Date	AG	Good	VG	Fine	VF	XF	Unc
1787	200	300	400	650	1,150	2,500	—

Machin Mill

KM# 13 • **Copper** • **Note:** Crude, lightweight imitations of the British Halfpenny were struck at Machin's Mill in large quantities bearing the obverse legends: GEORGVS II REX, GEORGIVS III REX, and GEORGIUS III REX, with the BRITANNIA reverse. There are many different mulings. These pieces, which have plain crosses in the shield of Britannia, are not to be confused with the very common British made imitations, which usually have outlined crosses in the shield. Some varieties are very rare.

Date	AG	Good	VG	Fine	VF	XF	Unc
(1747-88)	—	—	—	—	—	—	—

Note: Examples are dated: 1747, 1771, 1772, 1774, 1775, 1776, 1777, 1778, 1784, 1785, 1786, 1787 and 1788. Other dates may exist.

VERMONT

KM# 1 • **Copper** • **Rev. Legend:** IMMUNE COLUMBIA.

Date	AG	Good	VG	Fine	VF	XF	Unc
(1785)	1,250	2,000	3,000	5,000	9,000	—	—

KM# 2 • **Copper** • **Obv. Legend:** VERMONTIS.

Date	AG	Good	VG	Fine	VF	XF	Unc
1785	120	200	300	600	1,150	—	—

KM# 3 • Copper • Obv. Legend: VERMONTS.

Date	AG	Good	VG	Fine	VF	XF	Unc
1785	85.00	150	225	450	900	3,200	—

KM# 4 • Copper • Obv. Legend: VERMONTENSIUM.

Date	AG	Good	VG	Fine	VF	XF	Unc
1786	75.00	125	200	450	950	3,250	—

KM# 5 • Copper • Obv: "Baby head." Rev: AUCTORI: VERMONS.

Date	AG	Good	VG	Fine	VF	XF	Unc
1786	120	200	300	550	1,150	4,500	—

KM# 6 • Copper • Obv: Bust facing left. Obv. Legend: VERMON: AUCTORI:.

Date	AG	Good	VG	Fine	VF	XF	Unc
1786	60.00	100.00	185	300	750	2,250	—
1787 extremely rare	—	—	—	—	—	—	—

KM# 7 • Copper • Obv: Bust facing right. **Note:** Varieties exist.

Date	AG	Good	VG	Fine	VF	XF	Unc
1787	—	—	—	—	—	—	—

KM# 8 • Copper • Note: Britannia mule.

Date	AG	Good	VG	Fine	VF	XF	Unc
1787	25.00	40.00	65.00	140	285	950	—

KM# 9.1 • Copper • Rev. Legend: INDE ET LIB. **Note:** Varieties exist.

Date	AG	Good	VG	Fine	VF	XF	Unc
1788	40.00	65.00	120	220	550	1,850	—

KM# 9.2 • Copper • Obv: "C" backward in AUCTORI.

Date	AG	Good	VG	Fine	VF	XF	Unc
1788 extremely rare	—	—	—	—	—	—	—

Note: Stack's Americana, Fine, $9,775

KM# 10 • Copper • Rev. Legend: ET LIB INDE.

Date	AG	Good	VG	Fine	VF	XF	Unc
1788	75.00	125	300	600	1,100	—	—

KM# 11 • Copper • Note: George III Rex mule.

Date	AG	Good	VG	Fine	VF	XF	Unc
1788	85.00	145	325	650	1,250	2,750	—

EARLY AMERICAN TOKENS
Albany Church "Penny"

KM# Tn54.1 • Copper • Obv: Without "D" above church. **Note:** Uniface.

Date	AG	Good	VG	Fine	VF	XF	Unc
5 known	—	—	3,500	7,000	14,000	—	—

KM# Tn54.2 • Copper • Obv: With "D" above church. **Note:** Uniface.

Date	AG	Good	VG	Fine	VF	XF	Unc
rare	—	—	3,000	5,000	10,000	—	—

Auctori Plebis

KM# Tn50 • Copper •

Date	AG	Good	VG	Fine	VF	XF	Unc
1787	20.00	45.00	90.00	150	300	600	—

Bar "Cent"

KM# Tn49 • Copper •

Date	AG	Good	VG	Fine	VF	XF	Unc
ND(1785)	85.00	150	275	675	1,200	2,500	—

Castorland "Half Dollar"

KM# Tn87.1 • Silver • Edge: Reeded.

Date	AG	Good	VG	Fine	VF	XF	Unc
1796	—	—	—	—	—	3,550	—

KM# Tn87.1a • Copper • Edge: Reeded.

Date	AG	Good	VG	Fine	VF	XF	Unc
1796 3 known	—	—	—	—	—	1,650	—

KM# Tn87.1b • Brass • Edge: Reeded.

Date	AG	Good	VG	Fine	VF	XF	Unc
1796 unique	—	—	—	—	—	—	—

KM# Tn87.2 • Copper • Edge: Plain. **Note:** Thin planchet.

Date	AG	Good	VG	Fine	VF	XF	Unc
1796 unique	—	—	—	—	—	—	—

KM# Tn87.3 • Silver • Edge: Reeded. **Note:** Thin planchet. Restrike.

Date	Good	VG	Fine	VF	XF	Unc	Proof
1796	—	—	—	—	—	325	—

KM# Tn87.3a • Copper • Edge: Reeded. **Note:** Thin planchet. Restrike.

Date	Good	VG	Fine	VF	XF	Unc	Proof
1796	—	—	—	—	—	285	—

KM# Tn87.4 • Silver • Edge: Lettered. **Edge Lettering:** ARGENT. **Note:** Thin planchet. Restrike.

Date	Good	VG	Fine	VF	XF	Unc	Proof
1796	—	—	—	—	—	60.00	—

KM# Tn87.5 • Copper • Edge: Lettered. **Edge Lettering:** CUIVRE. **Note:** Thin planchet. Restrike.

Date	Good	VG	Fine	VF	XF	Unc	Proof
1796	—	—	—	—	—	40.00	—

Chalmers

3 PENCE

KM# Tn45 • Silver •

Date	AG	Good	VG	Fine	VF	XF	Unc
1783	250	500	1,000	1,500	2,650	5,500	—

6 PENCE

KM# Tn46.1 • Silver • Rev: Small date

Date	AG	Good	VG	Fine	VF	XF	Unc
1783	350	700	1,500	2,250	5,500	12,000	—

KM# Tn46.2 • Silver • Rev: Large date

Date	AG	Good	VG	Fine	VF	XF	Unc
1783	300	600	1,300	2,000	4,000	10,000	—

SHILLING

KM# Tn47.1 • **Silver** • **Rev:** Birds with long worm

Date	AG	Good	VG	Fine	VF	XF	Unc
1783	180	300	500	1,000	2,000	4,500	—

KM# Tn47.2 • **Silver** • **Rev:** Birds with short worm

Date	AG	Good	VG	Fine	VF	XF	Unc
1783	150	250	475	900	1,850	4,500	—

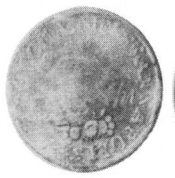

KM# Tn48 • **Silver** • **Rev:** Rings and stars

Date	AG	Good	VG	Fine	VF	XF	Unc
1783 4 known	—	—	—	—	—	—	—

Note: Garrett $75,000

Copper Company of Upper Canada

HALFPENNY

KM# Tn86 • **Copper** •

Date	Good	VG	Fine	VF	XF	Unc	Proof
1796	—	—	—	—	—	—	3,750

Franklin Press

KM# Tn73 • **Copper** • **Edge:** Plain.

Date	AG	Good	VG	Fine	VF	XF	Unc
1794	18.00	35.00	55.00	85.00	175	300	600

Kentucky Token

KM# Tn70.1 • **Copper** • **Edge:** Plain. **Note:** 1793 date is circa.

Date	AG	Good	VG	Fine	VF	XF	Unc
1793	12.00	25.00	40.00	60.00	100.00	265	575

KM# Tn70.2 • **Copper** • **Edge:** Engrailed.

Date	AG	Good	VG	Fine	VF	XF	Unc
	35.00	75.00	125	200	350	950	1,850

KM# Tn70.3 • **Copper** • **Edge:** Lettered. **Edge Lettering:** PAYABLE AT BEDWORTH.

Date	AG	Good	VG	Fine	VF	XF	Unc
unique	—	—	—	—	—	1,980	—

KM# Tn70.4 • **Copper** • **Edge:** Lettered. **Edge Lettering:** PAYABLE AT LANCASTER.

Date	AG	Good	VG	Fine	VF	XF	Unc
	14.00	28.00	45.00	65.00	110	285	725

KM# Tn70.5 • **Copper** • **Edge:** Lettered. **Edge Lettering:** PAYABLE AT I.FIELDING.

Date	AG	Good	VG	Fine	VF	XF	Unc
unique	—	—	—	—	—	—	—

KM# Tn70.6 • **Copper** • **Edge:** Lettered. **Edge Lettering:** PAYABLE AT W. PARKERS.

Date	AG	Good	VG	Fine	VF	XF	Unc
unique	—	—	—	—	1,800	—	—

KM# Tn70.7 • **Copper** • **Edge:** Ornamented branch with two leaves.

Date	AG	Good	VG	Fine	VF	XF	Unc
unique	—	—	—	—	—	—	—

Mott Token

KM# Tn52.1 • **Copper** • **Note:** Thin planchet.

Date	AG	Good	VG	Fine	VF	XF	Unc
1789	30.00	60.00	120	220	350	850	—

KM# Tn52.2 • **Copper** • **Note:** Thick planchet. Weight generally about 170 grams.

Date	AG	Good	VG	Fine	VF	XF	Unc
1789	25.00	50.00	100.00	175	300	700	—

KM# Tn52.3 • **Copper** • **Edge:** Fully engrailed. **Note:** Specimens struck with perfect dies are scarcer and generally command higher prices.

Date	AG	Good	VG	Fine	VF	XF	Unc
1789	40.00	85.00	175	350	600	1,250	—

Myddelton Token

KM# Tn85 • Copper •

Date	Good	VG	Fine	VF	XF	Unc	Proof
1796	—	—	—	—	—	—	6,500

KM# Tn85a • Silver •

Date	Good	VG	Fine	VF	XF	Unc	Proof
1796	—	—	—	—	—	—	5,500

New York Theatre

KM# Tn90 • Copper • Note: 1796 date is circa.

Date	AG	Good	VG	Fine	VF	XF	Unc
1796	—	—	300	900	2,000	3,250	8,000

North American

HALFPENNY

KM# Tn30 • Copper •

Date	AG	Good	VG	Fine	VF	XF	Unc
1781	6.50	12.50	25.00	75.00	135	365	750

Rhode Island Ship

KM# Tn27a • Brass • Obv: Without wreath below ship.

Date	AG	Good	VG	Fine	VF	XF	Unc
1779	50.00	100.00	175	275	500	1,000	2,000

KM# Tn27b • Pewter • Obv: Without wreath below ship.

Date	AG	Good	VG	Fine	VF	XF	Unc
1779	—	—	—	—	1,250	2,500	5,500

KM# Tn28a • Brass • Obv: Wreath below ship.

Date	AG	Good	VG	Fine	VF	XF	Unc
1779	60.00	120	200	325	600	1,150	2,200

KM# Tn28b • Pewter • Obv: Wreath below ship.

Date	AG	Good	VG	Fine	VF	XF	Unc
1779	—	—	—	—	1,500	3,000	6,500

KM# Tn29 • Brass • Obv: VLUGTENDE below ship

Date	AG	Good	VG	Fine	VF	XF	Unc
1779 unique	—	—	—	—	—	—	—

Note: Garrett $16,000

Standish Barry

3 PENCE

KM# Tn55 • Silver •

Date	AG	Good	VG	Fine	VF	XF	Unc
1790	850	1,350	2,000	3,000	6,500	12,000	—

Talbot, Allum & Lee

CENT

KM# Tn71.1 • Copper • Rev: NEW YORK above ship **Edge:** Lettered. **Edge Lettering:** PAYABLE AT THE STORE OF

Date	AG	Good	VG	Fine	VF	XF	Unc
1794	12.00	25.00	45.00	90.00	175	300	925

KM# Tn71.2 • Copper • Rev: NEW YORK above ship **Edge:** Plain. **Note:** Size of ampersand varies on obverse and reverse dies.

Date	AG	Good	VG	Fine	VF	XF	Unc
1794 4 known	—	—	—	—	2,350	3,000	—

KM# Tn72.1 • Copper • Rev: Without NEW YORK above ship **Edge:** Lettered. **Edge Lettering:** PAYABLE AT THE STORE OF

Date	AG	Good	VG	Fine	VF	XF	Unc
1794	100.00	200	350	650	1,000	2,250	4,550

KM# Tn72.2 • Copper • Edge: Lettered. **Edge Lettering:** WE PROMISE TO PAY THE BEARER ONE CENT.

Date	AG	Good	VG	Fine	VF	XF	Unc
1795	10.00	20.00	40.00	75.00	160	300	725

KM# Tn72.3 • Copper • Edge: Lettered. **Edge Lettering:** CURRENT EVERYWHERE.

Date	AG	Good	VG	Fine	VF	XF	Unc
1795 unique	—	—	—	—	—	—	—

KM# Tn72.4 • Copper • Edge: Olive leaf.

Date	AG	Good	VG	Fine	VF	XF	Unc
1795 unique	—	—	—	—	—	—	—

Note: Norweb $4,400

KM# Tn72.5 • Copper • Edge: Plain.

Date	AG	Good	VG	Fine	VF	XF	Unc
1795 plain edge, 2 known	—	—	—	—	—	—	—

Date	AG	Good	VG	Fine	VF	XF	Unc
1795 edge: Cambridge Bedford Huntington.X.X., unique	—	—	—	—	—	—	—

Note: Norweb, $3,960

Washington Pieces

KM# Tn35 • Copper • Obv. Legend: GEORGIVS TRIUMPHO.

Date	AG	Good	VG	Fine	VF	XF	Unc
1783	25.00	40.00	65.00	150	325	750	—

KM# Tn36 • Copper • Obv: Large military bust. **Note:** Varieties exist.

Date	AG	Good	VG	Fine	VF	XF	Unc
1783	8.00	15.00	25.00	50.00	110	280	—

KM# Tn37.1 • Copper • Obv: Small military bust. **Edge:** Plain.

Date	AG	Good	VG	Fine	VF	XF	Unc
1783	10.00	20.00	35.00	65.00	125	300	—

Note: One proof example is known. Value: $12,500

KM# Tn37.2 • Copper • Obv: Small military bust. **Edge:** Engrailed.

Date	AG	Good	VG	Fine	VF	XF	Unc
1783	18.00	35.00	50.00	80.00	175	345	—

KM# Tn38.1 • Copper • Obv: Draped bust, no button on drapery, small letter.

Date	AG	Good	VG	Fine	VF	XF	Unc
1783	10.00	20.00	35.00	65.00	125	285	—

KM# Tn38.2 • Copper • Obv: Draped bust, button on drapery, large letter.

Date	AG	Good	VG	Fine	VF	XF	Unc
1783	25.00	40.00	60.00	100.00	200	350	—

KM# Tn38.4 • Copper • Edge: Engrailed. **Note:** Restrike.

Date	Good	VG	Fine	VF	XF	Unc	Proof
1783	—	—	—	—	—	—	400

KM# Tn38.4a • Copper • Note: Bronzed. Restrike.

Date	Good	VG	Fine	VF	XF	Unc	Proof
1783	—	—	—	—	—	—	—

KM# Tn83.3 • Copper • Obv: Large modern lettering. **Edge:** Plain. **Note:** Restrike.

Date	Good	VG	Fine	VF	XF	Unc	Proof
1783	—	—	—	—	—	—	500

KM# Tn83.4b • Silver • Note: Restrike.

Date	Good	VG	Fine	VF	XF	Unc	Proof
1783	—	—	—	—	—	—	1,000

KM# Tn83.4c • Gold • Note: Restrike.

Date	AG	Good	VG	Fine	VF	XF	Unc
1783 2 known	—	—	—	—	—	—	—

KM# Tn60.1 • Copper • Obv. Legend: WASHINGTON PRESIDENT. **Edge:** Plain.

Date	AG	Good	VG	Fine	VF	XF	Unc
1792	850	1,450	3,250	5,000	7,500	—	—

Note: Steinberg $12,650. Garrett $15,500.

KM# Tn60.2 • Copper • Obv. Legend: WASHINGTON PRESIDENT. **Edge:** Lettered. **Edge Lettering:** UNITED STATES OF AMERICA.

Date	AG	Good	VG	Fine	VF	XF	Unc
1792	1,350	2,250	4,500	7,500	12,500	—	—

KM# Tn61.1 • Copper • Obv. Legend: BORN VIRGINIA. **Note:** Varieties exist.

Date	AG	Good	VG	Fine	VF	XF	Unc
	250	500	1,000	2,200	3,750	7,500	—

KM# Tn61.2 • Silver • Edge: Lettered. **Edge Lettering:** UNITED STATES OF AMERICA.

Date	AG	Good	VG	Fine	VF	XF	Unc
2 known	—	—	—	—	—	—	—

KM# Tn61.1a • Silver • Edge: Plain.

Date	AG	Good	VG	Fine	VF	XF	Unc
4 known	—	—	—	—	—	—	—

Note: Roper $16,500

KM# Tn62 • Silver • Rev: Heraldic eagle. 1792 half dollar. **Note:** Mule.

Date	AG	Good	VG	Fine	VF	XF	Unc
3 known	—	—	—	—	—	—	—

KM# Tn77.1 • Copper • Obv. Legend: LIBERTY AND SECURITY. **Edge:** Lettered. **Note:** "Penny."

Date	AG	Good	VG	Fine	VF	XF	Unc
	25.00	40.00	75.00	135	275	625	2,000

KM# Tn77.2 • Copper • Edge: Plain. **Note:** "Penny."

Date	AG	Good	VG	Fine	VF	XF	Unc
extremely rare	—	—	—	—	—	—	—

KM# Tn77.3 • Copper • Note: "Penny." Engine-turned borders.

Date	AG	Good	VG	Fine	VF	XF	Unc
12 known	—	—	—	—	—	—	3,750

KM# Tn78 • Copper • Note: Similar to "Halfpenny" with date on reverse.

Date	AG	Good	VG	Fine	VF	XF	Unc
1795 very rare	—	—	—	—	—	—	—

Note: Roper $6,600

KM# Tn81.2 • Copper • Obv. Legend: NORTH WALES. **Edge:** Lettered.

Date	AG	Good	VG	Fine	VF	XF	Unc
	120	250	400	600	950	2,000	4,500

HALFPENNY

KM# Tn56 • Copper • Obv. Legend: LIVERPOOL HALFPENNY

Date	AG	Good	VG	Fine	VF	XF	Unc
1791	300	450	550	850	1,650	2,350	—

KM# Tn66.1 • Copper • Rev: Ship **Edge:** Lettered.

Date	AG	Good	VG	Fine	VF	XF	Unc
1793	20.00	30.00	60.00	110	235	500	—

KM# Tn66.2 • Copper • Rev: Ship **Edge:** Plain.

Date	AG	Good	VG	Fine	VF	XF	Unc
1793 5 known	—	—	—	—	2,000	—	—

KM# Tn75.1 • Copper • Obv: Large coat buttons **Rev:** Grate **Edge:** Reeded.

Date	AG	Good	VG	Fine	VF	XF	Unc
1795	12.00	20.00	30.00	60.00	120	265	575

KM# Tn75.2 • Copper • Rev: Grate **Edge:** Lettered.

Date	AG	Good	VG	Fine	VF	XF	Unc
1795	45.00	85.00	165	225	300	625	1,200

KM# Tn75.3 • Copper • Obv: Small coat buttons **Rev:** Grate **Edge:** Reeded.

Date	AG	Good	VG	Fine	VF	XF	Unc
1795	10.00	35.00	60.00	100.00	175	375	850

KM# Tn76.1 • Copper • Obv. Legend: LIBERTY AND SECURITY. **Edge:** Plain.

Date	AG	Good	VG	Fine	VF	XF	Unc
1795	18.00	35.00	60.00	100.00	175	435	975

KM# Tn76.2 • Copper • Edge: Lettered. **Edge Lettering:** PAYABLE AT LONDON ...

Date	AG	Good	VG	Fine	VF	XF	Unc
1795	12.00	20.00	30.00	60.00	125	375	800

KM# Tn76.3 • Copper • Edge: Lettered. **Edge Lettering:** BIRMINGHAM ...

Date	AG	Good	VG	Fine	VF	XF	Unc
1795	14.00	22.00	35.00	70.00	150	425	950

KM# Tn76.4 • Copper • Edge: Lettered. **Edge Lettering:** AN ASYLUM ...

Date	AG	Good	VG	Fine	VF	XF	Unc
1795	18.00	35.00	60.00	100.00	225	450	1,000

KM# Tn76.5 • Copper • Edge: Lettered. **Edge Lettering:** PAYABLE AT LIVERPOOL ...

Date	AG	Good	VG	Fine	VF	XF	Unc
1795 unique	—	—	—	—	—	—	—

KM# Tn76.6 • Copper • Edge: Lettered. **Edge Lettering:** PAYABLE AT LONDON-LIVERPOOL.

Date	AG	Good	VG	Fine	VF	XF	Unc
1795 unique	—	—	—	—	—	—	—

KM# Tn81.1 • Copper • Obv. Legend: NORTH WALES. **Edge:** Plain.

Date	AG	Good	VG	Fine	VF	XF	Unc
(1795)	25.00	45.00	85.00	145	250	550	1,450

KM# Tn82 • Copper • Obv. Legend: NORTH WALES. **Rev:** Four stars at bottom

Date	AG	Good	VG	Fine	VF	XF	Unc
(1795)	200	400	700	1,500	2,850	5,500	—

CENT

KM# Tn39 • Copper • Obv. Legend: UNITY STATES

Date	AG	Good	VG	Fine	VF	XF	Unc
1783	12.00	22.00	40.00	70.00	160	325	—

KM# Tn40 • Copper • Note: Double head.

Date	AG	Good	VG	Fine	VF	XF	Unc
(1783)	10.00	20.00	35.00	65.00	135	300	—

KM# Tn41 • Copper • Obv: "Ugly head." **Note:** 3 known in copper, 1 in white metal.

Date	AG	Good	VG	Fine	VF	XF	Unc
1784	—	—	—	—	—	—	—

Note: Roper $14,850

KM# Tn57 • Copper • Rev: Small eagle

Date	AG	Good	VG	Fine	VF	XF	Unc
1791	30.00	60.00	125	250	335	675	—

KM# Tn58 • Copper • Rev: Large eagle

Date	AG	Good	VG	Fine	VF	XF	Unc
1791	35.00	65.00	145	275	375	725	—

KM# Tn65 • Copper • Obv: "Roman" head

Date	Good	VG	Fine	VF	XF	Unc	Proof
1792	—	—	—	—	—	—	17,600

HALF DOLLAR

KM# Tn59.1 • Copper • Edge: Lettered. **Edge Lettering:** UNITED STATES OF AMERICA

Date	AG	Good	VG	Fine	VF	XF	Unc
1792 2 known	—	—	—	—	—	—	—

Note: Roper $2,860. Benson, EF, $48,300

KM# Tn59.1a • Silver • Edge: Lettered. **Edge Lettering:** UNITED STATES OF AMERICA

Date	AG	Good	VG	Fine	VF	XF	Unc
1792 rare	—	—	—	—	—	—	—

Note: Roper $35,200

KM# Tn59.1b • Gold • Edge: Lettered. **Edge Lettering:** UNITED STATES OF AMERICA

Date	AG	Good	VG	Fine	VF	XF	Unc
1792 unique	—	—	—	—	—	—	—

KM# Tn59.2 • Copper • Edge: Plain.

Date	AG	Good	VG	Fine	VF	XF	Unc
1792 3 known	—	—	—	—	—	—	—

KM# Tn59.2a • Silver • Edge: Plain.

Date	AG	Good	VG	Fine	VF	XF	Unc
1792 rare	—	—	—	—	—	—	—

KM# Tn63.1 • Silver • Rev: Small eagle **Edge:** Plain.

Date	AG	Good	VG	Fine	VF	XF	Unc
1792	4,500	7,000	9,000	12,500	20,000	37,500	—

KM# Tn63.1a • Copper • Edge: Plain.

Date	AG	Good	VG	Fine	VF	XF	Unc
1792	750	1,500	3,500	5,750	8,500	—	—

Note: Garrett $32,000

KM# Tn63.2 • Silver • Edge: Ornamented, circles and squares.

Date	AG	Good	VG	Fine	VF	XF	Unc
1792 5 known	—	—	—	—	—	—	—

KM# Tn63.3 • Silver • Edge: Two olive leaves.

Date	AG	Good	VG	Fine	VF	XF	Unc
1792 unique	—	—	—	—	—	—	—

KM# Tn64 • Silver • Rev: Large heraldic eagle

Date	AG	Good	VG	Fine	VF	XF	Unc
1792 unique	—	—	—	—	—	—	—

Note: Garrett $16,500

EARLY AMERICAN PATTERNS
Confederatio

KM# EA22 • Copper • Rev: Small circle of stars.

Date	AG	Good	VG	Fine	VF	XF	Unc
1785	—	—	—	—	8,800	16,500	—

KM# EA23 • Copper • Rev: Large circle of stars. **Note:** The Confederatio dies were struck in combination with 13 other dies of the period. All surviving examples of these combinations are extremely rare.

Date	AG	Good	VG	Fine	VF	XF	Unc
extremely rare	—	—	—	—	—	—	—

Immune Columbia

KM# EA20 • Copper • Obv: George III.

Date	AG	Good	VG	Fine	VF	XF	Unc
1785	750	1,250	1,850	2,250	5,000	9,000	—

KM# EA21 • Copper • Obv: Vermon.

Date	AG	Good	VG	Fine	VF	XF	Unc
1785	600	1,000	1,650	2,000	4,750	8,500	—

KM# EA17 • Copper • Rev. Legend: CONSTELLATIO.

Date	AG	Good	VG	Fine	VF	XF	Unc
1785	—	—	—	—	—	14,375	—

KM# EA17a • Silver • Rev. Legend: CONSTELLATIO.

Date	AG	Good	VG	Fine	VF	XF	Unc
1785	—	—	—	—	—	20,700	—

KM# EA18 • Copper • Obv. Legend: Extra star in border. **Rev. Legend:** CONSTELLATIO.

Date	AG	Good	VG	Fine	VF	XF	Unc
1785	—	—	—	—	—	—	—

Note: Caldwell $4,675

KM# EA19 • Copper • Rev: Blunt rays.

Date	AG	Good	VG	Fine	VF	XF	Unc
1785 2 known	—	—	—	—	—	—	—

Note: Norweb $22,000

KM# EA19a • Gold • Rev. Legend: CONSTELATIO.

Date	AG	Good	VG	Fine	VF	XF	Unc
1785 unique	—	—	—	—	—	—	—

KM# EA24 • Copper • Obv: Washington.

Date	AG	Good	VG	Fine	VF	XF	Unc
1786 3 known	—	—	—	—	—	—	—

Note: Garrett $50,000. Steinberg $12,650

KM# EA25 • Copper • Obv: Eagle.

Date	AG	Good	VG	Fine	VF	XF	Unc
1786 unique	—	—	—	—	—	—	—

Note: Garrett $37,500

KM# EA26 • Copper • Obv: Washington. **Rev:** Eagle.

Date	AG	Good	VG	Fine	VF	XF	Unc
1786 2 known	—	—	—	—	—	—	—

KM# EA27 • Copper • Obv. Legend: IMMUNIS COLUMBIA.

Date	AG	Good	VG	Fine	VF	XF	Unc
1786 extremely rare	—	—	—	—	—	—	—

Note: Rescigno, AU, $33,000. Steinberg, VF, $11,000

KM# EA28 • Copper • Obv. Legend: IMMUNIS COLUMBIA. **Rev:** Eagle.

Date	AG	Good	VG	Fine	VF	XF	Unc
1786 3 known	—	—	—	—	—	—	—

Nova Constellatio

KM# EA6.1 • Copper • Obv: Pointed rays. **Obv. Legend:** CONSTELLATIO. **Rev:** Small "US".

Date	AG	Good	VG	Fine	VF	XF	Unc
1783	20.00	35.00	65.00	125	255	585	—

KM# EA6.2 • Copper • Obv: Pointed rays. **Obv. Legend:** CONSTALLATIO. **Rev:** Large "US".

Date	AG	Good	VG	Fine	VF	XF	Unc
1783	20.00	35.00	70.00	140	285	650	—

KM# EA7 • Copper • Obv: Blunt rays. **Obv. Legend:** CONSTELATIO.

Date	AG	Good	VG	Fine	VF	XF	Unc
1783	22.00	40.00	80.00	150	350	750	—

KM# EA8 • Copper • Obv: Blunt rays. **Obv. Legend:** CONSTELATIO.

Date	AG	Good	VG	Fine	VF	XF	Unc
1785	22.00	40.00	80.00	160	375	775	—

KM# EA9 • Copper • Obv: Pointed rays. **Obv. Legend:** CONSTELLATIO.

Date	AG	Good	VG	Fine	VF	XF	Unc
1785	20.00	35.00	70.00	140	285	650	—

KM# EA10 • Copper • Note: Contemporary circulating counterfeit. Similar to previously listed coin.

Date	AG	Good	VG	Fine	VF	XF	Unc
1786 extremely rare	—	—	—	—	—	—	—

5 UNITS

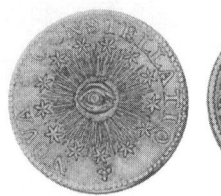

KM# EA12 • Copper •

Date	AG	Good	VG	Fine	VF	XF	Unc
1783 unique	—	—	—	—	—	—	—

100 (BIT)

KM# EA13.1 • Silver • Edge: Leaf.

Date	AG	Good	VG	Fine	VF	XF	Unc
1783 2 known	—	—	—	—	—	—	—

Note: Garrett $97,500. Stack's auction, May 1991, $72,500

KM# EA13.2 • Silver • Edge: Plain.

Date	AG	Good	VG	Fine	VF	XF	Unc
1783 unique	—	—	—	—	—	—	—

500 (QUINT)

KM# EA14 • Silver • Obv. Legend: NOVA CONSTELLATIO

Date	AG	Good	VG	Fine	VF	XF	Unc
1783 unique	—	—	—	—	—	—	—

Note: Garrett $165,000

KM# EA15 • Silver • Obv: Without legend

Date	AG	Good	VG	Fine	VF	XF	Unc
1783 unique	—	—	—	—	—	—	—

Note: Garrett $55,000

1000 (MARK)

KM# EA16 • Silver •

Date	AG	Good	VG	Fine	VF	XF	Unc
1783 unique	—	—	—	—	—	—	—

Note: Garrett $190,000

EARLY FEDERAL COINAGE

Brasher

KM# Tn51.1 • Gold • Rev: EB on wing.

Date	AG	Good	VG	Fine	VF	XF	Unc
1787 6 known	—	—	—	—	—	—	—

Note: Heritage FUN Sale, January 2005, AU-55, $2.415 million.

KM# Tn51.2 • Gold • Rev: EG on breast.

Date	AG	Good	VG	Fine	VF	XF	Unc
1787 unique	—	—	—	—	—	—	—

Note: Heritage FUN Sale, January 2005, XF-45, $2.99 million

Fugio "Cent"

KM# EA30.1 • Copper • Obv: Club rays, round ends.

Date	AG	Good	VG	Fine	VF	XF	Unc
1787	40.00	75.00	150	375	850	1,600	—

KM# EA30.2 • Copper • Obv: Club rays, concave ends.

Date	AG	Good	VG	Fine	VF	XF	Unc
1787	250	700	1,800	2,750	5,000	—	—

KM# EA30.3 • Copper • Obv. Legend: FUCIO.

Date	AG	Good	VG	Fine	VF	XF	Unc
1787	—	750	1,850	2,850	55,000	—	—

KM# EA31.1 • Copper • Obv: Pointed rays. **Rev:** UNITED above, STATES below.

Date	AG	Good	VG	Fine	VF	XF	Unc
1787	100.00	250	550	1,000	1,500	3,500	—

KM# EA31.2 • Copper • Rev: UNITED STATES at sides of ring.

Date	AG	Good	VG	Fine	VF	XF	Unc
1787	20.00	45.00	90.00	175	300	650	—

KM# EA31.3 • Copper • Rev: STATES UNITED at sides of ring.

Date	AG	Good	VG	Fine	VF	XF	Unc
1787	25.00	55.00	110	220	350	700	—

KM# EA31.4 • Copper • Rev: Eight-pointed stars on ring.

Date	AG	Good	VG	Fine	VF	XF	Unc
1787	30.00	65.00	120	250	400	800	—

KM# EA31.5 • Copper • Rev: Raised rims on ring, large lettering in center.

Date	AG	Good	VG	Fine	VF	XF	Unc
1787	35.00	75.00	135	275	450	950	—

KM# EA32.1 • Copper • Obv: No cinquefoils, cross after date. **Obv. Legend:** UNITED STATES.

Date	AG	Good	VG	Fine	VF	XF	Unc
1787	50.00	110	250	425	650	1,250	—

KM# EA32.2 • Copper • Obv: No cinquefoils, cross after date. **Obv. Legend:** STATES UNITED.

Date	AG	Good	VG	Fine	VF	XF	Unc
1787	60.00	110	250	425	650	1,250	—

KM# EA32.3 • Copper • Obv: No cinquefoils, cross after date. **Rev:** Raised rims on ring.

Date	AG	Good	VG	Fine	VF	XF	Unc
1787	—	—	—	—	2,600	—	—

KM# EA33 • Copper • Obv: No cinquefoils, cross after date. **Rev:** With rays. **Rev. Legend:** AMERICAN CONGRESS.

Date	AG	Good	VG	Fine	VF	XF	Unc
1787 extremely rare	—	—	—	—	—	—	—

Note: Norweb $63,800

KM# EA34 • Brass • Note: New Haven restrike.

Date	AG	Good	VG	Fine	VF	XF	Unc
	—	—	—	—	—	—	500

KM# EA34a • Copper • Note: New Haven restrike.

Date	AG	Good	VG	Fine	VF	XF	Unc
	—	—	—	—	—	500	—

KM# EA34b • Silver • Note: New Haven restrike.

Date	AG	Good	VG	Fine	VF	XF	Unc
	—	—	—	—	—	—	1,850

KM# EA34c • Gold • Note: New Haven restrike.

Date	AG	Good	VG	Fine	VF	XF	Unc
2 known	—	—	—	—	—	—	—

Note: Norweb (holed) $1,430

ISSUES OF 1792

CENT

KM# PnE1 • Copper Around Silver • Note: Silver plug in center.

Date	AG	Good	VG	Fine	VF	XF	Unc
1792 12 known	—	—	—	—	—	—	—

Note: Norweb, MS-60, $143,000

KM# PnF1 • Copper • Note: No silver center.

Date	AG	Good	VG	Fine	VF	XF	Unc
1792 8 known	—	—	—	—	—	—	—

Note: Norweb, EF-40, $35,200; Benson, VG-10, $57,500

KM# PnG1 • Copper • Edge: Plain **Note:** Commonly called "Birch cent."

Date	AG	Good	VG	Fine	VF	XF	Unc
1792 unique	—	—	—	—	—	—	—

KM# PnH1 • Copper • Obv: One star in edge legend **Note:** Commonly called "Birch cent."

Date	AG	Good	VG	Fine	VF	XF	Unc
1792 2 known	—	—	—	—	—	—	—

Note: Norweb, EF-40, $59,400

KM# PnI1 • Copper • Obv: Two stars in edge legend **Note:** Commonly called "Birch cent."

Date	AG	Good	VG	Fine	VF	XF	Unc
1792 6 known	—	—	—	—	—	—	—

Note: Hawn, strong VF, $57,750

KM# PnJ1 • **White Metal** • **Rev:** "G.W.Pt." below wreath tie **Note:** Commonly called "Birch cent."

Date	AG	Good	VG	Fine	VF	XF	Unc
1792 unique	—	—	—	—	—	—	—

Note: Garrett, $90,000

HALF DISME

KM# 5 • **Silver** •

Date	AG	Good	VG	Fine	VF	XF	Unc
1792	1,250	—	3,500	6,500	8,500	16,500	—

KM# PnA1 • **Copper** •

Date	AG	Good	VG	Fine	VF	XF	Unc
1792 unique	—	—	—	—	—	—	—

DISME

KM# PnB1 • **Silver** •

Date	AG	Good	VG	Fine	VF	XF	Unc
1792 3 known	—	—	—	—	—	—	—

Note: Norweb, EF-40, $28,600

KM# PnC1 • **Copper** • **Edge:** Reeded

Date	AG	Good	VG	Fine	VF	XF	Unc
1792 14 known	—	—	—	—	—	—	—

Note: Hawn, VF, $30,800; Benson, EF-45, $109,250

KM# PnD1 • **Copper** • **Edge:** Plain

Date	AG	Good	VG	Fine	VF	XF	Unc
1792 2 known	—	—	—	—	—	—	—

Note: Garrett, $45,000

QUARTER

KM# PnK1 • **Copper** • **Edge:** Reeded **Note:** Commonly called "Wright quarter."

Date	AG	Good	VG	Fine	VF	XF	Unc
1792 2 known	—	—	—	—	—	—	—

KM# PnL1 • **White Metal** • **Edge:** Plain **Note:** Commonly called "Wright quarter."

Date	AG	Good	VG	Fine	VF	XF	Unc
1792 2 known	—	—	—	—	—	—	—

Note: Norweb, VF-30 to EF-40, $28,600

KM# PnM1 • **White Metal** • **Note:** Commonly called "Wright quarter."

Date	AG	Good	VG	Fine	VF	XF	Unc
1792 die trial	—	—	—	—	—	—	—

Note: Garrett, $12,000

CIRCULATION COINAGE

HALF CENT

Liberty Cap
Head facing left obverse

KM# 10 • 6.7400 g., **Copper**, 22 mm. • **Designer:** Henry Voigt

Date	Mintage	G-4	VG-8	F-12	VF-20	XF-40	MS-60
1793	35,334	2,000	2,750	4,200	6,000	12,500	35,000

Head facing right obverse

KM# 14 • **Copper**, 6.74 g. (1794-95) and 5.44 g. (1795-97), 23.5 mm. • **Designer:** Robert Scot (1794) and John Smith Gardner (1795) **Notes:** The "lettered edge" varieties have "Two Hundred for a Dollar" inscribed around the edge. The "pole" varieties have a pole upon which the cap is hanging, resting on Liberty's shoulder. The "punctuated date" varieties have a comma after the 1 in the date. The 1797 "1 above 1" variety has a second 1 above the 1 in the date.

Date	Mintage	G-4	VG-8	F-12	VF-20	XF-40	MS-60
1794	81,600	375	650	850	1,600	3,500	18,000
1795 lettered edge, pole	25,600	425	500	850	1,500	4,250	17,500
1795 plain edge, no pole	109,000	375	475	800	1,400	3,500	16,000
1795 lettered edge, punctuated date	Inc. above	425	650	900	1,400	3,750	20,000
1795 plain edge, punctuated date	Inc. above	350	450	750	1,200	3,000	27,500
1796 pole	5,090	15,000	16,000	20,000	25,000	35,000	—
1796 no pole	1,390	27,000	32,500	47,500	90,000	—	—
1797 plain edge	119,215	400	575	950	1,900	6,000	27,500
1797 lettered edge	Inc. above	1,700	2,700	4,000	8,000	25,000	—
1797 1 above 1	Inc. above	375	475	950	1,600	3,250	20,000
1797 gripped edge	Inc. above	16,000	37,500	48,000	60,000	70,000	—

Draped Bust Half Cent

Stemless   Stems

KM# 33 • 5.4400 g., **Copper**, 23.5 mm. • **Designer:** Robert Scot **Notes:** The wreath on the reverse was redesigned slightly in 1802, resulting in "reverse of 1800" and "reverse of 1802" varieties. The "stems" varieties have stems extending from the wreath above and on both sides of the fraction on the reverse. On the 1804 "crosslet 4" variety, a serif appears at the far right of the crossbar on the 4 in the date. The "spiked chin" variety appears to have a spike extending from Liberty's chin, the result of a damaged die. Varieties of the 1805 strikes are distinguished by the size of the 5 in the date. Varieties of the 1806 strikes are distinguished by the size of the 6 in the date.

Date	Mintage	G-4	VG-8	F-12	VF-20	XF-40	MS-60
1800	211,530	50.00	75.00	100.00	200	500	2,500
1802/0 rev. 1800	14,366	15,000	22,000	30,000	—	—	—
1802/0 rev. 1802	Inc. above	800	1,200	2,750	6,500	17,000	—
1803	97,900	45.00	70.00	125	275	950	7,000
1804 plain 4, stemless wreath	1,055,312	50.00	60.00	85.00	130	250	1,400
1804 plain 4, stems	Inc. above	45.00	75.00	125	250	1,500	12,000
1804 crosslet 4, stemless	Inc. above	50.00	75.00	85.00	125	250	1,350

Date	Mintage	G-4	VG-8	F-12	VF-20	XF-40	MS-60
1804 crosslet 4, stems	Inc. above	47.00	75.00	110	175	300	1,200
1804 spiked chin	Inc. above	60.00	90.00	125	175	325	1,200
1805 small 5, stemless	814,464	50.00	75.00	90.00	135	400	3,500
1805 small 5, stems	Inc. above	675	1,200	2,400	4,500	8,000	—
1805 large 5, stems	Inc. above	49.00	65.00	85.00	125	400	3,000
1806 small 6, stems	356,000	175	325	600	1,000	2,750	—
1806 small 6, stemless	Inc. above	50.00	65.00	85.00	125	235	1,350
1806 large 6, stems	Inc. above	50.00	65.00	85.00	125	250	1,200
1807	476,000	50.00	80.00	120	175	300	1,400
1808/7	400,000	225	325	600	1,200	6,000	27,500
1808	Inc. above	50.00	65.00	90.00	135	350	5,000

Classic Head Half Cent

KM# 41 • 5.4400 g., **Copper**, 23.5 mm. • **Designer:** John Reich **Notes:** Restrikes listed were produced privately in the mid-1800s. The 1831 restrikes have two varieties with different-size berries in the wreath on the reverse. The 1828 strikes have either 12 or 13 stars on the obverse.

Date	Mintage	G-4	VG-8	F-12	VF-20	XF-40	MS-60
1809/6	1,154,572	50.00	80.00	110	150	215	1,000
1809	Inc. above	32.00	40.00	55.00	80.00	215	800
1809 circle in 0	—	35.00	45.00	60.00	110	250	2,100
1810	215,000	45.00	60.00	120	200	600	3,250
1811	63,140	200	275	550	1,350	4,000	—
1811 restrike, reverse of 1802, uncirculated	—	—	—	—	—	—	27,500
1825	63,000	35.00	40.00	55.00	90.00	175	950
1826	234,000	35.00	40.00	60.00	90.00	150	750
1828 13 stars	606,000	30.00	37.50	52.50	60.00	75.00	300
1828 12 stars	Inc. above	40.00	60.00	80.00	125	215	850
1829	487,000	35.00	40.00	65.00	90.00	150	500
1831 original	2,200	5,000	6,000	6,500	7,000	9,750	—
1831 1st restrike, lg. berries, reverse of 1836	—	—	—	—	—	—	6,500

1825 Half Cent
Grade F-12

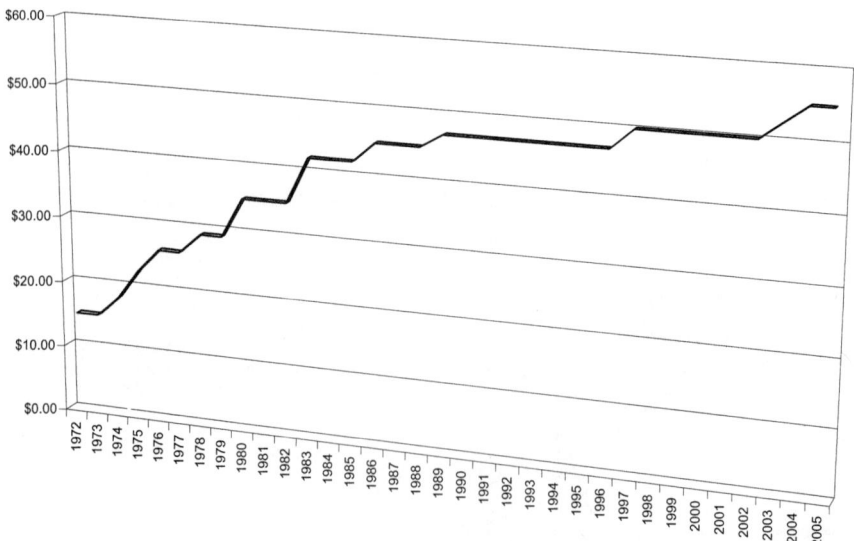
Retail Price

Date	Mintage	G-4	VG-8	F-12	VF-20	XF-40	MS-60
1831 2nd restrike, sm. berries, reverse of 1840, proof	—	—	—	—	—	—	25,000
1832	154,000	34.00	45.00	60.00	75.00	110	325
1833	120,000	34.00	45.00	60.00	75.00	110	325
1834	141,000	34.00	45.00	60.00	75.00	110	325
1835	398,000	34.00	45.00	60.00	75.00	110	325
1836 original, proof	—	—	—	—	—	—	5,000
1836 restrike, reverse of 1840, proof	—	—	—	—	—	—	18,000

Braided Hair Half Cent

KM# 70 • 5.4400 g., **Copper**, 23 mm. • **Designer:** Christian Gobrecht **Notes:** 1840-1849 and 1852 strikes, both originals and restrikes, are known in proof only; mintages are unknown. The small-date varieties of 1849, both originals and restrikes are known in proof only. The Restrikes were produced clandestinely by Philadelphia Mint personnel in the mid-1800s.

Date	Mintage	G-4	VG-8	F-12	VF-20	XF-40	MS-60	Prf-60
1840 original	—	1,000	1,200	1,500	2,000	3,000	—	5,500
1840 1st restrike	—	1,000	1,200	1,500	2,000	3,000	—	6,500
1840 2nd restrike	—	1,000	1,200	1,500	2,000	3,000	—	5,500
1841 original	—	1,000	1,200	1,500	2,000	3,000	—	5,500
1841 1st restrike	—	1,000	1,200	1,500	2,000	3,000	—	6,500
1841 2nd restrike	—	1,000	1,200	1,500	2,000	3,000	—	6,000
1842 original	—	1,000	1,200	1,500	2,000	3,000	—	6,000
1842 1st restrike	—	1,000	1,200	1,500	2,000	3,000	—	6,000
1842 2nd restrike	—	1,000	1,200	1,500	2,000	3,000	—	6,500
1843 original	—	1,000	1,200	1,500	2,000	3,000	—	6,000
1843 1st restrike	—	1,000	1,200	1,500	2,000	3,000	—	6,500
1843 2nd restrike	—	1,000	1,200	1,500	2,000	3,000	—	6,000
1844 original	—	1,000	1,200	1,500	2,000	3,000	—	6,000
1844 1st restrike	—	1,000	1,200	1,500	2,000	3,000	—	6,000
1844 2nd restrike	—	1,000	1,200	1,500	2,000	3,000	—	6,000
1845 original	—	1,000	1,200	1,500	2,000	3,000	—	6,000
1845 1st restrike	—	1,000	1,200	1,500	2,000	3,000	—	6,000
1845 2nd restrike	—	1,000	1,200	1,500	2,000	3,000	—	6,000
1846 original	—	1,000	1,200	1,500	2,000	3,000	—	6,000
1846 1st restrike	—	1,000	1,200	1,500	2,000	3,000	—	6,500
1846 2nd restrike	—	1,000	1,200	1,500	2,000	3,000	—	6,000
1847 original	—	1,000	1,200	1,500	2,000	3,000	—	6,000
1847 1st restrike	—	3,000	4,000	4,500	5,000	5,500	—	8,000
1847 2nd restrike	—	1,000	1,200	1,500	2,000	3,000	—	6,000
1848 original	—	1,000	1,200	1,500	2,000	3,000	—	6,000
1848 1st restrike	—	1,000	1,200	1,500	2,000	3,000	—	6,000
1848 2nd restrike	—	1,000	1,200	1,500	2,000	3,000	—	6,000
1849 original, small date	—	1,000	1,200	1,500	2,000	3,000	—	6,500
1849 1st restrike small date	—	1,000	1,200	1,500	2,000	3,000	—	6,000
1849 large date	39,864	40.00	45.00	75.00	100.00	150	275	—
1850	39,812	39.00	55.00	90.00	150	200	400	—
1851	147,672	30.00	40.00	55.00	65.00	100.00	175	—
1852 original	—	12,000	25,000	30,000	35,000	40,000	—	90,000
1852 1st restrike	—	1,000	1,200	1,500	2,000	3,000	—	5,000
1852 2nd restrike	—	1,000	1,200	1,500	2,000	3,000	—	7,000
1853	129,694	40.00	55.00	75.00	110	150	300	—
1854	55,358	40.00	55.00	75.00	110	150	300	—
1855	56,500	40.00	55.00	75.00	110	150	300	—
1856	40,430	40.00	55.00	75.00	110	150	300	—
1857	35,180	65.00	80.00	150	200	250	500	—

CENT

Flowing Hair Cent
Chain reverse

KM# 11 • 13.4800 g., **Copper**, 26-27 mm. • **Designer:** Henry Voigt

Date	Mintage	G-4	VG-8	F-12	VF-20	XF-40	MS-60
1793	36,103	7,750	11,000	15,000	23,000	33,000	135,000

Wreath reverse

KM# 12 • 13.4800 g., **Copper**, 26-28 mm. • **Designer:** Henry Voigt

Date	Mintage	G-4	VG-8	F-12	VF-20	XF-40	MS-60
1793	63,353	1,700	2,500	4,000	8,000	12,000	30,000

Liberty Cap Cent
Thick Planchet

KM# 13 • **Copper**, 13.48 g. (1793-95) and 10.89 g. (1795-96), 29 mm. • **Designer:** Joseph Wright (1793-1795) and John Smith Gardner (1795-1796) **Notes:** The heavier pieces were struck on a thicker planchet. The Liberty design on the obverse was revised slightly in 1794, but the 1793 design was used on some 1794 strikes. A 1795 "lettered edge" variety has "One Hundred for a Dollar" and a leaf inscribed on the edge.

Date	Mintage	G-4	VG-8	F-12	VF-20	XF-40	MS-60
1793 cap	11,056	5,000	6,000	9,000	20,000	26,000	—
1794	918,521	350	485	750	1,200	3,750	9,000
1794 head '93	Inc. above	1,500	2,600	4,000	7,900	12,000	—
1795	501,500	350	485	650	1,000	2,000	4,750

Thin Planchet

KM# 13a • 10.8900 g., **Copper**, 29 mm. • **Designer:** Joseph Wright (1793-1795) and John Smith Gardner (1795-1796)

Date	Mintage	G-4	VG-8	F-12	VF-20	XF-40	MS-60
1795 lettered edge, "One Cent" high in wreath	37,000	350	550	900	1,750	3,300	11,000

Date	Mintage	G-4	VG-8	F-12	VF-20	XF-40	MS-60
1796	109,825	350	500	800	1,400	3,750	21,000

Draped Bust Cent

Stemless   Stems

KM# 22 • 10.9800 g., **Copper**, 29 mm. • **Designer:** Robert Scot **Notes:** The "stemless" variety does not have stems extending from the wreath above and on both sides of the fraction on the reverse. The 1801 "3 errors" variety has the fraction on the reverse reading "1/000," has only one stem extending from the wreath above and on both sides of the fraction on the reverse, and "United" in "United States of America" appears as "Iinited."

Date	Mintage	G-4	VG-8	F-12	VF-20	XF-40	MS-60
1796	363,375	350	600	850	1,800	3,400	—
1797	897,510	130	175	250	335	1,150	3,300
1797 stemless	Inc. above	300	495	600	910	3,200	—
1798	1,841,745	90.00	130	200	350	1,300	3,100
1798/7	Inc. above	150	225	310	1,200	3,900	—
1799	42,540	3,250	4,500	7,500	16,000	35,000	—
1800	2,822,175	50.00	95.00	200	400	1,750	—
1801	1,362,837	60.00	87.00	180	325	1,000	—
1801 3 errors	Inc. above	100.00	250	700	1,500	5,500	—
1802	3,435,100	50.00	75.00	150	250	775	2,250
1803	2,471,353	50.00	80.00	150	250	775	2,250
1804	96,500	1,300	2,000	2,600	3,200	7,000	—
1804 Restrike of 1860	—	325	450	500	600	900	1,100
1805	941,116	60.00	90.00	160	300	875	2,450
1806	348,000	70.00	100.00	150	375	1,100	4,700
1807	727,221	60.00	80.00	160	300	800	2,250
1807/6 large 7/6	—	60.00	80.00	160	350	1,275	—
1807/6 small 7/6	—	1,900	2,900	4,200	6,000	19,000	—

1804 Cent
Grade F-12

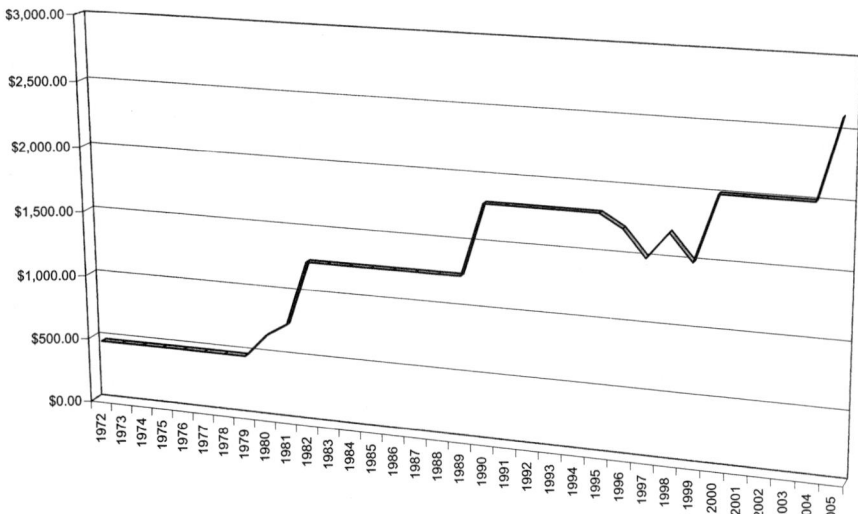

Retail Price

Classic Head Cent

KM# 39 • 10.8900 g., **Copper**, 29 mm. • **Designer:** John Reich

Date	Mintage	G-4	VG-8	F-12	VF-20	XF-40	MS-60
1808	1,109,000	125	200	325	575	1,200	3,600
1809	222,867	175	300	525	1,200	2,650	6,300
1810	1,458,500	75.00	95.00	210	550	1,100	3,850
1811	218,025	110	175	400	1,000	1,500	7,000
1811/10	Inc. above	130	200	440	1,200	2,200	—
1812	1,075,500	48.00	83.00	200	525	975	2,800
1813	418,000	60.00	95.00	375	600	1,200	—
1814	357,830	45.00	80.00	200	530	975	2,800

Coronet Cent

KM# 45 • 10.8900 g., **Copper**, 28-29 mm. • **Designer:** John Reich **Notes:** The 1817 strikes have either 13 or 15 stars on the obverse.

Date	Mintage	G-4	VG-8	F-12	VF-20	XF-40	MS-60
1816	2,820,982	25.00	30.00	50.00	100.00	175	420
1817 13 stars	3,948,400	20.00	26.00	30.00	60.00	120	470
1817 15 stars	Inc. above	27.50	32.50	45.00	125	350	1,600
1818	3,167,000	20.00	26.00	35.00	60.00	125	270
1819	2,671,000	20.00	26.00	35.00	63.00	120	285
1820	4,407,550	20.00	26.00	35.00	65.00	120	300
1821	389,000	32.50	55.00	250	400	1,500	6,000
1822	2,072,339	25.00	30.00	50.00	100.00	195	750
1823 Included in 1824 mintage	—	90.00	150	310	690	2,750	—
1823/22 Included in 1824 mintage	—	80.00	110	300	675	2,450	—
1823 Restrike	—	700	550	675	800	900	1,300
1824	1,262,000	20.00	26.00	38.00	160	350	950
1824/22	Inc. above	28.50	36.00	100.00	400	975	3,600
1825	1,461,100	20.00	26.00	40.00	110	300	960
1826	1,517,425	20.00	26.00	40.00	84.00	175	750
1826/25	Inc. above	21.00	40.00	75.00	175	600	2,000
1827	2,357,732	20.00	26.00	40.00	75.00	160	750
1828	2,260,624	20.00	26.00	40.00	90.00	175	450
1829	1,414,500	20.00	26.00	40.00	90.00	175	425
1830	1,711,500	20.00	26.00	40.00	90.00	175	400
1831	3,359,260	20.00	26.00	40.00	80.00	175	315
1832	2,362,000	20.00	26.00	40.00	80.00	175	380
1833	2,739,000	20.00	26.00	40.00	80.00	175	300
1834	1,855,100	20.00	26.00	40.00	80.00	175	300
1835	3,878,400	20.00	26.00	40.00	80.00	200	300
1836	2,111,000	20.00	26.00	40.00	80.00	175	300
1837	5,558,300	20.00	26.00	40.00	80.00	175	300
1838	6,370,200	20.00	26.00	40.00	80.00	175	300
1839	3,128,661	20.00	26.00	40.00	80.00	175	350
1839/36	Inc. above	400	500	700	1,500	3,900	—

1857 Cent
Grade XF-40

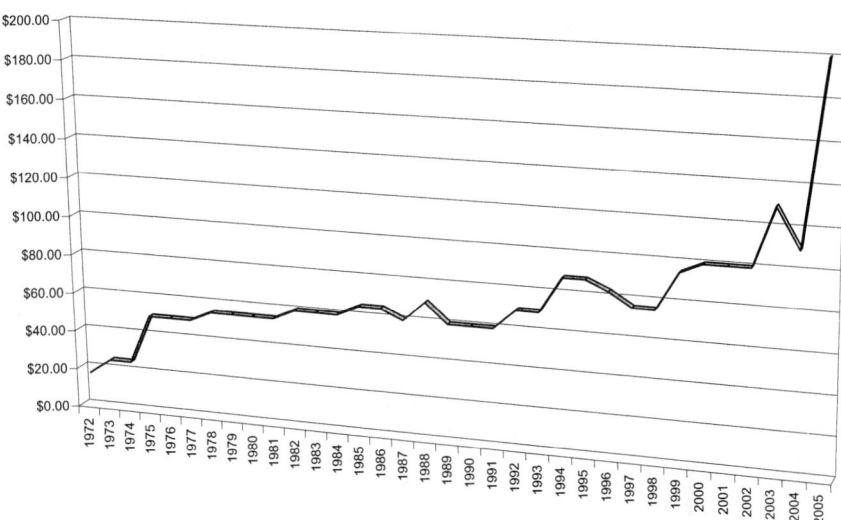

Retail Price

Braided Hair Cent

KM# 67 • 10.8900 g., **Copper**, 27.5 mm. • **Designer:** Christian Gobrecht **Notes:** 1840 and 1842 strikes are known with both small and large dates, with little difference in value. 1855 and 1856 strikes are known with both slanting and upright 5s in the date, with little difference in value. A slightly larger Liberty head and larger reverse lettering were used beginning in 1843. One 1843 variety uses the old obverse with the new reverse.

Date	Mintage	G-4	VG-8	F-12	VF-20	XF-40	MS-60
1840	2,462,700	20.00	30.00	40.00	50.00	70.00	475
1841	1,597,367	20.00	30.00	40.00	50.00	80.00	440
1842	2,383,390	20.00	30.00	40.00	50.00	70.00	425
1843	2,425,342	20.00	30.00	40.00	50.00	75.00	445
1843 obverse 1842 with reverse of 1844	Inc. above	20.00	30.00	40.00	50.00	80.00	350
1844	2,398,752	20.00	30.00	40.00	50.00	75.00	225
1844/81	Inc. above	30.00	75.00	125	175	225	600
1845	3,894,804	20.00	30.00	40.00	50.00	75.00	225
1846	4,120,800	20.00	30.00	40.00	50.00	75.00	225
1847	6,183,669	20.00	30.00	40.00	50.00	75.00	200
1848	6,415,799	20.00	30.00	40.00	50.00	75.00	200
1849	4,178,500	20.00	30.00	40.00	50.00	75.00	275
1850	4,426,844	20.00	30.00	40.00	50.00	75.00	250
1851	9,889,707	20.00	30.00	40.00	50.00	75.00	200
1851/81	Inc. above	27.00	39.00	75.00	125	290	600
1852	5,063,094	20.00	30.00	40.00	50.00	75.00	200
1853	6,641,131	20.00	30.00	40.00	50.00	75.00	200
1854	4,236,156	20.00	30.00	40.00	50.00	75.00	200
1855	1,574,829	20.00	30.00	40.00	50.00	75.00	200
1856	2,690,463	20.00	30.00	40.00	50.00	75.00	200
1857	333,456	60.00	90.00	120	150	200	400

Flying Eagle Cent

   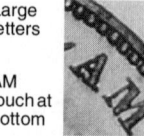 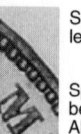

Large letters

AM touch at bottom

Small letters

Space between AM

KM# 85 • 4.6700 g., **Copper-Nickel**, 19 mm. • **Designer:** James B. Longacre **Notes:** On the large-letter variety of 1858, the "A" and "M" in "America" are connected at their bases; on the small-letter variety, the two letters are separated.

Date	Mintage	G-4	VG-8	F-12	VF-20	XF-40	AU-50	MS-60	MS-65	Prf-65
1856	Est. 2,500	6,250	7,250	8,000	9,900	11,000	12,800	16,500	58,000	24,500
1857	17,450,000	20.00	24.00	33.00	44.00	125	165	285	3,750	29,000
1858/7	—	65.00	90.00	175	390	750	1,500	2,500	75,000	—
1858 large letters	24,600,000	20.00	24.00	34.00	52.50	140	200	345	3,750	23,500
1858 small letters	Inc. above	20.00	24.00	33.00	44.00	125	175	290	3,800	30,000

Indian Head Cent

KM# 87 • 4.6700 g., **Copper-Nickel**, 19 mm. • **Designer:** James B. Longacre

Date	Mintage	G-4	VG-8	F-12	VF-20	XF-40	AU-50	MS-60	MS-65	Prf-65
1859	36,400,000	12.50	15.00	21.00	46.00	100.00	175	215	3,200	5,000

Shield added at top of wreath reverse

KM# 90 • 4.6700 g., **Copper-Nickel**, 19 mm. • **Designer:** James B. Longacre

Date	Mintage	G-4	VG-8	F-12	VF-20	XF-40	AU-50	MS-60	MS-65	Prf-65
1860	20,566,000(1,000)	10.00	13.50	19.00	27.50	53.50	80.00	185	1,000	3,900
1861	10,100,000	20.00	30.00	41.00	52.50	90.00	160	180	1,000	7,150
1862	28,075,000	7.50	9.00	10.00	14.50	27.50	55.00	80.00	1,000	2,100

1864-L Indian Cent
Grade F-12

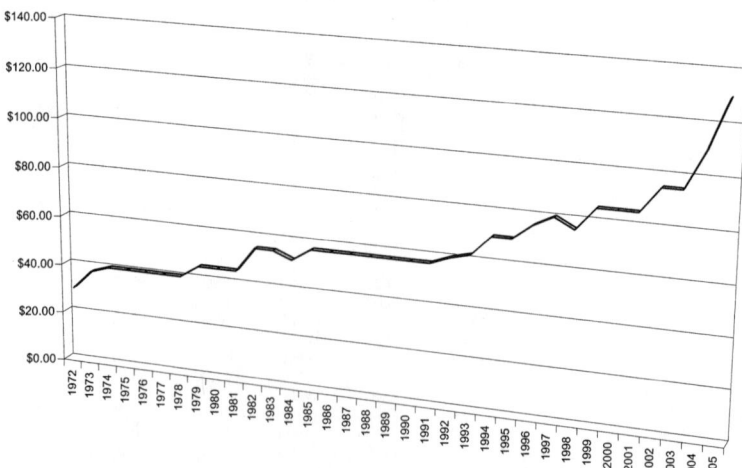

Retail Price

Date	Mintage	G-4	VG-8	F-12	VF-20	XF-40	AU-50	MS-60	MS-65	Prf-65
1863	49,840,000	7.50	9.00	10.00	11.00	24.00	54.00	72.50	1,000	3,200
1864	13,740,000	15.00	20.00	34.00	47.50	70.00	92.50	150	1,250	3,200

1864 "L"

KM# 90a • 3.1100 g., **Bronze**, 19 mm. • **Designer:** James B. Longacre **Notes:** The 1864 "L" variety has the designer's initial in Liberty's hair to the right of her neck.

Date	Mintage	G-4	VG-8	F-12	VF-20	XF-40	AU-50	MS-60	MS-65	Prf-65
1864	39,233,714	6.00	12.00	20.00	37.50	60.00	75.00	90.00	325	4,300
1864 L	Inc. above	50.00	65.00	130	170	260	310	400	1,650	110,000
1865	35,429,286	6.00	10.00	17.50	23.00	35.00	50.00	80.00	450	1,550
1866	9,826,500	40.00	48.00	60.00	95.00	180	215	250	1,250	950
1867	9,821,000	40.00	53.00	70.00	110	175	210	265	1,250	1,050
1868	10,266,500	37.50	40.00	65.00	100.00	150	180	220	1,000	985
1869/9	6,420,000	115	155	330	480	650	685	775	1,800	—
1869	Inc. above	60.00	85.00	215	300	400	475	510	1,650	950
1870	5,275,000	45.00	70.00	200	280	375	440	515	1,600	1,075
1871	3,929,500	60.00	100.00	230	285	380	400	425	2,550	1,100
1872	4,042,000	67.50	150	375	425	575	700	775	4,100	1,100
1873	11,676,500	21.00	30.00	46.00	75.00	150	190	215	1,300	850
1874	14,187,500	15.00	20.00	35.00	55.00	95.00	125	170	700	800
1875	13,528,000	15.00	27.50	47.50	62.50	95.00	135	175	800	1,500
1876	7,944,000	27.00	35.00	62.50	125	200	265	315	1,100	925
1877	852,500	590	780	1,250	1,600	2,100	2,650	2,850	8,750	4,900
1878	5,799,850	28.00	38.00	65.00	135	225	265	315	900	490
1879	16,231,200	7.00	11.00	16.00	33.00	65.00	72.50	75.00	350	450
1880	38,964,955	4.00	6.00	8.00	11.00	25.00	37.50	60.00	350	435
1881	39,211,575	4.00	5.00	7.00	10.00	18.00	30.00	40.00	330	425
1882	38,581,100	4.00	6.00	8.00	11.00	18.00	30.00	37.50	330	425
1883	45,589,109	3.00	4.50	7.00	10.00	16.00	24.00	38.50	330	425
1884	23,261,742	4.00	6.00	8.00	14.00	27.00	38.00	65.00	500	425
1885	11,765,384	6.00	8.00	15.00	29.00	54.00	65.00	95.00	750	425
1886	17,654,290	4.00	6.00	30.00	65.00	120	175	200	1,250	460
1887	45,226,483	2.00	3.00	4.00	6.00	15.00	28.00	50.00	395	475
1888	37,494,414	2.00	2.50	4.00	7.00	20.00	28.00	42.00	950	525
1889	48,869,361	1.75	2.20	2.50	4.00	10.00	27.00	35.00	395	450
1890	57,182,854	1.50	1.80	2.50	4.00	10.00	22.00	35.00	395	500
1891	47,072,350	1.70	2.25	3.00	4.50	10.00	22.00	35.00	400	520
1892	37,649,832	2.00	2.25	3.00	5.00	16.00	20.00	34.00	395	525
1893	46,642,195	1.70	2.25	3.00	5.00	10.00	22.00	30.00	340	540
1894	16,752,132	4.00	6.00	12.00	20.00	45.00	55.00	70.00	375	525
1895	38,343,636	1.75	2.00	3.00	6.00	12.00	22.00	32.00	200	475
1896	39,057,293	1.50	2.00	2.75	5.00	10.00	21.00	33.00	230	425
1897	50,466,330	1.50	2.00	2.25	4.00	10.00	20.00	30.00	200	425
1898	49,823,079	1.50	2.00	2.25	3.00	10.00	20.00	30.00	200	425
1899	53,600,031	1.50	1.80	2.00	3.00	10.00	18.00	27.50	140	415
1900	66,833,764	1.40	1.70	2.00	4.00	12.00	20.00	25.00	175	425
1901	79,611,143	1.35	1.65	1.85	3.00	7.50	17.00	25.00	140	425
1902	87,376,722	1.35	1.65	1.85	3.00	7.00	17.00	25.00	140	425
1903	85,094,493	1.35	1.65	1.85	3.00	7.00	17.00	25.00	140	425
1904	61,328,015	1.35	1.65	1.85	3.00	7.00	17.00	25.00	140	475
1905	80,719,163	1.35	1.65	1.85	3.00	7.00	17.00	25.00	140	475
1906	96,022,255	1.35	1.65	1.85	3.00	7.00	17.00	25.00	140	395
1907	108,138,618	1.35	1.65	1.85	3.00	7.00	17.00	25.00	145	485
1908	32,327,987	1.60	2.00	2.25	3.00	7.50	18.00	26.00	145	395
1908S	1,115,000	60.00	65.00	75.00	88.00	150	185	275	650	—
1909	14,370,645	3.00	3.50	4.00	5.00	15.00	24.00	30.00	150	400
1909S	309,000	350	375	425	475	550	635	750	1,500	—

Lincoln Cent
Wheat Ears reverse

KM# 132 • 3.1100 g., **Bronze**, 19 mm. • **Designer:** Victor D. Brenner **Notes:** The 1909 "VDB" varieties have the designer's initials inscribed at the 6 o'clock position on the reverse. The initials were removed until 1918, when they were restored on the obverse.

Date	Mintage	G-4	VG-8	F-12	VF-20	XF-40	AU-50	MS-60	MS-65	Prf-65
1909	72,702,618	1.35	1.60	1.90	2.10	3.40	9.00	13.50	80.00	520
1909 VDB	27,995,000	4.25	4.50	4.75	5.00	5.25	5.75	9.50	100.00	6,000
1909S	1,825,000	68.50	75.00	95.00	140	195	225	285	1,300	—
1909S VDB	484,000	550	675	780	800	1,100	1,200	1,300	6,750	—
1910	146,801,218	.25	.30	.40	.50	3.75	8.00	17.50	250	700
1910S	6,045,000	7.50	9.50	11.00	13.50	28.50	60.00	65.00	800	—
1911	101,177,787	16.00	.45	1.50	2.15	4.00	8.00	19.00	375	600
1911D	12,672,000	5.00	5.75	9.50	15.00	40.00	65.00	80.00	1,350	—
1911S	4,026,000	16.00	20.00	23.50	30.00	47.50	90.00	150	3,300	—
1912	68,153,060	1.25	1.50	2.20	5.50	11.00	20.00	30.00	550	950
1912D	10,411,000	6.75	7.75	9.50	22.00	50.00	85.00	150	1,900	—
1912S	4,431,000	13.50	16.75	20.00	25.00	55.00	85.00	130	4,250	—
1913	76,532,352	.65	.75	1.40	3.00	13.50	20.00	33.50	410	550
1913D	15,804,000	2.75	3.00	3.50	10.50	27.50	55.00	90.00	1,925	—
1913S	6,101,000	6.50	7.75	9.00	14.00	33.50	75.00	135	5,500	—
1914	75,238,432	.45	.70	2.00	5.25	13.50	32.50	47.50	415	600
1914D	1,193,000	125	180	260	335	575	1,250	1,600	21,000	—
1914S	4,137,000	12.50	15.00	17.00	27.00	60.00	150	275	9,800	—
1915	29,092,120	1.35	1.75	3.50	12.50	41.50	67.50	80.00	1,150	600
1915D	22,050,000	1.50	1.75	3.00	5.50	19.00	41.50	67.50	1,250	—
1915S	4,833,000	7.50	9.50	12.50	18.00	45.00	75.00	150	4,800	—
1916	131,833,677	.20	.25	.80	2.15	5.00	10.00	16.00	415	1,650
1916D	35,956,000	1.00	1.85	2.80	5.50	12.50	27.50	65.00	3,000	—
1916S	22,510,000	1.60	3.15	4.35	6.75	16.50	35.00	71.00	6,850	—
1917	196,429,785	.20	.25	.30	1.85	4.00	9.50	16.00	450	—
1917D	55,120,000	.70	1.00	2.20	4.25	14.00	30.00	60.00	3,000	—
1917S	32,620,000	.50	.80	1.25	2.15	9.50	21.50	56.00	6,850	—
1918	288,104,634	.20	.25	.30	.80	3.75	7.50	12.50	415	—
1918D	47,830,000	.80	1.30	2.20	4.00	12.50	26.00	62.50	3,550	—
1918S	34,680,000	.30	.75	1.00	2.75	8.50	30.00	57.50	6,850	—
1919	392,021,000	.20	.25	.30	.50	1.35	4.00	8.00	100.00	—
1919D	57,154,000	.80	1.00	1.25	2.75	7.00	30.00	47.50	2,500	—
1919S	139,760,000	.25	.40	1.40	2.50	4.50	16.00	41.50	4,000	—
1920	310,165,000	.20	.25	.35	.90	2.65	5.50	12.50	195	—
1920D	49,280,000	.80	1.00	1.85	2.80	12.50	31.00	62.50	2,750	—
1920S	46,220,000	.60	.65	1.50	2.15	8.50	32.50	80.00	8,000	—
1921	39,157,000	.40	.65	.80	2.15	6.75	20.00	38.00	235	—
1921S	15,274,000	1.50	1.95	2.50	4.40	25.00	67.00	100.00	5,500	—
1922D	7,160,000	10.00	12.00	14.00	17.00	27.50	47.50	75.00	2,350	—
1922 No D-T.2	Inc. above	480	645	970	1,550	3,500	6,850	7,500	180,000	—
1923	74,723,000	.35	.45	.65	.90	3.40	8.00	13.50	480	—
1923S	8,700,000	1.85	2.50	3.40	6.50	26.00	75.00	195	13,500	—

1914-D Cent
Grade F-12

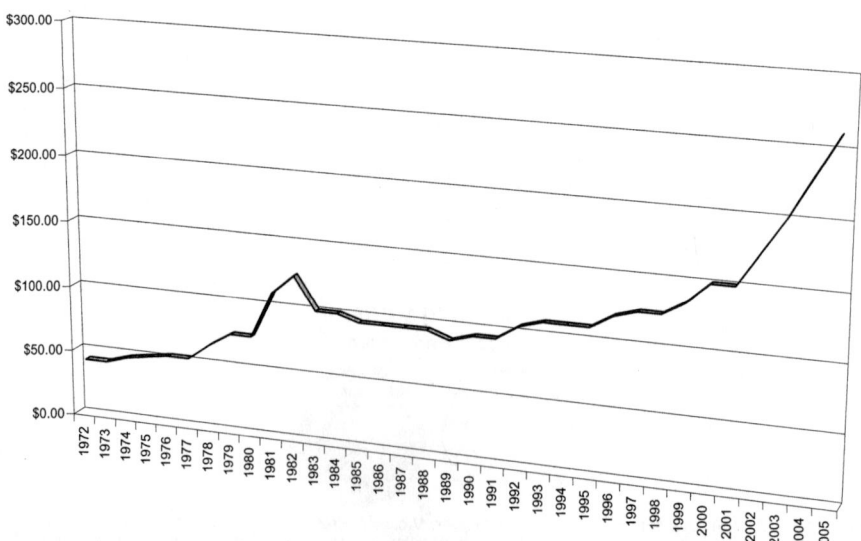

☐ Retail Price

Date	Mintage	G-4	VG-8	F-12	VF-20	XF-40	AU-50	MS-60	MS-65	Prf-65
1924	75,178,000	.20	.30	.40	.60	3.00	8.00	20.00	390	—
1924D	2,520,000	15.00	18.00	22.00	35.00	85.00	150	235	8,350	—
1924S	11,696,000	1.25	1.50	2.50	400	16.00	60.00	100.00	11,000	—
1925	139,949,000	.20	.25	.30	.50	2.50	6.00	8.50	100.00	—
1925D	22,580,000	.60	1.25	1.85	4.00	10.00	23.50	50.00	4,350	—
1925S	26,380,000	.60	.80	1.50	2.15	9.50	30.00	68.50	8,400	—
1926	157,088,000	.15	.20	.25	.50	1.35	4.00	7.00	66.00	—
1926D	28,020,000	.75	1.00	1.85	2.75	10.00	27.50	65.00	4,350	—
1926S	4,550,000	4.00	5.00	7.00	9.00	18.00	56.00	110	67,500	—
1927	144,440,000	.15	.20	.25	.50	1.35	3.25	7.00	95.00	—
1927D	27,170,000	.80	1.10	1.50	2.15	4.65	20.00	55.00	1,700	—
1927S	14,276,000	1.25	1.85	2.50	4.65	11.00	32.50	62.50	6,000	—
1928	134,116,000	.15	.20	.25	.45	1.10	3.00	7.50	90.00	—
1928D	31,170,000	.80	1.00	1.50	2.15	4.65	12.50	30.00	1,100	—
1928S	17,266,000	.90	1.40	2.50	3.00	6.25	20.00	65.00	4,800	—
1929	185,262,000	.15	.20	.25	.40	.70	4.25	6.00	85.00	—
1929D	41,730,000	.40	.80	1.10	2.15	4.65	11.00	21.50	550	—
1929S	50,148,000	.50	.85	1.50	2.15	4.00	6.75	17.50	415	—
1930	157,415,000	.15	.20	.25	.40	1.10	2.25	3.75	32.50	—
1930D	40,100,000	.20	.25	.40	.55	1.95	4.00	10.50	95.00	—
1930S	24,286,000	.25	.35	.50	.65	1.10	6.50	10.00	50.00	—
1931	19,396,000	.45	.50	.80	1.85	2.50	8.00	19.00	100.00	—
1931D	4,480,000	3.75	4.40	5.00	6.25	11.00	37.50	52.00	815	—
1931S	866,000	62.50	65.00	75.00	76.00	78.50	85.00	100.00	750	—
1932	9,062,000	1.30	1.75	2.75	3.25	4.25	11.50	19.00	72.50	—
1932D	10,500,000	1.10	1.85	2.35	2.75	3.75	8.50	17.50	80.00	—
1933	14,360,000	1.10	1.65	2.35	2.75	4.00	8.50	17.50	70.00	—
1933D	6,200,000	2.50	3.15	3.75	5.00	7.75	13.50	19.00	70.00	—
1934	219,080,000	—	.15	.20	.25	.75	1.50	4.00	27.00	—
1934D	28,446,000	.15	.20	.25	.45	1.50	5.00	16.50	52.00	—
1935	245,338,000	—	.10	.15	.25	.75	1.00	2.50	13.00	—
1935D	47,000,000	—	.15	.20	.30	.95	2.50	5.50	9.50	—
1935S	38,702,000	.10	.20	.30	.40	1.00	3.00	12.00	46.00	—
1936	309,637,569	—	.10	.15	.25	.75	1.00	2.00	6.00	1,200
1936D	40,620,000	—	.10	.15	.25	.75	1.50	2.75	8.50	—
1936S	29,130,000	.10	.15	.25	.35	.85	1.75	2.75	8.50	—
1937	309,179,320	—	.10	.15	.20	.70	.90	1.75	7.00	125
1937D	50,430,000	—	.10	.15	.25	.70	1.00	2.50	9.50	—
1937S	34,500,000	—	.10	.15	.25	.60	1.25	3.00	8.50	—
1938	156,696,734	—	.10	.15	.20	.50	1.00	2.00	8.00	85.00
1938D	20,010,000	.20	.25	.35	.45	.75	1.50	3.50	12.50	—
1938S	15,180,000	.30	.40	.50	.70	1.00	2.00	2.80	8.50	—
1939	316,479,520	—	.10	.15	.20	.30	.50	1.00	5.75	78.00
1939D	15,160,000	.35	.40	.35	.60	.85	1.90	2.25	8.50	—
1939S	52,070,000	—	.15	.20	.25	.45	.90	1.35	9.50	—
1940	586,825,872	—	.15	.20	.25	.30	.45	1.00	5.75	70.00
1940D	81,390,000	—	.15	.20	.25	.35	.50	1.20	5.75	—
1940S	112,940,000	—	.15	.20	.25	.30	.75	1.25	5.85	—
1941	887,039,100	—	—	.10	.15	.25	.40	.85	5.75	65.00
1941D	128,700,000	—	—	.15	.20	.25	1.00	2.00	8.50	—
1941S	92,360,000	—	—	.15	.20	.25	1.25	2.25	11.00	—
1942	657,828,600	—	—	.10	.15	.20	.25	.50	4.60	78.00
1942D	206,698,000	—	—	.10	.15	.20	.30	.50	5.75	—
1942S	85,590,000	—	—	.10	.20	.30	1.50	3.50	16.00	—

1943 Steel Cents

KM# 132a • 2.7000 g., **Zinc Coated Steel**, 19 mm. • **Designer:** Victor D. Brenner

Date	Mintage	G-4	VG-8	F-12	VF-20	XF-40	AU-50	MS-60	MS-65	Prf-65
1943	684,628,670	—	—	.25	.30	.50	.70	.85	4.75	—
1943D	217,660,000	—	—	.25	.35	.60	.65	1.00	6.50	—
1943S	191,550,000	—	.30	.35	.40	.70	1.00	3.00	12.50	—

KM# A132 • 3.1100 g., **Copper-Zinc**, 19 mm. • **Designer:** Victor D. Brenner **Notes:** KM#132 design and composition resumed.

Date	Mintage	XF-40	MS-65	Prf-65	Date	Mintage	XF-40	MS-65	Prf-65
1944	1,435,400,000	.20	2.00	—	1946	991,655,000	.20	2.00	—
1944D	430,578,000	.20	2.00	—	1946D	315,690,000	.20	4.50	—
1944D/S	—	180	1,600	—	1946S	198,100,000	.20	4.60	—
1944S	282,760,000	.20	5.50	—	1947	190,555,000	.20	2.25	—
1945	1,040,515,000	.20	2.00	—	1947D	194,750,000	.20	2.00	—
1945D	226,268,000	.20	2.00	—	1947S	99,000,000	.20	5.50	—
1945S	181,770,000	.20	5.50	—	1948	317,570,000	.20	2.00	—

Date	Mintage	XF-40	MS-65	Prf-65
1948D	172,637,000	.20	2.25	—
1948S	81,735,000	.20	5.50	—
1949	217,775,000	.20	3.50	—
1949D	153,132,000	.20	3.50	—
1949S	64,290,000	.25	6.00	—
1950	272,686,386	.20	1.75	40.00
1950D	334,950,000	.20	1.50	—
1950S	118,505,000	.20	2.50	—
1951	295,633,500	.20	2.00	40.00
1951D	625,355,000	.10	1.65	—
1951S	136,010,000	.15	3.00	—
1952	186,856,980	.15	3.00	34.00
1952D	746,130,000	.10	1.60	—
1952S	137,800,004	.15	5.00	—
1953	256,883,800	.10	1.25	28.00
1953D	700,515,000	.10	1.25	—
1953S	181,835,000	.15	1.75	—
1954	71,873,350	.15	1.25	9.00
1954D	251,552,500	.10	.50	—
1954S	96,190,000	.15	.75	—
1955	330,958,000	.10	.75	13.00
1955 doubled die	—	1,350	34,500	—

Note: The 1955 "doubled die" has distinct doubling of the date and lettering on the obverse.

Date	Mintage	XF-40	MS-65	Prf-65
1955D	563,257,500	.10	.75	—
1955S	44,610,000	.25	1.00	—
1956	421,414,384	—	.50	3.00
1956D	1,098,201,100	—	.50	—
1957	283,787,952	—	.50	2.00
1957D	1,051,342,000	—	.50	—
1958	253,400,652	—	.50	3.00
1958D	800,953,300	—	.50	—

Lincoln Memorial reverse

KM# 201 • 3.1100 g., **Copper-Zinc** • **Rev. Des.:** Frank Gasparro **Notes:** The dates were modified in 1960, 1970 and 1982, resulting in large-date and small-date varieties for those years. The 1972 "doubled die" shows doubling of "In God We Trust." The 1979-S and 1981-S Type II proofs have a clearer mint mark than the Type I proofs of those years. Some 1982 cents have the predominantly copper composition; others have the predominantly zinc composition. They can be distinguished by weight.

Date	Mintage	XF-40	MS-65	Prf-65
1959	610,864,291	—	.50	1.50
1959D	1,279,760,000	—	.50	—
1960 small date	588,096,602	2.10	7.00	16.00
1960 large date	Inc. above	—	.30	1.25
1960D small date	1,580,884,000	—	.30	—
1960D large date	Inc. above	—	.30	—
1961	756,373,244	—	.30	1.00
1961D	1,753,266,700	—	.30	—
1962	609,263,019	—	.30	1.00
1962D	1,793,148,400	—	.30	—
1963	757,185,645	—	.30	1.00
1963D	1,774,020,400	—	.30	—
1964	2,652,525,762	—	.30	1.00
1964D	3,799,071,500	—	.30	—
1965	1,497,224,900	—	.30	—
1966	2,188,147,783	—	.30	—
1967	3,048,667,100	—	.50	—
1968	1,707,880,970	—	.30	—
1968D	2,886,269,600	—	.40	—
1968S	261,311,510	—	.40	1.00
1969	1,136,910,000	—	.60	—
1969D	4,002,832,200	—	.40	—
1969S	547,309,631	—	.40	1.10
1970	1,898,315,000	—	.40	—
1970D	2,891,438,900	—	.40	—
1970S	693,192,814	—	.40	1.20

Date	Mintage	XF-40	MS-65	Prf-65
1970S small date	—	—	55.00	60.00
1971	1,919,490,000	—	.35	—
1971D	2,911,045,600	—	.40	—
1971S	528,354,192	—	.25	1.20
1972	2,933,255,000	—	.25	—
1972 doubled die	—	275	715	—
1972D	2,665,071,400	—	.25	—
1972S	380,200,104	—	.25	1.15
1973	3,728,245,000	—	.25	—
1973D	3,549,576,588	—	.25	—
1973S	319,937,634	—	.25	0.80
1974	4,232,140,523	—	.25	—
1974D	4,235,098,000	—	.25	—
1974S	412,039,228	—	.25	0.75
1975	5,451,476,142	—	.25	—
1975D	4,505,245,300	—	.25	—
1975S	(2,845,450)	—	—	5.50
1976	4,674,292,426	—	.25	—
1976D	4,221,592,455	—	.25	—
1976S	(4,149,730)	—	—	5.00
1977	4,469,930,000	—	.25	—
1977D	4,149,062,300	—	.25	—
1977S	(3,251,152)	—	—	3.00
1978	5,558,605,000	—	.25	—
1978D	4,280,233,400	—	.25	—
1978S	(3,127,781)	—	—	3.50
1979	6,018,515,000	—	.25	—
1979D	4,139,357,254	—	.25	—
1979S type I, proof	(3,677,175)	—	—	4.00
1979S type II, proof	Inc. above	—	—	4.25
1980	7,414,705,000	—	.25	—
1980D	5,140,098,660	—	.25	—
1980S	(3,554,806)	—	—	2.25
1981	7,491,750,000	—	.25	—
1981S type II, proof	Inc. above	—	—	60.00
1981D	5,373,235,677	—	.25	—
1981S type I, proof	(4,063,083)	—	—	3.50
1982 large date	10,712,525,000	—	.25	—
1982 small date	—	—	.25	—
1982D large date	6,012,979,368	—	.25	—

Lincoln Memorial reverse - 1982 Varieties

KM# 201a • 2.5000 g., **Copper Plated Zinc**, 19 mm.

Date	Mintage	XF-40	MS-65	Prf-65
1982 large date	—	—	.50	—
1982 small date	—	—	2.00	—
1982D large date	—	—	.30	—
1982D small date	—	—	.25	—

KM# 201b • **Copper Plated Zinc**, 19 mm. • **Notes:** The 1983 "doubled die reverse" shows doubling of "United States of America." The 1984 "doubled die" shows doubling of Lincoln's ear on the obverse.

Date	Mintage	XF-40	MS-65	Prf-65
1982S	(3,857,479)	—	—	3.00
1983	7,752,355,000	—	.25	—
1983 doubled die	—	—	400	—
1983D	6,467,199,428	—	.50	—
1983S	(3,279,126)	—	—	4.00
1984	8,151,079,000	—	.25	—
1984 doubled die	—	—	275	—
1984D	5,569,238,906	—	.75	—
1984S	(3,065,110)	—	—	4.50
1985	5,648,489,887	—	.25	—
1985D	5,287,399,926	—	.25	—
1985S	(3,362,821)	—	—	6.00
1986	4,491,395,493	—	1.50	—
1986D	4,442,866,698	—	1.25	—

Date	Mintage	XF-40	MS-65	Prf-65	Date	Mintage	XF-40	MS-65	Prf-65
1986S	(3,010,497)	—	—	7.50	1995D	7,128,560,000	—	.25	—
1987	4,682,466,931	—	.25	—	1995S	(2,707,481)	—	—	9.50
1987D	4,879,389,514	—	.25	—	1996	6,612,465,000	—	.25	—
1987S	(4,227,728)	—	—	5.00	1996D	6,510,795,000	—	.25	—
1988	6,092,810,000	—	.25	—	1996S	(2,915,212)	—	—	6.50
1988D	5,253,740,443	—	.25	—	1997	4,622,800,000	—	.25	—
1988S	(3,262,948)	—	—	12.50	1997D	4,576,555,000	—	.25	—
1989	7,261,535,000	—	.25	—	1997S	(2,796,678)	—	—	11.50
1989D	5,345,467,111	—	.25	—	1998	5,032,155,000	—	.25	—
1989S	(3,220,194)	—	—	12.50	1998D	5,255,353,500	—	.25	—
1990	6,851,765,000	—	.25	—	1998S	(2,957,286)	—	—	9.50
1990D	4,922,894,533	—	.25	—	1999	5,237,600,000	—	.25	—
1990S	(3,299,559)	—	—	5.75	1999D	6,360,065,000	—	.25	—
1990 no S	—	—	—	2,750	1999S	(3,362,462)	—	—	5.00
1991	5,165,940,000	—	.25	—	2000	5,503,200,000	—	.25	—
1991D	4,158,442,076	—	.25	—	2000D	8,774,220,000	—	.25	—
1991S	(2,867,787)	—	—	30.00	2000S	(4,063,361)	—	—	4.00
1992	4,648,905,000	—	.25	—	2001P	4,959,600,000	—	.25	—
1992D	4,448,673,300	—	.25	—	2001D	5,374,990,000	—	.25	—
1992S	(4,176,560)	—	—	5.50	2001S	(3,099,096)	—	—	4.00
1993	5,684,705,000	—	.25	—	2002P	3,260,800,000	—	.25	—
1993D	6,426,650,571	—	.25	—	2002D	4,028,055,000	—	.25	—
1993S	(3,394,792)	—	—	9.50	2002S	(3,157,739)	—	—	4.00
1994	6,500,850,000	—	.25	—	2003P	—	—	.25	—
1994D	7,131,765,000	—	.25	—	2003D	—	—	.25	—
1994S	(3,269,923)	—	—	8.50	2003S	(3,116,590)	—	—	4.00
1995	6,411,440,000	—	.25	—	2004S	—	—	—	—
1995 doubled die	—	20.00	50.00	—					

2 CENTS

Small motto   Large motto

KM# 94 • 6.2200 g., **Copper-Tin-Zinc**, 23 mm. • **Designer:** James B. Longacre **Notes:** The motto "In God We Trust" was modified in 1864, resulting in small-motto and large-motto varieties for that year.

Date	Mintage	G-4	VG-8	F-12	VF-20	XF-40	AU-50	MS-60	MS-65	Prf-65
1864 small motto	19,847,500	120	185	250	375	565	625	800	2,300	45,000
1864 large motto	Inc. above	14.50	15.00	18.50	25.00	34.00	65.00	70.00	500	1,400
1865	13,640,000	14.50	15.00	18.50	25.00	34.00	65.00	70.00	500	850
1866	3,177,000	14.50	17.00	20.00	28.00	34.00	65.00	70.00	630	850
1867	2,938,750	17.50	22.00	34.00	43.50	55.00	85.00	125	550	850
1868	2,803,750	17.50	22.00	34.00	43.50	57.50	95.00	135	625	850
1869	1,546,000	18.50	23.00	35.00	47.50	66.00	110	150	650	850
1870	861,250	23.50	30.00	41.50	46.00	100.00	150	235	750	850
1871	721,250	27.50	34.00	50.00	75.00	125	175	250	750	850
1872	65,000	315	360	445	625	780	860	1,200	3,900	900
1873 proof	Est. 1,100	1,175	1,300	1,400	1,475	1,525	1,600	—	—	2,850

SILVER 3 CENTS

Type 1
No outlines in star obverse

KM# 75 • 0.8000 g., 0.7500 **Silver**, 0.0193 oz. ASW, 14 mm. • **Designer:** James B. Longacre

Date	Mintage	G-4	VG-8	F-12	VF-20	XF-40	AU-50	MS-60	MS-65	Prf-65
1851	5,447,400	25.00	33.50	37.50	41.50	65.00	155	185	950	—
1851O	720,000	32.50	40.00	47.50	90.00	150	225	340	2,500	—
1852	18,663,500	23.50	33.50	37.50	41.50	62.50	145	160	950	—
1853	11,400,000	23.50	33.50	37.50	41.50	62.50	145	160	950	—

1851-O Silver Three-Cent Piece
Grade XF-40

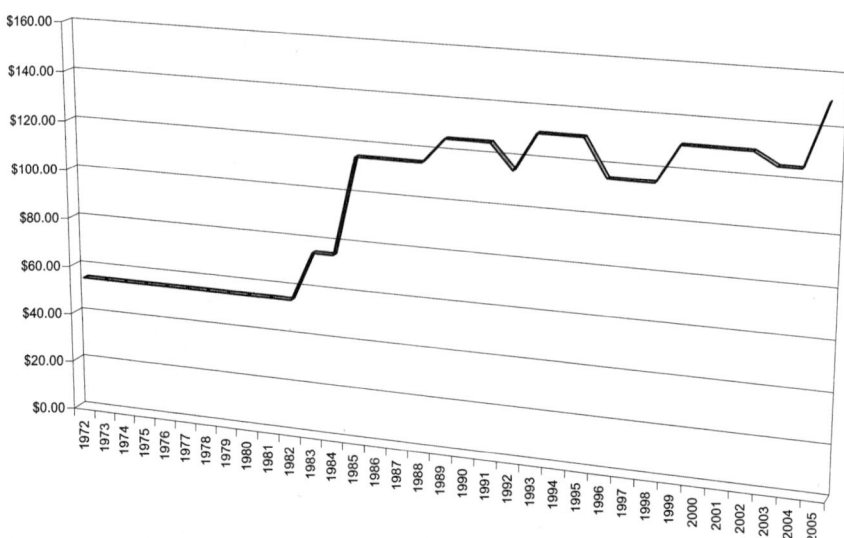

Retail Price

Type 2
Three outlines in star obverse

KM# 80 • 0.7500 g., 0.9000 **Silver**, 0.0218 oz. ASW, 14 mm. • **Designer:** James B. Longacre

Date	Mintage	G-4	VG-8	F-12	VF-20	XF-40	AU-50	MS-60	MS-65	Prf-65
1854	671,000	25.00	33.50	37.50	47.50	100.00	225	350	3,450	33,500
1855	139,000	37.50	50.00	65.00	110	185	300	525	8,500	15,000
1856	1,458,000	26.00	35.00	40.00	57.50	100.00	190	275	4,500	15,500
1857	1,042,000	25.00	33.50	37.50	48.50	95.00	240	300	3,300	13,500
1858	1,604,000	25.00	33.50	37.50	46.00	95.00	190	240	3,300	6,400

Type 3
Two outlines in star obverse

KM# 88 • 0.7500 g., 0.9000 **Silver**, 0.0218 oz. ASW, 14 mm. • **Designer:** James B. Longacre

Date	Mintage	G-4	VG-8	F-12	VF-20	XF-40	AU-50	MS-60	MS-65	Prf-65
1859	365,000	26.00	35.00	40.00	50.00	71.00	155	170	900	2,150
1860	287,000	26.00	36.00	41.50	52.50	75.00	155	170	900	4,000
1861	498,000	25.00	33.50	37.50	45.00	66.00	150	170	900	1,800
1862	343,550	30.00	40.00	42.50	57.50	75.00	180	230	900	1,400
1863	21,460	325	355	390	420	450	585	720	2,250	1,350
1863/62 proof only; Rare	Inc. above	470	500	560	650	685	720	—	—	5,000
1864	12,470	325	355	390	420	450	585	675	1,700	1,350
1865	8,500	390	420	450	480	520	560	750	1,700	1,350
1866	22,725	325	355	390	420	440	500	650	1,900	1,325
1867	4,625	390	420	450	480	520	560	720	2,750	1,300
1868	4,100	390	420	450	480	520	560	720	5,750	1,400
1869	5,100	390	420	450	480	520	560	720	2,350	1,400
1869/68 proof only; Rare	Inc. above	—	—	—	—	—	—	—	—	—
1870	4,000	390	420	450	480	520	560	900	5,500	1,350

Date	Mintage	G-4	VG-8	F-12	VF-20	XF-40	AU-50	MS-60	MS-65	Prf-65
1871	4,360	390	420	450	480	520	560	750	1,700	1,450
1872	1,950	400	440	460	500	520	600	775	5,500	1,350
1873 proof only	600	650	685	730	800	850	975	—	—	2,000

NICKEL 3 CENTS

KM# 95 • 1.9400 g., **Copper-Nickel**, 17.9 mm. • **Designer:** James B. Longacre

Date	Mintage	G-4	VG-8	F-12	VF-20	XF-40	AU-50	MS-60	MS-65	Prf-65
1865	11,382,000	14.00	15.50	16.50	23.50	32.50	55.00	100.00	675	6,500
1866	4,801,000	14.00	15.50	16.50	23.50	32.50	55.00	100.00	675	1,725
1867	3,915,000	14.00	15.50	16.50	23.50	32.50	55.00	100.00	850	1,575
1868	3,252,000	14.00	15.50	16.50	23.50	32.50	55.00	100.00	675	1,400
1869	1,604,000	14.00	16.00	17.50	25.00	34.00	60.00	115	775	1,000
1870	1,335,000	14.00	16.00	17.50	25.00	34.00	60.00	125	775	2,300
1871	604,000	14.00	16.00	19.00	26.00	35.00	62.50	135	800	1,200
1872	862,000	14.00	16.00	19.00	26.00	35.00	62.50	135	1,100	880
1873	1,173,000	14.00	16.00	19.00	26.00	35.00	62.50	135	1,400	1,050
1874	790,000	14.00	16.00	19.00	26.00	37.50	65.00	150	1,050	950
1875	228,000	15.00	17.50	20.00	27.50	41.50	75.00	170	825	1,700
1876	162,000	18.00	21.00	25.00	32.50	45.00	97.50	200	1,700	1,000
1877 proof	Est. 900	950	1,000	1,050	1,050	1,150	1,300	—	—	2,750
1878 proof	2,350	550	575	625	660	715	775	—	—	950
1879	41,200	60.00	70.00	90.00	100.00	110	150	250	850	580
1880	24,955	96.00	115	130	140	150	190	300	800	630
1881	1,080,575	15.00	15.50	18.00	25.00	34.00	55.00	100.00	715	580
1882	25,300	110	125	140	160	185	200	315	1,100	625
1883	10,609	185	200	260	285	330	375	480	4,350	580
1884	5,642	375	400	550	575	600	675	800	5,800	600
1885	4,790	435	480	640	660	700	775	850	2,300	650
1886 proof	4,290	320	330	345	385	385	415	—	—	615
1887/6 proof	7,961	350	390	415	450	450	485	—	—	750
1887	Inc. above	285	345	345	385	385	450	515	1,250	1,350
1888	41,083	47.50	57.50	62.50	70.00	90.00	135	235	725	580
1889	21,561	80.00	100.00	125	150	170	200	285	800	580

HALF DIME

Flowing Hair Half Dime

KM# 15 • 1.3500 g., 0.8920 **Silver**, 0.0388 oz. ASW, 16.5 mm. • **Designer:** Robert Scot

Date	Mintage	G-4	VG-8	F-12	VF-20	XF-40	MS-60
1794	86,416	1,000	1,250	1,750	2,700	4,800	13,500
1795	Inc. above	700	900	1,350	2,000	4,000	9,500

Draped Bust Half Dime
Small eagle reverse

KM# 23 • 1.3500 g., 0.8920 **Silver**, 0.0388 oz. ASW, 16.5 mm. • **Designer:** Robert Scot **Notes:** Some 1796 strikes have "Liberty" spelled as "Likerty." The 1797 strikes have either 13, 15 or 16 stars on the obverse.

Date	Mintage	G-4	VG-8	F-12	VF-20	XF-40	MS-60
1796	10,230	1,000	1,350	2,000	3,500	6,000	13,500
1796 "Likerty"	Inc. above	1,100	1,400	2,100	3,750	6,250	14,500
1796/5	Inc. above	1,000	1,350	2,200	4,000	7,000	25,000
1797 13 stars	44,527	1,750	2,300	3,000	5,500	9,000	25,000

1802 Half Dime
Grade F-12

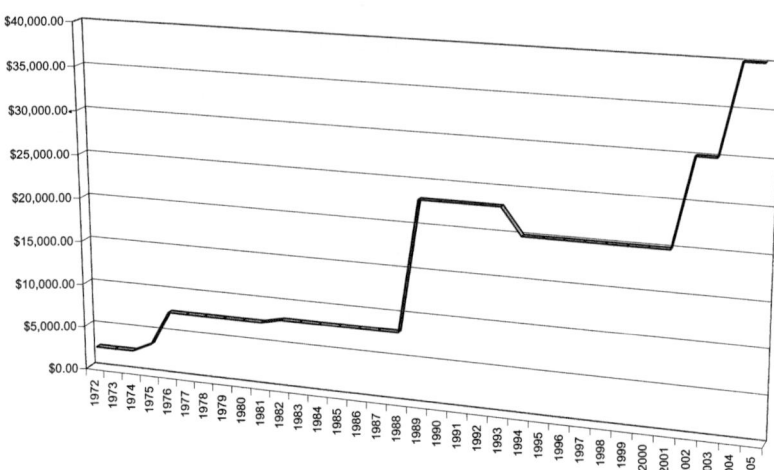

☐ Retail Price

Date	Mintage	G-4	VG-8	F-12	VF-20	XF-40	MS-60
1797 15 stars	Inc. above	1,000	1,250	1,900	3,250	5,750	12,500
1797 16 stars	Inc. above	1,050	1,350	2,100	3,650	6,250	13,750

Heraldic eagle reverse

KM# 34 • 1.3500 g., 0.8920 **Silver**, 0.0388 oz. ASW, 16.5 mm. • **Designer:** Robert Scot **Notes:** Some 1800 strikes have "Liberty" spelled as "Libekty."

Date	Mintage	G-4	VG-8	F-12	VF-20	XF-40	MS-60
1800	24,000	575	750	1,500	2,500	4,250	9,000
1800 "Libekty"	Inc. above	600	800	1,575	2,650	4,400	9,300
1801	33,910	775	1,150	1,600	2,800	5,000	15,000
1802	13,010	17,500	25,000	40,000	65,000	85,000	185,000
1803 Large 8	37,850	750	950	1,300	2,000	4,000	9,000
1803 Small 8	Inc. above	950	1,400	1,900	3,000	5,500	11,500
1805	15,600	900	1,250	1,650	2,500	5,500	27,500

Liberty Cap Half Dime

KM# 47 • 1.3500 g., 0.8920 **Silver**, 0.0388 oz. ASW, 15.5 mm. • **Designer:** William Kneass **Notes:** Design modifications in 1835, 1836 and 1837 resulted in variety combinations with large and small dates, and large and small "5C." inscriptions on the reverse.

Date	Mintage	G-4	VG-8	F-12	VF-20	XF-40	AU-50	MS-60	MS-65
1829	1,230,000	27.50	36.00	48.00	80.00	140	250	350	2,650
1830	1,240,000	25.00	36.00	48.00	75.00	140	250	350	2,650
1831	1,242,700	25.00	36.00	48.00	75.00	140	250	350	2,600
1832	965,000	25.00	36.00	48.00	75.00	140	250	350	2,600
1833	1,370,000	25.00	36.00	48.00	75.00	140	250	350	2,650
1834	1,480,000	25.00	36.00	48.00	75.00	140	250	350	2,600
1835 lg. dt., lg. 5C.	2,760,000	25.00	36.00	48.00	75.00	140	250	350	2,600
1835 lg. dt., sm. 5C	Inc. above	25.00	36.00	48.00	75.00	140	250	350	2,600
1835 sm. dt., lg. 5C	Inc. above	25.00	36.00	48.00	75.00	140	250	350	2,600
1835 sm. dt., sm. 5C	Inc. above	25.00	36.00	48.00	75.00	140	250	350	2,600
1836 lg. 5C.	1,900,000	25.00	36.00	48.00	75.00	140	250	350	2,600
1836 sm. 5C.	Inc. above	25.00	36.00	48.00	75.00	140	250	350	2,600

Date	Mintage	G-4	VG-8	F-12	VF-20	XF-40	AU-50	MS-60	MS-65
1837 lg. 5C.	2,276,000	27.50	36.00	48.00	80.00	140	250	350	3,500
1837 sm. 5C.	Inc. above	33.00	40.00	55.00	100.00	200	450	950	8,750

Seated Liberty Half Dime
No stars around rim obverse

KM# 60 • 1.3400 g., 0.9000 **Silver**, 0.0388 oz. ASW, 15.5 mm. • **Designer:** Christian Gobrecht **Notes:** A design modification in 1837 resulted in small-date and large-date varieties for that year.

Date	Mintage	G-4	VG-8	F-12	VF-20	XF-40	AU-50	MS-60	MS-65
1837 small date	Inc. above	30.00	42.00	62.50	115	190	485	800	3,900
1837 large date	Inc. above	34.00	46.00	70.00	125	200	375	625	3,250
1838O	70,000	80.00	125	225	400	750	1,450	2,000	25,000

Stars around rim. No drapery obverse

KM# 62.1 • 1.3400 g., 0.9000 **Silver**, 0.0388 oz. ASW, 15.5 mm. • **Designer:** Christian Gobrecht **Notes:** The two varieties of 1838 are distinguished by the size of the stars on the obverse. The 1839-O with reverse of 1838-O was struck from rusted reverse dies. The result is a bumpy surface on this variety's reverse.

Date	Mintage	G-4	VG-8	F-12	VF-20	XF-40	AU-50	MS-60	MS-65
1838 large stars	2,255,000	15.00	17.50	20.00	27.50	70.00	150	250	2,250
1838 small stars	Inc. above	18.00	27.50	45.00	100.00	175	315	650	3,850
1839	1,069,150	16.00	18.50	21.00	30.00	75.00	160	250	2,500
1839O	1,034,039	17.50	20.00	25.00	35.00	93.50	185	550	5,500
1839O reverse 1838O	—	375	575	750	1,200	2,250	3,500	—	—
1840	1,344,085	16.00	18.50	21.00	30.00	75.00	160	250	2,100
1840O	935,000	17.50	20.00	23.50	40.00	80.00	215	700	17,000

Drapery added to Liberty's left elbow obverse

KM# 62.2 • 1.3400 g., 0.9000 **Silver**, 0.0388 oz. ASW, 15.5 mm. • **Designer:** Christian Gobrecht **Notes:** In 1840 drapery was added to Liberty's left elbow. Varieties for the 1848 Philadelphia strikes are distinguished by the size of the numerals in the date.

Date	Mintage	G-4	VG-8	F-12	VF-20	XF-40	AU-50	MS-60	MS-65
1840	Inc. above	25.00	40.00	75.00	125	225	350	450	300
1840O	Inc. above	35.00	60.00	115	190	450	1,250	6,500	—
1841	1,150,000	15.00	17.50	21.00	28.50	56.00	115	160	1,250
1841O	815,000	17.50	20.00	25.00	43.50	110	280	650	6,500
1842	815,000	15.00	17.50	20.00	27.50	55.00	115	160	1,750
1842O	350,000	30.00	45.00	75.00	225	500	1,250	2,500	—
1843	1,165,000	15.00	17.50	20.00	27.50	55.00	110	160	1,350
1844	430,000	17.50	20.00	22.50	31.50	56.00	115	175	1,150
1844O	220,000	75.00	105	175	450	1,000	2,250	5,400	25,000
1845	1,564,000	15.00	17.50	20.00	33.50	56.00	110	160	1,150
1845/1845	Inc. above	16.00	20.00	22.50	35.00	60.00	115	160	1,200
1846	27,000	300	450	750	1,150	2,250	3,600	8,500	—
1847	1,274,000	15.00	17.50	20.00	27.50	55.00	110	160	1,150
1848 medium date	668,000	17.50	20.00	23.50	30.00	57.50	125	230	2,850
1848 large date	Inc. above	22.50	30.00	45.00	65.00	135	275	450	4,000
1848O	600,000	19.00	25.00	33.00	50.00	110	265	400	1,950
1849/8	1,309,000	28.50	35.00	47.50	62.50	125	250	625	2,600
1849/6	Inc. above	20.00	26.00	30.00	52.50	105	200	400	2,500
1849	Inc. above	16.00	18.50	27.50	50.00	65.00	125	180	1,700
1849O	140,000	29.00	40.00	95.00	225	475	975	1,950	14,000
1850	955,000	17.50	20.00	23.50	31.50	60.00	115	165	1,400
1850O	690,000	18.50	22.50	30.00	56.00	125	280	675	4,250
1851	781,000	15.00	17.50	20.00	27.50	56.00	110	160	1,500
1851O	860,000	17.50	20.00	25.00	41.50	110	220	500	4,350
1852	1,000,500	15.00	17.50	20.00	27.50	56.00	110	160	1,150
1852O	260,000	23.00	32.00	65.00	135	275	475	750	10,000
1853	135,000	32.50	43.50	67.50	125	220	385	750	3,000
1853O	160,000	225	265	375	675	1,350	2,750	500	25,000

1846 Half Dime Grade XF-40

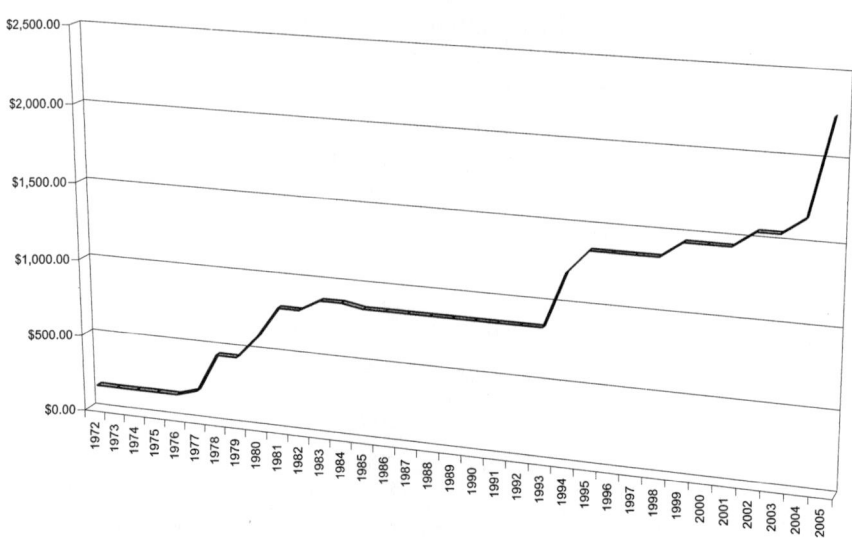

☐ Retail Price

Arrows at date obverse

KM# 76 • 1.2400 g., 0.9000 **Silver**, 0.0362 oz. ASW • **Designer:** Christian Gobrecht

Date	Mintage	G-4	VG-8	F-12	VF-20	XF-40	AU-50	MS-60	MS-65	Prf-65
1853	13,210,020	11.00	12.00	14.00	17.00	50.00	120	190	1,850	35,000
1853O	2,200,000	12.00	14.00	16.00	25.00	65.00	135	275	3,500	—
1854	5,740,000	10.50	12.00	14.00	17.00	45.00	110	185	1,850	16,000
1854O	1,560,000	11.00	13.00	15.00	23.00	60.00	145	250	4,250	—
1855	1,750,000	11.00	13.00	15.00	18.00	47.00	115	190	1,950	18,000
1855O	600,000	15.00	20.00	30.00	55.00	135	235	600	4,000	—

Arrows at date removed obverse

KM# A62.2 • 1.2400 g., 0.9000 **Silver**, 0.0362 oz. ASW • **Designer:** Christian Gobrecht **Notes:** On the 1858/inverted date variety, the date was engraved into the die upside down and then re-engraved right side up. Another 1858 variety has the date doubled.

Date	Mintage	G-4	VG-8	F-12	VF-20	XF-40	AU-50	MS-60	MS-65	Prf-65
1856	4,880,000	13.50	16.00	17.50	23.50	50.00	115	170	1,650	15,000
1856O	1,100,000	16.00	18.50	20.00	46.00	95.00	250	550	2,000	—
1857	7,280,000	13.50	16.00	17.50	23.50	50.00	110	170	1,550	5,500
1857O	1,380,000	15.00	16.00	18.50	37.50	60.00	185	325	1,800	—
1858	3,500,000	13.50	16.00	17.00	23.50	55.00	175	300	1,700	5,500
1858 inverted date	Inc. above	30.00	43.50	62.50	90.00	185	275	675	3,000	—
1858 double date	Inc. above	45.00	60.00	90.00	175	285	425	700	—	—
1858O	1,660,000	15.00	16.00	20.00	42.50	75.00	135	265	1,600	—
1859	340,000	16.00	17.50	21.50	34.00	70.00	135	225	1,550	4,000
1859O	560,000	17.50	20.00	28.50	43.50	115	200	260	1,850	—

"United States of America" replaced stars obverse

KM# 91 • 1.2400 g., 0.9000 **Silver**, 0.0362 oz. ASW • **Designer:** Christian Gobrecht **Notes:** In 1860 the legend "United States of America" replaced the stars on the obverse.

Date	Mintage	G-4	VG-8	F-12	VF-20	XF-40	AU-50	MS-60	MS-65	Prf-65
1860	799,000	13.50	16.00	17.50	21.00	40.00	72.50	125	1,150	1,850
1860O	1,060,000	13.50	16.00	18.50	25.00	43.50	93.50	180	1,450	—
1861	3,361,000	13.50	16.00	17.50	21.00	40.00	72.50	125	1,175	2,500
1861/0	Inc. above	25.00	32.50	59.00	125	260	435	560	4,000	—
1862	1,492,550	20.00	25.00	33.50	43.50	55.00	93.50	160	1,150	1,650
1863	18,460	190	225	275	375	475	550	700	1,650	1,700
1863S	100,000	25.00	35.00	50.00	75.00	150	295	700	2,500	—
1864	48,470	325	425	500	600	800	1,000	1,250	2,250	1,750
1864S	90,000	50.00	65.00	100.00	150	250	450	700	3,750	—
1865	13,500	325	400	450	550	650	875	1,000	1,950	1,750
1865S	120,000	25.00	35.00	50.00	75.00	135	375	800	—	—
1866	10,725	350	450	550	650	800	1,000	1,250	2,550	1,700
1866S	120,000	25.00	35.00	50.00	75.00	135	285	450	5,000	—
1867	8,625	450	550	675	800	900	1,100	1,300	2,250	1,750
1867S	120,000	25.00	35.00	50.00	75.00	135	295	550	3,850	—
1868	89,200	55.00	70.00	110	170	250	375	570	2,400	1,750
1868S	280,000	20.00	25.00	30.00	40.00	55.00	125	300	3,250	—
1869	208,600	20.00	25.00	30.00	40.00	55.00	125	235	1,500	1,750
1869S	230,000	18.00	22.00	29.00	35.00	50.00	115	325	4,000	—
1870	536,600	18.00	22.00	29.00	35.00	50.00	125	175	1,200	1,650
1870S unique	—	—	—	—	—	—	—	—	—	—

Note: 1870S, Superior Galleries, July 1986, brilliant uncirculated, $253,000.

Date	Mintage	G-4	VG-8	F-12	VF-20	XF-40	AU-50	MS-60	MS-65	Prf-65
1871	1,873,960	14.00	16.00	17.50	21.00	37.50	75.00	125	1,250	1,650
1871S	161,000	25.00	30.00	45.00	60.00	85.00	175	250	2,450	—
1872	2,947,950	14.00	16.00	17.50	21.00	37.50	75.00	125	1,200	1,650
1872S mint mark in wreath	837,000	14.00	16.00	17.50	21.00	37.50	75.00	125	1,200	—
1872S mint mark below wreath	Inc. above	14.00	16.00	17.50	21.00	37.50	75.00	125	1,200	—
1873	712,600	14.00	16.00	17.50	21.00	37.50	75.00	125	1,300	1,750
1873S	324,000	20.00	25.00	30.00	39.00	50.00	90.00	150	1,350	—

5 CENTS

Shield Nickel
Rays between stars reverse

KM# 96 • 5.0000 g., **Copper-Nickel**, 20.5 mm. • **Designer:** James B. Longacre

Date	Mintage	G-4	VG-8	F-12	VF-20	XF-40	AU-50	MS-60	MS-65	Prf-65
1866	14,742,500	27.50	38.50	50.00	70.00	155	235	250	2,700	3,400
1867	2,019,000	34.00	46.00	62.50	92.50	190	285	335	4,150	75,000

No rays between stars reverse

KM# 97 • 5.0000 g., **Copper-Nickel** •

Date	Mintage	G-4	VG-8	F-12	VF-20	XF-40	AU-50	MS-60	MS-65	Prf-65
1867	28,890,500	16.00	17.50	22.00	30.00	45.00	80.00	110	950	2,750
1868	28,817,000	16.00	17.50	22.00	30.00	45.00	80.00	110	1,000	1,400
1869	16,395,000	16.00	17.50	22.00	30.00	45.00	80.00	110	775	1,025
1870	4,806,000	22.00	26.00	43.50	55.00	75.00	115	177.5	1,650	1,275
1871	561,000	60.00	72.50	100.00	135	200	240	325	2,000	1,075
1872	6,036,000	22.00	27.50	46.00	55.00	67.50	110	165	1,350	750
1873	4,550,000	22.00	27.50	43.50	52.50	65.00	100.00	160	2,400	800

Date	Mintage	G-4	VG-8	F-12	VF-20	XF-40	AU-50	MS-60	MS-65	Prf-65
1874	3,538,000	25.00	34.00	57.50	67.50	85.00	115	185	1,500	850
1875	2,097,000	30.00	41.50	68.50	90.00	115	155	200	2,000	1,750
1876	2,530,000	30.00	38.50	62.50	85.00	110	140	200	1,900	950
1877 proof	Est. 900	1,350	1,500	1,650	1,900	2,000	2,000	—	—	4,100
1878 proof	2,350	650	700	825	970	1,050	1,200	—	—	1,700
1879	29,100	375	460	575	600	650	715	850	1,800	790
1880	19,995	500	600	700	850	1,250	1,750	3,450	40,000	650
1881	72,375	235	320	430	475	570	685	775	1,650	630
1882	11,476,600	16.00	17.50	22.00	30.00	45.00	80.00	110	750	600
1883	1,456,919	17.00	22.00	28.00	37.50	50.00	80.00	115	675	570
1883/2	—	160	220	285	345	600	750	920	3,800	—

Liberty Nickel
Without "Cents" below "V" reverse

KM# 111 • 5.0000 g., **Copper-Nickel**, 21.2 mm. • **Designer:** Charles E. Barber

Date	Mintage	G-4	VG-8	F-12	VF-20	XF-40	AU-50	MS-60	MS-65	Prf-65
1883	5,479,519	4.75	5.50	6.50	6.25	8.00	11.50	24.00	275	1,000

"Cents" below "V" reverse

KM# 112 • 5.0000 g., **Copper Nickel** •

Date	Mintage	G-4	VG-8	F-12	VF-20	XF-40	AU-50	MS-60	MS-65	Prf-65
1883	16,032,983	11.00	15.00	30.00	45.00	80.00	105	150	675	500
1884	11,273,942	17.50	27.50	38.50	52.50	80.00	125	185	2,000	575
1885	1,476,490	500	600	775	925	1,100	1,300	1,550	7,500	1,350

1884 Nickel Five-Cent
Grade F-12

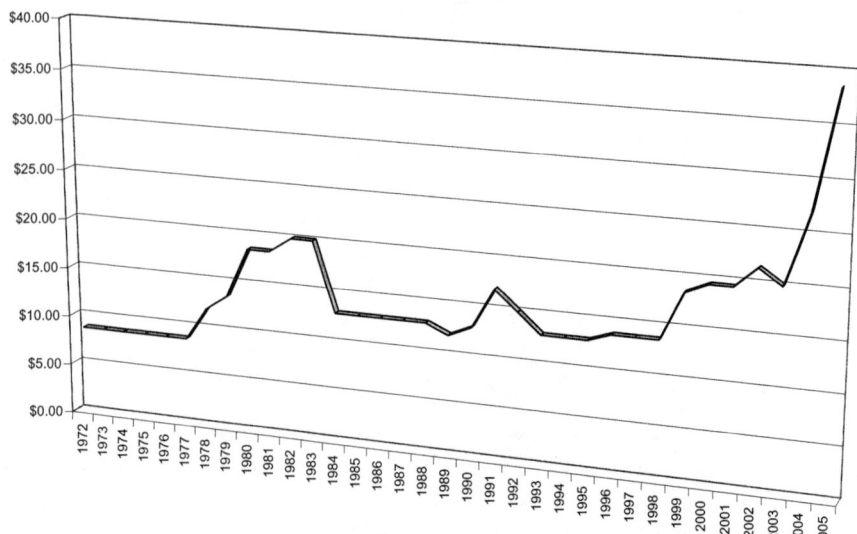

Retail Price

Date	Mintage	G-4	VG-8	F-12	VF-20	XF-40	AU-50	MS-60	MS-65	Prf-65
1886	3,330,290	195	250	375	480	630	765	850	9,000	850
1887	15,263,652	9.00	13.50	30.00	45.00	75.00	95.00	130	1,400	525
1888	10,720,483	22.50	32.50	57.50	110	160	220	275	2,000	525
1889	15,881,361	6.25	11.00	27.50	45.00	67.50	100.00	135	1,000	525
1890	16,259,272	7.00	16.00	27.50	41.50	65.00	110	160	1,950	650
1891	16,834,350	6.00	8.00	20.00	32.50	60.00	100.00	150	1,150	525
1892	11,699,642	7.00	10.00	22.00	35.00	60.00	115	150	1,500	525
1893	13,370,195	6.00	8.00	22.00	32.50	60.00	100.00	135	1,650	525
1894	5,413,132	12.00	27.00	83.50	140	200	275	330	1,500	525
1895	9,979,884	4.00	5.50	25.00	40.00	60.00	100.00	135	2,750	650
1896	8,842,920	8.00	16.00	39.00	58.50	80.00	135	190	2,400	620
1897	20,428,735	3.00	6.00	14.00	26.00	41.50	65.00	95.00	1,250	600
1898	12,532,087	2.00	4.50	10.00	21.00	36.00	70.00	140	1,250	500
1899	26,029,031	1.50	3.00	9.00	18.00	28.00	54.00	94.00	650	500
1900	27,255,995	1.50	3.00	8.00	18.00	35.00	70.00	88.00	675	500
1901	26,480,213	1.50	2.50	7.00	15.00	30.00	53.50	75.00	650	500
1902	31,480,579	1.50	2.50	5.00	15.00	27.00	53.50	77.50	650	500
1903	28,006,725	1.50	2.50	5.00	15.00	28.00	53.50	80.00	675	500
1904	21,404,984	1.50	2.50	5.00	11.00	26.00	53.50	72.50	700	725
1905	29,827,276	1.50	2.00	5.00	12.00	26.00	53.50	72.50	650	500
1906	38,613,725	1.50	2.00	5.00	12.00	26.00	53.50	70.00	1,000	500
1907	39,214,800	1.50	2.00	5.00	12.00	26.00	53.50	72.50	1,500	625
1908	22,686,177	1.50	2.00	5.00	12.00	26.00	53.50	72.50	1,250	500
1909	11,590,526	2.00	2.50	5.00	14.00	30.00	60.00	82.50	1,300	500
1910	30,169,353	1.50	2.00	5.00	11.00	27.50	48.50	65.00	750	500
1911	39,559,372	1.50	2.00	5.00	10.00	27.50	48.50	65.00	650	500
1912	26,236,714	1.50	2.00	5.00	10.00	27.50	48.50	65.00	675	575
1912D	8,474,000	2.00	3.00	9.50	32.50	65.00	150	275	2,200	—
1912S	238,000	140	170	240	480	800	1,250	1,500	6,750	—
1913 5 known	—	—	—	—	—	—	—	—	—	—

Note: 1913, Superior Sale, March 2001, Proof, $1,840,000.

Buffalo Nickel
Buffalo standing on a mound reverse

KM# 133 • 5.0000 g., **Copper-Nickel**, 21.2 mm. • **Designer:** James Earle Fraser

Date	Mintage	G-4	VG-8	F-12	VF-20	XF-40	AU-50	MS-60	MS-65	Prf-65
1913	30,993,520	7.50	9.50	10.00	11.50	18.50	23.50	32.50	150	3,500
1913D	5,337,000	12.50	15.00	19.00	25.00	35.00	50.00	62.50	315	—
1913S	2,105,000	35.00	42.00	50.00	60.00	75.00	92.50	125	700	—

Buffalo standing on a line reverse

   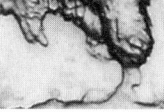

1918/17D   1937D 3-legged

KM# 134 • 5.0000 g., **Copper Nickel**, 21.2 mm. • **Designer:** James Earle Fraser **Notes:** In 1913 the reverse design was modified so the ground under the buffalo was represented as a line rather than a mound. On the 1937D 3-legged variety, the buffalo's right front leg is missing, the result of a damaged die.

Date	Mintage	G-4	VG-8	F-12	VF-20	XF-40	AU-50	MS-60	MS-65	Prf-65
1913	29,858,700	7.50	9.50	11.00	12.50	18.50	25.00	34.00	35.00	2,500
1913D	4,156,000	100.00	130	155	170	195	225	285	1,500	—
1913S	1,209,000	300	350	400	465	535	620	795	4,250	—
1914	20,665,738	15.00	16.50	19.00	21.50	27.50	37.50	45.00	450	2,350
1914D	3,912,000	75.00	100.00	140	185	275	340	415	1,750	—
1914S	3,470,000	23.50	33.50	43.50	62.50	90.00	135	150	2,350	—
1915	20,987,270	4.75	5.50	6.75	11.00	21.50	38.50	48.50	305	2,000
1915D	7,569,500	16.00	21.50	33.50	62.50	110	140	225	2,500	—
1915S	1,505,000	40.00	57.50	85.00	185	320	450	575	3,400	—
1916	63,498,066	3.75	5.00	5.50	6.75	12.50	19.00	41.00	350	3,850
1916/16	Inc. above	1,900	4,250	7,800	11,000	15,000	38,000	49,000	395,000	—
1916D	13,333,000	11.00	17.50	25.00	38.50	82.50	110	150	2,500	—
1916S	11,860,000	9.50	13.50	20.00	35.00	75.00	115	175	2,650	—
1917	51,424,029	3.75	5.00	6.25	8.50	13.50	31.00	55.00	540	—
1917D	9,910,800	16.00	23.00	47.50	80.00	130	255	330	4,400	—

Date	Mintage	G-4	VG-8	F-12	VF-20	XF-40	AU-50	MS-60	MS-65	Prf-65
1917S	4,193,000	23.00	35.00	70.00	110	170	285	380	5,250	—
1918	32,086,314	3.40	4.15	6.75	15.00	31.00	48.50	95.00	1,700	—
1918/17D	8,362,314	1,050	1,550	2,800	6,250	10,000	11,500	28,500	285,000	—
1918D	Inc. above	17.50	30.00	47.50	130	220	330	410	5,000	—
1918S	4,882,000	12.50	27.50	47.50	100.00	175	300	480	32,500	—
1919	60,868,000	1.35	2.10	3.25	7.00	15.00	30.00	55.00	595	—
1919D	8,006,000	12.50	23.50	55.00	115	235	335	540	8,000	—
1919S	7,521,000	8.00	20.00	47.50	110	225	360	510	19,000	—
1920	63,093,000	1.35	2.10	2.80	7.00	15.00	30.00	54.00	850	—
1920D	9,418,000	7.00	13.50	32.50	100.00	275	340	535	7,800	—
1920S	9,689,000	3.50	8.25	27.50	96.00	200	300	500	28,500	—
1921	10,663,000	3.75	6.25	8.50	25.00	53.50	70.00	115	850	—
1921S	1,557,000	65.00	110	200	545	845	1,100	1,500	8,000	—
1923	35,715,000	1.70	2.80	4.25	7.00	13.50	37.50	55.00	750	—
1923S	6,142,000	7.00	9.50	23.00	125	260	335	460	12,500	—
1924	21,620,000	1.00	1.60	4.15	9.60	19.00	41.00	70.00	950	—
1924D	5,258,000	7.50	11.00	30.00	85.00	200	285	340	5,600	—
1924S	1,437,000	16.00	32.50	96.00	470	1,100	1,700	2,250	12,000	—
1925	35,565,100	2.00	2.50	3.75	8.50	17.50	30.00	40.00	545	—
1925D	4,450,000	7.00	15.00	35.00	80.00	160	240	350	6,600	—
1925S	6,256,000	4.00	8.50	15.00	75.00	170	240	395	45,000	—
1926	44,693,000	.75	1.00	2.80	5.40	11.50	20.00	30.00	185	—
1926D	5,638,000	7.50	13.50	28.50	100.00	170	285	295	6,400	—
1926S	970,000	19.00	33.50	82.50	420	920	2,800	4,500	115,000	—
1927	37,981,000	.75	1.00	2.15	4.15	12.50	20.00	32.50	300	—
1927D	5,730,000	1.85	4.00	5.50	27.50	75.00	110	150	9,000	—
1927S	3,430,000	2.00	3.00	5.00	31.00	80.00	160	485	22,000	—
1928	23,411,000	.85	1.00	2.20	4.15	12.50	23.00	30.00	325	—
1928D	6,436,000	1.10	2.10	3.45	15.00	40.00	45.00	50.00	1,000	—
1928S	6,936,000	1.35	1.50	2.20	11.50	27.50	100.00	215	5,500	—
1929	36,446,000	.75	1.00	2.15	4.15	12.50	20.00	31.00	375	—
1929D	8,370,000	.85	1.10	3.00	6.75	32.50	42.50	55.00	2,000	—
1929S	7,754,000	.80	1.00	2.25	5.00	11.50	25.00	47.50	515	—
1930	22,849,000	.75	1.00	2.15	4.15	11.50	20.00	30.00	220	—
1930S	5,435,000	1.00	1.25	2.50	3.75	13.50	30.00	47.50	500	—
1931S	1,200,000	15.00	18.00	20.00	22.00	27.50	42.50	50.00	315	—
1934	20,213,003	.75	1.00	2.15	4.15	10.00	19.00	47.50	440	—
1934D	7,480,000	1.35	2.50	3.40	8.50	20.00	50.00	82.50	960	—
1935	58,264,000	.75	1.00	1.10	1.40	1.80	8.50	19.00	115	—
1935D	12,092,000	1.35	2.20	2.50	7.50	19.50	45.00	70.00	475	—
1935S	10,300,000	.75	1.00	1.10	1.40	3.00	15.00	50.00	185	—
1936	119,001,420	.75	1.00	1.10	1.40	1.75	6.50	15.00	100.00	1,100
1936D	24,814,000	.75	1.00	1.10	1.40	340	11.00	35.00	100.00	—

1921-S Nickel
Grade F-12

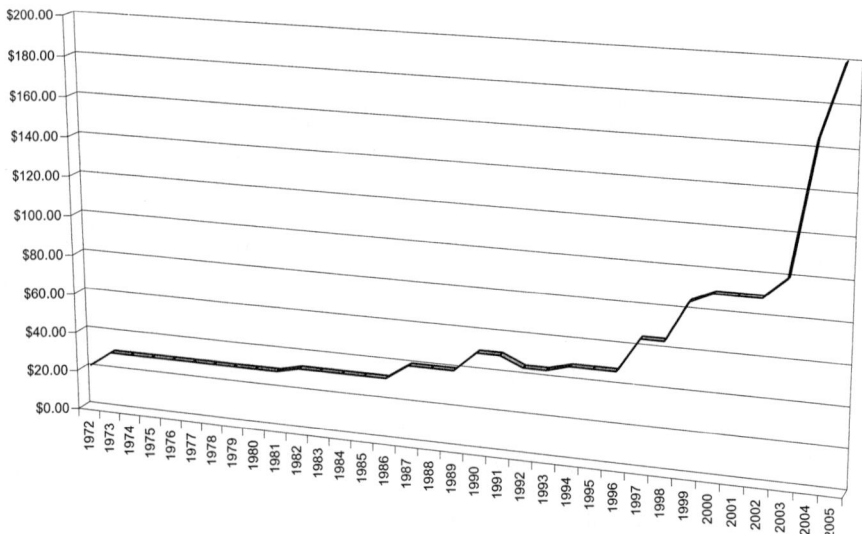

Retail Price

Date	Mintage	G-4	VG-8	F-12	VF-20	XF-40	AU-50	MS-60	MS-65	Prf-65
1936S	14,930,000	.75	1.00	1.10	1.40	1.75	9.50	35.00	110	—
1937	79,485,769	.75	1.00	1.10	1.40	1.50	6.50	14.50	27.50	850
1937D	17,826,000	.75	1.00	1.10	1.40	1.50	8.00	27.50	62.50	—
1937D 3-legged	Inc. above	470	530	850	980	1,150	1,300	2,550	27,500	—
1937S	5,635,000	.90	1.00	1.20	1.50	2.25	8.00	27.50	67.50	—
1938D	7,020,000	2.00	2.25	2.50	2.75	3.75	8.00	20.00	42.50	—
1938D/D	—	2.50	4.50	6.00	8.00	10.00	17.00	20.00	50.00	—
1938D/S	Inc. above	4.50	6.75	9.00	12.50	16.00	30.00	50.00	185	—

Jefferson Nickel
Monticello, mintmark to right side reverse

KM# 192 • 5.0000 g., **Copper-Nickel**, 21.2 mm. • **Designer:** Felix Schlag **Notes:** Some 1939 strikes have doubling of the word "Monticello" on the reverse.

Date	Mintage	VG-8	F-12	VF-20	XF-40	MS-60	MS-65	-65FS	Prf-65
1938	19,515,365	.25	.40	.80	1.25	4.00	8.50	125	70.00
1938D	5,376,000	.90	1.00	1.25	1.75	3.50	8.00	95.00	—
1938S	4,105,000	1.75	2.00	2.50	3.00	4.75	8.50	165	—
1939 T I	—	—	—	—	—	—	—	300	70.00
1939 T II	120,627,535	—	.20	.25	.30	1.75	3.50	40.00	300
1939 doubled Monticello T II	—	30.00	50.00	80.00	140	250	750	900	—
1939D T I	—	—	—	—	—	—	—	275	—
1939D T II	3,514,000	3.00	3.50	5.00	10.00	42.00	125	250	—
1939S T I	—	—	—	—	—	—	—	250	—
1939S T II	6,630,000	.45	.60	1.50	2.75	15.00	45.00	275	—
1940	176,499,158	—	—	—	.25	1.00	3.00	35.00	65.00
1940D	43,540,000	—	.20	.30	.40	1.50	2.75	25.00	—
1940S	39,690,000	—	.20	.25	.50	2.50	6.00	45.00	—
1941	203,283,720	—	—	—	.20	.75	2.50	40.00	60.00
1941D	53,432,000	—	.20	.30	.50	2.50	6.00	25.00	—
1941S	43,445,000	—	.20	.30	.50	3.75	6.75	60.00	—
1942	49,818,600	—	—	—	.40	5.00	8.50	75.00	55.00
1942D	13,938,000	.30	.40	1.00	2.00	27.00	60.00	70.00	—

Note: Fully Struck Full Step nickels command higher prices. Bright, Fully Struck coins command even higher prices. 1938 thru 1989 - 5 Full Steps. 1990 to date - 6 Full Steps. Without bag marks or nicks on steps.

Monticello, mint mark above reverse

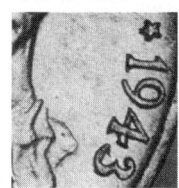

1943/2 P

KM# 192a • **Copper-Silver-Manganese**, 0 oz., 21.2 mm. • **Designer:** Felix Schlag **Notes:** War-time composition nickels have the mint mark above Monticello on the reverse. Composition: 0.350 Silver, .0563 oz. ASW.

Date	Mintage	VG-8	F-12	VF-20	XF-40	MS-60	MS-65	-65FS	Prf-65
1942P	57,900,600	.65	.85	1.00	1.75	6.00	22.50	70.00	140
1942S	32,900,000	.70	1.00	1.10	1.75	6.00	20.00	125	—
1943P	271,165,000	.50	.85	1.00	1.50	2.75	15.00	35.00	—
1943/2P	Inc. above	35.00	50.00	75.00	110	250	650	1,000	—
1943D	15,294,000	.90	1.20	1.50	1.75	4.00	13.00	30.00	—
1943S	104,060,000	.55	.70	1.00	1.50	3.00	13.00	55.00	—
1944P	119,150,000	.50	.70	1.00	1.50	4.00	22.50	100.00	—
1944D	32,309,000	.60	.80	1.00	1.75	6.50	17.50	30.00	—
1944S	21,640,000	.70	1.00	1.25	2.00	3.50	14.00	185	—
1945P	119,408,100	.50	.70	1.00	1.50	3.50	13.50	125	—
1945D	37,158,000	.55	.75	1.00	1.50	3.50	13.00	40.00	—
1945S	58,939,000	.50	.70	.80	.90	3.00	14.00	250	—

Note: Fully Struck Full Step nickels command higher prices. Bright, Fully Struck coins command higher prices. 1938 thru 1989 - 5 Full Steps. 1990 to date - 6 Full Steps. Without bag marks or nicks on steps.

Pre-war design resumed reverse

KM# A192 • 5.0000 g., **Copper-Nickel**, 21.2 mm. • **Designer:** Felix Schlag **Notes:** KM#192 design and composition resumed. The 1979-S and 1981-S Type II proofs have clearer mint marks than the Type I proofs of those years.

Date	Mintage	VG-8	F-12	VF-20	XF-40	MS-60	MS-65	-65FS	Prf-65
1946	161,116,000	—	—	.20	.25	.80	3.50	40.00	—
1946D	45,292,200	—	—	.25	.35	.95	3.50	30.00	—
1946S	13,560,000	—	—	.30	.40	.50	2.00	45.00	—
1947	95,000,000	—	—	.20	.25	.75	2.00	30.00	—
1947D	37,822,000	—	—	.20	.30	.90	2.50	30.00	—
1947S	24,720,000	—	—	.20	.25	1.00	2.25	55.00	—
1948	89,348,000	—	—	.20	.25	.50	2.50	60.00	—
1948D	44,734,000	—	—	.25	.35	1.20	4.50	30.00	—
1948S	11,300,000	—	—	.25	.50	1.20	3.50	45.00	—
1949	60,652,000	—	—	.25	.30	2.25	6.00	200	—
1949D	36,498,000	—	—	.30	.40	1.25	5.00	75.00	—
1949D/S	Inc. above	—	35.00	40.00	65.00	170	325	1,750	—
1949S	9,716,000	.25	.35	.45	.90	1.50	3.50	145	—
1950	9,847,386	.20	.30	.35	.75	1.50	4.75	150	45.00
1950D	2,630,030	11.00	11.50	12.00	12.50	22.00	30.00	45.00	—
1951	28,609,500	—	—	.40	.50	1.50	9.00	90.00	30.00
1951D	20,460,000	.25	.30	.40	.50	3.00	10.00	45.00	—
1951S	7,776,000	.30	.40	.50	1.10	1.75	5.00	150	—
1952	64,069,980	—	—	.20	.25	.85	4.50	125	26.00
1952D	30,638,000	—	—	.30	.45	2.00	7.00	65.00	—
1952S	20,572,000	—	—	.20	.25	.75	3.50	195	—
1953	46,772,800	—	—	.20	.25	.40	1.50	200	28.00
1953D	59,878,600	—	—	.20	.25	.40	1.50	100.00	—
1953S	19,210,900	—	—	.20	.25	.60	2.50	1,750	—
1954	47,917,350	—	—	—	—	.60	2.00	95.00	16.00
1954D	117,136,560	—	—	—	—	.35	2.00	175	—
1954S	29,384,000	—	—	—	.20	1.00	3.00	1,000	—
1954S/D	Inc. above	—	6.00	9.00	13.00	22.00	65.00	—	—
1955	8,266,200	.25	.35	.40	.45	.75	2.00	85.00	16.00
1955D	74,464,100	—	—	—	—	.20	1.00	150	—
1955D/S	Inc. above	—	5.00	8.50	13.00	33.00	75.00	—	—
1956	35,885,384	—	—	—	—	.30	.70	35.00	2.50
1956D	67,222,940	—	—	—	—	.25	.60	90.00	—
1957	39,655,952	—	—	—	—	.25	.60	40.00	1.50
1957D	136,828,900	—	—	—	—	.25	.60	55.00	—
1958	17,963,652	—	—	.15	.20	.30	.65	80.00	6.00
1958D	168,249,120	—	—	—	—	.25	.60	30.00	—

Note: Fully Struck Full Step nickels command higher prices. Bright, Fully Struck coins command even higher prices. 1938 thru 1989 - 5 Full Steps. 1990 to date - 6 Full Steps. Without bag marks or nicks on steps.

KM# A192 • 5.0000 g., **Copper-Nickel**, 21.2 mm. • **Designer:** Felix Schlag **Notes:** KM#192 design and composition resumed. The 1979-S and 1981-S Type II proofs have clearer mint marks than the Type I proofs of those years.

Date	Mintage	MS-65	-65FS	Prf-65	Date	Mintage	MS-65	-65FS	Prf-65
1959	28,397,291	.65	30.00	1.25	1970D	515,485,380	.50	500	—
1959D	160,738,240	.55	45.00	—	1970S	241,464,814	.50	125	0.75
1960	57,107,602	2.00	60.00	1.00	1971	106,884,000	2.00	35.00	—
1960D	192,582,180	.55	650	—	1971D	316,144,800	.50	25.00	—
1961	76,668,244	.55	100.00	1.00	1971S	(3,220,733)	—	—	2.00
1961D	229,342,760	.55	800	—	1972	202,036,000	.50	35.00	—
1962	100,602,019	1.50	75.00	1.00	1972D	351,694,600	.50	25.00	—
1962D	280,195,720	.55	600	—	1972S	(3,260,996)	—	—	2.00
1963	178,851,645	.55	45.00	1.00	1973	384,396,000	.50	20.00	—
1963D	276,829,460	.55	650	—	1973D	261,405,000	.50	20.00	—
1964	1,028,622,762	.55	55.00	1.00	1973S	(2,760,339)	—	—	1.75
1964D	1,787,297,160	.50	500	—	1974	601,752,000	.50	75.00	—
1965	136,131,380	.50	225	—	1974D	277,373,000	.50	50.00	—
1966	156,208,283	.50	350	—	1974S	(2,612,568)	—	—	2.00
1967	107,325,800	.50	275	—	1975	181,772,000	.75	65.00	—
1968 none minted	—	—	—	—	1975D	401,875,300	.50	60.00	—
1968D	91,227,880	.50	750	—	1975S	(2,845,450)	—	—	2.25
1968S	103,437,510	.50	300	0.75	1976	367,124,000	.75	150	—
1969 none minted	—	—	—	—	1976D	563,964,147	.60	55.00	—
1969D	202,807,500	.50	—	—	1976S	(4,149,730)	—	—	2.00
1969S	123,099,631	.50	450	0.75	1977	585,376,000	.40	65.00	—
1970 none minted	—	—	—	—	1977D	297,313,460	.55	35.00	—

Date	Mintage	MS-65-65FS	Prf-65
1977S	(3,251,152)	—	1.75
1978	391,308,000	.40 40.00	—
1978D	313,092,780	.40 35.00	—
1978S	(3,127,781)	—	1.75
1979	463,188,000	.40 95.00	—
1979D	325,867,672	.40 35.00	—
1979S type I, proof	(3,677,175)	—	1.50
1979S type II, proof	Inc. above	—	1.75
1980P	593,004,000	.40 30.00	—
1980D	502,323,448	.40 25.00	—
1980S	(3,554,806)	—	1.50
1981P	657,504,000	.40 70.00	—
1981D	364,801,843	.40 40.00	—
1981S type I, proof	(4,063,083)	—	2.00
1981S type II, proof	Inc. above	—	2.50
1982P	292,355,000	12.50 80.00	—
1982D	373,726,544	3.50 45.00	—
1982S	(3,857,479)	—	3.50
1983P	561,615,000	4.00 45.00	—
1983D	536,726,276	2.50 35.00	—
1983S	(3,279,126)	—	4.00
1984P	746,769,000	3.00 65.00	—
1984D	517,675,146	.85 30.00	—
1984S	(3,065,110)	—	5.00
1985P	647,114,962	.75 60.00	—
1985D	459,747,446	.75 35.00	—
1985S	(3,362,821)	—	4.00
1986P	536,883,483	1.00 70.00	—
1986D	361,819,140	2.00 60.00	—
1986S	(3,010,497)	—	7.00
1987P	371,499,481	.75 30.00	—
1987D	410,590,604	.75 25.00	—
1987S	(4,227,728)	—	3.50
1988P	771,360,000	.75 30.00	—
1988D	663,771,652	.75 25.00	—
1988S	(3,262,948)	—	6.50
1989P	898,812,000	.75 75.00	—
1989D	570,842,474	.75 25.00	—
1989S	(3,220,194)	—	5.50
1990P	661,636,000	.75 25.00	—
1990D	663,938,503	.75 25.00	—
1990S	(3,299,559)	—	5.50
1991P	614,104,000	.75 25.00	—
1991D	436,496,678	.75 25.00	—
1991S	(2,867,787)	—	5.00
1992P	399,552,000	2.00 25.00	—
1992D	450,565,113	.75 25.00	—
1992S	(4,176,560)	—	4.00
1993P	412,076,000	.75 25.00	—
1993D	406,084,135	.75 25.00	—
1993S	(3,394,792)	—	4.50
1994P	722,160,000	.75 25.00	—
1994P matte	167,703	.75	—
1994D	715,762,110	.75 25.00	—
1994S	(3,269,923)	—	4.00
1995P	774,156,000	.75 25.00	—
1995D	888,112,000	.85 25.00	—
1995S	(2,707,481)	—	7.50
1996P	829,332,000	.75 25.00	—
1996D	817,736,000	.75 25.00	—
1996S	(2,915,212)	—	4.00
1997P	470,972,000	.75 25.00	—
1997P matte	25,000	200 —	—
1997D	466,640,000	2.00 25.00	—
1997S	(1,975,000)	—	5.00
1998P	688,272,000	.80 25.00	—
1998D	635,360,000	.80 25.00	—
1998S	(2,957,286)	—	4.50
1999P	1,212,000,000	.80 20.00	—
1999D	1,066,720,000	.80 20.00	—
1999S	(3,362,462)	—	3.50
2000P	846,240,000	.80 20.00	—
2000D	1,509,520,000	.80 20.00	—
2000S	(4,063,361)	—	2.00
2001P	675,704,000	.50 20.00	—
2001D	627,680,000	.50 20.00	—

Date	Mintage	MS-65-65FS	Prf-65
2001S	(3,099,096)	—	2.00
2002P	539,280,000	.50	—
2002D	691,200,000	.50	—
2002S	(3,157,739)	—	2.00
2003P	441,840,000	.50	—
2003D	383,040,000	.50	—
2003S	3,116,590	—	2.00

Jefferson - Peace Reverse
Two clasp hands, pipe and hatchet reverse

KM# 360 • 5.0000 g., Copper Nickel, 21.2 mm.
•

Date	Mintage	MS-65	-65FS	Prf-65
2004P	—	.50	—	—
2004D	—	.50	—	—
2004S	—	—	—	2.00

Jefferson - Keelboat reverse
Lewis and Clark's Keelboat reverse

KM# 361 • 5.0000 g., Copper Nickel, 21.2 mm. •

Date	Mintage	MS-65	-65FS	Prf-65
2004P	—	.50	—	—
2004D	—	.50	—	—
2004S	—	—	—	2.00

Thomas Jefferson
large profile right obverse

KM# 368 • Copper Nickel, 0 oz., 21.2 mm. •
Obv. Designer: Joe Fitzgerald and Don Everhart
Rev. Designer: Jamie Franki and Norman E. Nemeth

Date	Mintage	MS-65	-65FS	Prf-65
2005P	—	.50	—	—
2005D	—	.50	—	—
2005S	—	—	—	2.00

Pacific coastline reverse

KM# 369 • 0.5000 g., Copper Nickel, 0 oz. •
Obv. Designer: Joe Fitzgerald and Don Everhart
Rev. Designer: Joe Fitzgerald and Donna Weaver

Date	Mintage	MS-65	-65FS	Prf-65
2005P	—	.50	—	—
2005D	—	.50	—	—
2005S	—	—	—	2.00

2006 D REQ

DIME

Draped Bust Dime
Small eagle reverse

KM# 24 • 2.7000 g., 0.8920 **Silver**, 0.0775 oz. ASW, 19 mm. • **Designer:** Robert Scot **Notes:** 1797 strikes have either 13 or 16 stars on the obverse.

Date	Mintage	G-4	VG-8	F-12	VF-20	XF-40	MS-60
1796	22,135	1,300	1,950	2,250	3,250	5,000	12,000
1797 13 stars	25,261	1,500	2,000	2,500	3,500	6,000	12,000
1797 16 stars	Inc. above	1,500	2,000	2,500	3,500	6,000	12,000

Heraldic eagle reverse

KM# 31 • 2.7000 g., 0.8920 **Silver**, 0.0775 oz. ASW, 19 mm. • **Designer:** Robert Scot **Notes:** The 1798 overdates have either 13 or 16 stars on the obverse. Varieties of the regular 1798 strikes are distinguished by the size of the 8 in the date. The 1805 strikes have either 4 or 5 berries on the olive branch held by the eagle.

Date	Mintage	G-4	VG-8	F-12	VF-20	XF-40	MS-60
1798	27,550	650	800	1,000	1,500	2,750	6,500
1798/97 13 stars	Inc. above	2,000	3,000	4,500	7,000	11,000	—
1798/97 16 stars	Inc. above	675	800	1,050	1,500	2,500	5,500
1798 small 8	Inc. above	900	1,150	1,700	2,400	3,600	9,500
1800	21,760	600	800	1,100	1,600	2,750	—
1801	34,640	650	850	1,300	2,500	4,500	—
1802	10,975	950	1,400	2,000	3,000	6,000	17,500
1803	33,040	550	700	950	1,500	3,600	—
1804 13 stars	8,265	1,400	1,900	2,650	5,500	13,500	—
1804 14 stars	Inc. above	1,600	2,100	3,000	6,000	15,000	—
1805 4 berries	120,780	450	650	800	1,050	2,100	5,000
1805 5 berries	Inc. above	700	1,000	1,300	1,800	2,700	5,250
1807	165,000	450	650	800	1,050	2,100	5,000

Liberty Cap Dime
Variety I

KM# 42 • 2.7000 g., 0.8920 **Silver**, .0775 oz. ASW, 18.8 mm. • **Designer:** John Reich **Notes:** Varieties of the 1814, 1821 and 1828 strikes are distinguished by the size of the numerals in the dates. The 1820 varieties are distinguished by the size of the 0 in the date. The 1823 overdates have either large E's or small E's in "United States of America" on the reverse.

Date	Mintage	G-4	VG-8	F-12	VF-20	XF-40	AU-50	MS-60	MS-65
1809	51,065	150	250	450	800	1,400	3,000	4,500	22,500
1811/9	65,180	90.00	165	275	650	1,100	2,000	4,000	22,500
1814 small date	421,500	60.00	70.00	120	475	700	1,000	2,000	8,000
1814 large date	Inc. above	29.00	35.00	55.00	200	400	800	1,100	8,000
1820 large O	942,587	26.00	33.00	55.00	150	375	750	1,050	8,000
1820 small O	Inc. above	26.00	33.00	55.00	175	425	750	1,050	8,000
1821 large date	1,186,512	26.00	33.00	60.00	150	375	750	1,050	8,000
1821 small date	Inc. above	26.00	33.00	55.00	175	400	750	1,050	8,000
1822	100,000	425	600	1,100	1,700	3,000	6,000	10,000	—
1823/22 large E's	440,000	26.00	33.00	50.00	150	375	750	1,050	8,000
1823/22 small E's	Inc. above	26.00	33.00	50.00	150	375	750	1,050	8,000
1824/22 mintage undetermined	—	30.00	50.00	150	400	750	1,500	2,500	—
1825	510,000	26.00	33.00	50.00	150	450	900	1,250	8,000
1827	1,215,000	26.00	33.00	50.00	140	375	775	1,050	8,000
1828 large date	125,000	80.00	110	175	375	750	1,275	3,000	—

1809 Dime
Grade F-12

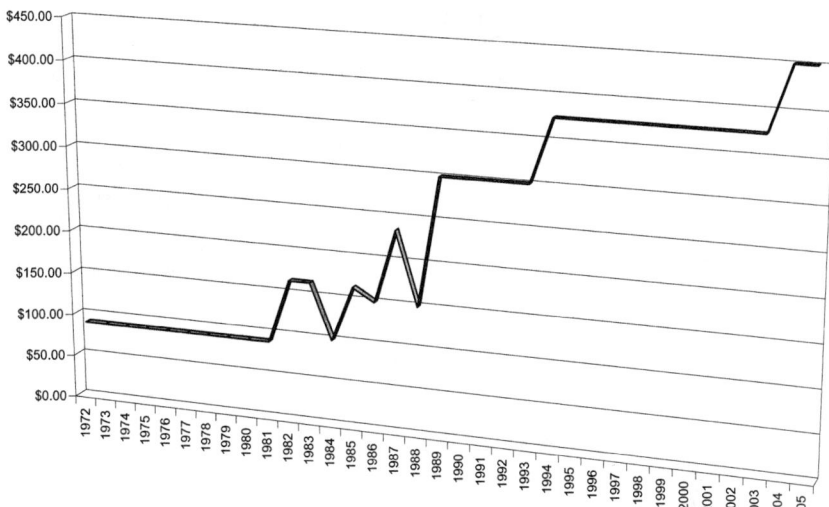

☐ Retail Price

Variety II

KM# 48 • **Silver**, 18.5 mm. • **Designer:** John Reich **Notes:** The three varieties of 1829 strikes and two varieties of 1830 strikes are distinguished by the size of "10C." on the reverse. On the 1833 "high 3" variety, the last 3 in the date is higher than the first 3. The two varieties of the 1834 strikes are distinguished by the size of the 4 in the date.

Date	Mintage	G-4	VG-8	F-12	VF-20	XF-40	AU-50	MS-60	MS-65
1828 small date	Inc. above	30.00	45.00	75.00	195	475	775	1,750	—
1829 very large 10C.	770,000	35.00	45.00	85.00	150	375	600	1,500	—
1829 large 10C.	—	26.00	30.00	40.00	75.00	270	400	725	8,000
1829 medium 10C.	Inc. above	26.00	30.00	40.00	70.00	270	400	725	8,000
1829 small 10C.	Inc. above	26.00	30.00	40.00	70.00	270	400	725	8,000
1829 curl base 2	—	3,200	5,000	7,500	—	—	—	—	—
1830 large 10C.	510,000	26.00	30.00	38.00	65.00	260	375	675	8,000
1830 small 10C.	Inc. above	26.00	30.00	38.00	65.00	260	375	675	8,000
1830/29	Inc. above	35.00	60.00	115	250	500	775	1,500	—
1831	771,350	26.00	30.00	38.00	65.00	260	375	675	6,000
1832	522,500	26.00	30.00	38.00	65.00	260	375	675	6,500
1833	485,000	26.00	30.00	38.00	65.00	260	375	675	6,700
1834	635,000	26.00	30.00	38.00	65.00	260	375	675	6,500
1835	1,410,000	26.00	30.00	38.00	65.00	260	375	675	6,500
1836	1,190,000	26.00	30.00	38.00	65.00	260	375	675	6,500
1837	1,042,000	26.00	30.00	38.00	65.00	260	375	675	6,600

Seated Liberty Dime
No stars around rim obverse

KM# 61 • 2.6700 g., 0.9000 **Silver**, 0.0773 oz. ASW, 17.9 mm. • **Designer:** Christian Gobrecht **Notes:** The two 1837 varieties are distinguished by the size of the numerals in the date.

Date	Mintage	G-4	VG-8	F-12	VF-20	XF-40	AU-50	MS-60	MS-65
1837 small date	Inc. above	40.00	50.00	85.00	290	550	750	1,100	6,500
1837 large date	Inc. above	32.50	43.50	75.00	275	550	750	1,100	6,500
1838O	406,034	40.00	60.00	110	375	725	1,250	3,500	21,000

Stars around rim. No drapery obverse

No drapery at elbow

KM# 63.1 • 2.6700 g., 0.9000 **Silver**, 0.0773 oz. ASW, 17.9 mm. • **Obv. Designer:** Christian Gobrecht
Notes: The two 1838 varieties are distinguished by the size of the stars on the obverse. The 1838 "partial drapery" variety has drapery on Liberty's left elbow. The 1839-O with reverse of 1838-O variety was struck from rusted dies. This variety has a bumpy surface on the reverse.

Date	Mintage	G-4	VG-8	F-12	VF-20	XF-40	AU-50	MS-60	MS-65
1838 small stars	1,992,500	25.00	30.00	50.00	80.00	165	350	600	—
1838 large stars	Inc. above	17.50	20.00	30.00	37.50	110	215	280	8,500
1838 partial drapery	Inc. above	30.00	45.00	65.00	125	195	325	550	—
1839	1,053,115	16.00	18.50	25.00	35.00	105	195	280	3,000
1839O	1,323,000	18.50	22.50	31.50	45.00	115	365	1,250	6,000
1839O reverse 1838O	—	145	200	350	550	950	—	—	—
1840	1,358,580	16.00	18.50	25.00	35.00	105	195	300	4,000
1840O	1,175,000	18.50	22.50	40.00	70.00	125	295	975	6,500

Drapery added to Liberty's left elbow obverse

Drapery at elbow

KM# 63.2 • 2.6700 g., 0.9000 **Silver**, 0.0773 oz. ASW, 17.9 mm. • **Designer:** Christian Gobrecht

Date	Mintage	G-4	VG-8	F-12	VF-20	XF-40	AU-50	MS-60	MS-65
1840	Inc. above	35.00	50.00	95.00	185	350	1,250	—	—
1841	1,622,500	16.00	18.50	21.50	27.50	50.00	175	260	2,700
1841O	2,007,500	18.50	22.50	28.50	42.50	75.00	250	1,500	5,000
1841O large O	Inc. above	600	900	1,200	2,500	—	—	—	—
1842	1,887,500	15.00	17.50	21.50	26.00	45.00	175	260	2,700
1842O	2,020,000	18.50	23.50	30.00	75.00	225	1,350	2,900	—
1843	1,370,000	15.00	17.50	21.50	26.00	45.00	175	260	3,000
1843/1843	—	16.00	18.50	22.50	30.00	75.00	200	295	—
1843O	150,000	35.00	65.00	125	275	800	2,250	—	—
1844	72,500	275	350	550	800	1,450	2,200	3,000	—
1845	1,755,000	16.00	18.50	21.50	27.50	45.00	120	260	2,600
1845/1845	Inc. above	17.00	20.00	35.00	55.00	100.00	175	—	—
1845O	230,000	22.00	35.00	70.00	200	550	1,350	—	—
1846	31,300	200	225	300	400	950	2,250	5,500	—
1847	245,000	19.00	25.00	40.00	75.00	150	350	950	9,000
1848	451,500	18.50	21.50	25.00	45.00	85.00	185	750	7,000
1849	839,000	17.50	19.50	23.50	33.50	60.00	140	500	4,000
1849O	300,000	21.50	30.00	45.00	120	275	750	2,200	—
1850	1,931,500	17.50	19.50	23.50	32.50	55.00	120	260	5,900
1850O	510,000	21.50	25.00	35.00	70.00	160	475	1,250	—
1851	1,026,500	17.50	20.00	22.50	30.00	60.00	120	325	5,000
1851O	400,000	21.50	25.00	35.00	75.00	175	500	1,850	—
1852	1,535,500	15.00	16.00	18.50	23.50	50.00	120	290	2,550
1852O	430,000	22.50	30.00	45.00	125	235	550	1,800	—
1853	95,000	70.00	100.00	130	195	300	475	800	—

Arrows at date obverse

KM# 77 • 2.4900 g., 0.9000 **Silver**, 0.0721 oz. ASW • **Designer:** Christian Gobrecht

Date	Mintage	G-4	VG-8	F-12	VF-20	XF-40	AU-50	MS-60	MS-65	Prf-65
1853	12,078,010	8.00	9.00	10.00	14.00	45.00	125	330	2,500	31,500
1853O	1,100,000	11.00	14.00	20.00	45.00	145	400	900	—	—
1854	4,470,000	8.75	9.25	10.00	15.00	45.00	125	330	2,500	31,500
1854O	1,770,000	10.00	11.00	14.00	25.00	75.00	175	600	—	—
1855	2,075,000	8.75	9.25	14.00	20.00	55.00	150	350	3,800	31,500

Seated Liberty Dime
Arrows at date removed obverse

KM# A63.2 • 2.4900 g., 0.9000 **Silver**, 0.0721 oz. ASW • **Designer:** Christian Gobrecht **Notes:** The two 1856 varieties are distinguished by the size of the numerals in the date.

Date	Mintage	G-4	VG-8	F-12	VF-20	XF-40	AU-50	MS-60	MS-65	Prf-65
1856 small date	5,780,000	14.00	15.00	18.00	22.00	37.50	115	250	7,050	38,000
1856 large date	Inc. above	16.00	18.50	19.50	25.00	65.00	175	475	—	—
1856O	1,180,000	16.00	18.50	19.50	35.00	85.00	215	625	5,250	—
1856S	70,000	160	225	325	500	1,200	1,750	—	—	—
1857	5,580,000	14.00	15.50	16.50	22.50	37.50	110	260	2,600	3,400
1857O	1,540,000	14.00	16.00	18.50	25.00	65.00	200	375	2,600	—
1858	1,540,000	14.00	15.50	16.50	22.50	55.00	145	260	2,600	3,400
1858O	290,000	19.00	25.00	40.00	85.00	165	280	800	5,000	—
1858S	60,000	135	200	300	425	975	1,400	—	—	—
1859	430,000	16.00	20.00	25.00	45.00	70.00	140	350	—	3,400
1859O	480,000	16.00	20.00	25.00	45.00	80.00	225	550	—	—
1859S	60,000	150	225	325	500	1,350	3,000	—	—	—
1860S	140,000	30.00	40.00	55.00	135	300	800	—	—	—

"United States of America" replaced stars obverse

KM# 92 • 2.4900 g., 0.9000 **Silver**, 0.0721 oz. ASW • **Obv. Designer:** Christian Gobrecht **Notes:** The 1873 "closed-3" and "open-3" varieties are distinguished by the amount of space between the upper left and lower left serifs of the 3 in the date.

Date	Mintage	G-4	VG-8	F-12	VF-20	XF-40	AU-50	MS-60	MS-65	Prf-65
1860	607,000	15.00	22.00	29.00	31.00	55.00	125	275	1,350	1,400
1860O	40,000	350	475	875	1,650	3,500	5,500	8,500	—	—
1861	1,884,000	12.50	15.00	17.00	20.00	35.00	72.50	135	1,250	1,400
1861S	172,500	50.00	85.00	145	275	400	900	1,400	—	—
1862	847,550	16.00	17.50	19.50	25.00	45.00	77.50	165	1,250	1,400
1862S	180,750	40.00	60.00	95.00	175	350	775	1,000	—	—
1863	14,460	350	450	600	700	875	1,100	1,300	—	1,400
1863S	157,500	34.00	44.00	75.00	125	275	550	1,200	—	—
1864	11,470	350	450	575	650	775	1,000	1,200	—	1,400
1864S	230,000	28.00	35.00	60.00	95.00	225	425	1,200	—	—
1865	10,500	400	500	650	750	900	1,100	1,250	—	1,400
1865S	175,000	35.00	45.00	75.00	125	300	850	—	—	—
1866	8,725	450	550	700	800	975	1,200	1,800	—	1,750
1866S	135,000	40.00	50.00	85.00	145	325	675	1,900	—	—
1867	6,625	550	700	950	1,100	1,450	1,600	1,800	—	1,750
1867S	140,000	40.00	50.00	85.00	145	295	625	1,200	—	—
1868	464,000	18.00	22.00	29.00	39.00	80.00	175	300	—	1,400
1868S	260,000	25.00	35.00	50.00	85.00	165	300	600	—	—
1869	256,600	25.00	35.00	45.00	75.00	135	250	600	—	1,400
1869S	450,000	20.00	25.00	35.00	45.00	75.00	175	400	—	—
1870	471,000	18.00	22.00	30.00	40.00	50.00	80.00	150	—	1,400
1870S	50,000	275	350	450	550	675	950	2,000	—	—
1871	907,710	16.00	20.00	25.00	33.00	55.00	160	300	—	1,400
1871CC	20,100	1,400	1,850	2,950	4,000	7,500	10,500	—	—	—
1871S	320,000	35.00	55.00	75.00	130	195	350	900	—	—
1872	2,396,450	12.00	15.00	17.00	20.00	31.00	95.00	175	—	1,400
1872CC	35,480	425	650	975	1,950	5,500	—	—	—	—
1872S	190,000	40.00	60.00	80.00	150	235	450	1,100	—	—
1873 closed 3	1,568,600	12.50	15.00	18.00	22.00	50.00	100.00	200	—	1,400
1873 open 3	Inc. above	22.00	30.00	40.00	60.00	110	225	650	—	—
1873CC	12,400	—	—	—	—	—	—	—	—	—

Note: 1873-CC, Heritage Sale, April 1999, MS-64, $632,500.

Arrows at date obverse

KM# 105 • 2.5000 g., 0.9000 **Silver**, 0.0724 oz. ASW • **Designer:** Christian Gobrecht

Date	Mintage	G-4	VG-8	F-12	VF-20	XF-40	AU-50	MS-60	MS-65	Prf-65
1873	2,378,500	15.00	18.50	25.00	55.00	150	350	500	4,500	4,500
1873CC	18,791	1,400	1,850	2,950	4,000	8,500	—	—	—	—
1873S	455,000	20.00	30.00	40.00	70.00	190	400	1,500	—	—
1874	2,940,700	13.50	17.50	22.50	50.00	150	315	500	4,500	4,500
1874CC	10,817	3,500	5,500	8,000	12,500	25,000	—	—	—	—
1874S	240,000	60.00	75.00	100.00	160	250	450	1,500	—	—

Arrows at date removed obverse

KM# A92 • 2.5000 g., 0.9000 **Silver**, 0.0724 oz. ASW • **Designer:** Christian Gobrecht **Notes:** On the 1876-CC doubled-obverse variety, doubling appears in the words "of America" in the legend.

Date	Mintage	G-4	VG-8	F-12	VF-20	XF-40	AU-50	MS-60	MS-65	Prf-65
1875	10,350,700	12.50	15.00	17.00	20.00	27.50	72.50	125	2,250	4,600
1875CC mint mark in wreath	4,645,000	15.00	16.00	18.50	26.00	42.50	90.00	190	2,700	—
1875CC mint mark under wreath	Inc. above	15.00	16.00	22.50	37.50	65.00	165	235	3,000	—
1875S mint mark in wreath	9,070,000	20.00	25.00	30.00	43.00	65.00	125	225	3,100	—
1875S mint mark under wreath	Inc. above	12.50	15.50	17.50	20.00	27.50	72.50	125	1,100	—
1876	11,461,150	12.00	15.00	17.00	20.00	24.00	72.50	125	1,100	1,200
1876CC	8,270,000	15.00	16.00	18.50	26.00	42.50	82.50	180	—	—
1876CC doubled obverse	Inc. above	16.00	20.00	30.00	80.00	135	300	500	—	—
1876S	10,420,000	12.50	15.00	17.00	20.00	35.00	72.50	125	1,750	—

1866-S Dime
Grade F-12

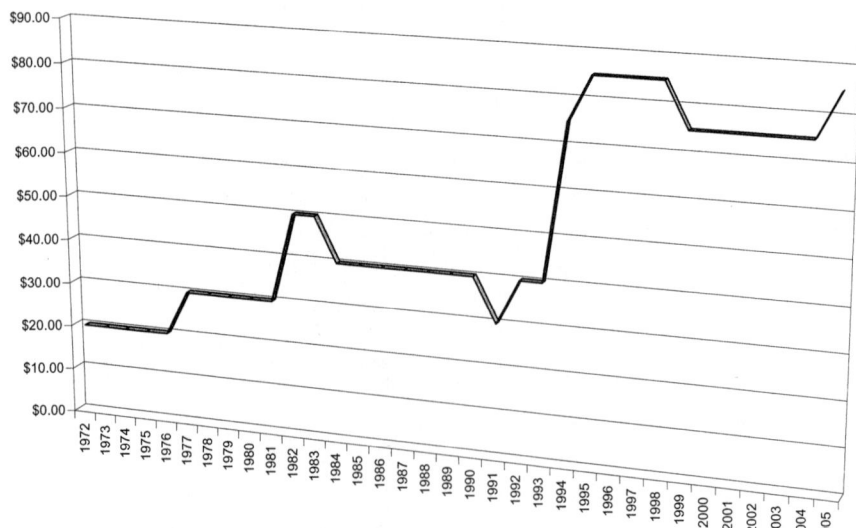

□ Retail Price

Date	Mintage	G-4	VG-8	F-12	VF-20	XF-40	AU-50	MS-60	MS-65	Prf-65
1877	7,310,510	12.00	15.00	17.00	20.00	27.50	72.50	125	1,100	1,200
1877CC	7,700,000	15.00	16.00	18.50	26.00	42.50	82.50	180	1,100	—
1877S	2,340,000	14.00	18.00	20.00	30.00	50.00	105	225	—	—
1878	1,678,800	12.50	15.00	17.00	20.00	36.00	72.50	125	1,500	1,200
1878CC	200,000	60.00	75.00	125	190	300	475	775	3,900	—
1879	15,100	225	250	300	350	425	525	675	1,750	1,500
1880	37,335	185	215	250	300	350	400	500	1,750	1,500
1881	24,975	200	225	275	325	400	500	650	2,500	1,600
1882	3,911,100	12.50	15.00	17.00	20.00	27.50	72.50	125	1,100	1,200
1883	7,675,712	12.50	15.00	17.00	20.00	27.50	72.50	125	1,100	1,200
1884	3,366,380	12.50	15.00	17.00	20.00	27.50	72.50	125	1,100	1,200
1884S	564,969	30.00	35.00	45.00	55.00	125	280	650	—	—
1885	2,533,427	12.50	15.00	17.00	20.00	27.50	72.50	125	1,100	1,200
1885S	43,690	375	525	725	1,450	2,200	3,600	5,000	—	—
1886	6,377,570	12.50	15.00	17.00	20.00	27.50	72.50	125	1,100	1,200
1886S	206,524	50.00	70.00	80.00	125	175	280	600	—	—
1887	11,283,939	12.50	15.00	17.00	20.00	27.50	72.50	125	1,100	1,200
1887S	4,454,450	12.50	15.00	17.00	20.00	38.00	80.00	125	1,100	—
1888	5,496,487	12.50	15.00	17.00	20.00	27.50	72.50	125	1,100	1,200
1888S	1,720,000	12.50	15.00	17.00	25.00	40.00	95.00	200	—	—
1889	7,380,711	12.50	15.00	17.00	20.00	27.50	72.50	125	1,100	1,200
1889S	972,678	14.00	18.00	25.00	45.00	70.00	150	475	4,500	—
1890	9,911,541	12.50	15.00	17.00	20.00	27.50	72.50	125	1,100	1,200
1890S	1,423,076	14.00	15.00	22.50	50.00	85.00	155	400	4,900	—
1891	15,310,600	12.50	15.00	17.00	20.00	27.50	72.50	125	1,100	1,200
1891O	4,540,000	12.50	15.00	17.00	20.00	27.50	72.50	175	1,750	—
1891O /horizontal O	Inc. above	65.00	95.00	125	175	225	400	—	—	—
1891S	3,196,116	13.50	15.00	17.50	20.00	30.00	75.00	225	1,650	—
1891S/S	Inc. above	25.00	30.00	40.00	85.00	135	250	—	—	—

Barber Dime

KM# 113 • 2.5000 g., 0.9000 **Silver**, 0.0724 oz. ASW, 17.9 mm. • **Designer:** Charles E. Barber

Date	Mintage	G-4	VG-8	F-12	VF-20	XF-40	AU-50	MS-60	MS-65	Prf-65
1892	12,121,245	4.25	5.75	16.00	23.50	27.50	70.00	110	750	1,450
1892O	3,841,700	8.50	13.00	30.00	47.50	57.50	82.50	152.5	1,275	—
1892S	990,710	60.00	105	185	200	260	295	400	4,000	—
1893	3,340,792	7.50	12.50	20.00	27.50	40.00	74.00	100.00	1,000	1,450
1893O	1,760,000	28.50	45.00	115	150	190	225	300	3,250	—
1893S	2,491,401	11.00	20.00	30.00	41.50	67.50	125	285	4,350	—
1894	1,330,972	20.00	38.50	110	135	160	375	275	1,200	1,450
1894O	720,000	62.50	95.00	200	260	370	650	1,550	14,500	—
1894S	24	—	—	—	—	—	—	—	1,300,000	—
Note: 1894S, Eliasberg Sale, May 1996, Prf-64, $451,000.										
1895	690,880	80.00	135	345	470	535	600	720	2,800	2,000
1895O	440,000	360	500	795	1,100	2,200	3,300	6,000	17,500	—
1895S	1,120,000	41.50	55.00	125	165	225	285	485	7,800	—
1896	2,000,762	10.00	22.00	55.00	75.00	95.00	115	160	1,500	1,450
1896O	610,000	75.00	150	275	345	445	700	1,000	8,400	—
1896S	575,056	82.50	150	275	315	385	515	770	4,600	—
1897	10,869,264	2.00	3.45	7.50	13.50	30.00	73.50	125	700	1,450
1897O	666,000	66.00	110	275	355	445	600	975	4,700	—
1897S	1,342,844	22.00	35.00	96.00	115	155	230	450	4,250	—
1898	16,320,735	2.00	2.75	6.75	11.00	25.00	72.50	110	720	1,450
1898O	2,130,000	11.00	25.00	80.00	115	175	230	450	4,150	—
1898S	1,702,507	6.75	13.50	28.50	41.50	67.50	150	370	3,850	—
1899	19,580,846	2.50	2.80	7.50	11.00	25.00	70.00	100.00	700	1,450
1899O	2,650,000	8.25	17.00	70.00	100.00	135	225	415	4,850	—
1899S	1,867,493	7.00	13.50	22.00	30.00	47.50	100.00	300	5,000	—
1900	17,600,912	2.80	4.00	7.00	11.00	23.50	780	100.00	825	1,450
1900O	2,010,000	17.50	35.00	110	150	215	355	595	6,000	—
1900S	5,168,270	4.25	5.50	11.50	16.00	27.50	75.00	155	1,900	—
1901	18,860,478	2.50	2.75	6.50	9.50	25.00	62.50	110	850	1,450
1901O	5,620,000	3.45	4.00	13.50	25.00	60.00	150	450	4,500	—
1901S	593,022	80.00	140	345	400	470	650	1,000	5,500	—
1902	21,380,777	3.00	3.45	5.50	8.00	22.00	62.50	100.00	700	1,450
1902O	4,500,000	3.45	5.00	13.50	27.50	55.00	130	125	4,650	—
1902S	2,070,000	7.00	19.50	55.00	75.00	115	195	385	4,000	—
1903	19,500,755	2.50	2.80	3.75	8.00	23.50	62.50	110	1,150	1,450
1903O	8,180,000	3.50	4.75	12.50	20.00	41.50	100.00	250	5,100	—
1903S	613,300	75.00	115	340	475	800	845	1,150	3,750	—
1904	14,601,027	2.75	3.00	6.25	9.50	25.00	62.50	110	1,950	1,450

1901-S Dime
Grade F-12

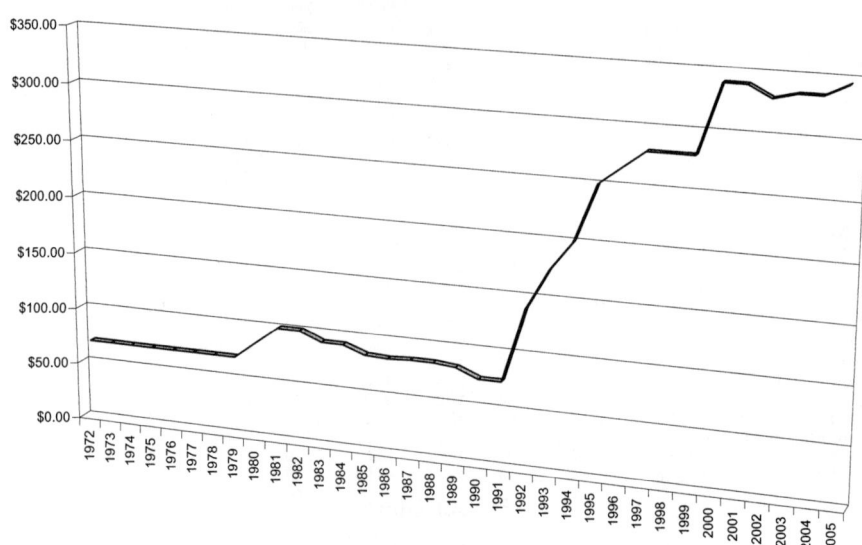

☑ Retail Price

Date	Mintage	G-4	VG-8	F-12	VF-20	XF-40	AU-50	MS-60	MS-65	Prf-65
1904S	800,000	40.00	65.00	150	225	320	480	750	4,500	—
1905	14,552,350	2.80	3.45	5.60	8.00	23.50	62.50	100.00	700	1,450
1905O	3,400,000	3.75	8.00	34.00	55.00	78.00	140	285	1,900	—
1905S	6,855,199	2.75	3.45	8.50	16.00	38.50	96.00	220	800	—
1906	19,958,406	1.75	2.20	3.75	6.75	22.00	62.50	100.00	700	1,450
1906D	4,060,000	2.75	3.45	6.25	15.00	35.00	80.00	175	1,600	—
1906O	2,610,000	4.80	12.50	47.50	68.50	96.00	135	200	1,300	—
1906S	3,136,640	2.50	4.65	11.50	20.00	43.50	110	240	1,300	—
1907	22,220,575	1.75	2.15	3.35	6.00	20.00	60.00	110	700	1,450
1907D	4,080,000	2.80	4.00	8.50	17.00	45.00	110	275	4,600	—
1907O	5,058,000	3.45	6.75	31.50	47.50	62.50	110	210	1,350	—
1907S	3,178,470	2.75	4.65	13.50	25.00	65.00	140	400	2,500	—
1908	10,600,545	2.15	2.50	3.40	6.75	22.00	62.50	110	700	1,450
1908D	7,490,000	2.15	2.50	4.65	9.50	30.00	62.50	130	1,000	—
1908O	1,789,000	4.65	11.00	42.50	57.50	90.00	140	300	1,700	—
1908S	3,220,000	2.80	4.45	11.00	20.00	41.50	175	325	2,750	—
1909	10,240,650	2.15	2.50	3.40	6.75	22.00	62.50	110	700	1,700
1909D	954,000	6.75	16.00	60.00	90.00	130	225	500	3,600	—
1909O	2,287,000	3.00	6.00	9.50	20.00	38.50	90.00	190	2,000	—
1909S	1,000,000	7.00	19.00	85.00	125	190	315	535	3,200	—
1910	11,520,551	1.85	2.15	3.40	8.50	22.00	62.50	100.00	700	1,450
1910D	3,490,000	2.50	4.00	8.50	18.50	43.50	110	175	1,550	—
1910S	1,240,000	5.00	10.00	48.50	71.00	100.00	200	435	2,600	—
1911	18,870,543	1.75	2.10	3.40	6.75	22.00	62.50	110	700	1,700
1911D	11,209,000	1.75	2.10	3.40	6.75	25.00	62.50	110	750	—
1911S	3,520,000	2.50	3.45	8.00	17.50	38.50	100.00	200	1,300	—
1912	19,350,700	1.75	2.10	3.40	6.75	22.00	62.50	110	700	1,700
1912D	11,760,000	1.75	2.10	3.75	6.75	22.00	62.50	110	700	—
1912S	3,420,000	2.20	2.75	5.60	12.50	32.50	92.50	160	850	—
1913	19,760,622	1.75	2.10	3.00	6.50	22.00	62.50	110	700	1,450
1913S	510,000	15.50	30.00	85.00	135	225	300	500	1,450	—
1914	17,360,655	1.75	2.10	3.00	6.50	22.00	62.50	110	700	1,700
1914D	11,908,000	1.75	2.10	3.40	6.50	22.00	62.50	110	700	—
1914S	2,100,000	3.00	4.00	8.00	17.50	38.50	80.00	150	1,350	—
1915	5,620,450	2.10	2.50	3.00	6.50	22.00	62.50	110	700	2,000
1915S	960,000	5.00	9.50	31.50	45.00	65.00	135	250	1,600	—
1916	18,490,000	1.75	2.15	3.40	8.00	22.00	62.50	110	700	—
1916S	5,820,000	1.75	2.15	4.00	8.00	23.50	65.00	110	850	—

Mercury Dime

Mint mark   1942/41

KM# 140 • 2.5000 g., 0.9000 **Silver**, 0.0724 oz. ASW, 17.9 mm. • **Designer:** Adolph A. Weinman **Notes:**
All specimens listed as -65FSB are for fully struck MS-65 coins with fully split and rounded horizontal bands
on the fasces.

Date	Mintage	G-4	VG-8	F-12	VF-20	XF-40	MS-60	MS-65	Prf-65	-65FSB
1916	22,180,080	3.45	4.70	6.25	6.75	9.50	30.00	90.00	—	120
1916D	264,000	775	1,100	2,100	3,450	5,500	9,350	22,500	—	44,500
1916S	10,450,000	4.00	4.35	9.00	10.00	18.50	35.00	155	—	600
1917	55,230,000	1.85	2.00	2.50	5.00	7.50	30.00	155	—	400
1917D	9,402,000	4.00	5.00	10.00	21.50	42.00	120	1,100	—	6,000
1917S	27,330,000	1.80	2.00	3.50	5.75	10.00	62.00	470	—	1,150
1918	26,680,000	2.50	2.75	5.50	10.00	25.00	70.00	420	—	1,150
1918D	22,674,800	2.65	3.00	4.50	10.00	21.50	105	600	—	33,500
1918S	19,300,000	2.40	2.75	3.50	8.50	16.00	90.00	660	—	6,600
1919	35,740,000	1.90	2.00	3.00	5.00	10.00	37.00	320	—	700
1919D	9,939,000	3.35	6.00	11.00	21.50	35.00	175	1,400	—	38,500
1919S	8,850,000	2.75	3.00	8.00	15.00	31.00	175	1,000	—	13,000
1920	59,030,000	1.35	1.45	2.00	3.50	6.50	27.50	235	—	515
1920D	19,171,000	2.40	2.75	4.00	7.00	18.00	105	750	—	4,000
1920S	13,820,000	2.40	2.75	4.00	7.50	15.00	110	1,300	—	8,000
1921	1,230,000	41.50	68.50	110	275	565	1,000	3,200	—	4,400
1921D	1,080,000	60.00	110	170	360	640	1,150	3,200	—	5,600
1923	50,130,000	1.20	1.60	2.00	3.50	6.00	27.50	110	—	295
1923S	6,440,000	2.40	2.75	7.00	12.50	65.00	160	1,150	—	6,900
1924	24,010,000	1.35	1.60	2.50	4.25	12.00	42.00	175	—	520
1924D	6,810,000	2.75	4.00	6.00	14.00	44.00	160	950	—	1,400
1924S	7,120,000	2.75	3.50	4.00	8.75	44.00	170	1,100	—	14,000
1925	25,610,000	1.15	1.45	2.00	3.75	7.50	27.00	195	—	1,000
1925D	5,117,000	4.00	4.25	11.50	38.00	110	350	1,750	—	3,500
1925S	5,850,000	2.40	2.75	7.00	12.50	65.00	175	1,400	—	4,400
1926	32,160,000	1.10	1.45	1.70	2.75	4.25	25.00	240	—	525
1926D	6,828,000	2.75	4.00	4.50	8.50	24.00	125	550	—	2,650
1926S	1,520,000	8.00	11.00	25.00	55.00	225	900	3,000	—	6,500
1927	28,080,000	1.10	1.45	1.75	3.50	4.50	26.00	125	—	400
1927D	4,812,000	2.75	5.00	7.25	18.50	65.00	175	1,200	—	8,500
1927S	4,770,000	2.10	3.50	4.75	8.00	23.00	280	1,400	—	7,700
1928	19,480,000	1.10	1.45	1.75	3.50	4.00	27.50	110	—	300

1916-D Dime
Grade F-12

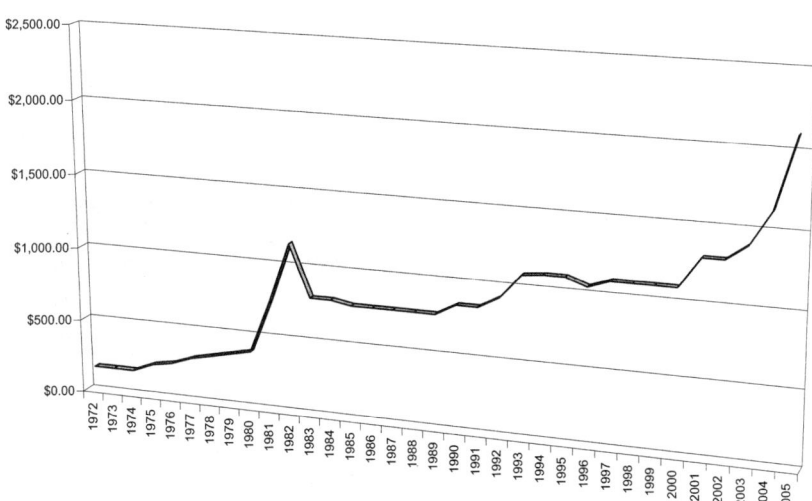

Retail Price

Date	Mintage	G-4	VG-8	F-12	VF-20	XF-40	MS-60	MS-65	Prf-65	-65FSB
1928D	4,161,000	3.00	3.25	8.00	18.50	44.00	170	875	—	2,500
1928S	7,400,000	1.80	2.10	2.75	5.50	16.00	125	425	—	1,900
1929	25,970,000	1.35	1.60	1.95	2.75	4.00	20.00	60.00	—	265
1929D	5,034,000	1.80	3.00	3.50	6.25	14.50	25.00	70.00	—	225
1929S	4,730,000	1.35	1.60	2.00	4.00	7.00	32.50	120	—	525
1930	6,770,000	1.35	1.50	2.00	3.50	7.00	26.00	115	—	525
1930S	1,843,000	2.50	3.50	4.80	6.25	15.00	75.00	200	—	565
1931	3,150,000	2.10	2.50	2.75	4.25	8.75	35.00	135	—	725
1931D	1,260,000	8.00	10.00	14.00	17.00	32.50	85.00	225	—	350
1931S	1,800,000	3.00	3.50	5.00	8.00	13.50	85.00	225	—	2,100
1934	24,080,000	1.00	1.45	1.75	3.00	5.00	21.50	40.00	—	150
1934D	6,772,000	1.60	2.10	2.75	4.00	8.00	50.00	72.00	—	360
1935	58,830,000	.80	1.00	1.50	2.15	4.25	8.00	30.00	—	70.00
1935D	10,477,000	1.25	1.75	2.50	3.75	7.50	34.00	72.00	—	600
1935S	15,840,000	1.00	1.50	1.75	3.00	5.50	24.00	31.50	—	500
1936	87,504,130	.80	1.00	1.50	2.25	3.50	8.00	25.00	2,000	90.00
1936D	16,132,000	1.00	1.25	1.50	3.00	6.50	26.00	42.00	—	295
1936S	9,210,000	1.00	1.25	1.50	2.50	3.00	20.00	31.50	—	85.00
1937	56,865,756	.80	1.00	1.50	2.00	3.25	8.00	23.00	800	42.00
1937D	14,146,000	1.00	1.25	1.50	3.00	5.50	21.00	43.00	—	100.00
1937S	9,740,000	1.00	1.25	1.50	3.00	5.50	24.00	34.00	—	195
1938	22,198,728	.80	1.00	1.50	2.25	3.50	13.00	27.50	450	80.00
1938D	5,537,000	1.50	1.75	2.00	3.50	6.00	16.00	28.00	—	65.00
1938S	8,090,000	1.35	1.55	1.75	2.35	3.75	20.00	35.00	—	135
1939	67,749,321	.80	1.00	1.50	2.00	3.25	8.50	25.00	425	170
1939D	24,394,000	1.00	1.25	1.50	2.00	3.50	7.50	26.00	—	45.00
1939S	10,540,000	1.25	1.50	2.00	2.50	4.25	21.00	35.00	—	750
1940	65,361,827	.60	.70	.90	1.10	2.50	6.00	26.00	385	57.50
1940D	21,198,000	.60	.70	.90	1.10	1.50	8.00	30.00	—	55.00
1940S	21,560,000	.60	.70	.90	1.10	1.50	8.50	30.00	—	95.00
1941	175,106,557	.60	.70	.90	1.10	1.50	5.00	30.00	385	42.00
1941D	45,634,000	.60	.70	.90	1.10	1.50	8.00	23.00	—	40.00
1941S	43,090,000	.60	.70	.90	1.10	1.50	7.00	30.00	—	50.00
1942	205,432,329	.60	.70	.90	1.10	1.50	5.50	24.00	385	52.50
1942/41	Inc. above	550	580	625	715	835	1,900	12,500	—	38,500
1942D	60,740,000	.60	.70	.90	1.10	1.50	8.00	27.50	—	40.00
1942/41D	Inc. above	500	560	625	750	850	2,250	5,600	—	19,500
1942S	49,300,000	.60	.70	.90	1.10	1.50	9.50	24.00	—	140
1943	191,710,000	.60	.70	.90	1.10	1.50	5.50	30.00	—	50.00
1943D	71,949,000	.60	.70	.90	1.10	1.50	7.50	27.50	—	40.00
1943S	60,400,000	.60	.70	.90	1.10	1.50	8.25	25.00	—	66.00
1944	231,410,000	.60	.70	.90	1.10	1.50	5.50	23.00	—	80.00
1944D	62,224,000	.60	.70	.90	1.10	1.50	6.50	23.00	—	40.00
1944S	49,490,000	.60	.70	.90	1.10	1.50	6.50	30.00	—	50.00
1945	159,130,000	.60	.70	.90	1.10	1.50	5.50	23.00	—	8,000
1945D	40,245,000	.60	.70	.90	1.10	1.50	6.00	24.00	—	40.00
1945S	41,920,000	.60	.70	.90	1.10	1.50	6.50	24.00	—	135
1945S micro S	Inc. above	1.00	1.25	1.50	3.00	4.25	26.00	85.00	—	650

Roosevelt Dime
Silver

  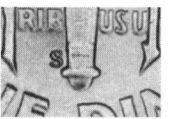

Mint mark 1946-64

KM# 195 • 2.5000 g., 0.9000 **Silver**, 0.0724 oz. ASW, 17.9 mm. • **Designer:** John R. Sinnock

Date	Mintage	G-4	VG-8	F-12	VF-20	XF-40	AU-50	MS-60	MS-65	Prf-65
1946	225,250,000	—	—	—	.50	.65	.95	3.10	9.00	—
1946D	61,043,500	—	—	—	.50	.65	1.10	3.50	8.00	—
1946S	27,900,000	—	—	—	.50	.65	.90	4.00	11.00	—
1947	121,520,000	—	—	—	.50	.65	.95	5.00	12.00	—
1947D	46,835,000	—	—	—	.50	.95	1.50	7.00	15.00	—
1947S	34,840,000	—	—	—	.50	.95	1.25	4.50	16.00	—
1948	74,950,000	—	—	—	.50	.95	1.50	3.00	14.00	—
1948D	52,841,000	—	—	—	.50	1.20	2.00	3.00	10.00	—
1948S	35,520,000	—	—	—	.50	.95	1.10	2.75	11.00	—
1949	30,940,000	—	—	—	1.00	1.50	4.00	23.50	42.00	—
1949D	26,034,000	—	—	.60	.80	1.25	2.00	9.50	22.00	—
1949S	13,510,000	—	1.00	1.25	1.50	2.75	6.00	33.50	60.00	—
1950	50,181,500	—	—	—	.50	.95	1.35	7.00	13.50	50.00
1950D	46,803,000	—	—	—	.50	.65	1.60	3.65	8.00	—
1950S	20,440,000	—	.85	1.00	1.10	1.25	6.00	34.50	50.00	—
1951	102,937,602	—	—	—	.50	.85	1.00	1.75	5.00	65.00
1951D	56,529,000	—	—	—	.50	.65	.95	1.75	5.00	—

Date	Mintage	G-4	VG-8	F-12	VF-20	XF-40	AU-50	MS-60	MS-65	Prf-65
1951S	31,630,000	—	—	—	.75	1.05	3.25	9.75	24.00	—
1952	99,122,073	—	—	—	.50	.90	1.10	1.35	5.00	30.00
1952D	122,100,000	—	—	—	.50	.65	.95	1.35	5.00	—
1952S	44,419,500	—	—	—	.75	1.05	1.50	4.25	11.00	—
1953	53,618,920	—	—	—	.50	.65	1.00	2.15	5.00	30.00
1953D	136,433,000	—	—	—	.50	.65	.95	2.15	5.00	—
1953S	39,180,000	—	—	—	.50	.65	.75	1.00	4.00	—
1954	114,243,503	—	—	—	.50	.65	.75	1.00	4.00	12.00
1954D	106,397,000	—	—	—	.50	.65	.75	1.00	3.25	—
1954S	22,860,000	—	—	—	.50	.65	.80	1.00	3.15	—
1955	12,828,381	—	—	—	.70	.80	.85	1.00	5.00	12.00
1955D	13,959,000	—	—	—	.50	.55	.60	1.00	4.00	—
1955S	18,510,000	—	—	—	.50	.60	.65	1.00	5.00	—
1956	109,309,384	—	—	—	.50	.50	.60	1.00	3.00	3.50
1956D	108,015,100	—	—	—	.50	.50	.60	1.00	3.25	—
1957	161,407,952	—	—	—	.50	.50	.60	1.00	3.00	2.75
1957D	113,354,330	—	—	—	.50	.50	.60	1.00	4.00	—
1958	32,785,652	—	—	—	.50	.50	.60	1.00	4.00	3.50
1958D	136,564,600	—	—	—	.50	.50	.60	1.00	4.00	—
1959	86,929,291	—	—	—	.50	.50	.60	1.00	3.00	2.50
1959D	164,919,790	—	—	—	.50	.50	.60	1.00	3.25	—
1960	72,081,602	—	—	—	.50	.50	.60	1.00	3.00	2.50
1960D	200,160,400	—	—	—	.50	.50	.60	1.00	3.00	—
1961	96,758,244	—	—	—	.50	.50	.60	1.00	3.00	2.00
1961D	209,146,550	—	—	—	.50	.50	.60	1.00	3.00	—
1962	75,668,019	—	—	—	.50	.50	.60	1.00	3.00	2.00
1962D	334,948,380	—	—	—	.50	.50	.60	1.00	3.00	—
1963	126,725,645	—	—	—	.50	.50	.60	1.00	3.00	2.00
1963D	421,476,530	—	—	—	.50	.50	.60	1.00	3.00	—
1964	933,310,762	—	—	—	.50	.50	.60	1.00	3.00	2.00
1964D	1,357,517,180	—	—	—	.50	.50	.60	1.00	3.00	—

Roosevelt Dime
Clad

Mint mark 1982 No mint mark
1968 - present

KM# 195a • 2.2700 g., **Copper-Nickel Clad Copper**, 17.9 mm. • **Designer:** John R. Sinnock **Notes:** The 1979-S and 1981-S Type II proofs have clearer mint marks than the Type I proofs of those years. On the 1982 no-mint-mark variety, the mint mark was inadvertently left off.

Date	Mintage	MS-65	Prf-65	Date	Mintage	MS-65	Prf-65
1965	1,652,140,570	1.00	—	1978	663,980,000	.70	—
1966	1,382,734,540	.80	—	1978D	282,847,540	.70	—
1967	2,244,007,320	.80	—	1978S	(3,127,781)	—	1.50
1968	424,470,000	.70	—	1979	315,440,000	.70	—
1968D	480,748,280	.80	—	1979D	390,921,184	.70	—
1968S	(3,041,506)	—	1.00	1979 type I	—	—	1.00
1969	145,790,000	2.00	—	1979S type I	(3,677,175)	—	1.00
1969D	563,323,870	1.00	—	1979S type II	Inc. above	—	1.25
1969S	(2,934,631)	—	0.80	1980P	735,170,000	.70	—
1970	345,570,000	.70	—	1980D	719,354,321	.70	—
1970D	754,942,100	.70	—	1980S	(3,554,806)	—	1.00
1970S	(2,632,810)	—	0.65	1981P	676,650,000	.70	—
1971	162,690,000	1.00	—	1981D	712,284,143	.70	—
1971D	377,914,240	.80	—	1981S type I	—	—	1.00
1971S	(3,220,733)	—	0.65	1981S type II	—	—	4.00
1972	431,540,000	.70	—	1982P	519,475,000	7.00	—
1972D	330,290,000	.70	—	1982 no mint mark	—	225	—
1972S	(3,260,996)	—	1.00	1982D	542,713,584	3.00	—
1973	315,670,000	.70	—	1982S	(3,857,479)	—	2.00
1973D	455,032,426	.75	—	1983P	647,025,000	8.00	—
1973S	(2,760,339)	—	1.00	1983D	730,129,224	2.00	—
1974	470,248,000	.70	—	1983S	(3,279,126)	—	1.25
1974D	571,083,000	.70	—	1984P	856,669,000	1.00	—
1974S	(2,612,568)	—	1.25	1984D	704,803,976	1.20	—
1975	585,673,900	.70	—	1984S	(3,065,110)	—	2.00
1975D	313,705,300	.75	—	1985P	705,200,962	.80	—
1975S	(2,845,450)	—	1.50	1985D	587,979,970	.80	—
1976	568,760,000	1.20	—	1985S	(3,362,821)	—	1.00
1976D	695,222,774	.80	—	1986P	682,649,693	1.70	—
1976S	(4,149,730)	—	1.50	1986D	473,326,970	1.60	—
1977	796,930,000	.70	—	1986S	(3,010,497)	—	2.75
1977D	376,607,228	.70	—	1987P	762,709,481	.75	—
1977S	(3,251,152)	—	1.75	1987D	653,203,402	.75	—

Date	Mintage	MS-65	Prf-65
1987S	(4,227,728)	—	1.25
1988P	1,030,550,000	.80	—
1988D	962,385,488	.80	—
1988S	(3,262,948)	—	3.00
1989P	1,298,400,000	1.00	—
1989D	896,535,597	.50	—
1989S	(3,220,194)	—	4.00
1990P	1,034,340,000	1.00	—
1990D	839,995,824	.80	—
1990S	(3,299,559)	—	2.75
1991P	927,220,000	.80	—
1991D	601,241,114	1.00	—
1991S	(2,867,787)	—	3.25
1992P	593,500,000	.75	—
1992D	616,273,932	.80	—
1992S	(2,858,981)	—	4.00
1993P	766,180,000	.80	—
1993D	750,110,166	.80	—
1993S	(2,633,439)	—	7.00
1994P	1,189,000,000	.80	—
1994D	1,303,268,110	.80	—
1994S	(2,484,594)	—	5.00
1995P	1,125,500,000	.80	—
1995D	1,274,890,000	1.20	—
1995S	(2,010,384)	—	20.00
1996P	1,421,163,000	1.00	—
1996D	1,400,300,000	1.00	—
1996W	1,457,949	25.00	—
1996S	(2,085,191)	—	3.50
1997P	991,640,000	1.00	—
1997D	979,810,000	.75	—
1997S	(1,975,000)	—	9.00
1998P	1,163,000,000	.80	—
1998D	1,172,250,000	.80	—
1998S	(2,078,494)	—	2.50
1999P	2,164,000,000	.80	—
1999D	1,397,750,000	.80	—
1999S	(2,557,897)	—	3.00
2000P	1,842,500,000	.80	—
2000D	1,818,700,000	.75	—
2000S	(3,097,440)	—	2.00
2001P	1,369,590,000	.80	—
2001D	1,412,800,000	.75	—
2001S	(2,249,496)	—	3.00
2002P	1,187,500,000	.75	—
2002D	1,379,500,000	.75	—
2002S	(2,268,913)	—	2.00
2003P	1,085,500,000	.75	—
2003D	986,500,000	.75	—
2003S	(2,076,165)	—	2.00
2004S	—	—	—

KM# A195 • Silver •

Date	Mintage	Prf-65
1992S	(1,317,579)	5.00
1993S	(761,353)	9.00
1994S	(785,329)	8.50
1995S	(838,953)	25.00
1996S	(830,021)	8.00
1997S	(821,678)	26.00
1998S	(878,792)	8.00
1999S	(804,565)	6.50
2000S	(965,921)	4.00
2001S	(849,600)	5.00
2002S	(888,826)	5.00
2003S	1,090,425	3.50

20 CENTS

KM# 109 • 5.0000 g., 0.9000 **Silver**, 0.1447 oz. ASW, 22 mm. • **Designer:** William Barber

Date	Mintage	G-4	VG-8	F-12	VF-20	XF-40	AU-50	MS-60	MS-65	Prf-65
1875	39,700	110	125	175	215	280	440	650	5,500	9,500
1875S	1,155,000	85.00	92.50	105	135	175	295	470	5,000	—
1875CC	133,290	160	185	250	315	400	580	850	10,000	—
1876	15,900	150	175	260	315	385	525	650	5,200	9,500
1876CC	10,000	—	—	—	—	—	—	—	—	—
Note: 1876CC, Eliasberg Sale, April 1997, MS-65, $148,500. Heritage 1999 ANA, MS-63, $86,500.										
1877 proof	510	1,600	1,800	2,250	2,600	280	3,150	—	—	10,500
1878 proof	600	1,350	1,525	1,850	2,000	2,300	2,600	—	—	9,700

QUARTER

Draped Bust Quarter

Small eagle reverse

KM# 25 • 6.7400 g., 0.8920 **Silver**, 0.1935 oz. ASW, 27.5 mm. • **Designer:** Robert Scot

Date	Mintage	G-4	VG-8	F-12	VF-20	XF-40	AU-50	MS-60	MS-65
1796	6,146	9,000	14,000	27,500	36,500	41,500	72,000	82,500	150,000

1876 20-Cent
Grade F-12

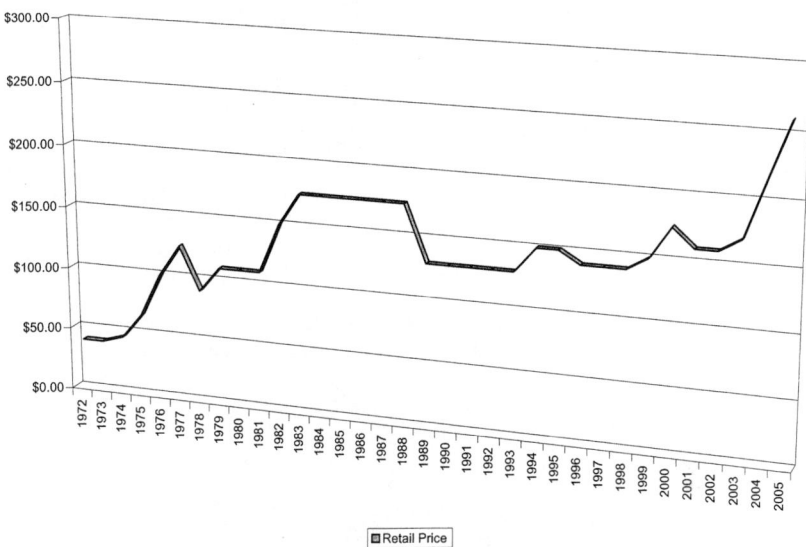

Retail Price

1804 Quarter
Grade XF-40

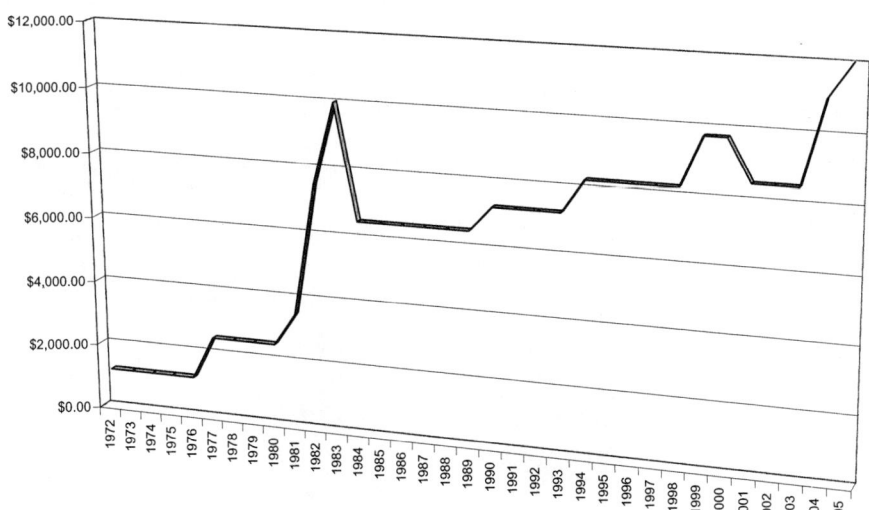

Retail Price

Heraldic eagle reverse

KM# 36 • 6.7400 g., 0.8920 **Silver**, .1935 oz. ASW, 27.5 mm. • **Designer:** Robert Scot

Date	Mintage	G-4	VG-8	F-12	VF-20	XF-40	AU-50	MS-60	MS-65
1804	6,738	2,750	3,300	4,750	6,000	12,000	23,000	45,000	120,000
1805	121,394	220	275	500	950	1,700	3,500	5,850	62,000
1806	206,124	220	275	500	900	1,650	3,300	5,300	46,500
1806/5	Inc. above	250	375	650	1,400	2,700	4,000	6,500	62,500
1807	220,643	220	275	500	925	1,650	3,400	5,300	48,500

Liberty Cap Quarter
"E Pluribus Unum" above eagle reverse

KM# 44 • 6.7400 g., 0.8920 **Silver**, 0.1935 oz. ASW, 27 mm. • **Designer:** John Reich **Notes:** Varieties of the 1819 strikes are distinguished by the size of the 9 in the date. Varieties of the 1820 strikes are distinguished by the size of the 0 in the date. One 1822 variety and one 1828 variety have "25" engraved over "50" in the denomination. The 1827 restrikes were produced privately using dies sold as scrap by the U.S. Mint.

Date	Mintage	G-4	VG-8	F-12	VF-20	XF-40	AU-50	MS-60	MS-65
1815	89,235	90.00	110	175	400	1,200	1,700	3,000	25,000
1818	361,174	80.00	100.00	150	375	1,100	1,500	2,750	16,000
1818/15	Inc. above	82.50	110	175	425	1,200	1,700	3,200	20,000
1819 small 9	144,000	80.00	100.00	150	375	1,100	1,500	2,900	22,000
1819 large 9	Inc. above	80.00	100.00	150	375	1,100	1,500	2,900	22,000
1820 small O	127,444	80.00	100.00	150	375	1,100	1,500	2,750	28,000
1820 large O	Inc. above	80.00	100.00	150	375	1,100	1,500	2,750	25,000
1821	216,851	92.50	110	160	385	1,175	1,600	2,700	16,500
1822	64,080	96.00	115	175	400	1,125	2,700	4,000	—
1822 25/50C.	Inc. above	1,500	3,000	4,600	6,500	12,500	20,000	—	—
1823/22	17,800	14,000	16,500	22,000	31,000	41,500	75,000	—	—

Note: 1823/22, Superior, Aug. 1990, Proof, $62,500.

Date	Mintage	G-4	VG-8	F-12	VF-20	XF-40	AU-50	MS-60	MS-65
1824/2 mintage unrecorded	—	170	240	350	750	2,000	3,900	7,500	—
1825/22	168,000	92.50	115	200	425	1,100	1,900	3,000	22,500
1825/23	Inc. above	82.50	110	165	375	11,000	1,650	2,750	16,500
1825/24	Inc. above	82.50	110	165	375	1,100	1,650	2,750	16,500
1827 original	4,000	—	—	—	70,000	75,000	80,000	85,000	—

Note: Eliasberg, April 1997, VF-20, $39,600.

Date	Mintage	G-4	VG-8	F-12	VF-20	XF-40	AU-50	MS-60	MS-65
1827 restrike	Inc. above	—	—	—	—	—	—	—	—

Note: 1827 restrike, Eliasberg, April 1997, Prf-65, $77,000.

Date	Mintage	G-4	VG-8	F-12	VF-20	XF-40	AU-50	MS-60	MS-65
1828	102,000	75.00	100.00	150	350	1,000	1,600	3,000	19,500
1828 25/50C.	Inc. above	125	250	475	1,100	1,925	3,500	8,500	—

"E Pluribus Unum" removed from above eagle reverse

KM# 55 • 0.8920 **Silver**, 24.3 mm. • **Designer:** William Kneass **Notes:** Varieties of the 1831 strikes are distinguished by the size of the lettering on the reverse.

Date	Mintage	G-4	VG-8	F-12	VF-20	XF-40	AU-50	MS-60	MS-65
1831 small letter	398,000	65.00	72.50	92.50	140	350	850	1,100	13,500
1831 large letter	Inc. above	65.00	72.50	92.50	140	350	850	1,100	18,500
1832	320,000	65.00	72.50	92.50	140	350	850	1,100	16,000
1833	156,000	67.50	77.50	100.00	165	400	925	1,400	13,500
1834	286,000	65.00	72.50	92.50	140	350	850	1,100	13,500
1835	1,952,000	65.00	72.50	92.50	140	350	850	1,100	13,500
1836	472,000	65.00	72.50	92.50	140	350	850	1,100	14,500
1837	252,400	65.00	72.50	92.50	140	350	850	1,100	13,500
1838	832,000	65.00	72.50	92.50	140	350	850	1,100	14,750

Seated Liberty Quarter
No drapery obverse

KM# 64.1 • 6.6800 g., 0.9000 **Silver**, 0.1934 oz. ASW, 24.3 mm. • **Designer:** Christian Gobrecht

Date	Mintage	G-4	VG-8	F-12	VF-20	XF-40	AU-50	MS-60	MS-65
1838	Inc. above	26.00	30.00	46.00	85.00	350	550	1,250	30,000
1839	491,146	25.00	29.00	44.00	75.00	350	550	1,250	34,000
1840O	425,200	28.50	35.00	60.00	400	375	575	1,350	38,500

Drapery added to Liberty's left elbow obverse

KM# 64.2 • 6.6800 g., 0.9000 **Silver**, 0.1934 oz. ASW, 24.3 mm. • **Designer:** Christian Gobrecht **Notes:** Two varieties for 1842 and 1842-O are distinguished by the size of the numerals in the date. 1852 obverse dies were used to strike the 1853 no-arrows variety, with the 2 being recut to form a 3.

Date	Mintage	G-4	VG-8	F-12	VF-20	XF-40	AU-50	MS-60	MS-65
1840	188,127	30.00	55.00	80.00	125	225	350	950	12,000
1840O	Inc. above	29.00	39.00	70.00	115	250	450	1,000	—
1841	120,000	75.00	90.00	120	185	300	385	750	11,000
1841O	452,000	21.50	27.50	50.00	85.00	165	350	700	10,000
1842 small date	88,000	—	—	—	—	—	—	—	—
Note: 1842 small date, Eliasberg, April 1997, Prf-63, $66,000.									
1842 large date	Inc. above	85.00	120	170	275	350	800	1,250	—
1842O small date	769,000	425	650	1,100	1,850	4,000	—	—	—
1842O large date	Inc. above	22.50	27.50	37.50	50.00	125	300	900	4,000
1843	645,600	20.00	25.00	31.50	40.00	70.00	150	400	6,750
1843O	968,000	25.00	31.50	47.50	100.00	250	750	2,000	11,000
1844	421,200	20.00	25.00	31.50	41.50	70.00	160	450	5,500
1844O	740,000	25.00	28.50	40.00	75.00	140	280	1,000	6,000
1845	922,000	20.00	25.00	31.50	40.00	70.00	150	465	5,000
1846	510,000	20.00	25.00	36.50	50.00	75.00	160	475	6,000
1847	734,000	20.00	25.00	31.50	40.00	70.00	150	450	5,000
1847O	368,000	27.50	40.00	60.00	120	275	700	1,900	—
1848	146,000	40.00	55.00	100.00	185	225	375	1,000	10,000
1849	340,000	20.00	25.00	36.00	65.00	125	275	750	9,000
1849O mintage unrecorded	—	425	600	1,000	1,700	2,900	5,750	—	—
1850	190,800	35.00	45.00	75.00	110	150	275	800	—
1850O	412,000	20.00	30.00	50.00	100.00	150	450	1,300	—
1851	160,000	60.00	75.00	125	225	285	400	850	8,500
1851O	88,000	150	265	375	575	1,000	2,250	4,000	—
1852	177,060	50.00	60.00	100.00	185	225	350	500	4,800
1852O	96,000	175	250	350	595	1,200	3,500	8,000	—
1853 recut date	44,200	350	500	700	900	1,200	1,600	2,600	9,000

Arrows at date obverse   Rays around eagle reverse

KM# 78 • 6.2200 g., 0.9000 **Silver**, 0.1800 oz. ASW, 24.3 mm. • **Designer:** Christian Gobrecht

Date	Mintage	G-4	VG-8	F-12	VF-20	XF-40	AU-50	MS-60	MS-65	Prf-65
1853	15,210,020	15.00	20.00	27.50	45.00	150	275	950	19,000	90,000
1853/4	Inc. above	40.00	65.00	100.00	200	275	750	1,750	—	—
1853O	1,332,000	18.00	35.00	50.00	100.00	275	1,100	2,750	—	—

Rays around eagle removed reverse

KM# 81 • 6.6800 g., 0.9000 **Silver**, .1934 oz. ASW, 24.3 mm. • **Designer:** Christian Gobrecht **Notes:** The 1854-O "huge O" variety has an oversized mint mark.

Date	Mintage	G-4	VG-8	F-12	VF-20	XF-40	AU-50	MS-60	MS-65	Prf-65
1854	12,380,000	15.00	20.00	27.50	35.00	75.00	225	440	7,500	17,500
1854O	1,484,000	17.00	24.00	35.00	60.00	125	300	1,750	—	—
1854O huge O	Inc. above	—	—	—	—	—	—	—	—	—
1855	2,857,000	15.00	20.00	27.50	35.00	75.00	225	440	8,500	18,500
1855O	176,000	50.00	75.00	110	240	475	950	2,750	—	—
1855S	396,400	40.00	60.00	80.00	225	500	1,250	2,000	—	—

Arrows at date removed obverse

KM# A64.2 • 6.2200 g., 0.9000 **Silver**, 0.1800 oz. ASW, 24.3 mm. • **Designer:** Christian Gobrecht

Date	Mintage	G-4	VG-8	F-12	VF-20	XF-40	AU-50	MS-60	MS-65	Prf-65
1856	7,264,000	15.00	20.00	27.50	35.00	60.00	145	290	4,250	15,000
1856O	968,000	20.00	30.00	40.00	60.00	110	250	1,000	8,500	—
1856S	286,000	45.00	65.00	110	250	450	900	2,200	—	—
1856S/S	Inc. above	70.00	100.00	185	375	875	1,250	—	—	—
1857	9,644,000	15.00	20.00	27.50	35.00	60.00	145	290	4,000	9,500
1857O	1,180,000	15.00	20.00	29.00	40.00	80.00	275	975	—	—
1857S	82,000	100.00	145	250	400	600	950	2,750	—	—
1858	7,368,000	15.00	20.00	27.50	35.00	60.00	160	300	4,000	6,500
1858O	520,000	25.00	30.00	45.00	70.00	135	360	1,350	—	—
1858S	121,000	60.00	100.00	175	275	650	1,250	—	—	—
1859	1,344,000	17.00	24.00	30.00	40.00	75.00	175	375	6,000	7,000
1859O	260,000	25.00	30.00	50.00	80.00	150	400	1,000	15,000	—
1859S	80,000	100.00	135	225	450	1,350	2,500	—	—	—
1860	805,400	18.00	22.00	28.00	33.00	60.00	160	500	—	5,250
1860O	388,000	20.00	30.00	40.00	55.00	100.00	275	1,200	—	—
1860S	56,000	175	325	575	900	3,500	6,000	—	—	—
1861	4,854,600	16.00	19.00	27.00	32.00	55.00	150	290	4,200	5,500
1861S	96,000	80.00	125	235	400	1,250	2,750	—	—	—
1862	932,550	18.00	22.00	33.00	40.00	65.00	165	300	4,350	5,350
1862S	67,000	80.00	125	200	300	700	1,600	2,750	—	—
1863	192,060	30.00	45.00	60.00	120	185	300	650	4,350	5,500
1864	94,070	75.00	100.00	135	200	300	400	650	5,000	5,500
1864S	20,000	375	575	875	1,250	2,350	3,750	7,000	—	—
1865	59,300	75.00	100.00	150	200	290	375	875	9,500	5,500
1865S	41,000	100.00	135	200	350	650	1,250	2,350	11,500	—
1866 unique	—	—	—	—	—	—	—	—	—	—

1856-S Quarter
Grade F-12

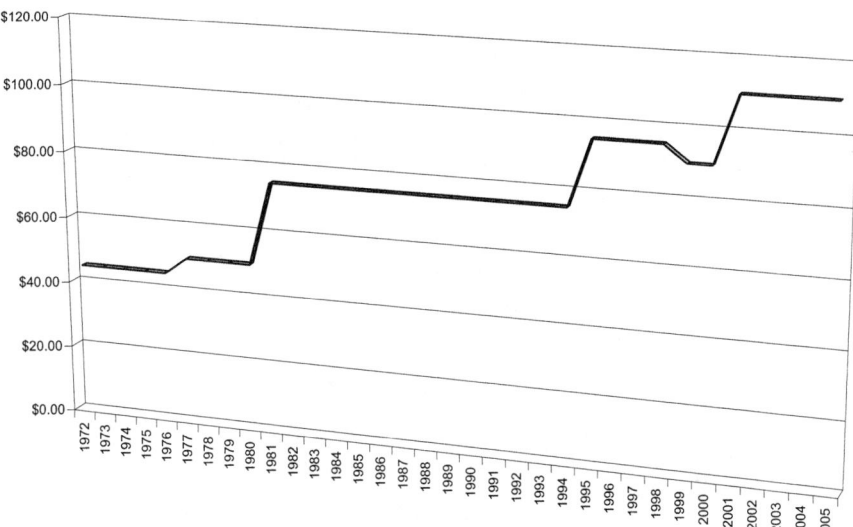

Retail Price

"In God We Trust" above eagle reverse

KM# 98 • 6.2200 g., 0.9000 **Silver**, 0.1800 oz. ASW, 24.3 mm. • **Designer:** Christian Gobrecht **Notes:** The 1873 closed-3 and open-3 varieties are distinguished by the amount of space between the upper left and lower left serifs in the 3.

Date	Mintage	G-4	VG-8	F-12	VF-20	XF-40	AU-50	MS-60	MS-65	Prf-65
1866	17,525	450	575	700	950	1,200	1,500	2,250	7,500	3,000
1866S	28,000	250	325	550	900	1,450	2,000	3,000	—	—
1867	20,625	225	300	450	625	800	975	1,200	—	2,450
1867S	48,000	275	350	600	900	1,350	1,700	—	—	—
1868	30,000	185	250	325	400	500	650	900	7,000	3,450
1868S	96,000	80.00	100.00	185	300	625	1,350	2,000	—	—
1869	16,600	325	425	550	675	775	950	1,275	—	2,500
1869S	76,000	90.00	115	225	375	700	1,400	2,400	16,000	—
1870	87,400	55.00	80.00	125	200	285	375	850	6,000	2,750
1870CC	8,340	3,800	5,500	8,000	12,000	16,000	25,000	35,000	—	—
1871	119,160	40.00	65.00	75.00	150	195	350	650	6,000	2,500
1871CC	10,890	2,250	3,800	5,500	9,500	14,500	25,000	40,000	—	—
1871S	30,900	300	450	550	800	1,100	1,850	3,000	10,000	—
1872	182,950	30.00	40.00	80.00	110	155	300	600	6,500	2,500
1872CC	22,850	650	850	1,500	2,950	5,900	7,500	14,000	—	—
1872S	83,000	900	1,250	1,650	2,100	3,500	4,500	7,500	—	—
1873 closed 3	212,600	150	225	325	525	600	1,000	2,000	—	2,600
1873 open 3	Inc. above	30.00	42.50	80.00	120	175	250	450	5,000	—
1873CC 6 known	4,000	—	75,000	—	—	—	—	—	—	—

Note: 1873CC, Heritage, April 1999, MS-62, $106,375.

Arrows at date obverse

KM# 106 • 6.2500 g., 0.9000 **Silver**, 0.1808 oz. ASW, 24.3 mm. • **Designer:** Christian Gobrecht

Date	Mintage	G-4	VG-8	F-12	VF-20	XF-40	AU-50	MS-60	MS-65	Prf-65
1873	1,271,700	16.00	23.00	30.00	60.00	200	400	775	4,250	8,000
1873CC	12,462	2,250	3,500	5,250	8,500	14,500	18,000	35,000	—	—
1873S	156,000	25.00	40.00	85.00	140	275	550	1,200	8,000	—
1874	471,900	20.00	26.00	40.00	70.00	220	420	850	4,000	6,750
1874S	392,000	23.00	30.00	50.00	110	240	425	900	4,500	—

Arrows at date removed obverse

KM# A98 • 6.2500 g., 0.9000 **Silver**, 0.1808 oz. ASW, 24.3 mm. • **Designer:** Christian Gobrecht **Notes:** The 1876-CC fine-reeding variety has a more finely reeded edge.

Date	Mintage	G-4	VG-8	F-12	VF-20	XF-40	AU-50	MS-60	MS-65	Prf-65
1875	4,293,500	14.00	17.00	25.00	30.00	50.00	135	225	1,600	2,300
1875CC	140,000	60.00	90.00	175	300	550	850	1,600	15,000	—
1875S	680,000	25.00	36.00	67.00	110	175	275	575	3,200	—
1876	17,817,150	14.00	17.00	25.00	30.00	50.00	135	225	1,600	2,250
1876CC	4,944,000	17.00	20.00	30.00	40.00	70.00	150	325	3,600	—
1876CC fine reeding	Inc. above	18.00	28.00	33.00	42.00	72.00	150	325	3,600	—
1876S	8,596,000	16.00	19.00	25.00	30.00	50.00	135	225	2,000	—
1877	10,911,710	14.00	17.00	25.00	30.00	50.00	135	225	1,600	2,250
1877CC	4,192,000	18.00	28.00	33.00	42.00	72.00	150	325	2,000	—
1877S	8,996,000	14.00	17.00	25.00	30.00	50.00	135	225	1,600	—
1877S /horizontal S	Inc. above	32.00	48.00	75.00	125	225	375	650	—	—
1878	2,260,800	16.00	18.00	28.00	34.00	55.00	145	250	2,750	2,300
1878CC	996,000	19.00	29.00	45.00	85.00	110	150	450	3,500	—
1878S	140,000	150	185	285	350	600	850	1,450	—	—
1879	14,700	190	235	285	325	400	485	575	1,700	2,250
1880	14,955	190	235	285	325	400	485	575	1,600	2,250
1881	12,975	200	250	300	350	425	500	600	1,650	2,200
1882	16,300	200	250	300	350	425	500	600	1,850	2,200
1883	15,439	210	265	315	365	435	525	625	2,450	2,200
1884	8,875	325	400	485	585	675	750	850	1,900	2,200
1885	14,530	210	265	315	365	435	525	625	2,600	2,200
1886	5,886	500	600	700	800	900	1,000	1,250	2,600	2,400
1887	10,710	300	350	400	485	585	625	750	2,350	2,200
1888	10,833	250	300	350	400	475	550	650	2,000	2,350
1888S	1,216,000	15.00	20.00	27.50	30.00	60.00	160	245	2,450	—
1889	12,711	225	285	325	385	450	500	625	1,750	2,350
1890	80,590	65.00	85.00	100.00	125	200	300	425	—	2,350
1891	3,920,600	15.00	20.00	27.50	30.00	60.00	160	245	1,750	2,350
1891O	68,000	150	225	325	550	950	1,250	3,000	14,500	—
1891S	2,216,000	16.00	22.00	29.00	65.00	52.50	185	275	2,400	—

Barber Quarter

KM# 114 • 6.2500 g., 0.9000 **Silver**, 0.1809 oz. ASW, 24.3 mm. • **Designer:** Charles E. Barber

Date	Mintage	G-4	VG-8	F-12	VF-20	XF-40	AU-50	MS-60	MS-65	Prf-65
1892	8,237,245	5.25	6.75	22.50	43.50	75.00	120	220	1,300	2,000
1892O	2,640,000	11.00	17.50	37.50	52.50	96.00	140	300	1,650	—

Date	Mintage	G-4	VG-8	F-12	VF-20	XF-40	AU-50	MS-60	MS-65	Prf-65
1892S	964,079	25.00	47.50	80.00	110	160	300	480	4,850	—
1893	5,484,838	5.00	7.00	26.00	38.50	71.00	120	210	1,750	2,000
1893O	3,396,000	6.75	11.00	27.50	50.00	90.00	160	275	1,900	—
1893S	1,454,535	15.00	30.00	60.00	105	135	300	480	8,400	—
1894	3,432,972	5.50	7.50	32.50	47.50	93.50	150	250	1,550	2,000
1894O	2,852,000	8.00	13.50	41.50	65.00	110	225	340	3,000	—
1894S	2,648,821	7.50	11.00	38.00	62.50	100.00	205	315	3,000	—
1895	4,440,880	5.50	8.00	30.00	41.50	78.50	135	230	1,900	2,000
1895O	2,816,000	10.00	15.00	41.50	67.50	115	225	400	2,750	—
1895S	1,764,681	13.50	22.00	52.50	85.00	125	250	400	4,000	—
1896	3,874,762	5.00	6.50	25.00	41.50	78.50	135	235	1,600	2,000
1896O	1,484,000	15.00	30.00	100.00	250	415	750	850	7,750	—
1896S	188,039	660	1,050	1,650	2,500	4,000	5,250	7,500	49,000	—
1897	8,140,731	5.00	6.25	21.50	33.50	71.50	120	220	1,300	2,000
1897O	1,414,800	13.50	32.50	100.00	220	375	625	800	4,150	—
1897S	542,229	85.00	110	250	300	430	700	1,000	7,000	—
1898	11,100,735	5.00	6.25	22.50	33.50	71.50	120	220	1,300	2,000
1898O	1,868,000	11.00	22.00	65.00	125	285	415	625	10,000	—
1898S	1,020,592	8.00	16.00	42.50	60.00	96.00	210	400	7,200	—
1899	12,624,846	5.00	6.25	22.50	33.50	71.50	120	215	1,300	2,000
1899O	2,644,000	9.50	16.00	32.50	55.00	110	275	400	3,350	—
1899S	708,000	15.00	27.50	70.00	85.00	135	275	440	3,700	—
1900	10,016,912	6.00	8.00	21.50	35.00	71.50	135	215	1,300	2,000
1900O	3,416,000	11.00	23.00	62.50	100.00	135	345	585	3,800	—
1900S	1,858,585	7.50	13.50	38.00	55.00	80.00	135	385	5,400	—
1901	8,892,813	8.00	11.00	22.50	38.00	80.00	125	215	2,250	2,200
1901O	1,612,000	38.50	55.00	130	250	440	685	900	6,000	—
1901S	72,664	5,500	10,000	13,500	16,000	19,500	22,000	26,000	55,000	—
1902	12,197,744	6.00	8.00	19.50	33.50	66.00	115	215	1,300	2,100
1902O	4,748,000	8.00	16.00	45.00	80.00	135	220	450	4,800	—
1902S	1,524,612	12.50	19.00	47.50	75.00	130	235	530	3,600	—
1903	9,670,064	5.75	8.00	19.00	33.50	66.00	115	215	2,600	2,000
1903O	3,500,000	7.00	11.00	38.00	60.00	105	250	450	5,800	—
1903S	1,036,000	14.00	23.00	45.00	75.00	125	275	450	2,900	—
1904	9,588,813	5.75	8.00	19.00	33.50	66.00	115	215	1,475	2,000
1904O	2,456,000	8.50	17.50	55.00	90.00	210	400	840	3,250	—
1905	4,968,250	7.50	9.50	27.50	33.50	72.50	125	215	1,650	2,000
1905O	1,230,000	15.00	30.00	80.00	150	230	375	515	6,600	—
1905S	1,884,000	8.50	15.00	40.00	62.50	105	225	350	3,650	—
1906	3,656,435	5.75	8.00	19.00	33.50	70.00	115	215	1,300	2,000
1906D	3,280,000	6.25	8.00	25.00	42.50	71.50	155	220	2,200	—
1906O	2,056,000	6.25	8.50	38.00	57.50	96.00	200	300	1,400	—
1907	7,192,575	5.25	8.00	17.50	33.50	66.00	115	215	1,300	2,000
1907D	2,484,000	6.00	9.00	29.00	52.50	80.00	180	250	2,750	—
1907O	4,560,000	5.25	8.00	17.50	38.50	70.00	135	220	2,600	—
1907S	1,360,000	8.50	15.00	42.50	62.50	125	265	480	3,500	—

1896-S Quarter
Grade F-12

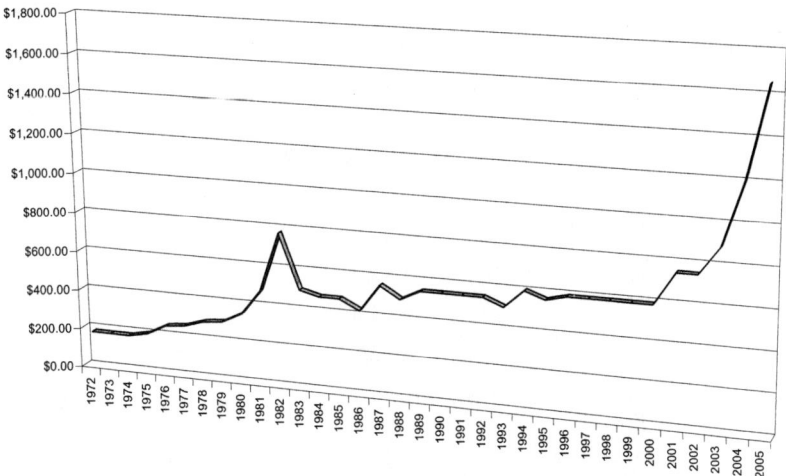

□ Retail Price

1913-S Quarter
Grade XF-40

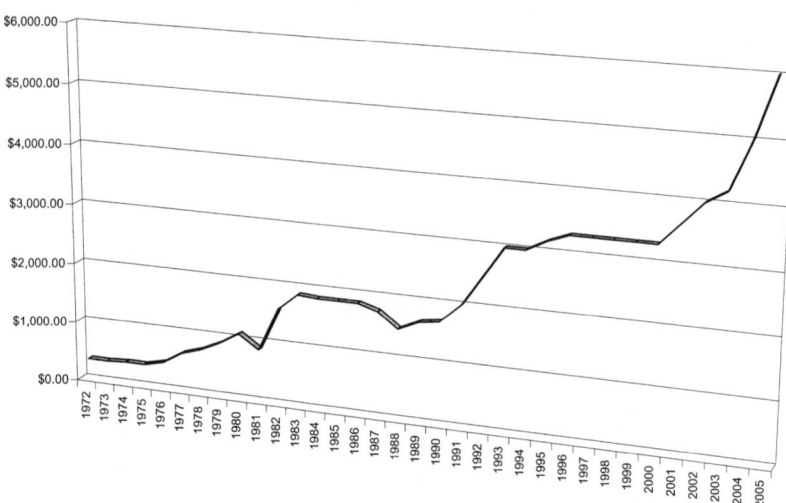

☒ Retail Price

Date	Mintage	G-4	VG-8	F-12	VF-20	XF-40	AU-50	MS-60	MS-65	Prf-65
1908	4,232,545	5.00	6.25	18.50	33.50	70.00	115	215	1,300	2,200
1908D	5,788,000	5.00	6.25	17.50	32.50	70.00	120	250	1,750	—
1908O	6,244,000	5.00	8.50	17.50	33.50	75.00	125	215	1,300	—
1908S	784,000	16.00	35.00	80.00	140	295	480	775	5,100	—
1909	9,268,650	5.00	6.25	17.50	33.50	66.00	115	215	1,300	2,000
1909D	5,114,000	6.25	7.50	20.50	38.50	75.00	162.5	215	2,350	—
1909O	712,000	16.00	38.50	90.00	185	330	520	825	9,000	—
1909S	1,348,000	7.00	9.50	33.50	47.50	80.00	200	300	2,400	—
1910	2,244,551	7.00	8.50	28.50	46.00	78.50	140	215	1,300	2,000
1910D	1,500,000	7.00	9.00	42.50	65.00	110	260	375	2,250	—
1911	3,720,543	5.25	8.00	17.50	33.50	72.50	125	215	1,300	2,000
1911D	933,600	7.50	19.00	95.00	215	310	500	700	6,250	—
1911S	988,000	6.25	12.00	51.50	75.00	150	300	400	1,500	—
1912	4,400,700	5.75	8.00	17.50	33.50	70.00	115	215	1,300	2,000
1912S	708,000	8.00	10.00	42.50	75.00	115	230	390	2,750	—
1913	484,613	12.50	21.50	71.50	160	415	535	960	4,250	2,200
1913D	1,450,800	7.50	12.00	34.00	55.00	85.00	185	275	1,400	—
1913S	40,000	990	1,600	3,500	3,500	5,250	6,000	6,500	7,300	16,000	—
1914	6,244,610	5.00	6.25	17.50	30.00	57.50	115	215	1,300	2,200
1914D	3,046,000	5.00	6.25	17.50	30.00	57.50	115	215	1,300	—
1914S	264,000	66.00	96.00	190	300	500	700	930	3,550	—
1915	3,480,450	5.00	6.25	17.50	30.00	66.00	115	215	1,300	2,200
1915D	3,694,000	5.00	6.25	17.50	30.00	66.00	115	215	1,300	—
1915S	704,000	8.00	11.00	32.50	52.50	96.00	220	255	1,300	—
1916	1,788,000	5.00	9.50	17.50	27.50	57.50	115	215	1,300	—
1916D	6,540,800	5.00	6.25	17.50	30.00	57.50	115	215	1,300	—

Standing Liberty Quarter
Type 1 obverse

Right breast exposed

KM# 141 • 6.2500 g., 0.9000 **Silver**, 0.1809 oz. ASW, 24.3 mm. • **Designer:** Hermon A. MacNeil

Date	Mintage	G-4	VG-8	F-12	VF-20	XF-40	AU-50	MS-60	MS-65	-65FH
1916	52,000	3,500	6,000	8,500	9,500	11,500	13,500	15,000	27,500	35,000
1917	8,792,000	22.00	38.00	50.00	65.00	95.00	185	250	1,200	1,500
1917D	1,509,200	28.00	39.00	55.00	70.00	115	195	275	950	2,500
1917S	1,952,000	30.00	39.00	60.00	80.00	160	220	400	1,600	3,500

Type 2 obverse
Three stars below eagle reverse

Right breast covered   Mint mark

KM# 145 • 6.2500 g., 0.9000 **Silver**, 0.1809 oz. ASW, 24.3 mm. • **Designer:** Hermon A. MacNeil

Date	Mintage	G-4	VG-8	F-12	VF-20	XF-40	AU-50	MS-60	MS-65	-65FH
1917	13,880,000	25.00	25.00	30.00	35.00	48.00	85.00	150	650	1,200
1917D	6,224,400	39.00	50.00	80.00	90.00	100.00	160	225	1,400	3,500
1917S	5,522,000	35.00	44.00	60.00	71.50	85.00	125	180	1,150	4,100
1918	14,240,000	18.50	30.00	30.00	38.00	48.00	90.00	140	625	1,800
1918D	7,380,000	28.00	36.00	57.00	65.00	90.00	150	220	1,450	5,500
1918S	11,072,000	18.00	24.00	35.00	44.00	60.00	120	225	1,500	14,500
1918/17S	Inc. above	1,500	2,150	3,750	4,200	7,000	11,500	1,500	110,000	300,000
1919	11,324,000	35.00	55.00	62.50	65.00	75.00	110	175	625	1,800
1919D	1,944,000	85.00	145	185	275	440	575	1,000	2,900	27,500
1919S	1,836,000	85.00	200	250	325	520	725	1,100	4,500	30,000
1920	27,860,000	16.00	21.00	30.00	35.00	45.00	75.00	120	540	1,950
1920D	3,586,400	55.00	60.00	88.00	120	160	200	300	2,600	6,750
1920S	6,380,000	20.00	29.00	35.00	45.00	66.00	125	250	2,400	27,500
1921	1,916,000	180	240	325	400	480	650	800	1,850	4,750
1923	9,716,000	15.00	21.00	35.00	40.00	50.00	80.00	125	700	4,500
1923S	1,360,000	260	390	550	660	900	1,050	1,500	2,200	4,600
1924	10,920,000	16.00	20.00	25.00	30.00	36.00	75.00	120	540	1,800
1924D	3,112,000	55.00	75.00	100.00	140	180	215	280	650	4,600
1924S	2,860,000	28.00	33.00	41.50	55.00	105	240	375	2,000	5,750
1925	12,280,000	3.00	4.00	7.00	15.00	35.00	72.50	125	540	1,200
1926	11,316,000	3.00	4.00	7.00	15.00	35.00	75.00	125	540	2,000
1926D	1,716,000	7.00	9.00	16.00	30.00	65.00	100.00	140	550	26,000
1926S	2,700,000	3.00	4.00	12.00	30.00	110	275	345	2,200	28,000
1927	11,912,000	3.00	4.00	6.00	15.00	40.00	80.00	125	540	1,200
1927D	976,400	12.50	17.50	23.00	60.00	130	175	220	700	3,100
1927S	396,000	25.00	30.00	90.00	300	1,250	3,000	4,000	16,000	175,000
1928	6,336,000	3.00	4.00	5.00	15.00	35.00	75.00	105	540	2,500
1928D	1,627,600	4.00	6.00	8.00	18.00	40.00	100.00	150	550	6,250
1928S	2,644,000	4.00	5.00	6.00	15.00	32.00	72.00	150	540	1,050
1929	11,140,000	3.00	4.00	6.00	11.50	36.00	75.00	130	540	1,250
1929D	1,358,000	4.00	5.00	8.00	14.00	34.00	72.00	150	540	6,750
1929S	1,764,000	3.00	4.00	5.00	15.00	35.00	75.00	150	540	900
1930	5,632,000	3.00	4.00	4.50	12.50	35.00	75.00	125	540	900
1930S	1,556,000	4.00	5.00	6.00	16.00	39.00	80.00	130	540	1,000

Washington Quarter

Mint mark
1932-64

KM# 164 • 6.2500 g., 0.9000 **Silver**, 0.1809 oz. ASW, 24.3 mm. • **Designer:** John Flanagan

Date	Mintage	G-4	VG-8	F-12	VF-20	XF-40	AU-50	MS-60	MS-65	Prf-65
1932	5,404,000	4.00	5.50	6.00	7.25	9.50	15.00	24.00	415	—
1932D	436,800	140	160	185	170	275	550	1,000	26,500	—
1932S	408,000	140	160	175	165	190	235	500	7,800	—
1934	31,912,052	2.00	2.50	3.00	3.50	5.00	9.00	25.00	90.00	—
1934D	3,527,200	3.75	5.50	6.50	10.00	22.00	80.00	220	1,500	—
1935	32,484,000	1.75	2.00	2.25	2.50	4.00	8.00	20.00	110	—
1935D	5,780,000	2.25	3.00	5.00	10.00	20.00	115	220	975	—
1935S	5,660,000	2.00	2.50	4.50	6.00	13.00	32.00	85.00	330	—
1936	41,303,837	1.75	1.85	2.00	2.50	4.00	8.50	20.00	95.00	1,050
1936D	5,374,000	3.75	4.40	5.65	20.00	47.50	260	600	1,850	—
1936S	3,828,000	2.25	2.50	3.50	5.00	12.00	45.00	100.00	425	—
1937	19,701,542	2.00	2.25	3.00	3.50	4.50	16.00	22.00	90.00	380
1937D	7,189,600	2.00	2.50	3.25	5.00	12.50	28.00	60.00	140	—
1937S	1,652,000	4.00	4.50	6.00	13.50	27.50	85.00	120	345	—
1938	9,480,045	3.75	4.50	5.00	6.00	14.00	41.50	85.00	250	225
1938S	2,832,000	4.50	5.00	5.50	7.00	19.00	52.50	95.00	235	—
1939	33,548,795	1.65	1.75	2.10	2.50	3.25	7.00	20.00	60.00	150

1932-D Quarter
Grade F-12

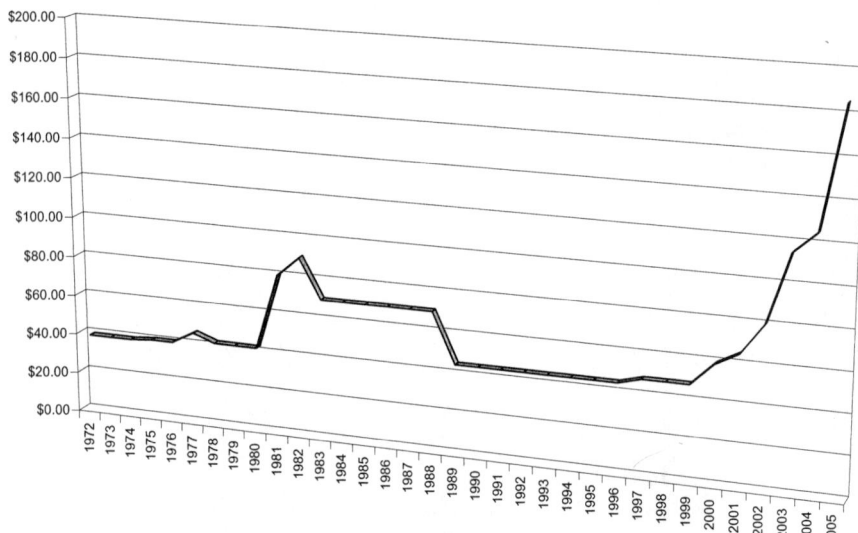

☐ Retail Price

Date	Mintage	G-4	VG-8	F-12	VF-20	XF-40	AU-50	MS-60	MS-65	Prf-65
1939D	7,092,000	2.00	2.25	3.00	4.50	8.50	16.00	37.50	100.00	—
1939S	2,628,000	3.50	3.75	4.00	6.75	16.00	45.00	100.00	325	—
1940	35,715,246	1.65	1.75	2.00	2.50	3.25	6.00	25.00	65.00	150
1940D	2,797,600	2.50	3.00	6.00	10.00	23.50	55.00	115	325	—
1940S	8,244,000	2.25	2.50	5.00	6.00	8.00	14.00	20.00	53.00	—
1941	79,047,287	—	—	1.65	2.00	2.50	3.50	12.50	45.00	110
1941D	16,714,800	—	—	2.25	3.00	4.50	12.50	35.00	95.00	—
1941S	16,080,000	—	—	2.00	2.50	3.50	10.00	30.00	80.00	—
1942	102,117,123	—	—	1.65	2.00	3.00	3.50	7.00	40.00	110
1942D	17,487,200	—	—	1.75	2.50	3.75	8.00	15.00	45.00	—
1942S	19,384,000	—	—	2.00	3.00	5.00	20.00	75.00	190	—
1943	99,700,000	—	—	1.50	2.00	2.25	3.00	5.00	45.00	—
1943D	16,095,600	—	—	2.00	3.50	6.00	12.50	27.50	70.00	—
1943S	21,700,000	—	—	3.00	5.00	7.50	15.00	30.00	70.00	—
1944	104,956,000	—	—	1.50	2.00	2.25	3.00	5.00	42.00	—
1944D	14,600,800	—	—	1.75	2.50	3.75	8.50	15.00	45.00	—
1944S	12,560,000	—	—	2.00	2.75	4.00	9.00	15.00	40.00	—
1945	74,372,000	—	—	1.50	1.75	2.00	2.50	5.00	42.00	—
1945D	12,341,600	—	—	2.00	3.50	6.50	11.00	17.50	44.00	—
1945S	17,004,001	—	—	1.75	2.50	3.50	6.00	10.00	42.00	—
1946	53,436,000	—	—	1.50	1.75	2.00	2.50	5.00	42.00	—
1946D	9,072,800	—	—	1.50	2.00	2.50	4.00	8.00	41.50	—
1946S	4,204,000	—	—	2.50	2.75	3.00	3.50	8.00	43.00	—
1947	22,556,000	—	—	1.65	2.10	2.75	4.00	10.00	45.00	—
1947D	15,338,400	—	—	1.65	2.25	3.00	4.00	10.00	45.00	—
1947S	5,532,000	—	—	2.25	2.50	2.75	4.00	10.00	45.00	—
1948	35,196,000	—	—	1.65	2.00	2.25	3.00	4.00	43.00	—
1948D	16,766,800	—	—	1.75	2.10	2.75	5.50	10.00	55.00	—
1948S	15,960,000	—	—	1.75	2.10	2.50	4.00	11.00	70.00	—
1949	9,312,000	—	—	2.00	3.00	6.50	14.00	35.00	75.00	—
1949D	10,068,400	—	—	2.25	2.50	5.00	7.00	25.00	50.00	—
1950	24,971,512	—	—	1.50	1.75	2.25	3.00	5.50	30.00	55.00
1950D	21,075,600	—	—	1.65	2.00	2.50	3.00	5.00	32.00	—
1950D/S	Inc. above	30.00	33.00	40.00	60.00	140	215	275	2,250	—
1950S	10,284,004	—	—	2.25	2.50	3.25	4.50	9.00	40.00	—
1950S/D	Inc. above	32.00	36.00	44.00	70.00	180	315	400	850	—
1951	43,505,602	—	—	1.50	1.75	2.25	3.50	6.00	32.00	40.00
1951D	35,354,800	—	—	1.50	2.00	2.50	3.50	7.00	38.00	—
1951S	9,048,000	—	—	3.00	4.50	6.00	9.00	24.00	52.00	—
1952	38,862,073	—	—	1.50	1.75	2.75	3.50	5.50	35.00	37.00
1952D	49,795,200	—	—	1.50	1.65	2.75	3.25	5.00	32.00	—
1952S	13,707,800	—	—	2.50	4.00	6.00	9.00	21.00	42.00	—

Date	Mintage	G-4	VG-8	F-12	VF-20	XF-40	AU-50	MS-60	MS-65	Prf-65
1953	18,664,920	—	—	1.50	1.65	1.75	3.00	5.50	30.00	25.00
1953D	56,112,400	—	—	1.50	1.65	1.75	2.75	4.25	29.00	—
1953S	14,016,000	—	—	1.50	1.75	2.10	2.75	5.00	30.00	—
1954	54,645,503	—	—	—	1.50	1.75	2.75	5.00	30.00	13.00
1954D	42,305,500	—	—	—	1.50	1.75	2.75	4.75	30.00	—
1954S	11,834,722	—	—	—	1.50	1.75	2.75	4.00	25.00	—
1955	18,558,381	—	—	—	1.65	1.75	2.75	3.50	25.00	14.00
1955D	3,182,400	—	—	2.00	2.25	2.50	2.75	3.25	45.00	—
1956	44,813,384	—	—	—	1.65	2.00	2.75	4.00	22.00	4.00
1956D	32,334,500	—	—	—	1.75	2.00	2.50	3.00	26.00	—
1957	47,779,952	—	—	—	1.65	1.75	2.25	3.50	23.00	4.00
1957D	77,924,160	—	—	—	1.65	1.75	2.00	2.25	26.00	—
1958	7,235,652	—	—	—	2.00	2.25	2.50	2.75	20.00	6.00
1958D	78,124,900	—	—	—	1.65	1.75	2.00	2.50	20.00	—
1959	25,533,291	—	—	—	1.65	1.75	2.00	2.75	20.00	4.25
1959D	62,054,232	—	—	—	1.65	1.75	2.00	2.75	25.00	—
1960	30,855,602	—	—	—	1.65	1.75	2.00	2.50	17.00	3.75
1960D	63,000,324	—	—	—	1.65	1.75	2.00	2.50	17.00	—
1961	40,064,244	—	—	—	1.65	1.75	2.00	2.75	19.00	3.50
1961D	83,656,928	—	—	—	1.65	1.75	2.00	2.50	16.00	—
1962	39,374,019	—	—	—	1.65	1.75	2.00	2.50	18.00	3.50
1962D	127,554,756	—	—	—	1.65	1.75	2.00	2.50	16.00	—
1963	77,391,645	—	—	—	1.50	1.60	2.00	2.50	15.00	3.50
1963D	135,288,184	—	—	—	1.50	1.60	2.00	2.50	15.00	—
1964	564,341,347	—	—	—	1.50	1.60	2.00	2.50	15.00	3.50
1964D	704,135,528	—	—	—	1.50	1.60	2.00	2.50	15.00	—

Clad type

KM# 164a • 5.6700 g., Copper-Nickel Clad Copper, 24.3 mm. • Designer: John Flanagan

Date	Mintage	MS-65	Prf-65	Date	Mintage	MS-65	Prf-65
1965	1,819,717,540	8.00	—	1971S	(3,220,733)	—	3.00
1966	821,101,500	4.50	—	1972	215,048,000	4.00	—
1967	1,524,031,848	6.50	—	1972D	311,067,732	5.50	—
1968	220,731,500	7.50	—	1972S	(3,260,996)	—	3.00
1968D	101,534,000	5.00	—	1973	346,924,000	7.00	—
1968S	(3,041,506)	—	3.50	1973D	232,977,400	9.00	—
1969	176,212,000	7.50	—	1973S	(2,760,339)	—	3.00
1969D	114,372,000	6.50	—	1974	801,456,000	6.50	—
1969S	(2,934,631)	—	3.50	1974D	353,160,300	10.00	—
1970	136,420,000	6.50	—	1974S	(2,612,568)	—	3.00
1970D	417,341,364	6.00	—	1975 none minted	—	—	—
1970S	(2,632,810)	—	3.00	1975D none minted	—	—	—
1971	109,284,000	6.00	—	1975S none minted	—	—	—
1971D	258,634,428	2.50	—				

Bicentennial design, drummer boy reverse

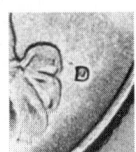

Mint mark
1968 - present

KM# 204 • 5.6700 g., Copper-Nickel Clad Copper, 24.3 mm. • Rev. Designer: Jack L. Ahr

Date	Mintage	G-4	VG-8	F-12	VF-20	XF-40	MS-60	MS-65	Prf-65
1976	809,784,016	—	—	—	—	—	.60	3.50	—
1976D	860,118,839	—	—	—	—	—	.60	4.00	—
1976S	(4,149,730)	—	—	—	—	—	—	—	3.00

Bicentennial design, drummer boy reverse

KM# 204a • 5.7500 g., Silver Clad, 0.074 oz., 24.3 mm. • Rev. Designer: Jack L. Ahr

Date	Mintage	G-4	VG-8	F-12	VF-20	XF-40	MS-60	MS-65	Prf-65
1976S	4,908,319 (3,998,621)	—	—	—	—	—	1.25	3.00	3.00

Regular design resumed reverse

KM# A164a • 5.6700 g., Copper-Nickel Clad Copper, 24.3 mm. • Notes: KM#164 design and composition resumed. The 1979-S and 1981 Type II proofs have clearer mint marks than the Type I proofs for those years.

Date	Mintage	MS-65	Prf-65	Date	Mintage	MS-65	Prf-65
1977	468,556,000	6.50	—	1979	515,708,000	6.00	—
1977D	256,524,978	4.00	—	1979D	489,789,780	4.00	—
1977S	(3,251,152)	—	1.50	1979S T-I	—	—	2.00
1978	521,452,000	6.00	—	1979S T-II	—	—	3.00
1978D	287,373,152	8.00	—	1980P	635,832,000	5.00	—
1978S	(3,127,781)	—	3.00	1980D	518,327,487	4.75	—

Date	Mintage	MS-65	Prf-65
1980S	(3,554,806)	—	2.00
1981P	601,716,000	6.00	—
1981D	575,722,833	4.00	—
1981S T-I	—	—	1.75
1981S T-II	—	—	5.00
1982P	500,931,000	18.50	—
1982D	480,042,788	10.00	—
1982S	(3,857,479)	—	2.75
1983P	673,535,000	45.00	—
1983D	617,806,446	30.00	—
1983S	(3,279,126)	—	2.75
1984P	676,545,000	10.00	—
1984D	546,483,064	7.00	—
1984S	(3,065,110)	—	2.75
1985P	775,818,962	10.00	—
1985D	519,962,888	6.00	—
1985S	(3,362,821)	5.00	1.75
1986P	551,199,333	7.00	—
1986D	504,298,660	10.00	—
1986S	(3,010,497)	—	3.00
1987P	582,499,481	7.00	—
1987D	655,594,696	5.00	—
1987S	(4,227,728)	—	1.75
1988P	562,052,000	9.00	—
1988D	596,810,688	8.00	—
1988S	(3,262,948)	—	2.25
1989P	512,868,000	9.00	—
1989D	896,535,597	3.00	—
1989S	(3,220,194)	—	2.25
1990P	613,792,000	9.00	—
1990D	927,638,181	3.00	—
1990S	(3,299,559)	—	6.00
1991P	570,968,000	8.00	—

Date	Mintage	MS-65	Prf-65
1991D	630,966,693	7.00	—
1991S	(2,867,787)	—	2.50
1992P	384,764,000	12.00	—
1992D	389,777,107	15.00	—
1992S	(2,858,981)	—	3.00
1993P	639,276,000	6.00	—
1993D	645,476,128	7.50	—
1993S	(2,633,439)	—	4.50
1994P	825,600,000	12.00	—
1994D	880,034,110	7.00	—
1994S	(2,484,594)	—	4.00
1995P	1,004,336,000	10.00	—
1995D	1,103,216,000	9.00	—
1995S	(2,010,384)	—	16.50
1996P	925,040,000	5.00	—
1996S	—	—	4.00
1996D	906,868,000	5.00	—
1997P	595,740,000	4.00	—
1997D	599,680,000	4.00	—
1997S	(1,975,000)	—	9.50
1998P	896,268,000	4.00	—
1998D	821,000,000	4.00	—
1998S	—	—	11.00

KM# A164b • Silver • Notes: Resumption of silver.

Date	Mintage	Prf-65
1992S	(1,317,579)	3.50
1993S	(761,353)	6.50
1994S	(785,329)	12.50
1995S	(838,953)	18.00
1996S	—	11.50
1997S	—	19.00
1998S	—	10.00

50 State Quarters

Connecticut

KM# 297 • Copper-Nickel Clad Copper •

Date	Mintage	MS-63	MS-65	Prf-65
1999P	688,744,000	.75	1.00	—
1999D	657,480,000	.75	1.00	—
1999S	(3,713,359)	—	—	10.00

KM# 297a • 0.9000 Silver •

Date	Mintage	MS-63	MS-65	Prf-65
1999S	(804,565)	—	—	40.00

Georgia

KM# 296 • Copper-Nickel Clad Copper •

Date	Mintage	MS-63	MS-65	Prf-65
1999P	451,188,000	.75	1.00	—
1999D	488,744,000	.75	1.00	—
1999S	(3,713,359)	—	—	10.00

KM# 296a • 0.9000 Silver •

Date	Mintage	MS-63	MS-65	Prf-65
1999S	(804,565)	—	—	40.00

Delaware

KM# 293 • 5.6700 g., Copper-Nickel Clad Copper, 24.3 mm. •

Date	Mintage	MS-63	MS-65	Prf-65
1999P	373,400,000	1.25	1.50	—
1999D	401,424,000	1.25	1.50	—
1999S	(3,713,359)	—	—	10.00

KM# 293a • 0.9000 Silver •

Date	Mintage	MS-63	MS-65	Prf-65
1999S	(804,565)	—	—	40.00

New Jersey

KM# 295 • Copper-Nickel Clad Copper •

Date	Mintage	MS-63	MS-65	Prf-65
1999P	363,200,000	1.00	1.50	—
1999D	299,028,000	1.00	1.75	—
1999S	(3,713,359)	—	—	10.00

KM# 295a • 0.9000 Silver •

Date	Mintage	MS-63	MS-65	Prf-65
1999S	(804,565)	—	—	40.00

Pennsylvania

KM# 294 • 5.6700 g., Copper-Nickel Clad Copper, 24.3 mm. •

Date	Mintage	MS-63	MS-65	Prf-65
1999P	349,000,000	1.50	2.00	—
1999D	358,332,000	1.25	1.50	—
1999S	(3,713,359)	—	—	10.00

KM# 294a • 0.9000 Silver •

Date	Mintage	MS-63	MS-65	Prf-65
1999S	(804,565)	—	—	40.00

Maryland

KM# 306 • Copper-Nickel Clad Copper •

Date	Mintage	MS-63	MS-65	Prf-65
2000P	678,200,000	.75	1.00	—
2000D	556,526,000	.75	1.00	—
2000S	(4,078,747)	—	—	5.00

KM# 306a • 0.9000 Silver •

Date	Mintage	MS-63	MS-65	Prf-65
2000S	(965,921)	—	—	7.50

Massachusetts

KM# 305 • Copper-Nickel Clad Copper •

Date	Mintage	MS-63	MS-65	Prf-65
2000P	629,800,000	.75	1.00	—
2000D	535,184,000	.75	1.00	—
2000S	(4,078,747)	—	—	5.00

KM# 305a • 0.9000 Silver •

Date	Mintage	MS-63	MS-65	Prf-65
2000S	(965,921)	—	—	7.50

New Hampshire

KM# 308 • Copper-Nickel Clad Copper •

Date	Mintage	MS-63	MS-65	Prf-65
2000P	673,040,000	.75	1.00	—
2000D	495,976,000	.75	1.00	—
2000S	(4,078,747)	—	—	5.00

KM# 308a • 0.9000 Silver •

Date	Mintage	MS-63	MS-65	Prf-65
2000S	(965,921)	—	—	7.50

South Carolina

KM# 307 • Copper-Nickel Clad Copper •

Date	Mintage	MS-63	MS-65	Prf-65
2000P	742,756,000	.75	1.00	—
2000D	566,208,000	.75	1.00	—
2000S	(4,078,747)	—	—	5.00

KM# 307a • 0.9000 Silver •

Date	Mintage	MS-63	MS-65	Prf-65
2000S	(965,921)	—	—	7.50

Virginia

KM# 309 • Copper-Nickel Clad Copper •

Date	Mintage	MS-63	MS-65	Prf-65
2000P	943,000,000	.75	1.00	—
2000D	651,616,000	.75	1.00	—
2000S	(4,078,747)	—	—	5.00

KM# 309a • 0.9000 Silver •

Date	Mintage	MS-63	MS-65	Prf-65
2000S	(965,921)	—	—	7.50

Kentucky

KM# 322 • Copper-Nickel Clad Copper •

Date	Mintage	MS-63	MS-65	Prf-65
2001P	353,000,000	.75	1.00	—
2001D	370,564,000	.75	1.00	—
2001S	(3,009,800)	—	—	6.50

KM# 322a • 0.9000 Silver •

Date	Mintage	MS-63	MS-65	Prf-65
2001S	(849,500)	—	—	22.50

14

New York

KM# 318 • Copper-Nickel Clad Copper •

Date	Mintage	MS-63	MS-65	Prf-65
2001P	655,400,000	.75	1.00	—
2001D	619,640,000	.75	1.00	—
2001S	(3,009,800)	—	—	6.50

KM# 318a • 0.9000 Silver •

Date	Mintage	MS-63	MS-65	Prf-65
2001S	(849,600)	—	—	22.50

North Carolina

KM# 319 • Copper-Nickel Clad Copper •

Date	Mintage	MS-63	MS-65	Prf-65
2001P	627,600,000	.75	1.00	—
2001D	427,876,000	.75	1.00	—
2001S	(3,009,800)	—	—	6.50

KM# 319a • 0.9000 Silver •

Date	Mintage	MS-63	MS-65	Prf-65
2001S	(849,600)	—	—	22.50

Rhode Island

KM# 320 • Copper-Nickel Clad Copper •

Date	Mintage	MS-63	MS-65	Prf-65
2001P	423,000,000	.75	1.00	—
2001D	447,100,000	.75	1.00	—
2001S	(3,009,800)	—	—	6.50

KM# 320a • 0.9000 Silver •

Date	Mintage	MS-63	MS-65	Prf-65
2001S	(849,600)	—	—	22.50

Vermont

KM# 321 • Copper-Nickel Clad Copper •

Date	Mintage	MS-63	MS-65	Prf-65
2001P	423,400,000	.75	1.00	—
2001D	459,404,000	.75	1.00	—
2001S	(3,009,800)	—	—	6.50

KM# 321a • 0.9000 Silver •

Date	Mintage	MS-63	MS-65	Prf-65
2001S	(849,600)	—	—	22.50

Indiana

KM# 334 • Copper-Nickel Clad Copper •

Date	Mintage	MS-63	MS-65	Prf-65
2002P	362,600,000	.75	1.00	—
2002D	327,200,000	.75	1.00	—
2002S	(3,084,185)	—	—	6.00

KM# 334a • 0.9000 Silver •

Date	Mintage	MS-63	MS-65	Prf-65
2002S	(892,229)	—	—	18.00

Louisiana

KM# 333 • Copper-Nickel Clad Copper •

Date	Mintage	MS-63	MS-65	Prf-65
2002P	362,000,000	.75	1.00	—
2002D	402,204,000	.75	1.00	—
2002S	(3,084,185)	—	—	6.00

KM# 333a • 0.9000 Silver •

Date	Mintage	MS-63	MS-65	Prf-65
2002S	(892,229)	—	—	18.00

Mississippi

KM# 335 • Copper-Nickel Clad Copper •

Date	Mintage	MS-63	MS-65	Prf-65
2002P	290,000,000	.75	1.00	—
2002D	289,600,000	.75	1.00	—
2002S	(3,084,185)	—	—	6.00

KM# 335a • 0.9000 Silver •

Date	Mintage	MS-63	MS-65	Prf-65
2002S	(892,229)	—	—	18.00

KM# 321a • 0.9000 Silver •

Date	Mintage	MS-63	MS-65	Prf-65
2001S	(849,600)	—	—	22.50

Ohio

KM# 332 • Copper-Nickel Clad Copper •

Date	Mintage	MS-63	MS-65	Prf-65
2002P	217,200,000	.75	1.00	—
2002D	414,832,000	.75	1.00	—
2002S	(3,084,185)	—	—	6.00

KM# 332a • 0.9000 Silver •

Date	Mintage	MS-63	MS-65	Prf-65
2002S	(892,229)	—	—	18.00

Tennessee

KM# 331 • Copper-Nickel Clad Copper •

Date	Mintage	MS-63	MS-65	Prf-65
2002P	361,600,000	1.25	2.00	—
2002D	286,468,000	.85	1.25	—
2002S	(3,084,185)	—	—	6.00

KM# 331a • 0.9000 Silver •

Date	Mintage	MS-63	MS-65	Prf-65
2002S	(892,229)	—	—	18.00

Alabama

KM# 344 • Copper-Nickel Clad Copper •

Date	Mintage	MS-63	MS-65	Prf-65
2003P	225,000,000	.75	1.00	—
2003D	232,400,000	.75	1.00	—
2003S	(3,270,603)	—	—	5.00

KM# 344a • 0.9000 Silver •

Date	Mintage	MS-63	MS-65	Prf-65
2003S	—	—	—	9.00

Arkansas

KM# 347 • Copper-Nickel Clad Copper •

Date	Mintage	MS-63	MS-65	Prf-65
2003P	228,000,000	.75	1.00	—
2003D	229,800,000	.75	1.00	—
2003S	(3,270,603)	—	—	5.00

KM# 347a • 0.9000 Silver •

Date	Mintage	MS-63	MS-65	Prf-65
2003S	—	—	—	9.00

Illinois

KM# 343 • Copper-Nickel Clad Copper •

Date	Mintage	MS-63	MS-65	Prf-65
2003P	225,800,000	.75	1.00	—
2003D	237,400,000	.75	1.00	—
2003S	(3,270,603)	—	—	5.00

KM# 343a • 0.9000 Silver •

Date	Mintage	MS-63	MS-65	Prf-65
2003S	—	—	—	9.00

Maine

KM# 345 • Copper-Nickel Clad Copper •

Date	Mintage	MS-63	MS-65	Prf-65
2003P	217,400,000	.75	1.00	—
2003D	213,400,000	.75	1.00	—
2003S	(3,270,603)	—	—	5.00

KM# 345a • 0.9000 Silver •

Date	Mintage	MS-63	MS-65	Prf-65
2003S	—	—	—	9.00

Missouri

KM# 346 • Copper-Nickel Clad Copper •

Date	Mintage	MS-63	MS-65	Prf-65
2003P	225,000,000	.75	1.00	—
2003D	228,200,000	.75	1.00	—
2003S	(3,270,603)	—	—	5.00

KM# 346a • 0.9000 Silver •

Date	Mintage	MS-63	MS-65	Prf-65
2003S	—	—	—	9.00

Florida

KM# 356   •   **Copper-Nickel Clad Copper** •

Date	Mintage	MS-63	MS-65	Prf-65
2004P	240,200,000	.75	1.00	—
2004D	241,600,000	.75	1.00	—
2004S	—	—	—	—

KM# 356a   •   **0.9000 Silver** •

Date	Mintage	MS-63	MS-65	Prf-65
2004S	—	—	—	—

Iowa

KM# 358   •   **Copper-Nickel Clad Copper** •

Date	Mintage	MS-63	MS-65	Prf-65
2004P	213,800,000	—	—	—
2004D	251,800,000	—	—	—
2004S	—	—	—	—

KM# 358a   •   **0.9000 Silver** •

Date	Mintage	MS-63	MS-65	Prf-65
2004S	—	—	—	—

Michigan

KM# 355   •   **Copper-Nickel Clad Copper** •

Date	Mintage	MS-63	MS-65	Prf-65
2004P	233,800,000	.75	1.00	—
2004D	225,800,000	.75	1.00	—
2004S	—	—	—	—

KM# 355a   •   **0.9000 Silver** •

Date	Mintage	MS-63	MS-65	Prf-65
2004S	—	—	—	—

Texas

KM# 357   •   **Copper-Nickel Clad Copper** •

Date	Mintage	MS-63	MS-65	Prf-65
2004P	278,800,000	—	—	—
2004D	263,000,000	—	—	—
2004S	—	—	—	—

KM# 357a   •   **0.9000 Silver** •

Date	Mintage	MS-63	MS-65	Prf-65
2004S	—	—	—	—

Wisconsin

KM# 359   •   **Copper-Nickel Clad Copper** •

Date	Mintage	MS-63	MS-65	Prf-65
2004P	226,400,000	—	—	—
2004D	226,800,000	—	—	—
2004S	—	—	—	—

KM# 359a   •   **0.9000 Silver** •

Date	Mintage	MS-63	MS-65	Prf-65
2004S	—	—	—	—

California

KM# 370   •   **Copper-Nickel Clad Copper** •

Date	Mintage	MS-63	MS-65	Prf-65
2005P	—	—	—	—
2005D	—	—	—	—
2005S	—	—	—	—

KM# 370a oz. ASW   •   **6.2500 g., 0.9000 Silver, 0.1808** •

Date	Mintage	MS-63	MS-65	Prf-65
2005S Proof	—	—	—	—

Kansas

KM# 373   •   **Copper-Nickel Clad Copper** •

Date	Mintage	MS-63	MS-65	Prf-65
2005P	—	—	—	—
2005D	—	—	—	—
2005S	—	—	—	—

KM# 373a oz. ASW   •   **6.2500 g., 0.9000 Silver, 0.1808** •

Date	Mintage	MS-63	MS-65	Prf-65
2005S	—	—	—	—

Minnesota

KM# 371 • **Copper-Nickel Clad Copper** •

Date	Mintage	MS-63	MS-65	Prf-65
2005P	—	—	—	—
2005D	—	—	—	—
2005S	—	—	—	—

KM# 371a • 6.2500 g., 0.9000 **Silver,** 0.1808 oz. ASW •

Date	Mintage	MS-63	MS-65	Prf-65
2005S	—	—	—	—

Oregon

KM# 372 • **Copper-Nickel Clad Copper** •

Date	Mintage	MS-63	MS-65	Prf-65
2005P	—	—	—	—
2005D	—	—	—	—

KM# 372a • 6.2500 g., 0.9000 **Silver,** 0.1808 oz. ASW •

Date	Mintage	MS-63	MS-65	Prf-65
2005S	—	—	—	—

West Virginia

KM# 374a • 6.2500 g., 0.9000 **Silver,** 0.1808 oz. ASW •

Date	Mintage	MS-63	MS-65	Prf-65
2005S	—	—	—	—

KM# 374 • **Copper-Nickel Clad Copper** •

Date	Mintage	MS-63	MS-65	Prf-65
2005P	—	—	—	—
2005D	—	—	—	—

HALF DOLLAR

Flowing Hair Half Dollar

KM# 16 • 13.4800 g., 0.8920 **Silver,** 0.3869 oz. ASW, 32.5 mm. • **Designer:** Robert Scot **Notes:** The 1795 "recut date" variety had the date cut into the dies twice, so both sets of numbers are visible on the coin. The 1795 "3 leaves" variety has three leaves under each of the eagle's wings on the reverse.

Date	Mintage	G-4	VG-8	F-12	VF-20	XF-40	MS-60
1794	23,464	2,400	4,000	6,000	13,000	20,000	90,000
1795	299,680	650	900	1,700	3,500	7,500	22,000
1795 recut date	Inc. above	700	950	1,750	3,750	7,750	25,000
1795 3 leaves	Inc. above	1,050	1,800	3,000	6,000	12,500	—

1797 Half Dollar
Grade F-12

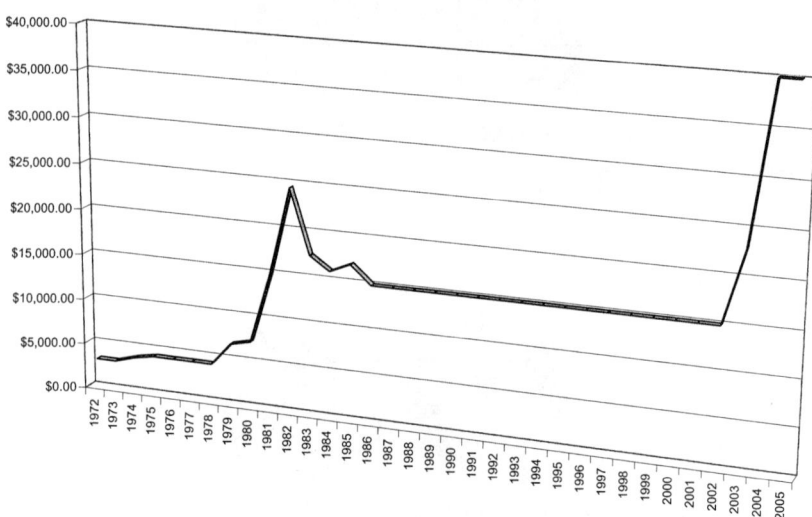

[Retail Price]

Draped Bust Half Dollar
Small eagle reverse

KM# 26 • 13.4800 g., 0.8920 **Silver**, 0.3869 oz. ASW, 32.5 mm. • **Designer:** Robert Scot **Notes:** The 1796 strikes have either 15 or 16 stars on the obverse.

Date	Mintage	G-4	VG-8	F-12	VF-20	XF-40	MS-60
1796 15 stars	3,918	29,000	35,000	40,000	55,000	80,000	175,000
1796 16 stars	Inc. above	30,000	36,000	42,000	60,000	85,000	200,000
1797	Inc. above	29,000	35,000	40,000	55,000	80,000	175,000

Heraldic eagle reverse

KM# 35 • 13.4800 g., 0.8920 **Silver**, 0.3869 oz. ASW, 32.5 mm. • **Designer:** Robert Scot **Notes:** The two varieties of the 1803 strikes are distinguished by the size of the 3 in the date. The several varieties of the 1806 strikes are distinguished by the style of 6 in the date, size of the stars on the obverse, and whether the stem of the olive branch held by the reverse eagle extends through the claw.

Date	Mintage	G-4	VG-8	F-12	VF-20	XF-40	MS-60
1801	30,289	225	300	700	1,500	5,000	35,000

Date	Mintage	G-4	VG-8	F-12	VF-20	XF-40	MS-60
1802	29,890	225	300	700	1,500	4,500	40,000
1803 small 3	188,234	150	170	300	600	1,500	8,500
1803 large 3	Inc. above	125	150	250	500	1,000	9,000
1805	211,722	125	150	250	550	1,050	9,000
1805/4	Inc. above	190	300	500	1,000	2,500	26,000
1806 round-top 6, large stars	839,576	125	150	190	450	1,100	6,000
1806 round-top 6, small stars	Inc. above	125	140	180	450	1,100	6,250
1806 knobbed 6, stem not through claw	—	—	35,000	40,000	50,000	65,000	—
1806 pointed-top 6, stem not through claw	Inc. above	115	130	250	340	1,000	5,750
1806 pointed-top 6, stem through claw	Inc. above	120	150	250	340	1,000	5,750
1806/5	Inc. above	125	160	275	500	1,400	8,000
1806 /inverted 6	Inc. above	200	350	600	1,200	2,100	15,000
1807	301,076	120	150	250	340	1,000	5,750

Bust Half Dollar
"50 C." below eagle reverse

KM# 37 • 13.4800 g., 0.8920 **Silver**, 0.3869 oz. ASW, 32.5 mm. • **Designer:** John Reich **Notes:** There are three varieties of the 1807 strikes. Two are distinguished by the size of the stars on the obverse. The third was struck from a reverse die that had a 5 cut over a 2 in the "50C" denomination. Two varieties of the 1811 are distinguished by the size of the 8 in the date. A third has a period between the 8 and second 1 in the date. One variety of the 1817 has a period between the 1 and 7 in the date. Two varieties of the 1819/18 overdate are distinguished by the size of the 9 in the date. Two varieties of the 1820 are distinguished by the size of the date. On the 1823 varieties, the "broken 3" appears to be almost separated in the middle of the 3 in the date; the "patched 3" has the error repaired; the "ugly 3" has portions of its detail missing. The 1827 "curled-2" and "square-2" varieties are distinguished by the numeral's base -- either curled or square. Among the 1828 varieties, "knobbed 2" and "no knob" refers to whether the upper left serif of the digit is rounded. The 1830 varieties are distinguished by the size of the 0 in the date. The four 1834 varieties are distinguished by the sizes of the stars, date and letters in the inscriptions. The 1836 "50/00" variety was struck from a reverse die that had "50" recut over "00" in the denomination.

Date	Mintage	G-4	VG-8	F-12	VF-20	XF-40	AU-50	MS-60	MS-65
1807 small stars	750,500	65.00	105	200	475	800	3,500	5,900	35,000
1807 large stars	Inc. above	60.00	100.00	180	475	800	3,500	5,500	—
1807 50/20 C.	Inc. above	55.00	92.50	140	250	500	2,100	4,000	30,000
1807 bearded goddess	—	300	500	900	1,500	2,750	7,500	—	—
1808	1,368,600	50.00	57.50	65.00	100.00	260	600	1,800	15,000
1808/7	Inc. above	52.50	62.50	92.50	160	330	900	1,850	17,500
1809	1,405,810	50.00	57.50	65.00	100.00	210	525	1,600	15,000
1810	1,276,276	52.50	57.50	66.00	100.00	175	475	1,550	13,000
1811 small 8	1,203,644	52.50	60.00	65.00	100.00	140	375	800	7,500
1811 large 8	Inc. above	50.00	57.50	62.50	95.00	150	500	1,000	8,500
1811 dated 18.11	Inc. above	55.00	60.00	80.00	150	300	800	2,100	12,000
1812	1,628,059	52.50	60.00	65.00	100.00	150	340	775	7,500
1812/1 small 8	Inc. above	53.50	61.00	90.00	160	250	700	2,000	12,000
1812/1 large 8	Inc. above	1,350	1,900	3,500	4,850	7,500	15,500	—	—
1813	1,241,903	52.50	60.00	65.00	100.00	165	500	1,250	11,000
1813 50/UNI reverse	1,241,903	55.00	62.50	92.50	135	300	900	1,900	12,000
1814	1,039,075	52.50	60.00	66.00	100.00	165	500	1,350	9,800
1814/3	Inc. above	62.50	75.00	110	150	275	850	2,000	16,500
1815/2	47,150	840	11,500	1,550	1,900	3,000	4,750	11,000	60,000
1817	1,215,567	52.50	60.00	66.00	90.00	160	385	900	10,000
1817/3	Inc. above	80.00	125	175	385	800	1,800	3,750	43,500
1817/4	—	50,000	60,000	115,000	145,000	190,000	240,000	—	—
1817 dated 181.7	Inc. above	54.00	62.50	70.00	100.00	175	650	1,500	12,500
1818	1,960,322	52.50	60.00	66.00	85.00	135	375	900	8,500
1818/7	Inc. above	60.00	72.50	85.00	105	160	700	1,500	11,000
1819	2,208,000	52.50	60.00	66.00	85.00	125	375	900	9,000
1819/8 small 9	Inc. above	57.50	62.50	75.00	100.00	200	550	1,300	1,150
1819/8 large 9	Inc. above	57.50	62.50	75.00	100.00	200	550	1,300	11,500
1820 small date	751,122	53.50	61.00	75.00	145	260	650	1,500	12,500
1820 large date	Inc. above	53.50	61.00	75.00	125	250	660	1,350	12,000
1820/19	Inc. above	62.50	75.00	85.00	150	300	900	2,000	15,000
1821	1,305,797	52.50	60.00	66.00	80.00	140	525	1,200	9,750
1822	1,559,573	52.50	60.00	66.00	85.00	125	300	750	7,700
1822/1	Inc. above	60.00	68.50	92.50	150	250	800	1,750	11,000

Date	Mintage	G-4	VG-8	F-12	VF-20	XF-40	AU-50	MS-60	MS-65
1823	1,694,200	47.50	52.50	57.50	66.00	110	300	825	7,500
1823 broken 3	Inc. above	55.00	66.00	92.50	140	360	900	1,750	12,000
1823 patched 3	Inc. above	52.50	62.50	85.00	115	180	400	1,300	13,500
1823 ugly 3	Inc. above	53.50	67.50	88.00	135	235	900	1,700	14,000
1824	3,504,954	47.50	52.50	66.00	75.00	110	260	650	7,500
1824/21	Inc. above	52.50	60.00	66.00	85.00	150	400	1,000	8,000
1824 1824/various dates	Inc. above	52.50	60.00	70.00	125	200	750	1,750	12,000
1825	2,943,166	47.50	52.50	66.00	75.00	110	260	550	7,000
1826	4,004,180	47.50	52.50	66.00	75.00	110	260	550	7,000
1827 curled 2	5,493,400	47.50	52.50	66.00	100.00	130	345	900	8,500
1827 square 2	Inc. above	47.50	52.50	60.00	75.00	110	260	650	7,500
1827/6	Inc. above	57.50	68.50	80.00	100.00	150	375	975	9,000
1828 curled-base 2, no knob	3,075,200	47.50	52.50	66.00	75.00	110	260	650	7,000
1828 curled-base 2, knobbed 2	Inc. above	47.50	52.50	66.00	85.00	120	270	700	7,250
1828 small 8s, square-base 2, large letters	Inc. above	47.50	52.50	66.00	75.00	110	260	550	6,250
1828 small 8s, square-base 2, small letters	Inc. above	52.50	70.00	95.00	135	220	720	1,200	9,500
1828 large 8s, square-base 2	Inc. above	48.50	52.50	66.00	75.00	110	260	750	9,000
1829	3,712,156	45.00	50.00	53.50	60.00	100.00	250	600	9,000
1829/7	Inc. above	47.50	57.50	67.50	85.00	165	330	925	11,750
1830 small letter rev.	4,764,800	45.00	50.00	53.50	60.00	100.00	250	500	7,000
1830 large letter rev.	Inc. above	1,250	1,850	2,250	3,300	4,500	7,500	—	—
1831	5,873,660	45.00	50.00	53.50	60.00	100.00	250	500	7,000
1832 small letters	4,797,000	45.00	50.00	53.50	60.00	100.00	250	575	7,000
1832 large letters	Inc. above	45.00	50.00	64.00	90.00	155	315	700	7,500
1833	5,206,000	45.00	50.00	53.50	60.00	100.00	250	575	7,000
1834 small date, large stars, small letters	6,412,004	45.00	50.00	53.50	60.00	100.00	250	575	7,000
1834 small date, small stars, small letters	Inc. above	45.00	50.00	53.50	60.00	100.00	250	575	7,000
1834 large date, small letters	Inc. above	45.00	50.00	53.50	60.00	100.00	250	575	7,000
1834 large date, large letters	Inc. above	45.00	50.00	53.50	60.00	100.00	250	575	7,000
1835	5,352,006	45.00	50.00	53.50	60.00	100.00	275	600	9,000
1836	6,545,000	45.00	50.00	53.50	60.00	100.00	250	500	7,000
1836 50/00	Inc. above	55.00	80.00	100.00	185	300	800	1,750	10,000

"50 Cents" below eagle reverse

KM# 58 • 13.3600 g., 0.9000 **Silver**, 0.3867 oz. ASW, 30 mm. • **Designer:** Christian Gobrecht **Edge Desc:** Reeded.

Date	Mintage	G-4	VG-8	F-12	VF-20	XF-40	AU-50	MS-60	MS-65
1836	1,200	700	1,000	1,200	1,500	2,250	3,200	6,000	40,000
1837	3,629,820	50.00	60.00	75.00	110	165	325	750	12,500

"Half Dol." below eagle reverse

KM# 65 • 13.3600 g., 0.9000 **Silver**, 0.3867 oz. ASW, 30 mm. • **Designer:** Christian Gobrecht

Date	Mintage	G-4	VG-8	F-12	VF-20	XF-40	AU-50	MS-60	MS-65
1838	3,546,000	50.00	60.00	75.00	110	165	475	825	17,000
1838O proof only	Est. 20	85,000	105,000	115,000	125,000	150,000	180,000	—	—
1839	1,392,976	56.00	66.00	82.50	115	185	375	990	30,000
1839O	178,976	135	215	300	400	675	1,200	2,500	45,000

Seated Liberty Half Dollar

KM# 68 • 13.3600 g., 0.9000 **Silver**, .3867 oz. ASW, 30.6 mm. • **Designer:** Christian Gobrecht **Notes:** The 1839 varieties are distinguished by whether there's drapery extending from Liberty's left elbow. One variety of the 1840 strikes has smaller lettering; another used the old reverse of 1838. Varieties of 1842 and 1846 are distinguished by the size of the numerals in the date.

Date	Mintage	G-4	VG-8	F-12	VF-20	XF-40	AU-50	MS-60	MS-65
1839 no drapery from elbow	Inc. above	38.00	65.00	110	315	725	1,650	4,500	150,000
1839 drapery	Inc. above	20.00	30.00	50.00	75.00	145	265	450	—
1840 small letters	1,435,008	23.00	32.00	47.50	67.00	110	350	575	8,250
1840 reverse 1838	Inc. above	125	175	250	325	575	1,100	2,900	12,000
1840O	855,100	23.00	28.00	45.00	80.00	125	275	430	—
1841	310,000	39.00	49.00	80.00	130	200	300	1,100	5,700
1841O	401,000	19.00	28.00	44.00	75.00	125	250	550	5,900
1842 small date	2,012,764	35.00	42.00	60.00	110	185	325	1,300	12,000
1842 large date	Inc. above	18.00	28.00	43.00	52.00	100.00	175	1,250	12,000
1842O small date	957,000	650	850	1,400	2,250	4,000	—	—	—
1842O large date	Inc. above	22.00	29.00	48.00	115	225	750	1,750	—
1843	3,844,000	17.00	28.00	43.00	52.00	100.00	180	350	4,500
1843O	2,268,000	17.00	28.00	43.00	60.00	115	250	550	—
1844	1,766,000	17.00	28.00	43.00	52.00	100.00	210	350	4,500
1844O	2,005,000	18.00	28.00	43.00	52.00	100.00	225	525	—
1844/1844O	Inc. above	500	775	1,000	1,375	2,300	4,900	—	—
1845	589,000	30.00	40.00	60.00	110	200	375	900	—
1845O	2,094,000	18.00	28.00	43.00	52.00	125	240	550	—
1845O no drapery	Inc. above	25.00	35.00	65.00	115	185	375	750	—
1846 medium date	2,210,000	18.00	28.00	43.00	52.00	100.00	200	500	9,000
1846 tall date	Inc. above	22.00	30.00	60.00	85.00	145	250	650	12,000
1846 /horizontal 6	Inc. above	175	235	300	400	575	1,000	2,500	—
1846O medium date	2,304,000	18.00	28.00	43.00	52.00	100.00	225	550	12,000
1846O tall date	Inc. above	135	245	325	575	950	2,000	3,600	—
1847/1846	1,156,000	2,000	2,750	3,200	4,250	6,500	—	—	—
1847	Inc. above	25.00	35.00	55.00	70.00	115	250	480	9,000
1847O	2,584,000	18.00	28.00	43.00	52.00	95.00	250	640	7,000
1848	580,000	40.00	60.00	85.00	170	265	475	1,000	9,000
1848O	3,180,000	18.00	28.00	43.00	52.00	110	285	750	9,000
1849	1,252,000	26.00	40.00	55.00	90.00	150	365	1,250	9,000
1849O	2,310,000	17.00	28.00	43.00	60.00	110	250	650	9,000
1850	227,000	275	325	400	500	675	1,000	1,500	—
1850O	2,456,000	20.00	28.00	45.00	80.00	135	275	650	9,000
1851	200,750	425	500	700	900	1,000	1,250	1,950	—
1851O	402,000	37.00	45.00	75.00	105	175	300	675	9,000
1852	77,130	400	500	650	850	1,000	1,200	1,650	—
1852O	144,000	100.00	125	200	350	525	1,050	1,850	—
1853O mintage unrecorded	—	—	—	—	—	—	—	—	—

Note: 1853O, Eliasberg Sale, 1997, VG-8, $154,000.

Arrows at date obverse   Rays around eagle reverse

KM# 79 • 12.4400 g., 0.9000 **Silver**, 0.3600 oz. ASW • **Designer:** Christian Gobrecht

Date	Mintage	G-4	VG-8	F-12	VF-20	XF-40	AU-50	MS-60	MS-65	Prf-65
1853	3,532,708	17.00	27.00	40.00	90.00	250	505	1,700	21,500	—
1853O	1,328,000	21.00	32.00	50.00	125	290	700	2,100	21,500	—

Rays around eagle removed reverse

KM# 82 • 12.4400 g., 0.9000 **Silver**, 0.3600 oz. ASW • **Designer:** Christian Gobrecht

Date	Mintage	G-4	VG-8	F-12	VF-20	XF-40	AU-50	MS-60	MS-65	Prf-65
1854	2,982,000	17.00	28.00	43.00	55.00	100.00	270	675	8,000	—
1854O	5,240,000	17.00	28.00	43.00	55.00	100.00	270	600	8,000	—
1855	759,500	23.00	33.00	45.00	75.00	150	325	1,200	8,000	22,500
1855/4	Inc. above	35.00	60.00	80.00	125	225	400	1,500	—	—
1855O	3,688,000	17.00	28.00	43.00	55.00	100.00	270	650	8,000	—
1855S	129,950	250	350	600	1,300	2,400	6,000	—	—	—

Arrows at date removed obverse

KM# A68 • 12.4400 g., 0.9000 **Silver**, 0.3600 oz. ASW • **Designer:** Christian Gobrecht

Date	Mintage	G-4	VG-8	F-12	VF-20	XF-40	AU-50	MS-60	MS-65	Prf-65
1856O	2,658,000	17.00	28.00	43.00	52.00	90.00	190	385	12,500	—
1856	938,000	19.00	31.00	43.00	55.00	90.00	195	425	6,500	12,500
1856S	211,000	85.00	120	160	260	475	1,250	3,500	19,000	—
1857	1,988,000	17.00	28.00	43.00	52.00	90.00	190	385	5,150	12,500
1857O	818,000	21.00	31.00	43.00	65.00	125	275	885	12,500	—
1857S	158,000	100.00	120	145	285	575	975	3,500	19,000	—
1858	4,226,000	17.00	28.00	43.00	52.00	90.00	190	385	6,500	12,500

1855-S Half Dollar
Grade XF-40

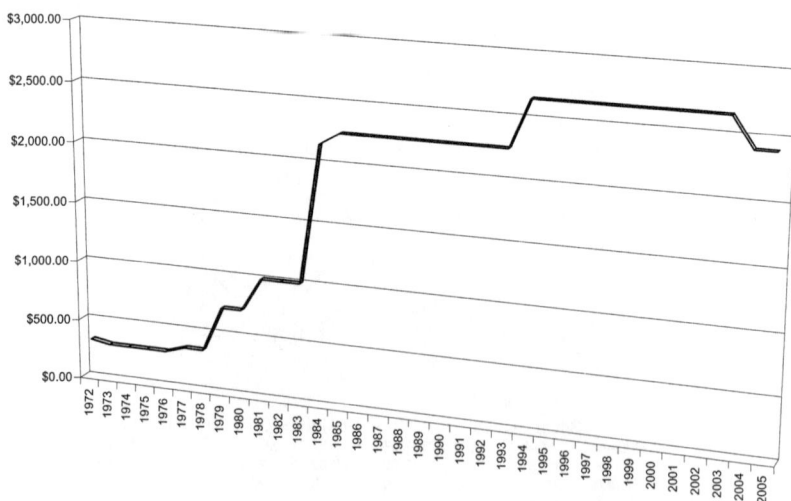

Retail Price

Date	Mintage	G-4	VG-8	F-12	VF-20	XF-40	AU-50	MS-60	MS-65	Prf-65
1858O	7,294,000	17.00	28.00	43.00	52.00	90.00	190	385	12,500	—
1858S	476,000	25.00	35.00	50.00	95.00	185	400	950	12,500	—
1859	748,000	17.00	28.00	43.00	60.00	110	200	650	6,600	5,500
1859O	2,834,000	17.00	28.00	43.00	50.00	90.00	190	450	6,500	—
1859S	566,000	25.00	38.00	55.00	85.00	215	375	750	12,500	—
1860	303,700	25.00	35.00	47.50	80.00	110	350	1,000	6,500	5,500
1860O	1,290,000	17.00	28.00	43.00	52.00	90.00	190	450	5,150	—
1860S	472,000	20.00	30.00	50.00	75.00	130	245	850	12,500	—
1861	2,888,400	17.00	28.00	43.00	52.00	90.00	190	440	5,150	5,500
1861O	2,532,633	18.00	29.00	50.00	65.00	100.00	190	450	5,150	—
1861S	939,500	18.00	29.00	43.00	60.00	110	195	975	9,500	—
1862	253,550	28.00	40.00	55.00	95.00	175	285	750	5,150	5,500
1862S	1,352,000	18.00	29.00	43.00	65.00	110	195	460	9,000	—
1863	503,660	20.00	32.00	43.00	75.00	130	250	750	5,150	5,500
1863S	916,000	18.00	29.00	43.00	60.00	100.00	195	460	9,000	—
1864	379,570	29.00	35.00	60.00	95.00	175	250	750	5,150	5,500
1864S	658,000	18.00	28.00	45.00	60.00	115	215	675	9,000	—
1865	511,900	28.00	37.00	55.00	85.00	135	275	750	5,150	5,500
1865S	675,000	18.00	29.00	43.00	60.00	100.00	235	500	9,000	—
1866 proof, unique	—	—	—	—	—	—	—	—	—	—
1866S	60,000	90.00	135	215	375	795	1,500	5,000	—	—

"In God We Trust" above eagle reverse

KM# 99 • 12.4400 g., 0.9000 **Silver**, 0.3600 oz. ASW • **Designer:** Christian Gobrecht **Notes:** In 1866 the motto "In God We Trust" was added to the reverse. The "closed-3" and "open-3" varieties are distinguished by the amount of space between the upper and lower left serifs of the 3.

Date	Mintage	G-4	VG-8	F-12	VF-20	XF-40	AU-50	MS-60	MS-65	Prf-65
1866	745,625	18.00	27.00	45.00	70.00	110	225	350	4,800	3,750
1866S	994,000	19.00	29.00	45.00	60.00	100.00	275	650	5,000	—
1867	449,925	25.00	35.00	55.00	90.00	145	250	350	4,800	3,750
1867S	1,196,000	19.00	29.00	40.00	60.00	100.00	250	350	7,000	—
1868	418,200	35.00	49.00	80.00	135	225	300	525	7,100	3,750
1868S	1,160,000	19.00	29.00	41.00	60.00	110	250	350	7,000	—
1869	795,900	19.00	29.00	41.00	60.00	110	190	385	4,600	3,750
1869S	656,000	20.00	29.00	41.00	60.00	120	265	600	7,000	—
1870	634,900	21.00	31.00	42.00	70.00	125	250	475	7,000	3,750
1870CC	54,617	800	1,200	1,750	2,900	10,000	—	—	—	—
1870S	1,004,000	19.00	31.00	45.00	70.00	125	275	575	7,000	—
1871	1,204,560	18.00	29.00	41.00	60.00	110	165	350	7,000	3,750
1871CC	153,950	200	325	600	1,200	1,950	10,000	15,000	—	—
1871S	2,178,000	18.00	29.00	41.00	55.00	110	215	400	7,000	—
1872	881,550	18.00	29.00	40.00	55.00	110	195	430	2,850	3,750
1872CC	272,000	70.00	100.00	200	325	1,500	4,000	8,000	50,000	—
1872S	580,000	28.00	33.00	60.00	110	185	375	975	7,000	—
1873 closed 3	801,800	23.00	30.00	50.00	90.00	135	250	500	4,500	3,750
1873 open 3	Inc. above	2,200	2,700	4,100	5,500	7,500	—	—	—	—
1873CC	122,500	170	225	325	800	1,500	2,500	4,100	9,000	3,750
1873S no arrows	5,000	—	—	—	—	—	—	—	—	—

Note: 1873S no arrows, no specimens known to survive.

Arrows at date obverse

KM# 107 • 12.5000 g., 0.9000 **Silver**, 0.3618 oz. ASW • **Designer:** Christian Gobrecht

Date	Mintage	G-4	VG-8	F-12	VF-20	XF-40	AU-50	MS-60	MS-65	Prf-65
1873	1,815,700	18.00	27.00	40.00	85.00	210	400	850	17,500	9,000
1873CC	214,560	115	220	335	725	1,700	2,400	5,700	42,000	—
1873S	233,000	42.50	62.50	100.00	200	375	675	2,200	40,000	—
1874	2,360,300	18.00	27.00	40.00	85.00	210	400	850	12,750	9,000
1874CC	59,000	400	550	950	1,500	2,500	4,500	8,000	—	—
1874S	394,000	30.00	40.00	70.00	160	315	600	1,600	—	—

Arrows at date removed obverse

KM# A99 • 12.5000 g., 0.9000 **Silver**, 0.3618 oz. ASW • **Designer:** Christian Gobrecht

Date	Mintage	G-4	VG-8	F-12	VF-20	XF-40	AU-50	MS-60	MS-65	Prf-65
1875	6,027,500	17.00	25.00	39.00	47.00	70.00	160	425	3,500	3,200
1875CC	1,008,000	20.00	34.00	53.00	95.00	185	300	540	5,450	—
1875S	3,200,000	17.00	26.00	40.00	47.00	80.00	165	340	2,700	—
1876	8,419,150	17.00	25.00	39.00	45.00	70.00	160	340	5,300	3,200
1876CC	1,956,000	18.00	30.00	48.00	85.00	175	275	560	4,200	—
1876S	4,528,000	17.00	25.00	39.00	45.00	70.00	160	340	2,700	—
1877	8,304,510	17.00	25.00	39.00	45.00	70.00	160	340	2,700	3,750
1877CC	1,420,000	18.00	33.00	43.00	75.00	145	275	630	3,250	—
1877S	5,356,000	17.00	25.00	39.00	45.00	70.00	160	340	2,700	—
1878	1,378,400	20.00	28.00	36.00	55.00	115	170	425	3,650	3,200
1878CC	62,000	375	525	875	1,250	2,750	5,000	7,000	42,500	—
1878S	12,000	15,000	17,500	22,000	27,500	33,000	40,000	52,500	125,000	—
1879	5,900	295	325	375	425	525	600	825	2,900	3,250
1880	9,755	275	310	365	415	500	575	800	2,900	3,250
1881	10,975	275	300	350	400	485	550	800	2,900	3,250
1882	5,500	350	400	425	500	585	650	850	3,600	3,250
1883	9,039	275	310	365	415	500	575	800	2,900	3,250
1884	5,275	375	425	450	550	600	675	825	2,900	3,250
1885	6,130	350	400	425	500	585	650	800	2,900	3,250
1886	5,886	375	425	475	575	625	700	850	4,800	3,250
1887	5,710	450	500	575	650	750	800	900	2,900	3,250

1878-S Half Dollar
Grade F-12

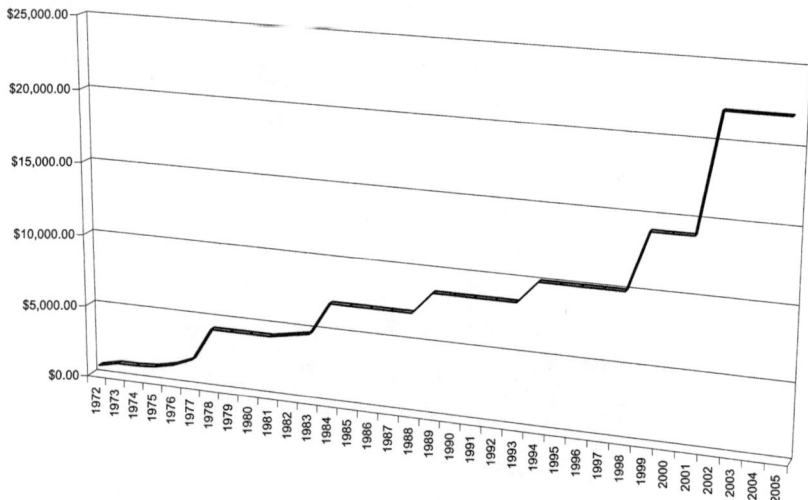

Date	Mintage	G-4	VG-8	F-12	VF-20	XF-40	AU-50	MS-60	MS-65	Prf-65
1888	12,833	280	310	365	400	485	550	800	2,900	3,250
1889	12,711	275	300	350	400	485	550	800	2,900	3,250
1890	12,590	285	310	365	415	500	550	800	3,250	3,250
1891	200,600	50.00	60.00	80.00	115	165	290	500	3,250	3,250

Barber Half Dollar

Mint mark

KM# 116 • 12.5000 g., 0.9000 **Silver**, 0.3618 oz. ASW, 30.6 mm. • **Designer:** Charles E. Barber

Date	Mintage	G-4	VG-8	F-12	VF-20	XF-40	AU-50	MS-60	MS-65	Prf-65
1892	935,245	27.50	38.50	65.00	125	190	295	475	3,400	3,300
1892O	390,000	285	375	480	535	570	635	850	4,750	—
1892O micro O	—	2,000	3,750	4,500	7,000	10,000	17,500	—	55,000	—
1892S	1,029,028	235	330	400	520	580	650	925	5,500	—
1893	1,826,792	19.00	27.50	75.00	135	205	325	535	5,500	3,300
1893O	1,389,000	35.00	62.50	125	220	360	450	650	10,500	—
1893S	740,000	140	195	300	475	550	625	1,200	27,500	—
1894	1,148,972	30.00	47.50	110	185	290	380	500	3,900	3,300
1894O	2,138,000	22.00	31.00	90.00	170	275	345	525	7,250	—
1894S	4,048,690	15.00	22.00	65.00	115	220	350	500	12,250	—
1895	1,835,218	16.00	22.00	67.50	150	200	325	595	3,500	3,300
1895O	1,766,000	21.00	37.50	125	230	300	415	595	7,850	—
1895S	1,108,086	30.00	50.00	115	220	285	385	575	9,000	—
1896	950,762	20.00	25.00	85.00	150	250	340	565	6,000	3,400
1896O	924,000	38.50	52.50	170	275	455	715	1,500	15,500	—
1896S	1,140,948	85.00	130	190	350	495	750	1,400	11,750	—
1897	2,480,731	12.50	15.00	47.50	100.00	160	325	485	4,300	3,300
1897O	632,000	155	225	480	825	1,100	1,275	1,700	10,000	—
1897S	933,900	150	205	355	550	840	1,050	1,500	8,500	—
1898	2,956,735	12.50	15.00	38.50	88.50	160	325	485	3,850	3,300
1898O	874,000	32.50	75.00	225	355	500	625	1,250	12,000	—
1898S	2,358,550	25.00	47.50	80.00	155	280	425	970	10,500	—
1899	5,538,846	13.50	15.00	38.50	100.00	155	310	485	4,800	3,900
1899O	1,724,000	23.00	34.00	75.00	155	275	395	650	8,500	—
1899S	1,686,411	22.00	32.50	72.50	135	225	360	660	7,000	—
1900	4,762,912	13.50	15.50	37.50	96.00	155	310	485	4,300	3,300
1900O	2,744,000	16.00	20.00	56.00	165	285	375	850	16,500	—
1900S	2,560,322	15.00	18.00	47.50	100.00	205	320	650	12,500	—
1901	4,268,813	13.50	16.00	38.50	96.00	180	300	510	4,500	3,500
1901O	1,124,000	16.00	27.50	75.00	205	310	475	1,350	17,000	—
1901S	847,044	30.00	52.50	160	355	600	1,000	1,850	22,000	—
1902	4,922,777	12.50	13.50	32.50	85.00	210	295	485	4,250	3,700
1902O	2,526,000	13.00	16.00	52.50	105	215	360	725	15,000	—
1902S	1,460,670	15.00	19.00	62.50	140	250	430	750	9,350	—
1903	2,278,755	13.50	16.00	47.50	100.00	205	340	500	11,000	3,825
1903O	2,100,000	12.50	16.00	55.00	115	215	345	680	10,000	—
1903S	1,920,772	13.50	16.00	53.50	115	235	380	610	5,750	—
1904	2,992,670	12.00	13.50	34.00	85.00	155	310	1,300	6,600	4,100
1904O	1,117,600	19.00	31.00	80.00	220	400	600	1,100	13,300	—
1904S	553,038	35.00	62.50	255	550	1,000	1,525	6,250	37,500	—
1905	662,727	19.00	26.00	90.00	170	260	345	575	8,500	3,900
1905O	505,000	25.00	43.50	125	235	340	440	760	5,250	—
1905S	2,494,000	12.50	15.00	48.50	115	235	380	565	10,000	—
1906	2,638,675	12.00	16.00	31.00	85.00	170	300	485	3,100	3,300
1906D	4,028,000	12.00	13.50	34.00	93.50	160	300	485	4,750	—
1906O	2,446,000	12.00	13.50	44.00	100.00	180	325	625	6,700	—
1906S	1,740,154	12.50	16.00	57.50	110	220	310	610	6,250	—
1907	2,598,575	12.00	13.50	30.00	85.00	155	300	485	3,000	4,000
1907D	3,856,000	12.00	13.50	30.00	78.50	155	300	485	3,400	—
1907O	3,946,000	12.00	13.50	31.00	93.50	155	325	595	3,700	—
1907S	1,250,000	16.00	22.00	80.00	170	325	650	1,275	13,500	—
1908	1,354,545	12.00	13.50	30.00	85.00	155	295	485	4,500	4,000
1908D	3,280,000	12.00	13.50	30.00	85.00	155	295	485	3,000	—
1908O	5,360,000	12.00	13.50	30.00	93.50	155	325	550	3,000	—
1908S	1,644,828	18.00	23.50	71.00	155	275	415	830	6,850	—
1909	2,368,650	12.50	16.00	31.00	85.00	160	295	485	3,000	4,000
1909O	925,400	15.00	20.00	60.00	130	300	525	775	5,250	—

Date	Mintage	G-4	VG-8	F-12	VF-20	XF-40	AU-50	MS-60	MS-65	Prf-65
1909S	1,764,000	12.00	13.50	35.00	100.00	200	350	595	5,000	—
1910	418,551	18.00	27.50	90.00	170	330	420	625	4,000	4,250
1910S	1,948,000	12.50	16.00	34.00	100.00	190	350	650	6,850	—
1911	1,406,543	12.00	13.50	30.00	85.00	155	300	485	3,000	3,300
1911D	695,080	12.50	15.00	41.00	96.00	200	295	575	3,350	—
1911S	1,272,000	12.50	16.00	41.00	100.00	180	330	580	6,000	—
1912	1,550,700	12.00	13.50	30.00	85.00	160	300	485	4,200	4,000
1912D	2,300,800	12.00	13.50	30.00	85.00	155	325	485	3,000	—
1912S	1,370,000	13.50	18.00	41.50	100.00	200	340	550	6,000	—
1913	188,627	46.00	65.00	190	375	535	825	1,100	4,850	3,800
1913D	534,000	13.00	15.00	46.00	100.00	200	315	500	5,500	—
1913S	604,000	16.00	22.50	55.00	110	230	375	625	5,250	—
1914	124,610	110	130	290	540	750	1,000	1,350	7,500	4,300
1914S	992,000	15.00	19.00	41.00	96.00	190	315	580	5,000	—
1915	138,450	62.50	90.00	225	375	550	850	1,200	6,500	4,250
1915D	1,170,400	12.00	13.50	30.00	78.50	155	295	485	3,000	—
1915S	1,604,000	15.00	19.00	38.50	93.50	160	295	485	3,050	—

Walking Liberty Half Dollar

Obverse
mint mark

Reverse
mint mark

KM# 142 • 12.5000 g., 0.9000 **Silver**, 0.3618 oz. ASW, 30.6 mm. • **Designer:** Adolph A. Weinman **Notes:** The mint mark appears on the obverse below the word "Trust" on 1916 and some 1917 issues. Starting with some 1917 issues and continuing through the remainder of the series, the mint mark was changed to the reverse, at about the 8 o'clock position near the rim.

Date	Mintage	G-4	VG-8	F-12	VF-20	XF-40	AU-50	MS-60	MS-65	Prf-65
1916	608,000	41.50	47.50	96.00	170	235	275	350	1,800	—
1916D	1,014,400	38.50	43.50	78.50	130	210	265	375	2,250	—
1916S	508,000	110	125	275	455	625	750	1,100	6,250	—
1917D obv.	765,400	20.00	30.00	75.00	150	220	330	625	8,000	—
1917S obv.	952,000	25.00	41.50	115	350	700	1,200	2,250	19,000	—
1917	12,292,000	4.00	5.25	8.75	20.00	40.00	75.00	135	1,000	—
1917D rev.	1,940,000	10.00	16.50	45.00	135	275	575	925	18,500	—
1917S rev.	5,554,000	4.50	8.00	16.50	33.00	54.00	160	340	13,000	—
1918	6,634,000	4.50	6.50	16.00	60.00	150	275	580	3,800	—
1918D	3,853,040	8.00	12.50	33.50	85.00	220	500	1,100	25,000	—
1918S	10,282,000	4.50	5.75	15.00	32.00	62.50	200	525	18,000	—
1919	962,000	19.00	30.00	75.00	260	515	900	1,300	7,500	—
1919D	1,165,000	14.50	32.50	90.00	300	725	1,550	6,000	130,000	—
1919S	1,552,000	16.50	27.50	70.00	290	800	1,800	3,300	19,000	—
1920	6,372,000	4.50	5.50	16.00	38.50	75.00	150	350	5,250	—
1920D	1,551,000	10.00	16.00	65.00	235	435	950	1,500	12,000	—
1920S	4,624,000	5.00	7.50	20.00	67.50	235	500	850	12,500	—
1921	246,000	170	210	320	760	1,525	2,750	4,325	17,750	—
1921D	208,000	260	320	515	900	2,150	3,250	4,800	23,500	—
1921S	548,000	45.00	66.00	200	730	4,800	8,600	13,500	85,000	—
1923S	2,178,000	8.50	11.50	25.00	100.00	275	700	1,400	15,000	—
1927S	2,392,000	6.25	6.75	13.50	45.00	150	385	1,000	10,000	—
1928S	1,940,000	6.25	6.75	15.00	65.00	180	470	1,000	10,500	—
1929D	1,001,200	8.00	12.00	16.00	45.00	110	210	415	3,500	—
1929S	1,902,000	5.75	7.25	12.50	28.50	110	230	415	3,550	—
1933S	1,786,000	7.50	12.00	14.00	20.00	55.00	250	600	4,600	—
1934	6,964,000	3.25	3.50	3.75	4.00	9.50	26.00	85.00	475	—
1934D	2,361,400	5.00	5.50	6.00	9.50	29.00	90.00	155	1,250	—
1934S	3,652,000	3.75	4.00	4.25	5.50	27.00	105	395	5,200	—
1935	9,162,000	3.25	3.50	3.75	4.50	6.75	22.50	45.00	485	—
1935D	3,003,800	3.75	4.00	5.50	10.00	31.50	67.50	140	2,500	—
1935S	3,854,000	3.25	3.50	3.75	8.00	28.50	100.00	295	2,700	—
1936	12,617,901	3.25	3.50	3.75	4.00	6.00	22.00	38.50	220	6,600
1936D	4,252,400	3.25	3.50	4.00	6.75	20.00	55.00	80.00	530	—
1936S	3,884,000	3.25	3.50	4.00	6.50	21.50	62.50	135	800	—
1937	9,527,728	3.25	3.50	3.75	4.00	8.00	22.50	40.00	265	1,700
1937D	1,676,000	6.00	7.00	8.00	13.50	33.50	110	225	600	—
1937S	2,090,000	3.50	4.00	4.75	7.75	25.00	62.50	165	600	—
1938	4,118,152	4.25	5.50	5.50	6.00	9.50	41.50	70.00	420	1,275
1938D	491,600	68.50	75.00	90.00	105	135	260	525	1,425	—
1939	6,820,808	3.25	3.50	3.75	4.00	5.50	22.50	42.50	160	1,150
1939D	4,267,800	3.25	3.50	3.75	4.00	7.25	23.50	43.50	200	—

1923-S Half Dollar
Grade XF-40

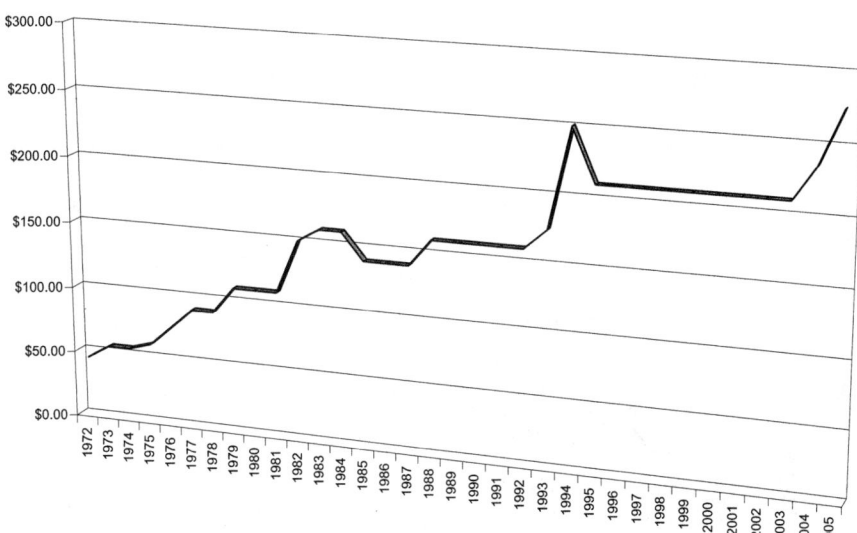

Retail Price

Date	Mintage	G-4	VG-8	F-12	VF-20	XF-40	AU-50	MS-60	MS-65	Prf-65
1939S	2,552,000	5.00	6.00	7.00	10.00	23.00	75.00	150	330	—
1940	9,167,279	3.25	3.50	3.75	4.00	4.75	11.00	30.00	150	1,000
1940S	4,550,000	3.30	3.60	3.85	4.00	10.00	22.00	52.50	435	—
1941	24,207,412	3.25	3.50	3.75	4.00	4.50	11.00	32.00	160	850
1941D	11,248,400	3.25	3.50	3.75	4.00	6.50	18.00	38.50	280	—
1941S	8,098,000	3.25	3.50	3.75	4.00	5.50	27.50	75.00	1,500	—
1942	47,839,120	3.25	3.50	3.75	4.00	4.50	11.00	32.00	150	850
1942D	10,973,800	3.25	3.50	3.75	4.00	6.50	19.00	38.50	380	—
1942S	12,708,000	3.25	3.50	3.75	4.00	5.50	17.50	38.50	850	—
1943	53,190,000	3.25	3.50	3.75	4.00	4.50	11.00	33.50	150	—
1943D	11,346,000	3.25	3.50	3.75	4.00	7.50	25.00	43.50	350	—
1943S	13,450,000	3.25	3.50	3.75	4.00	5.50	18.50	43.50	560	—
1944	28,206,000	3.25	3.50	3.75	4.00	4.50	11.00	33.00	175	—
1944D	9,769,000	3.25	3.50	3.75	4.00	6.50	20.00	36.00	195	—
1944S	8,904,000	3.25	3.50	3.75	4.00	5.50	16.00	38.50	775	—
1945	31,502,000	3.25	3.50	3.75	4.00	4.50	11.00	32.00	160	—
1945D	9,966,800	3.25	3.50	3.75	4.00	6.50	19.00	34.00	160	—
1945S	10,156,000	3.25	3.50	3.75	4.00	5.50	17.50	35.00	235	—
1946	12,118,000	3.25	3.50	3.75	4.00	5.00	11.00	32.00	235	—
1946D	2,151,000	4.00	5.50	6.50	9.00	25.00	38.50	50.00	125	—
1946S	3,724,000	3.25	3.50	3.75	4.00	7.50	19.00	43.50	160	—
1947	4,094,000	3.25	4.00	4.75	5.50	9.00	22.00	50.00	250	—
1947D	3,900,600	3.25	4.00	4.75	6.25	11.00	31.50	50.00	165	—

Franklin Half Dollar

Mint mark

KM# 199 • 12.5000 g., 0.9000 **Silver**, 0.3618 oz. ASW, 30.6 mm. • **Designer:** John R. Sinnock

Date	Mintage	G-4	VG-8	F-12	VF-20	XF-40	AU-50	MS-60	MS-65	-65FBL	-65CAM
1948	3,006,814	—	4.00	4.50	5.00	6.50	10.00	15.00	80.00	200	—
1948D	4,028,600	—	3.50	3.75	4.50	5.50	11.00	15.00	130	200	—

Date	Mintage	G-4	VG-8	F-12	VF-20	XF-40	AU-50	MS-60	MS-65	-65FBL	-65CAM
1949	5,614,000	—	3.75	4.00	4.50	6.00	12.00	38.50	145	300	—
1949D	4,120,600	—	3.50	3.75	4.25	8.00	25.00	43.50	850	1,750	—
1949S	3,744,000	—	3.75	4.25	7.00	11.00	30.00	62.50	155	650	—
1950	7,793,509	—	—	3.25	3.75	6.00	10.00	26.00	110	250	3,700
1950D	8,031,600	—	—	3.50	4.00	7.50	11.50	22.00	425	1,150	—
1951	16,859,602	—	—	3.00	3.50	4.50	5.50	11.00	75.00	235	2,200
1951D	9,475,200	—	—	3.75	4.75	7.50	17.50	26.00	170	525	—
1951S	13,696,000	—	—	3.50	3.75	4.00	15.00	23.50	125	775	—
1952	21,274,073	—	—	2.75	3.25	3.75	4.50	8.50	80.00	200	1,100
1952D	25,395,600	—	—	2.75	3.25	3.75	5.50	7.75	135	450	—
1952S	5,526,000	—	4.00	4.50	5.50	10.00	28.50	46.00	75.00	1,250	—
1953	2,796,920	—	4.00	4.50	5.00	6.00	15.00	23.50	125	850	475
1953D	20,900,400	—	—	2.75	3.50	4.00	5.25	8.00	160	400	—
1953S	4,148,000	—	3.50	4.00	4.75	6.00	15.00	25.00	65.00	16,000	—
1954	13,421,503	—	—	2.50	3.50	4.00	5.00	7.00	80.00	250	250
1954D	25,445,580	—	—	2.50	3.25	3.50	4.25	7.00	110	200	—
1954S	4,993,400	—	3.50	4.00	4.75	6.00	8.50	13.50	105	425	—
1955	2,876,381	20.00	21.00	22.00	23.00	24.00	25.00	26.00	62.50	185	195
1955 Bugs Bunny	—	16.00	17.00	18.00	19.00	20.00	24.00	27.00	100.00	750	—
1956	4,701,384	6.50	7.00	7.50	8.00	8.50	9.00	14.00	50.00	95.00	75.00
1957	6,361,952	—	4.00	4.25	4.50	4.75	5.60	7.00	47.50	95.00	135
1957D	19,966,850	—	—	—	2.75	3.25	4.40	6.25	50.00	65.00	—
1958	4,917,652	—	4.00	4.25	4.50	4.75	5.00	6.25	50.00	100.00	250
1958D	23,962,412	—	—	—	2.50	3.25	4.40	6.25	50.00	75.00	—
1959	7,349,291	—	4.00	4.25	4.50	4.75	5.00	6.25	105	250	475
1959D	13,053,750	—	—	—	2.50	2.75	4.40	6.25	135	190	—
1960	7,715,602	—	—	4.00	4.25	4.50	4.75	5.95	135	350	75.00
1960D	18,215,812	—	—	—	2.50	2.75	4.40	5.95	475	1,250	—
1961	11,318,244	—	—	—	2.50	2.75	4.40	5.95	145	1,750	75.00
1961D	20,276,442	—	—	—	2.50	2.75	4.40	5.95	200	875	—
1962	12,932,019	—	—	—	2.50	2.75	4.40	5.95	160	1,850	50.00
1962D	35,473,281	—	—	—	2.50	2.75	4.40	5.95	225	775	—
1963	25,239,645	—	—	—	2.50	2.75	4.40	5.95	55.00	775	50.00
1963D	67,069,292	—	—	—	2.50	2.75	4.40	5.95	70.00	125	—

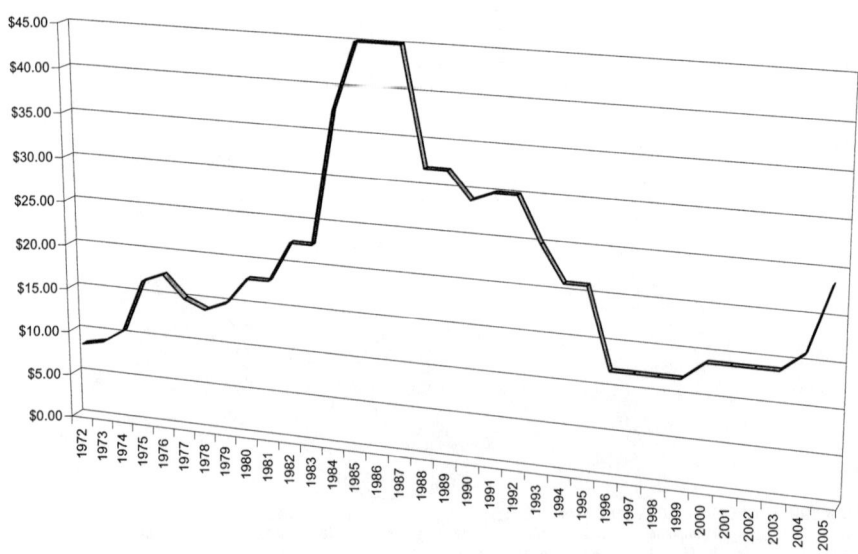

1953 Half Dollar
Grade MS-60

Retail Price

Kennedy Half Dollar
90% silver type

Mint mark 1964

KM# 202 • 12.5000 g., **0.9000 Silver**, 0.3618 oz. ASW, 30.6 mm. • **Obv. Designer:** Gilroy Roberts **Rev. Designer:** Frank Gasparro

Date	Mintage	G-4	VG-8	F-12	VF-20	XF-40	MS-60	MS-65	Prf-65
1964	277,254,766	—	—	—	—	—	3.00	9.00	10.00
1964D	156,205,446	—	—	—	—	—	3.50	12.00	—

40% silver type

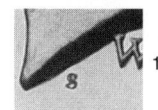

Mint mark
1968 - present

KM# 202a • 11.5000 g., **0.4000 Silver**, 0.1480 oz. ASW, 30.6 mm. • **Obv. Designer:** Gilroy Roberts **Rev. Designer:** Frank Gasparro

Date	Mintage	G-4	VG-8	F-12	VF-20	XF-40	MS-60	MS-65	Prf-65
1965	65,879,366	—	—	—	—	—	1.25	9.50	—
1965 SMS	2,360,000	—	—	—	—	—	—	9.50	—
1966	108,984,932	—	—	—	—	—	1.40	11.00	—
1966 SMS	2,261,583	—	—	—	—	—	—	11.00	—
1967	295,046,978	—	—	—	—	—	1.50	9.50	—
1967 SMS	18,633,440	—	—	—	—	—	—	9.50	—
1968D	246,951,930	—	—	—	—	—	1.25	9.00	—
1968S	3,041,506	—	—	—	—	—	—	—	5.00
1969D	129,881,800	—	—	—	—	—	1.25	7.50	—
1969S	2,934,631	—	—	—	—	—	—	—	5.00
1970D	2,150,000	—	—	—	—	—	10.00	32.00	—
1970S	2,632,810	—	—	—	—	—	—	—	10.00

Clad type

KM# 202b • 11.3400 g., **Copper-Nickel Clad Copper**, 30.6 mm. • **Obv. Designer:** Gilroy Roberts **Rev. Designer:** Frank Gasparro

Date	Mintage	G-4	VG-8	F-12	VF-20	XF-40	MS-60	MS-65	Prf-65
1971	155,640,000	—	—	—	—	—	1.50	12.00	—
1971D	302,097,424	—	—	—	—	—	1.00	5.00	—
1971S	3,244,183	—	—	—	—	—	—	—	3.00
1972	153,180,000	—	—	—	—	—	1.00	9.00	—
1972D	141,890,000	—	—	—	—	—	1.00	6.00	—
1972S	3,267,667	—	—	—	—	—	—	—	2.50
1973	64,964,000	—	—	—	—	—	1.00	6.00	—
1973D	83,171,400	—	—	—	—	—	—	5.50	—
1973S	(2,769,624)	—	—	—	—	—	—	—	2.50
1974	201,596,000	—	—	—	—	—	1.00	5.00	—
1974D	79,066,300	—	—	—	—	—	1.00	6.00	—
1974S	(2,617,350)	—	—	—	—	—	—	—	3.00
1975	—	—	—	—	—	—	—	—	—
1975D none minted	—	—	—	—	—	—	—	—	—
1975S none minted	—	—	—	—	—	—	—	—	—

Bicentennial design, Independence Hall reverse

KM# 205 • **Copper-Nickel Clad Copper** • **Rev. Designer:** Seth Huntington

Date	Mintage	G-4	VG-8	F-12	VF-20	XF-40	MS-60	MS-65	Prf-65
1976	234,308,000	—	—	—	—	—	1.00	10.00	—
1976D	287,565,248	—	—	—	—	—	1.00	7.00	—
1976S	(7,059,099)	—	—	—	—	—	—	—	2.00

Bicentennial design, Independence Hall reverse

KM# 205a • 11.5000 g., **0.4000 Silver**, 0.1480 oz. ASW • **Rev. Designer:** Seth Huntington

Date	Mintage	G-4	VG-8	F-12	VF-20	XF-40	MS-60	MS-65	Prf-65
1976S	4,908,319(3,998,621)	—	—	—	—	—	—	13.00	5.00

Regular design resumed reverse

KM# A202b • 11.3400 g., **Copper-Nickel Clad Copper**, 30.6 mm. • **Notes:** KM#202b design and composition resumed. The 1979-S and 1981-S Type II proofs have clearer mint marks than the Type I proofs of those years.

Date	Mintage	MS-65	Prf-65	Date	Mintage	MS-65	Prf-65
1977	43,598,000	6.50	—	1990S	(3,299,559)	—	5.00
1977D	31,449,106	6.00	—	1991P	14,874,000	10.00	—
1977S	(3,251,152)	—	2.00	1991D	15,054,678	12.00	—
1978	14,350,000	6.50	—	1991S	(2,867,787)	—	11.50
1978D	13,765,799	6.50	—	1992P	17,628,000	7.00	—
1978S	(3,127,788)	—	2.00	1992D	17,000,106	8.00	—
1979	68,312,000	5.50	—	1992S	(2,858,981)	—	10.00
1979D	15,815,422	6.00	—	1993P	15,510,000	8.00	—
1979S type I, proof	(3,677,175)	—	2.00	1993D	15,000,006	12.00	—
1979S type II, proof	Inc. above	—	18.00	1993S	(2,633,439)	—	14.00
1980P	44,134,000	5.00	—	1994P	23,718,000	6.00	—
1980D	33,456,449	4.50	—	1994D	23,828,110	6.00	—
1980S	(3,547,030)	—	2.00	1994S	(2,484,594)	—	8.00
1981P	29,544,000	6.00	—	1995P	26,496,000	6.00	—
1981D	27,839,533	5.50	—	1995D	26,288,000	6.00	—
1981S type I, proof	(4,063,083)	—	2.00	1995S	(2,010,384)	—	47.50
1981S type II, proof	Inc. above	—	14.50	1996P	24,442,000	6.00	—
1982P	10,819,000	5.00	—	1996D	24,744,000	6.00	—
1982D	13,140,102	7.00	—	1996S	2,085,191	—	10.00
1982S	(38,957,479)	—	3.50	1997P	20,882,000	7.00	—
1983P	34,139,000	10.00	—	1997D	19,876,000	6.00	—
1983D	32,472,244	10.00	—	1997S	(1,975,000)	—	25.00
1983S	(3,279,126)	—	3.00	1998P	15,646,000	9.00	—
1984P	26,029,000	6.50	—	1998D	15,064,000	8.00	—
1984D	26,262,158	7.00	—	1998S	(2,078,494)	—	14.00
1084S	(3,065,110)	—	4.00	1998S matte	62,350	—	400
1985P	18,706,962	10.00	—	1999P	8,900,000	6.00	—
1985D	19,814,034	12.00	—	1999D	10,682,000	6.00	—
1985S	(3,962,138)	—	4.50	1999S	(2,557,897)	—	10.00
1986P	13,107,633	16.00	—	2000P	22,600,000	6.00	—
1986D	15,336,145	12.00	—	2000D	19,466,000	6.00	—
1986S	(2,411,180)	—	7.50	2000S	(3,082,944)	—	4.50
1987P	2,890,758	12.00	—	2001P	21,200,000	6.00	—
1987D	2,890,758	10.00	—	2001D	19,504,000	6.00	—
1987S	(4,407,728)	—	3.50	2001S	(2,235,000)	—	10.00
1988P	13,626,000	10.00	—	2002P	3,100,000	15.00	—
1988D	12,000,096	10.00	—	2002D	2,500,000	10.00	—
1988S	(3,262,948)	—	7.00	2002S	(2,268,913)	—	7.00
1989P	24,542,000	10.00	—	2003P	2,500,000	10.00	—
1989D	23,000,216	8.00	—	2003D	2,500,000	10.00	—
1989S	(3,220,194)	—	7.00	2003S	2,076,165	—	7.00
1990P	22,780,000	15.00	—	2004S	—	—	—
1990D	20,096,242	15.00	—				

KM# B202b • **Silver** •

Date	Mintage	Prf-65	Date	Mintage	Prf-65
1992S	(1,317,579)	15.00	1998S	(878,792)	30.00
1993S	(761,353)	25.00	1999S	(804,565)	15.00
1994S	(785,329)	35.00	2000S	(965,921)	12.50
1995S	(838,953)	100.00	2001S	(849,600)	12.50
1996S	(830,021)	50.00	2002S	(888,816)	—
1997S	(821,678)	100.00	2003S	1,040,425	—

1794 Silver Dollar
Grade XF-40

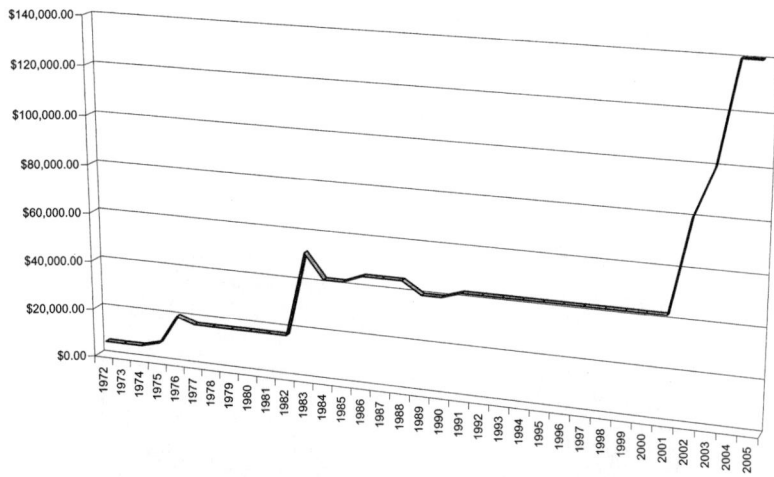

☐ Retail Price

DOLLAR
Flowing Hair Dollar

KM# 17 • 26.9600 g., 0.8920 **Silver**, 0.7737 oz. ASW, 39-40 mm. • **Designer:** Robert Scot **Notes:** The two 1795 varieties have either two or three leaves under each of the eagle's wings on the reverse.

Date	Mintage	F-12	VF-20	XF-40	AU-50	MS-60	MS-63
1794	1,758	45,000	80,000	140,000	250,000	—	—
1795 2 leaves	203,033	3,250	5,750	10,000	17,000	38,000	58,000
1795 3 leaves	Inc. above	3,000	5,500	9,500	15,000	34,000	55,000

Draped Bust Dollar
Small eagle reverse

KM# 18 • 26.9600 g., 0.8920 **Silver**, 0.7737 oz. ASW, 39-40 mm. • **Designer:** Robert Scot **Notes:** The 1796 varieties are distinguished by the size of the numerals in the date and letters in "United States of

America." The 1797 varieties are distinguished by the number of stars to the left and right of the word "Liberty" and by the size of the letters in "United States of America." The 1798 varieties have either 13 or 15 stars on the obverse.

Date	Mintage	F-12	VF-20	XF-40	AU-50	MS-60	MS-63
1795	Inc. above	2,000	3,300	5,900	7,800	24,500	57,500
1796 small date, small letters	72,920	2,000	3,300	5,900	7,800	24,500	—
1796 small date, large letters	Inc. above	2,050	11,350	6,000	8,000	25,500	—
1796 large date, small letters	Inc. above	1,975	3,250	5,850	7,750	27,000	65,000
1797 9 stars left, 7 stars right, small letters	7,776	3,000	4,800	9,000	16,500	42,500	70,000
1797 9 stars left, 7 stars right, large letters	Inc. above	2,050	3,350	6,000	7,750	28,500	60,000
1797 10 stars left, 6 stars right	Inc. above	1,975	3,250	5,850	7,750	24,500	60,000
1798 13 stars	327,536	1,875	3,350	6,250	9,500	28,500	—
1798 15 stars	Inc. above	2,350	3,800	8,000	12,500	33,500	—

Heraldic eagle reverse

KM# 32 • 26.9600 g., 0.8920 **Silver**, 0.7737 oz. ASW, 39-40 mm. • **Designer:** Robert Scot **Notes:** The 1798 "knob 9" variety has a serif on the lower left of the 9 in the date. The 1798 varieties are distinguished by the number of arrows held by the eagle on the reverse and the number of berries on the olive branch. On the 1798 "high-8" variety, the 8 in the date is higher than the other numerals. The 1799 varieties are distinguished by the number and positioning of the stars on the obverse and by the size of the berries in the olive branch on the reverse. On the 1700 "irregular date" variety, the first 9 in the date is smaller than the other numerals. Some varieties of the 1800 strikes had letters in the legend cut twice into the dies; as the dies became worn, the letters were touched up. On the 1800 "very wide date, low 8" variety, the spacing between the numerals in the date are wider than other varieties and the 8 is lower than the other numerals. The 1800 "small berries" variety refers to the size of the berries in the olive branch on the reverse. The 1800 "12 arrows" and "10 arrows" varieties refer to the number of arrows held by the eagle. The 1800 "Americai" variety appears to have the faint outline of an "I" after "America" in the reverse legend. The "close" and "wide" varieties of 1802 refer to the amount of space between the numerals in the date. The 1800 large-3 and small-3 varieties are distinguished by the size of the 3 in the date.

Date	Mintage	F-12	VF-20	XF-40	AU-50	MS-60	MS-63
1798 knob 9	Inc. above	1,125	1,775	2,850	4,200	16,750	34,500
1798 10 arrows	Inc. above	1,125	1,775	2,850	4,200	16,750	34,500
1798 4 berries	Inc. above	1,125	1,775	2,850	4,200	16,750	34,500
1798 5 berries, 12 arrows	Inc. above	1,125	1,775	2,850	4,200	16,750	34,500
1798 high 8	Inc. above	1,125	1,775	2,850	7,200	18,750	34,500
1798 13 arrows	Inc. above	1,125	1,775	2,850	4,200	16,750	34,500
1799/98 13-star reverse	423,515	1,350	2,050	3,300	6,000	18,500	36,000
1799/98 15-star reverse	Inc. above	1,225	1,825	3,000	6,200	19,500	36,000
1799 irregular date, 13-star reverse	Inc. above	1,200	1,850	2,900	4,650	18,500	38,500
1799 irregular date, 15-star reverse	Inc. above	1,175	1,825	2,850	4,600	16,500	36,000
1799 perfect date, 7- and 6-star obverse, no berries	Inc. above	1,100	1,750	2,750	4,800	13,500	33,500
1799 perfect date, 7- and 6-star obverse, small berries	Inc. above	1,100	1,350	2,750	4,200	13,500	33,500
1799 perfect date, 7- and 6-star obverse, medium large berries	Inc. above	1,125	1,350	2,750	4,200	13,500	33,500
1799 perfect date, 7- and 6-star obverse, extra large berries	Inc. above	1,125	1,350	2,750	4,200	13,500	33,500
1799 8 stars left, 5 stars right on obverse	Inc. above	1,200	1,850	2,900	4,650	19,000	42,500
1800 "R" in "Liberty" double cut	220,920	1,175	1,825	2,850	4,600	16,500	36,000
1800 first "T" in "States" double cut	Inc. above	1,175	1,825	2,850	4,600	16,500	36,000
1800 both letters double cut	Inc. above	1,175	1,825	2,850	4,600	16,500	36,000
1800 "T" in "United" double cut	Inc. above	1,175	1,825	2,850	4,600	16,500	36,000
1800 very wide date, low 8	Inc. above	1,175	1,825	2,850	4,600	16,500	36,000
1800 small berries	Inc. above	1,200	1,850	2,900	4,650	17,000	—
1800 dot date	Inc. above	1,350	2,050	3,300	6,000	16,500	39,500
1800 12 arrows	Inc. above	1,175	1,825	2,850	4,600	16,500	36,000
1800 10 arrows	Inc. above	1,175	1,825	2,850	4,600	16,500	36,000
1800 "Americai"	Inc. above	1,350	2,050	3,300	6,000	16,500	39,500
1801	54,454	1,300	2,100	3,000	4,600	20,000	40,000
1801 proof restrike	—	—	—	—	—	—	—

Date	Mintage	F-12	VF-20	XF-40	AU-50	MS-60	MS-63
1802/1 close	Inc. above	1,350	2,050	3,300	6,000	15,500	—
1802/1 wide	Inc. above	1,350	2,050	3,300	6,000	15,500	—
1802 close, perfect date	Inc. above	1,200	1,850	2,900	4,650	15,500	—
1802 wide, perfect date	Inc. above	1,175	1,825	2,850	4,600	16,500	—
1802 proof restrike, mintage unrecorded	—	—	—	—	—	—	—
1803 large 3	85,634	1,225	1,925	3,000	5,400	15,500	37,500
1803 small 3	Inc. above	1,350	2,050	3,300	6,000	16,500	38,500
1803 proof restrike, mintage unrecorded	—	—	—	—	—	—	—
1804 15 known	—	—	—	—	1,000,000	—	—

Note: 1804, Childs Sale, Aug. 1999, Prf-68, $4,140,000.

Gobrecht Dollar

"C. Gobrecht F." below base obverse   Eagle flying left amid stars reverse

KM# 59.1 • 26.7300 g., 0.9000 **Silver**, 0.7736 oz. ASW, 38.1 mm. • **Obv. Designer:** Christian Gobrecht
Edge Desc: Plain.

Date	Mintage	VF-20	XF-40	AU-50	Prf-60
1836	1,000	3,750	4,750	—	12,500

"C. Gobrecht F." below base obverse   Eagle flying in plain field reverse
KM# 59.2 • 26.7300 g., 0.9000 **Silver**, 0.7736 oz. ASW, 38.1 mm. • **Obv. Designer:** Christian Gobrecht.
Edge Desc: Plain.

Date	Mintage	VF-20	XF-40	AU-50	Prf-60
1836 Restrike	—	—	—	—	—

"C. Gobrecht F." on base obverse
KM# 59a.1 • 26.7300 g., 0.9000 **Silver**, 0.7736 oz. ASW, 38.1 mm. • **Obv. Legend**Eagle flying left amid
stars. **Edge Desc:** Plain.

Date	Mintage	VF-20	XF-40	AU-50	Prf-60
1836	600	—	—	—	—

"C. Gobrecht F." on base obverse   Eagle flying left amid stars reverse
KM# 59a.2 • 26.7300 g., 0.9000 **Silver**, 0.7736 oz. ASW, 38.1 mm. • **Edge Desc:** Reeded.

Date	Mintage	VF-20	XF-40	AU-50	Prf-60
1836 Restrike	—	—	—	—	—

Designer's name omitted obverse   Eagle in plain field reverse
KM# 59a.3 • 26.7300 g., 0.9000 **Silver**, 0.7736 oz. ASW, 38.1 mm. • **Edge Desc:** Reeded.

Date	Mintage	VF-20	XF-40	AU-50	Prf-60
1839	300	—	—	—	—

Seated Liberty Dollar
No motto above eagle reverse

KM# 71 • 26.7300 g., 0.9000 **Silver**, 0.7736 oz. ASW, 38.1 mm. • **Designer:** Christian Gobrecht

Date	Mintage	G-4	VG-8	F-12	VF-20	XF-40	AU-50	MS-60	MS-63	MS-65	Prf-65
1840	61,005	160	180	225	300	525	750	1,750	12,500	—	—
1841	173,000	145	165	210	250	360	625	1,500	4,200	42,500	—

Date	Mintage	G-4	VG-8	F-12	VF-20	XF-40	AU-50	MS-60	MS-63	MS-65	Prf-65
1842	184,618	145	165	210	250	350	600	1,100	3,750	24,000	—
1843	165,100	145	165	210	250	350	625	1,400	4,350	24,000	—
1844	20,000	180	245	300	385	500	850	3,000	7,000	44,500	—
1845	24,500	200	260	285	350	550	800	4,850	17,000	—	—
1846	110,600	145	165	225	275	385	625	1,450	4,650	30,000	—
1846O	59,000	150	250	300	475	1,250	3,000	12,000	24,500	—	—
1847	140,750	145	165	210	250	350	600	950	3,500	26,500	—
1848	15,000	250	300	425	550	750	1,500	3,000	7,500	40,000	—
1849	62,600	165	190	250	325	400	700	1,650	4,600	32,500	—
1850	7,500	500	675	800	900	1,000	2,000	4,500	13,000	47,500	—
1850O	40,000	250	300	375	650	1,275	2,850	6,250	15,500	55,000	—
1851	1,300	4,000	5,000	8,000	9,500	13,500	21,500	27,500	35,000	60,000	—
1852	1,100	3,800	4,800	7,500	8,500	11,500	21,500	26,500	33,500	55,000	—
1853	46,110	185	235	285	375	600	850	2,350	6,500	26,500	—
1854	33,140	1,000	1,200	1,600	2,350	3,650	4,850	7,000	9,800	24,500	—
1855	26,000	900	1,150	1,400	1,900	2,950	3,800	6,500	15,000	—	—
1856	63,500	400	500	600	750	975	1,650	3,450	6,500	—	—
1857	94,000	375	475	550	750	950	1,300	2,750	4,200	27,500	—
1858 proof	Est. 800	2,250	2,650	3,350	4,200	5,500	6,250	9,000	12,000	—	—

Note: Proof Only restruck in later years.

Date	Mintage	G-4	VG-8	F-12	VF-20	XF-40	AU-50	MS-60	MS-63	MS-65	Prf-65
1859	256,500	180	220	300	450	600	850	1,800	5,000	15,000	13,500
1859O	360,000	145	175	220	275	375	600	950	2,600	32,000	—
1859S	20,000	235	300	400	600	1,350	3,000	8,000	25,500	60,000	—
1860	218,930	165	200	275	350	475	600	1,100	2,600	26,000	13,500
1860O	515,000	145	165	210	250	350	550	900	2,500	15,000	—
1861	78,500	440	500	650	800	1,000	1,500	2,800	4,600	22,500	13,500
1862	12,090	450	525	675	850	1,100	1,600	2,750	5,000	34,500	13,500
1863	27,660	375	425	500	650	1,200	2,350	3,800	11,250	1,400	13,500
1864	31,170	240	265	315	425	600	1,200	2,300	4,600	20,000	13,500
1865	47,000	225	245	290	400	560	1,150	2,150	4,450	32,500	13,500
1866 2 known without motto	—	—	—	—	—	—	—	—	—	—	—

"In God We Trust" above eagle reverse

KM# 100 • 26.7300 g., 0.9000 **Silver**, 0.7736 oz. ASW, 38.1 mm. • **Designer:** Christian Gobrecht **Notes:** In 1866 the motto "In God We Trust" was added to the reverse above the eagle.

Date	Mintage	G-4	VG-8	F-12	VF-20	XF-40	AU-50	MS-60	MS-63	MS-65	Prf-65
1866	49,625	175	220	285	400	550	900	1,650	2,900	23,500	7,000
1867	47,525	170	215	265	415	525	875	1,500	3,000	24,500	7,000
1868	162,700	165	205	245	375	475	850	1,600	6,000	33,500	7,000
1869	424,300	155	195	235	325	440	650	1,450	3,350	24,500	7,000
1870	416,000	165	185	225	320	440	600	1,400	2,750	24,500	7,000
1870CC	12,462	275	345	500	800	1,450	3,000	9,500	20,000	38,500	—
1870S 12-15 known	—	50,000	—	—	—	—	—	—	—	—	—

Note: 1870S, Eliasberg Sale, April 1997, EF-45 to AU-50, $264,000.

Date	Mintage	G-4	VG-8	F-12	VF-20	XF-40	AU-50	MS-60	MS-63	MS-65	Prf-65
1871	1,074,760	155	190	265	340	425	600	1,100	2,600	21,500	7,000
1871CC	1,376	2,000	2,600	4,000	6,000	9,000	18,500	41,000	96,000	150,000	—
1872	1,106,450	150	190	265	340	425	600	1,100	2,600	21,500	7,000
1872CC	3,150	900	1,250	1,750	2,850	4,250	8,500	18,500	35,000	—	—
1872S	9,000	250	325	450	650	1,100	2,750	8,500	23,500	—	—
1873	293,600	145	165	215	240	350	575	1,125	2,750	21,500	7,000
1873CC	2,300	3,250	4,750	6,500	9,000	16,000	30,000	63,500	110,000	—	—
1873S none known	700	—	—	—	—	—	—	—	—	—	—

Trade Dollar

KM# 108 • 27.2200 g., 0.9000 **Silver**, 0.7878 oz. ASW, 38.1 mm. • **Designer:** William Barber

Date	Mintage	G-4	VG-8	F-12	VF-20	XF-40	AU-50	MS-60	MS-65	Prf-65
1873	397,500	100.00	110	125	165	250	325	1,000	12,000	12,000
1873CC	124,500	175	200	300	450	700	1,200	2,100	80,000	—
1873S	703,000	130	145	160	220	280	400	1,200	25,000	—
1874	987,800	120	130	150	185	240	340	700	15,000	12,000
1874CC	1,373,200	80.00	90.00	105	165	240	350	1,000	40,000	—
1874S	2,549,000	70.00	80.00	95.00	120	165	250	675	30,000	—
1875	218,900	260	350	425	525	675	800	1,850	13,000	6,500
1875CC	1,573,700	80.00	90.00	105	130	200	375	900	40,000	—
1875S	4,487,000	60.00	70.00	85.00	100.00	120	210	500	7,000	—
1875S/CC	Inc. above	275	325	400	525	695	1,100	1,900	—	—
1876	456,150	70.00	80.00	100.00	125	165	400	675	7,500	6,500
1876CC	509,000	200	240	260	290	375	500	2,100	75,000	—
1876S	5,227,000	60.00	70.00	85.00	100.00	120	210	475	10,000	—
1877	3,039,710	60.00	70.00	85.00	105	130	210	525	16,000	19,000
1877CC	534,000	150	175	210	290	400	600	1,275	70,000	—
1877S	9,519,000	60.00	70.00	85.00	100.00	120	210	475	8,000	—
1878 proof	900	—	—	—	1,100	1,300	1,500	—	—	22,000
1878CC	97,000	425	525	675	850	1,750	2,100	5,500	67,500	—
1878S	4,162,000	60.00	70.00	85.00	100.00	120	210	475	7,000	—
1879 proof	1,541	—	—	—	900	950	1,100	—	—	22,000
1880 proof	1,987	—	—	—	900	950	1,100	—	—	19,500
1881 proof	960	—	—	—	950	1,000	1,250	—	—	20,000
1882 proof	1,097	—	—	—	950	1,000	1,250	—	—	20,000

1875 Trade Dollar
Grade F-12

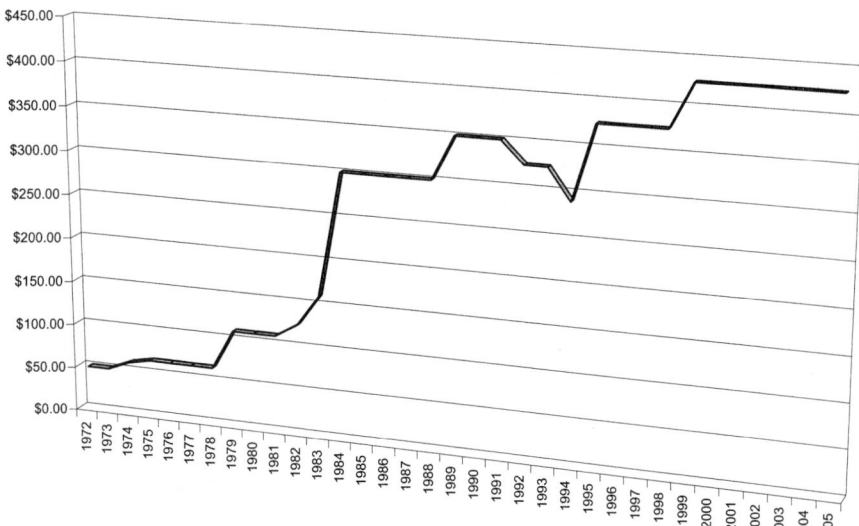

Date	Mintage	G-4	VG-8	F-12	VF-20	XF-40	AU-50	MS-60	MS-65	Prf-65
1883 proof	979	—	—	—	1,100	1,200	1,400	—	—	20,000
1884 proof	10	—	—	—	—	—	—	—	—	—

Note: 1884, Eliasberg Sale, April 1997, Prf-66, $396,000.

| 1885 proof | 5 | — | — | — | — | — | — | — | — | — |

Note: 1885, Eliasberg Sale, April 1997, Prf-65, $907,500.

Morgan Dollar

8 tail feathers

7 tail feathers

7/8 tail feathers

KM# 110 • 26.7300 g., 0.9000 **Silver**, 0.7736 oz. ASW, 38.1 mm. • **Designer:** George T. Morgan **Notes:** "65DMPL" values are for coins grading MS-65 deep-mirror prooflike. The 1878 "8 tail feathers" and "7 tail feathers" varieties are distinguished by the number of feathers in the eagle's tail. On the "reverse of 1878" varieties, the top of the top feather in the arrows held by the eagle is straight across and the eagle's breast is concave. On the "reverse of 1879 varieties," the top feather in the arrows held by the eagle is slanted and the eagle's breast is convex. The 1890-CC "tail-bar variety has a bar extending from the arrow feathers to the wreath on the reverse, the result of a die gouge.

Date	Mintage	VG-8	F-12	VF-20	XF-40	AU-50	MS-60	MS-63	MS-64	MS-65	65DMPL	Prf-65
1878 8 tail feathers	750,000	25.00	27.50	34.00	41.50	65.00	125	165	400	1,300	6,300	7,500
1878 7 tail feathers, reverse of 1878	Inc. above	16.00	17.50	20.00	22.00	40.00	56.00	95.00	390	1,500	6,300	—
1878 7 tail feathers, reverse of 1879	Inc. above	16.00	17.50	19.50	22.00	40.00	67.50	140	640	2,650	8,800	9,000
1878 7 over 8 tail feathers	9,759,550	20.00	22.00	23.00	31.50	55.00	130	350	550	2,750	14,500	—
1878CC	2,212,000	96.00	98.00	105	100.00	110	220	400	640	2,000	3,450	—
1878S	9,744,000	15.50	17.50	19.50	21.50	33.00	46.00	70.00	105	285	2,250	—
1879	14,807,100	14.50	14.75	15.75	17.50	21.00	30.00	60.00	135	1,250	6,950	6,000
1879CC	756,000	110	122.5	180	640	1,350	3,500	8,000	10,500	26,000	65,000	—
1879O	2,887,000	14.50	14.75	15.75	17.50	21.50	72.50	180	480	3,250	16,500	—
1879S reverse of 1878	9,110,000	16.50	17.00	18.00	21.00	34.50	94.00	360	1,450	8,300	22,000	—
1879S reverse of 1879	9,110,000	14.50	14.75	16.00	17.50	21.50	40.00	42.50	63.50	165	450	—
1880	12,601,335	14.50	14.75	15.75	17.50	21.25	30.00	55.00	115	800	3,450	5,900
1880CC reverse of 1878	591,000	100.00	125	150	185	250	495	640	1,100	3,000	11,000	—
1880CC reverse of 1879	591,000	115	150	165	225	300	495	515	800	1,450	3,650	—
1880O	5,305,000	14.50	14.75	15.75	17.50	21.50	60.00	385	2,000	24,000	70,000	—
1880S	8,900,000	14.50	14.75	15.75	17.50	21.50	33.00	46.00	65.00	165	450	—
1881	9,163,975	14.50	14.75	15.75	17.50	21.25	30.00	55.00	150	850	13,750	6,250
1881CC	296,000	320	330	345	370	430	500	560	625	850	1,450	—
1881O	5,708,000	14.50	14.75	15.75	17.50	21.25	30.00	48.00	160	1,650	15,000	—
1881S	12,760,000	14.50	14.75	15.75	17.50	21.25	30.00	46.00	58.50	165	450	—
1882	11,101,100	14.50	14.75	15.75	17.50	21.25	30.00	46.00	63.50	450	4,100	5,900
1882CC	1,133,000	90.00	92.50	95.00	96.00	100.00	215	245	270	500	725	—
1882O	6,090,000	14.50	14.75	15.75	17.50	21.25	32.50	46.00	75.00	800	4,200	—
1882S	9,250,000	14.50	14.75	15.75	17.50	25.00	33.00	46.00	63.50	165	1,100	—
1883	12,291,039	14.50	14.75	15.75	17.50	21.25	30.00	46.00	63.50	170	760	5,900
1883CC	1,204,000	95.00	97.50	105	115	120	220	230	280	500	830	—
1883O	8,725,000	14.50	14.75	15.75	17.50	20.00	30.00	46.00	65.00	165	575	—
1883S	6,250,000	14.50	16.00	17.00	33.00	155	660	230	5,250	22,000	94,500	—
1884	14,070,875	14.50	14.75	15.75	17.50	21.25	30.00	46.00	63.50	300	2,200	5,900
1884CC	1,136,000	100.00	110	120	130	160	220	230	275	550	600	—
1884O	9,730,000	14.50	14.75	16.00	17.50	20.00	30.00	46.00	63.50	165	670	—
1884S	3,200,000	15.00	15.00	17.50	41.50	21.25	6,000	31,500	110,000	200,000	220,000	—
1885	17,787,767	14.50	14.75	15.75	17.50	21.25	30.00	46.00	60.00	165	570	5,900
1885CC	228,000	395	415	460	480	575	615	670	780	1,500	1,450	—
1885O	9,185,000	14.50	14.75	15.75	17.50	21.25	30.00	46.00	63.50	165	490	—
1885S	1,497,000	17.50	21.50	34.00	57.50	130	200	250	650	1,800	16,500	—
1886	19,963,886	14.50	14.75	15.75	17.50	21.25	30.00	46.00	62.00	165	575	5,900
1886O	10,710,000	14.50	14.75	15.75	18.00	80.00	660	4,400	10,000	215,000	283,500	—
1886S	750,000	30.00	36.00	58.50	65.00	125	285	470	715	3,250	16,500	—
1887	20,290,710	14.50	15.00	15.75	17.50	21.25	30.00	46.00	63.50	165	530	5,900
1887O	11,550,000	14.50	15.00	15.75	17.50	22.00	54.00	105	425	4,100	8,500	—

1889-O Silver Dollar
Grade F-12

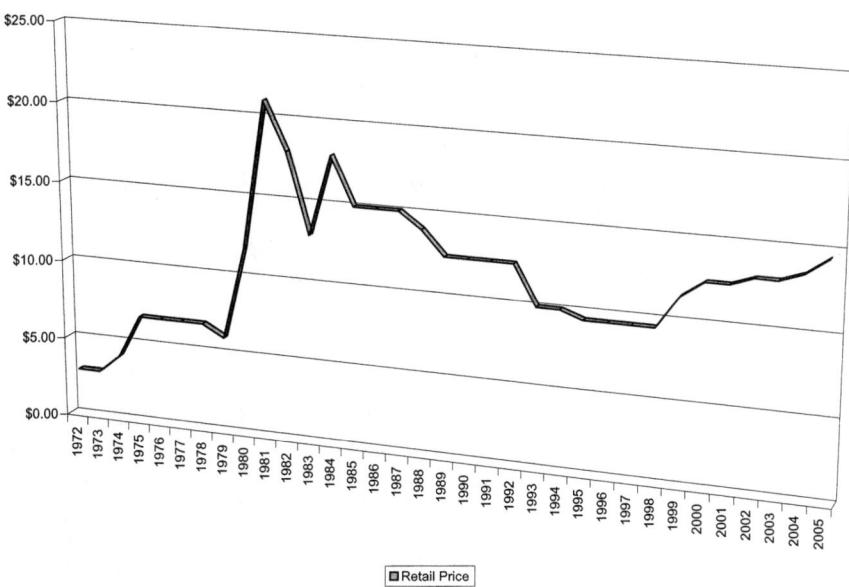

Retail Price

1897-O Dollar
Grade MS-60

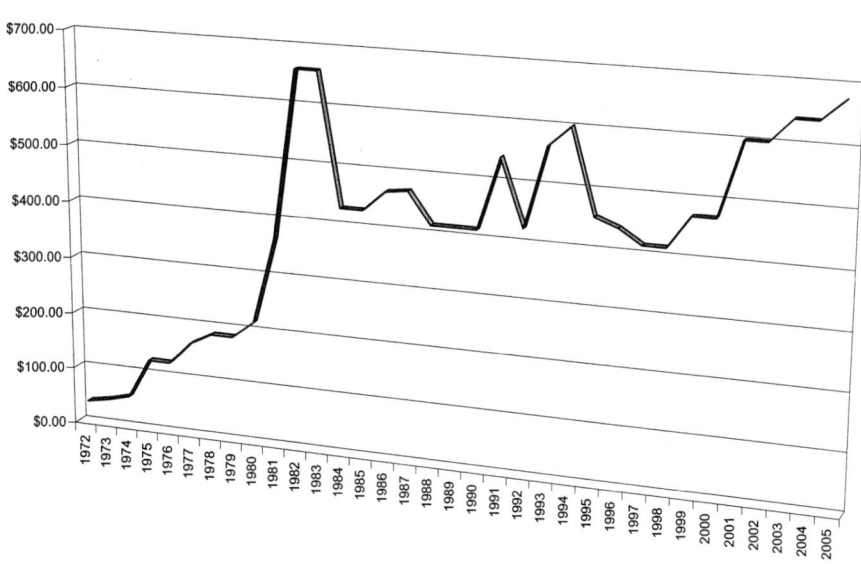

Retail Price

Date	Mintage	VG-8	F-12	VF-20	XF-40	AU-50	MS-60	MS-63	MS-64	MS-65	65DMPL	Prf-65
1887S	1,771,000	15.00	15.50	17.50	20.00	39.00	100.00	285	750	4,000	27,000	—
1888	19,183,833	14.50	14.75	15.75	17.50	21.25	30.00	46.00	63.50	215	2,350	6,000
1888O	12,150,000	14.50	15.00	16.00	17.50	21.25	30.00	46.00	64.50	460	1,600	—
1888S	657,000	50.00	150	180	190	200	250	440	850	3,500	10,500	—
1889	21,726,811	14.50	14.75	15.75	17.50	21.25	29.00	46.00	62.00	310	2,950	5,900
1889CC	350,000	625	900	1,700	3,500	7,500	22,000	34,000	51,500	315,000	285,000	—
1889O	11,875,000	14.50	14.75	15.75	17.50	30.00	140	465	840	5,000	14,500	—
1889S	700,000	33.50	46.00	57.50	77.50	100.00	200	440	550	1,950	7,550	—
1890	16,802,590	14.50	14.75	15.75	17.50	21.25	30.00	50.00	115	2,300	12,500	5,900
1890CC	2,309,041	90.00	92.50	115	160	210	350	850	2,300	6,300	9,750	—
1890CC tail bar	Inc. above	135	145	180	500	900	1,600	4,000	8,500	—	9,800	—
1890O	10,701,000	14.50	14.75	15.75	18.00	24.00	56.00	110	340	1,750	7,500	—
1890S	8,230,373	14.50	14.75	15.75	17.50	21.25	56.00	110	270	1,050	8,200	—
1891	8,694,206	14.50	14.75	15.75	18.50	23.50	52.50	180	560	7,200	25,000	5,900
1891CC	1,618,000	90.00	92.50	95.00	160	210	345	950	1,350	5,000	20,000	—
1891O	7,954,529	14.50	14.75	15.75	18.00	34.00	135	350	750	7,350	21,500	—
1891S	5,296,000	14.50	14.75	15.75	19.50	24.00	60.00	125	275	1,300	7,250	—
1892	1,037,245	17.00	19.00	21.00	30.00	72.50	150	400	1,000	4,000	15,750	5,900
1892CC	1,352,000	125	135	225	440	575	1,050	2,650	3,700	11,000	27,000	—
1892O	2,744,000	17.50	19.00	19.50	30.00	60.00	160	325	700	5,250	27,000	—
1892S	1,200,000	20.00	27.50	66.00	200	1,750	35,000	57,500	96,000	170,000	170,000	—
1893	378,792	160	185	220	250	330	645	1,400	2,600	7,750	38,000	5,900
1893CC	677,000	195	265	550	1,800	2,300	3,800	8,000	14,750	54,500	85,000	—
1893O	300,000	180	240	350	600	1,000	1,850	6,750	20,000	220,000	201,500	—
1893S	100,000	2,900	4,300	6,300	11,000	27,000	85,000	130,000	250,000	415,000	380,000	—
1894	110,972	1,300	1,340	1,700	2,500	3,000	4,500	6,250	10,500	40,000	44,000	6,500
1894O	1,723,000	43.50	50.00	60.00	110	315	550	4,000	10,500	50,000	56,500	—
1894S	1,260,000	37.50	50.00	75.00	130	525	715	1,150	1,850	5,750	19,000	—
1895 proof only	12,880	21,000	27,500	29,000	33,500	37,000	—	—	—	—	—	67,500
1895O	450,000	330	440	580	850	1,400	14,000	55,000	100,000	225,000	—	—
1895S	400,000	200	275	340	690	1,700	3,500	5,900	8,500	21,000	40,500	—
1896	9,967,762	14.50	16.00	16.25	17.50	21.25	29.00	46.00	67.50	200	975	5,900
1896O	4,900,000	14.50	16.00	16.50	18.00	190	1,050	7,350	46,000	185,000	170,000	—
1896S	5,000,000	17.50	27.00	47.50	200	750	1,400	3,250	4,400	16,000	25,000	—
1897	2,822,731	14.50	16.00	16.25	17.50	21.25	30.00	46.00	63.50	260	2,900	5,900
1897O	4,004,000	14.50	16.00	16.50	24.00	110	740	5,500	15,500	50,000	56,500	—
1897S	5,825,000	14.50	16.00	16.50	17.50	24.00	56.00	115	170	600	1,700	—
1898	5,884,735	16.00	16.50	17.00	18.00	21.25	30.00	46.00	63.50	265	1,075	5,900
1898O	4,440,000	17.00	21.00	22.00	23.00	25.00	30.00	46.00	63.50	165	510	—
1898S	4,102,000	20.00	23.00	27.50	37.50	95.00	260	465	890	2,500	11,250	—
1899	330,846	48.50	66.00	80.00	110	150	200	285	440	850	2,250	6,000
1899O	12,290,000	15.00	16.00	16.50	21.50	22.00	30.00	45.00	63.50	165	825	—
1899S	2,562,000	18.00	22.00	32.50	48.50	100.00	330	480	800	2,200	8,600	—
1900	8,880,938	14.50	15.00	16.00	18.00	21.25	30.00	46.00	63.50	210	11,000	5,900
1900O	12,590,000	14.50	25.00	16.00	20.00	24.00	32.00	46.00	63.50	165	3,000	—

1903-O Dollar
Grade MS-60

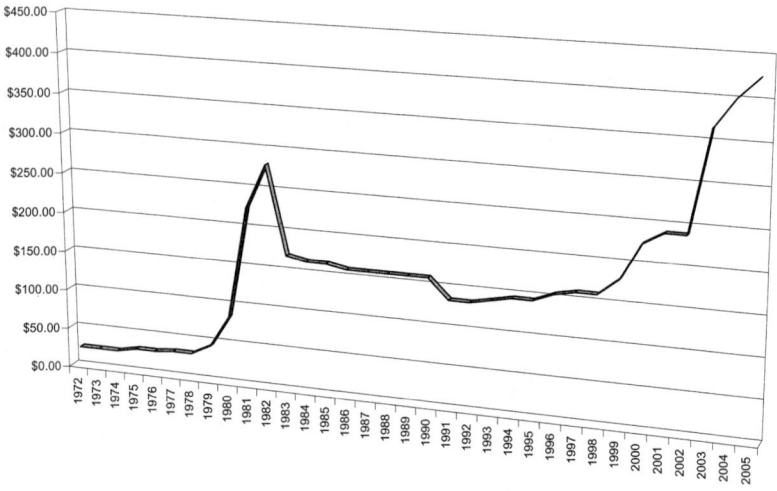

1921 Silver Dollar
Grade MS-60

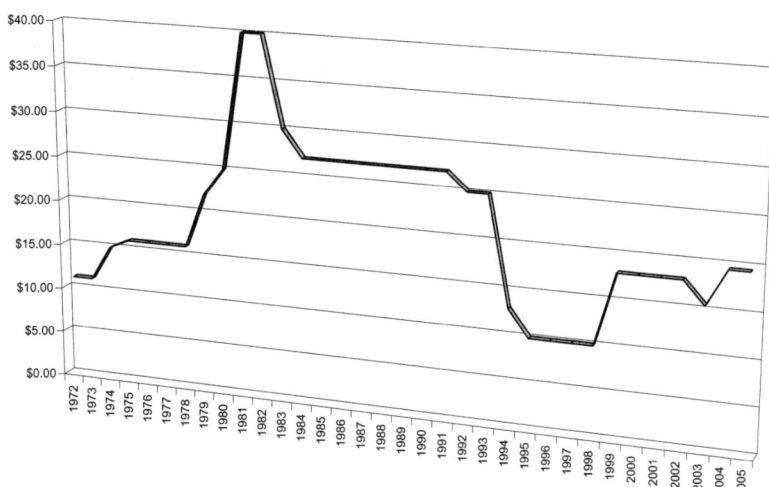

□ Retail Price

Date	Mintage	VG-8	F-12	VF-20	XF-40	AU-50	MS-60	MS-63	MS-64	MS-65	65DMPL	Prf-65
1900O/CC	Inc. above	30.00	39.00	52.50	82.50	170	3,158	895	1,525	3,500	19,000	—
1900S	3,540,000	16.00	17.00	19.50	36.00	83.00	275	400	500	1,575	9,450	—
1901	6,962,813	25.00	30.00	41.50	85.00	360	2,050	16,000	56,000	220,000	220,000	6,500
1901O	13,320,000	14.50	14.75	16.00	21.50	22.00	32.00	46.00	67.50	200	3,800	—
1901S	2,284,000	15.00	20.00	31.00	45.00	220	400	695	960	4,000	12,500	—
1902	7,994,777	16.50	17.50	18.00	19.00	23.00	42.50	105	140	525	15,750	5,900
1902O	8,636,000	14.50	17.50	18.00	20.00	21.50	30.00	46.00	63.50	165	3,600	—
1902S	1,530,000	51.00	67.90	130	180	285	415	600	1,000	3,350	15,000	—
1903	4,652,755	45.00	47.50	50.00	57.50	65.00	77.50	93.50	115	285	9,150	5,900
1903O	4,450,000	275	300	320	345	400	425	450	500	720	4,650	—
1903S	1,241,000	50.00	67.50	130	285	1,800	4,150	6,500	7,500	8,500	40,000	—
1904	2,788,650	19.50	20.00	20.50	21.50	33.00	80.00	265	680	4,500	38,000	5,900
1904O	3,720,000	19.50	20.00	20.50	21.00	24.00	33.00	46.00	72.50	165	550	—
1904S	2,304,000	30.00	41.50	68.50	220	550	1,150	3,400	4,300	8,000	19,000	—
1921	44,690,000	11.00	11.50	11.75	12.00	15.00	19.50	32.50	50.00	130	8,800	—
1921D	20,345,000	11.00	11.50	11.75	12.25	15.50	40.00	66.00	135	315	15,000	—
1921S	21,695,000	11.00	11.50	11.75	12.50	15.50	40.00	68.50	175	1,450	22,000	—

Peace Dollar

Mint mark

KM# 150 • 26.7300 g., 0.9000 **Silver**, 0.7736 oz. ASW, 38.1 mm. • **Designer:** Anthony DeFrancisci
Notes: Commonly called Peace dollars.

Date	Mintage	G-4	VG-8	F-12	VF-20	XF-40	AU-50	MS-60	MS-63	MS-64	MS-65
1921	1,006,473	70.00	90.00	100.00	105	115	160	225	385	825	2,550
1922	51,737,000	8.00	9.00	9.25	9.50	9.75	10.00	16.00	33.50	52.50	160
1922D	15,063,000	8.00	9.00	9.25	10.00	11.00	12.00	24.00	48.00	85.00	365
1922S	17,475,000	8.00	9.00	9.25	10.25	12.00	13.00	23.00	67.50	230	2,250
1923	30,800,000	8.00	9.00	9.25	9.50	9.75	10.00	16.00	33.50	52.50	160
1923D	6,811,000	8.00	9.00	10.00	10.50	11.00	18.00	53.00	120	260	925

1927-S Dollar
Grade MS-60

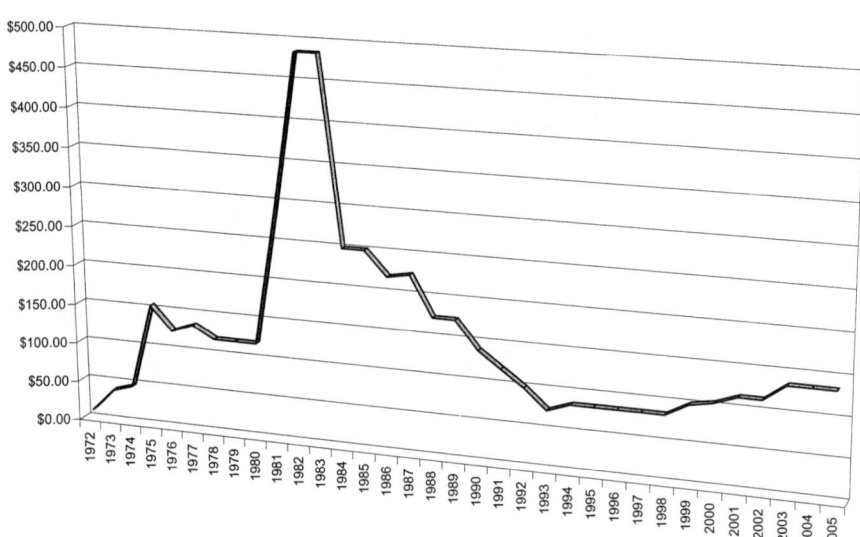

Retail Price

Date	Mintage	G-4	VG-8	F-12	VF-20	XF-40	AU-50	MS-60	MS-63	MS-64	MS-65
1923S	19,020,000	8.00	9.00	10.00	10.50	11.00	13.00	28.00	67.50	200	5,750
1924	11,811,000	8.00	9.00	9.50	10.00	10.50	11.00	16.00	33.50	52.50	160
1924S	1,728,000	11.00	17.50	27.50	34.00	40.00	57.50	200	625	1,100	9,000
1925	10,198,000	8.00	9.00	9.25	9.50	9.75	12.50	16.00	33.50	52.50	160
1925S	1,610,000	9.00	13.50	17.50	22.00	27.50	41.50	75.00	160	550	20,000
1926	1,939,000	9.00	13.00	14.50	15.00	17.50	23.00	41.50	77.50	110	360
1926D	2,348,700	8.00	14.00	15.50	16.50	20.00	31.50	66.00	135	275	600
1926S	6,980,000	8.00	12.50	15.00	15.25	15.50	19.00	41.50	80.00	235	925
1927	848,000	13.00	25.00	32.50	34.00	35.00	55.00	70.00	140	280	2,550
1927D	1,268,900	11.00	24.50	25.00	25.50	27.50	84.00	150	300	625	5,100
1927S	866,000	14.00	25.00	30.00	31.50	32.50	80.00	135	415	940	11,700
1928	360,649	250	375	420	430	460	485	505	800	1,300	4,600
1928S	1,632,000	13.00	32.50	34.00	35.00	41.50	68.50	140	580	1,250	19,000
1934	954,057	12.00	18.50	19.00	22.00	23.00	47.50	105	250	425	1,000
1934D	1,569,500	11.00	18.50	19.00	19.50	21.50	47.50	110	375	530	1,850
1934S	1,011,000	12.00	27.50	37.50	68.50	180	500	1,800	4,150	5,300	7,500
1935	1,576,000	11.00	16.00	20.00	21.50	23.00	30.00	62.50	100.00	165	670
1935S	1,964,000	11.00	16.00	16.50	17.00	25.00	96.00	250	365	525	1,250

Eisenhower Dollar
Clad type

KM# 203 • 22.6800 g., **Copper-Nickel Clad Copper**, 38.1 mm. • **Designer:** Frank Gasparro

Date	Mintage	Proof	MS-63	Prf-65	Date	Mintage	Proof	MS-63	Prf-65
1971	47,799,000	—	3.75	—	1972	75,890,000	—	2.75	—
1971D	68,587,424	—	2.00	—	1972D	92,548,511	—	2.25	—

Date	Mintage	Proof	MS-63	Prf-65
1973	2,000,056	—	11.00	—
1973D	2,000,000	—	11.00	—
1973S	2,769,624	—	—	11.00
1974	27,366,000	—	3.00	—
1974D	35,466,000	—	2.75	—
1974S	—	(2,617,350)	—	6.50

Silver type

KM# 203a • 24.5900 g., **Silver**, 38.1 mm. •
Designer: Frank Gasparro

Date	Mintage	Proof	MS-63	Prf-65
1971S	6,868,530	(4,265,234)	6.00	7.00
1972S	2,193,056	(1,811,631)	7.50	7.00
1973S	1,833,140	(1,005,617)	8.50	30.00
1974S	1,720,000	(1,306,579)	7.50	7.25

Clad type
Bicentennial design,
moon behind Liberty Bell reverse

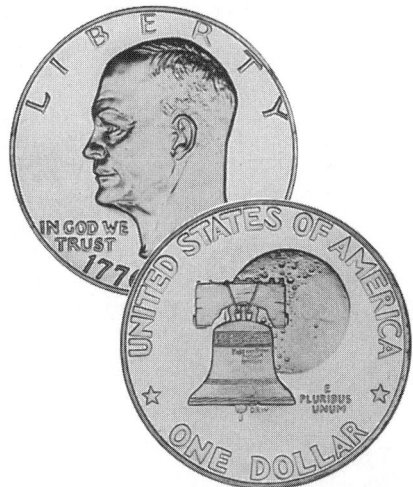

Type I

Type II

KM# 206 • 22.6800 g., **Copper-Nickel Clad
Copper**, 38.1 mm. • **Rev. Designer:** Dennis R.
Williams **Notes:** In 1976 the lettering on the reverse
was changed to thinner letters, resulting in the Type
II variety for that year. The Type I variety was
minted 1975 and dated 1976.

Date	Mintage	Proof	MS-63	Prf-65
1976 type I	117,337,000	—	4.00	—
1976 type II	Inc. above	—	2.00	—
1976D type I	103,228,274	—	3.25	—
1976D type II	Inc. above	—	2.00	—
1976S type I	—	(2,909,369)	—	5.75
1976S type II	—	(4,149,730)	—	5.75

Silver type
Bicentennial design,
moon behind Liberty Bell reverse

KM# 206a • 24.5900 g., 0.4000 **Silver**, 0.3162 oz.
ASW • **Rev. Designer:** Dennis R. Williams

Date	Mintage	Proof	MS-63	Prf-65
1976S	4,908,319	(3,998,621)	14.00	12.50

Clad type
Regular design resumed reverse

KM# A203 • **Copper-Nickel Clad Copper**,
38.1 mm. •

Date	Mintage	Proof	MS-63	Prf-65
1977	12,596,000	—	4.25	—
1977D	32,983,006	—	3.25	—
1977S	—	(3,251,152)	—	8.00
1978	25,702,000	—	2.75	—
1978D	33,012,890	—	3.00	—
1978S	—	(3,127,788)	—	10.00

Susan B. Anthony Dollar

Susan B. Anthony bust right. Obverse
Eagle landing on moon, symbolic of
Apollo manned moon landing reverse

KM# 207 • 8.1000 g., **Copper-Nickel Clad
Copper**, 0 oz., 26.5 mm. • **Designer:** Frank
Gasparro **Edge Desc:** Reeded **Notes:** The 1979-S
and 1981-S Type II coins have a clearer mint mark
than the Type I varieties for those years.

Date	Mintage	MS-63	Prf-65
1979P	360,222,000	2.00	—
1979P Near date	Inc. above	12.00	—
1979D	288,015,744	1.75	—
1979S	109,576,000	2.00	—
1979S Proof, Type I	(3,677,175)	—	8.00
1979S Proof, Type II	Inc. above	—	110
1980P	27,610,000	2.00	—
1980D	41,628,708	2.00	—
1980S	20,422,000	2.00	—
1980S Proof	3,547,030	—	8.00
1981P	3,000,000	5.75	—
1981D	3,250,000	5.75	—
1981S	3,492,000	6.00	—
1981S Proof, Type I	4,063,083	—	8.00
1981S Proof, Type II	Inc. above	—	230
1999P	29,592,000	1.50	—
1999D	11,776,000	1.75	—
1999P Proof; *maximum mintage	(750,000)	—	25.00

Sacagawea Dollar

Sacagawea bust right, with baby on back
obverse. Eagle in flight left reverse

KM# 310 • 8.0700 g., **Copper-Zinc-Manganese-
Nickel Clad Copper**, 26.4 mm. •

Date	Mintage	MS-63	Prf-65
2000P	767,140,000	2.00	—
2000D	518,916,000	2.00	—
2000S	(4,048,865)	—	10.00
2001P	62,468,000	4.00	—
2001D	70,909,500	4.00	—
2001S	(3,084,600)	—	100.00
2002P	3,865,610	2.00	—

Date	Mintage	MS-63	Prf-65	Date	Mintage	MS-63	Prf-65
2002D	3,732,000	2.00	—	2003D	3,090,000	2.50	—
2002S	(3,157,739)	—	28.50	2003S	(3,116,590)	—	20.00
2003P	3,090,000	2.50	—	2004S	—	—	22.50

ONE DOLLAR GOLD

Liberty Head - Type 1

KM# 73 • 1.6720 g., 0.9000 **Gold**, 0.0484 oz. AGW, 13 mm. • **Designer:** James B. Longacre **Notes:** On the "closed wreath" varieties of 1849, the wreath on the reverse extends closer to the numeral 1.

Date	Mintage	F-12	VF-20	XF-40	AU-50	MS-60
1849 open wreath	688,567	100.00	140	190	225	450
1849 closed wreath	Inc. above	100.00	135	185	210	365
1849C closed wreath	11,634	800	950	1,250	1,900	8,000
1849C open wreath	Inc. above	—	—	—	—	—
1849D open wreath	21,588	950	1,150	1,600	1,950	5,000
1849O open wreath	215,000	120	150	230	310	700
1850	481,953	100.00	135	190	200	340
1850C	6,966	800	950	1,250	2,250	7,500
1850D	8,382	950	1,150	1,650	2,600	8,500
1850O	14,000	185	245	350	725	2,700
1851	3,317,671	100.00	135	190	200	250
1851C	41,267	800	950	1,250	1,600	4,900
1851D	9,882	950	1,150	1,600	2,000	5,400
1851O	290,000	135	160	200	230	725
1852	2,045,351	100.00	135	190	200	245
1852C	9,434	800	950	1,250	1,600	3,800
1852D	6,360	950	1,150	1,600	2,150	8,500
1852O	140,000	115	140	230	320	1,100
1853	4,076,051	100.00	135	190	200	245
1853C	11,515	800	950	1,250	1,750	5,000
1853D	6,583	950	1,150	1,600	2,400	8,500
1853O	290,000	130	160	210	225	600
1854	736,709	100.00	135	190	200	250
1854D	2,935	950	1,150	2,000	5,300	11,000
1854S	14,632	245	290	420	700	2,100

Indian Head - Type 2

KM# 83 • 1.6720 g., 0.9000 **Gold**, 0.0484 oz. AGW, 15 mm. • **Designer:** James B. Longacre

Date	Mintage	F-12	VF-20	XF-40	AU-50	MS-60
1854	902,736	210	280	415	550	3,300
1855	758,269	210	280	415	550	3,300
1855C	9,803	800	1,100	3,000	8,500	24,500
1855D	1,811	3,000	4,250	8,250	22,000	48,000
1855O	55,000	330	400	540	1,250	6,750
1856S	24,600	440	725	1,200	2,200	7,700

Indian Head - Type 3

KM# 86 • 1.6720 g., 0.9000 **Gold**, 0.0484 oz. AGW, 15 mm. • **Designer:** James B. Longacre **Notes:** The 1856 varieties are distinguished by whether the 5 in the date is slanted or upright. The 1873 varieties are distinguished by the amount of space between the upper left and lower left serifs in the 3.

Date	Mintage	F-12	VF-20	XF-40	AU-50	MS-60	Prf-65
1856 upright 5	1,762,936	125	145	195	225	465	—
1856 slanted 5	Inc. above	130	140	190	210	260	50,000
1856D	1,460	2,200	3,400	5,400	7,500	30,000	—
1857	774,789	110	135	190	210	260	31,000
1857C	13,280	800	950	1,400	2,750	10,500	—
1857D	3,533	950	1,150	1,750	3,650	10,000	—

Date	Mintage	F-12	VF-20	XF-40	AU-50	MS-60	Prf-65
1857S	10,000	250	500	600	1,100	5,600	—
1858	117,995	110	135	190	215	265	27,500
1858D	3,477	950	1,150	1,500	2,750	10,000	—
1858S	10,000	280	375	500	1,150	5,000	—
1859	168,244	110	135	190	205	260	16,000
1859C	5,235	800	950	1,500	3,100	9,000	—
1859D	4,952	950	1,150	1,500	2,850	10,000	—
1859S	15,000	185	225	480	1,000	5,000	—
1860	36,668	110	135	190	205	280	14,500
1860D	1,566	2,000	2,500	3,800	6,000	15,000	—
1860S	13,000	280	325	465	700	2,250	—
1861	527,499	110	135	190	205	265	13,500
1861D mintage unrecorded	—	4,600	6,400	9,000	16,500	28,000	—
1862	1,361,390	110	135	190	205	260	14,500
1863	6,250	370	425	825	1,600	3,650	16,500
1864	5,950	270	350	440	750	950	16,000
1865	3,725	270	350	550	700	1,450	16,000
1866	7,130	275	360	425	650	900	16,000
1867	5,250	300	400	485	600	1,100	16,000
1868	10,525	250	275	400	465	900	16,500
1869	5,925	315	335	520	800	1,000	15,000
1870	6,335	245	270	385	475	850	14,000
1870S	3,000	280	440	725	1,100	2,150	—
1871	3,930	245	270	365	450	700	16,500
1872	3,530	245	275	350	440	850	16,500
1873 closed 3	125,125	300	400	750	900	1,600	—
1873 open 3	Inc. above	110	135	190	200	260	—
1874	198,820	110	135	190	200	260	16,500
1875	420	1,600	1,850	3,650	4,700	5,900	32,500
1876	3,245	220	275	345	440	600	15,500
1877	3,920	140	175	330	440	900	16,500
1878	3,020	175	200	350	450	600	14,000
1879	3,030	160	180	270	315	500	12,500
1880	1,636	140	160	200	225	440	12,500
1881	7,707	140	160	200	225	425	10,500
1882	5,125	150	170	200	225	425	8,500
1883	11,007	140	160	200	225	425	8,500
1884	6,236	135	150	200	225	415	8,500
1885	12,261	140	160	200	225	400	8,500
1886	6,016	140	160	200	225	400	8,500
1887	8,543	140	160	200	225	400	8,500
1888	16,580	140	160	200	225	400	8,500
1889	30,729	140	160	200	225	400	8,500

$2.50 (QUARTER EAGLE) GOLD

Liberty Cap

KM# 27 • 4.3700 g., 0.9160 **Gold**, 0.1289 oz. AGW, 20 mm. • **Designer:** Robert Scot **Notes:** The 1796 "no stars" variety does not have stars on the obverse. The 1804 varieties are distinguished by the number of stars on the obverse.

Date	Mintage	F-12	VF-20	XF-40	MS-60
1796 no stars	963	25,000	37,500	70,000	110,000
1796 stars	432	22,500	33,500	60,000	140,000
1797	427	14,000	16,500	21,500	100,000
1798	1,094	4,350	6,250	7,750	49,000
1802/1	3,035	4,350	6,250	7,500	20,000
1804 13-star reverse	3,327	23,500	31,250	70,000	200,000
1804 14-star reverse	Inc. above	4,350	6,250	7,250	20,000
1805	1,781	4,350	6,250	7,250	20,000
1806/4	1,616	4,500	6,350	7,500	21,000
1806/5	Inc. above	5,600	8,000	11,500	70,000
1807	6,812	4,350	6,250	7,250	18,500

Turban Head

KM# 40 • 4.3700 g., 0.9160 **Gold**, 0.1289 oz. AGW, 20 mm. • **Designer:** John Reich

Date	Mintage	F-12	VF-20	XF-40	MS-60
1808	2,710	22,500	28,000	34,000	80,000

KM# 46 • 4.3700 g., 0.9160 **Gold**, 0.1289 oz. AGW, 18.5 mm. • **Designer:** John Reich

Date	Mintage	F-12	VF-20	XF-40	MS-60
1821	6,448	5,000	6,250	7,500	20,000
1824/21	2,600	5,000	6,250	7,250	18,500
1825	4,434	5,000	6,250	7,250	15,500
1826/25	760	5,250	6,500	8,000	31,500
1827	2,800	5,350	7,000	8,500	19,000

KM# 49 • 4.3700 g., 0.9160 **Gold**, 0.1289 oz. AGW, 18.2 mm. • **Designer:** John Reich

Date	Mintage	F-12	VF-20	XF-40	MS-60
1829	3,403	4,600	5,500	6,500	12,500
1830	4,540	4,600	5,500	6,500	12,500
1831	4,520	4,600	5,500	6,500	12,500
1832	4,400	4,600	5,500	6,500	12,500
1833	4,160	4,600	5,500	6,600	12,750
1834	4,000	7,000	9,750	15,500	33,500

Classic Head

KM# 56 • 4.1800 g., 0.8990 **Gold**, 0.1209 oz. AGW, 18.2 mm. • **Designer:** William Kneass

Date	Mintage	VF-20	XF-40	AU-50	MS-60	MS-65
1834	112,234	325	465	700	2,000	24,000
1835	131,402	325	465	700	2,250	31,000
1836	547,986	325	465	700	2,000	27,500
1837	45,080	415	650	1,175	3,250	32,500
1838	47,030	325	465	800	2,000	27,000
1838C	7,880	1,200	2,000	6,100	23,500	50,000
1839	27,021	360	650	1,440	4,250	—
1839C	18,140	1,100	2,200	3,500	22,500	—
1839D	13,674	1,125	2,800	6,000	21,000	—
1839O	17,781	500	925	1,500	5,600	—

Coronet Head

1848 'Cal.' reverse

KM# 72 • 4.1800 g., 0.9000 **Gold**, 0.121 oz. AGW, 18 mm. • **Designer:** Christian Gobrecht **Notes:** Varieties for 1843 are distinguished by the size of the numerals in the date. One 1848 variety has "Cal." inscribed on the reverse, indicating it was made from California gold. The 1873 "closed-3" and "open-3" varieties are distinguished by the amount of space between the upper left and lower left serifs in the 3 in the date.

Date	Mintage	F-12	VF-20	XF-40	AU-50	MS-60	Prf-65
1840	18,859	150	180	850	2,950	6,000	—
1840C	12,822	650	1,100	1,600	4,700	13,000	—
1840D	3,532	800	2,400	8,000	15,500	35,000	—
1840O	33,580	225	270	800	1,700	10,000	—
1841	—	—	50,000	90,000	95,000	—	—
1841C	10,281	650	1,100	1,600	3,250	18,500	—
1841D	4,164	850	1,650	3,850	9,900	25,000	—
1842	2,823	500	900	2,900	6,500	20,000	140,000
1842C	6,729	700	1,300	2,800	7,500	27,000	—
1842D	4,643	900	1,650	3,350	11,750	36,500	—
1842O	19,800	220	350	1,100	2,400	11,000	—
1843	100,546	150	170	220	325	1,150	140,000
1843C small date	26,064	1,100	2,150	5,000	8,400	22,000	—
1843C large date	Inc. above	600	1,100	1,600	3,100	8,500	—
1843D small date	36,209	700	1,250	1,850	2,750	9,500	—
1843O small date	288,002	150	180	240	350	1,600	—
1843O large date	76,000	200	250	450	1,600	7,000	—
1844	6,784	225	400	850	1,900	7,250	140,000
1844C	11,622	600	1,100	1,850	6,250	19,000	—
1844D	17,332	650	1,250	1,850	2,650	7,800	—
1845	91,051	180	245	300	440	1,150	140,000
1845D	19,460	650	1,250	1,850	2,750	13,000	—
1845O	4,000	525	950	2,000	5,900	16,000	—
1846	21,598	200	275	500	850	5,500	140,000
1846C	4,808	650	1,250	3,500	8,500	18,750	—
1846D	19,303	650	1,250	1,850	2,500	10,500	—
1846O	66,000	170	280	400	1,050	6,100	—
1847	29,814	140	220	360	825	3,400	—
1847C	23,226	600	1,100	1,600	2,300	6,500	—
1847D	15,784	650	1,250	1,850	2,500	10,000	—
1847O	124,000	150	220	375	1,000	3,500	—
1848	7,497	315	500	850	1,700	6,000	125,000
1848 "Cal."	1,389	6,000	10,000	20,000	29,000	40,000	—
1848C	16,788	600	1,100	1,650	2,800	14,000	—
1848D	13,771	650	1,250	1,850	2,750	10,000	—
1849	23,294	200	275	475	900	2,500	—
1849C	10,220	600	1,100	1,750	5,000	23,500	—
1849D	10,945	650	1,250	1,850	3,500	16,000	—
1850	252,923	140	170	215	350	1,100	—
1850C	9,148	600	1,100	1,600	2,400	17,500	—
1850D	12,148	650	1,250	1,850	3,150	11,500	—
1850O	84,000	160	225	450	1,150	4,750	—
1851	1,372,748	135	170	200	225	325	—
1851C	14,923	600	1,100	1,600	4,400	12,000	—
1851D	11,264	650	1,250	1,850	3,800	12,000	—
1851O	148,000	140	185	215	900	4,650	—
1852	1,159,681	135	170	200	225	325	—
1852C	9,772	600	1,100	1,700	4,250	19,000	—
1852D	4,078	700	1,300	2,550	7,250	17,000	—
1852O	140,000	145	185	300	950	5,000	—
1853	1,404,668	135	170	200	225	350	—
1853D	3,178	950	1,700	3,250	4,900	18,500	—
1854	596,258	135	170	200	225	350	—
1854C	7,295	600	1,100	2,000	5,000	14,750	—
1854D	1,760	1,750	2,750	5,000	11,000	27,500	—
1854O	153,000	140	170	215	415	1,500	—
1854S	246	32,500	43,500	80,000	185,000	300,000	—
1855	235,480	135	170	200	225	350	—
1855C	3,677	700	1,350	3,000	6,000	25,000	—
1855D	1,123	1,750	3,250	7,500	18,500	48,500	—
1856	384,240	135	170	200	225	380	9,500
1856C	7,913	650	1,150	2,200	4,400	15,500	—
1856D	874	3,500	6,400	9,800	2,500	72,500	—
1856O	21,100	150	200	700	1,250	7,700	—
1856S	71,120	145	195	360	900	4,400	—
1857	214,130	135	170	200	225	380	78,000
1857D	2,364	650	1,250	2,500	3,750	13,000	—
1857O	34,000	145	195	350	1,000	4,400	—
1857S	69,200	145	195	330	850	5,500	—
1858	47,377	135	170	235	350	1,250	62,500
1858C	9,056	600	1,100	1,600	2,900	9,250	—
1859	39,444	135	170	250	400	1,250	62,500
1859D	2,244	900	1,650	2,900	4,750	20,000	—
1859S	15,200	180	425	900	2,500	6,500	—
1860	22,675	135	170	245	450	1,100	33,500
1860C	7,469	600	1,100	1,800	3,650	22,500	—
1860S	35,600	160	250	675	1,150	4,000	—

Date	Mintage	F-12	VF-20	XF-40	AU-50	MS-60	Prf-65
1861	1,283,878	135	170	200	230	325	33,000
1861S	24,000	175	350	900	2,900	7,250	—
1862	98,543	145	190	300	500	1,250	33,000
1862/1	Inc. above	450	900	1,750	3,300	8,000	—
1862S	8,000	400	850	2,100	4,250	17,000	—
1863	30	—	—	—	—	—	80,000
1863S	10,800	300	500	1,500	3,200	13,500	—
1864	2,874	2,500	5,500	11,000	22,000	37,500	27,000
1865	1,545	2,400	4,650	7,250	19,000	36,500	31,500
1865S	23,376	150	215	610	1,200	4,400	—
1866	3,110	650	1,200	3,500	6,000	11,500	25,000
1866S	38,960	170	300	650	1,500	6,250	—
1867	3,250	185	365	800	1,150	4,800	27,000
1867S	28,000	150	250	600	1,600	4,000	—
1868	3,625	170	220	400	650	1,600	27,000
1868S	34,000	135	190	290	1,000	4,000	—
1869	4,345	150	230	450	715	3,000	23,000
1869S	29,500	135	215	440	775	5,000	—
1870	4,555	150	220	400	725	3,650	23,500
1870S	16,000	135	200	400	750	4,750	—
1871	5,350	150	230	325	575	2,200	23,500
1871S	22,000	135	185	275	525	2,200	—
1872	3,030	200	400	750	1,000	4,650	22,000
1872S	18,000	135	190	400	900	4,300	—
1873 closed 3	178,025	135	170	200	250	515	22,500
1873 open 3	Inc. above	135	165	195	240	285	—
1873S	27,000	135	225	400	850	2,750	—
1874	3,940	150	240	365	700	2,100	33,000
1875	420	1,750	3,500	5,000	8,000	12,500	43,500
1875S	11,600	135	180	300	750	3,350	—
1876	4,221	160	275	6,400	900	3,300	21,000
1876S	5,000	145	225	500	950	3,300	—
1877	1,652	250	380	750	1,050	3,000	21,500
1877S	35,400	135	160	195	230	615	—
1878	286,260	135	160	195	225	275	34,000
1878S	178,000	135	160	195	225	340	—
1879	88,990	135	160	195	225	275	21,500
1879S	43,500	135	195	275	525	215	—
1880	2,996	160	200	335	600	1,300	21,000
1881	691	850	1,850	2,800	4,350	9,000	19,000
1882	4,067	150	210	290	400	675	15,000
1883	2,002	150	220	440	975	2,300	15,500
1884	2,023	150	210	400	590	1,500	16,000
1885	887	400	700	1,750	2,350	4,400	15,500
1886	4,088	150	190	260	425	1,100	16,500
1887	6,282	150	175	245	325	700	16,500
1888	16,098	140	165	225	270	325	15,000
1889	17,648	150	165	200	250	325	17,500
1890	8,813	150	180	225	280	500	14,000
1891	11,040	150	165	200	230	400	14,000
1892	2,545	155	175	235	325	725	15,000
1893	30,106	145	165	190	225	280	14,000
1894	4,122	155	170	225	325	750	13,500
1895	6,199	135	160	205	275	395	12,500
1896	19,202	135	160	195	225	285	12,500
1897	29,904	135	160	195	225	285	12,500
1898	24,165	135	160	195	225	285	12,500
1899	27,350	135	160	195	225	285	12,500
1900	67,205	135	160	250	340	425	12,500
1901	91,322	135	160	195	220	275	12,500
1902	133,733	135	160	195	220	275	12,500
1903	201,257	135	160	195	220	275	13,000
1904	160,960	135	160	195	225	275	12,500
1905	217,944	135	160	195	225	275	12,500
1906	176,490	135	160	195	225	275	12,500
1907	336,448	135	160	195	225	275	12,500

Indian Head

KM# 128 • 4.1800 g., 0.9000 **Gold**, 0.121 oz. AGW, 18 mm. • **Designer:** Bela Lyon Pratt

Date	Mintage	VF-20	XF-40	AU-50	MS-60	MS-63	MS-65	Prf-65
1908	565,057	165	200	225	285	1,750	7,600	16,000

1911-D $2.50 Gold
Grade MS-60

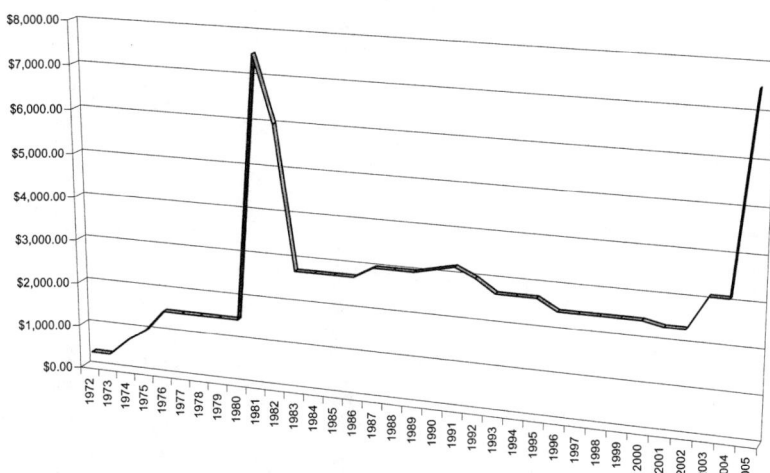

Retail Price

Date	Mintage	VF-20	XF-40	AU-50	MS-60	MS-63	MS-65	Prf-65
1909	441,899	165	200	225	275	2,300	9,600	30,000
1910	492,682	165	200	225	265	2,300	10,000	18,000
1911	704,191	165	200	225	275	1,725	10,500	16,000
1911D	55,680	2,100	2,700	3,400	7,500	25,000	95,000	16,000
1912	616,197	165	200	225	275	2,600	14,500	16,000
1913	722,165	165	200	225	280	1,725	12,500	16,500
1914	240,117	165	210	235	450	8,000	22,000	16,500
1914D	448,000	165	200	225	300	2,500	28,000	23,000
1915	606,100	165	200	225	260	1,650	10,750	15,250
1925D	578,000	165	200	225	260	1,450	7,600	—
1926	446,000	165	200	225	260	1,450	7,600	—
1927	388,000	165	200	225	260	1,450	7,600	—
1928	416,000	165	200	225	260	1,450	7,600	—
1929	532,000	165	200	225	260	1,450	9,350	—

$3 GOLD

KM# 84 • 5.0150 g., 0.9000 **Gold**, 0.1452 oz. AGW, 20.5 mm. • **Designer:** James B. Longacre **Notes:** The 1873 "closed-3" and "open-3" varieties are distinguished by the amount of space between the upper left and lower left serifs of the 3 in the date.

Date	Mintage	VF-20	XF-40	AU-50	MS-60	MS-65	Prf-65
1854	138,618	675	1,000	1,350	2,450	15,500	125,000
1854D	1,120	8,000	14,000	25,500	65,000	—	—
1854O	24,000	950	1,750	3,000	16,500	55,000	—
1855	50,555	700	1,000	1,300	2,400	30,000	125,000
1855S	6,600	1,000	2,000	5,000	22,000	—	—
1856	26,010	700	1,000	1,400	2,400	27,000	85,000
1856S	34,500	750	1,150	2,000	9,000	50,000	—
1857	20,891	700	1,000	1,400	3,000	32,500	62,500
1857S	14,000	800	1,750	4,500	15,500	—	—
1858	2,133	800	1,450	2,600	7,000	35,000	62,500
1859	15,638	700	1,000	1,400	2,550	18,500	45,000
1860	7,155	750	1,000	1,400	3,150	21,000	46,000
1860S	7,000	850	1,550	6,100	14,000	—	—

Date	Mintage	VF-20	XF-40	AU-50	MS-60	MS-65	Prf-65
1861	6,072	750	1,025	1,600	3,300	27,000	46,000
1862	5,785	750	1,000	1,600	3,300	28,000	46,500
1863	5,039	800	1,150	1,600	3,400	20,000	40,000
1864	2,680	800	1,050	1,600	3,300	29,000	40,000
1865	1,165	1,150	2,200	4,500	7,500	40,000	40,000
1866	4,030	850	1,000	1,600	3,300	27,500	40,000
1867	2,650	850	1,000	1,800	3,350	28,000	40,000
1868	4,875	700	950	1,500	2,800	22,000	38,000
1869	2,525	825	1,000	1,700	3,650	34,500	40,000
1870	3,535	725	1,000	1,750	3,700	40,000	47,000
1870S unique	—	—	—	—	—	—	—
Note: Est. value, $1.25 million, AU50 cleaned, Bass Collection.							
1871	1,330	825	1,000	1,700	3,700	27,500	47,000
1872	2,030	750	1,000	1,500	3,250	35,000	33,000
1873 open 3, proof only	25	3,300	5,000	8,700	—	—	65,000
1873 closed 3, mintage unknown		4,000	6,000	10,000	—	—	40,000
1874	41,820	650	950	1,300	2,300	12,500	38,000
1875 proof only	20	20,000	28,000	47,500	—	—	175,000
1876	45	5,500	10,000	14,000	—	—	50,000
1877	1,488	1,200	2,700	5,000	11,500	67,000	42,000
1878	82,324	650	1,000	1,300	2,500	11,000	47,500
1879	3,030	700	1,000	1,500	2,400	12,000	32,000
1880	1,036	750	1,600	2,000	2,800	15,500	31,000
1881	554	1,200	2,250	4,000	5,250	22,500	25,000
1882	1,576	850	1,000	1,750	3,000	20,000	25,000
1883	989	800	1,300	20,000	3,200	18,000	24,000
1884	1,106	1,150	1,500	2,200	2,750	22,000	24,000
1885	910	1,150	1,500	2,250	3,300	22,500	25,000
1886	1,142	1,100	1,700	2,100	4,000	35,000	24,000
1887	6,160	700	1,000	1,600	2,800	14,000	24,000
1888	5,291	750	1,000	1,500	2,450	13,000	24,000
1889	2,429	725	1,000	1,400	2,500	13,500	24,000

$5 (HALF EAGLE) GOLD

Liberty Cap

KM# 19 • 8.7500 g., 0.9160 **Gold**, 0.258 oz. AGW, 25 mm. • **Designer:** Robert Scot **Notes:** From 1795 through 1798, varieties exist with either a "small eagle" or a "large (heraldic) eagle" on the reverse. After 1798, only the heraldic eagle was used. Two 1797 varieties are distinguished by the size of the 8 in the date. 1806 varieties are distinguished by whether the top of the 6 has a serif.

Date	Mintage	F-12	VF-20	XF-40	MS-60
1795 small eagle	8,707	11,500	17,000	20,000	40,000
1795 large eagle	Inc. above	8,800	13,500	20,000	89,000
1796/95 small eagle	6,196	12,000	17,500	22,500	67,500
1797/95 large eagle	3,609	8,600	12,500	21,000	165,000
1797 15 stars, small eagle	Inc. above	13,500	19,000	33,000	150,000
1797 16 stars, small eagle	Inc. above	12,000	17,500	27,500	137,500
1798 small eagle	—	96,000	165,000	300,000	—
1798 large eagle, small 8	24,867	2,800	3,600	4,900	22,000
1798 large eagle, large 8, 13-star reverse	Inc. above	2,750	3,500	4,500	17,500
1798 large eagle, large 8, 14-star reverse	Inc. above	2,900	3,850	7,000	25,000
1799	7,451	2,850	3,450	4,500	16,500
1800	37,628	2,750	3,300	3,700	8,700
1802/1	53,176	2,750	3,300	3,700	8,700
1803/2	33,506	2,750	3,300	3,700	8,700
1804 small 8	30,475	2,750	3,300	3,700	8,700
1804 large 8	Inc. above	2,750	3,300	3,700	9,600
1805	33,183	2,750	3,300	3,700	8,600
1806 pointed 6	64,093	2,800	3,350	3,750	9,000
1806 round 6	Inc. above	2,750	3,300	3,700	8,600
1807	32,488	2,750	3,300	3,700	8,700

Turban Head
Capped draped bust obverse

KM# 38 • 8.7500 g., 0.9160 **Gold**, 0.258 oz. AGW, 25 mm. • **Designer:** John Reich **Notes:** The 1810 varieties are distinguished by the size of the numerals in the date and the size of the 5 in the "5D." on the reverse. The 1811 varieties are distinguished by the size of the 5 in the "5D." on the reverse.

Date	Mintage	F-12	VF-20	XF-40	MS-60
1807	51,605	2,000	2,400	3,150	6,800
1808	55,578	2,000	2,400	3,150	6,900
1808/7	Inc. above	3,100	3,300	3,750	12,000
1809/8	33,875	2,000	2,400	3,150	6,900
1810 small date, small 5	100,287	9,600	22,500	35,000	102,500
1810 small date, large 5	Inc. above	2,100	2,400	3,200	7,000
1810 large date, small 5	Inc. above	13,500	25,000	37,000	124,000
1810 large date, large 5	Inc. above	2,000	2,400	3,150	6,800
1811 small 5	99,581	2,000	2,400	3,150	6,800
1811 large 5	Inc. above	1,950	2,350	3,100	7,000
1812	58,087	2,000	2,400	3,150	6,800

Capped head obverse

KM# 43 • 8.7500 g., 0.9160 **Gold**, 0.258 oz. AGW, 25 mm. • **Designer:** John Reich **Notes:** 1820 varieties are distinguished by whether the 2 in the date has a curved base or square base and by the size of the letters in the reverse inscriptions. 1832 varieties are distinguished by whether the 2 in the date has a curved base or square base and by the number of stars on the reverse. 1834 varieties are distinguished by whether the 4 has a serif at its far right.

Date	Mintage	F-12	VF-20	XF-40	MS-60
1813	95,428	2,400	2,750	3,400	7,800
1814/13	15,454	2,500	2,800	3,500	9,800
1815	635	—	—	—	—
Note: 1815, private sale, Jan. 1994, MS-61, $150,000					
1818	48,588	2,475	2,750	3,400	8,000
1819	51,723	9,600	16,500	275,000	62,000
1820 curved-base 2, small letters	263,806	2,450	2,800	3,600	10,500
1820 curved-base 2, large letters	Inc. above	2,500	3,000	3,750	20,000
1820 square-base 2	Inc. above	2,450	2,800	3,600	10,500
1821	34,641	5,800	13,500	20,000	72,000
1822 3 known	—	55,000	1,000,000	1,500,000	—
Note: 1822, private sale, 1993, VF-30, $1,000,000.					
1823	14,485	2,500	3,400	4,700	16,000
1824	17,340	5,000	10,000	16,000	38,000
1825/21	29,060	5,150	8,250	12,000	38,000
1825/24	Inc. above	—	—	250,000	350,000
Note: 1825/4, Bowers & Merena, March 1989, XF, $148,500.					
1826	18,069	3,600	7,500	9,300	25,000
1827	24,913	5,600	9,600	12,250	34,000
1828/7	28,029	15,000	27,500	41,000	125,000
Note: 1828/7, Bowers & Merena, June 1989, XF, $20,900.					
1828	Inc. above	5,500	12,500	19,000	65,000
1829 large planchet	57,442	15,000	27,500	50,000	110,000
Note: 1829 large planchet, Superior, July 1985, MS-65, $104,500.					
1829 small planchet	Inc. above	37,500	50,000	82,500	140,000
Note: 1829 small planchet, private sale, 1992 (XF-45), $89,000.					
1830 small "5D."	126,351	14,500	17,500	21,000	40,000
1830 large "5D."	Inc. above	14,500	17,500	21,000	40,000
1831	140,594	14,500	17,500	21,000	42,500
1832 curved-base 2, 12 stars	157,487	45,000	65,000	125,000	—
1832 square-base 2, 13 stars	Inc. above	14,500	17,500	21,000	40,000
1833	193,630	14,500	17,500	21,000	40,000

Date	Mintage	F-12	VF-20	XF-40	MS-60
1834 plain 4	50,141	14,500	17,500	21,000	40,000
1834 crosslet 4	Inc. above	14,500	17,500	21,000	40,000

Classic Head

KM# 57 • 8.3600 g., 0.8990 **Gold**, 0.2418 oz. AGW, 22.5 mm. • **Designer:** William Kneass **Notes:** 1834 varieties are distinguished by whether the 4 has a serif at its far right.

Date	Mintage	VF-20	XF-40	AU-50	MS-60	MS-65
1834 plain 4	658,028	390	550	890	2,850	48,000
1834 crosslet 4	Inc. above	1,650	2,750	5,500	20,000	—
1835	371,534	390	560	960	3,150	70,000
1836	553,147	390	550	890	2,900	70,000
1837	207,121	390	585	1,200	3,500	75,000
1838	286,588	390	5,500	890	3,700	58,000
1838C	17,179	1,900	3,850	12,500	38,500	—
1838D	20,583	1,500	3,400	8,250	23,000	—

Coronet Head
No motto above eagle reverse

KM# 69 • 8.3590 g., 0.9000 **Gold**, 0.242 oz. AGW, 21.6 mm. • **Designer:** Christian Gobrecht **Notes:** Varieties for the 1842 Philadelphia strikes are distinguished by the size of the letters in the reverse inscriptions. Varieties for the 1842-C and -D strikes are distinguished by the size of the numerals in the date. Varieties for the 1843-O strikes are distinguished by the size of the letters in the reverse inscriptions.

Date	Mintage	F-12	VF-20	XF-40	MS-60	Prf-65
1839	118,143	250	275	480	4,000	—
1839/8 curved date	Inc. above	275	325	700	2,250	—
1839C	17,205	700	1,450	2,700	24,000	—
1839D	18,939	700	1,450	2,200	22,000	—
1840	137,382	190	235	360	3,700	—
1840C	18,992	700	1,450	2,600	25,000	—
1840D	22,896	700	1,450	2,000	15,000	—
1840O	40,120	200	325	850	11,000	—
1841	15,833	210	375	1,750	10,500	—
1841C	21,467	650	1,400	1,925	18,500	—
1841D	30,495	700	1,450	1,925	14,500	—
1841O 2 known	50	—	—	—	—	—
1842 small letters	27,578	165	345	1,100	1,375	—
1842 large letters	Inc. above	300	750	2,000	11,000	—
1842C small date	28,184	4,500	9,000	23,000	125,000	—
1842C large date	Inc. above	650	1,400	2,000	18,000	—
1842D small date	59,608	700	1,450	1,925	15,000	—
1842D large date	Inc. above	1,000	2,200	5,800	48,000	—
1842O	16,400	450	1,000	3,000	22,000	—
1843	611,205	170	220	260	1,850	—
1843C	44,201	650	1,375	1,925	12,500	—
1843D	98,452	650	1,450	1,925	12,500	—
1843O small letters	19,075	250	500	1,400	20,000	—
1843O large letters	82,000	175	250	1,125	12,000	—
1844	340,330	150	220	240	2,000	—
1844C	23,631	650	1,375	3,000	22,000	—
1844D	88,982	700	1,450	1,925	11,000	—
1844O	364,600	175	250	375	4,000	—
1845	417,099	150	220	240	2,000	—
1845D	90,629	700	1,450	1,925	12,000	—
1845O	41,000	200	410	750	9,900	—
1846	395,942	150	220	240	2,400	—
1846C	12,995	700	1,450	2,900	22,500	—
1846D	80,294	700	1,450	1,925	12,000	—
1846O	58,000	200	375	960	11,500	—

Date	Mintage	F-12	VF-20	XF-40	MS-60	Prf-65
1847	915,981	150	220	250	1,650	—
1847C	84,151	650	1,375	1,925	13,000	—
1847D	64,405	700	1,450	1,925	10,000	—
1847O	12,000	1,925	7,500	9,600	26,000	—
1848	260,775	150	225	275	1,500	—
1848C	64,472	650	1,375	1,925	19,250	—
1848D	47,465	700	1,450	1,925	14,500	—
1849	133,070	150	220	270	2,750	—
1849C	64,823	650	1,375	1,925	13,500	—
1849D	39,036	700	1,450	1,925	14,000	—
1850	64,491	185	275	600	3,700	—
1850C	63,591	650	1,375	1,925	12,000	—
1850D	43,984	700	1,450	1,925	27,500	—
1851	377,505	150	220	240	2,800	—
1851C	49,176	650	1,375	1,925	16,500	—
1851D	62,710	700	1,450	1,925	15,000	—
1851O	41,000	275	565	1,500	12,000	—
1852	573,901	150	220	245	1,250	—
1852C	72,574	650	1,375	1,925	6,750	—
1852D	91,584	700	1,450	1,925	12,500	—
1853	305,770	150	220	240	1,500	—
1853C	65,571	650	1,375	1,925	8,500	—
1853D	89,678	700	1,450	1,925	10,000	—
1854	160,675	150	220	250	2,000	—
1854C	39,283	650	1,375	1,925	14,000	—
1854D	56,413	700	1,450	1,925	10,500	—
1854O	46,000	200	300	525	8,250	—
1854S	268	—	—	—	—	—
Note: 1854S, Bowers & Merena, Oct. 1982, AU-55, $170,000.						
1855	117,098	140	220	235	1,800	—
1855C	39,788	650	1,375	2,000	15,000	—
1855D	22,432	700	1,450	1,925	16,500	—
1855O	11,100	275	650	2,100	20,000	—
1855S	61,000	200	390	975	15,500	—
1856	197,990	150	220	240	2,300	—
1856C	28,457	650	1,375	1,925	20,000	—
1856D	19,786	700	1,450	1,925	11,000	—
1856O	10,000	330	650	1,250	12,500	—
1856S	105,100	175	300	625	6,900	—
1857	98,188	150	220	240	1,600	123,500
1857C	31,360	650	1,375	1,925	9,000	—
1857D	17,046	700	1,450	1,925	13,000	—
1857O	13,000	325	640	1,400	17,000	—
1857S	87,000	180	300	525	9,600	—
1858	15,136	150	240	550	3,850	190,000
1858C	38,856	650	1,375	1,925	10,000	—

1852-C $5 Gold
Grade MS-60

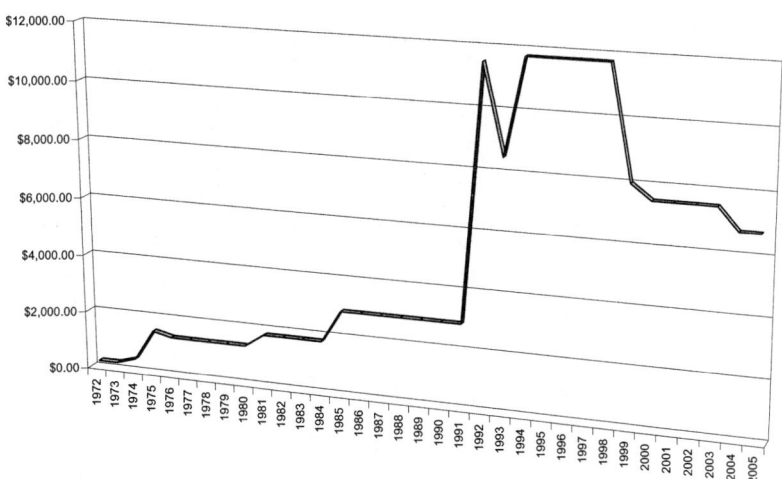

☐ Retail Price

Date	Mintage	F-12	VF-20	XF-40	MS-60	Prf-65
1858D	15,362	700	1,450	1,925	12,500	—
1858S	18,600	300	700	2,350	30,000	—
1859	16,814	185	325	625	7,250	—
1859C	31,847	650	1,375	1,925	15,000	—
1859D	10,366	700	1,450	1,925	14,500	—
1859S	13,220	500	1,250	3,500	29,000	—
1860	19,825	175	275	575	2,700	100,000
1860C	14,813	650	1,375	2,200	15,000	—
1860D	14,635	700	1,450	2,000	17,000	—
1860S	21,200	400	1,100	2,100	25,000	—
1861	688,150	150	220	245	1,200	100,000
1861C	6,879	700	1,850	3,900	25,000	—
1861D	1,597	2,400	4,400	7,000	53,500	—
1861S	18,000	450	1,000	4,500	36,500	—
1862	4,465	300	700	1,850	20,000	96,000
1862S	9,500	1,600	3,000	6,300	62,000	—
1863	2,472	450	1,200	3,750	27,500	90,000
1863S	17,000	600	1,450	3,900	35,500	—
1864	4,220	350	630	1,850	14,500	72,000
1864S	3,888	2,300	5,000	16,000	55,000	—
1865	1,295	500	1,300	4,100	20,000	82,500
1865S	27,612	450	1,300	2,400	20,000	—
1866S	9,000	700	1,650	4,000	40,000	—

"In God We Trust" above eagle reverse

KM# 101 • 8.3590 g., 0.9000 **Gold**, 0.242 oz. AGW, 21.6 mm. • **Designer:** Christian Gobrecht **Notes:** The 1873 "closed-3" and "open-3" varieties are known and are distinguished by the amount of space between the upper left and lower left serifs of the 3 in the date.

Date	Mintage	VF-20	XF-40	AU-50	MS-60	MS-63	MS-65	Prf-65
1866	6,730	800	1,650	3,500	16,500	—	—	70,000
1866S	34,920	900	2,600	8,000	25,000	—	—	—
1867	6,920	500	1,700	3,700	11,500	—	—	70,000
1867S	29,000	1,300	2,700	8,000	34,500	—	—	—
1868	5,725	650	1,000	3,500	11,000	—	—	70,000
1868S	52,000	400	1,550	4,000	20,000	—	—	—
1869	1,785	925	2,400	3,500	17,500	33,500	—	65,000
1869S	31,000	500	1,750	4,000	26,000	—	—	—
1870	4,035	800	2,000	2,850	18,000	—	—	75,000
1870CC	7,675	5,000	13,000	26,000	110,000	137,500	200,000	—
1870S	17,000	950	2,600	8,250	29,000	—	—	—
1871	3,230	950	1,850	3,300	12,500	—	—	70,000
1871CC	20,770	1,100	3,300	11,000	60,000	—	—	—
1871S	25,000	500	1,000	3,150	13,000	—	—	—
1872	1,690	850	1,925	3,000	15,000	20,000	—	60,000
1872CC	16,980	1,100	4,800	20,000	60,000	—	—	—
1872S	36,400	445	800	3,600	13,000	—	—	—
1873 closed 3	49,305	180	225	400	1,175	6,500	24,000	70,000
1873 open 3	63,200	180	215	350	850	3,800	—	—
1873CC	7,416	2,200	12,500	27,500	60,000	—	—	—
1873S	31,000	525	1,400	3,250	22,000	—	—	—
1874	3,508	660	1,675	2,500	12,500	26,000	—	66,000
1874CC	21,198	800	1,700	9,500	38,000	—	—	—
1874S	16,000	640	2,100	4,600	22,500	—	—	—
1875	220	34,000	45,000	60,000	200,000	—	—	185,000
1875CC	11,828	1,400	4,400	11,500	52,000	—	—	—
1875S	9,000	675	2,250	4,800	16,500	32,500	—	—
1876	1,477	1,100	2,500	4,125	11,000	14,500	55,000	60,000
1876CC	6,887	1,200	5,000	14,000	46,500	82,500	165,000	—
1876S	4,000	2,000	3,600	9,500	30,000	—	—	—
1877	1,152	900	2,750	4,000	13,750	29,000	—	75,000
1877CC	8,680	1,000	3,300	11,000	52,500	—	—	—
1877S	26,700	400	650	1,400	9,200	—	—	—
1878	131,740	160	190	240	425	2,000	—	50,000
1878CC	9,054	3,000	7,200	20,000	60,000	—	—	—
1878S	144,700	165	190	3,000	675	4,250	—	—
1879	301,950	165	180	225	400	2,000	12,000	55,000
1879CC	17,281	525	1,375	3,000	2,200	—	—	—
1879S	426,200	180	225	240	825	3,300	—	—
1880	3,166,436	160	175	180	220	840	7,500	54,000
1880CC	51,017	425	770	1,375	9,900	—	—	—

Date	Mintage	VF-20	XF-40	AU-50	MS-60	MS-63	MS-65	Prf-65
1880S	1,348,900	160	175	180	220	800	5,750	—
1881	5,708,802	160	175	180	220	775	4,800	54,000
1881/80	Inc. above	330	600	750	1,500	4,500	—	—
1881CC	13,886	515	1,400	6,750	22,500	60,000	—	—
1881S	969,000	160	175	180	220	775	7,150	—
1882	2,514,568	160	175	180	220	800	6,150	54,000
1882CC	82,817	390	550	800	7,500	40,000	—	—
1882S	969,000	160	175	180	220	800	4,500	—
1883	233,461	160	175	200	260	1,200	—	40,000
1883CC	12,958	450	1,000	3,200	18,000	—	—	—
1883S	83,200	200	240	300	1,000	2,950	—	—
1884	191,078	170	200	220	650	2,250	—	35,000
1884CC	16,402	550	975	3,000	17,000	—	—	—
1884S	177,000	170	200	215	360	2,000	—	—
1885	601,506	160	175	180	220	825	4,800	35,000
1885S	1,211,500	160	175	180	220	790	4,000	—
1886	388,432	160	175	180	230	1,100	5,600	44,000
1886S	3,268,000	160	175	180	220	790	4,500	—
1887	87	—	14,500	20,000	—	—	—	130,000
1887S	1,912,000	160	175	180	220	825	4,800	—
1888	18,296	175	230	300	550	1,550	—	28,000
1888S	293,900	175	200	320	1,200	4,000	—	—
1889	7,565	280	4,400	515	1,100	2,400	—	29,000
1890	4,328	400	475	550	2,200	6,500	—	27,000
1890CC	53,800	330	385	560	1,175	5,000	55,000	—
1891	61,413	170	200	225	450	1,900	5,400	28,000
1891CC	208,000	315	415	525	750	3,150	31,500	—
1892	753,572	160	175	180	220	880	7,000	30,000
1892CC	82,968	315	400	575	1,500	6,000	33,500	—
1892O	10,000	515	1,000	1,375	3,300	—	—	—
1892S	298,400	180	195	220	525	3,300	—	—
1893	1,528,197	160	175	180	220	790	3,900	34,000
1893CC	60,000	315	450	770	1,400	6,350	—	—
1893O	110,000	225	315	480	950	6,500	—	—
1893S	224,000	170	200	210	230	825	9,000	—
1894	957,955	160	175	180	220	790	2,000	35,000
1894O	16,600	200	360	570	1,300	5,500	—	—
1894S	55,900	240	375	575	2,900	10,000	—	—
1895	1,345,936	160	175	180	220	790	4,500	29,000
1895S	112,000	200	275	400	3,150	6,500	26,000	—
1896	59,063	160	175	175	235	9,750	4,500	30,000
1896S	155,400	200	240	300	1,150	6,000	24,500	—
1897	867,883	160	175	180	220	825	4,500	35,000
1897S	354,000	175	210	235	865	5,150	—	—
1898	633,495	160	175	180	225	885	6,000	30,000
1898S	1,397,400	175	200	210	230	950	—	—
1899	1,710,729	160	175	180	220	790	3,600	30,000
1899S	1,545,000	170	180	185	230	1,000	9,600	—
1900	1,405,730	160	175	180	220	790	3,600	30,000
1900S	329,000	170	190	200	230	900	14,000	—
1901	616,040	160	175	180	220	790	3,650	12,500
1901S	3,648,000	160	175	180	220	790	3,600	—
1902	172,562	160	175	180	220	790	4,400	22,000
1902S	939,000	160	175	180	220	790	3,600	—
1903	227,024	160	175	180	220	790	4,000	22,000
1903S	1,855,000	160	175	180	220	790	3,600	—
1904	392,136	160	175	180	220	790	3,600	25,000
1904S	97,000	175	215	285	900	3,850	9,600	—
1905	302,308	160	175	180	220	790	4,000	25,000
1905S	880,700	175	200	235	550	1,500	9,600	—
1906	348,820	160	175	180	220	790	3,600	22,000
1906D	320,000	160	175	180	220	790	400	—
1906S	598,000	165	185	200	230	1,000	4,500	—
1907	626,192	160	175	180	220	790	3,600	23,000
1907D	888,000	160	175	180	220	790	3,600	—
1908	421,874	160	175	180	220	790	3,600	—

Indian Head

KM# 129 • 8.3590 g., 0.9000 **Gold**, .2420 oz. AGW, 21.6 mm. • **Designer:** Bela Lyon Pratt

Date	Mintage	VF-20	XF-40	AU-50	MS-60	MS-63	MS-65	Prf-65
1908	578,012	230	250	275	330	2,000	17,250	25,500
1908D	148,000	230	250	275	330	2,000	27,500	—
1908S	82,000	240	250	480	1,275	3,000	17,750	—
1909	627,138	230	250	275	340	2,000	17,500	36,000
1909D	3,423,560	230	250	275	330	2,000	17,250	—
1909O	34,200	1,100	3,350	4,750	14,500	56,250	260,000	—
1909S	297,200	240	275	315	1,375	10,500	45,000	—
1910	604,250	230	250	275	330	2,000	18,000	37,000
1910D	193,600	230	250	275	380	2,050	42,500	—
1910S	770,200	230	285	315	1,000	5,500	44,000	—
1911	915,139	230	250	275	330	2,000	17,500	28,500
1911D	72,500	450	495	625	4,125	32,000	200,000	—
1911S	1,416,000	240	275	285	560	2,600	41,250	—
1912	790,144	230	250	275	330	2,000	17,500	28,500
1912S	392,000	280	330	360	1,700	13,750	93,500	—
1913	916,099	230	250	275	330	2,000	17,500	28,000
1913S	408,000	250	295	325	1,400	11,500	120,000	—
1914	247,125	230	250	275	350	2,000	17,500	28,500
1914D	247,000	235	250	275	345	2,750	25,000	—
1914S	263,000	275	315	345	1,375	13,750	100,000	—
1915	588,075	230	250	275	330	2,000	17,500	39,000
1915S	164,000	300	410	450	2,000	17,000	110,000	—
1916S	240,000	275	300	330	560	2,750	20,000	—
1929	662,000	3,600	8,250	8,900	9,500	11,000	42,500	—

$10 (EAGLE) GOLD

Liberty Cap
Small eagle reverse

KM# 21 • 17.5000 g., 0.9160 **Gold**, 0.5159 oz. AGW, 33 mm. • **Designer:** Robert Scot

Date	Mintage	F-12	VF-20	XF-40	MS-60
1795 13 leaves	5,583	17,000	22,000	31,500	60,000
1795 9 leaves	Inc. above	22,500	37,500	60,000	190,000
1796	4,146	18,500	24,000	34,500	37,500
1797 small eagle	3,615	24,000	30,000	38,500	185,000

Heraldic eagle reverse

KM# 30 • 17.5000 g., 0.9160 **Gold**, 0.5159 oz. AGW, 33 mm. • **Designer:** Robert Scot **Notes:** The 1798/97 varieties are distinguished by the positioning of the stars on the obverse.

Date	Mintage	F-12	VF-20	XF-40	MS-60
1797 large eagle	10,940	8,250	10,000	12,500	3,150
1798/97 9 stars left, 4 right	900	9,600	14,500	26,500	90,000
1798/97 7 stars left, 6 right	842	17,500	27,500	60,000	—
1799	37,449	7,500	8,900	10,000	20,000
1800	5,999	7,500	8,900	10,000	26,000
1801	44,344	7,500	8,900	10,000	20,000

Date	Mintage	F-12	VF-20	XF-40	MS-60
1803	15,017	7,500	9,000	10,000	21,000
1804	3,757	7,700	9,250	10,250	34,500

Coronet Head
Old-style head obverse   No motto above eagle reverse

KM# 66.1 • 16.7180 g., 0.9000 **Gold**, 0.4839 oz. AGW, 27 mm. • **Designer:** Christian Gobrecht

Date	Mintage	F-12	VF-20	XF-40	MS-60	Prf-65
1838	7,200	800	1,100	2,900	35,500	—
1839 large letters	38,248	800	1,000	1,950	30,000	—

New-style head obverse   No motto above eagle reverse

KM# 66.2 • 16.7180 g., 0.9000 **Gold**, 0.4839 oz. AGW, 27 mm. • **Designer:** Christian Gobrecht **Notes:** The 1842 varieties are distinguished by the size of the numerals in the date.

Date	Mintage	F-12	VF-20	XF-40	MS-60	Prf-65
1839 small letters	Inc. above	800	1,500	3,500	30,000	—
1840	47,338	300	400	650	10,000	—
1841	63,131	300	385	500	9,500	—
1841O	2,500	1,100	2,200	5,000	30,000	—
1842 small date	81,507	275	375	650	16,500	—
1842 large date	Inc. above	250	325	475	9,200	—
1842O	27,400	250	370	500	22,500	—
1843	75,462	250	370	500	19,000	—
1843O	175,162	250	370	475	11,500	—
1844	6,361	800	1,350	2,700	16,750	—
1844O	118,700	245	325	475	15,000	—
1845	26,153	290	600	775	14,000	—
1845O	47,500	250	380	650	16,500	—
1846	20,095	410	625	900	20,000	—
1846O	81,780	250	425	770	14,750	—
1847	862,258	240	300	350	3,000	—
1847O	571,500	250	325	375	4,850	—
1848	145,484	260	340	375	4,300	—
1848O	38,850	325	525	1,050	14,000	—
1849	653,618	240	300	350	3,400	—
1849O	23,900	375	710	2,100	21,000	—
1850	291,451	240	300	380	3,600	—
1850O	57,500	285	380	880	—	—
1851	176,328	275	325	475	5,150	—
1851O	263,000	250	315	440	5,750	—
1852	263,106	240	300	350	4,200	—
1852O	18,000	375	650	1,100	19,000	—
1853	201,253	240	300	350	3,500	—
1853O	51,000	285	325	485	12,500	—
1854	54,250	290	320	400	6,000	—
1854O small date	52,500	290	375	675	10,500	—
1854O large date	Inc. above	375	475	875	—	—
1854S	123,826	275	325	410	5,500	—
1855	121,701	250	300	350	4,150	—
1855O	18,000	400	625	1,250	20,000	—
1855S	9,000	700	1,250	2,100	29,500	—
1856	60,490	250	300	350	4,200	—
1856O	14,500	375	725	1,250	9,800	—
1856S	68,000	250	320	500	8,500	—
1857	16,606	325	490	850	12,000	—
1857O	5,500	600	975	1,850	18,000	—

1853 $10 Gold
Grade XF-40

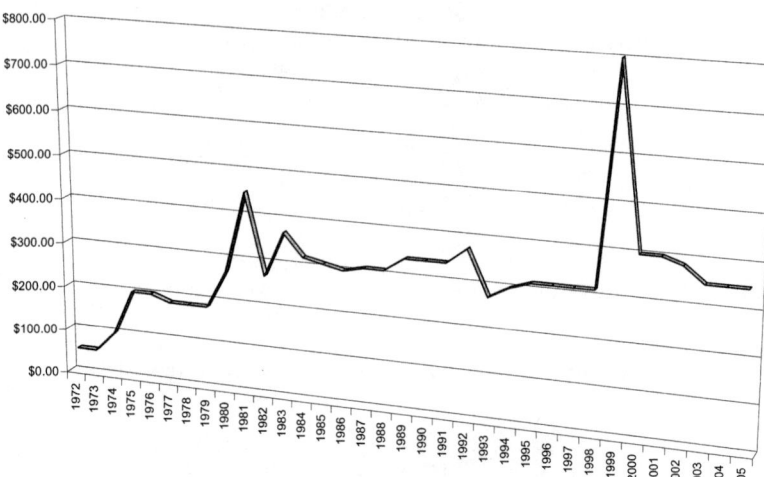

☐ Retail Price

Date	Mintage	F-12	VF-20	XF-40	MS-60	Prf-65
1857S	26,000	300	375	950	9,500	—
1858	2,521	2,600	4,650	7,250	32,000	—
1858O	20,000	300	440	750	9,000	—
1858S	11,800	825	1,450	3,100	34,000	—
1859	16,093	325	390	750	10,500	—
1859O	2,300	1,850	3,800	8,200	47,500	—
1859S	7,000	1,000	1,800	4,500	40,000	—
1860	15,105	300	420	775	8,000	—
1860O	11,100	410	575	1,100	8,250	—
1860S	5,000	1,400	3,250	6,100	40,500	—
1861	113,233	250	300	350	3,600	—
1861S	15,500	690	1,600	2,950	32,500	—
1862	10,995	265	515	1,000	13,500	—
1862S	12,500	675	1,750	2,950	37,000	—
1863	1,248	2,400	3,650	10,000	42,500	—
1863S	10,000	625	1,600	3,350	24,000	—
1864	3,580	775	1,600	4,200	17,500	—
1864S	2,500	2,300	4,900	12,500	50,000	—
1865	4,005	875	1,950	3,500	31,500	—
1865S	16,700	1,700	5,350	10,500	45,000	—
1865S /inverted 186	—	1,250	2,850	6,100	47,000	—
1866S	8,500	950	2,400	3,300	44,000	—

New-style head obverse　"In God We Trust" above eagle reverse

KM# 102 • 16.7180 g., 0.9000 **Gold**, 0.4839 oz. AGW, 27 mm. • **Designer:** Christian Gobrecht **Notes:** The 1873 "closed-3" and "open-3" varieties are distinguished by the amount of space between the upper left and lower left serifs of the 3 in the date.

Date	Mintage	VF-20	XF-40	AU-50	MS-60	MS-63	MS-65	Prf-65
1866	3,780	775	1,650	3,500	15,500	—	—	75,000
1866S	11,500	1,550	3,400	6,400	23,000	—	—	—
1867	3,140	1,500	2,600	4,800	26,000	—	—	75,000
1867S	9,000	2,000	5,200	8,900	40,000	—	—	—
1868	10,655	500	750	1,700	15,000	—	—	60,000
1868S	13,500	1,250	2,100	3,800	24,000	—	—	—

Date	Mintage	VF-20	XF-40	AU-50	MS-60	MS-63	MS-65	Prf-65
1869	1,855	1,400	2,800	5,400	27,500	—	—	—
1869S	6,430	1,500	2,500	6,250	25,000	—	—	—
1870	4,025	800	1,175	2,350	17,000	—	—	60,000
1870CC	5,908	9,000	22,000	42,000	90,000	—	—	—
1870S	8,000	1,100	2,500	6,500	32,000	—	—	—
1871	1,820	1,450	2,400	4,000	19,500	—	—	75,000
1871CC	8,085	2,150	4,950	16,500	53,500	—	—	—
1871S	16,500	1,075	1,500	5,700	26,000	—	—	—
1872	1,650	2,200	3,600	9,500	16,500	32,000	—	60,000
1872CC	4,600	3,000	8,800	20,000	55,000	—	—	—
1872S	17,300	550	850	1,800	22,000	—	—	—
1873 closed 3	825	4,500	9,500	17,500	55,000	—	—	60,000
1873CC	4,543	5,000	12,000	26,000	57,500	—	—	—
1873S	12,000	950	1,950	4,750	24,500	—	—	—
1874	53,160	240	265	315	1,850	8,750	—	60,000
1874CC	16,767	850	2,500	8,000	40,000	—	—	—
1874S	10,000	1,150	3,250	6,800	39,500	—	—	—
1875	120	38,000	53,000	80,000	95,000	—	—	185,000

Note: 1875, Akers, Aug. 1990, Proof, $115,000.

Date	Mintage	VF-20	XF-40	AU-50	MS-60	MS-63	MS-65	Prf-65
1875CC	7,715	3,700	8,800	25,000	65,000	—	—	—
1876	732	3,500	4,750	15,000	55,000	—	—	60,000
1876CC	4,696	3,200	6,500	20,500	50,000	—	—	—
1876S	5,000	1,250	2,000	5,500	38,000	—	—	—
1877	817	2,100	3,800	8,500	—	—	—	—
1877CC	3,332	2,300	4,750	14,000	47,000	—	—	—
1877S	17,000	500	700	2,200	22,500	—	—	—
1878	73,800	220	265	285	900	4,800	—	60,000
1878CC	3,244	3,600	7,500	14,000	47,000	—	—	—
1878S	26,100	450	550	1,650	15,000	—	—	—
1879	384,770	200	220	315	665	2,850	—	50,000
1879/78	Inc. above	300	400	700	800	900	—	—
1879CC	1,762	6,500	12,000	21,750	60,000	—	—	—
1879O	1,500	2,300	3,750	10,000	28,750	—	—	—
1879S	224,000	200	220	250	1,100	7,750	—	—
1880	1,644,876	210	225	250	280	2,250	—	45,000
1880CC	11,190	475	700	1,450	12,500	—	—	—
1880O	9,200	415	700	1,200	12,750	—	—	—
1880S	506,250	200	230	315	415	3,300	—	—
1881	3,877,260	200	225	240	275	800	—	45,000
1881CC	24,015	360	515	950	6,500	18,500	—	—
1881O	8,350	375	650	1,250	6,750	—	—	—
1881S	970,000	200	225	240	350	—	—	—
1882	2,324,480	200	225	240	270	800	—	41,500
1882CC	6,764	950	1,300	3,000	13,000	35,000	—	—
1882O	10,820	375	575	1,200	7,700	16,750	—	—
1882S	132,000	200	230	240	350	4,200	—	—
1883	208,740	200	225	240	300	1,300	—	41,500
1883CC	12,000	425	700	2,350	12,500	35,000	—	—
1883O	800	2,950	6,800	9,500	33,500	—	—	—
1883S	38,000	200	250	340	1,100	6,900	—	—
1884	76,905	190	225	250	750	2,600	—	46,000
1884CC	9,925	600	950	2,250	10,750	34,000	—	—
1884S	124,250	210	220	235	525	6,500	—	—
1885	253,527	210	220	230	375	2,750	—	43,000
1885S	228,000	210	225	250	375	3,600	6,500	—
1886	236,160	210	225	250	375	1,800	—	42,500
1886S	826,000	200	225	250	340	1,000	—	—
1887	53,680	200	225	295	800	3,800	—	37,000
1887S	817,000	200	225	240	315	1,950	—	—
1888	132,996	225	235	315	700	4,500	—	38,500
1888O	21,335	225	250	275	515	4,500	—	—
1888S	648,700	210	225	240	300	1,950	—	—
1889	4,485	575	700	1,100	2,700	6,800	—	43,000
1889S	425,400	210	220	240	350	1,400	4,200	—
1890	58,043	225	275	300	700	3,900	7,750	37,500
1890CC	17,500	385	450	650	2,000	13,500	—	—
1891	91,868	225	250	275	325	1,900	—	32,500
1891CC	103,732	350	400	515	750	4,200	—	—
1892	797,552	210	225	250	285	1,150	12,000	37,500
1892CC	40,000	350	450	625	3,100	8,000	—	—
1892O	28,688	250	275	300	400	2,500	—	—
1892S	115,500	210	220	250	360	2,950	—	—
1893	1,840,895	200	210	235	275	695	—	34,500
1893CC	14,000	425	625	1,450	6,200	14,500	—	—
1893O	17,000	260	315	350	625	5,100	—	—
1893S	141,350	220	230	250	440	2,750	—	—
1894	2,470,778	210	225	250	265	725	11,500	35,000
1894O	107,500	225	260	360	900	4,750	—	—
1894S	25,000	260	385	875	3,500	8,800	—	—

Date	Mintage	VF-20	XF-40	AU-50	MS-60	MS-63	MS-65	Prf-65
1895	567,826	200	210	240	280	775	8,800	33,000
1895O	98,000	220	230	280	480	3,500	—	—
1895S	49,000	225	300	600	2,250	9,000	—	—
1896	76,348	200	220	260	300	1,475	—	31,500
1896S	123,750	215	265	450	2,500	10,500	—	—
1897	1,000,159	200	215	250	285	685	6,500	35,000
1897O	42,500	225	265	335	700	2,000	—	—
1897S	234,750	200	250	335	870	3,300	—	—
1898	812,197	200	215	255	285	900	3,800	35,000
1898S	473,600	205	235	250	350	2,200	—	—
1899	1,262,305	200	220	245	285	650	2,800	31,000
1899O	37,047	230	275	325	550	2,700	—	—
1899S	841,000	200	235	265	320	1,300	—	—
1900	293,960	200	225	230	300	650	7,750	30,500
1900S	81,000	210	275	350	850	3,800	—	—
1901	1,718,825	200	215	240	285	615	2,800	30,500
1901O	72,041	225	250	285	400	1,850	—	—
1901S	2,812,750	200	215	240	285	615	2,500	—
1902	82,513	230	260	295	330	1,175	—	30,500
1902S	469,500	230	250	260	400	615	2,700	—
1903	125,926	215	260	290	315	850	—	30,000
1903O	112,771	225	250	295	375	1,875	—	—
1903S	538,000	200	225	250	290	640	2,650	—
1904	162,038	215	230	260	325	900	—	31,500
1904O	108,950	220	250	285	360	1,975	—	—
1905	201,078	200	220	250	285	850	4,800	30,000
1905S	369,250	210	230	300	1,100	4,500	—	—
1906	165,497	225	230	250	295	950	7,750	30,000
1906D	981,000	230	245	275	325	615	3,850	—
1906O	86,895	235	250	330	450	2,350	—	—
1906S	457,000	220	250	300	475	3,100	12,500	—
1907	1,203,973	195	210	220	275	615	—	30,000
1907D	1,030,000	230	240	250	310	850	—	—
1907S	210,500	240	260	280	600	2,400	—	—

Indian Head
No motto next to eagle reverse

KM# 125 • 16.7180 g., 0.9000 **Gold**, 0.4839 oz. AGW, 27 mm. • **Designer:** Augustus Saint-Gaudens
Notes: 1907 varieties are distinguished by whether the edge is rolled or wired, and whether the legend "E Pluribus Unum" has periods between each word.

Date	Mintage	VF-20	XF-40	AU-50	MS-60	MS-63	MS-65	Prf-65
1907 wire edge, periods before and after legend	500	7,500	12,000	13,000	17,500	23,500	47,000	—
1907 same, without stars on edge, unique	—	—	—	—	—	—	—	—
1907 rolled edge, periods	42	15,000	24,000	27,000	32,500	54,000	95,000	—
1907 without periods	239,406	350	375	400	550	2,500	7,200	—
1908 without motto	33,500	350	390	450	835	4,000	14,000	—
1908D without motto	210,000	335	375	400	700	6,400	40,000	—

"In God We Trust" left of eagle reverse

KM# 130 • 16.7180 g., 0.9000 **Gold**, 0.4839 oz. AGW, 27 mm. • **Designer:** Augustus Saint-Gaudens

Date	Mintage	VF-20	XF-40	AU-50	MS-60	MS-63	MS-65	Prf-65
1908	341,486	315	360	400	475	1,700	5,700	37,000
1908D	836,500	320	360	400	725	6,300	20,000	—

1933 $10 Gold
Grade MS-60

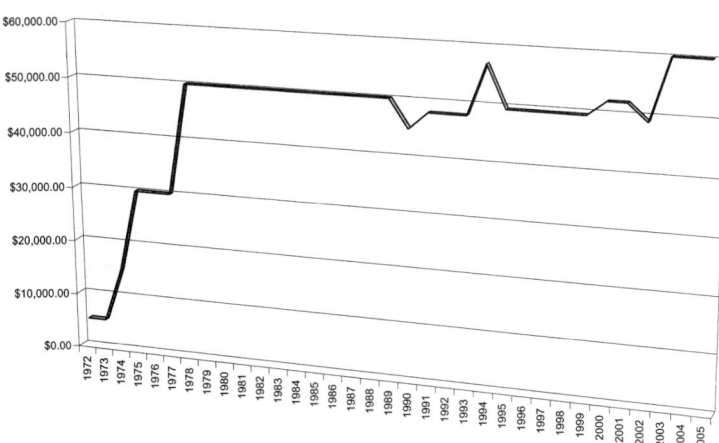

☑ Retail Price

Date	Mintage	VF-20	XF-40	AU-50	MS-60	MS-63	MS-65	Prf-65
1908S	59,850	360	390	400	1,675	5,800	20,000	—
1909	184,863	320	335	400	485	2,150	8,500	43,500
1909D	121,540	320	335	400	575	3,600	48,000	—
1909S	292,350	330	350	400	610	4,000	11,500	—
1910	318,704	335	375	400	480	1,125	5,700	43,500
1910D	2,356,640	330	365	400	465	1,100	5,700	—
1910S	811,000	330	370	400	600	6,000	45,000	—
1911	505,595	325	365	390	480	1,200	6,000	37,500
1911D	30,100	425	725	800	3,900	16,500	100,000	—
1911S	51,000	365	550	640	1,100	6,750	10,500	—
1912	405,083	330	335	400	450	1,200	7,500	37,500
1912S	300,000	330	350	400	715	5,150	48,500	—
1913	442,071	320	335	400	440	1,200	5,400	37,500
1913S	66,000	550	640	800	3,550	25,000	100,000	—
1914	151,050	325	340	390	520	1,700	7,000	37,500
1914D	343,500	320	340	390	545	1,700	10,500	—
1914S	208,000	320	340	390	675	5,400	38,000	—
1915	351,075	320	340	390	530	1,300	6,000	45,000
1915S	59,000	550	700	800	2,900	9,500	60,000	—
1916S	138,500	330	350	415	720	3,600	17,500	—
1920S	126,500	5,000	7,250	8,250	17,000	54,000	195,000	—
1926	1,014,000	290	325	380	415	1,000	4,300	—
1930S	96,000	4,000	6,000	8,000	9,500	17,500	28,000	—
1932	4,463,000	290	325	380	430	615	4,200	—
1933	312,500	10,000	30,000	42,500	60,000	110,000	400,000	—

$20 (DOUBLE EAGLE) GOLD

Liberty
"Twenty D." below eagle. No motto above eagle reverse

KM# 74.1 • 33.4360 g., 0.9000 **Gold**, 0.9677 oz. AGW, 34 mm. • **Designer:** James B. Longacre

Date	Mintage	VF-20	XF-40	AU-50	MS-60	MS-63	MS-65	Prf-65
1849 unique, in Smithsonian collection	1	—	—	—	—	—	—	—
1850	1,170,261	700	1,150	6,000	6,700	46,500	—	—
1850O	141,000	850	1,400	7,500	33,000	—	—	—
1851	2,087,155	650	700	925	3,200	20,000	—	—
1851O	315,000	750	925	1,650	17,000	—	—	—
1852	2,053,026	650	720	900	3,300	13,000	—	—
1852O	190,000	775	925	1,800	15,000	—	—	—
1853	1,261,326	650	720	925	4,400	21,000	—	—
1853O	71,000	750	1,200	2,500	25,000	—	—	—
1854	757,899	650	715	925	5,850	21,000	—	—
1854O	3,250	29,000	57,500	110,000	330,000	—	—	—
1854S	141,468	700	825	1,300	3,800	12,000	40,000	—
1855	364,666	650	725	1,150	8,250	—	—	—
1855O	8,000	2,350	5,750	17,500	75,000	—	—	—
1855S	879,675	650	675	1,100	7,200	15,000	—	—
1856	329,878	675	725	1,150	8,900	22,500	—	—
1856O	2,250	41,500	75,000	120,000	425,000	—	—	—
1856S	1,189,750	650	725	1,150	5,500	11,500	33,000	—
1857	439,375	650	675	900	3,400	26,000	—	—
1857O	30,000	1,050	1,750	4,250	27,500	115,000	—	—
1857S	970,500	650	700	950	4,800	7,150	—	—
1858	211,714	700	925	1,250	4,950	36,000	—	—
1858O	35,250	1,375	2,000	1,800	26,500	—	—	—
1858S	846,710	650	725	1,000	9,250	—	—	—
1859	43,597	960	2,100	4,000	31,500	—	—	—
1859O	9,100	3,400	6,750	17,000	82,500	—	—	—
1859S	636,445	650	675	1,000	4,950	—	—	—
1860	577,670	650	675	950	4,000	20,000	—	—
1860O	6,600	3,200	6,000	17,500	89,000	—	—	—
1860S	544,950	650	675	1,000	6,000	20,000	—	—
1861	2,976,453	650	675	950	2,500	9,500	36,000	—
1861O	17,741	2,400	4,000	13,750	90,000	—	—	—
1861S	768,000	650	720	1,600	8,500	30,000	—	—

Paquet design reverse

KM# 93 • 33.4360 g., 0.9000 **Gold**, 0.9677 oz. AGW • **Notes:** In 1861 the reverse was redesigned by Anthony C. Paquet, but it was withdrawn soon after its release. The letters in the inscriptions on the Paquet-reverse variety are taller than on the regular reverse.

Date	Mintage	VF-20	XF-40	AU-50	MS-60	MS-63	MS-65	Prf-65
1861 2 Known	—	—	—	—	—	—	—	—
Note: 1861 Paquet reverse, Bowers & Merena, Nov. 1988, MS-67, $660,000.								
1861S	—	11,000	22,500	34,000	170,000	—	—	—
Note: Included in mintage of 1861S, KM#74.1								

Longacre design resumed reverse

KM# A74.1 • 33.4360 g., 0.9000 **Gold**, 0.9677 oz. AGW •

Date	Mintage	VF-20	XF-40	AU-50	MS-60	MS-63	MS-65	Prf-65
1862	92,133	925	1,450	2,900	15,500	33,000	—	—
1862S	854,173	650	775	1,600	10,000	—	—	—
1863	142,790	720	880	1,850	17,000	35,000	—	—
1863S	966,570	650	800	1,400	7,500	30,000	—	—
1864	204,285	775	1,000	1,750	14,000	—	—	—
1864S	793,660	650	675	1,700	6,600	—	—	—
1865	351,200	650	700	1,000	6,000	25,000	—	—
1865S	1,042,500	650	715	1,000	4,000	6,600	17,500	—
1866S	Inc. below	1,650	2,850	11,000	60,000	—	—	—

"Twenty D." below eagle. "In God We Trust" above eagle reverse

KM# 74.2 • 33.4360 g., 0.9000 **Gold**, 0.9677 oz. AGW, 34 mm. • **Designer:** James B. Longacre **Notes:** The 1873 "closed-3" and "open-3" varieties are known and are distinguished by the amount of space between the upper left and lower left serif in the 3 in the date.

Date	Mintage	VF-20	XF-40	AU-50	MS-60	MS-63	MS-65	Prf-65
1866	698,775	675	825	1,300	4,800	28,500	—	—
1866S	842,250	625	700	1,250	15,500	—	—	—
1867	251,065	625	650	925	2,400	20,000	—	—
1867S	920,750	625	725	1,600	14,000	—	—	—
1868	98,600	925	1,150	2,000	10,000	40,000	—	—
1868S	837,500	625	750	1,200	8,500	—	—	—
1869	175,155	700	950	1,250	6,000	21,000	—	—
1869S	686,750	625	650	1,100	5,300	30,000	—	—
1870	155,185	750	1,000	1,650	9,000	—	—	—
1870CC	3,789	85,000	115,000	240,000	675,000	—	—	—
1870S	982,000	650	675	925	5,000	24,000	—	—
1871	80,150	825	960	1,500	4,000	26,000	—	—
1871CC	17,387	6,000	9,600	19,000	50,000	—	—	—
1871S	928,000	625	750	750	4,400	22,000	—	—
1872	251,880	650	675	740	2,700	25,000	—	—
1872CC	26,900	1,900	2,400	5,500	27,500	—	—	—
1872S	780,000	625	740	715	3,000	24,000	—	—
1873 closed 3	Est. 208,925	675	800	1,100	2,600	—	—	—
1873 open 3	Est. 1,500,900	625	650	660	990	11,000	—	—
1873CC	22,410	2,250	3,500	6,000	30,000	100,000	—	—
1873S	1,040,600	625	650	660	1,500	21,000	—	—
1874	366,800	625	650	660	1,150	20,000	—	—
1874CC	115,085	1,100	1,500	2,400	8,500	—	—	—
1874S	1,214,000	625	650	660	1,375	26,000	—	—
1875	295,740	625	650	660	1,000	11,000	—	—
1875CC	111,151	1,100	1,300	1,500	2,300	17,500	—	—
1875S	1,230,000	625	650	660	1,000	16,500	—	—
1876	583,905	625	650	660	990	11,500	—	—
1876CC	138,441	1,100	1,300	1,650	4,500	35,000	—	—
1876S	1,597,000	625	650	660	990	11,500	—	—

"Twenty Dollars" below eagle reverse

KM# 74.3 • 33.4360 g., 0.9000 **Gold**, 0.9677 oz. AGW •

Date	Mintage	VF-20	XF-40	AU-50	MS-60	MS-63	MS-65	Prf-65
1877	397,670	585	590	600	825	5,250	—	—
1877CC	42,565	1,250	1,550	2,300	16,500	—	—	—
1877S	1,735,000	585	590	600	750	12,500	—	—
1878	543,645	585	590	600	675	5,600	—	—
1878CC	13,180	2,000	2,800	4,600	26,000	—	—	—
1878S	1,739,000	585	590	600	750	22,000	—	—
1879	207,630	585	590	600	1,000	125,000	—	—
1879CC	10,708	2,000	3,000	5,750	30,000	—	—	—
1879O	2,325	4,500	6,750	15,000	75,000	120,000	—	—
1879S	1,223,800	585	590	600	1,375	—	—	—
1880	51,456	585	590	600	3,000	16,500	—	—

Date	Mintage	VF-20	XF-40	AU-50	MS-60	MS-63	MS-65	Prf-65
1880S	836,000	585	590	600	950	16,000	—	—
1881	2,260	4,500	6,750	13,750	44,000	—	—	105,000
1881S	727,000	585	590	600	850	17,500	—	—
1882	630	7,000	15,000	28,000	66,000	135,000	—	—
1882CC	39,140	1,150	1,375	1,900	6,500	—	—	—
1882S	1,125,000	585	590	600	750	16,000	—	—
1883 proof only	92	—	—	10,000	—	—	—	—
1883CC	59,962	1,100	1,250	1,650	4,000	20,000	—	—
1883S	1,189,000	585	590	600	675	8,500	—	—
1884 proof only	71	—	—	10,000	—	—	—	150,000
1884CC	81,139	1,100	1,300	1,600	2,750	—	—	—
1884S	916,000	585	590	600	675	7,000	—	—
1885	828	6,500	8,500	11,000	35,000	—	—	—
1885CC	9,450	2,100	3,000	5,500	11,000	—	—	—
1885S	683,500	585	590	600	675	7,000	—	—
1886	1,106	8,250	11,500	30,000	45,000	55,000	—	67,000
1887	121	—	—	8,000	—	—	—	85,000
1887S	283,000	585	590	600	675	14,000	—	—
1888	226,266	585	590	600	675	4,500	32,000	—
1888S	859,600	585	590	600	675	5,500	—	—
1889	44,111	625	650	700	750	11,000	—	57,500
1889CC	30,945	1,250	1,450	2,100	3,400	15,000	—	—
1889S	774,700	585	590	600	675	6,750	—	—
1890	75,995	585	590	600	675	5,500	—	27,000
1890CC	91,209	1,100	1,400	1,400	2,300	27,500	—	—
1890S	802,750	585	590	600	675	8,500	—	—
1891	1,442	3,300	5,000	8,500	40,000	—	—	62,500
1891CC	5,000	3,500	5,000	7,500	15,000	44,000	—	—
1891S	1,288,125	585	590	600	650	3,350	—	—
1892	4,523	1,150	1,650	2,600	5,500	18,500	—	55,000
1892CC	27,265	1,200	1,400	2,000	3,300	25,000	—	—
1892S	930,150	585	590	600	650	4,000	—	—
1893	344,339	585	590	600	650	2,400	—	60,000
1893CC	18,402	1,400	1,750	2,000	3,000	15,000	—	—
1893S	996,175	585	590	600	650	3,850	—	—
1894	1,368,990	585	590	600	650	1,500	—	55,000
1894S	1,048,550	585	590	600	650	2,400	—	—
1895	1,114,656	585	590	600	650	1,300	11,500	54,000
1895S	1,143,500	585	590	600	650	2,400	12,500	—
1896	792,663	585	590	600	650	2,000	11,500	49,000
1896S	1,403,925	585	590	600	650	2,150	—	—
1897	1,383,261	585	590	600	650	1,350	—	55,000
1897S	1,470,250	585	590	600	650	1,350	9,600	—
1898	170,470	585	590	625	675	4,800	—	49,000
1898S	2,575,175	585	590	600	650	1,300	12,000	—
1899	1,669,384	585	590	600	650	1,000	8,500	49,000
1899S	2,010,300	585	590	600	650	1,800	12,500	—
1900	1,874,584	585	590	600	650	900	6,000	49,000
1900S	2,459,500	585	590	600	650	2,300	—	—
1901	111,526	585	590	600	650	975	6,000	—
1901S	1,596,000	585	590	600	650	3,850	—	—
1902	31,254	585	590	600	900	10,000	—	—
1902S	1,753,625	585	590	600	650	4,000	—	—
1903	287,428	585	590	600	650	900	6,000	51,500
1903S	954,000	585	590	600	650	1,800	10,000	—
1904	6,256,797	585	590	600	650	900	5,500	50,000
1904S	5,134,175	585	590	600	650	950	6,600	—
1905	59,011	585	590	600	1,000	14,000	—	—
1905S	1,813,000	585	590	600	650	3,850	16,500	—
1906	69,690	585	590	600	650	6,600	15,000	52,500
1906D	620,250	585	590	600	650	2,000	13,000	—
1906S	2,065,750	585	590	600	650	2,300	19,000	—
1907	1,451,864	585	590	600	650	960	7,500	—
1907D	842,250	585	590	600	650	2,000	7,000	—
1907S	2,165,800	585	590	600	650	2,400	13,500	—

1907-S $20 Gold
Grade VF-20

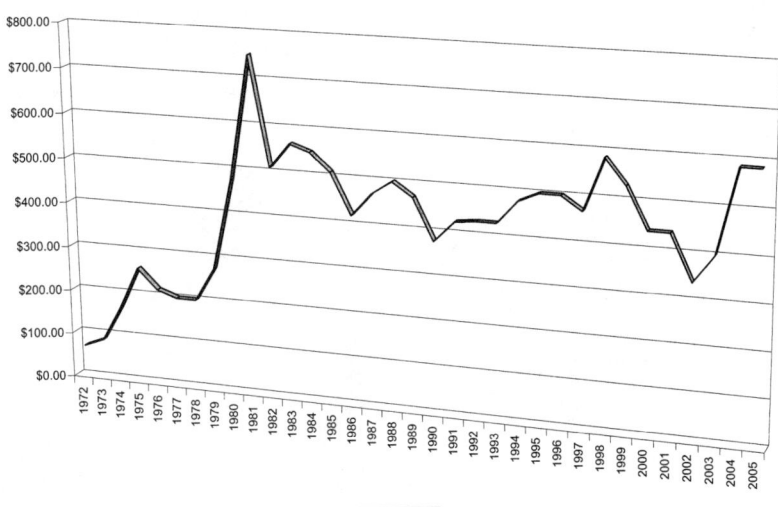

☐ Retail Price

Saint-Gaudens
Roman numerals in date obverse   No motto below eagle reverse

KM# 126 • 33.4360 g., 0.9000 **Gold**, 0.9677 oz. AGW, 34 mm. • **Designer:** Augustus Saint-Gaudens
Edge Desc: Plain.

Date	Mintage	VF-20	XF-40	AU-50	MS-60	MS-63	MS-65	Prf-65
MCMVII (1907) high relief, unique, AU-55, $150,000	—	—	—	—	—	—	—	—
MCMVII (1907) high relief, wire rim	11,250	6,100	6,700	7,900	10,000	17,000	32,500	—
MCMVII (1907) high relief, flat rim	Inc. above	6,250	6,900	8,250	10,500	17,750	35,000	—

Arabic numerals in date obverse   No motto below eagle reverse

KM# 127 • 33.4360 g., 0.9000 **Gold**, 0.9677 oz. AGW, 34 mm. • **Designer:** Augustus Saint-Gaudens
Edge Desc: Lettered; large letters.

Date	Mintage	VF-20	XF-40	AU-50	MS-60	MS-63	MS-65	Prf-65
1907 large letters on edge, unique	—	—	—	—	—	—	—	—

Date	Mintage	VF-20	XF-40	AU-50	MS-60	MS-63	MS-65	Prf-65
1907 small letters on edge	361,667	465	475	485	565	950	2,500	—
1908	4,271,551	455	465	475	560	675	1,200	—
1908D	663,750	460	475	490	565	900	10,500	—

Roman numerals in date obverse   No motto below eagle reverse

KM# Pn1874 • 33.4360 g., 0.9000 **Gold**, 0.9677 oz. AGW, 34 mm. • **Designer:** Augustus Saint-Gaudens
Edge Desc: Plain. **Notes:** The "Roman numerals" varieties for 1907 use Roman numerals for the date instead of Arabic numerals. The lettered-edge varieties have "E Pluribus Unum" on the edge, with stars between the words.

Date	Mintage	VF-20	XF-40	AU-50	MS-60	MS-63	MS-65	Prf-65
1907 extremely high relief, unique	—	—	—	—	—	—	—	—
1907 extremely high relief, lettered edge	—	—	—	—	—	—	—	—

Note: 1907 extremely high relief, lettered edge, Prf-68, private sale, 1990, $1,500,000.

"In God We Trust" below eagle reverse

KM# 131 • 33.4360 g., 0.9000 **Gold**, 0.9677 oz. AGW, 34 mm. • **Designer:** Augustus Saint-Gaudens

Date	Mintage	VF-20	XF-40	AU-50	MS-60	MS-63	MS-65	Prf-65
1908	156,359	465	510	585	595	1,350	20,000	49,500
1908D	349,500	460	470	495	560	990	5,300	—
1908S	22,000	750	1,400	1,750	4,400	11,000	37,500	—
1909/8	161,282	525	580	700	1,150	5,850	29,000	—
1909	Inc. above	470	560	625	775	3,350	37,500	49,000
1909D	52,500	500	690	775	1,200	6,750	35,000	—
1909S	2,774,925	470	485	525	700	1,550	5,750	—
1910	482,167	465	475	510	595	700	7,350	49,000
1910D	429,000	465	475	500	595	700	3,450	—
1910S	2,128,250	460	485	500	610	850	8,850	—
1911	197,350	455	465	495	580	1,850	14,000	39,500
1911D	846,500	455	465	485	565	680	1,600	—
1911S	775,750	460	470	500	600	750	6,200	—
1912	149,824	455	485	495	585	1,200	17,500	44,000
1913	168,838	455	465	495	585	2,750	31,000	44,000

1908-D $20 Gold
Grade MS-60

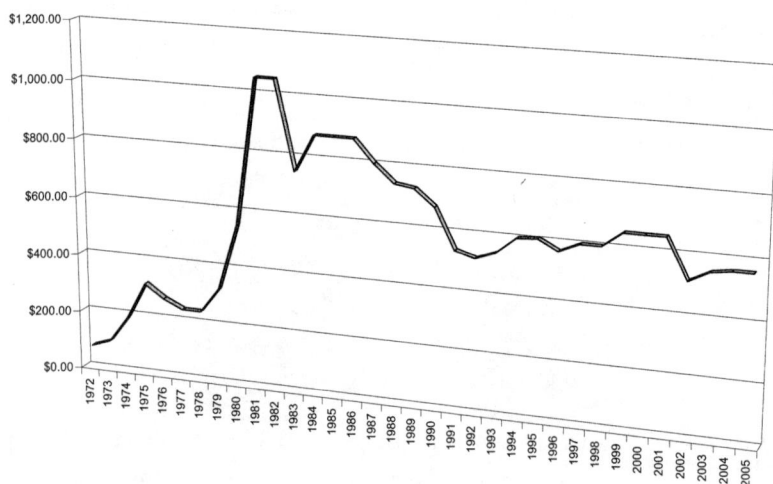

Retail Price

Date	Mintage	VF-20	XF-40	AU-50	MS-60	MS-63	MS-65	Prf-65
1913D	393,500	465	475	495	575	900	6,200	—
1913S	34,000	550	800	840	1,350	3,650	38,500	—
1914	95,320	460	515	530	625	1,650	15,200	41,500
1914D	453,000	465	475	495	585	750	3,250	—
1914S	1,498,000	465	475	495	580	725	2,150	—
1915	152,050	465	485	520	665	2,100	24,500	47,500
1915S	567,500	465	475	485	585	725	2,150	—
1916S	796,000	465	475	495	675	900	2,500	—
1920	228,250	465	475	450	610	825	36,500	—
1920S	558,000	4,950	8,000	10,500	25,000	48,500	185,000	—
1921	528,500	8,000	14,400	20,000	36,000	125,000	285,000	—
1922	1,375,500	455	465	485	560	680	3,900	—
1922S	2,658,000	500	750	800	975	1,450	39,500	—
1923	566,000	455	465	495	545	650	6,250	—
1923D	1,702,250	165	475	495	560	775	1,650	—
1924	4,323,500	455	465	495	545	650	1,500	—
1924D	3,049,500	800	1,325	1,500	2,000	6,200	56,000	—
1924S	2,927,500	750	1,200	1,440	2,600	6,100	36,500	—
1925	2,831,750	455	465	485	545	650	1,550	—
1925D	2,938,500	1,000	1,750	2,300	4,400	8,250	55,000	—
1925S	3,776,500	900	1,350	1,550	5,800	18,500	86,500	—
1926	816,750	455	465	485	545	650	1,575	—
1926D	481,000	1,100	2,850	3,200	7,900	21,000	105,000	—
1926S	2,041,500	700	1,250	1,375	1,850	4,000	35,000	—
1927	2,946,750	455	465	485	545	650	1,550	—
1927D	180,000	—	195,000	245,000	300,000	485,000	785,000	—
1927S	3,107,000	2,500	4,400	4,550	12,500	50,000	105,000	—
1928	8,816,000	455	465	485	550	655	1,550	—
1929	1,779,750	4,750	7,000	8,000	13,000	20,000	35,000	—
1930S	74,000	6,000	8,500	9,300	25,000	44,500	115,000	—
1931	2,938,250	4,850	8,000	9,250	18,500	27,500	52,000	—
1931D	106,500	5,500	8,000	8,500	25,500	32,500	64,500	—
1932	1,101,750	7,000	10,000	11,500	19,000	26,000	44,500	—
1933 Sotheby/Stack Sale, July 2002	445,500	—	—	—	—	—	7,590,000	—

MINT SETS

Mint, or uncirculated, sets contain one uncirculated coin of each denomination from each mint produced for circulation that year. Values listed here are only for those sets sold by the U.S. Mint. Sets were not offered in years not listed. In years when the Mint did not offer the sets, some private companies compiled and marketed uncirculated sets. Mint sets from 1947 through 1958 contained two examples of each coin mounted in cardboard holders, which caused the coins to tarnish. Beginning in 1959, the sets have been packaged in sealed Pliofilm packets and include only one specimen of each coin struck for that year (both P & D mints). Listings for 1965, 1966 and 1967 are for "special mint sets," which were of higher quality than regular mint sets and were prooflike. They were packaged in plastic cases. The 1970 large-date and small-date varieties are distinguished by the size of the date on the coin. The 1976 three-piece set contains the quarter, half dollar and dollar with the Bicentennial design. The 1971 and 1972 sets do not include a dollar coin; the 1979 set does not include an S-mint-marked dollar.

Date	Sets Sold	Issue Price	Value	Date	Sets Sold	Issue Price	Value
1947 Est. 5,000	—	4.87	1,400	1976 3 coins	4,908,319	9.00	18.00
1948 Est. 6,000	—	4.92	650	1976	1,892,513	6.00	10.00
1949 Est. 5,200	—	5.45	940	1977	2,006,869	7.00	7.25
1950 None issued	—	—	—	1978	2,162,609	7.00	8.50
1951	8,654	6.75	1,000	1979	2,526,000	8.00	5.50
1952	11,499	6.14	900	1980	2,815,066	9.00	6.25
1953	15,538	6.14	575	1981	2,908,145	11.00	14.00
1954	25,599	6.19	290	1982 & 1983 None issued	—	—	—
1955	49,656	3.57	175	1984	1,832,857	7.00	6.25
1956	45,475	3.34	165	1985	1,710,571	7.00	7.00
1957	32,324	4.40	285	1986	1,153,536	7.00	20.00
1958	50,314	4.43	160	1987	2,890,758	7.00	6.50
1959	187,000	2.40	56.00	1988	1,646,204	7.00	6.50
1960	260,485	2.40	27.50	1989	1,987,915	7.00	5.50
1961	223,704	2.40	45.00	1990	1,809,184	7.00	6.50
1962	385,285	2.40	19.00	1991	1,352,101	7.00	8.50
1963	606,612	2.40	14.00	1992	1,500,143	7.00	6.50
1964	1,008,108	2.40	11.50	1993	1,297,094	8.00	9.50
1965 Special Mint Set	2,360,000	4.00	12.50	1994	1,234,813	8.00	9.00
1966 Special Mint Set	2,261,583	4.00	14.00	1995	1,038,787	8.00	26.00
1967 Special Mint Set	1,863,344	4.00	21.00	1996	1,457,949	8.00	30.00
1968	2,105,128	2.50	5.50	1997	950,473	8.00	36.00
1969	1,817,392	2.50	6.50	1998	1,187,325	8.00	13.00
1970 large date	2,038,134	2.50	23.00	1999	1,421,625	14.95	31.00
1970 small date	Inc. above	2.50	56.00	2000	1,490,160	14.95	13.50
1971	2,193,396	3.50	6.50	2001	1,066,900	14.95	19.00
1972	2,750,000	3.50	6.25	2002	1,139,388	14.95	13.00
1973	1,767,691	6.00	25.00	2003	1,002,555	14.95	24.50
1974	1,975,981	6.00	7.50	2004	—	16.95	70.00
1975	1,921,488	6.00	11.00				

PROOF SETS

Proof coins are produced through a special process involving specially selected, highly polished planchets and dies. They usually receive two strikings from the coin press at increased pressure. The result is a coin with mirrorlike surfaces and, in recent years, a cameo effect on its raised design surfaces. Proof sets have been sold off and on by the U.S. Mint since 1858. Listings here are for sets from what is commonly called the modern era, since 1936. Values for earlier proofs are included in regular date listings. Sets were not offered in years not listed. Since 1968, proof coins have been produced at the San Francisco Mint; before that they were produced at the Philadelphia Mint. In 1942 the five-cent coin was struck in two compositions. Some proof sets for that year contain only one type (five-coin set); others contain both types. Two types of packaging were used in 1955 -- a box and a flat, plastic holder. The 1960 large-date and small-date sets are distinguished by the size of the date on the cent. Some 1968 sets are missing the mint mark on the dime, the result of an error in the preparation of an obverse die. The 1970 large-date and small-date sets are distinguished by the size of the date on the cent. Some 1970 sets are missing the mint mark on the dime, the result of an error in the preparation of an obverse die. Some 1971 sets are missing the mint mark on the five-cent piece, the result of an error in the preparation of an obverse die. The 1976 three-piece set contains the quarter, half dollar and dollar with the Bicentennial designs. The 1979 and 1981 Type II sets have clearer mint marks than the Type I sets for those years. Some 1983 sets are missing the mint mark on the dime, the result of an error in the preparation of an obverse die. Prestige sets contain the five regular-issue coins plus a commemorative silver dollar from that year.

Date	Sets Sold	Issue Price	Value	Date	Sets Sold	Issue Price	Value
1936	3,837	1.89	8,000	1950	51,386	2.10	785
1937	5,542	1.89	4,400	1951	57,500	2.10	675
1938	8,045	1.89	2,000	1952	81,980	2.10	385
1939	8,795	1.89	1,850	1953	128,800	2.10	335
1940	11,246	1.89	1,550	1954	233,300	2.10	180
1941	15,287	1.89	1,550	1955 box	378,200	2.10	150
1942 6 coins	21,120	1.89	1,550	1955 flat pack	Inc. above	2.10	185
1942 5 coins	Inc. above	1.89	1,400	1956	669,384	2.10	72.50

Date	Sets Sold	Issue Price	Value	Date	Sets Sold	Issue Price	Value
1957	1,247,952	2.10	32.50	1990S Prestige Set, no S 1¢	Inc. above	45.00	8,000
1958	875,652	2.10	78.50	1991S	2,610,833	11.00	13.50
1959	1,149,291	2.10	28.50	1991S Prestige Set	256,954	59.00	85.00
1960 large date	1,691,602	2.10	21.00	1992S	2,675,618	12.00	7.50
1960 small date	Inc. above	2.10	38.50	1992S Prestige Set	183,285	59.00	135
1961	3,028,244	2.10	11.50	1992S Silver	1,009,585	21.00	18.00
1962	3,218,019	2.10	11.50	1992S Silver premier	308,055	37.00	18.00
1963	3,075,645	2.10	15.50	1993S	2,337,819	12.50	13.50
1964	3,950,762	2.10	11.00	1993S Prestige Set	224,045	57.00	62.50
1968S	3,041,509	5.00	7.50	1993S Silver	570,213	21.00	45.00
1968S no mint mark dime	Inc. above	5.00	11,000	1993S Silver premier	191,140	37.00	45.00
1969S	2,934,631	5.00	7.50	1994S	2,308,701	13.00	16.50
1970S large date	2,632,810	5.00	16.00	1994S Prestige Set	175,893	57.00	80.00
1970S small date	Inc. above	5.00	95.00	1994S Silver	636,009	21.00	52.50
1970S no mint mark dime	Inc. above	5.00	1,550	1994S Silver premier	149,320	37.50	52.50
1971S	3,224,138	5.00	6.00	1995S	2,010,384	12.50	73.50
1971S no mint mark nickel				1995S Prestige Set	107,112	57.00	355
Est. 1,655	1,655	5.00	1,350	1995S Silver	549,878	21.00	135
1972S	3,267,667	5.50	4.75	1995S Silver premier	130,107	37.50	135
1973S	2,769,624	7.00	11.00	1996S	2,085,191	16.00	18.50
1974S	2,617,350	7.00	8.00	1996S Prestige Set	55,000	57.00	750
1975S	2,909,369	7.00	13.00	1996S Silver	623,655	21.00	62.50
1975S no mint mark dime	Inc. above	7.00	50,000	1996S Silver premier	151,366	37.50	62.50
1976S 3 coins	3,998,621	12.00	17.50	1997S	1,975,000	12.50	59.00
1976S	4,149,730	7.00	8.50	1997S Prestige Set	80,000	57.00	350
1977S	3,251,152	9.00	8.00	1997S Silver	605,473	21.00	110
1978S	3,127,788	9.00	9.00	1997S Silver premier	136,205	37.50	110
1979S Type I	3,677,175	9.00	8.00	1998S	2,078,494	12.50	31.00
1979S Type II	Inc. above	9.00	135	1998S Silver	638,134	21.00	55.00
1980S	3,547,030	10.00	6.50	1998S Silver premier	240,658	37.50	55.00
1981S Type I	4,063,083	11.00	8.50	1999S	2,557,899	19.95	80.00
1981S Type II	Inc. above	11.00	390	1999S 5 quarter set	1,169,958	13.95	77.50
1982S	3,857,479	11.00	4.75	1999S Silver	804,565	31.95	370
1983S	3,138,765	11.00	5.50	2000S	3,097,442	19.95	26.00
1983S Prestige Set	140,361	59.00	135	2000S 5 quarter set	995,803	13.95	14.00
1983S no mint mark dime	Inc. above	11.00	1,000	2000S Silver	965,421	31.95	35.00
1984S	2,748,430	11.00	8.00	2001S	2,249,498	19.95	155
1984S Prestige Set	316,680	59.00	35.00	2001S 5 quarter set	774,800	13.95	55.00
1985S	3,362,821	11.00	4.75	2001S Silver	849,600	31.95	175
1986S	2,411,180	11.00	18.00	2002S	2,319,766	19.95	47.00
1986S Prestige Set	599,317	48.50	50.00	2002S 5 quarter set	764,419	13.95	25.00
1987S	3,972,233	11.00	4.50	2002S Silver	892,229	31.95	68.50
1987S Prestige Set	435,495	45.00	37.50	2003 X#207, 208, 209.2	—	44.00	45.00
1988S	3,031,287	11.00	7.75	2003S	—	19.95	34.00
1988S Prestige Set	231,661	45.00	43.50	2003S 5 quarter set	—	13.95	22.50
1989S	3,009,107	11.00	7.50	2003S Silver	—	31.95	35.00
1989S Prestige Set	211,087	45.00	60.00	2004S 11 pieces	—	22.95	80.00
1990S	2,793,433	11.00	7.50	2004S 5 quarter set	—	15.95	34.00
1990S no S 1¢	3,555	11.00	8,000	2004S 5 silver quarter set	600,000	23.95	35.00
1990S Prestige Set	506,126	45.00	36.00	2004S Silver 11 pieces	—	37.95	50.00

1952 Proof Set

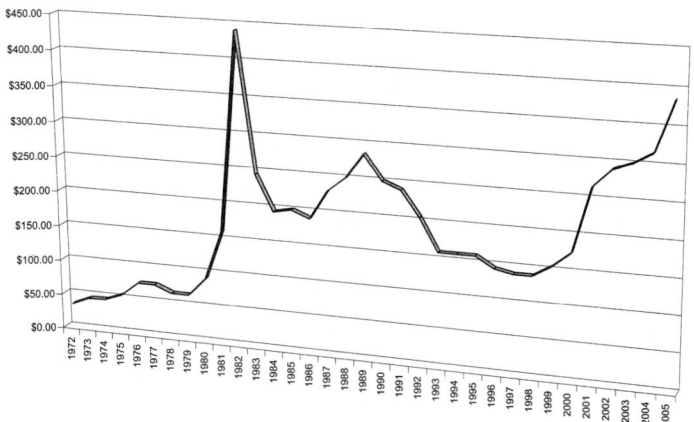

□ Retail Price

UNCIRCULATED ROLLS

Listings are for rolls containing uncirculated coins. Large date and small date varieties for 1960 and 1970 apply to the one cent coins.

Date	Cents	Nickels	Dimes	Quarters	Halves
1938	235	250	1,000	3,250	1,900
1938D	340	210	900	—	—
1938S	215	280	1,250	3,400	—
1939	88.00	80.00	600	1,125	1,200
1939D	190	3,400	540	1,800	2,000
1939S	135	1,150	1,350	3,250	2,400
1940	110	60.00	470	1,675	1,000
1940D	125	94.00	630	4,400	—
1940S	120	145	600	1,300	1,200
1941	88.00	68.00	385	750	725
1941D	165	170	635	2,900	1,200
1941S	200	165	400	2,200	3,200
1942	50.00	245	385	420	700
1942P	—	400	—	—	—
1942D	30.00	1,700	580	1,000	1,300
1942S	485	400	850	4,700	1,400
1943	70.00	220	390	415	700
1943D	115	260	475	2,000	1,800
1943S	350	175	575	2,000	1,400
1944	22.00	530	400	415	700
1944D	19.50	400	470	800	1,200
1944S	22.00	240	415	850	1,250
1945	32.00	270	380	380	700
1945D	40.00	210	380	1,100	1,000
1945S	22.00	210	380	650	950
1946	15.00	80.00	155	420	1,000
1946D	18.00	80.00	160	415	850
1946S	22.00	38.00	190	400	880
1947	85.00	46.00	250	825	1,000
1947D	16.00	52.00	335	740	950
1947S	30.00	52.00	180	670	—
1948	30.00	52.00	185	280	475
1948D	36.50	110	175	675	340
1948S	95.00	80.00	165	460	—
1949	72.50	160	1,300	2,200	1,700
1949D	44.00	96.00	550	1,500	1,425
1949S	110	90.00	2,000	—	2,350
1950	32.00	110	440	360	880
1950D	29.00	540	210	300	920
1950S	39.00	—	1,800	520	—
1951	36.50	140	130	450	420
1951D	13.50	270	100.00	430	780
1951S	41.50	125	550	1,200	650
1952	95.00	52.00	80.00	430	380
1952D	13.50	190	115	370	250
1952S	135	35.00	250	1,100	1,100
1953	18.00	13.50	130	465	390
1953D	15.00	16.50	130	230	190
1953S	24.00	38.00	56.00	340	575
1954	15.00	44.00	55.00	365	240
1954D	15.00	30.00	48.50	360	225
1954S	17.50	78.00	37.50	215	225
1955	15.00	24.00	40.00	150	440
1955D	12.50	7.50	40.00	120	—
1955S	20.00	—	35.00	—	—
1956	11.00	7.50	35.00	225	230
1956D	11.00	7.00	35.00	165	—
1957	10.00	13.00	35.00	145	150
1957D	10.00	7.00	40.00	80.00	170
1958	10.00	7.00	35.00	60.00	110
1958D	10.00	4.25	35.00	60.00	150
1959	1.50	4.25	35.00	60.00	125
1959D	1.50	5.40	35.00	60.00	140
1960 large date	1.50	4.25	35.00	60.00	125
1960 small date	225	—	—	—	—
1960D large date	1.50	4.25	35.00	60.00	125
1960D small date	2.00	—	35.00	—	—
1961	1.50	4.25	35.00	60.00	130
1961D	1.50	5.00	35.00	60.00	105
1962	1.50	6.50	35.00	60.00	100.00
1962D	1.50	7.00	35.00	60.00	95.00
1963	1.50	5.00	35.00	60.00	95.00
1963D	1.50	5.40	35.00	60.00	95.00
1964	1.50	4.25	35.00	60.00	70.00
1964D	1.50	4.25	35.00	60.00	70.00

Date	Cents	Nickels	Dimes	Quarters	Halves
1965	2.70	4.60	9.50	26.00	30.00
1966	4.50	4.25	11.00	27.00	30.00
1967	10.00	8.00	11.00	27.00	30.00
1968	4.00	—	8.50	40.00	—
1968D	2.50	5.40	10.00	34.00	30.00
1968S	1.75	4.25	—	—	—
1969	8.00	—	42.00	95.00	—
1969D	1.50	4.80	12.50	60.00	30.00
1969S	3.25	4.70	—	—	—
1970	4.50	—	8.00	25.00	—
1970D	3.25	4.25	9.00	16.00	375
1970S	3.25	4.25	—	—	—
1970S small date	1,350	—	—	—	—
1971	7.00	30.00	13.00	40.00	27.50
1971D	7.00	6.00	9.50	21.00	17.50
1971S	5.00	—	—	—	—
1972	2.75	6.00	9.50	23.00	30.00
1972D	2.75	4.25	11.00	21.00	30.00
1972S	2.75	—	—	—	—
1973	1.50	4.25	9.50	21.00	32.00
1973D	1.40	6.00	8.50	23.50	23.00
1973S	2.75	—	—	—	—
1974	1.20	4.25	8.00	21.50	21.50
1974D	1.20	6.00	7.50	18.00	23.00
1974S	3.00	—	—	—	—
1975	2.00	11.00	10.00	—	—
1975D	2.00	4.25	12.50	—	—
1976	1.80	15.00	20.00	22.00	21.00
1976D	4.25	12.50	16.00	22.00	21.00
1977	2.00	4.25	12.50	17.00	28.50
1977D	2.00	6.00	8.50	17.50	35.00
1978	2.00	4.25	7.50	16.00	44.00
1978D	2.00	5.00	8.00	17.00	78.00
1979	1.75	5.00	8.50	17.00	27.50
1979D	1.75	5.40	8.00	18.50	28.50
1980	1.75	4.25	8.50	17.00	20.00
1980D	1.75	4.25	8.00	18.50	22.50
1981	1.75	4.25	8.00	16.00	30.00
1981D	1.50	4.25	8.50	16.00	26.00
1982	1.75	160	275	210	62.50
1982D	1.75	48.00	58.00	90.00	60.00
1983	2.25	80.00	185	1,150	80.00
1983D	10.50	36.00	30.00	500	58.00
1984	3.50	25.00	9.50	17.50	37.50
1984D	15.00	5.00	21.50	30.00	47.50
1985	7.00	10.00	9.50	37.50	75.00
1985D	3.50	8.00	9.50	13.50	70.00
1986	35.00	8.00	27.50	125	130
1986D	33.00	28.00	26.00	285	115
1987	4.00	6.00	7.50	16.00	92.50
1987D	3.50	4.25	7.50	16.00	80.00
1988	7.00	5.40	10.25	40.00	90.00
1988D	7.00	8.00	9.50	23.50	57.50
1989	2.40	5.40	11.50	20.00	57.50
1989D	2.40	8.00	11.00	21.00	42.00
1990	2.40	10.00	13.00	26.00	50.00
1990D	2.40	11.00	12.50	30.00	70.00
1991	2.40	12.00	10.50	35.00	70.00
1991D	2.40	12.00	13.50	35.00	110
1992	2.60	48.00	8.00	26.00	30.00
1992D	2.60	8.00	10.00	34.00	55.00
1993	2.60	11.50	9.50	42.00	42.00
1993D	2.60	12.50	12.50	37.50	65.00
1994	2.25	7.00	8.50	42.00	15.00
1994D	2.25	6.00	8.50	42.00	23.00
1995	2.25	7.50	12.50	42.00	16.00
1995D	2.25	20.00	17.50	42.00	13.00
1996	2.00	5.40	11.00	22.00	15.00
1996D	2.00	7.50	11.50	28.00	13.00
1997	2.00	12.50	27.50	23.50	15.00
1997D	2.00	28.00	8.50	34.00	16.00
1998	2.00	12.50	10.50	30.00	15.00
1998D	2.00	13.50	9.50	25.00	15.00
1999P	1.75	4.25	13.50	—	18.50
1999D	1.75	5.40	9.50	—	17.50
2000P	1.75	5.40	9.00	—	14.00
2000D	1.75	3.40	7.00	—	15.00
2001P	1.75	4.25	9.00	—	18.00
2001D	1.75	4.25	7.00	—	15.00

Date	Cents	Nickels	Dimes	Quarters	Halves
2002P	1.50	3.40	7.50	—	42.00
2002D	1.50	3.40	7.50	—	42.00
2003 P	1.50	3.50	8.00	—	27.50
2003D	1.50	3.50	8.00	—	27.50
2004 P	1.50	—	8.00	—	27.50
2004D	1.50	—	8.00	—	27.50
2004 P Peace medal	—	4.00	—	—	—
2004 D Peace medal	—	4.00	—	—	—
2004 P Keelboat	—	4.00	—	—	—
2004 D Keelboat	—	4.00	—	—	—
2005 P	1.50	—	8.00	—	27.50
2005 D	1.50	—	8.00	—	27.50
2005 P Bison	—	4.00	—	—	—
2005 D Bison	—	4.00	—	—	—
2005 P Ocean	—	4.00	—	—	—
2005 D Ocean	—	4.00	—	—	—

COMMEMORATIVE COINAGE
1892-1954

All commemorative half dollars of 1892-1954 have the following specifications: diameter -- 30.6 millimeters; weight -- 12.5000 grams; composition -- 0.9000 silver, 0.3617 ounces actual silver weight. Values for PDS sets contain one example each from the Philadelphia, Denver and San Francisco mints. Type coin prices are the most inexpensive single coin available from the date and mint-mark combinations listed.

QUARTER

KM# 115 COLUMBIAN EXPOSITION Weight: 6.2500 g. **Composition:** 0.9000 Silver, 0.1808 oz. ASW **Diameter:** 24.3mm. **Obv:** Queen Isabella

Date	Mintage	AU-50	MS-60	MS-63	MS-64	MS-65
1893	24,214	685	720	960	1,400	3,125

HALF DOLLAR

KM# 117 COLUMBIAN EXPOSITION Obv. Designer: Charles E. Barber **Rev. Designer:** George T. Morgan

Date	Mintage	AU-50	MS-60	MS-63	MS-64	MS-65
1892	950,000	19.00	28.00	80.00	200	700
1893	1,550,405	16.00	27.50	80.00	200	950

1892 Columbian Expo Half
Grade MS-60

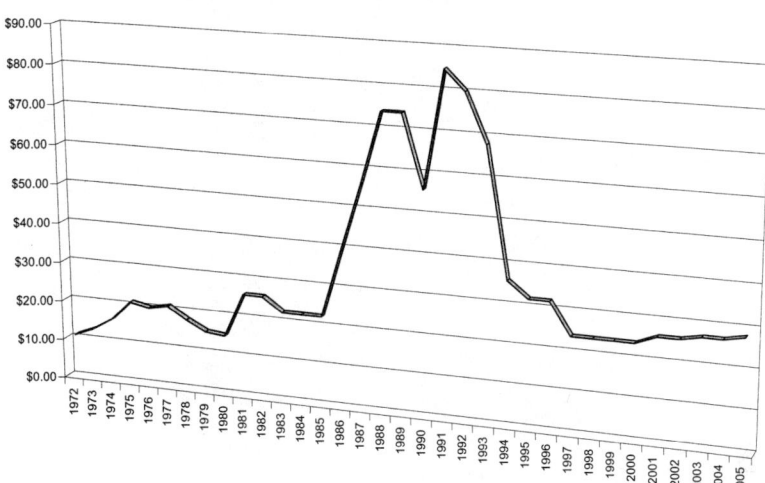

Retail Price

KM# 135 PANAMA-PACIFIC EXPOSITION **Designer:** Charles E. Barber

Date	Mintage	AU-50	MS-60	MS-63	MS-64	MS-65
1915S	27,134	470	550	795	1,600	2,850

KM# 143 LINCOLN-ILLINOIS **Obv. Designer:** George T. Morgan **Rev. Designer:** John R. Sinnock

Date	Mintage	AU-50	MS-60	MS-63	MS-64	MS-65
1918	100,058	135	155	170	265	500

KM# 146 MAINE CENTENNIAL **Designer:** Anthony de Francisci

Date	Mintage	AU-50	MS-60	MS-63	MS-64	MS-65
1920	50,028	135	170	225	340	615

KM# 147.1 PILGRIM TERCENTENARY **Designer:** Cyrus E. Dallin

Date	Mintage	AU-50	MS-60	MS-63	MS-64	MS-65
1920	152,112	78.50	100.00	115	160	450

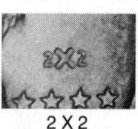

2 X 2

KM# 148.1 ALABAMA CENTENNIAL **Obv:** "2x2" at right above stars **Designer:** Laura G. Fraser

Date	Mintage	AU-50	MS-60	MS-63	MS-64	MS-65
1921	6,006	325	340	625	1,050	2,525

KM# 148.2 ALABAMA CENTENNIAL **Obv. Designer:** Laura G. Fraser

Date	Mintage	AU-50	MS-60	MS-63	MS-64	MS-65
1921	59,038	205	225	550	825	2,400

KM# 149.1 MISSOURI CENTENNIAL **Designer:** Robert Aitken

Date	Mintage	AU-50	MS-60	MS-63	MS-64	MS-65
1921	15,428	420	730	960	1,800	6,150

2 ★ 4

KM# 149.2 MISSOURI CENTENNIAL Obv: 2 star 4 in field at left **Designer:** Robert Aitken

Date	Mintage	AU-50	MS-60	MS-63	MS-64	MS-65
1921	5,000	650	825	1,150	2,000	5,600

KM# 147.2 PILGRIM TERCENTENARY Obv: 1921 date next to Pilgrim **Designer:** Cyrus E. Dallin

Date	Mintage	AU-50	MS-60	MS-63	MS-64	MS-65
1921	20,053	180	210	225	300	605

KM# 151.1 GRANT MEMORIAL Designer: Laura G. Fraser

Date	Mintage	AU-50	MS-60	MS-63	MS-64	MS-65
1922	67,405	115	130	170	325	850

KM# 151.2 GRANT MEMORIAL Obv: Star above the word "Grant" **Designer:** Laura G. Fraser

Date	Mintage	AU-50	MS-60	MS-63	MS-64	MS-65
1922	4,256	975	1,350	1,900	2,700	8,000

KM# 153 MONROE DOCTRINE CENTENNIAL   Designer: Chester Beach

Date	Mintage	AU-50	MS-60	MS-63	MS-64	MS-65
1923S	274,077	55.00	72.50	155	555	3,700

KM# 154 HUGUENOT-WALLOON TERCENTENARY   Obv: Huguenot leader Gaspard de Coligny and William I of Orange Designer: George T. Morgan

Date	Mintage	AU-50	MS-60	MS-63	MS-64	MS-65
1924	142,080	140	153	185	270	560

KM# 155 CALIFORNIA DIAMOND JUBILEE   Designer: Jo Mora

Date	Mintage	AU-50	MS-60	MS-63	MS-64	MS-65
1925S	86,594	180	205	250	445	1,240

KM# 158 FORT VANCOUVER CENTENNIAL   Designer: Laura G. Fraser

Date	Mintage	AU-50	MS-60	MS-63	MS-64	MS-65
1925	14,994	345	445	450	625	1,500

KM# 156 LEXINGTON-CONCORD SESQUICENTENNIAL Designer: Chester Beach

Date	Mintage	AU-50	MS-60	MS-63	MS-64	MS-65
1925	162,013	93.50	110	115	200	645

KM# 157.1 STONE MOUNTAIN MEMORIAL Designer: Gutzon Borglum

Date	Mintage	AU-50	MS-60	MS-63	MS-64	MS-65
1925	1,314,709	62.50	71.00	75.00	92.50	275

KM# 159 OREGON TRAIL MEMORIAL Designer: James E. and Laura G. Fraser

Date	Mintage	AU-50	MS-60	MS-63	MS-64	MS-65
1926	47,955	145	175	185	205	350
1926S	83,055	140	175	185	205	320
Type coin	—	140	175	185	205	300
1928	6,028	220	253	275	280	390
1933D	5,008	390	400	405	410	580
1934D	7,006	205	220	230	235	345
1936	10,006	155	190	200	205	315
1936S	5,006	170	190	210	215	375
1937D	12,008	180	210	215	220	300
1938 PDS set	6,005	515	565	675	700	950
1939 PDS set	3,004	1,600	1,850	1,875	1,900	2,300

KM# 160 U.S. SESQUICENTENNIAL Designer: John R. Sinnock

Date	Mintage	AU-50	MS-60	MS-63	MS-64	MS-65
1926	141,120	91.50	115	160	615	4,300

1926 Oregon Trail Half
Grade MS-60

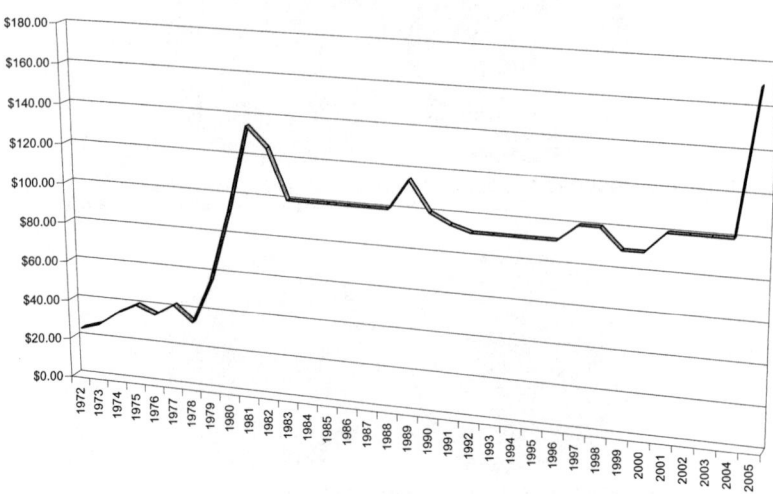

☑ Retail Price

KM# 162 VERMONT SESQUICENTENNIAL   Obv. Designer: Charles Keck

Date	Mintage	AU-50	MS-60	MS-63	MS-64	MS-65
1927	28,142	230	275	280	355	970

KM# 163 HAWAIIAN SESQUICENTENNIAL   Designer: Juliette M. Fraser

Date	Mintage	AU-50	MS-60	MS-63	MS-64	MS-65
1928	10,008	1,775	2,550	3,050	4,150	6,850

KM# 165.1 DANIEL BOONE BICENTENNIAL   Designer: Augustus Lukeman

Date	Mintage	AU-50	MS-60	MS-63	MS-64	MS-65
1934	10,007	125	130	140	145	220
1935 PDS set	2,003	920	1,000	1,025	1,150	2,150

KM# 165.2 DANIEL BOONE BICENTENNIAL Rev: "1934" added above the word "Pioneer." **Designer:** Augustus Lukeman

Date	Mintage	AU-50	MS-60	MS-63	MS-64	MS-65
1935 PDS set	5,005	375	395	430	440	660
Type coin	—	125	130	143	145	220
1936 PDS set	5,005	375	395	430	440	660
Type coin	—	—	110	—	—	—
1937 PDS set	2,506	840	930	945	960	1,325
1938 PDS set	2,100	1,100	1,250	1,260	1,280	1,825

KM# 166 MARYLAND TERCENTENARY Designer: Hans Schuler

Date	Mintage	AU-50	MS-60	MS-63	MS-64	MS-65
1934	25,015	155	180	185	220	390

KM# 167 TEXAS CENTENNIAL Designer: Pompeo Coppini

Date	Mintage	AU-50	MS-60	MS-63	MS-64	MS-65
1934	61,463	135	150	155	160	240
Type coin	—	135	150	155	160	240
1935 PDS set	9,994	415	450	470	490	725
1936 PDS set	8,911	415	450	470	490	725
1937 PDS set	6,571	415	450	470	490	725
1938 PDS set	3,775	725	800	850	925	1,560

KM# 168 ARKANSAS CENTENNIAL Designer: Edward E. Burr

Date	Mintage	AU-50	MS-60	MS-63	MS-64	MS-65
Type coin	—	100.00	105	115	125	215
1935 PDS set	5,505	315	325	350	385	825
1936 PDS set	9,600	315	325	350	385	850
1937 PDS set	5,505	315	325	350	385	1,050

Date	Mintage	AU-50	MS-60	MS-63	MS-64	MS-65
1938 PDS set	3,155	485	575	595	625	2,000
1939 PDS set	—	980	1,200	1,250	1,265	3,500

KM# 169 CONNECTICUT TERCENTENARY Designer: Henry Kreiss

Date	Mintage	AU-50	MS-60	MS-63	MS-64	MS-65
1935	25,018	260	295	305	390	635

KM# 170 HUDSON, N.Y., SESQUICENTENNIAL Designer: Chester Beach

Date	Mintage	AU-50	MS-60	MS-63	MS-64	MS-65
1935	10,008	750	850	1,050	1,330	2,050

KM# 172 OLD SPANISH TRAIL Designer: L.W. Hoffecker

Date	Mintage	AU-50	MS-60	MS-63	MS-64	MS-65
1935	10,008	1,200	1,300	1,350	1,425	1,550

KM# 171 SAN DIEGO, CALIFORNIA - PACIFIC EXPOSITION Designer: Robert Aitken

Date	Mintage	AU-50	MS-60	MS-63	MS-64	MS-65
1935S	70,132	97.50	133	135	140	185
1936D	30,092	97.50	148	160	160	185

KM# 173 ALBANY, N.Y., CHARTER ANNIVERSARY **Designer:** Gertrude K. Lathrop

Date	Mintage	AU-50	MS-60	MS-63	MS-64	MS-65
1936	17,671	325	330	350	375	405

KM# 187 ARKANSAS CENTENNIAL **Obv:** Sen. Joseph T. Robinson **Obv. Designer:** Henry Kreiss **Rev. Designer:** Edward E. Burr

Date	Mintage	AU-50	MS-60	MS-63	MS-64	MS-65
1936	25,265	148	155	165	170	430

KM# 181 BATTLE OF GETTYSBURG 75TH ANNIVERSARY **Designer:** Frank Vittor

Date	Mintage	AU-50	MS-60	MS-63	MS-64	MS-65
1936	26,928	420	455	480	500	750

KM# 175 BRIDGEPORT, CONN., CENTENNIAL **Designer:** Henry Kreiss

Date	Mintage	AU-50	MS-60	MS-63	MS-64	MS-65
1936	25,015	175	180	200	205	270

KM# 176 CINCINNATI MUSIC CENTER Designer: Constance Ortmayer

Date	Mintage	AU-50	MS-60	MS-63	MS-64	MS-65
Type coin	—	325	330	360	470	700
1936 PDS set	5,005	975	1,000	1,050	1,400	2,850

 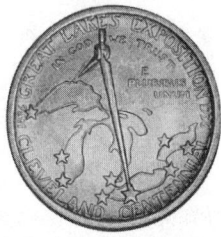

KM# 177 CLEVELAND-GREAT LAKES EXPOSITION Designer: Brenda Putnam

Date	Mintage	AU-50	MS-60	MS-63	MS-64	MS-65
1936	50,030	138	140	155	170	255

KM# 178 COLUMBIA, S.C., SESQUICENTENNIAL Designer: A. Wolfe Davidson

Date	Mintage	AU-50	MS-60	MS-63	MS-64	MS-65
1936 PDS set	9,007	785	800	880	900	920
Type coin	—	268	270	300	305	320

KM# 179 DELAWARE TERCENTENARY Designer: Carl L. Schmitz

Date	Mintage	AU-50	MS-60	MS-63	MS-64	MS-65
1936	20,993	320	350	375	380	455

KM# 180 ELGIN, ILL., CENTENNIAL Designer: Trygve Rovelstad

Date	Mintage	AU-50	MS-60	MS-63	MS-64	MS-65
1936	20,015	235	265	280	285	305

KM# 182 LONG ISLAND TERCENTENARY Designer: Howard K. Weinman

Date	Mintage	AU-50	MS-60	MS-63	MS-64	MS-65
1936	81,826	90.00	100.00	110	125	435

KM# 183 LYNCHBURG, VA., SESQUICENTENNIAL Designer: Charles Keck

Date	Mintage	AU-50	MS-60	MS-63	MS-64	MS-65
1936	20,013	240	275	280	290	355

KM# 184 NORFOLK, VA., BICENTENNIAL Designer: William M. and Marjorie E. Simpson

Date	Mintage	AU-50	MS-60	MS-63	MS-64	MS-65
1936	16,936	540	555	595	605	615

KM# 185 RHODE ISLAND TERCENTENARY   Designer: Arthur G. Carey and John H. Benson

Date	Mintage	AU-50	MS-60	MS-63	MS-64	MS-65
1936 PDS set	15,010	290	315	345	375	840
Type coin	—	97.50	105	110	125	275

KM# 174 SAN FRANCISCO-OAKLAND BAY BRIDGE   Designer: Jacques Schnier

Date	Mintage	AU-50	MS-60	MS-63	MS-64	MS-65
1936	71,424	175	180	205	210	315

KM# 188 WISCONSIN TERRITORIAL CENTENNIAL   Designer: David Parsons

Date	Mintage	AU-50	MS-60	MS-63	MS-64	MS-65
1936	25,015	235	260	285	315	375

KM# 189 YORK COUNTY, MAINE, TERCENTENARY   Designer: Walter H. Rich

Date	Mintage	AU-50	MS-60	MS-63	MS-64	MS-65
1936	25,015	230	235	263	275	315

KM# 190 BATTLE OF ANTIETAM 75TH ANNIVERSARY Designer: William M. Simpson

Date	Mintage	AU-50	MS-60	MS-63	MS-64	MS-65
1937	18,028	720	725	730	775	850

KM# 186 ROANOKE ISLAND, N.C. Designer: William M. Simpson

Date	Mintage	AU-50	MS-60	MS-63	MS-64	MS-65
1937	29,030	255	300	315	320	340

KM# 191 NEW ROCHELLE, N.Y. Designer: Gertrude K. Lathrop

Date	Mintage	AU-50	MS-60	MS-63	MS-64	MS-65
1938	15,266	415	430	440	470	525

KM# 198 BOOKER T. WASHINGTON Designer: Isaac S. Hathaway

Date	Mintage	AU-50	MS-60	MS-63	MS-64	MS-65
1946 PDS set	200,113	45.00	50.00	67.50	75.00	160
Type coin	—	15.00	16.00	17.50	18.50	56.00
1947 PDS set	100,017	52.50	75.00	85.00	120	300
1948 PDS set	8,005	85.00	150	155	165	225
1949 PDS set	6,004	160	230	245	250	355
1950 PDS set	6,004	75.00	130	135	140	230
1951 PDS set	7,004	85.00	110	140	150	220

KM# 197 IOWA STATEHOOD CENTENNIAL Designer: Adam Pietz

Date	Mintage	AU-50	MS-60	MS-63	MS-64	MS-65
1946	100,057	105	125	129	130	190

KM# 200 BOOKER T. WASHINGTON AND GEORGE WASHINGTON CARVER Designer: Isaac S. Hathaway

Date	Mintage	AU-50	MS-60	MS-63	MS-64	MS-65
1951 PDS set	10,004	68.50	85.00	95.00	125	585
Type coin	—	13.50	16.00	18.50	20.00	52.50
1952 PDS set	8,006	68.50	82.50	110	130	415
1953 PDS set	8,003	58.50	82.50	110	135	600
1954 PDS set	12,006	55.00	80.00	92.50	110	445

DOLLAR

KM# 118 LAFAYETTE Weight: 26.7300 g. Composition: 0.9000 Silver, 0.7736 oz. ASW Diameter: 38.1mm. Designer: Charles E. Barber

Date	Mintage	AU-50	MS-60	MS-63	MS-64	MS-65
1900	36,026	650	975	2,100	4,400	10,500

KM# 120 LOUISIANA PURCHASE EXPOSITION Weight: 1.6720 g. Composition: 0.9000 Gold, 0.0484 oz. AGW Diameter: 15mm. Obv: William McKinley Obv. Designer: Charles E. Barber

Date	Mintage	AU-50	MS-60	MS-63	MS-64	MS-65
1903	17,500	740	780	970	2,050	3,000

KM# 119 LOUISIANA PURCHASE EXPOSITION Weight: 1.6720 g. **Composition:** 0.9000 Gold, 0.0484 oz. AGW **Diameter:** 15mm. **Obv:** Jefferson **Designer:** Charles E. Barber

Date	Mintage	AU-50	MS-60	MS-63	MS-64	MS-65
1903	17,500	735	780	1,100	2,100	3,200

KM# 121 LEWIS AND CLARK EXPOSITION Weight: 1.6720 g. **Composition:** 0.9000 Gold, 0.7736 oz. AGW **Diameter:** 15mm. **Obv. Designer:** Charles E. Barber

Date	Mintage	AU-50	MS-60	MS-63	MS-64	MS-65
1904	10,025	1,050	1,100	2,300	5,150	10,500
1905	10,041	1,350	1,550	2,950	7,000	16,000

KM# 136 PANAMA-PACIFIC EXPOSITION Weight: 1.6720 g. **Composition:** 0.9000 Gold, 0.0484 oz. AGW **Diameter:** 15mm. **Obv. Designer:** Charles Keck

Date	Mintage	AU-50	MS-60	MS-63	MS-64	MS-65
1915S	15,000	675	770	925	1,350	2,600

KM# 144 MCKINLEY MEMORIAL Weight: 1.6720 g. **Composition:** 0.9000 Gold, 0.0484 oz. AGW **Diameter:** 15mm. **Obv. Designer:** Charles E. Barber **Rev. Designer:** George T. Morgan

Date	Mintage	AU-50	MS-60	MS-63	MS-64	MS-65
1916	9,977	650	705	850	1,275	2,600
1917	10,000	800	845	1,250	2,300	3,600

KM# 152.1 GRANT MEMORIAL Weight: 1.6720 g. **Composition:** 0.9000 Gold, 0.0484 oz. AGW **Diameter:** 15mm. **Obv:** Without a star above the word "Grant" **Obv. Designer:** Laura G. Fraser **Notes:** Without an incuse "star" above the word GRANT on the obverse.

Date	Mintage	AU-50	MS-60	MS-63	MS-64	MS-65
1922	5,016	1,950	2,000	2,250	3,500	4,200

Grant w/star

KM# 152.2 GRANT MEMORIAL Weight: 1.6720 g. **Composition:** 0.9000 Gold, 0.0484 oz. AGW **Diameter:** 15mm. **Obv. Designer:** Laura G. Fraser **Notes:** Variety with an incuse "star" above the wrod GRANT on the obverse.

Date	Mintage	AU-50	MS-60	MS-63	MS-64	MS-65
1922	5,000	1,800	1,900	2,250	3,500	4,000

$2.50 (QUARTER EAGLE)

KM# 137 PANAMA PACIFIC EXPOSITION   Weight: 4.1800 g. **Composition:** 0.9000 Gold, 0.121 oz. AGW
Diameter: 18mm. **Obv. Designer:** Charles E. Barber **Rev. Designer:** George T. Morgan

Date	Mintage	AU-50	MS-60	MS-63	MS-64	MS-65
1915S	6,749	1,850	1,950	3,750	5,200	6,600

KM# 161 PHILADELPHIA SESQUICENTENNIAL   Weight: 4.1800 g. **Composition:** 0.9000 Gold, 0.121
oz. AGW **Diameter:** 18mm. **Obv. Designer:** John R. Sinnock

Date	Mintage	AU-50	MS-60	MS-63	MS-64	MS-65
1926	46,019	550	575	825	1,550	4,850

$50

KM# 138 PANAMA-PACIFIC EXPOSITION   Weight: 83.5900 g. **Composition:** 0.9000 Gold, 2.419 oz.
AGW **Diameter:** 44mm. **Obv. Designer:** Robert Aitken

Date	Mintage	AU-50	MS-60	MS-63	MS-64	MS-65
1915S	483	31,500	40,000	65,000	75,000	135,000

KM# 139 PANAMA-PACIFIC EXPOSITION   Weight: 83.5900 g. **Composition:** 0.9000 Gold, 2.419 oz.
AGW **Diameter:** 44mm. **Obv. Designer:** Robert Aitken

Date	Mintage	AU-50	MS-60	MS-63	MS-64	MS-65
1915S	645	30,000	35,000	57,500	70,000	125,000

COMMEMORATIVE COINAGE
1982-PRESENT

All commemorative silver dollar coins of 1982-present have the following specifications: diameter -- 38.1 millimeters; weight -- 26.7300 grams; composition -- 0.9000 silver, 0.7736 ounces actual silver weight. All commemorative $5 coins of 1982-present have the following specificiations: diameter -- 21.6 millimeters; weight -- 8.3590 grams; composition: 0.9000 gold, 0.242 ounces actual gold weight.

Note: In 1982, after a hiatus of nearly 20 years, coinage of commemorative half dollars resumed. Those designated with a 'W' were struck at the West Point Mint. Some issues were struck in copper--nickel. Those struck in silver have the same size, weight and composition as the prior commemorative half--dollar series.

HALF DOLLAR

KM# 208 GEORGE WASHINTON, 250TH BIRTH ANNIVERSARY Weight: 12.5000 g. **Composition:** 0.9000 Silver, 0.3618 oz. ASW **Diameter:** 30.6mm. **Obv. Designer:** Elizabeth Jones

Date	Mintage	Proof	MS-65	Prf-65
1982D	2,210,458	—	5.50	—
1982S	—	(4,894,044)	—	5.75

KM# 212 STATUE OF LIBERTY CENTENNIAL Weight: 11.3400 g. **Composition:** Copper-Nickel Clad Copper **Obv. Designer:** Edgar Z. Steever **Rev. Designer:** Sherl Joseph Winter

Date	Mintage	Proof	MS-65	Prf-65
1986D	928,008	—	6.75	—
1986S	—	(6,925,627)	—	6.50

KM# 224 BICENTENNIAL OF THE CONGRESS Weight: 11.3400 g. **Composition:** Copper-Nickel Clad Copper **Obv. Designer:** Patricia L. Verani **Rev. Designer:** William Woodward and Edgar Z. Steever

Date	Mintage	Proof	MS-65	Prf-65
1989D	163,753	—	8.00	—
1989S	—	—	—	8.00

KM# 228 MOUNT RUSHMORE 50TH ANNIVERSARY Weight: 11.3400 g. Composition: Copper-Nickel Clad Copper Obv. Designer: Marcel Jovine Rev. Designer: T. James Ferrell

Date	Mintage	Proof	MS-65	Prf-65
1991D	172,754	—	21.50	—
1991S	—	—	—	22.00

KM# 233 1992 OLYMPICS Weight: 11.3400 g. Composition: Copper-Nickel Clad Copper Obv. Designer: William Cousins Rev. Designer: Steven M. Bieda

Date	Mintage	Proof	MS-65	Prf-65
1992P	161,607	—	8.50	—
1992S	—	(519,645)	—	8.50

KM# 237 500TH ANNIVERSARY OF COLUMBUS DISCOVERY Weight: 11.3400 g. Composition: Copper-Nickel Clad Copper Designer: T. James Ferrell

Date	Mintage	Proof	MS-65	Prf-65
1992D	135,702	—	11.50	—
1992S	—	(390,154)	—	11.50

KM# 240 JAMES MADISON AND BILL OF RIGHTS Weight: 12.5000 g. Composition: 0.9000 Silver, 0.3618 oz. ASW Obv. Designer: T. James Ferrell Rev. Designer: Dean McMullen

Date	Mintage	Proof	MS-65	Prf-65
1993W	173,224	—	20.50	—
1993S	—	(559,758)	—	16.50

KM# 243 WORLD WAR II 50TH ANNIVERSARY Weight: 11.3400 g. **Composition:** Copper-Nickel Clad Copper **Obv. Designer:** George Klauba **Rev. Designer:** William J. Leftwich

Date	Mintage	Proof	MS-65	Prf-65
1993P	192,968	(290,343)	38.50	37.50

KM# 246 1994 WORLD CUP SOCCER Weight: 11.3400 g. **Composition:** Copper-Nickel Clad Copper **Obv. Designer:** Richard T. LaRoche **Rev. Designer:** Dean McMullen

Date	Mintage	Proof	MS-65	Prf-65
1994D	168,208	—	10.25	—
1994P	122,412	(609,354)	—	9.75

KM# 257 ATLANTA OLYMPICS Weight: 11.3400 g. **Composition:** Copper-Nickel Clad Copper **Obv:** Basketball

Date	Mintage	Proof	MS-65	Prf-65
1995S	171,001	(169,655)	22.50	18.50

KM# 262 ATLANTA OLYMPICS Weight: 11.3400 g. **Composition:** Copper-Nickel Clad Copper **Obv:** Baseball **Obv. Designer:** Edgar Z. Steever

Date	Mintage	Proof	MS-65	Prf-65
1995S	164,605	(118,087)	23.50	19.00

KM# 254 CIVIL WAR Weight: 11.3400 g. **Composition:** Copper-Nickel Clad Copper **Obv. Designer:** Don Troiani **Rev. Designer:** T. James Ferrell

Date	Mintage	Proof	MS-65	Prf-65
1995S	119,510	(330,099)	47.50	43.50

KM# 271 ATLANTA OLYMPICS Weight: 11.3400 g. **Composition:** Copper-Nickel Clad Copper **Obv:** Soccer

Date	Mintage	Proof	MS-65	Prf-65
1996S	52,836	(122,412)	90.00	105

KM# 267 ATLANTA OLYMPICS Weight: 11.3400 g. **Composition:** Copper-Nickel Clad Copper **Obv:** Swimming

Date	Mintage	Proof	MS-65	Prf-65
1996S	49,533	(114,315)	170	37.50

KM# 323 U. S. CAPITOL VISITOR CENTER Weight: 11.3400 g. **Composition:** Copper-Nickel Clad Copper **Obv. Designer:** Dean McMullen **Rev. Designer:** Alex Shagin and Marcel Jovine

Date	Mintage	Proof	MS-65	Prf-65
2001	99,157	(77,962)	13.50	18.00

KM# 348 FIRST FLIGHT CENTENNIAL Weight: 11.3400 g. **Composition:** Copper-Nickel Clad Copper **Obv. Designer:** John Mercanti **Rev. Designer:** Donna Weaver

Date	Mintage	Proof	MS-65	Prf-65
2003P	—	—	—	—

DOLLAR

KM# 209 LOS ANGELES XXIII OLYMPIAD   Obv. Designer: Elizabeth Jones

Date	Mintage	Proof	MS-65	Prf-65
1983P	294,543	—	11.50	—
1983D	174,014	—	12.00	—
1983S	174,014	(1,577,025)	11.50	13.00

KM# 210 LOS ANGELES XXIII OLYMPIAD   Obv. Designer: Robert Graham

Date	Mintage	Proof	MS-65	Prf-65
1984P	217,954	—	13.50	—
1984D	116,675	—	18.00	—
1984S	116,675	(1,801,210)	19.00	13.00

KM# 214 STATUE OF LIBERTY CENTENNIAL   Obv. Designer: John Mercanti **Rev. Designer:** John
Mercanti and Matthew Peloso

Date	Mintage	Proof	MS-65	Prf-65
1986P	723,635	—	15.00	—
1986S	—	(6,414,638)	—	15.50

KM# 220 CONSTITUTION BICENTENNIAL   Obv. Designer: Patricia L. Verani

Date	Mintage	Proof	MS-65	Prf-65
1987P	451,629	—	11.00	—
1987S	—	(2,747,116)	—	11.00

KM# 222 OLYMPICS   Obv. Designer: Patricia L. Verani **Rev. Designer:** Sherl Joseph Winter

Date	Mintage	Proof	MS-65	Prf-65
1988D	191,368	—	11.50	—
1988S	—	(1,359,366)	—	11.50

KM# 225 BICENTENNIAL OF THE CONGRESS   Designer: William Woodward and Chester Y. Martin

Date	Mintage	Proof	MS-65	Prf-65
1989D	135,203	—	16.00	—
1989S	—	(762,198)	—	21.50

KM# 227 EISENHOWER CENTENNIAL Obv. Designer: John Mercanti **Rev. Designer:** Marcel Jovine and John Mercanti

Date	Mintage	Proof	MS-65	Prf-65
1990W	241,669	—	18.00	—
1990P	—	(638,335)	—	22.50

KM# 231 KOREAN WAR Obv. Designer: John Mercanti **Rev. Designer:** T. James Ferrell

Date	Mintage	Proof	MS-65	Prf-65
1991D	213,049	—	16.00	—
1991P	—	(618,488)	—	19.00

KM# 229 MOUNT RUSHMORE GOLDEN ANNIVERSARY Obv. Designer: Marika Somogyi **Rev. Designer:** Frank Gasparro

Date	Mintage	Proof	MS-65	Prf-65
1991P	133,139	—	34.00	—
1991S	—	(738,419)	—	41.50

KM# 232 USO 50TH ANNIVERSARY Obv. Designer: Robert Lamb **Rev. Designer:** John Mercanti

Date	Mintage	Proof	MS-65	Prf-65
1991D	124,958	—	16.00	—
1991S	—	(321,275)	—	22.50

KM# 238 COLUMBUS QUINCENTENARY Obv. Designer: John Mercanti **Rev. Designer:** Thomas D. Rogers, Sr.

Date	Mintage	Proof	MS-65	Prf-65
1992D	106,949	—	31.00	—
1992P	—	(385,241)	—	46.00

KM# 234 OLYMPICS Obv. Designer: John R. Deecken and Chester Y. Martin **Rev. Designer:** Marcel Jovine

Date	Mintage	Proof	MS-65	Prf-65
1992D	187,552	—	26.00	—
1992S	—	(504,505)	—	28.50

KM# 236 WHITE HOUSE BICENTENNIAL Obv. Designer: Edgar Z. Steever **Rev. Designer:** Chester Y. Martin

Date	Mintage	Proof	MS-65	Prf-65
1992D	123,803	—	38.50	—
1992W	—	(375,851)	—	46.00

KM# 241 JAMES MADISON AND BILL OF RIGHTS Obv. Designer: William Krawczewicz and Thomas D. Rogers, Sr. **Rev. Designer:** Dean McMullen and Thomas D. Rogers, Sr.

Date	Mintage	Proof	MS-65	Prf-65
1993D	98,383	—	21.00	—
1993S	—	(534,001)	—	22.00

KM# 249 THOMAS JEFFERSON 250TH BIRTH ANNIVERSARY Designer: T. James Ferrell

Date	Mintage	Proof	MS-65	Prf-65
1993P	266,927	—	27.50	—
1993S	—	(332,891)	—	31.00

KM# 244 WORLD WAR II 50TH ANNIVERSARY Designer: Thomas D. Rogers, Sr.

Date	Mintage	Proof	MS-65	Prf-65
1993D	94,708	—	35.00	—
1993W	—	(322,422)	—	42.50

KM# 251 NATIONAL PRISONER OF WAR MUSEUM Obv. Designer: Thomas Nielson and Alfred Maletsky **Rev. Designer:** Edgar Z. Steever

Date	Mintage	Proof	MS-65	Prf-65
1994W	54,790	—	96.00	—
1994P	—	(220,100)	—	80.00

KM# 253 U.S. CAPITOL BICENTENNIAL

Date	Mintage	Proof	MS-65	Prf-65
1994D	68,352	—	23.00	—
1994S	—	(279,416)	—	30.00

KM# 250 VIETNAM VETERANS MEMORIAL **Obv. Designer:** John Mercanti **Rev. Designer:** Thomas D. Rogers, Sr.

Date	Mintage	Proof	MS-65	Prf-65
1994W	57,317	—	85.00	—
1994P	—	(226,262)	—	100.00

KM# 252 WOMEN IN MILITARY SERVICE MEMORIAL **Obv. Designer:** T. James Ferrell **Rev. Designer:** Thomas D. Rogers, Sr.

Date	Mintage	Proof	MS-65	Prf-65
1994W	53,054	—	62.50	—
1994P	—	(213,201)	—	59.00

KM# 247 WORLD CUP SOCCER **Obv. Designer:** Dean McMullen and T. James Ferrell

Date	Mintage	Proof	MS-65	Prf-65
1994D	81,698	—	27.50	—
1994S	—	(576,978)	—	31.00

KM# 260 ATLANTA OLYMPICS Obv: Gymnastics

Date	Mintage	Proof	MS-65	Prf-65
1995D	42,497	—	77.50	—
1995P	—	(182,676)	—	62.50

KM# 264 ATLANTA OLYMPICS   Obv: Track and field **Obv. Designer:** John Mercanti

Date	Mintage	Proof	MS-65	Prf-65
1995D	24,796	—	96.00	—
1995P	—	(136,935)	—	57.50

KM# 263 ATLANTA OLYMPICS Obv: Cycling **Obv. Designer:** John Mercanti

Date	Mintage	Proof	MS-65	Prf-65
1995D	19,662	—	150	—
1995P	—	(118,795)	—	47.50

KM# 259 ATLANTA OLYMPICS, PARALYMPICS   Obv: Blind runner

Date	Mintage	Proof	MS-65	Prf-65
1995D	28,649	—	97.50	—
1995P	—	(138,337)	—	66.00

KM# 255 CIVIL WAR   Obv. Designer: Don Troiani and Edgar Z. Steever **Rev. Designer:** John Mercanti

Date	Mintage	Proof	MS-65	Prf-65
1995P	45,866	—	77.50	—
1995S	—	(437,114)	—	90.00

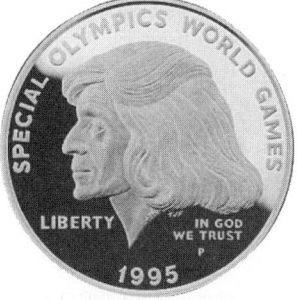

KM# 266 SPECIAL OLYMPICS WORLD GAMES   Obv. Designer: Jamie Wyeth and T. James Ferrell **Rev. Designer:** Thomas D. Rogers, Sr.

Date	Mintage	Proof	MS-65	Prf-65
1995W	89,301	—	25.00	—
1995P	—	(351,764)	—	27.50

KM# 269 ATLANTA OLYMPICS   Obv: Tennis **Rev. Designer:** Thomas D. Rogers, Sr.

Date	Mintage	Proof	MS-65	Prf-65
1996D	15,983	—	330	—
1996P	—	(92,016)	—	96.00

KM# 272 ATLANTA OLYMPICS   Obv: Rowing **Rev. Designer:** Thomas D. Rogers, Sr.

Date	Mintage	Proof	MS-65	Prf-65
1996D	16,258	—	360	—
1996P	—	(151,890)	—	75.00

KM# 272A ATLANTA OLYMPICS   Obv: High jumper **Rev. Designer:** Thomas D. Rogers, Sr.

Date	Mintage	Proof	MS-65	Prf-65
1996D	15,697	—	415	—
1996P	—	(124,502)	—	62.50

KM# 268 ATLANTA OLYMPICS, PARALYMPICS Obv: Wheelchair racer **Rev. Designer:** Thomas D. Rogers, Sr.

Date	Mintage	Proof	MS-65	Prf-65
1996D	14,497	—	415	—
1996P	—	(84,280)	—	90.00

KM# 275 NATIONAL COMMUNITY SERVICE Obv. Designer: Thomas D. Rogers, Sr. **Rev. Designer:** William C. Cousins

Date	Mintage	Proof	MS-65	Prf-65
1996S	23,500	—	285	—
1996S	—	(101,543)	—	96.00

KM# 276 SMITHSONIAN 150TH ANNIVERSARY Obv. Designer: Thomas D. Rogers, Sr. **Rev. Designer:** John Mercanti

Date	Mintage	Proof	MS-65	Prf-65
1996D	31,230	—	150	—
1996P	—	(129,152)	—	72.50

KM# 279 JACKIE ROBINSON 50TH ANNIVERSARY   Obv. Designer: Alfred Maletsky **Rev. Designer:** T.
James Ferrell

Date	Mintage	Proof	MS-65	Prf-65
1997S	30,007	(110,495)	103	85.00

KM# 281 NATIONAL LAW ENFORCEMENT OFFICERS MEMORIAL   Designer: Alfred Maletsky

Date	Mintage	Proof	MS-65	Prf-65
1997P	28,575	(110,428)	190	165

KM# 278 U.S. BOTANIC GARDENS 175TH ANNIVERSARY   Designer: Edgar Z. Steever

Date	Mintage	Proof	MS-65	Prf-65
1997P	57,272	(264,528)	47.50	46.00

KM# 288 BLACK REVOLUTIONARY WAR PATRIOTS   Obv: Crispus Attucks **Obv. Designer:** John
Mercanti **Rev. Designer:** Ed Dwight

Date	Mintage	Proof	MS-65	Prf-65
1998S	37,210	(75,070)	178	123

KM# 287 ROBERT F. KENNEDY Obv. Designer: Thomas D. Rogers, Sr. **Rev. Designer:** James M. Peed and Thomas D. Rogers, Sr.

Date	Mintage	Proof	MS-65	Prf-65
1998S	106,422	(99,020)	32.50	51.00

KM# 298 DOLLEY MADISON Obv. Designer: T. James Ferrell **Rev. Designer:** Thomas D. Rogers, Sr. **Designer:** Tiffany & Co.

Date	Mintage	Proof	MS-65	Prf-65
1999P	22,948	(158,247)	60.00	57.50

KM# 299 YELLOWSTONE Obv. Designer: Edgar Z. Steever **Rev. Designer:** William C. Cousins

Date	Mintage	Proof	MS-65	Prf-65
1999P	23,614	(128,646)	57.50	60.00

KM# 313 LEIF ERICSON   Obv. Designer: John Mercanti **Rev. Designer:** T. James Ferrell

Date	Mintage	Proof	MS-65	Prf-65
2000P	28,150	(58,612)	92.50	72.50
2000 Iceland	—	(15,947)	—	72.50

KM# 311 LIBRARY OF CONGRESS BICENTENNIAL   Obv. Designer: Thomas D. Rogers, Sr. **Rev. Designer:** John Mercanti

Date	Mintage	Proof	MS-65	Prf-65
2000P	52,771	(196,900)	45.00	45.00

KM# 325 AMERICAN BUFFALO   Designer: James E. Fraser

Date	Mintage	Proof	MS-65	Prf-65
2001	197,131	(272,869)	130	150

KM# 324 CAPITOL VISITOR CENTER Obv. Designer: Marika Somogyi **Rev. Designer:** John Mercanti

Date	Mintage	Proof	MS-65	Prf-65
2001	66,636	(143,793)	41.50	46.00

KM# 338 WEST POINT MILITARY ACADEMY BICENTENNIAL   Obv. Designer: T. James Ferrell **Rev. Designer:** John Mercanti

Date	Mintage	Proof	MS-65	Prf-65
2002	103,201	(288,293)	32.50	36.00

KM# 336 WINTER OLYMPICS - SALT LAKE CITY Obv. Designer: John Mercanti **Rev. Designer:** Donna Weaver

Date	Mintage	Proof	MS-65	Prf-65
2002	35,388	(142,873)	—	40.00

KM# 349 FIRST FLIGHT CENTENNIAL   Obv: Orville and Wilbur Wright **Obv. Designer:** T. James Ferrell
Rev: Wright Brothers airplane **Rev. Designer:** Norman E. Nemeth

Date	Mintage	Proof	MS-65	Prf-65
2003P	—	—	38.50	42.50

KM# 362 125TH ANNIVERSARY OF EDISON'S ELECTRIC LIGHT   Obv. Designer: Donna Weaver **Rev. Designer:** John Mercanti

Date	Mintage	Proof	MS-65	Prf-65
2004P	—	—	43.50	46.00

KM# 363 LEWIS AND CLARK CORPS OF DISCOVERY BICENTENNIAL

Date	Mintage	Proof	MS-65	Prf-65
2004P	—	—	—	—

KM# 375   CHIEF JUSTICE JOHN MARSHALL, 250TH BIRTH ANNIVERSARY   Obv. Designer: John Mercanti **Rev. Designer:** Donna Weaver

Date	Mintage	Proof	MS-65	Prf-65
2005P	—	—	—	—

KM# 376 U.S. MARINE CORPS, 230TH ANNIVERSARY

Date	Mintage	Proof	MS-65	Prf-65
2005P	—	—	—	—

$5 (HALF EAGLE)

KM# 215 STATUE OF LIBERTY CENTENNIAL   Designer: Elizabeth Jones

Date	Mintage	Proof	MS-65	Prf-65
1986W	95,248	(404,013)	140	140

KM# 221 CONSTITUTION BICENTENNIAL   Designer: Marcel Jovine

Date	Mintage	Proof	MS-65	Prf-65
1987W	214,225	(651,659)	140	140

KM# 223 OLYMPICS   Obv. Designer: Elizabeth Jones **Rev. Designer:** Marcel Jovine

Date	Mintage	Proof	MS-65	Prf-65
1988W	62,913	(281,456)	140	140

KM# 226 BICENTENNIAL OF THE CONGRESS **Obv. Designer:** John Mercanti

Date	Mintage	Proof	MS-65	Prf-65
1989W	46,899	(164,690)	140	140

KM# 230 MOUNT RUSHMORE GOLDEN ANNIVERSARY **Obv. Designer:** John Mercanti **Rev. Designer:** Robert Lamb and William C. Cousins

Date	Mintage	Proof	MS-65	Prf-65
1991W	31,959	(111,991)	185	165

KM# 239 COLUMBUS QUINCENTENARY **Obv. Designer:** T. James Ferrell **Rev. Designer:** Thomas D. Rogers, Sr.

Date	Mintage	Proof	MS-65	Prf-65
1992W	24,329	(79,730)	220	185

KM# 235 OLYMPICS **Obv. Designer:** James C. Sharpe and T. James Ferrell **Rev. Designer:** James M. Peed

Date	Mintage	Proof	MS-65	Prf-65
1992W	27,732	(77,313)	175	155

KM# 242 JAMES MADISON AND BILL OF RIGHTS **Obv. Designer:** Scott R. Blazek **Rev. Designer:** Joseph D. Peña

Date	Mintage	Proof	MS-65	Prf-65
1993W	22,266	(78,651)	215	185

KM# 245 WORLD WAR II 50TH ANNIVERSARY **Obv. Designer:** Charles J. Madsen **Rev. Designer:** Edward S. Fisher

Date	Mintage	Proof	MS-65	Prf-65
1993W	23,089	(65,461)	220	215

KM# 248 WORLD CUP SOCCER **Obv. Designer:** William J. Krawczewicz **Rev. Designer:** Dean McMullen

Date	Mintage	Proof	MS-65	Prf-65
1994W	22,464	(89,619)	200	165

KM# 256 CIVIL WAR **Obv. Designer:** Don Troiani **Rev. Designer:** Alfred Maletsky

Date	Mintage	Proof	MS-65	Prf-65
1995W	12,735	(55,246)	585	385

KM# 261 OLYMPICS **Obv:** Torch runner

Date	Mintage	Proof	MS-65	Prf-65
1995W	14,675	(57,442)	350	250

KM# 265 OLYMPICS **Obv:** Stadium

Date	Mintage	Proof	MS-65	Prf-65
1995W	10,579	(43,124)	385	290

KM# 270 1996 ATLANTA OLYMPICS Obv: Cauldron

Date	Mintage	Proof	MS-65	Prf-65
1996W	9,210	(38,555)	465	375

KM# 274 OLYMPICS Obv: Flag bearer

Date	Mintage	Proof	MS-65	Prf-65
1996W	9,174	(32,886)	485	375

KM# 277 SMITHSONIAN INSTITUTION 150TH ANNIVERSARY Obv. Designer: Alfred Maletsky **Rev. Designer:** T. James Ferrell

Date	Mintage	Proof	MS-65	Prf-65
1996W	9,068	(21,772)	950	2.00

KM# 282 FRANKLIN DELANO ROOSEVELT Obv. Designer: T. James Ferrell **Rev. Designer:** James M. Peed and Thomas D. Rogers, Sr.

Date	Mintage	Proof	MS-65	Prf-65
1997W	11,894	(29,474)	350	375

KM# 280 JACKIE ROBINSON 50TH ANNIVERSARY Obv. Designer: William C. Cousins **Rev. Designer:** James M. Peed

Date	Mintage	Proof	MS-65	Prf-65
1997W	5,202	(24,546)	3,150	625

KM# 300 GEORGE WASHINGTON DEATH BICENTENNIAL   Designer: Laura G. Fraser

Date	Mintage	Proof	MS-65	Prf-65
1999W	22,511	(41,693)	315	320

KM# 326 CAPITOL VISITOR CENTER   Designer: Elizabeth Jones

Date	Mintage	Proof	MS-65	Prf-65
2001	6,761	(27,652)	650	285

KM# 337   2002 SALT LAKE CITY WINTER OLYMPICS   Designer: Donna Weaver

Date	Mintage	Proof	MS-65	Prf-65
2002	10,585	(32,877)	345	300

$10 (EAGLE)

KM# 211 LOS ANGELES XXIII OLYMPIAD   Weight: 16.7180 g. **Composition:** 0.9000 Gold, 0.4839 oz. AGW **Diameter:** 27mm. **Obv. Designer:** James M. Peed and John Mercanti **Rev. Designer:** John Mercanti

Date	Mintage	Proof	MS-65	Prf-65
1984W	75,886	(381,085)	275	275
1984P	33,309	—	—	275
1984D	34,533	—	—	290
1984S	48,551	—	—	275

KM# 312 LIBRARY OF CONGRESS Weight: 16.2590 g. **Composition:** Platinum-Gold-Alloy **Obv. Designer:** John Mercanti **Rev. Designer:** Thomas D. Rogers, Sr. **Notes:** Composition is 48 percent platinum, 48 percent gold, and 4 percent alloy.

Date	Mintage	Proof	MS-65	Prf-65
2000W	6,683	(27,167)	1,600	650

KM# 350 FIRST FLIGHT CENTENNIAL Weight: 16.7180 g. **Composition:** 0.9000 Gold, .4839 oz. AGW **Designer:** Donna Weaver

Date	Mintage	Proof	MS-65	Prf-65
2003P	—	—	—	—

MODERN COMMEMORATIVE COIN SETS

Olympic • 1983-1984

Date	Price
1983 & 1984 proof dollars	26.00
1983 & 1984 gold and silver uncirculated set: One 1983 and one 1984 uncirculated dollar and one 1984P uncirculated gold $10; KM209, 210, 211.	300
1983 & 1984S gold and silver proof set: One 1983 and one 1984 proof dollar and one 1984 proof gold $10; KM209, 210, 211.	305
1983 & 1984 6 coin set: One 1983 and one 1984 uncirculated and proof dollar, one uncirculated and one proof gold $10; KM209, 210, 211.	605
1983 collectors set: 1983 PDS uncirculated dollars; KM209.	36.50
1984 collectors set: 1984 PDS uncirculated dollars; KM210.	42.50

Statue of Liberty

Date	Price
1986 3 coin set: proof silver dollar, clad half dollar and gold $5; KM212, 214, 215.	160
1986 2 coin set: uncirculated silver dollar and clad half dollar; KM212, 214.	21.50
1986 2 coin set: proof silver dollar and clad half dollar; KM212, 214.	21.50
1986 3 coin set: uncirculated silver dollar, clad half dollar and gold $5; KM212, 214, 215.	160
1986 6 coin set: 1 each of the proof and uncirculated issues; KM212, 214, 215.	350

Constitution

Date	Price
1987 2 coin set: uncirculated silver dollar and gold $5; KM220, 221.	145
1987 2 coin set: proof silver dollar and gold $5; KM220, 221.	150
1987 4 coin set: 1 each of the proof and uncirculated issues; KM220, 221.	300

Olympic • 1988

Date	Price
1988 2 coin set: uncirculated silver dollar and gold $5; KM222, 223.	150
1988 2 coin set: Proof silver dollar and gold $5; KM222, 223.	155
1988 4 coin set: 1 each of proof and uncirculated issues; KM222, 223.	300

Congress

Date	Price
1989 2 coin set: uncirculated silver dollar and clad half dollar; KM224, 225.	24.00
1989 2 coin set: proof silver dollar and clad half dollar; KM224, 225.	29.50
1989 3 coin set: uncirculated silver dollar, clad half and gold $5; KM224, 225, 226.	170
1989 3 coin set: proof silver dollar, clad half and gold $5; KM224, 225, 226.	170
1989 6 coin set: 1 each of the proof and uncirculated issues; KM224, 225, 226.	325

Mt. Rushmore

Date	Price
1991 2 coin set: uncirculated half dollar and silver dollar; KM228, 229.	55.00
1991 2 coin set: proof half dollar and silver dollar; KM228, 229.	63.00
1991 3 coin set: uncirculated half dollar, silver dollar and gold $5; KM228, 229, 230.	240
1991 3 coin set: proof half dollar, silver dollar and gold $5; KM228, 229, 230.	200
1991 6 coin set: 1 each of proof and uncirculated issues; KM228, 229, 230.	440

Olympic • 1992

Date	Price
1992 2 coin set: uncirculated half dollar and silver dollar; KM233, 234.	37.00

Date	Price
1992 2 coin set: proof half dollar and silver dollar; KM233, 234.	34.50
1992 3 coin set: uncirculated half dollar, silver dollar and gold $5; KM233, 234, 235.	210
1992 3 coin set: proof half dollar, silver dollar and gold $5; KM233, 234, 235.	200
1992 6 coin set: 1 each of proof and uncirculated issues; KM233, 234, 235.	410

Columbus Quincentenary

Date	Price
1992 2 coin set: uncirculated half dollar and silver dollar; KM237, 238.	42.50
1992 2 coin set: proof half dollar and silver dollar; KM237, 238.	57.50
1992 3 coin set: uncirculated half dollar, silver dollar and gold $5; KM237, 238, 239.	263
1992 3 coin set: proof half dollar, silver dollar and gold $5; KM237, 238, 239.	243
1992 6 coin set: 1 each of proof and uncirculated issues; KM237, 238, 239.	505

Jefferson

Date	Price
1993 Jefferson: dollar, nickel and $2 note; KM249, 192.	105

Madison / Bill of Rights

Date	Price
1993 2 coin set: uncirculated half dollar and silver dollar; KM240, 241.	37.50
1993 2 coin set: proof half dollar and silver dollar; KM240, 241.	39.00
1993 3 coin set: uncirculated half dollar, silver dollar and gold $5; KM240, 241, 242.	253
1993 3 coin set: proof half dollar, silver dollar and gold $5; KM240, 241, 242.	225
1993 6 coin set: 1 each of proof and uncirculated issues; KM240, 241, 242.	480

World War II

Date	Price
1993 2 coin set: uncirculated half dollar and silver dollar; KM243, 244.	73.50
1993 2 coin set: proof half dollar and silver dollar; KM243, 244.	80.00
1993 3 coin set: uncirculated half dollar, silver dollar and gold $5; KM243, 244, 245.	295
1993 3 coin set: proof half dollar, silver dollar and gold $5; KM243, 244, 245.	295
1993 6 coin set: 1 each of proof and uncirculated issues; KM243, 244, 245.	510

World Cup

Date	Price
1994 2 coin set: uncirculated half dollar and silver dollar; KM246, 247.	37.00
1994 2 coin set: proof half dollar and silver dollar; KM246, 247.	40.00
1994 3 coin set: uncirculated half dollar, silver dollar and gold $5; KM246, 247, 248.	220
1994 3 coin set: proof half dollar, silver dollar and gold $5; KM246, 247, 248.	235
1994 6 coin set: 1 each of proof and uncirculated issues; KM246, 247, 248.	440

U.S. Veterans

Date	Price
1994 3 coin set: uncirculated POW, Vietnam, Women dollars; KM250, 251, 252.	245
1994 3 coin set: proof POW, Vietnam, Women dollars; KM250, 251, 252.	240

Olympic • 1995-96

Date	Price
1995 4 coin set: uncirculated basketball half, $1 gymnast & blind runner, $5 torch runner; KM257, 259, 260, 261.	650
1995 4 coin set: proof basketball half, $1 gymnast & blind runner, $5 torch runner; KM257, 259, 260, 261.	410
1995P 2 coin set: proof $1 gymnast & blind runner; KM259, 260.	143
1995P 2 coin set: proof $1 track & field, cycling; KM263, 264.	80.00
1995-96 4 coin set: proof halves, basketball, baseball, swimming, soccer; KM257, 262, 267, 271.	180
1996P 2 coin set: proof $1 wheelchair & tennis; KM268, 269.	185
1996P 2 coin set: proof $1 rowing & high jump; KM272, 272A.	138

Civil War

Date	Price
1995 2 coin set: uncirculated half and dollar; KM254, 255.	125
1995 2 coin set: proof half and dollar; KM254, 255.	135
1995 3 coin set: uncirculated half, dollar and gold $5; KM254, 255, 256.	710
1995 3 coin set: proof half, dollar and gold $5; KM254, 255, 256.	520
1995 6 coin set: 1 each of proof and uncirculated issues; KM254, 255, 256.	1,230

Smithsonian

Date	Price
1996 2 coin set: proof dollar and $5 gold; KM276, 277.	465
1996 4 coin set: proof and B.U. ; KM276, 277.	1,550

Botanic Garden

Date	Price
1997 2 coin set: dollar, Jefferson nickel and $1 note; KM278, 192.	240

Franklin Delano Roosevelt

Date	Price
1997W 2 coin set: uncirculated and proof; KM282.	725

Jackie Robinson

Date	Price
1997 2 coin set: proof dollar & $5 gold; KM279, 280.	700
1997 4 coin set: proof & BU; KM279, 280.	4,500
1997 legacy set.	650

Kennedy

Date	Price
1998 2 coin set: proof; KM287.	92.50
1998 2 coin collectors set: Robert Kennedy dollar and John Kennedy half dollar; KM287, 202b. Matte finished.	325

Black Patriots

Date	Price
1998S 2 coin set: uncirculated and proof; KM288.	300

George Washington

Date	Price
1999 2 coin set: proof and uncirculated gold $5; KM300.	635

Dolley Madison

Date	Price
1999 2 coin set: proof and uncirculated silver dollars; KM298.	118

Yellowstone National Park

Date	Price
1999 2 coin set: proof and uncirculated silver dollars; KM299.	118

Millennium Coin & Currency

Date	Price
2000 2 coin set: uncirculated Sacagewea $1, silver Eagle & $1 note	70.00

Leif Ericson

Date	Price
2000 2 coin set: proof and uncirculated silver dollars; KM313.	145

American Buffalo

Date	Price
2001 2 coin set: 90% Silver unc. & proof $1.; KM325.	280
2001 coin & currency set 90% unc. dollar & replicas of 1899 $5 silver cert.; KM325.	145

Capitol Visitor Center

Date	Price
2001 3 coin set: proof half, silver dollar, gold $5; KM323, 324, 326.	380

Winter Olympics - Salt Lake City

Date	Price
2002 2 coin set: Proof 90% silver dollar; KM336 & $5.00 Gold; KM337	340
2002 4 coin set: 90% Silver unc. & proof $1, KM336 & unc. & proof gold $5, KM337.	725

First Flight Centennial

Date	Price
2003 3-coin set includes Proof Gold Ten Dollar KM#350 , Proof Silver Dollar KM#349 & Proof Clad Half Dollar KM#348	475

AMERICAN EAGLE BULLION COINS

SILVER DOLLAR

KM# 273 • 31.1010 g., 0.9993 **Silver**, 1 oz. , 40.6mm. • **Obv. Designer:** Adolph A. Weinman **Rev. Designer:** John Mercanti

Date	Mintage	Unc	Prf.	Date	Mintage	Unc	Prf.
1986	5,393,005	17.50	—	1995W 10th Anniversary	(30,125)	—	3,000
1986S	(1,446,778)	—	35.00	1996	3,603,386	38.00	—
1987	11,442,335	10.00	—	1996P	(473,021)	—	60.00
1987S	(904,732)	—	35.00	1997	4,295,004	11.00	—
1988	5,004,646	11.00	—	1997P	(429,682)	—	90.00
1988S	(557,370)	—	90.00	1998	4,847,549	10.50	—
1989	5,203,327	11.00	—	1998P	(452,319)	—	62.50
1989S	(617,694)	—	47.50	1999	7,408,640	10.50	—
1990	5,840,210	12.00	—	1999P	(549,769)	—	82.50
1990S	(695,510)	—	42.50	2000P	(600,000)	—	41.00
1991	7,191,066	10.50	—	2000	9,239,132	10.50	—
1991S	(511,924)	—	60.00	2001	9,001,711	10.50	—
1992	5,540,068	13.00	—	2001W	(746,154)	—	35.00
1992S	(498,552)	—	55.00	2002	10,539,026	10.50	—
1993	6,763,762	10.50	—	2002W	(647,342)	—	35.00
1993P	(403,625)	—	210	2003	8,495,008	10.50	—
1994	4,227,319	11.00	—	2003W	—	—	38.50
1994P	(372,168)	—	200	2004	—	10.50	—
1995	4,672,051	11.00	—	2004W	—	—	—
1995P	(395,400)	—	200				

GOLD $5

KM# 216 • 3.3930 g., 0.9167 **Gold**, 0.1 oz. , 16.5mm. • **Obv. Designer:** Augustus Saint-Gaudens **Rev. Designer:** Miley Busiek

Date	Mintage	Unc	Prf.	Date	Mintage	Unc	Prf.
MCMLXXXVI (1986)	912,609	60.00	—	1996W	(58,440)	—	80.00
MCMLXXXVII (1987)	580,266	60.00	—	1997	528,515	56.00	—
MCMLXXXVIII (1988)	159,500	192	—	1997W	(35,000)	—	91.00
MCMLXXXVIII (1988)P	(143,881)	—	80.00	1998	1,344,520	53.00	—
MCMLXXXIX (1989)	264,790	96.00	—	1998W	(39,653)	—	80.00
MCMLXXXIX (1989)P	(82,924)	—	80.00	1999	2,750,338	53.00	—
MCMXC (1990)	210,210	72.00	—	1999W	(48,426)	—	80.00
MCMXC (1990)P	(99,349)	—	80.00	2000	569,153	56.00	—
MCMXCI (1991)	165,200	125	—	2000W	(50,000)	—	90.00
MCMXCI (1991)P	(70,344)	—	80.00	2001	269,147	56.00	—
1992	209,300	60.00	—	2001W	(37,547)	—	80.00
1992P	(64,902)	—	80.00	2002	230,027	56.00	—
1993	210,709	70.00	—	2002W	(40,864)	—	80.00
1993P	(58,649)	—	80.00	2003	245,029	56.00	—
1994	206,380	56.00	—	2003W	—	—	85.00
1994W	(62,100)	—	80.00	2004	—	56.00	—
1995	223,025	56.00	—	2004W	—	—	—
1995W	(62,650)	—	80.00				
1996	401,964	56.00	—				

GOLD $10

KM# 217 • 8.4830 g., 0.9167 **Gold**, 0.25 oz. , 22mm. • **Obv. Designer:** Augustus Saint-Gaudens **Rev. Designer:** Miley Busiek

Date	Mintage	Unc	Prf.	Date	Mintage	Unc	Prf.
MCMLXXXVI (1986)	726,031	160	—	1996	60,318	145	—
MCMLXXXVII (1987)	269,255	160	—	1996W	(39,190)	—	160
MCMLXXXVIII (1988)	49,000	170	—	1997	108,805	145	—
MCMLXXXVIII (1988)P	(98,028)	—	160	1997W	(29,800)	—	160
MCMLXXXIX (1989)	81,789	135	—	1998	309,829	135	—
MCMLXXXIX (1989P)	(53,593)	—	160	1998W	(29,733)	—	160
MCMXC (1990)	41,000	160	—	1999	564,232	135	—
MCMXC (1990)P	(62,674)	—	160	1999W	(34,416)	—	160
MCMXCI (1991)	36,100	290	—	2000	128,964	135	—
MCMXCI (1991)P	(50,839)	—	160	2000W	(36,000)	—	160
1992	59,546	150	—	2001	71,280	150	—
1992P	(46,290)	—	160	2001W	(25,630)	—	160
1993	71,864	150	—	2002	62,027	135	—
1993P	(46,271)	—	150	2002W	(29,242)	—	160
1994	72,650	145	—	2003	74,029	150	—
1994W	(47,600)	—	160	2003W	—	—	165
1995	83,752	145	—	2004	—	135	—
1995W	(47,545)	—	160	2004W	—	—	—

GOLD $25

KM# 218 • 16.9660 g., 0.9167 **Gold**, 0.5 oz. , 27mm. • **Obv. Designer:** Augustus Saint-Gaudens **Rev. Designer:** Miley Busiek

Date	Mintage	Unc	Prf.	Date	Mintage	Unc	Prf.
MCMLXXXVI (1986)	599,566	335	—	1996	39,287	325	—
MCMLXXXVII (1987)	131,255	300	—	1996W	(35,937)	—	320
MCMLXXXVII (1987)P	(143,398)	—	320	1997	79,605	265	—
MCMLXXXVIII (1988)	45,000	385	—	1997W	(26,350)	—	320
MCMLXXXVIII (1988)P	(76,528)	—	320	1998	169,029	260	—
MCMLXXXIX (1989)	44,829	480	—	1998W	(25,896)	—	320
MCMLXXXIX (1989)P	(44,264)	—	320	1999	263,013	260	—
MCMXC (1990)	31,000	500	—	1999W	(30,452)	—	320
MCMXC (1990)P	(51,636)	—	320	2000	79,287	280	—
MCMXCI (1991)	24,100	800	—	2000W	(32,000)	—	320
MCMXCI (1991)P	(53,125)	—	320	2001	48,047	325	—
1992	54,404	360	—	2001W	(23,261)	—	320
1992P	(40,982)	—	320	2002	70,027	275	—
1993	73,324	280	—	2002W	(26,646)	—	320
1993P	(43,319)	—	320	2003	79,029	265	—
1994	62,400	280	—	2003W	—	—	320
1994W	(44,100)	—	320	2004	—	260	—
1995	53,474	325	—	2004W	—	—	—
1995W	(45,511)	—	320				

GOLD $50

KM# 219 • 33.9310 g., 0.9167 **Gold**, 1 oz. , 32.7mm. • **Obv. Designer:** Augustus Saint-Gaudens **Rev. Designer:** Miley Busiek

Date	Mintage	Unc	Prf.	Date	Mintage	Unc	Prf.
MCMLXXXVI (1986)	1,362,650	525	—	1995W	(46,553)	—	620
MCMLXXXVI (1986)W	(446,290)	—	620	1996	189,148	525	—
MCMLXXXVII (1987)	1,045,500	525	—	1996W	(37,302)	—	620
MCMLXXXVII (1987)W	(147,498)	—	620	1997	664,508	525	—
MCMLXXXVIII (1988)	465,000	525	—	1997W	(28,000)	—	620
MCMLXXXVIII (1988)W	(87,133)	—	620	1998	1,468,530	525	—
MCMLXXXIX (1989)	415,790	525	—	1998W	(26,060)	—	620
MCMLXXXIX (1989)W	(53,960)	—	620	1999	1,505,026	525	—
MCMXC (1990)	373,210	525	—	1999W	(31,446)	—	620
MCMXC (1990)W	(62,401)	—	620	2000	433,319	525	—
MCMXCI (1991)	243,100	252	—	2000W	(33,000)	—	620
MCMXCI (1991)W	(50,411)	—	620	2001	143,605	525	—
1992	275,000	525	—	2001W	(24,580)	—	—
1992W	(44,835)	—	620	2002	222,029	525	—
1993	480,192	525	—	2002W	(24,242)	—	620
1993W	(34,389)	—	620	2003	416,032	525	—
1994	221,633	525	—	2003W	—	—	620
1994W	(36,300)	—	620	2004	—	525	—
1995	200,636	525	—	2004W	—	—	—

PLATINUM $10

KM# 283 • 3.1100 g., 0.9995 **Platinum**, .1000 oz. • **Obv. Designer:** John Mercanti **Rev. Designer:** Thomas D. Rogers Sr

Date	Mintage	Unc	Prf.
1997	70,250	125	—
1997W	(36,996)	—	125
1998	39,525	138	—
1999	55,955	125	—
2000	34,027	125	—
2001	52,017	125	—
2002	23,005	150	—
2003	22,007	132	—
2004	—	125	—

KM# 289 • 3.1100 g., 0.9995 **Platinum**, .1000 oz. • **Obv. Designer:** John Mercanti

Date	Mintage	Unc	Prf.
1998W	(19,832)	—	125

KM# 301 • 3.1100 g., 0.9995 **Platinum**, .1000 oz. • **Obv. Designer:** John Mercanti

Date	Mintage	Unc	Prf.
1999W	(19,123)	—	125

KM# 314 • 3.1100 g., 0.9995 **Platinum**, .1000 oz. • **Obv. Designer:** John Mercanti

Date	Mintage	Unc	Prf.
2000W	(15,651)	—	125

KM# 327 • 3.1100 g., 0.9995 **Platinum**, .1000 oz. • **Obv. Designer:** John Mercanti

Date	Mintage	Unc	Prf.
2001W	(12,193)	—	125

KM# 339 • 3.1100 g., 0.9995 **Platinum**, .1000 oz. • **Obv. Designer:** John Mercanti

Date	Mintage	Unc	Prf.
2002W	(12,365)	—	135

KM# 351 • 3.1100 g., 0.9995 **Platinum**, .1000 oz. • **Obv. Designer:** John Mercanti **Rev. Designer:** Al Maletsky

Date	Mintage	Unc	Prf.
2003W	—	—	135

KM# 364 • 3.1100 g., 0.9995 **Platinum**, .1000 oz. • **Obv. Designer:** John Mercanti

Date	Mintage	Unc	Prf.
2004W	6,846	—	—

PLATINUM $25

KM# 284 • 7.7857 g., 0.9995 **Platinum**, 0.2500 oz. • **Obv. Designer:** John Mercanti **Rev. Designer:** Thomas D. Rogers Sr

Date	Mintage	Unc	Prf.
1997	27,100	300	—
1997W	(18,628)	—	300
1998	38,887	300	—
1999	39,734	300	—
2000	20,054	300	—
2001	21,815	325	—
2002	27,405	290	—
2003	25,207	325	—
2004	—	305	—

KM# 290 • 7.7857 g., 0.9995 **Platinum**, .2500 oz. • **Obv. Designer:** John Mercanti

Date	Mintage	Unc	Prf.
1998W	(14,860)	—	300

KM# 302 • 7.7857 g., 0.9995 **Platinum**, .2500 oz. • **Obv. Designer:** John Mercanti

Date	Mintage	Unc	Prf.
1999W	(13,514)	—	300

KM# 315 • 7.7857 g., 0.9995 **Platinum**, .2500 oz. • **Obv. Designer:** John Mercanti

Date	Mintage	Unc	Prf.
2000W	(11,995)	—	300

KM# 328 • 7.7857 g., 0.9995 **Platinum**, .2500 oz. • **Obv. Designer:** John Mercanti

Date	Mintage	Unc	Prf.
2001W	(8,858)	—	300

KM# 340 • 7.7857 g., 0.9995 **Platinum**, .2500 oz. • **Obv. Designer:** John Mercanti

Date	Mintage	Unc	Prf.
2002W	(9,282)	—	385

KM# 352 • 7.7857 g., 0.9995 **Platinum**, .2500 oz. • **Obv. Designer:** John Mercanti **Rev. Designer:** Al Maletsky

Date	Mintage	Unc	Prf.
2003W	—	—	385

KM# 365 • 7.7857 g., 0.9995 **Platinum**, .2500 oz. • **Obv. Designer:** John Mercanti

Date	Mintage	Unc	Prf.
2004W	5,035	—	—

PLATINUM $50

KM# 285 • 15.5520 g., 0.9995 **Platinum**, 0.5000 oz. • **Obv. Designer:** John Mercanti **Rev. Designer:** Thomas D. Rogers Sr

Date	Mintage	Unc	Prf.
1997	20,500	575	—
1997W	(15,432)	—	575
1998	32,415	575	—
1999	32,309	575	—
2000	18,892	575	—
2001	12,815	600	—
2002	24,005	565	—
2003	17,409	575	—
2004	—	575	—

KM# 291 • 15.5520 g., 0.9995 **Platinum**, .5000 oz. • **Obv. Designer:** John Mercanti

Date	Mintage	Unc	Prf.
1998W	(13,821)	—	575

KM# 303 • 15.5520 g., 0.9995 **Platinum**, .5000 oz. • **Obv. Designer:** John Mercanti

Date	Mintage	Unc	Prf.
1999W	(11,098)	—	575

KM# 316 • 15.5520 g., 0.9995 **Platinum**, .5000 oz. • **Obv. Designer:** John Mercanti

Date	Mintage	Unc	Prf.
2000W	(11,049)	—	575

KM# 329 • 15.5520 g., 0.9995 **Platinum**, .5000 oz. • **Obv. Designer:** John Mercanti

Date	Mintage	Unc	Prf.
2001W	(8,268)	—	575

KM# 341 • 15.5520 g., 0.9995 **Platinum**, .5000 oz. • **Obv. Designer:** John Mercanti

Date	Mintage	Unc	Prf.
2002W	(8,772)	—	630

KM# 353 • 15.5520 g., 0.9995 **Platinum**, .5000 oz. • **Obv. Designer:** John Mercanti **Rev. Designer:** Al Maletsky

Date	Mintage	Unc	Prf.
2003W	—	—	630

KM# 366 • 15.5520 g., 0.9995 **Platinum**, .5000 oz. • **Obv. Designer:** John Mercanti

Date	Mintage	Unc	Prf.
2004W	4,886	—	—

PLATINUM $100

KM# 286 • 31.1050 g., 0.9995 **Platinum**, 1.000
oz. • **Obv. Designer:** John Mercanti **Rev.**
Designer: Thomas D. Rogers Sr

Date	Mintage	Unc	Prf.
1997	56,000	1,115	—
1997W	(15,885)	—	1,115
1998	133,002	1,115	—
1999	56,707	1,115	—
2000	18,892	1,115	—
2001	14,070	1,115	—
2002	11,502	1,115	—
2003	8,007	1,115	—
2004	—	1,115	—

KM# 292 • 31.1050 g., 0.9995 **Platinum**, 1.000
oz. • **Obv. Designer:** John Mercanti

Date	Mintage	Unc	Prf.
1998W	(14,203)	—	1,115

KM# 304 • 31.1050 g., 0.9995 **Platinum**, 1.000
oz. • **Obv. Designer:** John Mercanti

Date	Mintage	Unc	Prf.
1999W	—	—	1,115

KM# 317 • 31.1050 g., 0.9995 **Platinum**, 1.000
oz. • **Obv. Designer:** John Mercanti

Date	Mintage	Unc	Prf.
2000W	—	—	1,115

KM# 330 • 31.1050 g., 0.9995 **Platinum**, 1.000
oz. • **Obv. Designer:** John Mercanti

Date	Mintage	Unc	Prf.
2001W	(8,990)	—	1,115

KM# 342 • 31.1050 g., 0.9995 **Platinum**, 1.000
oz. • **Obv. Designer:** John Mercanti

Date	Mintage	Unc	Prf.
2002W	(9,834)	—	1,115

KM# 354 • 31.1050 g., 0.9995 **Platinum**, 1.000
oz. • **Obv. Designer:** John Mercanti **Rev.**
Designer: Al Maletsky

Date	Mintage	Unc	Prf.
2003W	—	—	1,215

KM# 367 • 31.1050 g., 0.9995 **Platinum**, 1.000
oz. • **Obv. Designer:** John Mercanti **Rev.**
Designer: Donna Weaver

Date	Mintage	Unc	Prf.
2004W	(5,833)	—	1,215

CANADA

CIRCULATION COINAGE

CENT

KM# 1 Weight: 3.2400 g. **Composition:** Bronze

Date	Mintage	VG-8	F-12	VF-20	XF-40	MS-60	MS-63	Proof
1858	421,000	50.00	60.00	80.00	120	300	1,250	—
1859/8 Wide 9	Inc. above	25.00	35.00	60.00	90.00	250	1,350	—
1859 Narrow 9	9,579,000	2.25	3.00	5.00	7.00	35.00	175	—
1859 Double punched narrow 9 type I	Inc. above	175	250	350	540	1,150	3,000	—
1859 Double punched narrow 9 type II	Inc. above	35.00	70.00	95.00	150	325	1,600	—

KM# 7 Obv. Designer: Leonard C. Wyon **Edge:** Plain **Weight:** 3.2400 g. **Composition:** Bronze

Date	Mintage	VG-8	F-12	VF-20	XF-40	MS-60	MS-63	Proof
1876H	4,000,000	2.00	2.75	4.00	7.50	45.00	190	—
1881H	2,000,000	3.00	4.00	9.00	14.00	60.00	250	—
1882H	4,000,000	2.00	2.75	4.00	7.50	32.00	170	—
1884	2,500,000	2.25	3.00	5.00	8.50	60.00	225	—
1886	1,500,000	3.75	5.00	10.00	20.00	90.00	350	—
1887	1,500,000	2.75	4.00	6.00	11.00	55.00	215	—
1888	4,000,000	2.00	3.00	5.00	7.50	35.00	160	—
1890H	1,000,000	5.00	8.00	13.00	25.00	100.00	400	—
1891 Large date	1,452,000	5.50	9.00	13.50	30.00	125	420	—
1891 S.D.L.L.	Inc. above	50.00	75.00	110	160	620	2,150	—
1891 S.D.S.L.	Inc. above	35.00	50.00	65.00	95.00	225	650	—
1892	1,200,000	4.00	7.00	10.00	13.50	55.00	220	—
1893	2,000,000	2.50	3.00	5.00	7.50	35.00	125	—
1894	1,000,000	8.00	12.00	17.00	30.00	90.00	265	—
1895	1,200,000	4.00	7.00	10.00	16.00	55.00	225	—
1896	2,000,000	2.00	2.75	5.00	7.50	40.00	150	—
1897	1,500,000	2.50	4.00	5.00	9.00	45.00	165	—
1898H	1,000,000	5.00	7.00	12.00	18.00	75.00	250	—
1899	2,400,000	2.25	3.00	4.00	7.00	35.00	100.00	—
1900	1,000,000	5.00	9.00	15.00	22.00	85.00	400	—
1900H	2,600,000	2.00	2.50	4.00	5.50	30.00	75.00	—
1901	4,100,000	2.25	3.00	4.50	5.50	35.00	85.00	—

KM# 8 Obv. Designer: G. W. DeSaulles **Edge:** Plain **Weight:** 3.2400 g. **Composition:** Bronze

Date	Mintage	VG-8	F-12	VF-20	XF-40	MS-60	MS-63	Proof
1902	3,000,000	1.25	2.25	3.50	6.00	23.00	50.00	—
1903	4,000,000	1.25	2.25	3.00	6.00	25.00	55.00	—
1904	2,500,000	2.00	2.25	3.25	8.00	30.00	85.00	—
1905	2,000,000	2.50	4.00	5.00	7.00	40.00	100.00	—
1906	4,100,000	1.25	2.25	3.00	6.00	30.00	125	—
1907	2,400,000	1.25	2.25	3.00	6.00	30.00	125	—

Date	Mintage	VG-8	F-12	VF-20	XF-40	MS-60	MS-63	Proof
1907H	800,000	8.00	11.00	20.00	35.00	150	350	—
1908	2,401,506	2.00	2.25	3.00	8.00	30.00	90.00	150
1909	3,973,339	1.25	2.25	2.00	4.00	25.00	70.00	—
1910	5,146,487	1.25	1.50	2.00	3.00	26.00	70.00	—

KM# 15 Obv. Designer: E. B. MacKennal **Edge:** Plain **Weight:** 3.2400 g. **Composition:** Bronze

Date	Mintage	VG-8	F-12	VF-20	XF-40	MS-60	MS-63	Proof
1911	4,663,486	0.80	1.30	1.75	3.50	22.00	50.00	250

KM# 21 Obv. Designer: E. B. MacKennal **Edge:** Plain **Weight:** 3.2400 g. **Composition:** Bronze

Date	Mintage	VG-8	F-12	VF-20	XF-40	MS-60	MS-63	Proof
1912	5,107,642	0.75	1.00	1.50	2.50	21.00	55.00	—
1913	5,735,405	0.75	1.00	1.50	2.50	23.00	80.00	—
1914	3,405,958	0.75	1.50	1.75	4.00	30.00	95.00	—
1915	4,932,134	0.75	1.00	1.50	2.50	25.00	70.00	—
1916	11,022,367	0.50	0.65	0.90	2.00	16.00	50.00	—
1917	11,899,254	0.50	0.65	0.90	1.50	8.00	45.00	—
1918	12,970,798	0.50	0.65	0.90	1.50	8.00	45.00	—
1919	11,279,634	0.50	0.65	0.90	1.50	8.00	45.00	—
1920	6,762,247	0.60	0.75	1.00	2.00	15.00	55.00	—

KM# 28 Obv. Designer: E. B. MacKennal **Rev. Designer:** Fred Lewis **Edge:** Plain **Weight:** 3.2400 g. **Composition:** Bronze

Date	Mintage	VG-8	F-12	VF-20	XF-40	MS-60	MS-63	Proof
1920	15,483,923	0.20	0.50	1.00	2.00	11.00	35.00	—
1921	7,601,627	0.50	0.75	1.75	3.00	30.00	125	—
1922	1,243,635	8.75	10.00	21.00	35.00	175	650	—
1923	1,019,002	19.00	21.00	30.00	45.00	275	1,200	—
1924	1,593,195	3.00	4.00	5.00	15.00	100.00	375	—
1925	1,000,622	18.00	21.00	27.00	40.00	175	550	—
1926	2,143,372	2.25	3.00	4.50	8.75	90.00	325	—
1927	3,553,928	0.90	1.25	2.25	6.00	35.00	125	—
1928	9,144,860	0.15	0.30	0.65	1.50	15.00	55.00	—
1929	12,159,840	0.15	0.30	0.65	1.50	15.00	55.00	—
1930	2,538,613	1.35	1.80	3.00	5.00	45.00	125	—
1931	3,842,776	0.65	1.00	1.75	3.50	35.00	125	—
1932	21,316,190	0.15	0.20	0.50	1.50	9.00	45.00	—
1933	12,079,310	0.15	0.20	0.50	1.50	9.00	45.00	—
1934	7,042,358	0.20	0.30	0.75	1.50	9.00	45.00	—
1935	7,526,400	0.20	0.30	0.75	1.50	9.00	40.00	—
1936	8,768,769	0.15	0.30	0.75	1.50	9.00	30.00	—
1936 dot below date; Rare	678,823	—	—	—	—	—	—	—

Note: Only one possible business strike is known to exist. No other examples (or possible business strikes) have ever surfaced.

1936 dot below date, specimen, 3 known	—	—	—	—	—	—	—	—

Note: At the David Akers auction of the John Jay Pittman collection (Part 1, 10-97), a gem specimen realized $121,000. At the David Akers auction of the John Jay Pittman collection (Part 3, 10-99), a near choice specimen realized $115,000.

KM# 32 Obv. Designer: T. H. Paget **Rev. Designer:** George E. Kruger-Gray **Edge:** Plain **Weight:** 3.2400 g. **Composition:** Bronze

Date	Mintage	VG-8	F-12	VF-20	XF-40	MS-60	MS-63	Proof
1937	10,040,231	0.50	0.65	1.25	1.50	3.00	9.00	—
1938	18,365,608	0.15	0.20	0.35	0.75	2.00	6.50	—
1939	21,600,319	0.15	0.20	0.35	0.70	1.75	5.00	—
1940	85,740,532	0.10	0.15	0.25	0.50	1.50	5.50	—
1941	56,336,011	0.10	0.15	0.25	0.50	6.00	50.00	—
1942	76,113,708	0.10	0.15	0.25	0.50	6.00	40.00	—
1943	89,111,969	0.10	0.15	0.25	0.45	2.50	25.00	—
1944	44,131,216	0.15	0.20	0.30	0.60	9.50	70.00	—
1945	77,268,591	0.10	0.15	0.20	0.30	1.50	14.00	—
1946	56,662,071	0.10	0.15	0.20	0.30	1.50	5.00	—
1947	31,093,901	0.10	0.15	0.20	0.30	1.50	6.00	—
1947 maple leaf	47,855,448	0.10	0.15	0.20	0.30	1.50	5.00	—

KM# 41 Obv: Modified legend **Obv. Designer:** T. H. Paget **Rev. Designer:** George E. Kruger-Gray **Edge:** Plain **Weight:** 3.2400 g. **Composition:** Bronze

Date	Mintage	VG-8	F-12	VF-20	XF-40	MS-60	MS-63	Proof
1948	25,767,779	—	0.15	0.25	0.70	2.25	20.00	—
1949	33,128,933	—	0.10	0.15	0.25	1.25	6.00	—
1950	60,444,992	—	0.10	0.15	0.25	0.85	6.00	—
1951	80,430,379	—	0.10	0.15	0.20	0.85	8.00	—
1952	67,631,736	—	0.10	0.15	0.20	0.85	4.00	—

   No strap  With strap

KM# 49 Obv: Elizabeth II effigy **Obv. Designer:** Mary Gillick **Rev. Designer:** George E. Kruger-Gray **Weight:** 3.2400 g. **Composition:** Bronze

Date	Mintage	VG-8	F-12	VF-20	XF-40	MS-60	MS-63	Proof
1953 without strap	67,806,016	0.10	0.15	0.20	0.25	0.65	1.50	—
1953 with strap	Inc. above	0.50	1.00	1.50	2.50	10.00	35.00	—
1954 with strap	22,181,760	0.10	0.15	0.25	0.40	1.00	4.00	—
1954 without strap, proof-like only	Inc. above	—	—	—	—	150	300	—
1955 with strap	56,403,193	—	0.10	0.15	0.20	0.35	1.00	—
1955 without strap	Inc. above	85.00	125	150	250	500	1,100	—
1956	78,658,535	—	—	—	0.10	0.50	0.90	—
1957	100,601,792	—	—	—	0.10	0.20	0.35	—
1958	59,385,679	—	—	—	0.10	0.20	0.35	—
1959	83,615,343	—	—	—	0.10	0.15	0.25	—
1960	75,772,775	—	—	—	0.10	0.15	0.25	—
1961	139,598,404	—	—	—	—	0.15	0.20	—
1962	227,244,069	—	—	—	—	0.10	0.20	—
1963	279,076,334	—	—	—	—	0.10	0.20	—
1964	484,655,322	—	—	—	—	0.10	0.20	—

KM# 59.1 Obv: Elizabeth II effigy **Obv. Designer:** Arnold Machin **Rev. Designer:** George E. Kruger-Gray **Edge:** Plain **Weight:** 3.2400 g. **Composition:** Bronze

Date	Mintage	VG-8	F-12	VF-20	XF-40	MS-60	MS-63	Proof
1965 sm. beads, pointed 5	304,441,082	—	—	—	0.40	1.00	4.00	—
1965 sm. beads, blunt 5	Inc. above	—	—	—	—	0.15	0.20	—
1965 lg. beads, pointed 5	Inc. above	—	—	3.00	5.00	12.00	35.00	—
1965 lg. beads, blunt 5	Inc. above	—	—	—	0.10	0.15	0.20	—
1966	184,151,087	—	—	—	—	0.10	0.20	—
1968	329,695,772	—	—	—	—	0.10	0.15	—
1969	335,240,929	—	—	—	—	0.10	0.15	—
1970	311,145,010	—	—	—	—	0.10	0.15	—
1971	298,228,936	—	—	—	—	0.10	0.15	—
1972	451,304,591	—	—	—	—	0.10	0.15	—
1973	457,059,852	—	—	—	—	0.10	0.15	—
1974	692,058,489	—	—	—	—	0.10	0.15	—
1975	642,318,000	—	—	—	—	0.10	0.15	—

Date	Mintage	VG-8	F-12	VF-20	XF-40	MS-60	MS-63	Proof
1976	701,122,890	—	—	—	—	0.10	0.15	—
1977	453,762,670	—	—	—	—	0.10	0.15	—
1978	911,170,647	—	—	—	—	0.10	0.15	—

KM# 59.2   Obv: Elizabeth II effigy. Smaller bust **Obv. Designer:** Arnold Machin **Rev. Designer:** George E. Kruger-Gray **Edge:** Plain **Weight:** 3.2400 g. **Composition:** Bronze

Date	Mintage	VG-8	F-12	VF-20	XF-40	MS-60	MS-63	Proof
1979	754,394,064	—	—	—	—	0.10	0.15	—

KM# 127   Obv: Elizabeth II effigy **Obv. Designer:** Arnold Machin **Rev. Designer:** George E. Kruger-Gray **Edge:** Plain **Weight:** 2.8000 g. **Composition:** Bronze **Note:** Reduced weight.

Date	Mintage	VG-8	F-12	VF-20	XF-40	MS-60	MS-63	Proof
1980	912,052,318	—	—	—	—	0.10	0.15	—
1981	1,209,468,500	—	—	—	—	0.10	0.15	—
1981 Proof	199,000	—	—	—	—	—	—	1.50

KM# 132   Obv: Elizabeth II effigy **Obv. Designer:** Arnold Machin **Rev. Designer:** George E. Kruger-Gray **Edge:** Plain **Weight:** 2.5000 g. **Composition:** Bronze **Shape:** Multi-sided **Note:** Reduced weight.

Date	Mintage	VG-8	F-12	VF-20	XF-40	MS-60	MS-63	Proof
1982	911,001,000	—	—	—	—	0.10	0.15	—
1982 Proof	180,908	—	—	—	—	—	—	1.50
1983	975,510,000	—	—	—	—	0.10	0.15	—
1983 Proof	168,000	—	—	—	—	—	—	1.50
1984	838,225,000	—	—	—	—	0.10	0.15	—
1984 Proof	161,602	—	—	—	—	—	—	1.50
1985 pointed 5	771,772,500	—	—	—	4.00	10.00	19.00	—
1985 blunt 5	Inc. above	—	—	—	—	0.10	0.15	—
1985 blunt 5, proof	157,037	—	—	—	—	—	—	1.50
1986	740,335,000	—	—	—	—	0.10	0.15	—
1986 Proof	175,745	—	—	—	—	—	—	1.50
1987	774,549,000	—	—	—	—	0.10	0.15	—
1987 Proof	179,004	—	—	—	—	—	—	1.50
1988	482,676,752	—	—	—	—	0.10	0.15	—
1988 Proof	175,259	—	—	—	—	—	—	1.50
1989	1,077,347,200	—	—	—	—	0.10	0.15	—
1989 Proof	170,928	—	—	—	—	—	—	1.50

KM# 181   Obv: Elizabeth II effigy **Obv. Designer:** Dora dePedery-Hunt **Rev. Designer:** George E. Kruger-Gray **Edge:** Plain **Weight:** 2.5000 g. **Composition:** Bronze

Date	Mintage	VG-8	F-12	VF-20	XF-40	MS-60	MS-63	Proof
1990	218,035,000	—	—	—	—	0.10	0.15	—
1990 Proof	140,649	—	—	—	—	—	—	2.50
1991	831,001,000	—	—	—	—	0.10	0.15	—
1991 Proof	131,888	—	—	—	—	—	—	3.50
1993	752,034,000	—	—	—	—	0.10	0.15	—
1993 Proof	145,065	—	—	—	—	—	—	2.00
1994	639,516,000	—	—	—	—	0.10	0.15	—
1994 Proof	146,424	—	—	—	—	—	—	2.50
1995	624,983,000	—	—	—	—	0.10	0.15	—
1996	445,746,000	—	—	—	—	0.10	0.15	—
1996 Proof	—	—	—	—	—	—	—	2.50

KM# 289   Edge: Round and plain. **Composition:** Copper Plated Zinc

Date	Mintage	VG-8	F-12	VF-20	XF-40	MS-60	MS-63	Proof
1997	549,868,000	—	—	—	—	0.10	0.15	—
1997 Proof	—	—	—	—	—	—	—	2.75
1998	999,578,000	—	—	—	—	0.10	0.15	—
1998 Proof	—	—	—	—	—	—	—	3.00
1998W	—	—	—	—	—	—	1.75	—
1999P Plated planchet, set only	—	—	—	—	—	—	6.00	—
1999	1,089,625,000	—	—	—	—	0.10	0.15	—
1999W	—	—	—	—	—	—	—	—
1999 Proof	—	—	—	—	—	—	—	4.00
2000	761,970,000	—	—	—	—	0.10	0.15	—
2000W	—	—	—	—	—	—	1.75	—
2000 Proof	—	—	—	—	—	—	—	4.00
2001	919,359,000	—	—	—	—	0.10	—	—
2001 Proof	—	—	—	—	—	—	—	4.00

Date	Mintage	VG-8	F-12	VF-20	XF-40	MS-60	MS-63	Proof
2003	—	—	—	—	—	—	0.10	—
2003 Proof	—	—	—	—	—	—	—	4.00

KM# 289a Composition: Bronze

Date	Mintage	VG-8	F-12	VF-20	XF-40	MS-60	MS-63	Proof
1998 In Specimen sets only	—	—	—	—	—	—	0.75	—

KM# 445 Subject: Elizabeth II Golden Jubilee Obv: Queen, Jubilee commemorative dates 1952-2002 Edge: Plain Composition: Bronze-Plated Zinc

Date	Mintage	VG-8	F-12	VF-20	XF-40	MS-60	MS-63	Proof
ND(2002)	716,366,000	—	—	—	—	—	0.75	—
ND(2002)P	114,212,000	—	—	—	—	—	1.00	—
ND(2002) In proof sets only	32,642	—	—	—	—	—	—	2.50

KM# 490 Obv: New effigy of Queen Elizabeth II Obv. Designer: Susanna Blunt Edge: Plain Composition: Bronze-Plated Zinc

Date	Mintage	VG-8	F-12	VF-20	XF-40	MS-60	MS-63	Proof
2003W	—	—	—	—	—	—	0.25	—

5 CENTS

     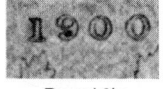

Oval 0's   Round 0's

KM# 2 Designer: Leonard C. Wyon Weight: 1.1620 g. Composition: 0.9250 Silver 0.0346 oz. ASW

Date	Mintage	VG-8	F-12	VF-20	XF-40	MS-60	MS-63	Proof
1858 Small date	1,500,000	12.00	20.00	35.00	55.00	250	525	—
1858 Large date over small date	Inc. above	125	200	325	550	1,350	3,000	—
1870 Flat rim	2,800,000	13.50	22.50	40.00	60.00	250	650	—
1870 Wire rim	Inc. above	10.00	20.00	35.00	55.00	225	525	—
1871	1,400,000	13.50	22.50	40.00	70.00	275	600	—
1872H	2,000,000	9.00	16.00	35.00	55.00	250	750	—
1874H Plain 4	800,000	15.00	35.00	75.00	120	400	950	—
1874H Crosslet 4	Inc. above	14.00	30.00	60.00	120	450	1,100	—
1875H Large date	1,000,000	170	275	425	875	2,750	7,000	—
1875H Small date	Inc. above	90.00	175	285	500	1,750	4,550	—
1880H	3,000,000	5.00	8.00	18.00	40.00	250	600	—
1881H	1,500,000	6.00	10.00	20.00	45.00	265	650	—
1882H	1,000,000	8.00	15.00	25.00	55.00	275	700	—
1883H	600,000	15.00	30.00	70.00	150	750	2,000	—
1884	200,000	85.00	165	275	650	2,850	7,250	—
1885 Small 5	1,000,000	10.00	20.00	40.00	90.00	500	1,800	—
1885 Large 5	Inc. above	11.50	22.50	45.00	100.00	550	2,000	—
1885 Large 5 over small 5	Inc. above	50.00	100.00	175	450	2,850	2,750	—
1886 Small 6	1,700,000	7.00	15.00	25.00	50.00	300	900	—
1886 Large 6	Inc. above	9.00	16.00	28.00	60.00	350	1,000	—
1887	500,000	16.00	30.00	55.00	120	400	825	—
1888	1,000,000	5.00	9.00	18.00	35.00	165	425	—
1889	1,200,000	20.00	35.00	75.00	125	475	1,200	—
1890H	1,000,000	6.00	12.00	22.00	50.00	200	450	—
1891	1,800,000	5.00	8.00	15.00	30.00	150	385	—
1892	860,000	6.00	10.00	20.00	50.00	250	675	—
1893	1,700,000	4.00	7.00	14.00	30.00	175	400	—
1894	500,000	12.00	25.00	50.00	100.00	300	1,100	—
1896	1,500,000	5.00	7.00	14.00	35.00	175	375	—
1897	1,319,283	4.50	6.50	13.50	30.00	150	325	—
1898	580,717	10.00	20.00	35.00	70.00	250	750	—
1899	3,000,000	4.50	6.50	12.00	25.00	115	300	—
1900 Oval 0's	1,800,000	4.50	6.50	12.00	25.00	115	325	—
1900 Round 0's	Inc. above	15.00	35.00	50.00	110	300	800	—
1901	2,000,000	4.50	6.50	12.00	35.00	150	400	—

KM# 9 Obv. Designer: G. W. DeSaulles Rev. Designer: Leonard C. Wyon Weight: 1.1620 g. Composition: 0.9250 Silver 0.0346 oz. ASW

Date	Mintage	VG-8	F-12	VF-20	XF-40	MS-60	MS-63	Proof
1902	2,120,000	1.50	2.00	3.25	7.00	35.00	55.00	—
1902 lg. broad H	2,200,000	1.50	2.00	3.25	7.00	35.00	60.00	—
1902 sm. narrow H	Inc. above	5.00	9.00	24.00	40.00	100.00	175	—

KM# 13 Weight: 1.1620 g. Composition: 0.9250 Silver 0.0346 oz. ASW

Date	Mintage	VG-8	F-12	VF-20	XF-40	MS-60	MS-63	Proof
1903 22 leaves	1,000,000	4.00	7.00	17.00	35.00	150	350	—
1903H 21 leaves	2,640,000	1.75	3.00	7.00	16.00	100.00	300	—
1904	2,400,000	1.75	3.00	7.00	23.00	175	500	—

Date	Mintage	VG-8	F-12	VF-20	XF-40	MS-60	MS-63	Proof
1905	2,600,000	1.75	3.00	6.00	16.00	100.00	225	—
1906	3,100,000	1.50	2.00	4.00	8.00	85.00	225	—
1907	5,200,000	1.50	2.00	4.00	7.00	55.00	150	—
1908	1,220,524	4.00	6.50	23.00	35.00	100.00	175	—
1909 round leaves	1,983,725	3.00	4.00	10.00	30.00	175	500	—
1909 pointed leaves	Inc. above	12.00	18.00	35.00	95.00	550	1,300	—
1910 pointed leaves	3,850,325	1.50	1.75	3.25	7.00	50.00	95.00	—
1910 round leaves	Inc. above	10.00	17.00	30.00	85.00	400	1,300	—

KM# 16 Obv. Designer: E. B. MacKennal **Rev. Designer:** Leonard C. Wyon **Weight:** 1.1620 g. **Composition:** 0.9250 Silver 0.0346 oz. ASW

Date	Mintage	VG-8	F-12	VF-20	XF-40	MS-60	MS-63	Proof
1911	3,692,350	1.25	3.00	4.00	8.00	60.00	100.00	—

KM# 22 Obv. Designer: E. B. MacKennal **Rev. Designer:** Leonard C. Wyon **Weight:** 1.1620 g. **Composition:** 0.9250 Silver 0.0346 oz. ASW

Date	Mintage	VG-8	F-12	VF-20	XF-40	MS-60	MS-63	Proof
1912	5,863,170	1.25	2.00	3.00	6.00	50.00	150	—
1913	5,488,048	1.25	1.75	2.50	5.00	26.00	50.00	—
1914	4,202,179	1.25	2.00	3.00	6.00	50.00	125	—
1915	1,172,258	7.50	15.00	26.00	50.00	225	600	—
1916	2,481,675	2.75	5.00	9.00	20.00	225	175	—
1917	5,521,373	1.25	1.75	3.00	6.00	30.00	80.00	—
1918	6,052,298	1.25	1.75	3.00	4.00	30.00	65.00	—
1919	7,835,400	1.25	1.75	3.00	4.00	30.00	65.00	—

KM# 22a Obv. Designer: E. B. MacKennal **Rev. Designer:** Leonard C. Wyon **Weight:** 1.1664 g. **Composition:** 0.8000 Silver .0300 oz. ASW

Date	Mintage	VG-8	F-12	VF-20	XF-40	MS-60	MS-63	Proof
1920	10,649,851	1.25	1.75	3.00	4.00	26.00	50.00	—
1921	2,582,495	1,700	2,500	3,500	4,500	9,000	16,000	—

Note: Approximately 460 known; balance remelted. Stack's A.G. Carter Jr. Sale (12-89) choice BU, finest known, realized $57,200.

KM# 29 Obv. Designer: E. B. MacKennal **Rev. Designer:** W. H. J. Blakemore **Composition:** Nickel

Date	Mintage	VG-8	F-12	VF-20	XF-40	MS-60	MS-63	Proof
1922	4,794,119	0.20	0.75	1.75	7.00	45.00	95.00	—
1923	2,502,279	0.40	1.25	3.50	16.00	100.00	275	—
1924	3,105,839	0.25	0.70	2.50	10.00	85.00	200	—
1925	201,921	55.00	70.00	100.00	200	1,200	3,600	—
1926 near 6	938,162	2.25	4.00	16.00	60.00	375	1,300	—
1926 far 6	Inc. above	80.00	130	200	400	1,500	4,300	—
1927	5,285,627	0.20	0.65	2.75	6.50	60.00	125	—
1928	4,577,712	0.20	0.65	2.75	6.50	55.00	100.00	—
1929	5,611,911	0.20	0.65	2.75	6.50	60.00	150	—
1930	3,704,673	0.20	0.65	2.75	10.00	90.00	200	—
1931	5,100,830	0.20	0.65	3.25	15.00	125	475	—
1932	3,198,566	0.20	0.65	3.25	10.50	100.00	350	—
1933	2,597,867	0.40	1.50	4.00	18.00	175	650	—
1934	3,827,304	0.20	0.65	3.00	10.75	100.00	375	—
1935	3,900,000	0.20	0.65	2.75	11.00	95.00	250	—
1936	4,400,450	0.20	0.65	1.75	6.00	50.00	100.00	—

KM# 33 Obv. Designer: T. H. Paget **Rev. Designer:** George E. Kruger-Gray **Composition:** Nickel

Date	Mintage	VG-8	F-12	VF-20	XF-40	MS-60	MS-63	Proof
1937 dot	4,593,263	0.15	0.25	1.25	2.50	9.00	22.00	—
1938	3,898,974	0.20	0.90	2.00	7.00	50.00	100.00	—
1939	5,661,123	0.15	0.30	1.25	3.00	30.00	55.00	—
1940	13,920,197	0.15	0.20	0.75	2.25	18.00	35.00	—
1941	8,681,785	0.10	0.20	0.75	2.25	23.00	42.00	—
1942 round	6,847,544	0.15	0.20	0.75	1.75	18.00	35.00	—

KM# 39 Obv. Designer: T. H. Paget **Rev. Designer:** George E. Kruger-Gray **Composition:** Tombac

Date	Mintage	VG-8	F-12	VF-20	XF-40	MS-60	MS-63	Proof
1942 - 12 sided	3,396,234	0.40	0.65	1.25	1.75	3.00	9.00	—

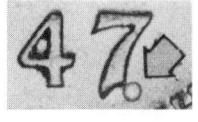

KM# 39a Obv. Designer: T. H. Paget **Rev. Designer:** George E. Kruger-Gray **Composition:** Nickel

Date	Mintage	VG-8	F-12	VF-20	XF-40	MS-60	MS-63	Proof
1946	6,952,684	0.15	0.20	0.50	2.00	8.00	18.00	—
1947	7,603,724	0.15	0.20	0.50	1.25	6.50	12.50	—
1947 dot	Inc. above	12.00	20.00	27.00	60.00	175	300	—
1947 maple leaf	9,595,124	0.15	0.20	0.45	1.25	6.00	12.00	—

KM# 42 Obv: Modified legend **Obv. Designer:** T. H. Paget **Rev. Designer:** George E. Kruger-Gray **Composition:** Nickel

Date	Mintage	VG-8	F-12	VF-20	XF-40	MS-60	MS-63	Proof
1948	1,810,789	0.40	0.50	1.00	3.00	12.00	20.00	—
1949	13,037,090	0.15	0.20	0.35	0.75	4.00	11.00	—
1950	11,970,521	0.15	0.20	0.35	0.75	4.00	11.00	—

KM# 42a Obv. Designer: T. H. Paget **Rev. Designer:** George E. Kruger-Gray **Composition:** Chromium And Nickel-Plated Steel

Date	Mintage	VG-8	F-12	VF-20	XF-40	MS-60	MS-63	Proof
1951 Low relief	4,313,410	0.15	0.25	0.50	0.80	2.50	4.50	—
Note: "A" in GRATIA points between denticles								
1951 High relief	Inc. above	400	525	700	1,000	1,900	3,100	—
Note: "A" in GRATIA points to a denticle								
1952	10,891,148	0.15	0.20	0.45	0.80	3.00	5.00	—

KM# 50 Obv: Elizabeth II effigy **Obv. Designer:** Mary Gillick **Rev. Designer:** George E. Kruger-Gray **Composition:** Chromium And Nickel-Plated Steel **Shape:** 12-sided

Date	Mintage	VG-8	F-12	VF-20	XF-40	MS-60	MS-63	Proof
1953 without strap	16,635,552	0.15	0.20	0.40	0.90	3.00	4.50	—
1953 without strap, near leaf	Inc. above	200	350	500	750	1,300	2,300	—
1953 with strap, far leaf	Inc. above	150	225	300	475	1,100	2,300	—
1953 with strap	Inc. above	0.15	0.20	0.40	0.90	3.50	7.00	—
1954	6,998,662	0.15	0.25	0.50	1.00	4.00	8.00	—

KM# 50a **Obv. Designer:** Mary Gillick **Rev. Designer:** George E. Kruger-Gray **Composition:** Nickel

Date	Mintage	VG-8	F-12	VF-20	XF-40	MS-60	MS-63	Proof
1955	5,355,028	0.15	0.25	0.40	0.75	2.50	4.50	—
1956	9,399,854	—	0.20	0.30	0.45	2.25	3.50	—
1957	7,387,703	—	—	0.25	0.30	1.25	3.00	—
1958	7,607,521	—	—	0.25	0.30	1.25	3.00	—
1959	11,552,523	—	—	—	0.20	0.40	1.00	—
1960	37,157,433	—	—	—	0.15	0.55	1.00	—
1961	47,889,051	—	—	—	—	0.30	0.80	—
1962	46,307,305	—	—	—	—	0.30	0.80	—

KM# 57 **Obv. Designer:** Mary Gillick **Rev. Designer:** George E. Kruger-Gray **Composition:** Nickel **Shape:** Round

Date	Mintage	VG-8	F-12	VF-20	XF-40	MS-60	MS-63	Proof
1963	43,970,320	—	—	—	—	0.20	0.50	—
1964	78,075,068	—	—	—	—	0.20	0.50	—
1964 extra water line	—	8.00	10.00	12.00	17.00	30.00	60.00	—

KM# 60.1 **Obv:** Elizabeth II effigy **Obv. Designer:** Arnold Machin **Rev. Designer:** George E. Kruger-Gray **Composition:** Nickel

Date	Mintage	VG-8	F-12	VF-20	XF-40	MS-60	MS-63	Proof
1965	84,876,018	—	—	—	—	0.20	0.30	—
1966	27,976,648	—	—	—	—	0.20	0.30	—
1968	101,930,379	—	—	—	—	0.20	0.30	—
1969	27,830,229	—	—	—	—	0.20	0.30	—
1970	5,726,010	—	—	—	0.20	0.35	0.75	—
1971	27,312,609	—	—	—	—	0.20	0.30	—
1972	62,417,387	—	—	—	—	0.20	0.30	—
1973	53,507,435	—	—	—	—	0.20	0.30	—
1974	94,704,645	—	—	—	—	0.20	0.30	—
1975	138,882,000	—	—	—	—	0.20	0.30	—
1976	55,140,213	—	—	—	—	0.20	0.30	—
1977	89,120,791	—	—	—	—	0.20	0.30	—
1978	137,079,273	—	—	—	—	0.20	0.30	—

KM# 60.2 **Obv:** Smaller bust **Obv. Designer:** Arnold Machin **Rev. Designer:** George E. Kruger-Gray **Composition:** Nickel

Date	Mintage	VG-8	F-12	VF-20	XF-40	MS-60	MS-63	Proof
1979	186,295,825	—	—	—	—	0.20	0.30	—
1980	134,878,000	—	—	—	—	0.20	0.30	—
1981	99,107,900	—	—	—	—	0.20	0.30	—
1981 Proof	199,000	—	—	—	—	—	—	1.50
1982	—	—	—	—	—	—	—	—
1982 Proof	—	—	—	—	—	—	—	—

KM# 60.2a **Obv. Designer:** Arnold Machin **Rev. Designer:** George E. Kruger-Gray **Composition:** Copper-Nickel

Date	Mintage	VG-8	F-12	VF-20	XF-40	MS-60	MS-63	Proof
1982	64,924,400	—	—	—	—	0.20	0.30	—
1982 Proof	180,908	—	—	—	—	—	—	1.50
1983	72,596,000	—	—	—	—	0.20	0.30	—
1983 Proof	168,000	—	—	—	—	—	—	1.50
1984	84,088,000	—	—	—	—	0.20	0.30	—
1984 Proof	161,602	—	—	—	—	—	—	1.50
1985	126,618,000	—	—	—	—	0.20	0.30	—
1985 Proof	157,037	—	—	—	—	—	—	1.50
1986	156,104,000	—	—	—	—	0.20	0.30	—
1986 Proof	175,745	—	—	—	—	—	—	1.50

Date	Mintage	VG-8	F-12	VF-20	XF-40	MS-60	MS-63	Proof
1987	106,299,000	—	—	—	—	0.15	0.30	—
1987 Proof	179,004	—	—	—	—	—	—	1.50
1988	75,025,000	—	—	—	—	0.15	0.30	—
1988 Proof	175,259	—	—	—	—	—	—	1.50
1989	141,570,538	—	—	—	—	0.15	0.30	—
1989 Proof	170,928	—	—	—	—	—	—	1.50

KM# 182 Obv: Elizabeth II effigy **Obv. Designer:** Dora dePedery-Hunt **Rev. Designer:** George E. Kruger-Gray **Composition:** Copper-Nickel

Date	Mintage	VG-8	F-12	VF-20	XF-40	MS-60	MS-63	Proof
1990	42,537,000	—	—	—	—	0.15	0.30	—
1990 Proof	140,649	—	—	—	—	—	—	2.50
1991	10,931,000	—	—	—	—	0.30	0.55	—
1991 Proof	131,888	—	—	—	—	—	—	7.00
1993	86,877,000	—	—	—	—	0.15	0.30	—
1993 Proof	143,065	—	—	—	—	—	—	2.50
1994	99,352,000	—	—	—	—	0.15	0.30	—
1994 Proof	146,424	—	—	—	—	—	—	3.00
1995	78,528,000	—	—	—	—	0.15	0.30	—
1995 Proof	50,000	—	—	—	—	—	—	2.50
1996 far 6	36,686,000	—	—	—	—	0.75	1.50	—
1996 near 6	Inc. above	—	—	—	—	0.45	1.25	—
1996 Proof	—	—	—	—	—	—	—	6.00
1997 Proof	—	—	—	—	—	—	—	5.00
1997	27,354,000	—	—	—	—	0.15	0.30	—
1998	156,873,000	—	—	—	—	0.15	0.30	—
1998 Proof	—	—	—	—	—	—	—	5.00
1998W	—	—	—	—	—	—	1.50	—
1999	124,861,000	—	—	—	—	0.15	0.30	—
1999 Proof	—	—	—	—	—	—	—	5.00
1999W	—	—	—	—	—	—	—	—
2000	108,514,000	—	—	—	—	0.15	0.30	—
2000 Proof	—	—	—	—	—	—	—	5.00
2000W	—	—	—	—	—	—	1.50	—
2001	166,672,000	—	—	—	—	0.15	0.30	—
2001 Proof	—	—	—	—	—	—	—	5.00
2002	—	—	—	—	—	0.15	0.30	—
2003	—	—	—	—	—	0.15	0.30	—

KM# 182b Obv: Queen's head right **Obv. Designer:** Dora dePedery-Hunt **Rev:** Beaver **Rev. Designer:** George E. Kruger-Gray **Edge:** Plain **Weight:** 3.9000 g. **Composition:** Nickel Plated Steel **Size:** 21.2 mm.

Date	Mintage	VG-8	F-12	VF-20	XF-40	MS-60	MS-63	Proof
1999 P	Est. 20,000	—	—	—	—	—	15.00	—
2000 P	Est. 2,300,000	—	—	—	—	1.50	2.25	—
2001 P	136,650	—	—	—	—	0.20	0.35	—
2002 P	—	—	—	—	—	—	0.25	—

KM# 182a Obv. Designer: Dora dePedery-Hunt **Rev. Designer:** George E. Kruger-Gray **Weight:** 5.3500 g. **Composition:** 0.9250 Silver 0.1591 oz. ASW

Date	Mintage	VG-8	F-12	VF-20	XF-40	MS-60	MS-63	Proof
1999	—	—	—	—	—	—	—	5.00
2000	—	—	—	—	—	—	—	5.00
2001	—	—	—	—	—	—	—	5.00
2002 Proof	—	—	—	—	—	—	—	5.00
2003 Proof	—	—	—	—	—	—	—	5.00

KM# 446 Subject: Elizabeth II Golden Jubilee **Obv:** Queen, Jubilee commemorative dates 1952-2002 **Obv. Designer:** Dora dePedery-Hunt **Rev. Designer:** George E. Kruger-Gray **Composition:** Copper-Nickel

Date	Mintage	VG-8	F-12	VF-20	XF-40	MS-60	MS-63	Proof
ND(2002)P	134,362,000	—	—	—	—	—	0.75	—
ND(2002) Proof	32,642	—	—	—	—	—	—	5.00

KM# 445a Subject: Elizabeth II Golden Jubilee **Obv:** Queen, Jubilee commemorative dates 1952-2002 **Obv. Designer:** Dora dePedery-Hunt **Rev. Designer:** George E. Kruger-Gray **Composition:** 0.9250 Silver

Date	Mintage	VG-8	F-12	VF-20	XF-40	MS-60	MS-63	Proof
ND(2002) In sets only	100,000	—	—	—	—	—	—	2.50

KM# 491   Obv: New effigy of Queen Elizabeth II **Obv. Designer:** Susanna Blunt **Rev. Designer:** George E. Kruger-Gray **Composition:** Copper-Nickel

Date	Mintage	VG-8	F-12	VF-20	XF-40	MS-60	MS-63	Proof
2003W	—	—	—	—	—	—	1.50	—

10 CENTS

KM# 3   Obv: Victoria head left **Designer:** Leonard C. Wyon **Edge:** Reeded **Weight:** 2.3240 g. **Composition:** 0.9250 Silver 0.0691 oz. ASW

Date	Mintage	VG-8	F-12	VF-20	XF-40	MS-60	MS-63	Proof
1858/5		475	775	1,250	1,850	4,550	—	—
1858	1,250,000	20.00	35.00	65.00	100.00	325	850	—
1870 Narrow 0	1,600,000	18.00	30.00	75.00	125	375	900	—
1870 Wide 0	Inc. above	25.00	50.00	100.00	200	500	1,150	—
1871	800,000	22.00	40.00	90.00	175	500	1,800	—
1871H	1,870,000	22.00	40.00	95.00	200	550	1,250	—
1872H	1,000,000	90.00	150	300	550	1,750	3,350	—
1874H	600,000	12.00	22.00	45.00	100.00	350	900	—
1875H	1,000,000	200	375	650	1,350	4,500	9,500	—
1880H	1,500,000	12.00	22.00	45.00	85.00	300	800	—
1881H	950,000	17.50	30.00	60.00	110	375	1,000	—
1882H	1,000,000	17.50	30.00	60.00	110	385	1,100	—
1883H	300,000	45.00	85.00	185	325	900	2,000	—
1884	150,000	165	345	635	1,400	5,150	12,000	—
1885	400,000	40.00	75.00	185	425	1,700	4,500	—
1886 Small 6	800,000	20.00	40.00	85.00	185	800	2,250	—
1886 Large 6	Inc. above	30.00	50.00	100.00	215	925	2,150	—
1887	350,000	45.00	85.00	175	375	1,150	3,000	—
1888	500,000	10.00	22.00	45.00	85.00	300	800	—
1889	600,000	450	900	1,550	3,200	10,000	18,500	—
1890H	450,000	20.00	35.00	80.00	175	425	950	—
1891 21 leaves	800,000	20.00	35.00	85.00	175	450	1,150	—
1891 22 leaves	Inc. above	20.00	35.00	85.00	175	435	1,000	—
1892/1	520,000	120	220	425	675	2,350	3,250	—
1892	Inc. above	20.00	35.00	75.00	145	425	950	—
1893 Flat-top 3	500,000	30.00	55.00	110	200	675	1,750	—
1893 Round-top 3	Inc. above	500	975	1,800	3,200	8,000	17,500	—
1894	500,000	25.00	45.00	85.00	150	400	1,150	—
1896	650,000	12.00	22.00	40.00	75.00	275	650	—
1898	720,000	12.00	24.00	45.00	80.00	300	700	—
1899 Small 9's	1,200,000	8.50	16.00	35.00	75.00	210	575	—
1899 Large 9's	Inc. above	16.00	28.00	60.00	120	400	1,100	—
1900	1,100,000	8.50	18.00	40.00	85.00	225	650	—
1901	1,200,000	8.50	18.00	40.00	85.00	225	650	—

KM# 10   Obv: Edward VII bust right **Obv. Designer:** G. W. DeSaulles **Rev. Designer:** Leonard C. Wyon **Edge:** Reeded **Weight:** 2.3240 g. **Composition:** 0.9250 Silver 0.0691 oz. ASW

Date	Mintage	VG-8	F-12	VF-20	XF-40	MS-60	MS-63	Proof
1902	720,000	5.50	16.00	30.00	80.00	325	1,100	—
1902H	1,100,000	4.00	8.00	18.00	40.00	100.00	250	—
1903	500,000	14.00	30.00	75.00	200	1,000	2,100	—
1903H	1,320,000	4.50	11.00	30.00	65.00	250	550	—
1904	1,000,000	7.50	24.00	45.00	100.00	325	700	—
1905	1,000,000	6.50	24.00	55.00	100.00	475	1,100	—
1906	1,700,000	4.25	12.00	30.00	60.00	275	750	—
1907	2,620,000	4.25	7.50	23.00	40.00	200	425	—
1908	776,666	8.00	24.00	55.00	95.00	200	400	—
1909 "Victorian" leaves, similar to 1902-08 coins	1,697,200	6.00	18.00	40.00	95.00	375	1,000	—
1909 Broad leaves, similar to 1910-12 coins	Inc. above	10.00	27.00	55.00	125	500	1,300	—
1910	4,468,331	4.00	8.00	18.00	35.00	125	300	—

KM# 17 Obv. Designer: E. B. MacKennal **Rev. Designer:** Leonard C. Wyon **Edge:** Reeded **Weight:** 2.3240 g. **Composition:** 0.9250 Silver 0.0691 oz. ASW

Date	Mintage	VG-8	F-12	VF-20	XF-40	MS-60	MS-63	Proof
1911	2,737,584	4.50	7.00	18.00	40.00	100.00	200	—

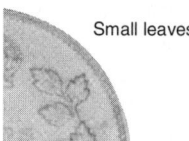
Small leaves

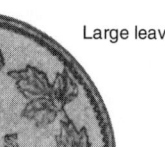
Large leaves

KM# 23 Obv. Designer: E. B. MacKennal **Rev. Designer:** Leonard C. Wyon **Edge:** Reeded **Weight:** 2.3240 g. **Composition:** 0.9250 Silver 0.0691 oz. ASW

Date	Mintage	VG-8	F-12	VF-20	XF-40	MS-60	MS-63	Proof
1912	3,235,557	1.75	2.50	9.00	30.00	175	500	—
1913 sm. leaves	3,613,937	1.50	2.25	5.00	23.00	125	325	—
1913 lg. leaves	Inc. above	95.00	175	350	900	5,600	20,000	—
1914	2,549,811	1.50	2.50	5.50	25.00	125	375	—
1915	688,057	4.00	10.00	30.00	100.00	325	650	—
1916	4,218,114	1.25	1.50	4.00	11.00	75.00	225	—
1917	5,011,988	1.00	1.50	3.00	8.75	50.00	95.00	—
1918	5,133,602	1.00	1.50	3.00	6.00	45.00	80.00	—
1919	7,877,722	1.00	1.50	3.00	6.00	45.00	80.00	—

KM# 23a Obv. Designer: Leonard C. Wyon **Edge:** Reeded **Weight:** 2.3328 g. **Composition:** 0.8000 Silver 0.0600 oz. ASW

Date	Mintage	VG-8	F-12	VF-20	XF-40	MS-60	MS-63	Proof
1920	6,305,345	1.00	1.50	3.00	8.00	50.00	125	—
1921	2,469,562	1.25	2.00	4.00	12.50	55.00	150	—
1928	2,458,602	1.00	1.75	4.00	12.00	55.00	125	—
1929	3,253,888	1.00	2.00	3.50	12.00	55.00	100.00	—
1930	1,831,043	1.00	2.50	4.50	14.00	60.00	125	—
1931	2,067,421	1.00	1.75	4.00	12.00	55.00	100.00	—
1932	1,154,317	1.50	2.50	9.00	23.00	90.00	150	—
1933	672,368	2.00	3.00	12.00	35.00	125	350	—
1934	409,067	3.00	6.00	22.00	60.00	250	500	—
1935	384,056	3.50	6.00	19.00	60.00	250	500	—
1936	2,460,871	0.60	1.25	3.00	6.00	45.00	80.00	—
1936 dot on rev. Specimen, 4 known	—	—	—	—	—	—	—	—

Note: At the David Akers sale of the John Jay Pittman collection, Part 1, 10-97, a gem specimen realized $120,000.

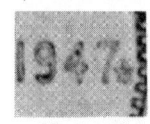
Maple leaf

KM# 34 Obv. Designer: T. H. Paget **Rev. Designer:** Emanuel Hahn **Edge:** Reeded **Weight:** 2.3328 g. **Composition:** 0.8000 Silver 0.0600 oz. ASW

Date	Mintage	VG-8	F-12	VF-20	XF-40	MS-60	MS-63	Proof
1937	2,500,095	0.50	1.00	2.00	3.75	12.00	18.00	—
1938	4,197,323	0.80	1.75	3.25	6.50	40.00	55.00	—
1939	5,501,748	0.65	1.25	2.50	5.00	30.00	40.00	—
1940	16,526,470	BV	0.50	1.50	3.00	15.00	20.00	—
1941	8,716,386	BV	1.25	2.50	6.00	25.00	60.00	—
1942	10,214,011	BV	0.50	1.25	4.00	20.00	45.00	—
1943	21,143,229	BV	0.50	1.25	4.00	11.00	20.00	—
1944	9,383,582	BV	0.50	1.50	4.50	15.00	25.00	—
1945	10,979,570	BV	0.50	1.25	4.00	11.00	23.00	—
1946	6,300,066	0.50	1.00	2.00	4.50	20.00	45.00	—
1947	4,431,926	0.60	1.25	2.50	6.00	20.00	45.00	—
1947 maple leaf	9,638,793	BV	0.50	1.50	3.00	10.00	15.00	—

KM# 43 Obv: Modified legend **Obv. Designer:** T. H. Paget **Rev. Designer:** Emanuel Hahn **Weight:** 2.3328 g.
Composition: 0.8000 Silver 0.0600 oz. ASW

Date	Mintage	VG-8	F-12	VF-20	XF-40	MS-60	MS-63	Proof
1948	422,741	2.00	3.50	7.50	13.00	30.00	45.00	—
1949	11,336,172	—	0.60	0.85	2.00	9.00	12.00	—
1950	17,823,075	—	BV	0.65	1.50	5.00	10.00	—
1951	15,079,265	—	BV	0.50	1.50	4.00	7.00	—
1951 Doubled die	—	—	1.50	2.50	7.00	22.00	—	—
1952	10,474,455	—	BV	0.50	1.50	3.00	5.00	—

KM# 51 Obv: Elizabeth II effigy **Obv. Designer:** Mary Gillick **Rev. Designer:** Emanuel Hahn **Weight:** 2.3328 g.
Composition: 0.8000 Silver 0.0600 oz. ASW

Date	Mintage	VG-8	F-12	VF-20	XF-40	MS-60	MS-63	Proof
1953 without straps	17,706,395	—	BV	0.80	1.25	3.00	6.00	—
1953 with straps	Inc. above	—	BV	0.80	1.25	3.00	8.00	—
1954	4,493,150	BV	0.60	1.00	2.25	5.00	8.00	—
1955	12,237,294	—	BV	0.60	0.75	3.00	4.50	—
1956	16,732,844	—	BV	0.60	0.75	2.00	3.50	—
1956 dot below date	Inc. above	—	2.25	3.00	4.50	8.00	15.00	—
1957	16,110,229	—	—	BV	0.65	1.50	2.25	—
1958	10,621,236	—	—	BV	0.65	1.50	2.25	—
1959	19,691,433	—	—	—	BV	1.25	2.00	—
1960	45,446,835	—	—	—	BV	1.00	1.50	—
1961	26,850,859	—	—	—	BV	0.75	1.50	—
1962	41,864,335	—	—	—	BV	0.50	1.00	—
1963	41,916,208	—	—	—	BV	0.50	1.00	—
1964	49,518,549	—	—	—	BV	0.50	1.00	—

KM# 61   Obv: Elizabeth II effigy **Obv. Designer:** Arnold Machin **Weight:** 2.3328 g. **Composition:** 0.8000
Silver 0.0600 oz. ASW

Date	Mintage	VG-8	F-12	VF-20	XF-40	MS-60	MS-63	Proof
1965	56,965,392	—	—	—	BV	0.50	1.00	—
1966	34,567,898	—	—	—	BV	0.50	1.00	—

Ottawa

KM# 72   Obv. Designer: Arnold Machin **Rev. Designer:** Emanuel Hahn **Weight:** 2.3328 g. **Composition:**
0.5000 Silver 0.0375 oz. ASW

Date	Mintage	VG-8	F-12	VF-20	XF-40	MS-60	MS-63	Proof
1968 Ottawa reeding	70,460,000	—	—	—	BV	0.45	0.90	—

Ottawa

KM# 72a   Composition: Nickel

Date	Mintage	VG-8	F-12	VF-20	XF-40	MS-60	MS-63	Proof
1968 Ottawa reeding	87,412,930	—	—	—	0.15	0.20	0.35	—

Philadelphia

KM# 73 Obv. Designer: Arnold Machin **Rev. Designer:** Emanuel Hahn **Composition:** Nickel

Date	Mintage	VG-8	F-12	VF-20	XF-40	MS-60	MS-63	Proof
1968 Philadelphia reeding	85,170,000	—	—	—	0.15	0.25	0.35	—
1969 lg. date, lg. ship, 10-20 known	—	—	6,100	8,300	11,000	19,000	—	—

KM# 77.1 Obv. Designer: Arnold Machin **Rev:** Redesigned smaller ship **Rev. Designer:** Emanuel Hahn **Composition:** Nickel

Date	Mintage	VG-8	F-12	VF-20	XF-40	MS-60	MS-63	Proof
1969	55,833,929	—	—	—	0.15	0.25	0.35	—
1970	5,249,296	—	—	—	0.25	0.40	0.90	—
1971	41,016,968	—	—	—	0.15	0.20	0.35	—
1972	60,169,387	—	—	—	0.15	0.20	0.35	—
1973	167,715,435	—	—	—	0.15	0.20	0.35	—
1974	201,566,565	—	—	—	0.15	0.20	0.35	—
1975	207,680,000	—	—	—	0.15	0.20	0.35	—
1976	95,018,533	—	—	—	0.15	0.20	0.35	—
1977	128,452,206	—	—	—	0.15	0.20	0.35	—
1978	170,366,431	—	—	—	0.15	0.20	0.35	—

KM# 77.2 Obv: Smaller bust **Obv. Designer:** Arnold Machin **Rev. Designer:** Emanuel Hahn **Composition:** Nickel

Date	Mintage	VG-8	F-12	VF-20	XF-40	MS-60	MS-63	Proof
1979	237,321,321	—	—	—	0.15	0.20	0.35	—
1980	170,111,533	—	—	—	0.15	0.20	0.35	—
1981	123,912,900	—	—	—	0.15	0.20	0.35	—
1981 Proof	199,000	—	—	—	—	—	—	1.50
1982	93,475,000	—	—	—	0.15	0.20	0.35	—
1982 Proof	180,908	—	—	—	—	—	—	1.50
1983	111,065,000	—	—	—	0.15	0.20	0.35	—
1983 Proof	168,000	—	—	—	—	—	—	1.50
1984	121,690,000	—	—	—	0.15	0.20	0.35	—
1984 Proof	161,602	—	—	—	—	—	—	1.50
1985	143,025,000	—	—	—	0.15	0.20	0.35	—
1985 Proof	157,037	—	—	—	—	—	—	1.50
1986	168,620,000	—	—	—	0.15	0.20	0.35	—
1986 Proof	175,745	—	—	—	—	—	—	1.50
1987	147,309,000	—	—	—	0.15	0.20	0.35	—
1987 Proof	179,004	—	—	—	—	—	—	1.50
1988	162,998,558	—	—	—	0.15	0.20	0.35	—
1988 Proof	175,259	—	—	—	—	—	—	1.50
1989	199,104,414	—	—	—	0.15	0.20	0.35	—
1989 Proof	170,528	—	—	—	—	—	—	1.50

KM# 183 Obv: Elizabeth II effigy **Obv. Designer:** Dora dePedery-Hunt **Rev. Designer:** Emanuel Hahn **Composition:** Nickel

Date	Mintage	VG-8	F-12	VF-20	XF-40	MS-60	MS-63	Proof
1990	65,023,000	—	—	—	0.15	0.20	0.35	—
1990 Proof	140,649	—	—	—	—	—	—	2.50
1991	50,397,000	—	—	—	0.15	0.30	0.45	—
1991 Proof	131,888	—	—	—	—	—	—	4.00
1993	135,569,000	—	—	—	0.15	0.20	0.35	—
1993 Proof	143,065	—	—	—	—	—	—	2.00
1994	145,800,000	—	—	—	0.15	0.20	0.35	—
1994 Proof	146,424	—	—	—	—	—	—	2.50
1995	123,875,000	—	—	—	0.15	0.20	0.35	—
1995 Proof	50,000	—	—	—	—	—	—	2.50
1996	51,814,000	—	—	—	0.15	0.20	0.35	—
1996 Proof	—	—	—	—	—	—	—	2.50
1997	43,126,000	—	—	—	0.15	0.20	0.35	—
1997 Proof	—	—	—	—	—	—	—	2.50

Date	Mintage	VG-8	F-12	VF-20	XF-40	MS-60	MS-63	Proof
1998 Proof	—	—	—	—	—	—	—	2.50
1998	203,514,000	—	—	—	0.15	0.20	0.35	—
1998W	—	—	—	—	—	—	1.50	—
1999	258,462,000	—	—	—	0.15	0.20	0.35	—
1999 Proof	—	—	—	—	—	—	—	2.50
2000 Proof	—	—	—	—	—	—	—	2.50
2000	159,125,000	—	—	—	0.15	0.20	0.35	—
2000W	—	—	—	—	—	—	1.50	—
2001	270,792,000	—	—	—	—	—	0.25	—
2002	—	—	—	—	—	—	0.25	—
2003	—	—	—	—	—	—	0.25	—

KM# 183a Weight: 2.4000 g. **Composition:** 0.9250 Silver 0.0713 oz. ASW

Date	Mintage	VG-8	F-12	VF-20	XF-40	MS-60	MS-63	Proof
1998 Proof	—	—	—	—	—	—	—	4.00
1998O Proof	—	—	—	—	—	—	—	4.00
1999 Proof	—	—	—	—	—	—	—	5.00
2000 Proof	—	—	—	—	—	—	—	5.00
2001 Proof	—	—	—	—	—	—	—	5.00
2002 Proof	—	—	—	—	—	—	—	5.00
2003 Proof	—	—	—	—	—	—	—	5.00

KM# 183b Obv: Queen's head right **Obv. Designer:** Dora dePedery-Hunt **Rev:** Sailboat **Rev. Designer:** Emanuel Hahn **Edge:** Reeded **Composition:** Nickel Plated Steel **Size:** 18 mm.

Date	Mintage	VG-8	F-12	VF-20	XF-40	MS-60	MS-63	Proof
1999 P	Est. 20,000	—	—	—	—	—	15.00	—
2000 P	Est. 200	—	—	—	—	350	600	—
2001 P	266,000,000	—	—	—	—	0.20	0.45	—
2002 P	—	—	—	—	—	—	0.20	—

KM# 447 Subject: Elizabeth II Golden Jubilee **Obv:** Queen, Jubilee commemorative dates 1952-2002 **Composition:** Nickel Plated Steel

Date	Mintage	VG-8	F-12	VF-20	XF-40	MS-60	MS-63	Proof
ND(2002)P	251,278,000	—	—	—	—	—	1.00	—
ND(2002) Proof	32,642	—	—	—	—	—	—	2.50

KM# 492 Obv: New effigy of Queen Elizabeth II **Obv. Designer:** Susanna Blunt **Composition:** Nickel

Date	Mintage	VG-8	F-12	VF-20	XF-40	MS-60	MS-63	Proof
2003W	—	—	—	—	—	—	1.50	—

20 CENTS

KM# 4 Weight: 4.6480 g. **Composition:** 0.9250 Silver 0.1382 oz. ASW

Date	Mintage	VG-8	F-12	VF-20	XF-40	MS-60	MS-63	Proof
1858	750,000	45.00	60.00	90.00	170	725	1,950	—

25 CENTS

KM# 5 Obv. Designer: Leonard C. Wyon **Weight:** 5.8100 g. **Composition:** 0.9250 Silver 0.1728 oz. ASW

Date	Mintage	VG-8	F-12	VF-20	XF-40	MS-60	MS-63	Proof
1870	900,000	14.00	30.00	75.00	150	550	1,500	—
1871	400,000	22.00	40.00	90.00	225	800	2,100	—
1871H	748,000	25.00	45.00	115	250	700	1,650	—
1872H	2,240,000	10.00	20.00	40.00	90.00	425	1,250	—

Date	Mintage	VG-8	F-12	VF-20	XF-40	MS-60	MS-63	Proof
1874H	1,600,000	10.00	20.00	40.00	90.00	375	1,100	—
1875H	1,000,000	275	550	1,350	2,750	10,000	17,500	—
1880H Narrow 0	400,000	40.00	85.00	220	400	1,150	2,750	—
1880H Wide 0	Inc. above	60.00	185	350	800	2,350	4,750	—
1880H Wide/narrow 0	Inc. above	100.00	225	400	950	2,800	—	—
1881H	820,000	20.00	45.00	90.00	250	1,000	2,300	—
1882H	600,000	20.00	45.00	110	265	1,000	2,150	—
1883H	960,000	16.00	32.00	70.00	150	500	1,250	—
1885	192,000	100.00	200	450	950	3,500	7,500	—
1886/3	540,000	35.00	80.00	150	375	1,500	3,200	—
1886	Inc. above	20.00	40.00	110	285	1,100	2,800	—
1887	100,000	85.00	225	450	1,000	4,250	8,000	—
1888	400,000	20.00	40.00	80.00	185	650	1,550	—
1889	66,324	100.00	250	500	1,000	3,500	8,500	—
1890H	200,000	25.00	50.00	125	275	950	2,250	—
1891	120,000	65.00	125	320	625	1,600	2,500	—
1892	510,000	15.00	25.00	65.00	175	675	1,600	—
1893	100,000	90.00	185	375	700	1,750	3,000	—
1894	220,000	20.00	40.00	90.00	250	700	1,600	—
1899	415,580	8.00	20.00	55.00	150	600	1,350	—
1900	1,320,000	7.00	20.00	45.00	100.00	525	1,200	—
1901	640,000	7.00	21.00	50.00	150	550	1,200	—

KM# 11 Obv. Designer: G. W. DeSaulles **Weight:** 5.8100 g. **Composition:** 0.9250 Silver 0.1728 oz. ASW

Date	Mintage	VG-8	F-12	VF-20	XF-40	MS-60	MS-63	Proof
1902	464,000	10.00	27.00	65.00	175	750	1,900	—
1902H	800,000	6.50	16.00	45.00	100.00	250	500	—
1903	846,150	10.00	29.00	75.00	200	800	1,900	—
1904	400,000	20.00	55.00	150	350	1,600	5,000	—
1905	800,000	10.00	30.00	100.00	225	1,400	4,600	—
1906 large crown	1,237,843	8.00	21.00	55.00	150	500	1,700	—
1906 small crown; Rare	Inc. above	1,600	2,300	3,000	3,500	—	—	—
1907	2,088,000	6.50	16.00	55.00	125	425	1,200	—
1908	495,016	15.00	35.00	95.00	200	400	750	—
1909	1,335,929	9.00	26.00	70.00	175	600	1,700	—

KM# 11a Weight: 5.8319 g. **Composition:** 0.9250 Silver 0.1734 oz. ASW

Date	Mintage	VG-8	F-12	VF-20	XF-40	MS-60	MS-63	Proof
1910	3,577,569	5.50	16.00	40.00	85.00	275	600	—

KM# 18 Obv. Designer: E. B. MacKennal **Weight:** 5.8319 g. **Composition:** 0.9250 Silver 0.1734 oz. ASW

Date	Mintage	VG-8	F-12	VF-20	XF-40	MS-60	MS-63	Proof
1911	1,721,341	6.50	18.00	35.00	85.00	250	425	—

KM# 24 Obv. Designer: E. B. MacKennal **Weight:** 5.8319 g. **Composition:** 0.9250 Silver 0.1734 oz. ASW

Date	Mintage	VG-8	F-12	VF-20	XF-40	MS-60	MS-63	Proof
1912	2,544,199	3.75	6.00	20.00	55.00	350	1,200	—
1913	2,213,595	3.25	5.50	17.00	50.00	300	950	—
1914	1,215,397	3.25	6.50	23.00	60.00	500	1,600	—
1915	242,382	16.00	45.00	150	425	2,200	6,100	—
1916	1,462,566	2.75	5.00	18.00	40.00	225	700	—
1917	3,365,644	1.75	3.00	11.00	30.00	125	225	—
1918	4,175,649	1.75	3.00	9.00	26.00	95.00	175	—
1919	5,852,262	1.75	3.00	6.00	25.00	95.00	175	—

Dot

KM# 24a   Obv. Designer: E. B. MacKennal **Weight:** 5.8319 g. **Composition:** 0.8000 Silver 0.1500 oz. ASW

Date	Mintage	VG-8	F-12	VF-20	XF-40	MS-60	MS-63	Proof
1920	1,975,278	1.75	4.50	12.00	30.00	150	400	—
1921	597,337	7.00	24.00	80.00	225	1,100	2,700	—
1927	468,096	27.00	50.00	100.00	225	750	1,600	—
1928	2,114,178	2.75	4.50	13.00	35.00	125	325	—
1929	2,690,562	1.75	2.75	13.00	35.00	125	325	—
1930	968,748	1.75	3.50	18.00	40.00	200	500	—
1931	537,815	1.75	3.50	20.00	50.00	200	500	—
1932	537,994	2.50	6.00	25.00	50.00	200	500	—
1933	421,282	3.00	6.50	28.00	65.00	175	325	—
1934	384,350	3.50	6.00	30.00	70.00	225	500	—
1935	537,772	3.50	5.00	22.00	50.00	150	325	—
1936	972,094	1.75	3.50	8.00	21.00	95.00	175	—
1936 dot	153,322	26.00	65.00	150	300	800	1,800	—

Note: David Akers John Jay Pittman sale Part Three, 10-99, nearly Choice Unc. realized $6,900; considered a possible specimen example

Maple leaf

KM# 35   Obv. Designer: T. H. Paget **Rev. Designer:** Emanuel Hahn **Weight:** 5.8319 g. **Composition:** 0.8000 Silver 0.1500 oz. ASW

Date	Mintage	VG-8	F-12	VF-20	XF-40	MS-60	MS-63	Proof
1937	2,690,176	1.00	2.00	4.00	6.00	10.00	25.00	—
1938	3,149,245	1.00	3.00	5.00	10.00	40.00	85.00	—
1939	3,532,495	1.00	2.00	5.00	7.00	35.00	75.00	—
1940	9,583,650	BV	1.00	1.50	2.50	15.00	30.00	—
1941	6,654,672	BV	1.00	1.50	2.50	16.00	30.00	—
1942	6,935,871	BV	1.00	1.50	2.50	17.00	30.00	—
1943	13,559,575	BV	1.00	1.50	2.50	16.00	30.00	—
1944	7,216,237	BV	1.00	1.50	2.50	17.00	35.00	—
1945	5,296,495	BV	1.00	1.50	2.00	16.00	30.00	—
1946	2,210,810	BV	2.00	4.00	8.00	30.00	70.00	—
1947	1,524,554	BV	1.50	4.00	8.00	30.00	55.00	—
1947 Dot after 7	Inc. above	30.00	40.00	70.00	100.00	250	500	—
1947 Maple leaf	4,393,938	BV	1.00	2.00	3.00	10.00	20.00	—

KM# 44   Obv: Modified legend **Obv. Designer:** T. H. Paget **Rev. Designer:** Emanuel Hahn **Weight:** 5.8319 g. **Composition:** 0.8000 Silver 0.1500 oz. ASW

Date	Mintage	VG-8	F-12	VF-20	XF-40	MS-60	MS-63	Proof
1948	2,564,424	BV	1.50	3.00	9.00	35.00	70.00	—
1949	7,988,830	—	BV	1.25	2.00	5.50	18.00	—
1950	9,673,335	—	BV	1.25	1.50	4.50	14.00	—
1951	8,290,719	—	BV	1.25	1.50	4.50	10.00	—
1952	8,859,642	—	BV	1.25	1.50	4.50	10.00	—

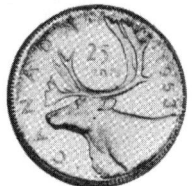

KM# 52 Obv: Elizabeth II effigy **Obv. Designer:** Mary Gillick **Rev. Designer:** Emanuel Hahn **Weight:** 5.8319 g. **Composition:** 0.8000 Silver 0.1500 oz. ASW

Date	Mintage	VG-8	F-12	VF-20	XF-40	MS-60	MS-63	Proof
1953 without strap	10,546,769	—	BV	1.25	1.50	3.00	7.00	—
1953 with strap	Inc. above	—	BV	1.25	1.50	6.50	12.00	—
1954	2,318,891	BV	1.25	2.00	4.00	15.00	25.00	—
1955	9,552,505	—	BV	1.25	1.50	4.50	10.00	—
1956	11,269,353	—	—	BV	1.25	3.25	6.50	—
1957	12,770,190	—	—	—	BV	1.50	3.00	—
1958	9,336,910	—	—	—	BV	1.50	3.00	—
1959	13,503,461	—	—	—	BV	1.50	2.50	—
1960	22,835,327	—	—	—	BV	1.15	2.50	—
1961	18,164,368	—	—	—	BV	1.15	2.50	—
1962	29,559,266	—	—	—	BV	1.15	2.50	—
1963	21,180,652	—	—	—	BV	1.15	1.25	—
1964	36,479,343	—	—	—	BV	1.15	1.25	—

KM# 62 Obv: Elizabeth II effigy **Obv. Designer:** Arnold Machin **Rev. Designer:** Emanuel Hahn **Weight:** 5.8319 g. **Composition:** 0.8000 Silver 0.1500 oz. ASW

Date	Mintage	VG-8	F-12	VF-20	XF-40	MS-60	MS-63	Proof
1965	44,708,869	—	—	—	BV	1.00	1.25	—
1966	25,626,315	—	—	—	BV	1.00	1.25	—

KM# 62a Obv: Elizabeth II effigy **Obv. Designer:** Machin **Weight:** 5.8319 g. **Composition:** 0.5000 Silver 0.0937 oz. ASW

Date	Mintage	VG-8	F-12	VF-20	XF-40	MS-60	MS-63	Proof
1968	71,464,000	—	—	—	BV	0.75	1.25	—

KM# 62b Obv: Elizabeth II effigy **Obv. Designer:** Machin **Composition:** Nickel

Date	Mintage	VG-8	F-12	VF-20	XF-40	MS-60	MS-63	Proof
1968	88,686,931	—	—	—	0.30	0.45	0.75	—
1969	133,037,929	—	—	—	0.30	0.45	0.75	—
1970	10,302,010	—	—	—	0.30	1.00	2.00	—
1971	48,170,428	—	—	—	0.30	0.45	0.75	—
1972	43,743,387	—	—	—	0.30	0.45	0.75	—
1973 Small Bust	135,958,589	—	—	—	0.30	0.50	1.00	—
1973 Large Bust	Inc. above	—	35.00	60.00	75.00	110	200	—
1974	192,360,598	—	—	—	0.30	0.45	0.75	—
1975	141,148,000	—	—	—	0.30	0.45	0.75	—
1976	86,898,261	—	—	—	0.30	0.45	0.75	—
1977	99,634,555	—	—	—	0.30	0.45	0.75	—
1978	176,475,408	—	—	—	0.30	0.45	0.75	—

KM# 74 Obv: Elizabeth II effigy, smaller bust **Obv. Designer:** Machin **Rev. Designer:** Emanuel Hahn **Composition:** Nickel

Date	Mintage	VG-8	F-12	VF-20	XF-40	MS-60	MS-63	Proof
1979	131,042,905	—	—	—	0.30	0.45	0.75	—
1980	76,178,000	—	—	—	0.30	0.45	0.75	—
1981	131,580,272	—	—	—	0.30	0.45	0.75	—
1981 Proof	199,000	—	—	—	—	—	—	2.00
1982	171,926,000	—	—	—	0.30	0.45	0.75	—
1982 Proof	180,908	—	—	—	—	—	—	2.00

Date	Mintage	VG-8	F-12	VF-20	XF-40	MS-60	MS-63	Proof
1983	13,162,000	—	—	—	0.30	0.75	1.50	—
1983 Proof	168,000	—	—	—	—	—	—	3.00
1984	121,668,000	—	—	—	0.30	0.45	0.75	—
1984 Proof	161,602	—	—	—	—	—	—	2.00
1985	158,734,000	—	—	—	0.30	0.45	0.75	—
1985 Proof	157,037	—	—	—	—	—	—	2.00
1986	132,220,000	—	—	—	0.30	0.45	0.75	—
1986 Proof	175,745	—	—	—	—	—	—	2.00
1987	53,408,000	—	—	—	0.30	0.60	1.25	—
1987 Proof	179,004	—	—	—	—	—	—	2.00
1988	80,368,473	—	—	—	0.30	0.45	1.00	—
1988 Proof	175,259	—	—	—	—	—	—	2.00
1989	119,796,307	—	—	—	0.30	0.45	0.75	—
1989 Proof	170,928	—	—	—	—	—	—	2.00

KM# 184 Obv: Elizabeth II effigy **Obv. Designer:** Dora dePedery-Hunt **Rev. Designer:** Emanuel Hahn **Composition:** Nickel

Date	Mintage	VG-8	F-12	VF-20	XF-40	MS-60	MS-63	Proof
1990	31,258,000	—	—	—	0.30	0.45	0.90	—
1990 Proof	140,649	—	—	—	—	—	—	2.50
1991	459,000	—	—	2.00	3.50	6.00	12.00	—
1991 Proof	131,888	—	—	—	—	—	—	20.00
1993	73,758,000	—	—	—	0.25	0.35	0.70	—
1993 Proof	143,065	—	—	—	—	—	—	2.00
1994	77,670,000	—	—	—	0.25	0.35	0.70	—
1994 Proof	146,424	—	—	—	—	—	—	3.00
1995	89,210,000	—	—	—	0.25	0.35	0.70	—
1995 Proof	50,000	—	—	—	—	—	—	3.00
1996	28,106,000	—	—	—	—	—	0.70	—
1996 Proof	—	—	—	—	—	—	—	6.00
1997 Proof	—	—	—	—	—	—	—	6.00
1997	—	—	—	—	—	—	0.70	—
1998W	—	—	—	—	—	—	5.00	—
1999	258,888,000	—	—	—	—	—	0.75	—
1999 Proof	—	—	—	—	—	—	—	6.00
2000 Proof	—	—	—	—	—	—	—	6.00
2000	434,087,000	—	—	—	—	—	0.75	—
2000W	—	—	—	—	—	—	5.00	—
2001	64,182,000	—	—	—	—	—	0.60	—
2001 Proof	—	—	—	—	—	—	—	6.00
2002	152,485,000	—	—	—	—	—	0.50	—
2003	—	—	—	—	—	—	0.50	—

KM# 184a Weight: 5.9000 g. **Composition:** 0.9250 Silver 0.1754 oz. ASW

Date	Mintage	VG-8	F-12	VF-20	XF-40	MS-60	MS-63	Proof
1996 Proof	—	—	—	—	—	—	—	6.50
1997 Proof	—	—	—	—	—	—	—	6.50
1998 Proof	—	—	—	—	—	—	—	5.50
1998O Proof	—	—	—	—	—	—	—	5.50
1999 Proof	—	—	—	—	—	—	—	5.50
2001 Proof	—	—	—	—	—	—	—	6.50
2002 Proof	—	—	—	—	—	—	—	10.00
2003 Proof	—	—	—	—	—	—	—	6.50

KM# 184b Composition: Nickel Plated Steel **Note:** No 2000 dated coins of this type were minted.

Date	Mintage	VG-8	F-12	VF-20	XF-40	MS-60	MS-63	Proof
1999 P	Est. 20,000	—	—	—	—	—	20.00	—
2000 P 3-5 Known	—	—	—	—	—	—	2,000	—
2001 P	52,153,000	—	—	—	—	0.35	0.70	—
2002 P	—	—	—	—	—	—	0.50	—

KM# 493 Obv: New effigy of Queen Elizabeth II **Obv. Designer:** Susanna Blunt **Composition:** Nickel

Date	Mintage	VG-8	F-12	VF-20	XF-40	MS-60	MS-63	Proof
2003W	—	—	—	—	—	—	3.00	—

50 CENTS

KM# 6 Obv. Designer: Leonard C. Wyon **Weight:** 11.6200 g. **Composition:** 0.9250 Silver .3456 oz. ASW

Date	Mintage	VG-8	F-12	VF-20	XF-40	MS-60	MS-63	Proof
1870	450,000	500	850	1,700	3,400	15,500	38,500	—
1870 LCW	Inc. above	45.00	75.00	165	375	3,500	10,000	—
1871	200,000	50.00	120	250	500	4,200	11,500	—
1871H	45,000	90.00	175	375	850	6,700	14,000	—
1872H	80,000	45.00	75.00	175	400	3,800	10,250	—
1872H Inverted A for V in Victoria	Inc. above	150	400	900	2,200	7,750	13,500	—
1881H	150,000	45.00	85.00	200	450	4,250	10,500	—
1888	60,000	175	300	600	1,100	5,600	13,500	—
1890H	20,000	650	1,250	2,000	4,000	12,250	22,500	—
1892	151,000	50.00	95.00	320	500	6,000	11,500	—
1894	29,036	250	450	950	2,100	9,000	17,500	—
1898	100,000	50.00	120	250	450	4,750	11,500	—
1899	50,000	100.00	200	450	1,100	9,000	17,500	—
1900	118,000	45.00	75.00	165	375	4,000	10,500	—
1901	80,000	55.00	100.00	225	550	5,700	15,000	—

Victorian leaves

KM# 12 Obv. Designer: G. W. DeSaulles **Weight:** 11.6200 g. **Composition:** 0.9250 Silver .3456 oz. ASW

Date	Mintage	VG-8	F-12	VF-20	XF-40	MS-60	MS-63	Proof
1902	120,000	15.00	35.00	100.00	250	1,300	3,500	—
1903H	140,000	22.00	45.00	125	300	1,400	3,700	—
1904	60,000	100.00	200	400	900	3,300	9,500	—
1905	40,000	150	275	600	1,400	6,000	15,000	—
1906	350,000	12.00	35.00	95.00	250	1,300	3,500	—
1907	300,000	12.00	35.00	95.00	250	1,400	3,900	—
1908	128,119	21.00	65.00	175	375	1,000	2,000	—
1909	302,118	17.00	60.00	175	475	2,400	7,600	—
1910 Victorian leaves	649,521	15.00	40.00	100.00	350	1,500	4,000	—

Edwardian leaves

KM# 12a Obv. Designer: G. W. DeSaulles **Weight:** 11.6638 g. **Composition:** 0.9250 Silver .3461 oz. ASW

Date	Mintage	VG-8	F-12	VF-20	XF-40	MS-60	MS-63	Proof
1910 Edwardian leaves	Inc. above	8.00	29.00	85.00	250	1,200	3,300	—

KM# 19 Obv. Designer: E. B. MacKennal **Weight:** 11.6638 g. **Composition:** 0.9250 Silver .3461 oz. ASW

Date	Mintage	VG-8	F-12	VF-20	XF-40	MS-60	MS-63	Proof
1911	209,972	12.00	70.00	250	550	1,400	3,200	—

KM# 25 Obv: Modified legend **Obv. Designer:** E. B. MacKennal **Weight:** 11.6638 g. **Composition:** 0.9250 Silver .3461 oz. ASW

Date	Mintage	VG-8	F-12	VF-20	XF-40	MS-60	MS-63	Proof
1912	285,867	4.50	24.00	100.00	225	1,100	2,900	—
1913	265,889	6.00	24.00	100.00	300	1,400	4,800	—
1914	160,128	14.00	55.00	150	500	2,800	7,800	—
1916	459,070	4.50	14.00	55.00	125	650	2,100	—
1917	752,213	3.00	11.00	40.00	100.00	475	1,100	—
1918	754,989	3.00	10.00	30.00	90.00	400	1,000	—
1919	1,113,429	3.00	10.00	30.00	90.00	375	1,200	—

KM# 25a Obv. Designer: E. B. MacKennal **Weight:** 11.6638 g. **Composition:** 0.8000 Silver .3000 oz. ASW

Date	Mintage	VG-8	F-12	VF-20	XF-40	MS-60	MS-63	Proof
1920	584,691	5.00	13.00	35.00	125	500	1,200	—
1921 75 to 100 known	—	15,000	21,000	27,000	30,000	45,000	60,000	—
Note: David Akers John Jay Pittman sale, Part Three, 10-99, Gem Unc. realized $63,250								
1929	228,328	3.00	13.00	35.00	100.00	475	1,100	—
1931	57,581	11.00	29.00	80.00	225	800	1,800	—
1932	19,213	100.00	175	375	800	3,600	8,300	—
1934	39,539	15.00	30.00	80.00	225	650	1,300	—
1936	38,550	15.00	29.00	70.00	175	500	1,000	—

KM# 36 Obv. Designer: T. H. Paget **Rev. Designer:** George E. Kruger-Gray **Weight:** 11.6638 g. **Composition:** 0.8000 Silver .3000 oz. ASW

Date	Mintage	VG-8	F-12	VF-20	XF-40	MS-60	MS-63	Proof
1937	192,016	3.00	4.00	7.00	10.00	30.00	50.00	—
1938	192,018	3.00	5.00	10.00	25.00	90.00	275	—
1939	287,976	2.50	5.00	8.00	17.00	60.00	170	—
1940	1,996,566	BV	2.50	3.00	6.00	27.00	60.00	—

Date	Mintage	VG-8	F-12	VF-20	XF-40	MS-60	MS-63	Proof
1941	1,714,874	BV	2.50	3.00	6.00	27.00	60.00	—
1942	1,974,164	BV	2.50	3.00	6.00	27.00	60.00	—
1943	3,109,583	BV	2.50	3.00	6.00	27.00	60.00	—
1944	2,460,205	BV	2.50	3.00	6.00	27.00	60.00	—
1945	1,959,528	BV	2.50	3.00	6.00	30.00	60.00	—
1946	950,235	BV	2.50	3.50	7.00	40.00	110	—
1946 hoof in 6	Inc. above	15.00	28.00	45.00	150	1,100	2,800	—
1947 straight 7	424,885	BV	2.50	5.00	10.00	65.00	175	—
1947 curved 7	Inc. above	BV	2.50	6.00	15.00	75.00	200	—
1947 maple leaf, straight 7	38,433	18.00	23.00	30.00	60.00	150	275	—
1947 maple leaf, curved 7	Inc. above	1,000	1,300	1,700	2,200	3,900	7,000	—

KM# 45 Obv: Modified legend **Obv. Designer:** T. H. Paget **Rev. Designer:** George E. Kruger-Gray **Weight:** 11.6638 g. **Composition:** 0.8000 Silver .3000 oz. ASW

Date	Mintage	VG-8	F-12	VF-20	XF-40	MS-60	MS-63	Proof
1948	37,784	45.00	55.00	70.00	95.00	150	225	—
1949	858,991	BV	2.50	3.50	7.00	25.00	100.00	—
1949 hoof over 9	Inc. above	7.00	12.00	25.00	60.00	325	750	—
1950 no lines	2,384,179	2.50	7.00	11.00	25.00	125	225	—
1950 lines in 0	Inc. above	BV	2.00	2.75	3.50	8.00	20.00	—
1951	2,421,730	BV	2.00	2.50	3.00	6.00	17.00	—
1952	2,596,465	BV	2.00	2.50	3.00	6.00	11.00	—

KM# 53 Obv: Elizabeth II Effigy **Obv. Designer:** Mary Gillick **Weight:** 11.6638 g. **Composition:** 0.8000 Silver .3000 oz. ASW

Date	Mintage	VG-8	F-12	VF-20	XF-40	MS-60	MS-63	Proof
1953 small date	1,630,429	—	BV	2.00	2.50	4.50	10.00	—
1953 lg. date, straps	Inc. above	—	BV	2.50	4.00	15.00	30.00	—
1953 lg. date without straps	Inc. above	BV	2.00	3.50	9.00	50.00	90.00	—
1954	506,305	BV	2.00	3.50	7.00	18.00	30.00	—
1955	753,511	—	BV	2.50	3.50	10.00	20.00	—
1956	1,379,499	—	BV	2.00	2.50	4.50	9.00	—
1957	2,171,689	—	—	BV	2.00	3.50	6.00	—
1958	2,957,266	—	—	BV	2.00	3.00	5.50	—

KM# 56 Obv. Designer: Mary Gillick **Rev:** New shield **Rev. Designer:** Thomas Shingles **Weight:** 11.6638 g. **Composition:** 0.8000 Silver .3000 oz. ASW

Date	Mintage	VG-8	F-12	VF-20	XF-40	MS-60	MS-63	Proof
1959 horizontal shading	3,095,535	—	—	BV	2.00	2.50	4.50	—
1960	3,488,897	—	—	—	BV	2.25	3.25	—
1961	3,584,417	—	—	—	BV	2.00	3.00	—
1962	5,208,030	—	—	—	BV	2.00	3.00	—
1963	8,348,871	—	—	—	BV	2.00	3.00	—
1964	9,377,676	—	—	—	BV	2.00	3.00	—

KM# 63 Obv: Elizabeth II effigy **Obv. Designer:** Arnold Machin **Rev. Designer:** Thomas Shingles **Weight:** 11.6638 g. **Composition:** 0.8000 Silver .3000 oz. ASW

Date	Mintage	VG-8	F-12	VF-20	XF-40	MS-60	MS-63	Proof
1965	12,629,974	—	—	—	BV	2.00	3.00	—
1966	7,920,496	—	—	—	BV	2.00	3.00	—

KM# 75.1 Obv. Designer: Arnold Machin **Rev. Designer:** Thomas Shingles **Composition:** Nickel

Date	Mintage	VG-8	F-12	VF-20	XF-40	MS-60	MS-63	Proof
1968	3,966,932	—	—	—	0.50	0.65	1.00	—
1969	7,113,929	—	—	—	0.50	0.65	1.00	—
1970	2,429,526	—	—	—	0.50	0.65	1.00	—
1971	2,166,444	—	—	—	0.50	0.65	1.00	—
1972	2,515,632	—	—	—	0.50	0.65	1.00	—
1973	2,546,096	—	—	—	0.50	0.65	1.00	—
1974	3,436,650	—	—	—	0.50	0.65	1.00	—
1975	3,710,000	—	—	—	0.50	0.65	1.00	—
1976	2,940,719	—	—	—	0.50	0.65	1.00	—

KM# 75.2 Obv: Smaller bust **Obv. Designer:** Arnold Machin **Rev. Designer:** Thomas Shingles **Composition:** Nickel

Date	Mintage	VG-8	F-12	VF-20	XF-40	MS-60	MS-63	Proof
1977	709,839	—	—	0.50	0.75	1.35	2.00	—

KM# 75.3 Obv. Designer: Arnold Machin **Rev:** Redesigned arms **Rev. Designer:** Thomas Shingles **Composition:** Nickel

Date	Mintage	VG-8	F-12	VF-20	XF-40	MS-60	MS-63	Proof
1978 square jewels	3,341,892	—	—	—	0.50	0.65	1.00	—
1978 round jewels	Inc. above	—	—	0.50	2.50	3.00	4.00	—
1979	3,425,000	—	—	—	0.50	0.65	1.00	—
1980	1,574,000	—	—	—	0.50	0.65	1.00	—
1981	2,690,272	—	—	—	0.50	0.65	1.00	—
1981 Proof	199,000	—	—	—	—	—	—	3.00
1982 small beads	2,236,674	—	—	—	20.00	40.00	60.00	—
1982 small beads; Proof	180,908	—	—	—	—	—	—	3.00
1982 large beads	Inc. above	—	—	—	0.50	0.65	1.00	—
1983	1,177,000	—	—	—	0.50	0.65	1.00	—
1983 Proof	168,000	—	—	—	—	—	—	3.00
1984	1,502,989	—	—	—	0.50	0.65	1.00	—
1984 Proof	161,602	—	—	—	—	—	—	3.00
1985	2,188,374	—	—	—	0.50	0.65	1.00	—
1985 Proof	157,037	—	—	—	—	—	—	3.00
1986	781,400	—	—	—	0.50	1.00	1.25	—
1986 Proof	175,745	—	—	—	—	—	—	3.00
1987	373,000	—	—	—	0.50	1.00	1.25	—
1987 Proof	179,004	—	—	—	—	—	—	3.50
1988	220,000	—	—	—	0.50	1.00	1.25	—

Date	Mintage	VG-8	F-12	VF-20	XF-40	MS-60	MS-63	Proof
1988 Proof	175,259	—	—	—	—	—	—	3.00
1989	266,419	—	—	—	0.50	1.00	1.25	—
1989 Proof	170,928	—	—	—	—	—	—	3.00

KM# 185 Obv: Elizabeth II effigy **Obv. Designer:** Dora dePedery-Hunt **Rev. Designer:** Thomas Shingles **Composition:** Nickel

Date	Mintage	VG-8	F-12	VF-20	XF-40	MS-60	MS-63	Proof
1990	207,000	—	—	—	0.50	1.00	1.25	—
1990 Proof	140,649	—	—	—	—	—	—	5.00
1991	490,000	—	—	—	0.50	0.85	1.00	—
1991 Proof	131,888	—	—	—	—	—	—	7.00
1993	393,000	—	—	—	0.50	0.85	1.00	—
1993 Proof	143,065	—	—	—	—	—	—	3.00
1994	987,000	—	—	—	0.50	0.75	1.00	—
1994 Proof	146,424	—	—	—	—	—	—	4.00
1995	626,000	—	—	—	0.50	0.75	1.00	—
1995 Proof	50,000	—	—	—	—	—	—	4.00
1996	458,000	—	—	—	0.50	0.65	1.00	—
1996 Proof	—	—	—	—	—	—	—	—

KM# 185a Weight: 11.6380 g. **Composition:** 0.9250 Silver .3461 oz. ASW

Date	Mintage	VG-8	F-12	VF-20	XF-40	MS-60	MS-63	Proof
1996 Proof	—	—	—	—	—	—	—	9.00

KM# 290 Obv. Designer: Dora dePedery-Hunt **Rev:** Redesigned arms **Rev. Designer:** Cathy Bursey-Sabourin **Composition:** Nickel

Date	Mintage	VG-8	F-12	VF-20	XF-40	MS-60	MS-63	Proof
1997 Proof	—	—	—	—	—	—	—	—
1997	387,000	—	—	—	0.50	0.65	1.00	—
1998	308,000	—	—	—	0.50	0.65	1.00	—
1998 Proof	—	—	—	—	—	—	—	—
1998W	—	—	—	—	—	—	2.00	—
1999	496,000	—	—	—	0.50	0.65	1.00	—
1999 Proof	—	—	—	—	—	—	—	—
2000 Proof	—	—	—	—	—	—	—	—
2000	559,000	—	—	—	0.50	0.65	1.00	—
2000W	—	—	—	—	—	—	1.50	—
2003	—	—	—	—	—	—	1.00	—

KM# 290a Weight: 11.6380 g. **Composition:** 0.9250 Silver .3461 oz. ASW

Date	Mintage	VG-8	F-12	VF-20	XF-40	MS-60	MS-63	Proof
1997 Proof	—	—	—	—	—	—	—	10.00
1998 Proof	—	—	—	—	—	—	—	10.00
1999 Proof	—	—	—	—	—	—	—	10.00
2000 Proof	—	—	—	—	—	—	—	10.00
2001 Proof	—	—	—	—	—	—	—	10.00
2002 Proof	—	—	—	—	—	—	—	10.00
2003 Proof	—	—	—	—	—	—	—	10.00

KM# 290b Rev: Redesigned arms **Composition:** Nickel Plated Steel

Date	Mintage	VG-8	F-12	VF-20	XF-40	MS-60	MS-63	Proof
1999	Est. 20,000	—	—	—	—	—	15.00	—
2000P	Est. 50	—	—	—	—	1,500	2,000	—
Note: Available only in RCM presentation coin clocks								
2001	389,000	—	—	—	—	1.00	1.25	—
2002	—	—	—	—	—	1.00	1.25	—
2002P	—	—	—	—	—	—	1.00	—

KM# 494 Obv: New effigy of Queen Elizabeth II **Obv. Designer:** Susanna Blunt **Rev. Designer:** Cathy Bursey-Sabourin **Composition:** Nickel

Date	Mintage	VG-8	F-12	VF-20	XF-40	MS-60	MS-63	Proof
2003W	—	—	—	—	—	—	1.50	—

DOLLAR

KM# 31 Obv. Designer: E. B. MacKennal **Rev:** Voyageur **Rev. Designer:** Emanuel Hahn **Weight:** 23.3276 g.
Composition: 0.8000 Silver 0.6000 oz. ASW

Date	Mintage	F-12	VF-20	XF-40	AU-50	MS-60	MS-63	Proof
1936	339,600	8.50	12.50	16.50	21.50	35.00	75.00	5,000

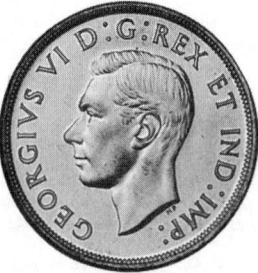 

 Pointed 7

Blunt 7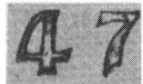

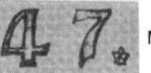 Maple leaf

KM# 37 Obv. Designer: T. H. Paget **Rev:** Voyageur **Rev. Designer:** Emanuel Hahn **Weight:** 23.3276 g.
Composition: 0.8000 Silver 0.6000 oz. ASW

Date	Mintage	F-12	VF-20	XF-40	AU-50	MS-60	MS-63	Proof
1937	207,406	9.00	10.00	12.00	15.00	25.00	65.00	—
1937 Mirror Proof	1,295	—	—	—	—	—	—	650
1937 Matte Proof	Inc. above	—	—	—	—	—	—	250
1938	90,304	25.00	35.00	45.00	55.00	70.00	175	6,000
1945	38,391	75.00	100.00	125	150	200	475	2,000
1946	93,055	15.00	25.00	35.00	45.00	65.00	225	1,800
1947 pointed 7		65.00	80.00	100.00	125	265	850	3,500
1947 blunt 7	65,595	45.00	60.00	80.00	95.00	125	250	4,500
1947 maple leaf	21,135	125	150	175	200	250	475	1,800

KM# 46 Obv: Modified left legend **Obv. Designer:** T. H. Paget **Rev:** Voyageur **Rev. Designer:** Emanuel
Hahn **Weight:** 23.3276 g. **Composition:** 0.8000 Silver 0.6000 oz. ASW

Date	Mintage	F-12	VF-20	XF-40	AU-50	MS-60	MS-63	Proof
1948	18,780	500	600	650	750	850	1,200	3,000
1950 with 3 water lines	261,002	6.00	8.00	10.00	12.00	16.00	35.00	800
1950 with 4 water lines, 1 known, Matte Proof	—	—	—	—	—	—	—	—
1950 arnprior with 2-1/2 water lines	Inc. above	7.00	9.00	12.50	17.00	28.00	90.00	1,500
1951 with 3 water lines	416,395	4.50	5.50	6.50	8.00	9.00	23.00	650
1951 arnprior with 1-1/2 water lines	Inc. above	20.00	35.00	50.00	70.00	125	275	2,000
1952 with 3 water lines	406,148	4.50	5.50	6.50	8.00	10.00	23.00	1,000
1952 short water lines, arnprior type	Inc. above	8.00	12.00	15.00	18.00	40.00	60.00	1,250
1952 without water lines	Inc. above	5.50	6.50	8.00	10.00	16.50	30.00	—

KM# 54 **Obv:** Elizabeth II effigy **Obv. Designer:** Mary Gillick **Rev:** Voyageur **Rev. Designer:** Emanuel Hahn **Weight:** 23.3276 g. **Composition:** 0.8000 Silver 0.6000 oz. ASW **Note:** All genuine circulation strike 1955 Arnprior dollars have a die break running along the top of TI in the word GRATIA on the obverse.

Date	Mintage	F-12	VF-20	XF-40	AU-50	MS-60	MS-63	Proof
1953 without strap, wire rim	1,074,578	BV	4.50	5.00	5.50	7.00	15.00	400
1953 with strap, flat rim	Inc. above	BV	4.50	5.00	5.50	7.00	15.00	—
1954	246,606	4.50	6.50	8.00	10.00	16.00	35.00	—
1955 with 3 water lines	268,105	5.00	6.50	8.00	10.00	15.00	29.00	—
1955 arnprior with 1-1/2 water lines* and die break	Inc. above	45.00	50.00	60.00	70.00	85.00	175	—
1956	209,092	7.50	9.50	13.00	16.00	20.00	50.00	—
1957 with 3 water lines	496,389	—	BV	5.00	5.50	7.50	11.00	—
1957 with 1 water line	Inc. above	4.50	5.50	7.50	8.50	10.00	21.00	—
1959	1,443,502	—	—	BV	5.00	5.50	7.00	—
1960	1,420,486	—	—	BV	5.00	5.50	7.00	—
1961	1,262,231	—	—	BV	5.00	5.50	7.00	—
1962	1,884,789	—	—	BV	5.00	5.50	7.00	—
1963	4,179,981	—	—	BV	5.00	5.50	7.00	—

Small beads

Medium beads

Large beads

KM# 64.1 **Obv:** Elizabeth II effigy **Obv. Designer:** Arnold Machin **Rev:** Voyageur **Rev. Designer:** Emanual Hahn **Weight:** 23.3276 g. **Composition:** 0.8000 Silver 0.6000 oz. ASW

Date	Mintage	F-12	VF-20	XF-40	AU-50	MS-60	MS-63	Proof
1965 small beads, pointed 5	10,768,569	—	—	BV	5.00	5.50	6.50	—
1965 small beads, blunt 5	Inc. above	—	—	BV	5.00	5.50	6.50	—
1965 large beads, blunt 5	Inc. above	—	—	BV	5.00	5.50	6.50	—
1965 large beads, pointed 5	Inc. above	—	—	BV	5.00	5.50	6.50	—
1965 medium beads, pointed 5	Inc. above	4.50	5.00	7.00	9.00	12.00	25.00	—
1966 large beads	9,912,178	—	—	BV	5.00	5.50	6.50	—
1966 small beads	485	—	—	1,200	1,500	1,800	2,200	—

Date	Mintage	MS-63	P/L	Proof
1968 Small island	—	5.00	—	—
1968 No island	—	—	4.00	—
1968 Doubled die	—	—	25.00	—
Note: Exhibits extra water lines				
1969	4,809,313	1.25	—	—
1969	594,258	—	2.00	—
1972	2,676,041	1.50	—	—
1972	405,865	—	2.50	—

KM# 64.2a **Obv:** Smaller bust **Obv. Designer:** Arnold Machin **Rev:** Voyageur **Rev. Designer:** Emanuel Hahn **Weight:** 23.3276 g. **Composition:** 0.5000 Silver 0.3750 oz. ASW **Size:** 36 mm.

Date	Mintage	MS-63	P/L	Proof
1972 Proof	341,598	—	—	5.00

Note: Specimen $5.50.

KM# 76.2 **Obv:** Smaller bust **Obv. Designer:** Arnold Machin **Rev:** Voyageur **Rev. Designer:** Emanuel Hahn **Composition:** Nickel **Size:** 32 mm.

Date	Mintage	MS-63	P/L	Proof
1975	3,256,000	1.50	—	—
1975	322,325	—	2.50	—

KM# 76.1 **Obv:** Large bust **Obv. Designer:** Arnold Machin **Rev:** Voyageur **Rev. Designer:** Emanuel Hahn **Composition:** Nickel **Size:** 32 mm.

Date	Mintage	MS-63	P/L	Proof
1968	5,579,714	1.25	—	—
1968	1,408,143	—	1.75	—

Date	Mintage	MS-63	P/L	Proof
1976	2,498,204	1.50	—	—
1976	274,106	—	2.50	—

KM# 76.3 Obv. Designer: Arnold Machin **Rev:** Voyageur **Rev. Designer:** Emanuel Hahn **Composition:** Nickel **Size:** 32 mm. **Note:** Only known in prooflike sets with 1976 obverse slightly modified.

Date	Mintage	MS-63	P/L	Proof
1975 mule w/1976 obv. Inc. above	—	—	3.00	—

KM# 117 Obv. Designer: Arnold Machin **Rev:** Voyageur modified **Rev. Designer:** Emanuel Hahn **Composition:** Nickel **Size:** 32 mm.

Date	Mintage	MS-63	P/L	Proof
1977	1,393,745	2.25	—	—

KM# 120.1 Obv. Designer: Arnold Machin **Rev:** Voyageur **Rev. Designer:** Emanuel Hahn **Comp.:** Nickel **Size:** 32 mm. **Note:** Modified design.

Date	Mintage	MS-63	P/L	Proof
1978	2,948,488	1.50	—	—
1979	2,954,842	1.50	—	—
1980	3,291,221	1.50	—	—
1981	2,778,900	1.50	—	—
1981 Proof	—	—	—	—
1982	1,098,500	1.50	2.50	—
1982 Proof	180,908	—	—	5.25
1983	2,267,525	1.50	4.00	—
1983 Proof	166,779	—	—	5.25
1984	1,223,486	1.50	—	—
1984 Proof	161,602	—	—	6.00
1985	3,104,092	1.50	3.50	—
1985 Proof	153,950	—	—	7.00
1986	3,089,225	2.00	4.00	—
1986 Proof	176,224	—	—	7.50
1987	287,330	3.50	5.00	—
1987 Proof	175,686	—	—	7.50

KM# 120.2 Rev: Voyageur **Composition:** Nickel **Size:** 32 mm. **Note:** Modified design.

Date	Mintage	MS-63	P/L	Spec.
1985 mule w/New Zealand 50 cent, KM-37 obverse	—	1,900	—	—

KM# 157 Obv: Elizabeth II effigy **Obv. Designer:** Arnold Machin **Rev:** Loon **Rev. Designer:** Robert R. Carmichael **Composition:** Aureate-Bronze Plated Nickel **Shape:** 11-sided

Date	Mintage	MS-63	P/L	Proof
1987	205,405,000	2.25	—	—
1987 Proof	178,120	—	—	8.00
1988	138,893,539	2.25	4.00	—
1988 Proof	175,259	—	—	6.75
1989	184,773,902	3.00	4.00	—
1989 Proof	170,928	—	—	6.75

KM# 186 Obv: Elizabeth II effigy **Obv. Designer:** Dora dePedery-Hunt **Rev:** Loon **Rev. Designer:** Robert R. Carmichael **Composition:** Aureate-Bronze Plated Nickel **Shape:** 11-sided

Date	Mintage	MS-63	P/L	Proof
1990	68,402,000	1.75	4.00	—
1990 Proof	140,649	—	—	7.00
1991	23,156,000	1.75	6.50	—
1991 Proof	—	—	—	13.00
1993	33,662,000	2.00	3.00	—
1993 Proof	—	—	—	6.00
1994	36,237,000	2.00	3.50	—
1994 Proof	—	—	—	7.00
1995	41,813,000	3.00	4.50	—
1995 Proof	—	—	—	7.00
1996	17,101,000	2.00	6.00	—
1996 Proof	—	—	—	7.50
1997	—	5.00	6.00	—
1997 Proof	—	—	—	8.00
1998	—	2.50	6.00	—
1998 Proof	—	—	—	10.00
1998W	—	—	4.50	—
1999	—	2.00	6.00	—
1999 Proof	—	—	—	8.00
2000	—	2.00	6.00	—
2000 Proof	—	—	—	8.00
2001	—	2.00	6.00	—
2001 Proof	—	—	—	8.00
2002	—	6.00	—	—
2002 Proof	—	—	12.00	—
2003	—	6.00	—	—
2003 Proof	100,000	—	—	12.00

KM# 186a Subject: Olympic Win **Composition:** Gold Plated

Date	Mintage	MS-63	P/L	Proof
2002 Proof	—	—	—	40.00

KM# 495 Obv: New effigy of Queen Elizabeth II **Obv. Designer:** Susanna Blunt **Rev. Designer:** Robert R. Carmichael **Composition:** Aureate-Bronze Plated Nickel

Date	Mintage	MS-63	P/L	Proof
2003W	—	6.00	—	—

2 DOLLARS

KM# 270 Obv. Designer: Dora dePedery-Hunt **Rev:** Polar bear **Rev. Designer:** Brent Townsend **Composition:** Bi-Metallic **Size:** 28 mm.

Date	Mintage	MS-63	P/L	Proof
1996	375,483,000	3.25	5.00	10.00
1997	16,942,000	3.25	—	—
1998	4,926,000	3.25	—	—
1998W	—	3.25	—	—
1999	25,130,000	3.25	—	—
2000	29,847,000	3.25	—	—
2000W	—	3.25	—	—
2001	27,008,000	3.25	—	—

Date	Mintage	MS-63	P/L	Proof
2002	11,910,000	3.25	—	—
2003	—	3.25	—	—

KM# 270a Rev: Polar bear **Composition:** Bi-Metallic Gold And Silver **Size:** 32 mm. **Note:** Silver ring, 5.0958 g., .1638 ASW; Gold Center, 5.7456 g., .1847 AGW.

Date	Mintage	MS-63	P/L	Proof
1996 Proof	5,000	—	—	125

KM# 270b Rev: Polar bear **Composition:** Bi-Metallic Gold And Silver **Note:** Silver ring, .925; Gold plated silver center.

Date	Mintage	MS-63	P/L	Proof
1996 Proof	10,000	—	—	55.00
1998 Proof	—	—	—	—

KM# 270c Rev: Polar bear **Composition:** Bi-Metallic Gold And Silver **Note:** Silver ring; Gold plated silver center. 8.83g., .925 silver, .2626 ASW.

Date	Mintage	MS-63	P/L	Proof
1996 Proof	10,000	—	—	12.00
1997 Proof	—	—	—	10.00
1998O Proof	—	—	—	12.00
1999 Proof	—	—	—	12.00
2000 Proof	—	—	—	12.00
2001 Proof	—	—	—	12.00

KM# 270d Subject: 100th Anniversary of the Cobalt Silver Strike **Composition:** Bi-Metallic

Date	Mintage	MS-63	P/L	Proof
2003 In proof sets only	100,000	—	—	25.00

KM# 496 Obv: New effigy of Queen Elizabeth II **Obv. Designer:** Susanna Blunt **Rev. Designer:** Brent Townsend **Composition:** Bi-Metallic

Date	Mintage	MS-63	P/L	Proof
2003W	—	3.50	—	—

5 DOLLARS

KM# 26 Obv. Designer: E. B. MacKennal **Rev. Designer:** W. H. J. Blakemore **Weight:** 8.3592 g. **Composition:** 0.9000 Gold 0.2419 oz. AGW

Date	Mintage	F-12	VF-20	XF-40	AU-50	MS-60	MS-63
1912	165,680	130	150	175	200	250	550
1913	98,832	130	150	175	200	250	600
1914	31,122	175	275	350	425	650	2,000

10 DOLLARS

KM# 27 Obv. Designer: E. B. MacKennal **Rev. Designer:** W. H. J. Blackmore **Weight:** 16.7185 g. **Composition:** 0.9000 Gold 0.4838 oz. AGW

Date	Mintage	F-12	VF-20	XF-40	AU-50	MS-60	MS-63
1912	74,759	250	300	350	400	550	2,000
1913	149,232	265	325	375	400	600	2,600
1914	140,068	265	325	400	450	700	2,750

SOVEREIGN

KM# 14 Rev: St. George slaying dragon, mint mark below horse's rear hooves **Weight:** 7.9881 g. **Composition:** 0.9170 Gold .2354 oz. AGW

Date	Mintage	VG-8	F-12	VF-20	XF-40	MS-60	MS-63	Proof
1908C	636	—	1,250	1,850	2,350	2,850	4,000	—
1909C	16,273	—	145	200	245	500	1,600	—
1910C	28,012	—	135	185	225	500	2,000	—

KM# 20 Rev: St. George slaying dragon, mint mark below horse's rear hooves **Weight:** 7.9881 g. **Composition:** 0.9170 Gold 0.2354 oz. AGW

Date	Mintage	VG-8	F-12	VF-20	XF-40	MS-60	MS-63	Proof
1911C	256,946	—	—	BV	115	150	175	—
1913C	3,715	—	375	475	600	1,500	2,000	—
1914C	14,871	—	175	225	285	375	950	—
1916C about 20 known	—	—	8,000	12,500	15,750	20,000	27,500	—
Note: Stacks' A.G. Carter Jr. Sale 12-89 Gem BU realized $82,500.								
1917C	58,845	—	BV	115	130	175	500	—
1918C	106,514	—	BV	115	130	175	750	—
1919C	135,889	—	BV	115	130	175	650	—

COMMEMORATIVE COINAGE

CENT

KM# 65 Subject: Confederation Centennial **Obv. Designer:** Arnold Machin **Rev:** Dove with wings spread **Rev. Designer:** Alex Coville **Comp.:** Bronze

Date	Mintage	MS-63	Proof
ND(1967)	345,140,645	0.20	1.00

KM# 204 Subject: Confederation 125 **Obv. Designer:** Dora dePedery-Hunt **Rev. Designer:** George E. Kruger-Gray **Composition:** Bronze

Date	Mintage	MS-63	Proof
ND(1992)	673,512,000	0.15	—
ND(1992) Proof	147,061	—	2.50

KM# 309 Subject: 90th Anniversary Royal Canadian Mint - 1908-1998 **Obv. Designer:** Dora dePedery-Hunt **Rev. Designer:** G. W. DeSaulles **Weight:** 5.6700 g. **Composition:** 0.9250 Copper-Plated Silver 0.1677 oz.

Date	Mintage	MS-63	Proof
ND(1998)	25,000	16.00	—
Note: Antique finish			
ND(1998) Proof	—	—	—

KM# 332 Subject: 90th Anniversary Royal Canadian Mint - 1908-1998 **Obv:** With "Canada" added to bust **Obv. Designer:** Dora dePedery-Hunt **Rev. Designer:** G. W. DeSaulles **Weight:** 5.6700 g. **Composition:** 0.9250 Silver .1677 oz. ASW

Date	Mintage	MS-63	Proof
ND(2000) Proof	25,000	—	16.00
Note: Mirror finish			

KM# 468 Subject: 50th Anniversary of the Coronation of Elizabeth II **Obv:** 1953 effigy of the Queen, Jubilee commemorative dates 1952-2002 **Composition:** Copper

Date	Mintage	MS-63	Proof
ND(2003)			
In Coronation			
Proof sets only	—	2.50	—

3 CENTS

KM# 410 Subject: 1st Canadian Postage Stamp **Obv:** Queen's head right **Obv. Designer:** Dora dePedery-Hunt **Rev:** Partial stamp design **Rev. Designer:** Sandford Fleming **Edge:** Plain **Weight:** 3.1100 g. **Composition:** 0.9250 Gold Plated Silver .1600 oz. ASW AGW **Size:** 21.1 mm.

Date	Mintage	MS-63	Proof
2001 Proof	90,000	—	20.00

5 CENTS

KM# 40 Subject: Victory **Obv. Designer:** T. H. Paget **Rev. Designer:** Thomas Shingles **Composition:** Tombac

Date	Mintage	VG-8	F-12	VF-20	XF-40	MS-60	MS-63	Proof
1943	24,760,256	0.20	0.30	0.40	0.80	2.00	9.00	—
1944 1 known	8,000	—	—	—	—	—	—	—

KM# 40a Composition: Chrome Plated Steel

Date	Mintage	VG-8	F-12	VF-20	XF-40	MS-60	MS-63	Proof
1944	11,532,784	0.15	0.20	0.40	0.90	2.00	4.00	—
1945	18,893,216	0.15	0.20	0.40	0.80	2.00	4.00	—

KM# 48 Subject: Nickel Bicentennial **Obv. Designer:** T. H. Paget **Rev. Designer:** Stephen Trenka **Composition:** Nickel

Date	Mintage	VG-8	F-12	VF-20	XF-40	MS-60	MS-63	Proof
ND(1951)	9,028,507	0.15	0.20	0.25	0.45	1.75	5.50	—

KM# 66 Subject: Confederation Centennial **Obv. Designer:** Arnold Machin **Rev:** Snowshoe rabbit bounding left **Rev. Designer:** Alex Coville **Composition:** Copper Nickel

Date	Mintage	MS-63	Proof
ND(1967)	36,876,574	0.40	1.00

KM# 205 Subject: Confederation 125 **Obv. Designer:** Dora dePedery-Hunt **Rev. Designer:** George E. Kruger-Gray **Composition:** Copper-Nickel

Date	Mintage	MS-63	Proof
ND(1992)	53,732,000	0.30	—
ND(1992) Proof	147,061	—	4.00

KM#310 Subject: 90th Anniversary Royal Canadian Mint **Obv. Designer:** Dora dePedery-Hunt **Rev. Designer:** W. H. J. Blackmore **Weight:** 1.1670 g. **Composition:** 0.9250 Silver .0347 oz. ASW

Date	Mintage	MS-63	Proof
ND(1998)	25,000	12.00	—
ND(1998) Proof	25,000	—	12.00

KM# 400 Subject: First French-Canadian Regiment **Obv:** Queen's portrait **Obv. Designer:** Dora dePedery-Hunt **Rev:** Regimental drums, sash and baton **Rev. Designer:** R. C. M. Staff **Edge:** Plain **Composition:** 0.9250 Silver **Size:** 21.2 mm.

Date	Mintage	MS-63	Proof
2000 Proof	—	—	9.00

KM# 413 Subject: Royal Military College **Obv:** Queen's head right **Rev:** Marching cadets and arch **Rev. Designer:** Gerald T. Locklin **Edge:** Plain **Weight:** 5.3500 g. **Composition:** 0.9250 Silver .1591 oz. ASW **Size:** 21.2 mm.

Date	Mintage	MS-63	Proof
2001 Proof	25,834	—	8.50

KM# 453 Subject: Vimy Ridge - WWI **Obv:** Queen's head right **Rev:** Vimy Ridge Memorial, allegorical figure and dates 1917-2003 **Rev. Designer:** S. A. Allward **Composition:** 0.9250 Silver

Date	Mintage	MS-63	Proof
ND(2003) Proof	22,646	—	12.50

KM# 446a Subject: Elizabeth II Golden Jubilee **Obv:** Queen, Jubilee commemorative dates 1952-2002 **Composition:** 0.9250 Silver

Date	Mintage	MS-63	Proof
ND(2002) In proof sets only	100,000	—	11.50

KM# 469 Subject: 50th Anniversary of the Coronation of Elizabeth II **Obv:** 1953 effigy of the Queen, Jubilee commemorative dates 1952-2002 **Composition:** 0.9250 Silver

Date	Mintage	MS-63	Proof
ND(2003) In Coronation Proof sets only	30,000	11.50	—

10 CENTS

KM# 67 Subject: Confederation Centennial **Rev:** Atlantic mackeral left **Rev. Designer:** Alex Colville **Weight:** 2.3328 g. **Composition:** 0.8000 Silver 0.0600 oz. ASW

Date	Mintage	MS-63	Proof
ND(1967)	62,998,215	1.00	2.00

KM# 67a Subject: Confederation Centennial **Weight:** 2.3328 g. **Composition:** 0.5000 Silver 0.0372 oz. ASW

Date	Mintage	MS-63	Proof
ND(1967)	Inc. above	1.00	—

KM# 206   Subject: Confederation 125 **Composition:** Nickel

Date	Mintage	MS-63	Proof
ND(1992)	174,476,000	0.35	—
ND(1992) Proof	147,061	—	3.00

KM# 299   Subject: John Cabot **Rev. Designer:** Donald H. Curley **Weight:** 2.4000 g. **Composition:** 0.9250 Silver .0714 oz. ASW

Date	Mintage	MS-63	Proof
ND(1997) Proof	49,848	—	17.50

KM# 311   Subject: 90th Anniversary Royal Canadian Mint **Weight:** 2.3200 g. **Composition:** 0.9250 Silver .0690 oz. ASW

Date	Mintage	MS-63	Proof
ND(1998) Matte	25,000	—	10.00
ND(1998) Proof	25,000	—	10.00

KM# 409   Subject: First Canadian Credit Union **Obv:** Queen's head right **Rev:** Alphonse Desjardins' house, (founder of the first credit union in Canada) **Edge:** Reeded **Weight:** 2.4000 g. **Composition:** 0.9250 Silver .0714 oz. ASW **Size:** 18 mm.

Date	Mintage	MS-63	Proof
ND(2000) Proof	66,336	—	8.00

KM# 412   Subject: Year of the Volunteer **Obv:** Queen's head right **Rev:** Three portraits and radiant sun **Rev. Designer:** R. C. M. Staff **Edge:** Reeded **Weight:** 1.7700 g. **Composition:** Nickel Plated Steel **Size:** 18 mm.

Date	Mintage	MS-63	Proof
2001P Proof	—	—	7.50

KM# 412a   Subject: Year of the Volunteer **Obv:** Queen's head right **Rev:** 3 conjoined busts above banner, radiant sun below **Edge:** Reeded **Weight:** 2.4000 g. **Composition:** 0.9250 Silver .0714 oz. ASW **Size:** 18 mm.

Date	Mintage	MS-63	Proof
2001P Proof	50,000	—	12.50

KM# 447a   Subject: Elizabeth II Golden Jubilee **Obv:** Queen, Jubilee commemorative dates 1952-2002 **Composition:** 0.9250 Silver

Date	Mintage	MS-63	Proof
ND(2002) In proof sets only	100,000	—	12.50

KM# 470   Subject: 50th Anniversary of the Coronation of Elizabeth II **Composition:** 0.9250 Silver

Date	Mintage	MS-63	Proof
ND(2003) In Coronation Proof sets only	30,000	12.00	—

25 CENTS

KM# 68   Subject: Confederation Centennial **Rev:** Lynx striding left **Rev. Designer:** Alex Colville **Weight:** 5.8319 g. **Composition:** 0.8000 Silver 0.1500 oz. ASW

Date	Mintage	MS-63	Proof
ND(1967)	48,855,500	1.75	—

KM# 68a   Subject: Confederation Centennial **Weight:** 5.8319 g. **Composition:** 0.5000 Silver 0.0937 oz. ASW

Date	Mintage	MS-63	Proof
ND(1967)	Inc. above	1.75	—

KM# 81.1   Subject: Royal Candian Mounted Police Centennial **Rev. Designer:** Paul Cedarberg **Composition:** Nickel **Note:** 120 beads.

Date	Mintage	MS-63	Proof
ND(1973)	134,958,587	1.00	—

KM# 81.2   Subject: RCMP Centennial **Composition:** Nickel **Note:** 132 beads.

Date	Mintage	MS-63	Proof
ND(1973)	Inc. above	200	—

KM# 207   Subject: Confederation 125 **Obv. Designer:** Dora dePedery-Hunt **Rev. Designer:** Emanuel Hahn **Composition:** Nickel

Date	Mintage	MS-63	Proof
ND(1992)	442,986	12.50	—
ND(1992) Proof	147,061	—	20.00

KM# 203 Subject: 125th Anniversary of Confederation, New Brunswick **Rev:** Covered bridge in Newton **Rev. Designer:** Ronald Lambert **Composition:** Nickel

Date	Mintage	MS-63	Proof
ND(1992)	12,174,000	0.70	—

KM# 203a Subject: 125th Anniversary of Confederation, New Brunswick **Weight:** 5.8319 g. **Composition:** 0.9250 Silver 0.1734 oz. ASW

Date	Mintage	MS-63	Proof
ND(1992) Proof	149,579	—	5.50

KM# 212 Subject: 125th Anniversary of Confederation, North West Territories **Rev. Designer:** Beth McEachen **Composition:** Nickel

Date	Mintage	MS-63	Proof
ND(1992)	12,582,000	0.70	—

KM# 212a Subject: 125th Anniversary of Confederation, North West Territories **Weight:** 5.8319 g. **Composition:** 0.9250 Silver 0.1734 oz. ASW

Date	Mintage	MS-63	Proof
ND(1992) Proof	149,579	—	5.50

KM# 213 Subject: 125th Anniversary of Confederation, Newfoundland **Rev:** Firsherman rowing a dory **Rev. Designer:** Christopher Newhook **Composition:** Nickel

Date	Mintage	MS-63	Proof
ND(1992)	11,405,000	0.70	—

KM# 213a Subject: 125th Anniversary of Confederation, Newfoundland **Weight:** 5.8319 g. **Composition:** 0.9250 Silver 0.1734 oz. ASW

Date	Mintage	MS-63	Proof
ND(1992) Proof	149,579	—	5.50

KM# 214 Subject: 125th Anniversary of Confederation, Manitoba **Rev. Designer:** Muriel Hope **Composition:** Nickel

Date	Mintage	MS-63	Proof
ND(1992)	11,349,000	0.70	—

KM# 214a Subject: 125th Anniversary of Confederation, Manitoba **Weight:** 5.8319 g. **Composition:** 0.9250 Silver 0.1734 oz. ASW

Date	Mintage	MS-63	Proof
ND(1992) Proof	149,579	—	5.50

KM# 220 Subject: 125th Anniversary of Confederation, Yukon **Rev. Designer:** Libby Dulac **Composition:** Nickel

Date	Mintage	MS-63	Proof
ND(1992)	10,388,000	0.70	—

KM# 220a Subject: 125th Anniversary of Confederation, Yukon **Weight:** 5.8319 g. **Composition:** 0.9250 Silver 0.1734 oz. ASW

Date	Mintage	MS-63	Proof
ND(1992) Proof	149,579	—	5.50

KM# 221 Subject: 125th Anniversary of Confederation, Alberta **Rev:** Rock formations in the badlands near Drumhelter **Rev. Designer:** Mel Heath **Composition:** Nickel

Date	Mintage	MS-63	Proof
ND(1992)	12,133,000	0.70	—

KM# 221a Subject: 125th Anniversary of Confederation, Alberta **Weight:** 5.8319 g. **Composition:** 0.9250 Silver 0.1734 oz. ASW

Date	Mintage	MS-63	Proof
ND(1992) Proof	—	—	5.50

KM# 222 Subject: 125th Anniversary of Confederation, Prince Edward Island **Rev. Designer:** Nigel Roe **Composition:** Nickel

Date	Mintage	MS-63	Proof
ND(1992)	13,001,000	0.70	—

KM# 222a Subject: 125th Anniversary of Confederation, Prince Edward Island **Weight:** 5.8319 g. **Composition:** 0.9250 Silver 0.1734 oz. ASW

Date	Mintage	MS-63	Proof
ND(1992) Proof	149,579	—	5.50

KM# 223 Subject: 125th Anniversary of Confederation, Ontario **Rev:** Jack pine **Rev. Designer:** Greg Salmela **Composition:** Nickel

Date	Mintage	MS-63	Proof
ND(1992)	14,263,000	0.70	—

KM# 223a Subject: 125th Anniversary of Confederation, Ontario **Weight:** 5.8319 g. **Composition:** 0.9250 Silver 0.1734 oz. ASW

Date	Mintage	MS-63	Proof
ND(1992) Proof	149,579	—	5.50

KM# 231 Subject: 125th Anniversary of Confederation, Nova Scotia **Rev:** Lighthouse **Rev. Designer:** Bruce Wood **Composition:** Nickel

Date	Mintage	MS-63	Proof
ND(1992)	13,600,000	0.70	—

KM# 231a Subject: 125th Anniversary of Confederation, Nova Scotia **Weight:** 5.8319 g. **Composition:** 0.9250 Silver 0.1734 oz. ASW

Date	Mintage	MS-63	Proof
ND(1992) Proof	149,579	—	5.50

KM# 232 Subject: 125th Anniversary of Confederation, British Columbia **Rev. Designer:** Carla Herrera Egan **Composition:** Nickel

Date	Mintage	MS-63	Proof
ND(1992)	14,001,000	0.70	—

KM# 232a Subject: 125th Anniversary of Confederation, British Columbia **Weight:** 5.8319 g. **Composition:** 0.9250 Silver 0.1734 oz. ASW

Date	Mintage	MS-63	Proof
ND(1992) Proof	149,579	—	5.50

KM# 233 Subject: 125th Anniversary of Confederation, Saskatchewan **Rev. Designer:** Brian Cobb **Composition:** Nickel

Date	Mintage	MS-63	Proof
ND(1992)	14,165,000	0.70	—

KM# 233a Subject: 125th Anniversary of Confederation, Saskatchewan **Weight:** 5.8319 g. **Composition:** 0.9250 Silver 0.1734 oz. ASW

Date	Mintage	MS-63	Proof
ND(1992) Proof	149,579	—	5.50

KM# 234 Subject: 125th Anniversary of Confederation, Quebec **Rev. Designer:** Romualdas Bukauskas **Composition:** Nickel

Date	Mintage	MS-63	Proof
ND(1992)	13,607,000	0.70	—

KM# 234a Subject: 125th Anniversary of Confederation, Quebec **Weight:** 5.8319 g. **Composition:** 0.9250 Silver 0.1734 oz. ASW

Date	Mintage	MS-63	Proof
ND(1992) Proof	149,579	—	5.50

KM# 342 Subject: Millennium, January - A country unfolds **Rev:** Totem pole, portraits **Rev. Designer:** P. Ka-Kin Poon **Composition:** Nickel

Date	Mintage	MS-63	Proof
1999	—	0.65	—

KM# 342a Subject: Millennium, January **Rev:** Totem pole, portraits **Weight:** 5.8319 g. **Composition:** 0.9250 Silver 0.1734 oz. ASW

Date	Mintage	MS-63	Proof
1999 Proof	—	—	8.00

KM# 343 Subject: Millennium, February - Etched in stone **Rev:** Native petroglyphs **Rev. Designer:** L. Springer **Composition:** Nickel

Date	Mintage	MS-63	Proof
1999	—	0.65	—

KM# 343a Subject: Millennium, February **Rev:** Native petroglyphs **Weight:** 5.8319 g. **Composition:** 0.9250 Silver 0.1734 oz. ASW

Date	Mintage	MS-63	Proof
1999 Proof	—	—	8.00

KM# 344 Subject: Millennium, March - The log drive **Rev:** Lumberjack **Rev. Designer:** M. Lavoie **Composition:** Nickel

Date	Mintage	MS-63	Proof
1999	—	0.65	—

KM# 344a Subject: Millennium, March **Rev:** Lumberjack **Weight:** 5.8319 g. **Composition:** 0.9250 Silver 0.1734 oz. ASW

Date	Mintage	MS-63	Proof
1999 Proof	—	—	8.00

KM# 345 Subject: Millennium, April - Our Northern Heritage **Rev:** Owl, polar bear **Rev. Designer:** Ken Ojnak Ashevac **Comp.:** Nickel

Date	Mintage	MS-63	Proof
1999	—	0.65	—

KM# 345a Subject: Millennium, April **Rev:** Owl, polar bear **Weight:** 5.8319 g. **Composition:** 0.9250 Silver 0.1734 oz. ASW

Date	Mintage	MS-63	Proof
1999 Proof	—	—	8.00

KM# 346 Subject: Millennium, May - The Voyageures **Rev:** Voyageurs in canoe **Rev. Designer:** S. Mineok **Composition:** Nickel

Date	Mintage	MS-63	Proof
1999	—	0.65	—

KM# 346a Subject: Millennium, May **Rev:** Voyageurs in canoe **Weight:** 5.8319 g. **Composition:** 0.9250 Silver 0.1734 oz. ASW

Date	Mintage	MS-63	Proof
1999 Proof	—	—	8.00

KM# 347 Subject: Millennium, June - from Coast to Coast **Rev:** 19th-century locomotive **Rev. Designer:** G. Ho **Composition:** Nickel

Date	Mintage	MS-63	Proof
1999	—	0.65	—

KM# 347a Subject: Millennium, June **Rev:** 19th-century locomotive **Weight:** 5.8319 g. **Composition:** 0.9250 Silver 0.1734 oz. ASW

Date	Mintage	MS-63	Proof
1999 Proof	—	—	8.00

KM# 348 Subject: Millennium, July - A Nation of people **Rev:** 6 stylized portraits **Rev. Designer:** M. H. Sarkany **Composition:** Nickel

Date	Mintage	MS-63	Proof
1999	—	0.65	—

KM# 348a Subject: Millennium, July **Rev:** 6 stylized portraits **Weight:** 5.8319 g. **Composition:** 0.9250 Silver 0.1734 oz. ASW

Date	Mintage	MS-63	Proof
1999 Proof	—	—	8.00

KM# 349 Subject: Millennium, August - the Pioneer Spirit **Rev:** Hay harvesting **Rev. Designer:** A. Botelho **Composition:** Nickel

Date	Mintage	MS-63	Proof
1999	—	0.65	—

KM# 349a Subject: Millennium, August **Rev:** Hay harvesting **Weight:** 5.8319 g. **Composition:** 0.9250 Silver 0.1734 oz. ASW

Date	Mintage	MS-63	Proof
1999 Proof	—	—	8.00

KM# 350 Subject: Millennium, September - Canada through a child's eye **Rev:** Childlike artwork **Rev. Designer:** Claudia Bertrand **Comp.:** Nickel

Date	Mintage	MS-63	Proof
1999	—	0.65	—

KM# 350a Subject: Millennium, September **Rev:** Childlike artwork **Weight:** 5.8319 g. **Composition:** 0.9250 Silver 0.1734 oz. ASW

Date	Mintage	MS-63	Proof
1999 Proof	—	—	8.00

KM# 351 Subject: Millennium, October - tribute to the First Nations **Rev:** Aboriginal artwork **Rev. Designer:** J. E. Read **Composition:** Nickel

Date	Mintage	MS-63	Proof
1999	—	0.65	—

KM# 351a Subject: Millennium, October **Rev:** Aboriginal artwork **Weight:** 5.8319 g. **Composition:** 0.9250 Silver 0.1734 oz. ASW

Date	Mintage	MS-63	Proof
1999 Proof	—	—	8.00

KM# 352 Subject: Millennium, November - The airplane opens the North **Rev:** Bush plane with landing skis **Rev. Designer:** B. R. Brown **Composition:** Nickel

Date	Mintage	MS-63	Proof
1999	—	0.65	—

KM# 352a Subject: Millennium, November **Rev:** Bush plane with landing skis **Weight:** 5.8319 g. **Composition:** 0.9250 Silver 0.1734 oz. ASW

Date	Mintage	MS-63	Proof
1999 Proof	—	—	8.00

KM# 353 Subject: Millennium, December - This is Canada **Rev:** Eclectic geometric design **Rev. Designer:** J. L. P. Provencher **Composition:** Nickel

Date	Mintage	MS-63	Proof

KM# 353a Subject: Millennium, December **Rev:** Eclectic geometric design **Weight:** 5.8319 g. **Composition:** 0.9250 Silver 0.1734 oz. ASW

Date	Mintage	MS-63	Proof
1999 Proof	—	—	8.00

KM# 373 Subject: Health **Rev:** Ribbon and caduceus **Rev. Designer:** Anny Wassef **Composition:** Nickel

Date	Mintage	MS-63	Proof
2000	—	0.65	—

KM# 373a Subject: Health **Rev:** Ribbon and caduceus **Composition:** 0.9250 Silver

Date	Mintage	MS-63	Proof

KM# 374 Subject: Freedom **Rev:** 2 children and rising sun **Rev. Designer:** Kathy Vinish **Composition:** Nickel

Date	Mintage	MS-63	Proof
2000	—	0.65	—

KM# 376 Subject: Community **Rev:** Map on globe **Rev. Designer:** Michelle Thibodeau **Comp.:** Nickel

Date	Mintage	MS-63	Proof
2000	—	0.65	—

KM# 376a Subject: Community **Rev:** Map on globe **Composition:** 0.9250 Silver

Date	Mintage	MS-63	Proof
2000 Proof	—	—	6.00

KM# 377 Subject: Harmony **Rev:** Maple leaf **Rev. Designer:** Haver Demirer **Comp.:** Nickel

Date	Mintage	MS-63	Proof
2000	—	0.65	—

KM# 377a Subject: Harmony **Rev:** Maple leaf **Composition:** 0.9250 Silver

Date	Mintage	MS-63	Proof
2000 Proof	—	—	6.00

KM# 378 Subject: Wisdom **Rev:** Man with young child **Rev. Designer:** Cezar Serbanescu **Composition:** Nickel

Date	Mintage	MS-63	Proof
2000	—	0.65	—

KM# 378a Subject: Wisdom **Rev:** Man with young child **Composition:** 0.9250 Silver

Date	Mintage	MS-63	Proof
2000 Proof	—	—	6.00

KM# 379 Subject: Creativity **Rev:** Canoe full of children **Rev. Designer:** Kong Tat Hui **Composition:** Nickel

Date	Mintage	MS-63	Proof
2000	—	0.65	—

KM# 379a Subject: Creativity **Rev:** Canoe full of children **Composition:** 0.9250 Silver

Date	Mintage	MS-63	Proof
2000 Proof	—	—	6.00

KM# 380 Subject: Ingenuity **Rev:** Crescent-shaped city views **Rev. Designer:** John Jaciw **Composition:** Nickel

Date	Mintage	MS-63	Proof
2000	—	0.65	—

KM# 380a Subject: Ingenuity **Rev:** Crescent-shaped city view **Composition:** 0.9250 Silver

Date	Mintage	MS-63	Proof
2000 Proof	—	—	6.00

KM# 381 Subject: Achievement **Rev:** Rocket above jagged design **Rev. Designer:** Daryl Dorosz **Composition:** Nickel

Date	Mintage	MS-63	Proof
2000	—	0.65	—

KM# 381a Subject: Achievement **Rev:** Rocket above jagged design **Composition:** 0.9250 Silver

Date	Mintage	MS-63	Proof
2000 Proof	—	—	6.00

KM# 382 Subject: Natural legacy **Rev:** Environmental elements **Rev. Designer:** Randy Trantau **Composition:** Nickel

Date	Mintage	MS-63	Proof
2000	—	0.65	—

KM# 382a Subject: Natural legacy **Rev:** Environmental elements **Comp.:** 0.9250 Silver

Date	Mintage	MS-63	Proof
2000 Proof	—	—	6.00

KM# 383 Subject: Celebration **Rev:** Fireworks, children behind flag **Rev. Designer:** Laura Paxton **Composition:** Nickel

Date	Mintage	MS-63	Proof
2000	—	0.65	—

KM# 383a Subject: Celebration **Rev:** Fireworks, children behind flag **Composition:** 0.9250 Silver

Date	Mintage	MS-63	Proof
2000 Proof	—	—	6.00

KM# 384.1 Subject: Pride **Obv:** Queen's portrait **Rev:** Red with 3 small maple leaves on large maple leaf **Rev. Designer:** Donald F. Warkentin **Edge:** Reeded **Composition:** Nickel **Size:** 23.9 mm. **Note:** Colorized version.

Date	Mintage	MS-63	Proof
2000	—	6.50	—

KM# 384.2 Subject: Pride **Rev:** 2 with three small maple leaves on large maple leaf **Rev. Designer:** Donald F. Warkentin **Composition:** Nickel

Date	Mintage	MS-63	Proof
2000	—	0.65	—

KM# 384.2a Subject: Pride **Rev:** 2 with 3 small maple leaves on large maple leaf **Composition:** 0.9250 Silver

Date	Mintage	MS-63	Proof
2000 Proof	—	—	6.00

KM# 374a Subject: Freedom **Rev:** 2 children and rising sun **Composition:** 0.9250 Silver

Date	Mintage	MS-63	Proof
2000 Proof	—	—	6.00

KM# 375 Subject: Family **Rev:** Circular native carvings **Rev. Designer:** Wade Stephen Baker **Composition:** Nickel

Date	Mintage	MS-63	Proof
2000	—	0.65	—

KM# 375a Subject: Family **Rev:** Circular native carvings **Composition:** 0.9250 Silver

Date	Mintage	MS-63	Proof
2000 Proof	—	—	6.00

KM# 419 Subject: Spirit of Canada **Obv:** Queen's head right **Rev:** Maple leaf at center, children holding hands below **Rev. Designer:** Silke Ware **Edge:** Reeded **Weight:** 5.0600 g. **Composition:** Nickel Plated Steel **Size:** 23.9 mm.

Date	Mintage	MS-63	Proof
2001	96,352	7.00	—

KM# 448 Subject: Elizabeth II Golden Jubilee **Composition:** Nickel Plated Steel **Note:** Double-dated 1952-2002.

Date	Mintage	MS-63	Proof
ND(2002)P	152,485,000	2.00	—
ND(2002) Proof	32,642	—	6.00

KM# 448a Subject: Elizabeth II Golden Jubilee **Obv:** Queen, Jubilee commemorative dates 1952-2002 **Composition:** 0.9250 Silver

Date	Mintage	MS-63	Proof
ND(2002) In proof sets only	100,000	—	12.50

KM# 471 Subject: 50th Anniversary of the Coronation of Elizabeth II **Obv:** 1953 effigy of the Queen, Jubilee commemorative dates 1952-2002 **Composition:** 0.9250 Silver

Date	Mintage	MS-63	Proof
ND(2003) In coronation proof sets only	30,000	12.50	—

KM# 474 Obv: Queen's head right **Rev:** Polar bear and red maple leaves **Composition:** 0.9250 Silver

Date	Mintage	MS-63	Proof
2003 Proof	—	—	7.50

50 CENTS

KM# 69 Subject: Confederation Centennial **Rev:** Seated wolf howling **Rev. Designer:** Alex Colville **Weight:** 11.6638 g. **Composition:** 0.8000 Silver .3000 oz. ASW

Date	Mintage	XF-40	MS-60	MS-63	Proof
ND(1967)	4,211,392	2.50	3.00	6.00	8.50

KM# 208 Subject: Confederation 125 **Obv. Designer:** Dora dePedery-Hunt **Rev. Designer:** Thomas Shingles **Comp.:** Nickel

Date	Mintage	XF-40	MS-60	MS-63	Proof
ND(1992)	445,000	0.50	0.75	1.00	—
ND(1992) Proof	147,061	—	—	—	5.00

KM# 261 Subject: Atlantic puffin **Rev. Designer:** Sheldon Beveridge **Weight:** 11.6638 g. **Composition:** 0.9250 Silver .3461 oz. ASW

Date	Mintage	MS-63	Proof
1995 Proof	—	—	20.00

KM# 262 Subject: Whooping crane **Rev. Designer:** Stan Witten **Weight:** 11.6638 g. **Composition:** 0.9250 Silver .3461 oz. ASW

Date	Mintage	MS-63	Proof
1995 Proof	—	—	20.00

KM# 263 Subject: Gray jays **Rev. Designer:** Sheldon Beveridge **Weight:** 11.6638 g. **Composition:** 0.9250 Silver .3461 oz. ASW

Date	Mintage	MS-63	Proof
1995 Proof	—	—	20.00

KM# 264 Subject: White-tailed ptarmigans **Rev. Designer:** Cosme Saffioti **Weight:** 11.6638 g. **Composition:** 0.9250 Silver .3461 oz. ASW

Date	Mintage	MS-63	Proof
1995 Proof	—	—	20.00

KM# 283 Subject: Moose calf **Rev. Designer:** Ago Aarand **Weight:** 11.6638 g. **Composition:** 0.9250 Silver .3461 oz. ASW

Date	Mintage	MS-63	Proof
1996 Proof	—	—	15.00

KM# 284 Subject: Wood ducklings **Rev. Designer:** Sheldon Beveridge **Weight:** 11.6638 g. **Comp.:** 0.9250 Silver .3461 oz. ASW

Date	Mintage	MS-63	Proof
1996 Proof	—	—	15.00

KM# 285 Subject: Cougar kittens **Rev. Designer:**
Stan Witten **Weight:** 11.6638 g. **Composition:**
0.9250 Silver .3461 oz. ASW

Date	Mintage	MS-63	Proof
1996 Proof	—	—	15.00

KM# 286 Subject: Black bear cubs
Rev. Designer: Sheldon Beveridge **Weight:**
11.6638 g. **Comp.:** 0.9250 Silver .3461 oz. ASW

Date	Mintage	MS-63	Proof
1996 Proof	—	—	15.00

KM# 292 Subject: Duck tolling retriever
Rev. Designer: Stan Witten **Weight:** 11.6638 g.
Composition: 0.9250 Silver .3461 oz. ASW

Date	Mintage	MS-63	Proof
1997 Proof	—	—	14.00

KM# 293 Subject: Labrador retriever
Rev. Designer: Sheldon Beveridge **Weight:**
11.6638 g. **Comp.:** 0.9250 Silver .3461 oz. ASW

Date	Mintage	MS-63	Proof
1997 Proof	—	—	15.00

KM# 294 Subject: Newfoundland **Rev. Designer:**
William Woodruff **Weight:** 11.6638 g.
Composition: 0.9250 Silver .3461 oz. ASW

Date	Mintage	MS-63	Proof
1997 Proof	—	—	14.00

KM# 295 Subject: Eskimo dog **Rev. Designer:**
Cosme Saffioti **Weight:** 11.6638 g. **Composition:**
0.9250 Silver .3461 oz. ASW

Date	Mintage	MS-63	Proof
1997 Proof	—	—	14.00

KM# 313 Subject: 90th Anniversary Royal
Canadian Mint **Rev. Designer:** W. H. J. Blakemore
Weight: 11.6638 g. **Composition:** 0.9250 Silver
.3461 oz. ASW

Date	Mintage	MS-63	Proof
ND(1998) Matte	25,000	—	15.00
ND(1998) Proof	25,000	—	15.00

KM# 314 Subject: 110 years Canadian speed and
figure skating **Rev. Designer:** Sheldon Beveridge
Weight: 11.6638 g. **Composition:** 0.9250 Silver
.3461 oz. ASW

Date	Mintage	MS-63	Proof
ND(1998) Proof	—	—	9.00

KM# 315 Subject: 100 years Canadian ski racing
Rev. Designer: Ago Aarand **Weight:** 11.6638 g.
Composition: 0.9250 Silver .3461 oz. ASW

Date	Mintage	MS-63	Proof
ND(1998) Proof	—	—	9.00

KM# 318 Subject: Killer whales **Rev. Designer:** William Woodruff **Weight:** 11.6638 g. **Composition:** 0.9250 Silver .3461 oz. ASW

Date	Mintage	MS-63	Proof
1998 Proof	—	—	12.50

KM# 319 Subject: Humpback whale **Rev. Designer:** Sheldon Beveridge **Weight:** 11.6638 g. **Comp.:** 0.9250 Silver .3461 oz. ASW

Date	Mintage	MS-63	Proof
1998 Proof	—	—	12.50

KM# 320 Subject: Beluga whale **Rev. Designer:** Cosme Saffioti **Weight:** 11.6638 g. **Composition:** 0.9250 Silver .3461 oz. ASW

Date	Mintage	MS-63	Proof
1998 Proof	—	—	12.50

KM# 321 Subject: Blue whale **Rev. Designer:** Stan Witten **Weight:** 11.6638 g. **Composition:** 0.9250 Silver .3461 oz. ASW

Date	Mintage	MS-63	Proof
1998 Proof	—	—	12.50

KM# 327 Subject: 110 years Canadian soccer **Rev. Designer:** Stan Witten **Weight:** 11.6638 g. **Composition:** 0.9250 Silver .3461 oz. ASW

Date	Mintage	MS-63	Proof
ND(1998) Proof	—	—	9.00

KM# 328 Subject: 20 years Canadian auto racing **Rev. Designer:** Cosme Saffioti **Weight:** 11.6638 g. **Composition:** 0.9250 Silver .3461 oz. ASW

Date	Mintage	MS-63	Proof
ND(1998) Proof	—	—	9.00

KM# 333 Subject: 1904 Canadian open **Rev. Designer:** William Woodruff **Weight:** 11.6638 g. **Comp.:** 0.9250 Silver .3461 oz. ASW

Date	Mintage	MS-63	Proof
ND(1999) Proof	—	—	13.50

KM# 334 Subject: First U.S.-Canadian yacht race **Rev. Designer:** Stan Witten **Weight:** 11.6638 g. **Composition:** 0.9250 Silver .3461 oz. ASW

Date	Mintage	MS-63	Proof
ND(1999) Proof	—	—	9.00

KM# 335 Subject: Canadian cats, Cymric **Rev. Designer:** Susan Taylor **Weight:** 11.6638 g. **Composition:** 0.9250 Silver .3461 oz. ASW

Date	Mintage	MS-63	Proof
1999 Proof	—	—	15.00

KM# 336 Subject: Canadian cats, Tonkinese
Rev. Designer: Susan Taylor **Weight:** 11.6638 g.
Composition: 0.9250 Silver .3461 oz. ASW

Date	Mintage	MS-63	Proof
1999 Proof	—	—	15.00

KM# 337 Subject: Canadian cats, Cougar
Rev. Designer: Susan Taylor **Weight:** 11.6638 g.
Composition: 0.9250 Silver .3461 oz. ASW

Date	Mintage	MS-63	Proof
1999 Proof	—	—	15.00

KM# 338 Subject: Canadian cats, Lynx
Rev. Designer: Susan Taylor **Weight:** 11.6638 g.
Composition: 0.9250 Silver .3461 oz. ASW

Date	Mintage	MS-63	Proof
1999 Proof	—	—	15.00

KM#371 Subject: Basketball **Obv:** Queen's portrait
Rev: Basketball players **Rev. Designer:** Sheldon
Beveridge **Edge:** Reeded **Weight:** 9.3600 g. **Comp.:**
0.9250 Silver 0.2784 oz. ASW **Size:** 27.1 mm.

Date	Mintage	MS-63	Proof
ND(1999) Proof	—	—	9.00

KM# 372 Obv: Queen's portrait **Rev:** Football
players **Rev. Designer:** Cosme Saffioti **Edge:**
Reeded **Weight:** 9.3600 g. **Composition:** 0.9250
Silver 0.2784 oz. ASW **Size:** 27.1 mm.

Date	Mintage	MS-63	Proof
ND(1999) Proof	—	—	9.00

KM#385 Subject: Ice hockey **Rev:** 4 hockey players
Rev. Designer: Stanley Witten **Comp.:** 0.9250 Silver

Date	Mintage	MS-63	Proof
ND(2000) Proof	—	—	12.00

KM# 386 Subject: Curling **Rev:** Motion study of a
curler **Rev. Designer:** Cosme Saffioti
Composition: 0.9250 Silver

Date	Mintage	MS-63	Proof
ND(2000) Proof	—	—	9.00

KM# 389 Sub.: Great horned owl **Rev. Des.:** Susan
Taylor **Weight:** 9.3500 g. **Comp.:** 0.9250 Silver

Date	Mintage	MS-63	Proof
2000 Proof	—	—	15.00

KM# 390 Subject: Red-tail hawk **Weight:**
9.3500 g. **Composition:** 0.9250 Silver

Date	Mintage	MS-63	Proof
2000 Proof	—	—	15.00

KM#391 Subject: Osprey **Rev. Designer:** Susan
Taylor **Weight:** 9.3500 g. **Comp.:** 0.9250 Silver

Date	Mintage	MS-63	Proof
2000 Proof	—	—	15.00

KM# 392 Subject: Bald eagle **Rev. Des.:** William
Woodruff **Weight:** 9.3500 g. **Comp.:** 0.9250 Silver

Date	Mintage	MS-63	Proof
2000 Proof	—	—	12.00

KM# 393 Subject: Steeplechase **Rev. Designer:** Susan Taylor **Composition:** 0.9250 Silver

Date	Mintage	MS-63	Proof
2000 Proof	—	—	9.00

KM# 394 Subject: Bowling **Rev. Designer:** William Woodruff **Composition:** 0.9250 Silver

Date	Mintage	MS-63	Proof
2000 Proof	—	—	9.00

KM# 420 Subject: Festivals - Quebec, **Obv:** Queen's head right **Rev:** Snowman and Chateau Frontenac **Rev. Designer:** Sylvie Daigneault **Edge:** Reeded **Weight:** 9.3000 g. **Composition:** 0.9250 Silver .2766 oz. ASW **Size:** 27.13 mm.

Date	Mintage	MS-63	Proof
2001 Proof	58,123	—	11.50

KM# 421 Subject: Festivals - Nunavut, **Obv:** Queen's head right **Rev:** Dancer, dog sled and snowmobiles **Rev. Designer:** John Mardon **Edge:** Reeded **Weight:** 9.3000 g. **Composition:** 0.9250 Silver .2766 oz. ASW **Size:** 27.13 mm.

Date	Mintage	MS-63	Proof
2001 Proof	58,123	—	11.50

KM# 422 Subject: Festivals - Newfoundland, **Obv:** Queen's head right **Rev:** Sailor and musical people **Rev. Designer:** David Craig **Edge:** Reeded **Weight:** 9.3000 g. **Composition:** 0.9250 Silver .2766 oz. ASW **Size:** 27.13 mm.

Date	Mintage	MS-63	Proof
2001 Proof	58,123	—	11.50

KM#423 Subject: Festivals - Prince Edward Island, **Obv:** Queen's head right **Rev:** Family, juggler and building **Rev. Designer:** Brenda Whiteway **Edge:**

Reeded **Weight:** 9.3000 g. **Comp.:** 0.9250 Silver .2766 oz. ASW **Size:** 27.13 mm.

Date	Mintage	MS-63	Proof
2001 Proof	58,123	—	11.50

KM# 424 Subject: Folklore - The Sled, **Obv:** Queen's head right **Rev:** Family scene **Rev. Designer:** Valentina Hotz-Entin **Edge:** Reeded **Weight:** 9.3000 g. **Composition:** 0.9250 Silver .2766 oz. ASW **Size:** 27.13 mm.

Date	Mintage	MS-63	Proof
2001 Proof	28,979	—	12.50

KM# 425 Subject: Folklore - The Maiden's Cave, **Obv:** Queen's head right **Rev:** Woman shouting **Rev. Designer:** Peter Kiss **Edge:** Reeded **Weight:** 9.3000 g. **Composition:** 0.9250 Silver .2766 oz. ASW **Size:** 27.13 mm.

Date	Mintage	MS-63	Proof
2001 Proof	28,979	—	12.50

KM# 426 Subject: Folklore - The Small Jumpers, **Obv:** Queen's head right **Rev:** Jumping children on seashore **Rev. Designer:** Miynki Tanobe **Edge:** Reeded **Weight:** 9.3000 g. **Composition:** 0.9250 Silver .2766 oz. ASW **Size:** 27.13 mm.

Date	Mintage	MS-63	Proof
2001 Proof	28,979	—	12.50

KM# 444 Subject: Queen's Golden Jubilee **Obv:** Bust of Queen Elizabeth II right and monogram **Rev:** Canadian arms **Rev. Designer:** Bursey Sabourin **Edge:** Reeded **Weight:** 6.8300 g. **Composition:** Nickel Plated Steel **Size:** 27 mm.

Date	Mintage	MS-63	Proof
ND(2002)P	1,440,000	2.00	—

KM# 461   Subject: Canadian Folklore and Legends, The Pig That Wouldn't Get Over the Stile **Rev. Designer:** Laura Jolicoeur **Composition:** 0.9250 Silver

Date	Mintage	MS-63	Proof
2002 Proof	19,267	—	13.50

KM# 458   Subject: Squamish Days Logger Sports **Rev. Designer:** Jose Osio **Comp.:** 0.9250 Silver

Date	Mintage	MS-63	Proof
2002 Proof	59,998	—	12.00

KM# 456   Subject: Folklorama **Rev. Designer:** William Woodruff **Composition:** 0.9250 Silver

Date	Mintage	MS-63	Proof
2002 Proof	59,998	—	12.00

KM# 460   Subject: Canadian Folklore and Legends, The Ghost Ship **Rev. Designer:** Colette Boivin **Composition:** 0.9250 Silver

Date	Mintage	MS-63	Proof
2002 Proof	19,267	—	13.50

KM# 457   Subject: Calgary Stampede **Rev. Designer:** Stan Witten **Comp.:** 0.9250 Silver

Date	Mintage	MS-63	Proof
2002 Proof	59,998	—	12.00

KM# 454   Subject: Annapolis Valley Apple Blossom Festival **Rev. Designer:** Bonnie Ross **Composition:** 0.9250 Silver

Date	Mintage	MS-63	Proof
2002 Proof	59,998	—	12.00

KM# 459   Subject: Canadian Folklore and Legends, **Obv:** Queen's head right **Rev:** The Shoemaker in Heaven **Rev. Designer:** Francine Gravel **Composition:** 0.9250 Silver

Date	Mintage	MS-63	Proof
2002 Proof	19,267	—	13.50

KM# 455   Subject: Stratford Festival **Obv:** Queen's head right **Rev:** Couple with building in background **Rev. Designer:** Laurie McGaw **Composition:** 0.9250 Silver

Date	Mintage	MS-63	Proof
2002 Proof	59,998	—	12.00

KM# 444a   Subject: Elizabeth II Golden Jubilee **Obv:** Queen, Jubilee commemorative dates 1952-2002 **Composition:** 0.9250 Silver

Date	Mintage	MS-63	Proof
ND(2002) In proof sets only	100,000	—	17.50

KM# 444b   Subject: Queen's Golden Jubilee **Obv:** Bust of Queen Elizabeth II right and monogram **Rev:** Canadian arms **Edge:** Reeded **Composition:** Gold Plated Silver **Size:** 27 mm. **Note:** Special 24 karat gold plated issue of KM#444, issued in sets only.

Date	Mintage	MS-63	Proof
ND(2002) Proof	32,642	—	—

KM# 479   Subject: Great Northern Arts Festival **Composition:** 0.9250 Silver

Date	Mintage	MS-63	Proof
2003 Proof	—	—	16.50

KM# 476   Subject: Yukon International Storytelling Festival **Composition:** 0.9250 Silver

Date	Mintage	MS-63	Proof
2003 Proof	—	—	16.50

KM# 477   Subject: Festival Acadien de Caraquet **Obv:** Queen's head right **Rev:** Sailboat and couple **Composition:** 0.9250 Silver

Date	Mintage	MS-63	Proof
2003 Proof	—	—	16.50

KM# 478   Subject: Back to batoche **Composition:** 0.9250 Silver

Date	Mintage	MS-63	Proof
2003 Proof	—	—	16.50

KM# 475   Rev: Golden daffodil **Composition:** 0.9250 Silver

Date	Mintage	MS-63	Proof
2003 Proof	55,000	—	25.00

KM# 472   Subject: 50th Anniversary of the Coronation of Elizabeth II **Obv:** 1953 effigy of the Queen, Jubilee commemorative dates 1952-2002 **Composition:** 0.9250 Silver

Date	Mintage	MS-63	Proof
ND(2003) In coronation proof sets only	30,000	15.00	—

DOLLAR

KM# 30   Subject: Silver Jubilee **Obv. Designer:** Percy Metcalfe **Rev. Designer:** Emanuel Hahn **Weight:** 23.3276 g. **Composition:** 0.8000 Silver 0.6000 oz. ASW

Date	Mintage	F-12	VF-20	XF-40	AU-50	MS-60	MS-63	Proof
1935	428,707	12.00	18.00	28.00	32.00	37.50	60.00	4,500

KM# 38   Subject: Royal Visit **Obv. Designer:** T. H. Paget **Rev. Designer:** Emanuel Hahn **Weight:** 23.3276 g. **Composition:** 0.8000 Silver 0.6000 oz. ASW

Date	Mintage	F-12	VF-20	XF-40	AU-50	MS-60	MS-63	Proof
1939	1,363,816	5.00	6.00	7.50	9.00	11.50	20.00	—
1939 Matte specimen	—	—	—	—	—	—	—	475

KM# 47 Subject: Newfoundland **Obv. Designer:** T. H. Paget **Rev:** The Matthew, John Cabot's ship
Rev. Designer: Thomas Shingles **Weight:** 23.3276 g. **Composition:** 0.8000 Silver 0.6000 oz. ASW

Date	Mintage	F-12	VF-20	XF-40	AU-50	MS-60	MS-63	Proof
1949	672,218	7.00	11.00	16.50	18.50	22.50	27.50	—
1949 Specimen proof	—	—	—	—	—	—	—	1,200

KM# 55 Subject: British Columbia **Obv. Designer:** Mary Gillick **Rev. Designer:** Stephan Trenka **Weight:**
23.3276 g. **Composition:** 0.8000 Silver 0.6000 oz. ASW

Date	Mintage	F-12	VF-20	XF-40	AU-50	MS-60	MS-63	Proof
ND(1958)	3,039,630	4.50	5.00	5.50	6.00	6.50	10.00	—

KM# 58 Subject: Charlottetown **Rev. Designer:** Dinko Voldanovic **Weight:** 23.3276 g. **Composition:** 0.8000
Silver 0.6000 oz. ASW

Date	Mintage	F-12	VF-20	XF-40	AU-50	MS-60	MS-63	Proof
ND(1964)	7,296,832	—	—	BV	5.00	5.50	8.00	—
ND(1964) Specimen proof	Inc. above	—	—	—	—	—	—	250

KM# 70 Subject: Confederation Centennial **Obv. Designer:** Arnold Machin **Rev:** Goose **Rev. Designer:** Alex
Colville **Weight:** 23.3276 g. **Composition:** 0.8000 Silver 0.6000 oz. ASW

Date	Mintage	MS-63	P/L	Proof
ND(1967)	6,767,496	6.50	7.50	10.00

KM# 78 Subject: Manitoba **Rev:** Pasque flower
Rev. Designer: Raymond Taylor **Composition:**
Nickel **Size:** 32 mm.

Date	Mintage	MS-63	P/L	Proof
1970	4,140,058	2.00	—	—
1970	645,869	—	2.50	—

KM#79 Subject: British Columbia **Rev. Designer:**
Thomas Shingles **Comp.:** Nickel **Size:** 32 mm.

Date	Mintage	MS-63	P/L	Proof
1971	4,260,781	2.00	—	—
1971	468,729	—	2.25	—

KM#80 Subject: British Columbia **Rev. Designer:**
Patrick Brindley **Weight:** 23.3276 g. **Composition:**
0.5000 Silver 0.3750 oz. ASW **Size:** 36 mm.

Date	Mintage	MS-63	P/L	Spec.
1971	585,674	—	—	5.75

KM# 82 Subject: Prince Edward Island **Rev.
Designer:** Terry Manning **Comp.:** Nickel **Size:** 32 mm.

Date	Mintage	MS-63	P/L	Proof
1973	3,196,452	2.00	—	—
1973 (c)	466,881	—	2.50	—

KM# 83 Subject: Mountie **Rev. Designer:** Paul
Cedarberg **Weight:** 23.3276 g. **Composition:**
0.5000 Silver 0.3750 oz. ASW **Size:** 36 mm.

Date	Mintage	MS-63	P/L	Spec.
1973	1,031,271	—	—	6.50

KM# 88 Subject: Winnipeg Centennial
Rev. Designer: Paul Pederson and Patrick Brindley
Composition: Nickel **Size:** 32 mm.

Date	Mintage	MS-63	P/L	Proof
1974	2,799,363	2.00	—	—
1974 (c)	363,786	—	2.50	—

KM# 88a Subject: Winnipeg Centennial
Rev. Designer: Paul Pederson and Patrick Brindley
Composition: 0.5000 Silver **Size:** 36 mm.

Date	Mintage	MS-63	P/L	Spec.
1974	728,947	—	—	5.75

KM# 97 Subject: Calgary **Rev. Designer:** Donald D. Paterson **Weight:** 23.3276 g. **Composition:** 0.5000 Silver 0.3750 oz. ASW **Size:** 36 mm.

Date	Mintage	MS-63	P/L	Spec.
1975	930,956	—	—	5.75

KM# 106 Subject: Parliament Library **Rev. Designer:** Walter Ott and Patrick Brindley **Weight:** 23.3276 g. **Composition:** 0.5000 Silver 0.3750 oz. ASW **Size:** 36 mm.

Date	Mintage	MS-63	P/L	Spec.
1976	578,708	—	—	6.50
1976 blue case VIP	Inc. above	—	—	15.00

KM# 118 Subject: Silver Jubilee **Rev. Designer:** Raymond Lee **Weight:** 23.3276 g. **Composition:** 0.5000 Silver 0.3750 oz. ASW **Size:** 36 mm.

Date	Mintage	MS-63	P/L	Spec.
1977	744,848	—	—	5.50
1977 red case VIP	Inc. above	—	—	25.00

KM# 121 Subject: XI Commonwealth Games **Rev. Designer:** Raymond Taylor **Weight:** 23.3276 g. **Composition:** 0.5000 Silver 0.3750 oz. ASW **Size:** 36 mm.

Date	Mintage	MS-63	P/L	Spec.
1978	709,602	—	—	5.50

KM# 124 Subject: Griffon **Rev. Designer:** Walter Schluep **Weight:** 23.3276 g. **Composition:** 0.5000 Silver 0.3750 oz. ASW **Size:** 36 mm.

Date	Mintage	MS-63	P/L	Spec.
1979	826,695	—	—	8.50

KM# 128 Subject: Arctic Territories **Rev. Designer:** Donald D. Paterson **Weight:** 23.3276 g. **Composition:** 0.5000 Silver 0.3750 oz. ASW **Size:** 36 mm.

Date	Mintage	MS-63	P/L	Spec.
1980	539,617	—	—	17.50

KM# 130 Subject: Transcontinental Railroad **Rev. Designer:** Christopher Gorey **Weight:** 23.3276 g. **Composition:** 0.5000 Silver 0.3750 oz. ASW **Size:** 36 mm.

Date	Mintage	MS-63	P/L	Proof
1981	699,494	7.50	—	—
1981 Proof	—	—	—	13.50

KM# 133 Subject: Regina **Rev. Designer:** Huntley Brown **Weight:** 23.3276 g. **Composition:** 0.5000 Silver 0.3750 oz. ASW **Size:** 36 mm.

Date	Mintage	MS-63	P/L	Proof
1982	144,930	7.50	—	—
1982 Proof	758,958	—	—	6.00

KM# 134 Subject: Constitution **Rev. Designer:** Ago Aarand **Composition:** Nickel **Size:** 32 mm.

Date	Mintage	MS-63	P/L	Proof
1982	9,709,422	3.00	6.00	—

KM# 138 Subject: Edmonton University Games **Rev. Designer:** Carola Tietz **Weight:** 23.3276 g. **Comp.:** 0.5000 Silver 0.3750 oz. ASW **Size:** 36 mm.

Date	Mintage	MS-63	P/L	Proof
1983	159,450	7.00	—	—
1983 Proof	506,847	—	—	6.00

KM# 140 Subject: Toronto Sesquicentennial **Rev. Designer:** D. J. Craig **Weight:** 23.3276 g. **Comp.:** 0.5000 Silver 0.3750 oz. ASW **Size:** 36 mm.

Date	Mintage	MS-63	P/L	Proof
1984	133,610	7.50	—	—
1984 Proof	732,542	—	—	6.00

KM# 141 Subject: Jacques Cartier **Rev. Designer:** Hector Greville **Comp.:** Nickel **Size:** 32 mm.

Date	Mintage	MS-63	P/L	Proof
1984	7,009,323	2.25	—	—
1984 Proof	87,760	—	—	6.00

KM# 143 Subject: National Parks / Moose **Rev. Designer:** Karel Rohlicek **Weight:** 23.3276 g. **Comp.:** 0.5000 Silver 0.3750 oz. ASW **Size:** 36 mm.

Date	Mintage	MS-63	P/L	Proof
1985	163,314	7.50	—	—
1985 Proof	733,354	—	—	6.50

KM# 149 Subject: Vancouver **Rev. Designer:** Elliot John Morrison **Weight:** 23.3276 g. **Comp.:** 0.5000 Silver 0.3750 oz. ASW **Size:** 36 mm.

Date	Mintage	MS-63	P/L	Proof
1986	125,949	8.00	—	—
1986 Proof	680,004	—	—	7.00

KM# 154 Subject: John Davis **Rev. Designer:** Christopher Gorey **Weight:** 23.3276 g. **Comp.:** 0.5000 Silver 0.3750 oz. ASW **Size:** 36 mm.

Date	Mintage	MS-63	P/L	Proof
1987	118,722	8.00	—	—
1987 Proof	602,374	—	—	9.00

KM# 161 Subject: Ironworks **Rev. Designer:** Robert R. Carmichael **Weight:** 23.3276 g. **Comp.:** 0.5000 Silver 0.3750 oz. ASW **Size:** 36 mm.

Date	Mintage	MS-63	P/L	Proof
1988	106,872	8.00	—	—
1988 Proof	255,013	—	—	15.00

KM# 168 Subject: MacKenzie River **Rev. Designer:** John Mardon **Weight:** 23.3276 g. **Comp.:** 0.5000 Silver 0.3750 oz. ASW **Size:** 36 mm.

Date	Mintage	MS-63	P/L	Proof
1989	99,774	8.00	—	—
1989 Proof	244,062	—	—	15.00

KM# 170 Subject: Henry Kelsey **Rev. Designer:** D. J. Craig **Weight:** 23.3276 g. **Composition:** 0.5000 Silver 0.3750 oz. ASW **Size:** 36 mm.

Date	Mintage	MS-63	P/L	Proof
1990	99,455	8.00	—	—
1990 Proof	254,959	—	—	14.00

KM# 179 Subject: S.S. Frontenac **Rev. Designer:** D. J. Craig **Weight:** 23.3276 g. **Comp.:** 0.5000 Silver 0.3750 oz. ASW **Size:** 36 mm.

Date	Mintage	MS-63	P/L	Proof
1991	73,843	8.00	—	—
1991 Proof	195,424	—	—	20.00

KM# 210 Subject: Stagecoach service
Rev. Designer: Karsten Smith **Weight:** 25.1750 g.
Comp.: 0.9250 Silver 0.7487 oz. ASW **Size:** 36 mm.

Date	Mintage	MS-63	P/L	Proof
1992	78,160	8.00	—	—
1992 Proof	187,612	—	—	12.50

KM# 209 Subject: Loon **Rev. Designer:** Robert
R. Carmichael **Comp.:** Aureate **Size:** 32 mm.

Date	Mintage	MS-63	P/L	Proof
ND(1992)	4,242,085	2.00	4.00	—
ND(1992) Proof	—	—	—	8.00

KM# 218 Subject: Parliament **Rev. Designer:**
Rita Swanson **Composition:** Aureate **Size:** 26 mm.

Date	Mintage	MS-63	P/L	Proof
ND(1992)	23,915,000	2.25	5.00	—
ND(1992) Proof	24,227	—	—	9.00

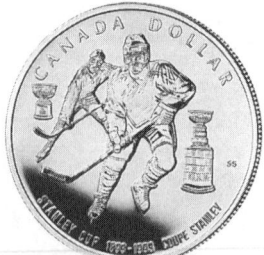

KM# 235 Subject: Stanley Cup hockey **Rev.
Designer:** Stewart Sherwood **Weight:** 25.1750 g.
Comp.: 0.9250 Silver 0.7487 oz. ASW **Size:** 36 mm.

Date	Mintage	MS-63	P/L	Proof
1993	88,150	8.00	—	—
1993 Proof	294,314	—	—	12.50

KM# 251 Subject: Last RCMP sled-dog patrol
Rev. Designer: Ian Sparks **Weight:** 25.1750 g.
Composition: 0.9250 Silver 0.7487 oz. ASW
Size: 36 mm.

Date	Mintage	MS-63	P/L	Proof
1994	61,561	9.00	—	—
1994 Proof	170,374	—	—	24.50

KM# 248 Subject: War Memorial **Rev. Designer:**
R. C. M. Staff **Composition:** Aureate **Size:** 26 mm.

Date	Mintage	MS-63	P/L	Proof
1994	15,000,000	2.25	—	—
1994 Proof	54,524	—	—	7.50

KM# 258 Subject: Peacekeeping Monument in
Ottawa **Rev. Designer:** J. K. Harmon, R. G. Hen-
riquez and C. H. Oberlander **Composition:** Aureate
Size: 26 mm. **Note:** Mintage included with KM#186.

Date	Mintage	MS-63	P/L	Proof
1995	—	2.25	—	—
1995 Proof	43,293	—	—	7.50

KM# 259 Subject: Hudson Bay Co.
Rev. Designer: Vincent McIndoe **Weight:**
25.1750 g. **Composition:** 0.9250 Silver 0.7487 oz.
ASW **Size:** 36 mm.

Date	Mintage	MS-63	P/L	Proof
1995	61,819	9.00	—	—
1995 Proof	166,259	—	—	18.00

KM# 274 Subject: McIntosh Apple
Rev. Designer: Roger Hill **Weight:** 25.1750 g.
Composition: 0.9250 Silver 0.7487 oz. ASW **Size:**
36 mm.

Date	Mintage	MS-63	P/L	Proof
1996	58,834	9.00	—	—
1996 Proof	133,779	—	—	20.00

KM# 282 Subject: 25th Anniversary Hockey Victory
Rev: The winning goal by Paul Aenderson. Based on
a painting by Andre l'Archeveque **Rev. Designer:**
Walter Burden **Weight:** 25.1750 g. **Composition:**
0.9250 Silver 0.7487 oz. ASW **Size:** 36 mm.

Date	Mintage	MS-63	P/L	Proof
ND(1997)	155,252	9.00	—	—
ND(1997) Proof	184,965	—	—	24.00

KM# 291 Subject: Loon Dollar 10th Anniversary
Rev. Designer: Jean-Luc Grondin **Composition:**
Aureate **Size:** 26 mm.

Date	Mintage	MS-63	P/L	Proof
1997	—	—	20.00	—

KM# 296 Subject: Loon Dollar 10th Anniversary
Rev. Designer: Jean-Luc Grondin **Weight:**
25.1750 g. **Composition:** 0.9250 Silver 0.7487 oz.
ASW **Size:** 36 mm.

Date	Mintage	MS-63	P/L	Proof
1997 Proof	24,995	—	—	75.00

KM# 306 Subject: 120th Anniversary Royal Canadian Mounted Police **Rev. Designer:** Adeline
Halvorson **Weight:** 25.1750 g. **Composition:**
0.9250 Silver 0.7487 oz. ASW **Size:** 36 mm. **Note:**
Individually cased prooflikes, proofs or specimens
are from broken-up prooflike or specimen sets.

Date	Mintage	MS-63	P/L	Proof
1998	79,777	—	10.00	—
1998 Proof	120,172	—	—	19.00

KM# 355 Subject: International Year of Old Per-
sons **Rev. Designer:** S. Armstrong-Hodgson
Weight: 25.1750 g. **Composition:** 0.9250 Silver
0.7487 oz. ASW **Size:** 36 mm.

Date	Mintage	MS-63	P/L	Proof
1999 Proof	24,976	—	—	32.50

KM#356 Subject: Discovery of Queen Charlotte Isle **Rev. Designer:** D. J. Craig **Weight:** 25.1750 g. **Composition:** 0.9250 Silver 0.7487 oz. **ASW Size:** 36 mm.

Date	Mintage	MS-63	P/L	Proof
ND(1999)	67,655	—	10.00	—
ND(1999) Proof	126,435	—	—	22.50

KM# 401 Subject: Voyage of Discovery **Obv:** Queen's portrait **Rev:** Human and space shuttle **Rev. Designer:** D. F. Warkentine **Weight:** 25.1750 g. **Composition:** 0.9250 Silver 0.7487 oz. **ASW Size:** 36 mm.

Date	Mintage	MS-63	P/L	Proof
2000	60,100	—	10.00	—
2000 Proof	114,130	—	—	22.50

KM# 443 Subject: Queen's Royal Jubilee **Obv:** Queen's portrait with anniversary date **Rev:** Queen in her coach and a view of the coach **Edge:** Reeded **Weight:** 25.1750 g. **Composition:** 0.9250 Silver 0.7487 oz. **ASW Size:** 36 mm.

Date	Mintage	MS-63	P/L	Proof
ND(2000) Proof	125,000	—	—	20.00
ND(2002)	—	—	12.00	—
ND(2002) Proof	—	—	—	21.50

KM# 443a Subject: Queen's Royal Jubilee **Obv:** Queen's portrait with anniversary date **Rev:** Queen in her coach and a view of the coach **Edge:** Reeded **Composition:** Gold Plated Silver **Size:** 36 mm. **Note:** Special 24 karat gold plated issue of KM#443, issued in sets only.

Date	Mintage	MS-63	Proof
ND(2002) Proof	32,642	—	—

KM# 414 Subject: National Ballet **Obv:** Queen's head right **Rev:** Ballet dancers **Rev. Designer:** Scott McKowen **Edge:** Reeded **Weight:** 25.1750 g. **Composition:** 0.9250 Silver 0.7487 oz. **ASW Size:** 36 mm.

Date	Mintage	MS-63	P/L	Proof
2001	65,000	8.50	12.00	—
2001 Proof	225,000	—	—	21.50

KM# 434 Obv: Bust of Queen Elizabeth II right. **Rev:** Recycled 1911 pattern dollar design: denomination, country name and dates in crowned wreath. **Edge:** Reeded. **Weight:** 25.1750 g. **Composition:** 0.9250 Silver 0.7487 oz. ASW **Size:** 36 mm.

Date	Mintage	MS-63	P/L	Proof
ND(2001) Proof	25,000	—	—	50.00

KM# 503 Subject: Queen Mother **Obv:** Queen's head right **Obv. Designer:** Dora de Pedery-Hunt **Rev:** Queen Mother facing **Weight:** 25.1750 g. **Composition:** 0.9250 Silver 0.7487 oz. ASW **Size:** 36 mm.

Date	Mintage	MS-63	P/L	Proof
2002 Proof	9,984	—	—	150

KM# 467 Subject: Elizabeth II Golden Jubilee **Obv:** Queen, Jubilee commemorative dates 1952-2002 **Composition:** Nickel

Date	Mintage	MS-63	P/L	Proof
ND(2002)	—	2.50	—	—
ND(2002) In proof sets only	—	—	—	8.00

KM# 462 Obv: Commemorative dates 1952-2002 **Rev:** Family of Loons **Composition:** Aureate-Bronze Plated Nickel

Date	Mintage	MS-63	P/L	Proof
ND(2002) In Specimen Sets only	75,000	10.00	—	—

KM# 450 Subject: Cobalt Mining Centennial **Obv:** Queen's portrait **Rev:** Mine tower and fox **Edge:** Reeded **Weight:** 25.1750 g. **Composition:** 0.9999 Silver 0.8093 oz. ASW **Size:** 36 mm.

Date	Mintage	MS-63	Proof
ND(2003)	75,000	20.00	—
ND(2003) Proof	125,000	—	27.50

KM# 480 Subject: Coronation of Queen Elizabeth II **Composition:** 0.9999 Silver

Date	Mintage	MS-63	Proof
2003 Proof	30,000	—	38.00

KM# 473 Subject: 50th Anniversary of the Coronation of Elizabeth II **Obv:** 1953 effigy of the Queen, Jubilee commemorative dates 1952-2002 **Rev:** Voyageur design similar to KM#54 **Composition:** 0.9999 Silver

Date	Mintage	MS-63	Proof
ND(2003) In coronation proof sets only	30,000	30.00	—

2 DOLLARS

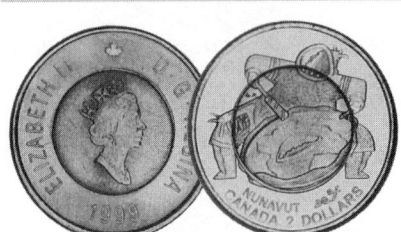

KM# 357 Subject: Nunavut **Rev. Designer:** G. Arnaktavyok **Composition:** Bi-Metallic

Date	Mintage	MS-63	P/L	Proof
1999	—	3.50	—	—

KM# 357a Subject: Nunavut **Obv:** Queen's head right. **Rev:** Drum dancer. **Edge:** Interrupted reeding. **Weight:** 8.5200 g. **Composition:** 0.9250 Gold Plated Silver **Size:** 28 mm.

Date	Mintage	MS-63	P/L	Proof
1999 Proof	—	—	—	15.00

KM# 357b Subject: Nunavut **Obv:** Queen's head right. **Rev:** Drum dancer. **Composition:** Gold

Date	Mintage	MS-63	P/L	Proof
1999 Proof	10,000	—	—	150

KM# 399 Subject: Knowledge **Rev:** Polar bear and 2 cubs **Rev. Designer:** Tony Bianco **Edge:**

Reeded and plain sections **Composition:** Bi-Metallic **Size:** 28 mm.

Date	Mintage	MS-63	P/L	Proof
2000	—	3.50	5.00	—

KM# 399a Subject: Knowledge **Rev:** Polar bear and 2 cubs **Composition:** 0.9250 Gold Plated Silver

Date	Mintage	MS-63	P/L	Proof
2000 Proof	40,000	—	—	15.00

KM# 399b Subject: Knowledge **Rev:** Polar bear and two cubs right. **Weight:** 6.3100 g. **Composition:** 0.9160 Gold

Date	Mintage	MS-63	P/L	Proof
2000 Proof	—	—	—	150

KM# 449 Subject: Elizabeth II Golden Jubilee **Obv:** Queen, Jubilee commemorative dates 1952-2002 **Weight:** 7.3000 g. **Composition:** Bi-Metallic

Date	Mintage	MS-63	Proof
ND(2002)	27,008,000	4.00	—

KM# 449a Subject: Elizabeth II Golden Jubilee **Obv:** Queen, Jubilee commemorative dates 1952-2002 **Composition:** Bi-Metallic

Date	Mintage	MS-63	Proof
ND(2002) In proof sets only	100,000	—	14.00

5 DOLLARS

KM# 84 Subject: 1976 Montreal Olympics **Rev:** Sailboat "Kingston" **Rev. Designer:** Georges Huel **Weight:** 24.3000 g. **Composition:** 0.9250 Silver 0.7227 oz. ASW **Size:** 38 mm. **Note:** Series I.

Date	Mintage	MS-63	Proof
1973	—	6.00	—
1973 Proof	165,203	—	6.50

KM# 85 Subject: 1976 Montreal Olympics **Rev:** North American map **Rev. Designer:** Georges Huel **Composition:** 0.9250 Silver 0.7227 oz. ASW **Note:** Series I.

Date	Mintage	MS-63	Proof
1973	—	6.00	—
1973 Proof	165,203	—	6.50

KM# 89 Subject: 1976 Montreal Olympics **Rev:** Olympic rings **Rev. Designer:** Anthony Mann **Weight:** 24.3000 g. **Composition:** 0.9250 Silver 0.7227 oz. ASW **Size:** 38 mm. **Note:** Series II.

Date	Mintage	MS-63	Proof
1974	—	6.00	—
1974 Proof	97,431	—	6.50

KM# 90 Subject: 1976 Montreal Olympics **Rev:** Athlete with torch **Rev. Designer:** Anthony Mann **Weight:** 24.3000 g. **Composition:** 0.9250 Silver 0.7227 oz. ASW **Size:** 38 mm. **Note:** Series II.

Date	Mintage	MS-63	Proof
1974	—	6.00	—
1974 Proof	97,431	—	6.50

KM# 91 Subject: 1976 Montreal Olympics **Rev:** Rowing **Rev. Designer:** Ken Danby **Weight:** 24.3000 g. **Composition:** 0.9250 Silver 0.7227 oz. ASW **Size:** 38 mm. **Note:** Series III.

Date	Mintage	MS-63	Proof
1974	—	6.00	—
1974 Proof	104,684	—	6.50

KM# 92 Subject: 1976 Montreal Olympics **Rev:** Canoeing **Rev. Designer:** Ken Danby **Weight:** 24.3000 g. **Composition:** 0.9250 Silver 0.7227 oz. ASW **Size:** 38 mm. **Note:** Series III.

Date	Mintage	MS-63	Proof
1974	—	6.00	—
1974 Proof	104,684	—	6.50

KM# 98 Subject: 1976 Montreal Olympics **Rev:** Marathon **Rev. Designer:** Leo Yerxa **Weight:** 24.3000 g. **Composition:** 0.9250 Silver 0.7227 oz. ASW **Size:** 38 mm. **Note:** Series IV.

Date	Mintage	MS-63	Proof
1975	—	6.00	—
1975 Proof	89,155	—	6.50

KM# 99 Subject: Montreal 1976 - 21st Summer Olympic Games **Rev:** Women's javelin event **Rev. Designer:** Leo Yerxa **Weight:** 24.3000 g. **Composition:** 0.9250 Silver 0.7227 oz. ASW **Size:** 38 mm. **Note:** Series IV.

Date	Mintage	MS-63	Proof
1975	—	6.00	—
1975 Proof	89,155	—	6.50

KM# 100 Subject: 1976 Montreal Olympics **Rev:** Swimmer **Rev. Designer:** Lynda Cooper **Weight:** 24.3000 g. **Composition:** 0.9250 Silver 0.7227 oz. ASW **Size:** 38 mm. **Note:** Series V.

Date	Mintage	MS-63	Proof
1975	—	6.00	—
1975 Proof	89,155	—	6.50

KM# 108 Subject: 1976 Montreal Olympics **Obv. Legend:** Boxing **Rev. Designer:** Shigeo Fukada **Weight:** 24.3000 g. **Composition:** 0.9250 Silver 0.7227 oz. ASW **Size:** 38 mm. **Note:** Series VI.

Date	Mintage	MS-63	Proof
1976	—	6.00	—
1976 Proof	82,302	—	6.50

KM# 101 Subject: Montreal 1976 - 21st Summer Olympic Games **Rev:** Platform Diver
Rev. Designer: Lynda Cooper **Weight:** 24.3000 g. **Composition:** 0.9250 Silver 0.7227 oz. ASW **Size:** 38 mm. **Note:** Series V.

Date	Mintage	MS-63	Proof
1975	—	6.00	—
1975 Proof	89,155	—	6.50

KM# 109 Subject: 1976 Montreal Olympics **Rev:** Olympic village **Rev. Designer:** Elliot John Morrison **Weight:** 24.3000 g. **Composition:** 0.9250 Silver 0.7227 oz. ASW **Size:** 38 mm. **Note:** Series VII.

Date	Mintage	MS-63	Proof
1976	—	6.00	—
1976 Proof	76,908	—	6.50

KM# 107 Subject: 1976 Montreal Olympics **Rev:** Fencing **Rev. Designer:** Shigeo Fukada **Weight:** 24.3000 g. **Composition:** 0.9250 Silver 0.7227 oz. ASW **Size:** 38 mm. **Note:** Series VI.

Date	Mintage	MS-63	Proof
1976	—	6.00	—
1976 Proof	82,302	—	6.50

KM# 110 Subject: 1976 Montreal Olympics **Rev:** Olympic flame **Rev. Designer:** Elliott John Morrison **Weight:** 24.3000 g. **Composition:** 0.9250 Silver 0.7227 oz. ASW **Size:** 38 mm. **Note:** Series VII.

Date	Mintage	MS-63	Proof
1976	—	6.00	—
1976 Proof	79,102	—	6.50

KM# 316 Subject: Dr. Norman Bethune
Rev. Designer: Harvey Chan **Weight:** 31.3900 g.
Composition: 0.9999 Silver 1.0091 oz. ASW

Date	Mintage	MS-63	Proof
1998 Proof	61,000	—	35.00

KM# 398 Rev: Viking ship under sail
Rev. Designer: Donald Curley **Composition:** Cop-per-Zinc-Nickel **Note:** Sold in sets with Norway 20 kroner, KM#465.

Date	Mintage	MS-63	Proof
1999 Proof	—	—	18.50

KM# 435 Subject: Guglielmo Marconi **Obv:** Bust of Queen Elizabeth II right **Rev:** Gold-plated cameo portrait of Marconi **Rev. Designer:** Cosme Saffioti **Edge:** Reeded **Weight:** 16.8600 g. **Composition:** 0.9250 Silver 0.5014 oz. ASW **Size:** 28.4 mm. **Note:** Only issued in two coin set with British 2 pounds KM#1014a.

Date	Mintage	MS-63	Proof
ND(2001) Proof	30,000	—	33.50

10 DOLLARS

KM# 86.1 Subject: 1976 Montreal Olympics **Rev:** World map **Rev. Designer:** Georges Huel **Weight:** 48.6000 g. **Composition:** 0.9250 Silver 1.4454 oz. ASW **Size:** 45 mm. **Note:** Series I.

Date	Mintage	MS-63	Proof
1973	103,426	11.00	—
1973 Proof	165,203	—	12.00

KM# 87 Subject: 1976 Montreal Olympics **Rev:** Montreal skyline **Rev. Designer:** Georges Huel **Weight:** 48.6000 g. **Composition:** 0.9250 Silver 1.4454 oz. ASW **Size:** 87 mm. **Note:** Series I.

Date	Mintage	MS-63	Proof
1973	—	11.00	—
1973 Proof	165,203	—	12.00

KM# 86.2 Subject: 1976 Montreal Olympics **Rev:** World map **Rev. Designer:** Georges Huel **Weight:** 48.6000 g. **Composition:** 0.9250 Silver 1.4454 oz. ASW **Size:** 45 mm. **Note:** Series I.

Date	Mintage	MS-63	Proof
1974 Error: mule	320	275	—

KM# 93 Subject: 1976 Montreal Olympics **Rev:** Head of Zeus **Rev. Designer:** Anthony Mann **Weight:** 48.6000 g. **Composition:** 0.9250 Silver 1.4454 oz. ASW **Size:** 45 mm. **Note:** Series II.

Date	Mintage	MS-63	Proof
1974	—	11.00	—
1974 Proof	104,684	—	12.00

KM# 94 Subject: 1976 Montreal Olympics **Rev:**
Temple of Zeus **Rev. Designer:** Anthony Mann
Weight: 48.6000 g. **Composition:** 0.9250 Silver
1.4454 oz. ASW **Size:** 45 mm. **Note:** Series II.

Date	Mintage	MS-63	Proof
1974	—	11.00	—
1974 Proof	104,684	—	12.00

KM# 95 Subject: 1976 Montreal Olympics **Rev:**
Cycling **Rev. Designer:** Ken Danby **Weight:**
48.6000 g. **Composition:** 0.9250 Silver 1.4454 oz.
ASW **Size:** 45 mm. **Note:** Series III.

Date	Mintage	MS-63	Proof
1974	—	11.00	—
1974 Proof	97,431	—	12.00

KM# 96 Subject: 1976 Montreal Olympics **Rev:**
Lacrosse **Rev. Designer:** Ken Danby **Weight:**
48.6000 g. **Composition:** 0.9250 Silver 1.4454 oz.
ASW **Size:** 45 mm. **Note:** Series III.

Date	Mintage	MS-63	Proof
1974	—	11.00	—
1974 Proof	97,431	—	12.00

KM# 102 Subject: 1976 Montreal Olympics **Rev:**
Men's hurdles **Rev. Designer:** Leo Yerxa **Weight:**
48.6000 g. **Composition:** 0.9250 Silver 1.4454 oz.
ASW **Size:** 45 mm. **Note:** Series IV.

Date	Mintage	MS-63	Proof
1975	—	11.00	—
1975 Proof	82,302	—	12.00

KM# 103 Subject: Montreal 1976 - 21st Summer
Olympic Games **Rev:** Women's shot put
Rev. Designer: Leo Yerxa **Weight:** 48.6000 g.
Composition: 0.9250 Silver 1.4454 oz. ASW **Size:**
45 mm. **Note:** Series IV.

Date	Mintage	MS-63	Proof
1975	—	11.00	—
1975 Proof	82,302	—	12.00

KM# 104 Subject: 1976 Montreal Olympics **Rev:**
Sailing **Rev. Designer:** Lynda Cooper **Weight:**
48.6000 g. **Composition:** 0.9250 Silver 1.4454 oz.
ASW **Size:** 45 mm. **Note:** Series V.

Date	Mintage	MS-63	Proof
1975	—	11.00	—
1975 Proof	89,155	—	12.00

KM# 105 Subject: 1976 Montreal Olympics **Rev:** Canoeing **Rev. Designer:** Lynda Cooper **Weight:** 48.6000 g. **Composition:** 0.9250 Silver 1.4454 oz. ASW **Size:** 45 mm. **Note:** Series V.

Date	Mintage	MS-63	Proof
1975	—	11.00	—
1975 Proof	89,155	—	12.00

KM# 111 Subject: 1976 Montreal Olympics **Rev:** Football **Rev. Designer:** Shigeo Fukada **Weight:** 48.6000 g. **Composition:** 0.9250 Silver 1.4454 oz. ASW **Size:** 45 mm. **Note:** Series VI.

Date	Mintage	MS-63	Proof
1976	—	11.00	—
1976 Proof	76,908	—	12.00

KM# 112 Subject: 1976 Montreal Olympics **Rev:** Field hockey **Rev. Designer:** Shigeo Fukada **Weight:** 48.6000 g. **Composition:** 0.9250 Silver 1.4454 oz. ASW **Size:** 45 mm. **Note:** Series VI.

Date	Mintage	MS-63	Proof
1976	—	11.00	—
1976 Proof	76,908	—	12.00

KM# 113 Subject: 1976 Montreal Olympics **Rev:** Olympic Stadium **Rev. Designer:** Elliott John Mor-

rison **Weight:** 48.6000 g. **Composition:** 0.9250 Silver 1.4454 oz. ASW **Size:** 45 mm. **Note:** Series VII.

Date	Mintage	MS-63	Proof
1976	—	11.00	—
1976 Proof	79,102	—	12.00

KM# 114 Subject: 1976 Montreal Olympics **Rev:** Olympic Velodrome **Rev. Designer:** Elliott John Morrison **Weight:** 48.6000 g. **Composition:** 0.9250 Silver 1.4454 oz. ASW **Size:** 45 mm. **Note:** Series VII.

Date	Mintage	MS-63	Proof
1976	—	11.00	—
1976 Proof	79,102	—	12.00

15 DOLLARS

KM# 215 Subject: 1992 Olympics **Rev:** Coaching track **Rev. Designer:** Stewart Sherwood **Weight:** 33.6300 g. **Composition:** 0.9250 Silver 1.0000 oz. ASW **Size:** 39 mm.

Date	Mintage	MS-63	Proof
1992 Proof	275,000	—	28.00

KM#216 Subject: 1992 Olympics **Rev:** High jump, rings, speed skating **Rev. Designer:** David Craig **Weight:** 33.6300 g. **Composition:** 0.9250 Silver 1.0000 oz. ASW

Date	Mintage	MS-63	Proof
1992 Proof	275,000	—	28.00

KM# 304 Subject: Year of the Tiger **Rev. Designer:** Harvey Chain **Size:** 40 mm.

Date	Mintage	MS-63	Proof
1998 Proof	68,888	—	275
1998 Proof	68,888	—	275

KM# 331 Subject: Year of the Rabbitt **Rev. Designer:** Harvey Chain

Date	Mintage	MS-63	Proof
1999 Proof	—	—	35.00
1999 Proof	—	—	35.00

KM# 387 Subject: Year of the Dragon **Rev. Designer:** Harvey Chain

Date	Mintage	MS-63	Proof
2000 Proof	—	—	125
2000 Proof	—	—	125

KM# 415 Subject: Year of the Snake **Obv:** Queen's head right **Rev:** Snake within circle of lunar calendar signs **Rev. Designer:** Harvey Chain **Edge:** Reeded **Weight:** 33.6300 g. **Composition:** 0.9250 Silver 1 oz. ASW **Size:** 40 mm.

Date	Mintage	MS-63	Proof
2001 Proof	60,754	—	37.50
2001 Proof	60,754	—	37.50

KM# 463 Subject: Year of the Horse **Rev. Designer:** Harvey Chain **Composition:** 0.9250 Silver

Date	Mintage	MS-63	Proof
2002 Proof	59,395	—	60.00

KM# 481 Subject: Year of the Sheep **Rev. Designer:** Harvey Chain **Composition:** 0.9250 Silver **Size:** 32 mm.

Date	Mintage	MS-63	Proof
2003 Proof	68,888	—	60.00

20 DOLLARS

KM# 71 Subject: Centennial **Rev:** Arms **Weight:** 18.2733 g. **Comp.:** 0.9000 Gold 0.5288 oz. AGW

Date	Mintage	MS-63	Proof
1967 Proof	337,688	—	275

KM# 145 Subject: 1988 Calgary Olympics **Rev:** Downhill skier **Rev. Designer:** Ian Stewart **Edge:** Lettered **Weight:** 33.6300 g. **Composition:** 0.9250 Silver 1.0000 oz. ASW **Size:** 40 mm.

Date	Mintage	MS-63	Proof
1985 Proof	406,360	—	21.50
1985 Plain edge; Proof	Inc. above	—	175

KM# 146 Subject: 1988 Calgary Olympics **Rev:** Speed skater **Rev. Designer:** Friedrich Peter **Edge:** Lettered **Weight:** 33.6300 g. **Composition:** 0.9250 Silver 1.0000 oz. ASW **Size:** 40 mm.

Date	Mintage	MS-63	Proof
1985 Proof	354,222	—	21.50
1985 Plain edge; Proof	Inc. above	—	175

KM# 150 Subject: Calgary 1988 - 15th Winter Olympic Games **Rev:** Cross-country skier **Rev. Designer:** Ian Stewart **Edge:** Lettered **Weight:** 33.6300 g. **Composition:** 0.9250 Silver 1.0000 oz. ASW **Size:** 40 mm.

Date	Mintage	MS-63	Proof
1986 Proof	303,199	—	21.50

KM# 147 Subject: 1988 Calgary Olympics **Rev:** Biathlon **Rev. Designer:** John Mardon **Edge:** Lettered **Weight:** 33.6300 g. **Composition:** 0.9250 Silver 1.0000 oz. ASW **Size:** 40 mm.

Date	Mintage	MS-63	Proof
1986 Proof	308,086	—	21.50
1986 Plain edge; Proof	Inc. above	—	175

KM# 151 Subject: 1988 Calgary Olympics **Rev:** Free-style skier **Rev. Designer:** Walter Ott **Edge:** Lettered **Weight:** 33.6300 g. **Composition:** 0.9250 Silver 1.0000 oz. ASW **Size:** 40 mm.

Date	Mintage	MS-63	Proof
1986 Proof	294,322	—	21.50
1986 Plain edge; Proof	Inc. above	—	175

KM# 148 Subject: 1988 Calgary Olympics **Rev:** Hockey **Rev. Designer:** Ian Stewart **Edge:** Lettered **Weight:** 33.6300 g. **Composition:** 0.9250 Silver 1.0000 oz. ASW **Size:** 40 mm.

Date	Mintage	MS-63	Proof
1986 Proof	396,602	—	21.50
1986 Plain edge; Proof	Inc. above	—	175

KM# 155 Subject: Calgary 1988 - 15th Winter Olympic Games **Rev:** Figure skating pairs event **Rev. Designer:** Raymond Taylor **Edge:** Lettered **Weight:** 34.1070 g. **Composition:** 0.9250 Silver 1.0000 oz. ASW **Size:** 40 mm.

Date	Mintage	MS-63	Proof
1987 Proof	334,875	—	21.50

KM# 156 Subject: 1988 Calgary Olympics **Rev:** Curling **Rev. Designer:** Ian Stewart **Edge:** Lettered **Weight:** 34.1070 g. **Composition:** 0.9250 Silver 1.0000 oz. ASW **Size:** 40 mm.

Date	Mintage	MS-63	Proof
1987 Proof	286,457	—	21.50

KM# 159 Subject: 1988 Calgary Olympics **Rev:** Ski jumper **Rev. Designer:** Raymond Taylor **Edge:** Lettered **Weight:** 34.1070 g. **Composition:** 0.9250 Silver 1.0000 oz. ASW **Size:** 40 mm.

Date	Mintage	MS-63	Proof
1987 Proof	290,954	—	21.50

KM# 160 Subject: 1988 Calgary Olympics **Rev:** Bobsled **Rev. Designer:** John Mardon **Edge:** Lettered **Weight:** 34.1070 g. **Composition:** 0.9250 Silver 1.0000 oz. ASW **Size:** 40 mm.

Date	Mintage	MS-63	Proof
1987 Proof	274,326	—	21.50

KM# 172 Subject: Aviation **Rev:** Lancaster, Fauquier in cameo **Rev. Designer:** Robert R. Carmichael **Weight:** 31.1030 g. **Composition:** 0.9250 Silver 0.9743 oz. ASW **Size:** 38 mm.

Date	Mintage	MS-63	Proof
1990 Proof	43,596	—	100
1990 Proof	43,596	—	100

KM# 173 Subject: Aviation **Rev:** Anson and Harvard, Air Marshal robert Leckie in cameo **Rev. Designer:** Geoff Bennett **Weight:** 31.1030 g. **Comp.:** 0.9250 Silver 0.9743 oz. ASW **Size:** 38 mm.

Date	Mintage	MS-63	Proof
1990 Proof	41,844	—	35.00
1990 Proof	41,844	—	35.00

KM# 196 Subject: Aviation **Rev:** Silver Dart, John A. D. McCurdy and F. W. "Casey" Baldwin in cameo **Rev. Designer:** George Velinger **Weight:** 31.1030 g. **Composition:** 0.9250 Silver 0.9743 oz. ASW **Size:** 38 mm.

Date	Mintage	MS-63	Proof
1991 Proof	28,791	—	30.00
1991 Proof	28,791	—	30.00

KM# 197 Subject: Aviation **Rev:** de Haviland Beaver, Philip C. Garratt in cameo **Rev. Designer:** Peter Massman **Weight:** 31.1030 g. **Composition:** 0.9250 Silver 0.9742 oz. ASW **Size:** 38 mm.

Date	Mintage	MS-63	Proof
1991 Proof	29,399	—	30.00
1991 Proof	29,399	—	30.00

KM# 236 Subject: Aviation **Rev:** Fairchild 71C float plane, James A. Richardson, Sr. in cameo **Rev. Designer:** Robert R. Carmichael **Weight:** 31.1030 g. **Composition:** 0.9250 Silver 0.0257 oz. ASW **Size:** 38 mm.

Date	Mintage	MS-63	Proof
1993 Proof	32,199	—	30.00
1993 Proof	32,199	—	30.00

KM# 224 Subject: Aviation **Rev:** Curtiss JN-4 Canick ("Jenny"), Sir Frank W. Baillie in cameo **Rev. Designer:** George Velinger **Weight:** 31.1030 g. **Composition:** 0.9250 Silver 0.9743 oz. ASW **Size:** 38 mm.

Date	Mintage	MS-63	Proof
1992 Proof	33,105	—	30.00
1992 Proof	33,105	—	30.00

KM# 237 Subject: Aviation **Rev:** Lockheed 14, Zebulon Lewis Leigh in cameo **Rev. Designer:** Robert R. Carmichael **Weight:** 31.1030 g. **Composition:** 0.9250 Silver 0.9743 oz. ASW **Size:** 38 mm.

Date	Mintage	MS-63	Proof
1993 Proof	32,550	—	30.00
1993 Proof	32,550	—	30.00

KM# 225 Subject: Aviation **Rev:** de Haviland Gypsy Moth, Murton A. Seymour in cameo **Rev. Designer:** John Mardon **Weight:** 31.1030 g. **Composition:** 0.9250 Silver 0.9743 oz. ASW **Size:** 38 mm.

Date	Mintage	MS-63	Proof
1992 Proof	32,537	—	30.00
1992 Proof	32,537	—	30.00

KM# 246 Subject: Aviation **Rev:** Curtiss HS-2L seaplane, Stewart Graham in cameo **Rev. Designer:** John Mardon **Weight:** 31.1030 g. **Composition:** 0.9250 Silver 0.9743 oz. ASW **Size:** 38 mm.

Date	Mintage	MS-63	Proof
1994 Proof	31,242	—	30.00
1994 Proof	31,242	—	30.00

KM# 247 Subject: Aviation **Rev:** Vickers Vedette, Wilfred T. Reid in cameo **Rev. Designer:** Robert R. Carmichael **Weight:** 31.1030 g. **Composition:** 0.9250 Silver 0.9743 oz. ASW **Size:** 38 mm.

Date	Mintage	MS-63	Proof
1994 Proof	30,880	—	30.00
1994 Proof	30,880	—	30.00

KM# 276 Subject: Aviation **Rev:** CF-100 Cannuck **Rev. Designer:** Jim Bruce **Weight:** 31.1030 g. **Composition:** 0.9250 Silver 0.9743 oz. ASW **Size:** 38 mm.

Date	Mintage	MS-63	Proof
1996 Proof	18,508	—	32.50
1996 Proof	18,508	—	32.50

KM# 271 Subject: Aviation **Rev:** C-FEA1 Fleet Cannuck **Rev. Designer:** Robert Bradford **Weight:** 31.1030 g. **Composition:** 0.9250 Silver 0.9743 oz. ASW **Size:** 38 mm.

Date	Mintage	MS-63	Proof
1995 Proof	17,438	—	30.00
1995 Proof	17,438	—	30.00

KM# 277 Subject: Aviation **Obv. Legend:** CF-105 Arrow **Rev. Designer:** Jim Bruce **Weight:** 31.1030 g. **Composition:** 0.9250 Silver 0.9743 oz. ASW **Size:** 38 mm.

Date	Mintage	MS-63	Proof
1996 Proof	27,163	—	65.00
1996 Proof	27,163	—	65.00

KM# 272 Subject: Aviation **Rev:** DHC-1 Chipmunk **Rev. Designer:** Robert Bradford **Weight:** 31.1030 g. **Composition:** 0.9250 Silver 0.9743 oz. ASW **Size:** 38 mm.

Date	Mintage	MS-63	Proof
1995 Proof	17,722	—	30.00
1995 Proof	17,722	—	30.00

KM# 297 Subject: Aviation **Rev:** Canadair F-86 Sabre **Rev. Designer:** Ross Buckland **Weight:** 31.1030 g. **Composition:** 0.9250 Silver 0.9743 oz. ASW **Size:** 38 mm.

Date	Mintage	MS-63	Proof
1997 Proof	14,389	—	30.00
1997 Proof	14,389	—	30.00

KM# 298 Subject: Aviation **Rev:** Canadair CT-114 Tutor **Rev. Designer:** Ross Buckland **Weight:** 31.1030 g. **Composition:** 0.9250 Silver 0.9743 oz. ASW **Size:** 38 mm.

Date	Mintage	MS-63	Proof
1997 Proof	15,669	—	30.00
1997 Proof	15,669	—	30.00

KM# 329 Subject: Aviation **Rev:** CP-107 Argus **Weight:** 31.1030 g. **Composition:** 0.9250 Silver 0.9743 oz. ASW **Size:** 38 mm.

Date	Mintage	MS-63	Proof
1998 Proof	50,000,000	—	37.50
1998 Proof	50,000,000	—	37.50

KM# 330 Subject: Aviation **Rev:** CP-215 Waterbomber **Rev. Designer:** Peter Mossman **Weight:** 31.1030 g. **Composition:** 0.9250 Silver 0.9743 oz. ASW **Size:** 38 mm.

Date	Mintage	MS-63	Proof
1998 Proof	50,000,000	—	37.50
1998 Proof	50,000,000	—	37.50

KM# 339 Subject: Aviation **Rev:** DHC-6 Twin Otter **Rev. Designer:** Neil Aird **Weight:** 31.1030 g. **Composition:** 0.9250 Silver 0.9743 oz. ASW **Size:** 38 mm.

Date	Mintage	MS-63	Proof
1999 Proof	50,000,000	—	37.50
1999 Proof	50,000,000	—	37.50

KM# 340 Subject: Aviation **Rev:** DHC-8 Dash 8 **Weight:** 31.1030 g. **Composition:** 0.9250 Silver 0.9743 oz. ASW **Size:** 38 mm.

Date	Mintage	MS-63	Proof
1999 Proof	50,000,000	—	37.50
1999 Proof	50,000,000	—	37.50

KM# 395 Subject: First Canadian locomotive **Rev:** Locomotive below multicolored cameo **Composition:** 0.9250 Silver **Size:** 38 mm.

Date	Mintage	MS-63	Proof
2000 Proof	—	—	40.00

KM# 396 Subject: First Canadian self-propelled car **Rev:** Car below multicolored cameo **Composition:** 0.9250 Silver **Size:** 38 mm.

Date	Mintage	MS-63	Proof
2000 Proof	—	—	40.00

KM# 397 Subject: Bluenose sailboat **Rev:** Boat below multicolored cameo **Composition:** 0.9250 Silver **Size:** 38 mm.

Date	Mintage	MS-63	Proof
2000 Proof	—	—	150

KM# 411 Subject: First Canadian Steel Boiler Steam Locomotive **Obv:** Queen's head right **Rev:** Locomotive and cameo hologram **Rev. Designer:** Don Curely **Edge:** Reeded and plain sections **Weight:** 31.1035 g. **Composition:** 0.9250 Silver .9250 oz. ASW **Size:** 38 mm.

Date	Mintage	MS-63	Proof
2001 Proof	15,000	—	40.00

KM# 427 Subject: Transportation - The Marco Polo, **Obv:** Queen's head right **Rev:** Sailship with hologram cameo **Rev. Designer:** J. Franklin Wright **Edge:** Reeded and plain sections **Weight:** 31.1030 g. **Composition:** 0.9250 Silver .9250 oz. ASW **Size:** 38 mm.

Date	Mintage	MS-63	Proof
2001 Proof	15,000	—	40.00

KM# 428 Subject: Transportation - Russell Touring Car, **Obv:** Queen's head right **Rev:** Russell touring car with hologram cameo **Rev. Designer:** John Mardon **Edge:** Reeded and plain sections **Weight:** 31.1030 g. **Composition:** 0.9250 Silver .9250 oz. ASW **Size:** 38 mm.

Date	Mintage	MS-63	Proof
2001 Proof	15,000	—	40.00

KM# 464 Obv: Queen's head right **Rev:** Gray-Dort Model 25-SM with cameo hologram **Rev. Designer:** John Mardon **Composition:** 0.9250 Silver

Date	Mintage	MS-63	Proof
2002 Proof	Est. 15,000	—	45.00

KM# 465 Rev: Sailing ship William D. Lawrence **Rev. Designer:** Bonnie Ross **Composition:** 0.9250 Silver

Date	Mintage	MS-63	Proof
2002 Proof	15,000	—	45.00

KM# 484 Subject: Canadian National FA-1 diesel-electric locomotive **Composition:** 0.9250 Silver

Date	Mintage	MS-63	Proof
2003 Proof	15,000	—	45.00

KM# 485 Obv: Queens head right **Rev:** The Bricklin SV-1 **Comp.:** Silver With Partial Gold Plating

Date	Mintage	MS-63	Proof
2003 Proof	Est. 15,000	—	50.00

KM# 482 Obv: Queens head right **Rev:** Niagara Falls hologram **Composition:** 0.9999 Silver

Date	Mintage	MS-63	Proof
2003 Proof	Est. 30,000	—	60.00

KM# 483 Subject: The HMCS Bras d'or (FHE-400) **Composition:** 0.9250 Silver

Date	Mintage	MS-63	Proof
2003 Proof	15,000	—	45.00

100 DOLLARS

KM# 115 Subject: 1976 Montreal Olympics **Obv:** Beaded borders **Rev. Designer:** Dora dePedery-Hunt **Weight:** 13.3375 g. **Composition:** 0.5830 Gold 0.2500 oz. AGW **Size:** 27 mm.

Date	Mintage	MS-63	Proof
1976	650,000	125	—

KM# 116 Subject: 1976 Montreal Olympics **Obv:** Plain borders **Rev. Designer:** Dora dePedery-Hunt **Weight:** 16.9655 g. **Composition:** 0.9170 Gold 0.5000 oz. AGW **Size:** 25 mm.

Date	Mintage	MS-63	Proof
1976 Proof	337,342	—	250

KM# 119 Subject: Queen's silver jubilee **Rev:** Bouquet of provincial flowers **Rev. Designer:** Raymond Lee **Weight:** 16.9655 g. **Composition:** 0.9170 Gold 0.5000 oz. AGW

Date	Mintage	MS-63	Proof
ND(1977) Proof	180,396	—	250

KM# 122 Subject: Canadian unification **Rev:** Geese (representing the provinces) in flight formation **Rev. Designer:** Roger Savage **Weight:** 16.9655 g. **Comp.:** 0.9170 Gold 0.5000 oz. AGW

Date	Mintage	MS-63	Proof
1978 Proof	200,000	—	250

KM# 126 Subject: International Year of the Child **Rev. Designer:** Carola Tietz **Weight:** 16.9655 g. **Composition:** 0.9170 Gold 0.5000 oz. AGW

Date	Mintage	MS-63	Proof
1979 Proof	250,000	—	250

KM# 129 Subject: Arctic Territories **Rev. Designer:** Arnaldo Marchetti **Weight:** 16.9655 g. **Comp.:** 0.9170 Gold 0.5000 oz. AGW

Date	Mintage	MS-63	Proof
1980 Proof	300,000	—	250

KM# 131 Subject: National anthem **Rev. Designer:** Roger Savage **Weight:** 16.9655 g. **Composition:** 0.9170 Gold 0.5000 oz. AGW

Date	Mintage	MS-63	Proof
1981 Proof	102,000	—	250

KM# 137 Subject: New Constitution **Rev. Designer:** Friedrich Peter **Weight:** 16.9655 g. **Composition:** 0.9170 Gold 0.5000 oz. AGW

Date	Mintage	MS-63	Proof
1982 Proof	121,708	—	250

KM#139 Subject: 400th Anniversary of St. John's, Newfoundland **Rev. Designer:** John Jaciw **Weight:** 16.9655 g. **Comp.:** 0.9170 Gold 0.5000 oz. AGW

Date	Mintage	MS-63	Proof
ND(1983) Proof	83,128	—	250

KM# 142 Subject: Jacques Cartier
Rev. Designer: Carola Tietz **Weight:** 16.9655 g.
Composition: 0.9170 Gold 0.5000 oz. AGW

Date	Mintage	MS-63	Proof
ND(1984) Proof	67,662	—	250

KM# 144 Subject: National Parks **Rev:** Big-horn sheep **Rev. Designer:** Hector Greville **Weight:** 16.9655 g. **Comp.:** 0.9170 Gold 0.5000 oz. AGW

Date	Mintage	MS-63	Proof
ND(1985) Proof	61,332	—	250

KM# 152 Subject: Peace **Rev. Designer:** Dora dePedery-Hunt **Weight:** 16.9655 g. **Composition:** 0.9170 Gold 0.5000 oz. AGW

Date	Mintage	MS-63	Proof
1986 Proof	76,409	—	250

KM# 158 Subject: 1988 Calgary Olympics **Rev:** Torch and logo **Rev. Designer:** Friedrich Peter **Edge:** Lettered in English and French **Weight:** 13.3375 g. **Comp.:** 0.5830 Gold 0.2500 oz. AGW

Date	Mintage	MS-63	Proof
1987 lettered edge; Proof	142,750	—	125
1987 plain edge; Proof	Inc. above	—	350

KM# 162 Subject: Bowhead Whales, balaera mysticetus **Rev. Designer:** Robert R. Carmichael **Weight:** 13.3375 g. **Composition:** 0.5830 Gold 0.2500 oz. AGW

Date	Mintage	MS-63	Proof
1988 Proof	52,594	—	125

KM# 169 Subject: Sainte-Marie **Rev:** Huron Indian, Missionary and Mission building
Rev. Designer: D. J. Craig **Weight:** 13.3375 g.
Composition: 0.5830 Gold 0.2500 oz. AGW

Date	Mintage	MS-63	Proof
ND(1989) Proof	59,657	—	125

KM# 171 Subject: International Literacy Year
Rev. Designer: John Mardon **Weight:** 13.3375 g.
Composition: 0.5830 Gold 0.2500 oz. AGW

Date	Mintage	MS-63	Proof
1990 Proof	49,940	—	125

KM# 180 Subject: S.S. Empress of India
Rev. Designer: Karsten Smith **Weight:** 13.3375 g.
Composition: 0.5830 Gold 0.2500 oz. AGW

Date	Mintage	MS-63	Proof
1991 Proof	33,966	—	125

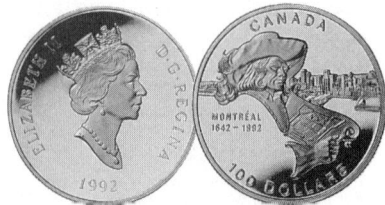

KM# 211 Subject: Montreal **Rev. Designer:**
Stewart Sherwood **Weight:** 13.3375 g. **Composition:** 0.5830 Gold 0.2500 oz. AGW

Date	Mintage	MS-63	Proof
1992 Proof	28,162	—	125

KM# 245 Subject: Antique Automobiles **Rev:** German Bene Victoria; Simmonds Steam Carriage; French Panhard-Levassor's Daimler; American Duryea. Canadian Featherston Haugh in center.
Rev. Designer: John Mardon **Weight:** 13.3375 g.
Composition: 0.5830 Gold 0.2500 oz. AGW

Date	Mintage	MS-63	Proof
1993 Proof	25,971	—	125

KM# 249 Subject: World War II Home Front
Rev. Designer: Paraskeva Clark **Weight:**
13.3375 g. **Comp.:** 0.5830 Gold 0.2500 oz. AGW

Date	Mintage	MS-63	Proof
1994 Proof	16,201	—	150

KM# 260 Subject: Louisbourg **Rev. Designer:**
Lewis Parker **Weight:** 13.3375 g. **Composition:**
0.5830 Gold 0.2500 oz. AGW

Date	Mintage	MS-63	Proof
1995 Proof	16,916	—	150

KM# 273 Subject: Klondike Gold Rush Centennial
Rev: Scene of Kate Carmack panning for gold
Rev. Designer: John Mantha **Weight:** 13.3375 g.
Composition: 0.5830 Gold 0.2500 oz. AGW

Date	Mintage	MS-63	Proof
ND(1996) Proof	17,973	—	150

KM# 287 Subject: Alexander Graham Bell
Rev. Designer: Donald H. Carley **Weight:**
13.3375 g. **Comp.:** 0.5830 Gold 0.2500 oz. AGW

Date	Mintage	MS-63	Proof
1997 Proof	14,775	—	150

KM# 307 Subject: Discovery of Insulin
Rev. Designer: Robert R. Carmichael **Weight:**
13.3375 g. **Comp.:** 0.5830 Gold 0.2500 oz. AGW

Date	Mintage	MS-63	Proof
1998 Proof	11,220	—	150

KM# 341 Subject: 50th Anniversary Newfoundland Unity With Canada **Rev. Designer:** Jackie Gale-Vaillancourt **Weight:** 13.3375 g. **Composition:** 0.5830 Gold 0.2500 oz. AGW

Date	Mintage	MS-63	Proof
1999 Proof	10,242	—	175

KM# 402 Subject: McClure's Arctic expedition **Obv:** Queen's portrait **Rev:** Six men pulling supply sled to an icebound ship **Rev. Designer:** John Mardon **Edge:** Reeded **Weight:** 13.3375 g. **Composition:** 0.5830 Gold 0.2500 oz. AGW **Size:** 27 mm.

Date	Mintage	MS-63	Proof
2000 Proof	9,767	—	170

KM# 416 Subject: Library of Parliament **Obv:** Queen's portrait **Rev:** Statue in domed building **Rev. Designer:** Robert R. Carmichael **Edge:** Reeded **Weight:** 13.3375 g. **Composition:** 0.5830 Gold 0.2500 oz. AGW **Size:** 27 mm.

Date	Mintage	MS-63	Proof
2001 Proof	8,080	—	170

KM# 486 Subject: 100th Anniversary of the Discovery of Marquis Wheat **Composition:** Gold

Date	Mintage	MS-63	Proof
2003 Proof	10,000	—	225

150 DOLLARS

KM# 388 Subject: Year of the Dragon **Rev. Designer:** Harvey Chan **Weight:** 13.6100 g. **Composition:** 0.7500 Gold .3282 oz. AGW

Date	Mintage	MS-63	Proof
2000 Proof	8,851	—	650

KM# 417 Subject: Year of the Snake **Obv:** Queen's head right **Rev:** Multicolor snake hologram **Edge:** Reeded **Weight:** 13.6100 g. **Composition:** 0.7500 Gold .3282 oz. AGW **Size:** 28 mm.

Date	Mintage	MS-63	Proof
2001 Proof	6,571	—	260

KM# 487 Subject: Year of the Sheep **Rev. Designer:** Harvey Chan **Composition:** Gold

Date	Mintage	MS-63	Proof
2003 Proof	6,888	—	325

175 DOLLARS

KM# 217 Subject: 1992 Olympics **Rev:** Passing the torch **Rev. Designer:** Stewart Sherwood **Edge:** Lettered **Weight:** 16.9700 g. **Composition:** 0.9170 Gold 0.5000 oz. AGW

Date	Mintage	MS-63	Proof
1992 Proof	22,092	—	250

200 DOLLARS

KM# 178 Subject: Canadian flag silver jubilee **Rev. Designer:** Stewart Sherwood **Weight:** 17.1350 g. **Composition:** 0.9170 Gold 0.5115 oz. AGW **Size:** 29 mm.

Date	Mintage	MS-63	Proof
1990 Proof	20,980	—	250

KM# 202 Subject: Hockey **Rev. Designer:** Stewart Sherwood **Weight:** 17.1350 g. **Composition:** 0.9170 Gold 0.5115 oz. AGW **Size:** 29 mm.

Date	Mintage	MS-63	Proof
1991 Proof	10,215	—	250

KM# 265 Subject: Maple-syrup production **Rev. Designer:** J. D. Mantha **Weight:** 17.1350 g. **Comp.:** 0.9170 Gold 0.5115 oz. AGW **Size:** 29 mm.

Date	Mintage	MS-63	Proof
1995 Proof	6,579	—	275

KM# 230 Subject: Niagara Falls **Rev. Designer:** John Marden **Weight:** 17.1350 g. **Composition:** 0.9170 Gold 0.5115 oz. AGW **Size:** 29 mm.

Date	Mintage	MS-63	Proof
1992 Proof	9,465	—	275

KM# 275 Subject: Transcontinental Canadian Railway **Rev. Designer:** Suzanne Duranceau **Weight:** 17.1350 g. **Composition:** 0.9170 Gold 0.5115 oz. AGW **Size:** 29 mm.

Date	Mintage	MS-63	Proof
1996 Proof	8,047	—	275

KM# 244 Subject: Mounted police **Rev. Designer:** Stewart Sherwood **Weight:** 17.1350 g. **Composition:** 0.9170 Gold 0.5115 oz. AGW **Size:** 29 mm.

Date	Mintage	MS-63	Proof
1993 Proof	10,807	—	250

KM# 288 Subject: Haida mask **Rev. Designer:** Robert Davidson **Weight:** 17.1350 g. **Composition:** 0.9170 Gold 0.5115 oz. AGW **Size:** 29 mm.

Date	Mintage	MS-63	Proof
1997 Proof	11,610	—	450

KM# 250 Subject: Interpretation of 1908 novel by Lucy Maud Montgomery, 1874-1942, Anne of Green Gables **Rev. Designer:** Phoebe Gilman **Weight:** 17.1350 g. **Composition:** 0.9170 Gold 0.5115 oz. AGW **Size:** 29 mm.

Date	Mintage	MS-63	Proof
1994 Proof	10,655	—	250

KM# 317 Subject: Legendary white buffalo **Rev. Designer:** Alex Janvler **Weight:** 17.1350 g. **Comp.:** 0.9170 Gold 0.5115 oz. AGW **Size:** 29 mm.

Date	Mintage	MS-63	Proof
1998 Proof	7,149	—	300

KM# 358 Subject: Mikmaq butterfly
Rev. Designer: Alan Syliboy **Weight:** 17.1350 g.
Comp.: 0.9170 Gold 0.5115 oz. AGW **Size:** 29 mm.

Date	Mintage	MS-63	Proof
1999 Proof	6,510	—	300

KM# 403 Subject: Motherhood **Rev:** Inuit mother
with infant **Rev. Designer:** Germaine Arnaktauyak
Edge: Reeded **Weight:** 17.1350 g. **Composition:**
0.9170 Gold 0.5115 oz. AGW **Size:** 29 mm.

Date	Mintage	MS-63	Proof
2000 Proof	6,284	—	300

KM# 418 Obv: Queen's head right **Rev:** The Ha-
bitant farm **Rev. Designer:** Cornelius D. Krieghoff
Edge: Reeded **Weight:** 17.1350 g. **Composition:**
0.9170 Gold 0.5115 oz. AGW **Size:** 29 mm.

Date	Mintage	MS-63	Proof
2001 Proof	5,406	—	300

KM# 466 Rev: The Jack Pine (1916-1917)
Rev. Designer: Thomas Thompson **Weight:**
17.1350 g. **Comp.:** 0.9170 Gold .5115 oz. AGW

Date	Mintage	MS-63	Proof
2002 Proof	5,264	—	325

KM# 488 Subject: Houses (1929) **Weight:**
17.1350 g. **Comp.:** 0.9170 Gold .5115 oz. AGW

Date	Mintage	MS-63	Proof
2003 Proof	10,000	—	350

300 DOLLARS

KM# 501 Obv: Triple cameo portraits of Queen Elizabeth II by Gillick, Machin and de Pedery-Hunt, each
in 14K gold, rose in center **Rev:** Dates "1952-2002"
and denomination in legend, rose in center **Weight:**
60.0000 g. **Comp.:** Bi-Metallic Gold And Silver **Size:**
50 mm. **Note:** Housed in anodized gold-colored aluminum box with cherrywood stained siding

Date	Mintage	MS-63	Proof
ND(2002)	993	—	450

350 DOLLARS

KM# 308 Subject: Flowers of Canada's Coat of
Arms **Rev. Designer:** Pierre Leduc **Weight:**
38.0500 g. **Comp.:** 0.9999 Gold 1.2233 oz. AGW

Date	Mintage	MS-63	Proof
1998 Proof	664	—	850

KM# 370 Subject: Lady's slipper **Rev. Designer:**
Henry Purdy **Weight:** 38.0500 g. **Composition:**
0.9999 Gold 1.2233 oz. AGW

Date	Mintage	MS-63	Proof
1999 Proof	1,990	—	750

KM# 404 Subject: Pacific Dogwood **Obv:** Queen's
portrait **Rev:** Three flowers **Rev. Designer:** Caren
Heine **Edge:** Reeded **Weight:** 38.0500 g. **Composition:** 0.9999 Gold 1.2233 oz. AGW **Size:** 34 mm.

Date	Mintage	MS-63	Proof
2000 Proof	1,506	—	750

KM# 433 Subject: The Mayflower Flower **Obv:**
Queen's portrait **Rev:** Two flowers **Rev. Designer:**
Bonnie Ross **Edge:** Reeded **Weight:** 38.0500 g.
Comp.: 0.9999 Gold 1.2233 oz. AGW **Size:** 34 mm.

Date	Mintage	MS-63	Proof
2001 Proof	—	—	750

KM# 502 Subject: The Wild Rose **Obv:** Queen's portrait **Obv. Designer:** Dora de Pedery-Hunt **Rev:** Wild rose plant **Rev. Designer:** Dr. Andreas Kare Hellum **Weight:** 38.0500 g. **Composition:** 0.9999 Gold 1.2232 oz. AGW **Size:** 34 mm.

Date	Mintage	MS-63	Proof
2002 Proof	1,803	—	800

KM# 504 Subject: The White Trillium **Obv:** Queen's portrait **Obv. Designer:** Dora de Pedery-Hunt **Rev:** White Trillium **Weight:** 38.0500 g. **Composition:** 9999.0000 Gold 12232.1 oz. AGW **Size:** 34 mm.

Date	Mintage	MS-63	Proof
2003 Proof	3,003	—	850

SILVER BULLION COINAGE

5 DOLLARS

Date	Mintage	MS-63	Proof
1997	100,970	12.00	—
1998 Tiger privy mark	25,000	16.50	—
1998 Titanic privy mark	26,000	75.00	—
1998 R.C.M.P. privy mark	25,000	32.50	—
1998 90th Anniversary R.C.M. privy mark	13,025	16.50	—
1998	591,359	10.00	—
1999	1,229,442	9.00	—
1999 Rabbit privy mark	25,000	19.00	—
1999 "Y2K" privy mark	9,999	25.00	—
2000	403,652	9.00	—
2000 Dragon privy mark	25,000	22.00	—
2000 Expo Hanover privy mark	—	35.00	—
2001 Snake privy mark	25,000	21.00	—
2001	398,563	9.00	—
2002	576,196	9.00	—
2002 Horse privy mark	25,000	21.00	—
2003	—	9.00	—
2003 Sheep privy mark	25,000	13.50	—

KM# 363 Rev: Maple leaf with fireworks privy mark **Weight:** 31.1000 g. **Comp.:** 0.9999 Silver 1 oz. ASW

Date	Mintage	MS-63	Proof
1999/2000	298,775	11.00	—

KM# 163 Obv: Elizabeth II effigy **Obv. Designer:** Arnold Machin **Rev:** Maple leaf **Weight:** 31.1000 g. **Composition:** 0.9999 Silver 1.0000 oz. ASW

Date	Mintage	MS-63	Proof
1988	1,155,931	8.50	—
1989	3,332,200	7.50	—
1989 Proof	29,999	—	30.00

KM# 436 Obv: Queen's portrait **Rev:** Three maple leaves in fall colors **Rev. Designer:** Debbie Adams **Edge:** Reeded **Weight:** 31.1035 g. **Composition:** 0.9999 Silver 0.9999 oz. ASW **Size:** 38 mm.

Date	Mintage	MS-63	Proof
2001	49,900	32.50	—

KM# 187 Obv: New Elizabeth II effigy **Obv. Designer:** Dora de Pedery-Hunt **Rev:** Maple leaf **Weight:** 31.1000 g. **Composition:** 0.9999 Silver 1.0000 oz. ASW

Date	Mintage	MS-63	Proof
1990	1,708,800	8.00	—
1991	644,300	10.00	—
1992	343,800	9.50	—
1993	889,946	8.00	—
1994	1,133,900	8.50	—
1995	326,244	9.00	—
1996	250,445	32.50	—

KM# 437 Subject: Multicolor Holographic Maple Leaf **Obv:** Queen's portrait **Rev:** Radiant maple leaf hologram ith date privy mark **Edge:** Reeded **Weight:** 31.1035 g. **Composition:** 0.9999 Silver 0.9999 oz. ASW **Size:** 38 mm.

Date	Mintage	MS-63	Proof
2001	29,906	75.00	—

50 DOLLARS

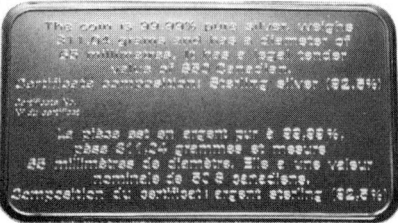

KM# 326 Subject: 10th Anniversary Silver Maple Leaf **Edge:** 10th ANNIVERSARY 10e ANNIVERSAIRE **Weight:** 311.0350 g. **Composition:** 0.9999 Silver 10.0000 oz. ASW

Date	Mintage	MS-63	Proof
1998 Proof	25,000	—	150

GOLD BULLION COINAGE

DOLLAR

KM# 238 Weight: 1.5551 g. **Composition:** 0.9999 Gold 0.05 oz. AGW

Date	Mintage	MS-63	Proof
1993	37,080	BV+37%	—
1994	78,860	BV+37%	—
1995	85,920	BV+37%	—
1996	56,520	BV+37%	—
1997	59,720	BV+37%	—
1998	44,260	BV+37%	—
1999 Maple leaf with oval "20 Years ANS" privy mark	—	BV+46%	—
2000 Maple leaf with oval "2000" privy mark	—	—	—

KM# 365 Rev: Maple leaf hologram **Weight:** 1.5551 g. **Composition:** 0.9999 Gold 0.05 oz. AGW

Date	Mintage	MS-63	Proof
1999	500	70.00	—

2 DOLLARS

KM# 256 Rev: Maple leaf **Weight:** 2.0735 g. **Composition:** 0.9999 Gold 0.0666 oz. AGW

Date	Mintage	MS-63	Proof
1994	5,493	65.00	—

5 DOLLARS

KM# 135 Obv: Elizabeth II effigy **Obv. Designer:** Arnold Machin **Rev:** Maple leaf **Weight:** 3.1200 g. **Composition:** 0.9999 Gold .1000 oz. AGW

Date	Mintage	MS-63	Proof
1982	246,000	BV+14%	—
1983	304,000	BV+14%	—
1984	262,000	BV+14%	—
1985	398,000	BV+14%	—
1986	529,516	BV+14%	—
1987	459,000	BV+14%	—
1988	506,500	BV+14%	—
1989	539,000	BV+14%	—
1989 Proof	16,992	—	60.00

KM# 188 Obv: Elizabeth II effigy **Obv. Designer:** Dora dePedery-Hunt **Rev:** Maple leaf **Weight:** 3.1200 g. **Comp.:** 0.9999 Gold 0.1000 oz. AGW

Date	Mintage	MS-63	Proof
1990	476,000	BV+14%	—
1991	322,000	BV+14%	—
1992	384,000	BV+14%	—
1993	248,630	BV+14%	—
1994	313,150	BV+14%	—
1995	294,890	BV+14%	—
1996	179,220	BV+14%	—
1997	188,540	BV+14%	—
1998	301,940	BV+14%	—
1999 Maple leaf with oval "20 Years ANS" privy mark	—	BV+19%	—
2000	—	BV+19%	—

KM# 366 Rev: Maple leaf hologram **Weight:** 3.1200 g. **Comp.:** 0.9999 Gold 0.1000 oz. AGW

Date	Mintage	MS-63	Proof
1999	500	150	—

KM# 439 Subject: Holographic Maple Leaves **Obv:** Queen's portrait **Rev:** Three maple leaves multicolor hologram **Edge:** Reeded **Weight:** 3.1310 g. **Composition:** 0.9999 Gold 0.1007 oz. AGW **Size:** 16 mm.

Date	Mintage	MS-63	Proof
2001 in sets only	600	150	—

10 DOLLARS

KM# 136 Obv: Elizabeth II effigy **Obv. Designer:** Arnold Machin **Rev:** Maple leaf **Weight:** 7.7850 g. **Composition:** 0.9999 Gold 0.2500 oz. AGW

Date	Mintage	MS-63	Proof
1982	184,000	BV+10%	—
1983	308,800	BV+10%	—
1984	242,400	BV+10%	—
1985	620,000	BV+10%	—
1986	915,200	BV+10%	—
1987	376,000	BV+10%	—
1988	436,000	BV+10%	—
1989	328,800	BV+10%	—
1989 Proof	6,998	—	150

KM# 189 Obv: Elizabeth II effigy **Obv. Designer:** Dora dePedery-Hunt **Rev:** Maple leaf **Weight:** 7.7850 g. **Composition:** 0.9999 Gold 0.2500 oz. AGW

Date	Mintage	MS-63	Proof
1990	253,600	BV+10%	—
1991	166,400	BV+10%	—
1992	179,600	BV+10%	—
1993	158,452	BV+10%	—
1994	148,792	BV+10%	—
1995	127,596	BV+10%	—
1996	89,148	BV+10%	—
1997	98,104	BV+10%	—
1998	85,472	BV+10%	—
1999 Maple leaf with oval "20 Years ANS" privy mark	—	BV+15%	—
2000 Maple leaf with oval "2000" privy mark	—	BV+15%	—

KM# 367 Rev: Maple leaf hologram **Weight:** 7.7850 g. **Comp.:** 0.9999 Gold 0.2500 oz. AGW

Date	Mintage	MS-63	Proof
1999	—	200	—

KM# 440 Subject: Holographic Maples Leaves **Obv:** Queen's portrait **Rev:** Three maple leaves multicolor hologram **Edge:** Reeded **Weight:** 7.7970 g. **Composition:** 0.9999 Gold 0.2507 oz. AGW **Size:** 20 mm.

Date	Mintage	MS-63	Proof
2001	15,000	175	—

20 DOLLARS

KM# 153 Obv: Elizabeth II effigy **Obv. Designer:** Arnold Machin **Weight:** 15.5515 g. **Composition:** 0.9999 Gold 0.5000 oz. AGW **Size:** 32 mm.

Date	Mintage	MS-63	Proof
1986	529,200	BV+7%	—
1987	332,800	BV+7%	—
1988	538,400	BV+7%	—
1989	259,200	BV+7%	—
1989 Proof	6,998	—	275

KM# 190 Obv: Elizabeth II effigy **Obv. Designer:** Dora dePedery-Hunt **Rev:** Maple leaf **Weight:** 15.5515 g. **Comp.:** 0.9999 Gold 0.5000 oz. AGW

Date	Mintage	MS-63	Proof
1990	174,400	BV+7%	—
1991	96,200	BV+7%	—
1992	108,000	BV+7%	—
1993	99,492	BV+7%	—
1994	104,766	BV+7%	—
1995	103,162	BV+7%	—
1996	66,246	BV+7%	—
1997	63,354	BV+7%	—
1998	65,366	BV+7%	—
1999 Maple leaf with oval "20 Years ANS" privy mark	—	BV+12%	—
2000	—	BV+12%	—

KM# 368 Rev: Maple leaf hologram **Weight:** 15.5515 g. **Comp.:** 0.9999 Gold 0.5000 oz. AGW

Date	Mintage	MS-63	Proof
1999	500	675	—

KM# 441 Subject: Holographic Maples Leaves **Obv:** Queen's portrait **Rev:** Three maple leaves multicolor hologram **Edge:** Reeded **Weight:** 15.5840 g. **Composition:** 0.9999 Gold 0.501 oz. AGW **Size:** 25 mm.

Date	Mintage	MS-63	Proof
2001 in set only	600	675	—

50 DOLLARS

KM# 125.1 Rev: Maple leaf flanked by .999 **Weight:** 31.1030 g. **Composition:** 0.9990 Gold 1.0000 oz. AGW

Date	Mintage	MS-63	Proof
1979	1,000,000	BV+4%	—
1980	1,251,500	BV+4%	—
1981	863,000	BV+4%	—
1982	883,000	BV+4%	—

KM# 125.2 Rev: Maple leaf flanked by .9999
Weight: 31.1030 g. **Composition:** 0.9999 Gold
1.0000 oz. AGW

Date	Mintage	MS-63	Proof
1983	843,000	BV+4%	—
1984	1,067,500	BV+4%	—
1985	1,908,000	BV+4%	—
1986	779,115	BV+4%	—
1987	978,000	BV+4%	—
1988	826,500	BV+4%	—
1989	856,000	BV+4%	—
1989 Proof	17,781	—	550

KM# 191 Obv: Elizabeth II effigy **Obv. Designer:**
Dora dePedery-Hunt **Rev:** Maple leaf flanked by
.9999 **Weight:** 31.1030 g. **Composition:** 0.9999
Gold 1.000 oz. AGW

Date	Mintage	MS-63	Proof
1990	815,000	BV+4%	—
1991	290,000	BV+4%	—
1992	368,900	BV+4%	—
1993	321,413	BV+4%	—
1994	180,357	BV+4%	—
1995	208,729	BV+4%	—
1996	143,682	BV+4%	—
1997	478,211	BV+4%	—
1998	593,704	BV+4%	—
1999 Maple leaf with oval "20 Years ANS" privy mark	—	BV+7%	—
2000 Maple leaf with oval	—	BV+7%	—

KM# 305 Rev: Mounted Mountie at gallop right
Rev. Designer: Ago Aarand **Weight:** 31.1030 g.
Comp.: 0.9999 Gold 1 oz. AGW **Shape:** 10-sided

Date	Mintage	MS-63	Proof
1997	12,913	450	—

KM# 369 Rev: Maple leaf hologram **Weight:**
31.1030 g. **Comp.:** 0.9999 Gold 1.0000 oz. AGW

Date	Mintage	MS-63	Proof
2000	500	1,350	—

KM# 364 Rev: Maple leaf with fireworks privy mark
Weight: 31.1030 g. **Composition:** 0.9999 Gold
1.0000 oz. AGW

Date	Mintage	MS-63	Proof
2000	—	750	—

KM# 442 Subject: Holographic Maples Leaves
Obv: Queen's portrait **Rev:** Three maple leaves
multicolor hologram **Edge:** Reeded **Weight:**
31.1500 g. **Composition:** 0.9999 Gold 1.0014 oz.
AGW **Size:** 30 mm.

Date	Mintage	MS-63	Proof
2001 in set only	600	1,350	—

PLATINUM BULLION COINAGE

DOLLAR

KM# 239 Rev: Maple leaf **Weight:** 1.5552 g. **Composition:** 0.9995 Platinum 0.0500 oz. APW

Date	Mintage	MS-63	Proof
1993	2,120	BV+35%	—
1994	4,260	BV+35%	—
1995	460	100.00	—
1996	1,640	BV+35%	—
1997	1,340	BV+35%	—
1998	2,000	BV+35%	—
1999	2,000	BV+35%	—

2 DOLLARS

KM# 257 Rev: Maple leaf **Weight:** 2.0735 g. **Composition:** 0.9995 Platinum 0.0666 oz. APW

Date	Mintage	MS-63	Proof
1994	1,470	225	—

5 DOLLARS

KM# 164   Obv: Elizabeth II effigy **Obv. Designer:** Arnold Machin **Weight:** 3.1203 g. **Composition:** 0.9995 Platinum 0.1000 oz. APW

Date	Mintage	MS-63	Proof
1988	74,000	BV+18%	—
1989	18,000	BV+18%	—
1989 Proof	11,999	—	100

KM# 192   Obv: Elizabeth II effigy **Obv. Designer:** dePedery-Hunt **Weight:** 3.1203 g. **Composition:** 0.9995 Platinum 0.1000 oz. APW

Date	Mintage	MS-63	Proof
1990	9,000	BV+18%	—
1991	13,000	BV+18%	—
1992	16,000	BV+18%	—
1993	14,020	BV+18%	—
1994	19,190	BV+18%	—
1995	8,940	BV+18%	—
1996	8,820	BV+18%	—
1997	7,050	BV+18%	—
1998	5,710	BV+18%	—
1999	2,000	BV+18%	—

10 DOLLARS

KM# 165   Obv: Elizabeth II effigy **Obv. Designer:** Machin **Rev:** Maple leaf **Weight:** 7.7857 g. **Composition:** 0.9995 Platinum 0.2500 oz. APW

Date	Mintage	MS-63	Proof
1988	93,600	BV+13%	—
1989	3,200	BV+13%	—
1989 Proof	1,999	—	250

KM# 193   Obv: Elizabeth II effigy **Obv. Designer:** dePedery-Hunt **Rev:** Maple leaf **Weight:** 7.7857 g. **Composition:** 0.9995 Platinum 0.2500 oz. APW

Date	Mintage	MS-63	Proof
1990	1,600	BV+13%	—
1991	7,200	BV+13%	—
1992	11,600	BV+13%	—
1993	8,048	BV+13%	—
1994	9,456	BV+13%	—
1995	6,524	BV+13%	—
1996	6,160	BV+13%	—
1997	4,552	BV+13%	—
1998	3,816	BV+13%	—
1999	2,000	BV+13%	—

20 DOLLARS

KM# 166   Obv: Elizabeth II effigy **Obv. Designer:** Machin **Rev:** Maple leaf **Weight:** 15.5519 g. **Composition:** 0.9995 Platinum 0.5000 oz. APW

Date	Mintage	MS-63	Proof
1988	23,600	BV+9%	—
1989	4,800	BV+9%	—
1989 Proof	1,999	—	500

KM# 194   Obv: Elizabeth II effigy **Obv. Designer:** dePedery-Hunt **Rev:** Maple leaf **Weight:** 15.5519 g. **Composition:** 0.9995 Platinum 0.5000 oz. APW

Date	Mintage	MS-63	Proof
1990	2,600	BV+9%	—
1991	5,600	BV+9%	—
1992	12,800	BV+9%	—
1993	6,022	BV+9%	—
1994	6,710	BV+9%	—
1995	6,308	BV+9%	—
1996	5,490	BV+9%	—
1997	3,990	BV+9%	—
1998	5,486	BV+9%	—
1999	500	BV+15%	—

30 DOLLARS

KM# 174   Rev: Polar bear swimming **Rev. Designer:** Robert Bateman **Weight:** 3.1100 g. **Comp.:** 0.9990 Platinum 0.1000 oz. APW

Date	Mintage	MS-63	Proof
1990 Proof	2,629	—	125

KM# 198   Rev: Snowy owl **Rev. Designer:** Glen Loates **Weight:** 3.1100 g. **Composition:** 0.9990 Platinum 0.1000 oz. APW

Date	Mintage	MS-63	Proof
1991 Proof	3,500	—	125

KM# 226   Rev: Cougar head and shoulders **Rev. Designer:** George McLean **Weight:** 3.1100 g. **Composition:** 0.9990 Platinum 0.1000 oz. APW

Date	Mintage	MS-63	Proof
1992 Proof	3,500	—	125

KM# 240   Rev: Arctic fox **Rev. Designer:** Claude D'Angelo **Weight:** 3.1100 g. **Composition:** 0.9990 Platinum 0.1000 oz. APW

Date	Mintage	MS-63	Proof
1993 Proof	3,500	—	135

KM# 252   Rev: Sea otter **Rev. Designer:** Ron S. Parker **Weight:** 3.1100 g. **Composition:** 0.9990 Platinum 0.1000 oz. APW

Date	Mintage	MS-63	Proof
1994 Proof	1,500	—	135

KM# 266 Rev: Canadian lynx **Rev. Designer:** Michael Dumas **Weight:** 3.1100 g. **Composition:** 0.9990 Platinum 0.1000 oz. APW

Date	Mintage	MS-63	Proof
1995 Proof	620	—	135

KM# 278 Rev: Falcon portrait **Rev. Designer:** Dwayne Harty **Weight:** 3.1100 g. **Composition:** 0.9990 Platinum 0.1000 oz. APW

Date	Mintage	MS-63	Proof
1996 Proof	489	—	135

KM# 300 Rev: Bison head **Rev. Designer:** Chris Bacon **Weight:** 3.1100 g. **Composition:** 0.9995 Platinum 0.1000 oz. APW

Date	Mintage	MS-63	Proof
1997 Proof	5,000	—	100

KM# 322 Rev: Grey wolf **Rev. Designer:** Kerr Burnett **Weight:** 3.1100 g. **Composition:** 0.9990 Platinum 0.1000 oz. APW

Date	Mintage	MS-63	Proof
ND(1998) Proof	2,000	—	135

KM# 359 Rev: Musk ox **Rev. Designer:** Mark Hobson **Weight:** 3.1100 g. **Composition:** 0.9995 Platinum 0.1000 oz. APW

Date	Mintage	MS-63	Proof
1999 Proof	1,500	—	135

KM# 405 Obv: Queen's portrait **Rev:** Pronghorn antelope head **Rev. Designer:** Mark Hobson **Edge:** Reeded **Weight:** 3.1100 g. **Composition:** 0.9995 Platinum .1000 oz. APW **Size:** 16 mm.

Date	Mintage	MS-63	Proof
2000 Proof	600	—	135

KM# 429 Obv: Queen's head right **Rev:** Harlequin duck's head **Rev. Designer:** Cosme Saffioti and Susan Taylor **Edge:** Reeded **Weight:** 3.1100 g. **Comp.:** 0.9995 Platinum .1000 oz. APW **Size:** 16 mm.

Date	Mintage	MS-63	Proof
2001 Proof	448	—	135

50 DOLLARS

KM# 167 Obv: Elizabeth II effigy **Obv. Designer:** Machin **Rev:** Maple leaf **Weight:** 31.1030 g. **Composition:** 0.9995 Platinum 1.0000 oz. APW

Date	Mintage	MS-63	Proof
1988	37,500	BV+4%	—
1989	10,000	BV+4%	—
1989 Proof	5,965	—	100

KM# 195 Obv: Elizabeth II effigy **Obv. Designer:** dePedery-Hunt **Rev:** Maple leaf **Weight:** 31.1030 g. **Composition:** 0.9995 Platinum 1.0000 oz. APW

Date	Mintage	MS-63	Proof
1990	15,100	BV+4%	—
1991	31,900	BV+4%	—
1992	40,500	BV+4%	—
1993	17,666	BV+4%	—
1994	36,245	BV+4%	—
1995	25,829	BV+4%	—
1996	62,273	BV+4%	—
1997	25,480	BV+4%	—
1998	10,403	BV+4%	—
1999	1,300	BV+10%	—

75 DOLLARS

KM# 175 Rev: Polar bear resting **Rev. Designer:** Robert Bateman **Weight:** 7.7760 g. **Composition:** 0.9990 Platinum 0.2500 oz. APW

Date	Mintage	MS-63	Proof
1990 Proof	2,629	—	275

KM# 199 Rev: Snowy owls perched on branch **Rev. Designer:** Glen Loates **Weight:** 7.7760 g. **Composition:** 0.9990 Platinum 0.2500 oz. APW

Date	Mintage	MS-63	Proof
1991 Proof	3,500	—	275

KM# 227 Rev: Cougar prowling **Rev. Designer:** George McLean **Weight:** 7.7760 g. **Composition:** 0.9990 Platinum 0.2500 oz. APW

Date	Mintage	MS-63	Proof
1992 Proof	3,500	—	300

KM# 241   Rev: Two Arctic foxes **Rev. Designer:** Claude D'Angelo **Weight:** 7.7760 g. **Composition:** 0.9990 Platinum 0.2500 oz. APW

Date	Mintage	MS-63	Proof
1993 Proof	3,500	—	300

KM# 253   Rev: Sea otter eating urchin **Rev. Designer:** Ron S. Parker **Weight:** 7.7760 g. **Composition:** 0.9990 Platinum 0.2500 oz. APW

Date	Mintage	MS-63	Proof
1994 Proof	1,500	—	300

KM# 267   Rev: Two lynx kittens **Rev. Designer:** Michael Dumas **Weight:** 7.7760 g. **Composition:** 0.9990 Platinum 0.2500 oz. APW

Date	Mintage	MS-63	Proof
1995 Proof	1,500	—	300

KM# 279   Rev: Peregrine falcon, diving falcon **Rev. Designer:** Dwayne Harty **Weight:** 7.7760 g. **Composition:** 0.9990 Platinum 0.2500 oz. APW

Date	Mintage	MS-63	Proof
1996 Proof	1,500	—	300

KM# 301   Rev: Two bison calves **Rev. Designer:** Chris Bacon **Weight:** 7.7760 g. **Composition:** 0.9990 Platinum 0.2500 oz. APW

Date	Mintage	MS-63	Proof
1997 Proof	1,500	—	300

KM# 323   Rev: Gray wolf **Rev. Designer:** Kerr Burnett **Weight:** 7.7760 g. **Composition:** 0.9990 Platinum 0.2500 oz. APW

Date	Mintage	MS-63	Proof
1998 Proof	1,000	—	300

KM# 360   Rev: Musk ox **Rev. Designer:** Mark Hobson **Weight:** 7.7760 g. **Composition:** 0.9990 Platinum 0.2500 oz. APW

Date	Mintage	MS-63	Proof
1999 Proof	500	—	325

KM# 406   Obv: Queen's portrait **Rev:** Standing pronghorn antelope **Rev. Designer:** Mark Hobson **Edge:** Reeded **Weight:** 7.7760 g. **Composition:** 0.9990 Platinum .2500 oz. APW **Size:** 20 mm.

Date	Mintage	MS-63	Proof
2000 Proof	600	—	325

KM# 430   Obv: Queen's head right **Rev:** Harlequin duck in flight **Rev. Designer:** Cosme Saffioti and Susan Taylor **Edge:** Reeded **Weight:** 7.7760 g. **Composition:** 0.9995 Platinum .2500 oz. APW **Size:** 20 mm.

Date	Mintage	MS-63	Proof
2001 Proof	448	—	325

150 DOLLARS

KM# 176   Rev: Polar bear walking **Rev. Designer:** Robert Bateman **Weight:** 15.5520 g. **Composition:** 0.9990 Platinum 0.5000 oz. APW

Date	Mintage	MS-63	Proof
1990 Proof	2,629	—	550

KM# 200   Rev: Snowy owl flying **Rev. Designer:** Glen Loates **Weight:** 15.5520 g. **Composition:** 0.9990 Platinum 0.5000 oz. APW

Date	Mintage	MS-63	Proof
1991 Proof	3,500	—	550

KM# 228   Rev: Cougar mother and cub **Rev. Designer:** George McLean **Weight:** 15.5520 g. **Composition:** 0.9990 Platinum 0.5000 oz. APW

Date	Mintage	MS-63	Proof
1992 Proof	3,500	—	575

KM# 242 Rev: Arctic fox by lake **Rev. Designer:** Claude D'Angelo **Weight:** 15.5520 g. **Composition:** 0.9990 Platinum 0.5000 oz. APW

Date	Mintage	MS-63	Proof
1993 Proof	3,500	—	575

KM# 254 Rev: Sea otter mother carrying pup **Rev. Designer:** Ron S. Parker **Weight:** 15.5520 g. **Composition:** 0.9990 Platinum 0.5000 oz. APW

Date	Mintage	MS-63	Proof
1994 Proof	—	—	600

KM# 268 Rev: Prowling lynx **Rev. Designer:** Michael Dumas **Weight:** 15.5520 g. **Composition:** 0.9990 Platinum 0.5000 oz. APW

Date	Mintage	MS-63	Proof
1995 Proof	226	—	575

KM# 280 Rev: Peregrine falcon - falcon on branch **Rev. Designer:** Dwayne Harty **Weight:** 15.5520 g. **Composition:** 0.9990 Platinum 0.5000 oz. APW

Date	Mintage	MS-63	Proof
1996 Proof	100	—	575

KM# 302 Rev: Bison bull **Rev. Designer:** Chris Bacon **Weight:** 15.5520 g. **Composition:** 0.9990 Platinum 0.5000 oz. APW

Date	Mintage	MS-63	Proof
1997 Proof	4,000	—	575

KM# 324 Rev: Two gray wolf cubs **Rev. Designer:** Kerr Burnett **Weight:** 15.5520 g. **Composition:** 0.9990 Platinum 0.5000 oz. APW

Date	Mintage	MS-63	Proof
1998 Proof	2,000	—	575

KM# 361 Rev: Musk ox **Rev. Des.:** Mark Hobson **Weight:** 15.5520 g. **Comp.:** 0.99 Plat. 0.50 oz. APW

Date	Mintage	MS-63	Proof
1999 Proof	500	—	600

KM# 407 Obv: Queen's portrait **Rev:** Two pronghorn antelope **Rev. Designer:** Mark Hobson **Edge:** Reeded **Weight:** 15.5500 g. **Composition:** 0.9990 Platinum .5000 oz. APW **Size:** 25 mm.

Date	Mintage	MS-63	Proof
2000 Proof	600	—	600

KM# 431 Obv: Queen's head right **Rev:** Two harlequin ducks **Rev. Designer:** Cosme Saffioti and Susan Taylor **Edge:** Reeded **Weight:** 15.5500 g. **Comp.:** 0.9995 Platinum .5000 oz. APW **Size:** 25 mm.

Date	Mintage	MS-63	Proof
2001 Proof	448	—	600

300 DOLLARS

KM# 177   Rev: Polar bear mother and cub
Rev. Designer: Robert Bateman **Weight:**
31.1035 g. **Comp.:** 0.9990 Platinum 1.00 oz. APW

Date	Mintage	MS-63	Proof
1990 Proof	2,629	—	1,000

KM# 201   Rev: Snowy owl with chicks
Rev. Designer: Glen Loates **Weight:** 31.1035 g.
Composition: 0.9990 Platinum 1.0000 oz. APW

Date	Mintage	MS-63	Proof
1991 Proof	3,500	—	1,000

KM# 229   Rev: Cougar resting in tree
Rev. Designer: George McLean **Weight:**
31.1035 g. **Comp.:** 0.9990 Platinum 1.00 oz. APW

Date	Mintage	MS-63	Proof
1992 Proof	3,500	—	1,000

KM# 243   Rev: Mother fox and three kits
Rev. Designer: Claude D'Angelo **Weight:**
31.1035 g. **Comp.:** 0.9990 Platinum 1.00 oz. APW

Date	Mintage	MS-63	Proof
1993 Proof	3,500	—	1,000

KM# 255   Rev: Two otters swimming
Rev. Designer: Ron S. Parker **Weight:** 31.1035 g.
Composition: 0.9990 Platinum 1.0000 oz. APW

Date	Mintage	MS-63	Proof
1994 Proof	—	—	1,100

KM# 269   Rev: Female lynx and three kittens
Rev. Designer: Michael Dumas **Weight:**
31.1035 g. **Comp.:** 0.9990 Platinum 1.00 oz. APW

Date	Mintage	MS-63	Proof
1995 Proof	1,500	—	1,000

KM# 281   Rev: Peregrine falcon feeding nestlings
Rev. Designer: Dwayne Harty **Weight:** 31.1035 g.
Composition: 0.9990 Platinum 1.0000 oz. APW

Date	Mintage	MS-63	Proof
1996 Proof	1,500	—	950

KM# 303   Rev: Bison family **Rev. Designer:** Chris
Bacon **Weight:** 31.1035 g. **Composition:** 0.9990
Platinum 1.0000 oz. APW

Date	Mintage	MS-63	Proof
1997 Proof	1,500	—	950

KM# 325   Rev: Gray wolf and two cubs
Rev. Designer: Kerr Burnett **Weight:** 31.1035 g.
Composition: 0.9990 Platinum 1.0000 oz. APW

Date	Mintage	MS-63	Proof
1998 Proof	—	—	950

KM# 362   Rev: Musk ox **Rev. Designer:** Mark
Hobson **Weight:** 31.1035 g. **Composition:** 0.9990
Platinum 1.0000 oz. APW

Date	Mintage	MS-63	Proof
1999 Proof	500	—	950

KM# 408 Obv: Queen's portrait **Rev:** Four prong-horn antelope **Rev. Designer:** Mark Hobson **Edge:** Reeded **Weight:** 31.1035 g. **Composition:** 0.9990 Platinum 1.0000 oz. APW **Size:** 30 mm.

Date	Mintage	MS-63	Proof
2000 Proof	600	—	950

KM# 432 Obv: Queen's head right **Rev:** Two standing harlequin ducks **Rev. Designer:** Cosme Saffioti and Susan Taylor **Edge:** Reeded **Weight:** 31.1035 g. **Composition:** 0.9995 Platinum 1.0000 oz. APW **Size:** 30 mm.

Date	Mintage	MS-63	Proof
2001 Proof	448	—	950

SETS

Custom Proof-Like Sets (CPL)

KM#	Date	Mintage	Identification	Issue Price	Mkt. Value
CPL1	1971 (7)	33,517	KM59.1 (2 pcs.), 60.1, 62b-75.1, 77.1 ,79	6.50	6.00
CPL2	1971 (7)	38,198	KM59.1 (2 pcs.), 60.1, 62b, 75.1-77.1	6.50	6.00
CPL3	1973 (7)	35,676	KM59.1 (2 pcs.), 60.1, 75.1, 77.1, 81.1 obv. 120 beads, 82	6.50	7.00
CPL4	1973 (7)	Inc. above	KM59.1 (2 pcs.), 60.1, 75.1, 77.1, 81.1 obv. 132 beads, 82	6.50	140
CPL5	1974 (7)	44,296	KM59.1 (2 pcs.), 60.1, 62b-75.1, 88	8.00	6.00
CPL6	1975 (7)	36,851	KM59.1 (2 pcs.), 60.1, 62b-75.1, 76.2, 77.1	8.00	6.00
CPL7	1976 (7)	28,162	KM59.1 (2 pcs.), 60.1, 62b-75.1, 76.2, 77.1	8.00	7.00
CPL8	1977 (7)	44,198	KM59.1 (2 pcs.), 60.1, 62b-75.2, 77.1, 117	8.15	5.50
CPL9	1978 (7)	41,000	KM59.1 (2 pcs.), 60.1, 62b-75.3, 77.1, 120.1	—	5.50
CPL10	1979 (7)	31,174	KM59.2 (2 pcs.), 60.2, 74, 75.3, 77.2, 120.1	10.75	5.50
CPL11	1980 (7)	41,447	KM60.2, 74, 75.3, 77.2, 120.1, 127 (2 pcs.)	10.75	6.00

Mint Sets

KM#	Date	Mintage	Identification	Issue Price	Mkt. Value
MS1	1973 (4)	Inc. above	KM84-85, 86.1, 87; Olympic Commemoratives, Series I	45.00	32.50
MS2	1974 (4)	Inc. above	KM89-90, 93-94; Olympic Commemoratives, Series II	48.00	32.50
MS3	1974 (4)	Inc. above	KM91-92, 95-96; Olympic Commemorative, Series III	48.00	32.50
MS4	1975 (4)	Inc. above	KM98-99, 102-103; Olympic Commemoratives, Series IV	48.00	32.50
MS5	1975 (4)	Inc. above	KM100-101, 104-105; Olympic Commemoratives, Series V	60.00	32.50
MS6	1976 (4)	Inc. above	KM107-108, 111-112; Olympic Commemoratives, Series VI	60.00	32.50
MS7	1976 (4)	Inc. above	KM109-110, 113-114; Olympic Commemoratives, Series VII	60.00	32.50
MS8	2001 (5)	600	KM438-442	1,996	2,400
MS12	2003 (7)	135,000	KM#289, 182-184, 290, 186, 270	12.00	12.00
MS13	2003 (7)	75,000	KM#490-496	13.25	14.00

Olympic Commemoratives (OCP)

KM#	Date	Mintage	Identification	Issue Price	Mkt. Value
OCP1	1973 (4)	Inc. above	KM84-87, Series I	78.50	40.00
OCP2	1974 (4)	Inc. above	KM89-90, 93-94, Series II	88.50	40.00
OCP3	1974 (4)	Inc. above	KM91-92, 95-96, Series III	88.50	40.00
OCP4	1975 (4)	Inc. above	KM98-99, 102-103, Series IV	88.50	40.00
OCP5	1975 (4)	Inc. above	KM100-101, 104-105, Series V	88.50	40.00
OCP6	1976 (4)	Inc. above	KM107-108, 111-112, Series VI	88.50	40.00
OCP7	1976 (4)	Inc. above	KM109-110, 113-114, Series VII	88.50	40.00

Proof Sets

KM#	Date	Mintage	Identification	Issue Price	Mkt. Value
XPS1	1980 (6)	1,500	X#51-56	—	110
PS1	1981 (7)	199,000	KM60.2, 74, 75.3, 77.2, 120.1, 127, 130	36.00	17.50
PS2	1982 (7)	180,908	KM60.2a, 74, 75.3, 77.2, 120.1, 132-133	36.00	12.00
PS3	1983 (7)	166,779	KM60.2a, 74, 75.3, 77.2, 120.1, 132, 138	36.00	13.00
PS4	1984 (7)	161,602	KM60.2a, 74, 75.3, 77.2, 120.1, 132, 140	30.00	15.00
PS5	1985 (7)	157,037	KM60.2a, 74, 75.3, 77.2, 120.1, 132, 143	30.00	15.00
PS6	1986 (7)	175,745	KM60.2a, 74, 75.3, 77.2, 120.1, 132, 149	30.00	15.00
PS7	1987 (7)	179,004	KM60.2a, 74, 75.3, 77.2, 120.1, 132, 154	34.00	15.00
PS8	1988 (7)	175,259	KM60.2a, 74, 75.3, 77.2, 132, 157, 161	37.50	23.00
PS10	1989 (4)	6,823	KM125.2, 135-136, 153	1,190	1,000
PS11	1989 (4)	1,995	KM164-167	1,700	1,350
PS12	1989 (3)	2,550	KM125.2, 163, 167	1,530	1,400
PS13	1989 (3)	9,979	KM135, 163-164	165	155
PS9	1989 (7)	170,928	KM60.2a, 74, 75.3, 77.2, 132, 157, 168	40.00	23.00

KM#	Date	Mintage	Identification	Issue Price	Mkt. Value
PS14	1990 (7)	158,068	KM170, 181, 182, 183, 184, 185, 186	41.00	23.00
PS15	1990 (4)	2,629	KM174-177	1,720	2,000
PS16	1991 (7)	14,629	KM179, 181, 182, 183, 184, 185, 186	—	45.00
PS17	1991 (4)	873	KM198-201	1,760	2,200
PS18	1992 (13)	84,397	KM203a, 212a-214a, 218, 220a-223a, 231a-234a	—	60.00
PS19	1992 (7)	147,061	KM204-210	42.75	26.00
PS20	1992 (4)	3,500	KM226-229	1,680	2,200
PS21	1993 (7)	143,065	KM181, 182, 183, 184, 185, 186, 235	42.75	19.00
PS22	1993 (4)	3,500	KM240-243	1,329	2,100
PS23	1994 (7)	47,303	KM181-186, 248	47.50	28.00
PS24	1994 (7)	99,121	KM181, 182, 183, 184, 185, 186, 251	43.00	28.00
PS25	1994 (4)	1,500	KM252-255	915	2,200
PS26	1995 (7)	Inc. above	KM181, 182, 183, 184, 185, 186, 259	37.45	25.00
PS27	1995 (7)	50,000	KM181, 182, 183, 184, 185, 258-259	49.45	22.00
PS28	1995 (4)	Inc. above	KM261-264	42.00	60.00
PS29	1995 (4)	682	KM266-269	1,555	2,300
PS30	1995 (2)	Inc. above	KM261-262	22.00	21.00
PS31	1995 (2)	Inc. above	KM263-264	22.00	30.00
PS32	1996 (4)	423	KM278-281	1,555	2,300
PS33	1996 (7)	Inc. above	KM181a, 182a, 183a, 184a, 185a, 186, 274	49.00	35.00
PS34	1996 (4)	Inc. above	KM283-286	44.45	45.00
PS35	1997 (8)	Inc. above	KM182a, 183a, 184a, 209, 270c, 282, 289,	60.00	30.00
PS36	1997 (4)	Inc. above	KM292-295	44.45	35.00
PS37	1997 (4)	Inc. above	KM300-303	1,530	2,300
PS38	1998 (8)	Inc. above	KM182a, 183a, 184a, 186, 270b, 289, 290a, 306	59.45	50.00
PS39	1998 (5)	25,000	KM309-313	73.50	55.00
PS40	1998 (0)	61,000	KM316 w/China Y-727	72.50	30.00
PS41	1998 (4)	Inc. above	KM318-321	44.45	38.00
PS42	1998 (4)	1,000	KM322-325	1,552	2,300
PS43	1998 (5)	25,000	KM310-313, 332	73.50	30.00
PS44	1999 (8)	Inc. above	KM182a-184a, 186, 270c, 289, 290a,	59.45	60.00
PS45	1999 (4)	Inc. above	KM335-338	39.95	40.00
PS46	1999 (12)	Inc. above	KM342a-353a	99.45	75.00
PS47	1999 (4)	Inc. above	KM359-362	1,425	2,300
PS48	2000 (12)	—	KM373a, 374a, 375a, 376a, 377a, 378a, 379a, 380a, 381a, 382a, 383a, 384.2a	101	90.00
PS49	2000 (4)	—	KM389-392	44.00	40.00
PS50	2000 (4)	600	KM405-408	1,416	2,300
PS51	2001 (4)	—	KM429, 430, 431, 432	—	2,300

Proof-Like Dollars

KM#	Date	Mintage	Identification	Issue Price	Mkt. Value
D1.1	1951 (0)	Inc. above	KM46, Canoe		175
D1.2	1951 (0)	Inc. above	KM46, Arnprior		700
D2.1	1952 (0)	Inc. above	KM46, water lines		1,200
D2.2	1952 (0)	Inc. above	KM46, without water lines		175
D3	1953 (1)	1,200	KM54, Canoe w/shoulder fold	—	300
D4	1954 (1)	5,300	KM54, Canoe	1.25	125
D5	1955 (1)	7,950	KM54, Canoe	1.25	100.00
D5a	1955 (1)	Inc. above	KM54, Arnprior	1.25	150
D6	1956 (0)	10,212	KM54, Canoe	1.25	55.00
D7	1957 (1)	16,241	KM54, Canoe	1.25	28.00
D8	1958 (1)	33,237	KM55, British Columbia	1.25	23.00
D9	1959 (1)	45,160	KM54, Canoe	1.25	11.00
D10	1960 (1)	82,728	KM54, Canoe	1.25	7.50
D11	1961 (1)	120,928	KM54, Canoe	1.25	7.50
D12	1962 (1)	248,901	KM54, Canoe	1.25	7.00
D13	1963 (1)	963,525	KM54, Canoe	1.25	6.00
D14	1964 (1)	2,862,441	KM58, Charlottetown	1.25	6.00
D15	1965 (1)	2,904,352	KM64.1, Canoe	—	6.00
D16	1966 (1)	672,514	KM64.1, Canoe	—	6.00
D17	1967 (1)	1,036,176	KM70, Confederation	—	7.50

Proof-Like Sets (PL)

KM#	Date	Mintage	Identification	Issue Price	Mkt. Value
PL1	1953 (6)	1,200	KM49 w/o shoulder fold, 50-54	2.20	1,250
PL3	1954 (6)	3,000	KM49-54	2.50	350
PL4	1954 (6)	Inc. above	KM49 w/o shoulder fold, 50-54	2.50	850
PL5	1955 (6)	6,300	KM49, 50a, 51-54	2.50	250
PL6	1955 (6)	Inc. above	KM49, 50a, 51-54, Arnprior	2.50	375
PL7	1956 (6)	6,500	KM49, 50a, 51-54	2.50	150
PL8	1957 (6)	11,862	KM49, 50a, 51-54	2.50	100.00
PL9	1958 (6)	18,259	KM49, 50a, 51-53, 55	2.50	70.00
PL10	1959 (6)	31,577	KM49, 50a, 51, 52, 54, 56	2.50	30.00
PL11	1960 (6)	64,097	KM49, 50a, 51, 52, 54, 56	3.00	24.00
PL12	1961 (6)	98,373	KM49, 50a, 51, 52, 54, 56	3.00	16.00
PL13	1962 (6)	200,950	KM49, 50a, 51, 52, 54, 56	3.00	10.00
PL14	1963 (6)	673,006	KM49, 51, 52, 54, 56, 57	3.00	8.50
PL15	1964 (6)	1,653,162	KM49, 51, 52, 56-58	3.00	8.50
PL16	1965 (6)	2,904,352	KM59.1-60.1, 61-63, 64.1	4.00	8.50
PL17	1966 (6)	672,514	KM59.1-60.1, 61-63, 64.1	4.00	8.50
PL18	1967 (6)	961,887	KM65-70 (pliofilm flat pack)	4.00	12.00

KM#	Date	Mintage	Identification	Issue Price	Mkt. Value
PL18A	1967 (6)	70,583	KM65-70 and Silver Medal (red box)	12.00	16.00
PL18B	1967 (7)	337,688	KM65-71 (black box)	40.00	250
PL19	1968 (6)	521,641	KM59.1-60.1, 62b, 72a, 75.1-76.1	4.00	2.25
PL20	1969 (6)	326,203	KM59.1-60.1, 62b, 75.1-77.1	4.00	2.75
PL21	1970 (6)	349,120	KM59.1-60.1, 62b, 75.1, 77.1, 78	4.00	3.25
PL22	1971 (6)	253,311	KM59.1-60.1, 62b, 75.1, 77.1, 79	4.00	2.75
PL23	1972 (6)	224,275	KM59.1-60.1, 62b-77.1	4.00	2.75
PL24	1973 (6)	243,695	KM59.1-60.1, 62b-75.1 obv. 120 beads, 77.1, 81.1, 82	4.00	4.00
PL25	1973 (6)	Inc. above	KM59.1-60.1, 62b-75.1 obv. 132 beads, 77.1, 81.2, 82	4.00	150
PL26	1974 (6)	213,589	KM59.1-60.1, 62b-75.1, 77.1, 88	5.00	3.00
PL27.1	1975 (6)	197,372	KM59.1, 60.1, 62b-75.1, 76.2, 77.1	5.00	2.50
PL27.2	1975 (6)	Inc. above	KM59.1, 60.1, 62b-75.1, 76.3, 77.1	5.00	5.00
PL28	1976 (6)	171,737	KM59.1, 60.1, 62b-75.1, 76.2, 77.1	5.15	2.75
PL29	1977 (6)	225,307	KM59.1, 60.1, 62b, 75.2, 77.1, 117.1	5.15	2.75
PL30	1978 (6)	260,000	KM59.1-60.1, 62b, 75.3, 77.1, 120.1	5.25	2.75
PL31	1979 (6)	187,624	KM59.2-60.2, 74, 75.3, 77.2, 120.1	6.25	2.75
PL32	1980 (6)	410,842	KM60.2, 74, 75.3, 77.2, 120.1, 127	6.50	4.50
PL33	1981 (6)	186,250	KM60.2, 74, 75.3, 77.2, 120.1, 123	5.00	3.25
PL34	1982 (6)	203,287	KM60.2, 74, 75.3, 77.2, 120.1, 123	6.00	2.50
PL36	1983 (6)	190,838	KM60.2a, 74, 75.3, 77.2, 120.1, 132	5.00	5.00
PL36.1	1983 (6)	Inc. above	KM60.2a, 74, 75.3, 77.2, 120.1, 132; set in folder packaged by British Royal Mint Coin Club	—	—
PL37	1984 (6)	181,249	KM60.2a, 74, 75.3, 77.2, 120.1, 132	5.25	5.00
PL38	1985 (6)	173,924	KM60.2a, 74, 75.3, 77.2, 120.1, 132	5.25	6.00
PL39	1986 (6)	167,338	KM60.2a, 74, 75.3, 77.2, 120.1, 132	5.25	6.50
PL40	1987 (6)	212,136	KM60.2a, 74, 75.3, 77.2, 120.1, 132	5.25	5.00
PL41	1988 (6)	182,048	KM60.2a, 74, 75.3, 77.2, 132, 157	6.05	5.00
PL42	1989 (6)	173,622	KM60.2a, 74, 75.3, 77.2, 132, 157	6.60	8.00
PL43	1990 (6)	170,791	KM181-186	7.40	8.00
PL44	1991 (6)	147,814	KM181-186	7.40	25.00
PL45	1992 (6)	217,597	KM204-209	8.25	11.00
PL46	1993 (6)	171,680	KM181-186	8.25	4.00
PL47	1994 (6)	141,676	KM181-185, 258	8.50	5.50
PL48	1994 (6)	18,794	KM181-185, 258 (Oh Canada holder)	—	8.50
PL49	1995 (6)	143,892	KM181-186	6.95	6.00
PL50	1995 (6)	50,927	KM181-186 (Oh Canada holder)	14.65	8.50
PL51	1995 (6)	36,443	KM181-186 (Baby Gift holder)	—	9.00
PL52	1996 (6)	116,736	KM181-186	—	14.00
PL53	1996 (6)	29,747	KM181-186 (Baby Gift holder)	—	14.00
PL54	1996 (6)	Inc. above	KM181a-185a, 186	8.95	16.00
PL55	1996 (6)	Inc. above	KM181a-185a, 186 (Oh Canada holder)	14.65	12.00
PL56	1996 (6)	Inc. above	KM181a-185a, 186 (Baby Gift holder)	—	12.00
PL57	1997 (7)	Inc. above	KM182a-184a, 209, 270, 289-290	10.45	8.00
PL58	1997 (7)	Inc. above	KM182a-184a, 270, 289-291 (Oh Canada holder)	16.45	20.00
PL59	1997 (7)	Inc. above	KM182a-184a, 209, 270, 289-290 (Baby Gift holder)	18.50	9.50
PL60	1998 (7)	Inc. above	KM182-184, 186, 270, 289-290	10.45	10.00
PL61	1998 (7)	Inc. above	KM182-184, 186, 270, 289-290 (Oh Canada holder)	16.45	12.00
PL62	1998 (7)	Inc. above	KM182-184, 186, 270, 289-290 (Tiny Treasures holder)	16.45	12.00
PL63	1999 (12)	Inc. above	KM342-353	16.95	10.00
PL64	2000 (12)	—	KM373-384	16.95	10.00

Specimen Sets (SS)

KM#	Date	Mintage	Identification	Issue Price	Mkt. Value
SS1	1858 (4)	Inc. above	KM1-4, Reeded edge	—	9,000
SS2	1858 (4)	Inc. above	KM1-4, Plain edge	—	6,000
SS3	1858 (8)	Inc. above	KM1-4; Double Set	—	15,000
SS4	1858 (8)	Inc. above	KM1 (overdate), 2-4; Double Set	—	15,000
SS5	1870 (4)	100	KM2, 3, 5, 6 (reeded edges)	—	28,500
SS6	1870 (8)	Inc. above	KM2, 3, 5, 6; Double Set (plain edges)	—	55,000
SS7	1872 (4)	Inc. above	KM2, 3, 5, 6	—	12,500
SS8	1875 (3)	Inc. above	KM2 (Large date), 3, 5	—	65,000
SS9	1880 (3)	Inc. above	KM2, 3, 5 (Narrow 0)	—	35,000
SS10	1881 (5)	Inc. above	KM7, 2, 3, 5, 6	—	26,500
SS11	1892 (2)	Inc. above	KM3, 5	—	10,000
SS12	1902 (5)	100	KM8-12	—	25,000
SS13	1902 (3)	Inc. above	KM9 (Large H), 10, 11	—	6,500
SS14	1903 (3)	Inc. above	KM10, 12, 13	—	7,000
SS15	1908 (5)	1,000	KM8, 10-13	—	2,200
SS16	1911 (5)	1,000	KM15-19	—	5,500
SS17	1911/12 (0)	5	KM15-20, 26-27	—	52,250
SS18	1921 (5)	Inc. above	KM22-25, 28	—	120,000
SS19	1922 (2)	Inc. above	KM28, 29	—	2,500
SS20	1923 (2)	Inc. above	KM28, 29	—	5,000
SS21	1924 (2)	Inc. above	KM28, 29	—	4,000
SS22	1925 (2)	Inc. above	KM28, 29	—	7,000
SS23	1926 (2)	Inc. above	KM28, 29 (Near 6)	—	5,000
SS24	1927 (3)	Inc. above	KM24a, 28, 29	—	8,000
SS25	1928 (4)	Inc. above	KM23a, 24a, 28, 29	—	12,000
SS26	1929 (5)	Inc. above	KM23a,-25a, 28, 29	—	22,500
SS27	1930 (4)	Inc. above	KM23a, 24a. 28, 29	—	16,000
SS28	1931 (5)	Inc. above	KM23a-25a, 28, 29	—	26,500
SS29	1932 (5)	Inc. above	KM23a-25a, 28, 29	—	20,000
SS30	1934 (5)	Inc. above	KM23-25, 28, 29	—	23,000
SS31	1936 (5)	Inc. above	KM23-25, 28, 29	—	12,000

KM#	Date	Mintage	Identification	Issue Price	Mkt. Value
SS32	1936 (6)	Inc. above	KM23a(dot), 24a(dot), 25a, 28(dot), 29, 30	—	400,000
SS33	1937 (6)	1,025	KM32-37, Matte Finish	—	750
SS34	1937 (4)	Inc. above	KM32-35, Mirror Fields	—	1,350
SS35	1937 (6)	75	KM32-37, Mirror Fields	—	3,900
SS36	1938 (6)	Inc. above	KM32-37	—	18,250
SS-A36	1939 (6)	Inc. above	KM32-35, 38, Matte Finish	—	—
SS-B36	1939 (6)	Inc. above	KM32-35, 38, Mirror Fields	—	—
SS-C36	1942 (2)	Inc. above	KM32, 33	—	1,000
SS-D36	1943 (2)	Inc. above	KM32, 40	—	1,000
SS-A37	1944 (2)	Inc. above	KM32, 40a	—	1,000
SS37	1944 (5)	3	KM32, 34-37, 40a	—	11,300
SS-A38	1945 (2)	Inc. above	KM32, 40a	—	1,000
SS38	1945 (6)	6	KM32, 34-37, 40a	—	4,650
SS39	1946 (6)	15	KM32, 34-37, 39a	—	4,000
SS40	1947 (6)	Inc. above	KM32, 34-37(7 curved), 37(7 pointed),	—	8,500
SS41	1947 (6)	Inc. above	KM32, 34-36(7 curved), 37(blunt 7), 39a	—	6,200
SS42	1947 (6)	Inc. above	KM32, 34-36(7 curved right), 37, 39a	—	4,250
SS43	1948 (6)	30	KM41-46	—	6,000
SS44	1949 (6)	20	KM41-45, 47	—	6,400
SS44A	1949 (2)	Inc. above	KM47	—	1,550
SS45	1950 (6)	12	KM41-46	—	1,650
SS46	1950 (6)	Inc. above	KM41-45, 46 (Arnprior)	—	3,175
SS47	1951 (7)	12	KM41, 48, 42a, 43-46 (w/water lines)	—	2,725
SS48	1952 (6)	2,317	KM41, 42a, 43-46 (water lines)	—	3,175
SS48A	1952 (6)	Inc. above	KM41, 42a, 43-46 (w/o water lines)	—	3,175
SS49	1953 (6)	28	KM49 w/o straps, 50-54	—	1,850
SS50	1953 (6)	Inc. above	KM49 w/ straps, 50-54	—	875
SS51	1964 (6)	Inc. above	KM49, 51, 52, 56-58	—	850
SS52	1965 (6)	Inc. above	KM59.1-60.1, 61-63, 64.1	—	850
SS56	1971 (7)	66,860	KM59.1-60.1, 62b-75.1, 77.1, 79 (2 pcs.); Double Dollar Prestige Sets	12.00	9.50
SS57	1972 (7)	36,349	KM59.1,-60.1, 62b-75.1, 76.1 (2 pcs.), 77; Double Dollar Prestige Sets	12.00	18.00
SS58	1973 (7)	119,819	KM59.1-60.1, 75.1, 77.1, 81.1, 82, 83; Double Dollar Prestige Sets	12.00	10.00
SS59	1973 (7)	Inc. above	KM59.1-60.1, 75.1, 77.1, 81.2, 82, 83; Double Dollar Prestige Sets	—	150
SS60	1974 (7)	85,230	KM59.1-60.1, 62b-75.1, 77.1, 88, 88a; Double Dollar Prestige Sets	15.00	10.00
SS61	1975 (7)	97,263	KM59.1-60.1, 62b-75.1, 76.2, 77.1, 97; Double Dollar Prestige Sets	15.00	10.00
SS62	1976 (7)	87,744	KM59.1-60, 62b-75.1, 76.2, 77.1, 106; Double Dollar Prestige Sets	16.00	10.00
SS63	1977 (7)	142,577	KM59.1-60.1, 62b, 75.2, 77.1, 117.1, 118; Double Dollar Prestige Sets	16.50	10.00
SS64	1978 (7)	147,000	KM59.1-60.1, 62b, 75.3, 77.1, 120.1, 121; Double Dollar Prestige Sets	16.50	10.00
SS65	1979 (7)	155,698	KM59.2-60.2, 74, 75.3, 77.2, 120, 124; Double Dollar Prestige Sets	18.50	11.50
SS66	1980 (7)	162,875	KM60.2, 74-75.3, 77.2, 120, 127, 128; Double Dollar Prestige Sets	30.50	22.50
SS67	1981 (6)	71,300	KM60.2, 74, 75.3, 77.2, 120.1, 127; Regular Specimen Sets Resumed	10.00	5.50
SS68	1982 (6)	62,298	KM60.2a, 74, 75.3, 77.2, 120.1, 132; Regular Specimen Sets Resumed	11.50	5.50
SS69	1983 (6)	60,329	KM60.2a, 74, 75.3, 77.2, 120.1, 132; Regular Specimen Sets Resumed	12.75	5.50
SS70	1984 (6)	60,400	KM60.2a, 74, 75.3, 77.2, 120.1, 132; Regular Specimen Sets Resumed	10.00	5.50
SS71	1985 (6)	61,553	KM60.2a, 74, 75.3, 77.2, 120.1, 132; Regular Specimen Sets Resumed	10.00	6.00
SS72	1986 (6)	67,152	KM60.2a, 74, 75.3, 77.2, 120.1, 132; Regular Specimen Sets Resumed	10.00	6.00
SS72A	1987 (6)	75,194	KM60.2a, 74, 75.3, 77.2, 120.1, 132; Regular Specimen Sets Resumed	11.00	6.50
SS73	1988 (6)	70,205	KM60.2a, 74, 75.3, 77.2, 132, 157; Regular Specimen Sets Resumed	12.30	6.50
SS74	1989 (6)	75,306	KM60.2a, 74, 75.3, 77.2, 132, 157; Regular Specimen Sets Resumed	14.50	8.50
SS75	1990 (6)	76,611	KM181-186; Regular Specimen Sets Resumed	15.50	8.50
SS76	1991 (6)	68,552	KM181-186; Regular Specimen Sets Resumed	15.50	22.00
SS77	1992 (6)	78,328	KM204-209; Regular Specimen Sets Resumed	16.25	13.00
SS78	1993 (6)	77,351	KM181-186; Regular Specimen Sets Resumed	16.25	6.50
SS79	1994 (6)	77,349	KM181-186; Regular Specimen Sets Resumed	16.50	9.50
SS80	1995 (6)	Inc. above	KM181-186; Regular Specimen Sets Resumed	13.95	9.50
SS82	1996 (6)	Inc. above	KM181a-185a, 186; Regular Specimen Sets Resumed	18.95	12.00
SS83	1997 (6)	Inc. above	KM182a-184a, 270, 289-291; Regular Specimen Sets Resumed	19.95	25.00
SS84	1998 (7)	Inc. above	KM182-184, 186, 270, 289, 290; Regular Specimen Sets Resumed	19.95	11.00
SS85	1999 (7)	Inc. above	KM182-184, 186, 270, 289a, 290; Regular Specimen Sets Resumed	19.95	11.00
SS91	2003 (7)	75,000	KM#182-184, 186, 270, 289, 290	30.00	27.50

V.I.P. Specimen Sets (VS)

KM#	Date	Mintage	Identification	Issue Price	Mkt. Value
VS1	1969 (0)	4		—	2,000
VS2	1970 (0)	100	KM59.1-60.1, 74.1-75.1, 77.1, 78	—	525
VS3	1971 (0)	69	KM59.1-60.1, 74.1-75.1, 77.1, 79(2 pcs.)	—	525
VS4	1972 (0)	25	KM59.1-60.1, 74.1-75.1, 76.1, (2 pcs.), 77.1	—	650
VS5	1973 (0)	26	KM59.1-60.1, 75.1, 77.1, 81.1, 82, 83	—	650
VS6	1974 (0)	72	KM59.1-60.1, 74.1-75.1, 77.1, 88, 88a	—	525
VS7	1975 (0)	94	KM59.1-60.1, 74.1-75.1, 76.2, 77.1, 97	—	525
VS8	1976 (0)	Inc. above	KM59.1-60.1, 74.1-75.1, 76.2, 77.1, 106	—	525

NEW BRUNSWICK
COLONIAL

STERLING COINAGE

HALFPENNY TOKEN

KM# 1 Composition: Copper

Date	Mintage	VG-8	F-12	VF-20	XF-40	MS-60	MS-63	Proof
1843	480,000	4.00	6.00	11.50	30.00	110	265	—
1843 Proof	—	—	—	—	—	—	—	750

KM# 3 Composition: Copper

Date	Mintage	VG-8	F-12	VF-20	XF-40	MS-60	MS-63	Proof
1854	864,000	4.00	6.00	11.50	30.00	100.00	265	—

KM# 3a Composition: Bronze

Date	Mintage	VG-8	F-12	VF-20	XF-40	MS-60	MS-63	Proof
1854 Proof	—	—	—	—	—	—	—	400

1 PENNY TOKEN

KM# 2 Composition: Copper

Date	Mintage	VG-8	F-12	VF-20	XF-40	MS-60	MS-63	Proof
1843	480,000	3.75	7.50	15.00	45.00	165	325	—
1843 Proof	—	—	—	—	—	—	—	800

KM# 4   Composition: Copper

Date	Mintage	VG-8	F-12	VF-20	XF-40	MS-60	MS-63	Proof
1854	432,000	3.75	7.50	15.00	50.00	175	350	—

DECIMAL COINAGE

HALF CENT

KM# 5   Composition: Bronze

Date	Mintage	VG-8	F-12	VF-20	XF-40	MS-60	MS-63	Proof
1861	222,800	80.00	100.00	175	225	450	900	—
1861 Proof	—	—	—	—	—	—	—	2,200

CENT

KM# 6   Composition: Bronze

Date	Mintage	VG-8	F-12	VF-20	XF-40	MS-60	MS-63	Proof
1861	1,000,000	2.25	4.00	8.00	13.00	100.00	275	—
1861 Proof	—	—	—	—	—	—	—	450
1864 short 6	1,000,000	2.25	4.00	8.00	13.00	110	275	—
1864 long 6	Inc. above	2.25	4.00	8.00	13.00	110	275	—

5 CENTS

KM# 7   Weight: 1.1620 g. **Composition:** 0.9250 Silver .0346 oz. ASW

Date	Mintage	VG-8	F-12	VF-20	XF-40	MS-60	MS-63	Proof
1862	100,000	45.00	80.00	175	375	1,700	3,200	—
1862 Proof	—	—	—	—	—	—	—	3,500
1864 large 6	Inc. above	45.00	80.00	175	375	1,700	3,200	—
1864 small 6	100,000	45.00	80.00	175	375	1,700	3,200	—

10 CENTS

KM# 8 Weight: 2.3240 g. **Composition:** 0.9250 Silver .0691 oz. ASW

Date	Mintage	VG-8	F-12	VF-20	XF-40	MS-60	MS-63	Proof
1862	150,000	45.00	80.00	175	350	1,200	2,450	—
1862 recut 2	Inc. above	60.00	125	275	550	2,200	4,400	—
1862 Proof	—	—	—	—	—	—	—	2,850
1864	100,000	45.00	80.00	175	350	1,500	2,750	—

20 CENTS

KM# 9 Weight: 4.6480 g. **Composition:** 0.9250 Silver .1382 oz. ASW

Date	Mintage	VG-8	F-12	VF-20	XF-40	MS-60	MS-63	Proof
1862	150,000	19.00	35.00	80.00	225	1,050	2,500	—
1862 Proof	—	—	—	—	—	—	—	2,850
1864	150,000	19.00	35.00	80.00	225	1,050	2,500	—

NEWFOUNDLAND

BRITISH COLONY

CIRCULATION COINAGE

CENT (Large)

KM# 1 Composition: Bronze

Date	Mintage	VG-8	F-12	VF-20	XF-40	MS-60	MS-63	Proof
1865	240,000	2.25	3.50	7.00	20.00	120	550	—
1872H	200,000	2.50	4.00	7.00	17.00	70.00	160	—
1872H Proof	—	—	—	—	—	—	—	800
1873	200,025	2.50	4.50	13.00	40.00	300	1,100	—
1873 Proof	—	—	—	—	—	—	—	3,000
1876H	200,000	2.50	7.00	15.00	40.00	300	1,100	—
1876H Proof, reported not confirmed	—	—	—	—	—	—	—	—
1880 round O, even date	400,000	2.25	3.50	7.00	20.00	90.00	300	—
1880 round O, low O	Inc. above	2.25	8.00	20.00	50.00	400	1,300	—
1880 oval 0	Inc. above	125	225	325	500	1,300	2,700	—
1880 oval O Proof	—	—	—	—	—	—	—	2,500
1885	40,000	25.00	50.00	75.00	125	500	1,800	—
1885 Proof	—	—	—	—	—	—	—	2,500
1888	50,000	30.00	50.00	80.00	175	750	3,000	—
1890	200,000	2.25	6.00	15.00	45.00	300	1,100	—
1894	200,000	2.25	5.00	10.00	25.00	140	700	—
1894 Proof	—	—	—	—	—	—	—	1,500
1896	200,000	2.25	3.50	7.00	18.00	120	350	—
1896 Proof	—	—	—	—	—	—	—	1,500

KM# 9 Obv. Designer: G.W. DeSaulles **Rev. Designer:** Horace Morehen **Composition:** Bronze

Date	Mintage	VG-8	F-12	VF-20	XF-40	MS-60	MS-63	Proof
1904H	100,000	4.00	8.00	20.00	37.50	300	700	—
1904H Proof	—	—	—	—	—	—	—	4,000
1907	200,000	1.50	2.50	4.00	20.00	220	650	—
1909	200,000	1.50	2.50	4.00	10.50	75.00	150	—
1909 Proof	—	—	—	—	—	—	—	400

KM# 16 Obv: George V bust facing left **Obv. Designer:** E.B. MacKennal **Rev:** Similar to KM#9 **Rev. Designer:** Horace Morehen **Composition:** Bronze

Date	Mintage	VG-8	F-12	VF-20	XF-40	MS-60	MS-63	Proof
1913	400,000	0.75	1.50	2.00	4.00	40.00	75.00	—
1917C	702,350	0.75	1.50	2.00	4.00	75.00	200	—
1917C Proof	—	—	—	—	—	—	—	800
1919C	300,000	0.80	1.60	2.25	5.00	125	300	—
1919C Proof	—	—	—	—	—	—	—	1,000
1920C	302,184	0.75	1.50	3.50	12.00	300	1,000	—
1929	300,000	0.75	1.50	2.00	4.00	55.00	100.00	—
1929C Proof	—	—	—	—	—	—	—	1,000
1936	300,000	0.75	1.25	1.75	3.00	28.00	75.00	—

CENT (Small)

KM# 18 Obv. Designer: Percy Metcalfe **Rev:** Pitcher plant **Rev. Designer:** Walter J. Newman **Composition:** Bronze

Date	Mintage	VG-8	F-12	VF-20	XF-40	MS-60	MS-63	Proof
1938	500,000	0.50	0.75	1.50	2.50	16.00	40.00	—
1938 Proof	—	—	—	—	—	—	—	1,000
1940	300,000	1.25	2.00	3.00	10.00	50.00	250	—
1940 re-engraved date	—	20.00	35.00	40.00	70.00	300	500	—
1940 Proof	—	—	—	—	—	—	—	1,000
1941C	827,662	0.35	0.45	0.70	1.50	20.00	120	—
1941C re-engraved date	—	9.00	13.00	20.00	35.00	100.00	400	—
1942	1,996,889	0.35	0.45	0.70	1.50	30.00	125	—
1943C	1,239,732	0.35	0.45	0.70	1.50	13.50	70.00	—
1944C	1,328,776	1.00	2.00	10.00	20.00	250	550	—
1947C	313,772	0.90	1.65	5.00	12.00	50.00	200	—
1947C Proof	—	—	—	—	—	—	—	2,000

5 CENTS

KM# 2 Weight: 1.1782 g. **Composition:** 0.9250 Silver .0350 oz. ASW

Date	Mintage	VG-8	F-12	VF-20	XF-40	MS-60	MS-63	Proof
1865	80,000	25.00	50.00	100.00	200	775	1,500	—
1865 Proof	—	—	—	—	—	—	—	4,000
1870	40,000	45.00	85.00	150	300	1,100	2,000	—
1870 Proof	—	—	—	—	—	—	—	4,000
1872H	40,000	22.00	45.00	85.00	175	600	1,400	—
1873	44,260	75.00	125	300	800	2,900	4,500	—
1873H	Inc. above	750	1,100	2,000	3,700	9,700	14,000	—
1873 Proof	—	—	—	—	—	—	—	10,000
1876H	20,000	80.00	125	225	425	1,200	2,750	—
1880	40,000	30.00	65.00	100.00	200	1,000	1,850	—
1880 Proof	—	—	—	—	—	—	—	5,000
1881	40,000	30.00	65.00	100.00	300	1,200	2,200	—
1881 Proof	—	—	—	—	—	—	—	5,000
1882H	60,000	15.00	27.00	50.00	125	800	1,500	—
1882H Proof	—	—	—	—	—	—	—	2,000
1885	16,000	125	200	325	700	2,400	4,500	—
1885 Proof	—	—	—	—	—	—	—	7,500
1888	40,000	40.00	75.00	150	375	1,900	3,200	—
1888 Proof	—	—	—	—	—	—	—	7,500
1890	160,000	6.00	12.00	30.00	85.00	800	1,500	—
1890 Proof	—	—	—	—	—	—	—	5,000
1894	160,000	6.50	12.50	30.00	75.00	800	1,500	—

Date	Mintage	VG-8	F-12	VF-20	XF-40	MS-60	MS-63	Proof
1894 Proof	—	—	—	—	—	—	—	5,000
1896	400,000	4.00	8.00	20.00	50.00	700	1,350	—
1896 Proof	—	—	—	—	—	—	—	5,000

KM# 7 Designer: G.W. DeSaulles **Weight:** 1.1782 g. **Composition:** 0.9250 Silver .0350 oz. ASW

Date	Mintage	VG-8	F-12	VF-20	XF-40	MS-60	MS-63	Proof
1903	100,000	3.00	6.00	18.00	45.00	435	1,350	—
1903 Proof	—	—	—	—	—	—	—	2,000
1904H	100,000	2.00	5.00	14.00	35.00	160	285	—
1904H Proof	—	—	—	—	—	—	—	1,200
1908	400,000	3.00	6.00	11.50	30.00	260	750	—

KM# 13 Obv: George V bust facing left **Obv. Designer:** E.B. MacKennal **Rev:** Similar to KM#7 **Rev. Designer:** G.W. DeSaulles **Weight:** 1.1782 g. **Composition:** 0.9250 Silver .0350 oz. ASW

Date	Mintage	VG-8	F-12	VF-20	XF-40	MS-60	MS-63	Proof
1912	300,000	1.00	2.00	5.00	20.00	125	275	—
1912 Proof	—	—	—	—	—	—	—	2,000
1917C	300,319	1.00	2.00	4.00	25.00	250	650	—
1917C Proof	—	—	—	—	—	—	—	2,000
1919C	100,844	3.00	6.00	15.00	75.00	950	1,750	—
1919C Proof	—	—	—	—	—	—	—	2,000
1929	300,000	1.00	1.75	3.25	12.00	165	350	—

KM# 19 Obv. Designer: Percy Metcalfe **Rev. Designer:** G.W. DeSaulles **Weight:** 1.1782 g. **Composition:** 0.9250 Silver .0350 oz. ASW

Date	Mintage	VG-8	F-12	VF-20	XF-40	MS-60	MS-63	Proof
1938	100,000	0.80	0.90	1.50	4.00	70.00	225	—
1938 Proof	—	—	—	—	—	—	—	1,000
1940C	200,000	0.80	0.90	1.50	4.00	85.00	300	—
1940C Proof	—	—	—	—	—	—	—	2,000
1941C	621,641	0.60	0.90	1.50	2.50	15.00	35.00	—
1942C	298,348	0.85	0.90	2.00	2.50	17.50	40.00	—
1943C	351,666	0.55	0.85	1.25	2.50	15.00	30.00	—

KM# 19a Obv. Designer: Percy Metcalfe **Rev. Designer:** G.W. DeSaulles **Weight:** 1.1664 g. **Composition:** 0.8000 Silver .0300 oz. ASW

Date	Mintage	VG-8	F-12	VF-20	XF-40	MS-60	MS-63	Proof
1944C	286,504	1.25	1.75	3.00	5.00	50.00	125	—
1945C	203,828	0.55	0.85	1.25	2.50	14.00	32.00	—
1946C	2,041	200	225	325	400	1,150	1,850	—
1946C Prooflike	—	—	—	—	—	—	2,500	—
1947C	38,400	2.00	3.00	5.00	10.00	65.00	120	—
1947C Prooflike	—	—	—	—	—	—	375	—

10 CENTS

KM# 3 Weight: 2.3564 g. **Composition:** 0.9250 Silver .0701 oz. ASW

Date	Mintage	VG-8	F-12	VF-20	XF-40	MS-60	MS-63	Proof
1865	80,000	15.00	30.00	75.00	180	1,100	2,250	—
1865 plain edge, Proof	—	—	—	—	—	—	—	5,500
1870	30,000	120	190	335	725	2,350	5,000	—
1870 Proof	—	—	—	—	—	—	—	10,000
1872H	40,000	13.50	20.00	50.00	135	800	1,700	—
1873 flat 3	23,614	35.00	70.00	175	425	2,200	4,500	—
1873 round 3	Inc. above	35.00	70.00	175	425	2,200	4,500	—
1873 Proof	—	—	—	—	—	—	—	12,000
1876H	10,000	35.00	70.00	150	350	1,400	2,500	—
1880/70	10,000	35.00	70.00	175	400	1,800	2,950	—
1880 Proof	—	—	—	—	—	—	—	7,500
1882H	20,000	30.00	55.00	150	475	2,200	4,500	—
1882H Proof	—	—	—	—	—	—	—	3,000
1885	8,000	65.00	125	225	550	2,200	4,250	—
1885 Proof	—	—	—	—	—	—	—	8,000
1888	30,000	35.00	70.00	200	700	2,500	4,200	—
1888 Proof	—	—	—	—	—	—	—	8,000
1890	100,000	5.50	11.50	35.00	100.00	1,100	1,550	—
1890 Proof	—	—	—	—	—	—	—	5,000
1894	100,000	5.50	11.50	25.00	90.00	700	1,550	—
1894 Proof	—	—	—	—	—	—	—	5,000
1896	230,000	5.00	10.00	25.00	90.00	700	1,500	—
1896 Proof	—	—	—	—	—	—	—	5,000

KM# 8   Designer: G.W. DeSaulles **Weight:** 2.3564 g. **Composition:** 0.9250 Silver .0701 oz. ASW

Date	Mintage	VG-8	F-12	VF-20	XF-40	MS-60	MS-63	Proof
1903	100,000	5.00	15.00	45.00	135	1,200	2,800	—
1903 Proof	—	—	—	—	—	—	—	2,500
1904H	100,000	2.50	6.50	20.00	60.00	200	350	—
1904H Proof	—	—	—	—	—	—	—	1,500

KM# 14   Obv. Designer: E.B. MacKennal **Rev. Designer:** G.W. DeSaulles **Weight:** 2.3564 g. **Composition:** 0.9250 Silver .0701 oz. ASW

Date	Mintage	VG-8	F-12	VF-20	XF-40	MS-60	MS-63	Proof
1912	150,000	0.75	1.50	6.00	25.00	165	300	—
1917C	250,805	0.50	1.25	7.50	30.00	400	1,500	—
1919C	54,342	1.00	2.25	6.00	25.00	175	350	—

KM# 20   Obv. Designer: Percy Metcalfe **Rev. Designer:** G.W. DeSaulles **Weight:** 2.3564 g. **Composition:** 0.9250 Silver .0701 oz. ASW

Date	Mintage	VG-8	F-12	VF-20	XF-40	MS-60	MS-63	Proof
1938	100,000	0.75	1.50	2.75	7.00	80.00	300	—
1938 Proof	—	—	—	—	—	—	—	2,000
1940	100,000	0.65	1.20	2.50	6.00	80.00	300	—
1940 Proof	—	—	—	—	—	—	—	2,500
1941C	483,630	0.60	1.40	2.20	3.50	27.00	125	—
1942C	293,736	0.60	1.50	2.20	3.50	30.00	130	—
1943C	104,706	0.60	1.50	2.40	3.50	60.00	200	—
1944C	151,471	2.50	3.50	10.00	20.00	200	800	—

KM# 20a   Obv. Designer: Percy Metcalfe **Rev. Designer:** G.W. DeSaulles **Weight:** 2.3328 g. **Composition:** 0.8000 Silver .0600 oz. ASW

Date	Mintage	VG-8	F-12	VF-20	XF-40	MS-60	MS-63	Proof
1945C	175,833	0.65	1.25	2.00	4.00	45.00	225	—
1946C	38,400	2.00	4.00	7.00	15.00	60.00	275	—
1946C Proof	—	—	—	—	—	—	—	750
1947C	61,988	1.50	3.00	4.50	9.00	65.00	275	—

20 CENTS

KM# 4   Weight: 4.7127 g. Composition: 0.9250 Silver .1401 oz. ASW

Date	Mintage	VG-8	F-12	VF-20	XF-40	MS-60	MS-63	Proof
1865	100,000	11.00	20.00	60.00	150	950	2,000	—
1865 plain edge, Proof	—	—	—	—	—	—	—	6,500
1865 reeded edge, Proof	—	—	—	—	—	—	—	10,000
1870	50,000	12.00	30.00	100.00	250	1,250	2,500	—
1870 plain edge, Proof	—	—	—	—	—	—	—	6,500
1870 reeded edge, Proof	—	—	—	—	—	—	—	6,500
1872H	90,000	7.00	14.00	40.00	140	750	1,800	—
1873	45,797	21.00	45.00	125	350	2,800	7,000	—
1873 Proof	—	—	—	—	—	—	—	12,000
1876H	50,000	15.00	30.00	80.00	200	1,350	2,700	—
1880/70	30,000	15.00	35.00	100.00	250	1,350	3,000	—
1880 Proof	—	—	—	—	—	—	—	8,000
1881	60,000	12.00	25.00	80.00	200	1,200	1,900	—
1881 Proof	—	—	—	—	—	—	—	8,000
1882H	100,000	5.00	12.00	35.00	140	1,000	1,900	—
1882H Proof	—	—	—	—	—	—	—	3,500
1885	40,000	14.00	30.00	80.00	225	1,900	3,500	—
1885 Proof	—	—	—	—	—	—	—	10,000
1888	75,000	6.00	15.00	45.00	150	900	2,200	—
1888 Proof	—	—	—	—	—	—	—	10,000
1890	100,000	6.00	15.00	45.00	150	700	1,600	—
1890 Proof	—	—	—	—	—	—	—	6,500
1894	100,000	15.00	30.00	100.00	300	1,200	—	—
1894 Proof	—	—	—	—	—	—	—	6,500
1896 large 96	Inc. above	7.00	15.00	50.00	200	725	1,900	—
1896 small 96	125,000	5.00	10.00	30.00	100.00	700	1,800	—
1896 large 96, Proof	—	—	—	—	—	—	—	6,500
1899 hook 99	125,000	18.00	35.00	90.00	250	1,000	3,100	—
1899 large 99	Inc. above	5.00	8.00	30.00	125	700	1,900	—
1900	125,000	5.00	8.00	25.00	80.00	700	1,900	—
1900 Proof	—	—	—	—	—	—	—	6,500

KM# 10   Obv. Designer: G.W. DeSaulles Rev. Designer: W.H.J. Blakemore Weight: 4.7127 g. Composition: 0.9250 Silver .1401 oz. ASW

Date	Mintage	VG-8	F-12	VF-20	XF-40	MS-60	MS-63	Proof
1904H	75,000	10.00	20.00	55.00	275	2,500	6,000	—
1904H Proof	—	—	—	—	—	—	—	1,750

KM# 15   Obv: George V bust facing left Obv. Designer: E.B. MacKennal Rev: Similar to KM#10 Rev. Designer: W.H.J. Blakemore Weight: 4.7127 g. Composition: 0.9250 Silver .1401 oz. ASW

Date	Mintage	VG-8	F-12	VF-20	XF-40	MS-60	MS-63	Proof
1912	350,000	2.00	3.00	8.00	35.00	325	850	—
1912 Proof	—	—	—	—	—	—	—	2,500

25 CENTS

KM# 17   Obv. Designer: E.B. MacKennal **Rev. Designer:** W.H.J. Blakemore **Weight:** 5.8319 g. **Composition:** 0.9250 Silver .1734 oz. ASW

Date	Mintage	VG-8	F-12	VF-20	XF-40	MS-60	MS-63	Proof
1917C	464,779	1.50	2.00	4.00	8.00	140	300	—
1917C Proof	—	—	—	—	—	—	—	2,500
1919C	163,939	1.50	2.25	7.00	20.00	325	1,200	—
1919C Proof	—	—	—	—	—	—	—	2,500

50 CENTS

KM# 6   Weight: 11.7818 g. **Composition:** 0.9250 Silver .3504 oz. ASW

Date	Mintage	VG-8	F-12	VF-20	XF-40	MS-60	MS-63	Proof
1870	50,000	12.00	30.00	100.00	600	1,600	3,600	—
1870 plain edge, Proof	—	—	—	—	—	—	—	25,000
1870 reeded edge, Proof	—	—	—	—	—	—	—	25,000
1872H	48,000	10.00	20.00	50.00	225	1,600	3,600	—
1873	37,675	40.00	75.00	200	650	5,700	10,000	—
1873 Proof	—	—	—	—	—	—	—	40,000
1874	80,000	25.00	45.00	125	550	4,300	8,000	—
1874 Proof	—	—	—	—	—	—	—	40,000
1876H	28,000	35.00	55.00	150	450	2,250	5,250	—
1880	24,000	30.00	60.00	175	600	4,000	9,500	—
1880 Proof	—	—	—	—	—	—	—	40,000
1881	50,000	20.00	35.00	135	400	2,250	5,250	—
1881 Proof	—	—	—	—	—	—	—	40,000
1882H	100,000	12.00	17.00	55.00	200	1,600	3,600	—
1882H Proof	—	—	—	—	—	—	—	8,000
1885	40,000	25.00	40.00	150	450	2,800	7,100	—
1885 Proof	—	—	—	—	—	—	—	40,000
1888	20,000	40.00	80.00	225	900	5,600	12,000	—
1888 Proof	—	—	—	—	—	—	—	40,000
1894	40,000	7.00	17.00	75.00	300	2,000	3,800	—
1896	60,000	7.00	15.00	65.00	225	1,600	3,600	—
1896 Proof	—	—	—	—	—	—	—	25,000
1898	76,607	7.00	12.00	60.00	200	1,700	3,600	—
1899 wide 9's	150,000	7.00	12.00	60.00	200	1,600	3,600	—
1899 narrow 9's	Inc. above	7.00	12.00	45.00	150	1,600	3,600	—
1900	150,000	7.00	12.00	45.00	175	1,600	3,600	—

KM# 11   Obv. Designer: G.W. DeSaulles **Rev. Designer:** W.H.J. Blakemore **Weight:** 11.7800 g. **Composition:** 0.9250 Silver .3504 oz. ASW

Date	Mintage	VG-8	F-12	VF-20	XF-40	MS-60	MS-63	Proof
1904H	140,000	3.25	5.00	13.00	35.00	275	850	—
1904H Proof	—	—	—	—	—	—	—	5,000

Date	Mintage	VG-8	F-12	VF-20	XF-40	MS-60	MS-63	Proof
1907	100,000	3.00	5.00	13.00	45.00	350	1,000	—
1908	160,000	3.25	4.50	12.50	32.50	225	700	—
1909	200,000	3.25	4.50	12.50	35.00	300	800	—

KM# 12 Obv. Designer: E.B. MacKennal **Rev. Designer:** W.H.J. Blakemore **Weight:** 11.7800 g. **Composition:** 0.9250 Silver .3504 oz. ASW

Date	Mintage	VG-8	F-12	VF-20	XF-40	MS-60	MS-63	Proof
1911	200,000	2.75	3.25	6.00	20.00	200	550	—
1917C	375,560	2.75	3.25	6.00	16.50	145	350	—
1917C Proof	—	—	—	—	—	—	—	2,500
1918C	294,824	2.75	3.25	6.00	16.50	145	350	—
1919C	306,267	2.75	3.25	6.00	16.50	325	1,150	—
1919C Proof	—	—	—	—	—	—	—	2,500

2 DOLLARS

KM# 5 Weight: 3.3284 g. **Composition:** 0.9170 Gold .0981 oz. AGW

Date	Mintage	F-12	VF-20	XF-40	AU-50	MS-60	MS-63
1865	10,000	150	175	225	375	1,100	5,000
1865 plain edge, Specimen-63, $15,000.	Est. 10	—	—	—	—	—	—
1870	10,000	150	175	250	375	1,100	5,850
1870 reeded edge, Specimen-63 $20,000.	Est. 5	—	—	—	—	—	—
1872	6,050	150	275	325	600	2,100	8,650
1872 Specimen-63 $12,500.	Est. 10	—	—	—	—	—	—
1880	2,500	800	1,000	1,200	2,300	4,650	14,250
1880/70	—	—	—	—	—	—	—
Note: Specimen. Bowers and Merena Norweb sale 11-96, specimen 64 realized $70,400.							
1881 Specimen; Rare	—	—	—	—	—	—	—
1881	10,000	125	150	200	325	1,200	5,400
1882H	25,000	125	150	200	225	425	1,600
1882H Specimen $4,250.	—	—	—	—	—	—	—
1885	10,000	125	150	200	225	425	1,800
1885 Specimen	—	—	—	—	—	—	—
Note: Bowers and Merena Norweb sale 11-96, specimen 66 realized $44,000							
1888	25,000	105	140	175	200	365	1,550
1888 Specimen; Rare	—	—	—	—	—	—	—

NOVA SCOTIA

PROVINCE

STERLING COINAGE

HALFPENNY TOKEN

KM# 1a Composition: Copper

Date	Mintage	VG-8	F-12	VF-20	XF-40	MS-60	MS-63	Proof
1382 1382 (error)	—	500	700	1,650	—	—	—	—
1832/1382	—	6.00	15.00	50.00	100.00	—	—	—
1832 (imitation)	—	3.00	6.00	18.00	40.00	50.00	100.00	—

KM# 1 Composition: Copper

Date	Mintage	VG-8	F-12	VF-20	XF-40	MS-60	MS-63	Proof
1823	400,000	3.00	6.00	13.00	40.00	125	250	—
1823 without hyphen	Inc. above	5.00	10.00	20.00	50.00	170	350	—
1824	118,636	4.00	8.00	18.00	45.00	150	275	—
1832	800,000	3.00	5.00	7.50	21.00	80.00	175	—

KM# 3 Composition: Copper

Date	Mintage	VG-8	F-12	VF-20	XF-40	MS-60	MS-63	Proof
1840 small 0	300,000	3.50	10.00	15.00	35.00	125	250	—
1840 medium 0	Inc. above	2.50	9.00	14.00	30.00	125	250	—
1840 large 0	Inc. above	4.00	10.00	15.00	35.00	125	250	—
1843	300,000	3.00	6.00	16.00	40.00	125	250	—

KM# 5 Composition: Copper

Date	Mintage	VG-8	F-12	VF-20	XF-40	MS-60	MS-63	Proof
1856 without LCW	720,000	2.00	4.00	7.50	15.00	70.00	175	—
1856 without LCW, Proof	—	—	—	—	—	—	—	600
1856 without LCW, inverted A for V in PROVINCE, Proof	—	—	—	—	—	—	—	600

KM# 5a Composition: Bronze

Date	Mintage	VG-8	F-12	VF-20	XF-40	MS-60	MS-63	Proof
1856 with LCW, Proof	—	—	—	—	—	—	—	600

1 PENNY TOKEN

KM# 2 Composition: Copper

Date	Mintage	VG-8	F-12	VF-20	XF-40	MS-60	MS-63	Proof
1824	217,776	4.00	10.00	17.00	55.00	175	350	—
1832	200,000	4.00	8.00	15.00	35.00	125	250	—

KM# 2a Composition: Copper

Date	Mintage	VG-8	F-12	VF-20	XF-40	MS-60	MS-63	Proof
1832 (imitation)	—	3.75	7.50	22.50	42.50	—	—	—

KM# 4 Composition: Copper **Size:** 32 mm.

Date	Mintage	VG-8	F-12	VF-20	XF-40	MS-60	MS-63	Proof
1840	150,000	2.50	6.00	14.00	40.00	150	250	—
1843/0	150,000	12.00	20.00	40.00	80.00	175	—	—
1843	Inc. above	4.00	8.00	15.00	40.00	175	275	—

KM# 6 Composition: Copper

Date	Mintage	VG-8	F-12	VF-20	XF-40	MS-60	MS-63	Proof
1856 without LCW	360,000	2.50	5.00	8.50	19.00	110	200	—
1856 with LCW	Inc. above	2.50	5.00	8.00	25.00	100.00	175	—

KM# 6a Composition: Bronze

Date	Mintage	VG-8	F-12	VF-20	XF-40	MS-60	MS-63	Proof
1856 Proof	—	—	—	—	—	—	—	400

DECIMAL COINAGE

HALF CENT

KM# 7 Composition: Bronze

Date	Mintage	VG-8	F-12	VF-20	XF-40	MS-60	MS-63	Proof
1861	400,000	3.00	5.00	8.00	13.00	60.00	175	—
1864	400,000	3.00	5.00	8.00	13.00	55.00	175	—
1864 Proof	—	—	—	—	—	—	—	300

CENT

KM# 8 Composition: Bronze **Note:** The Royal Mint report records mintage of 1 million for 1862, which is considered incorrect.

Date	Mintage	VG-8	F-12	VF-20	XF-40	MS-60	MS-63	Proof
1861	800,000	2.00	3.00	5.00	11.00	250	215	—
1862	Est. 1,000,000	25.00	40.00	90.00	175	850	2,900	—
1864	800,000	2.00	3.00	5.00	11.00	250	225	—

PRINCE EDWARD ISLAND
PROVINCE

DECIMAL COINAGE

CENT

KM# 4 Composition: Bronze

Date	Mintage	VG-8	F-12	VF-20	XF-40	MS-60	MS-63	Proof
1871	2,000,000	1.75	2.50	4.50	11.00	75.00	185	—
1871 Proof	—	—	—	—	—	—	—	2,000

CUT & COUNTERMARKED COINAGE
ca. 1813

SHILLING

KM# 1 Composition: Silver **Note:** Countermark on center plug of Spanish or Spanish Colonial 8 Reales.

Date	Mintage	VG-8	F-12	VF-20	XF-40	MS-60	MS-63	Proof
ND	1,000	2,000	3,000	5,000	—	—	—	—

5 SHILLING

KM# 2 Composition: Silver **Note:** Countermark on holed Mexico City 8 Reales, KM#109.

Date	Mintage	VG-8	F-12	VF-20	XF-40	MS-60	MS-63	Proof
1791-1808	—	800	1,350	2,250	—	—	—	—

KM# 3 Composition: Silver **Note:** Countermark on holed Lima 8 Reales, C#96.

Date	Mintage	VG-8	F-12	VF-20	XF-40	MS-60	MS-63	Proof
ND	1,000	1,000	1,750	3,000	—	—	—	—

MEXICO

The United States of Mexico, located immediately south of the United States has an area of 759,529 sq. mi. (1,967,183 sq. km.) and an estimated population of 88 million. Capital: Mexico City. The economy is based on agriculture, manufacturing and mining. Oil, cotton, silver, coffee, and shrimp are exported.

Mexico was the site of highly advanced Indian civilizations 1,500 years before conquistador Hernando Cortes conquered the wealthy Aztec empire of Montezuma,1519-21, and founded a Spanish colony which lasted for nearly 300 years. During the Spanish period, Mexico, then called New Spain, stretched from Guatemala to the present states of Wyoming and California, its present northern boundary having been established by the secession of Texas during 1836 and the war of 1846-48 with the United States.

Independence from Spain was declared by Father Miguel Hidalgo on Sept. 16, 1810, (Mexican Independence Day) and was achieved by General Agustin de Iturbide in1821. Iturbide became emperor in 1822 but was deposed when a republic was established a year later. For more than fifty years following the birth of the republic, the political scene of Mexico was characterized by turmoil which saw two emperors (including the unfortunate Maximilian), several dictators and an average of one new government every nine months passing swiftly from obscurity to oblivion. The land, social, economic and labor reforms promulgated by the Reform Constitution of Feb. 5, 1917 established the basis for sustained economic development and participative democracy that have made Mexico one of the most politically stable countries of modern Latin America.

RULERS
Philip V, 1700-1746
Luis I, 1724
Ferdinand VI, 1746-59
Charles III, 1760-88
Charles IV, 1788-1808

MINT MARKS
Mo, Mxo – Mexico City Mint

Initials	Date	Name
L	1678-1703	Martin Lopez
J	1708-23	Jose E. de Leon
D	1724-27	?
R	1729-30	Nicolas de Roxas
G	1730	
F	1730-33	Felipe Rivas de Angulo
F	1733-84	Francisco de la Pena
M	1733-63	Manuel de la Pena
M	1754-70	Manuel Assorin
F	1762-70	Francisco de Rivera
M	1770-77	Manuel de Rivera
F	1777-1803	Francisco Arance Cobos
M	1784-1801	Mariano Rodriguez

COLONIAL

COB COINAGE

KM# 24 1/2 REAL
1.6900 g., 0.9310 Silver **Ruler:** Philip V **Obv:** Legend around crowned PHILIPVS monogram **Rev:** Legend around cross, lions and castles **Note:** Struck at Mexico City Mint, mint mark M, Mo.

Date	Mintage	Good	VG	F	VF	XF
ND(1701-28) Date off flan	—	—	20.00	35.00	65.00	—
1701 L	—	—	100	125	225	—
1702 L	—	—	100	125	225	—
1703 L	—	—	100	125	225	—
1704 L	—	—	100	125	225	—
1705 L	—	—	100	125	225	—
1706 J	—	—	100	125	225	—
1707 J	—	—	100	125	225	—
1708 J	—	—	100	125	175	—
1709 J	—	—	100	125	175	—
1710 J	—	—	100	125	175	—
1711 J	—	—	100	125	175	—
1712 J	—	—	100	125	175	—
1714 J	—	—	100	125	175	—
1715 J	—	—	100	125	175	—
1716 J	—	—	100	125	175	—
1717 J	—	—	100	125	175	—
1718 J	—	—	100	125	175	—
1719 J	—	—	100	125	175	—
1720 J	—	—	100	125	175	—
1721 J	—	—	100	125	175	—
1722 J	—	—	100	125	175	—
1723 J	—	—	100	125	175	—
1724 J	—	—	100	125	175	—
1724 D	—	—	100	125	175	—
1725 D	—	—	100	125	175	—
1726 D	—	—	100	125	175	—
1727 D	—	—	100	125	175	—
1728 D	—	—	100	125	175	—

KM# 25 1/2 REAL
1.6900 g., 0.9310 Silver **Ruler:** Luis I **Obv:** Legend around crowned LVDOVICVS monogram **Rev:** Legend around cross, lions and castles **Note:** Struck at Mexico City Mint, mint mark M, Mo.

Date	Mintage	Good	VG	F	VF	XF
ND(1724-25) Date off flan	—	—	125	200	250	—
1724 D	—	—	325	450	550	—
1725 D	—	—	325	450	550	—

KM# 24a 1/2 REAL
1.6900 g., 0.9160 Silver **Ruler:** Philip V **Obv:** Legend around crowned PHILIPVS monogram **Rev:** Legend around cross, lions and castles **Note:** Struck at Mexico City Mint, mint mark M, Mo.

Date	Mintage	Good	VG	F	VF	XF
ND(1729-33) Date off flan	—	—	20.00	35.00	60.00	—
1729 R	—	—	90.00	120	150	—
1730 R	—	—	90.00	120	150	—
1731 F	—	—	90.00	120	150	—
1732/1 F	—	—	90.00	120	150	—
1732 F	—	—	90.00	120	150	—
1733/2 F	—	—	90.00	120	150	—
1733 F	—	—	90.00	120	150	—

KM# 30 REAL
3.3800 g., 0.9310 Silver **Ruler:** Philip V **Obv:** Legend and date around crowned arms **Obv. Legend:** PHILIPVS V DEI G **Note:** Struck at Mexico City Mint, mint mark M, Mo.

Date	Mintage	Good	VG	F	VF	XF
ND(1701-28) Date off flan	—	—	30.00	50.00	70.00	—
1701 L	—	—	125	175	275	—
1702 L	—	—	125	175	275	—
1703 L	—	—	125	175	275	—
1704 L	—	—	125	175	275	—
1705 L	—	—	125	175	275	—
1706 J	—	—	125	175	275	—
1707 J	—	—	125	175	275	—
1708 J	—	—	125	175	275	—
1709 J	—	—	125	175	275	—
1710 J	—	—	125	175	275	—
1711 J	—	—	125	175	275	—
1712 J	—	—	125	175	275	—
1713 J	—	—	125	175	275	—
1714 J	—	—	125	175	275	—
1715 J	—	—	100	175	275	—
1716 J	—	—	100	175	275	—
1717 J	—	—	100	175	275	—

Date	Mintage	Good	VG	F	VF	XF
1718 J	—	—	100	175	275	—
1719 J	—	—	100	175	275	—
1720/19 J	—	—	100	175	275	—
1720 J	—	—	100	175	275	—
1721 J	—	—	100	175	275	—
1722 J	—	—	100	175	275	—
1723 J	—	—	100	175	275	—
1726 D	—	—	100	175	275	—
1727 D	—	—	100	175	275	—
1728 D	—	—	100	175	275	—

KM# 30a   REAL
3.3800 g., 0.9160 Silver **Ruler:** Philip V **Obv:** Legend and date around crowned arms **Obv. Legend:** PHILIPVS V DEI G **Note:** Struck at Mexico City Mint, mint mark M, Mo.

Date	Mintage	Good	VG	F	VF	XF
ND(1729-32) Date off flan	—	—	25.00	40.00	65.00	—
1729 R	—	—	90.00	125	175	—
1730 R	—	—	90.00	125	175	—
1730 F	—	—	90.00	125	175	—
1730 G	—	—	90.00	125	175	—
1731 F	—	—	90.00	125	175	—
1732 F	—	—	90.00	125	175	—

KM# A31   REAL
3.3834 g., 0.9310 Silver .1013 oz. ASW **Ruler:** Luis I **Note:** A significant portion of the legend must be visibile for proper attribution. Struck at Mexico City Mint, mint mark M, Mo.

Date	Mintage	Good	VG	F	VF	XF
1/24 D Rare	—	—	—	—	—	—
1725 D Rare	—	—	—	—	—	—

KM# 35   2 REALES
6.7700 g., 0.9310 Silver **Ruler:** Philip V **Obv:** Legend and date around crowned arms **Obv. Legend:** PHILIPVS V DEI G **Note:** Struck at Mexico City Mint, mint mark M, Mo.

Date	Mintage	Good	VG	F	VF	XF
ND(1701-28) Date off flan	—	—	45.00	65.00	100	—
1701 L	—	—	125	150	250	—
1702 L	—	—	125	150	250	—
1703 L	—	—	125	150	250	—
1704 L	—	—	125	150	250	—
1705 L	—	—	125	150	250	—
1706 J	—	—	125	150	250	—
1707 J	—	—	125	150	250	—
1708 J	—	—	125	150	250	—
1710 J	—	—	125	150	250	—
1711 J	—	—	125	150	250	—
1712 J	—	—	125	150	250	—
1713 J	—	—	125	150	250	—
1714 J	—	—	150	185	300	—
1715 J	—	—	150	185	300	—
1716 J	—	—	150	185	300	—
1717 J	—	—	150	185	300	—
1718 J	—	—	150	185	300	—
1719 J	—	—	150	185	300	—
1720 J	—	—	150	185	300	—
1721 J	—	—	150	185	300	—
1722 J	—	—	150	185	300	—
1723 J	—	—	150	185	300	—
1724 J	—	—	150	185	300	—
1726 D	—	—	150	185	300	—
1727 D	—	—	150	185	300	—
1728 D	—	—	150	185	300	—

KM# 35a   2 REALES
6.7700 g., 0.9160 Silver **Ruler:** Philip V **Obv:** Legend and date around crowned arms **Obv. Legend:** PHILIPVS V DEI G **Note:** Struck at Mexico City Mint, mint mark M, Mo.

Date	Mintage	Good	VG	F	VF	XF
ND(1729-32) Date off flan	—	—	40.00	60.00	90.00	—
1729 R	—	—	100	125	150	—

Date	Mintage	Good	VG	F	VF	XF
1730 R	—	—	100	125	150	—
1731 F	—	—	100	125	150	—
1731/0 F	—	—	100	125	150	—
1732 F	—	—	100	125	150	—

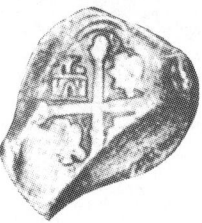

KM# 40   4 REALES
13.5400 g., 0.9310 Silver **Ruler:** Philip V **Obv:** Legend and date around crowned arms **Obv. Legend:** PHILIPVS V DEI G **Note:** Struck at Mexico City Mint, mint mark M, Mo.

Date	Mintage	Good	VG	F	VF	XF
1701 L	—	—	175	250	375	—
1702 L	—	—	175	250	375	—
1703 L	—	—	175	250	375	—
1704 L	—	—	175	250	375	—
1705 L	—	—	175	250	375	—
1706 J	—	—	175	250	375	—
1707 J	—	—	175	250	375	—
1708 J	—	—	175	250	375	—
1709 J	—	—	175	250	375	—
1710 J	—	—	175	250	375	—
1711 J	—	—	175	250	375	—
1712 J	—	—	175	250	375	—
1713 J	—	—	175	250	375	—
1714 J	—	—	175	250	375	—
1715 J	—	—	125	225	375	—
1716 J	—	—	200	300	500	—
1717 J	—	—	200	300	500	—
1718 J	—	—	200	300	500	—
1719 J	—	—	200	300	500	—
1720 J	—	—	200	300	500	—
1721 J	—	—	200	300	500	—
1722 J	—	—	200	300	500	—
1723 J	—	—	200	300	500	—
1726 D	—	—	200	300	500	—
1727 D	—	—	200	300	500	—
1728 D	—	—	200	300	500	—

KM# 40a   4 REALES
13.5400 g., 0.9160 Silver **Ruler:** Philip V **Obv:** Legend and date around crowned arms **Obv. Legend:** PHILIPVS V DEI G **Note:** Struck at Mexico City Mint, mint mark M, Mo.

Date	Mintage	Good	VG	F	VF	XF
ND(1729-33) Date off flan	—	—	50.00	70.00	100	—
1729 D	—	—	125	200	275	—
1730 R	—	—	125	200	275	—
1730 G	—	—	125	200	275	—
1731 F	—	—	125	200	275	—
1732/1 F	—	—	125	175	250	—
1732 F	—	—	125	175	250	—
1733/2 F	—	—	125	175	250	—

KM# 42 4 REALES
13.5400 g., 0.9310 Silver **Ruler:** Luis I **Obv:** Legend around crowned arms **Obv. Legend:** LVDOVICUS I DEI G **Rev:** Legend around cross, lions and castles **Note:** A significant portion of the legend must be visible for proper attribution. Struck at Mexico City Mint, mint mark M, Mo.

Date	Mintage	Good	VG	F	VF	XF
1724 D Rare	—	—	—	—	—	—
1725 D Rare	—	—	—	—	—	—

KM# 41 4 REALES
13.5400 g., 0.9160 Silver **Ruler:** Philip V **Obv:** Legend and date around crowned arms **Obv. Legend:** PHILIPVS V DEI G **Rev:** Legend around cross, lions and castles **Note:** Klippe. Similar to KM#40a. Struck at Mexico City Mint, mint mark M, Mo.

Date	Mintage	Good	VG	F	VF	XF
1733 F	—	—	450	600	750	—
1733 MF	—	—	450	600	750	—
1734/3 MF	—	—	450	600	750	—

KM# 46 8 REALES
27.0700 g., 0.9310 Silver **Ruler:** Charles II **Obv:** Legend and date around crowned arms **Obv. Legend:** CAROLVS II DEI G **Rev:** Legend around cross, lions and castles **Note:** Struck at Mexico City Mint, mint mark M, Mo.

Date	Mintage	Good	VG	F	VF	XF
1697 L	—	—	600	900	1,500	—
1701 L	—	—	700	1,000	1,700	—

KM# 47 8 REALES
27.0700 g., 0.9310 Silver **Ruler:** Philip V **Obv:** Legend and date around crowned arms **Obv. Legend:** PHILIPVS V DEI G **Rev:** Legend around cross, lions and castles **Note:** Struck at Mexico City Mint, mint mark M, Mo.

Date	Mintage	Good	VG	F	VF	XF
ND(1702-28) Date off flan	—	—	70.00	90.00	120	—
1702 L	—	—	200	350	500	—
1703 L	—	—	200	350	500	—
1704 L Rare	—	—	—	—	—	—
1705 L	—	—	200	350	600	—
1706 J	—	—	200	350	600	—
1707 J	—	—	200	350	500	—
1708 J	—	—	200	350	500	—
1709 J	—	—	200	350	500	—
1710 J	—	—	200	350	500	—
1711 J	—	—	175	300	475	—
1712 J	—	—	175	300	475	—
1713 J	—	—	175	300	475	—
1714 J	—	—	175	300	475	—
1715 J	—	—	175	300	475	—
1716 J	—	—	375	575	800	—
1717 J	—	—	375	575	800	—
1718/7 J	—	—	375	575	800	—
1718 J	—	—	350	500	800	—
1719 J	—	—	350	500	800	—
1720 J	—	—	350	500	800	—
1721 J	—	—	350	500	800	—
1722 J	—	—	350	500	800	—
1723 J	—	—	350	500	800	—
1724 D	—	—	350	500	800	—
1725 D	—	—	350	500	800	—
1726 D	—	—	350	500	800	—
1727 D	—	—	350	500	800	—
1728 D	—	—	400	600	1,000	—

KM# 47a 8 REALES
27.0700 g., 0.9160 Silver **Ruler:** Philip V **Obv:** Legend and date around crowned arms **Obv. Legend:** PHILIPVS V DEI G **Rev:** Legend around cross, lions and castles **Note:** Struck at Mexico City Mint, mint mark M, Mo.

Date	Mintage	Good	VG	F	VF	XF
ND(1729-33) Date off flan	—	—	70.00	90.00	110	—
1729 R	—	—	150	250	400	—
1730 G/R	—	—	150	250	400	—
1730 R	—	—	150	250	400	—
1730 G	—	—	150	250	400	—
1730 F	—	—	150	250	400	—
1731/0 F	—	—	150	250	400	—
1731 F	—	—	150	250	400	—
1732/1 F	—	—	150	250	400	—
1732 F	—	—	150	250	400	—
1733/2 F	—	—	150	250	400	—
1733 F	—	—	150	250	400	—

KM# 49 8 REALES
27.0700 g., 0.9310 Silver **Ruler:** Luis I **Obv:** Legend and date around crowned arms **Obv. Legend:** LVDOVICVS I DEI G **Rev:** Legend around cross, lions and castles **Note:** A significant portion of the legend must be visible for proper attribution. Struck at Mexico City Mint, mint mark M, Mo.

Date	Mintage	Good	VG	F	VF	XF
ND(1724-25) Date off flan; Rare	—	—	—	—	—	—
1724 D Rare	—	—	—	—	—	—
1725 D Rare	—	—	—	—	—	—

KM# 48   8 REALES
0.9160 g., Silver **Ruler:** Philip V **Note:** Klippe. Similar to KM#47a. Mint mark M, Mo.

Date	Mintage	Good	VG	F	VF	XF
ND(1733-34) Date off flan	—	—	150	200	300	—
1733 F	—	—	550	750	1,150	—
1733 MF	—	—	350	500	650	—
1734/3 MF	—	—	500	750	1,000	—
1734 MF	—	—	500	750	1,000	—

KM# 50   ESCUDO
3.3800 g., 0.9170 Gold **Ruler:** Charles II **Obv:** Legend and date around crowned arms **Obv. Legend:** CAROLVS II DEI G **Rev:** Legend around cross, lions and castles **Note:** Struck at Mexico City Mint, mint mark MXo.

Date	Mintage	VG	F	VF	XF	Unc
1701/0MXo L	—	—	3,000	4,000	5,000	—

KM# 51.1   ESCUDO
3.3800 g., 0.9170 Gold .0997 oz. AGW **Ruler:** Philip V **Obv:** Legend and date around crowned arms **Obv. Legend:** PHILIPVS V DEI G **Rev:** Legend around cross, lions and castles **Note:** Struck at Mexico City Mint, mint mark MXo.

Date	Mintage	VG	F	VF	XF	Unc
ND(1702-13) Date off flan	—	—	1,000	1,350	1,500	—
1702MXo L	—	—	1,500	2,500	3,500	—
1703/2MXo L	—	—	1,500	2,500	3,500	—
1704MXo L	—	—	1,500	2,500	3,500	—
1707MXo J	—	—	1,500	2,500	3,500	—
1708MXo J	—	—	1,500	2,500	3,500	—
1709MXo J	—	—	1,500	2,500	3,500	—
1710MXo J	—	—	1,500	2,500	3,500	—
1711MXo J	—	—	1,500	2,500	3,500	—
1712MXo J	—	—	1,500	2,500	3,500	—
1713MXo J	—	—	1,500	2,500	3,500	—

KM# 51.2   ESCUDO
3.3800 g., 0.9170 Gold .0997 oz. AGW **Ruler:** Philip V **Obv:** Legend and date around crowned arms **Obv. Legend:** PHILIPVS V DEI G **Rev:** Legend around cross, lions and castles **Note:** Struck at Mexico City Mint, mint mark Mo.

Date	Mintage	VG	F	VF	XF	Unc
ND(1702-13) Date off flan	—	—	1,200	1,500	1,750	—
1712Mo J	—	—	2,000	3,000	4,000	—
1714Mo J	—	—	1,400	2,000	3,000	—
1714Mo J J's 1's (J7J4J)	—	—	2,000	3,000	4,000	—
1715Mo J	—	—	2,000	3,000	4,000	—
1727Mo J Rare	—	—	—	—	—	—
1728Mo J Rare	—	—	—	—	—	—

Note: Die-struck counterfiets of 1731 F exist

KM# 52   2 ESCUDOS
6.7700 g., 0.9170 Gold .1996 oz. AGW **Ruler:** Philip V **Obv:** Legend and date around crowned arms **Obv. Legend:** CAROLVS II DEI G **Rev:** Legend around cross **Note:** Struck at Mexico City Mint, mint mark MXo.

Date	Mintage	VG	F	VF	XF	Unc
1701MXo L	—	—	4,000	2,200	6,000	—

KM# 53.1   2 ESCUDOS
6.7700 g., 0.9170 Gold .1996 oz. AGW **Ruler:** Philip V **Obv:** Legend and date around crowned arms **Obv. Legend:** PHILIPVS V DEI G **Rev:** Legend around cross **Note:** Struck at Mexico City Mint, mint mark MXo.

Date	Mintage	VG	F	VF	XF	Unc
ND(1704-13) Date off flan	—	—	1,200	1,500	1,750	—
1704MXo L	—	—	2,750	3,750	4,750	—
1708MXo J	—	—	2,750	3,750	4,750	—
1710MXo J	—	—	2,750	3,750	4,750	—
1711MXo J	—	—	2,750	3,750	4,750	—
1712MXo J	—	—	2,750	3,750	4,750	—
1713MXo J	—	—	2,750	3,750	4,750	—

KM# 53.2   2 ESCUDOS
6.7700 g., 0.9170 Gold .1996 oz. AGW **Ruler:** Philip V **Obv:** Legend and date around crowned arms **Obv. Legend:** PHILIPVS V DEI G **Rev:** Legend around cross **Note:** Struck counterfeits exist for 1731. Struck at Mexico City Mint, mint mark Mo.

Date	Mintage	VG	F	VF	XF	Unc
ND(1714-31) Date off flan	—	—	1,500	1,750	2,500	—
1714Mo J	—	—	—	2,500	3,500	—

Date	Mintage	VG	F	VF	XF	Unc
1717Mo J Rare	—	—	—	—	—	—
1722Mo J Rare	—	—	—	—	—	—
1729Mo R Rare	—	—	—	—	—	—
1731Mo F Rare	.	—	—	—	—	—

KM# A54 2 ESCUDOS
6.7700 g., 0.9170 Gold .1996 oz. AGW **Ruler:** Luis I **Obv:** Legend and date around crowned arms **Obv. Legend:** LVDOVICVS I DEI G. **Rev:** Legend around cross **Note:** A significant portion of the legend must be visible for proper attribution. Struck at Mexico City Mint, mint mark MXo.

Date	Mintage	VG	F	VF	XF	Unc
NDMXo F Rare	—	—	—	—	—	—

KM# 55.1 4 ESCUDOS
13.5400 g., 0.9170 Gold .3992 oz. AGW **Ruler:** Philip V **Obv:** Legend and date around crowned arms **Obv. Legend:** PHILIPVS V DEI G **Rev:** Legend around cross **Note:** Struck at Mexico City Mint, mint mark MXo.

Date	Mintage	VG	F	VF	XF	Unc
ND(1705-13)	—	—	2,500	3,000	4,000	—
Date off flan						
1705MXo J	—	—	4,000	5,750	6,750	—
1706MXo L	—	—	4,000	5,750	6,750	—
1711MXo J	—	—	4,000	5,750	6,750	—
1712MXo J	—	—	4,000	5,750	6,750	—
1713MXo J	—	—	4,000	5,750	6,750	—

KM# 55.2 4 ESCUDOS
13.5400 g., 0.9170 Gold .3992 oz. AGW **Ruler:** Philip V **Obv:** Legend and date around crowned arms **Obv. Legend:** PHILIPVS V DEI G **Rev:** Legend around cross **Note:** Struck at Mexico City Mint, mint mark Mo.

Date	Mintage	VG	F	VF	XF	Unc
ND(1714-20)	—	—	2,500	3,750	5,000	—
Date off flan						
1714Mo J	—	—	—	5,750	7,500	—
1715Mo J	—	—	—	5,750	7,500	—
1720Mo J Rare	—	—	—	—	—	—

KM# 57.1 8 ESCUDOS
27.0700 g., 0.9170 Gold .7980 oz. AGW **Ruler:** Philip V **Obv:** Legend and date around crowned arms **Obv. Legend:**

PHILIPVS V DEI G Rev: Legend around cross **Note:** Struck at Mexico City Mint, mint mark MXo.

Date	Mintage	VG	F	VF	XF	Unc
ND(1701-13)	—	2,000	3,000	4,000	—
Date off flan					
1701MXo L	—	—	6,000	7,500	9,000	—
1703MXo L	—	—	6,000	7,500	9,000	—
1706MXo J	—	—	6,000	7,500	9,000	—
1708MXo J	—	—	6,000	7,500	9,000	—
1709MXo J	—	—	6,000	7,500	9,000	—
1710MXo J	—	—	6,000	7,500	9,000	—
1711MXo J	—	—	3,500	4,000	5,750	—
1712MXo J	—	—	3,500	4,000	5,750	—
1713MXo J	—	—	3,500	4,000	5,750	—

KM# 57.2 8 ESCUDOS
27.0700 g., 0.9170 Gold .7980 oz. AGW **Ruler:** Philip V **Obv:** Legend and date around crowned arms **Obv. Legend:** PHILIPVS V DEI G **Rev:** Legend around cross **Note:** Struck at Mexico City Mint, mint mark Mo.

Date	Mintage	VG	F	VF	XF	Unc
ND(1714-32)Mo	—	—	2,750	3,750	4,750	—
Date off flan						
1714Mo J	—	—	5,000	6,000	7,500	—
1714Mo Date over	—	—	6,000	7,500	9,000	—
GRAT on obverse						
1715Mo J Rare	—	—	—	—	—	—
1717/6Mo J Rare	—	—	—	—	—	—
1720/19Mo J Rare	—	—	—	—	—	—
1723Mo J Rare	—	—	—	—	—	—
1727/6Mo D Rare	—	—	—	—	—	—
1728/7Mo D Rare	—	—	—	—	—	—
1729Mo R Rare	—	—	—	—	—	—
1730Mo R Rare	—	—	—	—	—	—
1730Mo F Rare	—	—	—	—	—	—
1731Mo F Rare	—	—	—	—	—	—
1732Mo F Rare	—	—	—	—	—	—

KM# 57.3 8 ESCUDOS
27.0700 g., 0.9170 Gold .7980 oz. AGW **Obv:** Date around crowned arms **Obv. Legend:** PHILIPVS V DEI G **Rev:** Legend and date around cross **Note:** Struck at Mexico City Mint, mint mark Mo.

Date	Mintage	VG	F	VF	XF	Unc
1714Mo J Date	—	—	6,000	7,500	9,000	—
on reverse						

KM# 58 8 ESCUDOS
27.0700 g., 0.9170 Gold .7980 oz. AGW **Ruler:** Luis I **Obv:** Legend and date around crowned arms **Obv. Legend:** LVDOVICVS I DEI G **Rev:** Legend around cross **Note:** A significant portion of the legend must be visible for proper attribution. Struck at Mexico City Mint, mint mark Mo.

Date	Mintage	VG	F	VF	XF	Unc
ND(1724-25)	—	—	—	—	—	—
Mo D Rare						

ROYAL COINAGE

Struck on specially prepared round planchets using well centered dies in excellent condition to prove the quality of the minting to the Viceroy or even to the King.

KM# R24 1/2 REAL
1.6917 g., 0.9130 Silver .0506 oz. ASW **Ruler:** Philip V **Note:** Normally found holed. Struck at Mexico City Mint, mint mark Mo.

Date	Mintage	Good	VG	F	VF	XF
1715Mo J	—	—	250	500	750	—
1719Mo J	—	—	250	500	750	—
1721Mo J	—	—	250	500	750	—
1726Mo D	—	—	250	500	750	—
1727Mo D	—	—	250	500	750	—

KM# R24a 1/2 REAL
1.6917 g., 0.9170 Silver .0498 oz. ASW **Ruler:** Philip V **Note:** Normally found holed. Struck at Mexico City Mint, mark mark Mo.

Date	Mintage	Good	VG	F	VF	XF
1730Mo D	—	—	250	500	750	—

KM# R25 1/2 REAL
1.6917 g., 0.9310 Silver .0506 oz. ASW **Ruler:** Luis I **Note:** Struck at Mexico City Mint, mint mark Mo.

Date	Mintage	Good	VG	F	VF	XF
1724Mo D Rare	—	—	—	—	—	—

KM# R29 REAL
3.3834 g., 0.9310 Silver .1013 oz. ASW **Ruler:** Charles II **Obv. Legend:** CAROLVS II DEI G **Note:** Struck at Mexico City Mint, mint mark Mo.

Date	Mintage	Good	VG	F	VF	XF
1699Mo L Rare	—	—	—	—	—	—

KM# R30　REAL
3.3834 g., 0.9310 Silver .1013 oz. ASW　**Ruler:** Philip V **Obv.**
Legend: PHILIPVS V DEI G **Note:** Struck at Mexico City Mint,
mint mark Mo.

Date	Mintage	Good	VG	F	VF	XF
1715Mo J Rare	—	—	—	—	—	—
1716Mo J Rare	—	—	—	—	—	—
1718Mo J Rare	—	—	—	—	—	—

KM# R35　2 REALES
6.7668 g., 0.9310 Silver .2026 oz. ASW　**Ruler:** Philip V **Obv.**
Legend: PHILIPVS V DEI G **Note:** Struck at Mexico City Mint,
mint mark Mo.

Date	Mintage	Good	VG	F	VF	XF
1715Mo J Rare	—	—	—	—	—	—

KM# R35a　2 REALES
6.7668 g., 0.9170 Silver .1995 oz. ASW　**Ruler:** Philip V **Note:**
Struck at Mexico City Mint, mint mark Mo.

Date	Mintage	Good	VG	F	VF	XF
1730Mo R Rare	—	—	—	—	—	—

KM# R40　4 REALES
13.5337 g., 0.9310 Silver .4051 oz. ASW　**Ruler:** Philip V
Obv. Legend: PHILIPVS V DEI G **Note:** Struck at Mexico
City Mint, mint mark Mo.

Date	Mintage	Good	VG	F	VF	XF
1716Mo J Rare	—	—	—	—	—	—
1719Mo J Rare	—	—	—	—	—	—
1721Mo J Rare	—	—	—	—	—	—
1722Mo J Rare	—	—	—	—	—	—
1723Mo J Rare	—	—	—	—	—	—

KM# R47　8 REALES
27.0674 g., 0.9310 Silver .8102 oz. ASW　**Ruler:** Philip V
Obv. Legend: PHILIPVS V DEI G **Note:** Struck at Mexico
City Mint, mint mark Mo.

Date	Mintage	Good	VG	F	VF	XF
1702Mo L Rare	—	—	—	—	—	—
1703Mo L Rare	—	—	—	—	—	—
1705Mo J Rare	—	—	—	—	—	—
1706Mo J Rare	—	—	—	—	—	—
1709Mo J Rare	—	—	—	—	—	—
1711Mo J Rare	—	—	—	—	—	—
1714Mo J Rare	—	—	—	—	—	—
1715Mo J Rare	—	—	—	—	—	—
1716Mo J Rare	—	—	—	—	—	—
1717Mo J Rare	—	—	—	—	—	—
1719Mo J Rare	—	—	—	—	—	—
1721Mo J Rare	—	—	—	—	—	—
1722Mo J Rare	—	—	—	—	—	—
1723Mo J Rare	—	—	—	—	—	—
1724Mo D Rare	—	—	—	—	—	—
1725Mo D Rare	—	—	—	—	—	—
1726/5Mo D Rare	—	—	—	—	—	—
1726Mo D Rare	—	—	—	—	—	—
1727Mo D Rare	—	—	—	—	—	—

KM# R47a　8 REALES
27.0674 g., 0.9170 Silver .7980 oz. ASW　**Note:** Struck at
Mexico City Mint, mint mark Mo.

Date	Mintage	Good	VG	F	VF	XF
1729 R Rare	—	—	—	—	—	—
1730 R/D Rare	—	—	—	—	—	—
1730 G Rare	—	—	—	—	—	—

KM# R49　8 REALES
27.0674 g., 0.9310 Silver .8102 oz. ASW　**Ruler:** Luis I **Note:**
Struck at Mexico City Mint, mint mark Mo.

Date	Mintage	Good	VG	F	VF	XF
1724 D Rare	—	—	—	—	—	—
1725 D Rare	—	—	—	—	—	—

KM# R51.2　ESCUDO
3.3834 g., 0.9170 Gold .0997 oz. AGW　**Note:** Struck at
Mexico City Mint, mint mark Mo.

Date	Mintage	Good	VG	F	VF	XF
1714Mo J Rare	—	—	—	—	—	—
1715Mo J Rare	—	—	—	—	—	—

KM# R53.1　2 ESCUDOS
6.7668 g., 0.9170 Gold .1995 oz. AGW　**Note:** Struck at
Mexico City Mint, mint mark MXo.

Date	Mintage	Good	VG	F	VF	XF
1711MXo J Rare	—	—	—	—	—	—
1712MXo J Rare	—	—	—	—	—	—

KM# R55.1　4 ESCUDOS
13.5337 g., 0.9170 Gold .3990 oz. AGW　**Note:** Struck at
Mexico City Mint, mint mark M, Mo.

Date	Mintage	Good	VG	F	VF	XF
1711 Rare	—	—	—	—	—	—

KM# R55.2　4 ESCUDOS
13.5337 g., 0.9170 Gold .3990 oz. AGW　**Note:** Struck at
Mexico City Mint, mint mark M, Mo.

Date	Mintage	Good	VG	F	VF	XF
1714 Rare	—	—	—	—	—	—

KM# R56　8 ESCUDOS
27.0674 g., 0.9170 Gold .7980 oz. AGW　**Note:** Fully struck
sample specimens referred to as "Royal" strikes are seldom
encountered. Struck at Mexico City Mint, mint mark MXo.

Date	Mintage	Good	VG	F	VF	XF
1695MXo L Rare	—	—	—	—	—	—
1698MXo L Rare	—	—	—	—	—	—

KM# R57.1　8 ESCUDOS
27.0674 g., 0.9170 Gold .7980 oz. AGW　**Ruler:** Philip V
Note: Struck at Mexico City Mint, mint mark MXo.

Date	Mintage	Good	VG	F	VF	XF
1702MXo L Rare	—	—	—	—	—	—
1711MXo J Rare	—	—	—	—	—	—
1712MXo J Rare	—	—	—	—	—	—
1713MXo J Rare	—	—	—	—	—	—

KM# R57.3　8 ESCUDOS
27.0674 g., 0.9170 Gold .7980 oz. AGW　**Note:** Struck at
Mexico City Mint, mint mark Mo.

Date	Mintage	Good	VG	F	VF	XF
1714Mo J Rare	—	—	—	—	—	—
1715Mo J Rare	—	—	—	—	—	—
1717Mo J Rare	—	—	—	—	—	—
1718Mo J Rare	—	—	—	—	—	—
1723Mo J Rare	—	—	—	—	—	—

MILLED COINAGE
100 Centavos = 1 Peso

KM# 59　1/16 REAL (1/8 Pilon)
Copper　**Obv:** Crowned F VII monogram **Rev:** Castles and
lions in wreath **Note:** Mint mark M, Mo.

Date	Mintage	VG	F	VF	XF	Unc
1814	—	10.00	20.00	45.00	120	—
1815	—	10.00	20.00	45.00	120	—

KM# 63   1/8 REAL (1/4 Tlaco)
Copper   **Obv:** Legend around crowned F. VII **Obv. Legend:**
FERDIN. VII... **Note:** Mint mark M, Mo.

Date	Mintage	VG	F	VF	XF	Unc
1814	—	12.00	25.00	50.00	150	—
1815	—	12.00	25.00	50.00	150	—
1816	—	12.00	25.00	50.00	150	—

KM# 62   1/4 REAL
0.8458 g., 0.8960 Silver .0244 oz. ASW   **Obv:** Castle **Rev:**
Lion **Note:** Mint mark M, Mo.

Date	Mintage	VG	F	VF	XF	Unc
1796	—	15.00	30.00	55.00	90.00	—
1797	—	15.00	30.00	55.00	90.00	—
1798	—	12.50	22.00	50.00	75.00	—
1799/8	—	12.50	22.00	50.00	75.00	—
1799	—	10.00	20.00	40.00	70.00	—
1800	—	10.00	25.00	55.00	90.00	—
1801/0	—	10.00	20.00	40.00	70.00	—
1801	—	10.00	20.00	40.00	70.00	—
1802	—	10.00	20.00	40.00	70.00	—
1803	—	10.00	20.00	40.00	70.00	—
1804	—	10.00	20.00	40.00	75.00	—
1805/4	—	12.50	25.00	55.00	85.00	—
1805	—	10.00	22.00	50.00	75.00	—
1806	—	10.00	22.00	50.00	80.00	—
1807/797	—	15.00	30.00	55.00	85.00	—
1807	—	12.50	25.00	50.00	80.00	—
1808	—	12.50	25.00	50.00	80.00	—
1809/8	—	12.50	25.00	50.00	80.00	—
1809	—	12.50	25.00	50.00	80.00	—
1810	—	12.50	25.00	50.00	75.00	—
1811	—	12.50	25.00	50.00	75.00	—
1812	—	12.50	25.00	50.00	75.00	—
1813	—	10.00	20.00	40.00	70.00	—
1815	—	12.50	22.00	50.00	75.00	—
1816	—	10.00	20.00	40.00	70.00	—

KM# 64   1/4 REAL (2/4 2 Tlaco)
Copper   **Obv:** Legend around crowned F. VII **Obv. Legend:**
FERDIN. VII... **Note:** Mint mark M, Mo.

Date	Mintage	VG	F	VF	XF	Unc
1814	—	12.00	25.00	50.00	150	—
1815/4	—	15.00	30.00	60.00	165	—
1815	—	12.00	25.00	50.00	150	—
1816	—	12.00	25.00	50.00	150	—
1821	—	20.00	40.00	75.00	200	—

KM# 65   1/2 REAL
1.6917 g., 0.9170 Silver .0498 oz. ASW   **Ruler:** Philip V **Obv.
Legend:** PHILIP. V. D. G. HISPAN. ET IND. REX **Note:**
Mint mark M, Mo.

Date	Mintage	VG	F	VF	XF	Unc
1732 Rare	—	—	—	—	—	—
1732 F	—	500	800	1,200	2,000	—
1733 MF (MX)	—	400	600	1,000	1,500	—
1733 F	—	200	325	550	800	—
1733/2 MF	—	300	400	600	800	—
1733 MF	—	300	400	600	800	—
1734/3 MF	—	12.00	25.00	45.00	85.00	—
1734 MF	—	12.00	25.00	45.00	85.00	—
1735/4 MF	—	10.00	20.00	45.00	85.00	—
1735 MF	—	10.00	20.00	45.00	85.00	—
1736/5 MF	—	10.00	20.00	45.00	85.00	—
1736 MF	—	10.00	20.00	45.00	85.00	—
1737/6 MF	—	10.00	20.00	45.00	85.00	—
1737 MF	—	10.00	20.00	45.00	85.00	—
1738/7 MF	—	10.00	20.00	45.00	85.00	—
1738 MF	—	10.00	20.00	45.00	85.00	—
1739 MF	—	10.00	20.00	45.00	85.00	—
1740/30 MF	—	8.00	18.00	40.00	75.00	—
1740 MF	—	8.00	18.00	40.00	75.00	—
1741 MF	—	8.00	18.00	40.00	75.00	—

KM# 66   1/2 REAL
1.6900 g., 0.9170 Silver .0498 oz. ASW   **Obv. Legend:** PHS.
V. D. G. HISP. ET IND. R **Note:** Struck at Mexico City Mint,
mint mark M, Mo.

Date	Mintage	VG	F	VF	XF	Unc
1742 M	—	8.00	18.00	40.00	75.00	—
1743 M	—	8.00	18.00	40.00	75.00	—
1744/3 M	—	8.00	18.00	40.00	75.00	—
1744 M	—	8.00	18.00	40.00	75.00	—
1745 M Rare	—	—	—	—	—	—

Note: Legend variation: PHS. V. D. G. HISP. EST IND. R

Date	Mintage	VG	F	VF	XF	Unc
1745 M	—	8.00	18.00	40.00	75.00	—
1746/5 M	—	8.00	18.00	40.00	75.00	—
1746 M	—	8.00	18.00	40.00	75.00	—
1747 M	—	8.00	18.00	40.00	75.00	—

KM# 67.1   1/2 REAL
1.6900 g., 0.9170 Silver .0498 oz. ASW   **Obv:** Royal crown
Obv. Legend: FRD. VI. D. G. HIPS. ET IND. R **Note:** Struck
at Mexico City Mint, mint mark M, Mo.

Date	Mintage	VG	F	VF	XF	Unc
1747/6 M	—	—	—	—	—	—
1747 M	—	8.00	18.00	40.00	75.00	—
1748/7 M	—	8.00	18.00	40.00	75.00	—
1748 M	—	8.00	18.00	40.00	75.00	—
1749 M	—	8.00	18.00	40.00	75.00	—
1750 M	—	8.00	18.00	40.00	75.00	—
1751 M	—	10.00	20.00	45.00	85.00	—
1752 M	—	8.00	18.00	40.00	75.00	—
1753 M	—	8.00	18.00	40.00	75.00	—
1754 M	—	12.00	25.00	55.00	100	—
1755/6 M	—	12.00	25.00	55.00	100	—
1755 M	—	8.00	18.00	40.00	75.00	—
1756/5 M	—	8.00	18.00	40.00	75.00	—
1756 M	—	8.00	18.00	40.00	75.00	—
1757/6 M	—	8.00	18.00	40.00	75.00	—
1757 M	—	8.00	18.00	40.00	75.00	—

KM# 67.2   1/2 REAL
1.6917 g., 0.9170 Silver .0498 oz. ASW   **Obv:** Different crown
Note: Struck at Mexico City Mint, mint mark M, Mo.

Date	Mintage	VG	F	VF	XF	Unc
1757 M	—	8.00	18.00	40.00	75.00	—
1758/7 M	—	8.00	18.00	40.00	75.00	—

Date	Mintage	VG	F	VF	XF	Unc
1758 M	—	8.00	18.00	40.00	75.00	—
1759 M	—	8.00	18.00	40.00	75.00	—
1760/59 M	—	8.00	18.00	40.00	75.00	—
1760 M	—	8.00	18.00	40.00	75.00	—

KM# 68   1/2 REAL
1.6900 g., 0.9170 Silver .0498 oz. ASW **Obv. Legend:** CAR. III. D. G. HISP. ET IND. R **Note:** Struck at Mexico City Mint, mint mark M, Mo.

Date	Mintage	VG	F	VF	XF	Unc
1760/59 M	—	8.00	18.00	40.00	75.00	—
1760 M	—	8.00	18.00	40.00	75.00	—
1761 M	—	8.00	18.00	40.00	75.00	—
1762 M	—	8.00	18.00	40.00	75.00	—
1763/2 M	—	8.00	18.00	40.00	75.00	—
1763 M	—	8.00	18.00	40.00	75.00	—
1764 M	—	8.00	18.00	40.00	75.00	—
1765/4 M	—	10.00	20.00	42.00	80.00	—
1765 M	—	8.00	18.00	40.00	75.00	—
1766 M	—	8.00	18.00	40.00	75.00	—
1767 M	—	10.00	20.00	45.00	85.00	—
1768/6 M	—	10.00	20.00	42.00	80.00	—
1768 M	—	8.00	18.00	40.00	75.00	—
1769 M	—	10.00	20.00	42.00	80.00	—
1770 M	—	10.00	20.00	42.00	80.00	—
1770 F	—	15.00	30.00	60.00	100	—
1771 F	—	10.00	20.00	42.00	80.00	—

KM# 69.2   1/2 REAL
1.6917 g., 0.9030 Silver .0491 oz. ASW **Obv. Legend:** CAROLUS. III. DEI. GRATIA **Rev:** Normal initials and mint mark **Note:** Struck at Mexico City Mint, mint mark Mo.

Date	Mintage	VG	F	VF	XF	Unc
1772Mo FF	—	9.00	18.00	35.00	80.00	—
1773Mo FM	—	4.50	10.00	25.00	60.00	—
1773Mo FM CAROLS (error)	—	75.00	150	250	400	—
1774Mo FM	—	4.50	10.00	25.00	55.00	—
1775Mo FM	—	4.50	10.00	25.00	55.00	—
1776Mo FM	—	4.50	10.00	25.00	55.00	—
1777/6Mo FM	—	10.00	18.00	35.00	75.00	—
1777Mo FM	—	7.00	15.00	30.00	65.00	—
1778Mo FF	—	4.50	10.00	25.00	55.00	—
1779Mo FF	—	4.50	10.00	25.00	55.00	—
1780/79Mo FF	—	6.00	12.50	30.00	75.00	—
1780Mo FF	—	4.50	10.00	25.00	55.00	—
1781Mo FF	—	4.50	10.00	25.00	55.00	—
1782/1Mo FF	—	6.00	12.50	30.00	75.00	—
1782Mo FF	—	4.50	10.00	25.00	55.00	—
1783Mo FF	—	4.50	10.00	25.00	55.00	—
1783Mo FM	—	125	300	450	—	—
1784Mo FF	—	4.50	10.00	25.00	55.00	—
1784Mo FM	—	7.00	15.00	35.00	80.00	—

KM# 69.1   1/2 REAL
1.6900 g., 0.9030 Silver .0490 oz. ASW **Obv. Legend:** CAROLUS. III. DEI. GRATIA **Rev:** Inverted FM and mint mark **Note:** Struck at Mexico City Mint, mint mark Mo.

Date	Mintage	VG	F	VF	XF	Unc
1772Mo FM	—	5.00	12.00	27.00	65.00	—
1773Mo FM	—	4.50	10.00	25.00	55.00	—

KM# 69.2a   1/2 REAL
1.6917 g., 0.8960 Silver .0487 oz. ASW **Rev:** Normal initials and mint mark **Note:** Struck at Mexico City Mint, mint mark M, Mo.

Date	Mintage	VG	F	VF	XF	Unc
1785/4 FM	—	7.00	15.00	35.00	80.00	—
1785 FM	—	5.00	12.00	27.00	60.00	—
1786 FM	—	4.50	10.00	25.00	55.00	—
1787 FM	—	4.50	10.00	25.00	55.00	—

Date	Mintage	VG	F	VF	XF	Unc
1788 FM	—	4.50	10.00	25.00	55.00	—
1789 FM	—	8.00	16.00	40.00	100	—

KM# 70   1/2 REAL
1.6917 g., 0.8960 Silver .0487 oz. ASW **Obv:** Armored bust of Charles III **Obv. Legend:** CAROLUS. IV... **Note:** Struck at Mexico City Mint, mint mark M, Mo.

Date	Mintage	VG	F	VF	XF	Unc
1789 FM	—	12.00	25.00	50.00	100	—
1790 FM	—	12.00	25.00	50.00	100	—

KM# 71   1/2 REAL
1.6917 g., 0.8960 Silver .0487 oz. ASW **Obv:** Armored bust of Charles III **Obv. Legend:** CAROLUS IIII... **Note:** Struck at Mexico City Mint, mint mark M, Mo.

Date	Mintage	VG	F	VF	XF	Unc
1790 FM	—	12.00	25.00	50.00	100	—

KM# 72   1/2 REAL
1.6900 g., 0.9030 Silver .0490 oz. ASW **Obv:** Armored bust of Charles IIII **Rev:** Pillars and arms **Note:** Mint mark M, Mo.

Date	Mintage	VG	F	VF	XF	Unc
1792 FM	—	6.00	12.00	25.00	50.00	—
1793 FM	—	6.00	12.00	25.00	50.00	—
1794/3 FM	—	7.50	15.00	30.00	75.00	—
1794 FM	—	5.00	10.00	22.00	45.00	—
1795 FM	—	4.00	10.00	22.00	45.00	—
1796 FM	—	4.00	10.00	22.00	45.00	—
1797 FM	—	4.00	10.00	22.00	45.00	—
1798/7 FM	—	5.00	11.50	25.00	50.00	—
1798 FM	—	4.00	10.00	22.00	45.00	—
1799 FM	—	4.00	10.00	22.00	45.00	—
1800/799 FM	—	5.00	11.50	25.00	50.00	—
1800 FM	—	4.00	10.00	22.00	45.00	—
1801 FM	—	7.50	15.00	30.00	80.00	—
1801 FT	—	4.00	10.00	22.00	45.00	—
1802 FT	—	4.00	10.00	22.00	45.00	—
1803 FT	—	5.00	11.50	25.00	50.00	—
1804 TH	—	4.00	10.00	22.00	45.00	—
1805 TH	—	4.00	10.00	22.00	45.00	—
1806 TH	—	4.00	10.00	22.00	45.00	—
1807/6 TH	—	5.00	11.50	25.00	50.00	—
1807 TH	—	4.00	10.00	22.00	45.00	—
1808/7 TH	—	5.00	11.50	25.00	50.00	—
1808 TH	—	4.00	10.00	22.00	45.00	—

KM# 73   1/2 REAL
1.6900 g., 0.9030 Silver .0490 oz. ASW **Obv:** Armored bust of Ferdinand VII **Rev:** Pillars and arms **Note:** Mint mark M, Mo.

Date	Mintage	VG	F	VF	XF	Unc
1808 TH	—	3.50	8.00	20.00	35.00	—
1809 TH	—	3.50	8.00	20.00	35.00	—

Date	Mintage	VG	F	VF	XF	Unc
1810 TH	—	5.00	10.00	22.00	45.00	—
1810 HJ	—	3.50	8.00	20.00	35.00	—
1811 HJ	—	3.50	8.00	20.00	35.00	—
1812/1 HJ	—	7.50	15.00	35.00	80.00	—
1812 HJ	—	3.50	8.00	20.00	35.00	—
1812 JJ	—	12.00	25.00	45.00	100	—
1813/2 JJ	—	12.00	25.00	45.00	100	—
1813 JJ	—	6.00	12.00	25.00	75.00	—
1813 TH	—	3.50	8.00	20.00	35.00	—
1813 HJ	—	7.50	15.00	35.00	90.00	—
1814/3 JJ	—	7.50	15.00	35.00	90.00	—
1814 JJ	—	5.00	10.00	22.00	45.00	—

KM# 74 1/2 REAL
1.6900 g., 0.9030 Silver .0490 oz. ASW **Obv:** Draped bust of Ferdinand VII **Rev:** Pillars and arms **Note:** Mint mark M, Mo.

Date	Mintage	VG	F	VF	XF	Unc
1815 JJ	—	3.50	8.00	20.00	40.00	—
1816 JJ	—	3.50	8.00	20.00	40.00	—
1817/6 JJ	—	12.00	25.00	50.00	120	—
1817 JJ	—	3.50	8.00	28.00	45.00	—
1818/7 JJ	—	3.50	8.00	25.00	50.00	—
1818 JJ	—	3.50	8.00	25.00	50.00	—
1819/8 JJ	—	6.00	12.00	35.00	90.00	—
1819 JJ	—	3.50	8.00	20.00	40.00	—
1820 JJ	—	3.50	8.00	25.00	50.00	—
1821 JJ	—	3.50	8.00	20.00	40.00	—

KM# 75.1 REAL
3.3834 g., 0.9170 Silver .0997 oz. ASW **Obv. Legend:** PHILIP. V. D. G. HISPAN. ET IND. REX **Rev:** Pillars and arms **Note:** Struck at Mexico City Mint, mint mark M, Mo, (MX).

Date	Mintage	VG	F	VF	XF	Unc
1732 Rare	—	—	—	—	—	—
1732 F	—	—	—	—	—	—
1733 F (MX)	—	150	350	425	750	—
1733 MF (MX)	—	150	350	425	750	—
1733 F Rare	—	—	—	—	—	—
1733 MF	—	100	200	300	500	—
1734/3 MF	—	15.00	30.00	65.00	150	—
1734 MF	—	12.00	25.00	60.00	140	—
1735 MF	—	12.00	25.00	60.00	140	—
1736 MF	—	12.00	25.00	60.00	140	—
1737 MF	—	12.00	25.00	60.00	140	—
1738 MF	—	12.00	25.00	60.00	140	—
1739 MF	—	12.00	25.00	60.00	140	—
1740 MF	—	12.00	25.00	60.00	140	—
1741 MF	—	12.00	25.00	60.00	140	—

KM# 75.2 REAL
3.3834 g., 0.9170 Silver .0997 oz. ASW **Obv. Legend:** PHS. V. D. G. HISP. ET. IND. R **Note:** Struck at Mexico City Mint, mint mark M, Mo.

Date	Mintage	VG	F	VF	XF	Unc
1742 M	—	10.00	20.00	50.00	120	—
1743 M	—	10.00	20.00	50.00	120	—
1744/3 M	—	10.00	20.00	50.00	120	—
1744 M	—	10.00	20.00	50.00	120	—
1745 M	—	8.00	18.00	50.00	120	—
1746/5 M	—	12.00	25.00	75.00	200	—
1746 M	—	10.00	20.00	55.00	125	—
1747 M	—	10.00	20.00	55.00	125	—

KM# 76.1 REAL
3.3800 g., 0.9170 Silver .0996 oz. ASW **Obv:** Royal crowns **Obv. Legend:** FRD. VI. D. G. HISP. ET IND. R **Note:** Struck at Mexico City Mint, mint mark M, Mo.

Date	Mintage	VG	F	VF	XF	Unc
1747 M	—	10.00	20.00	50.00	100	—
1748/7 M	—	10.00	20.00	50.00	100	—
1748 M	—	10.00	20.00	50.00	100	—
1749 M	—	10.00	20.00	50.00	100	—
1750/40 M	—	10.00	20.00	50.00	100	—
1750 M	—	10.00	20.00	50.00	100	—
1751 M	—	10.00	20.00	55.00	110	—
1752 M	—	10.00	20.00	50.00	100	—
1753 M	—	10.00	20.00	50.00	100	—
1754 M	—	10.00	20.00	55.00	110	—
1755/4 M	—	10.00	20.00	50.00	100	—
1755 M	—	10.00	20.00	50.00	100	—
1756 M	—	10.00	20.00	55.00	110	—
1757 M	—	10.00	20.00	55.00	110	—
1758/5 M	—	10.00	20.00	50.00	100	—
1758 M	—	10.00	20.00	50.00	100	—

KM# 76.2 REAL
3.3834 g., 0.9170 Silver .0997 oz. ASW **Obv:** Royal and Imperial crowns **Note:** Struck at Mexico City Mint, mint mark M, Mo.

Date	Mintage	VG	F	VF	XF	Unc
1757 M	—	10.00	20.00	50.00	100	—
1758/7 M	—	10.00	20.00	50.00	100	—
1758 M	—	10.00	20.00	50.00	100	—
1759 M	—	10.00	20.00	55.00	110	—
1760 M	—	15.00	30.00	70.00	140	—

KM# 77 REAL
3.3800 g., 0.9170 Silver .0996 oz. ASW **Obv. Legend:** CAR. III. D. G. HISP. ET IND. R **Note:** Struck at Mexico City Mint, mint mark M, Mo.

Date	Mintage	VG	F	VF	XF	Unc
1760 M	—	10.00	20.00	50.00	100	—
1761/0 M	—	10.00	20.00	55.00	125	—
1761 M	—	10.00	20.00	50.00	100	—
1762 M	—	10.00	20.00	50.00	100	—
1763/2 M	—	12.00	25.00	60.00	120	—
1763 M	—	10.00	20.00	50.00	100	—
1764 M	—	10.00	20.00	55.00	110	—
1765 M	—	10.00	20.00	55.00	110	—
1766 M	—	10.00	20.00	50.00	100	—
1767 M	—	10.00	20.00	55.00	110	—
1768 M	—	10.00	20.00	50.00	100	—
1769 M	—	10.00	20.00	50.00	100	—
1769/70 M	—	10.00	20.00	55.00	125	—
1770 M	—	10.00	20.00	55.00	125	—
1770 F	—	20.00	40.00	90.00	250	—
1771 F	—	20.00	40.00	90.00	250	—

KM# 78.1 REAL
3.3834 g., 0.9030 Silver .0982 oz. ASW **Obv. Legend:** CAROLUS. III. DEI. GRATIA **Rev:** Inverted FM and mint mark **Note:** Struck at Mexico City Mint, mint mark M, Mo.

Date	Mintage	VG	F	VF	XF	Unc
1772 FM	—	5.00	10.00	25.00	60.00	—
1773 FM	—	5.00	10.00	25.00	60.00	—

KM# 78.2 REAL
3.3800 g., 0.9030 Silver .0981 oz. ASW **Obv:** Draped bust of Ferdinand VII **Obv. Legend:** CAROLUS. III. DEI. GRATIA **Rev. Legend:** Normal initials and mint mark **Note:** Struck at Mexico City Mint, mint mark M, Mo.

Date	Mintage	VG	F	VF	XF	Unc
1774 FM	—	5.00	10.00	25.00	60.00	—
1775/4 FM	—	6.00	12.00	28.00	75.00	—
1775 FM	—	5.00	10.00	25.00	60.00	—
1776 FM	—	5.00	10.00	25.00	60.00	—
1777 FM	—	5.00	10.00	25.00	60.00	—
1778 FF/M	—	6.00	12.00	28.00	75.00	—
1778 FF	—	5.00	10.00	25.00	60.00	—
1779 FF	—	5.00	10.00	25.00	60.00	—
1780 FF	—	5.00	10.00	25.00	60.00	—
1780 F F/M	—	5.00	10.00	25.00	60.00	—
1781 FF	—	5.00	10.00	25.00	60.00	—
1782 FF	—	5.00	10.00	25.00	60.00	—
1783 FF	—	5.00	10.00	25.00	60.00	—
1784 FF	—	5.00	10.00	25.00	60.00	—

KM# 78.2a REAL
3.3834 g., 0.8960 Silver .0975 oz. ASW **Rev:** Normal initials and mint mark **Note:** Struck at Mexico City Mint, mint mark M, Mo.

Date	Mintage	VG	F	VF	XF	Unc
1785 FF	—	6.00	12.00	28.00	75.00	—
1785 FM	—	6.00	12.00	28.00	75.00	—
1786 FM	—	6.00	12.00	28.00	75.00	—
1787 FF	—	15.00	30.00	60.00	125	—
1787 FM	—	12.00	25.00	50.00	100	—
1788 FF	—	50.00	100	200	—	—
1788 FM	—	5.00	10.00	25.00	60.00	—
1789 FM	—	6.00	12.00	28.00	75.00	—

KM# 79 REAL
3.3800 g., 0.9030 Silver .0981 oz. ASW **Obv:** Armored bust of Charles III **Obv. Legend:** CAROLUS. IV... **Note:** Struck at Mexico City Mint, mint mark M, Mo.

Date	Mintage	VG	F	VF	XF	Unc
1789 FM	—	15.00	30.00	60.00	150	—
1790 FM	—	15.00	30.00	60.00	150	—

KM# 80 REAL
3.3800 g., 0.9030 Silver .0981 oz. ASW **Obv:** Armored bust of Charles III **Obv. Legend:** CAROLUS. IIII **Note:** Struck at Mexico City Mint, mint mark M, Mo.

Date	Mintage	VG	F	VF	XF	Unc
1790 FM	—	17.00	35.00	70.00	165	—

KM# 81 REAL
3.3834 g., 0.8960 Silver .0975 oz. ASW **Obv:** Armored bust of Charles IIII **Note:** Mint mark M, Mo.

Date	Mintage	VG	F	VF	XF	Unc
1792 FM	—	10.00	20.00	35.00	90.00	—
1793 FM	—	15.00	30.00	60.00	150	—
1794 FM	—	25.00	50.00	100	250	—
1795 FM	—	15.00	30.00	60.00	150	—
1796 FM	—	5.00	10.00	25.00	65.00	—
1797/6 FM	—	8.00	15.00	28.00	80.00	—
1797 FM	—	5.00	10.00	25.00	60.00	—
1798/7 FM	—	5.00	10.00	25.00	65.00	—
1798 FM	—	5.00	10.00	25.00	60.00	—
1799 FM	—	5.00	10.00	25.00	60.00	—
1800 FM	—	5.00	10.00	25.00	60.00	—
1801 FT/M	—	5.00	10.00	25.00	60.00	—
1801 FM	—	8.00	15.00	28.00	80.00	—
1801 FT	—	5.00	10.00	25.00	60.00	—
1802 FM	—	5.00	10.00	25.00	60.00	—
1802 FT	—	5.00	10.00	25.00	60.00	—
1802/1 FT	—	5.00	10.00	25.00	60.00	—
1802 FT/M	—	5.00	10.00	25.00	60.00	—
1803 FT	—	5.00	10.00	25.00	60.00	—
1804 TH	—	5.00	10.00	25.00	60.00	—
1805 TH	—	5.00	10.00	25.00	60.00	—
1806 TH	—	5.00	10.00	25.00	60.00	—
1807/6 TH	—	5.00	10.00	25.00	65.00	—
1807 TH	—	5.00	10.00	25.00	60.00	—
1808/7 TH	—	5.00	10.00	25.00	65.00	—
1808 FM	—	5.00	10.00	25.00	60.00	—

KM# 82 REAL
3.3800 g., 0.9030 Silver .0981 oz. ASW **Obv:** Armored bust of Ferdinand VII **Note:** Mint mark M, Mo.

Date	Mintage	VG	F	VF	XF	Unc
1809 TH	—	8.00	15.00	28.00	90.00	—
1810/09 TH	—	8.00	15.00	28.00	90.00	—
1810 TH	—	8.00	15.00	28.00	90.00	—
1811 TH	—	25.00	35.00	60.00	250	—
1811 HJ	—	8.00	15.00	28.00	90.00	—
1812 HJ	—	4.00	9.00	28.00	80.00	—
1812 JJ	—	10.00	20.00	40.00	120	—
1813 HJ	—	10.00	20.00	40.00	120	—
1813 JJ	—	50.00	100	150	250	—
1814 HJ	—	15.00	30.00	150	150	—
1814 JJ	—	50.00	100	175	300	—

KM# 83 REAL
3.3800 g., 0.9030 Silver .0981 oz. ASW **Obv:** Draped bust of Ferdinand VII **Note:** Mint mark M, Mo.

Date	Mintage	VG	F	VF	XF	Unc
1814 JJ	—	25.00	50.00	100	350	—
1815 HJ	—	15.00	30.00	60.00	150	—
1815 JJ	—	10.00	20.00	40.00	120	—
1816 JJ	—	5.00	10.00	25.00	70.00	—
1817 JJ	—	5.00	10.00	25.00	70.00	—

Date	Mintage	VG	F	VF	XF	Unc
1818 JJ	—	30.00	60.00	125	500	—
1819 JJ	—	5.00	10.00	25.00	70.00	—
1820 JJ	—	5.00	10.00	25.00	70.00	—
1821/0 JJ	—	8.00	15.00	30.00	110	—
1821 JJ	—	5.00	10.00	25.00	50.00	—

KM# 84   2 REALES
6.7668 g., 0.9170 Silver .1995 oz. ASW   **Obv. Legend:**
PHILIP. V. D. G. HISPAN. ET IND. REX **Note:** Struck at
Mexico City Mint, mint mark M, Mo, (MX).

Date	Mintage	VG	F	VF	XF	Unc
1732 Rare	—	—	—	—	—	—
1732 F	—	800	1,300	1,750	2,750	—
1733 F	—	600	800	1,350	2,250	—
1733 MF (MX)	—	350	600	1,000	1,650	—
1733 MF	—	600	900	1,500	2,500	—
1734/3 MF	—	20.00	40.00	85.00	170	—
1734 MF	—	20.00	40.00	85.00	170	—
1735/3 MF	—	15.00	30.00	75.00	150	—
1735/4 MF	—	15.00	30.00	75.00	150	—
1735 MF	—	15.00	30.00	75.00	150	—
1736/3 MF	—	18.00	35.00	80.00	160	—
1736/4 MF	—	18.00	35.00	80.00	160	—
1736/5 MF	—	18.00	35.00	80.00	160	—
1736 MF	—	18.00	35.00	80.00	160	—
1737/3 MF	—	18.00	35.00	80.00	160	—
1737 MF	—	18.00	35.00	80.00	160	—
1738/7 MF	—	18.00	35.00	80.00	160	—
1738 MF	—	18.00	35.00	80.00	160	—
1739 MF	—	18.00	35.00	80.00	160	—
1740/30 MF	—	18.00	35.00	80.00	160	—
1740 MF	—	18.00	35.00	80.00	160	—
1741 MF	—	18.00	35.00	80.00	160	—

KM# 85   2 REALES
6.7700 g., 0.9170 Silver .1996 oz. ASW   **Obv. Legend:** PHS.
V. D. G. HISP. ET IND. R **Note:** Struck at Mexico City Mint,
mint mark M, Mo.

Date	Mintage	F	VF	XF	Unc	BU
1742 M	—	30.00	75.00	125	—	—
1743/2 M	—	30.00	75.00	125	—	—
1743 M	—	30.00	75.00	125	—	—
1744/3 M	—	30.00	75.00	125	—	—
1744 M	—	30.00	75.00	125	—	—
1745/4 M	—	30.00	75.00	125	—	—
1745 M	—	30.00	75.00	125	—	—
1745 M HIP	—	400	—	—	—	—
1746/5 M	—	30.00	75.00	125	—	—
1746 M	—	30.00	75.00	125	—	—
1747 M	—	30.00	75.00	125	—	—
1750 M	—	450	650	1,000	—	—

KM# 86.1   2 REALES
6.7668 g., 0.9170 Silver .1995 oz. ASW   **Obv:** Royal crowns
Obv. Legend: FRD. VI. D. G. HISP. ET IND. R **Note:** Struck
at Mexico City Mint, mint mark M, Mo.

Date	Mintage	VG	F	VF	XF	Unc
1747 M	—	16.00	32.00	78.00	135	—
1748/7 M	—	16.00	32.00	78.00	135	—

Date	Mintage	VG	F	VF	XF	Unc
1748 M	—	15.00	30.00	75.00	125	—
1749 M	—	15.00	30.00	75.00	125	—
1750 M	—	15.00	30.00	75.00	125	—
1751/41 M	—	18.00	35.00	80.00	150	—
1751 M	—	15.00	30.00	75.00	125	—
1752 M	—	15.00	30.00	75.00	125	—
1753/2 M	—	18.00	35.00	80.00	150	—
1753 M	—	18.00	35.00	80.00	150	—
1754 M	—	18.00	35.00	80.00	150	—
1755/4 M	—	18.00	35.00	80.00	150	—
1755 M	—	18.00	35.00	80.00	150	—
1756/55 M	—	18.00	35.00	80.00	150	—
1756 M	—	18.00	35.00	80.00	140	—
1757/6 M	—	15.00	30.00	75.00	125	—
1757 M	—	18.00	35.00	80.00	150	—

KM# 86.2   2 REALES
6.7668 g., 0.9170 Silver .1995 oz. ASW **Obv:** Royal and Imperial
crowns **Note:** Struck at Mexico City Mint, mint mark M, Mo.

Date	Mintage	VG	F	VF	XF	Unc
1757 M	—	15.00	30.00	75.00	125	—
1758 M	—	15.00	30.00	75.00	125	—
1759/8 M	—	15.00	30.00	75.00	125	—
1759 M	—	20.00	40.00	90.00	175	—
1760 M	—	20.00	40.00	90.00	175	—

KM# 87   2 REALES
6.7700 g., 0.9170 Silver .1996 oz. ASW **Obv. Legend:** CAR.
III. D. G. HISP. ET IND. R **Note:** Struck at Mexico City Mint,
mint mark M, Mo.

Date	Mintage	VG	F	VF	XF	Unc
1760 M	—	15.00	30.00	75.00	125	—
1761 M	—	15.00	30.00	75.00	125	—
1762/1 M	—	15.00	30.00	75.00	125	—
1762 M	—	15.00	30.00	75.00	125	—
1763/2 M	—	15.00	30.00	75.00	125	—
1763 M	—	15.00	30.00	75.00	125	—
1764 M	—	15.00	30.00	75.00	125	—
1765 M	—	15.00	30.00	75.00	125	—
1766 M	—	12.00	35.00	80.00	160	—
1767 M	—	15.00	30.00	75.00	125	—
1768/6 M	—	15.00	30.00	75.00	125	—
1768 M	—	15.00	30.00	75.00	125	—
1769 M	—	15.00	30.00	75.00	125	—
1770 M	—	350	550	—	—	—
1770 F Rare	—	—	—	—	—	—
1771 F	—	15.00	30.00	75.00	125	—

KM# 88.1   2 REALES
6.7668 g., 0.9170 Silver .1964 oz. ASW **Obv. Legend:**
CAROLUS. III. DEI. GRATIA **Rev:** Inverted FM and mint mark
Note: Struck at Mexico City Mint, mint mark M, Mo.

Date	Mintage	VG	F	VF	XF	Unc
1772 FM	—	7.00	15.00	30.00	100	—
1773 FM	—	7.00	15.00	30.00	100	—

KM# 88.2   2 REALES
6.7700 g., 0.9030 Silver .1965 oz. ASW   **Rev:** Normal initials
and mint mark **Note:** Struck at Mexico City Mint, mint mark M, Mo.

Date	Mintage	VG	F	VF	XF	Unc
1773 FM	—	7.00	15.00	30.00	100	—
1774 FM	—	7.00	15.00	30.00	100	—
1775 FM	—	7.00	15.00	30.00	100	—
1776 FM	—	7.00	15.00	30.00	100	—
1777 FM	—	7.00	15.00	30.00	100	—
1778/7 FF	—	7.00	15.00	30.00	100	—
1778 FF	—	7.00	15.00	30.00	100	—
1779/8 FF	—	7.00	15.00	30.00	100	—
1779 FF	—	7.00	15.00	30.00	100	—
1780 FF	—	7.00	15.00	30.00	100	—
1781 FF	—	7.00	15.00	30.00	100	—
1782/1 FF	—	7.00	15.00	30.00	100	—
1782 FF	—	7.00	15.00	30.00	100	—
1783 FF	—	7.00	15.00	30.00	100	—
1784 FF	—	7.00	15.00	30.00	100	—
1784 FF DEI GRTIA (error)	—	100	150	250	600	—
1784 FF	—	70.00	120	225	575	—

KM# 88.2a 2 REALES
6.7668 g., 0.8960 Silver .1949 oz. ASW **Note:** Struck at Mexico City Mint, mint mark Mo.

Date	Mintage	VG	F	VF	XF	Unc
1785Mo FM	—	7.00	15.00	30.00	100	—
1786Mo FF	—	200	350	550	950	—
1786Mo FM	—	7.00	15.00	30.00	100	—
1787Mo FM	—	7.00	15.00	30.00	100	—
1788/98Mo FM	—	7.00	15.00	30.00	100	—
1788Mo FM	—	7.00	15.00	30.00	100	—
1789Mo FM	—	12.00	25.00	50.00	150	—

KM# 89 2 REALES
6.7700 g., 0.9030 Silver .1965 oz. ASW **Obv:** Armored bust of Charles III **Obv. Legend:** CAROLUS. IV... **Note:** Struck at Mexico City Mint, mint mark M, Mo.

Date	Mintage	VG	F	VF	XF	Unc
1789 FM	—	15.00	30.00	75.00	200	—
1790 FM	—	15.00	30.00	75.00	200	—

KM# 90 2 REALES
6.7700 g., 0.9030 Silver .1965 oz. ASW **Obv:** Armored bust of Charles III **Obv. Legend:** CAROLUS. IIII... **Note:** Struck at Mexico City Mint, mint mark M, Mo.

Date	Mintage	VG	F	VF	XF	Unc
1790 FM	—	17.00	35.00	80.00	200	—

KM# 91 2 REALES
6.7668 g., 0.8960 Silver .1949 oz. ASW **Obv:** Armored bust of Carolus IIII **Note:** Mint mark M, Mo.

Date	Mintage	VG	F	VF	XF	Unc
1792 FM	—	15.00	30.00	60.00	200	—
1793 FM	—	15.00	30.00	60.00	200	—
1794/3 FM	—	50.00	100	200	450	—
1794 FM	—	40.00	75.00	150	400	—
1795 FM	—	7.00	15.00	30.00	85.00	—
1796 FM	—	7.00	15.00	30.00	85.00	—
1797 FM	—	7.00	15.00	30.00	85.00	—
1798 FM	—	7.00	15.00	30.00	85.00	—
1799/8 FM	—	7.00	15.00	32.00	90.00	—
1799 FM	—	7.00	15.00	30.00	85.00	—

Date	Mintage	VG	F	VF	XF	Unc
1800 FM	—	7.00	15.00	30.00	85.00	—
1801 FT/M	—	7.00	15.00	30.00	85.00	—
1801 FT	—	7.00	15.00	30.00	85.00	—
1801 FM	—	20.00	40.00	75.00	250	—
1802 FT	—	7.00	15.00	30.00	85.00	—
1803 FT	—	7.00	15.00	30.00	85.00	—
1804/3 TH	—	7.00	15.00	30.00	85.00	—
1804 TH	—	7.00	15.00	30.00	85.00	—
1805 TH	—	7.00	15.00	30.00	85.00	—
1806/5 TH	—	7.00	15.00	32.00	90.00	—
1806 TH	—	7.00	15.00	30.00	85.00	—
1807/5 TH	—	7.00	15.00	32.00	90.00	—
1807/6 TH	—	15.00	30.00	60.00	200	—
1807 TH	—	7.00	15.00	30.00	85.00	—
1808/7 TH	—	7.00	15.00	32.00	90.00	—
1808 TH	—	7.00	15.00	30.00	85.00	—

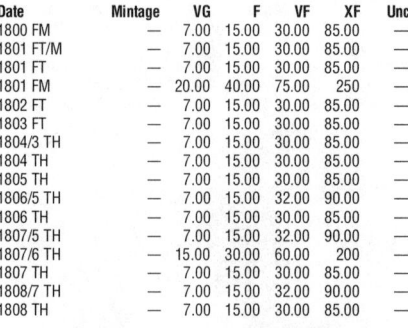

KM# 92 2 REALES
6.7700 g., 0.9030 Silver .1965 oz. ASW **Obv:** Armored bust of Ferdinand VII **Note:** Mint mark M, Mo.

Date	Mintage	VG	F	VF	XF	Unc
1809 TH	—	15.00	30.00	75.00	200	—
181/00 TH	—	15.00	30.00	75.00	200	—
181/00 HJ/TH	—	15.00	30.00	75.00	200	—
1810 TH	—	15.00	30.00	75.00	200	—
181/00 HJ	—	15.00	30.00	75.00	200	—
1810 HJ	—	15.00	30.00	75.00	200	—
1811 TH	—	150	250	350	750	—
1811 HJ/TH	—	40.00	80.00	150	300	—
1811 HJ	—	15.00	30.00	75.00	200	—

KM# 93 2 REALES
6.7700 g., 0.9030 Silver .1965 oz. ASW **Obv:** Draped bust of Ferdinand VII **Note:** Mint mark M, Mo.

Date	Mintage	VG	F	VF	XF	Unc
1812 TH	—	60.00	125	250	550	—
1812 HJ	—	40.00	100	200	500	—
1812 JJ	—	10.00	20.00	60.00	200	—
1813 TH	—	15.00	30.00	100	400	—
1813 JJ	—	20.00	60.00	125	350	—
1813 HJ	—	40.00	100	200	500	—
1814/2 JJ	—	15.00	30.00	100	400	—
1814 JJ	—	15.00	30.00	100	400	—
1815 JJ	—	6.00	12.00	28.00	85.00	—
1816 JJ	—	6.00	12.00	28.00	85.00	—
1817 JJ	—	6.00	12.00	28.00	85.00	—
1818 JJ	—	6.00	12.00	28.00	85.00	—
1819/8 JJ	—	5.50	12.00	30.00	85.00	—
1819 JJ	—	6.00	12.00	28.00	85.00	—
1820 JJ	—	175	—	—	—	—

Date	Mintage	VG	F	VF	XF	Unc
1821/0 JJ	—	7.00	15.00	30.00	90.00	—
1821 JJ	—	6.00	12.00	28.00	85.00	—

KM# 94   4 REALES
13.5337 g., 0.9170 Silver .3990 oz. ASW **Obv. Legend:** PHILLIP. V. D. G. HISPAN. ET IND. REX **Note:** Mint mark M, Mo, (MX).

Date	Mintage	VG	F	VF	XF	Unc
1732 Rare; Specimen	—	—	—	—	—	—
1732 F	—	2,000	3,000	5,000	10,000	—
1733/2 F	—	1,500	2,000	4,000	6,500	—
1733 MF	—	1,100	1,650	2,250	4,250	—
1733 MF (MX)	—	1,500	2,200	3,250	5,500	—
1733 MX/XM	—	1,500	2,200	3,250	5,500	—
1734/3 MF	—	150	300	600	1,200	—
1734 MF	—	150	300	600	1,200	—
1735/4 MF	—	100	175	300	600	—
1735 MF	—	100	175	300	600	—
1736 MF	—	100	175	300	600	—
1737 MF	—	100	175	300	600	—
1738/7 MF	—	100	175	300	600	—
1738 MF	—	100	175	300	600	—
1739 MF	—	100	175	300	600	—
1740/30 MF	—	100	200	325	625	—
1740 MF	—	100	175	300	600	—
1741 MF	—	100	175	300	600	—
1742/1 MF	—	100	175	300	600	—
1742/32 MF	—	100	175	300	600	—
1742 MF	—	100	175	300	600	—
1743 MF	—	100	175	300	600	—
1744/3 MF	—	100	200	325	625	—
1744 MF	—	100	175	300	600	—
1745 MF	—	100	175	300	600	—
1746 MF	—	100	175	300	600	—
1747 MF	—	150	275	400	650	—

KM# 95   4 REALES
13.5400 g., 0.9170 Silver .3992 oz. ASW **Obv. Legend:** FERDND. VI. D. G. HISPAN. ET IND. REX **Note:** Struck at Mexico City Mint, mint mark M, Mo.

Date	Mintage	VG	F	VF	XF	Unc
1747 MF	—	100	150	300	550	—
1748/7 MF	—	100	150	300	550	—
1748 MF	—	100	125	250	500	—
1749 MF	—	150	225	350	650	—
1750/40 MF	—	100	125	250	500	—

Date	Mintage	VG	F	VF	XF	Unc
1751/41 MF	—	100	125	250	500	—
1751 MF	—	100	125	250	500	—
1752 MF	—	100	125	250	500	—
1753 MF	—	100	125	300	550	—
1754 MF	—	250	375	500	850	—
1755 MM	—	100	125	250	500	—
1756 MM	—	100	150	300	550	—
1757 MM	—	100	150	300	550	—
1758 MM	—	100	125	250	500	—
1759 MM	—	100	125	250	500	—
1760/59 MM	—	100	175	350	600	—
1760 MM	—	100	175	350	600	—

KM# 96   4 REALES
13.5400 g., 0.9170 Silver .3992 oz. ASW **Obv. Legend:** CAROLVS. III. D. G. HISPAN. ET IND. REX **Note:** Struck at Mexico City Mint, mint mark M, Mo.

Date	Mintage	VG	F	VF	XF	Unc
1760 MM	—	100	150	250	900	—
1761 MM	—	100	150	250	900	—
1761 MM Cross between H and I	—	100	150	250	900	—
1762 MM	—	75.00	125	250	500	—
1763/1 MM	—	100	150	300	600	—
1763 MM	—	100	150	300	600	—
1764 MM	—	400	600	1,000	2,000	—
1764 MF	—	350	500	1,000	2,000	—
1765 MF	—	350	500	1,000	2,000	—
1766 MF	—	250	350	550	1,250	—
1767 MF	—	100	150	300	600	—
1768 MF	—	75.00	125	250	500	—
1769 MF	—	75.00	125	250	500	—
1770 MF	—	75.00	125	250	500	—
1771 MF	—	125	200	325	700	—

KM# 97.1   4 REALES
13.5337 g., 0.9030 Silver .3929 oz. ASW **Obv. Legend:** CAROLUS. III. DEI. GRATIA **Rev:** Inverted FM and mint mark **Note:** Struck at Mexico City Mint, mint mark M, Mo.

Date	Mintage	VG	F	VF	XF	Unc
1772 FM	—	90.00	125	250	500	—
1773 FM	—	100	175	300	650	—

KM# 97.2   4 REALES
13.5400 g., 0.9030 Silver .3931 oz. ASW **Obv. Legend:**
CAROLUS. III. DEI. GRATIA **Rev:** Normal initials and mint
mark **Note:** Struck at Mexico City Mint, mint mark M, Mo.

Date	Mintage	VG	F	VF	XF	Unc
1774 FM	—	50.00	100	200	500	—
1775 FM	—	50.00	100	200	500	—
1776 FM	—	50.00	100	200	500	—
1777 FM	—	50.00	100	200	500	—
1778 FF	—	50.00	100	200	500	—
1779 FF	—	50.00	100	200	500	—
1780 FF	—	50.00	100	200	500	—
1781 FF	—	50.00	100	200	500	—
1782 FF	—	50.00	100	200	500	—
1783 FF	—	50.00	100	200	500	—
1784 FF	—	50.00	100	200	500	—
1784 FM	—	100	200	350	600	—

KM# 97.2a   4 REALES
13.5337 g., 0.8960 Silver .3899 oz. ASW **Rev:** Normal initials
and mint mark **Note:** Struck at Mexico City Mint, mint mark M, Mo.

Date	Mintage	VG	F	VF	XF	Unc
1785 FM	—	100	200	350	600	—
1786 FM	—	50.00	100	200	500	—
1787 FM	—	50.00	100	200	500	—
1788 FM	—	50.00	100	200	500	—
1789 FM	—	50.00	100	200	500	—

KM# 98   4 REALES
13.5400 g., 0.9030 Silver .3931 oz. ASW **Obv:** Armored bust
of Charles III **Obv. Legend:** CAROLUS. IV... **Note:** Struck at
Mexico City Mint, mint mark M, Mo.

Date	Mintage	VG	F	VF	XF	Unc
1789 FM	—	65.00	125	250	550	—
1790 FM	—	50.00	100	200	500	—

KM# 99   4 REALES
13.5400 g., 0.9030 Silver .3931 oz. ASW **Obv:** Armored bust
of Charles III **Obv. Legend:** CAROLUS. IIII... **Note:** Struck at
Mexico City Mint, mint mark M, Mo.

Date	Mintage	VG	F	VF	XF	Unc
1790 FM	—	65.00	125	250	550	—

KM# 100   4 REALES
13.5337 g., 0.8960 Silver .3899 oz. ASW **Obv:** Armored bust
of Charles IIII **Rev:** Pillars, arms **Note:** Mint mark M, Mo.

Date	Mintage	VG	F	VF	XF	Unc
1792 FM	—	35.00	65.00	150	400	—
1793 FM	—	75.00	125	200	500	—
1794/3 FM	—	35.00	65.00	150	400	—
1794 FM	—	35.00	65.00	150	400	—
1795 FM	—	35.00	65.00	150	400	—
1796 FM	—	150	250	400	800	—
1797 FM	—	60.00	120	200	500	—
1798/7 FM	—	35.00	65.00	150	400	—
1798 FM	—	35.00	65.00	150	400	—
1799 FM	—	35.00	65.00	150	400	—
1800 FM	—	35.00	65.00	150	400	—
1801 FM	—	35.00	65.00	150	400	—
1801 FT	—	60.00	120	200	500	—
1802 FT	—	200	300	500	1,000	—
1803 FT	—	75.00	135	225	550	—
1803 FM	—	200	300	500	1,000	—

Date	Mintage	VG	F	VF	XF	Unc
1804 TH	—	40.00	75.00	175	450	—
1805 TH	—	35.00	65.00	150	400	—
1806 TH	—	35.00	65.00	150	400	—
1807 TH	—	35.00	65.00	150	400	—
1808/7 TH	—	40.00	75.00	175	450	—
1808 TH	—	40.00	75.00	175	450	—

KM# 101 4 REALES
13.5400 g., 0.9030 Silver .3931 oz. ASW **Obv:** Armored bust of Ferdinand VII **Note:** Mint mark M, Mo.

Date	Mintage	VG	F	VF	XF	Unc
1809 HJ	—	75.00	135	250	750	—
1810 HJ	—	75.00	135	250	750	—
1811 HJ	—	75.00	135	250	750	—
1812 HJ	—	400	650	900	1,850	—

KM# 102 4 REALES
13.5400 g., 0.9030 Silver .3931 oz. ASW **Obv:** Draped bust of Ferdinand VII **Note:** Mint mark M, Mo.

Date	Mintage	VG	F	VF	XF	Unc
1816 JJ	—	150	200	325	700	—
1817 JJ	—	250	400	500	1,000	—
1818/7 JJ	—	250	400	500	1,000	—
1819 JJ	—	175	250	325	700	—
1820 JJ	—	175	250	325	700	—
1821 JJ	—	75.00	135	250	650	—

KM# 103 8 REALES
27.0674 g., 0.9170 Silver .7980 oz. ASW **Obv. Legend:** PHILIP. V. D. G. HISPAN. ET IND. REX **Note:** Struck at Mexico City Mint, mint mark M, Mo, (MX).

Date	Mintage	VG	F	VF	XF	Unc
1732 F	—	2,750	4,750	8,000	—	—
1733/2 F (MX)	—	3,000	5,250	9,000	—	—
1733 F	—	2,000	3,000	5,000	9,000	—
1733 MF Large crown; Rare	—	—	—	—	—	—
1733 F (MX) Rare	—	—	—	—	—	—
Note: Rare; Bonhams Patterson sale 7-96 VF 1733 F (MX) realized $11,710						
1733 MF (MX) Rare	—	—	—	—	—	—
1733 MF Small crown	—	700	1,500	2,500	4,250	—
1734/3 MF	—	100	150	275	575	—
1734 MF	—	100	150	250	450	—
1735 MF	—	100	150	250	450	—
1736/5 MF	—	100	150	275	575	—
1736 MF Small planchet	—	100	150	250	450	—
1736 MF	—	100	150	250	450	—
1737 MF	—	65.00	100	200	400	—
1738/6 MF	—	65.00	100	200	400	—
1738/7 MF	—	65.00	100	200	400	—
1738 MF	—	65.00	100	200	400	—
1739/6 MF 9 over inverted 6	—	65.00	100	200	400	—
1739 MF	—	65.00	100	200	400	—
1740/30 MF	—	100	150	275	500	—
1740/39 MF	—	100	150	275	500	—
1740 MF	—	65.00	100	200	400	—
1741/31 MF	—	65.00	100	200	400	—
1741 MF	—	65.00	100	200	400	—
1742/32 MF	—	75.00	125	220	500	—
1742/1 MF	—	65.00	100	200	400	—
1742 MF	—	65.00	100	200	400	—
1743/2 MF	—	65.00	100	200	400	—
1743 MF	—	65.00	100	200	400	—
1744/34 MF	—	65.00	100	200	400	—
1744/3 MF	—	65.00	100	200	400	—
1744 MF	—	65.00	100	200	400	—
1745/4 MF	—	65.00	100	200	425	—
1745 MF	—	65.00	100	200	400	—
1746/5 MF	—	100	150	275	575	—
1746 MF	—	65.00	100	200	400	—
1747 MF	—	65.00	100	200	400	—

KM# 104.1   8 REALES
27.0674 g., 0.9170 Silver .7980 oz. ASW **Obv. Legend:**
FERDND. VI. D. G. HISPAN. ET IND. REX **Rev:** With Royal
crown on left pillar **Note:** Struck at Mexico City Mint, mint mark
M, Mo.

Date	Mintage	VG	F	VF	XF	Unc
1747 MF	—	55.00	100	175	300	—
1748/7 MF	—	60.00	120	250	450	—
1748 MF	—	50.00	75.00	125	250	—
1749 MF	—	50.00	75.00	125	250	—
1749/8 MF	—	50.00	75.00	125	250	—
1750 MF	—	50.00	75.00	125	250	—
1751/0 MF	—	55.00	100	165	275	—
1751 MF	—	50.00	75.00	125	250	—
1752/1 MF	—	55.00	100	165	275	—
1752 MF	—	50.00	75.00	125	250	—
1753/2 MF	—	50.00	75.00	125	250	—
1753 MF	—	55.00	100	165	275	—
1754/3 MF	—	55.00	100	185	325	—
1754 MF	—	50.00	75.00	125	250	—
1754 MM/MF	—	300	700	1,500	3,500	—
1754 MM	—	300	700	1,500	3,500	—

KM# 104.2   8 REALES
27.0674 g., 0.9170 Silver .7980 oz. ASW **Obv. Legend:**
FERDND. VI. D. G. HISPAN. ET IND. REX **Rev:** Imperial crown
on left pillar **Note:** Struck at Mexico City Mint, mint mark M, Mo.

Date	Mintage	VG	F	VF	XF	Unc
1754 MM	—	60.00	110	200	375	—
1754 MM/MF	—	75.00	125	250	500	—
1754 MF	—	150	285	550	950	—
1755/4 MM	—	55.00	100	185	325	—
1755 MM	—	50.00	75.00	125	250	—
1756/5 MM	—	55.00	100	165	275	—
1756 MM	—	50.00	75.00	125	250	—
1757/6 MM	—	50.00	75.00	125	250	—
1757 MM	—	55.00	100	185	325	—
1758 MM	—	50.00	75.00	125	250	—
1759 MM	—	50.00	75.00	125	250	—
1760/59 MM	—	55.00	100	165	275	—
1760 MM	—	50.00	75.00	125	250	—

KM# 105   8 REALES
27.0674 g., 0.9170 Silver .7980 oz. ASW **Obv. Legend:**
CAROLUS. III. D. G. HISPAN. ET IND. REX **Note:** Struck at
Mexico City Mint, mint mark M, Mo.

Date	Mintage	VG	F	VF	XF	Unc
1760/59 MM CAROLUS. III/Ferdin. Vi	—	450	700	—	—	—
1760 MM CAROLUS. III/FERDIN. VI. recut die	—	60.00	100	150	325	—
1760 MM	—	60.00	100	150	300	—
1761/50 MM Tip of cross between I and S in legend	—	65.00	110	165	325	—
1761/51 MM Tip of cross between I and S in legend	—	65.00	110	165	325	—
1761/0 MM Tip of cross between H and I in legend	—	65.00	110	165	325	—
1761 MM Cross under I in legend	—	60.00	100	150	275	—
1761 MM Tip of cross between H and I in legend	—	60.00	100	150	275	—
1761 MM Tip of cross between I and S in legend	—	65.00	110	165	325	—
1762/1 MM Tip of cross between H and I in legend	—	70.00	120	175	450	—
1762/1 MM	—	70.00	120	175	450	—
1762 MM Tip of cross between H and I in legend	—	60.00	100	150	275	—
1762 MM Tip of cross between I and S in legend	—	50.00	75.00	125	250	—
1762 MF	—	500	750	1,250	2,300	—
1763/2 MM	—	300	450	750	1,350	—
1763 MM	—	450	650	1,150	2,250	—
1763/1 MF	—	50.00	75.00	125	250	—
1763/2 MF	—	50.00	75.00	125	250	—
1763 MF	—	50.00	75.00	125	250	—
1764 MF CAR/CRA	—	50.00	75.00	125	250	—

Date	Mintage	VG	F	VF	XF	Unc
1764 MF	—	50.00	75.00	125	250	—
1765 MF	—	50.00	75.00	125	250	—
1766/5 MF	—	75.00	150	225	575	—
1766 MF	—	50.00	75.00	125	250	—
1767/6 MF	—	50.00	75.00	125	250	—
1767 MF	—	50.00	75.00	125	250	—
1768/7 MF	—	85.00	165	250	600	—
1768 MF	—	50.00	75.00	125	250	—
1769 MF	—	50.00	75.00	125	250	—
1770/60 MF	—	100	185	300	650	—
1770 MF	—	50.00	75.00	125	250	—
1770/60 FM	—	100	185	300	650	—
1770/69 FM	—	100	185	300	650	—
1770 FM/F	—	50.00	75.00	125	250	—
1770 FM	—	50.00	75.00	125	250	—
1771/0 FM	—	50.00	75.00	125	250	—
1771 FM	—	50.00	75.00	125	250	—

Date	Mintage	VG	F	VF	XF	Unc
1784 FF	—	150	300	500	1,250	—
1784 FM	—	25.00	45.00	75.00	150	—

KM# 106.2a 8 REALES
27.0674 g., 0.8960 Silver .7797 oz. ASW **Obv. Legend:**
CAROLUS.III.DEI.GRATIA **Rev:** Normal initials and mint
mark **Note:** Struck at Mexico City Mint, mint mark M, Mo.

Date	Mintage	VG	F	VF	XF	Unc
1785 FM	—	25.00	45.00	75.00	150	—
1786/5 FM	—	50.00	100	200	400	—
1786 FM	—	25.00	45.00	75.00	150	—
1787/6 FM	—	100	250	450	1,200	—
1787 FM	—	25.00	45.00	75.00	150	—
1788 FM	—	25.00	45.00	75.00	150	—
1789 FM	—	50.00	100	150	225	—

KM# 106.1 8 REALES
27.0674 g., 0.9030 Silver .7858 oz. ASW **Obv. Legend:**
CAROLUS. III. DEI. GRATIA **Rev:** Inverted initials and mint
mark **Note:** Two varieties exist, one with inverted initials "F.M."
(left), and one with normal presentation (right). Struck at
Mexico City Mint, mint mark M, Mo.

Date	Mintage	VG	F	VF	XF	Unc
1772 FM	—	25.00	50.00	120	250	—
1772 MF	—	150	350	750	1,250	—
1773 FM	—	25.00	50.00	100	175	—

KM# 106.2 8 REALES
27.0674 g., 0.9030 Silver .7858 oz. ASW **Obv. Legend:**
CAROLUS. III. DEI. GRATIA **Rev:** Normal initials and mint
mark **Note:** Struck at Mexico City Mint, mint mark M, Mo.

Date	Mintage	VG	F	VF	XF	Unc
1773 FM	—	25.00	50.00	80.00	160	—
1774 FM	—	25.00	45.00	75.00	150	—
1775 FM	—	25.00	45.00	75.00	150	—
1776 FM	—	25.00	45.00	75.00	150	—
1777/6 FM	—	35.00	65.00	180	300	—
1777 FM	—	25.00	45.00	75.00	150	—
1777 FF	—	35.00	50.00	100	250	—
1778 FM	—	—	—	—	—	—

Note: Superior Casterline sale 5-89 VF realized $17,600

Date	Mintage	VG	F	VF	XF	Unc
1778/7 FF	—	25.00	45.00	75.00	150	—
1778 FF	—	25.00	45.00	75.00	150	—
1779 FF	—	25.00	45.00	75.00	150	—
1780 FF	—	25.00	45.00	75.00	150	—
1781 FF	—	25.00	45.00	75.00	150	—
1782 FF	—	25.00	45.00	75.00	150	—
1783 FF	—	25.00	45.00	75.00	150	—
1783 FM	—	4,000	6,000	9,000	—	—

KM# 107 8 REALES
27.0674 g., 0.9030 Silver .7858 oz. ASW **Obv:** Armored bust
of Charles III **Obv. Legend:** CAROLUS. IV... **Note:** Struck at
Mexico City Mint, mint mark M, Mo.

Date	Mintage	VG	F	VF	XF	Unc
1789 FM	—	40.00	65.00	120	250	—
1790 FM	—	30.00	50.00	100	200	—

KM# 108   8 REALES
27.0674 g., 0.9030 Silver .7858 oz. ASW **Obv:** Armored bust of Charles III **Obv. Legend:** CAROLUS. IIII **Note:** Struck at Mexico City Mint, mint mark M, Mo.

Date	Mintage	VG	F	VF	XF	Unc
1790 FM	—	30.00	50.00	100	200	—

KM# 109   8 REALES
27.0674 g., 0.8960 Silver .7797 oz. ASW **Obv:** Armored bust of Charles IIII **Note:** Mint mark M, Mo.

Date	Mintage	VG	F	VF	XF	Unc
1791 FM	—	20.00	35.00	50.00	100	—
1792 FM	—	20.00	35.00	50.00	100	—
1793 FM	—	20.00	35.00	50.00	100	—
1794 FM	—	20.00	35.00	50.00	100	—
1795/4 FM	—	20.00	35.00	50.00	100	—
1795 FM	—	20.00	35.00	50.00	100	—
1796 FM	—	20.00	35.00	50.00	100	—
1797 FM	—	20.00	35.00	50.00	100	—
1798 FM	—	20.00	35.00	50.00	100	—
1799 FM	—	20.00	35.00	50.00	100	—
1800/700 FM	—	20.00	35.00	50.00	100	—
1800 FM	—	20.00	35.00	50.00	100	—
1801/0 FT/FM	—	20.00	35.00	50.00	100	—
1801/791 FM	—	35.00	60.00	100	250	—
1801/0 FM	—	35.00	60.00	100	250	—
1801 FM	—	20.00	40.00	100	250	—
1801 FT/M	—	35.00	60.00	100	250	—
1801 FT	—	20.00	35.00	50.00	100	—
1802/1 FT	—	35.00	60.00	100	250	—
1802 FT	—	20.00	35.00	50.00	100	—
1802 FT/M	—	20.00	35.00	50.00	100	—
1803 FT	—	20.00	35.00	50.00	110	—
1803 FT/M	—	20.00	35.00	50.00	100	—
1803 TH	—	75.00	150	250	500	—
1804/3 TH	—	35.00	60.00	100	250	—
1804 TH CARLUS (error)	—	20.00	35.00	50.00	100	—
1805/4 TH	—	40.00	80.00	125	275	—
1805 TH Narrow date	—	20.00	35.00	50.00	100	—
1805 Wide date	—	20.00	35.00	50.00	100	—
1806 TH	—	20.00	35.00	50.00	100	—
1807/6 TH	—	150	250	350	700	—
1807 TH	—	20.00	35.00	50.00	100	—
1808/7 TH	—	20.00	35.00	50.00	100	—
1808 TH	—	20.00	35.00	50.00	100	—

KM# 110   8 REALES
27.0674 g., 0.8960 Silver .7797 oz. ASW **Obv:** Armored bust of Ferdinand VII **Note:** Mint mark M, Mo.

Date	Mintage	VG	F	VF	XF	Unc
1808 TH	—	25.00	40.00	75.00	145	—
1809/8 TH	—	25.00	40.00	75.00	145	—
1809 TH	—	20.00	35.00	55.00	120	—
1809 HJ	—	25.00	40.00	75.00	145	—
1809 HJ/TH	—	20.00	35.00	55.00	120	—
1810/09 HJ	—	25.00	40.00	75.00	145	—
1810 TH	—	75.00	150	300	600	—
1810 HJ/TH	—	25.00	40.00	75.00	145	—
1810 HJ	—	25.00	40.00	75.00	145	—
1811/0 HJ	—	20.00	35.00	55.00	120	—
1811 HJ	—	20.00	35.00	55.00	120	—
1811 HJ/TH	—	20.00	35.00	50.00	100	—

KM# 111   8 REALES
27.0700 g., 0.9030 Silver .7859 oz. ASW **Obv:** Draped bust of Ferdinand VII **Note:** Mint mark M, Mo.

Date	Mintage	VG	F	VF	XF	Unc
1811 HJ	—	20.00	40.00	60.00	125	—
1812 HJ	—	50.00	75.00	125	250	—
1812 JJ/HJ	—	20.00	35.00	50.00	100	—
1812 JJ	—	20.00	35.00	50.00	100	—
1813 HJ	—	50.00	75.00	125	250	—
1813 JJ	—	20.00	35.00	50.00	100	—
1814/3 HJ	—	1,200	2,500	5,000	—	—
1814/3 JJ	—	20.00	35.00	50.00	100	—
1814 JJ	—	20.00	35.00	50.00	100	—
1815/4 JJ	—	20.00	35.00	50.00	100	—
1815 JJ	—	20.00	35.00	50.00	100	—
1816/5 JJ	—	20.00	35.00	50.00	90.00	—
1816 JJ	—	20.00	35.00	50.00	90.00	—
1817 JJ	—	20.00	35.00	50.00	90.00	—
1818 JJ	—	20.00	35.00	50.00	90.00	—
1819 JJ	—	20.00	35.00	50.00	90.00	—
1820 JJ	—	20.00	35.00	50.00	90.00	—
1821 JJ	—	20.00	35.00	50.00	90.00	—

KM# 112   1/2 ESCUDO
1.6917 g., 0.8750 Gold .0476 oz. AGW **Obv. Legend:** FERD. VII. D. G. HISP. ET IND **Note:** Mint mark M, Mo.

Date	Mintage	VG	F	VF	XF	Unc
1814 JJ	—	100	150	225	375	—
1815/4 JJ	—	150	200	250	400	—
1815 JJ	—	150	200	250	400	—
1816 JJ	—	100	150	225	375	—
1817 JJ	—	150	200	250	400	—
1818 JJ	—	150	200	250	400	—
1819 JJ	—	150	200	250	400	—
1820 JJ	—	200	300	400	550	—

KM# 113   ESCUDO
3.3834 g., 0.9170 Gold .0997 oz. AGW **Obv. Legend:** PHILIP. V. D. G. HISPAN. ET IND. REX **Note:** Struck at Mexico City Mint, mint mark M, Mo.

Date	Mintage	VG	F	VF	XF	Unc
1732 F	—	1,000	2,000	3,000	4,000	—
1733/2 F	—	1,000	2,000	3,000	4,000	—
1734/3 MF	—	150	250	400	850	—
1735/4 MF	—	150	250	400	850	—
1735 MF	—	150	250	400	850	—
1736/5 MF	—	150	250	400	850	—
1736 MF	—	150	250	400	850	—
1737 MF	—	200	300	600	1,200	—
1738/7 MF	—	200	300	600	1,200	—
1738 MF	—	200	300	600	1,200	—
1739 MF	—	200	300	600	1,200	—
1740/30 MF	—	200	300	600	1,200	—
1741 MF	—	200	300	600	1,200	—
1742 MF	—	200	300	600	1,200	—
1743/2 MF	—	150	275	450	800	—
1743 MF	—	150	250	400	700	—
1744/3 MF	—	150	250	400	700	—
1744 MF	—	150	250	400	700	—
1745 MF	—	150	250	400	700	—
1746/5 MF	—	150	250	400	700	—
1747 MF Rare	—	—	—	—	—	—

KM# 114   ESCUDO
3.3834 g., 0.9170 Gold .0997 oz. AGW **Obv:** Long bust **Obv. Legend:** FERD. VI. D. G. HISPAN. ET IND. REX **Note:** Struck at Mexico City Mint, mint mark M, Mo.

Date	Mintage	VG	F	VF	XF	Unc
1747 MF	—	1,650	3,000	5,000	7,500	—

KM# 115.1   ESCUDO
3.3834 g., 0.9170 Gold .0997 oz. AGW **Obv:** Short bust **Obv. Legend:** FERD. VI. D. G. HISPAN. ET IND. REX **Note:** Struck at Mexico City Mint, mint mark M, Mo.

Date	Mintage	VG	F	VF	XF	Unc
1748 MF	—	250	350	550	950	—
1749 MF	—	300	450	700	1,150	—
1750 MF	—	150	250	400	800	—
1751 MF	—	150	250	400	800	—

KM# 115.2   ESCUDO
3.3834 g., 0.9170 Gold .0997 oz. AGW **Obv:** Short bust **Obv. Legend:** FERD. VI. D. G. HISPAN. ET IND. REX **Rev:** Without 1 S flanking arms **Note:** Struck at Mexico City Mint, mint mark M, Mo.

Date	Mintage	VG	F	VF	XF	Unc
1752 MF	—	125	225	375	750	—
1753/2 MF	—	150	250	400	800	—
1753 MF	—	150	250	400	800	—
1754 MF	—	150	250	400	800	—
1755 MM	—	150	250	400	800	—
1756 MM	—	150	250	400	800	—

KM# A116   ESCUDO
3.3834 g., 0.9170 Gold .0997 oz. AGW **Obv:** Armored bust **Note:** Struck at Mexico City Mint, mint mark M, Mo.

Date	Mintage	VG	F	VF	XF	Unc
1757 MM	—	150	250	400	800	—
1759 MM	—	150	250	400	800	—

KM# 116   ESCUDO
3.3834 g., 0.9170 Gold .0997 oz. AGW **Obv. Legend:** CAROLVS. III. D. G. HISPAN. ET IND. REX **Rev. Legend:** NOMINA MAGNA SEQUOR **Note:** Struck at Mexico City Mint, mint mark M, Mo.

Date	Mintage	VG	F	VF	XF	Unc
1760 MM	—	400	800	1,500	2,500	—
1761/0 MM	—	400	800	1,500	2,500	—
1761 MM	—	400	800	1,500	2,500	—

KM# 117 ESCUDO
3.3834 g., 0.9170 Gold .0997 oz. AGW **Obv:** Large bust
Obv. Legend: CAR. III. D. G. HISP. ET IND. R **Rev. Legend:**
IN. UTROQ. FELIX **Note:** Mint mark M, Mo.

Date	Mintage	VG	F	VF	XF	Unc
1762 MM	—	250	375	600	1,000	—
1763 MM	—	275	425	700	1,100	—
1764 MM	—	250	375	600	1,000	—
1765 MF	—	250	375	600	1,000	—
1766 MF	—	250	375	600	1,000	—
1767 MF	—	250	375	600	1,000	—
1768 MF	—	250	375	600	1,000	—
1769 MF	—	250	375	600	1,000	—
1770 MF	—	250	375	600	1,000	—
1771 MF	—	250	375	600	1,000	—

KM# 118.1 ESCUDO
3.3834 g., 0.9010 Gold .0980 oz. AGW **Obv:** Large bust
Obv. Legend: CAROL. III. D. G. HISPAN. ET IND. R **Rev:**
Initials and mint mark upright **Rev. Legend:** FELIX. A. D **Note:**
Mint mark M, Mo.

Date	Mintage	VG	F	VF	XF	Unc
1772 MF	—	125	150	275	475	—
1772 FM	—	125	150	275	475	—
1773 FM	—	125	150	275	475	—

KM# 118.2 ESCUDO
3.3834 g., 0.9010 Gold .0980 oz. AGW **Obv:** Large bust
Obv. Legend: CAROL. III. D. G. HISPAN. ET IND. R **Rev:**
Initials and mint mark inverted **Rev. Legend:** FELIX. A. D
Note: Mint mark M, Mo.

Date	Mintage	VG	F	VF	XF	Unc
1773 FM	—	125	150	275	475	—
1774 FM	—	125	150	275	475	—
1775 FM	—	125	150	275	475	—
1776 FM	—	125	150	275	475	—
1777 FM	—	125	150	275	475	—
1778 FF	—	125	150	275	475	—
1779 FF	—	125	150	275	475	—
1780 FF	—	125	150	275	475	—
1781 FF	—	125	150	275	475	—
1782 FF	—	125	150	275	475	—
1783/2 FF	—	125	150	275	475	—
1783 FF	—	125	150	275	475	—
1784/3 FF	—	125	150	275	475	—
1784/3 FM/F	—	125	150	275	475	—

KM# 118.2a ESCUDO
3.3800 g., 0.8750 Gold .0950 oz. AGW **Obv:** Large bust
Obv. Legend: CAROL. III. D. G. HISPAN. ET IND. R. **Rev:**
Initials and mint mark inverted **Rev. Legend:** FELIX. A. D.
Note: Mint mark M, Mo.

Date	Mintage	VG	F	VF	XF	Unc
1785 FM	—	125	150	275	475	—
1786 FM	—	125	150	275	475	—
1787 FM	—	125	150	275	475	—
1788 FM	—	125	150	275	475	—

KM# 118.1a ESCUDO
3.3834 g., 0.8750 Gold .0952 oz. AGW **Obv:** Large bust
Obv. Legend: CAROL. III. D. G. HISPAN. ET IND. R **Rev:**
Initial letters and mint mark upright **Rev. Legend:** FELIX. A.
D **Note:** Mint mark M, Mo.

Date	Mintage	VG	F	VF	XF	Unc
1788 FM	—	125	150	275	475	—

KM# 119 ESCUDO
3.3834 g., 0.8750 Gold .0952 oz. AGW **Obv:** Bust of Charles
III **Obv. Legend:** CAROL. IIII. D. G... **Rev:** Initial letters and mint
mark upright **Rev. Legend:** FELIX. A. D **Note:** Mint mark M, Mo.

Date	Mintage	VG	F	VF	XF	Unc
1789 FM	—	300	550	1,000	2,000	—
1790 FM	—	300	550	1,000	2,000	—

KM# 120 ESCUDO
3.3834 g., 0.8750 Gold .0952 oz. AGW **Obv:** Armored bust
of Charles IV **Obv. Legend:** CAROL. IIII. D. G... **Rev:** Initial
letters and mint mark upright **Rev. Legend:** FELIX. A. D **Note:**
Mint mark M, Mo.

Date	Mintage	VG	F	VF	XF	Unc
1792 MF	—	125	165	235	345	—
1793 FM	—	125	165	235	345	—
1794 FM	—	125	165	235	345	—
1795 FM	—	125	165	235	345	—
1796 FM	—	125	165	235	345	—
1797 FM	—	125	165	235	345	—
1798 FM	—	125	165	235	345	—
1799 FM	—	125	165	235	345	—
1800 FM	—	125	165	235	345	—
1801 FM	—	125	165	235	345	—
1801 FT	—	125	165	235	345	—
1802 FT	—	125	165	235	345	—
1803 FT	—	125	165	235	345	—
1804/3 TH	—	125	165	235	345	—
1804 TH	—	125	165	235	345	—
1805 TH	—	125	165	235	345	—
1806/5 TH	—	125	165	235	345	—
1806 TH	—	125	165	235	345	—
1807 TH	—	125	165	235	345	—
1808 TH	—	125	165	235	345	—

KM# 121 ESCUDO
3.3834 g., 0.8750 Gold .0952 oz. AGW **Obv:** Armored bust
of Ferdinand VII **Obv. Legend:** FERDIN. VII. D. G... **Rev:**
Initial letters and mint mark upright **Rev. Legend:** FELIX. A.
D **Note:** Mint mark M, Mo.

Date	Mintage	VG	F	VF	XF	Unc
1809 HJ/TH	—	125	165	235	400	—
1809 HJ	—	125	165	235	400	—
1811/0 HJ	—	125	165	235	400	—
1812 HJ	—	150	250	300	500	—

KM# 122 ESCUDO
3.3834 g., 0.8750 Gold .0952 oz. AGW **Obv:** Undraped bust of Ferdinand VII **Obv. Legend:** FERDIN. VII. D. G... **Rev:** Initial letters and mint mark upright **Rev. Legend:** FELIX. A. D **Note:** Mint mark M, Mo.

Date	Mintage	VG	F	VF	XF	Unc
1814 HJ	—	150	250	300	500	—
1815 HJ	—	150	250	300	500	—
1815 JJ	—	150	250	300	500	—
1816 JJ	—	175	275	325	550	—
1817 JJ	—	150	250	300	500	—
1818 JJ	—	150	250	300	500	—
1819 JJ	—	150	250	300	500	—
1820 JJ	—	150	250	300	500	—

KM# 124 2 ESCUDOS
6.7660 g., 0.9170 Gold .1995 oz. AGW **Obv. Legend:** PHILIP. V. D. G. HISPAN. ET IND. REX **Rev. Legend:** INITIUM SAPIENTIAE TIMOR DOMINI **Note:** Mint mark M, Mo.

Date	Mintage	VG	F	VF	XF	Unc
1732 F	—	1,000	1,500	2,000	3,000	—
1733 F	—	750	1,000	1,500	2,500	—
1734/3 MF	—	400	500	900	1,400	—
1735 MF	—	400	500	900	1,400	—
1736/5 MF	—	400	500	900	1,400	—
1736 MF	—	400	500	900	1,400	—
1737 MF	—	400	500	900	1,400	—
1738/7 MF	—	400	500	900	1,400	—
1739 MF	—	400	500	900	1,400	—
1740/30 MF	—	400	500	900	1,400	—
1741 MF	—	400	500	900	1,400	—
1742 MF	—	400	500	900	1,400	—
1743 MF	—	400	500	900	1,400	—
1744/2 MF	—	400	500	900	1,400	—
1744 MF	—	400	500	900	1,400	—
1745 MF	—	400	500	900	1,400	—
1746/5 MF	—	400	500	900	1,400	—
1747 MF	—	400	500	900	1,400	—

KM# 125 2 ESCUDOS
6.7660 g., 0.9170 Gold .1995 oz. AGW **Obv:** Large bust **Obv. Legend:** FERD. VI. D. G... **Rev. Legend:** INITIUM... **Note:** Mint mark M, Mo.

Date	Mintage	VG	F	VF	XF	Unc
1747 MF	—	3,000	5,500	9,000	15,000	—

KM# 126.1 2 ESCUDOS
6.7660 g., 0.9170 Gold .1995 oz. AGW **Obv:** Small young bust **Obv. Legend:** FERD. VI. D. G... **Rev. Legend:** NOMINA MAGNA SEQUOR **Note:** Mint mark M, Mo.

Date	Mintage	VG	F	VF	XF	Unc
1748 MF	—	450	750	1,500	3,000	—
1749/8 MF	—	450	750	1,500	3,000	—
1750 MF	—	400	700	1,400	2,850	—
1751 MF	—	400	700	1,400	2,850	—

KM# 126.2 2 ESCUDOS
6.7660 g., 0.9170 Gold .1995 oz. AGW **Obv:** Small young bust **Obv. Legend:** FERD. VI. D. G... **Rev:** Without 2 S by arms **Rev. Legend:** NOMINA MAGNA SEQUOR **Note:** Mint mark M, Mo.

Date	Mintage	VG	F	VF	XF	Unc
1752 MF	—	400	700	1,400	2,850	—
1753 MF	—	400	700	1,400	2,850	—
1754 MF	—	600	850	1,750	3,500	—
1755 MM	—	400	700	1,400	2,850	—
1756 MM	—	600	850	1,750	3,500	—

KM# 127 2 ESCUDOS
6.7660 g., 0.9170 Gold .1995 oz. AGW **Obv:** Armored bust **Obv. Legend:** FERDND. VI. D. G... **Rev:** Without 2 S by arms **Rev. Legend:** NOMINA MAGNA SEQUOR **Note:** Mint mark M, Mo.

Date	Mintage	VG	F	VF	XF	Unc
1757 MM	—	450	750	1,500	3,000	—
1759 MM	—	450	750	1,500	3,000	—

KM# 128 2 ESCUDOS
6.7660 g., 0.9170 Gold .1995 oz. AGW **Obv:** Young bust **Obv. Legend:** CAROLVS. III. D. G... **Rev:** Without 2 S by arms **Rev. Legend:** NOMINA MAGNA SEQUOR **Note:** Mint mark M, Mo.

Date	Mintage	VG	F	VF	XF	Unc
1760 MM	—	550	1,000	2,000	4,000	—
1761 MM	—	550	1,000	2,000	4,000	—

KM# 129 2 ESCUDOS
6.7668 g., 0.9170 Gold .1995 oz. AGW **Obv:** Large young bust **Obv. Legend:** CAROLUS. III. D. G... **Rev:** Without 2 S by arms **Rev. Legend:** IN. UTROQ. FELIX. AUSPICE. DEO **Note:** Mint mark M, Mo.

Date	Mintage	VG	F	VF	XF	Unc
1762 MF	—	500	900	1,850	3,750	—
1763 MF	—	500	900	1,850	3,750	—

Date	Mintage	VG	F	VF	XF	Unc
1764/3 MF	—	500	900	1,850	3,750	—
1765 MF	—	500	900	1,850	3,750	—
1766 MF	—	500	900	1,850	3,750	—
1767 MF	—	500	900	1,850	3,750	—
1768 MF	—	500	900	1,850	3,750	—
1769 MF	—	500	900	1,850	3,750	—
1770 MF	—	500	900	1,850	3,750	—
1771 MF	—	500	900	1,850	3,750	—

KM# 130.1 2 ESCUDOS
6.7668 g., 0.9010 Gold .1960 oz. AGW **Obv:** Older bust **Obv. Legend:** CAROLUS. III. D. G... **Rev:** Initials and mint mark upright **Rev. Legend:** IN. UTROQ. FELIX. AUSPICE. DEO **Note:** Mint mark M, Mo.

Date	Mintage	VG	F	VF	XF	Unc
1772 FM	—	200	375	550	1,000	—
1773 FM	—	200	375	550	1,000	—

KM# 130.2 2 ESCUDOS
6.7668 g., 0.9010 Gold .1960 oz. AGW **Obv:** Older bust **Obv. Legend:** CAROLUS. III. D. G... **Rev:** Initials and mint mark inverted **Rev. Legend:** IN. UTROQ. FELIX. AUSPICE. DEO **Note:** Mint mark M, Mo.

Date	Mintage	VG	F	VF	XF	Unc
1773 FM	—	200	375	550	1,000	—
1774 FM	—	200	375	550	1,000	—
1775 FM	—	200	375	550	1,000	—
1776 FM	—	200	375	550	1,000	—
1777 FM	—	175	300	450	900	—
1778 FF	—	175	300	450	900	—
1779 FF	—	175	300	450	900	—
1780 FF	—	175	300	450	900	—
1781 FM/M	—	175	300	450	900	—
1781 FF	—	175	300	450	900	—
1782 FF	—	175	300	450	900	—
1783 FF	—	175	300	450	900	—
1784 FF	—	175	300	450	900	—
1784 FM/F	—	175	300	450	900	—

KM# 130.2a 2 ESCUDOS
6.7668 g., 0.8750 Gold .1904 oz. AGW **Obv:** Older bust **Obv. Legend:** CAROLUS. III. D. G... **Rev:** Initials and mint mark inverted **Rev. Legend:** IN. UTROQ. FELIX. AUSPICE. DEO **Note:** Mint mark M, Mo.

Date	Mintage	VG	F	VF	XF	Unc
1785 FM	—	175	300	450	900	—
1786 FM	—	175	300	450	900	—
1787 FM	—	175	300	450	900	—
1788 FM	—	175	300	450	900	—

KM# 130.1a 2 ESCUDOS
6.7668 g., 0.8750 Gold .1904 oz. AGW **Obv:** Older bust **Obv. Legend:** CAROLUS. III. D. G... **Rev:** Initials and mint mark upright **Rev. Legend:** IN. UTROQ. FELIX. AUSPICE. DEO **Note:** Mint mark M, Mo.

Date	Mintage	VG	F	VF	XF	Unc
1788 FM	—	175	300	450	900	—

KM# 131 2 ESCUDOS
6.7668 g., 0.8750 Gold .1904 oz. AGW **Obv:** Bust of Charles III **Obv. Legend:** CAROL. IV. D. G... **Rev:** Initials and mint mark upright **Rev. Legend:** IN. UTROQ. FELIX. AUSPICE. DEO **Note:** Mint mark M, Mo.

Date	Mintage	VG	F	VF	XF	Unc
1789 FM	—	650	1,200	2,000	3,500	—
1790 FM	—	650	1,200	2,000	3,500	—

KM# 132 2 ESCUDOS
6.7668 g., 0.8750 Gold .1904 oz. AGW **Obv:** Armored bust of Charles IV **Obv. Legend:** CAROL. IIII. D. G... **Rev:** Initials and mint mark upright **Rev. Legend:** IN. UTROQ. FELIX. AUSPICE. DEO **Note:** Mint mark M, Mo.

Date	Mintage	VG	F	VF	XF	Unc
1791 FM Mo over inverted Mo	—	300	375	600	950	—
1792 FM	—	125	225	350	575	—
1793 FM	—	125	225	350	575	—
1794 FM	—	125	225	350	575	—
1795 FM	—	125	225	350	575	—
1796 FM	—	125	225	350	575	—
1797 FM	—	125	225	350	575	—
1798 FM	—	125	225	350	575	—
1799 FM	—	125	225	350	575	—
1800 FM	—	125	225	350	575	—
1801 FT	—	125	225	350	575	—
1802 FT	—	125	225	350	575	—
1803 FT	—	125	225	350	575	—
1804 TH	—	125	225	350	575	—
1805 TH	—	125	225	350	575	—
1806/5 TH	—	125	225	350	575	—
1807 TH	—	125	225	350	575	—
1808 TH	—	125	225	350	575	—

KM# 134 2 ESCUDOS
6.7668 g., 0.8750 Gold .1904 oz. AGW **Obv:** Undraped bust of Ferdinand VII **Obv. Legend:** FERDIN. VII. D. G... **Rev:** Initials and mint mark upright **Rev. Legend:** IN. UTROQ. FELIX. AUSPICE. DEO **Note:** Mint mark M, Mo.

Date	Mintage	VG	F	VF	XF	Unc
1814 JJ	—	250	425	700	1,200	—
1815 JJ	—	250	425	700	1,200	—
1816 JJ	—	250	425	700	1,200	—
1817 JJ	—	250	425	700	1,200	—
1818 JJ	—	250	425	700	1,200	—
1819 JJ	—	250	425	700	1,200	—
1820 JJ	—	250	425	700	1,200	—
1821 JJ	—	250	425	700	1,200	—

KM# 135 4 ESCUDOS
13.5337 g., 0.9170 Gold .3990 oz. AGW **Obv. Legend:** PHILIP. V. D. G. HISPAN. ET IND. REX **Rev. Legend:** INITIUM SAPIENTIAE TIMOR DOMINI **Note:** Mint mark M, Mo.

Date	Mintage	VG	F	VF	XF	Unc
1732 Rare	—	—	—	—	—	—
1732 F Rare	—	—	—	—	—	—
1733 F Rare	—	—	—	—	—	—
1734/3 F	—	1,000	1,500	2,800	4,500	—
1734 MF	—	850	1,350	2,500	4,250	—
1735 MF	—	850	1,350	2,500	4,500	—
1736 MF	—	850	1,350	2,500	4,500	—
1737 MF	—	750	1,250	2,400	4,000	—
1738/7 MF	—	750	1,250	2,400	4,000	—
1738 MF	—	750	1,250	2,400	4,000	—
1739 MF	—	750	1,250	2,400	4,000	—
1740/30 MF	—	750	1,250	2,400	4,000	—
1740 MF	—	750	1,250	2,400	4,000	—
1741 MF	—	750	1,250	2,400	4,000	—

Date	Mintage	VG	F	VF	XF	Unc
1742/32 MF	—	750	1,250	2,400	4,000	—
1743 MF	—	750	1,250	2,400	4,000	—
1744 MD	—	750	1,250	2,400	4,000	—
1745 MF	—	750	1,250	2,400	4,000	—
1746 MF	—	750	1,250	2,400	4,000	—
1747 MF	—	750	1,250	2,400	4,000	—
1746/5 MF	—	750	1,250	2,400	4,000	—

KM# 136   4 ESCUDOS
13.5337 g., 0.9170 Gold .3990 oz. AGW   **Obv:** Large bust
Obv. Legend: FERDND. VI. D. G...   **Rev. Legend:** INITIUM
SAPIENTIAE TIMOR DOMINI **Note:** Mint mark M, Mo.

Date	Mintage	VG	F	VF	XF	Unc
1747 MF	—	7,500	13,500	20,000	30,000	—

KM# 137   4 ESCUDOS
13.5337 g., 0.9170 Gold .3990 oz. AGW   **Obv:** Small bust
Obv. Legend: FERDND. VI. D. G...   **Rev:** 4S divided by arms
Rev. Legend: NOMINA MAGNA...   **Note:** Mint mark M, Mo.

Date	Mintage	VG	F	VF	XF	Unc
1748 MF	—	1,500	3,000	5,000	8,000	—
1749 MF	—	1,500	3,000	5,000	8,000	—
1750/48 MF	—	1,500	3,000	5,000	8,000	—
1750 MF	—	1,500	3,000	5,000	8,000	—
1751 MF	—	1,500	3,000	5,000	8,000	—

KM# 138   4 ESCUDOS
13.5337 g., 0.9170 Gold .3990 oz. AGW   **Obv:** Small bust
Obv. Legend: FERDND. VI. D. G...   **Rev:** Without value **Rev.
Legend:** NOMINA MAGNA...   **Note:** Mint mark M, Mo.

Date	Mintage	VG	F	VF	XF	Unc
1752 MF	—	1,000	2,000	3,500	6,000	—
1753 MF	—	1,000	2,000	3,500	6,000	—
1754 MF	—	1,000	2,000	3,500	6,000	—
1755 MM	—	1,000	2,000	3,500	6,000	—
1756 MM	—	1,000	2,000	3,500	6,000	—

KM# 139   4 ESCUDOS
13.5337 g., 0.9170 Gold .3990 oz. AGW   **Obv:** Large full bust
Obv. Legend: FERDND. VI. D. G...   **Rev:** Without value **Rev.
Legend:** NOMINA MAGNA...   **Note:** Mint mark M, Mo.

Date	Mintage	VG	F	VF	XF	Unc
1757 MM	—	1,250	2,500	4,000	6,500	—
1759 MM	—	1,250	2,500	4,000	6,500	—

KM# 140   4 ESCUDOS
13.5337 g., 0.9170 Gold .3990 oz. AGW   **Obv:** Young bust
Obv. Legend: CAROLVS. III. D. G...   **Rev:** Without value **Rev.
Legend:** NOMINA MAGNA SEQUOR **Note:** Mint mark M, Mo.

Date	Mintage	VG	F	VF	XF	Unc
1760 MM	—	3,500	6,500	10,000	20,000	—
1761 MM	—	3,500	6,500	10,000	20,000	—

KM# 141   4 ESCUDOS
13.5337 g., 0.9170 Gold .3990 oz. AGW   **Obv:** Large young
bust **Obv. Legend:** CAROLUS. III. D. G...   **Rev:** Without value
Rev. Legend: IN. UTROQ. FELIX. AUSPICE. DEO **Note:**
Mint mark M, Mo.

Date	Mintage	VG	F	VF	XF	Unc
1762 MF	—	2,500	4,500	7,500	15,000	—
1763 MF	—	2,500	4,500	7,500	15,000	—
1764 MF	—	2,500	4,500	7,500	15,000	—
1765 MF	—	2,500	4,500	7,500	15,000	—
1766/5 MF	—	2,500	4,500	7,500	15,000	—
1767 MF	—	2,500	4,500	7,500	15,000	—
1768 MF	—	2,500	4,500	7,500	15,000	—
1769 MF	—	2,500	4,500	7,500	15,000	—
1770 MF	—	2,500	4,500	7,500	15,000	—
1771 MF	—	2,500	4,500	7,500	15,000	—

KM# 142.1   4 ESCUDOS
13.5337 g., 0.9010 Gold .3920 oz. AGW   **Obv:** Large young
bust **Obv. Legend:** CAROL. III. D. G...   **Rev:** Initials and mint
mark upright **Rev. Legend:** IN. UTROQ. FELIX. AUSPICE.
DEO **Note:** Mint mark M, Mo.

Date	Mintage	VG	F	VF	XF	Unc
1772 FM	—	400	650	1,000	2,000	—
1773 FM	—	400	650	1,000	2,000	—

KM# 142.2   4 ESCUDOS
13.5337 g., 0.9010 Gold .3920 oz. AGW **Obv:** Large young
bust **Obv. Legend:** CAROL. III. D. G... **Rev:** Initials and mint
mark inverted **Rev. Legend:** IN. UTROQ. FELIX. AUSPICE.
DEO **Note:** Mint mark M, Mo.

Date	Mintage	VG	F	VF	XF	Unc
1773 FM	—	400	600	900	1,850	—
1774 FM	—	400	600	900	1,850	—
1775 FM	—	400	600	900	1,850	—
1776 FM	—	400	600	900	1,850	—
1777 FM	—	400	600	900	1,850	—
1778 FF	—	400	600	900	1,850	—
1779 FF	—	400	600	900	1,850	—
1780 FF	—	400	600	900	1,850	—
1781 FF	—	400	600	900	1,850	—
1782 FF	—	400	600	900	1,850	—
1783 FF	—	400	600	900	1,850	—
1784 FF	—	400	600	900	1,850	—
1784/3 FM/F	—	400	600	900	1,850	—

KM# 142.2a   4 ESCUDOS
13.5337 g., 0.8750 Gold .3807 oz. AGW **Obv:** Large young
bust **Obv. Legend:** CAROL. III. D. G... **Rev:** Initials and mint
mark inverted **Rev. Legend:** IN. UTROQ. FELIX. AUSPICE.
DEO **Note:** Mint mark M, Mo.

Date	Mintage	VG	F	VF	XF	Unc
1785 FM	—	400	600	900	1,850	—
1786 FM/F	—	400	600	900	1,850	—
1786 FM	—	400	600	900	1,850	—
1787 FM	—	400	600	900	1,850	—
1788 FM	—	400	600	900	1,850	—

KM# 142.1a   4 ESCUDOS
13.5337 g., 0.8750 Gold .3807 oz. AGW **Obv:** Large young
bust **Obv. Legend:** CAROL. III. D. G... **Rev:** Initials and mint
mark upright **Rev. Legend:** IN. UTROQ. FELIX. AUSPICE.
DEO **Note:** Mint mark M, Mo.

Date	Mintage	VG	F	VF	XF	Unc
1788 FM	—	400	650	1,000	2,000	—

KM# 143.1   4 ESCUDOS
13.5337 g., 0.8750 Gold .3807 oz. AGW **Obv:** Bust of
Charles III **Obv. Legend:** CAROL. IV. D. G **Rev:** Initials and
mint mark upright **Rev. Legend:** IN. UTROQ. FELIX.
AUSPICE. DEO **Note:** Mint mark M, Mo.

Date	Mintage	VG	F	VF	XF	Unc
1789 FM	—	500	700	1,100	2,150	—
1790 FM	—	500	700	1,100	2,150	—

KM# 143.2   4 ESCUDOS
13.5337 g., 0.8750 Gold .3807 oz. AGW **Obv:** Bust of
Charles III **Obv. Legend:** CAROL. IIII D. G... **Rev:** Initials and
mint mark upright **Rev. Legend:** IN. UTROQ. FELIX.
AUSPICE. DEO **Note:** Mint mark M, Mo.

Date	Mintage	VG	F	VF	XF	Unc
1790 FM	—	600	1,000	1,800	3,000	—

KM# 144   4 ESCUDOS
13.5337 g., 0.8750 Gold .3807 oz. AGW **Obv:** Armored bust
of Charles IIII **Obv. Legend:** CAROL. IIII D. G... **Rev:** Initials

and mint mark upright **Rev. Legend:** IN. UTROQ. FELIX.
AUSPICE. DEO **Note:** Mint mark M, Mo.

Date	Mintage	VG	F	VF	XF	Unc
1792 FM	—	300	500	750	1,500	—
1793 FM	—	300	500	750	1,500	—
1794/3 FM	—	300	500	750	1,500	—
1795 FM	—	300	500	750	1,500	—
1796 FM	—	300	500	750	1,500	—
1797 FM	—	300	500	750	1,500	—
1798/7 FM	—	300	500	750	1,500	—
1798 FM	—	300	500	750	1,500	—
1799 FM	—	300	500	750	1,500	—
1800 FM	—	300	500	750	1,500	—
1801 FM	—	300	500	750	1,500	—
1801 FT	—	300	500	750	1,500	—
1802 FT	—	300	500	750	1,500	—
1803 FT	—	300	500	750	1,500	—
1804/3 TH	—	300	500	750	1,500	—
1804 TH	—	300	500	750	1,500	—
1805 TH	—	300	500	750	1,500	—
1806/5 TH	—	300	500	750	1,500	—
1807 TH	—	300	500	750	1,500	—
1808/0 TH	—	300	500	750	1,500	—
1808 TH	—	300	500	750	1,500	—

KM# 145   4 ESCUDOS
13.5337 g., 0.8750 Gold .3807 oz. AGW **Obv:** Armored bust
of Ferdinand VII **Obv. Legend:** FERDIN. VII D. G...
Initials and mint mark upright **Rev. Legend:** IN. UTROQ.
FELIX. AUSPICE. DEO **Note:** Mint mark M, Mo.

Date	Mintage	VG	F	VF	XF	Unc
1810 HJ	—	350	500	850	1,700	—
1811 HJ	—	350	500	850	1,700	—
1812 HJ	—	350	500	850	1,700	—

KM# 146   4 ESCUDOS
13.5337 g., 0.8750 Gold .3807 oz. AGW **Obv:** Undraped
bust of Ferdinand VII **Obv. Legend:** FERDIN. VII D. G... **Rev:**
Initials and mint mark upright **Rev. Legend:** IN. UTROQ.
FELIX. AUSPICE. DEO **Note:** Mint mark M, Mo.

Date	Mintage	VG	F	VF	XF	Unc
1814 HJ	—	400	700	1,200	2,700	—
1815 HJ	—	400	700	1,200	2,700	—
1815 JJ	—	400	700	1,200	2,700	—
1816 JJ	—	400	700	1,200	2,700	—
1817 JJ	—	400	700	1,200	2,700	—
1818 JJ	—	400	700	1,200	2,700	—
1819 JJ	—	400	700	1,200	2,700	—
1820 JJ	—	400	700	1,200	2,700	—

KM# 149   8 ESCUDOS
27.0674 g., 0.9170 Gold .7980 oz. AGW **Obv:** Young bust
Obv. Legend: FERDND. VI. D. G... **Rev. Legend:** INITIUM
SAPIENTIAE TIMOR DOMINI **Note:** Mint mark M, Mo.

Date	Mintage	VG	F	VF	XF	Unc
1747 MF	—	9,000	15,000	22,000	35,000	—

KM# 148   8 ESCUDOS
27.0674 g., 0.9170 Gold .7980 oz. AGW **Obv. Legend:**
PHILIP. V. D. G. HISPAN. ET IND. REX **Rev. Legend:** INITIUM
SAPIENTIAE TIMOR DOMINI **Note:** Mint mark M, Mo.

Date	Mintage	VG	F	VF	XF	Unc
1732 Rare	—	—	—	—	—	—
1732 F Rare	—	—	—	—	—	—
1733 F Rare	—	—	—	—	—	—
1734 MF	—	1,000	1,650	2,750	4,850	—
1734 MF/F	—	1,000	1,650	2,750	4,850	—
1735 MF	—	1,000	1,500	2,500	4,500	—
1736 MF	—	1,000	1,500	2,500	4,500	—
1737 MF	—	1,000	1,500	2,500	4,500	—
1738/7 MF	—	1,000	1,500	2,500	4,500	—
1738 MF	—	1,000	1,500	2,500	4,500	—
1739 MF	—	1,000	1,500	2,500	4,500	—
1740 MF	—	1,000	1,500	2,500	4,500	—
1740/30 MF	—	1,000	1,500	2,500	4,500	—
1741 MF	—	1,000	1,500	2,500	4,500	—
1742 MF	—	1,000	1,500	2,500	4,500	—
1743 MF	—	1,000	1,500	2,500	4,500	—
1744 MF	—	1,000	1,500	2,500	4,500	—
1744/3 MF	—	1,000	1,500	2,500	4,500	—
1745/4 MF	—	1,000	1,500	2,500	4,500	—
1745 MF	—	1,000	1,500	2,500	4,500	—
1746/5 MF	—	1,000	1,500	2,500	4,500	—
1746 MF	—	1,000	1,500	2,500	4,500	—
1747 MF	—	1,100	1,750	2,850	5,000	—

KM# 150   8 ESCUDOS
27.0674 g., 0.9170 Gold .7980 oz. AGW **Obv:** Small bust
Obv. Legend: FERDND. VI. D. G... **Rev. Legend:** NOMINA
MAGNA SEQUOR **Note:** Mint mark M, Mo.

Date	Mintage	VG	F	VF	XF	Unc
1748 MF	—	1,200	2,000	3,500	6,000	—
1749/8 MF	—	1,200	2,000	3,500	6,000	—
1749 MF	—	1,200	2,000	3,500	6,000	—
1750 MF	—	1,200	2,000	3,500	6,000	—
1751/0 MF	—	1,500	2,000	3,500	6,000	—
1751 MF	—	1,200	2,000	3,500	6,000	—

KM# 151   8 ESCUDOS
27.0674 g., 0.9170 Gold .7980 oz. AGW **Obv:** Large bust
Obv. Legend: FERDND. VI. D. G... **Rev:** Without 8 S divided
by arms **Rev. Legend:** NOMINA MAGNA SEQUOR **Note:**
Mint mark M, Mo.

Date	Mintage	VG	F	VF	XF	Unc
1752 MF	—	1,200	2,000	3,500	6,000	—
1753 MF	—	1,200	2,000	3,500	6,000	—

Date	Mintage	VG	F	VF	XF	Unc
1754 MF	—	1,200	2,000	3,500	6,000	—
1755 MM	—	1,200	2,000	3,500	6,000	—
1756 MM	—	1,200	2,000	3,500	6,000	—

KM# 152   8 ESCUDOS
27.0674 g., 0.9170 Gold .7980 oz. AGW   **Obv:** Medium, full bust **Obv. Legend:** FERDND. VI. D. G... **Rev:** Without 8 S divided by arms **Rev. Legend:** NOMINA MAGNA SEQUOR **Note:** Mint mark M, Mo.

Date	Mintage	VG	F	VF	XF	Unc
1757 MM	—	1,200	2,000	3,500	6,000	—
1758 MM	—	1,200	2,000	3,500	6,000	—
1759 MM	—	1,200	2,000	3,500	6,000	—

KM# 153   8 ESCUDOS
27.0674 g., 0.9170 Gold .7980 oz. AGW   **Obv:** Young bust with Order of the Golden Fleece at date **Obv. Legend:** CAROLVS. III. D. G... **Rev:** Without 8 S divided by arms **Rev. Legend:** NOMINA MAGNA SEQUOR **Note:** Mint mark M, Mo.

Date	Mintage	VG	F	VF	XF	Unc
1760 MM	—	1,750	3,000	5,000	9,000	—
1761/0 MM	—	2,000	3,500	5,500	10,000	—
1761 MM	—	2,000	3,500	5,500	10,000	—

KM# 154   8 ESCUDOS
27.0674 g., 0.9170 Gold .7980 oz. AGW   **Obv:** Young bust with Order of the Golden Fleece on chest **Obv. Legend:** CAROLVS. III. D. G... **Rev:** Without 8 S divided by arms **Rev. Legend:** NOMINA MAGNA SEQUOR **Note:** Mint mark M, Mo.

Date	Mintage	VG	F	VF	XF	Unc
1/61 MM	—	1,750	3,000	5,250	9,500	—

KM# 155   8 ESCUDOS
27.0674 g., 0.9170 Gold .7980 oz. AGW   **Obv:** Large bust **Obv. Legend:** CAROLUS. III. D. G... **Rev:** Without 8 S divided by arms **Rev. Legend:** IN. UTROQ. FELIX. AUSPICE **Note:** Mint mark M, Mo.

Date	Mintage	VG	F	VF	XF	Unc
1762 MM	—	1,600	2,750	4,500	8,500	—
1763 MM	—	1,600	2,750	4,500	8,500	—
1764 MF	—	1,750	3,000	5,000	9,000	—
1764/2 MF	—	1,750	3,000	5,000	9,000	—
1764 MM	—	1,750	3,000	5,000	9,000	—
1765/4 MF	—	1,750	3,000	5,000	9,000	—
1765/4 MM	—	1,750	3,000	5,000	9,000	—
1765 MF	—	1,750	3,000	5,000	9,000	—
1765 MM	—	1,500	2,500	4,000	7,500	—
1766 MF	—	1,500	2,500	4,000	7,500	—
1767/6 MF	—	1,500	2,500	4,000	7,500	—
1767 MF	—	1,500	2,500	4,000	7,500	—
1768/7 MF	—	1,500	2,500	4,000	7,500	—
1768 MF	—	1,500	2,500	4,000	7,500	—
1769 MF	—	1,500	2,500	4,000	7,500	—
1770 MF	—	1,500	2,500	4,000	7,500	—
1771 MF	—	1,750	3,000	5,000	9,000	—

KM# 156.1   8 ESCUDOS
27.0674 g., 0.9010 Gold .7840 oz. AGW **Obv:** Mature bust **Obv. Legend:** CAROL. III. D. G... **Rev:** Initials and mint mark upright **Rev. Legend:** ... AUSPICE. DEO **Note:** Mint mark M, Mo.

Date	Mintage	VG	F	VF	XF	Unc
1772 FM	—	500	750	1,250	2,000	—
1773 FM	—	550	850	1,350	2,250	—

KM# 156.2 8 ESCUDOS
27.0674 g., 0.9010 Gold .7840 oz. AGW **Obv:** Mature bust **Obv. Legend:** CAROL. III. D. G... **Rev:** Initials and mint mark inverted **Rev. Legend:** ... AUSPICE. DEO **Note:** Mint mark M, Mo.

Date	Mintage	VG	F	VF	XF	Unc
1773 FM	—	500	700	1,100	1,650	—
1774 FM	—	500	700	1,100	1,650	—
1775 FM	—	500	700	1,100	1,650	—
1776 FM	—	500	700	1,100	1,650	—
1777/6 FM	—	500	700	1,100	1,650	—
1777 FM	—	500	700	1,100	1,650	—
1778 FF	—	500	700	1,100	1,650	—
1779 FF	—	500	700	1,100	1,650	—
1780 FF	—	500	700	1,100	1,650	—
1781 FF	—	500	700	1,100	1,650	—
1782 FF	—	500	700	1,100	1,650	—
1783 FF	—	500	700	1,100	1,650	—
1784 FF	—	500	700	1,100	1,650	—
1784 FM/F	—	500	700	1,100	1,650	—
1784 FM	—	500	700	1,100	1,650	—
1785 FM	—	500	700	1,100	1,650	—

KM# 156.2a 8 ESCUDOS
27.0674 g., 0.8750 Gold .7615 oz. AGW **Obv:** Mature bust **Obv. Legend:** CAROL. III. D. G... **Rev:** Initials and mint mark inverted **Rev. Legend:** ... AUSPICE. DEO **Note:** Mint mark M, Mo.

Date	Mintage	VG	F	VF	XF	Unc
1786 FM	—	500	700	1,100	1,650	—
1787 FM	—	500	700	1,100	1,650	—
1788 FM	—	500	700	1,100	1,650	—

KM# 156.1a 8 ESCUDOS
27.0674 g., 0.8750 Gold .7615 oz. AGW **Obv:** Mature bust **Obv. Legend:** CAROL. III. D. G... **Rev:** Initials and mint mark upright **Rev. Legend:** ... AUSPICE. DEO **Note:** Mint mark M, Mo.

Date	Mintage	VG	F	VF	XF	Unc
1788 FM	—	500	700	1,100	1,650	—

KM# 157 8 ESCUDOS
27.0674 g., 0.8750 Gold .7615 oz. AGW **Obv:** Bust of Charles III **Obv. Legend:** CAROL. IV. D. G... **Rev:** Arms, Order chain **Rev. Legend:** IN UTROQ... A. D **Note:** Mint mark M, Mo.

Date	Mintage	VG	F	VF	XF	Unc
1789 FM	—	500	700	1,150	2,000	—
1790 FM	—	500	700	1,150	2,000	—

KM# 158 8 ESCUDOS
27.0674 g., 0.8750 Gold .7615 oz. AGW **Obv:** Bust of Charles III **Obv. Legend:** CAROL. IIII. D. G... **Rev:** Arms, Order chain **Rev. Legend:** IN UTROQ... A. D **Note:** Mint mark M, Mo.

Date	Mintage	VG	F	VF	XF	Unc
1790 FM	—	500	700	1,150	2,000	—

KM# 159 8 ESCUDOS
27.0674 g., 0.8750 Gold .7615 oz. AGW **Obv:** Armored bust of Charles IIII **Obv. Legend:** CAROL. IIII. D. G... **Rev:** Arms, Order chain **Rev. Legend:** IN UTROQ. FELIX **Note:** Mint mark M, Mo.

Date	Mintage	VG	F	VF	XF	Unc
1791 FM	—	350	450	625	1,000	—
1792 FM	—	350	450	625	1,000	—
1793 FM	—	350	450	625	1,000	—
1794 FM	—	350	450	625	1,000	—
1795 FM	—	350	450	625	1,000	—
1796/5 FM	—	400	500	700	1,150	—
1796 FM	—	350	450	625	1,000	—
1797 FM	—	350	450	625	1,000	—
1797 FM EPLIX	—	400	500	700	1,150	—
1798 FM	—	350	450	625	1,000	—
1799 FM	—	350	450	625	1,000	—
1800 FM	—	350	450	625	1,000	—
1801/0 FT	—	400	500	700	1,150	—
1801 FM	—	350	450	625	1,000	—
1801 FT	—	350	450	625	1,000	—
1802 FT	—	350	450	625	1,000	—

Date	Mintage	VG	F	VF	XF	Unc
1803 FT	—	350	450	625	1,000	—
1804/3 TH	—	400	500	700	1,150	—
1804 TH	—	350	450	625	1,000	—
1805 TH	—	350	450	625	1,000	—
1806 TH	—	350	450	625	1,000	—
1807/6 TH	—	400	500	700	1,150	—
1807 TH Mo over inverted Mo	—	400	500	700	1,150	—
1808/7 TH	—	450	600	800	1,250	—
1807 TH	—	350	450	625	1,000	—
1808 TH	—	450	600	800	1,250	—

Date	Mintage	VG	F	VF	XF	Unc
1814 JJ	—	360	465	650	1,000	—
1815/4 JJ	—	400	500	700	1,150	—
1815/4 HJ	—	400	500	700	1,150	—
1815 JJ	—	360	465	650	1,000	—
1815 HJ	—	360	465	650	1,000	—
1816 JJ	—	360	465	650	1,000	—
1817 JJ	—	400	500	700	1,150	—
1818/7 JJ	—	360	465	675	1,100	—
1818 JJ	—	360	465	675	1,100	—
1819 JJ	—	360	465	675	1,100	—
1820 JJ	—	360	465	675	1,100	—
1821 JJ	—	400	500	750	1,300	—

KM# 160 8 ESCUDOS
27.0674 g., 0.8750 Gold .7615 oz. AGW **Obv:** Armored bust of Ferdinand VII **Obv. Legend:** FERDIN. VII. D. G... **Rev:** Arms, Order chain **Rev. Legend:** IN UTROQ. FELIX **Note:** Mint mark M, Mo.

Date	Mintage	VG	F	VF	XF	Unc
1808 TH	—	400	500	750	1,250	—
1809 HJ	—	400	500	750	1,350	—
1810 HJ	—	375	475	700	1,200	—
1811/0 HJ	—	425	525	800	1,350	—
1811 HJ H/T	—	425	525	800	1,350	—
1811 HJ	—	425	525	800	1,350	—
1811 JJ	—	375	475	700	1,200	—
1812 JJ	—	375	475	700	1,200	—

KM# 161 8 ESCUDOS
27.0674 g., 0.8750 Gold .7615 oz. AGW **Obv:** Undraped bust of Ferdinand VII **Obv. Legend:** FERDIN. VII. D. G... **Rev:** Arms, Order chain **Rev. Legend:** IN UTROQ. FELIX **Note:** Mint mark M, Mo.

PROCLAMATION MEDALLIC COINAGE

The Q used in the following listings refer to Standard Catalog of Mexican Coins, Paper Money, Stocks, Bonds, and Medals by Krause Publications, Inc.,©1981.

KM# Q22 1/2 REAL
1.6000 g., Silver **Issuer:** Mexico City **Obv. Legend:** A CARLOS IV REY DE ESPANA Y DE LAS YNDIAS **Rev. Legend:** PROCLAMADO EN MEXICO ANO DE 1789

Date	Mintage	F	VF	XF	Unc	BU
1789	—	20.00	28.50	40.00	—	—

KM# Q22a 1/2 REAL
Bronze **Issuer:** Mexico City **Obv. Legend:** A CARLOS IV REY DE ESPANA Y DE LAS YNDIAS **Rev. Legend:** PROCLAMADO EN MEXICO ANO DE 1709

Date	Mintage	F	VF	XF	Unc	BU
1789	—	22.50	35.00	50.00	—	—

KM# Q23 1/2 REAL
Silver **Issuer:** Mexico City **Obv:** Crowned arms in double-lined circle **Obv. Legend:** A CARLOS IV REY DE ESPANA Y DE LAS YNDIAS **Rev. Legend:** PROCLAMADO EN MEXICO ANO DE 1789

Date	Mintage	F	VF	XF	Unc	BU
1789	—	20.00	28.50	40.00	—	—

KM# Q23a 1/2 REAL
Bronze **Issuer:** Mexico City **Obv:** Crowned arms in double-lined circle **Obv. Legend:** A CARLOS IV REY DE ESPANA Y DE LAS YNDIAS **Rev. Legend:** PROCLAMADO EN MEXICO ANO DE 1789

Date	Mintage	F	VF	XF	Unc	BU
1789	—	22.50	35.00	50.00	—	—

KM# Q24 REAL
Silver **Issuer:** Mexico City **Obv. Legend:** A CARLOS IV REY DE ESPANA Y DE LAS YNDIAS **Rev. Legend:** PROCLAMADO EN MEXICO ANO DE 1789

Date	Mintage	F	VF	XF	Unc	BU
1789	—	20.00	28.50	40.00	—	—

KM# Q24a REAL
Bronze **Issuer:** Mexico City **Obv. Legend:** A CARLOS IV REY DE ESPANA Y DE LAS YNDIAS **Rev. Legend:** PROCLAMADO EN MEXICO ANO DE 1789

Date	Mintage	F	VF	XF	Unc	BU
1789	—	22.50	35.00	50.00	—	—

KM# Q-A24 REAL
Silver **Issuer:** Mexico City **Obv:** Crowned arms in double-lined circle **Obv. Legend:** A CARLOS IV REY DE ESPANA Y DE LAS YNDIAS **Rev. Legend:** PROCLAMADO EN MEXICO ANO DE 1789

Date	Mintage	F	VF	XF	Unc	BU
1789	—	20.00	28.50	40.00	—	—

KM# Q-A24a REAL
Copper **Issuer:** Mexico City **Obv:** Crowned arms in double-lined circle **Obv. Legend:** A CARLOS IV REY DE ESPANA Y DE LAS YNDIAS **Rev. Legend:** PROCLAMADO EN MEXICO ANO DE 1789

Date	Mintage	F	VF	XF	Unc	BU
1789	—	22.50	35.00	50.00	—	—

KM# Q8 REAL
Silver **Issuer:** Chiapa **Obv:** Crowned arms between pillars, IR below **Obv. Legend:** FERNANDO VII REY DE ESPANA Y DE SUS INDIAS **Rev:** Legend in 5 lines within wreath **Rev. Legend:** PROCLA/MADO/ENCIUD/R. DECHIAPPA/1808

Date	Mintage	F	VF	XF	Unc	BU
1808	—	20.00	32.50	47.50	75.00	—

KM# Q25 2 REALES
6.7000 g., Silver **Issuer:** Mexico City **Obv. Legend:** A CARLOS IV REY DE ESPANA Y DE LAS YNDIAS **Rev. Legend:** PROCLAMADO EN MEXICO ANO DE 1789

Date	Mintage	F	VF	XF	Unc	BU
1789	—	35.00	50.00	75.00	—	—

KM# Q25a 2 REALES
6.7000 g., Bronze **Issuer:** Mexico City **Obv. Legend:** A
CARLOS IV REY DE ESPANA Y DE LAS YNDIAS **Rev.**
Legend: PROCLAMADO EN MEXICO ANO DE 1789

Date	Mintage	F	VF	XF	Unc	BU
1789	—	30.00	45.00	60.00	—	—

KM# Q64 2 REALES
Silver **Issuer:** Queretaro **Obv. Legend:** FERNANDO VII
REY DE ESPANA

Date	Mintage	F	VF	XF	Unc	BU
1808	—	20.00	37.50	67.50	100	—

KM# Q10 2 REALES
Silver **Issuer:** Chiapa **Obv. Legend:** FERNANDO VII REY
DE ESPANA Y DE SUS INDIAS

Date	Mintage	F	VF	XF	Unc	BU
1808	—	37.50	57.50	78.50	115	—

KM# Q27 4 REALES
13.6000 g., Silver **Issuer:** Mexico City **Obv. Legend:** A
CARLOS IV REY DE ESPANA Y DE LAS YNDIAS **Rev.**
Legend: PROCLAMADO EN MEXICO ANO DE 1789

Date	Mintage	F	VF	XF	Unc	BU
1789	—	100	150	225	—	—

KM# Q27a 4 REALES
13.6000 g., Bronze **Issuer:** Mexico City **Obv. Legend:** A
CARLOS IV REY DE ESPANA Y DE LAS YNDIAS **Rev.**
Legend: PROCLAMADO EN MEXICO ANO DE 1789

Date	Mintage	F	VF	XF	Unc	BU
1789	—	70.00	100	150	—	—

KM# Q-A66 4 REALES
Silver **Issuer:** Queretaro **Obv. Legend:** FERNANDO VII
REY DE ESPANA

Date	Mintage	F	VF	XF	Unc	BU
1808	—	85.00	135	200	325	—

KM# Q28 8 REALES
27.0000 g., Silver **Issuer:** Mexico City **Obv. Legend:** A
CARLOS IV REY DE ESPANA Y DE LAS YNDIAS **Rev.**
Legend: PROCLAMADO EN MEXICO ANO DE 1789

Date	Mintage	F	VF	XF	Unc	BU
1789	—	200	275	400	—	—

KM# Q28a 8 REALES
27.0000 g., Bronze **Issuer:** Mexico City **Obv. Legend:** A
CARLOS IV REY DE ESPANA Y DE LAS YNDIAS **Rev.**
Legend: PROCLAMADO EN MEXICO ANO DE 1789

Date	Mintage	F	VF	XF	Unc	BU
1789	—	70.00	100	150	—	—

KM# Q68 8 REALES
Silver **Issuer:** Queretaro **Obv. Legend:** FERNANDO VII
REY DE ESPANA

Date	Mintage	F	VF	XF	Unc	BU
1808	—	185	350	475	625	—

EMPIRE OF ITURBIDE

RULERS
Augustin I Iturbide, 1822-1823
MINT MARKS
Mo - Mexico City
ASSAYERS INITIALS
JA - Jose Garcia Ansaldo, 1812-1833
JM - Joaquin Davila Madrid, 1809-1833

MILLED COINAGE

16 Pilones = 1 Real; 8 Tlaco = 1 Real;
16 Reales = 1 Escudo

Mint: Durango
KM# 299 1/8 REAL
Copper **Rev. Inscription:** DE LA PROVINCIA DE NUEVA
VISCAYA

Date	Good	VG	F	VF	XF
1821D	22.50	50.00	85.00	150	—
1822D	7.50	13.50	28.50	60.00	—
1823D	7.50	12.50	25.00	50.00	—

Mint: Durango
KM# 300 1/4 REAL
Copper **Rev. Inscription:** DE LA PROVINCIA DE NUEVA
VISCAYA

Date	Good	VG	F	VF	XF
1822D	160	275	400	550	—

Mint: Mexico City
KM# 301 1/2 REAL
0.9030 Silver

Date	F	VF	XF	Unc
1822Mo JM	20.00	40.00	80.00	300
1823Mo JM	15.00	30.00	60.00	250

Mint: Mexico City
KM# 302 REAL
0.9030 Silver

Date	VG	F	VF	XF	Unc
1822Mo JM	100	175	350	550	900

Mint: Mexico City
KM# 303 2 REALES
6.7667 g., 0.9030 Silver

Date	F	VF	XF	Unc
1822Mo JM	50.00	100	350	1,000
1823Mo JM	40.00	80.00	250	850

Mint: Mexico City
KM# 304   8 REALES
27.0674 g., 0.9030 Silver

Date	F	VF	XF	Unc
1822Mo JM	75.00	150	300	950
1822Mo JM Proof, 3 known	—	—	—	—

Note: Ponterio & Associates Sale #86, 04-97, choice AU Proof realized $12,650.

Mint: Mexico City
KM# 305   8 REALES
0.9030 Silver   **Obv:** Bust similar to 8 Escudos, KM#131 **Rev:** Similar to KM#304

Date	F	VF	XF	Unc
1822Mo JM Rare	—	—	—	—

Mint: Mexico City
KM# 306.1   8 REALES
0.9030 Silver   **Obv:** Legend divided **Rev:** 8 R.J.M. at upper left of eagle **Note:** Type I.

Date	F	VF	XF	Unc
1822Mo JM	90.00	170	450	1,300

Mint: Mexico City
KM# 306.2   8 REALES
0.9030 Silver   **Obv:** Legend divided **Rev:** Cross on crown **Note:** Type I.

Date	F	VF	XF	Unc
1822Mo JM	650	1,000	—	—

Mint: Mexico City
KM# 307   8 REALES
0.9030 Silver   **Obv:** Similar to KM#306 **Rev:** Similar to KM#310 **Note:** Type II.

Date	F	VF	XF	Unc
1822Mo JM	150	350	650	2,250

Mint: Mexico City
KM# 308   8 REALES
0.9030 Silver   **Obv:** Continous legend with long smooth truncation **Rev:** Similar to KM#306 **Note:** Type III.

Date	F	VF	XF	Unc
1822Mo JM	175	500	950	2,250

Note: Variety with long, straight truncation is valued at $5,000 in uncirculated condition

Mint: Mexico City
KM# 309   8 REALES
0.9030 Silver   **Obv:** Similar to KM#308 **Rev:** Similar to KM#310 **Note:** Type IV.

Date	F	VF	XF	Unc
1822Mo JM	50.00	120	250	850

Mint: Mexico City
KM# 310   8 REALES
0.9030 Silver   **Obv:** Continuous legend with short irregular truncation **Rev:** 8 R.J.M. below eagle **Note:** Type V.

Date	F	VF	XF	Unc
1822Mo JM	50.00	120	225	900
1823Mo JM	50.00	120	225	900

Mint: Mexico City
KM# 311   8 REALES
0.9030 Silver   **Obv:** Bust with long truncation **Rev:** Similar to KM#310 **Note:** Type VI.

Date	F	VF	XF	Unc
1822Mo JM Rare	—	—	—	—

Mint: Mexico City
KM# 312   4 SCUDOS
13.5334 g., 0.8750 Gold   **Obv:** Bust **Rev:** Eagle in shield

Date	F	VF	XF	Unc
1823Mo JM	1,000	1,750	2,850	5,500

Mint: Mexico City
KM# 313.1   8 SCUDOS
27.0674 g., 0.8750 Gold   **Obv. Legend:** AUGUSTINUS

Date	F	VF	XF	Unc
1822Mo JM	1,200	2,000	3,750	—

Note: Superior Casterline sale 5-89 choice AU realized $11,000

Mint: Mexico City
KM# 313.2   8 SCUDOS
0.8750 Gold   **Obv:** Error in legend **Obv. Legend:** AUGSTINUS

Date	F	VF	XF	Unc
1822Mo JM	1,250	2,250	4,200	—

Mint: Mexico City
KM# 314   8 SCUDOS
0.8750 Gold   **Obv:** Large bust **Rev:** Eagle in shield

Date	F	VF	XF	Unc
1823Mo JM	1,000	1,800	3,250	6,000

REPUBLIC
First

MINT MARKS
A, AS - Alamos
CE - Real de Catorce
CA,CH - Chihuahua
C, Cn, Gn(error) - Culiacan
D, Do - Durango
EoMo - Estado de Mexico
Ga - Guadalajara
GC - Guadalupe y Calvo
G, Go - Guanajuato
H, Ho - Hermosillo
M, Mo - Mexico City
O, OA - Oaxaca
SLP, PI, P, I/P - San Luis Potosi
Z, Zs – Zacatecas

ASSAYERS' INITIALS

ALAMOS MINT

PG	1862-68	Pascual Gaxiola
DL, L	1866-79	Domingo Larraguibel
AM	1872-74	Antonio Moreno
ML, L	1878-95	Manuel Larraguibel

REAL DE CATORCE MINT

ML	1863	Mariano Cristobal Ramirez

CHIHUAHUA MINT

MR	1831-34	Mariano Cristobal Ramirez
AM	1833-39	Jose Antonio Mucharraz
MJ	1832	Jose Mariano Jimenez
RG	1839-56	Rodrigo Garcia
JC	1856-65	Joaquin Campa
BA	1858	Bruno Arriada
FP	1866	Francisco Potts
JC	1866-1868	Jose Maria Gomez del Campo
MM, M	1868-95	Manuel Merino
AV	1873-80	Antonio Valero
EA	1877	Eduardo Avila
JM	1877	Jacobo Mucharraz
GR	1877	Guadalupe Rocha
MG	1880-82	Manuel Gameros

CULIACAN MINT

CE	1846-70	Clemente Espinosa de los Monteros
C	1870	???
PV	1860-61	Pablo Viruega
MP, P	1871-76	Manuel Onofre Parodi
GP	1876	Celso Gaxiola & Manuel Onofre Parodi
CG, G	1876-78	Celso Gaxiola
JD, D	1878-82	Juan Dominguez
AM, M	1882-1899	Antonio Moreno
F	1870	Fernando Ferrari
JQ, Q	1899-1903	Jesus S. Quiroz

DURANGO MINT

RL	1825-1832	???
RM	1830-48	Ramon Mascarenas
OMC	1840	Octavio Martinez de Castro
CM	1848-76	Clemente Moron
JMR	1849-52	Jose Maria Ramirez
CP, P	1853-64, 1867-73	Carlos Leon de la Pena
LT	1864-65	???
JMP, P	1877	Carlos Miguel de la Palma
PE, E	1878	Pedro Espejo
TB, B	1878-80	Trinidad Barrera
JP	1880-94	J. Miguel Palma
MC, C,	1882-90	Manuel M. Canseco or Melchor Calderon
JB	1885	Jocobo Blanco
ND, D	1892-95	Norberto Dominguez

ESTADO DE MEXICO MINT

L	1828-30	Luis Valazquez de la Cadena
F	1828-30	Francisco Parodi

GUADALAJARA MINT

FS	1818-35	Francisco Suarez
JM	1830-32	???
JG	1836-39, 1842-67	Juan de Dios Guzman
MC	1839-46	Manuel Cueras
JM	1867-69	Jesus P. Manzano
IC, C	1869-77	Ignacio Canizo y Soto
MC	1874-75	Manuel Contreras
JA, A	1877-81	Julio Arancivia
FS, S	1880-82	Fernando Sayago
TB, B	1883-84	Trinidad Barrera
AH, H	1884-85	Antonio Hernandez y Prado
JS, S	1885-95	Jose S. Schiafino

GUADALUPE Y CALVO MINT

MP	1844-52	Manuel Onofre Parodi

GUANAJUATO MINT

JJ	1825-26	Jose Mariano Jimenez
MJ, MR, JM, PG, PJ, PF		???
PM	1841-48, 1853-61	Patrick Murphy
YF	1862-68	Yldefonso Flores
YE	1862-63	Ynocencio Espinoza
FR	1870-78	Faustino Ramirez
SB, RR		???
RS	1891-1900	Rosendo Sandoval

HERMOSILLO MINT

PP	1835-36	Pedro Peimbert
FM	1871-76	Florencio Monteverde
MP	1866	Manuel Onofre Parodi
PR	1866-75	Pablo Rubio
R	1874-75	Pablo Rubio
GR	1877	Guadalupe Rocha
AF, F	1876-77	Alejandro Fourcade
JA, A	1877-83	Jesus Acosta
FM, M	1883-86	Fernando Mendez
FG, G	1886-95	Fausto Gaxiola

MEXICO CITY MINT

Because of the great number of assayers for this mint (Mexico City is a much larger mint than any of the others)there is much confusion as to which initial stands for which assayer at any one time. Therefore we feel that it would be of no value to list the assayers.

OAXACA MINT

AE	1859-91	Agustin Endner
E	1889-90	Agustin Endner
FR	1861-64	Francisco de la Rosa
EN	1890	Eduardo Navarro Luna
N	1890	Eduardo Navarro Luna

POTOSI MINT

JS	1827-42	Juan Sanabria
AM	1838, 1843-49	Jose Antonio Mucharraz
PS	1842-43, 1848-49, 1857-61, 1867-70	Pompaso Sanabria
S	1869-70	Pomposo Sanabria
MC	1849-59	Mariano Catano
RO	1859-65	Romualdo Obregon
MH, H	1870-85	Manuel Herrera Razo
O	1870-73	Juan R. Ochoa
CA, G	1867-70	Carlos Aguirre Gomez
BE, E	1879-81	Blas Escontria
LC, C	1885-86	Luis Cuevas
MR, R	1886-93	Mariano Reyes

ZACATECAS MINT

A	1825-29	Adalco
Z	1825-26	Mariano Zaldivar
V	1824-31	Jose Mariano Vela
O	1829-67	Manuel Ochoa
M	1831-67	Manuel Miner
VL	1860-66	Vicente Larranaga
JS	1867-68, 1876-86	J.S. de Santa Ana
YH	1868-74	Ygnacio Hierro
JA	1874-76	Juan H. Acuna
FZ	18861905	Francisco de P. Zarate

Die Varieties

Similar basic designs were utilized by all the Mexican mints, but many variations are noticeable, particularly in the eagle, cactus and sprays.

1835 Durango, 8 Escudos
Illustration enlarged.

A large winged eagle was portrayed on the earlier coinage of the new republic.

1849 Mexico City, 8 Escudos
Illustration enlarged.
The later eagle featured undersized wings.

1844 Durango, 8 Escudos
Illustration enlarged.
The early renditions of the hand held Liberty cap over open book were massive in the gold escudo series.

1864 Durango, 8 Escudos
Illustration enlarged.
A finer, more petite style was adopted later on in the gold escudo series.

PROFILE EAGLE COINAGE

The first coins of the Republic were of the distinctive Profile Eagle style, sometimes called the "Hooked Neck Eagle". They were struck first in Mexico City in 1823 in denominations of eight reales and eight escudos. In 1824, they were produced at the Durango and Guanajuato mints in addition to Mexico City. Denominations included the one half, one, two and eight reales. No gold escudos of this design were struck in 1824. In 1825, only the eight reales were struck briefly at the Guanajuato mint.

NOTE: For a more extensive examination of Profile Eagle Coinage, please refer to "Hookneck - El Aguilade Perfil" by Clyde Hubbard and David O Harrow.

Mint: Mexico City
KM# 369   1/2 REAL
1.6900 g., 0.9030 Silver .0490 oz. ASW **Obv:** Full breast Profile eagle **Rev:** Cap and rays **Note:** Die varieties exist.

Date	F	VF	XF	Unc
1824Mo JM	45.00	75.00	150	600

Mint: Durango
KM# 371.1   REAL
3.3800 g., 0.9030 Silver .081 oz. ASW **Obv:** Thin Profile eagle **Rev:** Superscript S reversed

Date	F	VF	XF	Unc
1824Do RL	3,750	7,500	10,000	15,000

Mint: Durango
KM# 371.2   REAL
3.3800 g., 0.9030 Silver .081 oz. ASW **Obv:** Thin Profile eagle **Rev:** Superscript S normal

Date	F	VF	XF	Unc
1824Do RL 3 known	—	—	—	—

Mint mark: Do

Mint: Durango
KM# 373.1   2 REALES
6.7600 g., 0.9030 Silver .1962 oz. ASW **Obv:** Profile eagle **Rev:** Cap and rays **Note:** Die varieties exist.

Date	F	VF	XF	Unc
1824Do RL	50.00	125	850	2,200

Mint: Durango
KM# 373.2   2 REALES
6.7600 g., 0.9030 Silver .1962 oz. ASW **Obv:** Thin Profile eagle **Rev:** Type I, dot before 2R in legend

Date	F	VF	XF	Unc
1824D RL	100	200	1,000	3,000

Mint: Durango
KM# 373.3   2 REALES
6.7600 g., 0.9030 Silver .1962 oz. ASW **Obv:** Thin Profile eagle **Rev:** Type II, no dot before 2R in legend

Date	F	VF	XF	Unc
1824D RL	100	200	1,000	3,000

Mint: Mexico City
KM# 373.4   2 REALES
   Obv: Profile eagle **Note:** Varieties exist.

Date	F	VF	XF	Unc
1824Mo JM	30.00	70.00	450	2,000

   Note: No coins are known with visible feather details on the eagle's breast

Mint: Durango
KM# 376.2   8 REALES
27.0700 g., 0.9030 Silver .7859 oz. ASW **Obv:** Thin profile eagle, defiant snake **Rev:** Small Libertad

Date	F	VF	XF	Unc
1824Do RL	300	400	1,600	3,500

   Note: Eleven die varieties are known, some are rare

Typical Submissive
Snake Obverse

Typical Folded
Snake Obverse

NOTE: Legible Libertads on the Cap are common on Durango eight reales.

Med. Libertad	Small Libertad	Large Libertad
Cap Reverse	Cap Reverse	Cap Reverse

NOTE: The three styles of obverses and the three styles of reverses were combined   to make six distinct varieties of coins.

Mint: Durango
KM# 376.1   8 REALES
27.0700 g., 0.9030 Silver .7859 oz. ASW **Obv:** Thin profile eagle, defiant snake **Rev:** Medium Libertad

Date	F	VF	XF	Unc
1824Do RL	500	1,200	4,500	7,000

   Note: Five die varieties are known, all are rare

Mint: Durango
KM# 376.3   8 REALES
27.0700 g., 0.9030 Silver .7859 oz. ASW **Obv:** Thin profile eagle, submissive snake **Rev:** Small Libertad

Date	F	VF	XF	Unc
1824Do RL	200	350	1,250	2,750

   Note: Seven die varieties are known, some are rare

Mint: Durango
KM# 376.4   8 REALES
27.0700 g., 0.9030 Silver .7859 oz. ASW **Obv:** Thin profile eagle, submissive snake **Rev:** Large Libertad

Date	F	VF	XF	Unc
1824Do RL	200	350	1,250	2,750

   Note: Twelve die varieties known, some are rare

Mint: Durango
KM# 376.5   8 REALES
27.0700 g., 0.9030 Silver .7859 oz. ASW **Obv:** Thin profile eagle, folded snake **Rev:** Small Libertad

Date	F	VF	XF	Unc
1824Do RL	200	350	1,200	2,500

   Note: Only one die variety is known

Mint: Durango
KM# 376.6   8 REALES
27.0700 g., 0.9030 Silver .7859 oz. ASW **Obv:** Thin profile eagle, folded snake **Rev:** Large Libertad

Date	F	VF	XF	Unc
1824Do RL	200	400	1,500	3,000

   Note: Eleven die varieties known, some are rare

Mint: Guanajuato
KM# A376.1   8 REALES
27.0700 g., 0.9030 Silver .7859 oz. ASW **Obv:** Full breast profile eagle

Date	F	VF	XF	Unc
1824Go JM	250	400	1,100	3,500
1825/4Go JJ	600	1,200	2,750	7,000
1825Go JJ	500	750	1,400	5,500

Type I Obverse/Reverse

NOTE: The cap on the reverse of the curved tail Type I points to the "A" of LIBERTAD.

Mint: Mexico City
KM# 382.1 8 ESCUDOS
27.0700 g., 0.8750 Gold .7616 oz. AGW **Obv:** Profile eagle, snakes tail curved **Rev:** Cap points to "A" of LIBERTAD

Date	F	VF	XF	Unc
1823Mo JM	6,000	9,000	12,500	20,000

Type II Obverse/Reverse

NOTE: The cap on the reverse of the looped tail Type II points to the "T" of LIBERTAD.

Mint: Mexico City
KM# 382.2 8 ESCUDOS
27.0700 g., 0.8750 Gold .7616 oz. AGW **Obv:** Profile eagle, snake's tail looped **Rev:** Cap points to "T" of LIBERTAD

Date	F	VF	XF	Unc
1823Mo JM	5,000	8,000	12,000	18,000

Note: The quality of the strikes of Type I coins is almost always superior to that of the Type II. Details of the eagle feathers, cactus and lettering on the open book are better on most Type I coins but the Type II coins are scarcer. Type I coins outnumber Type II coins by about two to one

Mint: Mexico City
KM# A376.2 8 REALES
27.0700 g., 0.9030 Silver .7859 oz. ASW **Obv:** Full breast profile eagle **Edge:** Standard or Republic

Date	F	VF	XF	Unc
1823Mo JM	150	300	800	4,500
1824Mo JM	125	250	700	4,000

Mint: Mexico City
KM# A376.3 8 REALES
27.0700 g., 0.9030 Silver .7859 oz. ASW **Obv:** Full breast profile eagle **Edge:** Colonial or circle and rectangle

Date	F	VF	XF	Unc
1823Mo JM Rare	—	—	—	—

The Round-Topped Three

Mint: Mexico City
KM# A376.4 8 REALES
27.0700 g., 0.9030 Silver .7859 oz. ASW **Obv:** Full breast profile eagle **Rev:** Round topped three **Edge:** Standard or Republic

Date	F	VF	XF	Unc
1823Mo JM	2,000	4,000	6,000	8,000

Note: Many die varieties exist. Illustrations of one of the die differences is the size of the snake loop at the eagle's beak. This difference is not apparent except on the 1824 Mo 8 Reales

Mint: Mexico City
KM# A376.5 8 REALES
27.0700 g., 0.9030 Silver .7859 oz. ASW **Obv:** REPULICA (error)

Date	F	VF	XF	Unc
1824Mo JM	6,000	9,000	11,000	—

Note: Legible Libertads on the cap are not as prevalent on the Mexico City 8 Reales as on the Durango 8 Reales. They are much more numerous than on the Guanajuato 8 Reales

STATE COINAGE

Mint: Guadalajara
KM# 316 1/16 REAL
4.7500 g., Copper, 21 mm. **Obv. Legend:** DEPARTMENTO DE JALISCO **Edge:** Oblique reeding

Date	Good	VG	F	VF	XF
1860	3.00	8.00	17.50	55.00	—

Mint: Guadalajara
KM# 317 1/16 REAL
4.7500 g., Copper, 21 mm. **Obv. Legend:** ESTADO LIBRE
DE JALISCO **Edge:** Oblique reeding

Date	Good	VG	F	VF	XF
1861	2.50	6.00	13.50	32.50	—

Mint: Alamos
KM# 335 1/8 REAL
Copper **Obv. Legend:** ESTADO DE OCCIDENTE **Edge:**
Oblique reeding **Note:** Size varies: 17-18mm, weight varies:
2-3 g. The C before date on reverse may be a mint mark
standing for Concepcion de Alamos.

Date	Good	VG	F	VF	XF
1828 Reverse S	35.00	65.00	120	—	—
1829	30.00	60.00	110	—	—

Mint: Chihuahua
KM# 318 1/8 REAL
3.5400 g., Copper, 20 mm. **Obv. Legend:** ESTADO
SOBERANO DE CHIHUAHUA **Edge:** Plain

Date	Good	VG	F	VF	XF
1833	350	750	—	—	—
1834	350	750	—	—	—
1835/3	350	750	—	—	—

Mint: Chihuahua
KM# 319 1/8 REAL
3.5400 g., Copper, 20 mm. **Obv. Legend:** ESTADO DE
CHIHUAHUA **Edge:** Plain

Date	Good	VG	F	VF	XF
1855	5.00	8.50	25.00	75.00	—

Mint: Durango
KM# 320 1/8 REAL
Copper **Rev. Legend:** LIBERTAD **Edge:** Oblique reeding
Note: Size varies 17-18mm. Weight varies 2.5-4 g. These
pieces were frequently struck over 1/8 Real, dated 1821-23
of Nueva Vizcaya. All known examples struck over these coins
are believed to be contemporary counterfeits.

Date	Good	VG	F	VF	XF
1824D	5.00	12.50	35.00	85.00	—
1828D	150	250	400	1,000	—

Mint: Durango
KM# 321 1/8 REAL
3.3000 g., Copper **Rev:** Date **Rev. Legend:** OCTo. DE. R.
DE DO **Edge:** Oblique reeding **Note:** Size varies 18-19mm.

Date	Good	VG	F	VF	XF
1828D	7.50	18.50	40.00	115	—

Mint: Durango
KM# 322 1/8 REAL
3.50 g., Copper, 20 mm. **Obv. Legend:** ESTADO DE
DURANGO

Date	Good	VG	F	VF	XF
1833 Rare	—	—	—	—	—

Mint: Durango
KM# 323 1/8 REAL
3.5000 g., Copper **Obv. Legend:** REPUBLICA MEXICANA
Note: Size varies: 19-23mm.

Date	Good	VG	F	VF	XF
1842/33	12.50	22.50	42.50	115	—
1842	8.50	15.00	32.50	100	—

Mint: Durango
KM# 324 1/8 REAL
Copper, 19 mm. **Obv. Legend:** REPUBLICA MEXICANA
Rev. Legend: DEPARTAMENTO DE DURANGO **Edge:**
Ornamented with arc and dot pattern **Note:** Weight varies:
3.5-3.8 g.

Date	Good	VG	F	VF	XF
1845	22.50	55.00	115	250	—
1846 Rare	—	—	—	—	—
1847	3.50	7.50	17.50	37.50	—

Mint: Durango
KM# 325 1/8 REAL
Copper, 19 mm. **Obv. Legend:** REPUBLICA MEXICANA
Rev. Legend: ESTADO DE DURANGO **Edge:** Ornamented
with arc and dot pattern **Note:** Weight varies: 3.5-3.8 g.

Date	Good	VG	F	VF	XF
1851	3.50	8.00	12.50	33.50	—
1852/1	3.50	6.50	11.00	33.50	—
1852	3.00	5.00	8.00	30.00	—
1854	7.00	13.50	28.50	62.50	—

Mint: Guanajuato
KM# 326 1/8 REAL
3.5000 g., Copper, 21 mm. **Obv. Legend:** ESTADO LIBRE
DE GUANAJUATO **Edge:** Ornamented with incuse dots

Date	Good	VG	F	VF	XF
1829	3.00	5.00	10.00	26.50	—
1829 error w/GUANJUATO	4.00	6.50	12.50	28.50	—
1830	8.00	13.50	28.50	62.50	—

Mint: Guanajuato
KM# 327 1/8 REAL
7.2000 g., Brass, 29 mm. **Obv. Legend:** ESTADO LIBRE
DE GUANAJUATO **Edge:** Plain

Date	Good	VG	F	VF	XF
1856	7.50	12.00	20.00	75.00	—

Mint: Guanajuato
KM# 328   1/8 REAL
Brass, 25 mm.   **Obv. Legend:** ESTADO LIBRE DE
GUANAJUATO **Edge:** Plain **Note:** Weight varies: 7.1-7.2 g.

Date	Good	VG	F	VF	XF
1856	4.00	7.50	12.50	35.00	—
1857	3.50	6.00	10.00	30.00	—

Mint: Guanajuato
KM# 328a   1/8 REAL
Copper, 25 mm.   **Obv. Legend:** ESTADO LIBRE DE
GUANAJUATO **Edge:** Plain **Note:** Weight varies: 7.1-7.2 g.

Date	Good	VG	F	VF	XF
1857	7.00	16.50	32.50	55.00	—

Mint: Guadalajara
KM# 329   1/8 REAL
4.8000 g., Copper, 21 mm.   **Obv. Legend:** ESTADO LIBRE
DE JALISCO **Edge:** Oblique reeding

Date	Good	VG	F	VF	XF
1828	3.00	5.00	8.00	22.50	—
1831	62.50	100	185	275	—
1832/28	4.50	6.50	11.00	27.50	—
1832	4.50	6.00	10.00	25.00	—
1833	3.50	5.50	9.00	23.50	—
1834	37.50	80.00	150	235	—

Mint: Guadalajara
KM# 330   1/8 REAL
9.5000 g., Copper, 28 mm.   **Obv. Legend:** ESTADO LIBRE
DE JALISCO **Edge:** Oblique reeding

Date	Good	VG	F	VF	XF
1856	3.00	6.00	9.00	18.50	—
1857	3.00	6.00	9.00	18.50	—
1858	3.00	6.00	9.00	18.50	—
1861	75.00	135	200	300	—
1862/1	4.00	7.00	10.00	22.50	—
1862	4.00	7.00	10.00	22.50	—

Mint: Guadalajara
KM# 331   1/8 REAL
9.5000 g., Copper, 28 mm.   **Obv. Legend:** DEPARTMENTO
DE JALISCO **Edge:** Oblique reeding

Date	Good	VG	F	VF	XF
1858	4.00	7.00	13.50	28.50	—
1859	3.00	5.75	8.00	20.00	—
1860/59	3.25	6.00	9.00	22.50	—
1860	3.25	6.00	9.00	22.50	—
1862	4.00	8.00	17.50	37.50	—

Mint: Hermosillo
KM# 337   1/8 REAL
6.7000 g., Copper, 28 mm.   **Obv. Legend:** ESTO LIBE Y
SOBO DE SONORA **Edge:** Reeded

Date	Good	VG	F	VF	XF
1859 Rare	—	—	—	—	—

Mint: San Luis Potosi
KM# 336   1/8 REAL
Copper, 21 mm.   **Obv. Legend:** ESTADO LIBRE DE SAN
LUIS POTOSI **Edge:** Oblique reeding **Note:** Weight varies
(1829-31) 4.5-5.5 g; (1859) 4-4.5 g.

Date	Good	VG	F	VF	XF
1829	6.00	11.00	26.50	62.50	—
1830	8.50	15.00	30.00	70.00	—
1831	6.00	9.50	18.50	47.50	—
1859	5.00	8.00	16.50	45.00	—
1865/1 Reported, not confirmed	—	—	—	—	—

Mint: Zacatecas
KM# 338   1/8 REAL
4.0000 g., Brass, 21 mm.   **Obv. Legend:** ESTo LIBe FEDo
DE ZACATECAS **Edge:** Oblique reeding

Date	Good	VG	F	VF	XF
1825	3.00	5.50	12.00	25.00	—
1827	3.00	5.50	12.00	25.00	—
1827 Inverted A for V in OCTAVO	12.00	20.00	40.00	100	—
1827 OCTAVA (error)	15.00	25.00	50.00	120	—
1827 Inverted 1	12.00	20.00	40.00	100	—
1829 Rare	—	—	—	—	—
1830	2.75	5.00	8.00	20.00	—
1831	4.50	6.75	13.50	27.50	—
1832	2.75	5.00	8.00	20.00	—
1833	2.75	5.00	8.00	20.00	—
1835	3.50	6.00	10.00	25.00	—
1846	3.50	6.00	10.00	25.00	—
1851	38.00	70.00	115	220	—
1852	3.50	6.00	10.00	25.00	—
1858	2.75	5.00	8.00	20.00	—
1859	2.75	5.00	8.00	20.00	—
1862	2.75	5.00	8.00	20.00	—
1863 Reversed 6 in date	2.75	5.00	8.00	20.00	—

Mint: Zacatecas
KM# 339   1/8 REAL
4.0000 g., Copper, 21 mm. **Obv. Legend:** DEPARTMENTO
DE ZACATECAS **Edge:** Oblique reeding

Date	Good	VG	F	VF	XF
1836	5.00	8.50	17.50	40.00	—
1845	7.50	12.50	22.50	50.00	—
1846	8.50	10.00	20.00	45.00	—

Mint: Chihuahua
KM# 340   1/4 REAL
Copper, 27 mm. **Obv. Legend:** ESTADO SOBERANO DE
CHIHUAHUA **Edge:** Herringbone pattern

Date	Good	VG	F	VF	XF
1833	7.50	16.50	37.50	85.00	—
1834	6.50	13.50	28.00	55.00	—
1835	5.00	10.00	22.00	50.00	—
1835 Plain edge	5.00	8.00	12.00	50.00	—

Mint: Chihuahua
KM# 341   1/4 REAL
7.0800 g., Copper, 27 mm. **Obv. Legend:** ESTADO LIBRE
DE CHIHUAHUA **Edge:** Plain

Date	Good	VG	F	VF	XF
1846 With fraction bar	3.50	6.00	12.00	37.50	—
1846 Without fraction bar	5.00	8.50	15.00	45.00	—

Mint: Chihuahua
KM# 342   1/4 REAL
7.0800 g., Copper, 27 mm. **Obv. Legend:** ESTADO DE
CHIHUAHUA **Edge:** Plain

Date	Good	VG	F	VF	XF
1855	2.50	5.75	13.50	40.00	—
1856	2.50	5.75	13.50	40.00	—

Mint: Chihuahua
KM# 343   1/4 REAL
7.0800 g., Copper, 27 mm. **Obv. Legend:** DEPARTMENTO
DE CHIHUAHUA **Edge:** Plain

Date	Good	VG	F	VF	XF
1855	3.00	5.75	13.00	36.50	—
1855 DE (reversed D)	4.50	8.50	17.50	40.00	—

Mint: Chihuahua
KM# 344   1/4 REAL
Copper, 28 mm. **Obv. Legend:** E. CHIHA LIBERTAD **Edge:**
Plain **Note:** Weight varies 11-11.5 g.

Date	Good	VG	F	VF	XF
1860	2.00	4.00	11.00	25.00	—
1861	2.00	4.00	11.00	25.00	—
1865/1	2.50	5.50	13.50	30.00	—
1865	6.00	14.00	28.50	65.00	—
1866/5	5.00	9.50	25.00	60.00	—
1866 Coin rotation	2.00	4.00	11.00	25.00	—
1866 Medal rotation	2.00	4.00	11.00	25.00	—

Mint: Culiacan
KM# 363   1/4 REAL
27.0000 g., Copper, 27 mm. **Obv. Legend:** ESTADO LIBRE
Y SOBERANO DE SINALOA **Edge:** Reeded

Date	Mintage	Good	VG	F	VF	XF
1847	—	3.50	5.50	12.00	23.50	—
1848	—	3.50	5.50	11.00	22.00	—
1859	—	3.00	4.50	7.50	16.50	—
1861	—	1.75	3.00	4.00	10.00	—
1862	—	1.75	3.00	4.00	11.00	—
1863	—	2.50	4.00	5.00	11.00	—
1864/3	—	2.50	4.00	5.00	11.00	—
1864	—	1.75	3.00	4.75	10.00	—
1865	—	3.00	5.50	8.50	18.50	—
1866/5	7,401,000	2.50	3.50	5.00	11.00	—
1866	Inc. above	1.75	3.00	4.00	10.00	—

Mint: Culiacan
KM# 363a   1/4 REAL
7.0000 g., Brass, 27 mm. **Obv. Legend:** ESTADO LIBRE
Y SOBERANO DE SINALOA **Edge:** Reeded

Date	Good	VG	F	VF	XF
1847	5.00	10.00	18.50	40.00	—

Mint: Durango
KM# 345   1/4 REAL
7.0000 g., Copper, 27 mm. **Obv. Legend:** REPUBLICA
MEXICANA **Rev:** DURANGO above in wreath

Date	Good	VG	F	VF	XF
1845 Rare	—	—	—	—	—

Mint: Durango
KM# 346 1/4 REAL
7.5000 g., Copper, 27 mm. **Obv. Legend:** REPUBLICA
MEXICANA **Rev:** Date, value **Rev. Legend:** DURANGO
Edge: Ornamented with arc and dot pattern

Date	Good	VG	F	VF	XF
1858 Rare	—	—	—	—	—

Mint: Durango
KM# 347 1/4 REAL
7.5000 g., Copper, 27 mm. **Obv. Legend:** ESTADO DE
DURANGO **Rev. Legend:** CONSTITUCION **Edge:**
Ornamented wiht arc and dot pattern **Note:** Brass examples
have been reported, but not confirmed.

Date	Good	VG	F	VF	XF
1858	4.00	8.50	22.00	50.00	—

Mint: Durango
KM# 348 1/4 REAL
Copper, 27 mm. **Obv. Legend:** DEPARTMENTO DE
DURANGO **Rev. Legend:** LIBERTAD EN EL ORDEN **Edge:**
Ornamented wiht arc and dot pattern **Note:** Weight varies: 7-7.5 g.

Date	Good	VG	F	VF	XF
1860	2.25	6.00	15.00	38.50	—
1866	3.00	7.50	16.50	42.50	—

Mint: Durango
KM# 349 1/4 REAL
7.0000 g., Copper **Obv. Legend:** ESTADO DE DURANGO
Rev. Legend: INDEPENDENCIA Y LIBERTAD **Edge:**
Ornamented with arc and dot pattern **Note:** Size varies: 26-
27mm.

Date	Good	VG	F	VF	XF
1866	3.75	8.50	22.00	50.00	—

Mint: Durango
KM# 350 1/4 REAL
7.5000 g., Copper, 27 mm. **Obv. Legend:** ESTADO DE
DURANGO **Rev. Legend:** SUFRAGIO LIBRE **Edge:**
Ornamented with arc and dot pattern **Note:** Brass examples
have been reported, but not confirmed.

Date	Good	VG	F	VF	XF
1872	2.00	3.75	8.50	18.50	—

Mint: Guadalajara
KM# 353 1/4 REAL
9.3500 g., Copper, 28 mm. **Obv:** Oblique reeding **Obv.
Legend:** ESTADO LIBRE DE JALISCO

Date	Good	VG	F	VF	XF
1828	3.75	7.00	15.00	37.50	—
1829/8	3.00	6.00	13.00	33.00	—
1829	3.00	6.00	13.00	33.00	—
1830/20	3.00	5.00	10.00	28.50	—
1830/29	3.00	5.00	10.00	28.50	—
1830	3.00	5.00	10.00	28.50	—
1831 Rare	—	—	—	—	—
1832/20	3.00	5.00	10.00	28.50	—
1832/28	3.00	5.00	10.00	28.50	—
1832	2.50	5.00	9.00	27.50	—
1833/2	3.00	5.00	9.00	27.50	—
1834	2.50	5.00	9.00	27.50	—
1835/3	3.00	5.00	9.00	27.50	—
1835	2.50	5.00	9.00	27.50	—
1836 Rare	—	—	—	—	—

Mint: Guadalajara
KM# 354 1/4 REAL
9.3500 g., Copper, 28 mm. **Obv. Legend:** DEPARTMENTO
DE JALISCO **Edge:** Oblique reeding

Date	Good	VG	F	VF	XF
1836 Rare	—	—	—	—	—

Mint: Guadalajara
KM# 355 1/4 REAL
19.0000 g., Copper, 32 mm. **Obv. Legend:** ESTADO LIBRE
DE JALISCO **Edge:** Oblique reeding

Date	Good	VG	F	VF	XF
1858	3.00	5.50	10.00	22.50	—
1861	3.50	7.50	15.00	30.00	—
1862	3.00	5.50	10.00	22.50	—

Mint: Guadalajara
KM# 356   1/4 REAL
19.0000 g., Copper, 32 mm. **Obv. Legend:**
DEPARTMENTO DE JALISCO **Edge:** Oblique reeding

Date	Good	VG	F	VF	XF
1858	2.75	5.00	8.50	18.50	—
1859/8	2.75	5.00	8.50	18.50	—
1859	2.75	5.00	8.50	18.50	—
1860	2.75	5.00	8.50	18.50	—

Mint: Guanajuato
KM# 351   1/4 REAL
7.0000 g., Copper, 27 mm. **Obv. Legend:** ESTADO LIBRE
DE GUANAJUATO **Edge:** Ornamented with incuse dots

Date	Good	VG	F	VF	XF
1828	3.75	8.00	18.50	40.00	—
1828 Error with GUANJUATO	4.00	9.00	20.00	42.50	—
1829	5.50	12.00	22.50	47.50	—

Mint: Guanajuato
KM# 352   1/4 REAL
14.0000 g., Copper, 32 mm. **Obv. Legend:** EST. LIB. DE
GUANAXUATO **Rev. Legend:** OMNIA VINCIT LABOR
Edge: Plain

Date	Good	VG	F	VF	XF
1856	7.50	18.50	37.50	65.00	—
1857	6.50	13.50	27.50	48.00	—

Mint: Guanajuato
KM# 352a   1/4 REAL
14.0000 g., Brass, 32 mm. **Obv. Legend:** EST. LIB. DE
GUANAXUATO **Rev. Legend:** OMNIA VINCIT LABOR
Edge: Plain

Date	Good	VG	F	VF	XF
1856	3.25	6.75	13.50	30.00	—
1857	3.25	6.75	13.50	30.00	—

Mint: Hermosillo
KM# 364   1/4 REAL
Copper **Obv. Legend:** EST. D. SONORA UNA CUART
Edge: Oblique reeding **Note:** Size varies: 21-22mm. Weight
varies: 2.3-5.5 g.

Date	Good	VG	F	VF	XF
1831 L.S. Rare	—	—	—	—	—
1832 L.S.	2.75	5.50	15.00	50.00	—
1833/2 L.S.	2.00	4.00	12.50	37.50	—
1833 L.S.	2.00	4.00	12.50	37.50	—
1834 L.S.	2.00	4.00	12.50	37.50	—
1835/3 L.S.	2.50	5.50	15.00	40.00	—
1835 L.S.	2.00	4.00	12.50	37.50	—
1836 L.S.	2.00	4.00	12.50	37.50	—

Mint: Hermosillo
KM# 365   1/4 REAL
14.3000 g., Copper, 32 mm. **Obv. Legend:** ESTO. LIBE. Y
SOBO. DE SONORA **Edge:** Reeded

Date	Good	VG	F	VF	XF
1859	2.00	5.00	8.00	20.00	—
1861/59	2.75	6.50	11.00	25.00	—
1861	2.00	5.00	8.00	20.00	—
1862	2.00	5.00	8.00	20.00	—
1863/2	5.00	12.50	25.00	55.00	—

Mint: San Luis Potosi
KM# 359   1/4 REAL
Copper **Obv. Legend:** ESTADO LIBRE DE SAN LUIS
POTOSI **Rev. Legend:** MEXICO LIBRE **Edge:** Oblique
reeding **Note:** Size varies: 25-31mm, weight varies: (1828-
32) 9-10 g.; (1859-60) 8-9 g.

Date	Good	VG	F	VF	XF
1828	2.00	3.50	8.00	17.50	—
1829	3.00	4.50	8.50	18.50	—
1830	2.00	3.50	7.00	15.00	—
1832	3.25	5.00	9.00	20.00	—
1859 Large LIBRE	2.50	4.00	7.50	16.50	—
1859 Small LIBRE	2.50	4.00	7.50	16.50	—
1860	2.50	4.00	7.00	16.50	—

Mint: San Luis Potosi
KM# 360   1/4 REAL
Copper   **Obv. Legend:** ESTADO LIBRE DE SAN LUIS
POTOSI **Rev. Legend:** REPUBLICA MEXICANA **Edge:**
Oblique reeding **Note:** Size varies: 25-31mm.

Date	Mintage	Good	VG	F	VF	XF
1862	1,367	2.50	4.00	7.00	15.00	—
1862 LIBR	Inc. above	3.25	5.00	8.00	16.50	—

Mint: San Luis Potosi
KM# 361   1/4 REAL
Copper   **Obv. Legend:** ESTADO LIBRE Y SOBERANO DE
S.L. POTOSI **Rev. Legend:** LIBERTAD Y REFORMA **Edge:**
Reeded or plain **Note:** Size varies: 27-28mm. Weight varies:
9-10 g.

Date	Mintage	Good	VG	F	VF	XF
1867	3,177,000	2.50	3.75	6.50	15.00	—
1867 AFG		2.50	3.75	6.50	15.00	—

Note: AFG are the coin designer/engraver initials

Mint: San Luis Potosi
KM# 362   1/4 REAL
Copper   **Obv. Legend:** ESTADO LIBRE Y SOBERANO DE
S.L. POTOSI **Rev. Legend:** LIBERTAD Y REFORMA **Edge:**
Plain

Date	Good	VG	F	VF	XF
1867	2.50	3.75	6.50	15.00	—
1867 AFG	2.50	3.75	6.50	15.00	—

Note: AFG are the coin designer/engraver initials

Mint: Zacatecas
KM# 366   1/4 REAL
8.0000 g., Brass   **Obv. Legend:** ESTO LIBE FEDO DE
ZACATECAS **Edge:** Oblique reeding **Note:** Size varies: 28-
29mm.

Date	Good	VG	F	VF	XF
1824 Rare	—	—	—	—	—
1825	2.50	5.00	10.00	20.00	—
1826	75.00	130	220	325	—
1827/17	2.50	5.00	9.00	20.00	—
1829	2.50	5.00	9.00	20.00	—
1830	2.50	5.00	8.50	20.00	—
1831	40.00	85.00	140	220	—
1832	2.50	5.00	9.00	20.00	—
1833	2.50	5.00	9.00	20.00	—
1834 Rare	—	—	—	—	—
1835	2.50	5.00	9.00	20.00	—

Date	Good	VG	F	VF	XF
1846	2.50	5.00	8.50	20.00	—
1847	2.50	5.00	8.50	20.00	—
1852	2.50	5.00	8.50	20.00	—
1853	2.50	5.00	8.50	20.00	—
1855	4.50	10.00	25.00	65.00	—
1858	2.50	5.00	8.50	20.00	—
1859	2.50	5.00	8.50	20.00	—
1860	75.00	125	200	310	—
1862/57	2.50	5.00	8.50	20.00	—
1862/59/7	8.00	18.00	37.50	75.00	—
1862	2.50	5.00	8.50	20.00	—
1863/2	2.50	5.00	8.00	20.00	—
1863	2.50	5.00	8.00	20.00	—
1864	4.00	11.00	25.00	60.00	—

Mint: Zacatecas
KM# 367   1/4 REAL
8.0000 g., Brass   **Obv. Legend:** DEPARTMENTO DE
ZACATECAS **Edge:** Oblique reeding **Note:** Size varies: 28-
29mm.

Date	Good	VG	F	VF	XF
1836	4.00	8.50	13.50	25.00	—
1845 Rare	—	—	—	—	—
1846	3.50	6.75	9.00	20.00	—

\Mint: Mexico City
KM# 315   1/16 REAL
1.7500 g., Copper, 17 mm.   **Obv. Legend:** REPUBLICA
MEXICANA **Edge:** Ornamented with small incuse rectangles

Date	VG	F	VF	XF	Unc
1831	10.00	20.00	50.00	100	—
1832/1	12.00	22.00	55.00	125	—
1832	10.00	20.00	50.00	100	—
1833	10.00	20.00	50.00	100	—

Mint: Mexico City
KM# 315a   1/16 REAL
1.7500 g., Brass, 17 mm.   **Obv. Legend:** REPUBLICA
MEXICANA **Edge:** Ornamented with small incuse rectangles

Date	VG	F	VF	XF	Unc
1832	13.50	22.50	60.00	165	—
1833	10.00	17.50	50.00	135	—
1835	400	800	1,250	2,500	—

Mint: Mexico City
KM# 332   1/8 REAL
7.0000 g., Copper, 27 mm.   **Obv. Legend:** REPUBLICA
MEXICANA **Edge:** Ornamented with small incuse rectangles

Date	VG	F	VF	XF	Unc
1829	450	900	1,500	2,500	—

Mint: Mexico City
KM# 333   1/8 REAL
3.5000 g., Copper, 21 mm.   **Obv. Legend:** REPUBLICA
MEXICANA **Edge:** Ornamented wiht small incuse rectangles

Date	Good	VG	F	VF	XF
1829	7.50	12.00	25.00	55.00	—
1830	1.00	2.00	6.00	20.00	—
1831	1.50	3.50	7.00	25.00	—
1832	1.50	3.50	7.00	25.00	—
1833/2	1.50	3.50	7.00	25.00	—
1833	1.50	2.75	6.00	20.00	—

Date	Good	VG	F	VF	XF
1834	1.50	2.75	6.00	20.00	—
1835/4	1.75	3.50	7.00	25.00	—
1835	1.50	2.75	6.00	20.00	—

Mint: Mexico City
KM# 334   1/8 REAL
14.0000 g., Copper **Obv. Legend:** LIBERTAD **Edge:**
Lettered (1841-41); Plain (1850-61) **Edge Lettering:**
REPUBLICA MEXICANA **Note:** Size varies: 29-30mm.

Date	Good	VG	F	VF	XF
1841	6.00	15.00	30.00	75.00	—
1842	2.50	5.00	10.00	30.00	—
1850	12.50	20.00	30.00	80.00	—
1861	5.00	12.00	25.00	70.00	—

Mint: Mexico City
KM# 357   1/4 REAL
14.0000 g., Copper, 33 mm. **Obv. Legend:** REPUBLICA
MEXICANA **Edge:** Ornamented with small incuse rectangles

Date	VG	F	VF	XF	Unc
1829	8.00	30.00	75.00	250	—

Mint: Mexico City
KM# 358   1/4 REAL
7.0000 g., Copper, 27 mm. **Obv. Legend:** REPUBLICA
MEXICANA **Edge:** Ornamented with small incuse rectangles
Note: Reduced size.

Date	VG	F	VF	XF	Unc
1829	12.00	25.00	50.00	150	—
1830	1.50	2.75	5.00	10.00	—
1831	1.50	2.75	5.00	10.00	—
1832	5.50	10.00	20.00	35.00	—
1833	1.50	2.75	5.00	10.00	—
1834/3	1.75	3.00	6.00	12.00	—
1834	1.50	2.75	5.00	10.00	—
1835	1.50	2.75	5.00	10.00	—
1836	1.50	2.75	5.00	10.00	—
1837	6.50	13.50	22.50	45.00	—

Mint: Mexico City
KM# 358a.1   1/4 REAL
7.0000 g., Brass, 27 mm. **Countermark:** JM **Obv. Legend:**
REPUBLICA MEXICANA **Edge:** Ornamented with small
incuse rectangles **Note:** Reduced size.

Date	VG	F	VF	XF	Unc
1831	8.00	13.50	27.50	50.00	—

Mint: Mexico City
KM# 358a.2   1/4 REAL
7.0000 g., Brass, 27 mm. **Obv. Legend:** REPUBLICA
MEXICANA **Edge:** Ornamented with small incuse rectangles
Note: Without countermark.

Date	VG	F	VF	XF	Unc
1831	—	—	—	—	—

Mint: Chihuahua
KM# 368   1/4 REAL
0.8450 g., 0.9030 Silver .0245 oz. ASW **Note:** Mint mark CA.

Date	VG	F	VF	XF	Unc
1843CA RG	75.00	125	300	500	—

Mint: Culiacan
KM# 368.1   1/4 REAL
0.8450 g., 0.9030 Silver .0245 oz. ASW **Note:** Mint mark C.

Date	VG	F	VF	XF	Unc
1855C LR	50.00	100	200	400	—

Mint: Durango
KM# 368.2   1/4 REAL
0.8450 g., 0.9030 Silver .0245 oz. ASW **Note:** Struck at
Durango Mint, mint mark Do.

Date	VG	F	VF	XF	Unc
1842Do LR	12.00	20.00	40.00	125	—
1843Do	20.00	25.00	60.00	150	—

Mint: Guadalajara
KM# 368.3   1/4 REAL
0.8450 g., 0.9030 Silver .0245 oz. ASW **Note:** Mint mark Ga.

Date	VG	F	VF	XF	Unc
1842Ga JG	2.50	5.50	8.00	20.00	—
1843/2Ga JG	—	—	—	—	—
1843Ga JG	6.00	9.00	12.50	30.00	—
1843Ga MC	4.00	6.50	9.00	25.00	—
1844Ga MC	4.00	6.50	9.00	25.00	—
1844Ga LR	2.50	5.00	7.50	15.00	—
1845Ga LR	2.50	4.50	7.50	15.00	—
1846Ga LR	5.00	8.00	10.00	25.00	—
1847Ga LR	4.00	6.50	9.00	25.00	—
1848Ga LR Rare	—	—	—	—	—
1850Ga LR Rare	—	—	—	—	—
1851Ga LR	6.00	10.00	20.00	50.00	—
1852Ga LR	50.00	100	135	200	—
1854/3Ga LR	50.00	100	135	200	—
1854Ga LR	5.00	10.00	12.50	30.00	—
1855Ga LR	5.00	8.00	10.00	30.00	—
1857Ga LR	6.50	10.00	15.00	27.50	—
1862Ga LR	5.50	10.00	15.00	30.00	—

Mint: Guadalupe y Calvo
KM# 368.4   1/4 REAL
0.8450 g., 0.9030 Silver .0245 oz. ASW **Note:** Mint mark GC.

Date	VG	F	VF	XF	Unc
1844GC LR	50.00	75.00	125	300	—

Mint: Guanajuato
KM# 368.5   1/4 REAL
0.8450 g., 0.9030 Silver .0245 oz. ASW **Note:** Mint mark Go.

Date	VG	F	VF	XF	Unc
1842Go PM	4.00	6.00	10.00	20.00	—
1842Go LR	2.00	4.00	8.00	15.00	—
1843/2Go LR	4.00	6.00	10.00	20.00	—
1843Go LR	2.00	4.00	8.00	15.00	—
1844/3Go LR	—	—	—	—	—
1844Go LR	2.00	4.00	8.00	15.00	—
1845Go LR	8.00	15.00	30.00	60.00	—
1846/5Go LR	—	—	—	—	—
1846Go LR	4.00	6.00	10.00	20.00	—
1847Go LR	2.00	4.00	8.00	15.00	—
1848/7Go LR	2.00	4.00	8.00	15.00	—
1848Go LR	2.00	4.00	8.00	15.00	—
1849/7Go LR	8.00	15.00	30.00	60.00	—
1849Go LR	2.00	4.00	8.00	15.00	—
1850Go LR	2.00	4.00	8.00	15.00	—
1851Go LR	2.00	4.00	8.00	15.00	—

Date	VG	F	VF	XF	Unc
1852Go LR	2.00	4.00	8.00	15.00	—
1853Go LR	2.00	4.00	8.00	15.00	—
1855Go LR	4.00	8.00	15.00	30.00	—
1856/4Go LR	—	—	—	—	—
1856Go LR	5.00	10.00	20.00	35.00	—
1862/1Go LR	3.00	5.00	10.00	20.00	—
1862Go LR	2.00	4.00	8.00	15.00	—
1863Go	2.00	4.00	8.00	15.00	—

Mint: Mexico City
KM# 368.6   1/4 REAL
0.8450 g., 0.9030 Silver .0245 oz. ASW **Note:** Mint mark Mo.

Date	VG	F	VF	XF	Unc
1842Mo LR	2.00	4.00	8.00	15.00	—
1843Mo LR	2.00	4.00	8.00	15.00	—
1844/3Mo LR	8.00	12.00	20.00	40.00	—
1844Mo LR	4.00	6.00	10.00	20.00	—
1845Mo LR	4.00	6.00	10.00	20.00	—
1846Mo LR	2.00	4.00	8.00	15.00	—
1850Mo LR	5.00	10.00	20.00	35.00	—
1858Mo LR	4.00	8.00	15.00	30.00	—
1859Mo LR	4.00	6.00	10.00	20.00	—
1860Mo LR	4.00	6.00	10.00	20.00	—
1861Mo LR	4.00	6.00	10.00	20.00	—
1862Mo LR	4.00	6.00	10.00	20.00	—
1863/53Mo LR	—	—	—	—	—
1863Mo LR	4.00	6.00	10.00	20.00	—

Mint: San Luis Potosi
KM# 368.7   1/4 REAL
0.8450 g., 0.9030 Silver .0245 oz. ASW   **Note:** Mint mark SLP, PI, P, I/P.

Date	VG	F	VF	XF	Unc
1842S.L.Pi	2.00	4.00	8.00	15.00	—
1843/2S.L.Pi	4.00	6.00	10.00	20.00	—
1843S.L.Pi	2.00	4.00	8.00	15.00	—
1844S.L.Pi	2.00	4.00	8.00	15.00	—
1845/3S.L.Pi	4.00	6.00	10.00	25.00	—
1845/4S.L.Pi	4.00	6.00	10.00	25.00	—
1845S.L.Pi	2.00	4.00	8.00	15.00	—
1847/5S.L.Pi	4.00	6.00	10.00	20.00	—
1847S.L.Pi	2.00	4.00	8.00	15.00	—
1851/47S.L.Pi	4.00	8.00	15.00	30.00	—
1854S.L.Pi	125	200	275	400	—
1856S.L.Pi	4.00	8.00	15.00	30.00	—
1857S.L.Pi	5.00	10.00	20.00	35.00	—
1862/57S.L.Pi	10.00	20.00	40.00	85.00	—

Mint: Zacatecas
KM# 368.8   1/4 REAL
0.8450 g., 0.9030 Silver .0245 oz. ASW **Note:** Mint mark Zs.

Date	VG	F	VF	XF	Unc
1842/1Zs LR	4.00	8.00	15.00	30.00	—
1842Zs LR	4.00	6.00	10.00	20.00	—

Mint: Alamos
KM# 370   1/2 REAL
1.6900 g., 0.9030 Silver .0490 oz. ASW **Obv:** Hook-necked eagle

Date	F	VF	XF	Unc
1862A PG Rare	—	—	—	—

Mint: Chihuahua
KM# 370.1   1/2 REAL
1.6900 g., 0.9030 Silver .0490 oz. ASW   **Obv:** Facing eagle

Date	F	VF	XF	Unc
1844 Ca RG	75.00	125	175	275
1845 Ca RG	75.00	125	150	250

Mint: Culiacan
KM# 370.2   1/2 REAL
1.6900 g., 0.9030 Silver .0490 oz. ASW   **Obv:** Facing eagle
Note: Mint mark C, Co.

Date	F	VF	XF	Unc
1846 CE	30.00	50.00	75.00	150
1848/7 CE	15.00	25.00	45.00	90.00
1849/8 CE	15.00	25.00	45.00	90.00
1849 CE	—	—	—	—
1852 CE	12.50	20.00	40.00	80.00

Date	F	VF	XF	Unc
1853/1 CE	12.50	20.00	40.00	80.00
1854 CE	20.00	35.00	50.00	100
1856 CE	12.50	20.00	40.00	80.00
1857/6 CE	20.00	35.00	50.00	100
1857 CE	15.00	25.00	45.00	90.00
1858 CE Error 1 for 1/2	12.50	20.00	40.00	80.00
1860/59 PV	20.00	35.00	50.00	100
1860 PV	12.50	20.00	40.00	80.00
1861 PV	12.50	20.00	40.00	80.00
1863 CE Error 1 for 1/2	15.00	25.00	45.00	90.00
1867 CE	12.50	20.00	40.00	80.00
1869 6/5 CE Error 1 for 1/2	12.50	20.00	40.00	80.00

Mint: Durango
KM# 370.3   1/2 REAL
1.6900 g., 0.9030 Silver .0490 oz. ASW **Obv:** Facing eagle
Note: Mint mark D, Do.

Date	F	VF	XF	Unc
1832 RM	125	225	350	600
1832 RM/L	—	—	—	—
1833/2 RM/L	75.00	100	150	225
1833/1 RM/L	12.50	20.00	40.00	80.00
1833 RM	25.00	40.00	75.00	150
1834/1 RM	25.00	40.00	75.00	150
1834 RM	12.50	20.00	40.00	80.00
1837/1 RM	12.50	30.00	60.00	200
1837/4 RM	12.50	30.00	60.00	200
1837/6 RM	12.50	30.00	60.00	200
1841/33 RM	15.00	30.00	60.00	250
1842/32 RM	12.50	20.00	40.00	80.00
1842 RM	12.50	20.00	40.00	80.00
1842 8R RM Error	12.50	20.00	40.00	80.00
1842 1/2/8R RM	12.50	20.00	40.00	80.00
1843/33 RM	15.00	25.00	50.00	100
1843 RM	15.00	25.00	50.00	100
1845/31 RM	12.50	20.00	40.00	80.00
1845/34 RM	12.50	20.00	40.00	80.00
1845/35 RM	12.50	20.00	40.00	80.00
1845 RM	15.00	25.00	50.00	100
1846 RM	30.00	50.00	80.00	200
1848/5 RM	35.00	55.00	110	250
1848/36 RM	25.00	40.00	75.00	200
1849 JMR	25.00	40.00	75.00	200
1850 RM Rare	—	—	—	—
1850 JMR	25.00	40.00	75.00	200
1851 JMR	20.00	35.00	50.00	100
1852/1 JMR	65.00	125	250	600
1852 JMR	30.00	50.00	80.00	200
1853 CP	12.50	20.00	40.00	80.00
1854 CP	25.00	40.00	75.00	200
1855 CP	25.00	40.00	60.00	150
1856/5 CP	20.00	35.00	50.00	100
1857 CP	20.00	35.00	50.00	100
1858/7 CP	20.00	35.00	50.00	100
1859 CP	20.00	35.00	50.00	100
1860/59 CP	40.00	65.00	135	300
1861 CP	125	250	400	700
1862 CP	25.00	40.00	60.00	125
1864 LT	100	300	500	1,000
1869 CP	40.00	65.00	125	275

Mint: Estado de Mexico
KM# 370.4   1/2 REAL
1.6900 g., 0.9030 Silver .0490 oz. ASW **Obv:** Facing eagle

Date	F	VF	XF	Unc
1829EoMo LF	175	300	500	1,400

Mint: Guadalajara
KM# 370.5   1/2 REAL
1.6900 g., 0.9030 Silver .0490 oz. ASW **Obv:** Facing eagle

Date	F	VF	XF	Unc
1825Ga FS	25.00	40.00	75.00	200
1826Ga FS	10.00	15.00	35.00	80.00
1828/7Ga FS	12.50	20.00	40.00	90.00
1829Ga FS	7.50	15.00	30.00	70.00
1830/29Ga FS	40.00	60.00	100	200
1831Ga LP Rare	—	—	—	—
1832Ga FS	10.00	20.00	35.00	80.00
1834/3Ga FS	65.00	100	175	250
1834Ga FS	10.00	20.00	35.00	80.00
1835/4/3Ga FS/LP	15.00	25.00	40.00	90.00
1837/6Ga JG	100	250	500	1,000
1838/7Ga JG	15.00	25.00	40.00	90.00

Date	F	VF	XF	Unc
1839/8Ga JG/FS	35.00	75.00	150	250
1839Ga MC	10.00	20.00	35.00	80.00
1840/39Ga MC/JG	—	—	—	—
1840Ga MC	15.00	25.00	40.00	90.00
1841Ga MC	20.00	35.00	50.00	100
1842/1Ga JG	15.00	25.00	40.00	90.00
1842Ga JG	10.00	20.00	35.00	80.00
1843/2Ga JG	15.00	30.00	50.00	100
1843Ga JG	10.00	20.00	35.00	80.00
1843Ga MC/JG	10.00	20.00	35.00	80.00
1843Ga MC	10.00	20.00	35.00	80.00
1844Ga MC	10.00	20.00	35.00	80.00
1845Ga MC	10.00	20.00	35.00	80.00
1845Ga JG	10.00	20.00	35.00	80.00
1846Ga MC	10.00	20.00	35.00	80.00
1846Ga JG	10.00	20.00	35.00	80.00
1847Ga JG	10.00	20.00	35.00	80.00
1848/7Ga JG	10.00	20.00	35.00	80.00
1849Ga JG	10.00	20.00	35.00	80.00
1850/49Ga JG	—	—	—	—
1850Ga JG	10.00	20.00	35.00	80.00
1851/0Ga JG	10.00	20.00	35.00	80.00
1852Ga JG	10.00	20.00	35.00	80.00
1853Ga JG	10.00	20.00	35.00	80.00
1854Ga JG	10.00	20.00	35.00	80.00
1855/4Ga JG	10.00	20.00	35.00	80.00
1855Ga JG	10.00	20.00	35.00	80.00
1856Ga JG	10.00	20.00	35.00	80.00
1857Ga JG	10.00	20.00	35.00	80.00
1858/7Ga JG	10.00	20.00	35.00	80.00
1858Ga JG	10.00	20.00	35.00	80.00
1859/7Ga JG	10.00	20.00	35.00	80.00
1860/59Ga JG	10.00	20.00	35.00	80.00
1861Ga JG	5.00	12.50	25.00	60.00
1862/1Ga JG	15.00	25.00	40.00	90.00

Mint: Guadalupe y Calvo
KM# 370.6   1/2 REAL
1.6900 g., 0.9030 Silver .0490 oz. ASW **Obv:** Facing eagle

Date	F	VF	XF	Unc
1844GC MP	50.00	100	150	350
1845GC MP	25.00	50.00	100	200
1846GC MP	25.00	50.00	100	200
1847GC MP	25.00	50.00	100	300
1848GC MP	20.00	40.00	75.00	150
1849GC MP	25.00	50.00	100	200
1850GC MP	30.00	60.00	125	250
1851GC MP	25.00	50.00	100	200

Mint: Guanajuato
KM# 370.7   1/2 REAL
1.6900 g., 0.9030 Silver .0490 oz. ASW **Obv:** Facing eagle
Note: Varieties exist.

Date	F	VF	XF	Unc
1826Go MJ	125	250	400	1,000
1827/6Go MJ	7.50	15.00	30.00	75.00
1828/7Go MJ	7.50	15.00	30.00	75.00
1828Go MJ Denomination 2/1	—	—	—	—
1828Go JG	—	—	—	—
1828Go MR	50.00	100	150	250
1829/8Go MJ	5.00	10.00	25.00	50.00
1829Go MJ	5.00	10.00	25.00	50.00
1829Go MJ Reversed N in MEXICANA	5.00	10.00	25.00	50.00
1830Go MJ	5.00	10.00	25.00	50.00
1831/29Go MJ	15.00	30.00	60.00	150
1831Go MJ	10.00	20.00	40.00	80.00
1832/1Go MJ	7.50	15.00	30.00	75.00
1832Go MJ	7.50	15.00	30.00	75.00
1833Go MJ Round top 3	10.00	20.00	40.00	80.00
1833Go MJ Flat top 3	10.00	20.00	40.00	80.00
1834Go PJ	5.00	10.00	25.00	50.00
1835Go PJ	5.00	10.00	25.00	50.00
1836/5Go PJ	7.50	15.00	30.00	75.00
1836Go PJ	5.00	10.00	25.00	50.00
1837Go PJ	5.00	10.00	25.00	50.00
1838/7Go PJ	5.00	10.00	25.00	50.00
1839Go PJ	5.00	10.00	25.00	50.00
1839Go PJ Error: REPUBLIGA	5.00	10.00	25.00	50.00
1840/39Go PJ	7.50	10.00	25.00	75.00
1840Go PJ Straight J	5.00	10.00	25.00	50.00
1840Go PJ Curved J	5.00	10.00	25.00	50.00

Date	F	VF	XF	Unc
1841/31Go PJ	5.00	10.00	25.00	50.00
1841Go PJ	5.00	10.00	25.00	50.00
1842/1Go PJ	5.00	10.00	25.00	50.00
1842/1Go PM	5.00	10.00	25.00	50.00
1842Go PM/J	5.00	10.00	25.00	50.00
1842Go PJ	5.00	10.00	25.00	50.00
1842Go PM	5.00	10.00	25.00	50.00
1843/33Go PM 1/2 over 8	5.00	10.00	25.00	50.00
1843Go PM Convex wings	5.00	10.00	25.00	50.00
1843Go PM Concave wings	5.00	10.00	25.00	50.00
1844/3Go PM	5.00	10.00	25.00	50.00
1844Go PM	10.00	20.00	40.00	90.00
1845/4Go PM	5.00	10.00	25.00	50.00
1845Go PM	5.00	10.00	25.00	50.00
1846/4Go PM	5.00	10.00	25.00	50.00
1846/5Go PM	5.00	10.00	25.00	50.00
1846Go PM	5.00	10.00	25.00	50.00
1847/6Go PM	7.50	15.00	30.00	60.00
1847Go PM	7.50	15.00	30.00	60.00
1848/35Go PM	5.00	10.00	25.00	50.00
1848Go PM	5.00	10.00	25.00	50.00
1848Go PF/M	5.00	10.00	25.00	50.00
1849/39Go PF	5.00	10.00	25.00	50.00
1849Go PF	5.00	10.00	25.00	50.00
1849Go PF Error: MEXCANA	5.00	10.00	25.00	50.00
1850Go PF	5.00	10.00	25.00	50.00
1851Go PF	5.00	10.00	25.00	50.00
1852/1Go PF	5.00	10.00	25.00	50.00
1852Go PF	2.50	7.50	17.50	40.00
1853Go PF/R	5.00	10.00	25.00	50.00
1853Go PF	5.00	10.00	25.00	50.00
1854Go PF	5.00	10.00	25.00	50.00
1855Go PF	5.00	10.00	25.00	50.00
1856/4Go PF	5.00	10.00	25.00	50.00
1856/5Go PF	5.00	10.00	25.00	50.00
1856Go PF	5.00	10.00	25.00	50.00
1857/6Go PF	5.00	10.00	25.00	50.00
1857Go PF	5.00	10.00	25.00	50.00
1858/7Go PF	7.50	15.00	30.00	60.00
1858Go PF	5.00	10.00	25.00	50.00
1859Go PF	5.00	10.00	25.00	50.00
1860Go PF Small 1/2	5.00	10.00	25.00	50.00
1860Go PF Large 1/2	5.00	10.00	25.00	50.00
1860/59Go PF	5.00	10.00	25.00	50.00
1861Go PF Small 1/2	5.00	10.00	25.00	50.00
1861Go PF Large 1/2	5.00	10.00	25.00	50.00
1862/1Go YE	5.00	10.00	25.00	50.00
1862Go YE	2.50	7.50	17.50	40.00
1862Go YF	5.00	10.00	25.00	50.00
1867Go YF	2.50	7.50	17.50	40.00
1868Go YF	2.50	7.50	17.50	40.00

Mint: Hermosillo
KM# 370.8   1/2 REAL
1.6900 g., 0.9030 Silver .0490 oz. ASW **Obv:** Facing eagle

Date	F	VF	XF	Unc
1839Ho PP Unique	—	—	—	—
1862Ho FM	500	650	1,000	—
1867Ho PR/FM Inverted 6, and 7/1	100	175	250	500

Mint: Mexico City
KM# 370.9   1/2 REAL
1.6900 g., 0.9030 Silver .0490 oz. ASW **Obv:** Facing eagle

Date	F	VF	XF	Unc
1825Mo JM Short top 5	10.00	20.00	40.00	80.00
1825Mo JM Long top 5	10.00	20.00	40.00	80.00
1826/5Mo JM	10.00	20.00	40.00	80.00
1826Mo JM	5.00	10.00	20.00	60.00
1827/6Mo JM	5.00	10.00	20.00	60.00
1827Mo JM	5.00	10.00	20.00	60.00
1828/7Mo JM	7.50	15.00	25.00	85.00
1828Mo JM	10.00	20.00	40.00	90.00
1829Mo JM	7.50	15.00	25.00	75.00
1830Mo JM	5.00	10.00	20.00	60.00
1831Mo JM	5.00	10.00	20.00	60.00
1832Mo JM	7.50	12.50	27.50	60.00
1833Mo MJ	7.50	12.50	27.50	60.00
1834Mo ML	5.00	10.00	20.00	60.00
1835Mo ML	5.00	10.00	20.00	60.00
1836/5Mo ML/MF	7.50	15.00	25.00	65.00
1836Mo ML	7.50	15.00	25.00	65.00

Date	F	VF	XF	Unc
1838Mo ML	5.00	10.00	20.00	60.00
1839/8Mo ML	5.00	10.00	25.00	65.00
1839Mo ML	5.00	10.00	20.00	50.00
1840Mo ML	5.00	10.00	20.00	50.00
1841Mo ML	5.00	10.00	20.00	50.00
1842Mo ML	5.00	10.00	20.00	50.00
1842Mo MM	5.00	10.00	20.00	50.00
1843Mo MM	10.00	20.00	40.00	80.00
1844Mo MF	5.00	10.00	20.00	50.00
1845/4Mo MF	5.00	10.00	25.00	60.00
1845Mo MF	5.00	10.00	20.00	50.00
1846Mo MF	5.00	10.00	20.00	50.00
1847Mo RC	10.00	20.00	40.00	80.00
1847Mo RC R/M	10.00	20.00	40.00	80.00
1848/7Mo GC/RC	5.00	10.00	20.00	50.00
1849Mo GC	5.00	10.00	20.00	50.00
1850Mo GC	5.00	10.00	20.00	50.00
1851Mo GC	5.00	10.00	20.00	50.00
1852Mo GC	5.00	10.00	20.00	50.00
1853Mo GC	5.00	10.00	20.00	50.00
1854Mo GC	5.00	10.00	20.00	50.00
1855Mo GC	5.00	10.00	20.00	50.00
1855Mo GF/GC	7.50	12.50	25.00	65.00
1856/5Mo GF	7.50	12.50	25.00	65.00
1857Mo GF	5.00	10.00	20.00	50.00
1858Mo FH	3.00	5.00	12.50	40.00
1858Mo FH F/G	5.00	10.00	20.00	50.00
1858/9Mo FH	5.00	10.00	20.00	50.00
1859Mo FH	3.00	6.00	15.00	50.00
1860Mo FH/GC	5.00	10.00	20.00	50.00
1860Mo FH	3.00	6.00	15.00	50.00
1860Mo TH	25.00	50.00	100	200
1860/59Mo FH	7.50	12.50	25.00	65.00
1861Mo CH	3.00	6.00	15.00	45.00
1862/52Mo CH	5.00	10.00	20.00	50.00
1862Mo CH	3.00	6.00	15.00	45.00
1863/55Mo TH/GC	5.00	10.00	20.00	50.00
1863Mo CH/GC	5.00	10.00	20.00	50.00
1863Mo CH	3.00	6.00	15.00	45.00

Mint: San Luis Potosi
KM# 370.10   1/2 REAL
1.6900 g., 0.9030 Silver .0490 oz. ASW **Obv:** Facing eagle

Date	F	VF	XF	Unc
1831 Pi JS	7.50	12.50	25.00	65.00
1841/36 Pi JS	20.00	40.00	75.00	125
1842/1 Pi PS	20.00	40.00	75.00	125
1842/1 Pi PS P/J	60.00	80.00	150	300
1842 Pi PS/PJ	50.00	75.00	125	250
1842 PS	60.00	80.00	150	300
1842 Pi JS	20.00	40.00	75.00	125
1843/2 Pi PS	17.50	25.00	40.00	80.00
1843 Pi PS	15.00	25.00	35.00	70.00
1843 Pi AM	10.00	15.00	25.00	60.00
1844 Pi AM	10.00	15.00	30.00	65.00
1845 Pi AM	250	375	500	1,500
1846/5 Pi AM	40.00	75.00	125	200
1847/6 Pi AM	15.00	25.00	40.00	80.00
1848 Pi AM	15.00	25.00	40.00	80.00
1849 Pi MC/AM	15.00	25.00	40.00	80.00
1849 Pi MC	12.50	20.00	35.00	70.00
1850/49 Pi MC	—	—	—	—
1850 Pi MC	10.00	15.00	25.00	60.00
1850P MC	—	—	—	—
1851 Pi MC	10.00	15.00	25.00	60.00
1852 Pi MC	10.00	20.00	30.00	65.00
1853 Pi MC	7.50	12.50	20.00	60.00
1854 Pi MC	7.50	12.50	20.00	60.00
1855 Pi MC	15.00	20.00	35.00	70.00
1856 Pi MC	15.00	25.00	50.00	100
1856PI (no I)	—	—	—	—
1857 Pi MC	7.50	12.50	20.00	60.00
1857 Pi PS	10.00	15.00	30.00	65.00
1858 Pi MC	12.50	20.00	35.00	70.00
1858 Pi PS	12.50	20.00	35.00	70.00
1859 Pi MC Rare	—	—	—	—
1860/59 Pi PS	125	200	600	—
1861 Pi RO	10.00	15.00	30.00	60.00
1862/1 Pi RO	15.00	25.00	50.00	125

Date	F	VF	XF	Unc
1862 Pi RO	15.00	25.00	50.00	125
1863/2 Pi RO	15.00	25.00	45.00	100

Mint: Zacatecas
KM# 370.11   1/2 REAL
1.6900 g., 0.9030 Silver .0490 oz. ASW **Obv:** Facing eagle
Note: Mint mark Z, Zs.

Date	F	VF	XF	Unc
1826 AZ	5.00	10.00	20.00	60.00
1826 AO	5.00	10.00	20.00	60.00
1827 AO	5.00	10.00	20.00	60.00
1828/7 AO	5.00	10.00	20.00	60.00
1829 AO	5.00	10.00	20.00	60.00
1830 OV	5.00	10.00	20.00	60.00
1831 OV	25.00	50.00	75.00	150
1831 OM	5.00	10.00	20.00	60.00
1832 OM	5.00	10.00	20.00	60.00
1833 OM	5.00	10.00	20.00	60.00
1834 OM	5.00	10.00	20.00	60.00
1835/4 OM	5.00	10.00	20.00	60.00
1835 OM	5.00	10.00	20.00	60.00
1836 OM	5.00	10.00	20.00	60.00
1837 OM	10.00	20.00	40.00	80.00
1838 OM	5.00	10.00	20.00	60.00
1839 OM	7.50	15.00	30.00	65.00
1840 OM	10.00	25.00	45.00	90.00
1841 OM	10.00	25.00	45.00	90.00
1842/1 OM	5.00	10.00	20.00	60.00
1842 OM	5.00	10.00	20.00	60.00
1843 OM	40.00	75.00	115	250
1844 OM	5.00	10.00	20.00	60.00
1845 OM	5.00	10.00	20.00	60.00
1846 OM	7.50	15.00	30.00	65.00
1847 OM	5.00	10.00	20.00	50.00
1848 OM	5.00	10.00	20.00	50.00
1849 OM	5.00	10.00	20.00	50.00
1850 OM	5.00	10.00	20.00	50.00
1851 OM	5.00	10.00	20.00	50.00
1852 OM	5.00	10.00	20.00	50.00
1853 OM	5.00	10.00	20.00	50.00
1854/3 OM	5.00	10.00	20.00	50.00
1854 OM	5.00	10.00	20.00	50.00
1855/3 OM	7.50	15.00	30.00	65.00
1855 OM	5.00	10.00	20.00	50.00
1856 OM	5.00	10.00	20.00	50.00
1857 MO	5.00	10.00	20.00	50.00
1858 MO	5.00	10.00	20.00	50.00
1859 MO	6.00	8.50	17.50	35.00
1859 VL	6.00	8.50	17.50	40.00
1860/50 VL Inverted A for V	5.00	10.00	20.00	50.00
1860/59 VL Inverted A for V	5.00	10.00	20.00	50.00
1860 MO	5.00	10.00	20.00	50.00
1860 VL	5.00	10.00	20.00	50.00
1861/0 VL Inverted A for V	7.50	15.00	30.00	65.00
1861 VL Inverted A for V	5.00	10.00	20.00	50.00
1862 VL Inverted A for V	5.00	10.00	20.00	50.00
1863/1 VL Inverted A for V	7.50	15.00	30.00	65.00
1863 VL Inverted A for V	5.00	10.00	20.00	50.00
1869 YH	5.00	10.00	20.00	50.00

Mint: Chihuahua
KM# 372   REAL
3.3800 g., 0.9030 Silver .0981 oz. ASW

Date	F	VF	XF	Unc
1844 Ca RG	500	1,000	1,500	2,750
1845 Ca RG	500	1,000	1,500	2,750
1855 Ca RG	100	150	225	450

Mint: Culiacan
KM# 372.1   REAL
3.3800 g., 0.9030 Silver .0981 oz. ASW

Date	F	VF	XF	Unc
1846C CE	12.50	25.00	40.00	110
1848C CE	12.50	25.00	40.00	110
1850C CE	12.50	25.00	40.00	110
1851/0C CE	12.50	25.00	40.00	110
1852/1C CE	7.50	15.00	30.00	100
1853/2C CE	7.50	15.00	30.00	100
1854C CE	7.50	15.00	30.00	100
1856C CE	40.00	65.00	100	225
1857/4C CE	10.00	20.00	35.00	100
1857/6C CE	10.00	20.00	35.00	100
1858C CE	5.00	7.50	15.00	100

Date	F	VF	XF	Unc
1859C CE	—	—	—	—
1860C PV	5.00	7.50	15.00	100
1861C PV	5.00	7.50	15.00	100
1863C CE 3 known	—	—	1,650	2,250
1869C CE	—	7.50	15.00	100

Mint: Durango
KM# 372.2 REAL
3.3800 g., 0.9030 Silver .0981 oz. ASW

Date	F	VF	XF	Unc
1832/1Do RM	5.00	10.00	20.00	90.00
1832Do RM/RL	10.00	15.00	30.00	100
1832Do RM	5.00	10.00	20.00	100
1834/24Do RM/RL	15.00	25.00	50.00	150
1834/3Do RM/RL	15.00	25.00	50.00	150
1834Do RM	10.00	20.00	40.00	110
1836/4Do RM	5.00	7.50	15.00	100
1836Do RM	5.00	7.50	15.00	100
1837Do RM 3/2	12.50	20.00	40.00	110
1837Do RM	12.50	20.00	40.00	110
1841Do RM	7.50	15.00	30.00	100
1842/32Do RM	10.00	20.00	40.00	110
1842Do RM	7.50	15.00	30.00	100
1843Do RM	5.00	7.50	15.00	100
1844/34Do RM	15.00	25.00	45.00	125
1845Do RM	5.00	7.50	15.00	100
1846Do RM	7.50	15.00	30.00	100
1847Do RM	10.00	15.00	35.00	100
1848/31Do RM	10.00	15.00	35.00	100
1848/33Do RM	10.00	15.00	35.00	100
1848/5Do RM	10.00	15.00	35.00	100
1848Do RM	7.50	12.50	20.00	100
1849/8Do CM	10.00	15.00	30.00	100
1850Do JMR	20.00	40.00	75.00	175
1851Do JMR	20.00	40.00	75.00	175
1852Do JMR	20.00	40.00	75.00	175
1853Do CP	12.50	20.00	35.00	100
1854/1Do CP	10.00	15.00	25.00	100
1854Do CP	7.50	12.50	20.00	100
1855Do CP	10.00	15.00	25.00	100
1856Do CP	12.50	20.00	35.00	100
1857Do CP	12.50	20.00	35.00	100
1858Do CP	12.50	20.00	35.00	100
1859Do CP	7.50	12.50	20.00	100
1860/59Do CP	10.00	15.00	25.00	100
1861Do CP	15.00	25.00	40.00	110
1862/1Do CP	225	300	450	1,250
1864Do LT	15.00	25.00	40.00	110

Mint: Estado de Mexico
KM# 372.3 REAL
3.3800 g., 0.9030 Silver .0981 oz. ASW

Date	F	VF	XF	Unc
1828EoMo LF	200	300	450	1,500

Mint: Guadalajara
KM# 372.4 REAL
3.3800 g., 0.9030 Silver .0981 oz. ASW

Date	F	VF	XF	Unc
1826Ga FS	15.00	30.00	50.00	125
1828/7Ga FS	15.00	30.00	50.00	125
1829/8/7Ga FS	—	—	—	—
1829Ga FS	15.00	30.00	50.00	125
1830Ga FS	250	425	600	—
1831Ga LP	15.00	30.00	50.00	125
1831Ga LP/FS	300	450	600	—
1832Ga FS	250	350	500	—
1833/2Ga G FS	100	150	275	550
1833Ga FS	75.00	125	225	500
1834/3Ga FS	75.00	125	225	500
1835Ga FS	—	—	—	—
1837/6Ga JG/FS	12.50	20.00	35.00	100
1838/7Ga JG/FS	100	200	400	—
1839Ga JG	250	350	500	—
1840Ga JG	12.50	20.00	35.00	100
1840Ga MC	7.50	12.50	25.00	70.00
1841Ga MC	50.00	75.00	125	250
1842/0Ga JG/MC	10.00	15.00	30.00	100
1842Ga JG	7.50	12.50	20.00	100
1843Ga JG	150	200	300	750
1843Ga MC	5.00	7.50	15.00	100
1844Ga MC	7.50	12.50	20.00	100
1845Ga MC	10.00	15.00	25.00	100

Date	F	VF	XF	Unc
1845Ga JG	5.00	7.50	20.00	100
1846Ga JG	12.50	20.00	35.00	100
1847/6Ga JG	10.00	15.00	25.00	100
1847Ga JG	10.00	15.00	25.00	100
1848Ga JG	400	550	700	—
1849Ga JG	7.50	12.50	20.00	100
1850Ga JG	175	275	400	—
1851Ga JG	10.00	15.00	25.00	100
1852Ga JG	10.00	15.00	25.00	100
1853/2Ga JG	10.00	15.00	25.00	100
1854Ga JG	10.00	15.00	25.00	100
1855Ga JG	15.00	25.00	40.00	100
1856Ga JG	7.50	12.50	20.00	100
1857/6Ga JG	12.50	20.00	35.00	100
1858/7Ga JG	15.00	25.00	40.00	110
1859/8Ga JG	25.00	50.00	75.00	150
1860/59Ga JG	30.00	60.00	90.00	225
1861/0Ga JG	20.00	30.00	50.00	125
1861Ga JG	25.00	50.00	100	250
1862Ga JG	7.50	12.50	20.00	100

Mint: Guadalupe y Calvo
KM# 372.5 REAL
3.3800 g., 0.9030 Silver .0981 oz. ASW

Date	F	VF	XF	Unc
1844GC MP	40.00	60.00	100	250
1845GC MP	40.00	60.00	100	250
1846GC MP	40.00	60.00	100	250
1847GC MP	40.00	60.00	100	250
1848GC MP	40.00	60.00	100	250
1849/7GC MP	40.00	60.00	100	250
1849/8GC MP	40.00	60.00	100	250
1849GC MP	40.00	60.00	100	250
1850GC MP	40.00	60.00	100	250
1851GC MP	40.00	60.00	100	250

Mint: Guanajuato
KM# 372.6 REAL
3.3800 g., 0.9030 Silver .0981 oz. ASW

Date	F	VF	XF	Unc
1826/5Go JJ	5.00	7.50	15.00	85.00
1826Go MJ	4.00	6.00	15.00	85.00
1827Go MJ	4.00	6.00	15.00	65.00
1827Go JM	10.00	15.00	25.00	75.00
1828/7Go MR	4.00	6.00	15.00	85.00
1828Go MJ	4.00	6.00	15.00	85.00
Note: Straight J, small 8				
1828Go MJ	4.00	6.00	15.00	85.00
Note: Full J, large 8				
1828G MR/JJ	4.00	6.00	15.00	85.00
1828Go MR	4.00	6.00	15.00	85.00
1829/8Go MG Small eagle	4.00	6.00	15.00	85.00
1829Go MJ Small eagle	4.00	6.00	15.00	85.00
1829Go MJ Large eagle	4.00	6.00	15.00	85.00
1830Go MJ Small initials	4.00	6.00	15.00	85.00
1830Go MJ Medium initials	4.00	6.00	15.00	85.00
1830Go MJ Large initials	4.00	6.00	15.00	85.00
1830Go MJ	4.00	6.00	15.00	85.00
Note: Reversed N in MEXICANA				
1830GC MJ 3/2	4.00	6.00	15.00	85.00
1831/0Go MJ	4.00	6.00	15.00	85.00
Note: Reversed N in MEXICANA				
1831Go MJ	4.00	6.00	15.00	85.00
1832/1Go MJ	15.00	30.00	50.00	125
1832Go MJ	15.00	30.00	50.00	125
1833Go MJ Top of 3 round	4.00	6.00	15.00	85.00
1833Go MJ Top of 3 flat	4.00	6.00	15.00	85.00
1834Go PJ	4.00	6.00	15.00	85.00
1835Go PJ	7.50	12.50	20.00	85.00
1836Go PJ	4.00	6.00	15.00	85.00
1837Go PJ	15.00	30.00	50.00	125
1838/7Go PJ	10.00	20.00	35.00	85.00

Date	F	VF	XF	Unc
1839Go PJ	4.00	6.00	15.00	85.00
1840/39Go PJ	4.00	6.00	15.00	85.00
1840Go PJ	4.00	6.00	15.00	85.00
1841/31Go PJ	10.00	20.00	35.00	85.00
1841Go PJ	4.00	6.00	15.00	85.00
1842Go PJ	4.00	6.00	15.00	85.00
1842Go PM	4.00	6.00	15.00	85.00
1843Go PM Convex wings	4.00	6.00	15.00	85.00
1843Go PM Concave wings	4.00	6.00	15.00	85.00
1844Go PM	4.00	6.00	15.00	85.00
1845/4Go PM	4.00	6.00	15.00	85.00
1845Go PM	4.00	6.00	15.00	85.00
1846/5Go PM	7.50	12.50	20.00	85.00
1846Go PM	4.00	6.00	15.00	85.00
1847/6Go PM	4.00	6.00	15.00	85.00
1847Go PM	4.00	6.00	15.00	85.00
1848Go PM	4.00	6.00	15.00	85.00
1849Go PF	10.00	20.00	35.00	85.00
1850Go PF	4.00	6.00	15.00	85.00
1851Go PF	10.00	20.00	35.00	100
1853/2Go PF	7.50	12.50	20.00	75.00
1853Go PF	4.00	6.00	15.00	75.00
1853Go PF/M 5/4	7.50	12.50	20.00	75.00
1854/3Go PF	4.00	6.00	15.00	75.00
1854Go PF Large eagle	4.00	6.00	15.00	75.00
1854Go PF Small eagle	4.00	6.00	15.00	75.00
1855/3Go PF	4.00	6.00	15.00	75.00
1855/4Go PF	4.00	6.00	15.00	75.00
1855Go PF	4.00	6.00	15.00	75.00
1856/5Go PF	4.00	6.00	15.00	75.00
1856Go PF	4.00	6.00	15.00	75.00
1857/6Go PF	4.00	6.00	15.00	75.00
1857Go PF	4.00	6.00	15.00	75.00
1858Go PF	4.00	6.00	15.00	75.00
1859Go PF	4.00	6.00	15.00	75.00
1860/50Go PF	4.00	6.00	15.00	75.00
1860Go PF	4.00	6.00	15.00	75.00
1861Go PF	4.00	6.00	15.00	75.00
1862Go YE	4.00	6.00	15.00	75.00
1862/1Go YF	7.50	12.50	20.00	75.00
1862Go YF	4.00	6.00	15.00	75.00
1867Go YF	4.00	6.00	15.00	75.00
1868/7Go YF	4.00	6.00	15.00	75.00

Mint: Hermosillo
KM# 372.7 REAL
3.3800 g., 0.9030 Silver .0981 oz. ASW

Date	F	VF	XF	Unc
1867Ho PR	38.50	75.00	120	250
Note: Small 7/1				
1867Ho PR	38.50	75.00	120	250
Note: Large 7/ small 7				
1868Ho PR	38.50	75.00	120	250

Mint: Mexico City
KM# 372.8 REAL
3.3800 g., 0.9030 Silver .0981 oz. ASW

Date	F	VF	XF	Unc
1825Mo JM	10.00	20.00	40.00	110
1826Mo JM	7.50	15.00	30.00	100
1827/6Mo JM	7.50	15.00	30.00	75.00
1827Mo JM	5.00	10.00	20.00	70.00
1828Mo JM	7.50	15.00	30.00	100
1830/29Mo JM	5.00	10.00	20.00	100
1830Mo JM	5.00	12.50	25.00	100
1831Mo JM	100	200	300	750
1832Mo JM	5.00	10.00	20.00	100
1833/2Mo MJ	5.00	10.00	20.00	100
1850Mo GC	5.00	10.00	20.00	100
1852Mo GC	275	425	575	—
1854Mo GC	10.00	20.00	40.00	100
1855Mo GF	5.00	10.00	20.00	80.00
1856Mo GF	5.00	10.00	20.00	80.00
1857Mo GF	5.00	10.00	20.00	80.00
1858Mo FH	5.00	10.00	20.00	80.00
1859Mo FH	5.00	10.00	20.00	80.00
1861Mo CH	5.00	10.00	20.00	80.00
1862Mo CH	5.00	10.00	20.00	80.00
1863/2Mo CH	7.50	12.50	25.00	80.00

Mint: San Luis Potosi
KM# 372.9 REAL
3.3800 g., 0.9030 Silver .0981 oz. ASW

Date	F	VF	XF	Unc
1831 Pi JS	5.00	10.00	20.00	125
1837 Pi JS	600	750	1,000	—
1838/7 Pi JS	250	300	375	—
1838 Pi JS	20.00	35.00	60.00	125
1840/39 Pi JS	7.50	15.00	30.00	125
1840 Pi JS	7.50	15.00	30.00	125
1841 Pi JS	7.50	15.00	30.00	125
1842 Pi JS	15.00	30.00	55.00	150
1842 Pi PS	5.00	10.00	20.00	125
1843 Pi PS	12.50	20.00	35.00	125
1843 Pi AM	40.00	60.00	80.00	150
1844 Pi AM	40.00	60.00	80.00	150
1845 Pi AM	7.50	15.00	30.00	125
1846/5 Pi AM	7.50	15.00	30.00	125
1847/6 Pi AM	7.50	15.00	30.00	125
1847 Pi AM	7.50	15.00	30.00	125
1848/7 Pi AM	7.50	15.00	30.00	125
1849 Pi PS	7.50	15.00	30.00	125
1849/8 Pi SP	60.00	100	150	—
1849 Pi SP	15.00	25.00	40.00	125
1850 Pi MC	5.00	10.00	20.00	125
1851/0 Pi MC	7.50	15.00	30.00	125
1851 Pi MC	7.50	15.00	30.00	125
1852/1/0 Pi MC	10.00	20.00	35.00	125
1852 Pi MC	7.50	15.00	30.00	125
1853/1 Pi MC	12.50	20.00	35.00	125
1853 Pi MC	10.00	20.00	35.00	125
1854/2 Pi MO	30.00	60.00	100	—
1854/3 Pi MC	20.00	40.00	60.00	150
1855/4 Pi MC	20.00	40.00	60.00	150
1855 Pi MC	15.00	25.00	45.00	125
1856 Pi MC	15.00	25.00	45.00	125
1857 Pi PS	20.00	35.00	55.00	135
1857 Pi MC	20.00	40.00	60.00	150
1858 Pi MC	12.50	20.00	35.00	125
1859 Pi PS	10.00	15.00	30.00	125
1860/59 Pi PS	10.00	15.00	30.00	125
1861 Pi PS	7.50	12.50	20.00	125
1861 Pi RO	12.50	20.00	35.00	125
1862/1 Pi RO	12.50	20.00	35.00	90.00
1862 Pi RO	7.50	12.50	20.00	125

Mint: Zacatecas
KM# 372.10 REAL
3.3800 g., 0.9030 Silver .0981 oz. ASW

Date	F	VF	XF	Unc
1826Zs AZ	5.00	12.50	35.00	120
1826Zs AO	5.00	12.50	35.00	120
1827Zs AO	5.00	12.50	35.00	120
1828/7Zs AO	5.00	12.50	35.00	120
1828Zs AO	5.00	12.50	35.00	120
1828Zs AO Inverted V for A	5.00	12.50	35.00	120
1829Zs AO	5.00	12.50	35.00	120
1830Zs ZsOV	5.00	12.50	35.00	120
1830Zs ZOV	5.00	12.50	35.00	120
1831Zs OV	5.00	12.50	35.00	120
1831Zs OM	5.00	12.50	30.00	120
1832Zs OM	5.00	12.50	30.00	120
1833/2Zs OM	5.00	12.50	30.00	120
1833/2Zs OM/V	5.00	12.50	30.00	120
1833Zs OM	5.00	12.50	30.00	120
1834/3Zs OM	5.00	12.50	30.00	120
1834Zs OM	5.00	12.50	30.00	120
1835/4Zs OM	20.00	35.00	60.00	150
1835Zs OM	4.00	8.00	20.00	65.00
1836/5Zs OM	4.00	8.00	20.00	85.00
1836Zs OM	4.00	8.00	20.00	85.00
1837Zs OM	4.00	8.00	20.00	85.00
1838Zs OM	4.00	8.00	20.00	85.00
1839Zs OM	4.00	8.00	20.00	85.00
1840Zs OM	4.00	8.00	20.00	85.00
1841Zs OM	20.00	40.00	60.00	150
1842/1Zs OM	4.00	8.00	20.00	85.00
1842Zs OM	4.00	8.00	20.00	85.00
1843Zs OM	4.00	8.00	20.00	85.00
1844Zs OM	4.00	8.00	20.00	85.00
1845/4Zs OM	5.00	12.50	30.00	100
1845Zs OM	4.00	8.00	20.00	85.00

Date	F	VF	XF	Unc
1846Zs OM	4.00	8.00	20.00	85.00
Note: Old font and obverse				
1846Zs OM	4.00	8.00	20.00	85.00
Note: New font and obverse				
1847Zs OM	4.00	8.00	20.00	85.00
1848Zs OM	4.00	8.00	20.00	85.00
1849Zs OM	10.00	25.00	50.00	125
1850Zs OM	4.00	6.00	15.00	85.00
1851Zs OM	4.00	6.00	15.00	85.00
1852Zs OM	4.00	6.00	15.00	85.00
1853Zs OM	4.00	6.00	15.00	85.00
1854/2Zs OM	4.00	6.00	15.00	85.00
1854/3Zs OM	4.00	6.00	15.00	85.00
1854Zs OM	4.00	6.00	15.00	85.00
1855/4Zs OM	4.00	6.00	15.00	85.00
1855Zs OM	4.00	6.00	15.00	85.00
1855Zs MO	4.00	6.00	15.00	85.00
1856Zs MO	4.00	6.00	15.00	85.00
1856Zs MO/OM	4.00	6.00	15.00	85.00
1857Zs MO	4.00	6.00	15.00	85.00
1858Zs MO	4.00	6.00	15.00	85.00
1859Zs MO	4.00	6.00	15.00	75.00
1860 MO	250	—	—	—
1860Zs VL	4.00	6.00	15.00	75.00
1860Zs VL Inverted A for V	4.00	6.00	15.00	75.00
1861Zs VL	4.00	6.00	15.00	75.00
1861Zs VL Inverted A for V	4.00	6.00	15.00	75.00
1862Zs VL	5.00	12.50	30.00	100
1868Zs JS	25.00	45.00	90.00	175
1869Zs YH	4.00	8.00	20.00	75.00

Mint: Alamos
KM# 374   2 REALES
6.7600 g., 0.9030 Silver .1962 oz. ASW   Obv: Facing eagle
Edge: Reeded

Date	Mintage	F	VF	XF	Unc
1872A AM	15,000	50.00	115	225	550

Mint: Real de Catorce
KM# 374.1   2 REALES
6.7600 g., 0.9030 Silver .1962 oz. ASW   Obv: Facing eagle
Edge: Reeded

Date	F	VF	XF	Unc
1863 Ce ML	125	200	325	675

Mint: Chihuahua
KM# 374.2   2 REALES
6.7600 g., 0.9030 Silver .1962 oz. ASW   Obv: Facing eagle
Edge: Reeded

Date	F	VF	XF	Unc
1832 Ca MR	30.00	60.00	100	200
1833 Ca MR	30.00	60.00	125	500
1834 Ca MR	35.00	75.00	125	500
1834 Ca AM	35.00	75.00	125	500
1835 Ca AM	35.00	75.00	125	500
1836 Ca AM	20.00	40.00	80.00	200
1844 Ca AM Rare	—	—	—	—
1844 Ca RG Unique	—	—	—	—
1845 Ca RG	20.00	40.00	80.00	200
1855 Ca RG	20.00	40.00	80.00	200

Mint: Culiacan
KM# 374.3   2 REALES
6.7600 g., 0.9030 Silver .1962 oz. ASW   Obv: Facing eagle
Edge: Reeded

Date	F	VF	XF	Unc
1846/1146C CE	25.00	50.00	100	225
1847C CE	12.50	20.00	40.00	200
1848C CE	12.50	20.00	40.00	200
1850C CE	25.00	50.00	75.00	200
1851C CE	12.50	20.00	40.00	200
1852/1C CE	12.50	20.00	40.00	200
1853/2C CE	12.50	20.00	40.00	200
1854C CE	15.00	30.00	50.00	200
1856C CE	20.00	35.00	70.00	200
1857C CE	12.50	20.00	40.00	200
1860C PV	12.50	20.00	40.00	200
1861C PV	12.50	20.00	40.00	200
1869C CE	12.50	20.00	40.00	200

Mint: Durango
KM# 374.4   2 REALES
6.7600 g., 0.9030 Silver .1962 oz. ASW   Obv: Facing eagle
Edge: Reeded

Date	F	VF	XF	Unc
1826Do RL	20.00	40.00	60.00	200
1832Do RM	20.00	40.00	60.00	200
Note: Style of pre-1832				
1832Do RM	20.00	40.00	60.00	200
Note: Style of post-1832				
1834/2Do RM	20.00	40.00	60.00	200
1834/3Do RM	20.00	40.00	60.00	200
1835/4Do RM/RL	200	300	500	—
1841/31Do RM	50.00	75.00	125	250
1841Do RM	50.00	75.00	125	250
1842/32Do RM	12.50	20.00	40.00	200
1843Do RM/RL	12.50	20.00	40.00	200
1844Do RM	35.00	50.00	80.00	200
1845/34Do RM/RL	12.50	20.00	40.00	200
1846/36Do RM	100	150	200	350
1848/36Do RM	12.50	20.00	40.00	200
1848/37Do RM	12.50	20.00	40.00	200
1848/7Do RM	12.50	20.00	40.00	200
1848Do RM	12.50	20.00	40.00	200
1849Do CM/RM	12.50	20.00	40.00	200
1849Do CM	12.50	20.00	40.00	200
1851Do JMR/RL	12.50	20.00	40.00	200
1852Do JMR	12.50	20.00	40.00	200
1854Do CP/CR	30.00	50.00	80.00	200
1855Do CP	250	350	500	—
1856Do CP	100	150	250	500
1858Do CP	12.50	20.00	40.00	200
1859/8Do CP	12.50	20.00	40.00	200
1861Do CP	12.50	20.00	40.00	200

Mint: Estado de Mexico
KM# 374.5   2 REALES
6.7600 g., 0.9030 Silver .1962 oz. ASW   Obv: Facing eagle
Edge: Reeded

Date	F	VF	XF	Unc
1828EoMo LF	325	525	900	2,500

Mint: Guadalajara
KM# 374.6   2 REALES
6.7600 g., 0.9030 Silver .1962 oz. ASW   Obv: Facing eagle
Edge: Reeded

Date	F	VF	XF	Unc
1825Ga FS	20.00	40.00	80.00	200
1826Ga FS	20.00	40.00	80.00	200
1828/7Ga FS	100	150	225	400
1829Ga FS Rare	—	—	—	—
1832/0Ga FS/LP	100	150	225	350
1832Ga FS	12.50	20.00	40.00	200
1833/2Ga FS/LP	12.50	20.00	40.00	200
1834/27Ga FS Rare	—	—	—	—
1834Ga FS	12.50	20.00	40.00	200
1835Ga FS	2,100	—	—	—
1837Ga JG	12.50	20.00	40.00	200
1838Ga JG	12.50	20.00	40.00	200
1840/30Ga MC	12.50	20.00	40.00	200
1841Ga MC	30.00	50.00	200	500
1842/32Ga JG/MC	35.00	50.00	100	200
1842Ga JG	20.00	40.00	80.00	200
1843Ga JG	12.50	20.00	40.00	200
1843Ga MC/JG	12.50	20.00	40.00	200
1844Ga MC	12.50	20.00	40.00	200
1845/3Ga MC/JG	12.50	20.00	40.00	200
1845/4Ga MC/JG	12.50	20.00	40.00	200
1845Ga JG	12.50	20.00	40.00	200
1846Ga JG	12.50	20.00	40.00	200
1847/6Ga JG	25.00	40.00	80.00	200
1848/7Ga JG	12.50	20.00	40.00	200
1849Ga JG	12.50	20.00	40.00	200
1850/40Ga JG	12.50	20.00	40.00	200
1851Ga JG	250	350	500	—
1852Ga JG	12.50	20.00	40.00	200
1853/1Ga JG	12.50	20.00	40.00	200
1854/3Ga JG	250	350	500	—
1855Ga JG	35.00	50.00	80.00	200
1856Ga JG	12.50	20.00	40.00	200
1857Ga JG	250	350	500	—
1859/8Ga JG	12.50	20.00	40.00	200
1859Ga JG	12.50	20.00	40.00	200
1862/1Ga JG	12.50	20.00	40.00	200

Mint: Guadalupe y Calvo
KM# 374.7 2 REALES
6.7600 g., 0.9030 Silver .1962 oz. ASW **Obv:** Facing eagle
Edge: Reeded

Date	F	VF	XF	Unc
1844GC MP	40.00	60.00	125	275
1845GC MP	40.00	60.00	125	275
1846GC MP	50.00	100	150	300
1847GC MP	35.00	50.00	100	250
1848GC MP	50.00	100	150	300
1849GC MP	50.00	100	150	300
1850GC MP	125	250	—	—
1851/0GC MP	50.00	100	150	300
1851GC MP	50.00	100	150	300

Mint: Guanajuato
KM# 374.8 2 REALES
6.7600 g., 0.9030 Silver .1962 oz. ASW **Obv:** Facing eagle
Edge: Reeded **Note:** Varieties exist.

Date	F	VF	XF	Unc
1825Go JJ	7.50	15.00	30.00	150
1826/5Go JJ	7.50	15.00	30.00	150
1826Go JJ	7.50	10.00	25.00	150
1826Go MJ	7.50	10.00	25.00	150
1827/6Go MJ	7.50	10.00	25.00	150
1827Go MJ	7.50	10.00	25.00	150
1828/7Go MR	7.50	15.00	30.00	150
1828Go MJ	7.50	10.00	20.00	150
1828Go JM	7.50	10.00	20.00	150
1829Go MJ	7.50	10.00	20.00	150
1831Go MJ	7.50	10.00	20.00	150
1832Go MJ	7.50	10.00	20.00	150
1833Go MJ	7.50	10.00	20.00	150
1834Go PJ	7.50	10.00	20.00	150
1835/4Go PJ	7.50	15.00	30.00	150
1835Go PJ	7.50	10.00	20.00	150
1836Go PJ	7.50	10.00	20.00	150
1837/6Go PJ	7.50	10.00	20.00	150
1837Go PJ	7.50	10.00	20.00	150
1838/7Go PJ	7.50	10.00	20.00	150
1838Go PJ	7.50	10.00	20.00	150
1839/8Go PJ	7.50	15.00	30.00	150
1839Go PJ	7.50	10.00	20.00	150
1840Go PJ	7.50	10.00	20.00	150
1841Go PJ	7.50	10.00	20.00	150
1842Go PJ	7.50	10.00	20.00	150
1842Go PM/PJ	7.50	10.00	20.00	150
1842Go PM	7.50	10.00	20.00	150
1843/2Go PM	7.50	10.00	20.00	150

Note: Concave wings, thin rays, small letters

1843Go PM	7.50	10.00	20.00	150

Note: Convex wings, thick rays, large letters

1844Go PM	7.50	10.00	20.00	150
1845/4Go PM	7.50	10.00	20.00	150
1845Go PM	7.50	10.00	20.00	150
1846/5Go PM	10.00	15.00	35.00	150
1846Go PM	7.50	10.00	20.00	150
1847Go PM	7.50	10.00	20.00	150
1848/7Go PM	7.50	15.00	30.00	150
1848Go PM	7.50	15.00	30.00	150
1848Go PF	100	150	250	500
1849/8Go PF/PM	7.50	10.00	20.00	150
1849Go PF	7.50	10.00	20.00	150
1850/40Go PF	7.50	10.00	20.00	150
1850Go PF	7.50	10.00	20.00	150
1851Go PF	7.50	10.00	20.00	150
1852/1Go PF	7.50	10.00	20.00	150
1852Go PF	7.50	10.00	20.00	150
1853Go PF	7.50	10.00	20.00	150
1854/3Go PF	7.50	10.00	20.00	150
1854Go PF	7.50	10.00	20.00	150

Note: Old font and obverse

1854Go PF	7.50	10.00	20.00	150

Note: New font and obverse

1855Go PF	7.50	10.00	20.00	150
1855Go PF	7.50	10.00	20.00	150

Note: Star in G of mint mark

1856/5Go PF	10.00	15.00	35.00	150
1856Go PF	10.00	15.00	25.00	150
1857/6Go PF	7.50	10.00	20.00	150
1857Go PF	7.50	10.00	20.00	150
1858/7Go PF	7.50	10.00	20.00	150

Date	F	VF	XF	Unc
1858Go PF	7.50	10.00	20.00	150
1859/7Go PF	7.50	10.00	20.00	150
1859Go PF	7.50	10.00	20.00	150
1860/7Go PF	7.50	10.00	20.00	150
1860/50Go PF	7.50	10.00	20.00	150
1860/59Go PF	7.50	10.00	20.00	150
1860Go PF	7.50	10.00	20.00	150
1861/51Go PF	7.50	10.00	20.00	150
1861/57Go PF	7.50	10.00	20.00	150
1861/0Go PF	7.50	10.00	20.00	150
1861Go PF	7.50	10.00	20.00	150
1862/1Go YE	7.50	10.00	20.00	125
1862Go YE	7.50	10.00	20.00	125
1862/57Go YE	7.50	10.00	20.00	125
1862Go YE/PF	7.50	10.00	20.00	125
1862Go YF	7.50	10.00	20.00	125
1863/52Go YF	7.50	10.00	20.00	125
1863Go YF	7.50	10.00	20.00	125
1867/57Go YF	7.50	10.00	20.00	125
1868/57Go YF	10.00	15.00	25.00	125

Mint: Hermosillo
KM# 374.9 2 REALES
6.7600 g., 0.9030 Silver .1962 oz. ASW **Obv:** Facing eagle
Edge: Reeded

Date	F	VF	XF	Unc
1861Ho FM	200	300	400	650
1862/52Ho FM/C. CE	250	350	500	—
1867/1Ho PR/FM	75.00	150	250	500

Mint: Mexico City
KM# 374.10 2 REALES
6.7600 g., 0.9030 Silver .1962 oz. ASW **Obv:** Facing eagle
Edge: Reeded **Note:** Varieties exist.

Date	F	VF	XF	Unc
1825Mo JM	10.00	15.00	30.00	175
1826Mo JM	10.00	15.00	30.00	175
1827Mo JM	10.00	15.00	30.00	175
1828Mo JM	10.00	15.00	30.00	175
1829/8Mo JM	10.00	15.00	30.00	175
1829Mo JM	10.00	15.00	30.00	175
1830Mo JM	40.00	60.00	125	250
1831Mo JM	10.00	15.00	30.00	175
1832Mo JM	100	200	400	—
1833/2Mo MJ/JM	10.00	15.00	30.00	175
1834Mo ML	50.00	100	200	400
1836Mo MF	10.00	15.00	30.00	175
1837Mo ML	10.00	15.00	30.00	175
1840/7Mo ML	150	225	350	—
1840Mo ML	150	225	350	—
1841Mo ML	15.00	40.00	100	250
1842 ML Rare	—	—	—	—
1847Mo RC Narrow date	10.00	15.00	30.00	175
1847Mo RC Wide date	10.00	15.00	30.00	175
1848Mo GC	10.00	15.00	30.00	175
1849Mo GC	10.00	15.00	30.00	175
1850Mo GC	10.00	15.00	30.00	175
1851Mo GC	40.00	60.00	125	250
1852Mo GC	10.00	15.00	30.00	175
1853Mo GC	10.00	15.00	30.00	175
1854/44Mo GC	10.00	15.00	30.00	175
1855Mo GC	10.00	15.00	30.00	175
1855Mo GF/GC	10.00	15.00	30.00	175
1855Mo GF	10.00	15.00	30.00	175
1856/5Mo GF/GC	10.00	15.00	30.00	175
1857Mo GF	10.00	15.00	30.00	175
1858Mo FH	7.50	12.50	25.00	150
1858Mo FH/GF	7.50	12.50	25.00	150
1859Mo FH	7.50	12.50	25.00	150
1860Mo FH	7.50	12.50	25.00	150

Date	F	VF	XF	Unc
1860Mo TH	7.50	12.50	25.00	150
1861Mo CH	7.50	12.50	25.00	150
1862Mo CH	7.50	12.50	25.00	150
1863Mo CH	7.50	12.50	25.00	150
1863Mo TH	7.50	12.50	25.00	150
1867Mo CH	7.50	12.50	25.00	150
1868Mo CH	10.00	15.00	30.00	150
1868Mo PH	7.50	12.50	25.00	150

Mint: San Luis Potosi
KM# 374.11   2 REALES
6.7600 g., 0.9030 Silver .1962 oz. ASW **Obv:** Facing eagle
Edge: Reeded

Date	F	VF	XF	Unc
1829 Pi JS	10.00	15.00	30.00	200
1830/20 Pi JS	20.00	30.00	60.00	200
1837 Pi JS	10.00	15.00	30.00	200
1841 Pi JS	10.00	15.00	30.00	200
1842/1 Pi JS	10.00	15.00	30.00	200
1842 Pi JS	10.00	15.00	30.00	200
1842 Pi PS	20.00	35.00	60.00	200
1843 Pi PS	12.50	20.00	40.00	200
1843 Pi AM	10.00	15.00	30.00	200
1844 Pi AM	10.00	15.00	30.00	200
1845 Pi AM	10.00	15.00	30.00	200
1846 Pi AM	10.00	15.00	30.00	200
1849 Pi MC	10.00	15.00	30.00	200
1850 Pi MC	10.00	15.00	30.00	200
1856 Pi MC	40.00	60.00	125	250
1857 Pi MC	—	—	—	—
1858 Pi MC	12.50	20.00	40.00	200
1859 Pi MC	50.00	70.00	100	200
1861 Pi PS	10.00	15.00	30.00	200
1862 Pi RO	12.50	20.00	40.00	200
1863 Pi RO	100	250	350	500
1868 Pi PS	10.00	15.00	30.00	200
1869/8 Pi PS	10.00	15.00	30.00	200
1869 Pi PS	10.00	15.00	30.00	200

Mint: Zacatecas
KM# 374.12   2 REALES
6.7600 g., 0.9030 Silver .1962 oz. ASW **Obv:** Facing eagle
Edge: Reeded **Note:** Varieties exist.

Date	F	VF	XF	Unc
1825Zs AZ	10.00	15.00	30.00	150
1826Zs AV	7.50	10.00	25.00	150
Note: A is inverted V				
1826Zs AZ	7.50	10.00	25.00	150
Note: A is inverted V				
1826Zs AO	10.00	15.00	30.00	150
1827Zs AO	6.00	8.00	12.00	150
Note: A is inverted V				
1827Zs AO	6.00	8.00	12.00	150
1828/7Zs AO	15.00	30.00	60.00	175
1828Zs AO	7.50	10.00	25.00	100
1828Zs AO	7.50	10.00	25.00	150
Note: A is inverted V				
1829Zs AO	7.50	10.00	25.00	150
1829Zs OV	7.50	10.00	25.00	150
1830Zs OV	7.50	10.00	25.00	150
1831Zs OV	7.50	10.00	25.00	150
1831Zs OM/OV	7.50	10.00	25.00	150
1831Zs OM	7.50	10.00	25.00	150
1832/1Zs OM	15.00	30.00	60.00	150
1832Zs OM	7.50	10.00	25.00	150
1833/27Zs OM	7.50	10.00	25.00	150
1833/2Zs OM	7.50	10.00	25.00	150
1833Zs OM	7.50	10.00	25.00	150
1834Zs OM	40.00	60.00	125	200
1835Zs OM	7.50	10.00	25.00	150
1836Zs OM	7.50	10.00	25.00	150
1837Zs OM	7.50	10.00	25.00	150
1838Zs OM	15.00	30.00	60.00	150
1839Zs OM	7.50	10.00	20.00	150
1840Zs OM	7.50	10.00	20.00	150
1841/0Zs OM	7.50	10.00	20.00	150
1841Zs OM	7.50	10.00	20.00	150
1842Zs OM Narrow date	7.50	10.00	20.00	150
1842Zs OM Wide date	7.50	10.00	20.00	150
1843Zs OM	7.50	10.00	20.00	150
1844Zs OM	7.50	10.00	20.00	150
1845Zs OM	7.50	10.00	20.00	150

Date	F	VF	XF	Unc
Note: Small letters with leaves				
1845Zs OM	7.50	10.00	20.00	150
Note: Large letters with leaves				
1846Zs OM	7.50	10.00	20.00	150
1847Zs OM	7.50	10.00	20.00	150
1848Zs OM	7.50	10.00	20.00	150
1849Zs OM	7.50	10.00	20.00	150
1850Zs OM	7.50	10.00	20.00	150
1851Zs OM	7.50	10.00	20.00	150
1852Zs OM	7.50	10.00	20.00	150
1853Zs OM	7.50	10.00	20.00	150
1854/3Zs OM	7.50	10.00	20.00	150
1854Zs OM	7.50	10.00	20.00	150
1855/4Zs OM	7.50	10.00	20.00	150
1855Zs OM	7.50	10.00	20.00	150
1855Zs MO	7.50	10.00	20.00	150
1856/5Zs MO	7.50	10.00	20.00	150
1856Zs MO	7.50	10.00	20.00	150
1857Zs MO	7.50	10.00	20.00	150
1858Zs MO	7.50	10.00	20.00	150
1859Zs MO	7.50	10.00	20.00	150
1860/59Zs MO	7.50	10.00	20.00	150
1860Zs MO	7.50	10.00	20.00	100
1860Zs VL	7.50	10.00	20.00	150
1861Zs VL	7.50	10.00	20.00	150
1862Zs VL	7.50	10.00	20.00	100
1863Zs MO	12.50	20.00	40.00	150
1863Zs VL	7.50	10.00	20.00	150
1864Zs MO	7.50	10.00	20.00	150
1864Zs VL	7.50	10.00	20.00	150
1865Zs MO	7.50	10.00	20.00	150
1867Zs JS	7.50	10.00	20.00	150
1868Zs JS	10.00	15.00	35.00	150
1868Zs YH	7.50	10.00	20.00	150
1869Zs YH	7.50	10.00	20.00	150
1870Zs YH	7.50	10.00	20.00	150

Mint: Real de Catorce
KM# 375   4 REALES
13.5400 g., 0.9030 Silver .3925 oz. ASW **Obv:** Facing eagle

Date	F	VF	XF	Unc
1863 Ce ML Large C	200	500	850	4,000
1863 Ce ML Small C	225	650	1,500	6,000

Mint: Culiacan
KM# 375.1   4 REALES
13.5400 g., 0.9030 Silver .3925 oz. ASW **Obv:** Facing eagle

Date	F	VF	XF	Unc
1846C CE	400	550	900	—
1850C CE	75.00	125	250	700
1852C CE	200	300	500	1,250
1857C CE Rare	—	—	—	—
1858C CE	100	200	350	1,000
1860C PV	25.00	50.00	125	650

Mint: Guadalajara
KM# 375.2   4 REALES
13.5400 g., 0.9030 Silver .3925 oz. ASW **Obv:** Facing eagle

Date	F	VF	XF	Unc
1843Ga MC	20.00	40.00	80.00	600
1844/3Ga MC	30.00	60.00	125	600
1844Ga MC	20.00	40.00	80.00	600
1845Ga MC	20.00	40.00	80.00	600
1845Ga JG	20.00	40.00	80.00	600
1846Ga JG	20.00	40.00	80.00	600
1847Ga JG	40.00	80.00	150	600
1848/7Ga JG	40.00	80.00	150	600
1849Ga JG	40.00	80.00	150	600
1850Ga JG	65.00	125	250	650
1852Ga JG Rare	—	—	—	—
1854Ga JG Rare	—	—	—	—
1855Ga JG	100	200	400	1,250
1856Ga JG Rare	—	—	—	—
1857/6Ga JG	65.00	125	250	700
1858Ga JG	125	250	450	1,250
1859/8Ga JG	125	250	450	1,250
1860Ga JG	850	1,450	—	—
1863/2Ga JG	150	300	1,250	7,500
1863Ga JG	150	300	1,250	7,500

Mint: Guadalupe y Calvo
KM# 375.3 4 REALES
13.5400 g., 0.9030 Silver .3925 oz. ASW **Obv:** Facing eagle

Date	F	VF	XF	Unc
1844GC MP	3,000	5,000	6,000	—
1845GC MP	3,000	4,000	5,000	9,000
1846GC MP	1,700	2,800	—	—
1847GC MP	1,500	2,500	—	—
1849GC MP	2,000	3,000	—	—
1850GC MP	500	1,000	—	—

Mint: Guanajuato
KM# 375.4 4 REALES
13.5400 g., 0.9030 Silver .3925 oz. ASW **Obv:** Facing eagle
Note: Varieties exist. Some 1862 dates appear to be 1869 because of weak dies.

Date	F	VF	XF	Unc
1835Go PJ	12.50	25.00	60.00	600
1836/5Go PJ	15.00	30.00	75.00	600
1836Go PJ	15.00	30.00	75.00	600
1837Go PJ	12.50	25.00	60.00	600
1838/7Go PJ	15.00	30.00	75.00	600
1838Go PJ	12.50	30.00	75.00	600
1839Go PJ	12.50	25.00	60.00	600
1840/30Go PJ	20.00	50.00	100	600
1840 PJ	20.00	50.00	100	600
1841/30 PJ	200	325	600	1,500
1841/31Go PJ	150	250	450	1,250
1842Go PJ Rare	—	—	—	—
1842Go PM	15.00	30.00	75.00	400
1843/2Go PM	12.50	25.00	60.00	400
Note: Eagle with convex wings, thick rays				
1843Go PM	12.50	25.00	60.00	400
Note: Eagle with concave wings, thin rays				
1844/3Go PM	15.00	30.00	75.00	600
1844Go PM	20.00	50.00	100	600
1845/4Go PM	20.00	50.00	100	600
1845Go PM	20.00	50.00	100	600
1846/5Go PM	15.00	30.00	75.00	600
1846Go PM	15.00	30.00	75.00	600
1847/6Go PM	15.00	30.00	75.00	600
1847Go PM	15.00	30.00	75.00	600
1848/7Go PM	20.00	50.00	100	600
1848Go PM	20.00	50.00	100	600
1849Go PF	20.00	50.00	100	600
1850Go PF	12.50	25.00	60.00	600
1851Go PF	12.50	25.00	60.00	600
1852Go PF	15.00	30.00	75.00	600
1852Go PF 5/4	20.00	50.00	100	600
1853Go PF	15.00	30.00	75.00	600
1854Go PF Large eagle	15.00	30.00	75.00	600
1854Go PF Small eagle	15.00	30.00	75.00	600
1855/4Go PF	15.00	30.00	75.00	600
1855Go PF	12.50	25.00	60.00	600
1856Go PF	12.50	25.00	60.00	600
1857Go PF	20.00	50.00	100	600
1858Go PF	20.00	50.00	100	600
1859Go PF	20.00	50.00	100	600
1860/59Go PF	15.00	30.00	75.00	600
1860Go PF	15.00	30.00	75.00	600
1861/51Go PF	15.00	30.00	75.00	600
1861Go PF	20.00	50.00	100	600
1862/1Go YE	15.00	30.00	75.00	600
1862/1Go YF	15.00	30.00	75.00	600
1862Go YE/PF	15.00	30.00	75.00	600
1862Go YE	15.00	30.00	75.00	600
1862Go YF	15.00	30.00	75.00	600

Date	F	VF	XF	Unc
1863/53Go YF	15.00	30.00	75.00	600
1863Go YF/PF	15.00	30.00	75.00	600
1863Go YF	15.00	30.00	75.00	600
1867/57Go YF/PF	15.00	30.00	75.00	600
1868/58Go YF/PF	15.00	30.00	75.00	600
1870Go FR	15.00	30.00	75.00	600

Mint: Hermosillo
KM# 375.5 4 REALES
13.5400 g., 0.9030 Silver .3925 oz. ASW **Obv:** Facing eagle

Date	F	VF	XF	Unc
1861Ho FM	200	350	500	2,500
1867/1Ho PR/FM	150	275	400	2,500

Mint: Mexico City
KM# 375.6 4 REALES
13.5400 g., 0.9030 Silver .3925 oz. ASW **Obv:** Facing eagle

Date	F	VF	XF	Unc
1827/6Mo JM	200	400	800	—
1850Mo GC Rare	—	—	—	—
1852Mo GC Rare	—	—	—	—
1854Mo GC Rare	—	—	—	—
1855Mo GF/GC	50.00	100	200	1,250
1855Mo GF	100	200	350	1,500
1856Mo GF/GC	50.00	125	400	1,200
1856Mo GF Rare	—	—	—	—
1859Mo FH	20.00	50.00	150	1,000
1861Mo CH	15.00	35.00	125	1,000
1862Mo CH	20.00	50.00	150	1,000
1863/2Mo CH	20.00	50.00	150	1,000
1863Mo CH	75.00	150	300	1,500
1867Mo CH	20.00	50.00	150	1,000
1868Mo CH/PH	30.00	75.00	150	1,000
1868Mo CH	20.00	50.00	150	1,000
1868Mo PH	30.00	75.00	200	1,250

Mint: Oaxaca
KM# 375.7 4 REALES
13.5400 g., 0.9030 Silver .3925 oz. ASW **Obv:** Facing eagle

Date	F	VF	XF	Unc
1861O FR	225	450	750	2,750
Note: Ornamental edge				
1861O FR	300	550	850	2,850
Note: Herringbone edge				
1861O FR	200	400	700	—
Note: Obliquely reeded edge				

Mint: San Luis Potosi
KM# 375.8 4 REALES
13.5400 g., 0.9030 Silver .3925 oz. ASW **Obv:** Facing eagle

Date	F	VF	XF	Unc
1837 Pi JS	200	350	—	—
1838 Pi JS	150	250	400	650
1842 Pi PS	50.00	100	200	650
1843/2 Pi PS	50.00	100	200	650
1843/2 Pi PS	50.00	100	200	650
Note: 3 cut from 8 punch				
1843 Pi AM	30.00	75.00	150	650
1843 Pi PS	50.00	100	200	650
1844 Pi AM	30.00	75.00	150	650
1845/4 Pi AM	20.00	50.00	100	650
1845 Pi AM	20.00	50.00	100	650
1846 Pi AM	20.00	50.00	100	650
1847 Pi AM	75.00	150	250	700
1848 Pi AM Rare	—	—	—	—
1849 Pi MC/AM	20.00	50.00	100	650
1849 Pi MC	20.00	50.00	100	650
1849 Pi PS	20.00	50.00	100	650
1850 Pi MC	20.00	50.00	100	650
1851 Pi MC	20.00	50.00	100	650

Date	F	VF	XF	Unc
1852 Pi MC	20.00	50.00	100	650
1853 Pi MC	20.00	50.00	100	650
1854 Pi MC	100	200	400	1,100
1855 Pi MC	175	300	750	2,000
1856 Pi MC	250	400	700	—
1857 Pi MC Rare	—	—	—	—
1857 Pi PS Rare	—	—	—	—
1858 Pi MC	100	200	400	1,000
1859 Pi MC	2,000	3,000	—	—
1860 Pi PS	300	450	700	—
1861 Pi PS	30.00	75.00	150	650
1861 Pi RO/PS	30.00	75.00	150	650
1861 Pi RO	50.00	100	200	650
1862 Pi RO	30.00	75.00	150	650
1863 Pi RO	30.00	75.00	150	650
1864 Pi RO	1,600	2,600	—	—
1868 Pi PS	30.00	75.00	150	650
1869/8 Pi PS	30.00	75.00	150	650
1869 Pi PS	30.00	75.00	150	650

Mint: Zacatecas
KM# 375.9   4 REALES
13.5400 g., 0.9030 Silver .3925 oz. ASW **Obv:** Facing eagle

Date	F	VF	XF	Unc
1830Zs OM	20.00	50.00	100	600
1831Zs OM	15.00	30.00	75.00	600
1832/1Zs OM	20.00	50.00	100	600
1832Zs OM	20.00	50.00	100	600
1833/2Zs OM	20.00	50.00	100	600
1833/27Zs OM	15.00	30.00	75.00	600
1833Zs OM	15.00	30.00	75.00	600
1834/3Zs OM	20.00	50.00	100	600
1834Zs OM	15.00	30.00	75.00	600
1835Zs OM	15.00	30.00	75.00	600
1836Zs OM	15.00	30.00	75.00	600
1837/5Zs OM	20.00	50.00	100	600
1837/6Zs OM	20.00	50.00	100	600
1837Zs OM	20.00	50.00	100	600
1838/7Zs OM	15.00	30.00	75.00	600
1839Zs OM	250	375	500	—
1840Zs OM	500	1,300	—	—
1841Zs OM	15.00	30.00	75.00	600
1842Zs OM Small letters	15.00	40.00	85.00	600
1842Zs OM Large letters	15.00	30.00	75.00	600
1843Zs OM	15.00	30.00	75.00	600
1844Zs OM	20.00	50.00	100	600
1845Zs OM	20.00	50.00	100	600
1846/5Zs OM	25.00	60.00	125	600
1846Zs OM	20.00	50.00	100	600
1847Zs OM	15.00	30.00	75.00	600
1848/6Zs OM	50.00	75.00	125	600
1848Zs OM	20.00	50.00	100	600
1849Zs OM	20.00	50.00	100	600
1850Zs OM	20.00	50.00	100	600
1851Zs OM	15.00	30.00	75.00	600
1852Zs OM	15.00	30.00	75.00	600
1853Zs OM	20.00	50.00	100	600
1854/3Zs OM	30.00	75.00	150	600
1855/4Zs OM	20.00	50.00	100	600
1855Zs OM	15.00	30.00	75.00	600
1856Zs OM	15.00	30.00	75.00	600
1856Zs MO	20.00	50.00	100	600
1857/5Zs MO	20.00	50.00	100	600
1857Zs O/M	20.00	50.00	100	600
1857Zs MO	15.00	30.00	75.00	600
1858Zs MO	20.00	50.00	100	600
1859Zs MO	15.00	30.00	75.00	600
1860/59Zs MO	20.00	50.00	100	600
1860Zs MO	15.00	30.00	75.00	600
1860Zs VL	20.00	50.00	100	600
1861/0Zs VL	20.00	50.00	100	600
1861Zs VL	15.00	30.00	75.00	600
1861Zs VL 6/5	20.00	50.00	100	600
1862/1Zs VL	20.00	50.00	100	600
1862Zs VL	20.00	50.00	100	600
1863Zs VL	20.00	50.00	100	600
1863Zs MO	20.00	50.00	100	600
1864Zs VL	15.00	30.00	75.00	600
1868Zs JS	20.00	50.00	100	600
1868Zs YH	15.00	30.00	75.00	600

Date	F	VF	XF	Unc
1869Zs YH	15.00	30.00	75.00	600
1870Zs YH	15.00	30.00	75.00	600

Mint: Alamos
KM# 377   8 REALES
27.0700 g., 0.9030 Silver .7859 oz. ASW **Obv:** Facing eagle
Note: Mint mark A, As. Varieties exist.

Date	Mintage	F	VF	XF	Unc
1864 PG	—	750	1,250	2,000	—
1865/4 PG Rare	—	—	—	—	—
1865 PG	—	500	750	1,000	—
1866/5 PG Rare	—	—	—	—	—
1866 PG	—	1,250	2,250	—	—
1866 DL Rare	—	—	—	—	—
1867 DL	—	1,150	2,150	—	—
1868 DL	—	50.00	90.00	150	300
1869/8 DL	—	50.00	90.00	150	—
1869 DL	—	50.00	80.00	120	300
1870 DL	—	30.00	60.00	120	300
1871 DL	—	20.00	35.00	75.00	200
1872 AM/DL	—	25.00	50.00	100	300
1872 AM	—	25.00	50.00	100	250
1873 AM	509,000	15.00	25.00	50.00	150
1874/3 As DL	—	25.00	50.00	100	250
1874 DL	—	15.00	25.00	50.00	150
1875A DL 7/7	—	40.00	80.00	120	300
1875A DL	—	15.00	25.00	50.00	150
1875 As DL	—	30.00	60.00	110	250
1876 DL	—	15.00	25.00	50.00	150
1877 DL	515,000	15.00	25.00	50.00	150
1878 DL	513,000	15.00	25.00	50.00	150
1879 DL	—	20.00	35.00	75.00	175
1879 ML	—	30.00	60.00	125	350
1880 ML	—	12.00	15.00	30.00	140
1881 ML	966,000	12.00	15.00	30.00	140
1882 ML	480,000	12.00	15.00	30.00	140
1883 ML	464,000	12.00	15.00	30.00	140
1884 ML	—	12.00	15.00	30.00	140
1885 ML	280,000	12.00	15.00	30.00	140
1886 ML	857,000	12.00	15.00	25.00	110
1886/0As/Cn ML/JD	Inc. above	15.00	20.00	35.00	160
1887 ML	650,000	12.00	15.00	25.00	110
1888/7 ML	508,000	30.00	60.00	100	400
1888 ML	Inc. above	12.00	15.00	25.00	110
1889 ML	427,000	12.00	15.00	25.00	110
1890 ML	450,000	12.00	15.00	25.00	110
1891 ML	533,000	12.00	15.00	25.00	110
1892/0 ML	—	20.00	30.00	60.00	160
1892 ML	465,000	12.00	15.00	25.00	110
1893 ML	734,000	10.00	12.00	22.00	85.00
1894 ML	725,000	10.00	12.00	22.00	85.00
1895 ML	477,000	10.00	12.00	22.00	85.00

Mint: Real de Catorce
KM# 377.1 8 REALES
27.0700 g., 0.9030 Silver .7859 oz. ASW **Obv:** Facing eagle

Date	F	VF	XF	Unc
1863 Ce ME	425	700	1,350	3,000
1863 Ce /PI ML/MC	425	750	1,500	3,250

Mint: Chihuahua
KM# 377.2 8 REALES
27.0700 g., 0.9030 Silver .7859 oz. ASW **Obv:** Facing eagle
Note: Varieties exist.

Date	Mintage	F	VF	XF	Unc
1831 Ca MR	—	1,000	1,750	2,250	3,250
1832 Ca MR	—	125	200	300	600
1833 Ca MR	—	250	550	1,000	—
1834 Ca MR	—	300	600	1,150	—
1834 Ca AM	—	350	500	700	—
1835 Ca AM	—	150	250	475	900
1836 Ca AM	—	100	200	300	600
1837 Ca AM	—	550	1,150	—	—

Date	Mintage	F	VF	XF	Unc
1838 Ca AM	—	100	200	300	600
1839 Ca RG	—	750	1,250	2,500	—
1840 Ca RG	—	300	500	800	1,500
Note: 1 dot after date					
1840 Ca RG	—	300	500	800	1,500
Note: 3 dots after date					
1841 Ca RG	—	50.00	100	150	300
1842 Ca RG	—	25.00	40.00	75.00	150
1843 Ca RG	—	40.00	80.00	125	250
1844/1 Ca RG	—	35.00	70.00	100	200
1844 Ca RG	—	25.00	40.00	75.00	160
1845 Ca RG	—	25.00	40.00	75.00	160
1846 Ca RG	—	30.00	60.00	100	250
1847 Ca RG	—	40.00	80.00	125	250
1848 Ca RG	—	35.00	70.00	125	250
1849 Ca RG	—	30.00	60.00	100	200
1850/40 Ca RG	—	40.00	80.00	125	250
1850 Ca RG	—	30.00	60.00	100	200
1851/41 Ca RG	—	100	200	300	500
1851 Ca RG	—	150	250	400	750
1852/42 Ca RG	—	150	250	400	750
1852 Ca RG	—	150	250	400	750
1853/43 Ca RG	—	150	250	400	750
1853 Ca RG	—	150	250	350	700
1854/44 Ca RG	—	100	200	300	500
1854 Ca RG	—	50.00	100	150	300
1855/45 Ca RG	—	100	200	350	650
1855 Ca RG	—	50.00	100	150	300
1856/45 Ca RG	—	275	450	750	1,250
1856/5 Ca RG	—	400	700	1,500	3,500
1857 Ca JC/RG	—	40.00	80.00	125	250
1857 Ca JC	—	50.00	100	150	250
1858 Ca JC	—	35.00	70.00	125	250
1858 Ca BA	—	2,000	3,500	—	—
1859 Ca JC	—	40.00	80.00	125	250
1860 Ca JC	—	20.00	40.00	90.00	175
1861 Ca JC	—	15.00	25.00	55.00	125
1862 Ca JC	—	15.00	25.00	55.00	125
1863 Ca JC	—	20.00	35.00	75.00	150
1864 Ca JC	—	20.00	35.00	75.00	150
1865 Ca JC	—	100	200	350	600
1865 Ca FP	—	1,350	2,150	3,250	—
1866 Ca JC	—	750	1,150	2,250	—
1866 Ca FP	—	1,000	2,000	3,250	5,000
1866 Ca JG	—	850	1,650	2,750	4,250
1867 Ca JG	—	100	200	350	600
1868 Ca JG	—	75.00	150	250	400
1868 Ca MM	—	65.00	125	200	350
1869 Ca MM	—	20.00	35.00	65.00	135
1870 Ca MM	—	20.00	35.00	65.00	135
1871/0 Ca MM	—	15.00	25.00	55.00	125
1871 Ca MM	—	15.00	25.00	55.00	125
1871 Ca MM	—	20.00	35.00	65.00	135
Note: First M over inverted M					
1873 Ca MM	—	20.00	35.00	65.00	135
1873 Ca MM/T	—	15.00	25.00	55.00	125
1874 Ca MM	—	12.00	15.00	30.00	100
1875 Ca MM	—	12.00	15.00	30.00	100
1876 Ca MM	—	12.00	15.00	30.00	100
1877 Ca EA	472,000	20.00	40.00	85.00	200
1877 Ca GR	Inc. above	25.00	45.00	65.00	150
1877 Ca JM	Inc. above	12.00	15.00	30.00	100
1877 Ca AV	Inc. above	100	200	350	750
1878 Ca AV	439,000	12.00	15.00	25.00	80.00
1879 Ca AV	—	12.00	15.00	25.00	80.00
1880 Ca AV	—	200	350	600	1,250
1880 Ca PM	—	500	800	1,250	2,500
1880 Ca MG	—	12.00	15.00	25.00	100
Note: Normal initials					
1880 Ca MG	—	12.00	15.00	25.00	100
Note: Tall initials					
1880 Ca MM	—	12.00	15.00	25.00	100
1881 Ca MG	1,085,000	10.00	12.00	20.00	65.00
1882 Ca MG	779,000	10.00	12.00	20.00	65.00
1882 Ca MM	Inc. above	10.00	12.00	20.00	65.00
1882 Ca MM	Inc. above	20.00	45.00	100	175
Note: M sideways					
1883 Ca MM	818,000	—	—	—	—
Note: Sideways M					

Date	Mintage	F	VF	XF	Unc
1883/2 Ca MM/G	—	12.00	15.00	30.00	80.00
1883 Ca MM	Inc. above	10.00	12.00	20.00	65.00
1884/3 Ca MM	—	12.00	15.00	30.00	90.00
1884 Ca MM	—	10.00	12.00	20.00	65.00
1885/4 Ca MM	1,345,000	15.00	25.00	55.00	125
1885/6 Ca MM	Inc. above	15.00	25.00	55.00	125
1885 Ca MM	Inc. above	10.00	12.00	20.00	65.00
1886 Ca MM	2,483,000	10.00	12.00	20.00	65.00
1887 Ca MM	2,625,000	10.00	12.00	20.00	65.00
1888/7 Ca MM	2,434,000	15.00	25.00	65.00	135
1888 Ca MM	Inc. above	10.00	12.00	20.00	65.00
1889 Ca MM	2,681,000	10.00	12.00	20.00	65.00
1890/89 Ca MM	—	15.00	25.00	55.00	125
1890 Ca MM	2,137,000	10.00	12.00	20.00	65.00
1891/0 Ca MM	2,268,000	15.00	25.00	55.00	135
1891 Ca MM	Inc. above	10.00	12.00	20.00	80.00
1892 Ca MM	2,527,000	10.00	12.00	20.00	65.00
1893 Ca MM	2,632,000	10.00	12.00	20.00	65.00
1894 Ca MM	2,642,000	10.00	12.00	20.00	65.00
1895 Ca MM	1,112,000	10.00	12.00	20.00	65.00

Mint: Culiacan
KM# 377.3   8 REALES
27.0700 g., 0.9030 Silver .7859 oz. ASW **Obv:** Facing eagle
Note: Mint mark C, Cn. Varieties exist.

Date	Mintage	F	VF	XF	Unc
1846 CE	—	150	300	800	1,500
1846 CE	—	175	385	900	1,650
Note: Dot after G					
1846 CE	—	125	265	750	1,450
Note: No dot after G					
1847 CE	—	400	700	1,500	—
1848 CE	—	125	250	450	1,000
1849 CE	—	75.00	125	200	400
1850 CE	—	75.00	125	200	400
1851 CE	—	125	250	450	1,000
1852/1 CE	—	100	150	250	500
1852 CE	—	100	200	300	600
1853/0 CE	—	200	350	700	1,300
1853/2/0	—	200	400	750	1,400
1853 CE	—	100	175	300	600
Note: Thick rays					
1853 CE	—	200	350	650	—
Note: Error: MEXIGANA					
1854 CE	—	750	1,250	—	—
1854 CE	—	175	350	750	1,200
Note: Large eagle and hat					
1855/6 CE	—	40.00	60.00	100	200
1855 CE	—	25.00	40.00	75.00	150
1856 CE	—	50.00	100	175	350
1857 CE	—	20.00	35.00	75.00	150
1858 CE	—	30.00	40.00	75.00	150
1859 CE	—	20.00	35.00	75.00	150
1860/9 PV/CV	—	50.00	70.00	100	200
1860/9 PV/E	—	50.00	70.00	100	200
1860 CE	—	25.00	40.00	75.00	150
1860 PV	—	40.00	60.00	90.00	175
1861/0 CE	—	50.00	80.00	120	250
1861 PV/CE	—	75.00	125	200	350
1861 CE	—	20.00	35.00	60.00	150
1862 CE	—	20.00	35.00	60.00	150
1863/2 CE	—	30.00	50.00	75.00	200
1863 CE	—	20.00	30.00	60.00	150
1864 CE	—	30.00	60.00	100	300
1865 CE	—	125	200	325	650
1866 CE	—	400	750	1,250	2,250
1867 CE	—	125	200	350	700
1868/7 CE	—	30.00	40.00	75.00	150
1868/8	—	50.00	100	150	300
1868 CE	—	30.00	40.00	75.00	150
1869 CE	—	30.00	40.00	75.00	175
1870 CE	—	50.00	100	150	350
1873 MP	—	50.00	100	150	300
1874/3 MP	—	30.00	40.00	75.00	150
1874C MP	—	20.00	30.00	45.00	100
1874 CN MP	—	125	200	300	600
1875 MP	—	12.00	15.00	22.00	80.00
1876 GP	—	12.00	15.00	30.00	90.00
1876 CG	—	12.00	15.00	22.00	80.00
1877 CG	339,000	12.00	15.00	22.00	80.00

Date	Mintage	F	VF	XF	Unc
1877Gn CG Error	—	65.00	125	200	400
1877 JA	Inc. above	35.00	75.00	125	250
1878/7 CG	483,000	35.00	75.00	125	250
1878 CG	Inc. above	15.00	25.00	35.00	125
1878 JD/CG	—	25.00	35.00	50.00	150
1878 JD	Inc. above	15.00	20.00	30.00	125
1878 JD	Inc. above	20.00	30.00	40.00	150
Note: D over retrograde D					
1879 JD	—	12.00	15.00	30.00	135
1880/70 JD	—	15.00	20.00	30.00	90.00
1880 JD	—	12.00	15.00	22.00	120
1881/0 JD	1,032,000	15.00	20.00	30.00	90.00
1881C JD	Inc. above	12.00	15.00	22.00	80.00
1881Cn JD	Inc. above	40.00	60.00	90.00	150
1882 JD	397,000	12.00	15.00	22.00	80.00
1882 AM	Inc. above	12.00	15.00	22.00	80.00
1883 AM	333,000	12.00	15.00	22.00	125
1884 AM	—	12.00	15.00	22.00	80.00
1885/6 AM	227,000	20.00	30.00	45.00	110
1885C AM	Inc. above	35.00	70.00	150	350
1885Cn AM	Inc. above	12.00	15.00	22.00	80.00
1885Gn AM Error	Inc. above	25.00	50.00	100	275
1886 AM	571,000	12.00	15.00	22.00	80.00
1887 AM	732,000	12.00	15.00	22.00	80.00
1888 AM	768,000	12.00	15.00	22.00	80.00
1889 AM	1,075,000	12.00	15.00	22.00	80.00
1890 AM	874,000	10.00	12.00	20.00	65.00
1891 AM	777,000	10.00	12.00	20.00	65.00
1892 AM	681,000	10.00	12.00	20.00	65.00
1893 AM	1,144,000	10.00	12.00	20.00	65.00
1894 AM	2,118,000	10.00	12.00	20.00	65.00
1895 AM	1,834,000	10.00	12.00	20.00	65.00
1896 AM	2,134,000	10.00	12.00	20.00	65.00
1897 AM	1,580,000	10.00	12.00	20.00	65.00

Mint: Durango
KM# 377.4   8 REALES
27.0700 g., 0.9030 Silver .7859 oz. ASW **Obv:** Facing eagle
Note: Varieties exist.

Date	Mintage	F	VF	XF	Unc
1825Do RL	—	30.00	65.00	150	375
1826Do RL	—	40.00	85.00	200	475
1827/6Do RL	—	35.00	60.00	85.00	200
1827/8Do RL	—	150	275	500	—
1827Do RL	—	30.00	50.00	90.00	200
1828/7Do RL	—	35.00	60.00	90.00	200
1828Do RL	—	25.00	50.00	80.00	175
1829Do RL	—	25.00	50.00	80.00	175
1830Do RM	—	25.00	50.00	90.00	200
Note: B on eagle's claw					
1831Do RM	—	20.00	30.00	60.00	150
Note: B on eagle's claw					
1832Do RM	—	35.00	60.00	120	300
Note: Mexican dies, B on eagle's claw					
1832/1Do RM/RL	—	25.00	35.00	75.00	165
Note: French dies					
1833/2Do RM/RL	—	20.00	35.00	75.00	165
1833Do RM	—	15.00	30.00	60.00	150
1834/3/2Do RM/RL	—	20.00	35.00	75.00	165
1834Do RM	—	15.00	25.00	50.00	150
1835/4Do RM/RL	—	20.00	35.00	65.00	150
1835Do RM	—	20.00	35.00	65.00	150
1836/1Do RM/RL	—	20.00	35.00	65.00	150
1836/4Do RM	—	20.00	35.00	65.00	150
1836/5/4Do RM/RL	—	75.00	150	250	500
1836Do RM	—	20.00	30.00	55.00	150
1836Do RM	—	20.00	30.00	55.00	150
Note: M on snake					
1837/1Do RM	—	20.00	30.00	55.00	150
1837Do RM	—	20.00	30.00	55.00	150
1838/1Do RM	—	20.00	30.00	60.00	165
1838/7Do RM	—	20.00	30.00	60.00	165
1838Do RM	—	20.00	30.00	55.00	150
1839/1Do RM/RL	—	20.00	30.00	55.00	150
1839/1Do RM	—	20.00	30.00	55.00	150
1839Do RM	—	20.00	30.00	55.00	150
1840/38/31Do RM	—	20.00	30.00	55.00	150
1840/39Do RM	—	20.00	30.00	55.00	150
1840Do RM	—	20.00	30.00	55.00	150
1841/31Do RM	—	65.00	125	275	450

Date	Mintage	F	VF	XF	Unc
1841/39Do RM/L	—	25.00	50.00	85.00	200
1841/39Do RM	—	25.00	50.00	85.00	200
1842/31Do RM	—	125	250	400	750
Note: B below cactus					
1842/31Do RM	—	40.00	80.00	125	250
1842/32Do RM	—	40.00	80.00	125	250
1842Do RM	—	20.00	30.00	55.00	150
Note: Eagle of 1832-41					
1842Do RM	—	20.00	30.00	55.00	150
Note: Pre-1832 eagle resumed					
1842Do RM	—	40.00	80.00	125	250
1843/33Do RM	—	50.00	90.00	150	250
1843Do RM	—	50.00	90.00	150	250
1844/34Do RM	—	100	200	300	500
1844/35Do RM	—	100	200	300	500
1844/43Do RM	—	60.00	120	220	425
1845/31Do RM	—	100	200	300	500
1845/34Do RM	—	35.00	75.00	125	250
1845/35Do RM	—	35.00	75.00	125	250
1845Do RM	—	20.00	30.00	55.00	150
1846/31Do RM	—	20.00	30.00	55.00	150
1846/36Do RM	—	20.00	30.00	55.00	150
1846Do RM	—	20.00	30.00	55.00	150
1847Do RM	—	25.00	50.00	80.00	185
1848/7Do RM	—	125	250	400	750
1848/7Do CM/RM	—	100	200	350	700
1848Do CM/RM	—	100	200	350	700
1848Do RM	—	100	200	300	600
1848Do CM	—	50.00	100	200	400
1849/39Do CM	—	100	200	350	700
1849Do CM	—	65.00	125	250	550
1849Do JMR/CM Oval 0	—	200	400	450	800
1849Do JMR Oval 0	—	200	325	450	800
1849Do JMR Round 0	—	200	400	600	1,000
1850Do JMR	—	100	150	250	500
1851/0Do JMR	—	65.00	125	225	475
1851Do JMR	—	100	150	250	500
1852Do CP/JMR	—	450	800	1,500	—
1852Do CP	—	750	1,200	2,250	—
1852Do JMR	—	175	250	375	650
1853Do CP/JMR	—	125	235	350	600
1853Do CP	—	200	350	600	1,200
1854Do CP	—	25.00	35.00	65.00	300
1855Do CP	—	50.00	100	175	350
Note: Eagle type of 1854					
1855Do CP	—	50.00	100	175	350
Note: Eagle type of 1856					
1856Do CP	—	50.00	100	175	350
1857Do CP	—	35.00	65.00	125	250
1858/7Do CP	—	25.00	35.00	70.00	165
1858Do CP	—	20.00	30.00	60.00	165
1859Do CP	—	20.00	30.00	60.00	165
1860/59Do CP	—	30.00	50.00	100	200
1860Do CP	—	20.00	30.00	60.00	165
1861/0Do CP	—	20.00	30.00	60.00	165
1861Do CP	—	20.00	30.00	50.00	125
1862/1Do CP	—	25.00	35.00	50.00	125
1862Do CP	—	20.00	30.00	60.00	175
1863/1Do CP	—	30.00	60.00	90.00	200
1863/2Do CP	—	25.00	50.00	75.00	175
1863/53Do CP	—	30.00	60.00	90.00	200
1863Do CP	—	25.00	50.00	75.00	175
1864Do CP	—	100	150	250	500
1864Do LT	—	25.00	40.00	80.00	175
1864Do LT/T	—	25.00	40.00	80.00	175
1864Do LT/CP	—	50.00	100	175	350
1865Do LT Rare	—	—	—	—	—
1866/4Do CM	—	2,750	5,500	—	—
1866Do CM	—	1,750	3,250	5,500	8,000
1867Do CM	—	3,500	—	—	—
1867/6Do CP	—	200	400	600	1,200
1867Do CP	—	175	300	500	1,000
1867Do CP/CM	—	125	250	400	900
1867Do CP/LT	—	200	400	650	1,250
1868Do CP	—	25.00	40.00	80.00	175
1869Do CP	—	20.00	30.00	50.00	135
1870/69Do CP	—	20.00	30.00	50.00	125
1870/9Do CP	—	20.00	30.00	50.00	125
1870Do CP	—	20.00	30.00	50.00	125

Date	Mintage	F	VF	XF	Unc
1873Do CP	—	125	225	325	600
1873Do CM	—	30.00	50.00	100	200
1874/3Do CM	—	12.00	15.00	22.00	100
1874Do CM	—	10.00	15.00	22.00	80.00
1874Do JH	—	1,150	1,750	2,750	—
1875Do JH	—	10.00	15.00	22.00	80.00
1875Do JH	—	80.00	150	250	450
1876Do CM	—	10.00	15.00	22.00	80.00
1877Do CM	431,000	1,450	2,500	—	—
1877Do CP	Inc. above	10.00	15.00	22.00	80.00
1877Do JMP	Inc. above	750	1,250	2,000	—
1878Do PE	409,000	15.00	25.00	40.00	100
1878Do TB	Inc. above	10.00	15.00	25.00	90.00
1879Do TB	—	10.00	15.00	22.00	80.00
1880/70Do TB	—	60.00	100	175	350
1880/70Do TB/JP	—	150	250	375	650
1880/70Do JP	—	15.00	25.00	40.00	100
1880Do TB	—	150	250	375	650
1880Do JP	—	10.00	15.00	22.00	80.00
1881Do JP	928,000	10.00	15.00	25.00	90.00
1882Do JP	414,000	10.00	15.00	22.00	80.00
1882Do MC/JP	Inc. above	30.00	60.00	100	200
1882Do MC	Inc. above	25.00	50.00	75.00	150
1883/73Do MC	452,000	15.00	25.00	40.00	90.00
1883Do MC	Inc. above	10.00	15.00	22.00	80.00
1884/3Do MC	—	15.00	25.00	40.00	90.00
1884Do MC	—	10.00	15.00	22.00	80.00
1885Do MC	547,000	10.00	12.00	20.00	70.00
1885Do JB	Inc. above	25.00	35.00	50.00	125
1886/5Do MC	—	15.00	25.00	40.00	100
1886/3Do MC	955,000	15.00	25.00	40.00	100
1886Do MC	Inc. above	10.00	12.00	20.00	70.00
1887Do MC	1,004,000	10.00	12.00	20.00	70.00
1888/7Do MC	—	65.00	125	250	450
1888Do MC	996,000	10.00	12.00	20.00	70.00
1889Do MC	874,000	10.00	12.00	20.00	70.00
1890Do MC	1,119,000	10.00	12.00	20.00	70.00
1890Do JP	Inc. above	10.00	12.00	20.00	70.00
1891Do JP	1,487,000	10.00	12.00	20.00	70.00
1892Do JP	1,597,000	10.00	12.00	20.00	70.00
1892Do ND	Inc. above	25.00	50.00	100	200
1893Do ND	1,617,000	10.00	12.00	20.00	70.00
1894Do ND	1,537,000	10.00	12.00	20.00	70.00
1895/3Do ND	761,000	15.00	25.00	40.00	100
1895Do ND	Inc. above	10.00	12.00	20.00	70.00
1895Do ND/P	—	15.00	25.00	40.00	100

Mint: Estado de Mexico
KM# 377.5   8 REALES
27.0700 g., 0.9030 Silver .7859 oz. ASW **Obv:** Facing eagle

Date	F	VF	XF	Unc
1828EoMo LF/LP	350	850	2,150	—
1828EoMo LF	350	850	2,150	5,500
1829EoMo LF	300	750	1,850	4,500
1830/20EoMo LF	1,250	2,750	4,250	—
1830EoMo LF	1,000	2,000	3,250	6,000

Mint: Guadalajara
KM# 377.6   8 REALES
27.0700 g., 0.9030 Silver .7859 oz. ASW **Obv:** Facing eagle
Note: Varieties exist.

Date	Mintage	F	VF	XF	Unc
1825Ga FS	—	150	275	475	1,000
1826/5Ga FS	—	125	250	450	1,000
1826Ga FS	—	125	250	450	1,000
1827/87Ga FS	—	125	250	450	1,000
1827Ga FS	—	125	250	450	1,000
1287Ga FS Error	—	8,500	9,500	—	—
1828Ga FS	—	200	375	550	1,200
1829/8Ga FS	—	200	375	550	1,200
1829Ga FS	—	175	325	475	950
1830/29Ga FS	—	100	175	300	600
1830Ga FS	—	100	175	300	600
1830Ga LP/FS	—	800	1,450	—	—

Note: The 1830 LP/FS is currently only known with a Philippine countermark.

Date	Mintage	F	VF	XF	Unc
1831Ga LP	—	200	400	600	1,200
1831Ga FS/LP	—	300	500	750	1,500
1831Ga FS	—	125	275	400	—
1832/1Ga FS	—	50.00	100	175	300
1832/1Ga FS/LP	—	50.00	100	175	300
1832Ga FS/LP	—	75.00	150	285	550
1832Ga FS	—	25.00	50.00	100	225
1833/2/1Ga FS/LP	—	45.00	75.00	125	250
1833/2Ga FS	—	25.00	50.00	100	225
1834/2Ga FS	—	60.00	125	200	350
1834/3Ga FS	—	60.00	125	200	350
1834/0Ga FS	—	50.00	100	150	300
1834Ga FS	—	50.00	100	150	300
1835Ga FS	—	25.00	50.00	100	225
1836/5Ga FS	—	175	350	—	—
1836/1Ga JG/FS	—	40.00	80.00	125	250
1836Ga FS	—	275	450	750	—
1836Ga JG/FS	—	25.00	50.00	100	225
1836Ga JG	—	25.00	50.00	100	225
1837/6Ga JG/FS	—	50.00	100	175	300
1837/6Ga JG	—	45.00	90.00	160	285
1837Ga JG	—	40.00	80.00	125	250
1838/7Ga JG	—	100	175	300	550
1838Ga JG	—	100	150	275	500
1839Ga MC	—	100	200	350	600
1839Ga MC/JG	—	100	200	300	550
1839Ga JG	—	60.00	125	200	350
1840/30Ga MC	—	50.00	75.00	150	275
1840Ga MC	—	30.00	60.00	125	250
1841Ga MC	—	30.00	60.00	125	250
1842/1Ga JG/MG	—	100	150	250	450
1842/1Ga JG/MC	—	100	150	250	450
1842Ga JG	—	25.00	50.00	100	225

Date	Mintage	F	VF	XF	Unc
1842Ga JG/MG	—	25.00	50.00	100	225
1843/2Ga MC/JG	—	25.00	50.00	100	225
1843Ga MC/JG	—	25.00	50.00	100	225
1843Ga JG	—	400	600	900	1,650
1843Ga MC	—	50.00	100	150	300
1844Ga MC	—	50.00	100	150	300
1845Ga MC	—	75.00	150	300	700
1845Ga JG	—	500	850	1,250	1,850
1846Ga JG	—	40.00	80.00	150	300
1847Ga JG	—	100	150	225	400
1848/7Ga JG	—	55.00	85.00	125	250
1848Ga JG	—	50.00	75.00	100	225
1849Ga JG	—	90.00	125	175	325
1849/39Ga JG	—	250	500	—	—
1850Ga JG	—	50.00	100	150	300
1851Ga JG	—	125	200	350	650
1852Ga JG	—	100	150	250	450
1853/2Ga JG	—	125	175	250	475
1853Ga JG	—	90.00	125	175	300
1854/3Ga JG	—	65.00	90.00	125	250
1854Ga JG	—	50.00	75.00	110	225
1855/4Ga JG	—	50.00	100	150	275
1855Ga JG	—	25.00	50.00	100	225
1856/4Ga JG	—	60.00	125	175	300
1856/5Ga 56	—	60.00	125	175	300
1856Ga JG	—	50.00	100	150	275
1857Ga JG	—	50.00	100	225	450
1858Ga JG	—	100	150	300	500
1859/7Ga JG	—	25.00	50.00	110	225
1859/8Ga JG	—	25.00	50.00	100	200
1859Ga JG	—	20.00	40.00	80.00	175
1860Ga JG Without dot	—	350	750	1,200	2,250
1860Ga JG	—	2,000	3,250	4,500	—

Note: Dot in loop of snake's tail, base alloy

Date	Mintage	F	VF	XF	Unc
1861Ga JG	—	2,200	5,750	—	—
1862Ga JG	—	850	1,350	2,750	4,500
1863/52Ga JG	—	—	—	—	—
1863/59Ga JG	—	45.00	50.00	85.00	145
1863/2Ga JG	—	30.00	50.00	90.00	175
1863/4Ga JG	—	40.00	75.00	150	250
1863Ga JG	—	25.00	45.00	75.00	150
1863Ga FV Rare	—	—	—	—	—
1867Ga JM Rare	—	—	—	—	—
1868/7Ga JM	—	50.00	75.00	125	200
1868Ga JM	—	50.00	75.00	125	200
1869Ga JM	—	50.00	75.00	125	200
1869Ga IC	—	75.00	125	200	375
1870/60Ga IC	—	60.00	90.00	150	275
1870Ga IC	—	60.00	90.00	150	275
1873Ga IC	—	15.00	25.00	50.00	125
1874Ga IC	—	10.00	15.00	22.00	90.00
1874Ga MC	—	25.00	50.00	100	200
1875Ga IC	—	15.00	30.00	60.00	125
1875Ga MC	—	10.00	15.00	22.00	90.00
1876Ga IC	559,000	15.00	30.00	50.00	100
1876Ga MC	Inc. above	125	175	250	375
1877Ga IC	928,000	10.00	15.00	22.00	90.00
1877/6Ga JA	—	10.00	15.00	22.00	90.00
1877Ga JA	Inc. above	10.00	15.00	22.00	90.00
1878Ga JA	764,000	10.00	15.00	22.00	90.00
1879Ga JA	—	10.00	15.00	22.00	90.00
1880/70Ga FS	—	15.00	25.00	50.00	125
1880Ga JA	—	10.00	15.00	22.00	90.00
1880Ga FS	—	10.00	15.00	22.00	90.00
1881Ga FS	1,300,000	10.00	15.00	22.00	90.00
1882/1Ga FS	537,000	15.00	25.00	50.00	125
1882Ga FS	Inc. above	10.00	15.00	22.00	90.00
1882Ga TB/FS	Inc. above	50.00	100	175	300
1882Ga TB	Inc. above	50.00	100	175	300
1883Ga TB	561,000	15.00	25.00	40.00	125
1884Ga TB	—	10.00	12.00	20.00	85.00
1884Ga AH	—	10.00	12.00	20.00	85.00
1885Ga AH	443,000	10.00	12.00	20.00	90.00
1885Ga JS	Inc. above	30.00	60.00	100	200
1886Ga JS/H	—	10.00	12.00	20.00	85.00
1886Ga JS	1,038,999	10.00	12.00	20.00	85.00
1887Ga JS	878,000	10.00	12.00	20.00	85.00
1888Ga JS	1,159,000	10.00	12.00	20.00	85.00
1889Ga JS	1,583,000	10.00	12.00	20.00	85.00

Date	Mintage	F	VF	XF	Unc
1890Ga JS	1,658,000	10.00	12.00	20.00	85.00
1891Ga JS	1,507,000	10.00	12.00	20.00	85.00
1892/1Ga JS	1,627,000	15.00	25.00	50.00	125
1892Ga JS	Inc. above	10.00	12.00	20.00	80.00
1893Ga JS	1,952,000	10.00	12.00	20.00	80.00
1894Ga JS	2,045,999	10.00	12.00	20.00	80.00
1895/3Ga JS	—	12.00	20.00	35.00	100
1895Ga JS	1,146,000	10.00	12.00	20.00	65.00

Mint: Guadalupe y Calvo
KM# 377.7 8 REALES
27.0700 g., 0.9030 Silver .7859 oz. ASW **Obv:** Facing eagle

Date	F	VF	XF	Unc
1844GC MP	350	500	1,000	2,000
1844GC MP Error, reversed S in Ds, Gs	400	600	1,200	2,250
1845GC MP Eagle's tail square	125	200	325	700
1845GC MP Eagle's tail round	175	350	650	1,200
1846GC MP Eagle's tail square	175	350	750	1,650
1846GC MP Eagle's tail round	125	200	350	750
1847GC MP	150	250	400	800
1848GC MP	175	300	500	900
1849GC MP	175	300	525	1,000
1850GC MP	175	300	575	1,100
1851GC MP	300	500	900	1,600
1852GC MP	350	600	1,250	2,500

Mint: Guanajuato
KM# 377.8 8 REALES
27.0700 g., 0.9030 Silver .7859 oz. ASW **Obv:** Facing eagle
Note: Varieties exist.

Date	Mintage	F	VF	XF	Unc
1825Go JJ	—	40.00	70.00	150	300
1825G JJ	—	1,250	1,650	—	—
Note: Error mint mark G					
1826Go JJ	—	40.00	80.00	175	350
Note: Straight J's					
1826Go JJ	—	30.00	60.00	125	250
Note: Full J's					
1826Go MJ	—	250	450	850	—
1827Go MJ	—	40.00	75.00	125	250
1827Go MJ/JJ	—	—	—	—	—
1827Go MR	—	100	200	350	600
1828Go MJ	—	—	—	—	—
Note: Error mint mark Goo					
1828Go MJ	—	30.00	60.00	125	250
1828/7Go MR	—	150	300	600	1,200
1828Go MR	—	150	300	600	1,200
1829Go MJ	—	20.00	35.00	55.00	165
1830Go MJ	—	20.00	30.00	55.00	165
Note: Oblong beading and narrow J					
1830Go MJ	—	20.00	30.00	55.00	165
Note: Regular beading and wide J					
1831Go MJ	—	12.00	20.00	40.00	150
Note: Colon after date					
1831Go MJ	—	12.00	20.00	40.00	150
Note: 2 stars after date					
1832Go MJ	—	12.00	20.00	40.00	150
1832Go MJ	—	12.00	35.00	65.00	175
Note: 1 of date over inverted 1					
1833Go MJ/1	—	20.00	35.00	65.00	175
1833Go MJ	—	12.00	20.00	40.00	150
1833Go JM	—	400	750	1,250	2,500
1834Go PJ	—	12.00	20.00	40.00	150
1835Go PJ	—	12.00	20.00	40.00	150
Note: Star on cap					
1835Go PJ	—	12.00	20.00	40.00	150
Note: Dot on cap					
1836Go PJ	—	12.00	20.00	40.00	150
1837Go PJ	—	12.00	20.00	40.00	150
1838Go PJ	—	12.00	20.00	40.00	150
1839Go PJ/JJ	—	12.00	20.00	40.00	150
1839Go PJ	—	12.00	20.00	40.00	150
1840/30Go PJ	—	20.00	30.00	50.00	150
1840Go PJ	—	12.00	20.00	35.00	125
1841/31Go PJ	—	12.00	20.00	35.00	125
1841Go PJ	—	12.00	20.00	35.00	125
1842/1Go PM	—	20.00	30.00	50.00	150
1842/31Go PM/PJ	—	25.00	35.00	60.00	150
1842Go PJ	—	20.00	30.00	50.00	125
1842Go PM/PJ	—	12.00	20.00	35.00	125
1842Go PM	—	12.00	20.00	35.00	125
1843Go PM	—	12.00	20.00	35.00	125
Note: Dot after date					
1843Go PM	—	12.00	20.00	35.00	125
Note: Triangle of dots after date					
1844Go PM	—	12.00	20.00	35.00	125
1845Go PM	—	12.00	20.00	35.00	125
1846/5Go PM	—	20.00	30.00	50.00	150
Note: Eagle type of 1845					
1846Go PM	—	15.00	25.00	40.00	135
Note: Early type of 1847					
1847Go PM Narrow date	—	12.00	20.00	35.00	125
1847Go PM Wide date	—	12.00	20.00	35.00	125
1848/7Go PM	—	20.00	35.00	65.00	150
1848Go PM	—	20.00	35.00	65.00	150
1848Go PF	—	12.00	20.00	35.00	125
1849Go PF	—	12.00	20.00	35.00	125
1850Go PF	—	12.00	20.00	35.00	125
1851/0Go PF	—	20.00	30.00	50.00	150
1851Go PF	—	12.00	20.00	35.00	125
1852/1Go PF	—	20.00	30.00	50.00	150
1852Go PF	—	12.00	20.00	35.00	125
1853/2Go PF	—	20.00	30.00	50.00	150
1853Go PF	—	12.00	20.00	35.00	125
1854Go PF	—	12.00	20.00	35.00	125
1855Go PF Large letters	—	12.00	20.00	35.00	125

Date	Mintage	F	VF	XF	Unc
1855Go PF Small letters	—	12.00	20.00	35.00	125
1856/5Go PF	—	20.00	30.00	50.00	150
1856Go PF	—	12.00	20.00	35.00	125
1857/5Go PF	—	20.00	30.00	50.00	150
1857/6Go PF	—	20.00	35.00	70.00	200
1857Go PF	—	12.00	15.00	20.00	75.00
1858/7Go PI	—	12.00	20.00	35.00	125
1858Go PF	—	12.00	20.00	35.00	125
1859/7Go PF	—	12.00	20.00	35.00	125
1859/8Go PF	—	20.00	30.00	50.00	150
1859Go PF	—	12.00	20.00	35.00	125
1860/50Go PF	—	20.00	30.00	50.00	150
1860/59Go PF	—	12.00	18.00	25.00	85.00
1860Go PF	—	12.00	15.00	20.00	75.00
1861/51Go PF	—	15.00	20.00	30.00	100
1861/0Go PF	—	12.00	15.00	20.00	75.00
1861Go PF	—	12.00	15.00	20.00	75.00
186/52Go YE	—	—	—	—	—
1862Go YE/PF	—	12.00	15.00	20.00	75.00
1862Go YE	—	12.00	15.00	20.00	75.00
1862Go YF	—	12.00	15.00	20.00	75.00
1862Go YF/PF	—	12.00	15.00	20.00	75.00
1863/53Go YF	—	12.00	18.00	25.00	75.00
1863/54Go YF	—	15.00	20.00	30.00	100
1863Go YE Rare	—	—	—	—	—
1863Go YF	—	12.00	15.00	20.00	75.00
1867/57Go YF	—	15.00	20.00	30.00	100
1867Go YF	—	12.00	15.00	20.00	75.00
1868/58Go YF	—	15.00	20.00	30.00	100
1868/7Go YF	—	15.00	20.00	30.00	100
1868Go YF	—	12.00	15.00	20.00	75.00
1870/60Go FR	—	20.00	30.00	50.00	150
1870Go YF	—	1,800	3,000	5,000	7,500
1870Go FR/YF	—	20.00	35.00	70.00	200
1870Go FR	—	12.00	15.00	20.00	75.00
1873Go FR	—	12.00	15.00	20.00	75.00
1874/3Go FR	—	15.00	20.00	30.00	85.00
1874Go FR	—	15.00	25.00	35.00	100
1875/3Go FR	—	15.00	20.00	30.00	85.00
1875/6Go FR	—	15.00	20.00	30.00	85.00
1875Go FR	—	12.00	15.00	20.00	75.00

Note: Small circle with dot on eagle

Date	Mintage	F	VF	XF	Unc
1876/5Go FR	—	15.00	20.00	30.00	85.00
1876Go FR	—	12.00	15.00	20.00	60.00
1877Go FR	2,477,000	12.00	15.00	20.00	60.00
1878/7Go FR	2,273,000	15.00	20.00	30.00	75.00
1878/7Go SM	—	15.00	20.00	30.00	75.00
1878Go FR	Inc. above	12.00	15.00	20.00	65.00
1878Go SM, S/F	—	15.00	20.00	25.00	70.00
1878Go SM	—	12.00	15.00	20.00	65.00
1879/7Go SM	—	15.00	20.00	30.00	75.00
1879/8Go SM	—	15.00	20.00	30.00	75.00
1879/8Go SM/FR	—	15.00	20.00	30.00	75.00
1879Go SM	—	12.00	15.00	20.00	65.00
1879Go SM/FR	—	15.00	20.00	30.00	75.00
1880/70Go SB	—	15.00	20.00	30.00	75.00
1880Go SB/SM	—	12.00	15.00	20.00	65.00
1880Go SB	—	12.00	15.00	20.00	65.00
1881/71Go SB	3,974,000	15.00	20.00	30.00	75.00
1881/0Go SB	Inc. above	15.00	20.00	30.00	75.00
1881Go SB	Inc. above	12.00	15.00	20.00	65.00
1882Go SB	2,015,000	12.00	15.00	20.00	75.00
1883Go SB	2,100,000	35.00	75.00	125	250
1883Go BR	Inc. above	12.00	15.00	20.00	65.00
1883Go BR/SR	—	12.00	15.00	20.00	65.00
1883Go BR/SB	Inc. above	12.00	15.00	20.00	65.00
1884/73Go BR	—	20.00	30.00	40.00	100
1884/74Go BR	—	20.00	30.00	40.00	100
1884/3Go BR	—	20.00	30.00	60.00	150
1884Go BR	—	12.00	15.00	20.00	65.00
1884/74Go RR	—	50.00	100	175	350
1884Go RR	—	25.00	50.00	100	250
1885/75Go RR	2,363,000	15.00	20.00	30.00	75.00
1885Go RR	Inc. above	12.00	15.00	20.00	65.00
1886/75Go RR	4,127,000	15.00	20.00	25.00	70.00
1886/76Go RR	Inc. above	12.00	15.00	20.00	65.00
1886/3Go RR/BR	Inc. above	12.00	15.00	20.00	65.00
1886Go RR	Inc. above	12.00	15.00	20.00	65.00
1887Go RR	4,205,000	10.00	15.00	20.00	65.00

Date	Mintage	F	VF	XF	Unc
1888Go RR	3,985,000	10.00	15.00	20.00	65.00
1889Go RR	3,646,000	10.00	15.00	20.00	65.00
1890Go RR	3,615,000	10.00	15.00	20.00	65.00
1891Go RS/R	—	10.00	15.00	20.00	65.00
1891Go RS	3,197,000	10.00	15.00	20.00	65.00
1892/0Go RS	—	10.00	15.00	20.00	65.00
1892Go RS	3,672,000	10.00	15.00	20.00	65.00
1893Go RS	3,854,000	10.00	15.00	20.00	65.00
1894Go RS	4,127,000	10.00	15.00	20.00	65.00
1895/1Go RS	3,768,000	15.00	20.00	25.00	75.00
1895/3Go RS	Inc. above	15.00	20.00	25.00	75.00
1895Go RS	Inc. above	10.00	15.00	20.00	65.00
1896/1Go/As RS/ML	5,229,000	15.00	20.00	25.00	75.00
1896/1Go RS	Inc. above	12.00	15.00	20.00	65.00
1896Go/Ga RS	Inc. above	—	—	—	—
1896Go RS	Inc. above	10.00	12.00	18.00	60.00
1897Go RS	4,344,000	10.00	12.00	18.00	60.00

Mint: Hermosillo
KM# 377.9   8 REALES
27.0700 g., 0.9030 Silver .7859 oz. ASW **Obv:** Facing eagle
Note: Varieties exist.

Date	Mintage	F	VF	XF	Unc
1835Ho PP Rare	—	—	—	—	—
1836Ho PP Rare	—	—	—	—	—
1839Ho PR Unique	—	—	—	—	—
1861Ho FM Reeded edge	—	4,500	7,500	—	—
1862Ho FM Rare	—	—	—	—	—

Note: Plain edge, snakes tail left, long ray over *8R

1862Ho FM	—	1,550	2,700	—	—

Note: Plain edge, snake's tail left

1862Ho FM	—	1,650	2,750	—	—

Note: Reeded edge, snakes tail right

1863Ho FM	—	150	300	800	—
1864Ho FM	—	850	1,650	2,750	—
1864Ho PR/FM	—	1,200	2,200	—	—
1864Ho PR	—	650	1,250	2,150	3,350
1865Ho FM	—	250	500	950	1,850
1866Ho FM	—	1,150	2,150	3,500	5,500
1866Ho MP	—	950	1,750	3,000	4,650
1867Ho PR	—	100	175	275	500
1868Ho PR	—	20.00	35.00	65.00	175
1869Ho PR	—	40.00	60.00	125	250
1870Ho PR	—	100	175	275	550
1871/0Ho PR	—	50.00	75.00	125	250
1871Ho PR	—	30.00	50.00	90.00	200
1872/1Ho PR	—	35.00	60.00	90.00	200
1872Ho PR	—	30.00	50.00	75.00	175
1873Ho PR	351,000	30.00	50.00	85.00	150
1874Ho PR	—	15.00	20.00	40.00	125
1875Ho PR	—	15.00	20.00	40.00	125
1876Ho AF	—	15.00	20.00	40.00	125
1877Ho AF	410,000	20.00	30.00	50.00	150
1877Ho GR	Inc. above	100	150	225	400
1877Ho JA	Inc. above	25.00	50.00	85.00	175
1878Ho JA	451,000	15.00	20.00	40.00	120
1879Ho JA	—	15.00	20.00	40.00	120
1880Ho JA	—	15.00	20.00	40.00	120
1881Ho JA	586,000	15.00	20.00	40.00	120
1882Ho JA	240,000	25.00	40.00	65.00	125

Note: O above H

1882Ho JA	Inc. above	25.00	40.00	65.00	125

Date	Mintage	F	VF	XF	Unc
Note: O after H					
1883/2Ho JA	204,000	200	350	500	1,000
1883/2Ho FM/JA	Inc. above	25.00	40.00	75.00	150
1883Ho FM/JA	—	27.00	45.00	85.00	165
1883Ho FM	Inc. above	20.00	30.00	60.00	125
1883Ho JA	Inc. above	275	450	800	1,500
1884/3Ho FM	—	20.00	25.00	50.00	125
1884Ho FM	—	15.00	20.00	40.00	120
1885Ho FM	132,000	15.00	20.00	40.00	120
1886Ho FM	225,000	20.00	30.00	45.00	125
1886Ho FG	Inc. above	20.00	30.00	45.00	125
1887/6Ho FG	—	20.00	35.00	65.00	150
1887Ho FG	150,000	20.00	35.00	65.00	150
1888Ho FG	364,000	12.00	18.00	25.00	100
1889Ho FG	490,000	12.00	18.00	25.00	100
1890Ho FG	565,000	12.00	18.00	25.00	100
1891Ho FG	738,000	12.00	18.00	25.00	100
1892Ho FG	643,000	12.00	18.00	25.00	100
1893Ho FG	518,000	12.00	18.00	25.00	100
1894Ho FG	504,000	12.00	18.00	25.00	100
1895Ho FG	320,000	12.00	18.00	25.00	100

Mint: Mexico City
KM# 377.10   8 REALES
27.0700 g., 0.9030 Silver .7859 oz. ASW **Obv:** Facing eagle
Note: Varieties exist. 1874 CP is a die struck counterfeit.

Date	Mintage	F	VF	XF	Unc
1824Mo JM Round tail	—	75.00	125	250	500
1824Mo JM Square tail	—	75.00	125	250	500
1825Mo JM	—	25.00	40.00	75.00	200
1826/5Mo JM	—	25.00	40.00	75.00	200
1826Mo JM	—	20.00	30.00	55.00	165
1827Mo JM	—	25.00	35.00	60.00	175
Note: Medal alignment					
1827Mo JM	—	25.00	35.00	60.00	175
Note: Coin alignment					
1828Mo JM	—	30.00	60.00	100	250
1829Mo JM	—	20.00	30.00	90.00	220
1830/20Mo JM	—	35.00	5.00	150	300
1830Mo JM	—	30.00	50.00	90.00	220
1831Mo JM	—	30.00	50.00	100	240
1832/1Mo JM	—	25.00	40.00	65.00	180
1832Mo JM	—	20.00	30.00	55.00	165
1833Mo MJ	—	25.00	40.00	80.00	200
1833Mo ML	—	450	650	950	2,000
1834/3Mo ML	—	25.00	35.00	60.00	175
1834Mo ML	—	20.00	30.00	55.00	165
1835Mo ML Narrow date	—	20.00	30.00	55.00	165
1835Mo ML Wide date	—	20.00	30.00	55.00	165
1836Mo ML	—	50.00	100	150	325
1836Mo ML/MF	—	50.00	100	150	325

Date	Mintage	F	VF	XF	Unc
1836Mo MF	—	30.00	50.00	90.00	220
1836Mo MF/ML	—	35.00	60.00	100	240
1837/6Mo ML	—	30.00	50.00	80.00	200
1837/6Mo MM	—	30.00	50.00	80.00	200
1837/6Mo MM/ML	—	30.00	50.00	80.00	200
1837/6Mo MM/MF	—	30.00	50.00	80.00	200
1837Mo ML	—	30.00	50.00	80.00	200
1837Mo MM	—	75.00	125	175	325
1838Mo MM	—	30.00	50.00	80.00	200
1838Mo ML	—	20.00	35.00	60.00	180
1838Mo ML/MM	—	20.00	35.00	60.00	180
1839Mo ML Narow date	—	15.00	25.00	50.00	165
1839Mo ML Wide date	—	15.00	25.00	50.00	165
1840Mo ML	—	15.00	25.00	50.00	165
1841Mo ML	—	15.00	25.00	45.00	150
1842Mo ML	—	15.00	25.00	45.00	150
1842Mo MM	—	15.00	25.00	45.00	150
1843Mo MM	—	15.00	25.00	45.00	150
1844Mo MF/MM	—	—	—	—	—
1844Mo MF	—	15.00	25.00	45.00	150
1845/4Mo MF	—	15.00	25.00	45.00	150
1845Mo MF	—	15.00	25.00	45.00	150
1846/5Mo MF	—	15.00	25.00	50.00	165
1846Mo MF	—	15.00	25.00	50.00	165
1847/6Mo MF	—	2,000	3,550	—	—
1847Mo MF	—	1,650	3,000	5,000	7,500
1847Mo RC	—	20.00	30.00	55.00	165
1847Mo RC/MF	—	15.00	25.00	45.00	150
1848Mo GC	—	15.00	25.00	45.00	150
1849/8Mo GC	—	20.00	35.00	60.00	180
1849Mo GC	—	15.00	25.00	45.00	150
1850/40Mo GC	—	25.00	50.00	100	240
1850/49Mo GC	—	25.00	50.00	100	240
1850Mo GC	—	20.00	40.00	75.00	200
1851Mo GC	—	20.00	40.00	60.00	175
1852Mo GC	—	20.00	40.00	75.00	200
1853Mo GC	—	15.00	25.00	50.00	160
1854Mo GC	—	12.00	15.00	30.00	125
1855Mo GC	—	20.00	35.00	65.00	180
1855Mo GF	—	12.00	15.00	30.00	125
1855Mo GF/GC	—	12.00	15.00	30.00	125
1856/4Mo GF	—	15.00	25.00	45.00	145
1856/5Mo GF	—	15.00	25.00	45.00	145
1856Mo GF	—	12.00	15.00	30.00	125
1857Mo GF	—	10.00	15.00	30.00	125
1858/7Mo FH/GF	—	10.00	15.00	30.00	125
1858Mo FH Narrow date	—	10.00	15.00	30.00	125
1858Mo FH Wide date	—	10.00	15.00	30.00	125
1859Mo FH	—	10.00	15.00	30.00	125
1859/8Mo FH	—	25.00	50.00	100	240
1860/59Mo FH	—	15.00	20.00	30.00	125
1860Mo FH	—	10.00	15.00	30.00	125
1860Mo TH	—	12.00	18.00	40.00	145
1861Mo TH	—	12.00	18.00	40.00	145
1861Mo CH	—	10.00	15.00	20.00	75.00
1862Mo CH	—	10.00	15.00	20.00	75.00
1863Mo CH	—	10.00	15.00	20.00	75.00
1863Mo CH/TH	—	10.00	15.00	20.00	75.00
1863Mo TH	—	10.00	15.00	20.00	75.00
1867Mo CH	—	10.00	15.00	20.00	65.00
1867Mo CH/TH	—	20.00	45.00	70.00	185
1868Mo CH	—	10.00	15.00	20.00	65.00
1868Mo PH	—	10.00	15.00	20.00	65.00
1868Mo CH/PH	—	10.00	15.00	20.00	65.00
1868Mo PH Narrow date	—	10.00	15.00	20.00	65.00
1868Mo PH Wide date	—	10.00	15.00	20.00	65.00
1869Mo CH	—	10.00	15.00	20.00	65.00
1873Mo MH	—	10.00	15.00	20.00	65.00
1873Mo MH/HH	—	12.00	18.00	25.00	75.00
1874/69Mo MH	—	20.00	45.00	70.00	185
1874Mo MH	—	12.00	18.00	25.00	75.00
1874Mo BH/MH	—	12.00	18.00	25.00	75.00
1874Mo BH	—	12.00	18.00	25.00	85.00
1875Mo BH	—	10.00	15.00	20.00	65.00
1876/4Mo BH	—	12.00	18.00	25.00	75.00
1876/5Mo BH	—	12.00	18.00	25.00	75.00
1876Mo BH	—	10.00	15.00	20.00	65.00
1877Mo MH	898,000	10.00	15.00	20.00	65.00
1877Mo MH/BH	Inc. above	12.00	18.00	25.00	75.00

Date	Mintage	F	VF	XF	Unc
1878Mo MH	2,154,000	10.00	15.00	20.00	65.00
1879/8Mo MH	—	10.00	15.00	20.00	75.00
1879Mo MH	—	10.00	15.00	20.00	65.00
1880/79Mo MH	—	15.00	20.00	30.00	75.00
1880Mo MH	—	10.00	15.00	20.00	75.00
1881Mo MH	5,712,000	10.00	15.00	20.00	65.00
1882/1Mo MH	2,746,000	12.00	15.00	20.00	75.00
1882Mo MH	Inc. above	10.00	15.00	20.00	65.00
1883/2Mo MH	2,726,000	12.00	18.00	25.00	85.00
1883Mo MH Narrow date	Inc. above	10.00	15.00	20.00	65.00
1883Mo MH Wide date	—	10.00	15.00	20.00	65.00
1884/3Mo MH	—	15.00	20.00	30.00	75.00
1884Mo MH	—	10.00	15.00	20.00	65.00
1885Mo MH	3,649,000	10.00	15.00	20.00	65.00
1886Mo MH	7,558,000	10.00	12.00	18.00	60.00
1887Mo MH	7,681,000	10.00	12.00	18.00	60.00
1888Mo MH Narrow date	7,179,000	10.00	12.00	18.00	60.00
1888Mo MH Wide date	—	10.00	12.00	18.00	60.00
1889Mo MH	7,332,000	10.00	15.00	20.00	65.00
1890Mo MH Narrow date	7,412,000	10.00	12.00	18.00	60.00
1890Mo AM Wide date	—	10.00	12.00	18.00	60.00
1890Mo AM	Inc. above	10.00	12.00	18.00	60.00
1891Mo AM	8,076,000	10.00	12.00	18.00	60.00
1892Mo AM	9,392,000	10.00	12.00	18.00	60.00
1893Mo AM	10,773,000	10.00	12.00	18.00	55.00
1894Mo AM	12,394,000	10.00	12.00	18.00	45.00
1895Mo AM	10,474,000	10.00	12.00	18.00	45.00
1895Mo AB	Inc. above	10.00	12.00	18.00	60.00
1896Mo AB	9,327,000	10.00	12.00	18.00	60.00
1896Mo AM	Inc. above	10.00	12.00	18.00	60.00
1897Mo AM	8,621,000	10.00	12.00	18.00	60.00

Date	Mintage	F	VF	XF	Unc
1876 AE	140,000	20.00	35.00	55.00	200
1877 AE	139,000	20.00	30.00	50.00	200
1878 AE	125,000	20.00	30.00	50.00	200
1879 AE	153,000	20.00	30.00	50.00	200
1880 AE	143,000	15.00	30.00	45.00	150
1881 AE	134,000	20.00	35.00	60.00	150
1882 AE	100,000	20.00	35.00	60.00	150
1883 AE	122,000	15.00	30.00	45.00	150
1884 AE	142,000	15.00	30.00	50.00	150
1885 AE	158,000	15.00	25.00	40.00	135
1886 AE	120,000	15.00	30.00	45.00	150
1887/6 AE	115,000	25.00	50.00	80.00	200
1887 AE	Inc. above	15.00	25.00	40.00	135
1888 AE	145,000	15.00	25.00	40.00	135
1889 AE	150,000	20.00	30.00	60.00	175
1890 AE	181,000	20.00	30.00	60.00	175
1891 EN	160,000	15.00	25.00	40.00	135
1892 EN	120,000	15.00	25.00	40.00	135
1893 EN	66,000	45.00	75.00	115	300

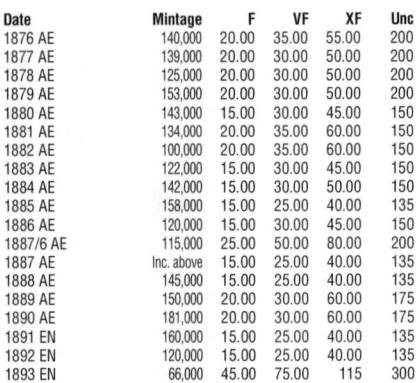

Mint: Oaxaca
KM# 377.11   8 REALES
27.0700 g., 0.9030 Silver .7859 oz. ASW **Obv:** Facing eagle
Note: Mint mark O, Oa. Varieties exist.

Date	Mintage	F	VF	XF	Unc
1858O AE	—	2,500	4,000	—	—
1858 Oa AE Unique	—	—	—	—	—
1859 AE	—	500	900	1,750	—
Note: A in O of mint mark					
1860 AE	—	200	450	800	—
Note: A in O of mint mark					
1861O FR	—	125	250	550	1,350
1861 Oa FR	—	150	350	700	—
1862O FR	—	40.00	80.00	200	375
1862 Oa FR	—	65.00	125	250	450
1863O FR	—	30.00	60.00	100	250
1863O AE	—	30.00	60.00	100	250
1863 Oa AE	—	100	150	250	450
Note: A in O of mint mark					
1863 Oa AE	—	1,000	1,750	2,750	—
Note: A above O in mint mark					
1864 FR	—	25.00	50.00	75.00	200
1865 AE	—	1,850	3,000	—	—
1867 AE	—	40.00	80.00	150	400
1868 AE	—	40.00	80.00	150	400
1869 AE	—	30.00	60.00	100	250
1873 AE	—	200	300	550	1,350
1874 AE	142,000	15.00	30.00	50.00	200
1875/4 AE	131,000	25.00	50.00	75.00	200
1875 AE	Inc. above	15.00	30.00	40.00	135

Mint: San Luis Potosi
KM# 377.12   8 REALES
27.0700 g., 0.9030 Silver .7859 oz. ASW **Obv:** Facing eagle
Note: Varieties exist.

Date	Mintage	F	VF	XF	Unc
1827 Pi JS	—	3,800	—	—	—
1827 Pi SA	—	6,000	9,000	—	—
1828/7 Pi JS	—	275	425	650	1,250
1828 Pi JS	—	225	375	550	1,100
1829 Pi JS	—	35.00	65.00	125	250
1830 Pi JS	—	30.00	50.00	100	200
1831/0 Pi JS	—	35.00	75.00	200	350
1831 Pi JS	—	25.00	35.00	75.00	200
1832/22 Pi JS	—	25.00	35.00	65.00	165
18/032 Pi JS	—	40.00	80.00	175	300
1832 Pi JS	—	25.00	35.00	65.00	165
1833/2 Pi JS	—	30.00	45.00	80.00	250
1833 Pi JS Narrow date	—	20.00	30.00	50.00	150
1833 Pi JS Wide date	—	20.00	30.00	50.00	150
1834/3 Pi JS	—	35.00	65.00	125	300
1834 Pi JS	—	15.00	25.00	50.00	150
1835/4 Pi JS	—	60.00	125	250	500
1835 Pi JS	—	20.00	30.00	65.00	175
Note: Denomination as 8R					
1835 Pi JS	—	15.00	25.00	50.00	150
Note: Denomination as 8Rs					
1836 Pi JS	—	20.00	30.00	55.00	150
1837 Pi JS	—	30.00	50.00	85.00	200
1838 Pi JS	—	20.00	30.00	55.00	150
1839 Pi JS	—	20.00	40.00	70.00	150
1840 Pi JS	—	20.00	30.00	60.00	150
1841 Pi JS	—	25.00	40.00	85.00	200

Date	Mintage	F	VF	XF	Unc
1841iP JS Error	—	200	350	550	—
1842/1 Pi JS	—	40.00	65.00	125	300
1842/1 Pi JS/PS	—	35.00	55.00	90.00	200
1842 Pi JS	—	30.00	50.00	80.00	175
Note: Eagle type of 1843					
1842 Pi PS	—	30.00	50.00	80.00	175
1842 Pi PS/JS	—	30.00	50.00	80.00	175
Note: Eagle type of 1841					
1843/2 Pi PS Round top 3	—	50.00	75.00	150	300
1843 Pi PS Flat top 3	—	60.00	100	200	475
1843 Pi AM Round top 3	—	20.00	30.00	55.00	150
1843 Pi AM Flat top 3	—	20.00	30.00	55.00	150
1844 Pi AM	—	20.00	30.00	55.00	150
1845/4 Pi AM	—	35.00	55.00	120	250
1845 Pi AM	—	25.00	50.00	100	225
1846/5 Pi AM	—	40.00	65.00	125	300
1846 Pi AM	—	15.00	25.00	50.00	150
1847 Pi AM	—	30.00	50.00	85.00	175
1848/7 Pi AM	—	30.00	60.00	100	200
1848 Pi AM	—	30.00	50.00	85.00	175
1849/8 Pi PS/AM	—	950	1,750	—	—
1849 Pi PS	—	950	1,750	—	—
1849 Pi MC/PS	—	60.00	125	250	500
1849 Pi AM	—	1,850	3,250	5,000	—
1849 Pi MC	—	60.00	125	250	500
1850 Pi MC	—	40.00	80.00	150	300
1851 Pi MC	—	75.00	150	275	550
1852 Pi MC	—	75.00	125	200	400
1853 Pi MC	—	150	275	400	850
1854 Pi MC	—	100	150	250	500
1855 Pi MC	—	100	150	250	500
1856 Pi MC	—	65.00	100	200	400
1857 Pi MC	—	400	700	1,250	—
1857 Pi PS/MC	—	150	250	450	1,000
1857 Pi PS	—	125	200	350	650
1858 Pi MC/PS	—	250	400	650	1,200
1858 Pi MC	—	250	400	650	1,200
1858 Pi PS	—	650	1,150	1,750	—
1859/8 Pi MC/PS	—	3,650	5,750	—	—
1859 Pi MC/PS	—	900	1,750	—	—
1859 Pi MC	—	2,000	3,500	5,000	—
1859 Pi PS/MC	—	800	1,500	2,500	—
1860 Pi FC Rare	—	—	—	—	—
1860 Pi FE Rare	—	—	—	—	—
1860 Pi MC	—	1,750	2,750	6,000	—
1860 Pi PS/FE	—	500	1,000	—	—
1860 Pi RO Rare	—	—	—	—	—
Note: Spink America Gerber sale 6-96 cleaned VF or better realized $33,000					
1860 Pi PS	—	400	600	900	1,750
1861 Pi PS	—	30.00	60.00	90.00	175
1861 Pi RO	—	25.00	35.00	55.00	125
1862/1 Pi RO	—	20.00	25.00	50.00	125
1862 Pi RO	—	15.00	20.00	40.00	100
1862 Pi RO	—	15.00	20.00	40.00	100
Note: Oval O in RO					
1862 Pi RO	—	20.00	30.00	50.00	125
Note: Round O in RO, 6 is an inverted 9					
1863/2 Pi RO	—	25.00	35.00	65.00	150
1863 Pi RO	—	15.00	20.00	40.00	125
1863	—	25.00	35.00	55.00	150
Note: 6 over inverted 6					
1863 Pi FC	—	2,750	4,750	—	—
1864 Pi RO Rare	—	—	—	—	—
1867 Pi CA	—	300	500	—	—
1867 Pi LR	—	250	400	650	—
1867 Pi PS/CA	—	850	—	—	—
1867 Pi PS	—	30.00	60.00	125	275
1868/7 Pi PS	—	30.00	60.00	125	250
1868 Pi PS	—	20.00	30.00	50.00	125
1869/8 Pi PS	—	20.00	25.00	45.00	125
1869 Pi PS	—	15.00	20.00	40.00	125
1870/69 Pi PS	—	750	1,450	3,500	—
1870 Pi PS	—	650	1,250	2,500	—
1873 Pi MH	—	18.00	25.00	45.00	150
1874/3 Pi MH	—	25.00	50.00	120	250
1874 Pi MH	—	10.00	12.00	22.00	120
1875 Pi MH	—	10.00	12.00	22.00	100

Date	Mintage	F	VF	XF	Unc
1876/5 Pi MH	—	18.00	25.00	45.00	150
1876 Pi MH	—	10.00	12.00	22.00	100
1877/6 Pi MH	—	165	325	550	—
1877 Pi MH	1,018,000	10.00	12.00	22.00	120
1878 Pi MH	1,046,000	15.00	30.00	100	225
1879/8 Pi MH	—	15.00	20.00	30.00	125
1879 Pi MH	—	10.00	12.00	22.00	100
1879 Pi BE	—	25.00	50.00	75.00	150
1879 Pi MR	—	30.00	50.00	100	200
1880 Pi MR	—	250	375	750	—
1880 Pi MH/R	—	10.00	12.00	22.00	100
1880 Pi MH	—	10.00	12.00	22.00	100
1881 Pi MH/R	—	10.00	12.00	22.00	100
1881 Pi MH	2,100,000	10.00	12.00	22.00	100
1882/1 Pi MH	1,602,000	15.00	20.00	30.00	125
1882 Pi MH	Inc. above	10.00	12.00	22.00	100
1883/2 Pi MH	—	15.00	20.00	30.00	125
1883 Pi MH	1,545,000	10.00	12.00	22.00	100
1884/3 Pi MH	—	15.00	20.00	30.00	125
1884 Pi MH/MM	—	12.00	15.00	22.00	90.00
1884 Pi MH	—	10.00	12.00	20.00	80.00
1885/4 Pi MH	1,736,000	10.00	20.00	30.00	125
1885/8 Pi MH	Inc. above	15.00	20.00	30.00	125
1885 Pi MH	Inc. above	10.00	12.00	20.00	80.00
1885 Pi LC	Inc. above	12.00	18.00	25.00	100
1886 Pi LC	3,347,000	10.00	12.00	20.00	80.00
1886 Pi MR	Inc. above	10.00	12.00	20.00	80.00
1887 Pi MR	2,922,000	10.00	12.00	20.00	80.00
1888/7 Pi MR	—	15.00	20.00	30.00	125
1888 Pi MR	2,438,000	10.00	12.00	20.00	70.00
1889 Pi MR	2,103,000	10.00	12.00	20.00	80.00
1890 Pi MR	1,562,000	10.00	12.00	20.00	70.00
1891 Pi MR	1,184,000	10.00	12.00	20.00	70.00
1892 Pi MR	1,336,000	10.00	12.00	20.00	70.00
1893 Pi MR	530,000	10.00	12.00	20.00	80.00

Mint: Zacatecas
KM# 377.13   8 REALES
27.0700 g., 0.9030 Silver .7859 oz. ASW **Obv:** Facing eagle
Note: Varieties exist.

Date	Mintage	F	VF	XF	Unc
1825Zs AZ	—	25.00	35.00	65.00	175
1826/5Zs AZ	—	25.00	45.00	85.00	200
1826Zs AZ	—	100	200	400	800
1826Zs AV	—	175	350	600	1,500
1826/5Zs AO/AZ	—	300	600	1,000	2,000
1826Zs AO	—	200	350	750	2,000
1827Zs AO/AZ	—	35.00	50.00	125	250
1827Zs AO	—	25.00	45.00	85.00	200
1828Zs AO	—	15.00	20.00	45.00	165
1829Zs AO	—	15.00	20.00	45.00	165
1829Zs OV	—	50.00	90.00	150	300
1830Zs OV	—	15.00	20.00	45.00	165
1831Zs OV	—	25.00	50.00	90.00	200
1831Zs OM	—	15.00	25.00	55.00	165
1832/1Zs OM	—	20.00	25.00	45.00	165
1832Zs OM	—	15.00	20.00	40.00	150
1833/2Zs OM	—	20.00	30.00	45.00	165
1833Zs OM/MM	—	15.00	25.00	40.00	150
1833Zs OM	—	15.00	20.00	35.00	150
1834Zs OM	—	15.00	20.00	35.00	150
1835Zs OM	—	15.00	20.00	40.00	150
1836/4Zs OM	—	20.00	30.00	50.00	165
1836/5Zs OM	—	20.00	30.00	50.00	165
1836Zs OM	—	15.00	20.00	35.00	150
1837Zs OM	—	15.00	20.00	35.00	150
1838/7Zs OM	—	20.00	30.00	45.00	165
1838Zs OM	—	15.00	20.00	35.00	150
1839Zs OM	—	15.00	20.00	35.00	150
1840Zs OM	—	15.00	20.00	35.00	150
1841Zs OM	—	15.00	20.00	35.00	150
1842Zs OM	—	15.00	20.00	35.00	150
Note: Eagle type of 1841					
1842Zs OM	—	15.00	20.00	35.00	150
Note: Eagle type of 1843					
1843Zs OM	—	15.00	20.00	35.00	150
1844Zs OM	—	15.00	20.00	35.00	150
1845Zs OM	—	15.00	20.00	35.00	150
1846Zs OM	—	15.00	20.00	35.00	150
1847Zs OM	—	15.00	20.00	35.00	150

Date	Mintage	F	VF	XF	Unc
1848/7Zs OM	—	20.00	30.00	45.00	165
1848Zs OM	—	15.00	20.00	35.00	150
1849Zs OM	—	15.00	20.00	35.00	150
1850Zs OM	—	15.00	20.00	35.00	150
1851Zs OM	—	15.00	20.00	35.00	150
1852Zs OM	—	15.00	20.00	35.00	150
1853Zs OM	—	30.00	45.00	75.00	200
1854/3Zs OM	—	20.00	30.00	60.00	175
1854Zs OM	—	15.00	25.00	45.00	165
1855Zs OM	—	20.00	30.00	60.00	175
1855Zs MO	—	30.00	60.00	90.00	200
1856/5Zs MO	—	20.00	30.00	45.00	165
1856Zs MO	—	15.00	20.00	35.00	150
1857/5Zs MO	—	20.00	30.00	45.00	165
1857Zs MO	—	15.00	20.00	35.00	150
1858/7Zs MO	—	15.00	20.00	35.00	150
1858Zs MO	—	15.00	20.00	35.00	150
1859/8Zs MO	—	15.00	20.00	35.00	150
1859Zs MO	—	15.00	20.00	35.00	150
1859Zs VL/MO	—	25.00	50.00	75.00	175
1859Zs VL	—	20.00	40.00	60.00	165
1860/50Zs MO	—	10.00	12.00	20.00	80.00
1860/59Zs MO	—	10.00	12.00	20.00	80.00
1860Zs MO	—	10.00	12.00	20.00	80.00
1860Zs VL/MO	—	10.00	12.00	20.00	80.00
1860Zs VL	—	10.00	12.00	20.00	80.00
1861/0Zs VL/MO	—	10.00	12.00	20.00	80.00
1861Zs VL	—	10.00	12.00	20.00	80.00
1861/0Zs VL	—	10.00	12.00	20.00	80.00
1862/1Zs VL	—	15.00	20.00	35.00	100
1862Zs VL	—	10.00	12.00	20.00	80.00
1863Zs VL	—	10.00	12.00	20.00	80.00
1863Zs MO	—	10.00	12.00	20.00	80.00
1864/3Zs VL	—	15.00	20.00	35.00	100
1864Zs VL	—	10.00	12.00	20.00	80.00
1864Zs MO	—	15.00	20.00	35.00	100
1865/4Zs MO	—	200	450	800	1,550
1865Zs MO	—	150	300	600	1,250
1866Zs VL	—	—	—	—	—
Note: Contemporary counterfeit					
1867Zs JS Rare	—	—	—	—	—
1868Zs JS	—	10.00	12.00	20.00	80.00
1868Zs YH	—	10.00	12.00	20.00	80.00
1869Zs YH	—	10.00	12.00	20.00	80.00
1870Zs YH Rare	—	—	—	—	—
1873Zs YH	—	10.00	12.00	20.00	80.00
1874Zs YH	—	10.00	12.00	20.00	80.00
1874Zs JA/YA	—	10.00	12.00	20.00	80.00
1874Zs JA	—	10.00	12.00	20.00	80.00
1875Zs JA	—	10.00	12.00	20.00	80.00
1876Zs JA	—	10.00	12.00	20.00	80.00
1876Zs JS	—	10.00	12.00	20.00	80.00
1877Zs JS	2,700,000	10.00	12.00	20.00	80.00
1878Zs JS	2,310,000	10.00	12.00	20.00	80.00
1879/8Zs JS	—	15.00	20.00	35.00	100
1879Zs JS	—	10.00	12.00	20.00	80.00
1880Zs JS	—	10.00	12.00	20.00	80.00
1881Zs JS	5,592,000	10.00	12.00	20.00	80.00
1882/1Zs JS	2,485,000	15.00	20.00	35.00	100
1882Zs JS Straight J	Inc. above	10.00	12.00	20.00	65.00
1882Zs JS Full J	Inc. above	10.00	12.00	20.00	65.00
1883/2Zs JS	2,563,000	15.00	20.00	35.00	100
1883Zs JS	Inc. above	10.00	12.00	20.00	80.00
1884Zs JS	—	10.00	12.00	20.00	65.00
1885Zs JS	2,252,000	10.00	12.00	20.00	65.00
1886/5Zs JS	5,303,000	15.00	20.00	35.00	100
1886/8Zs JS	Inc. above	15.00	20.00	35.00	100
1886Zs JS	Inc. above	10.00	12.00	20.00	65.00
1886Zs FZ	Inc. above	10.00	12.00	20.00	65.00
1887Zs FZ	4,733,000	10.00	12.00	20.00	65.00
1887Z FZ	Inc. above	20.00	30.00	50.00	100
1888/7Zs FZ	5,132,000	12.00	15.00	25.00	80.00
1888Zs FZ	Inc. above	10.00	12.00	20.00	65.00
1889Zs FZ	4,344,000	10.00	12.00	20.00	65.00
1890Zs FZ	3,887,000	10.00	12.00	20.00	65.00
1891Zs FZ	4,114,000	10.00	12.00	20.00	65.00
1892/1Zs FZ	4,238,000	12.00	15.00	25.00	80.00
1892Zs FZ Narrow date	Inc. above	10.00	12.00	20.00	65.00
1892Zs FZ Wide date	—	10.00	12.00	20.00	65.00

Date	Mintage	F	VF	XF	Unc
1893Zs FZ	3,872,000	10.00	12.00	20.00	65.00
1894Zs FZ	3,081,000	10.00	12.00	20.00	65.00
1895Zs FZ	4,718,000	10.00	12.00	20.00	65.00
1896Zs FZ	4,226,000	10.00	12.00	20.00	55.00
1897Zs FZ	4,877,000	10.00	12.00	20.00	55.00

Mint: Culiacan
KM# 378   1/2 ESCUDO
1.6900 g., 0.8750 Gold .0475 oz. AGW   **Obv:** Facing eagle

Date	VG	F	VF	XF	Unc
1848C CE	35.00	50.00	75.00	150	—
1853C CE	35.00	50.00	75.00	150	—
1854C CE Revised eagle	35.00	50.00	75.00	150	—
Note: Dates 1854-1870 of this type display the revised eagle					
1856C CE	50.00	100	150	250	—
1857C CE	35.00	50.00	75.00	150	—
1859C CE	35.00	50.00	75.00	150	—
1860C CE	35.00	50.00	75.00	150	—
1862C CE	35.00	50.00	75.00	125	—
1863C CE	35.00	50.00	75.00	125	—
1866C CE	35.00	50.00	75.00	125	—
1867C CE	35.00	50.00	75.00	125	—
1870C CE	75.00	150	275	450	—

Mint: Durango
KM# 378.1   1/2 ESCUDO
1.6900 g., 0.8750 Gold .0475 oz. AGW   **Obv:** Facing eagle

Date	VG	F	VF	XF	Unc
1833Do RM/RL	35.00	50.00	75.00	150	—
1834/1Do RM	35.00	50.00	75.00	150	—
1834/3Do RM	35.00	50.00	75.00	150	—
1835/2Do RM	35.00	50.00	75.00	150	—
1835/3Do RM	35.00	50.00	75.00	150	—
1835/4Do RM	35.00	50.00	75.00	150	—
1836/4Do RM	35.00	50.00	75.00	150	—
1837Do RM	35.00	50.00	75.00	150	—
1838Do RM	40.00	60.00	100	175	—
1843Do RM	40.00	60.00	100	175	—
1844/33Do RM	40.00	60.00	100	175	—
1844/33Do R,/RL	65.00	125	275	450	—
1845Do CM	40.00	60.00	100	175	—
1846Do RM	40.00	60.00	100	175	—
1848Do RM	40.00	60.00	100	175	—
1850/33Do JMR	40.00	60.00	100	175	—
1851Do JMR	40.00	60.00	100	200	—
1852Do JMR	40.00	60.00	100	175	—
1853/33Do CP	75.00	150	300	500	—
1853Do CP	35.00	50.00	75.00	150	—
1854Do CP	35.00	50.00	75.00	150	—
1855Do CP	35.00	50.00	75.00	150	—
1859Do CP	35.00	50.00	75.00	150	—
1861Do CP	35.00	50.00	75.00	150	—
1862Do CP	35.00	50.00	75.00	150	—
1864Do LT	75.00	125	250	400	—

Mint: Guadalajara
KM# 378.2   1/2 ESCUDO
1.6900 g., 0.8750 Gold .0475 oz. AGW   **Obv:** Facing eagle

Date	VG	F	VF	XF	Unc
1825Ga FS	40.00	60.00	100	175	—
1829Ga FS	40.00	60.00	100	175	—
1831Ga FS	40.00	60.00	100	175	—
1834Ga FS	40.00	60.00	100	175	—
1835Ga FS	40.00	60.00	100	175	—
1837Ga JG	40.00	60.00	100	175	—
1838Ga JG	40.00	60.00	100	175	—
1839Ga JG	—	—	—	—	—

Date	VG	F	VF	XF	Unc
1842Ga JG	—	—	—	—	—
1847Ga JG	40.00	60.00	100	175	—
1850Ga JG	35.00	50.00	75.00	150	—
1852Ga JG	35.00	50.00	75.00	150	—
1859Ga JG	40.00	60.00	100	175	—
1861Ga JG	35.00	50.00	75.00	150	—

Mint: Guadalupe y Calvo
KM# 378.3   1/2 ESCUDO
1.6900 g., 0.8750 Gold .0475 oz. AGW   **Obv:** Facing eagle

Date	VG	F	VF	XF	Unc
1846GC MP	50.00	75.00	100	175	—
1847GC MP	50.00	75.00	100	175	—
1848/7GC MP	50.00	75.00	100	200	—
1850GC MP	50.00	75.00	100	175	—
1851GC Revised eagle	50.00	75.00	100	175	—

Mint: Guanajuato
KM# 378.4   1/2 ESCUDO
1.6900 g., 0.8750 Gold .0475 oz. AGW   **Obv:** Facing eagle

Date	VG	F	VF	XF	Unc
1845Go PM	30.00	40.00	65.00	125	—
1849Go PF	30.00	40.00	65.00	125	—
1851/41Go PF	30.00	40.00	65.00	125	—
1851Go PF	30.00	40.00	65.00	125	—
1852Go PF	30.00	40.00	65.00	125	—
1853Go PF	30.00	40.00	65.00	125	—
1855Go PF	30.00	50.00	80.00	150	—
1857Go PF	30.00	40.00	65.00	125	—
1858/7Go PF	30.00	40.00	65.00	125	—
1859Go PF	30.00	40.00	65.00	125	—
1860Go PF	30.00	40.00	65.00	125	—
1861Go PF	30.00	40.00	65.00	125	—
1862/1Go YE	30.00	40.00	65.00	125	—
1863Go PF	30.00	50.00	80.00	150	—
1863Go YF	30.00	40.00	65.00	125	—

Mint: Mexico City
KM# 378.5   1/2 ESCUDO
1.6900 g., 0.8750 Gold .0475 oz. AGW   **Obv:** Facing eagle

Date	VG	F	VF	XF	Unc
1825/1Mo JM	50.00	75.00	125	200	—
1825/4Mo JM	50.00	75.00	125	200	—
1825Mo JM	30.00	40.00	80.00	150	—
1827/6Mo JM	30.00	40.00	80.00	150	—
1827Mo JM	30.00	40.00	80.00	150	—
1829Mo JM	30.00	40.00	80.00	150	—
1831/0Mo JM	30.00	40.00	80.00	150	—
1831Mo JM	30.00	40.00	60.00	125	—
1832Mo	30.00	40.00	60.00	125	—
1833Mo MJ Olive and oak branches reversed	30.00	50.00	90.00	175	—
1834Mo ML	30.00	40.00	60.00	125	—
1835Mo ML	30.00	40.00	80.00	150	—
1838Mo ML	30.00	50.00	90.00	175	—
1839Mo ML	30.00	50.00	90.00	175	—
1840Mo ML	30.00	40.00	60.00	125	—
1841Mo ML	30.00	40.00	60.00	125	—
1842Mo ML	30.00	40.00	80.00	150	—
1842Mo MM	30.00	40.00	80.00	150	—
1843Mo MM	30.00	40.00	60.00	125	—
1844Mo MF	30.00	40.00	60.00	125	—
1845Mo MF	30.00	40.00	60.00	125	—
1846/5Mo MF	30.00	40.00	60.00	125	—
1846Mo MF	30.00	40.00	60.00	125	—
1848Mo GC	30.00	40.00	60.00	125	—
1850Mo GC	30.00	40.00	60.00	125	—
1851Mo GC	30.00	40.00	60.00	125	—
1852Mo GC	30.00	40.00	60.00	125	—
1853Mo GC	30.00	40.00	60.00	125	—
1854Mo GC	30.00	40.00	60.00	125	—
1855Mo GF	30.00	40.00	60.00	125	—
1856/4Mo GF	30.00	40.00	60.00	125	—
1857Mo GF	30.00	40.00	60.00	125	—
1858/7Mo FH/GF	35.00	50.00	75.00	150	—
1858Mo FH	30.00	40.00	60.00	125	—

Date	VG	F	VF	XF	Unc
1859Mo FH	30.00	40.00	60.00	125	—
1860/59Mo FH	30.00	40.00	60.00	125	—
1861Mo CH/FH	30.00	40.00	80.00	150	—
1862Mo CH	30.00	40.00	60.00	125	—
1863/57Mo CH/GF	30.00	40.00	60.00	125	—
1868/58Mo PH	30.00	40.00	80.00	150	—
1869/59Mo CH	30.00	40.00	80.00	150	—

Mint: Zacatecas
KM# 378.6   1/2 ESCUDO
1.6900 g., 0.8750 Gold .0475 oz. AGW   **Obv:** Facing eagle

Date	VG	F	VF	XF	Unc
1860Zs VL	35.00	50.00	75.00	150	—
1862/1Zs VL	35.00	50.00	75.00	150	—
1862Zs VL	30.00	40.00	65.00	125	—

Mint: Culiacan
KM# 379   ESCUDO
3.3800 g., 0.8750 Gold .0950 oz. AGW   **Obv:** Facing eagle

Date	VG	F	VF	XF	Unc
1846C CE	75.00	100	200	350	—
1847C CE	50.00	75.00	125	175	—
1848C CE	50.00	75.00	125	175	—
1849/8C CE	60.00	100	150	225	—
1850C CE	50.00	75.00	125	175	—
1851C CE	60.00	100	150	225	—
1853/1C CE	60.00	100	150	225	—
1854C CE	50.00	75.00	125	175	—
1856/5/4C CE	60.00	100	150	225	—
1856C CE	50.00	75.00	125	175	—
1857/1C CE	60.00	100	150	225	—
1857C CE	50.00	75.00	125	175	—
1861C PV	50.00	75.00	125	175	—
1862C CE	50.00	75.00	125	175	—
1863C CE	50.00	75.00	125	175	—
1866C CE	50.00	75.00	125	175	—
1870C CE	50.00	75.00	125	175	—

Mint: Durango
KM# 379.1   ESCUDO
3.3800 g., 0.8750 Gold .0950 oz. AGW   **Obv:** Facing eagle

Date	VG	F	VF	XF	Unc
1832Do R.L.	—	—	—	—	—
1833/2Do RM/R.L.	75.00	125	200	300	—
1834Do RM	60.00	100	150	200	—
1835Do RM	—	—	—	—	—
1836Do RM/RL	60.00	100	150	200	—
1838Do RM	60.00	100	150	200	—
1846/38Do RM	75.00	125	200	300	—
1850Do JMR	75.00	125	175	225	—
1851/31Do JMR	75.00	125	200	300	—
1851Do JMR	75.00	125	175	225	—
1853Do CP	75.00	125	175	225	—
1854/34Do CP	75.00	125	175	225	—
1854/44Do CP/RP	75.00	125	175	225	—
1855Do CP	75.00	125	175	225	—
1859Do CP	75.00	125	175	225	—
1861Do CP	75.00	125	175	225	—
1864Do LT/CP Rare	—	—	—	—	—

Mint: Guadalajara
KM# 379.2 ESCUDO
3.3800 g., 0.8750 Gold .0950 oz. AGW **Obv:** Facing eagle

Date	VG	F	VF	XF	Unc
1825Ga FS	60.00	90.00	125	200	—
1826Ga FS	60.00	90.00	125	200	—
1829Ga FS	—	—	—	—	—
1831Ga FS	60.00	90.00	125	200	—
1834Ga FS	60.00	90.00	125	200	—
1835Ga JG	60.00	90.00	125	200	—
1842Ga JG/MC	60.00	90.00	125	200	—
1843Ga MC	60.00	90.00	125	200	—
1847Ga JG	60.00	90.00	125	200	—
1848/7Ga JG	60.00	90.00	125	200	—
1849Ga JG	60.00	90.00	125	200	—
1850/40Ga JG	65.00	125	225	325	—
1850Ga JG	60.00	90.00	125	200	—
1852/1Ga JG	60.00	90.00	125	200	—
1856Ga JG	60.00	90.00	125	200	—
1857Ga JG	60.00	90.00	125	200	—
1859/7Ga JG	60.00	90.00	125	200	—
1860/59Ga JG	65.00	100	175	275	—
1860Ga	60.00	90.00	125	200	—

Mint: Guadalupe y Calvo
KM# 379.3 ESCUDO
3.3800 g., 0.8750 Gold .0950 oz. AGW **Obv:** Facing eagle

Date	VG	F	VF	XF	Unc
1844GC MP	75.00	100	175	250	—
1845GC MP	75.00	100	175	250	—
1846GC MP	75.00	100	175	250	—
1847GC MP	75.00	100	175	250	—
1848GC MP	75.00	100	175	250	—
1849GC MP	75.00	100	175	250	—
1850GC MP	75.00	100	175	250	—
1851GC MP Revised eagle	75.00	100	175	250	—

Mint: Guanajuato
KM# 379.4 ESCUDO
3.3800 g., 0.8750 Gold .0950 oz. AGW **Obv:** Facing eagle

Date	VG	F	VF	XF	Unc
1845Go PM	60.00	75.00	125	200	—
1849Go PF	60.00	75.00	125	200	—
1851Go PF	60.00	75.00	125	200	—
1853Go PF	60.00	75.00	125	200	—
1860Go PF	75.00	125	200	300	—
1862Go PE	60.00	75.00	125	200	—

Mint: Mexico City
KM# 379.5 ESCUDO
3.3800 g., 0.8750 Gold .0950 oz. AGW **Obv:** Facing eagle

Date	VG	F	VF	XF	Unc
1825Mo JM	50.00	70.00	100	150	—
1827/6Mo JM	50.00	70.00	100	150	—
1827Mo JM	50.00	70.00	100	150	—
1830/29Mo JM	50.00	70.00	100	150	—
1831Mo JM	50.00	70.00	100	150	—
1832Mo JM	50.00	70.00	125	175	—
1833Mo MJ	50.00	70.00	100	150	—
1834Mo ML	50.00	70.00	125	175	—
1841Mo ML	50.00	70.00	125	175	—
1843Mo MM	50.00	70.00	100	150	—
1845Mo MF	50.00	70.00	100	150	—
1846/5Mo MF	50.00	70.00	100	150	—
1848Mo GC	50.00	70.00	125	175	—
1850Mo GC	50.00	70.00	125	175	—
1856/4Mo GF	50.00	70.00	100	150	—
1856/5Mo GF	50.00	70.00	100	150	—
1856Mo GF	50.00	70.00	100	150	—
1858Mo FH	50.00	70.00	125	175	—
1859Mo FH	50.00	70.00	100	150	—
1860Mo TH	50.00	70.00	125	175	—
1861Mo CH	50.00	70.00	100	150	—
1862Mo CH	50.00	70.00	125	175	—
1863Mo TH	50.00	70.00	100	150	—
1869Mo CH	50.00	70.00	100	150	—

Mint: Zacatecas
KM# 379.6 ESCUDO
3.3800 g., 0.8750 Gold .0950 oz. AGW **Obv:** Facing eagle
Note: Struck at Zacatecas Mint, mint mark Zs.

Date	VG	F	VF	XF	Unc
1853Zs OM	100	125	200	300	—
1860/59Zs VL V is inverted A	75.00	100	200	350	—
1860Zs VL	75.00	100	150	200	—
1862Zs VL	75.00	100	150	200	—

Mint: Culiacan
KM# 380 2 ESCUDOS
6.7700 g., 0.8750 Gold .1904 oz. AGW **Obv:** Facing eagle

Date	VG	F	VF	XF	Unc
1846C CE	100	150	225	325	—
1847C CE	100	150	225	325	—
1848C CE	100	150	225	325	—
1852C CE	100	150	225	325	—
1854C CE	100	175	250	375	—
1856/4C CE	100	175	250	375	—
1857C CE	100	150	225	325	—

Mint: Durango
KM# 380.1 2 ESCUDOS
6.7700 g., 0.8750 Gold .1904 oz. AGW **Obv:** Facing eagle

Date	VG	F	VF	XF	Unc
1833Do RM	300	450	700	1,200	—
1837/4Do RM	—	—	—	—	—
1837Do RM	—	—	—	—	—
1844Do RM	275	400	600	1,000	—

Mint: Estado de Mexico
KM# 380.2 2 ESCUDOS
6.7700 g., 0.8750 Gold .1904 oz. AGW **Obv:** Facing eagle

Date	VG	F	VF	XF	Unc
1828EoMo LF	700	1,000	1,750	2,500	—

Mint: Guadalajara
KM# 380.3 2 ESCUDOS
6.7700 g., 0.8750 Gold .1904 oz. AGW **Obv:** Facing eagle

Date	VG	F	VF	XF	Unc
1835Ga FS	100	150	225	325	—
1836/5Ga JG	125	200	400	500	—
1839/5Ga JG	—	—	—	—	—
1839Ga JG	100	150	200	285	—
1840Ga MC	100	150	200	285	—
1841Ga MC	100	150	250	400	—
1847/6Ga JG	100	150	225	300	—
1848/7Ga JG	100	150	225	300	—
1850/40Ga JG	100	150	200	285	—
1851Ga JG	100	150	200	285	—
1852Ga JG	100	150	225	325	—
1853Ga JG	100	150	200	285	—
1854/2Ga JG	—	—	—	—	—
1858Ga JG	100	150	200	285	—
1859/8Ga JG	100	150	225	300	—
1859Ga JG	100	150	200	285	—
1860/50Ga JG	100	150	225	300	—
1860Ga JG	100	150	225	300	—
1861/59Ga JG	100	150	200	285	—
1861/0Ga JG	100	150	200	285	—
1863/1Ga JG	100	150	200	285	—
1870Ga IC	100	150	200	285	—

Mint: Guadalupe y Calvo
KM# 380.4 2 ESCUDOS
6.7700 g., 0.8750 Gold .1904 oz. AGW **Obv:** Facing eagle

Date	VG	F	VF	XF	Unc
1844GC MP	150	200	275	400	—
1845GC MP	750	1,250	2,000	3,000	—
1846GC MP	750	1,250	2,000	3,000	—
1847GC MP	125	175	350	500	—
1848GC MP	150	200	350	450	—
1849GC MP	150	200	300	400	—
1850GC MP	150	200	300	400	—

Mint: Guanajuato
KM# 380.5   2 ESCUDOS
6.7700 g., 0.8750 Gold .1904 oz. AGW   **Obv:** Facing eagle

Date	VG	F	VF	XF	Unc
1845Go PM	100	150	250	400	—
1849Go PF	100	150	250	400	—
1853Go PF	100	150	250	400	—
1856Go PF	100	150	250	400	—
1859Go PF	100	150	250	400	—
1860/59Go PF	100	150	250	400	—
1860Go PF	100	150	250	400	—
1862Go YE	100	150	250	400	—

Mint: Hermosillo
KM# 380.6   2 ESCUDOS
6.7700 g., 0.8750 Gold .1904 oz. AGW   **Obv:** Facing eagle

Date	VG	F	VF	XF	Unc
1861Ho FM	500	1,000	1,500	2,000	—

Mint: Mexico City
KM# 380.7   2 ESCUDOS
6.7700 g., 0.8750 Gold .1904 oz. AGW   **Obv:** Facing eagle

Date	VG	F	VF	XF	Unc
1825Mo JM	100	150	200	285	—
1827/6Mo JM	100	150	200	285	—
1827Mo JM	100	150	200	285	—
1830/29Mo JM	100	150	200	285	—
1831Mo JM	100	150	200	285	—
1833Mo ML	100	150	200	285	—
1841Mo ML	100	150	200	285	—
1844Mo MF	100	150	200	285	—
1845Mo MF	100	150	200	285	—
1846Mo MF	125	200	400	600	—
1848Mo GC	100	150	200	285	—
1850Mo GC	100	150	200	285	—
1856/5Mo GF	100	150	200	285	—
1856Mo GF	100	150	200	285	—
1858Mo FH	100	150	200	285	—
1859Mo FH	100	150	200	285	—
1861Mo TH	100	150	200	285	—
1861Mo CH	100	150	200	300	—
1862Mo CH	100	150	200	300	—
1863Mo TH	100	150	200	300	—
1868Mo PH	100	150	200	300	—
1869Mo CH	100	150	200	300	—

Mint: Zacatecas
KM# 380.8   2 ESCUDOS
6.7700 g., 0.8750 Gold .1904 oz. AGW   **Obv:** Facing eagle

Date	VG	F	VF	XF	Unc
1860Zs VL	150	300	600	1,200	—
1862Zs VL	250	500	800	1,200	—
1864Zs MO	150	300	600	1,200	—

Mint: Culiacan
KM# 381   4 ESCUDOS
13.5400 g., 0.8750 Gold .3809 oz. AGW   **Obv:** Facing eagle

Date	VG	F	VF	XF	Unc
1846C CE	1,200	1,700	—	—	—
1847C CE	400	650	850	1,350	—
1848C CE	600	900	1,250	1,850	—

Mint: Durango
KM# 381.1   4 ESCUDOS
13.5400 g., 0.8750 Gold .3809 oz. AGW   **Obv:** Facing eagle

Date	VG	F	VF	XF	Unc
1832Do RM/LR Rare	—	—	—	—	—
1832Do RM	600	900	1,250	1,850	—
1833Do RM/RL Rare	—	—	—	—	—
1852Do JMR Rare	—	—	—	—	—

Mint: Guadalajara
KM# 381.2   4 ESCUDOS
13.5400 g., 0.8750 Gold .3809 oz. AGW   **Obv:** Facing eagle

Date	VG	F	VF	XF	Unc
1844Ga MC	500	750	1,000	1,600	—
1844Ga JG	400	650	850	1,350	—

Mint: Guadalupe y Calvo
KM# 381.3   4 ESCUDOS
13.5400 g., 0.8750 Gold .3809 oz. AGW   **Obv:** Facing eagle

Date	VG	F	VF	XF	Unc
1844GC MP	400	650	850	1,350	—
1845GC MP	350	500	700	1,000	—
1846GC MP	400	650	850	1,350	—
1848GC MP	400	650	850	1,350	—
1850GC MP	500	750	1,000	1,600	—

Mint: Guanajuato
KM# 381.4   4 ESCUDOS
13.5400 g., 0.8750 Gold .3809 oz. AGW   **Obv:** Facing eagle

Date	VG	F	VF	XF	Unc
1829/8Go MJ	200	300	450	850	—
1829Go JM	200	300	450	850	—
1829Go MJ	200	300	450	850	—
1831Go MJ	200	300	450	850	—
1832Go MJ	200	300	450	850	—
1833Go MJ	200	300	500	900	—
1834Go PJ	250	450	650	1,000	—
1835Go PJ	250	450	650	1,000	—
1836Go PJ	200	300	500	900	—
1837Go PJ	200	300	500	900	—
1838Go PJ	200	300	500	900	—
1839Go PJ	250	450	650	1,000	—
1840Go PJ	200	300	500	900	—
1841Go PJ	250	450	650	1,000	—
1845Go PM	200	300	500	900	—
1847/5Go YE	250	450	650	1,000	—
1847Go PM	250	450	650	1,000	—
1849Go PF	250	450	650	1,000	—
1851Go PF	250	450	650	1,000	—
1852Go PF	200	300	500	900	—
1855Go PF	200	300	500	900	—
1857/5Go PF	200	300	500	900	—
1858/7Go PF	200	300	500	900	—
1858Go PF	200	300	500	900	—
1859/7Go PF	250	450	650	1,000	—
1860Go PF	275	475	750	1,200	—
1862Go YE	200	300	500	900	—
1863Go YF	200	300	500	900	—

Mint: Hermosillo
KM# 381.5   4 ESCUDOS
13.5400 g., 0.8750 Gold .3809 oz. AGW   **Obv:** Facing eagle

Date	VG	F	VF	XF	Unc
1861Ho FM	1,000	1,500	2,500	3,750	—

Mint: Mexico City
KM# 381.6   4 ESCUDOS
13.5400 g., 0.8750 Gold .3809 oz. AGW   **Obv:** Facing eagle

Date	VG	F	VF	XF	Unc
1825Mo JM	200	300	525	950	—
1827/6Mo JM	200	300	500	900	—
1829Mo JM	200	350	650	1,000	—
1831Mo JM	200	350	650	1,000	—

Date	VG	F	VF	XF	Unc
1832Mo JM	275	475	750	1,200	—
1844Mo MF	200	350	650	1,000	—
1850Mo GC	200	350	650	1,000	—
1856Mo GF	200	300	500	900	—
1857/6Mo GF	200	300	500	900	—
1857Mo GF	200	300	500	900	—
1858Mo FH	200	350	650	1,000	—
1859/8Mo FH	200	350	650	1,000	—
1861Mo CH	400	800	1,200	1,750	—
1863Mo CH	200	350	650	1,000	—
1868Mo PH	200	300	500	900	—
1869Mo CH	200	300	500	900	—

Mint: Oaxaca
KM# 381.7   4 ESCUDOS
13.5400 g., 0.8750 Gold .3809 oz. AGW **Obv:** Facing eagle
Note: Mint mark O, Oa.

Date	VG	F	VF	XF	Unc
1861 FR	1,500	2,500	4,000	6,500	—

Mint: Zacatecas
KM# 381.8   4 ESCUDOS
13.5400 g., 0.8750 Gold .3809 oz. AGW **Obv:** Facing eagle

Date	VG	F	VF	XF	Unc
1860Zs VL Rare	—	—	—	—	—
1862Zs VL	750	1,250	2,250	3,750	—

Mint: Alamos
KM# 383   8 ESCUDOS
27.0700 g., 0.8750 Gold .7616 oz. AGW **Obv:** Facing eagle

Date	F	VF	XF	Unc
1864A PG	650	1,250	2,250	—
1866A DL	—	—	7,500	—
1868/7A DL	1,500	2,250	3,250	—
1869A DL	650	1,250	2,250	—
1870A DL	1,500	2,250	3,250	—
1872A AM Rare	—	—	—	—

Mint: Chihuahua
KM# 383.1   8 ESCUDOS
27.0700 g., 0.8750 Gold .7616 oz. AGW **Obv:** Facing eagle

Date	F	VF	XF	Unc
1841 Ca RG	400	750	1,250	1,750
1842 Ca RG	350	500	1,000	1,500
1843 Ca RG	350	500	1,000	1,500
1844 Ca RG	350	500	1,000	1,500
1845 Ca RG	350	500	1,000	1,500
1846 Ca RG	500	1,250	1,500	2,000
1847 Ca RG	1,000	2,500	—	—
1848 Ca RG	350	500	1,000	1,500
1849 Ca RG	350	500	1,000	1,500
1850/40 Ca RG	350	500	1,000	1,500
1851/41 Ca RG	50.00	500	1,000	1,500
1852/42 Ca RG	350	500	1,000	1,500
1853/43 Ca RG	350	500	1,000	1,500
1854/44 Ca RG	350	500	1,000	1,500
1855/43 Ca RG	350	500	1,000	1,500
1856/46 Ca RG	400	650	1,250	1,750
1857 Ca JC/RG	325	475	750	1,250
1858 Ca JC	325	475	750	1,250
1858 Ca BA/RG	325	475	750	1,250
1859 Ca JC/RG	325	475	750	1,250
1860 Ca JC/RG	350	500	1,000	1,500
1861 Ca JC	350	475	750	1,250
1862 Ca JC	350	475	750	1,250
1863 Ca JC	500	1,000	1,750	2,250
1864 Ca JC	400	750	1,250	1,750
1865 Ca JC	750	1,500	2,500	3,500
1866 Ca JC	350	500	1,000	1,500
1866 Ca FP	600	1,250	2,000	2,500
1866 Ca JG	350	500	1,000	1,500
1867 Ca JG	350	475	750	1,250
1868 Ca JG Concave wings	350	475	750	1,250
1869 Ca MM Regular eagle	350	475	750	1,250
1870/60 Ca MM	350	475	750	1,250
1871/61 Ca MM	350	475	750	1,250

Mint: Culiacan
KM# 383.2   8 ESCUDOS
27.0700 g., 0.8750 Gold .7616 oz. AGW **Obv:** Facing eagle

Date	F	VF	XF	Unc
1846C CE	350	500	1,000	1,750
1847C CE	350	500	800	1,250
1848C CE	350	500	1,000	1,750
1849C CE	325	450	700	1,250
1850C CE	325	450	700	1,250
1851C CE	350	500	800	1,250
1852C CE	350	500	800	1,250
1853/1C CE	325	450	700	1,250
1854C CE	325	450	700	1,250
1855/4C CE	350	500	1,000	1,750
1855C CE	350	500	800	1,250
1856C CE	325	450	700	1,250
1857C CE	325	450	700	1,250
1857C CE	—	—	—	—
Note: Without periods after C's				
1858C CE	325	450	700	1,250
1859C CE	325	450	700	1,250
1860/58C CE	350	500	800	1,250
1860C CE	350	500	800	1,250
1860C PV	325	450	700	1,250

Date	F	VF	XF	Unc
1861C PV	350	500	800	1,250
1861C CE	350	500	800	1,250
1862C CE	350	500	800	1,250
1863C CE	350	500	800	1,250
1864C CE	325	450	700	1,250
1865C CE	350	500	800	1,250
1866/5C CE	325	450	700	1,250
1866C CE	325	450	700	1,250
1867C CB Error	325	450	700	1,250
1867C CE/CB	325	450	700	1,250
1868C CB Error	350	500	800	1,250
1869C CE	350	500	800	1,250
1870C CE	350	500	800	1,250

Mint: Durango
KM# 383.3 8 ESCUDOS
27.0700 g., 0.8750 Gold .7616 oz. AGW **Obv:** Facing eagle

Date	F	VF	XF	Unc
1832Do RM	850	1,750	2,000	3,000
1833Do RM/RL	350	500	800	1,250
1834Do RM	350	500	800	1,250
1835Do RM	350	500	800	1,250
1836Do RM/RL	350	500	800	1,250
1836Do RM	350	500	800	1,250
Note: M on snake				
1837Do RM	350	500	800	1,250
1838/6Do RM	350	500	800	1,250
1838Do RM	350	500	800	1,250
1839Do RM	325	450	700	1,250
1840/30Do RM/RL	400	600	1,000	1,750
1841/30Do RM	550	750	1,250	2,000
1841/31Do RM	350	500	800	1,250
1841/34Do RM	350	500	800	1,250
1841Do RM/RL	350	500	800	1,250
1842/32Do RM	350	500	800	1,250
1843/33Do RM	550	750	1,250	2,000
1843/1Do RM	350	500	800	1,250
1843Do RM	350	500	800	1,250
1844/34Do RM/RL	500	1,000	1,500	2,500
1844Do RM	450	800	1,250	2,000
1845/36Do RM	400	600	1,000	1,750
1845Do RM	400	600	1,000	1,750
1846Do RM	350	500	800	1,250
1847/37Do RM	350	500	800	1,250
1848/37Do RM	—	—	—	—
1848/38Do CM	350	500	800	1,250
1849/39Do CM	350	500	800	1,250
1849Do J.M.R. Rare	—	—	—	—
1850Do JMR.	400	750	1,250	2,000
1851Do JMR	400	750	1,250	2,000
1852/1Do JMR	450	800	1,250	2,000
1852Do CP	450	800	1,250	2,000
1853Do CP	450	800	1,250	2,000
1854Do CP	400	600	1,000	1,750
1855/4Do CP	350	500	800	1,250
1855Do CP	350	500	800	1,250
1856Do CP	400	600	1,000	1,750

Date	F	VF	XF	Unc
1857Do CP	350	500	800	1,250
Note: French style eagle, 1832-57				
1857Do CP	350	500	800	1,250
Note: Mexican style eagle				
1858Do CP	350	500	800	1,250
1859Do CP	350	500	800	1,250
1860/59Do CP	450	700	1,250	2,200
1861/0Do CP	400	600	1,000	1,750
1862/52Do CP	350	500	800	1,250
1862/1Do CP	350	500	800	1,250
1862Do CP	350	500	800	1,250
1863/53Do CP	350	500	800	1,250
1864Do LT	350	500	800	1,250
1865/4Do LT	500	1,000	1,650	2,750
1866/4Do CM	1,250	2,000	2,500	—
1866Do CM	400	600	1,000	1,750
1867/56Do CP	400	600	1,000	1,750
1867/4Do CP	350	500	800	1,250
1868/4Do CP/LT	—	—	—	—
1869Do CP	500	1,250	1,750	2,750
1870Do CP	400	600	1,000	1,750

Mint: Estado de Mexico
KM# 383.4 8 ESCUDOS
27.0700 g., 0.8750 Gold .7616 oz. AGW **Obv:** Facing eagle

Date	F	VF	XF	Unc
1828EoMo LF	3,500	5,500	8,500	—
1829EoMo LF	3,500	5,500	8,500	—

Mint: Guadalajara
KM# 383.5 8 ESCUDOS
27.0700 g., 0.8750 Gold .7616 oz. AGW **Obv:** Facing eagle

Date	F	VF	XF	Unc
1825Ga FS	500	1,000	1,250	1,750
1826Ga FS	500	1,000	1,250	1,750
1830Ga FS	500	1,000	1,250	1,750
1836Ga FS	750	1,500	2,000	3,000
1836Ga JG	1,000	2,500	3,500	—
1837Ga JG	1,000	2,500	3,500	—
1840Ga MC	750	1,500	2,000	3,000
1841/31Ga MC	1,000	2,500	—	—
1841Ga MC	850	1,650	2,250	—
1842Ga JG	—	—	—	—
1843Ga MC	—	—	—	—
1845Ga MC	400	850	1,100	1,650
1847Ga JG	2,250	—	—	—
1849Ga JG	500	1,000	1,250	1,750
1850Ga JG	400	850	1,100	1,650
1851Ga JG	400	850	1,100	1,650
1852/1Ga JG	500	1,000	1,250	1,750
1855Ga JG	1,000	2,500	3,500	—
1856Ga JG	400	850	1,100	1,650
1857Ga JG	400	850	1,100	1,650
1861/0Ga JG	500	1,000	1,250	1,750
1861Ga JG	400	700	1,200	1,750
1863/1Ga JG	500	1,000	1,250	1,750
1866Ga JG	400	850	1,100	1,650

Mint: Guadalupe y Calvo
KM# 383.6   8 ESCUDOS
27.0700 g., 0.8750 Gold .7616 oz. AGW **Obv:** Facing eagle

Date	F	VF	XF	Unc
1844GC MP	550	750	1,250	2,000
1845GC MP	550	750	1,250	2,000
Note: Eagle's tail square				
1845GC MP	550	750	1,250	2,000
Note: Eagle's tail round				
1846GC MP	450	650	1,000	1,750
Note: Eagle's tail square				
1846GC MP	450	650	1,000	1,750
Note: Eagle's tail round				
1847GC MP	450	650	1,000	1,750
1848GC MP	550	750	1,250	2,000
1849GC MP	550	750	1,250	2,000
1850GC MP	450	650	1,000	1,750
1851GC MP	450	650	1,000	1,750
1852GC MP	550	750	1,250	2,000

Mint: Guanajuato
KM# 383.7   8 ESCUDOS
27.0700 g., 0.8750 Gold .7616 oz. AGW **Obv:** Facing eagle

Date	F	VF	XF	Unc
1828Go MJ	700	1,750	2,250	3,000
1829Go MJ	600	1,500	2,000	2,750
1830Go MJ	350	500	750	1,000
1831Go MJ	600	1,500	2,000	2,750
1832Go MJ	500	1,250	1,750	2,500
1833Go MJ	350	500	700	1,000
1834Go PJ	350	500	700	1,000
1835Go PJ	350	500	700	1,000
1836Go PJ	400	650	900	1,250
1837Go PJ	400	650	900	1,250
1838/7Go PJ	350	500	700	1,000
1838Go PJ	350	500	800	1,200
1839/8Go PJ	350	500	700	1,000
1839Go PJ	350	500	800	1,200
Note: Regular eagle				

Date	F	VF	XF	Unc
1840Go PJ	350	500	700	1,000
Note: Concave wings				
1841Go PJ	350	500	700	1,000
1842Go PJ	325	400	500	900
1842Go PM	350	500	700	1,000
1843Go PM	350	500	700	1,000
Note: Small eagle				
1844/3Go PM	400	650	900	1,250
1844Go PM	350	500	700	1,000
1845Go PM	350	500	700	1,000
1846/5Go PM	350	500	800	1,200
1846Go PM	350	500	700	1,000
1847Go PM	400	650	900	1,250
1848/7Go PM	350	500	700	1,000
1848Go PM	350	500	700	1,000
1848Go PF	350	500	700	1,000
1849Go PF	325	400	500	900
1850Go PF	325	400	500	900
1851Go PF	375	500	700	1,000
1852Go PF	375	500	700	1,000
1853Go PF	325	400	500	900
1854Go PF	350	500	700	1,000
Note: Eagle of 1853				
1854Go PF	350	500	700	1,000
Note: Eagle of 1855				
1855/4Go PF	400	650	900	1,250
1855Go PF	350	500	700	1,000
1856Go PF	350	500	700	1,000
1857Go PF	350	500	700	1,000
1858Go PF	350	500	700	1,000
1859Go PF	325	400	500	800
1860/50Go PF	325	400	500	900
1860/59Go PF	400	650	900	1,250
1860Go PF	375	500	700	1,100
1861/0Go PF	325	400	500	800
1861Go PF	325	400	500	800
1862/1Go YE	350	500	700	1,000
1862Go YE	350	500	700	1,000
1862Go YF	—	—	—	—
1863/53Go YF	350	500	700	1,000
1863Go PF	350	500	700	1,000
1867/57Go YF/PF	350	500	700	1,000
1867Go YF	350	500	700	1,000
1868/58Go YF	350	500	700	1,000
1870Go FR	325	400	500	900

Mint: Hermosillo
KM# 383.8   8 ESCUDOS
27.0700 g., 0.8750 Gold .7616 oz. AGW **Obv:** Facing eagle

Date	F	VF	XF	Unc
1863Ho FM	400	650	1,000	2,000
1864Ho FM	600	1,250	1,750	2,750
1864Ho PR/FM	400	650	1,000	2,000
1865Ho FM/PR	500	800	1,250	2,500
1867/57Ho PR	400	650	1,000	2,000
1868Ho PR	500	800	1,250	2,500
1868Ho PR/FM	500	800	1,250	2,500
1869Ho PR/FM	400	650	1,000	2,000
1869Ho PR	400	650	1,000	2,000
1870Ho PR	400	650	1,000	2,000
1871/0Ho PR	500	800	1,250	2,500
1871Ho PR	500	800	1,250	2,500
1872/1Ho PR	600	1,250	1,750	2,750
1873Ho PR	400	650	1,000	2,000

Date	F	VF	XF	Unc
1868Mo CH	325	400	500	900
1868Mo PH	325	400	500	900
1869Mo CH	325	400	500	900

Mint: Oaxaca
KM# 383.10 8 ESCUDOS
27.0700 g., 0.8750 Gold .7616 oz. AGW **Obv:** Facing eagle

Date	F	VF	XF	Unc
1858O AE	2,000	3,000	4,000	6,000
1859O AE	1,000	2,500	3,750	5,500
1860O AE	1,000	2,500	3,750	5,500
1861O FR	450	850	1,250	2,750
1862O FR	450	850	1,250	2,750
1863O FR	450	850	1,250	2,750
1864O FR	450	850	1,250	2,750
1867O AE	450	850	1,250	2,750
1868O AE	450	850	1,250	2,750
1869O AE	450	850	1,250	2,750

Mint: Mexico City
KM# 383.9 8 ESCUDOS
27.0700 g., 0.8750 Gold .7616 oz. AGW **Obv:** Facing eagle
Note: Formerly reported 1825/3 JM is merely a reworked 5.

Date	F	VF	XF	Unc
1824Mo JM	500	1,000	1,250	2,000
Note: Large book reverse				
1825Mo JM	325	400	500	1,000
Note: Small book reverse				
1826/5Mo JM	700	1,750	2,250	3,000
1827Mo JM	350	500	700	1,000
1828Mo JM	350	500	700	1,000
1829Mo JM	350	500	700	1,000
1830Mo JM	350	500	700	1,000
1831Mo JM	350	500	700	1,000
1832/1Mo JM	350	500	700	1,000
1832Mo JM	350	500	700	1,000
1833Mo MJ	400	750	1,000	1,500
1833Mo ML	325	400	500	900
1834Mo ML	400	750	1,000	1,500
1835/4Mo ML	500	1,000	1,250	2,000
1836Mo ML	325	400	500	900
1836Mo MF	500	700	1,200	2,000
1837/6Mo ML	325	400	500	900
1838Mo ML	325	400	500	900
1839Mo ML	325	400	500	900
1840Mo ML	325	400	500	900
1841Mo ML	325	400	500	900
1842/1Mo ML	—	—	—	—
1842Mo ML	325	400	500	900
1842Mo MM	—	—	—	—
1843Mo MM	325	400	500	900
1844Mo MF	325	400	500	900
1845Mo MF	325	400	500	900
1846Mo MF	500	1,000	1,250	2,000
1847Mo MF	950	2,250	—	—
1847Mo RC	325	500	800	1,250
1848Mo GC	325	400	500	900
1849Mo GC	325	400	500	900
1850Mo GC	325	400	500	900
1851Mo GC	325	400	500	900
1852Mo GC	325	400	500	900
1853Mo GC	325	400	500	900
1854/44Mo GC	325	400	500	900
1854/3Mo GC	325	400	500	900
1855Mo GF	325	400	500	900
1856/5Mo GF	325	400	500	900
1856Mo GF	325	400	500	900
1857Mo GF	325	400	500	900
1858Mo FH	325	400	500	900
1859Mo FH	400	750	1,000	1,500
1860Mo FH	325	400	500	900
1860Mo TH	325	400	500	900
1861/51Mo CH	325	400	500	900
1862Mo CH	325	400	500	900
1863/53Mo CH	325	400	500	900
1863/53Mo TH	325	400	500	900
1867Mo CH	325	400	500	900

Mint: Zacatecas
KM# 383.11 8 ESCUDOS
27.0700 g., 0.8750 Gold .7616 oz. AGW **Obv:** Facing eagle

Date	F	VF	XF	Unc
1858Zs MO	400	750	1,000	2,000
1859Zs MO	325	400	500	900
1860/59Zs VL/MO	2,000	3,000	4,000	
1860/9Zs MO	400	750	1,000	2,000
1860Zs MO	375	500	700	1,000
1861/0Zs VL	375	500	700	1,000
1861Zs VL	375	500	700	1,000
1862Zs VL	375	500	700	1,100
1863Zs VL	375	525	750	1,150
1863Zs MO	375	500	700	1,000
1864Zs MO	750	1,000	1,500	3,000
1865Zs MO	375	500	700	1,000
1865Zs MP	—	—	—	—
Note: Contemporary counterfeit				
1868Zs JS	400	600	800	1,250
1868Zs YH	400	600	800	1,250
1869Zs YH	400	600	800	1,250
1870Zs YH	400	600	800	1,250
1871Zs YH	400	600	800	1,250

EMPIRE OF MAXIMILIAN

RULER
Maximilian, Emperor, 1864-1867
MINT MARKS
Refer To Republic Coinage
MONETARY SYSTEM
100 Centavos = 1 Peso (8 Reales)

MILLED COINAGE

16 Pilones = 1 Real; 8 Tlaco = 1 Real;
16 Reales = 1 Escudo

Mint: Mexico City
KM# 384   CENTAVO
Copper

Date	F	VF	XF	Unc
1864M	40.00	75.00	225	1,100

Mint: Guanajuato
KM# 385   5 CENTAVOS
1.3537 g., 0.9030 Silver .0393 oz. ASW

Date	Mintage	F	VF	XF	Unc
1864G	90,000	17.50	35.00	75.00	320
1865G	—	20.00	30.00	55.00	285
1866G	—	75.00	150	300	1,800

Mint: Mexico City
KM# 385.1   5 CENTAVOS
1.3537 g., 0.9030 Silver .0393 oz. ASW

Date	F	VF	XF	Unc
1864M	12.50	20.00	55.00	285
1866/4M	25.00	40.00	75.00	385
1866M	20.00	35.00	65.00	375

Mint: San Luis Potosi
KM# 385.2   5 CENTAVOS
1.3537 g., 0.9030 Silver .0393 oz. ASW

Date	F	VF	XF	Unc
1864P	150	400	1,500	2,500

Mint: Zacatecas
KM# 385.3   5 CENTAVOS
1.3537 g., 0.9030 Silver .0393 oz. ASW

Date	F	VF	XF	Unc
1865Z	25.00	45.00	150	425

Mint: Guanajuato
KM# 386   10 CENTAVOS
2.7073 g., 0.9030 Silver .0786 oz. ASW

Date	Mintage	F	VF	XF	Unc
1864G	45,000	20.00	45.00	90.00	325
1865G	—	30.00	60.00	110	375

Mint: Mexico City
KM# 386.1   10 CENTAVOS
2.7073 g., 0.9030 Silver .0786 oz. ASW   **Note:** Struck at
Mexico City Mint, mint mark M.

Date	F	VF	XF	Unc
1864M	15.00	25.00	55.00	285
1866/4M	25.00	35.00	70.00	320
1866/5M	25.00	40.00	85.00	375
1866M	25.00	35.00	75.00	375

Mint: San Luis Potosi
KM# 386.2   10 CENTAVOS
2.7073 g., 0.9030 Silver .0786 oz. ASW

Date	F	VF	XF	Unc
1864P	70.00	150	300	600

Mint: Zacatecas
KM# 386.3   10 CENTAVOS
2.7073 g., 0.9030 Silver .0786 oz. ASW

Date	F	VF	XF	Unc
1865Z	25.00	55.00	165	475

Mint: Mexico City
KM# 387   50 CENTAVOS
13.5365 g., 0.9030 Silver .3929 oz. ASW

Date	Mintage	F	VF	XF	Unc
1866Mo	31,000	40.00	95.00	200	600

Mint: Guanajuato
KM# 388   PESO
27.0700 g., 0.9030 Silver .7857 oz. ASW

Date	F	VF	XF	Unc
1866Go	300	400	900	3,500

Mint: Mexico City
KM# 388.1   PESO
27.0700 g., 0.9030 Silver .7857 oz. ASW

Date	Mintage	F	VF	XF	Unc
1866Mo	2,148,000	30.00	45.00	125	375
1867Mo	1,238,000	40.00	65.00	175	425

Mint: San Luis Potosi
KM# 388.2 PESO
27.0700 g., 0.9030 Silver .7857 oz. ASW

Date		F	VF	XF	Unc
1866 Pi		45.00	90.00	275	725

Mint: San Luis Potosi
KM# 390.1 CENTAVO
Copper, 26.5 mm. **Obv:** Seated Liberty **Rev:** Thin wreath

Date	Mintage	F	VF	XF	Unc
1863SLP	1,024,999	15.00	30.00	60.00	400

Mint: Alamos
KM# 391 CENTAVO
Copper **Obv:** Standing eagle **Edge:** Reeded.

Date	Mintage	F	VF	XF	Unc
1875 As Rare	—	—	—	—	—
1876 As	50,000	100	200	300	650
1880 As	—	25.00	50.00	125	400
1881 As	—	30.00	60.00	125	350

Mint: Mexico City
KM# 389 20 PESOS
33.8400 g., 0.8750 Gold .9520 oz. AGW

Date	Mintage	F	VF	XF	Unc
1866Mo	8,274	500	900	1,350	2,500

REPUBLIC
Second

MINT MARKS
A, AS - Alamos
CE - Real de Catorce
CA,CH - Chihuahua
C, Cn, Gn(error) - Culiacan
D, Do - Durango
EoMo - Estado de Mexico
Ga - Guadalajara
GC - Guadalupe y Calvo
G, Go - Guanajuato
H, Ho - Hermosillo
M, Mo - Mexico City
O, OA - Oaxaca
SLP, PI, P, I/P - San Luis Potosi
Z, Zs – Zacatecas

ASSAYERS' INITIALS

CULIACAN MINT

Initials	Years	Mint Officials
JQ, Q	1899-1903	Jesus S. Quiroz
FV, V	1903	Francisco Valdez
MH, H	1904	Merced Hernandez
RP, P	1904-05	Ramon Ponce de Leon

MEXICO CITY MINT

Because of the great number of assayers for this mint (Mexico City is a much larger mint than any of the others) there is much confusion as to which initial stands for which assayer at any one time. Therefore we feel that it would be of no value to list the assayers.

ZACATECAS MINT

Initials	Years	Mint Officials
FZ	1886-1905	Francisco de P. Zarate
FM	1904-05	Francisco Mateos

DECIMAL COINAGE
100 Centavos = 1 Peso

Mint: Mexico City
KM# 390 CENTAVO
Copper, 25 mm. **Obv:** Seated Liberty **Rev:** Thick wreath.

Date	Mintage	F	VF	XF	Unc
1863Mo Round top 3, reeded edge	—	15.00	30.00	75.00	500
1863Mo Round top 3, plain edge	—	15.00	30.00	75.00	500
1863Mo Flat top 3, reeded edge	—	12.00	28.00	70.00	500

Mint: Culiacan
KM# 391.1 CENTAVO
Copper **Obv:** Standing eagle **Edge:** Plain

Date	Mintage	F	VF	XF	Unc
1874Cn	266,000	12.50	17.50	35.00	250
1875/4Cn	153,000	15.00	20.00	45.00	250
1875Cn	Inc. above	10.00	15.00	25.00	250
1876Cn	154,000	5.00	8.00	15.00	200
1877/6Cn	993,000	7.50	11.50	17.50	200
1877Cn	Inc. above	6.00	9.00	15.00	200
1880Cn	142,000	7.50	10.00	12.50	200
1881Cn	167,000	7.50	10.00	25.00	200
1897Cn Large N in mint mark	300,000	2.50	5.00	12.00	50.00
1897Cn Small N in mint mark	Inc. above	2.50	5.00	9.00	45.00

Mint: Durango
KM# 391.2 CENTAVO
Copper **Obv:** Standing eagle

Date	Mintage	F	VF	XF	Unc
1879Do	110,000	10.00	17.50	35.00	150
1880Do	69,000	40.00	90.00	175	500
1891Do	—	8.00	11.00	30.00	150
1891Do/Mo	—	8.00	11.00	30.00	150

Mint: Guadalajara
KM# 391.3 CENTAVO
Copper **Obv:** Standing eagle

Date	Mintage	F	VF	XF	Unc
1872Ga	263,000	15.00	30.00	60.00	200
1873Ga	333,000	6.00	9.00	25.00	150
1874Ga	76,000	15.00	25.00	50.00	175
1875Ga	—	10.00	15.00	30.00	150
1876Ga	303,000	3.00	6.00	17.50	150
1877Ga	108,000	4.00	6.00	20.00	150

Date	Mintage	F	VF	XF	Unc
1878Ga	543,000	4.00	6.00	15.00	150
1881/71Ga	975,000	7.00	9.00	20.00	175
1881Ga	Inc. above	7.00	9.00	20.00	175
1889Ga/Mo	—	3.50	5.00	25.00	125
1890Ga	—	4.00	7.50	20.00	100

Mint: Guanajuato
KM# 391.4 CENTAVO
Copper **Obv:** Standing eagle

Date	Mintage	F	VF	XF	Unc
1874Go	—	20.00	40.00	80.00	250
1875Go	190,000	11.50	20.00	60.00	200
1876Go	—	125	200	350	750
1877Go Rare	—	—	—	—	—
1878Go	576,000	8.00	11.00	30.00	175
1880Go	890,000	6.00	10.00	25.00	175

Mint: Hermosillo
KM# 391.5 CENTAVO
Copper **Obv:** Standing eagle

Date	Mintage	F	VF	XF	Unc
1875Ho	3,500	450	—	—	—
1876Ho	8,508	50.00	100	225	500
1880Ho Short H, round O	102,000	7.50	15.00	35.00	150
1880Ho Tall H, oval O	Inc. above	7.50	15.00	35.00	150
1881Ho	459,000	5.00	10.00	25.00	150

Mint: Mexico City
KM# 391.6 CENTAVO
Copper **Obv:** Standing eagle **Note:** Varieties exist.

Date	Mintage	F	VF	XF	Unc
1869Mo	1,874,000	7.50	25.00	60.00	200
1870/69Mo	1,200,000	10.00	25.00	60.00	225
1870Mo	Inc. above	8.00	20.00	50.00	200
1871Mo	918,000	8.00	15.00	40.00	200
1872/1Mo	1,625,000	6.50	10.00	30.00	200
1872Mo	Inc. above	6.00	9.00	25.00	200
1873Mo	1,605,000	4.00	7.50	20.00	200
1874/3Mo	1,700,000	5.00	7.00	15.00	100
1874Mo	Inc. above	3.00	5.50	15.00	100
1874Mo	Inc. above	5.00	10.00	25.00	200
1875Mo	1,495,000	6.00	8.00	30.00	100
1876Mo	1,600,000	3.00	5.50	12.50	100
1877Mo	1,270,000	3.00	5.50	13.50	100
1878/5Mo	1,900,000	7.50	11.00	22.50	125
1878/6Mo	Inc. above	7.50	11.00	22.50	125
1878/7Mo	Inc. above	7.50	11.00	20.00	125
1878Mo	Inc. above	6.00	9.00	13.50	100
1879/8Mo	1,505,000	4.50	6.50	13.50	100
1879Mo	Inc. above	3.00	5.50	12.50	75.00
1880/70Mo	1,130,000	5.50	7.50	15.00	100
1880/72Mo	Inc. above	20.00	50.00	100	250
1880/79Mo	Inc. above	15.00	35.00	75.00	175
1880Mo	Inc. above	4.25	6.00	12.50	75.00
1881Mo	1,060,000	4.50	7.00	15.00	75.00
1886Mo	12,687,000	1.50	2.00	10.00	40.00
1887Mo	7,292,000	1.50	2.00	10.00	35.00
1888/78Mo	9,984,000	2.50	3.00	10.00	30.00
1888/7Mo	Inc. above	2.50	3.00	10.00	30.00
1888Mo	Inc. above	1.50	2.00	10.00	30.00
1889Mo	19,970,000	2.00	3.00	10.00	30.00
1890/89Mo	18,726,000	2.50	3.00	12.00	40.00
1890/990Mo	Inc. above	2.50	3.00	12.00	40.00
1890Mo	Inc. above	1.50	2.00	10.00	30.00
1891Mo	14,544,000	1.50	2.00	10.00	30.00
1892Mo	12,908,000	1.50	2.00	10.00	30.00
1893/2Mo	5,078,000	2.50	3.00	12.00	35.00
1893Mo	Inc. above	1.50	2.00	10.00	30.00
1894/3Mo	1,896,000	3.00	6.00	15.00	50.00
1894Mo	Inc. above	2.00	3.00	12.00	35.00
1895/3Mo	3,453,000	3.00	4.50	12.50	35.00

Date	Mintage	F	VF	XF	Unc
1895/85Mo	Inc. above	3.00	6.00	15.00	50.00
1895Mo	Inc. above	2.00	3.00	10.00	30.00
1896Mo	3,075,000	2.00	3.00	10.00	30.00
1897Mo	4,150,000	1.50	2.00	10.00	30.00

Mint: Oaxaca
KM# 391.7 CENTAVO
Copper **Obv:** Standing eagle

Date	Mintage	F	VF	XF	Unc
1872 Oa	16,000	300	500	1,200	—
1873 Oa	11,000	350	600	—	—
1874 Oa	4,835	450	—	—	—
1875 Oa	2,860	500	—	—	—

Mint: San Luis Potosi
KM# 391.8 CENTAVO
Copper **Obv:** Standing eagle

Date	Mintage	F	VF	XF	Unc
1871 Pi Rare	—	—	—	—	—
1877 Pi	249,000	15.00	50.00	200	—
1878 Pi	751,000	12.50	25.00	50.00	200
1878 Pp error mintmark - rare	—	—	—	—	—
1891Pi/Mo	—	10.00	50.00	150	300
1891 Pi	—	8.00	25.00	125	250

Mint: Zacatecas
KM# 391.9 CENTAVO
Copper **Obv:** Standing eagle **Note:** Struck at Zacatecas Mint, mint mark Zs.

Date	Mintage	F	VF	XF	Unc
1872Zs	55,000	22.50	30.00	100	300
1873Zs	1,460,000	4.00	8.00	25.00	150
1874/3Zs	685,000	5.50	11.00	30.00	250
1874Zs	Inc. above	4.00	8.00	25.00	200
1875/4Zs	200,000	8.50	17.00	45.00	250
1875Zs	Inc. above	7.00	14.00	35.00	200
1876Zs	—	5.00	10.00	25.00	200
1877Zs	—	50.00	125	300	750
1878Zs	—	4.50	9.00	25.00	200
1880Zs	100,000	5.00	10.00	30.00	200
1881Zs	1,200,000	4.25	8.00	25.00	150

Mint: Mexico City
KM# 392 CENTAVO
Copper-Nickel

Date	Mintage	F	VF	XF	Unc
1882Mo	99,955,000	7.50	12.50	17.50	35.00
1883Mo	Inc. above	0.50	0.75	1.00	1.50

Mint: Mexico City
KM# 393 CENTAVO
Copper **Obv:** Restyled eagle **Note:** Varieties exist.

Date	Mintage	F	VF	XF	Unc
1898Mo	1,529,000	4.00	6.00	15.00	50.00

Mint: Culiacan
KM# 394 CENTAVO
Copper **Note:** Struck at Culiacan Mint, mint mark C, Cn. Reduced size. Varieties exist.

Date	Mintage	F	VF	XF	Unc
1901	220,000	15.00	22.50	35.00	65.00
1902	320,000	15.00	22.50	50.00	90.00
1903	536,000	7.50	12.50	20.00	50.00
1904/3	148,000	35.00	50.00	75.00	125
1905	110,000	100	150	250	550

Mint: Mexico City
KM# 394.1 CENTAVO
Copper **Note:** Mint mark M, Mo. Reduced size. Varieties exist.

Date	Mintage	F	VF	XF	Unc
1899M	51,000	150	175	300	800
1900M Wide date	4,010,000	2.50	4.00	8.00	28.00
1900M Narrow date	Inc. above	2.50	4.00	8.00	28.00
1901	1,494,000	3.00	8.00	17.50	50.00
1902/899	2,090,000	30.00	60.00	100	175
1902	Inc. above	2.25	4.00	10.00	40.00
1903	8,400,000	1.50	3.00	7.00	20.00
1904/3	10,250,000	1.50	10.00	20.00	55.00
1904	Inc. above	1.50	3.00	8.00	25.00
1905	3,643,000	2.25	4.00	10.00	40.00

Mint: Mexico City
KM# 395 2 CENTAVOS
Copper-Nickel

Date	Mintage	F	VF	XF	Unc
1882	50,023,000	2.00	3.00	7.50	15.00
1883/2	Inc. above	2.00	3.00	7.50	15.00
1883	Inc. above	0.50	0.75	1.00	2.50

Mint: Chihuahua
KM# 396 5 CENTAVOS
1.3530 g., 0.9030 Silver .0392 oz. ASW **Obv:** Facing eagle
Rev: Denomination in wreath

Date	Mintage	F	VF	XF	Unc
1868 Ca	—	40.00	65.00	125	450
1869 Ca	30,000	25.00	40.00	100	400
1870/69 Ca	—	35.00	55.00	120	425
1870 Ca	35,000	30.00	50.00	100	400

Mint: San Luis Potosi
KM# 396.1 5 CENTAVOS
1.3530 g., 0.9030 Silver .0392 oz. ASW **Obv:** Facing eagle
Rev: Deonomination in wreath

Date	Mintage	F	VF	XF	Unc
1863SLP	—	37.50	135	350	1,200

Mint: Mexico City
KM# 397 5 CENTAVOS
1.3530 g., 0.9030 Silver .0392 oz. ASW **Obv:** Facing eagle
Rev: Cap and rays **Note:** Varieties exist.

Date	Mintage	F	VF	XF	Unc
1867/3Mo	—	22.50	50.00	125	425
1867Mo	—	18.50	42.50	100	400
1868/7Mo	—	22.50	50.00	150	500
1868Mo	—	18.50	42.50	100	400

Mint: San Luis Potosi
KM# 397.1 5 CENTAVOS
1.3530 g., 0.9030 Silver .0392 oz. ASW **Obv:** Facing eagle
Rev: Cap and rays

Date	Mintage	F	VF	XF	Unc
1868/7P	34,000	25.00	50.00	125	450
1868P	Inc. above	20.00	45.00	100	400
1869P	14,000	200	300	600	—

Mint: Alamos
KM# 398 5 CENTAVOS
1.3530 g., 0.9030 Silver .0392 oz. ASW **Obv:** Standing eagle
Rev: Denomination in wreath

Date	Mintage	F	VF	XF	Unc
1874 As DL	—	10.00	20.00	40.00	150
1875 As DL	—	10.00	20.00	40.00	150
1876 As L	—	22.00	45.00	70.00	160
1878 As L Mule, gold peso reverse	—	250	350	650	—
1879 As L Mule, gold peso obverse	—	40.00	65.00	120	275
1880 As L Mule, gold peso obverse	12,000	55.00	85.00	165	325
1886 As L	43,000	12.00	25.00	50.00	165
1886 As L Mule, gold peso obverse	Inc. above	55.00	85.00	165	300
1887 As L	20,000	25.00	50.00	75.00	165
1888 As L	32,000	12.00	25.00	50.00	125
1889 As L	16,000	25.00	50.00	100	200
1890 As L	30,000	25.00	50.00	85.00	175
1891 As L	8,000	65.00	125	200	400
1892 As L	13,000	20.00	40.00	60.00	125
1893 As L	24,000	10.00	20.00	45.00	90.00
1895 As L	20,000	10.00	20.00	45.00	90.00

Mint: Chihuahua
KM# 398.1 5 CENTAVOS
1.3530 g., 0.9030 Silver .0392 oz. ASW **Obv:** Standing eagle
Rev: Denomination in wreath **Note:** Mint mark: *Ca or Ch*.

Date	Mintage	F	VF	XF	Unc
1871* M	14,000	20.00	40.00	100	250
1873* M Crude date	—	100	150	250	500
1874* M Crude date	—	25.00	50.00	75.00	150
1886* M	25,000	7.50	15.00	30.00	100
1887* M	37,000	7.50	15.00	30.00	100
1887* Ca/MoM	Inc. above	10.00	20.00	40.00	125
1888* M	145,000	1.50	3.00	6.00	25.00
1889* M	44,000	5.00	10.00	20.00	50.00
1890* M	102,000	1.50	3.00	6.00	25.00
1891* M	164,000	1.50	3.00	6.00	25.00
1892* M	85,000	1.50	3.00	6.00	25.00
1892* M 9/inverted 9	Inc. above	2.00	4.00	7.50	30.00
1893* M	133,000	1.50	3.00	6.00	25.00
1894* M	108,000	1.50	3.00	6.00	25.00
1895* M	74,000	2.00	4.00	7.50	30.00

Mint: Culiacan
KM# 398.2 5 CENTAVOS
1.3530 g., 0.9030 Silver .0392 oz. ASW **Obv:** Standing eagle
Rev: Denomination in wreath

Date	Mintage	F	VF	XF	Unc
1871Cn P	—	125	200	350	—
1873Cn P	4,992	50.00	100	200	400
1874Cn P	—	25.00	50.00	100	200
1875Cn P Rare	—	—	—	—	—
1876Cn P	—	25.00	50.00	100	200
1886Cn M	10,000	25.00	50.00	100	200
1887Cn M	10,000	25.00	50.00	100	200
1888Cn M	119,000	1.50	3.00	6.00	30.00
1889Cn M	66,000	4.00	7.50	15.00	50.00

Date	Mintage	F	VF	XF	Unc
1890Cn M	180,000	1.50	3.00	6.00	25.00
1890/9Cn M	—	2.00	4.00	8.00	40.00
1890Cn D Error	Inc. above	125	175	250	—
1891Cn M	87,000	2.00	4.00	7.50	25.00
1894Cn M	24,000	4.00	7.50	15.00	40.00
1896Cn M	16,000	7.50	12.50	25.00	75.00
1897Cn M	223,000	1.50	2.50	5.00	20.00

Mint: Durango
KM# 398.3　5 CENTAVOS
1.3530 g., 0.9030 Silver .0392 oz. ASW **Obv:** Standing eagle
Rev: Denomination in wreath

Date	Mintage	F	VF	XF	Unc
1874Do M	—	100	150	225	500
1877Do P	4,795	75.00	125	225	450
1878/7Do E/P	4,300	200	300	450	—
1879Do B	—	125	200	350	—
1880Do B Rare	—	—	—	—	—
1881Do P	3,020	300	500	800	—
1887Do C	42,000	5.00	8.00	17.50	60.00
1888/9Do C	91,000	6.00	10.00	20.00	70.00
1888Do C	Inc. above	4.00	7.50	15.00	55.00
1889Do C	49,000	3.50	6.00	12.50	50.00
1890Do C	136,000	4.00	7.50	15.00	55.00
1890Do P	Inc. above	5.00	8.00	17.50	60.00
1891/0Do P	48,000	3.50	6.00	12.50	50.00
1891Do P	Inc. above	3.00	5.00	10.00	45.00
1894Do D	38,000	3.50	6.00	12.50	50.00

Mint: Guadalajara
KM# 398.4　5 CENTAVOS
1.3530 g., 0.9030 Silver .0392 oz. ASW **Obv:** Standing eagle
Rev: Denomination in wreath

Date	Mintage	F	VF	XF	Unc
1877Ga A	—	15.00	30.00	60.00	150
1881Ga S	156,000	4.00	7.50	15.00	60.00
1886Ga S	87,000	2.00	4.00	7.50	25.00
1888Ga S Large G	262,000	2.00	4.00	10.00	30.00
1888Ga S Small G	Inc. above	2.00	4.00	10.00	30.00
1889Ga S	178,000	1.50	3.00	7.50	25.00
1890Ga S	68,000	4.00	7.50	12.50	35.00
1891Ga S	50,000	4.00	6.50	10.00	35.00
1892Ga S	78,000	2.00	4.00	7.50	25.00
1893Ga S	44,000	4.00	7.50	15.00	45.00

Mint: Guanajuato
KM# 398.5　5 CENTAVOS
1.3530 g., 0.9030 Silver .0392 oz. ASW **Obv:** Standing eagle
Rev: Denomination in wreath

Date	Mintage	F	VF	XF	Unc
1869Go S	80,000	15.00	30.00	75.00	175
1871Go S	100,000	5.00	10.00	25.00	75.00
1872Go S	30,000	30.00	60.00	125	250
1873Go S	40,000	30.00	60.00	125	250
1874Go S	—	7.00	12.00	25.00	75.00
1875Go S	—	8.00	15.00	30.00	75.00
1876Go S	—	8.00	15.00	30.00	75.00
1877Go S	—	7.00	12.00	20.00	75.00
1878/7Go S	20,000	8.00	15.00	25.00	75.00
1879Go S	—	8.00	15.00	25.00	75.00
1880Go S	55,000	15.00	30.00	60.00	200
1881/0Go S	160,000	5.00	8.00	17.50	60.00
1881Go S	Inc. above	4.00	6.00	12.00	45.00
1886Go R	230,000	1.50	3.00	6.00	30.00
1887Go R/S	—	1.50	3.00	6.00	30.00
1887Go R	230,000	1.50	2.50	5.00	20.00
1888Go R	320,000	1.50	2.50	5.00	20.00
1889Go R	60,000	4.00	6.00	12.00	45.00
1890/5Go R/S	—	1.50	3.00	6.00	30.00
1890Go R	250,000	1.50	2.50	5.00	20.00
1891/0Go R	168,000	1.80	3.00	6.00	30.00
1891Go R	Inc. above	1.50	2.50	5.00	20.00
1892Go R	138,000	1.50	3.00	6.00	25.00
1893Go R	200,000	1.25	2.50	5.00	20.00
1894Go R	200,000	1.25	2.50	5.00	20.00
1896Go R	525,000	1.25	2.00	4.00	15.00

Date	Mintage	F	VF	XF	Unc
1896Go R/S	—	1.50	3.00	6.00	25.00
1897Go R	596,000	1.50	2.00	4.00	15.00
1898Go R	—	—	—	—	—

Mint: Hermosillo
KM# 398.6　5 CENTAVOS
1.3530 g., 0.9030 Silver .0392 oz. ASW **Obv:** Standing eagle
Rev: Denomination in wreath

Date	Mintage	F	VF	XF	Unc
1874/69Ho R	—	125	225	350	—
1874Ho R	—	100	200	325	—
1878/7Ho A Rare	22,000	—	—	—	—
1878Ho A	Inc. above	20.00	40.00	80.00	175
1878Ho A Mule, gold peso obverse	Inc. above	40.00	80.00	150	300
1880Ho A	43,000	7.50	15.00	30.00	75.00
1886Ho G	44,000	5.00	10.00	20.00	75.00
1887Ho G	20,000	5.00	10.00	20.00	75.00
1888Ho G	12,000	7.50	15.00	30.00	85.00
1889Ho G	67,000	3.00	6.00	12.50	40.00
1890Ho G	50,000	3.00	6.00	12.50	40.00
1891Ho G	46,000	3.00	6.00	12.50	40.00
1893Ho G	84,000	2.50	5.00	10.00	30.00
1894Ho G	68,000	2.00	4.00	10.00	30.00

Mint: Mexico City
KM# 398.7　5 CENTAVOS
1.3530 g., 0.9030 Silver .0392 oz. ASW **Obv:** Standing eagle
Rev: Denomination in wreath **Note:** Struck at Mexico City
Mint, mint mark Mo. Varieties exist.

Date	Mintage	F	VF	XF	Unc
1869/8Mo C	40,000	8.00	15.00	40.00	120
1870Mo C	140,000	4.00	7.00	20.00	60.00
1871Mo C	103,000	9.00	20.00	40.00	100
1871Mo M	Inc. above	7.50	12.50	25.00	60.00
1872Mo M	266,000	5.00	8.00	20.00	55.00
1873Mo M	20,000	40.00	60.00	100	225
1874/69Mo M	—	7.50	15.00	30.00	75.00
1874Mo M	—	4.00	7.00	17.50	50.00
1874/3Mo M	—	5.00	8.00	22.50	55.00
1874Mo B	—	5.00	8.00	22.50	55.00
1875Mo B	—	4.00	7.00	15.00	50.00
1875Mo B/M	—	6.00	9.00	17.50	60.00
1876/5Mo B	—	4.00	7.00	15.00	50.00
1876Mo B	—	4.00	7.00	12.50	50.00
1877/6Mo M	80,000	4.00	7.00	15.00	60.00
1877Mo M	Inc. above	4.00	7.00	12.50	60.00
1878/7Mo M	100,000	4.00	7.00	15.00	55.00
1878Mo M	Inc. above	2.50	5.00	12.50	45.00
1879/8Mo M	—	8.00	12.50	22.50	55.00
1879Mo M	—	4.50	7.00	15.00	50.00
1879Mo M 9/inverted 9	—	10.00	15.00	25.00	75.00
1880/76Mo M/B	—	5.00	7.50	15.00	50.00
1880/76Mo M	—	5.00	7.50	15.00	50.00
1880Mo M	—	4.00	6.00	12.00	40.00
1881/0Mo M	180,000	4.00	6.00	10.00	35.00
1881Mo M	Inc. above	3.00	4.50	9.00	35.00
1886/0Mo M	398,000	2.00	2.75	7.50	25.00
1886/1Mo M	Inc. above	2.00	2.75	5.00	25.00
1886Mo M	Inc. above	1.75	2.25	6.00	20.00
1887Mo m	720,000	1.75	2.00	5.00	20.00
1887Mo M/m	Inc. above	1.75	2.00	6.00	20.00
1888/7Mo M	1,360,000	2.25	2.50	6.00	20.00
1888Mo M	Inc. above	1.75	2.00	5.00	20.00
1889/8Mo M	1,242,000	2.25	2.50	6.00	20.00
1889Mo M	Inc. above	1.75	2.00	5.00	20.00
1890/00Mo M	1,694,000	1.75	2.75	6.00	20.00
1890Mo M	Inc. above	1.50	2.00	5.00	20.00
1891Mo M	1,030,000	1.75	2.00	5.00	20.00
1892Mo M	1,400,000	1.75	2.00	5.00	20.00
1892Mo M 9/inverted 9	Inc. above	2.00	2.75	7.50	20.00
1893Mo M	220,000	1.75	2.00	5.00	15.00
1894Mo M	320,000	1.75	2.00	5.00	15.00
1895Mo M	78,000	3.00	5.00	8.00	25.00

Date	Mintage	F	VF	XF	Unc
1896Mo B	80,000	1.75	2.00	5.00	20.00
1897Mo B	160,000	1.75	2.00	5.00	15.00

Mint: Oaxaca
KM# 398.8 5 CENTAVOS
1.3530 g., 0.9030 Silver .0392 oz. ASW **Obv:** Standing eagle
Rev: Denomination in wreath

Date	Mintage	F	VF	XF	Unc
1890 Oa E Rare	48,000	—	—	—	—
1890 Oa N	Inc. above	65.00	125	200	350

Mint: San Luis Potosi
KM# 398.9 5 CENTAVOS
1.3530 g., 0.9030 Silver .0392 oz. ASW **Obv:** Standing eagle
Rev: Denomination in wreath **Note:** Varieties exist.

Date	Mintage	F	VF	XF	Unc
1869 Pi S	—	300	400	500	—
1870 Pi G/MoC Rare	20,000	150	250	400	—
1870 Pi O	Inc. above	200	300	450	—
1871 Pi O Rare	5,400	—	—	—	—
1872 Pi O	—	75.00	100	175	400
1873 Pi Rare	5,000	—	—	—	—
1874 Pi H	—	30.00	50.00	100	225
1875 Pi H	—	7.50	12.50	30.00	75.00
1876 Pi H	—	10.00	20.00	45.00	100
1877 Pi H	—	7.50	12.50	20.00	60.00
1878/7 Pi H Rare	—	—	—	—	—
1878 Pi H	—	60.00	90.00	150	300
1879 H	—	200	400	—	—
1880 Pi H Rare	6,200	—	—	—	—
1881 Pi H Rare	4,500	—	—	—	—
1886 Pi R	33,000	12.50	25.00	50.00	125
1887/0 Pi R	169,000	4.00	7.50	15.00	45.00
1887 Pi R	Inc. above	3.00	5.00	10.00	32.00
1888 Pi R	210,000	2.00	4.00	9.00	30.00
1889/7 Pi R	197,000	2.50	5.00	10.00	32.00
1889 Pi R	Inc. above	2.00	4.00	9.00	30.00
1890 Pi R	221,000	2.00	3.00	6.00	25.00
1891/89 Pi R/B	176,000	2.00	4.00	8.00	25.00
1891 Pi R	Inc. above	2.00	3.00	6.00	20.00
1892/89 Pi R	182,000	2.00	4.00	8.00	25.00
1892/0 Pi R	Inc. above	2.00	4.00	8.00	25.00
1892 Pi R	Inc. above	2.00	3.00	6.00	20.00
1893 Pi R	41,000	5.00	10.00	20.00	60.00

Mint: Zacatecas
KM# 398.10 5 CENTAVOS
1.3530 g., 0.9030 Silver .0392 oz. ASW **Obv:** Standing eagle
Rev: Denomination in wreath

Date	Mintage	F	VF	XF	Unc
1871Zs H	40,000	12.50	25.00	50.00	125
1872Zs H	40,000	12.50	25.00	50.00	125
1873/2Zs H	20,000	35.00	65.00	125	275
1873Zs H	Inc. above	25.00	50.00	100	250
1874Zs H	—	7.50	12.50	25.00	75.00
1874Zs A	—	40.00	75.00	150	300
1875Zs A	—	7.50	12.50	25.00	75.00
1876Zs A	—	50.00	75.00	150	500
1876/5Zs S	—	15.00	30.00	60.00	150
1876Zs S	—	12.50	25.00	50.00	125
1877Zs S	—	3.00	6.00	12.00	40.00
1878Zs S	60,000	3.00	6.00	12.00	40.00
1879/8Zs S	—	3.00	6.00	15.00	50.00
1879Zs S	—	3.00	6.00	12.00	40.00
1880/79Zs S	130,000	6.00	10.00	20.00	60.00
1880Zs S	Inc. above	5.00	8.00	16.00	45.00
1881Zs S	210,000	2.50	5.00	10.00	35.00
1886/4Zs S	360,000	6.00	10.00	20.00	60.00
1886Zs S	Inc. above	2.00	3.00	6.00	20.00
1886Zs Z	Inc. above	5.00	10.00	25.00	65.00
1887Zs Z	400,000	2.00	3.00	6.00	25.00
1888/7Zs Z	500,000	2.00	3.00	6.00	25.00
1888Zs Z	Inc. above	2.00	3.00	6.00	25.00
1889Zs Z	520,000	2.00	3.00	6.00	25.00
1889Zs Z 9/inverted 9	Inc. above	2.00	3.00	6.00	25.00
1889Zs Z/MoM	Inc. above	2.00	3.00	6.00	25.00

Date	Mintage	F	VF	XF	Unc
1890Zs Z	580,000	1.75	2.50	5.00	20.00
1890Zs Z/MoM	Inc. above	2.00	3.00	6.00	25.00
1890Zs ZsZ 9/8	—	2.00	3.00	6.00	25.00
1890Zs ZsZ 0/9 Z/M	—	2.00	3.00	6.00	25.00
1891Zs Z	420,000	1.75	2.50	5.00	20.00
1892Zs Z	346,000	1.75	2.50	5.00	20.00
1893Zs Z	258,000	1.75	2.50	5.00	20.00
1894Zs Z	228,000	1.75	2.50	5.00	20.00
1894Zs ZoZ Error	Inc. above	2.00	4.00	8.00	30.00
1895Zs Z	260,000	1.75	2.50	5.00	20.00
1895Zs Z	260,000	1.75	2.50	5.00	20.00
1895/4Zs ZsZ	—	2.00	3.00	6.00	25.00
1896Zs Z	200,000	1.75	2.50	5.00	20.00
1896Zs 6/inverted 6	Inc. above	2.00	3.00	6.00	25.00
1897/6Zs Z	200,000	2.00	3.00	6.00	25.00
1897Zs Z	Inc. above	1.75	2.50	5.00	20.00
1870Zs H	40,000	12.50	25.00	50.00	125

Mint: Mexico City
KM# 399 5 CENTAVOS
Copper-Nickel

Date	Mintage	F	VF	XF	Unc
1882	Inc. above	0.50	1.00	2.50	7.50
1883	Inc. above	25.00	50.00	80.00	250

Mint: Culiacan
KM# 400 5 CENTAVOS
0.9030 Silver **Obv:** Restyled eagle **Note:** Varieties exist.

Date	Mintage	F	VF	XF	Unc
1898Cn M	44,000	1.75	4.00	8.00	20.00
1899Cn M	111,000	5.50	8.50	20.00	50.00
1899Cn Q	Inc. above	1.75	2.50	4.50	15.00
1900/800Cn Q	239,000	3.50	5.00	12.50	30.00
1900Cn Q	Inc. above	1.75	3.00	6.00	16.50
Note: Round Q, single tail					
1900Cn Q	Inc. above	1.75	3.00	6.00	16.50
Note: Narrow C, oval Q					
1900Cn Q	Inc. above	1.75	3.00	6.00	16.50
Note: Wide C, oval Q					
1901Cn Q	148,000	1.75	2.50	4.50	15.00
1902Cn Q	262,000	1.75	3.00	6.00	16.50
Note: Narrow C, heavy serifs					
1902Cn Q	Inc. above	1.75	3.00	6.00	16.50
Note: Wide C, light serifs					
1903/1Cn Q	331,000	2.00	3.00	6.00	16.50
1903Cn Q	Inc. above	1.75	2.50	4.50	15.00
1903/1898Cn V	Inc. above	3.50	4.50	9.00	22.50
1903Cn V	Inc. above	1.75	2.50	4.50	15.00
1904Cn H	352,000	1.75	2.25	4.50	16.50
1904Cn H 0/9	—	1.75	3.00	5.00	16.50
1904Cn H/C	—	1.75	2.50	5.00	16.50

Mint: Guanajuato
KM# 400.1 5 CENTAVOS
0.9030 Silver **Obv:** Restyled eagle **Note:** Varieties exist.

Date	Mintage	F	VF	XF	Unc
1898Go R Mule, gold peso obverse	180,000	7.50	15.00	30.00	75.00
1899Go R	260,000	1.75	2.50	4.50	15.00
1900Go R	200,000	1.75	2.50	4.50	15.00

Mint: Mexico City
KM# 400.2 5 CENTAVOS
0.9030 Silver **Obv:** Restyled eagle

Date	Mintage	F	VF	XF	Unc
1898Mo M	80,000	2.00	4.00	7.00	25.00
1899Mo M	168,000	1.75	2.50	4.50	15.00

Date	Mintage	F	VF	XF	Unc
1900/800Mo M	300,000	4.50	6.50	10.00	30.00
1900Mo M	Inc. above	1.75	2.50	4.50	15.00
1901Mo M	100,000	1.75	2.50	4.50	15.00
1902Mo M	144,000	1.25	2.00	3.75	12.00
1902/1Mo MoM	—	1.75	3.00	7.00	16.50
1903Mo M	500,000	1.25	2.00	3.75	12.00
1904/804Mo M	1,090,000	1.75	3.50	8.50	16.50
1904/94Mo M	Inc. above	1.75	3.75	9.00	16.50
1904Mo M	Inc. above	1.75	3.00	6.00	15.00
1905Mo M	344,000	1.75	3.00	7.00	16.50

Mint: Zacatecas
KM# 400.3 5 CENTAVOS
0.9030 Silver **Obv:** Restyled eagle

Date	Mintage	F	VF	XF	Unc
1898Zs Z	100,000	1.75	2.25	4.50	12.50
1899Zs Z	50,000	2.00	3.00	7.00	20.00
1900Zs Z	55,000	1.75	2.50	5.00	16.50
1901Zs Z	40,000	1.75	2.50	5.00	16.50
1902/1Zs Z	34,000	2.00	4.50	9.00	22.50
1902Zs Z	Inc. above	1.75	3.75	7.50	18.50
1903Zs Z	217,000	1.25	2.00	5.00	16.50
1904Zs Z	191,000	1.75	2.50	5.00	12.50
1904Zs M	Inc. above	1.75	2.50	6.00	16.50
1905Zs M	46,000	2.00	4.50	9.00	22.50
1905Zs M Republica - Rare	Inc. above	—	—	—	—

Mint: Chihuahua
KM# 401.1 10 CENTAVOS
2.7070 g., 0.9030 Silver .0785 oz. ASW **Obv:** Eagle **Rev:** Value within wreath **Note:** Previous KM#401.

Date	Mintage	F	VF	XF	Unc
1868/7 Ca	—	30.00	60.00	150	550
1868 Ca	—	30.00	60.00	150	550
1869 Ca	15,000	25.00	50.00	125	600
1870 Ca	17,000	22.50	45.00	100	550

Mint: San Luis Potosi
KM# 401.2 10 CENTAVOS
2.7070 g., 0.9030 Silver .0785 oz. ASW **Obv:** Eagle **Rev:** Value within wreath

Date	Mintage	F	VF	XF	Unc
1863SLP	—	75.00	150	275	900

Mint: Mexico City
KM# 402 10 CENTAVOS
2.7070 g., 0.9030 Silver .0785 oz. ASW **Obv:** Eagle **Rev:** Cap and rays

Date	Mintage	F	VF	XF	Unc
1867/3Mo	—	50.00	100	200	550
1867Mo	—	20.00	50.00	150	450
1868/7Mo	—	20.00	50.00	175	500
1868Mo	—	20.00	55.00	175	500

Mint: San Luis Potosi
KM# 402.1 10 CENTAVOS
2.7070 g., 0.9030 Silver .0785 oz. ASW **Obv:** Eagle **Rev:** Cap and rays

Date	Mintage	F	VF	XF	Unc
1868/7P	38,000	45.00	90.00	175	650
1868P	Inc. above	20.00	40.00	100	550
1869/7P	4,900	55.00	125	250	800

Mint: Alamos
KM# 403 10 CENTAVOS
2.7070 g., 0.9030 Silver .0785 oz. ASW **Obv:** Eagle **Rev:** Value within wreath **Note:** Varieties exist.

Date	Mintage	F	VF	XF	Unc
1874 As DL	—	20.00	40.00	80.00	175
1875 As L	—	5.00	10.00	25.00	90.00
1876 As L	—	10.00	18.00	40.00	110

Date	Mintage	F	VF	XF	Unc
1878/7 As L	—	10.00	18.00	45.00	120
1878 As L	—	5.00	10.00	30.00	100
1879 As L	—	10.00	18.00	40.00	110
1880 As L	13,000	10.00	18.00	40.00	110
1882 As L	22,000	10.00	18.00	40.00	110
1883 As L	8,520	25.00	50.00	100	225
1884 As L	—	7.50	12.50	35.00	100
1885 As L	15,000	7.50	12.50	35.00	100
1886 As L	45,000	7.50	12.50	35.00	100
1887 As L	15,000	7.50	12.50	35.00	100
1888 As L	38,000	7.50	12.50	35.00	100
1889 As L	20,000	7.50	12.50	35.00	100
1890 As L	40,000	7.50	12.50	35.00	100
1891 As L	38,000	7.50	12.50	35.00	100
1892 As L	57,000	5.00	10.00	25.00	90.00
1893 As L	70,000	10.00	18.00	40.00	110

Note: An 1891 As L over 1889 HoG exists which was evidently produced at the Alamos Mint using dies sent from the Hermosillo Mint

Mint: Chihuahua
KM# 403.1 10 CENTAVOS
2.7070 g., 0.9030 Silver .0785 oz. ASW **Obv:** Eagle **Rev:** Value within wreath **Note:** Mint mark CH, Ca. Varieties exist.

Date	Mintage	F	VF	XF	Unc
1871 M	8,150	15.00	30.00	60.00	150
1873 M Crude date	—	35.00	75.00	125	175
1874 M	—	10.00	17.50	35.00	100
1880/70 G	7,620	20.00	40.00	80.00	175
1880 G/g	Inc. above	15.00	25.00	50.00	125
1881 Rare	340	—	—	—	—
1883 M	9,000	10.00	20.00	40.00	125
1884/73	—	5.00	30.00	60.00	150
1884 M	—	10.00	20.00	40.00	125
1886 M	45,000	7.50	12.50	30.00	100
1887/3 M/G	96,000	5.00	10.00	20.00	75.00
1887 M/G	—	2.00	4.00	8.00	75.00
1887 M	Inc. above	2.00	4.00	8.00	75.00
1888 M/G	—	2.00	4.00	8.00	75.00
1888 M	299,000	1.50	2.50	5.00	75.00
1888 Ca/Mo	Inc. above	1.50	2.50	5.00	75.00
1889/8 M	115,000	2.00	4.00	8.00	75.00
1889 M Small 89 (5 Centavo font)	Inc. above	2.00	4.00	8.00	75.00
1890/80 M	140,000	2.00	4.00	8.00	75.00
1890/89 M	Inc. above	2.00	4.00	8.00	75.00
1890 M	Inc. above	1.50	3.00	7.00	75.00
1891 M	163,000	1.50	3.00	7.00	75.00
1892 M	169,000	1.50	3.00	7.00	75.00
1892 M 9/inverted 9	Inc. above	2.00	4.00	8.00	75.00
1893 M	246,000	1.50	3.00	7.00	75.00
1894 M	163,000	1.50	3.00	7.00	75.00
1895 M	127,000	1.50	3.00	7.00	75.00

Mint: Culiacan
KM# 403.2 10 CENTAVOS
2.7070 g., 0.9030 Silver .0785 oz. ASW **Obv:** Eagle **Rev:** Value within wreath

Date	Mintage	F	VF	XF	Unc
1871Cn P Rare	—	—	—	—	—
1873Cn P	8,732	20.00	50.00	100	225
1881Cn D	9,440	75.00	175	325	500
1882Cn D	12,000	75.00	125	200	400
1885Cn M Mule, gold 2-1/2 peso obverse	18,000	25.00	50.00	100	200
1886Cn M Mule, gold 2-1/2 peso obverse	13,000	50.00	100	150	300
1887Cn M	11,000	20.00	40.00	75.00	175
1888Cn M	56,000	5.00	10.00	25.00	125
1889Cn M	42,000	5.00	10.00	20.00	75.00
1890Cn M	132,000	2.00	4.00	7.50	75.00
1891Cn M	84,000	5.00	10.00	20.00	75.00
1892/1Cn M	37,000	4.00	8.00	15.00	75.00
1892Cn M	Inc. above	2.50	5.00	10.00	75.00
1894Cn M	43,000	2.50	5.00	10.00	75.00
1895Cn M	23,000	2.50	5.00	10.00	60.00
1896Cn M	121,000	1.50	2.50	5.00	50.00

Mint: Durango
KM# 403.3 10 CENTAVOS
2.7070 g., 0.9030 Silver .0785 oz. ASW **Obv:** Eagle **Rev:** Value within wreath

Date	Mintage	F	VF	XF	Unc
1878Do E	2,500	100	175	300	600
1879Do B Rare	—	—	—	—	—
1880/70Do B Rare	—	—	—	—	—
1880/79Do B Rare	—	—	—	—	—
1884Do C	—	30.00	60.00	100	225
1886Do C	13,000	75.00	150	300	500
1887Do C	81,000	4.00	8.00	15.00	100
1888Do C	31,000	6.00	12.00	30.00	100
1889Do C	55,000	4.00	8.00	15.00	100
1890Do C	50,000	4.00	8.00	15.00	100
1891Do P	139,000	2.00	4.00	8.00	80.00
1892Do P	212,000	2.00	4.00	8.00	80.00
1892Do D	Inc. above	2.00	4.00	8.00	80.00
1893Do D	258,000	2.00	4.00	8.00	80.00
1893Do D/C	Inc. above	2.50	5.00	10.00	80.00
1894Do D	184,000	1.50	3.00	6.00	80.00
1894Do D/C	Inc. above	2.00	4.00	8.00	80.00
1895Do D	142,000	1.50	3.00	6.00	80.00

Mint: Guadalajara
KM# 403.4 10 CENTAVOS
2.7070 g., 0.9030 Silver .0785 oz. ASW **Obv:** Eagle **Rev:** Value within wreath **Note:** Varieties exist.

Date	Mintage	F	VF	XF	Unc
1871Ga C	4,734	75.00	125	200	500
1873/1Ga C	25,000	10.00	15.00	35.00	150
1873Ga C	Inc. above	10.00	15.00	35.00	150
1874Ga C	—	10.00	15.00	35.00	150
1877Ga A	—	10.00	15.00	30.00	150
1881Ga S	115,000	5.00	10.00	25.00	150
1883Ga B	90,000	4.00	8.00	15.00	90.00
1884Ga B	—	5.00	10.00	20.00	90.00
1884Ga B/S	—	6.00	12.50	25.00	90.00
1884Ga H	—	3.00	5.00	10.00	90.00
1885Ga H	93,000	3.00	5.00	10.00	90.00
1886Ga S	151,000	2.50	4.00	9.00	90.00
1887Ga S	162,000	1.50	3.00	6.00	90.00
1888Ga S	225,000	1.50	3.00	6.00	90.00
1888Ga GaS/HoG	Inc. above	1.50	3.00	6.00	90.00
1889Ga S	310,000	1.50	3.00	6.00	40.00
1890Ga S	303,000	1.50	3.00	6.00	40.00
1891Ga S	199,000	5.00	10.00	20.00	45.00
1892Ga S	329,000	1.50	3.00	6.00	40.00
1893Ga S	225,000	1.50	3.00	6.00	40.00
1894Ga S	243,000	3.00	6.00	12.00	40.00
1895Ga S	80,000	1.50	3.00	6.00	40.00

Mint: Guanajuato
KM# 403.5 10 CENTAVOS
2.7070 g., 0.9030 Silver .0785 oz. ASW **Obv:** Eagle **Rev:** Value within wreath **Note:** Varieties exist.

Date	Mintage	F	VF	XF	Unc
1869Go S	7,000	20.00	40.00	80.00	200
1871/0Go S	60,000	15.00	25.00	50.00	125
1872Go S	60,000	15.00	25.00	50.00	125
1873Go S	50,000	15.00	25.00	50.00	125
1874Go S	—	15.00	25.00	50.00	125
1875Go S	—	250	350	500	800
1876Go S	—	10.00	20.00	40.00	100
1877Go S	—	80.00	120	200	400
1878/7Go S	10,000	10.00	20.00	45.00	110
1878Go S	Inc. above	7.50	12.00	20.00	75.00
1879Go S	—	7.50	12.00	20.00	75.00
1880Go S	—	100	200	300	450
1881/71Go S	100,000	3.00	5.00	10.00	75.00
1881/0Go S	Inc. above	3.50	5.00	10.00	75.00
1881Go S	Inc. above	3.00	5.00	10.00	75.00
1882/1Go S	40,000	3.00	6.00	12.00	75.00
1883Go B	—	3.00	5.00	10.00	75.00
1884Go B	—	1.50	3.00	6.00	75.00
1884Go S	—	6.00	12.50	25.00	90.00
1885Go R	100,000	1.50	3.00	6.00	75.00
1886Go R	95,000	3.00	5.00	10.00	75.00
1887Go R	330,000	2.50	5.00	10.00	75.00
1888Go R	270,000	1.50	3.00	6.00	75.00
1889Go R	205,000	2.00	4.00	8.00	75.00
1889Go GoR/HoG	Inc. above	3.00	5.00	10.00	75.00
1890Go R	270,000	1.50	3.00	6.00	35.00
1890Go GoR/Cn M	Inc. above	1.50	3.00	6.00	35.00

Date	Mintage	F	VF	XF	Unc
1891Go R	523,000	1.50	3.00	6.00	35.00
1891Go R/G	—	1.50	3.00	6.00	35.00
1891Go GoR/HoG	Inc. above	1.50	3.00	6.00	35.00
1892Go R	440,000	1.50	3.00	6.00	35.00
1893/1Go R	389,000	3.00	5.00	10.00	35.00
1893Go R	Inc. above	1.50	3.00	6.00	35.00
1894Go R	400,000	1.50	2.50	5.00	35.00
1895Go R	355,000	1.50	2.50	5.00	35.00
1896Go R	190,000	1.50	2.50	5.00	35.00
1897Go R	205,000	1.50	2.50	5.00	35.00

Mint: Hermosillo
KM# 403.6 10 CENTAVOS
2.7070 g., 0.9030 Silver .0785 oz. ASW **Obv:** Eagle **Rev:** Value within wreath

Date	Mintage	F	VF	XF	Unc
1874Ho R	—	30.00	60.00	100	200
1876Ho F	3,140	200	300	450	750
1878Ho A	—	5.00	10.00	15.00	85.00
1879Ho A	—	25.00	50.00	90.00	175
1880Ho A	—	3.00	6.00	12.50	85.00
1881Ho A	28,000	4.00	7.00	15.00	85.00
1882/1Ho A	25,000	5.00	10.00	20.00	85.00
1882/1Ho a	Inc. above	6.00	12.50	25.00	85.00
1882Ho A	Inc. above	4.00	7.00	15.00	85.00
1883Ho	7,000	65.00	100	200	400
1884Ho A	—	35.00	75.00	150	300
1884/3Ho M	—	10.00	20.00	40.00	90.00
1884Ho M	—	7.50	15.00	30.00	85.00
1885Ho M	21,000	12.50	25.00	50.00	100
1886Ho M Rare	10,000	—	—	—	—
1886Ho G	Inc. above	7.50	12.50	25.00	85.00
1887Ho G	—	25.00	50.00	75.00	150
1888Ho G	25,000	6.00	12.50	25.00	85.00
1889Ho G	42,000	3.00	6.00	10.00	85.00
1890Ho G	48,000	3.00	6.00	10.00	85.00
1891/80Ho G	136,000	3.00	6.00	10.00	85.00
1891/0Ho G	Inc. above	4.00	6.00	10.00	85.00
1891Ho G	Inc. above	3.00	6.00	10.00	85.00
1892Ho G	67,000	3.00	6.00	10.00	85.00
1893Ho G	67,000	3.00	6.00	10.00	85.00

Mint: Mexico City
KM# 403.7 10 CENTAVOS
2.7070 g., 0.9020 Silver .0785 oz. ASW **Obv:** Eagle **Rev:** Value within wreath **Note:** Varieties exist.

Date	Mintage	F	VF	XF	Unc
1869/8Mo C	30,000	10.00	20.00	40.00	100
1869Mo C	Inc. above	8.00	17.50	35.00	90.00
1870Mo C	110,000	3.00	7.50	15.00	50.00
1871Mo C	84,000	50.00	75.00	125	250
1871Mo M	Inc. above	12.00	17.50	45.00	125
1872/69Mo M	198,000	10.00	20.00	35.00	100
1872Mo M	Inc. above	3.00	7.50	15.00	65.00
1873Mo M	40,000	10.00	15.00	30.00	75.00
1874Mo M	—	5.00	10.00	20.00	65.00
1874Mo M/C	—	5.00	10.00	20.00	65.00
1874/64Mo B	—	5.00	10.00	20.00	65.00
1874Mo B/M	—	20.00	40.00	60.00	125
1874Mo B	—	5.00	10.00	15.00	65.00
1875Mo B	—	20.00	40.00	60.00	125
1876/5Mo B	—	3.00	5.00	9.00	65.00
1876/5Mo B/M	—	3.00	5.00	9.00	65.00
1877/6Mo M	—	3.00	5.00	9.00	65.00
1877/6Mo M/B	—	3.00	5.00	9.00	65.00
1877Mo M	—	3.00	5.00	9.00	65.00
1878/7Mo M	100,000	3.00	5.00	9.00	65.00
1878Mo M	Inc. above	3.00	5.00	9.00	65.00
1879/69Mo M	—	3.00	5.00	9.00	65.00
1879Mo M/C	—	3.00	5.00	9.00	65.00
1880/79Mo M	—	3.00	5.00	9.00	65.00
1881/0Mo M	510,000	3.00	5.00	9.00	35.00
1881Mo M	Inc. above	3.00	5.00	9.00	35.00
1882/1Mo M	550,000	3.00	5.00	9.00	35.00

Date	Mintage	F	VF	XF	Unc
1882Mo M	Inc. above	3.00	5.00	9.00	35.00
1883/2Mo M	250,000	3.00	5.00	9.00	35.00
1884Mo M	—	3.00	5.00	9.00	35.00
1885Mo M	470,000	3.00	5.00	9.00	35.00
1886Mo M	603,000	3.00	5.00	9.00	35.00
1887Mo M	580,000	3.00	5.00	9.00	35.00
1888/7Mo MoM	710,000	3.00	5.00	9.00	35.00
1888Mo MoM	Inc. above	3.00	5.00	9.00	35.00
1888Mo MOM	Inc. above	3.00	5.00	9.00	35.00
1889/8Mo M	622,000	3.00	5.00	9.00	35.00
1889Mo M	Inc. above	3.00	5.00	9.00	35.00
1890/89Mo M	815,000	3.00	5.00	9.00	35.00
1890Mo M	Inc. above	3.00	5.00	9.00	35.00
1891Mo M	859,000	1.50	2.50	7.00	25.00
1892Mo M	1,030,000	1.50	2.50	7.00	25.00
1893Mo M	310,000	1.50	2.50	7.00	25.00
1893Mo M/C	Inc. above	1.50	2.50	7.00	25.00
1893Mo Mo/Ho M/G	—	1.50	2.50	7.00	25.00
1894/3Mo M	—	5.00	10.00	20.00	60.00
1894Mo M	350,000	5.00	10.00	20.00	60.00
1895Mo M	320,000	1.50	2.50	7.00	25.00
1896Mo B/G	340,000	1.50	2.50	7.00	25.00
1896Mo M	Inc. above	35.00	70.00	100	150
1897Mo M	170,000	1.50	2.50	5.00	20.00

Mint: Oaxaca
KM# 403.8   10 CENTAVOS
2.7070 g., 0.9030 Silver .0785 oz. ASW   **Obv:** Eagle **Rev:**
Value within wreath

Date	Mintage	F	VF	XF	Unc
1889 Oa E	21,000	200	400	600	—
1890 Oa N Rare	Inc. above	—	—	—	—
1890 Oa E	31,000	100	150	250	500

Mint: San Luis Potosi
KM# 403.9   10 CENTAVOS
2.7070 g., 0.9030 Silver .0785 oz. ASW   **Obv:** Eagle **Rev:**
Value within wreath **Note:** Varieties exist.

Date	Mintage	F	VF	XF	Unc
1869/8 Pi S Rare	4,000	—	—	—	—
1870/69 Pi O Rare	18,000	—	—	—	—
1870 Pi G	Inc. above	125	200	325	600
1871 Pi O	21,000	50.00	100	150	300
1872 Pi O	16,000	150	225	350	650
1873 Pi O Rare	4,750	—	—	—	—
1874 Pi H	—	25.00	50.00	100	200
1875 Pi H	—	75.00	125	200	400
1876 Pi H	—	75.00	125	200	400
1877 Pi H	—	75.00	125	200	400
1878 Pi H	—	250	500	750	—
1879 Pi H	—	—	—	—	—
1880 Pi H	—	150	250	350	—
1881 Pi H	7,600	250	350	500	—
1882 Pi H Rare	4,000	—	—	—	—
1883 Pi H	—	125	200	300	500
1884 Pi H	—	25.00	50.00	100	200
1885 Pi H	51,000	25.00	50.00	100	200
1885 Pi C Rare	Inc. above	—	—	—	—
1886 Pi C	52,000	15.00	30.00	60.00	150
1886 Pi R	Inc. above	5.00	10.00	20.00	65.00
1887 Pi R	118,000	2.50	5.00	10.00	50.00
1888 Pi R	136,000	2.50	5.00	10.00	50.00
1889/8 Pi R/G	—	7.50	12.50	20.00	60.00
1889/7 Pi R	131,000	7.50	12.50	20.00	60.00
1890 Pi R	204,000	1.50	3.00	7.50	40.00
1891/89 Pi R	163,000	2.50	5.00	10.00	40.00
1891 Pi R	Inc. above	1.50	3.50	6.00	30.00
1892/0 Pi R	200,000	2.00	4.00	8.00	40.00
1892 Pi R	Inc. above	1.50	2.50	5.00	40.00
1892 Pi R/G	—	2.00	4.00	8.00	40.00
1893 Pi R	48,000	7.50	10.00	17.50	60.00
1893 Pi R/G	—	1.50	10.00	17.50	60.00

Mint: Zacatecas
KM# 403.10   10 CENTAVOS
2.7070 g., 0.9030 Silver .0785 oz. ASW   **Obv:** Eagle **Rev:**
Value within wreath **Note:** Varieties exist.

Date	Mintage	F	VF	XF	Unc
1870Zs H	20,000	100	150	200	400
1871/0Zs H	10,000	—	—	—	—
1871Zs H	Inc. above	—	—	—	—
1872Zs H	10,000	150	200	275	500
1873Zs H	10,000	250	350	600	—
1874/3Zs H	—	50.00	75.00	150	300
1874Zs A	—	200	300	500	—
1875Zs A	—	5.00	10.00	25.00	100
1876Zs A	—	5.00	10.00	25.00	100
1876Zs S	—	100	200	300	500
1877Zs S Small S	—	7.50	12.50	25.00	100
1877Zs S Regular S	—	7.50	12.50	25.00	100
1878/7Zs S	30,000	5.00	10.00	20.00	80.00
1878Zs S	Inc. above	5.00	10.00	20.00	80.00
18797s S	—	5.00	10.00	20.00	80.00
1880Zs S	—	5.00	10.00	20.00	80.00
1881/0Zs S	120,000	3.00	6.00	12.50	50.00
1881Zs S	Inc. above	3.00	6.00	12.50	50.00
1882/1Zs S	64,000	12.50	25.00	50.00	125
1882Zs S	Inc. above	12.50	25.00	50.00	125
1883/73Zs S	102,000	2.00	4.00	8.00	50.00
1883Zs S	Inc. above	2.00	4.00	8.00	50.00
1884/3Zs S	—	2.00	4.00	8.00	50.00
1884Zs S	—	2.00	4.00	8.00	50.00
1885Zs S	297,000	1.50	2.50	5.00	50.00
1885Zs S Small S in mint mark	Inc. above	2.50	4.00	8.00	50.00
1885Zs Z Without assayers initials (error)	Inc. above	3.50	7.50	15.00	65.00
1886Zs S	274,000	1.50	2.50	5.00	30.00
1886Zs Z	Inc. above	12.50	25.00	50.00	125
1887Zs ZsZ	233,000	1.50	2.50	5.00	30.00
1887Zs Z Z (Error)	Inc. above	3.50	10.00	25.00	100
1888Zs ZsZ	270,000	1.50	2.50	5.00	30.00
1888Zs Z Z (Error)	Inc. above	3.50	10.00	25.00	100
1889/7Zs Z/S	240,000	4.00	8.00	12.50	40.00
1889Zs ZS	Inc. above	1.50	4.00	8.00	30.00
1889Zs Z/G	—	1.50	4.00	8.00	30.00
1889Zs Z	Inc. above	1.50	2.50	5.00	30.00
1890Zs ZsZ	410,000	1.50	2.50	5.00	30.00
1890Zs Z Z (Error)	Inc. above	3.75	10.00	25.00	100
1891Zs Z	1,105,000	1.50	2.50	5.00	30.00
1891Zs ZsZ Double s	Inc. above	2.00	4.00	7.00	30.00
1892Zs Z	1,102,000	1.50	2.50	5.00	30.00
1892Zs Z/G	—	2.00	4.00	7.00	30.00
1893/2Zs Z	—	2.00	4.00	8.00	40.00
1893Zs Z	1,010,999	1.50	2.50	5.00	25.00
1894Zs Z	892,000	1.50	2.50	5.00	30.00
1895Zs Z	920,000	1.50	2.50	5.00	30.00
1895Zs Z 9/5	—	2.00	4.00	7.00	30.00
1896/5Zs Z/G	—	1.50	2.50	5.00	30.00
1896Zs Z/G	—	1.50	2.50	5.00	30.00
1896/5Zs ZsZ	700,000	1.50	2.50	5.00	30.00
1896Zs ZsZ	Inc. above	1.50	2.50	5.00	30.00
1896Zs Z Z (Error)	Inc. above	3.75	10.00	25.00	100
1897/6Zs ZsZ	900,000	2.00	5.00	10.00	30.00
1897/6Zs Z Z (Error)	Inc. above	3.75	10.00	25.00	100
1897Zs Z	Inc. above	1.50	2.50	5.00	30.00

Mint: Culiacan
KM# 404   10 CENTAVOS
2.7070 g., 0.9030 Silver .0785 oz. ASW   **Obv:** Restyled eagle
Note: Varieties exist.

Date	Mintage	F	VF	XF	Unc
1898Cn M	9,870	50.00	100	200	500
1899Cn Q Round Q, single tail	80,000	5.00	7.50	25.00	100
1899Cn Q Oval Q, double tail	Inc. above	5.00	7.50	25.00	100

Date	Mintage	F	VF	XF	Unc
1900Cn Q	160,000	1.50	2.50	5.00	20.00
1901Cn Q	235,000	1.50	2.50	5.00	18.00
1902Cn Q	186,000	1.50	2.50	5.00	20.00
1903Cn Q	256,000	1.50	2.50	6.00	20.00
1903Cn V	Inc. above	1.50	2.50	5.00	15.00
1904Cn H	307,000	1.50	2.50	5.00	15.00

Mint: Guanajuato
KM# 404.1   10 CENTAVOS
2.7070 g., 0.9030 Silver .0785 oz. ASW **Obv:** Restyled eagle

Date	Mintage	F	VF	XF	Unc
1898Go R	435,000	1.50	2.50	5.00	20.00
1899Go R	270,000	1.50	2.50	5.00	25.00
1900Go R	130,000	7.50	12.50	25.00	60.00

Mint: Mexico City
KM# 404.2   10 CENTAVOS
2.7070 g., 0.9030 Silver .0785 oz. ASW **Obv:** Restyled eagle

Date	Mintage	F	VF	XF	Unc
1898Mo M	130,000	1.50	2.50	5.00	20.00
1899Mo M	190,000	1.50	2.50	5.00	20.00
1900Mo M	311,000	1.50	2.50	5.00	20.00
1901Mo M	80,000	2.50	3.50	7.00	22.50
1902Mo M	181,000	1.50	2.50	6.00	20.00
1903Mo M	581,000	1.50	2.50	6.00	20.00
1904Mo M	1,266,000	1.25	2.00	4.50	18.00
1904Mo MM (Error)	Inc. above	2.50	5.00	10.00	25.00
1905Mo M	266,000	2.00	3.75	7.50	20.00

Mint: Zacatecas
KM# 404.3   10 CENTAVOS
2.7070 g., 0.9020 Silver .0785 oz. ASW **Obv:** Restyled eagle

Date	Mintage	F	VF	XF	Unc
1898Zs Z	240,000	1.50	2.50	7.50	20.00
1899Zs Z	105,000	1.50	3.00	10.00	22.00
1900Zs Z	219,000	7.50	10.00	20.00	45.00
1901Zs Z	70,000	2.50	5.00	10.00	25.00
1902Zs Z	120,000	2.50	5.00	10.00	25.00
1903Zs Z	228,000	1.50	3.00	9.00	18.00
1904Zs Z	368,000	1.50	3.00	9.00	18.00
1904Zs M	Inc. above	1.50	3.00	9.00	22.00
1905Zs M	66,000	7.50	20.00	50.00	200

Mint: Culiacan
KM# 405   20 CENTAVOS
5.4150 g., 0.9030 Silver .1572 oz. ASW **Obv:** Restyled eagle

Date	Mintage	F	VF	XF	Unc
1898Cn M	114,000	5.00	12.50	35.00	140
1899Cn M	44,000	12.00	20.00	45.00	225
1899Cn Q	Inc. above	20.00	35.00	100	250
1900Cn Q	68,000	6.50	12.50	35.00	140
1901Cn Q	185,000	5.00	10.00	30.00	120
1902/802Cn Q	98,000	6.00	10.00	30.00	120
1902Cn Q	Inc. above	4.00	9.00	30.00	120
1903Cn Q	93,000	4.00	9.00	30.00	120
1904/3Cn H	258,000	—	—	—	—
1904Cn H	Inc. above	5.00	10.00	30.00	120

Mint: Guanajuato
KM# 405.1   20 CENTAVOS
5.4150 g., 0.9027 Silver .1572 oz. ASW **Obv:** Restyled eagle

Date	Mintage	F	VF	XF	Unc
1898Go R	135,000	4.00	8.00	20.00	100
1899Go R	215,000	4.00	8.00	20.00	100
1900/800Go R	38,000	10.00	20.00	60.00	250

Mint: Mexico City
KM# 405.2   20 CENTAVOS
5.4150 g., 0.9030 Silver .1572 oz. ASW **Obv:** Restyled eagle
Note: Varieties exist.

Date	Mintage	F	VF	XF	Unc
1898Mo M	150,000	4.00	8.00	20.00	90.00
1899Mo M	425,000	4.00	8.00	20.00	90.00
1900/800Mo M	295,000	4.00	8.00	20.00	90.00
1901Mo M	110,000	4.00	8.00	20.00	90.00
1902Mo M	120,000	4.00	8.00	20.00	90.00
1903Mo M	213,000	4.00	8.00	20.00	90.00
1904Mo M	276,000	4.00	8.00	20.00	90.00
1905Mo M	117,000	6.50	20.00	50.00	150

Mint: Zacatecas
KM# 405.3   20 CENTAVOS
5.4150 g., 0.9027 Silver .1572 oz. ASW **Obv:** Restyled eagle

Date	Mintage	F	VF	XF	Unc
1898Zs Z	195,000	5.00	10.00	20.00	100
1899Zs Z	210,000	5.00	10.00	20.00	100
1900/800Zs Z	97,000	5.00	10.00	20.00	100
1901Zs Z	Inc. above	5.00	10.00	20.00	100
1901/0Zs Z	130,000	25.00	50.00	100	250
1902Zs Z	105,000	5.00	10.00	20.00	100
1903Zs Z	143,000	5.00	10.00	20.00	100
1904Zs Z	246,000	5.00	10.00	20.00	100
1904Zs M	Inc. above	5.00	10.00	50.00	300
1905Zs M	59,000	10.00	20.00	50.00	400

Mint: Alamos
KM# 406   25 CENTAVOS
6.7680 g., 0.9030 Silver .1965 oz. ASW **Note:** Mint mark A, As.

Date	Mintage	F	VF	XF	Unc
1874 L	—	20.00	40.00	90.00	200
1875 L	—	15.00	30.00	70.00	200
1876 L	—	30.00	50.00	100	200
1877 L	11,000	200	300	500	—
1877.	Inc. above	10.00	25.00	60.00	200
1878 L	25,000	10.00	25.00	60.00	200
1879 L	—	10.00	25.00	60.00	200
1880 L	—	10.00	25.00	60.00	200
1880. L	—	10.00	25.00	60.00	200
1881 L	8,800	500	700	—	—
1882 L	7,777	15.00	35.00	80.00	200
1883 L	28,000	10.00	25.00	60.00	200
1884 L	—	10.00	25.00	60.00	200
1885 L	—	20.00	40.00	90.00	200
1886 L	46,000	15.00	30.00	70.00	200
1887 L	12,000	12.50	27.50	65.00	200
1888 L	20,000	12.50	27.50	65.00	200
1889 L	14,000	12.50	27.50	65.00	200
1890 L	23,000	10.00	25.00	60.00	200

Mint: Chihuahua
KM# 406.1   25 CENTAVOS
6.7680 g., 0.9030 Silver .1965 oz. ASW **Note:** Mint mark CA, CH, Ca.

Date	Mintage	F	VF	XF	Unc
1871 M	18,000	25.00	50.00	100	200
1872 M Very crude date	24,000	50.00	100	150	300
1883 M	12,000	10.00	25.00	50.00	175
1885/3 M	35,000	10.00	25.00	50.00	175
1885 M	Inc. above	10.00	25.00	50.00	175
1886 M	22,000	10.00	25.00	50.00	175
1887/6 M	26,000	10.00	15.00	30.00	175
1887 M	Inc. above	10.00	15.00	30.00	175
1888 M	14,000	10.00	25.00	50.00	175
1889 M	50,000	10.00	15.00	30.00	175

Mint: Culiacan
KM# 406.2   25 CENTAVOS
6.7680 g., 0.9030 Silver .1965 oz. ASW

Date	Mintage	F	VF	XF	Unc
1871Cn P	—	250	500	750	—
1872Cn P	2,780	300	550	800	—
1873Cn P	20,000	100	150	250	500

Date	Mintage	F	VF	XF	Unc
1874Cn P	—	20.00	50.00	125	250
1875Cn P	—	250	500	750	—
1876Cn P Rare	—	—	—	—	—
1878/7Cn D/S	—	100	150	250	500
1878Cn Cn/Go D/S	—	100	150	250	500
1878Cn D	—	100	150	250	500
1879Cn D	—	15.00	35.00	70.00	175
1880Cn D	—	250	500	750	—
1881/0Cn D	18,000	15.00	30.00	60.00	175
1882Cn D	—	200	350	600	—
1882Cn M Rare	—	—	—	—	—
1883Cn M	15,000	50.00	100	150	300
1884Cn M	—	20.00	40.00	80.00	175
1885/4Cn M	19,000	20.00	40.00	80.00	175
1886Cn M	22,000	12.50	20.00	50.00	175
1887Cn M	32,000	12.50	20.00	50.00	175
1888Cn M	86,000	7.50	15.00	30.00	175
1888Cn M Cn/Mo	—	—	—	—	—
1889Cn M	50,000	10.00	25.00	50.00	175
1890Cn M 9/8	—	7.50	17.50	40.00	175
1890Cn M	91,000	7.50	17.50	40.00	175
1892/0Cn M	16,000	20.00	40.00	80.00	200
1892Cn M	Inc. above	20.00	40.00	80.00	200

Mint: Durango
KM# 406.3   25 CENTAVOS
6.7680 g., 0.9030 Silver .1965 oz. ASW

Date	Mintage	F	VF	XF	Unc
1873Do P Rare	892	—	—	—	—
1877Do P	—	25.00	50.00	100	200
1878/7Do E	—	250	500	750	—
1878Do B Rare	—	—	—	—	—
1879Do B	—	50.00	75.00	125	250
1880Do B Rare	—	—	—	—	—
1882Do C	17,000	25.00	50.00	100	225
1884/3Do C	—	25.00	50.00	100	200
1885Do C	15,000	20.00	40.00	80.00	200
1885Do C/S	—	20.00	40.00	80.00	200
1886Do C	33,000	15.00	30.00	60.00	200
1887Do C	27,000	10.00	20.00	50.00	200
1888Do C	25,000	10.00	20.00	50.00	200
1889Do C	29,000	10.00	20.00	50.00	200
1890Do C	68,000	7.50	15.00	40.00	200

Mint: Guadalajara
KM# 406.4   25 CENTAVOS
6.7680 g., 0.9030 Silver .1965 oz. ASW

Date	Mintage	F	VF	XF	Unc
1880Ga A	38,000	25.00	50.00	100	200
1881/0Ga S	39,000	25.00	50.00	100	200
1881Ga S	Inc. above	25.00	50.00	100	200
1882Ga S	18,000	25.00	50.00	100	200
1883/2Ga B/S	—	50.00	100	150	300
1884Ga B	—	20.00	40.00	80.00	150
1889Ga S	30,000	20.00	40.00	80.00	150

Mint: Guanajuato
KM# 406.5   25 CENTAVOS
6.7680 g., 0.9030 Silver .1965 oz. ASW **Note:** Varieties exist.

Date	Mintage	F	VF	XF	Unc
1870Go S	128,000	10.00	20.00	50.00	125
1871Go S	172,000	10.00	20.00	50.00	125
1872/1Go S	178,000	10.00	20.00	50.00	125
1872Go S	Inc. above	10.00	20.00	50.00	125
1873Go S	120,000	10.00	20.00	50.00	125
1874Go S	—	15.00	30.00	60.00	150
1875/4Go S	—	15.00	30.00	60.00	150
1875Go S	—	10.00	20.00	50.00	125
1876Go S	—	20.00	40.00	80.00	175
1877Go S	124,000	10.00	20.00	50.00	125
1878Go S	146,000	10.00	20.00	50.00	125
1879Go S	—	10.00	20.00	50.00	125
1880Go S	—	20.00	40.00	80.00	175
1881Go S	408,000	7.50	17.50	45.00	125
1882Go S	204,000	7.50	17.50	45.00	125
1883Go B	168,000	7.50	17.50	45.00	125
1884/69Go B	—	7.50	17.50	45.00	125
1884/3Go B	—	7.50	17.50	45.00	125
1884/3Go B/R	—	7.50	17.50	45.00	125
1884Go B	—	7.50	17.50	45.00	125
1885/65Go R	300,000	7.50	17.50	45.00	125
1885/69Go R	Inc. above	7.50	17.50	45.00	125
1885Go R	Inc. above	7.50	17.50	45.00	125

Date	Mintage	F	VF	XF	Unc
1886/66Go R	322,000	7.50	17.50	45.00	125
1886/69Go R/S	Inc. above	7.50	17.50	45.00	125
1886/5/69Go R	Inc. above	7.50	15.00	45.00	125
1886Go R	Inc. above	7.50	15.00	45.00	125
1887Go R	254,000	7.50	15.00	45.00	125
1887Go/Cn R/D	Inc. above	7.50	15.00	45.00	125
1888Go R	312,000	7.50	15.00	45.00	125
1889/8Go R	304,000	7.50	15.00	45.00	125
1889/8Go/Cn R/D	Inc. above	7.50	15.00	45.00	125
1889Go R	Inc. above	7.50	15.00	45.00	125
1890Go R	236,000	7.50	15.00	45.00	125

Mint: Hermosillo
KM# 406.6   25 CENTAVOS
6.7680 g., 0.9030 Silver .1965 oz. ASW **Note:** Varieties exist.

Date	Mintage	F	VF	XF	Unc
1874/64Ho R	Inc. above	10.00	20.00	40.00	125
1874/69Ho R	—	10.00	20.00	40.00	125
1874Ho R	23,000	10.00	20.00	40.00	125
1875Ho R Rare	—	—	—	—	—
1876/4Ho F/R	34,000	10.00	20.00	50.00	150
1876Ho F/R	Inc. above	10.00	25.00	60.00	150
1876Ho F	Inc. above	10.00	25.00	55.00	135
1877Ho F	—	10.00	20.00	50.00	125
1878Ho A	23,000	10.00	20.00	50.00	125
1879Ho A	—	10.00	20.00	50.00	125
1880Ho A	—	15.00	30.00	60.00	125
1881Ho A	19,000	15.00	30.00	60.00	125
1882Ho A	8,120	20.00	40.00	80.00	150
1883Ho M	2,000	100	200	300	600
1884Ho M	—	12.50	25.00	50.00	150
1885Ho M	—	10.00	20.00	50.00	125
1886Ho G	6,400	30.00	60.00	125	250
1887Ho G	12,000	10.00	20.00	40.00	125
1888Ho G	20,000	10.00	20.00	40.00	125
1889Ho G	28,000	10.00	20.00	40.00	125
1890/80Ho G	18,000	25.00	50.00	100	125
1890Ho G	Inc. above	25.00	50.00	100	125

Mint: Mexico City
KM# 406.7   25 CENTAVOS
6.7680 g., 0.9027 Silver .1965 oz. ASW **Note:** Varieties exist.

Date	Mintage	F	VF	XF	Unc
1869Mo C	76,000	10.00	25.00	50.00	125
1870/69Mo C	—	6.00	12.00	30.00	125
1870/9Mo C	136,000	6.00	12.00	30.00	125
1870Mo C	Inc. above	6.00	12.00	30.00	125
1871Mo M	138,000	6.00	12.00	30.00	125
1872Mo M	220,000	6.00	12.00	30.00	125
1873/1Mo M	48,000	10.00	25.00	50.00	125
1873Mo M	Inc. above	10.00	25.00	50.00	125
1874/69Mo B/M	—	10.00	25.00	50.00	125
1874/3Mo M	—	10.00	25.00	50.00	125
1874/3Mo B	—	10.00	25.00	50.00	125
1874/3Mo B/M	—	10.00	25.00	50.00	125
1874Mo M	—	6.00	12.00	30.00	125
1874Mo B/M	—	10.00	25.00	50.00	125
1875Mo B	—	6.00	12.00	30.00	125
1876/5Mo B	—	7.50	15.00	40.00	125
1876Mo B	—	6.00	12.00	30.00	125
1877Mo M	56,000	10.00	25.00	50.00	125
1878/1Mo M	120,000	10.00	25.00	50.00	125
1878/7Mo M	Inc. above	10.00	25.00	50.00	125
1878Mo M	Inc. above	6.00	12.00	30.00	125
1879Mo M	—	10.00	20.00	40.00	125
1880Mo M	—	7.50	15.00	35.00	125
1881/0Mo M	300,000	10.00	25.00	50.00	125
1881Mo M	Inc. above	10.00	25.00	50.00	125
1882Mo M	212,000	7.50	15.00	35.00	125
1883Mo M	108,000	7.50	15.00	35.00	125

Date	Mintage	F	VF	XF	Unc
1884/3Mo M	—	10.00	25.00	50.00	125
1884Mo M	—	10.00	20.00	40.00	125
1885Mo M	216,000	10.00	20.00	40.00	125
1886/5Mo M	436,000	7.50	15.00	35.00	125
1886Mo M	Inc. above	7.50	15.00	35.00	125
1887Mo M	376,000	7.50	15.00	35.00	125
1888Mo M	192,000	7.50	15.00	35.00	125
1889Mo M	132,000	7.50	15.00	35.00	125
1890Mo M	60,000	10.00	20.00	40.00	125

Mint: San Luis Potosi
KM# 406.8   25 CENTAVOS
6.7680 g., 0.9030 Silver .1965 oz. ASW **Note:** Varieties exist.

Date	Mintage	F	VF	XF	Unc
1869 Pi S	—	25.00	75.00	150	300
1870 Pi G	50,000	10.00	30.00	75.00	150
1870 Pi O	Inc. above	15.00	35.00	85.00	175
1871 Pi O	30,000	10.00	30.00	75.00	150
1872 Pi O	46,000	10.00	30.00	75.00	150
1873 Pi O	13,000	15.00	40.00	90.00	175
1874 Pi H	—	15.00	40.00	90.00	200
1875 Pi H	—	10.00	20.00	60.00	150
1876/5 Pi H	—	15.00	30.00	80.00	175
1876 Pi H	—	10.00	25.00	65.00	150
1877 Pi H	19,000	10.00	25.00	65.00	150
1878 Pi H	—	15.00	30.00	60.00	150
1879/8 Pi H	—	10.00	25.00	60.00	150
1879 Pi H	—	10.00	25.00	60.00	150
1879 Pi E	—	100	200	300	600
1880 Pi H	—	20.00	40.00	100	200
1880 Pi H/M	—	20.00	40.00	100	200
1881 Pi H	50,000	20.00	40.00	80.00	175
1881 Pi E Rare	Inc. above	—	—	—	—
1882 Pi H	20,000	10.00	20.00	60.00	150
1883 Pi H	17,000	10.00	25.00	65.00	150
1884 Pi H	—	10.00	25.00	65.00	150
1885/4 Pi H	—	10.00	20.00	60.00	150
1885 Pi H	43,000	10.00	20.00	60.00	150
1886 Pi C	78,000	10.00	25.00	65.00	150
1886 Pi R	Inc. above	7.50	20.00	50.00	150
1886 Pi R 6/inverted 6	Inc. above	7.50	20.00	50.00	150
1887Pi/ZsR	92,000	7.50	20.00	50.00	150
1887Pi/ZsB	Inc. above	100	150	300	500
1887 Pi R	—	7.50	20.00	50.00	150
1888 Pi R	106,000	7.50	20.00	50.00	150
1888Pi/ZsR	Inc. above	10.00	20.00	50.00	150
1888 Pi R/B	Inc. above	10.00	20.00	50.00	150
1889 Pi R	115,000	7.50	15.00	40.00	150
1889Pi/ZsR	Inc. above	10.00	20.00	50.00	150
1889 Pi R/B	Inc. above	10.00	20.00	50.00	150
1890 Pi R	64,000	10.00	20.00	50.00	150
1890Pi/ZsR/B	Inc. above	7.50	15.00	40.00	150
1890 Pi R/B	Inc. above	10.00	20.00	50.00	150

Mint: Zacatecas
KM# 406.9   25 CENTAVOS
6.7680 g., 0.9030 Silver .1965 oz. ASW **Note:** Varieties exist.

Date	Mintage	F	VF	XF	Unc
1870Zs H	152,000	6.00	15.00	50.00	125
1871Zs H	250,000	6.00	15.00	50.00	125
1872Zs H	260,000	6.00	15.00	50.00	125
1872Zs H	—	—	—	—	—
1873Zs H	132,000	6.00	15.00	50.00	125
1874Zs H	—	10.00	20.00	60.00	125
1874Zs A	—	10.00	20.00	60.00	125
1875Zs A	—	7.00	20.00	60.00	125
1876Zs A	—	6.00	15.00	50.00	125
1876Zs S	—	6.00	15.00	50.00	125
1877Zs S	350,000	6.00	15.00	50.00	125
1878Zs S	252,000	6.00	15.00	50.00	125
1878/1Zs S	—	7.00	20.00	60.00	125
1878/7Zs S	—	7.00	20.00	60.00	125
1879Zs S	—	6.00	15.00	50.00	125
1880Zs S	—	6.00	15.00	50.00	125
1881/0Zs S	570,000	6.00	15.00	50.00	125
1881Zs S	Inc. above	6.00	15.00	50.00	125
1882/1Zs S	300,000	10.00	17.50	55.00	125
1882Zs S	Inc. above	6.00	15.00	50.00	125
1883/2Zs S	193,000	10.00	17.50	55.00	125
1883Zs S	Inc. above	6.00	15.00	50.00	125
1884/3Zs S	—	10.00	17.50	55.00	125

Date	Mintage	F	VF	XF	Unc
1884Zs S	—	6.00	15.00	50.00	125
1885Zs S	309,000	6.00	15.00	50.00	125
1886/2Zs S	—	10.00	17.50	55.00	125
1886/5Zs S	613,000	6.00	15.00	50.00	125
1886Zs S	Inc. above	6.00	15.00	50.00	125
1886Zs Z	Inc. above	6.00	15.00	55.00	125
1887Zs Z	389,000	6.00	15.00	50.00	125
1888Zs Z	408,000	6.00	15.00	50.00	125
1889Zs Z	400,000	6.00	15.00	50.00	125
1890Zs Z	269,000	6.00	15.00	50.00	125

Mint: Alamos
KM# 407   50 CENTAVOS
13.5360 g., 0.9030 Silver .3930 oz. ASW **Rev:** Balance scale
Note: Mint mark A, As.

Date	Mintage	F	VF	XF	Unc
1875 L	—	12.00	25.00	70.00	400
1876/5 L	—	25.00	50.00	120	450
1876 L	—	12.00	25.00	70.00	400
1876. L	—	—	—	—	—
1877 L	26,000	15.00	30.00	85.00	450
1878 L	—	12.00	25.00	70.00	400
1879 L	—	25.00	50.00	120	450
1880 L	57,000	12.00	25.00	70.00	400
1881 L	18,000	15.00	30.00	80.00	450
1884 L	6,286	65.00	120	250	650
1885As/HoL	21,000	15.00	35.00	90.00	450
1888 L	—	4,000	5,000	7,000	—

Mint: Chihuahua
KM# 407.1   50 CENTAVOS
13.5360 g., 0.9030 Silver .3930 oz. ASW **Rev:** Balance scale
Note: Mint mark Ca, CHa.

Date	Mintage	F	VF	XF	Unc
1883 M	12,000	30.00	60.00	125	500
1884 M	—	25.00	50.00	125	500
1885 M	13,000	15.00	35.00	90.00	400
1886 M	18,000	20.00	40.00	100	450
1887 M	26,000	25.00	65.00	150	500

Mint: Culiacan
KM# 407.2   50 CENTAVOS
13.5360 g., 0.9030 Silver .3930 oz. ASW **Rev:** Balance scale

Date	Mintage	F	VF	XF	Unc
1871Cn P	—	400	550	750	1,500
1873Cn P	—	400	550	750	1,500
1874Cn P	—	200	300	500	1,000
1875/4Cn P	—	20.00	40.00	75.00	450
1875Cn P	—	12.00	25.00	50.00	450
1876Cn P	—	15.00	30.00	60.00	450
1877/6Cn G	—	15.00	30.00	60.00	450
1877Cn G	—	12.00	25.00	50.00	450
1878Cn G	18,000	20.00	40.00	75.00	450
1878Cn/Mo D	Inc. above	30.00	60.00	100	450
1878Cn D	Inc. above	15.00	35.00	75.00	450
1879Cn D	—	12.00	25.00	50.00	450
1879Cn D/G	—	12.00	25.00	50.00	450
1880/8Cn D	—	15.00	30.00	60.00	450
1880Cn D	—	15.00	30.00	60.00	450
1881/0Cn D	188,000	15.00	30.00	60.00	450
1881Cn D	Inc. above	15.00	30.00	60.00	450
1881Cn G	Inc. above	125	175	275	550
1882Cn D	—	175	300	500	2,000
1882Gn G	—	100	250	300	1,000
1883 D	19,000	25.00	50.00	100	500
1885/3Cn M/H	9,254	30.00	60.00	100	500
1886Cn M/G	7,030	50.00	100	300	1,500
1886Cn M	Inc. above	40.00	80.00	150	800
1887Cn M	76,000	20.00	40.00	100	450
1888Cn M	—	4,000	6,000	—	—
1892Cn M	8,200	40.00	80.00	150	650

Mint: Durango
KM# 407.3　50 CENTAVOS
13.5360 g., 0.9030 Silver .3930 oz. ASW **Rev:** Balance scale

Date	Mintage	F	VF	XF	Unc
1871Do P Rare	591	—	—	—	—
1873Do P	4,010	150	250	500	1,250
1873Do M/P	Inc. above	150	250	500	1,250
1874Do M	—	20.00	40.00	175	750
1875Do M	—	20.00	40.00	80.00	350
1875Do H	—	150	250	450	1,000
1876/5Do M	—	35.00	70.00	150	500
1876Do M	—	35.00	70.00	150	500
1877Do P	2,000	30.00	45.00	150	1,250
1878Do B Rare	—	—	—	—	—
1879Do B Rare	—	—	—	—	—
1880Do P	—	30.00	60.00	125	500
1881Do P	10,000	40.00	80.00	150	550
1882Do C	8,957	30.00	75.00	200	800
1884/2Do C	—	20.00	50.00	125	600
1884Do C	—	—	—	—	—
1885Do B	—	15.00	40.00	100	500
1885Do B/P	—	15.00	40.00	100	500
1886Do C	16,000	15.00	40.00	100	500
1887Do/Mo C	28,000	15.00	40.00	100	500
1887Do C	—	15.00	40.00	100	500

Mint: Guanajuato
KM# 407.4　50 CENTAVOS
13.5360 g., 0.9030 Silver .3930 oz. ASW **Rev:** Balance scale
Note: Struck at Guanajuato Mint, mtn mark Go. Varieties exist.

Date	Mintage	F	VF	XF	Unc
1869Go S	—	15.00	35.00	75.00	550
1870Go S	166,000	12.00	25.00	50.00	450
1871Go S	148,000	12.00	25.00	50.00	450
1872/1Go S	144,000	15.00	30.00	60.00	500
1872Go S	Inc. above	12.00	25.00	50.00	450
1873Go S	50,000	12.00	25.00	50.00	450
1874Go S	—	12.00	25.00	50.00	450
1875Go S	—	15.00	35.00	75.00	450
1876/5Go S	—	12.00	25.00	50.00	450
1877Go S	76,000	12.00	25.00	60.00	450
1878Go S	37,000	15.00	30.00	75.00	550
1879/8Go S	—	15.00	30.00	60.00	500
1879Go S	—	12.00	25.00	50.00	450
1880Go S	—	12.00	25.00	50.00	450
1881/79Go S	32,000	15.00	30.00	60.00	500
1881Go S	Inc. above	12.00	25.00	50.00	450
1882Go S	18,000	12.00	25.00	50.00	450
1883/2Go B/S	—	15.00	30.00	60.00	500
1883Go B	—	12.00	25.00	50.00	450
1883Go S Rare	—	—	—	—	—
1884Go B/S	—	15.00	30.00	60.00	500
1885/4Go R/B	—	15.00	30.00	60.00	500
1885Go R	53,000	12.00	25.00	50.00	450
1886/5Go R/B	59,000	15.00	30.00	60.00	500
1886/5Go R/S	Inc. above	20.00	40.00	75.00	500
1886Go R	Inc. above	20.00	40.00	75.00	450
1887Go R	18,000	20.00	40.00	75.00	550
1888Go R 1 known; Rare	—	—	—	—	—

Mint: Hermosillo
KM# 407.5　50 CENTAVOS
13.5360 g., 0.9030 Silver .3930 oz. ASW **Rev:** Balance scale
Note: Varieties exist.

Date	Mintage	F	VF	XF	Unc
1874Ho R	—	20.00	40.00	100	600
1875/4Ho R	—	20.00	50.00	125	600
1875Ho R	—	20.00	50.00	125	600
1876/5Ho F/R	—	15.00	35.00	100	550
1876Ho F	—	15.00	35.00	100	550

Date	Mintage	F	VF	XF	Unc
1877Ho F	—	50.00	75.00	150	650
1880/70Ho A	—	15.00	35.00	100	550
1880Ho A	—	15.00	35.00	100	550
1881Ho A	13,000	15.00	35.00	100	550
1882Ho A	—	75.00	150	250	750
1888Ho G	—	2,000	3,000	6,000	—
1894Ho G	59,000	15.00	30.00	100	450
1895Ho G	8,000	250	350	700	1,500

Mint: Mexico City
KM# 407.6　50 CENTAVOS
13.5360 g., 0.9027 Silver .3930 oz. ASW **Rev:** Balance scale

Date	Mintage	F	VF	XF	Unc
1869Mo C	46,000	15.00	35.00	95.00	600
1870Mo C	52,000	15.00	30.00	90.00	550
1871Mo C	14,000	40.00	75.00	150	650
1871Mo M/C	Inc. above	35.00	75.00	150	600
1872/1Mo M	60,000	35.00	75.00	150	550
1872Mo M	Inc. above	35.00	75.00	150	550
1873Mo M	6,000	35.00	75.00	150	600
1874/3Mo M	—	200	400	600	1,250
1874/2Mo B	—	15.00	30.00	75.00	500
1874/2Mo B/M	—	15.00	30.00	75.00	500
1874/3Mo B/M	—	15.00	30.00	75.00	500
1874Mo B	—	15.00	30.00	75.00	500
1875Mo B	—	15.00	30.00	75.00	550
1876/5Mo B	—	15.00	30.00	75.00	500
1876Mo B	—	12.00	25.00	75.00	500
1877/2Mo M	—	20.00	40.00	100	550
1877Mo M	—	15.00	30.00	90.00	500
1878/7Mo M	8,000	25.00	50.00	125	600
1878Mo M	Inc. above	15.00	35.00	100	550
1879Mo M	—	25.00	50.00	125	550
1880Mo M	—	100	150	250	750
1881Mo M	16,000	25.00	50.00	125	600
1881/0Mo M	—	30.00	50.00	125	600
1882/1Mo M	2,000	30.00	60.00	150	750
1883/2Mo M	4,000	150	225	350	1,000
1884Mo M	—	150	225	350	1,000
1885Mo M	12,000	30.00	60.00	150	600
1886/5Mo M	66,000	15.00	35.00	90.00	475
1886Mo M	Inc. above	12.00	25.00	75.00	450
1887/6Mo M	88,000	15.00	35.00	90.00	475
1887Mo M	Inc. above	15.00	35.00	75.00	475
1888Mo M	—	3,000	4,000	6,000	—

Mint: San Luis Potosi
KM# 407.7　50 CENTAVOS
13.5360 g., 0.9030 Silver .3930 oz. ASW **Rev:** Balance scale

Date	Mintage	F	VF	XF	Unc
1870 Pi G	Inc. above	20.00	40.00	100	450
1870/780 Pi G	50,000	25.00	45.00	110	500
1870 Pi O	Inc. above	20.00	40.00	100	450
1871 Pi O	—	15.00	30.00	80.00	400
1871 Pi O/G	64,000	15.00	30.00	80.00	400
1872 Pi O	52,000	15.00	30.00	80.00	400
1872 Pi O/G	Inc. above	15.00	30.00	80.00	400
1873 Pi O	32,000	20.00	40.00	100	450
1873 Pi H	Inc. above	25.00	50.00	125	550
1874 Pi H/O	—	15.00	30.00	80.00	400
1875/3 Pi H	—	15.00	30.00	80.00	400
1875 Pi H	—	15.00	30.00	80.00	400
1876 Pi H	—	30.00	60.00	150	700
1877 Pi H	34,000	20.00	40.00	100	450
1878 Pi H	9,700	20.00	40.00	100	450
1879/7 Pi H	—	15.00	35.00	90.00	450
1879 Pi H	—	15.00	35.00	90.00	400
1880 Pi H	—	20.00	40.00	100	450
1881 Pi H	28,000	20.00	40.00	100	450

Date	Mintage	F	VF	XF	Unc
1882 Pi H	22,000	15.00	30.00	80.00	400
1883 Pi H 8/8	29,000	50.00	100	200	750
1883 Pi H	Inc. above	15.00	30.00	80.00	400
1884 Pi H	—	50.00	100	175	600
1885/3 Pi H	—	20.00	40.00	100	450
1885/0 Pi H	45,000	20.00	40.00	100	450
1885/4 Pi H	Inc. above	20.00	40.00	100	450
1885 Pi H	Inc. above	25.00	50.00	125	450
1885 Pi C	Inc. above	15.00	30.00	80.00	400
1886/1 Pi R	92,000	50.00	100	175	600
1886/1 Pi C	—	25.00	40.00	100	450
1886 Pi C	Inc. above	15.00	30.00	80.00	400
1886 Pi R	Inc. above	15.00	30.00	80.00	400
1887 Pi R	32,000	15.00	30.00	90.00	450

Mint: Zacatecas
KM# 407.8   50 CENTAVOS
13.5360 g., 0.9030 Silver .3930 oz. ASW **Rev:** Balance scale
Note: Varieties exist.

Date	Mintage	F	VF	XF	Unc
1870Zs H	86,000	12.00	25.00	60.00	450
1871Zs H	146,000	12.00	25.00	50.00	400
1872Zs H	132,000	12.00	25.00	50.00	400
1873Zs H	56,000	12.00	25.00	50.00	400
1874Zs H	—	12.00	25.00	50.00	400
1874Zs A Rare	—	—	—	—	—
1875Zs A	—	12.00	25.00	50.00	400
1876/5Zs A	—	15.00	30.00	60.00	450
1876Zs A	—	12.00	25.00	50.00	400
1876Zs S	—	100	200	350	750
1877Zs S	100,000	12.00	25.00	50.00	400
1878/7Zs S	254,000	15.00	30.00	60.00	450
1878Zs S	Inc. above	15.00	30.00	60.00	400
1879Zs S	—	12.00	25.00	50.00	400
1880Zs S	—	12.00	25.00	50.00	400
1881Zs S	201,000	12.00	25.00	50.00	400
1882/1Zs S	2,000	50.00	100	250	650
1882Zs S	Inc. above	50.00	100	250	650
1883Zs/Za S	31,000	30.00	60.00	100	450
1883Zs S	Inc. above	25.00	50.00	100	450
1884/3Zs S	—	15.00	30.00	60.00	450
1884Zs S	—	12.00	25.00	50.00	400
1885/4Zs S	2,000	25.00	50.00	125	450
1885Zs S	Inc. above	25.00	50.00	125	450
1886Zs Z	2,000	150	275	400	1,000
1887Zs Z	63,000	30.00	60.00	125	450

Mint: Chihuahua
KM# 408   PESO
27.0730 g., 0.9030 Silver .7860 oz. ASW **Rev:** Balance scale

Date	Mintage	F	VF	XF	Unc
1872CH M	Inc. above	17.50	25.00	50.00	250
1872CH P/M	747,000	750	1,500	3,500	—
1872CH P	Inc. above	350	700	1,500	—
1872/1CH M	Inc. above	25.00	40.00	75.00	400
1873CH M	320,000	20.00	30.00	60.00	265
1873CH M/P	Inc. above	25.00	40.00	75.00	350

Mint: Culiacan
KM# 408.1   PESO
27.0730 g., 0.9030 Silver .7860 oz. ASW **Rev:** Balance scale

Date	Mintage	F	VF	XF	Unc
1870Cn E	—	40.00	80.00	150	500
1871/11Cn P	478,000	25.00	45.00	100	450
1871Cn P	Inc. above	20.00	40.00	75.00	300
1872/1Cn P	—	20.00	40.00	75.00	300
1872Cn P	209,000	20.00	40.00	75.00	300
1873Cn P narrow date	527,000	20.00	40.00	75.00	300
1873Cn P wide date	Inc. above	20.00	40.00	75.00	300

Mint: Durango
KM# 408.2   PESO
27.0730 g., 0.9027 Silver .7860 oz. ASW **Rev:** Balance scale

Date	Mintage	F	VF	XF	Unc
1870Do P	—	50.00	100	175	450
1871Do P	427,000	25.00	50.00	75.00	300
1872Do P	296,000	20.00	40.00	75.00	350
1872Do PT	Inc. above	100	175	250	850
1873Do P	203,000	25.00	45.00	85.00	350

Mint: Guadalajara
KM# 408.3   PESO
27.0730 g., 0.9030 Silver .7860 oz. ASW **Rev:** Balance scale

Date	Mintage	F	VF	XF	Unc
1870Ga C	—	650	850	—	—
1871Ga C	829,000	25.00	65.00	135	600
1872Ga C	485,000	40.00	90.00	175	650
1873/2Ga C	277,000	40.00	90.00	175	700
1873Ga C	Inc. above	25.00	65.00	135	600

Mint: Guanajuato
KM# 408.4   PESO
27.0730 g., 0.9027 Silver .7860 oz. ASW **Rev:** Balance scale

Date	Mintage	F	VF	XF	Unc
1871/0Go S	3,946,000	30.00	50.00	90.00	350
1871/3Go S	Inc. above	20.00	35.00	70.00	275
1871Go S	Inc. above	12.00	20.00	40.00	220
1872Go S	4,067,000	12.00	20.00	40.00	250
1873/2Go S	1,560,000	15.00	25.00	50.00	250
1873Go S	Inc. above	12.00	20.00	45.00	250
1873Go/Mo/S/M	Inc. above	12.00	20.00	45.00	250

Mint: Mexico City
KM# 408.5 PESO
27.0730 g., 0.9030 Silver .7860 oz. ASW **Rev:** Balance scale

Date	Mintage	F	VF	XF	Unc
1869Mo C	—	35.00	65.00	135	600
1870/69Mo C	5,115,000	15.00	25.00	55.00	275
1870Mo C	Inc. above	12.00	20.00	40.00	250
1870Mo M/C	Inc. above	18.00	30.00	60.00	275
1870Mo M	Inc. above	18.00	30.00	60.00	275
1871/0Mo M	6,974,000	15.00	25.00	55.00	275
1871Mo M	Inc. above	12.00	20.00	40.00	250
1872/1Mo M	—	15.00	25.00	50.00	275
1872/1Mo M/C	4,801,000	15.00	25.00	50.00	275
1872Mo M	Inc. above	12.00	20.00	40.00	250
1873Mo M	1,765,000	12.00	20.00	40.00	250

Note: The 1869 C with large LEY on the scroll is a pattern

Mint: Oaxaca
KM# 408.6 PESO
27.0730 g., 0.9030 Silver .7860 oz. ASW **Rev:** Balance scale

Date	Mintage	F	VF	XF	Unc
1869 Oa E	—	275	400	600	2,000
1870 Oa E Small A	Inc. above	15.00	30.00	75.00	400
1870OA E Large A	Inc. above	100	150	300	900
1871/69 Oa E	140,000	30.00	50.00	125	550
1871 Oa E Small A	Inc. above	15.00	30.00	60.00	300
1871 Oa E Large A	Inc. above	15.00	30.00	75.00	400
1872 Oa E Small A	180,000	15.00	30.00	75.00	400
1872 Oa E Large A	Inc. above	50.00	100	200	450
1873 Oa E	105,000	15.00	30.00	75.00	350

Mint: San Luis Potosi
KM# 408.7 PESO
27.0730 g., 0.9030 Silver .7860 oz. ASW **Rev:** Balance scale
Note: Varieties exist.

Date	Mintage	F	VF	XF	Unc
1870 Pi S	1,967,000	200	350	500	1,000
1870 Pi S/A	Inc. above	200	350	550	1,200
1870 Pi G	Inc. above	25.00	40.00	75.00	550
1870 Pi H Contemporary counterfeits	Inc. above	—	—	—	—
1870 Pi O/G	Inc. above	25.00	40.00	75.00	550
1870 Pi O	Inc. above	20.00	30.00	100	400
1871/69 Pi O	2,103,000	75.00	100	200	500
1871 Pi O/G	Inc. above	15.00	30.00	60.00	500
1871 Pi O	—	15.00	30.00	60.00	500
1872 Pi O	1,873,000	15.00	30.00	60.00	500
1873 Pi O	893,000	15.00	30.00	60.00	500
1873 Pi H	Inc. above	15.00	30.00	60.00	500

Mint: Zacatecas
KM# 408.8 PESO
27.0730 g., 0.9030 Silver .7860 oz. ASW **Rev:** Balance scale
Note: Varieties exist.

Date	Mintage	F	VF	XF	Unc
1870Zs H	4,519,000	12.00	30.00	40.00	220
1871Zs H	4,459,000	12.00	20.00	40.00	220
1872Zs H	4,039,000	12.00	20.00	40.00	220
1873/1Zs H	Inc. above	12.00	20.00	40.00	220
1873Zs H	1,782,000	12.00	20.00	40.00	220

Mint: Culiacan
KM# 409 PESO
27.0730 g., 0.9030 Silver .7860 oz. ASW **Rev:** Liberty cap

Date	Mintage	F	VF	XF	Unc
1898Cn AM	1,720,000	10.00	15.00	25.00	65.00
1898Cn/MoAM	Inc. above	15.00	30.00	90.00	150
1899Cn AM	1,722,000	25.00	50.00	90.00	175
1899Cn JQ	Inc. above	10.00	15.00	50.00	125
1900Cn JQ	1,804,000	10.00	15.00	25.00	75.00
1901Cn JQ	1,473,000	10.00	15.00	25.00	75.00
1902Cn JQ	1,194,000	10.00	15.00	45.00	125
1903Cn JQ	1,514,000	10.00	15.00	30.00	85.00
1903Cn FV	Inc. above	25.00	50.00	100	225
1904Cn MH	1,554,000	10.00	15.00	25.00	75.00
1904Cn RP	Inc. above	50.00	100	150	350
1905Cn RP	598,000	25.00	50.00	100	250

Mint: Guanajuato
KM# 409.1 PESO
27.0730 g., 0.9030 Silver .7860 oz. ASW **Rev:** Liberty cap
Note: Varieties exist.

Date	Mintage	F	VF	XF	Unc
1898Go RS	4,256,000	10.00	15.00	35.00	75.00
1898Go/MoRS	Inc. above	20.00	30.00	60.00	125
1899Go RS	3,207,000	10.00	15.00	30.00	75.00
1900Go RS	1,489,000	25.00	50.00	100	250

Mint: Mexico City
KM# 409.2 PESO
27.0730 g., 0.9027 Silver .7860 oz. ASW **Rev:** Liberty cap
Note: Varieties exist.

Date	Mintage	F	VF	XF	Unc
1898Mo AM Original strike - reverse with 139 beads	10,156,000	9.00	11.50	18.50	60.00
1898Mo AM Restrike (1949) - reverse with 134 beads	10,250,000	9.00	11.50	16.50	40.00
1899Mo AM	7,930,000	10.00	12.50	20.00	70.00
1900Mo AM	8,226,000	10.00	12.50	20.00	70.00
1901Mo AM	14,505,000	9.00	11.50	20.00	70.00
1902/1Mo AM	16,224,000	150	300	500	950
1902Mo AM	Inc. above	9.00	11.50	20.00	70.00
1903Mo AM	22,396,000	9.00	11.50	20.00	70.00
1903Mo AM (Error)	Inc. above	1,500	2,500	3,500	7,500
1904Mo AM	14,935,000	9.00	11.50	20.00	70.00
1905Mo AM	3,557,000	15.00	25.00	55.00	125
1908Mo AM	7,575,000	10.00	12.50	20.00	60.00
1908Mo GV	Inc. above	10.00	12.50	18.50	40.00
1909Mo GV	2,924,000	10.00	12.50	18.50	40.00

Mint: Zacatecas
KM# 409.3 PESO
27.0730 g., 0.9030 Silver .7860 oz. ASW **Rev:** Liberty cap
Note: Struck at Zacatecas Mint, mint mark Zs. Varieties exist.

Date	Mintage	F	VF	XF	Unc
1898Zs FZ	5,714,000	10.00	12.50	20.00	60.00
1899Zs FZ	5,618,000	10.00	12.50	20.00	65.00
1900Zs FZ	5,357,000	10.00	12.50	20.00	60.00
1901Zs FZ	Inc. above	10.00	12.50	20.00	55.00
1901Zs AZ	5,706,000	4,000	6,500	10,000	—
1902Zs FZ	7,134,000	10.00	12.50	20.00	55.00
1903/2Zs FZ	3,080,000	12.50	15.00	50.00	125
1903Zs FZ	Inc. above	10.00	12.50	20.00	65.00
1904Zs FZ	2,423,000	10.00	15.00	25.00	85.00
1904Zs FM	Inc. above	10.00	15.00	25.00	75.00
1905Zs FM	995,000	20.00	40.00	60.00	150

Mint: Alamos
KM# 410 PESO
1.6920 g., 0.8750 Gold .0476 oz. AGW

Date	Mintage	F	VF	XF	Unc
1888AsL/MoM Rare	—	—	—	—	—
1888 As L Rare	—	—	—	—	—

Mint: Chihuahua
KM# 410.1 PESO
1.6920 g., 0.8750 Gold .0476 oz. AGW

Date	Mintage	F	VF	XF	Unc
1888Ca/MoM Rare	104	—	—	—	—

Mint: Culiacan
KM# 410.2 PESO
1.6920 g., 0.8750 Gold .0476 oz. AGW

Date	Mintage	F	VF	XF	Unc
1873Cn P	1,221	75.00	100	150	250
1875Cn P	—	85.00	125	150	250
1878Cn G	248	100	175	225	475
1879Cn D	—	100	150	175	285
1881/0Cn D	338	100	150	175	285
1882Cn D	340	100	150	175	285
1883Cn D	—	100	150	175	285
1884Cn M	—	100	150	175	285
1886/4Cn M	277	100	150	225	450
1888/7Cn M	2,586	100	175	225	450
1888Cn M	Inc. above	65.00	100	150	265
1889Cn M Rare	—	—	—	—	—
1891/89Cn M	969	75.00	100	150	265
1892Cn M	780	75.00	100	150	265
1893Cn M	498	85.00	125	150	265
1894Cn M	493	80.00	125	150	265
1895Cn M	1,143	65.00	100	150	250
1896/5Cn M	1,028	65.00	100	150	250
1897Cn M	785	65.00	100	150	250
1898Cn M	3,521	65.00	100	150	225
1898Cn/MoM	Inc. above	65.00	100	150	250
1899Cn Q	2,000	65.00	100	150	225
1901/0Cn Q	2,350	65.00	100	150	225
1902Cn Q	2,480	65.00	100	150	225
1902Cn/MoQ/C	Inc. above	65.00	100	150	225
1904Cn H	3,614	65.00	100	150	225
1904Cn/Mo/ H	Inc. above	65.00	100	150	250
1905Cn P	1,000	—	—	—	—

Note: Reported, not confirmed

Mint: Guanajuato
KM# 410.3 PESO
1.6920 g., 0.8750 Gold .0476 oz. AGW

Date	Mintage	F	VF	XF	Unc
1870Go S	—	100	125	150	265
1871Go S	500	100	175	225	475
1888Go R	210	125	200	250	550
1890Go R	1,916	75.00	100	150	265
1892Go R	533	100	150	175	350
1894Go R	180	150	200	250	550
1895Go R	676	100	150	175	325
1896/5Go R	4,671	65.00	100	150	250
1897/6Go R	4,280	65.00	100	150	250
1897Go R	Inc. above	65.00	100	150	250
1898Go R Regular obverse	5,193	65.00	100	150	250
1898Go R Mule, 5 Centavos obverse, normal reverse	Inc. above	75.00	100	150	250
1899Go R	2,748	65.00	100	150	250
1900/800Go R	864	75.00	125	150	285

Mint: Hermosillo
KM# 410.4 PESO
1.6920 g., 0.8750 Gold .0476 oz. AGW

Date	Mintage	F	VF	XF	Unc
1875Ho R Rare	310	—	—	—	—
1876Ho F Rare	—	—	—	—	—
1888Ho G/MoM Rare	—	—	—	—	—

Mint: Mexico City
KM# 410.5 PESO
1.6920 g., 0.8750 Gold .0476 oz. AGW

Date	Mintage	F	VF	XF	Unc
1870Mo C	2,540	40.00	60.00	90.00	185
1871Mo M/C	1,000	50.00	100	150	250

Date	Mintage	F	VF	XF	Unc
1872Mo M/C	3,000	40.00	60.00	90.00	185
1873/1Mo M	2,900	40.00	60.00	90.00	185
1873Mo M	Inc. above	40.00	60.00	90.00	185
1874Mo M	—	40.00	60.00	90.00	185
1875Mo B/M	—	40.00	60.00	90.00	185
1876/5Mo B/M	—	40.00	60.00	90.00	185
1877Mo M	—	40.00	60.00	90.00	185
1878Mo M	2,000	40.00	60.00	90.00	185
1879Mo M	—	40.00	60.00	90.00	185
1880/70Mo M	—	40.00	60.00	90.00	185
1881/71Mo M	1,000	40.00	60.00	90.00	185
1882/72Mo M	—	40.00	60.00	90.00	185
1883/72Mo M	1,000	40.00	60.00	90.00	185
1884Mo M	—	40.00	60.00	90.00	185
1885/71Mo M	—	40.00	60.00	90.00	185
1885Mo M	—	40.00	60.00	90.00	185
1886Mo M	1,700	40.00	60.00	90.00	185
1887Mo M	2,200	40.00	60.00	90.00	185
1888Mo M	1,000	40.00	60.00	90.00	185
1889Mo M	500	100	150	200	285
1890Mo M	570	100	150	200	285
1891Mo M	746	100	150	200	285
1892/0Mo M	2,895	40.00	60.00	90.00	185
1893Mo M	5,917	40.00	60.00	90.00	185
1894/3MMo	—	40.00	60.00	90.00	185
1894Mo M	6,244	40.00	60.00	90.00	185
1895Mo M	8,994	40.00	60.00	90.00	185
1895Mo B	Inc. above	40.00	60.00	90.00	185
1896Mo B	7,166	40.00	60.00	90.00	185
1896Mo M	Inc. above	40.00	60.00	90.00	185
1897Mo M	5,131	40.00	60.00	90.00	185
1898/7Mo M	5,368	40.00	60.00	90.00	185
1899Mo M	9,515	40.00	60.00	90.00	185
1900/800Mo M	9,301	40.00	60.00	90.00	185
1900/880Mo M	Inc. above	40.00	60.00	90.00	185
1900/890Mo M	Inc. above	40.00	60.00	90.00	185
1900Mo M	Inc. above	40.00	60.00	90.00	185
1901Mo M Small date	Inc. above	40.00	60.00	90.00	185
1901/801Mo M Large date	8,293	40.00	60.00	90.00	185
1902Mo M Large date	11,000	40.00	60.00	90.00	185
1902Mo M Small date	Inc. above	40.00	60.00	90.00	185
1903Mo M Large date	10,000	40.00	60.00	90.00	185
1903Mo M Small date	Inc. above	50.00	80.00	120	200
1904Mo M	9,845	40.00	60.00	90.00	185
1905Mo M	3,429	40.00	60.00	90.00	185

Mint: Zacatecas
KM# 410.6 PESO
1.6920 g., 0.8750 Gold .0476 oz. AGW

Date	Mintage	F	VF	XF	Unc
1872Zs H	2,024	125	150	175	275
1875/3Zs A	—	125	150	200	325
1878Zs S	—	125	150	175	275
1888Zs Z	280	175	225	325	700
1889Zs Z	492	150	175	225	450
1890Zs Z	738	150	175	225	450

Mint: Alamos
KM# 411 2-1/2 PESOS
4.2300 g., 0.8750 Gold .1190 oz. AGW

Date	Mintage	F	VF	XF	Unc
1888As/MoL Rare	—	—	—	—	—

Mint: Culiacan
KM# 411.1 2-1/2 PESOS
4.2300 g., 0.8750 Gold .1190 oz. AGW

Date	Mintage	F	VF	XF	Unc
1893Cn M	141	1,500	2,000	2,500	3,500

Mint: Durango
KM# 411.2 2-1/2 PESOS
4.2300 g., 0.8750 Gold .1190 oz. AGW

Date	Mintage	F	VF	XF	Unc
1888Do C Rare	—	—	—	—	—

Mint: Guanajuato
KM# 411.3 2-1/2 PESOS
4.2300 g., 0.8750 Gold .1190 oz. AGW

Date	Mintage	F	VF	XF	Unc
1871Go S	600	1,250	2,000	2,500	3,250
1888Go/MoR	110	1,750	2,250	2,750	3,500

Mint: Hermosillo
KM# 411.4   2-1/2 PESOS
4.2300 g., 0.8750 Gold .1190 oz. AGW

Date	Mintage	F	VF	XF	Unc
1874Ho R Rare	—	—	—	—	—
1888Ho G Rare	—	—	—	—	—

Mint: Mexico City
KM# 411.5   2-1/2 PESOS
4.2300 g., 0.8750 Gold .1190 oz. AGW

Date	Mintage	F	VF	XF	Unc
1870Mo C	820	150	250	350	750
1872Mo M/C	800	150	250	350	750
1873/2Mo M	—	200	350	750	1,350
1874Mo M	—	200	350	750	1,350
1874Mo B/M	—	200	350	750	1,350
1875Mo B	—	200	350	750	1,350
1876Mo B	—	250	500	1,000	1,600
1877Mo M	—	200	350	750	1,350
1878Mo M	400	200	350	750	1,350
1879Mo M	—	200	350	750	1,350
1880/79Mo M	—	200	350	750	1,350
1881Mo M	400	200	350	750	1,350
1882Mo M	—	200	350	750	1,350
1883/73Mo M	400	200	350	750	1,350
1884Mo M	—	250	500	1,000	1,600
1885Mo M	—	200	350	750	1,350
1886Mo M	400	200	350	750	1,350
1887Mo M	400	200	350	750	1,350
1888Mo M	540	200	350	750	1,350
1889Mo M	240	150	300	525	950
1890Mo M	420	200	350	750	1,350
1891Mo M	188	200	350	750	1,350
1892Mo M	240	200	350	750	1,350

Mint: Zacatecas
KM# 411.6   2-1/2 PESOS
4.2300 g., 0.8750 Gold .1190 oz. AGW

Date	Mintage	F	VF	XF	Unc
1872Zs H	1,300	200	350	500	1,200
1873Zs H	—	175	325	450	850
1875/3Zs A	—	200	350	750	1,350
1877Zs S	—	200	350	750	1,350
1878Zs S	300	200	350	750	1,350
1888Zs/MoS	80	300	500	1,000	1,800
1889Zs/Mo Z	184	250	450	950	1,600
1890Zs Z	326	200	350	750	1,350

Mint: Alamos
KM# 412   5 PESOS
8.4600 g., 0.8750 Gold .2380 oz. AGW

Date	Mintage	F	VF	XF	Unc
1875 As L	—	—	—	—	—
1878 As L	383	900	1,700	3,000	4,500

Mint: Chihuahua
KM# 412.1   5 PESOS
8.4600 g., 0.8750 Gold .2380 oz. AGW

Date	Mintage	F	VF	XF	Unc
1888 Ca M Rare	120	—	—	—	—

Mint: Culiacan
KM# 412.2   5 PESOS
8.4600 g., 0.8750 Gold .2380 oz. AGW

Date	Mintage	F	VF	XF	Unc
1873Cn P	—	300	600	1,000	1,500
1874Cn P	—	—	—	—	—
1875Cn P	—	300	500	700	1,250
1876Cn P	—	300	500	700	1,250
1877Cn G	—	300	500	700	1,250
1882Cn Rare	174	—	—	—	—
1888Cn M	—	500	1,000	1,350	2,000
1890Cn M	435	250	500	750	1,250
1891Cn M	1,390	250	400	500	1,000
1894Cn M	484	250	500	750	1,600
1895Cn M	142	500	750	1,500	2,500
1900Cn Q	1,536	150	300	400	900
1903Cn Q	1,000	150	300	400	750

Mint: Durango
KM# 412.3   5 PESOS
8.4600 g., 0.8750 Gold .2380 oz. AGW

Date	Mintage	F	VF	XF	Unc
1873/2Do P	—	700	1,250	1,800	3,000
1877Do P	—	700	1,250	1,800	3,000
1878Do E	—	700	1,250	1,800	3,000
1879/7Do B	—	700	1,250	1,800	3,000
1879Do B	—	700	1,250	1,800	3,000

Mint: Guanajuato
KM# 412.4   5 PESOS
8.4600 g., 0.8750 Gold .2380 oz. AGW

Date	Mintage	F	VF	XF	Unc
1871Go S	1,600	400	800	1,250	2,500
1887Go R	140	600	1,200	1,500	2,750
1888Go R Rare	65	—	—	—	—
1893Go R Rare	16	—	—	—	—

Mint: Hermosillo
KM# 412.5   5 PESOS
8.4600 g., 0.8750 Gold .2380 oz. AGW

Date	Mintage	F	VF	XF	Unc
1877Ho R	990	750	1,250	2,000	3,000
1877Ho A	Inc. above	650	1,100	1,750	2,750
1888Ho G Rare	—	—	—	—	—
1874Ho R	—	1,750	2,500	3,000	4,500

Mint: Mexico City
KM# 412.6   5 PESOS
8.4600 g., 0.8750 Gold .2380 oz. AGW

Date	Mintage	F	VF	XF	Unc
1870Mo C	550	200	400	550	900
1871/69Mo M	1,600	150	300	400	650
1871Mo M	Inc. above	150	300	400	650
1872Mo M	1,600	150	300	400	650
1873/2Mo M	—	200	400	550	850
1874Mo M	—	200	400	550	850
1875/3Mo B/M	—	200	400	550	950
1875Mo B	—	200	400	550	950
1876/5Mo B/M	—	200	400	550	1,000
1877Mo M	—	250	450	750	1,250
1878/7Mo M	400	200	400	550	1,250
1878Mo M	Inc. above	200	400	550	1,250
1879/8Mo M	—	200	400	550	1,250
1880Mo M	—	200	400	550	1,250
1881Mo M	—	200	400	550	1,250
1882Mo M	200	250	450	750	1,250
1883Mo M	200	250	450	750	1,250
1884Mo M	—	250	450	750	1,250
1886Mo M	200	250	450	750	1,250
1887Mo M	200	250	450	750	1,250
1888Mo M	250	200	400	550	1,250
1889Mo M	190	250	450	750	1,250
1890Mo M	149	250	450	750	1,250
1891Mo M	156	250	450	750	1,250
1892Mo M	214	250	450	750	1,250

Date	Mintage	F	VF	XF	Unc
1893Mo M	1,058	200	400	500	800
1897Mo M	370	200	400	550	1,000
1898Mo M	376	200	400	550	1,000
1900Mo M	1,014	150	300	400	650
1901Mo M	1,071	150	300	400	650
1902Mo M	1,478	150	300	400	650
1903Mo M	1,162	150	300	400	650
1904Mo M	1,415	150	300	400	650
1905Mo M	563	200	400	550	1,500

Mint: Zacatecas
KM# 412.7 5 PESOS
8.4600 g., 0.8750 Gold .2380 oz. AGW

Date	Mintage	F	VF	XF	Unc
1874Zs A	—	250	500	750	1,500
1875Zs A	—	200	400	500	1,000
1877Zs S/A	—	200	400	550	1,000
1878/7Zs S/A	—	200	400	550	1,000
1883Zs S	—	150	300	450	700
1888Zs Z	70	1,000	1,500	2,000	3,000
1889Zs Z	373	200	300	500	850
1892Zs Z	1,229	150	300	450	700

Mint: Alamos
KM# 413 10 PESOS
16.9200 g., 0.8750 Gold .4760 oz. AGW **Rev:** Balance scale

Date	Mintage	F	VF	XF	Unc
1874 As DL Rare	—	—	—	—	—
1875 As L	642	600	1,250	2,500	3,500
1878 As L	977	500	1,000	2,000	3,000
1879 As L	1,078	500	1,000	2,000	3,000
1880 As L	2,629	500	1,000	2,000	3,000
1881 As L	2,574	500	1,000	2,000	3,000
1882 As L	3,403	500	1,000	2,000	3,000
1883 As L	3,597	500	1,000	2,000	3,000
1884 As L Rare	—	—	—	—	—
1885 As L	4,562	500	1,000	2,000	3,000
1886 As L	4,643	500	1,000	2,000	3,000
1887 As L	3,667	500	1,000	2,000	3,000
1888 As L	4,521	500	1,000	2,000	3,000
1889 As L	5,615	500	1,000	2,000	3,000
1890 As L	4,920	500	1,000	2,000	3,000
1891 As L	568	500	1,000	2,000	3,000
1892 As L	—	—	—	—	—
1893 As L	817	500	1,000	2,000	3,000
1894/3 As L	1,658	—	—	—	—
1894 As L	Inc. above	500	1,000	2,000	3,000
1895 As L	1,237	500	1,000	2,000	3,000

Mint: Chihuahua
KM# 413.1 10 PESOS
16.9200 g., 0.8750 Gold .4760 oz. AGW **Rev:** Balance scale

Date	Mintage	F	VF	XF	Unc
1888 Ca M	175	—	—	7,500	—

Mint: Culiacan
KM# 413.2 10 PESOS
16.9200 g., 0.8750 Gold .4760 oz. AGW **Rev:** Balance scale

Date	Mintage	F	VF	XF	Unc
1881Cn D	—	400	600	1,000	1,750
1882Cn D	874	400	600	1,000	1,750
1882Cn E	Inc. above	400	600	1,000	1,750
1883Cn D	221	—	—	—	—
1883Cn M	Inc. above	400	600	1,000	1,750
1884Cn D	—	400	600	1,000	1,750
1884Cn M	—	400	600	1,000	1,750
1885Cn M	1,235	400	600	1,000	1,750
1886Cn M	981	400	600	1,000	1,750
1887Cn M	2,289	400	600	1,000	1,750
1888Cn M	767	400	600	1,000	1,750
1889Cn M	859	400	600	1,000	1,750
1890Cn M	1,427	400	600	1,000	1,750
1891Cn M	670	400	600	1,000	1,750
1892Cn M	379	400	600	1,000	1,750
1893Cn M	1,806	400	600	1,000	1,750
1895Cn M	179	500	1,000	1,500	2,500
1903Cn Q	774	400	600	1,000	1,750

Mint: Durango
KM# 413.3 10 PESOS
16.9200 g., 0.8750 Gold .4760 oz. AGW **Rev:** Balance scale

Date	Mintage	F	VF	XF	Unc
1872Do P	1,755	350	500	800	1,250
1873/2Do P	1,091	350	550	900	1,450
1873/2Do M/P	Inc. above	350	550	900	1,450
1874Do M	—	350	550	900	1,450
1875Do M	—	350	550	900	1,450
1876Do M	—	450	750	1,250	2,000
1877Do P	—	350	550	900	1,450
1878Do E	582	350	550	900	1,450
1879/8Do B	—	350	550	900	1,450
1879Do B	—	350	550	900	1,450
1880Do P	2,030	350	550	900	1,450
1881/79Do P	2,617	350	550	900	1,450
1882Do P Rare	1,528	—	—	—	—
1882Do C	Inc. above	350	550	900	1,450
1883Do C	793	450	750	1,250	2,000
1884Do C	108	450	750	1,250	2,000

Mint: Guadalajara
KM# 413.4 10 PESOS
16.9200 g., 0.8750 Gold .4760 oz. AGW **Rev:** Balance scale

Date	Mintage	F	VF	XF	Unc
1870Ga C	490	500	800	1,000	1,550
1871Ga C	1,910	400	800	1,500	2,250
1872Ga C	780	500	1,000	2,000	2,500
1873Ga C	422	500	1,000	2,000	3,000
1874/3Ga C	477	500	1,000	2,000	3,000
1875Ga C	710	500	1,000	2,000	3,000
1878Ga A	183	600	1,200	2,500	3,500
1879Ga A	200	600	1,200	2,500	3,500
1880Ga S	404	500	1,000	2,000	3,000
1881Ga S	239	600	1,200	2,500	3,500
1891Ga S	196	600	1,200	2,500	3,500

Mint: Guanajuato
KM# 413.5 10 PESOS
16.9200 g., 0.8750 Gold .4760 oz. AGW **Rev:** Balance scale

Date	Mintage	F	VF	XF	Unc
1872Go S	1,400	2,000	4,000	6,500	10,000
1887Go R Rare	80	—	—	—	—

Note: Stack's Rio Grande Sale 6-93, P/L AU realized, $12,650

1888Go R Rare	68	—	—	—	—

Mint: Hermosillo
KM# 413.6 10 PESOS
16.9200 g., 0.8750 Gold .4760 oz. AGW **Rev:** Balance scale

Date	Mintage	F	VF	XF	Unc
1874Ho R Rare	—	—	—	—	—
1876Ho F Rare	357	—	—	—	—
1878Ho A	814	1,750	3,000	3,500	5,500
1879Ho A	—	1,000	2,000	2,500	4,000
1880Ho A	—	1,000	2,000	2,500	4,000
1881Ho A Rare	—	—	—	—	—

Mint: Mexico City
KM# 413.7 10 PESOS
16.9200 g., 0.8750 Gold .4760 oz. AGW **Rev:** Balance scale

Date	Mintage	F	VF	XF	Unc
1870Mo C	480	500	900	1,200	2,000
1872/1Mo M/C	2,100	350	550	900	1,350
1873Mo M	—	400	600	950	1,450
1874/3Mo M	—	400	600	950	1,450
1875Mo B/M	—	400	600	950	1,450
1876Mo B Rare	—	—	—	—	—
1878Mo M	300	400	600	950	1,450
1879Mo M	—	—	—	—	—

Date	Mintage	F	VF	XF	Unc
1881Mo M	100	500	1,000	1,600	2,500
1882Mo M	—	400	600	950	1,450
1883Mo M	100	600	1,000	1,600	2,500
1884Mo M	—	600	1,000	1,600	2,500
1885Mo M	—	400	600	950	1,450
1886Mo M	100	600	1,000	1,600	2,500
1887Mo M	100	600	1,000	1,625	2,750
1888Mo M	144	450	750	1,200	2,000
1889Mo M	88	600	1,000	1,600	2,500
1890Mo M	137	600	1,000	1,600	2,500
1891Mo M	133	600	1,000	1,600	2,500
1892Mo M	45	600	1,000	1,600	2,500
1893Mo M	1,361	350	550	900	1,350
1897Mo M	239	400	600	950	1,450
1898/7Mo M	244	425	625	1,000	1,750
1900Mo M	733	400	600	950	1,450
1901Mo M	562	350	500	800	1,250
1902Mo M	719	350	500	800	1,250
1903Mo M	713	350	500	800	1,250
1904Mo M	694	350	500	800	1,250
1905Mo M	401	400	600	950	1,500

Mint: Oaxaca
KM# 413.8   10 PESOS
16.9200 g., 0.8750 Gold .4760 oz. AGW **Rev:** Balance scale

Date	Mintage	F	VF	XF	Unc
1870 Oa E	4,614	400	600	900	1,350
1871 Oa E	2,705	400	600	900	1,350
1872 Oa E	5,897	400	600	900	1,350
1873 Oa E	3,537	400	600	950	1,500
1874 Oa E	2,205	400	600	1,200	1,800
1875 Oa E	312	450	750	1,400	2,250
1876 Oa E	766	450	750	1,400	2,250
1877 Oa E	463	450	750	1,400	2,250
1878 Oa E	229	450	750	1,400	2,250
1879 Oa E	210	450	750	1,400	2,250
1880 Oa E	238	450	750	1,400	2,250
1881 Oa E	961	400	600	1,200	2,000
1882 Oa E	170	600	1,000	1,500	2,500
1883 Oa E	111	600	1,000	1,500	2,500
1884 Oa E	325	450	750	1,400	2,250
1885 Oa E	370	450	750	1,400	2,250
1886 Oa E	400	450	750	1,400	2,250
1887 Oa E	—	700	1,250	2,250	4,000
1888 Oa E	—	—	—	—	—

Mint: Zacatecas
KM# 413.9   10 PESOS
16.9200 g., 0.8750 Gold .4760 oz. AGW **Rev:** Balance scale

Date	Mintage	F	VF	XF	Unc
1871Zs H	2,000	350	500	800	1,250
1872Zs H	3,092	300	500	750	1,150
1873Zs H	936	400	600	950	1,450
1874Zs H	—	400	600	950	1,450
1875/3Zs A	—	400	600	1,000	1,750
1876/5Zs S	—	400	600	1,000	1,750
1877Zs S/H	506	400	600	1,000	1,750
1878Zs S	711	400	600	1,000	1,750
1879/8Zs S	—	450	750	1,400	2,250
1879Zs S	—	450	750	1,400	2,250
1880Zs S	2,089	350	550	950	1,450
1881Zs S	736	400	600	1,000	1,750
1882Zs S	1,599	350	550	950	1,450
1883/2Zs S	256	400	600	1,000	1,750
1884/3Zs S	—	350	550	950	1,600
1884Zs S	—	350	550	950	1,600
1885Zs S	1,588	350	550	950	1,450
1886Zs S	5,364	350	550	950	1,450
1887Zs Z	2,330	350	550	950	1,450

Date	Mintage	F	VF	XF	Unc
1888Zs Z	4,810	350	550	950	1,450
1889Zs Z	6,154	300	500	750	1,250
1890Zs Z	1,321	350	550	950	1,450
1891Zs Z	1,930	350	550	950	1,450
1892Zs Z	1,882	350	550	950	1,450
1893Zs Z	2,899	350	550	950	1,450
1894Zs Z	2,501	350	550	950	1,450
1895Zs Z	1,217	350	550	950	1,450

Mint: Alamos
KM# 414   20 PESOS
33.8400 g., 0.8750 Gold .9520 oz. AGW **Rev:** Balance scale

Date	Mintage	F	VF	XF	Unc
1876 As L Rare	276	—	—	—	—
1877 As L Rare	166	—	—	—	—
1878 As L	—	—	—	—	—
1888 As L Rare	—	—	—	—	—

Mint: Chihuahua
KM# 414.1   20 PESOS
33.8400 g., 0.8750 Gold .9520 oz. AGW **Rev:** Balance scale
Note: Mint mark CH, Ca.

Date	Mintage	F	VF	XF	Unc
1872 M	995	500	700	1,000	2,500
1873 M	950	500	700	1,000	2,500
1874 M	1,116	450	675	950	2,500
1875 M	750	500	700	1,000	2,500
1876 M	600	500	800	1,250	2,750
1877 Rare	55	—	—	—	—
1882 M	1,758	450	675	950	2,500
1883 M	161	600	1,000	1,500	3,000
1884 M	496	500	700	1,000	2,500
1885 M	122	600	1,000	1,500	3,000
1887 M	550	500	700	1,000	2,500
1888 M	351	500	700	1,000	2,500
1889 M	464	500	700	1,000	2,500
1890 M	1,209	450	675	950	2,500
1891 M	2,004	425	650	900	2,250
1893 M	418	500	700	950	2,500
1895 M	133	600	1,000	1,500	3,000

Mint: Culiacan
KM# 414.2   20 PESOS
33.8400 g., 0.8750 Gold .9520 oz. AGW **Rev:** Balance scale

Date	Mintage	F	VF	XF	Unc
1870Cn E	3,749	450	675	950	2,000
1871Cn P	3,046	450	675	950	2,000
1872Cn P	972	450	675	950	2,000
1873Cn P	1,317	450	675	950	2,000
1874Cn P	—	450	675	950	2,000
1875Cn P	—	600	1,200	1,800	2,500
1876Cn P	—	450	675	950	2,000
1876Cn G	—	450	675	950	2,000
1877Cn G	167	600	1,000	1,500	3,000
1878Cn Rare	842	—	—	—	—
1881/0Cn D	2,039	—	—	—	—
1881Cn D	Inc. above	450	675	950	2,000
1882/1Cn D	736	450	675	950	2,000
1883Cn M	1,836	450	675	950	2,000
1884Cn M	—	450	675	950	2,000
1885Cn M	544	450	675	950	2,000
1886Cn M	882	450	675	950	2,000
1887Cn M	837	450	675	950	2,000
1888Cn M	473	450	675	950	2,000
1889Cn M	1,376	450	675	950	2,000
1890Cn M	—	450	675	950	2,000
1891Cn M	237	500	900	1,200	2,250
1892Cn M	526	450	675	950	2,000
1893Cn M	2,062	450	675	950	2,000
1894Cn M	4,516	450	675	950	2,000
1895Cn M	3,193	450	675	950	2,000
1896Cn M	4,072	450	675	950	2,000
1897/6Cn M	959	450	675	950	2,000
1897Cn M	Inc. above	450	675	950	2,000
1898Cn M	1,660	450	675	950	2,000
1899Cn M	1,243	450	675	950	2,000
1899Cn Q	Inc. above	500	900	1,200	2,250
1900Cn Q	1,558	450	675	950	2,000
1901Cn Q	Inc. above	450	675	950	2,000
1901/0Cn Q	1,496	—	—	—	—
1902Cn Q	1,059	450	675	950	2,000
1903Cn Q	1,121	450	675	950	2,000

Date	Mintage	F	VF	XF	Unc
1904Cn H	4,646	450	675	950	2,000
1905Cn P	1,738	500	900	1,200	2,250

Mint: Durango
KM# 414.3 20 PESOS
33.8400 g., 0.8750 Gold .9520 oz. AGW **Rev:** Balance scale

Date	Mintage	F	VF	XF	Unc
1870Do P	416	1,000	1,500	2,000	2,500
1871/0Do P	1,073	1,000	1,750	2,250	2,750
1871Do P	Inc. above	1,000	1,500	2,000	2,500
1872/1Do PT	—	1,500	3,000	4,500	7,000
1876Do M	—	1,000	1,500	2,000	2,500
1877Do P	94	1,500	2,250	2,750	3,250
1878Do Rare	258	—	—	—	—

Mint: Guanajuato
KM# 414.4 20 PESOS
33.8400 g., 0.8750 Gold .9520 oz. AGW **Rev:** Balance scale

Date	Mintage	F	VF	XF	Unc
1870Go S	3,250	425	650	900	1,500
1871Go S	20,000	425	650	900	1,500
1872Go S	18,000	425	650	900	1,500
1873Go S	7,000	425	650	900	1,500
1874Go S	—	425	650	900	1,500
1875Go S	—	425	650	900	1,500
1876Go S	—	425	650	900	1,500
1876Go M/S	—	—	—	—	—
1877Go M/S Rare	15,000	—	—	—	—
1877Go R	Inc. above	425	650	900	1,500
1877Go S Rare	Inc. above	—	—	—	—
1878/7Go M/S	13,000	650	1,250	2,000	2,800
1878Go M	Inc. above	650	1,250	2,000	2,800
1878Go S	Inc. above	425	650	900	1,500
1879Go S	8,202	500	800	1,200	2,300
1880Go S	7,375	425	650	900	1,500
1881Go S	4,909	425	650	900	1,500
1882Go S	4,020	425	650	900	1,500
1883/2Go B	3,705	500	750	1,150	2,250
1883Go B	Inc. above	425	650	900	1,500
1884Go B	1,798	425	650	900	1,500
1885Go B	2,660	425	650	900	1,500
1886Go R	1,090	550	800	1,250	2,500
1887Go R	1,009	550	800	1,250	2,500
1888Go R	1,011	550	800	1,250	2,500
1889Go R	956	550	800	1,250	2,500
1890Go R	879	550	800	1,250	2,500
1891Go R	818	550	800	1,250	2,500
1892Go R	730	550	800	1,250	2,500
1893Go R	3,343	425	650	1,000	2,000
1894/3Go R	6,734	425	650	900	1,500
1894Go R	Inc. above	425	650	900	1,500
1895/3Go R	7,118	425	650	900	1,500
1895Go R	Inc. above	425	650	900	1,500
1896Go R	9,219	425	650	900	1,500
1897/6Go R	6,781	425	650	900	1,500
1897Go R	Inc. above	425	650	900	1,500
1898Go R	7,710	425	650	900	1,500
1899Go R	8,527	425	650	900	1,500
1900Go R	4,512	550	800	1,250	2,350

Mint: Hermosillo
KM# 414.5 20 PESOS
33.8400 g., 0.8750 Gold .9520 oz. AGW **Rev:** Balance scale

Date	Mintage	F	VF	XF	Unc
1874Ho R Rare	—	—	—	—	—
1875Ho R Rare	—	—	—	—	—
1876Ho F Rare	—	—	—	—	—
1888Ho g Rare	—	—	—	—	—

Mint: Mexico City
KM# 414.6 20 PESOS
33.8400 g., 0.8750 Gold .9520 oz. AGW **Rev:** Balance scale

Date	Mintage	F	VF	XF	Unc
1870Mo C	14,000	420	600	850	1,450
1871Mo M	21,000	420	600	850	1,450
1872/1Mo M	11,000	420	600	850	1,600
1872Mo M	Inc. above	420	600	850	1,450
1873Mo M	5,600	420	600	850	1,450
1874/2Mo M	—	420	600	850	1,450
1874/2Mo B	—	450	700	1,000	1,600
1875Mo B	—	435	650	900	1,500
1876Mo B	—	435	650	900	1,500
1876Mo M Reported, not confirmed	—	—	—	—	—
1877Mo M	2,000	450	700	1,100	2,000
1878Mo M	7,000	435	650	900	1,500
1879Mo M	—	435	650	900	1,750
1880Mo M	—	435	650	900	1,750
1881/0Mo M	11,000	425	600	850	1,450
1881Mo M	Inc. above	425	600	850	1,450
1882/1Mo M	5,800	425	600	850	1,450
1882Mo M	Inc. above	425	600	850	1,450
1883/1Mo M	4,000	425	600	850	1,450
1883Mo M	Inc. above	425	600	850	1,450
1884/3Mo M	—	435	650	900	1,500
1884Mo M	—	435	650	900	1,500
1885Mo M	6,000	435	650	900	1,750
1886Mo M	10,000	420	600	850	1,450
1887Mo M	12,000	600	800	1,500	2,500
1888Mo M	7,300	420	600	850	1,450
1889Mo M	6,477	420	600	900	1,650
1890Mo M	7,852	420	600	850	1,500
1891/0Mo M	8,725	420	600	850	1,500
1891Mo M	Inc. above	420	600	850	1,500
1892Mo M	11,000	420	600	850	1,450
1893Mo M	15,000	420	600	850	1,450
1894Mo M	14,000	420	600	850	1,450
1895Mo M	13,000	420	600	850	1,450
1896Mo B	14,000	420	600	850	1,450
1897/6Mo M	12,000	420	600	850	1,450
1897Mo M	Inc. above	420	600	850	1,450
1898Mo M	20,000	420	600	850	1,450
1899Mo M	23,000	420	600	850	1,450
1900Mo M	21,000	420	600	850	1,450
1901Mo M	29,000	420	600	850	1,450
1902Mo M	38,000	420	600	850	1,450
1903/2Mo M	31,000	420	600	850	1,450
1903Mo M	Inc. above	420	600	850	1,450
1904Mo M	52,000	420	600	850	1,450
1905Mo M	9,757	420	600	850	1,450

Mint: Oaxaca
KM# 414.7 20 PESOS
33.8400 g., 0.8750 Gold .9520 oz. AGW **Rev:** Balance scale

Date	Mintage	F	VF	XF	Unc
1870 Oa E	1,131	750	1,500	2,500	5,000
1871 Oa E	1,591	750	1,500	2,500	5,000
1872 Oa E	255	1,000	1,750	3,000	7,000
1888 Oa E	170	2,000	3,000	5,000	—

Mint: Zacatecas
KM# 414.8 20 PESOS
33.8400 g., 0.8750 Gold .9520 oz. AGW **Rev:** Balance scale

Date	Mintage	F	VF	XF	Unc
1871Zs H	1,000	3,500	6,500	7,000	9,000
1875Zs A	—	4,000	6,000	7,500	9,500
1878Zs S	441	4,000	6,000	7,500	9,500

Date	Mintage	F	VF	XF	Unc
1888Zs Z Rare	50	—	—	—	—
1889Zs Z	640	3,500	5,500	7,000	9,000

UNITED STATES

DECIMAL COINAGE
100 Centavos = 1 Peso

KM# 415   CENTAVO
Bronze, 20 mm. **Note:** Struck at Mexico City Mint, mint mark Mo.

Date	Mintage	F	VF	XF	Unc	BU
1905 Narrow date	6,040,000	4.00	6.50	14.00	90.00	—
1905 Wide date	—	4.00	6.50	14.00	90.00	—
1906 Narrow date	Est. 67,505,000	0.50	0.75	1.25	14.00	—

Note: 50,000,000 pcs. were struck at the Birmingham Mint

Date	Mintage	F	VF	XF	Unc	BU
1906 Wide date	Inc. above	0.75	1.50	2.50	20.00	—
1910 Narrow date	8,700,000	2.00	3.00	6.50	85.00	—
1910 Wide date	—	2.00	3.00	6.50	85.00	—
1911 Narrow date	16,450,000	0.60	1.00	2.75	22.50	—
1911 Wide date	Inc. above	0.75	1.00	4.00	32.00	—
1912	12,650,000	1.00	1.35	3.25	32.00	—
1913	12,850,000	0.75	1.25	3.00	35.00	—
1914 Narrow date	17,350,000	0.75	1.00	3.00	13.50	18.00
1914 Wide date	Inc. above	0.75	1.00	3.00	13.50	18.00
1915	2,277,000	11.00	25.00	67.50	250	—
1916	500,000	45.00	80.00	170	1,200	—
1920	1,433,000	22.00	50.00	110	400	—
1921	3,470,000	5.50	15.50	47.00	275	—
1922	1,880,000	9.00	17.00	50.00	250	—
1923	4,800,000	0.75	1.25	1.75	13.50	—
1924/3	2,000,000	65.00	170	285	525	—
1924	Inc. above	4.50	11.00	22.00	235	275
1925	1,550,000	4.50	10.00	25.00	220	—
1926	5,000,000	1.00	2.00	4.00	26.00	30.00
1927/6	6,000,000	30.00	45.00	70.00	150	—
1927	Inc. above	0.75	1.25	4.50	36.00	—
1928	5,000,000	0.75	1.00	3.25	16.50	25.00
1929	4,500,000	0.75	1.00	1.75	17.00	25.00
1930	7,000,000	0.75	1.00	2.50	19.00	—
1933	10,000,000	0.25	0.35	1.75	16.50	—
1934	7,500,000	0.25	0.95	3.25	30.00	—
1935	12,400,000	0.15	0.25	0.40	11.50	—
1936	20,100,000	0.15	0.20	0.30	8.00	—
1937	20,000,000	0.15	0.25	0.35	3.25	5.00
1938	10,000,000	0.10	0.15	0.30	2.00	2.75
1939	30,000,000	0.10	0.20	0.30	1.00	1.50
1940	10,000,000	0.20	0.30	0.60	5.50	7.50
1941	15,800,000	0.15	0.25	0.35	2.00	3.00
1942	30,400,000	0.15	0.20	0.30	1.25	2.00
1943	4,310,000	0.30	0.50	0.75	8.00	10.00
1944	5,645,000	0.15	0.25	0.50	6.00	7.50
1945	26,375,000	0.10	0.15	0.25	1.00	1.25
1946	42,135,000	—	0.15	0.20	0.60	1.00
1947	13,445,000	—	0.10	0.15	0.80	1.25
1948	20,040,000	0.10	0.15	0.30	1.10	2.00
1949	6,235,000	0.10	0.15	0.30	1.25	2.00

Note: Varieties exist.

KM# 416   CENTAVO
Bronze, 16 mm. **Note:** Zapata issue. Struck at Mexico City Mint, mint mark Mo. Reduced size.

Date	Mintage	F	VF	XF	Unc	BU
1915	179,000	18.00	30.00	50.00	75.00	—

KM# 417   CENTAVO
Brass, 16 mm. **Note:** Struck at Mexico City Mint, mint mark Mo.

Date	Mintage	F	VF	XF	Unc	BU
1950	12,815,000	—	0.15	0.35	1.65	2.00
1951	25,740,000	—	0.15	0.35	0.65	1.00
1952	24,610,000	—	0.10	0.25	0.40	0.75
1953	21,160,000	—	0.10	0.25	0.40	0.85
1954	25,675,000	—	0.10	0.15	0.85	1.20
1955	9,820,000	—	0.15	0.25	0.85	1.50
1956	11,285,000	—	0.15	0.25	0.80	1.25
1957	9,805,000	—	0.15	0.25	0.85	1.35
1958	12,155,000	—	0.10	0.25	0.45	0.75
1959	11,875,000	—	0.10	0.25	0.75	1.25
1960	10,360,000	—	0.10	0.15	0.40	0.65
1961	6,385,000	—	0.10	0.15	0.45	0.85
1962	4,850,000	—	0.10	0.15	0.55	0.90
1963	7,775,000	—	0.10	0.15	0.25	0.45
1964	4,280,000	—	0.10	0.15	0.20	0.30
1965	2,255,000	—	0.10	0.15	0.25	0.40
1966	1,760,000	—	0.10	0.25	0.60	0.75
1967	1,290,000	—	0.10	0.15	0.40	0.60
1968	1,000,000	—	0.10	0.20	0.85	1.25
1969	1,000,000	—	0.10	0.15	0.65	0.85

KM# 418   CENTAVO
Brass, 13 mm. **Note:** Reduced size.

Date	Mintage	F	VF	XF	Unc	BU
1970	1,000,000	—	0.20	0.40	1.45	1.75
1972	1,000,000	—	0.20	0.45	2.50	3.25
1972/2	—	—	0.50	1.25	3.50	5.00
1973	1,000,000	—	1.65	2.75	8.50	12.00

KM# 419   2 CENTAVOS
Bronze, 25 mm. **Note:** Struck at Mexico City Mint, mint mark Mo.

Date	Mintage	F	VF	XF	Unc	BU
1905	50,000	150	300	500	1,200	1,350
1906 Inverted 6	9,998,000	30.00	55.00	120	375	—
1906 Wide date	Inc. above	5.00	11.00	23.00	80.00	—
1906 Narrow date	Inc. above	6.50	14.00	28.00	85.00	—

Note: 5,000,000 pieces were struck at the Birmingham Mint

Date	Mintage	F	VF	XF	Unc	BU
1920	1,325,000	6.50	17.50	35.00	350	—
1921	4,275,000	2.50	4.75	10.00	90.00	—
1922	—	225	550	1,350	4,000	—
1924	750,000	8.50	22.50	55.00	450	—
1925	3,650,000	2.50	3.50	7.50	38.00	—
1926	4,750,000	1.00	2.25	5.50	35.00	—
1927	7,250,000	0.60	1.00	4.50	22.00	—
1928	3,250,000	0.75	1.50	4.75	30.00	—
1929	250,000	65.00	180	500	1,000	—
1935	1,250,000	4.25	9.25	22.50	200	—
1939	5,000,000	0.60	0.90	2.25	20.00	22.00
1941	3,550,000	0.45	0.60	1.25	18.00	20.00

Date	Mintage	F	VF	XF	Unc	BU
1934	10,000,000	1.25	1.75	2.75	25.00	40.00
1935	21,980,000	0.75	1.20	2.50	22.50	30.00

KM# 420   2 CENTAVOS
Bronze, 20 mm. **Note:** Zapata issue. Struck at Mexico City Mint, mint mark Mo. Reduced size.

Date	Mintage	F	VF	XF	Unc	BU
1915	487,000	7.50	9.00	17.50	75.00	—

KM# 421   5 CENTAVOS
Nickel   **Note:** Struck at Mexico City Mint, mint mark Mo. Varieties exist.

Date	Mintage	F	VF	XF	Unc	BU
1905	1,420,000	7.00	10.00	25.00	300	375
1906/5	10,615,000	13.00	30.00	70.00	375	—
1906	Inc. above	0.75	1.35	3.25	55.00	75.00
1907	4,000,000	1.25	4.00	12.00	350	—
1909	2,052,000	3.25	10.00	48.00	360	—
1910	6,181,000	1.30	3.50	6.00	78.00	115
1911 Narrow date	4,487,000	1.00	3.00	5.00	85.00	125
1911 Wide date	Inc. above	2.50	5.00	9.00	110	160
1912 Small mint mark	420,000	90.00	100	230	725	—
1912 Large mint mark	Inc. above	70.00	95.00	175	575	—
1913	2,035,000	1.75	4.25	9.00	100	150

Note: Wide and narrow dates exist for 1913

Date	Mintage	F	VF	XF	Unc	BU
1914	2,000,000	1.00	2.00	3.50	70.00	95.00

Note: 5,000,000 pieces appear to have been struck at the Birmingham Mint in 1914 and all of 1909-1911. The Mexican Mint report does not mention receiving the 1914 dated coins

KM# 422   5 CENTAVOS
Bronze   **Note:** Struck at Mexico City Mint, mint mark Mo.

Date	Mintage	F	VF	XF	Unc	BU
1914	2,500,000	10.00	23.00	50.00	240	—
1915	11,424,000	3.00	5.00	20.00	145	—
1916	2,860,000	15.00	35.00	150	645	—
1917	800,000	75.00	195	375	825	—
1918	1,332,000	35.00	90.00	200	625	—
1919	400,000	115	225	360	925	—
1920	5,920,000	3.00	8.00	40.00	265	—
1921	2,080,000	10.00	24.00	75.00	275	—
1924	780,000	40.00	95.00	260	625	—
1925	4,040,000	5.50	11.00	47.50	200	—
1926	3,160,000	5.50	11.00	48.00	300	—
1927	3,600,000	4.00	7.00	30.00	215	250
1928 Large date	1,740,000	11.00	18.00	65.00	250	—
1928 Small date	Inc. above	30.00	45.00	95.00	385	—
1929	2,400,000	5.50	11.00	48.00	195	—
1930	2,600,000	5.00	8.00	27.50	210	—

Note: Large oval O in date

Date	Mintage	F	VF	XF	Unc	BU
1930	Inc. above	60.00	125	250	565	—

Note: Small square O in date

Date	Mintage	F	VF	XF	Unc	BU
1931	—	475	750	1,150	3,000	—
1933	8,000,000	1.50	2.25	3.50	27.50	35.00

KM# 423   5 CENTAVOS
Copper-Nickel   **Note:** Struck at Mexico City Mint, mint mark Mo.

Date	Mintage	F	VF	XF	Unc	BU
1936	46,700,000	—	0.65	1.25	6.50	7.50
1937	49,060,000	—	0.50	1.00	6.00	7.00
1938	3,340,000	—	4.00	10.00	75.00	250
1940	22,800,000	—	0.75	1.25	8.00	10.00
1942	7,100,000	—	1.50	3.00	35.00	45.00

KM# 424   5 CENTAVOS
Ring Composition: Bronze   **Rev:** "Josefa" Ortiz de Dominguez **Note:** Struck at Mexico City Mint, mint mark Mo.

Date	Mintage	F	VF	XF	Unc	BU
1942	900,000	—	25.00	75.00	375	550
1943	54,660,000	—	0.50	0.75	2.50	3.50
1944	53,463,000	—	0.25	0.35	0.75	1.00
1945	44,262,000	—	0.25	0.35	0.75	1.25
1946	49,054,000	—	0.50	1.00	2.00	3.00
1951	50,758,000	—	0.75	0.90	3.00	5.00
1952	17,674,000	—	1.50	2.50	9.50	11.50
1953	31,568,000	—	1.25	2.00	6.00	9.00
1954	58,680,000	—	0.40	1.00	2.75	4.00
1955	31,114,000	—	2.00	3.00	11.00	14.00

KM# 425   5 CENTAVOS
Copper-Nickel   **Rev:** Josefa **Note:** Struck at Mexico City Mint, mint mark Mo.

Date	Mintage	F	VF	XF	Unc	BU
1950	5,700,000	—	0.75	1.50	6.00	7.00

Note: 5,600,000 pieces struck at Connecticut melted

KM# 426   5 CENTAVOS
Brass   **Rev:** Josefa **Note:** Struck at Mexico City Mint, mint mark Mo.

Date	Mintage	F	VF	XF	Unc	BU
1954 Dot	—	—	10.00	45.00	300	375
1954 Without dot	—	—	15.00	30.00	250	290
1955	12,136,000	—	0.75	1.50	9.00	12.50
1956	60,216,000	—	0.20	0.30	0.75	1.25
1957	55,288,000	—	0.15	0.20	0.90	1.50
1958	104,624,000	—	0.15	0.20	0.60	1.00
1959	106,000,000	—	0.15	0.25	0.75	1.25

Date	Mintage	F	VF	XF	Unc	BU
1960	99,144,000	—	0.10	0.15	0.50	0.75
1961	61,136,000	—	0.10	0.15	0.50	0.75
1962	47,232,000	—	0.10	0.15	0.25	0.35
1963	156,680,000	—	—	0.15	0.25	0.40
1964	71,168,000	—	—	0.15	0.20	0.40
1965	155,720,000	—	—	0.15	0.25	0.35
1966	124,944,000	—	—	0.15	0.40	0.65
1967	118,816,000	—	—	0.15	0.25	0.40
1968	189,588,000	—	—	0.15	0.50	0.75
1969	210,492,000	—	—	0.15	0.55	0.80

KM# 426a 5 CENTAVOS
Copper-Nickel **Rev:** Josefa **Note:** Struck at Mexico City Mint, mint mark Mo.

Date	Mintage	F	VF	XF	Unc	BU
1960	—	—	250	300	350	—
1962	19	—	250	300	350	—
1965	—	—	250	300	350	—

KM# 427 5 CENTAVOS
Brass, 18 mm. **Rev:** Josefa **Note:** Due to some minor alloy variations this type is often encountered with a bronze color toning. Reduced size.

Date	Mintage	F	VF	XF	Unc	BU
1970	163,368,000	—	0.10	0.15	0.35	0.45
1971	198,844,000	—	0.10	0.15	0.25	0.30
1972	225,000,000	—	0.10	0.15	0.25	0.30
1973 Flat top 3	595,070,000	—	0.10	0.15	0.25	0.40
1973 Round top 3	Inc. above	—	0.10	0.15	0.20	0.30
1974	401,584,000	—	0.10	0.15	0.30	0.40
1975	342,308,000	—	0.10	0.15	0.25	0.35
1976	367,524,000	—	0.10	0.15	0.40	0.60

KM# 428 10 CENTAVOS
2.5000 g., 0.8000 Silver .0643 oz. ASW **Note:** Struck at Mexico City Mint, mint mark Mo.

Date	Mintage	F	VF	XF	Unc	BU
1905	3,920,000	—	6.00	8.00	40.00	50.00
1906	8,410,000	—	5.50	7.50	27.00	35.00
1907/6	5,950,000	—	50.00	135	275	350
1907	Inc. above	—	5.50	6.25	35.00	42.50
1909	2,620,000	—	8.50	13.00	70.00	85.00
1910/00	3,450,000	—	10.00	40.00	75.00	85.00
1910	Inc. above	—	7.00	15.00	25.00	30.00
1911 Narrow date	2,550,000	—	11.00	17.00	88.00	125
1911 Wide date	Inc. above	—	7.50	10.00	42.00	60.00
1912	1,350,000	—	10.00	18.00	130	160
1912 Low 2	Inc. above	—	10.00	18.00	115	140
1913/2	1,990,000	—	10.00	25.00	40.00	70.00
1913	Inc. above	—	7.00	10.00	33.00	40.00
1914	3,110,000	—	5.50	7.00	15.00	20.00

Note: Wide and narrow dates exist for 1914

KM# 429 10 CENTAVOS
1.8125 g., 0.8000 Silver .0466 oz. ASW, 15 mm. **Note:** Struck at Mexico City Mint, mint mark Mo. Reduced size.

Date	Mintage	F	VF	XF	Unc	BU
1919	8,360,000	—	10.00	15.00	85.00	110

KM# 430 10 CENTAVOS
Bronze **Note:** Struck at Mexico City Mint, mint mark Mo.

Date	Mintage	F	VF	XF	Unc	BU
1919	1,232,000	—	25.00	70.00	450	525
1920	6,612,000	—	15.00	50.00	400	475
1921	2,255,000	—	35.00	80.00	650	800
1935	5,970,000	—	14.00	30.00	120	175

KM# 431 10 CENTAVOS
1.6600 g., 0.7200 Silver .0384 oz. ASW **Note:** Struck at Mexico City Mint, mint mark Mo.

Date	Mintage	F	VF	XF	Unc	BU
1925/15	5,350,000	—	30.00	75.00	125	175
1925/3	Inc. above	—	20.00	40.00	125	150
1925	Inc. above	—	2.00	5.00	40.00	45.00
1926/16	2,650,000	—	30.00	75.00	125	175
1926	Inc. above	—	3.50	7.50	65.00	85.00
1927	2,810,000	—	2.25	3.00	17.50	22.50
1928	5,270,000	—	2.00	2.75	13.50	16.50
1930	2,000,000	—	3.75	5.00	18.75	25.00
1933	5,000,000	—	1.50	3.00	10.00	11.50
1934	8,000,000	—	1.75	2.50	8.00	10.00
1935	3,500,000	—	2.75	5.00	11.00	12.50

KM# 432 10 CENTAVOS
Copper-Nickel **Note:** Struck at Mexico City Mint, mint mark Mo.

Date	Mintage	F	VF	XF	Unc	BU
1936	33,030,000	—	0.75	2.50	9.00	10.00
1937	3,000,000	—	8.00	45.00	215	250
1938	3,650,000	1.25	2.00	7.00	60.00	75.00
1939	6,920,000	—	1.00	3.50	27.50	30.00
1940	12,300,000	—	0.40	1.25	5.00	6.00
1942	14,380,000	—	0.60	1.50	7.00	9.00
1945	9,558,000	—	0.40	0.70	3.50	4.00
1946	46,230,000	—	0.40	0.60	2.50	3.00

KM# 433 10 CENTAVOS
Bronze **Rev:** Benito Juarez **Note:** Struck at Mexico City Mint, mint mark Mo.

Date	Mintage	F	VF	XF	Unc	BU
1955	1,818,000	—	0.75	3.25	23.00	30.00
1956	5,255,000	—	0.75	3.25	23.00	28.00

Date	Mintage	F	VF	XF	Unc	BU
1957	11,925,000	—	0.20	0.40	5.50	8.00
1959	26,140,000	—	0.30	0.45	0.75	1.25
1966	5,873,000	—	0.15	0.25	0.60	1.75
1967	32,318,000	—	0.10	0.15	0.30	0.40

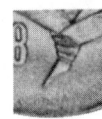

KM# 434.1 10 CENTAVOS
Copper-Nickel **Rev:** Five full rows of kernels, sharp stem, wide date **Note:** Variety I

Date	Mintage	F	VF	XF	Unc	BU
1974	6,000,000	—	—	0.35	0.75	1.00
1975	5,550,000	—	0.10	0.35	0.75	1.00
1976	7,680,000	—	0.10	0.20	0.30	0.40
1977	144,650,000	—	1.25	2.25	3.00	3.50
1978	271,870,000	—	—	1.00	1.50	2.25
1979	375,660,000	—	—	0.50	1.00	1.75
1980/79	21,290,000	—	2.45	3.75	6.00	7.00
1980	Inc. above	—	1.50	2.00	4.50	5.50

KM# 434.2 10 CENTAVOS
Copper-Nickel **Rev:** Five full, plus one partial row at left, blunt stem, narrow date **Note:** Variety II

Date	Mintage	F	VF	XF	Unc	BU
1974	Inc. above	—	—	0.10	0.20	0.30
1977	Inc. above	—	0.15	0.50	1.25	2.25
1978	Inc. above	—	—	0.10	0.30	0.40
1979	Inc. above	—	0.15	0.35	0.85	1.50
1980	Inc. above	—	—	0.10	0.20	0.30

KM# 434.4 10 CENTAVOS
Copper-Nickel **Rev:** Five full, plus one partial row, sharp stem and narrow date **Note:** Variety IV

Date	Mintage	F	VF	XF	Unc	BU
1974	—	—	—	—	1.50	2.50
1979	—	—	—	—	1.50	2.50

KM# 434.3 10 CENTAVOS
Copper-Nickel **Rev:** Five full, plus one partial row, blunt stem and wide date **Note:** Variety III

Date	Mintage	F	VF	XF	Unc	BU
1980/79	—	—	—	—	5.00	6.00

KM# 435 20 CENTAVOS
5.0000 g., 0.8000 Silver .1286 oz. ASW **Note:** Struck at Mexico City Mint, mint mark Mo.

Date	Mintage	F	VF	XF	Unc	BU
1905	2,565,000	—	12.00	20.00	145	175
1906	6,860,000	—	9.00	16.50	60.00	80.00
1907 Straight 7	4,000,000	—	11.50	20.00	70.00	100
1907 Curved 7	5,435,000	—	7.50	13.50	65.00	90.00
1908	350,000	50.00	90.00	225	1,500	—
1910	1,135,000	—	11.00	16.00	80.00	95.00
1911	1,150,000	12.00	15.00	35.00	125	150
1912	625,000	20.00	40.00	70.00	335	375
1913	1,000,000	—	14.50	30.00	95.00	115
1914	1,500,000	—	10.00	21.50	62.50	75.00

KM# 436 20 CENTAVOS
3.6250 g., 0.8000 Silver .0932 oz. ASW, 19 mm. **Note:** Struck at Mexico City Mint, mint mark Mo. Reduced size.

Date	Mintage	F	VF	XF	Unc	BU
1919	4,155,000	—	30.00	55.00	190	225

KM# 437 20 CENTAVOS
Bronze **Note:** Struck at Mexico City Mint, mint mark Mo.

Date	Mintage	F	VF	XF	Unc	BU
1920	4,835,000	—	45.00	140	650	750
1935	20,000,000	—	6.00	10.00	80.00	125

KM# 438 20 CENTAVOS
3.3333 g., 0.7200 Silver .0772 oz. ASW **Note:** Struck at Mexico City Mint, mint mark Mo.

Date	Mintage	F	VF	XF	Unc	BU
1920	3,710,000	—	6.00	17.50	165	200
1921	6,160,000	—	6.00	14.00	100	145
1925	1,450,000	—	12.00	20.00	125	150
1926/5	1,465,000	—	20.00	65.00	325	375
1926	Inc. above	—	3.25	7.50	80.00	110
1927	1,405,000	—	3.50	8.00	85.00	115
1928	3,630,000	—	4.00	5.25	14.50	19.50
1930	1,000,000	—	5.00	8.00	25.00	35.00
1933	2,500,000	—	2.25	3.00	10.00	11.50
1934	2,500,000	—	2.25	4.00	11.00	12.50
1935	2,460,000	—	2.25	4.00	11.00	12.50
1937	10,000,000	—	1.75	2.25	4.00	5.00
1939	8,800,000	—	1.75	2.25	4.00	5.00
1940	3,000,000	—	1.75	2.25	3.50	5.00
1941	5,740,000	—	1.50	2.25	3.00	4.00
1942	12,460,000	—	1.50	2.25	3.25	3.75
1943	3,955,000	—	2.00	2.50	3.50	4.25

KM# 439 20 CENTAVOS
Bronze **Note:** Struck at Mexico City Mint, mint mark Mo.

Date	Mintage	F	VF	XF	Unc	BU
1943	46,350,000	—	1.25	3.00	18.00	25.00
1944	83,650,000	—	0.40	0.65	8.00	10.00

Date	Mintage	F	VF	XF	Unc	BU
1945	26,801,000	—	1.25	3.50	9.50	12.00
1946	25,695,000	—	1.10	2.25	6.00	8.25
1951	11,385,000	—	3.00	8.75	90.00	110
1952	6,560,000	—	3.00	5.00	25.00	32.00
1953	26,948,000	—	0.35	0.80	8.25	12.00
1954	40,108,000	—	0.35	0.80	8.00	11.50
1955	16,950,000	—	2.75	7.00	60.00	75.00

KM# 440   20 CENTAVOS
Bronze **Note:** Struck at Mexico City Mint, mint mark Mo.

Date	Mintage	F	VF	XF	Unc	BU
1955	Inc. above	—	0.75	1.75	17.00	22.00
1956	22,431,000	—	0.30	0.35	3.00	4.00
1957	13,455,000	—	0.45	1.25	9.00	12.00
1959	6,017,000	—	4.50	9.00	75.00	100
1960	39,756,000	—	0.15	0.25	0.75	1.00
1963	14,869,000	—	0.25	0.35	0.80	1.00
1964	28,654,000	—	0.25	0.40	0.90	1.25
1965	74,162,000	—	0.20	0.35	0.80	1.00
1966	43,745,000	—	0.15	0.25	0.75	1.00
1967	46,487,000	—	0.20	0.50	1.00	1.25
1968	15,477,000	—	0.30	0.55	1.35	1.65
1969	63,647,000	—	0.20	0.35	0.80	1.00
1970	76,287,000	—	0.15	0.20	0.90	1.30
1971	49,892,000	—	0.30	0.50	1.25	1.50

KM# 441   20 CENTAVOS
Bronze

Date	Mintage	F	VF	XF	Unc	BU
1971	Inc. above	—	0.20	0.35	1.85	2.35
1973	78,398,000	—	0.25	0.35	0.95	1.50
1974	34,200,000	—	0.20	0.35	1.25	1.75

KM# 442   20 CENTAVOS
Copper-Nickel **Rev:** Francisco Madero

Date	Mintage	F	VF	XF	Unc	BU
1974	112,000,000	—	0.10	0.15	0.25	0.30
1975	611,000,000	—	0.10	0.15	0.30	0.35
1976	394,000,000	—	0.10	0.15	0.35	0.45
1977	394,350,000	—	0.10	0.15	0.40	0.45
1978	527,950,000	—	0.10	0.15	0.25	0.30
1979	524,615,000	—	0.10	0.15	0.25	0.30
1979	—	—	1.25	2.00	4.00	8.00

Note: Doubled die obv. small letters

| 1979 | — | — | 1.25 | 2.00 | 4.00 | 8.00 |

Note: Doubled die obv. large letters

| 1980 | 326,500,000 | — | 0.15 | 0.20 | 0.30 | 0.40 |
| 1981 Open 8 | 106,205,000 | — | 0.30 | 0.50 | 1.00 | 2.00 |

Date	Mintage	F	VF	XF	Unc	BU
1981 Closed 8, high date	248,500,000	—	0.30	0.50	1.00	2.00
1981 Closed 8, low date	—	—	1.00	1.50	3.50	4.25
1981/1982	—	—	40.00	75.00	175	195

Note: The 1981/1982 overdate is often mistaken as 1982/1981

1982	286,855,000	—	0.40	0.60	0.90	1.10
1983 Round top 3	100,930,000	—	0.25	0.40	1.75	2.25
1983 Flat top 3	Inc. above	—	0.25	0.50	1.25	1.75
1983 Proof	998	Value: 15.00				

KM# 491   20 CENTAVOS
Bronze **Subject:** Olmec Culture

Date	Mintage	F	VF	XF	Unc	BU
1983	260,000,000	—	0.20	0.25	1.25	1.75
1983 Proof	53	Value: 185				
1984	180,320,000	—	0.20	0.35	1.85	2.25

KM# 443   25 CENTAVOS
3.3330 g., 0.3000 Silver .0321 oz. ASW **Note:** Struck at Mexico City Mint, mint mark Mo.

Date	Mintage	F	VF	XF	Unc	BU
1950	77,060,000	—	0.50	0.75	1.60	2.00
1951	41,172,000	—	0.50	0.75	1.60	2.00
1952	29,264,000	—	0.75	1.10	1.75	2.25
1953	38,144,000	—	0.60	0.70	1.50	2.00

KM# 444   25 CENTAVOS
Copper-Nickel **Rev:** Francisco Madero

Date	Mintage	F	VF	XF	Unc	BU
1964	20,686,000	—	—	0.15	0.20	0.30
1966 Closed beak	180,000	—	0.65	1.00	2.25	2.50
1966 Open beak	Inc. above	—	1.75	3.50	10.00	13.50

KM# 445   50 CENTAVOS
12.5000 g., 0.8000 Silver .3215 oz. ASW **Note:** Struck at Mexico City Mint, mint mark Mo.

Date	Mintage	F	VF	XF	Unc	BU
1905	2,446,000	12.50	20.00	30.00	150	225
1906 Open 9	16,966,000	—	6.00	10.00	40.00	60.00
1906 Closed 9	Inc. above	—	5.00	9.00	35.00	50.00

Date	Mintage	F	VF	XF	Unc	BU
1907 Straight 7	18,920,000	—	5.00	9.00	25.00	28.50
1907 Curved 7	14,841,000	—	5.25	9.00	25.00	32.00
1908	488,000	—	80.00	190	545	650
1912	3,736,000	—	11.00	14.00	45.00	60.00
1913/07	10,510,000	—	40.00	90.00	240	275
1913/2	Inc. above	—	20.00	27.50	65.00	85.00
1913	Inc. above	—	5.50	8.50	27.50	35.00
1914	7,710,000	—	6.75	13.50	32.00	45.00
1916 Narrow date	480,000	—	60.00	85.00	200	290
1916 Wide date	Inc. above	—	60.00	85.00	200	290
1917	37,112,000	—	6.00	9.50	20.00	22.50
1918	1,320,000	—	70.00	135	250	335

KM# 446 50 CENTAVOS
9.0625 g., 0.8000 Silver .2331 oz. ASW, 27 mm. **Note:** Struck at Mexico City Mint, mint mark Mo. Reduced size.

Date	Mintage	F	VF	XF	Unc	BU
1918/7	2,760,000	—	525	675	1,250	—
1918	Inc. above	—	17.50	55.00	300	385
1919	29,670,000	—	9.50	22.50	95.00	125

KM# 447 50 CENTAVOS
8.3333 g., 0.7200 Silver .1929 oz. ASW **Note:** Struck at Mexico City Mint, mint mark Mo.

Date	Mintage	F	VF	XF	Unc	BU
1919	10,200,000	—	10.00	20.00	90.00	110
1920	27,166,000	—	8.00	14.00	70.00	80.00
1921	21,864,000	—	8.00	14.00	85.00	100
1925	3,280,000	—	17.50	30.00	125	160
1937	20,000,000	—	4.25	5.50	7.50	8.50
1938	100,000	—	50.00	85.00	225	300
1939	10,440,000	—	6.00	8.00	15.00	18.50
1942	800,000	—	6.00	9.00	16.00	20.00
1943	41,512,000	—	2.75	4.00	5.50	6.50
1944	55,806,000	—	3.00	4.25	5.50	6.50
1945	56,766,000	—	3.00	3.75	6.00	6.50

KM# 448 50 CENTAVOS
7.9730 g., 0.4200 Silver .1076 oz. ASW **Note:** Struck at Mexico City Mint, mint mark Mo.

Date	Mintage	F	VF	XF	Unc	BU
1935	70,800,000	—	2.50	3.25	5.50	7.00

KM# 449 50 CENTAVOS
6.6600 g., 0.3000 Silver .0642 oz. ASW **Rev:** Cuauhtemoc **Note:** Struck at Mexico City Mint, mint mark Mo.

Date	Mintage	F	VF	XF	Unc	BU
1950	13,570,000	—	1.50	1.85	3.00	4.50
1951	3,650,000	—	2.00	2.50	3.75	5.75

KM# 450 50 CENTAVOS
Bronze **Note:** Struck at Mexico City Mint, mint mark Mo.

Date	Mintage	F	VF	XF	Unc	BU
1955	3,502,000	—	1.50	3.00	29.00	35.00
1956	34,643,000	—	0.75	1.50	3.75	4.50
1957	9,675,000	—	1.00	2.00	6.50	7.50
1959	4,540,000	—	0.50	0.75	2.00	2.75

KM# 451 50 CENTAVOS
Copper-Nickel

Date	Mintage	F	VF	XF	Unc	BU
1964	43,806,000	—	0.15	0.20	0.40	0.60
1965	14,326,000	—	0.20	0.25	0.45	0.65
1966	1,726,000	—	0.20	0.40	1.30	1.75
1967	55,144,000	—	0.20	0.30	0.65	1.00
1968	80,438,000	—	0.15	0.30	0.65	0.90
1969	87,640,000	—	0.20	0.35	0.80	1.00

KM# 452 50 CENTAVOS
Copper-Nickel **Obv:** Stylized eagle **Note:** Coins dated 1975 and 1976 exist with and without dots in centers of three circles on plumage on reverse. Edge varieties exist.

Date	Mintage	F	VF	XF	Unc	BU
1970	76,236,000	—	0.15	0.20	0.80	1.00
1971	125,288,000	—	0.15	0.20	0.90	1.30
1972	16,000,000	—	1.25	2.00	3.00	4.75
1975 Dots	177,958,000	—	0.60	1.25	3.50	6.00
1975 No dots	Inc. above	—	0.15	0.20	0.75	1.00
1976 Dots	37,480,000	—	0.75	1.25	5.00	6.00

Date	Mintage	F	VF	XF	Unc	BU
1976 No dots	Inc. above	—	0.15	0.20	0.50	0.75
1977	12,410,000	—	6.50	10.00	32.50	42.50
1978	85,400,000	—	0.15	0.25	0.50	0.75
1979 Round 2nd 9 in date	229,000,000	—	0.15	0.25	0.50	0.65
1979 Square 9's in date	Inc. above	—	0.20	0.40	1.60	2.00
1980 Narrow date, square 9	89,978,000	—	0.45	0.75	1.75	2.50
1980 Wide date, round 9	178,188,000	—	0.20	0.25	1.00	1.15
1981 Rectangular 9, narrow date	142,212,000	—	0.50	0.75	1.75	2.50
1981 Round 9, wide date	Inc. above	—	0.30	0.50	1.25	1.75
1982	45,474,000	—	0.20	0.40	1.00	1.25
1983	90,318,000	—	0.50	0.75	2.00	2.50
1983 Proof	998	Value: 35.00				

KM# 492   50 CENTAVOS
Stainless Steel   **Subject:** Palenque Culture **Obv:** Stylized eagle **Rev:** Cuauhtemoc

Date	Mintage	F	VF	XF	Unc	BU
1983	99,540,000	—	—	0.30	1.50	2.50
1983 Proof	53	Value: 195				

KM# 453   PESO
27.0700 g., 0.9030 Silver .7859 oz. ASW   **Subject:** Caballito **Note:** Struck at Mexico City Mint, mint mark Mo.

Date	Mintage	F	VF	XF	Unc	BU
1910	3,814,000	—	45.00	50.00	160	250
1911 Long lower left ray on reverse	1,227,000	—	45.00	75.00	200	275
1911 Short lower left ray on reverse	Inc. above	—	145	210	600	800
1912	322,000	—	100	210	365	500
1913/2	2,880,000	—	45.00	75.00	270	400
1913	Inc. above	—	45.00	70.00	175	250
Note: 1913 coins exist with even and unevenly spaced date						
1914	120,000	—	600	950	2,800	—

KM# 454   PESO
18.1300 g., 0.8000 Silver .4663 oz. ASW   **Note:** Struck at Mexico City Mint, mint mark Mo.

Date	Mintage	F	VF	XF	Unc	BU
1918	3,050,000	—	35.00	125	1,350	2,100
1919	6,151,000	—	20.00	50.00	900	1,600

KM# 455   PESO
16.6600 g., 0.7200 Silver .3856 oz. ASW   **Note:** Struck at Mexico City Mint, mint mark Mo.

Date	Mintage	F	VF	XF	Unc	BU
1920/10	8,830,000	—	50.00	90.00	325	—
1920	Inc. above	—	8.00	25.00	185	300
1921	5,480,000	—	8.00	25.00	155	200
1922	33,620,000	—	3.25	5.00	20.00	26.00
1923	35,280,000	—	3.25	5.00	20.00	28.00
1924	33,060,000	—	3.25	5.00	20.00	26.00
1925	9,160,000	—	4.50	10.00	60.00	75.00
1926	28,840,000	—	3.25	5.00	20.00	25.00
1927	5,060,000	—	7.00	10.00	70.00	85.00
1932 Open 9	50,770,000	—	2.75	4.00	5.00	7.00
1932 Closed 9	Inc. above	—	2.75	4.00	5.00	7.00
1933/2	43,920,000	—	15.00	25.00	85.00	—
1933	Inc. above	—	2.75	4.25	5.50	7.50
1934	22,070,000	—	3.25	4.50	9.00	10.50
1935	8,050,000	—	4.50	6.00	11.50	13.50
1938	30,000,000	—	2.75	3.50	5.00	6.50
1940	20,000,000	—	2.75	3.75	6.00	7.50
1943	47,662,000	—	2.75	3.25	4.50	6.00
1944	39,522,000	—	2.75	3.50	5.00	6.50
1945	37,300,000	—	2.75	3.50	5.00	6.50

KM# 456   PESO
14.0000 g., 0.5000 Silver .2250 oz. ASW   **Rev:** Jose Morelos y Pavon **Note:** Struck at Mexico City Mint, mint mark Mo.

Date	Mintage	F	VF	XF	Unc	BU
1947	61,460,000	—	1.75	2.50	4.50	5.50
1948	22,915,000	—	2.25	3.50	5.50	6.50
1949	4,000,000	—	—	1,200	1,600	2,500

Date	Mintage	F	VF	XF	Unc	BU

Note: Not released for circulation
1949 Proof — Value: 4,000

KM# 457 PESO
13.3300 g., 0.3000 Silver .1285 oz. ASW **Rev:** Jose Morelos y Pavon **Note:** Struck at Mexico City Mint, mint mark Mo.

Date	Mintage	F	VF	XF	Unc	BU
1950	3,287,000	—	2.50	4.00	7.00	8.50

KM# 459 PESO
16.0000 g., 0.1000 Silver .0514 oz. ASW **Subject:** 100th Anniversary of Constitution **Rev:** Jose Morelos y Pavon **Edge Lettering:** INDEPENDENCIA Y LIBERTAD **Note:** Mint mark Mo.

Date	Mintage	F	VF	XF	Unc	BU
1957	28,273,000	—	0.65	1.00	2.50	10.00
1958	41,899,000	—	0.50	0.75	1.65	2.00
1959	27,369,000	—	1.25	2.00	5.50	8.00
1960	26,259,000	—	0.65	1.10	3.25	4.50
1961	52,601,000	—	0.50	0.90	2.25	3.00
1962	61,094,000	—	0.50	0.75	1.75	2.25
1963	26,394,000	—	BV	0.75	1.75	2.00
1964	15,615,000	—	BV	0.75	2.00	2.40
1965	5,004,000	—	BV	0.60	1.85	2.00
1966	30,998,000	—	BV	0.50	1.35	1.85
1967	9,308,000	—	BV	0.60	2.75	3.50

KM# 458 PESO
16.0000 g., 0.1000 Silver .0514 oz. ASW **Subject:** 100th Anniversary of Constitution **Obv. Designer:** Manuel L. Negrete **Edge Lettering:** INDEPENDENCIA Y LIBERTAD **Note:** Struck at Mexico City Mint, mint mark Mo.

Date	Mintage	F	VF	XF	Unc	BU
1957	500,000	—	3.50	5.00	12.50	15.00

Tall narrow date

Short wide date

KM# 460 PESO
Copper-Nickel **Rev:** Jose Morelos y Pavon

Date	Mintage	F	VF	XF	Unc	BU
1970 Narrow date	102,715,000	—	0.25	0.35	0.65	0.80
1970 Wide date	Inc. above	—	1.25	2.50	7.50	9.00
1971	426,222,000	—	0.20	0.25	0.55	0.75
1972	120,000,000	—	0.20	0.25	0.40	0.65
1974	63,700,000	—	0.20	0.25	0.65	0.90
1975 Tall narrow date	205,979,000	—	0.25	0.45	1.00	1.35
1975 Short wide date	Inc. above	—	0.30	0.40	0.75	1.00
1976	94,489,000	—	0.15	0.20	0.50	0.75
1977 Thick date close to rim	94,364,000	—	0.25	0.45	1.00	1.25
1977 Thin date, space between sideburns and collar	Inc. above	—	1.00	2.00	6.50	13.50
1978 Closed 8	208,300,000	—	0.20	0.30	1.00	1.50
1978 Open 8	55,140,000	—	0.75	1.75	12.00	15.00
1979 Thin date	117,884,000	—	0.20	0.30	1.15	1.50
1979 Thick date	Inc. above	—	0.20	0.30	1.25	1.75
1980 Closed 8	318,800,000	—	0.25	0.35	1.00	1.25
1980 Open 8	23,865,000	—	0.75	1.50	8.00	12.00
1981 Closed 8	413,349,000	—	0.20	0.30	0.75	0.90
1981 Open 8	58,616,000	—	0.50	1.25	6.50	8.00
1982 Closed 8	235,000,000	—	0.25	0.75	2.25	2.50
1982 Open 8	—	—	0.75	1.50	8.00	12.00
1983 Wide date	100,000,000	—	0.30	0.45	3.00	3.50
1983 Narrow date	Inc. above	—	0.30	0.45	3.00	3.50
1983 Proof	1,051,000	Value: 38.00				

KM# 496 PESO
Stainless Steel **Rev:** Jose Morelos y Pavon

Date	Mintage	F	VF	XF	Unc	BU
1984	722,802,000	—	0.10	0.25	0.65	1.00
1985	985,000,000	—	0.10	0.25	0.50	0.75
1986	740,000,000	—	0.10	0.25	0.50	0.75
1987	250,000,000	—	—	0.25	0.50	0.80
1987 Proof; 2 known	—	Value: 1,000				

KM# 461 2 PESOS
1.6666 g., 0.9000 Gold .0482 oz. AGW **Note:** Struck at Mexico City Mint, mint mark Mo.

Date	Mintage	F	VF	XF	Unc	BU
1919	1,670,000	—	BV	30.00	65.00	—
1920/10	—	22.00	30.00	55.00	100	—
1920	4,282,000	—	BV	30.00	50.00	—

Date	Mintage	F	VF	XF	Unc	BU
1944	10,000	22.00	30.00	50.00	70.00	—
1945	Est. 140,000	—	—	—	BV+20%	—
1946	168,000	22.00	30.00	50.00	75.00	—
1947	25,000	22.00	30.00	50.00	75.00	—
1948 No specimens known	45,000	—	—	—	—	—

Note: During 1951-1972 a total of 4,590,493 pieces were restruck, most likely dated 1945. In 1996 matte restrikes were produced

Date	Mintage	F	VF	XF	Unc	BU
1918	Inc. above	—	BV	55.00	265	—
1919	506,000	—	BV	55.00	100	—
1920	2,385,000	—	BV	55.00	100	—
1955	Est. 48,000	—	—	—	BV+11%	—

Note: During 1955-1972 a total of 1,767,645 pieces were restruck, most likely dated 1955. In 1996 matte restrikes were produced

KM# 462   2 PESOS
26.6667 g., 0.9000 Silver .7717 oz. ASW **Subject:** Centennial of Independence **Note:** Struck at Mexico City Mint, mint mark Mo.

Date	Mintage	F	VF	XF	Unc	BU
1921	1,278,000	—	40.00	55.00	325	450

KM# 463   2-1/2 PESOS
2.0833 g., 0.9000 Gold .0602 oz. AGW **Note:** Struck at Mexico City Mint, mint mark Mo.

Date	Mintage	F	VF	XF	Unc	BU
1918	1,704,000	—	BV	28.00	80.00	—
1919	984,000	—	BV	28.00	80.00	—
1920/10	607,000	—	BV	55.00	130	—
1920	Inc. above	—	BV	30.00	65.00	—
1944	20,000	—	BV	30.00	55.00	—
1945	Est. 180,000	—	—	—	BV+18%	—
1946	163,000	—	BV	30.00	55.00	—
1947	24,000	200	265	325	425	—
1948	63,000	—	BV	30.00	70.00	—

Note: During 1951-1972 a total of 5,025,087 pieces were restruck, most likely dated 1945. In 1996 matte restrikes were produced

KM# 464   5 PESOS
4.1666 g., 0.9000 Gold .1205 oz. AGW **Note:** Struck at Mexico City Mint, mint mark Mo.

Date	Mintage	F	VF	XF	Unc	BU
1905	18,000	120	175	245	570	—
1906	4,638,000	—	BV	55.00	85.00	—
1907	1,088,000	—	BV	55.00	90.00	—
1910	100,000	BV	55.00	60.00	120	—
1918/7	609,000	BV	55.00	70.00	200	—

KM# 465   5 PESOS
30.0000 g., 0.9000 Silver .8681 oz. ASW **Rev:** Head of Cuauhtemoc left **Note:** Struck at Mexico City Mint, mint mark Mo.

Date	Mintage	F	VF	XF	Unc	BU
1947	5,110,000	—	BV	6.25	8.75	10.00
1948	26,740,000	—	BV	6.00	8.00	9.50

KM# 466   5 PESOS
27.7800 g., 0.7200 Silver .06431 oz. ASW **Subject:** Opening of Southern Railroad **Edge Lettering:** COMMERCIO - AGRICULTURA - INDUSTRIA **Note:** Struck at Mexico City Mint, mint mark Mo.

Date	Mintage	F	VF	XF	Unc	BU
1950	200,000	—	22.50	40.00	50.00	55.00

Note: It is recorded that 100,000 pieces were melted to be used for the 1968 Mexican Olympic 25 Pesos

KM# 467 5 PESOS
27.7800 g., 0.7200 Silver .6431 oz. ASW **Rev:** Miguel
Hidalgo y Costilla **Edge Lettering:** COMMERCIO -
AGRICULTURA - INDUSTRIA **Note:** Struck at Mexico City
Mint, mint mark Mo.

Date	Mintage	F	VF	XF	Unc	BU
1951	4,958,000	—	BV	5.75	7.00	9.00
1952	9,595,000	—	BV	5.50	6.75	8.00
1953	20,376,000	—	BV	5.25	6.75	8.00
1954	30,000	—	30.00	60.00	70.00	85.00

KM# 468 5 PESOS
27.7800 g., 0.7200 Silver .6431 oz. ASW **Subject:**
Bicentennial of Hidalgo's Birth **Edge Lettering:**
COMMERCIO - AGRICULTURA - INDUSTRIA **Note:** Struck
at Mexico City Mint, mint mark Mo.

Date	Mintage	F	VF	XF	Unc	BU
1953	1,000,000	—	BV	5.50	8.00	10.00

KM# 469 5 PESOS
18.0500 g., 0.7200 Silver .4170 oz. ASW **Note:** Struck at
Mexico City Mint, mint mark Mo.

Date	Mintage	F	VF	XF	Unc	BU
1955	4,271,000	—	3.25	4.00	4.75	6.50
1956	4,596,000	—	3.25	4.00	4.75	6.50
1957	3,464,000	—	3.25	4.00	4.75	6.50

KM# 470 5 PESOS
18.0500 g., 0.7200 Silver .4170 oz. ASW **Subject:** 100th
Anniversary of Constitution **Edge Lettering:**
INDEPENDENCIA Y LIBERTDAD **Note:** Struck at Mexico
City Mint, mint mark Mo.

Date	Mintage	F	VF	XF	Unc	BU
1957	200,000	—	5.50	7.50	13.50	15.50

KM# 471 5 PESOS
18.0500 g., 0.7200 Silver .6431 oz. ASW **Subject:**
Centennial of Carranza's Birth **Edge:** Plain **Note:** Struck at
Mexico City Mint, mint mark Mo.

Date	Mintage	F	VF	XF	Unc	BU
1959	1,000,000	—	BV	4.50	6.50	8.50

Small date   Large date

KM# 472 5 PESOS
Copper-Nickel **Rev:** Vicente Guerrero **Edge Lettering:**
INDEPENDENCIA Y LIBERTDAD **Note:** Small date, large
date varieties.

Date	Mintage	F	VF	XF	Unc	BU
1971	28,457,000	—	0.50	0.95	2.50	3.25
1972	75,000,000	—	0.60	1.25	2.00	2.50
1973	19,405,000	—	1.25	2.00	4.50	5.50
1974	34,500,000	—	0.50	0.80	1.75	2.25
1976 Small date	26,121,000	—	0.75	1.45	3.25	4.00
1976 Large date	121,550,000	—	0.35	0.50	1.50	1.75
1977	102,000,000	—	0.35	0.50	1.50	1.75
1978	25,700,000	—	1.00	1.50	4.50	6.25

KM# 485 5 PESOS
Copper-Nickel **Subject:** Quetzalcoatl **Edge Lettering:**
LIBERTAD Y INDEPENDENCIA **Note:** Inverted and normal
edge legend varieties exist for the 1980 and 1981 dates.

Date	Mintage	F	VF	XF	Unc	BU
1980	266,899,999	—	0.25	0.50	1.75	2.25
1981	30,500,000	—	0.45	0.65	2.75	3.25
1982	20,000,000	—	—	1.50	2.35	4.25	5.25
1982 Proof	1,051	Value: 18.00				
1983 Proof; 7 known	—	Value: 1,200				
1984	16,300,000	—	1.25	2.00	4.75	6.00
1985	76,900,000	—	2.00	3.25	4.25	5.00

KM# 502 5 PESOS
Brass **Subject:** Quetzalcoatl **Note:** Circulation coinage.

Date	Mintage	F	VF	XF	Unc	BU
1985	30,000,000	—	—	0.15	0.35	0.50
1987	81,900,000	—	8.00	9.50	12.50	15.00
1988	76,600,000	—	—	0.10	0.25	0.35
1988 Proof; 2 known	—	Value: 600				

KM# 678 5 PESOS
27.0000 g., 0.9250 Silver 0.803 oz. ASW, 40 mm. **Subject:**
Ibero-America: Acapulco Galleon **Obv:** Mexican arms
encircled by ten coats of arms **Rev:** Spanish galleon with
Pacific Ocean background and trading scene in foreground
Edge: Reeded

Date	Mintage	F	VF	XF	Unc	BU
2003Mo Proof	5,000	Value: 65.00				

KM# 473 10 PESOS
8.3333 g., 0.9000 Gold .2411 oz. AGW **Rev:** Miguel Hidalgo
Note: Struck at Mexico City Mint, mint mark Mo.

Date	Mintage	F	VF	XF	Unc	BU
1905	39,000	110	125	155	225	—
1906	2,949,000	—	BV	110	175	—
1907	1,589,000	—	BV	110	175	—
1908	890,000	—	BV	110	175	—
1910	451,000	—	BV	110	175	—
1916	26,000	110	120	175	350	—
1917	1,967,000	—	BV	110	175	—
1919	266,000	—	BV	110	200	—
1920	12,000	150	250	425	650	—
1959	Est. 50,000	—	—	— BV+7%	—	—

Note: *During 1961-1972 a total of 954,983 pieces were
restruck, most likely dated 1959. In 1996 matte restrikes
were produced

KM# 474 10 PESOS
28.8800 g., 0.9000 Silver .8357 oz. ASW **Rev:** Miguel
Hidalgo **Note:** Struck at Mexico City Mint, mint mark Mo.

Date	Mintage	F	VF	XF	Unc	BU
1955	585,000	—	BV	6.00	8.50	11.00
1956	3,535,000	—	BV	5.50	8.00	10.00

KM# 475 10 PESOS
28.8800 g., 0.9000 Silver .8357 oz. ASW **Subject:** 100th Anniversary of Constutution **Edge Lettering:** INDEPENDENCIA Y LIBERTDAD **Note:** Struck at Mexico City Mint, mint mark Mo.

Date	Mintage	F	VF	XF	Unc	BU
1957	100,000	—	12.50	27.50	45.00	50.00

KM# 476 10 PESOS
28.8800 g., 0.9000 Silver .8357 oz. ASW **Subject:** 150th Anniversary - War of Independence **Note:** Struck at Mexico City Mint, mint mark Mo.

Date	Mintage	F	VF	XF	Unc	BU
1960	1,000,000	—	BV	6.00	9.00	12.50

KM# 477.1 10 PESOS
Copper-Nickel **Rev:** Miguel Hidalgo **Shape:** 7-sided **Note:** Thin flan - 1.6mm

Date	Mintage	F	VF	XF	Unc	BU
1974	3,900,000	—	0.50	1.00	3.00	4.00
1974 Proof	—	Value: 625				
1975	1,000,000	—	2.25	3.25	7.50	8.50
1976	74,500,000	—	0.25	0.75	1.75	2.25
1977	79,620,000	—	0.50	1.00	2.00	3.00

KM# 477.2 10 PESOS
Copper-Nickel **Rev:** Miguel Hidalgo **Note:** Thick flan - 2.3mm

Date	Mintage	F	VF	XF	Unc	BU
1978	124,850,000	—	0.50	0.75	2.50	2.75
1979	57,200,000	—	0.50	0.75	2.25	2.50

Date	Mintage	F	VF	XF	Unc	BU
1980	55,200,000	—	0.50	0.75	2.50	3.75
1981	222,768,000	—	0.40	0.60	2.25	2.65
1982	151,770,000	—	0.50	0.80	2.50	3.50
1982 Proof	1,051	Value: 40.00				
1983 Proof; 3 known	—	Value: 1,800				
1985	58,000,000	—	1.25	1.75	5.75	7.50

KM# 512 10 PESOS
Stainless Steel **Rev:** Miguel Hidalgo **Note:** Date varieties exist.

Date	Mintage	F	VF	XF	Unc	BU
1985	257,000,000	—	—	0.15	0.50	0.75
1986	392,000,000	—	—	0.15	0.50	1.50
1987	305,000,000	—	—	0.15	0.35	0.50
1988	500,300,000	—	—	0.15	0.25	0.35
1989	—	—	0.20	0.25	0.75	1.50
1990	—	—	—	0.25	0.75	1.25
1990 Proof; 2 known	—	Value: 550				

KM# 478 20 PESOS
16.6666 g., 0.9000 Gold .4823 oz. AGW **Note:** Struck at Mexico City Mint, mint mark Mo.

Date	Mintage	F	VF	XF	Unc	BU
1917	852,000	—	BV	200	250	—
1918	2,831,000	—	BV	200	250	—
1919	1,094,000	—	BV	200	250	—
1920/10	462,000	—	BV	200	250	—
1920	Inc. above	—	BV	200	250	—
1921/11	922,000	—	BV	200	250	—
1921/10	—	—	—	—	—	—
1921	Inc. above	—	BV	200	250	—
1959	Est. 13,000	—	—	—	—	—

Note: During 1960-1971 a total of 1,158,414 pieces were restruck, most likely dated 1959. In 1996 matte restrikes were produced

KM# 486 20 PESOS
Copper-Nickel

Date	Mintage	F	VF	XF	Unc	BU
1980	84,900,000	—	0.50	0.85	2.25	3.00
1981	250,573,000	—	0.60	0.80	2.25	3.25
1982	236,892,000	—	1.00	1.75	2.50	3.50
1982 Proof	1,051	Value: 45.00				
1983 Proof; 3 known	—	Value: 575				
1984	55,000,000	—	1.00	1.50	2.50	4.75

KM# 508   20 PESOS
Brass **Rev:** Guadalupe Victoria, First President

Date	Mintage	F	VF	XF	Unc	BU
1985 Wide date	25,000,000	—	0.10	0.20	1.00	1.25
1985 Narrow date	Inc. above	—	0.10	0.25	1.50	2.00
1986	10,000,000	—	1.00	1.75	5.00	5.50
1988	355,200,000	—	0.10	0.20	0.45	0.75
1989	—	—	0.15	0.30	1.50	2.00
1990	—	—	0.15	0.30	1.50	2.50
1990 Proof; 3 known	—	Value: 575				

Normal tongue

KM# 479.1   25 PESOS
22.5000 g., 0.7200 Silver .5209 oz. ASW **Obv:** Snake with straight tongue **Note:** Type I, Rings aligned.

Date	Mintage	F	VF	XF	Unc	BU
1968	27,182,000	—	BV	4.00	4.50	5.50

KM# 479.2   25 PESOS
22.5000 g., 0.7200 Silver .5209 oz. ASW **Subject:** Summer Olympics - Mexico City **Note:** Type II, center ring low.

Date	Mintage	F	VF	XF	Unc	BU
1968	Inc. above	—	4.00	5.00	8.50	10.00

Long curved tongue

KM# 479.3   25 PESOS
22.5000 g., 0.7200 Silver .5209 oz. ASW **Subject:** Summer Olympics - Mexico City **Note:** Snake with long curved or normal tongue. Type III, center rings low.

Date	Mintage	F	VF	XF	Unc	BU
1968	Inc. above	—	4.25	5.25	9.00	10.50

KM# 480   25 PESOS
22.5000 g., 0.7200 Silver .5209 oz. ASW **Rev:** Benito Juarez

Date	Mintage	F	VF	XF	Unc	BU
1972	2,000,000	—	—	4.00	5.50	7.50

KM# 497   25 PESOS
7.7760 g., 0.7200 Silver .1800 oz. ASW **Subject:** 1986 World Cup Soccer Games

Date	Mintage	F	VF	XF	Unc	BU
1985	354,000	—	—	—	—	7.50

KM# 503   25 PESOS
8.4060 g., 0.9250 Silver .2450 oz. ASW **Subject:** 1986 World Cup Soccer Games **Rev:** Pre-Columbian geroglyphs, ojo de bury, and soccer ball

Date	Mintage	F	VF	XF	Unc	BU
1985 Proof	277,000	Value: 12.00				

KM# 514   25 PESOS
8.4060 g., 0.9250 Silver .2450 oz. ASW **Subject:** 1986 World Cup Soccer Games

Date	Mintage	F	VF	XF	Unc	BU
1985 Proof	234,000	Value: 12.00				

KM# 497a 25 PESOS
8.4060 g., 0.9250 Silver .2450 oz. ASW **Subject:** 1986 World
Cup Soccer Games **Rev:** Without fineness statement

Date	Mintage	F	VF	XF	Unc	BU
1986 Proof	—	Value: 12.00				

KM# 519 25 PESOS
8.4060 g., 0.9250 Silver .2450 oz. ASW **Subject:** 1986 World
Cup Soccer Games

Date	Mintage	F	VF	XF	Unc	BU
1986 Proof	—	Value: 12.00				

KM# 481 50 PESOS
41.6666 g., 0.9000 Gold 1.2057 oz. AGW **Subject:**
Centennial of Independence **Edge:** Reeded **Note:** During
1949-1972 a total of 3,975,654 pieces were restruck, most
likely dated 1947. In 1996 matte restrikes were produced.
Struck at Mexico City Mint, mint mark Mo.

Date	Mintage	F	VF	XF	Unc	BU
1921	180,000	—	—	BV	725	—
1922	463,000	—	—	BV	525	—
1923	432,000	—	—	BV	525	—
1924	439,000	—	—	BV	525	—
1925	716,000	—	—	BV	525	—
1926	600,000	—	—	BV	525	—
1927	606,000	—	—	BV	525	—
1928	538,000	—	—	BV	525	—
1929	458,000	—	—	BV	525	—
1930	372,000	—	—	BV	525	—
1931	137,000	—	—	BV	575	—
1944	593,000	—	—	BV	525	—
1945	1,012,000	—	—	BV	525	—
1946	1,588,000	—	—	BV	525	—
1947	309,000	—	—	—	BV+3%	—
1947 Specimen	—	—	—	—	—	—

Note: Value, $6,500

KM# 482 50 PESOS
41.6666 g., 0.9000 Gold 1.2057 oz. AGW

Date	Mintage	F	VF	XF	Unc	BU
1943	89,000	—	—	—	BV	535

KM# 490 50 PESOS
Copper-Nickel **Subject:** Coyolxauhqui **Edge:** Reeded **Note:**
Doubled die examples of 1982 and 1983 dates exist.

Date	Mintage	F	VF	XF	Unc	BU
1982	222,890,000	—	1.00	2.50	5.00	6.00
1983	45,000,000	—	1.50	3.00	6.00	6.50
1983 Proof	1,051	Value: 40.00				
1984	73,537,000	—	1.00	1.35	3.50	4.00
1984 Proof; 4 known	—	Value: 750				

KM# 495 50 PESOS
Copper-Nickel **Subject:** Benito Juarez **Edge:** Reeded

Date	Mintage	F	VF	XF	Unc	BU
1984	94,216,000	—	0.65	1.25	2.70	3.00
1985	296,000,000	—	0.25	0.45	1.25	2.00
1986	50,000,000	—	6.00	10.00	12.00	14.00
1987	210,000,000	—	0.25	0.45	1.00	1.25
1988	80,200,000	—	6.25	9.00	13.50	15.50

KM# 495a 50 PESOS
Stainless Steel **Subject:** Benito Juarez **Edge:** Plain

Date	Mintage	F	VF	XF	Unc	BU
1988	353,300,000	—	—	0.20	1.25	1.75
1990	—	—	—	0.30	1.00	2.00
1992	—	—	—	0.25	1.00	2.75

KM# 498 50 PESOS
15.5520 g., 0.7200 Silver .3601 oz. ASW **Subject:** 1986
World Cup Soccer Games

Date	Mintage	F	VF	XF	Unc	BU
1985	347,000	—	—	—	—	6.50

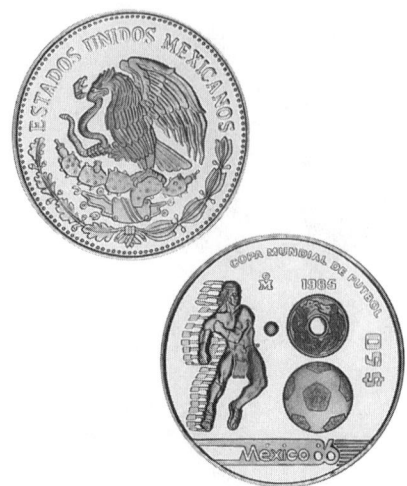

KM# 504 50 PESOS
16.8310 g., 0.9250 Silver .5000 oz. ASW **Subject:** 1986
World Cup Soccer Games **Rev:** Pre-Columbia athlete playing
pot-a-poke, or tlachco, the forerunners of soccer; without
fineness statement

Date	Mintage	F	VF	XF	Unc	BU
1985 Proof	347,000	Value: 20.00				

KM# 515 50 PESOS
16.8310 g., 0.9250 Silver .5000 oz. ASW **Subject:** 1986
World Cup Soccer Games

Date	Mintage	F	VF	XF	Unc	BU
1985 Proof	234,000	Value: 20.00				

KM# 523 50 PESOS
16.8310 g., 0.9250 Silver .5000 oz. ASW **Subject:** 1986
World Cup Soccer Games

Date	Mintage	F	VF	XF	Unc	BU
1986 Proof	190,000	Value: 20.00				

KM# 498a 50 PESOS
16.8310 g., 0.9250 Silver .5000 oz. ASW **Subject:** 1986
World Cup Soccer Games **Rev:** Without fineness statement

Date	Mintage	F	VF	XF	Unc	BU
1986 Proof	10,000	Value: 20.00				

KM# 532 50 PESOS
15.5500 g., 0.9990 Silver .5000 oz. ASW **Subject:** 50th
Anniversary - Nationalization of Oil Industry

Date	Mintage	F	VF	XF	Unc	BU
ND(1988)	30,000	—	—	—	20.00	22.00

Low 7's

KM# 483.1 100 PESOS
27.7700 g., 0.7200 Silver .6429 oz. ASW **Rev:** Jose Morelos
y Pavon **Edge:** Reeded

Date	Mintage	F	VF	XF	Unc	BU
1977 Low 7's, sloping right shoulder round left shoulder with no clothing folds	5,225,000	—	BV	4.00	6.00	10.00
1977 High 7's, sloping right shoulder, round right shoulder with no clothing folds	Inc. above	—	BV	4.00	6.00	10.50

High 7's

KM# 483.2   100 PESOS
27.7700 g., 0.7200 Silver .6429 oz. ASW **Rev:** Jose Morelos
y Pavon

Date	Mintage	F	VF	XF	Unc	BU
1977 Date in line, higher	—	—	BV	4.00	5.00	6.50
right shoulder, left						
shoulder with clothing						
folds. Mintage inc.						
KM#483.1						
1978	9,879,000	—	BV	4.00	6.50	8.50
1979	784,000	—	BV	4.00	6.50	8.50
1979 Proof	—	Value: 650				

KM# 493   100 PESOS
Aluminum-Bronze **Rev:** Venustiano Carranza

Date	Mintage	F	VF	XF	Unc	BU
1984	227,809,000	—	0.45	0.60	2.50	4.00
1985	377,423,000	—	0.30	0.50	2.00	3.00
1986	43,000,000	—	1.00	2.50	4.75	7.50
1987	165,000,000	—	0.60	1.25	2.25	3.00
1988	433,100,000	—	0.30	0.50	2.00	2.75
1989	—	—	0.35	0.65	2.00	2.75
1990	—	—	0.15	0.40	1.50	2.50
1990 Proof; 1	—	Value: 650				
known						
1991	—	—	0.15	0.25	1.00	2.50
1992	—	—	0.30	0.75	1.75	3.00

KM# 499   100 PESOS
31.1030 g., 0.7200 Silver .7201 oz. ASW **Subject:** 1986
World Cup Soccer Games

Date	Mintage	F	VF	XF	Unc	BU
1985	302,000	—	—	—	—	15.00

KM# 499a   100 PESOS
32.6250 g., 0.9250 Silver 1.0000 oz. ASW **Subject:** 1986
World Cup Soccer Games **Rev:** Without fineness statement

Date	Mintage	F	VF	XF	Unc	BU
1985 Proof	9,006	Value: 30.00				

KM# 505   100 PESOS
32.6250 g., 0.9250 Silver 1.0000 oz. ASW **Subject:** 1986
World Cup Soccer Games **Rev:** Defensive player shown
heading the ball away from the net, without fineness statement

Date	Mintage	F	VF	XF	Unc	BU
1985 Proof	9,006	Value: 30.00				

KM# 521   100 PESOS
32.6250 g., 0.9250 Silver 1.0000 oz. ASW **Subject:** 1986
World Cup Soccer Games **Rev:** Without fineness statement

Date	Mintage	F	VF	XF	Unc	BU
1986 Proof	208,000	Value: 30.00				

KM# 524   100 PESOS
32.6250 g., 0.9250 Silver 1.0000 oz. ASW **Subject:** 1986
World Cup Soccer Games **Rev:** Without fineness statement

Date	Mintage	F	VF	XF	Unc	BU
1986 Proof	190,000	Value: 30.00				

KM# 537   100 PESOS
32.6250 g., 0.9250 Silver 1.0000 oz. ASW **Subject:** World
Wildlife Fund **Rev:** Monarch butterflies

Date	Mintage	F	VF	XF	Unc	BU
1987 Proof	Est. 30,000	Value: 50.00				

KM# 533   100 PESOS
31.1030 g., 0.9990 Silver 1.0000 oz. ASW **Subject:** 50th
Anniversary - Nationalization of Oil Industry

Date	Mintage	F	VF	XF	Unc	BU
1988	10,000	—	—	—	27.00	40.00

KM# 539   100 PESOS
33.6250 g., 0.9250 Silver 1.0000 oz. ASW **Subject:** Save
the Children

Date	Mintage	F	VF	XF	Unc	BU
1991 Proof	30,000	Value: 45.00				

KM# 540   100 PESOS
27.0000 g., 0.9250 Silver .8029 oz. ASW **Subject:** Ibero -
American Series **Rev:** Pillars

Date	Mintage	F	VF	XF	Unc	BU
1991 Proof	50,000	Value: 55.00				
1992 Proof	75,000	Value: 45.00				

KM# 566 100 PESOS
31.1035 g., 0.9990 Silver 1.0000 oz. ASW **Subject:** Save the Vaquita Porpoise

Date	Mintage	F	VF	XF	Unc	BU
1992 Proof	—	Value: 45.00				

KM# 509 200 PESOS
Copper-Nickel **Subject:** 175th Anniversary of Independence **Rev:** Independence monument, heads of Allendi, Hidalgo, Morelos and Guerrero

Date	Mintage	F	VF	XF	Unc	BU
1985	75,000,000	—	—	0.25	3.00	4.00

KM# 510 200 PESOS
Copper-Nickel **Subject:** 175th Anniversary of 1910 Revolution **Rev:** Heads of Pancho Villa, Emiliano Zapata, Venustiano Carranza and Francisco Madera

Date	Mintage	F	VF	XF	Unc	BU
1985	98,590,000	—	—	0.25	3.25	4.50

KM# 525 200 PESOS
Copper-Nickel **Subject:** 1986 World Cup Soccer Games
Edge: Reeded

Date	Mintage	F	VF	XF	Unc	BU
1986	50,000,000	—	—	1.00	3.50	4.50

KM# 526 200 PESOS
62.2060 g., 0.9990 Silver 2.0000 oz. ASW **Subject:** 1986 World Cup Soccer Games

Date	Mintage	F	VF	XF	Unc	BU
1986	50,000	—	—	—	40.00	50.00

KM# 500.1 250 PESOS
8.6400 g., 0.9000 Gold .2500 oz. AGW **Subject:** 1986 World Cup Soccer Games

Date	Mintage	F	VF	XF	Unc	BU
1985	100,000	—	—	—	—	115
1986	—	—	—	—	—	115

KM# 500.2 250 PESOS
8.6400 g., 0.9000 Gold .2500 oz. AGW **Subject:** 1986 World Cup Soccer Games **Rev:** Without fineness statement

Date	Mintage	F	VF	XF	Unc	BU
1985 Proof	4,506	Value: 135				
1986 Proof	—	Value: 145				

KM# 506.1 250 PESOS
8.6400 g., 0.9000 Gold .2500 oz. AGW **Subject:** 1986 World Cup Soccer Games

Date	Mintage	F	VF	XF	Unc	BU
1985	88,000	—	—	—	—	115

KM# 506.2 250 PESOS
8.6400 g., 0.9000 Gold .2500 oz. AGW **Subject:** 1986 World Cup Soccer Games **Rev:** Without fineness statement

Date	Mintage	F	VF	XF	Unc	BU
1985 Proof	Est. 80,000	Value: 115				

KM# 501.1 500 PESOS
17.2800 g., 0.9000 Gold .5000 oz. AGW **Subject:** 1986
World Cup Soccer Games **Obv:** Eagle facing left with snake
in beak

Date	Mintage	F	VF	XF	Unc	BU
1985	102,000	—	—	—	—	225
1986	—	—	—	—	—	225

KM# 501.2 500 PESOS
17.2800 g., 0.9000 Gold .5000 oz. AGW **Subject:** 1986
World Cup Soccer Games **Obv:** Eagle facing left with snake
in beak **Rev:** Without fineness statement

Date	Mintage	F	VF	XF	Unc	BU
1985 Proof	5,506	Value: 235				
1986 Proof	—	Value: 235				

KM# 507.1 500 PESOS
17.2800 g., 0.9000 Gold .5000 oz. AGW **Subject:** 1986
World Cup Soccer Games **Obv:** Eagle facing left with snake
in beak

Date	Mintage	F	VF	XF	Unc	BU
1985	—	—	—	—	—	235

KM# 507.2 500 PESOS
17.2800 g., 0.9000 Gold .5000 oz. AGW **Subject:** 1986
World Cup Soccer Games **Obv:** Eagle facing left with snake
in beak **Rev:** Without fineness statement

Date	Mintage	F	VF	XF	Unc	BU
1985 Proof	—	Value: 235				

KM# 511 500 PESOS
33.4500 g., 0.9250 Silver 1.0000 oz. ASW **Subject:** 17th
Anniversary of 1910 Revolution **Obv:** Eagle facing left with
snake in beak

Date	Mintage	F	VF	XF	Unc	BU
1985 Proof	40,000	Value: 35.00				

KM# 529 500 PESOS
Copper-Nickel **Rev:** Francisco Madero

Date	Mintage	F	VF	XF	Unc	BU
1986	20,000,000	—	—	1.00	3.25	3.50
1987	180,000,000	—	—	0.75	2.25	2.50
1988	230,000,000	—	—	0.50	2.25	2.50
1988 Proof; 2 known	—	Value: 650				
1989	—	—	—	0.75	2.25	3.00
1992	—	—	—	1.00	2.25	3.50

KM# 534 500 PESOS
17.2800 g., 0.9000 Gold .5000 oz. AGW **Subject:** 50th
Anniversary - Nationalization of Oil Industry **Rev:** Monument
Note: Similar to 5000 Pesos, KM#531.

Date	Mintage	F	VF	XF	Unc	BU
1988	—	—	—	—	—	235

KM# 513 1000 PESOS
17.2800 g., 0.9000 Gold .5000 oz. AGW **Subject:** 175th
Anniversary of Independence

Date	Mintage	F	VF	XF	Unc	BU
1985 Proof	—	Value: 325				

KM# 527 1000 PESOS
31.1030 g., 0.9990 Gold 1.0000 oz. AGW **Subject:** 1986
World Cup Soccer Games

Date	Mintage	F	VF	XF	Unc	BU
1986	—	—	—	—	—	550

KM# 536 1000 PESOS
Aluminum-Bronze **Note:** Juana de Asbaje

Date	Mintage	F	VF	XF	Unc	BU
1988	229,300,000	—	0.85	2.00	4.25	5.75
1989	—	—	0.85	2.00	4.25	5.75

Date	Mintage	F	VF	XF	Unc	BU
1990	—	—	0.85	2.00	4.00	5.50
1990 Proof; 2 known	—	Value: 550				
1991	—	—	1.00	2.00	3.00	7.00
1992	—	—	1.00	2.00	3.00	7.00

KM# 535   1000 PESOS
34.5590 g., 0.9000 Gold 1.0000 oz. AGW **Subject:** 50th Anniversary - Nationalization of Oil Industry **Rev:** Portrait of Cardenas **Note:** Similar to 5000 Pesos, KM#531.

Date	Mintage	F	VF	XF	Unc	BU
1988 Proof	—	Value: 550				

KM# 528   2000 PESOS
62.2000 g., 0.9990 Gold 2.0000 oz. AGW **Subject:** 1986 World Cup Soccer Games

Date	Mintage	F	VF	XF	Unc	BU
1986	—	—	—	—	—	900

KM# 531   5000 PESOS
Copper-Nickel **Subject:** 50th Anniversary - Nationalization of Oil Industry

Date	Mintage	F	VF	XF	Unc	BU
ND(1988)	50,000,000	—	—	4.75	7.75	10.00

REFORM COINAGE
1 New Peso = 1000 Old Pesos

KM# 546   5 CENTAVOS
Stainless Steel

Date	Mintage	F	VF	XF	Unc	BU
1992	136,800,000	—	—	0.15	0.20	0.25
1993	234,000,000	—	—	0.15	0.20	0.25
1994	125,000,000	—	—	0.15	0.20	0.25
1995	195,000,000	—	—	0.15	0.20	0.25
1995 Proof	6,981	Value: 0.50				
1996	104,831,000	—	—	0.15	0.20	0.25
1997	153,675,000	—	—	0.15	0.20	0.25
1998	64,417,000	—	—	0.15	0.20	0.25
1999	9,949,000	—	—	0.15	0.20	0.25
2000Mo	10,871,000	—	—	0.15	0.20	0.25
2001Mo	34,811,000	—	—	0.15	0.20	0.25
2002Mo	14,901,000	—	—	0.15	0.20	0.25

KM# 547   10 CENTAVOS
Stainless Steel

Date	Mintage	F	VF	XF	Unc	BU
1992	121,250,000	—	—	0.20	0.30	0.35
1993	755,000,000	—	—	0.20	0.25	0.30
1994	557,000,000	—	—	0.20	0.25	0.30
1995	560,000,000	—	—	0.20	0.25	0.30
1995 Proof	6,981	Value: 0.50				
1996	594,216,000	—	—	0.20	0.25	0.30
1997	581,622,000	—	—	0.20	0.25	0.30
1998	602,667,000	—	—	0.20	0.25	0.30
1999	488,346,000	—	—	0.20	0.25	0.30
2000	577,546,000	—	—	0.20	0.30	0.35
2001	618,061,000	—	—	0.20	0.25	0.30
2002	463,968,000	—	—	0.20	0.25	0.30
2003Mo	378,938,000	—	—	0.20	0.25	0.30

KM# 548   20 CENTAVOS
Aluminum-Bronze

Date	Mintage	F	VF	XF	Unc	BU
1992	95,000,000	—	—	0.25	0.35	0.40
1993	95,000,000	—	—	0.25	0.35	0.40
1994	105,000,000	—	—	0.25	0.35	0.40
1995	180,000,000	—	—	0.25	0.35	0.40
1995 Proof	6,981	Value: 0.75				
1996	54,896,000	—	—	0.25	0.35	0.40
1997	178,807,000	—	—	0.25	0.35	0.40
1998	223,847,000	—	—	0.25	0.35	0.40
1999	233,753,000	—	—	0.25	0.35	0.40
2000	223,973,000	—	—	0.25	0.35	0.40
2001	234,360,000	—	—	0.25	0.35	0.40
2002Mo	229,256,000	—	—	0.25	0.35	0.40
2003Mo	149,518,000	—	—	0.25	0.35	0.40

KM# 549   50 CENTAVOS
Aluminum-Bronze **Shape:** Scalloped

Date	Mintage	F	VF	XF	Unc	BU
1992	120,150,000	—	—	0.45	0.85	1.00
1993	330,000,000	—	—	0.45	0.75	1.00
1994	100,000,000	—	—	0.45	0.75	1.00
1995	60,000,000	—	—	0.45	0.75	1.00
1995 Proof	6,981	Value: 0.90				
1996	69,956,000	—	—	0.45	0.75	1.00
1997	129,029,000	—	—	0.45	0.75	1.00
1998	223,605,000	—	—	0.45	0.75	1.00
1999	89,516,000	—	—	0.45	0.75	1.00
2000	135,112,000	—	—	0.45	0.75	1.00
2001	199,006,000	—	—	0.45	0.75	1.00
2002	94,552,000	—	—	0.45	0.75	1.00
2003Mo	124,522,000	—	—	0.45	0.75	1.00

KM# 550   NUEVO PESO
Bi-Metallic Aluminumn-Bronze center in Stainless Steel ring

Date	Mintage	F	VF	XF	Unc	BU
1992	144,000,000	—	—	0.60	1.50	2.25
1993	329,860,000	—	—	0.60	1.50	2.25
1994	221,000,000	—	—	0.60	1.50	2.25

Date	Mintage	F	VF	XF	Unc	BU
1995 Small date	125,000,000	—	—	0.60	1.50	2.25
1995 Large date	Inc. above	—	—	0.60	1.50	2.25
1995 Proof	6,981	Value: 2.75				

KM# 603   PESO
Note: Similar to KM#550 but without N.

Date	Mintage	F	VF	XF	Unc	BU
1996Mo	169,510,000	—	—	—	1.25	2.25
1997Mo	222,870,000	—	—	—	1.25	2.25
1998Mo	261,942,000	—	—	—	1.25	2.25
1999Mo	99,168,000	—	—	—	1.25	2.25
2000Mo	158,379,000	—	—	—	1.25	2.25
2001Mo	208,576,000	—	—	—	1.25	2.25
2002Mo	119,541,000	—	—	—	1.25	2.25
2003Mo	169,320,000	—	—	—	1.25	2.25

KM# 551   2 NUEVOS PESOS
Bi-Metallic Aluminumn-Bronze center in Stainless Steel ring

Date	Mintage	F	VF	XF	Unc	BU
1992	60,000,000	—	—	1.00	2.35	2.50
1993	77,000,000	—	—	1.00	2.35	2.50
1994	44,000,000	—	—	1.00	2.35	2.50
1995	20,000,000	—	—	1.00	2.35	2.50
1995 Proof	6,981	Value: 4.50				

KM# 604   2 PESOS
Bi-Metallic Aluminumn-Bronze center in Stainless Steel ring
Note: Similar to KM#551, but denomination without N.

Date	Mintage	F	VF	XF	Unc	BU
1996Mo	24,902,000	—	—	—	2.35	2.50
1997Mo	34,560,000	—	—	—	2.35	2.50
1998Mo	104,138,000	—	—	—	2.35	2.50
1999Mo	34,713,000	—	—	—	2.35	2.50
2000Mo	69,322,000	—	—	—	2.35	2.50
2001Mo	74,563,000	—	—	—	2.35	2.50
2002Mo	74,547,000	—	—	—	2.35	2.50
2003Mo	39,814,000	—	—	—	2.35	2.50

KM# 552   5 NUEVOS PESOS
Bi-Metallic Aluminumn-Bronze center in Stainless Steel ring

Date	Mintage	F	VF	XF	Unc	BU
1992	70,000,000	—	—	2.00	4.00	4.50
1993	168,240,000	—	—	2.00	4.00	4.50
1994	58,000,000	—	—	2.00	4.00	4.50
1995 Proof	6,981	Value: 25.00				

KM# 588   5 NUEVOS PESOS
27.0000 g., 0.9250 Silver .8030 oz. ASW **Subject:**
Environmental Protection **Rev:** Pacific Ridley Sea Turtle

Date	Mintage	F	VF	XF	Unc	BU
1994 Proof	20,000	Value: 50.00				

KM# 652   5 NUEVOS PESOS
31.1710 g., 0.9990 Silver 1.0012 oz. ASW, 40 mm. **Series:**
Endangered Wildlife **Subject:** Aguila Real **Obv:** National
arms past and present **Rev:** Eagle on branch

Date	Mintage	F	VF	XF	Unc	BU
2000	50,000	—	—	—	30.00	—

KM# 655   5 NUEVOS PESOS
31.1710 g., 0.9990 Silver 1.0012 oz. ASW, 40 mm. **Series:**
Endangered Wildlife **Subject:** Cocodrilo de Rio **Obv:** National
arms past and present **Rev:** Crocodile

Date	Mintage	F	VF	XF	Unc	BU
2000	50,000	—	—	—	30.00	—

KM# 657   5 NUEVOS PESOS
31.1710 g., 0.9990 Silver 1.0012 oz. ASW, 40 mm. **Series:**
Endangered Wildlife - Berrendo **Obv:** National arms past and
present **Rev:** Peninsula antelope, giant cardon cactus in back

Date	Mintage	F	VF	XF	Unc	BU
2000	50,000	—	—	—	30.00	—

KM# 658 5 NUEVOS PESOS
31.1710 g., 0.9990 Silver 1.0012 oz. ASW, 40 mm. **Series:**
Endangered Wildlife **Obv:** National arms past and present
Rev: Jaguar resting

Date	Mintage	F	VF	XF	Unc	BU
2001	50,000	—	—	—	30.00	—

KM# 653 5 NUEVOS PESOS
31.1710 g., 0.9990 Silver 1.0012 oz. ASW, 40 mm. **Subject:**
Aguila Arpia **Obv:** National arms past and present **Rev:**
Harpie Eagle

Date	Mintage	F	VF	XF	Unc	BU
2001	50,000	—	—	—	30.00	—

KM# 656 5 NUEVOS PESOS
31.1710 g., 0.9990 Silver 1.0012 oz. ASW, 40 mm. **Series:**
Endangered Wildlife **Subject:** Nutria de Rio **Obv:** National
arms past and present **Rev:** Nutria

Date	Mintage	F	VF	XF	Unc	BU
2000	50,000	—	—	—	30.00	—

KM# 654 5 NUEVOS PESOS
31.1710 g., 0.9990 Silver 1.0012 oz. ASW, 40 mm. **Series:**
Endangered Wildlife **Subject:** Oso Negro **Obv:** National arms
past and present **Rev:** Black bear

Date	Mintage	F	VF	XF	Unc	BU
2001	50,000	—	—	—	30.00	—

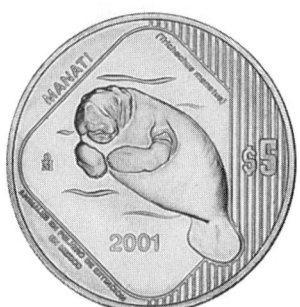

KM# 651 5 NUEVOS PESOS
31.1710 g., 0.9990 Silver 1.0012 oz. ASW, 40 mm. **Series:**
Endangered Wildlife **Obv:** National arms past and present
Rev: West Indian Manati **Edge:** Reeded

Date	Mintage	F	VF	XF	Unc	BU
2001	50,000	—	—	—	30.00	—

KM# 659 5 NUEVOS PESOS
31.1710 g., 0.9990 Silver 1.0012 oz. ASW, 40 mm. **Series:**
Endangered Wildlife **Obv:** National arms past and present
Rev: Black-tailed Prairie dog

Date	Mintage	F	VF	XF	Unc	BU
2001	50,000	—	—	—	30.00	—

KM# 660 5 NUEVOS PESOS
31.1710 g., 0.9990 Silver 1.0012 oz. ASW, 40 mm. **Series:** Endangered Wildlife **Obv:** National arms past and present **Rev:** Volcano Rabbit

Date	Mintage	F	VF	XF	Unc	BU
2001	50,000	—	—	—	30.00	—

KM# 629 5 PESOS
27.0000 g., 0.9250 Silver .8030 oz. ASW **Subject:** Jarabe Tapatio **Obv:** Mexican emblem within circle of arms **Rev:** Two dancers

Date	Mintage	F	VF	XF	Unc	BU
1997 Proof	20,000	Value: 275				
1998 Proof	—	Value: 275				

KM# 605 5 PESOS
Bi-Metallic Aluminumn-Bronze center in Stainless Steel ring **Note:** Similar to KM#552 but deonomination without N.

Date	Mintage	F	VF	XF	Unc	BU
1997Mo	39,468,000	—	—	3.00	4.00	5.00
1998Mo	103,729,000	—	—	3.00	4.00	5.00
1999Mo	59,427,000	—	—	3.00	4.00	5.00
2000Mo	20,869,000	—	—	3.00	4.00	5.00
2001Mo	79,169,000	—	—	3.00	4.00	5.00
2002Mo	34,754,000	—	—	3.00	4.00	5.00
2003Mo	54,676,000	—	—	3.00	4.00	5.00

KM# 627 5 PESOS
31.1035 g., 0.9990 Silver 1.0000 oz. ASW **Subject:** World Wildlife Fund **Obv:** Mexican eagle **Rev:** Wolf with pup

Date	Mintage	F	VF	XF	Unc	BU
1998 Proof	Est. 15,000	Value: 75.00				

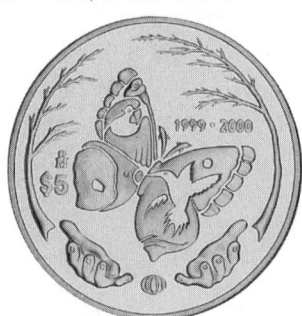

KM# 630 5 PESOS
31.1800 g., 0.9990 Silver 1.0025 oz. ASW **Subject:** Millennium Series **Obv:** Current national eagle within circle of obsolete versions **Rev:** Butterfly, dates **Rev. Designer:** Francisco Ortega Romero

Date	Mintage	F	VF	XF	Unc	BU
1999-2000 Proof	75,000	Value: 40.00				

KM# 631 5 PESOS
31.1800 g., 0.9990 Silver 1.0025 oz. ASW **Subject:** Millennium Series **Obv:** Current national eagle within circle of obsolete versions **Rev:** Stylized dove/hand of peace **Rev. Designer:** Omar Jiminez Torres

Date	Mintage	F	VF	XF	Unc	BU
1999-2000 Proof	75,000	Value: 40.00				

KM# 632 5 PESOS
31.1800 g., 0.9990 Silver 1.0025 oz. ASW **Subject:**
Millennium Series **Obv:** Current national eagle within circle
of obsolete versions **Rev:** Olga Maria Vega de Ochoa

Date	Mintage	F	VF	XF	Unc	BU
1999-2000 Proof	75,000	Value: 40.00				

KM# 635 5 PESOS
19.6000 g., 0.9250 Silver .6411 oz. ASW **Subject:**
Millennium Series **Obv:** Current national eagle within circle
of obsolete versions **Rev:** Naval training ship Cuauhtemoc

Date	Mintage	F	VF	XF	Unc	BU
1999	—	Value: 35.00				

KM# 640 5 PESOS
31.1030 g., 0.9990 Silver .9990 oz. ASW, 40 mm. **Subject:**
UNICEF **Obv:** National arms **Rev:** Two children flying kite
Edge: Reeded

Date	Mintage	F	VF	XF	Unc	BU
1999 Proof	—	Value: 45.00				

KM# 670 5 PESOS
27.0000 g., 0.9250 Silver 0.803 oz. ASW, 40 mm. **Series:**
Ibero-America **Obv:** Mexican arms within circle of other
national arms **Rev:** Cowboy trick riding two horses **Edge:**
Reeded

Date	Mintage	F	VF	XF	Unc	BU
2000 Proof	—	Value: 45.00				

KM# 553 10 NUEVOS PESOS
Bi-Metallic 0.925 Silver center%2C .1667 oz. ASW within
Aluminumn-Bronze ring

Date	Mintage	F	VF	XF	Unc	BU
1992	20,000,000	—	—	—	7.50	8.50
1993	47,981,000	—	—	—	7.50	8.50
1994	15,000,000	—	—	—	7.50	8.50
1995	15,000,000	—	—	—	7.50	8.50
1995 Proof	6,981	Value: 15.00				

KM# 576 10 NUEVOS PESOS
 Center Weight: 115.5175 g. **Center Composition:** 0.9990
Silver 4.9956 oz. ASW , 64 mm. **Subject:** Piramide del
Castillo **Note:** Illustration reduced.

Date	Mintage	F	VF	XF	Unc	BU
1994	20,000	—	—	—	—	55.00
1994 Proof	2,100	Value: 85.00				

KM# 606   10 PESOS
Bi-Metallic 0.925 Silver .1667 ASW center within Aluminumn-Bronze ring **Note:** Similar to KM#553, but denomination without N.

Date	Mintage	F	VF	XF	Unc	BU
1996 Reported not confirmed	—	—	—	—	—	—

KM# 616   10 PESOS
Bi-Metallic Copper-Nickel-Brass center within Brass ring **Obv:** National emblem **Rev:** Aztec design

Date	Mintage	F	VF	XF	Unc	BU
1997	44,837,000	—	—	—	5.00	6.50
1998	203,735,000	—	—	—	5.00	6.50
1998	—	—	—	—	5.00	6.50

Note: Small date, date on brass ring

1998	—	—	—	—	5.00	6.50

Note: Large date, date partially on copper-nickel center

1999	29,842,000	—	—	—	5.00	6.50
2000	—	—	—	—	5.00	6.50
2002	44,721,000	—	—	—	5.00	6.50

KM# 633   10 PESOS
62.0300 g., 0.9990 Silver 1.9923 oz. ASW **Subject:** Millennium Series **Obv:** Current national eagle within circle of obsolete versions **Rev:** Old and modern buildings, dates

Date	Mintage	F	VF	XF	Unc	BU
1999-2000 Proof	75,000	Value: 45.00				

KM# 636   10 PESOS
Bi-Metallic Copper-Nickel center in Brass ring **Subject:** Millennium Series **Rev:** Aztec carving

Date	Mintage	F	VF	XF	Unc	BU
2000Mo	24,839,000	—	—	—	5.00	6.50
2001Mo	44,768,000	—	—	—	5.00	6.50
2002Mo	—	—	—	—	5.00	6.50
2003Mo	—	—	—	—	5.00	6.50

KM# 561   20 NUEVOS PESOS
Bi-Metallic 0.925 Silver .2500 oz. ASW center within Aluminumn-Bronze ring

Date	Mintage	F	VF	XF	Unc	BU
1993	25,000,000	—	—	—	12.00	13.00
1994	5,000,000	—	—	—	12.00	13.00
1995	5,000,000	—	—	—	12.00	13.00

KM# 641   20 PESOS
6.2210 g., 0.9990 Gold .1998 oz. AGW, 21.9 mm. **Subject:** UNICEF **Obv:** National arms **Rev:** Child playing with lasso **Edge:** Reeded

Date	Mintage	F	VF	XF	Unc	BU
1999 Proof	—	Value: 275				

KM# 637   20 PESOS
Bi-Metallic Copper-Nickel center within Brass ring **Subject:** Xiuhtecuhtli **Rev:** Aztec with torch

Date	Mintage	F	VF	XF	Unc	BU
2000	14,890,000	—	—	—	15.00	17.50
2001	2,478,000	—	—	—	15.00	17.50

KM# 638   20 PESOS
Bi-Metallic Copper-Nickel center within Brass ring **Rev:** Octavio Paz

Date	Mintage	F	VF	XF	Unc	BU
2000	14,943,000	—	—	—	15.00	17.50
2001	2,515,000	—	—	—	15.00	17.50

KM# 571 50 NUEVOS PESOS
Bi-Metallic 0.925 Silver .5000 ASW center within Brass ring
Subject: Nino Heroes

Date	Mintage	F	VF	XF	Unc	BU
1993	2,000,000	—	—	—	25.00	28.00
1994	1,500,000	—	—	—	25.00	28.00
1995	1,500,000	—	—	—	25.00	28.00

KM# 608 50 PESOS
Bi-Metallic 0.925 Silver .5000 ASW center within Brass ring
Note: Similar to 50 New Pesos, KM#571 without "N" before denomination.

Date	Mintage	F	VF	XF	Unc	BU
1996 Reported not confirmed	—	—	—	—	—	—

SILVER BULLION COINAGE
Libertad Series

KM# 542 1/20 ONZA (1/20 Troy Ounce of Silver)
1.5551 g., 0.9990 Silver .0500 oz. ASW **Rev:** Winged Victory

Date	Mintage	F	VF	XF	Unc	BU
1991	50,017	—	—	—	—	4.50
1992	295,783	—	—	—	—	4.50
1992 Proof	5,000	Value: 10.00				
1993	100,000	—	—	—	—	4.50
1993 Proof	—	Value: 10.00				
1994	90,100	—	—	—	—	4.50
1994 Proof	10,000	Value: 10.00				
1995	50,000	—	—	—	—	4.50
1995 Proof	2,000	Value: 10.00				

KM# 609 1/20 ONZA (1/20 Troy Ounce of Silver)
1.5551 g., 0.9990 Silver .0500 oz. ASW **Obv:** Mexican eagle
Rev: Winged Victory

Date	Mintage	F	VF	XF	Unc	BU
1996	50,000	—	—	—	—	4.50
1996 Proof	1,000	Value: 10.00				
1997	20,000	—	—	—	—	5.00
1997 Proof	800	Value: 12.00				
1998	6,400	—	—	—	—	7.00
1998 Proof	300	Value: 12.00				
1999	8,001	—	—	—	—	7.00
1999 Proof	600	Value: 11.50				

Date	Mintage	F	VF	XF	Unc	BU
2000	57,500	—	—	—	—	5.00
2000 Proof	900	Value: 10.00				
2001	25,000	—	—	—	—	4.50
2001 Proof	1,500	Value: 10.00				
2002	45,000	—	—	—	—	4.50
2002 Proof	2,800	Value: 10.00				
2003	—	—	—	—	—	4.50
2003 Proof	—	Value: 10.00				
2004	—	—	—	—	—	4.50
2004 Proof	—	Value: 10.00				

KM# 543 1/10 ONZA (1/10 Troy Ounce of Silver)
3.1103 g., 0.9990 Silver .1000 oz. ASW **Obv:** Mexican eagle
Rev: Winged Victory

Date	Mintage	F	VF	XF	Unc	BU
1991	50,017	—	—	—	—	5.50
1992	299,983	—	—	—	—	5.50
1992 Proof	5,000	Value: 12.00				
1993	100,000	—	—	—	—	5.50
1993 Proof	—	Value: 12.00				
1994	90,100	—	—	—	—	5.50
1994 Proof	10,000	Value: 12.00				
1995	50,000	—	—	—	—	5.50
1995 Proof	2,000	Value: 12.00				

KM# 610 1/10 ONZA (1/10 Troy Ounce of Silver)
3.1103 g., 0.9990 Silver .1000 oz. ASW **Obv:** Mexican eagle
Rev: Winged Victory

Date	Mintage	F	VF	XF	Unc	BU
1996	50,000	—	—	—	—	5.50
1996 Proof	1,000	Value: 12.00				
1997	20,000	—	—	—	—	6.00
1997 Proof	800	Value: 14.00				
1998	6,400	—	—	—	—	8.00
1998 Proof	300	Value: 15.00				
1999	8,000	—	—	—	—	8.00
1999 Proof	600	Value: 13.50				
2000	27,500	—	—	—	—	6.00
2000 Proof	1,000	Value: 12.00				
2001	25,000	—	—	—	—	5.50
2001 Proof	1,500	Value: 12.00				
2002	35,000	—	—	—	—	5.50
2002 Proof	2,800	Value: 12.00				
2003	—	—	—	—	—	5.50
2003 Proof	—	Value: 12.00				
2004	—	—	—	—	—	5.50
2004 Proof	—	Value: 12.00				

KM# 544 1/4 ONZA (1/4 Troy Ounce of Silver)
7.7758 g., 0.9990 Silver .2500 oz. ASW **Obv:** Mexican eagle
Rev: Winged Victory

Date	Mintage	F	VF	XF	Unc	BU
1991	50,017	—	—	—	—	7.50
1992	104,000	—	—	—	—	7.50

Date	Mintage	F	VF	XF	Unc	BU
1992 Proof	5,000	Value: 15.00				
1993	86,500	—	—	—	—	7.50
1993 Proof	—	Value: 15.00				
1994	90,100	—	—	—	—	7.50
1994 Proof	15,000	Value: 15.00				
1995	50,000	—	—	—	—	7.50
1995 Proof	2,000	Value: 15.00				

KM# 611   1/4 ONZA (1/4 Troy Ounce of Silver)
7.7758 g., 0.9990 Silver .2500 oz. ASW **Obv:** Mexican eagle
Rev: Winged Victory

Date	Mintage	F	VF	XF	Unc	BU
1996	50,000	—	—	—	—	7.50
1996 Proof	1,000	Value: 15.00				
1997	20,000	—	—	—	—	8.00
1997 Proof	800	Value: 18.00				
1998	6,400	—	—	—	—	10.00
1998 Proof	300	Value: 20.00				
1999	7,000	—	—	—	—	10.00
1999 Proof	600	Value: 16.50				
2000	21,000	—	—	—	—	8.00
2000 Proof	700	Value: 15.00				
2001	25,000	—	—	—	—	7.50
2001 Proof	1,000	Value: 15.00				
2002	35,000	—	—	—	—	7.50
2002 Proof	2,800	Value: 15.00				
2003	—	—	—	—	—	7.50
2003 Proof	—	Value: 15.00				
2004	—	—	—	—	—	7.50
2004 Proof	—	Value: 15.00				

KM# 545   1/2 ONZA (1/2 Troy Ounce of Silver)
15.5517 g., 0.9990 Silver .5000 oz. ASW **Obv:** Mexican
eagle **Rev:** Winged Victory

Date	Mintage	F	VF	XF	Unc	BU
1991	50,618	—	—	—	—	9.00
1992	119,000	—	—	—	—	9.00
1992 Proof	5,000	Value: 17.50				
1993	71,500	—	—	—	—	9.00
1993 Proof	—	Value: 17.50				
1994	90,100	—	—	—	—	9.00
1994 Proof	15,000	Value: 17.50				
1995	50,000	—	—	—	—	9.00
1995 Proof	2,000	Value: 17.50				

KM# 612   1/2 ONZA (1/2 Troy Ounce of Silver)
15.5517 g., 0.9990 Silver .5000 oz. ASW **Obv:** Mexican
eagle **Rev:** Winged Victory

Date	Mintage	F	VF	XF	Unc	BU
1996	50,000	—	—	—	—	9.00
1996 Proof	1,000	Value: 17.50				
1997	20,000	—	—	—	—	10.00
1997 Proof	800	Value: 22.50				
1998	6,400	—	—	—	—	11.50
1998 Proof	300	Value: 25.00				
1999	7,000	—	—	—	—	11.50
1999 Proof	600	Value: 20.00				
2000	20,000	—	—	—	—	10.00
2000 Proof	700	Value: 17.50				
2001	20,000	—	—	—	—	9.00
2001 Proof	1,000	Value: 17.50				
2002	35,000	—	—	—	—	9.00
2002 Proof	2,800	Value: 17.50				
2003	—	—	—	—	—	9.00
2003 Proof	—	Value: 17.50				
2004	—	—	—	—	—	9.00
2004 Proof	—	Value: 17.50				

KM# 494.1   ONZA (Troy Ounce of Silver)   **Subject:** Libertad
31.1000 g., 0.9990 Silver 1.0000 oz. ASW

Date	Mintage	F	VF	XF	Unc	BU
1982	1,049,680	—	—	—	BV	12.50
1983	1,001,768	—	—	—	BV	12.50
1983 Proof	998	Value: 200				
1984	1,014,000	—	—	—	BV	12.50
1985	2,017,000	—	—	—	BV	12.50
1986	1,699,426	—	—	—	BV	12.50
1986 Proof	30,006	Value: 25.00				
1987	500,000	—	—	—	BV	35.00
1987 Proof	12,000	Value: 30.00				
1987 Proof doubled date	Inc. above	Value: 40.00				
1988	1,500,500	—	—	—	BV	35.00
1989	1,396,500	—	—	—	BV	20.00
1989 Proof	10,000	Value: 50.00				

KM# 494.2   ONZA (Troy Ounce of Silver)
31.1000 g., 0.9990 Silver 1.0000 oz. ASW **Edge:** Reeded

Date	Mintage	F	VF	XF	Unc	BU
1988 Proof	10,000	Value: 55.00				
1990	1,200,000	—	—	—	BV	12.50
1990 Proof	10,000	Value: 45.00				
1991	1,650,518	—	—	—	BV	15.00

KM# 494.5 ONZA (Troy Ounce of Silver)
31.1000 g., 0.9990 Silver 1.0000 oz. ASW **Subject:** Libertad
Obv: KM#494.3 **Rev:** KM#494.2 **Edge:** Reeded edge **Note:** Mule

Date	Mintage	F	VF	XF	Unc	BU
1991 Proof	10,000	Value: 40.00				

KM# 494.3 ONZA (Troy Ounce of Silver)
31.1000 g., 0.9990 Silver 1.0000 oz. ASW **Subject:** Libertad
Obv: Eight dots below eagle's left talons **Rev:** Revised design and lettering **Edge:** Reeded edge **Note:** Mule

Date	Mintage	F	VF	XF	Unc	BU
1991	Inc. above	—	—	—	BV	22.00
1992	2,458,000	—	—	—	BV	12.50
1992 Proof	10,000	Value: 40.00				

KM# 494.4 ONZA (Troy Ounce of Silver)
31.1000 g., 0.9990 Silver 1.0000 oz. ASW **Subject:** Libertad
Obv: Seven dots below eagle's left talons, dull claws on right talon, thick letters **Rev:** Revised design and lettering **Edge:** Reeded edge **Note:** Mule

Date	Mintage	F	VF	XF	Unc	BU
1993	1,000,000	—	—	—	BV	14.00
1993 Proof	—	Value: 35.00				
1994	400,000	—	—	—	BV	18.00
1994 Proof	10,000	Value: 35.00				
1995	500,000	—	—	—	BV	16.00
1995 Proof	2,000	Value: 35.00				

KM# 613 ONZA (Troy Ounce of Silver)
33.6250 g., 0.9250 Silver 1.0000 oz. ASW **Obv:** Mexican eagle **Rev:** Winged Victory

Date	Mintage	F	VF	XF	Unc	BU
1996	300,000	—	—	—	—	16.00
1996 Proof	2,000	Value: 40.00				

Date	Mintage	F	VF	XF	Unc	BU
1997	100,000	—	—	—	—	16.50
1997 Proof	1,500	Value: 42.00				
1998	67,000	—	—	—	—	40.00
1998 Proof	500	Value: 80.00				
1999	95,000	—	—	—	—	20.00
1999 Proof	600	Value: 50.00				

KM# 639 ONZA (Troy Ounce of Silver)
31.1000 g., 0.9990 Silver 1.0000 oz. ASW **Subject:** Libertad
Obv: Modern Mexican eagle within circle of obsolete versions **Edge:** Reeded edge **Note:** Mule

Date	Mintage	F	VF	XF	Unc	BU
2000	340,000	—	—	—	—	18.00
2000 Proof	1,600	Value: 40.00				
2001	650,000	—	—	—	—	12.50
2001 Proof	2,000	Value: 35.00				
2002	850,000	—	—	—	—	12.50
2002 Proof	3,800	Value: 35.00				
2003Mo	—	—	—	—	—	12.50
2003Mo Proof	—	Value: 35.00				
2004Mo	—	—	—	—	—	14.00
2004Mo Proof	—	Value: 39.00				

KM# 614 2 ONZAS (2 Troy Ounces of Silver)
62.2070 g., 0.9990 Silver 2.0000 oz. ASW **Subject:** Libertad
Obv: Mexican eagle within circle of obsolete versions **Rev:** Winged Victory

Date	Mintage	F	VF	XF	Unc	BU
1996	50,000	—	—	—	—	27.50
1996 Proof	1,200	Value: 47.50				
1997	15,000	—	—	—	—	27.50
1997 Proof	1,300	Value: 50.00				
1998	7,000	—	—	—	—	30.00
1998 Proof	400	Value: 100				
1999	5,000	—	—	—	—	32.50
1999 Proof	280	Value: 175				
2000	7,500	—	—	—	—	30.00

Date	Mintage	F	VF	XF	Unc	BU
2000 Proof	500	Value: 50.00				
2001	1,700	—	—	—	—	30.00
2001 Proof	500	Value: 50.00				
2002	8,700	—	—	—	—	27.50
2002 Proof	1,000	Value: 47.50				
2003	—	—	—	—	—	27.50
2003 Proof	—	Value: 47.50				
2004	—	—	—	—	—	29.00
2004 Proof	—	Value: 49.00				

KM# 615   5 ONZAS (5 Troy Ounces of Silver)
155.5175 g., 0.9990 Silver 5.0000 oz. ASW   **Subject:**
Libertad **Obv:** Mexican eagle within circle of obsolete versions
Rev: Winged Victory

Date	Mintage	F	VF	XF	Unc	BU
1996	20,000	—	—	—	—	55.00
1996 Proof	1,200	Value: 85.00				
1997	10,000	—	—	—	—	55.00
1997 Proof	1,300	Value: 85.00				
1998	3,500	—	—	—	—	100
1998 Proof	400	Value: 300				
1999	2,800	—	—	—	—	100
1999 Proof	100	Value: 500				
2000	4,000	—	—	—	—	55.00
2000 Proof	500	Value: 125				
2001	4,000	—	—	—	—	50.00
2001 Proof	600	Value: 80.00				
2002	5,200	—	—	—	—	50.00
2002 Proof	1,000	Value: 80.00				
2003	—	—	—	—	—	50.00
2003 Proof	—	Value: 80.00				
2004	—	—	—	—	—	59.00
2004 Proof	—	Value: 95.00				

KM# 677   KILO (32.15 Troy Ounces of Silver)
999.9775 g., 0.9990 Silver 32.1178 oz. ASW, 110 mm.
Subject: Collector Bullion **Obv:** Current Mexican emblem
within circle of obsolete versions **Rev:** Winged Victory statue
Edge: Reeded

Date	Mintage	F	VF	XF	Unc	BU
2002Mo Prooflike	1,100	—	—	—	—	650
2003Mo Proof	3,000	Value: 500				
2004Mo Prooflike	—	—	—	—	—	600

GOLD BULLION COINAGE

KM# 530   1/20 ONZA (1/20 Ounce of Pure Gold)
1.7500 g., 0.9000 Gold .0500 oz. AGW **Obv:** Winged Victory
Rev: Calendar stone

Date	Mintage	F	VF	XF	Unc	BU
1987	—	—	—	—	—	275
1988	—	—	—	—	—	—

KM# 589   1/20 ONZA (1/20 Ounce of Pure Gold)
1.5551 g., 0.9990 Gold .500 oz. AGW **Obv:** Winged Victory
Rev: Eagle and snake

Date	Mintage	F	VF	XF	Unc	BU
1991	10,000	—	—	—	—	BV+30%
1992	65,225	—	—	—	—	BV+30%
1993	10,000	—	—	—	—	BV+30%
1994	10,000	—	—	—	—	BV+30%

KM# 642   1/20 ONZA (1/20 Ounce of Pure Gold)
1.5551 g., 0.9990 Gold .500 oz. AGW **Obv:** Winged Victory
Rev: Teocuitlatl and an indian working

Date	Mintage	F	VF	XF	Unc	BU
2000 Proof	—	Value: 50.00				

KM# 671   1/20 ONZA (1/20 Ounce of Pure Gold)
1.5551 g., 0.9990 Gold 0.0499 oz. AGW, 16 mm.   **Obv:**
Mexican arms **Rev:** Winged Victory facing left **Edge:** Reeded
Note: Design similar to KM#609. Value estimates do not
include the high taxes and surcharges added to the issue
prices by the Mexican Government.

Date	Mintage	F	VF	XF	Unc	BU
2000	5,300	—	—	—	—	—
2002Mo	5,000	—	—	—	—	—

KM# 628   1/15 ONZA (1/15 Ounce of Pure Gold)
0.9990 Gold   **Obv:** Winged Victory above legend

Date	Mintage	F	VF	XF	Unc	BU
1987	—	—	—	—	—	275

KM# 541   1/10 ONZA (1/10 Ounce of Pure Gold)
3.1103 g., 0.9990 Gold .1000 oz. AGW

Date	Mintage	F	VF	XF	Unc	BU
1991	10,000	—	—	—	—	BV+20%
1992	50,777	—	—	—	—	BV+20%
1993	10,000	—	—	—	—	BV+20%
1994	10,000	—	—	—	—	BV+20%

KM# 672   1/10 ONZA (1/10 Ounce of Pure Gold)
3.1103 g., 0.9990 Gold 0.0999 oz. AGW, 20 mm.   **Obv:**
Mexican arms **Rev:** Winged Victory facing left **Edge:** Reeded
Note: Design similar to KM#610. Value estimates do not
include the high taxes and surcharges added to the issue
prices by the Mexican Government.

Date	Mintage	F	VF	XF	Unc	BU
2000	3,500	—	—	—	—	—
2002Mo	5,000	—	—	—	—	—

KM# 487   1/4 ONZA (1/4 Ounce of Pure Gold)
8.6396 g., 0.9000 Gold .2500 oz. AGW   **Note:** Similar to
KM#488.

Date	Mintage	F	VF	XF	Unc	BU
1981	313,000	—	—	—	—	BV+11%
1982	—	—	—	—	—	BV+11%

KM# 590   1/4 ONZA (1/4 Ounce of Pure Gold)
7.7758 g., 0.9990 Gold .2500 oz. AGW **Obv:** Winged Victory
above legend **Rev:** Eagle and snake

Date	Mintage	F	VF	XF	Unc	BU
1991	10,000	—	—	—	—	BV+11%
1992	28,106	—	—	—	—	BV+11%
1993	2,500	—	—	—	—	BV+11%
1994	2,500	—	—	—	—	BV+11%

KM# 673   1/4 ONZA (1/4 Ounce of Pure Gold)
7.7758 g., 0.9990 Gold 0.2497 oz. AGW, 26.9 mm.   **Obv:**
Mexican arms **Rev:** Winged Victory facing left **Edge:** Reeded
Note: Design similar to KM#611. Value estimates do not
include the high taxes and surcharges added to the issue
prices by the Mexican Government.

Date	Mintage	F	VF	XF	Unc	BU
2000	2,500	—	—	—	—	—
2002Mo	—	—	—	—	—	—

KM# 488 1/2 ONZA (1/2 Ounce of Pure Gold)
17.2792 g., 0.9000 Gold .5000 oz. AGW

Date	Mintage	F	VF	XF	Unc	BU
1981	193,000	—	—	—	—	BV+8%
1982	—	—	—	—	—	BV+8%
1989 Proof	704	Value: 500				

KM# 591 1/2 ONZA (1/2 Ounce of Pure Gold)
15.5517 g., 0.9990 Gold .5000 oz. AGW **Obv:** Winged
Victory above legend **Rev:** Eagle and snake

Date	Mintage	F	VF	XF	Unc	BU
1991	10,000	—	—	—	—	BV+8%
1992	25,220	—	—	—	—	BV+8%
1993	2,500	—	—	—	—	BV+8%
1994	2,500	—	—	—	—	BV+8%

KM# 674 1/2 ONZA (1/2 Ounce of Pure Gold)
15.5517 g., 0.9990 Gold 0.4995 oz. AGW, 32.9 mm. **Obv:**
Mexican arms **Rev:** Winged Victory facing left **Edge:** Reeded
Note: Design similar to KM#612. Value estimates do not
include the high taxes and surcharges added to the issue
prices by the Mexican Government.

Date	Mintage	F	VF	XF	Unc	BU
2000	1,500	—	—	—	—	BV+8%
2002Mo	—	—	—	—	—	BV+8%

KM# 489 ONZA (Ounce of Pure Gold)
34.5585 g., 0.9000 Gold 1.0000 oz. AGW **Note:** Similar to
KM#488.

Date	Mintage	F	VF	XF	Unc	BU
1981	596,000	—	—	—	—	BV+3%
1985	—	—	—	—	—	BV+3%
1988	—	—	—	—	—	BV+3%

KM# 592 ONZA (Ounce of Pure Gold)
31.1035 g., 0.9990 Gold 1.0000 oz. AGW **Obv:** Winged
Victory above legend **Rev:** Eagle and snake

Date	Mintage	F	VF	XF	Unc	BU
1991	109,193	—	—	—	—	BV+3%
1992	46,281	—	—	—	—	BV+3%
1993	10,000	—	—	—	—	BV+3%
1994	1,000	—	—	—	—	BV+3%

KM# 675 ONZA (Ounce of Pure Gold)
31.1035 g., 0.9990 Gold 0.999 oz. AGW, 40 mm. **Obv:**
Mexican arms **Rev:** Winged Victory facing left **Edge:** Reeded
Note: Design similar to KM#639. Value estimates do not
include the high taxes and surcharges added to the issue
prices by the Mexican Government.

Date	Mintage	F	VF	XF	Unc	BU
2000	2,730	—	—	—	—	BV+3%
2002Mo	—	—	—	—	—	BV+3%

PLATINUM BULLION COINAGE

KM# 538 1/4 ONZA (1/4 Ounce)
7.7775 g., 0.9990 Platinum .2500 oz. APW

Date	Mintage	F	VF	XF	Unc	BU
1989	704	Value: 350				

BULLION COINAGE
Pre-Colombian •
Azteca Series

KM# 644 NUEVO PESO
7.7700 g., 0.9990 Silver .2496 oz. ASW, 26.8 mm. **Subject:**
Eagle Warrior **Obv:** National arms **Rev:** Costumed warrior
Edge: Reeded

Date	Mintage	F	VF	XF	Unc	BU
1993Mo	1,500	—	—	—	—	10.00
1993 Proof	900	Value: 20.00				

KM# 645 2 NUEVOS PESOS
15.4200 g., 0.9990 Silver .4953 oz. ASW, 32.9 mm. **Subject:**
Eagle Warrior **Obv:** National arms **Rev:** Costumed warrior
Edge: Reeded

Date	Mintage	F	VF	XF	Unc	BU
1993Mo	1,500	—	—	—	—	10.00
1993 Proof	800	Value: 22.00				

KM# 646 5 NUEVOS PESOS
31.0500 g., 0.9990 Silver .9973 oz. ASW, 40 mm. **Subject:**
Eagle Warrior **Obv:** National arms **Rev:** Costumed warrior
Edge: Reeded

Date	Mintage	F	VF	XF	Unc	BU
1993	2,000	—	—	—	—	16.00
1993 Proof	1,000	Value: 45.00				

KM# 647 5 NUEVOS PESOS
31.0000 g., 0.9990 Silver .9957 oz. ASW, 40 mm. **Subject:**
Xochipilli **Obv:** National arms **Rev:** Seated figure sculpture
Edge: Reeded

Date	Mintage	F	VF	XF	Unc	BU
1993	2,000	—	—	—	—	15.00
1993 Proof	800	Value: 52.00				

KM# 649   5 NUEVOS PESOS
31.0000 g., 0.9990 Silver .9957 oz. ASW, 40 mm. **Subject:** Huchucteotl **Obv:** National arms **Rev:** Aztec sculpture **Edge:** Reeded

Date	Mintage	F	VF	XF	Unc	BU
1993	5,000	—	—	—	—	15.00
1993 Proof	800	Value: 45.00				

KM# 648   5 NUEVOS PESOS
31.00 g., 0.9990 Silver .9957 oz. ASW, 40 mm. **Subject:** Brasco Efigie **Obv:** National arms **Rev:** Sculpture **Edge:** Reeded

Date	Mintage	F	VF	XF	Unc	BU
1993	2,000	—	—	—	—	15.00
1993 Proof	500	Value: 40.00				

KM# 650   10 NUEVOS PESOS
155.3100 g., 0.9990 Silver 4.9883 oz. ASW, 64 mm. **Subject:** Piedra de Tizoc **Obv:** National arms **Rev:** Warrior capturing woman **Edge:** Reeded **Note:** Illustration reduced.

Date	Mintage	F	VF	XF	Unc	BU
1992 Proof	—	Value: 150				
1993	1,000	—	—	—	—	55.00
1993 Proof	1,000	Value: 85.00				

 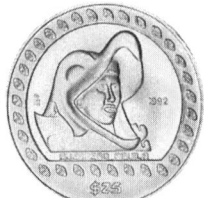

KM# 554   25 PESOS
7.7758 g., 0.9990 Silver .2500 oz. ASW   **Rev:** Eagle warrior

Date	Mintage	F	VF	XF	Unc	BU
1992	50,000	—	—	—	10.00	—
1992 Proof	3,000	Value: 15.00				

KM# 555   50 PESOS
15.5517 g., 0.9990 Silver .5000 oz. ASW   **Rev:** Eagle warrior

Date	Mintage	F	VF	XF	Unc	BU
1992	50,000	—	—	—	16.00	—
1992 Proof	3,000	Value: 24.00				

KM# 556   100 PESOS
31.1035 g., 0.9990 Silver 1.00 oz. ASW   **Rev:** Eagle warrior

Date	Mintage	F	VF	XF	Unc	BU
1992	205,000	—	—	—	16.00	—
1992	4,000	Value: 42.00				

KM# 562   100 PESOS
31.1035 g., 0.9990 Silver 1.0000 oz. ASW   **Rev:** Xochipilli - The God of Joy, Music and Dance

Date	Mintage	F	VF	XF	Unc	BU
1992 Proof	4,000	Value: 42.00				

KM# 563   100 PESOS
31.1035 g., 0.9990 Silver 1.0000 oz. ASW   **Rev:** Brasero Efigie - The God of Rain

Date	Mintage	F	VF	XF	Unc	BU
1992 Proof	4,000	Value: 40.00				

KM# 564   100 PESOS
31.1035 g., 0.9990 Silver 1.0000 oz. ASW   **Rev:** Huehueteotl - The God of Fire

Date	Mintage	F	VF	XF	Unc	BU
1992 Proof	4,000	Value: 42.00				

KM# 558   250 PESOS
7.7758 g., 0.9990 Gold .2500 oz. AGW   **Subject:** Native Culture **Rev:** Sculpture of jaguar head

Date	Mintage	F	VF	XF	Unc	BU
1992	10,000	—	—	—	140	—
1992 Proof	2,000	Value: 275				

KM# 559   500 PESOS
15.5517 g., 0.9990 Gold .5000 oz. AGW   **Subject:** Native Culture - Sculpture of Jaguar Head

Date	Mintage	F	VF	XF	Unc	BU
1992	10,000	—	—	—	265	—
1992 Proof	2,000	Value: 470				

KM# 560   1000 PESOS
31.1035 g., 0.9990 Gold 1.0000 oz. AGW **Subject:** Native
Culture **Rev:** Sculpture of jaguar head

Date	Mintage	F	VF	XF	Unc	BU
1992	17,850	—	—	—	425	—
1992 Proof	2,000	Value: 600				

KM# 557   10000 PESOS
155.5175 g., 0.9990 Silver 5.0000 oz. ASW, 64 mm.
Subject: Pieora De Tizoc **Rev:** Native warriors taking female
captive **Note:** Illustration reduced.

Date	Mintage	F	VF	XF	Unc	BU
1992	51,900	—	—	—	—	52.00
1992 Proof	3,000	Value: 150				

BULLION COINAGE
Pre-Colombian •
Central Veracruz Series

KM# 567   NUEVO PESO
7.7601 g., 0.9990 Silver .2498 oz. ASW **Subject:**
Bajorrelieve Del El Tajin

Date	Mintage	F	VF	XF	Unc	BU
1993	100,000	—	—	—	—	8.75
1993 Proof	3,300	Value: 20.00				

KM# 568   2 NUEVOS PESOS
15.5516 g., 0.9990 Silver .4995 oz. ASW **Subject:**
Bajorrelieve Del El Tajin

Date	Mintage	F	VF	XF	Unc	BU
1993	100,000	—	—	—	—	12.00
1993 Proof	3,000	Value: 20.00				

KM# 569   5 NUEVOS PESOS
31.1035 g., 0.9990 Silver .9991 oz. ASW **Subject:**
Bajorrelieve Del El Tajin **Obv:** Mexican eagle

Date	Mintage	F	VF	XF	Unc	BU
1993	100,000	—	—	—	—	15.00
1993 Proof	3,000	Value: 42.00				

KM# 582   5 NUEVOS PESOS
31.1035 g., 0.9990 Silver .9991 oz. ASW **Subject:** Palma
Con Cecodrilo **Obv:** National emblem **Rev:** Aerial view of
crocodile

Date	Mintage	F	VF	XF	Unc	BU
1993	4,500	—	—	—	—	15.00
1993 Proof	2,650	Value: 42.00				

BULLION COINAGE
Pre-Colombian •
Mayan Series

KM# 583 5 NUEVOS PESOS
31.1035 g., 0.9990 Silver .9991 oz. ASW **Subject:** Anciano
Con Brasero **Rev:** Kneeling figure sculpture

Date	Mintage	F	VF	XF	Unc	BU
1993	2,650	—	—	—	—	15.00
1993 Proof	1,500	Value: 42.00				

KM# 584 5 NUEVOS PESOS
31.1035 g., 0.9990 Silver .9991 oz. ASW **Subject:** Carita
Sonriente **Rev:** Sculptured head

Date	Mintage	F	VF	XF	Unc	BU
1993	4,500	—	—	—	—	15.00
1993 Proof	3,300	Value: 42.00				

KM# 572 NUEVO PESO
7.7601 g., 0.9990 Silver .2498 oz. ASW **Subject:** Chaac
Mool

Date	Mintage	F	VF	XF	Unc	BU
1994 Matte	30,000	—	—	—	—	10.00
1994 Proof	2,500	Value: 20.00				

KM# 573 2 NUEVOS PESOS
15.5516 g., 0.9990 Silver .4995 oz. ASW **Subject:** Chaac
Mool

Date	Mintage	F	VF	XF	Unc	BU
1994 Matte	30,000	—	—	—	—	12.00
1994 Proof	2,500	Value: 20.00				

KM# 570 10 NUEVOS PESOS
Center Weight: 115.5175 g. **Center Composition:** 0.9990
Silver 4.9956 oz. ASW , 64 mm. **Subject:** Piramide Del El
Tajin **Note:** Illustration reduced.

Date	Mintage	F	VF	XF	Unc	BU
1993	50,000	—	—	—	—	55.00
1993 Proof	3,100	Value: 85.00				

KM# 585 25 NUEVOS PESOS
7.7758 g., 0.9990 Gold .2500 oz. AGW **Subject:** Hacha
Ceremonial **Note:** Similar to 100 New Pesos, KM#587.

Date	Mintage	F	VF	XF	Unc	BU
1993	15,500	—	—	—	145	—
1993 Proof	800	Value: 275				

KM# 586 50 NUEVOS PESOS
15.5517 g., 0.9990 Gold .5000 oz. AGW **Subject:** Hacha
Ceremonial **Note:** Similar to 100 New Pesos, KM#587.

Date	Mintage	F	VF	XF	Unc	BU
1993	15,500	—	—	—	275	—
1993 Proof	500	Value: 475				

KM# 587 100 NUEVOS PESOS
31.1035 g., 0.9990 Gold 1.0000 oz. AGW **Subject:** Hacha
Ceremonial

Date	Mintage	F	VF	XF	Unc	BU
1993	7,150	—	—	—	475	—
1993 Proof	500	Value: 600				

KM# 574 5 NUEVOS PESOS
31.1035 g., 0.9990 Silver .9991 oz. ASW **Subject:** Chaac
Mool **Rev:** Reclining Sculpture

Date	Mintage	F	VF	XF	Unc	BU
1994 Matte	50,000	—	—	—	—	15.00
1994 Proof	3,000	Value: 42.00				

KM# 575 5 NUEVOS PESOS
31.1035 g., 0.9990 Silver .9991 oz. ASW **Subject:** Chaac
Mool **Rev:** Tomb of Palenque Memorial Stone

Date	Mintage	F	VF	XF	Unc	BU
1994	4,500	—	—	—	—	15.00
1994 Proof	2,800	Value: 42.00				

KM# 577 5 NUEVOS PESOS
31.1035 g., 0.9990 Silver .9991 oz. ASW **Subject:** Mascaron Del Dios Chaac **Rev:** Elaborately carved wall segment

Date	Mintage	F	VF	XF	Unc	BU
1994	4,500	—	—	—	—	15.00
1994 Proof	2,500	Value: 42.00				

KM# 578 5 NUEVOS PESOS
31.1035 g., 0.9990 Silver .9991 oz. ASW **Subject:** Dintel 26 **Rev:** Two seated figures wall carving

Date	Mintage	F	VF	XF	Unc	BU
1994	4,500	—	—	—	—	15.00
1994 Proof	2,600	Value: 42.00				

KM# 676 10 NUEVOS PESOS
155.5175 g., 0.9990 Silver 4.995 oz. ASW, 65 mm. **Subject:** Piramid Del Castillo **Obv:** National emblem above metal content statement **Rev:** Pyramid above two line inscription **Rev. Inscription:** PIRAMIDE DEL CASTILLO / CHICHEN-ITZA **Edge:** Reeded

Date	Mintage	F	VF	XF	Unc	BU
1993Mo Proof	—	Value: 325				

KM# 579 25 NUEVOS PESOS
7.7758 g., 0.9990 Gold .2500 oz. AGW **Subject:** Personaje de Jaina **Rev:** Seated figure

Date	Mintage	F	VF	XF	Unc	BU
1994	2,000	—	—	—	145	—
1994 Proof	500	Value: 275				

KM# 580 50 NUEVOS PESOS
15.5517 g., 0.9990 Gold .5000 oz. AGW **Subject:** Personaje de Jaina **Rev:** Seated figure

Date	Mintage	F	VF	XF	Unc	BU
1994	1,000	—	—	—	275	—
1994 Proof	500	Value: 475				

KM# 581 100 NUEVOS PESOS
31.1035 g., 0.9990 Gold 1.0000 oz. AGW **Subject:** Personaje de Jaina

Date	Mintage	F	VF	XF	Unc	BU
1994	1,000	—	—	—	475	—
1994 Proof	500	Value: 600				

BULLION COINAGE
Pre-Colombian •
Olmec Series

KM# 593 PESO
7.7750 g., 0.9990 Silver .2500 oz. ASW **Subject:** Senor De Las Limas **Note:** Similar to 5 Pesos, KM#595.

Date	Mintage	F	VF	XF	Unc	BU
1996	4,000	—	—	—	—	10.00
1996 Proof	2,200	Value: 20.00				
1998 Matte	2,400	—	—	—	—	12.00

KM# 594 2 PESOS
15.5517 g., 0.9990 Silver .5000 oz. ASW **Subject:** Senor De Las Limasl **Note:** Similar to 5 Pesos, KM#595.

Date	Mintage	F	VF	XF	Unc	BU
1996	4,000	—	—	—	—	12.00
1996 Proof	2,200	Value: 20.00				
1998 Matte	2,400	—	—	—	—	15.00

KM# 596 5 PESOS
31.1035 g., 0.9990 Silver 1.0000 oz. ASW **Subject:** Hombre Jaguar

Date	Mintage	F	VF	XF	Unc	BU
1996	1,500	—	—	—	—	15.00
1996 Proof	2,800	Value: 42.00				
1998 Matte	6,000	—	—	—	—	15.00
1998 Proof	4,800	Value: 42.00				

KM# 595 5 PESOS
31.1035 g., 0.9990 Silver 1.0000 oz. ASW **Subject:** Senor De Las Limas

Date	Mintage	F	VF	XF	Unc	BU
1996	4,000	—	—	—	—	15.00
1996 Proof	3,000	Value: 42.00				
1998 Matte	3,400	—	—	—	—	15.00

KM# 597   5 PESOS
31.1035 g., 0.9990 Silver 1.0000 oz. ASW **Subject:** El Luchador

Date	Mintage	F	VF	XF	Unc	BU
1996	4,500	—	—	—	—	15.00
1996 Proof	2,700	Value: 42.00				
1998 Matte	2,000	—	—	—	—	15.00

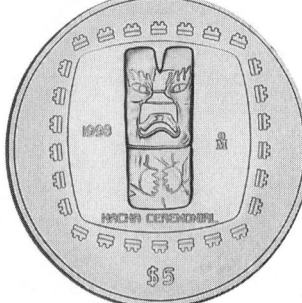

KM# 598   5 PESOS
31.1035 g., 0.9990 Silver 1.0000 oz. ASW **Subject:** Hacha Ceremonial

Date	Mintage	F	VF	XF	Unc	BU
1996	4,500	—	—	—	—	15.00
1996 Proof	2,700	Value: 42.00				
1998 Matte	2,000	—	—	—	—	15.00

KM# 599   10 PESOS
Center Weight: 1555.5175 g. **Center Composition:** 0.9990 Silver 5.0000 oz. ASW , 64 mm. **Subject:** Cabeza Olmeca
Note: Illustration reduced.

Date	Mintage	F	VF	XF	Unc	BU
1996	2,000	—	—	—	—	55.00
1996 Proof	2,750	Value: 85.00				
1998 Matte	2,150	—	—	—	—	55.00

KM# 600   25 PESOS
7.7758 g., 0.9990 Gold .2500 oz. AGW **Subject:** Sacerdote
Note: Similar to 100 Pesos, KM#602.

Date	Mintage	F	VF	XF	Unc	BU
1996	500	—	—	—	145	—
1996 Proof	750	Value: 275				

KM# 601   50 PESOS
15.5517 g., 0.9990 Gold .5000 oz. AGW **Subject:** Sacerdote
Note: Similar to 100 Pesos, KM#602.

Date	Mintage	F	VF	XF	Unc	BU
1996	500	—	—	—	275	—
1996 Proof	500	Value: 475				

KM# 602   100 PESOS
31.1035 g., 0.9990 Gold 1.0000 oz. AGW **Subject:** Sacerdote

Date	Mintage	F	VF	XF	Unc	BU
1996	500	—	—	—	475	—
1996 Proof	500	Value: 600				

BULLION COINAGE

Pre-Colombian •
Teotihuacan Series

KM# 617   PESO
7.7759 g., 0.9990 Silver .2500 oz. ASW **Subject:** Disco De La Muerte **Obv:** Mexican eagle

Date	Mintage	F	VF	XF	Unc	BU
1997	3,000	—	—	—	—	9.00
1997 Proof	1,600	Value: 17.50				
1998 Proof	500	Value: 20.00				
1998 Matte	2,400	—	—	—	—	10.00

KM# 618   2 PESOS
15.5517 g., 0.9990 Silver .5000 oz. ASW **Subject:** Disco De La Muerte **Obv:** Mexican eagle

Date	Mintage	F	VF	XF	Unc	BU
1997	3,000	—	—	—	—	10.00
1997 Proof	1,600	Value: 20.00				

Date	Mintage	F	VF	XF	Unc	BU
1998	2,400	—	—	—	—	10.00
1998 Proof	500	Value: 20.00				

KM# 621 5 PESOS
31.1035 g., 0.9990 Silver 1.0000 oz. ASW **Subject:**
Teohituacan - Vasija **Obv:** Eagle and snake

Date	Mintage	F	VF	XF	Unc	BU
1997	4,500	—	—	—	—	15.00
1997 Proof	Est. 1,800	Value: 42.00				
1998 Matte	2,000	—	—	—	—	15.00
1998 Proof	500	Value: 50.00				

KM# 622 5 PESOS
31.1035 g., 0.9990 Silver 1.0000 oz. ASW **Subject:**
Teohituacan - Jugador of Pelota **Obv:** Eagle and snake

Date	Mintage	F	VF	XF	Unc	BU
1997	4,500	—	—	—	—	15.00
1997 Proof	Est. 1,800	Value: 42.00				
1998 Matte	2,000	—	—	—	—	15.00
1998 Proof	500	Value: 50.00				

KM# 619 5 PESOS
31.1035 g., 0.9990 Silver 1.0000 oz. ASW **Subject:**
Teohituacan - Disco de la Muerte **Obv:** Eagle and snake

Date	Mintage	F	VF	XF	Unc	BU
1997	3,500	—	—	—	—	15.00
1997 Proof	Est. 1,800	Value: 42.00				
1998	3,400	—	—	—	—	15.00
1998 Proof	500	Value: 50.00				

KM# 620 5 PESOS
31.1035 g., 0.9990 Silver 1.0000 oz. ASW **Subject:**
Teohituacan - Mascara **Obv:** Eagle and snake

Date	Mintage	F	VF	XF	Unc	BU
1997	4,500	—	—	—	—	15.00
1997 Proof	Est. 1,800	Value: 42.00				
1998	2,000	—	—	—	—	15.00
1998 Proof	500	Value: 50.00				

KM# 623 10 PESOS
1555.5175 g., 0.9990 Silver 5.0000 oz. ASW, 64 mm.
Subject: Piramide Del Sol **Obv:** Mexican eagle **Note:**
Illustration reduced.

Date	Mintage	F	VF	XF	Unc	BU
1997	1,500	—	—	—	—	55.00
1997 Proof	2,100	Value: 85.00				
1998 Matte	2,150	—	—	—	—	55.00

KM# 624 25 PESOS
7.7758 g., 0.9990 Gold .2500 oz. AGW **Subject:** Serpiente
Emplumada **Obv:** Mexican eagle **Note:** Similar to 100 Pesos,
KM#626.

Date	Mintage	F	VF	XF	Unc	BU
1997	500	—	—	—	145	—
1997 Proof	200	Value: 275				

KM# 625 50 PESOS
15.5517 g., 0.9990 Gold .5000 oz. AGW **Subject:** Serpiente
Emplumada **Obv:** Mexican eagle **Note:** Similar to 100 Pesos,
KM#626.

Date	Mintage	F	VF	XF	Unc	BU
1997	500	—	—	—	275	—
1997 Proof	200	Value: 475				

KM# 626 100 PESOS
31.1035 g., 0.9990 Gold 1.0000 oz. AGW **Subject:**
Teohituacan - Serpiente Emplumada **Obv:** Eagle and snake

Date	Mintage	F	VF	XF	Unc	BU
1997	500	—	—	—	475	—
1997 Proof	Est. 200	Value: 600				

BULLION COINAGE

Pre-Colombian •
Tolteca Series

KM# 661   PESO
7.7759 g., 0.9990 Silver .2500 oz. ASW, 27 mm. **Subject:**
Jaguar **Obv:** National emblem **Rev:** Jaguar carving **Edge:**
Reeded

Date	Mintage	F	VF	XF	Unc	BU
1998	6,000	—	—	—	—	9.00
1998 Proof	4,800	Value: 15.00				

KM# 662   2 PESOS
15.5517 g., 0.9990 Silver .5000 oz. ASW, 33 mm. **Subject:**
Jaguar **Obv:** National emblem **Rev:** Jaguar carving **Edge:**
Reeded

Date	Mintage	F	VF	XF	Unc	BU
1998	6,000	—	—	—	—	10.00
1998 Proof	4,800	Value: 20.00				

KM# 663   5 PESOS
31.1035 g., 0.9990 Silver 1.0000 oz. ASW, 40 mm. **Subject:**
Jaguar **Obv:** National emblem **Rev:** Jaguar carving **Edge:**
Reeded

Date	Mintage	F	VF	XF	Unc	BU
1998	6,000	—	—	—	—	15.00
1998 Proof	4,800	Value: 42.00				

KM# 664   5 PESOS
31.1035 g., 0.9990 Silver 1.0000 oz. ASW, 40 mm. **Obv:**
National emblem **Rev:** Sacerdote sculpture **Edge:** Reeded

Date	Mintage	F	VF	XF	Unc	BU
1998	5,000	—	—	—	—	15.00
1998 Proof	4,800	Value: 42.00				

KM# 666   5 PESOS
31.1035 g., 0.9990 Silver 1.0000 oz. ASW, 40 mm. **Subject:**
Serpiente con Craneo **Obv:** National emblem **Rev:** Large
sculpture **Edge:** Reeded

Date	Mintage	F	VF	XF	Unc	BU
1998	5,000	—	—	—	—	15.00
1998 Proof	4,800	Value: 42.00				

KM# 665   5 PESOS
31.1035 g., 0.9990 Silver 1.0000 oz. ASW, 40 mm. **Subject:**
Quetzalcoatl **Obv:** National emblem **Rev:** Quetzalcoatl
sculpture **Edge:** Reeded

Date	Mintage	F	VF	XF	Unc	BU
1998	5,000	—	—	—	—	15.00
1998 Proof	4,800	Value: 42.00				

KM# 634   10 PESOS
155.7300 g., 0.9990 Silver 5.0018 oz. ASW **Subject:**
Atlantes **Obv:** National arms **Rev:** Three carved statues

Date	Mintage	F	VF	XF	Unc	BU
1998	3,500	—	—	—	—	55.00
1998 Proof	4,200	Value: 85.00				

KM# 667   25 PESOS
7.7759 g., 0.9990 Gold 0.2498 oz. AGW, 23 mm. **Subject:**
Aguila **Obv:** Mexican arms **Rev:** Eagle sculpture **Edge:**
Reeded

Date	Mintage	F	VF	XF	Unc	BU
1998	300	—	—	—	140	—
1998 Proof	300	Value: 270				

KM# 668   50 PESOS
15.5517 g., 0.9990 Gold 0.4995 oz. AGW, 29 mm. **Subject:**
Aguila **Obv:** Mexican arms **Rev:** Eagle sculpture **Edge:**
Reeded

Date	Mintage	F	VF	XF	Unc	BU
1998	300	—	—	—	275	—
1998 Proof	300	Value: 475				

KM# 669   100 PESOS
31.1035 g., 0.9990 Gold 0.999 oz. AGW, 34.5 mm. **Subject:**
Aguila **Obv:** Mexican arms **Rev:** Eagle sculpture **Edge:**
Reeded

Date	Mintage	F	VF	XF	Unc	BU
1998	300	—	—	—	475	—
1998 Proof	300	Value: 600				

MEDALLIC SILVER BULLION COINAGE

KM# M49a   ONZA
33.6250 g., 0.9250 Silver 1.0000 oz. ASW **Obv:** Mint mark
above coin press

Date	Mintage	F	VF	XF	Unc	BU
1949	1,000,000	—	10.00	12.50	17.50	27.50

KM# M49b.1   ONZA
33.6250 g., 0.9250 Silver 1.0000 oz. ASW **Obv:** Wide
spacing between DE MONEDA **Rev:** Mint mark below balance
scale **Note:** Type I

Date	Mintage	F	VF	XF	Unc	BU
1978	280,000	—	—	BV	8.50	12.50

KM# M49b.2   ONZA
33.6250 g., 0.9250 Silver 1.0000 oz. ASW **Obv:** Close
spacing between DE MONEDA **Rev:** Mint mark below balance
scale **Note:** Type II

Date	Mintage	F	VF	XF	Unc	BU
1978	Inc. above	—	—	BV	8.50	12.50

KM# M49b.3   ONZA
33.6250 g., 0.9250 Silver 1.0000 oz. ASW **Obv:** Close
spacing between DE MONEDA **Rev:** Left scale pan points to
U in UNA **Note:** Type III

Date	Mintage	F	VF	XF	Unc	BU
1979	4,508,000	—	—	BV	7.50	11.50

KM# M49b.4   ONZA
33.6250 g., 0.9250 Silver 1.0000 oz. ASW   **Obv:** Close
spacing between DE MONEDA **Rev:** Left scale pan points
between U and N of UNA **Note:** Type IV

Date	Mintage	F	VF	XF	Unc	BU
1979	Inc. above	—	—	BV	7.50	11.50

KM# M49b.5   ONZA
33.6250 g., 0.9250 Silver 1.0000 oz. ASW   **Obv:** Close
spacing between DE MONEDA **Rev:** Left scale pan points
between U and N of UNA **Note:** Type V

Date	Mintage	F	VF	XF	Unc	BU
1980	6,104,000	—	—	BV	7.50	11.50
1980/70	Inc. above	—	—	BV	7.50	14.50

MEDALLIC GOLD COINAGE

KM# M91a   10 PESOS
8.3333 g., 0.9000 Gold .2411 oz. AGW   **Subject:** 200th
Anniversary - Birth of Hidalgo

Date	Mintage	F	VF	XF	Unc	BU
1953	—	—	—	—	BV	125

KM# M123a   10 PESOS
8.3333 g., 0.9000 Gold .2411 oz. AGW   **Subject:** Centennial
of Constitution

Date	Mintage	F	VF	XF	Unc	BU
1957	Est. 73,000	—	—	—	BV	125

Note: Mintage includes #M122a

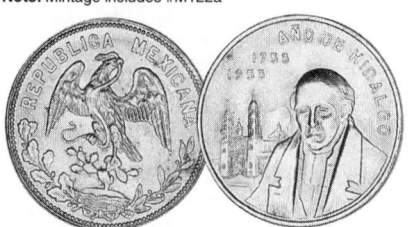

KM# M92a   20 PESOS
16.6666 g., 0.9000 Gold .4823 oz. AGW   **Subject:** 200th
Anniversary - Birth of Hidalgo

Date	Mintage	F	VF	XF	Unc	BU
1953	—	—	—	—	BV	225

KM# M122a   50 PESOS
41.6666 g., 0.9000 Gold 1.2057 oz. AGW   **Subject:**
Centennial of Constitution

Date	Mintage	F	VF	XF	Unc	BU
1957 Inc. M123a	—	—	—	—	BV	600

BANK SETS

Hard Case Sets unless otherwise noted.

KM#	Date	Mintage	Identification	Issue Price	Mkt Val
BS1	1972 (6)	—	KM#418, 427, 452, 460, 472, 480	—	30.00
BS2	1973 (5)	—	KM#418, 427 (2), 441, 472	—	20.00
BS3	1974 (7)	—	KM#427, 434.4, 441, 442, 460, 472, 477.1	—	30.00
BS4	1975 (7)	—	KM#427, 434.1, 442, 452, 460 (2), 477.1	—	20.00
BS5	1976 (9)	—	KM#427, 434.1, 442, 452 (2), 460, 472(2), 477.1	—	15.00
BS6	1977 (9)	—	KM#434.1, 434.2, 442, 452, 460 (2), 472, 477.1, 483.1	—	35.00
BS7	1977 (9)	—	KM#434.1, 434.2, 442, 452, 460 (2), 472, 477.1, 483.2 Type II for 3-ring binder	—	—
BS8	1978 (9)	500	KM#434.1, 434.2, 442, 452, 460 (2), 472, 477.2, 483.2, Type I, flat pack	—	35.00
BS9	1978 (9)	—	KM#434.1, 434.2, 442, 452, 460 (2), 472, 477.2, 483.2 Type II for 3-ring binder,	—	15.00

KM#	Date	Mintage	Identification	Issue Price	Mkt Val
BS10	1979 (9)	—	KM#434.1, 434.4, 442, 452 (2), 460 (2), 477.2, 483.2 Type I flat pack	11.00	25.00
BS11	1979 (8)	—	KM#434.1, 434.2, 442, 452 (2), 460, 477.2, 483.2 Type II for 3-ring binder	11.00	15.00
BS12	1980 (9)	—	KM#434.2, 442, 452 (2), 460 (2), 485, 486, 477.2	4.20	25.00
BS13	1981 (9)	—	KM#442 (2), 452 (2), 460 (2), 477.2, 485, 486	4.20	25.00
BS14	1982 (7)	—	KM#442, 452, 460, 477.2, 485, 486, 490	—	20.00
BS15	1983 (11)	—	KM#442 (2), 452 (2), 460 (2), 490, 491 (2), 492 (2)	—	20.00
BS16	1983 (11)	—	KM#442 (2), 452 (2), 460 (2), 490, 491 (2), 492 (2) 3-ring plastic page	—	12.50
BS17	1984 (8)	—	KM#485, 486, 490, 491, 493, 495 (2), 496,	—	25.00
BS22	1988 (8)	—	KM#493, 495a, 502, 508, 512, 529, 531, 536	—	20.00
BS18	1985 (12)	—	KM#477.2, 485, 493 (2), 495 (2), 496, 502, 508, 509, 510, 512	—	30.00
BS19	1985 (12)	—	KM#477.2, 485, 493 (2), 495 (2), 496, 502, 508, 509, 510, 512 3-ring plastic page	—	20.00
BS20	1986 (7)	—	KM#493, 495, 496, 508, 512, 525, 529 3-ring plastic page	—	20.00
BS21	1987 (9)	—	KM#493, 495 (2), 496, 502 (2), 512, 529 (2)	—	20.00
BS23	1989 (10)	—	KM#493 (3), 508 (3), 512, 529, 536 (2)	—	20.00
BS24	1990 (8)	—	KM#493 (2), 495a, 509 (2), 512, 536 (2)	—	20.00
BS25	1991 (4)	—	KM#493 (2), 536 (2)	—	15.00
BS26	1992 (5)	—	KM#493 (2), 495a, 529, 536	—	15.00
BS27	1992 (8)	—	KM#546-553	—	30.00
BS28	1993 (7)	—	KM#546-552	—	18.00
BS29	1993 (3)	—	KM#553, 561, 571	—	35.00
BS30	1994 (7)	—	KM#546-552	—	18.00
BS31	1994 (3)	—	KM#553, 561, 571	—	35.00
BS32	1995 (9)	—	KM#546-551, 553, 561, 571	—	45.00
BS33	1996 (6)	—	KM#546-549, 603, 604	12.00	30.00
BS34	1997 (8)	—	KM#546-549, 603-605, 616	—	30.00
BS35	1998 (8)	—	KM#546-549, 603-605, 616	—	30.00
BS36	1999 (8)	—	KM#546-549, 603-605, 616	—	35.00
BS37	2000 (7)	—	KM#547-549, 603-605, 636 Set in folder	—	30.00
BS38	2001 (10)	—	KM#546-549, 603-605, 636-638 Set in folder	—	30.00
BS39	2002 (8)	—	KM#546-549, 603-605, 616 Set in folder	—	30.00
BS40	2003 (6)	—	KM#547-549, 603-605 Set in folder	—	30.00

PROOF SETS

KM#	Date	Mintage	Identification	Issue Price	Mkt Val
PS1	1982/1983 (8)	998	KM442, 452, 460, 485, 477.2, 486, 490, 494.1	495	285
PS2	1982/1983 (8)	—	KM460, 477.2, 485, 486, 490, 491, 492, PnB169 (in white box with Mo. in gold)	—	—
PS3	1982/1983 (7)	23	KM460, 477.2, 485, 486, 490, 491, 492 (in white box with Mo in gold)	—	500
PS4	1982/1983 (7)	17	KM460, 477.2, 485, 486, 490, 491, 492 (in white box)	—	500
PS5	1982/1983 (7)	8	KM460, 477.2, 485, 486, 490, 491, 492 (in white box)	—	500
PS6	1983 (7)	3	KM460, 477.2, 485, 486, 490, 491, 492	—	—
PS10	1985 (3)	—	KM503-505 (in blue box)	—	60.00
PS11	1985 (2)	—	KM511, 513	—	350
PS7	1985/1986 (12)	—	KM497a-499a, 503-505, 514-515, 519, 521, 523-524	—	250
PS8	1985 (4)	—	KM500.2-501.2, 506.2, 507.2	—	700
PS9	1985 (3)	—	KM499a, 514, 515 (in blue box)	—	60.00
PS12	1989 (3)	704	KM488, 494.1, 538, Rainbow	730	850
PS13	1992 (5)	5,000	KM494.3, 542-545	—	87.50
PS14	1993 (5)	5,000	KM494.4, 542-545	—	87.50
PS15	1994 (5)	5,000	KM494.4, 542-545	—	85.00
PS16	1995 (7)	—	KM546-550, 552, 553, 555	45.00	48.00

CHIHUAHUA

The Chihuahua Mint was established by a decree of October 8, 1810 as a temporary mint. Their first coins were cast 8 Reales using Mexico City coins as patterns and obliterating/changing the mint mark and moneyer initials. Two c/m were placed on the obverse - on the left, a T designating receipt by the Royal Treasurer, crowned pillars of Hercules on the right with pomegranate beneath, the comptrollers symbol.

In 1814, standard dies were made available, thus machine struck 8 Reales were produced until 1822. Only the one denomination was made at Chihuahua.

Mint mark: CA.

WAR OF INDEPENDENCE

ROYALIST COINAGE

KM# 123   8 REALES
Cast Silver   **Ruler:** Ferdinand VII **Countermark:** T at left, pillars at right, pomegranate below **Obv:** Imaginary bust of Ferdinand VII **Obv. Legend:** FERDIN. VII. DEI. GRATIA

Date	Mintage	Good	VG	F	VF	XF
1810CA RP Rare	—	—	—	—	—	—
1811CA RP	—	45.00	60.00	100	150	—
1812CA RP	—	30.00	40.00	60.00	90.00	—
1813CA RP	—	30.00	40.00	60.00	90.00	—

KM# 111.1 8 REALES
27.0700 g., 0.9030 Silver .7860 oz. ASW **Ruler:**
Ferdinand VII **Obv:** Draped bust of Ferdinand VII **Obv.
Legend:** FERDIN. VII. DEI. GRATIA **Rev:** Similar to KM#123

Date	Mintage	VG	F	VF	XF	Unc
1815CA RP	—	200	275	350	500	—
1816CA RP	—	80.00	125	150	275	—
1817CA RP	—	100	150	185	275	—
1818CA RP	—	100	150	185	275	—
1819/8 RP	—	125	175	250	350	—
1819CA RP	—	125	175	250	350	—
1820CA RP	—	200	275	350	500	—
1821CA RP	—	200	275	350	500	—
1822CA RP	—	400	600	800	1,100	—

Note: KM#111.1 is normally found struck over earlier cast 8
Reales, KM#123 and Monclova (MVA) 1812 cast countermark 8 Reales, KM#202 and Zacatecas 8 Reales, KM#190

DURANGO

The Durango mint was authorized as a temporary mint
on the same day as the Chihuahua Mint, October 8, 1810. The
mint opened in 1811 and made coins of 6 denominations
between 1811 and 1822.
Mint mark: D.

WAR OF INDEPENDENCE

ROYALIST COINAGE

KM# 60 1/8 REAL
Copper **Ruler:** Ferdinand VII **Obv:** Crown above double F7
monogram **Rev:** EN DURANGO, value, date

Date	Mintage	VG	F	VF	XF	Unc
1812D	—	32.50	75.00	125	250	—
1813D Rare	—	—	—	—	—	—
1814D Rare	—	—	—	—	—	—

KM# 61 1/8 REAL
Copper **Ruler:** Ferdinand VII **Obv:** Crown above double F7
monogram **Rev:** Spray added above date

Date	Mintage	VG	F	VF	XF	Unc
1814D	—	15.00	30.00	50.00	90.00	—
1815D	—	18.00	35.00	60.00	100	—
1816D	—	18.00	35.00	60.00	100	—
1817D	—	15.00	30.00	50.00	90.00	—
1818D	—	15.00	30.00	50.00	90.00	—
1818D OCTAVO DD REAL (error)	—	45.00	80.00	125	225	—

KM# 74.1 1/2 REAL
1.6900 g., 0.9030 Silver .0491 oz. ASW **Ruler:** Ferdinand VII
Obv: Draped bust of Ferdinand VII

Date	Mintage	VG	F	VF	XF	Unc
1813D RM	—	250	450	750	1,800	—
1814D MZ	—	250	450	750	1,850	—
1816D MZ	—	250	450	750	1,850	—

KM# 83.1 REAL
3.3800 g., 0.9030 Silver .0981 oz. ASW **Ruler:** Ferdinand VII
Obv: Draped bust of Ferdinand VII

Date	Mintage	VG	F	VF	XF	Unc
1813D RM	—	250	450	650	1,650	—
1814D MZ	—	250	450	650	1,650	—
1815D MZ	—	250	450	650	1,650	—

KM# 92.2 2 REALES
6.7700 g., 0.9030 Silver .1966 oz. ASW **Ruler:** Ferdinand VII
Obv: Armored bust of Ferdinand VII **Rev. Legend:** MON
PROV DE DURANGO...

Date	Mintage	VG	F	VF	XF	Unc
1811D RM	—	375	450	850	1,750	—

KM# 92.3 2 REALES
6.7700 g., 0.9030 Silver .1966 oz. ASW **Ruler:** Ferdinand VII
Obv: Armored bust of Ferdinand VII **Rev. Legend:** HISPAN
ET IND REX...

Date	Mintage	VG	F	VF	XF	Unc
1812 RM	—	250	400	750	1,650	—

KM# 93.1 2 REALES
6.7700 g., 0.9030 Silver .1966 oz. ASW **Ruler:** Ferdinand VII
Obv: Draped bust of Ferdinand VII

Date	Mintage	VG	F	VF	XF	Unc
1812D RM	—	250	400	750	1,650	—
1813D RM	—	300	600	1,000	2,750	—
1813D MZ	—	300	600	1,000	2,750	—
1814D MZ	—	300	600	1,000	2,750	—
1815D MZ	—	300	600	1,000	2,750	—
1816D MZ	—	300	600	1,000	2,750	—
1817D MZ	—	300	600	1,000	2,750	—

KM# 102.1   4 REALES

13.5400 g., 0.9030 Silver .3931 oz. ASW **Ruler:** Ferdinand VII **Obv:** Draped bust of Ferdinand VII

Date	Mintage	VG	F	VF	XF	Unc
1814D MZ	—	550	1,000	1,650	4,500	—
1816D MZ	—	450	900	1,400	4,000	—
1817D MZ	—	450	900	1,400	4,000	—

KM# 110.1   8 REALES

27.0700 g., 0.9030 Silver .7860 oz. ASW **Ruler:** Ferdinand VII **Obv:** Armored bust of Ferdinand VII

Date	Mintage	VG	F	VF	XF	Unc
1811D RM	—	600	1,000	1,750	5,000	—
1812D RM	—	350	650	1,000	3,500	—
1814D MZ	—	350	650	1,000	3,500	—

KM# 111.2   8 REALES

27.0700 g., 0.9030 Silver .7860 oz. ASW **Ruler:** Ferdinand VII **Obv:** Draped bust of Ferdinand VII

Date	Mintage	VG	F	VF	XF	Unc
1812D RM	—	125	175	275	800	—
1813D RM	—	150	200	325	850	—
1813D MZ	—	125	175	275	750	—
1814/2D MZ	—	150	200	300	750	—

Date	Mintage	VG	F	VF	XF	Unc
1814D MZ	—	150	200	300	750	—
1815D MZ	—	75.00	125	225	600	—
1816D MZ	—	50.00	75.00	125	325	—
1817D MZ	—	30.00	50.00	90.00	250	—
1818D MZ	—	50.00	75.00	125	350	—
1818D RM	—	50.00	75.00	125	325	—
1818D CG/RM	—	100	125	150	350	—
1818D CG	—	50.00	75.00	125	325	—
1819D CG/RM	—	50.00	100	150	300	—
1819D CG	—	30.00	60.00	100	250	—
1820D CG	—	30.00	60.00	100	250	—
1821D CG	—	30.00	40.00	80.00	200	—
1822D CG	—	30.00	50.00	90.00	240	—

Note: Occasionally these are found struck over cast Chihuahua 8 reales and are very rare in general, specimens dated prior to 1816 are rather crudely struck

GUADALAJARA

The Guadalajara Mint made its first coins in 1812 and the mint operated until April 30, 1815. It was to reopen in 1818 and continue operations until 1822. It was the only Royalist mint to strike gold coins, both 4 and 8 Escudos. In addition to these it struck the standard 5 denominations in silver.
Mint mark: GA.

WAR OF INDEPENDENCE

ROYALIST COINAGE

KM# 74.2   1/2 REAL

1.6900 g., 0.9030 Silver .0491 oz. ASW **Ruler:** Ferdinand VII **Obv:** Draped bust of Ferdinand VII

Date	Mintage	VG	F	VF	XF	Unc
1812GA MR Rare	—	—	—	—	—	—
1814GA MR	—	40.00	100	200	300	—
1815GA MR	—	200	350	500	1,000	—

KM# 83.2   REAL

3.3800 g., 0.9030 Silver .0981 oz. ASW **Ruler:** Ferdinand VII **Obv:** Draped bust of Ferdinand VII

Date	Mintage	VG	F	VF	XF	Unc
1813GA MR	—	300	500	800	—	—
1814GA MR	—	150	200	350	650	—
1815GA MR	—	300	500	800	—	—

KM# 93.2   2 REALES

6.7700 g., 0.9030 Silver .1966 oz. ASW **Ruler:** Ferdinand VII **Obv:** Draped bust of Ferdinand VII

Date	Mintage	VG	F	VF	XF	Unc
1812GA MR	—	300	500	800	2,500	—
1814/2GA MR	—	75.00	125	250	600	—
1814GA MR	—	75.00	125	250	600	—
1815/4GA MR	—	425	725	1,100	3,600	—
1815GA MR	—	400	700	1,000	3,500	—
1821GA FS	—	200	250	350	900	—

KM# 102.2   4 REALES
13.5400 g., 0.9030 Silver .3931 oz. ASW **Ruler:**
Ferdinand VII **Obv:** Draped small bust of Ferdinand VII

Date	Mintage	VG	F	VF	XF	Unc
1814GA MR	—	40.00	65.00	150	250	—
1815GA MR	—	80.00	150	300	500	—

KM# 102.3   4 REALES
13.5400 g., 0.9030 Silver .3931 oz. ASW **Ruler:**
Ferdinand VII **Obv:** Large bust

Date	Mintage	VG	F	VF	XF	Unc
1814GA MR	—	50.00	100	200	400	—

KM# 102.4   4 REALES
13.5400 g., 0.9030 Silver .3931 oz. ASW **Ruler:**
Ferdinand VII **Obv:** Large bust with berries in laurel

Date	Mintage	VG	F	VF	XF	Unc
1814GA MR	—	60.00	120	250	450	—

KM# 111.3   8 REALES
27.0700 g., 0.9030 Silver .7860 oz. ASW **Ruler:**
Ferdinand VII **Obv:** Draped bust of Ferdinand VII

Date	Mintage	VG	F	VF	XF	Unc
1812GA MR	—	2,000	3,500	5,000	7,000	—
1813/2GA MR	—	60.00	100	150	400	—
1813GA MR	—	60.00	100	150	400	—
1814GA MR	—	20.00	35.00	60.00	180	—
Note: Several bust varieties exist for the 1814 issue						
1815GA MR	—	150	200	350	750	—
1818GA FS	—	30.00	50.00	75.00	200	—
1821/18GA FS	—	30.00	50.00	75.00	200	—
1821GA FS	—	25.00	35.00	60.00	165	—
1821/2GA FS	—	30.00	50.00	75.00	200	—
1822/1GA FS	—	30.00	50.00	75.00	200	—
1822GA FS	—	30.00	50.00	75.00	200	—

Note: Die varieties exist. Early dates are also encountered struck over other types

KM# 147   4 ESCUDOS
13.5400 g., 0.8750 Gold .3809 oz. AGW **Ruler:**
Ferdinand VII **Obv:** Uniformed bust of Ferdinand VII

Date	Mintage	VG	F	VF	XF	Unc
1812GA MR	—	—	—	—	—	—
Rare						

KM# 162   8 ESCUDOS
27.0700 g., 0.8750 Gold .7616 oz. AGW **Ruler:**
Ferdinand VII **Obv:** Large uniformed bust of Ferdinand VII

Date	Mintage	VG	F	VF	XF	Unc
1812GA MR	—	—	—	—	—	—
Rare						
1813GA MR	—	5,250	8,250	12,500	21,000	—

KM# 163   8 ESCUDOS
27.0700 g., 0.8750 Gold .7616 oz. AGW **Ruler:**
Ferdinand VII **Obv:** Small uniformed bust of Ferdinand VII

Date	Mintage	VG	F	VF	XF	Unc
1813GA MR	—	10,000	16,000	30,000	45,000	—

Note: Spink America Gerber sale 6-96 VF or better realized
$46,200

KM# 161.1   8 ESCUDOS
27.0700 g., 0.8750 Gold .7616 oz. AGW **Ruler:**
Ferdinand VII **Obv:** Undraped bust of Ferdinand VII

Date	Mintage	VG	F	VF	XF	Unc
1821GA FS	—	1,200	2,000	4,000	6,500	—

KM# 164   8 ESCUDOS
27.0700 g., 0.8750 Gold .7616 oz. AGW **Ruler:**
Ferdinand VII **Obv:** Draped bust of Ferdinand VII

Date	Mintage	VG	F	VF	XF	Unc
1821GA FS	—	5,000	7,500	14,000	23,000	—

GUANAJUATO

The Guanajuato Mint was authorized December 24,
1812 and started production shortly thereafter; closing for
unknown reasons on May 15, 1813. The mint was reopened in
April, 1821 by the insurgents, who struck coins of the old royal
Spanish design to pay their army, even after independence,
well into 1822.

Only the 2 and 8 Reales coins were made.
Mint mark: Go.

WAR OF INDEPENDENCE

ROYALIST COINAGE

KM# 93.3   2 REALES
6.7700 g., 0.9030 Silver .1966 oz. ASW **Ruler:** Ferdinand VII
Obv: Draped bust of Ferdinand VII

Date	Mintage	VG	F	VF	XF	Unc
1821Go JM	—	35.00	65.00	100	185	—
1822Go JM	—	30.00	50.00	75.00	145	—

KM# 111.4   8 REALES
27.0700 g., 0.9030 Silver .7860 oz. ASW   **Ruler:**
Ferdinand VII **Obv:** Draped bust of Ferdinand VII

Date	Mintage	VG	F	VF	XF	Unc
1812Go JJ	—	3,000	5,000	—	—	—
1813Go JJ	—	125	175	275	600	—
1821Go JM	—	25.00	50.00	75.00	200	—
1822Go JM	—	20.00	35.00	60.00	185	—

NUEVA GALICIA

(Later became Jalisco State)

In early colonial times, Nueva Galicia was an extensive
province which substantially combined later provinces of
Zacatecas and Jalisco. These are states of Mexico today
although the name was revived during the War of Independence. The only issue was 2 Reales of rather enigmatic origin.
No decrees or other authorization to strike this coin has yet
been located or reported.

WAR OF INDEPENDENCE
INSURGENT COINAGE

KM# 218   2 REALES
0.9030 Silver   **Obv:** N. G. in center, date **Obv. Legend:**
PROVYCIONAL... **Rev:** 2R in center **Rev. Legend:** ... A.
JUNIANA...

Date	Mintage	Good	VG	F	VF	XF
1813	—	1,000	2,500	4,500	—	—

Note: Excellent struck counterfeits exist

NUEVA VISCAYA

(Later became Durango State)

This 8 Reales, intended for the province of Nueva Vis-
caya, was minted in the newly-opened Durango Mint during
February and March of 1811, before the regular coinage of
Durango was started.

WAR OF INDEPENDENCE
ROYALIST COINAGE

KM# 181   8 REALES
27.0700 g., 0.9030 Silver .7860 oz. ASW   **Ruler:**
Ferdinand VII **Obv:** Arms of Durango **Obv. Legend:** MON.
PROV. DE NUEV. VIZCAYA **Rev:** Royal arms

Date	Mintage	Good	VG	F	VF	XF
1811 RM	—	1,000	2,250	2,850	5,500	—

Note: Several varieties exist.

OAXACA

The city of Oaxaca was in the midst of a coin shortage
when it became apparent the city would be taken by the Insurgents. Royalist forces under Lt. Gen. Saravia had coins made.
They were cast in a blacksmith shop. 1/2, 1, and 8 Reales
were made only briefly in 1812 before the Royalists surren-
dered the city.

WAR OF INDEPENDENCE
ROYALIST COINAGE

KM# 166   1/2 REAL
0.9030 Silver   **Ruler:** Ferdinand VII **Obv:** Cross separating
castle, lion, Fo, 7o **Rev:** Legend around shield **Rev. Legend:**
PROV. D. OAXACA

Date	Mintage	Good	VG	F	VF	XF
1812	—	1,000	1,500	2,500	3,500	—

KM# 167 REAL
0.9030 Silver **Ruler:** Ferdinand VII **Obv:** Cross separating castle, lion, Fo, 7o **Rev:** Legend around shield **Rev. Legend:** PROV. D. OAXACA

Date	Mintage	Good	VG	F	VF	XF
1812	—	350	650	1,200	2,500	—

KM# 168 8 REALES
0.9030 Silver **Obv:** Cross seperating castle, lion, Fo, 7o **Rev:** Shield, authorization mark above **Note:** These issues usually display a second mark 'O' between the crowned pillars on the obverse. Varieties of large and small lion in shield also exist.

Date	Mintage	Good	VG	F	VF	XF
1812 "A"	—	1,300	1,900	3,300	5,000	—
1812 "B"	—	1,300	1,900	3,300	5,000	—
1812 "C"	—	1,300	1,900	3,300	5,000	—
1812 "D"	—	1,300	1,900	3,300	5,000	—
1812 "K"	—	1,300	1,900	3,300	5,000	—
1812 "L"	—	1,300	1,900	3,300	5,000	—
1812 "Mo"	—	1,300	1,900	3,300	5,000	—
1812 "N"	—	1,300	1,900	3,300	5,000	—
1812 "O"	—	1,300	1,900	3,300	5,000	—
1812 "R"	—	1,300	1,900	3,300	5,000	—
1812 "V"	—	1,300	1,900	3,300	5,000	—
1812 "Z"	—	1,300	1,900	3,300	5,000	—

INSURGENT COINAGE

Oaxaca was the hub of Insurgent activity in the south where coinage started in July 1811 and continued until October 1814. The Oaxaca issues represent episodic strikings, usually under dire circumstances by various individuals. Coins were commonly made of copper due to urgency and were intended to be redeemed at face value in gold or silver once silver was available to the Insurgents. Some were later made in silver, but most appear to be of more recent origin, to satisfy collectors.

KM# 219 1/2 REAL
Struck Copper **Issuer:** SUD, Under General Morelos **Obv:** Bow, arrow, SUD **Rev:** Morelos monogram Mo, date

Date	Mintage	Good	VG	F	VF	XF
1811	—	6.75	11.50	20.00	35.00	—
1812	—	6.75	11.50	20.00	35.00	—
1813	—	5.50	9.00	17.50	30.00	—
1814	—	9.00	16.50	25.00	40.00	—

Note: Uniface strikes exist of #219

KM# 220.1 1/2 REAL
Struck Silver **Issuer:** SUD, Under General Morelos **Obv:** Bow, arrow, SUD **Rev:** Morelos monogram Mo, date

Date	Mintage	Good	VG	F	VF	XF
1811	—	—	—	—	—	—
1812	—	—	—	—	—	—
1813	—	—	—	—	—	—

KM# 220.2 1/2 REAL
Struck Silver **Issuer:** SUD, Under General Morelos **Obv:** Bow, arrow, SUD **Rev:** Morelos monogram Mo, date

Date	Mintage	Good	VG	F	VF	XF
1811	—	—	—	—	—	—
1812	—	—	—	—	—	—
1813	—	25.00	50.00	100	150	—

Note: Use caution as silver specimens appear questionable and may be considered spurious

KM# 221 1/2 REAL
Struck Silver **Issuer:** SUD, Under General Morelos **Obv:** Bow, arrow **Obv. Legend:** PROVICIONAL DE OAXACA **Rev:** Lion **Rev. Legend:** AMERICA MORELOS

Date	Mintage	Good	VG	F	VF	XF
1812	—	35.00	60.00	100	150	—
1813	—	35.00	60.00	100	150	—

KM# 221a 1/2 REAL
Struck Copper **Issuer:** SUD, Under General Morelos **Obv:** Bow, arrow **Obv. Legend:** PROVICIONAL DE OAXACA **Rev:** Lion **Rev. Legend:** AMERICA MORELOS

Date	Mintage	Good	VG	F	VF	XF
1812	—	27.50	42.50	70.00	100	—
1813	—	20.00	35.00	60.00	85.00	—

KM# A222 1/2 REAL
Struck Copper **Issuer:** SUD, Under General Morelos **Obv:** Similar to KM#220 **Rev:** Similar to KM#221 but with 1/2 at left of lion **Rev. Legend:** AMERICA MORELOS

Date	Mintage	Good	VG	F	VF	XF
1813	—	27.50	42.50	70.00	100	—

KM# 243 1/2 REAL
Struck Copper **Issuer:** Tierra Caliente (Hot Country), Under
General Morelos **Obv:** Bow, T.C., SUD **Rev:** Morelos
monogram, value, date

Date	Mintage	Good	VG	F	VF	XF
1813	—	37.50	70.00	125	200	—

KM# 222 REAL
Struck Copper **Issuer:** SUD, Under General Morelos **Obv:**
Bow, arrow, SUD **Rev:** Morelos monogram, 1 R., date

Date	Mintage	Good	VG	F	VF	XF
1811	—	4.75	9.00	18.00	38.00	—
1812	—	3.75	7.00	14.00	30.00	—
1813	—	3.75	7.00	14.00	30.00	—

KM# 222a REAL
Struck Silver **Issuer:** SUD, Under General Morelos **Obv:**
Bow, arrow, SUD **Rev:** Morelos monogram, 1 R., date

Date	Mintage	Good	VG	F	VF	XF
1812	—	—	—	—	—	—
1813	—	—	—	—	—	—

KM# 223 REAL
Cast Silver **Issuer:** SUD, Under General Morelos **Obv:** Bow,
arrow, SUD with floral ornaments **Rev:** Morelos monogram,
1 R., date

Date	Mintage	Good	VG	F	VF	XF
1812	—	—	—	—	—	—
1813	—	27.50	60.00	115	160	—

Note: Use caution as many silver specimens appear questionable and may be considered spurious

KM# 224 REAL
Struck Copper **Issuer:** SUD, Under General Morelos **Obv:**
Bow, arrow/SUD **Rev:** Lion **Rev. Legend:** AMERICA
MORELOS

Date	Mintage	Good	VG	F	VF	XF
1813	—	27.50	42.50	75.00	110	—

KM# 225 REAL
Silver **Issuer:** SUD, Under General Morelos **Obv:** Bow,
arrow/SUD **Rev:** Lion **Rev. Legend:** AMERICA MORELOS

Date	Mintage	Good	VG	F	VF	XF
1813 Rare	—	—	—	—	—	—

KM# 244 REAL
Struck Copper **Issuer:** Tierra Caliente (Hot Country), Under
General Morelos **Obv:** Bow, T.C., SUD **Rev:** Morelos
monogram, value, date

Date	Mintage	Good	VG	F	VF	XF
1813	—	13.50	25.00	50.00	80.00	—

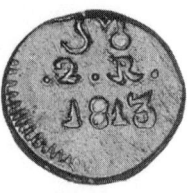

KM# 226.1 2 REALES
Struck Copper **Issuer:** SUD, Under General Morelos **Obv:**
Bow, arrow/SUD **Rev:** Morelos monogram, .2.R., date

Date	Mintage	Good	VG	F	VF	XF
1811	—	12.50	25.00	55.00	100	—
1811 inverted 2	—	15.00	30.00	60.00	120	—
1812	—	2.50	4.00	6.50	12.00	—
1813	—	3.00	5.00	8.00	15.00	—
1814	—	13.50	28.00	65.00	120	—

KM# 226.1a 2 REALES
Struck Silver **Issuer:** SUD, Under General Morelos **Obv:**
Bow, arrow/SUD **Rev:** Morelos monogram, .2.R., date

Date	Mintage	Good	VG	F	VF	XF
1812	—	175	300	500	750	—

KM# 229 2 REALES
Cast Silver **Issuer:** SUD, Under General Morelos **Obv:** Bow,
arrow, SUD **Rev:** Morelos monogram, value, date in center
with ornamentation around

Date	Mintage	Good	VG	F	VF	XF
1812	—	60.00	100	150	225	—
1812 Filled in D in SUD	—	60.00	100	150	225	—

Note: Use caution as many silver specimens appear questionable and may be considered spurious

KM# 245 2 REALES
Struck Copper **Issuer:** Tierra Caliente (Hot Country), Under
General Morelos **Obv:** Bow, T.C., SUD **Rev:** Morelos
monogram, value, date

Date	Mintage	Good	VG	F	VF	XF
1813	—	9.00	22.50	35.00	50.00	—

KM# 227 2 REALES
Struck Silver **Issuer:** SUD, Under General Morelos **Obv:**
Bow, arrow **Obv. Legend:** SUD-OXA **Rev:** Morelos
monogram, value, date

Date	Mintage	Good	VG	F	VF	XF
1813	—	60.00	100	200	300	—
1814	—	60.00	100	200	300	—

KM# 226.2 2 REALES
Struck Silver **Issuer:** SUD, Under General Morelos **Obv:**
Three large stars added **Rev:** Morelos monogram, .2.R., date

Date	Mintage	Good	VG	F	VF	XF
1814	—	10.00	20.00	40.00	60.00	—

KM# 246 2 REALES
Struck Copper **Issuer:** Tierra Caliente (Hot Country), Under General Morelos **Obv:** Bow, T.C., SUD **Rev:** Morelos monogram, value, date

Date	Mintage	Good	VG	F	VF	XF
1814	—	22.50	50.00	100	175	—

KM# 228 2 REALES
Struck Silver **Issuer:** SUD, Under General Morelos **Obv:** Bow, arrow **Obv. Legend:** SUD. OAXACA **Rev:** Morelos monogram, value, date

Date	Mintage	Good	VG	F	VF	XF
1814	—	60.00	100	200	325	—

KM# 234a 8 REALES
Struck Silver **Issuer:** SUD, under General Morelos **Obv:** Bow, arrow, SUD in floral ornamentation **Rev:** Morelos monogram, .8.R., date surrounded by ornate flowery fields

Date	Mintage	Good	VG	F	VF	XF
1811	—	—	—	2,500	4,000	—
1812	—	—	—	1,200	2,000	—

KM# 234 8 REALES
Copper **Issuer:** SUD, Under General Morelos **Obv:** Bow, arrow, SUD in floral ornamentation **Obv. Legend:** SUD-OXA **Rev:** Morelos monogram, .8.R., date surrounded by ornate flowery fields

Date	Mintage	Good	VG	F	VF	XF
1811	—	75.00	125	150	225	—
1812	—	4.00	6.00	10.00	20.00	—
1813	—	4.00	6.00	10.00	20.00	—
1814	—	10.00	15.00	25.00	50.00	—

KM# 235 8 REALES
Cast Silver **Issuer:** SUD, Under General Morelos **Obv:** Bow, arrow, SUD in floral ornamentation **Rev:** Morelos monogram, value, date surrounded by ornate flowery fields

Date	Mintage	Good	VG	F	VF	XF
1811	—	—	—	—	—	—
1812	—	75.00	125	200	350	—
1813	—	60.00	100	175	300	—
1814	—	—	—	—	—	—

Note: Most silver specimens available in today's market are considered spurious

KM# 236 8 REALES
0.9030 Struck Silver **Issuer:** SUD, Under General Morelos **Obv:** M monogram **Obv. Legend:** PROV. D. OAXACA **Rev:** Lion shield with or without bow above

Date	Mintage	Good	VG	F	VF	XF
1812 Rare	—	—	—	—	—	—

KM# 233.1 8 REALES
Copper **Issuer:** SUD, Under General Morelos **Obv:** Bow, arrow, SUD **Rev:** Morelos monogram, 8.R., date, plain fields

Date	Mintage	Good	VG	F	VF	XF
1812	—	15.00	30.00	60.00	90.00	—

KM# 233.5a 8 REALES
Silver **Issuer:** SUD, Under General Morelos **Obv:** 8 dots below bow, SUD, plain fields **Rev:** Morelos monogram, 8.R., date

Date	Mintage	Good	VG	F	VF	XF
1812	—	—	—	1,200	2,000	—

KM# 233.1a 8 REALES
Struck Silver **Issuer:** SUD, Under General Morelos **Obv:** Bow, arrow, SUD **Rev:** Morelos monogram, 8.R., date, plain fields

Date	Mintage	Good	VG	F	VF	XF
1812	—	100	150	250	450	—

KM# 233.2   8 REALES
Copper **Issuer:** SUD, Under General Morelos **Obv:** Bow, arrow, SUD **Rev:** Morelos monogram, 8 R, date, plain fields

Date	Mintage	Good	VG	F	VF	XF
1812	—	6.00	8.00	12.00	15.00	—
1813	—	6.00	8.00	12.00	15.00	—
1814	—	10.00	12.00	15.00	20.00	—

Note: Similar to KM#233.4 but lines below bow slant left

KM# 242   8 REALES
Copper **Issuer:** Huautla, Under General Morelos **Obv:** Legend around bow, arrow/SUD **Obv. Legend:** MONEDA PROVI. CIONAL PS. ES. **Rev. Legend:** FABRICADO EN HUAUTLA

Date	Mintage	Good	VG	F	VF	XF
1812	—	1,000	1,500	2,000	—	—

KM# 248   8 REALES
Struck Copper **Issuer:** Tierra Caliente (Hot Country), Under General Morelos **Obv:** Bow, T.C., SUD **Rev:** Morelos monogram, value, date

Date	Mintage	Good	VG	F	VF	XF
1813	—	9.00	20.00	40.00	75.00	—

KM# 249   8 REALES
Cast Silver **Issuer:** Tierra Caliente (Hot Country), Under General Morelos **Obv:** Bow, T.C., SUD **Rev:** Morelos monogram, value, date

Date	Mintage	Good	VG	F	VF	XF
1813	—	—	—	—	—	—

Note: Use caution as many silver specimens appear questionable and may be considered spurious

KM# 233.3   8 REALES
Struck Copper **Issuer:** SUD, Under General Morelos **Obv:** Bow, arrow, SUD, with left slant lines below bow **Rev:** Morelos monogram, 8.R., date, plain fields

Date	Mintage	Good	VG	F	VF	XF
1813	—	10.00	17.50	30.00	50.00	—

KM# 233.4   8 REALES
Struck Copper **Issuer:** SUD, Under General Morelos **Obv:** Bow, arrow, SUD, with right slant lines below bow **Rev:** Morelos monogram, 8.R., date, plain fields

Date	Mintage	Good	VG	F	VF	XF
1813	—	10.00	17.50	30.00	50.00	—

KM# 233.2a   8 REALES
Silver **Issuer:** SUD, Under General Morelos **Obv:** bow, arrow, SUD **Rev:** Morelos monogram, 8R, date, plain fields

Date	Mintage	Good	VG	F	VF	XF
1813	—	—	—	1,200	2,000	—

KM# 237   8 REALES
0.9030 Sterling Silver **Issuer:** SUD, Under General Morelos **Obv:** M monogram, without legend **Rev:** Lion shield with or without bow above

Date	Mintage	Good	VG	F	VF	XF
1813 Rare	—	—	—	—	—	—

KM# 238   8 REALES
0.9030 Struck Silver **Issuer:** SUD, Under General Morelos **Obv:** Bow/M/SUD **Rev:** PROV. DE. ... arms

Date	Mintage	Good	VG	F	VF	XF
1813 Rare	—	—	—	—	—	—

KM# 239   8 REALES
Cast Silver **Issuer:** SUD, Under General Morelos **Obv:** Bow, arrow **Obv. Legend:** SUD-OXA **Rev:** Morelos monogram

Date	Mintage	Good	VG	F	VF	XF
1814 Rare	—	—	—	—	—	—

KM# 240 8 REALES
Copper **Issuer:** SUD, Under General Morelos **Obv:** Bow, arrow **Obv. Legend:** SUD-OXA **Rev:** Morelos monogram, 8.R., date

Date	Mintage	Good	VG	F	VF	XF
1814	—	35.00	70.00	150	250	—

KM# 241 8 REALES
Copper **Issuer:** SUD, Under General Morelos **Obv:** Bow, arrow **Obv. Legend:** SUD-OAXACA **Rev:** Morelos monogram, 8.R., date

Date	Mintage	Good	VG	F	VF	XF
1814	—	100	200	350	550	—

PUEBLA

WAR OF INDEPENDENCE

INSURGENT COINAGE

KM# 250 1/2 REAL
Copper **Issuer:** Zacatlan, struck by General Osorno **Obv:** Osorno monogram, ZACATLAN, date **Rev:** Crossed arrows, wreath, value

Date	Mintage	Good	VG	F	VF	XF
1813 Rare	—	—	—	—	—	—

KM# 251 REAL
Copper **Issuer:** Zacatlan, struck by General Osorno **Obv:** Osorno monogram, ZACATLAN, date **Rev:** Crossed arrows, wreath, value

Date	Mintage	Good	VG	F	VF	XF
1813	—	100	150	225	450	—

KM# 252 2 REALES
Copper **Issuer:** Zacatlan, struck by General Osorno **Obv:** Osorno monogram, ZACATLAN, date **Rev:** Crossed arrows, wreath, value

Date	Mintage	Good	VG	F	VF	XF
1813	—	125	175	275	500	—

REAL DEL CATORCE

(City in San Luis Potosi)
Real del Catorce is an important mining center in the Province of San Luis Potosi. In 1811 an 8 Reales coin was issued under very primitive conditions while the city was still in Royalist hands. Few survive.

WAR OF INDEPENDENCE

ROYALIST COINAGE

KM# 169 8 REALES
0.9030 Silver **Ruler:** Ferdinand VII **Obv. Legend:** EL R. D. CATORC. POR FERNA. VII **Rev. Legend:** MONEDA. PROVISIONAL. VALE. 8R

Date	Mintage	VG	F	VF	XF	Unc
1811	—	7,000	15,000	35,000	65,000	—

Note: Spink America Gerber Sale 6-96 VF or XF realized $63,800

SAN FERNANDO DE BEXAR

WAR OF INDEPENDENCE

ROYALIST COINAGE

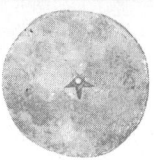

KM# Tn1 1/2 REAL (Jola)
Copper **Ruler:** Ferdinand VII **Note:** Prev. KM#170.

Date	Mintage	Good	VG	F	VF	XF
1818	8,000	—	—	—	25,000	30,000

KM# Tn2 1/2 REAL (Jola)
Copper **Ruler:** Ferdinand VII **Note:** Prev. KM#171.

Date	Mintage	Good	VG	F	VF	XF
1818	Inc. above	—	—	—	22,500	27,500

SAN LUIS POTOSI

Sierra de Pinos

WAR OF INDEPENDENCE

ROYALIST COINAGE

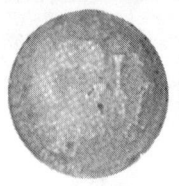

KM# A172   1/4 REAL
Copper   **Ruler:** Ferdinand VII **Issuer:** Sierra de Pinos, Villa

Date	Mintage	Good	VG	F	VF	XF
1814	—	75.00	125	200	350	—

KM# A172a   1/4 REAL
Silver   **Ruler:** Ferdinand VII

Date	Mintage	Good	VG	F	VF	XF
1814 Rare	—	—	—	—	—	—

SOMBRERETE

(Under Royalist Vargas)

The Sombrerete Mint opened on October 8, 1810 in an area that boasted some of the richest mines in Mexico. The mint operated only until July 16, 1811, only to reopen in 1812 and finally close for good at the end of the year. Mines Administrator Fernando Vargas, was also in charge of the coining, all coins bear his name.

WAR OF INDEPENDENCE

ROYALIST COINAGE

KM# 172   1/2 REAL
0.9030 Silver   **Ruler:** Ferdinand VII **Obv:** Legend around crowned globes **Obv. Legend:** FERDIN. VII. SOMBRERETE... **Rev:** Legend above lys in oval, sprays, date below **Rev. Legend:** VARGAS

Date	Mintage	Good	VG	F	VF	XF
1811	—	45.00	70.00	150	250	—
1812	—	50.00	90.00	175	275	—

KM# 173   REAL
0.9030 Silver   **Ruler:** Ferdinand VII **Obv:** Legend around crowned globes **Obv. Legend:** FERDIN. VII. SOMBRERETE... **Rev:** Legend above lys in oval with denomination flanking, sprays, date below **Rev. Legend:** VARGAS

Date	Mintage	Good	VG	F	VF	XF
1811	—	45.00	70.00	150	250	—

Note: For 1811, denomination reads as '1R' or 'R1'

1812	—	50.00	90.00	175	275	—

KM# 175   4 REALES
0.9030 Silver   **Ruler:** Ferdinand VII **Obv:** Crowned Royal arms **Obv. Legend:** R. CAXA. DE. SOMBRERETE. Large legend **Rev. Legend:** VARGAS/1811 **Note:** Prev. KM#172.

Date	Mintage	Good	VG	F	VF	XF
1812	—	50.00	100	200	450	—

KM# 176   8 REALES
0.9030 Silver   **Ruler:** Ferdinand VII **Countermark:** VARGAS, date, S **Obv:** Royal arms **Obv. Legend:** R. CAXA. DE SOMBRERETE **Rev:** Several countermarks between crowned pillars

Date	Mintage	Good	VG	F	VF	XF
1810	—	1,000	1,750	2,750	4,000	—
1811	—	225	325	450	600	—

KM# 177 8 REALES
0.9030 Silver **Ruler:** Ferdinand VII **Obv:** Crowned Royal
arms **Obv. Legend:** R. CAXA. DE SOMBRETE **Rev.
Legend:** VARGAS/date/3, S between crowned pillars

Date	Mintage	Good	VG	F	VF	XF
1811	—	125	185	245	500	—
1812	—	125	175	225	475	—

VALLADOLID MICHOACAN

WAR OF INDEPENDENCE

ROYALIST COINAGE

KM# 178 8 REALES
0.9030 Silver **Ruler:** Ferdinand VII **Obv:** Royal arms in
wreath, value at sides **Rev:** PROVISIONAL/DE
VALLADOLID/1813

Date	Mintage	Good	VG	F	VF	XF
1813 Rare	—	—	—	—	—	—

KM# 179 8 REALES
0.9030 Silver **Ruler:** Ferdinand VII **Obv:** Bust **Obv. Legend:**
FERDIN. VII. **Rev:** Arms, pillars, P. D. V. in legend

Date	Mintage	Good	VG	F	VF	XF
1813 Rare	—	—	—	—	—	—

Note: Spink America Gerber sale 6-96 good realized
$23,100

VERACRUZ

In Zongolica, in the province of Veracruz, 2 priests and a
lawyer decided to raise an army to fight for independence. Due
to isolation from other Insurgent forces, they decided to make
their own coins. Records show that they intended to mint coins
of 1/2, 1, 2, 4, and 8 Reales, but specimens are extant of only
the three higher denominations.

WAR OF INDEPENDENCE

INSURGENT COUNTERMARKED COINAGE
General Vicente Guerrero

The countermark of an eagle facing left within a pearl-
ed oval has been attributed by some authors as that of
General Vicente Guerrero, a leader of the insurgents in
the south, 1816-1821.

KM# 276 1/2 REAL
Silver **Issuer:** General Vicente Guerrero **Countermark:**
Eagle **Note:** Countermark on Mexico City KM#72.

CM Date	Host Date	Good	VG	F	VF	XF
ND	ND	40.00	60.00	80.00	175	—

KM# 277 REAL
Silver **Issuer:** General Vicente Guerrero **Countermark:**
Eagle **Note:** Countermark on Mexico City KM#78.

CM Date	Host Date	Good	VG	F	VF	XF
ND	1772 FM	35.00	50.00	75.00	165	—

KM# 278.1 2 REALES
Silver **Issuer:** General Vicente Guerrero **Countermark:**
Eagle **Note:** Countermark on Mexico City KM#88.

CM Date	Host Date	Good	VG	F	VF	XF
ND	1784 FM	40.00	60.00	100	225	—
ND	1798	40.00	60.00	100	225	—

KM# 278.2 2 REALES
Silver **Issuer:** General Vicente Guerrero **Countermark:**
Eagle **Note:** Countermark on Mexico City KM#91.

CM Date	Host Date	Good	VG	F	VF	XF
ND	1807 PJ	30.00	50.00	80.00	200	—

KM# 279 8 REALES
Silver **Issuer:** General Vicente Guerrero **Countermark:**
Eagle **Note:** Countermark on Zacatecas KM#191.

CM Date	Host Date	Good	VG	F	VF	XF
ND	1811	100	150	200	350	—

INSURGENT COUNTERMARKED COINAGE
ZMY

KM# 286 8 REALES
Silver **Issuer:** Unknown, presumed insurgent **Countermark:**
ZMY **Note:** Countermark on Zacatecas KM#191.

CM Date	Host Date	Good	VG	F	VF	XF
ND	1812	100	150	200	350	—

INSURGENT COINAGE

KM# 253 2 REALES
0.9030 Silver **Issuer:** Zongolica **Obv:** Bow and arrow **Obv.**
Legend: VIVA FERNANDO VII Y AMERICA **Rev:** Value,
crossed palm branch, sword, date **Rev. Legend:** ZONGOLICA

Date	Mintage	Good	VG	F	VF	XF
1812	—	85.00	175	300	500	—

KM# 255 8 REALES
0.9030 Silver **Issuer:** Zongolica **Obv:** Bow and arrow **Obv.**
Legend: VIVA FERNANDO VII Y AMERICA **Rev:** Value,
crossed palm branch, sword, date **Rev. Legend:**
ZONGOLICA **Note:** Similar to 2 Reales, KM#253.

Date	Mintage	Good	VG	F	VF	XF
1812 Rare	—	—	—	—	—	—

Note: Spink America Gerber sale 6-96 VF to XF realized
$57,200

INSURGENT COUNTERMARKED COINAGE
Congress of Chilpanzingo

Type A: Hand holding bow and arrow between quiver
with arrows, sword and bow.

Type B: Crowned eagle on bridge.

KM# 256.1 1/2 REAL
Silver **Issuer:** Congress of Chilpanzingo **Countermark:** Type
A hand holding bow and arrow between quiver with arrows,
sword and bow **Note:** Countermark on cast Mexico City KM#72.

CM Date	Host Date	Good	VG	F	VF	XF
ND	1812	42.50	70.00	90.00	120	—

KM# 256.2 1/2 REAL
Silver **Issuer:** Congress of Chilpanzingo **Countermark:** Type
A hand holding bow and arrow between quiver with arrows,
sword and bow **Note:** Countermark on Zacatecas KM#181.

CM Date	Host Date	Good	VG	F	VF	XF
ND	1811	50.00	75.00	100	125	—

KM# A257 REAL
Cast Silver **Issuer:** Congress of Chilpanzingo **Countermark:**
Type A hand holding bow and arrow between quiver with arrows,
sword and bow **Note:** Countermark on cast Mexico City KM#81.

CM Date	Host Date	Good	VG	F	VF	XF
ND	1803	18.50	30.00	50.00	80.00	—

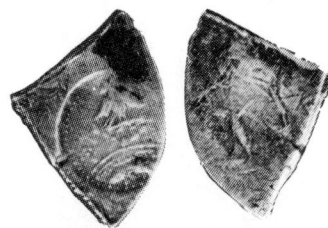

KM# 257.1 2 REALES
Silver **Issuer:** Congress of Chilpanzingo **Countermark:**
Type B crowned eagle on bridge **Note:** Countermark on 1/4
cut of 8 Reales.

CM Date	Host Date	Good	VG	F	VF	XF
	ND Unique	—	—	—	—	—

KM# 257.2 2 REALES
Silver **Issuer:** Congress of Chilpanzingo **Countermark:**
Type B crowned eagle on bridge **Note:** Countermark on
Zacatecas KM#186.

CM Date	Host Date	Good	VG	F	VF	XF
ND	1811 Unique	—	—	—	—	—

KM# 258.1 8 REALES
Silver **Issuer:** Congress of Chilpanzingo **Countermark:**
Type A hand holding bow and arrow between quiver with
arrows, sword and bow **Note:** Countermark on cast Mexico
City KM#109.

CM Date	Host Date	Good	VG	F	VF	XF
ND	1805	45.00	65.00	85.00	125	—

Note: A countermark appears on coins dated 1805 TH

KM# 258.2 8 REALES
Silver **Issuer:** Congress of Chilpanzingo **Countermark:**
Type A hand holding bow and arrow between quiver with
arrows, sword and bow **Note:** Countermark on cast Mexico
City KM#110.

CM Date	Host Date	Good	VG	F	VF	XF
ND	1810 HJ	50.00	75.00	100	150	—

KM# 258.3 8 REALES
Silver **Issuer:** Congress of Chilpanzingo **Countermark:**
Type A hand holding bow and arrow between quiver with
arrows, sword and bow **Note:** Countermark on cast Mexico
City KM#111.

CM Date	Host Date	Good	VG	F	VF	XF
ND	1811 HJ	45.00	65.00	85.00	125	—
ND	1812 HJ	100	125	175	275	—

KM# 259.1 8 REALES
Silver **Issuer:** Congress of Chilpanzingo **Countermark:**
Type B crowned eagle on bridge **Note:** Countermark on
Chihuahua KM#111.1.

CM Date	Host Date	Good	VG	F	VF	XF
ND	1816 RP	200	250	300	350	—

KM# 259.2 8 REALES
Silver **Issuer:** Congress of Chilpanzingo **Countermark:**
Type B crowned eagle on bridge **Note:** Countermark on cast
Mexico City KM#111.

CM Date	Host Date	Good	VG	F	VF	XF
ND	1811 HJ	130	140	150	175	—

KM# 259.3 8 REALES
Silver **Issuer:** Congress of Chilpanzingo **Countermark:**
Type B crowned eagle on bridge **Note:** Countermark on
Valladolid KM#178.

CM Date	Host Date	Good	VG	F	VF	XF
ND	1813	1,000	2,000	3,000	5,000	—

KM# 259.4   8 REALES
Silver **Issuer:** Congress of Chilpanzingo **Countermark:**
Type B crowned eagle on bridge **Note:** Countermark on
Zacatecas KM#190.

CM Date	Host Date	Good	VG	F	VF	XF
ND	1810	400	500	600	750	—

INSURGENT COUNTERMARKED COINAGE

Don Jose Maria De Linares

KM# 263.1   8 REALES
Silver **Issuer:** Don Jose Maria De Linares **Countermark:**
LINA/RES* **Note:** Countermark on Mexico City KM#110.

CM Date	Host Date	Good	VG	F	VF	XF
ND	1808 TH	250	300	375	500	—

KM# 263.2   8 REALES
Silver **Issuer:** Don Jose Maria De Linares **Countermark:**
LINA/RES * **Note:** Countermark on Zacatecas KM#190.

CM Date	Host Date	Good	VG	F	VF	XF
ND	1811	300	375	450	575	—

KM# 263.3   8 REALES
Silver **Issuer:** Don Jose Maria De Linares **Countermark:**
LINA/RES* **Note:** Countermark on Zacatecas KM#191.

CM Date	Host Date	Good	VG	F	VF	XF
ND	1812	250	300	375	500	—

INSURGENT COUNTERMARKED COINAGE

Ensaie

KM# 260.3   8 REALES
Silver **Issuer:** Ensaie **Countermark:** Eagle over ENSAIE,
crude sling below **Note:** Countermark on Zacatecas KM#190.

CM Date	Host Date	Good	VG	F	VF	XF
ND	1810	—	—	—	—	—
ND	1811	100	150	200	300	—

KM# 260.4   8 REALES
Silver **Issuer:** Ensaie **Countermark:** Eagle over ENSAIE,
crude sling below **Note:** Countermark on Zacatecas KM#191.

CM Date	Host Date	Good	VG	F	VF	XF
ND	1810	500	700	900	1,200	—
ND	1811	250	300	375	500	—
ND	1812	200	250	285	400	—

KM# 260.1   8 REALES
Silver **Issuer:** Ensaie **Countermark:** Eagle over ENSAIE,
crude sling below **Note:** Countermark on Mexico City
KM#110.

CM Date	Host Date	Good	VG	F	VF	XF
ND	1811 HJ	150	200	275	350	—

KM# 260.2   8 REALES
Silver **Issuer:** Ensaie **Countermark:** Eagle over ENSAIE,
crude sling below **Note:** Countermark on Zacatecas KM#189.

CM Date	Host Date	Good	VG	F	VF	XF
ND	1811	200	400	600	800	—

INSURGENT COUNTERMARKED COINAGE

Jose Maria Liceaga

J.M.L. with banner on cross, crossed olive branches.

(J.M.L./V., D.s, S.M., S.Y.S.L., Ve, A.P., s.r.a., Sea,
P.G., S., S.M., El)

KM# A260   1/2 REAL
Silver **Issuer:** Jose Maria Liceaga **Countermark:** JML/SM
with banner on cross, crossed olive branches **Note:**
Countermark on cast Mexico City 1/2 Real.

CM Date	Host Date	Good	VG	F	VF	XF
ND	ND	100	150	200	275	—

KM# 261.6   2 REALES
Silver **Issuer:** Jose Maria Liceaga **Countermark:** J.M.L./V.
with banner on cross, crossed olive branches **Note:**
Countermark on Zacatecas KM#187.

CM Date	Host Date	Good	VG	F	VF	XF
ND	1811	200	225	250	300	—

KM# 261.7 2 REALES
Silver **Issuer:** Jose Maria Liceaga **Countermark:** J.M.L./DS
with banner on cross, crossed olive branches **Note:**
Countermark on Zacatecas KM#187.

CM Date	Host Date	Good	VG	F	VF	XF
ND	1811	200	235	275	325	—

KM# 261.8 2 REALES
Silver **Issuer:** Jose Maria Liceaga **Countermark:** J.M.L./
S.M. with banner on cross, crossed olive branches **Note:**
Countermark on Zacatecas KM#187.

CM Date	Host Date	Good	VG	F	VF	XF
ND	1811	200	235	275	325	—

KM# 261.9 2 REALES
Silver **Issuer:** Jose Maria Liceaga **Countermark:** J.M.L./
S.Y. with banner on cross, crossed olive branches **Note:**
Countermark on Zacatecas KM#187.

CM Date	Host Date	Good	VG	F	VF	XF
ND	1811	200	235	275	325	—

KM# 261.1 2 REALES
Silver **Issuer:** Jose Maria Liceaga **Countermark:** J.M.L./Ve
with banner on cross, crossed olive branches **Note:**
Countermark on 1/4 cut of 8 Reales.

CM Date	Host Date	Good	VG	F	VF	XF
ND	ND	175	225	300	—	—

KM# 261.2 2 REALES
Silver **Issuer:** Jose Maria Liceaga **Countermark:** J.M.L./V
with banner on cross, crossed olive branchs **Note:**
Countermark on Zacatecas KM#186.

CM Date	Host Date	Good	VG	F	VF	XF
ND	1811	200	225	250	300	—

KM# 261.3 2 REALES
Silver **Issuer:** Jose Maria Liceaga **Countermark:** J.M.L./DS
with banner on cross, crossed olive branches **Note:**
Countermark on Zacatecas KM#186.

CM Date	Host Date	Good	VG	F	VF	XF
ND	1811	200	235	275	325	—

KM# 261.4 2 REALES
Silver **Issuer:** Jose Maria Liceaga **Countermark:** J.M.L./
S.M. with banner on cross, crossed olive branches **Note:**
Countermark on Zacatecas KM#186.

CM Date	Host Date	Good	VG	F	VF	XF
ND	1811	200	235	275	325	—

KM# 261.5 2 REALES
Silver **Issuer:** Jose Maria Liceaga **Countermark:** J.M.L./
S.Y. with banner on cross, crossed olive branches **Note:**
Countermark on Zacatecas KM#186.

CM Date	Host Date	Good	VG	F	VF	XF
ND	1811	200	235	275	325	—

KM# 262.1 8 REALES
Silver **Issuer:** Jose Maria Liceaga **Countermark:** J.M.L./
D.S. with banner on cross, crossed olive branches **Note:**
Countermark on Zacatecas KM#190.

CM Date	Host Date	Good	VG	F	VF	XF
ND	1811	250	325	425	550	—

KM# 262.4 8 REALES
Silver **Issuer:** Jose Maria Liceaga **Countermark:** J.M.L./
S.F. with banner on cross, crossed olive branches **Note:**
Countermark on Zacatecas KM#190.

CM Date	Host Date	Good	VG	F	VF	XF
ND	1811	200	275	375	525	—

KM# 262.2 8 REALES
Silver **Issuer:** Jose Maria Liceaga **Countermark:** J.M.L./E
with banner on cross, crossed olive branches **Note:**
Countermark on Zacatecas KM#190.

CM Date	Host Date	Good	VG	F	VF	XF
ND	1811	225	300	400	550	—

KM# 262.3 8 REALES
Silver **Issuer:** Jose Maria Liceaga **Countermark:** J.M.L./
P.G. with banner on cross, crossed olive branches **Note:**
Countermark on Durango KM#111.2.

CM Date	Host Date	Good	VG	F	VF	XF
ND	1813 RM	200	275	375	525	—

KM# 262.5 8 REALES
Silver **Issuer:** Jose Maria Liceaga **Countermark:** J.M.L./
S.M. with banner on cross, crossed olive branches **Note:**
Countermark on Zacatecas KM#190.

CM Date	Host Date	Good	VG	F	VF	XF
ND	1811	200	275	375	525	—

KM# 262.6 8 REALES
Silver **Issuer:** Jose Maria Liceaga **Countermark:** J.M.L./
V.E. with banner on cross, cross olive branches **Note:**
Countermark on Zacatecas KM#190.

CM Date	Host Date	Good	VG	F	VF	XF
ND	1811	200	275	375	525	—

INSURGENT COUNTERMARKED COINAGE

L.V.S. - Labor Vincit Semper

Some authorities believe L.V.S. is for
La Villa de Sombrerete.

KM# 264.1 8 REALES
Cast Silver **Issuer:** Labor Vincit Semper, Some authorities
believe L.V.S. is for "La Villa de Sombrerete" **Countermark:**
L.V.S. **Note:** Countermark on Chihuahua KM#123.

CM Date	Host Date	Good	VG	F	VF	XF
ND	1811 RP	275	350	450	550	—
ND	1812 RP	200	250	300	375	—

KM# 264.2 8 REALES
Silver **Issuer:** Labor Vincit Semper, Some authorities believe
L.V.S. is for "La Villa de Sombrerete" **Countermark:** L.V.S.
Note: Countermark on Chihuahua KM#111.1 overstruck on
KM#123.

CM Date	Host Date	Good	VG	F	VF	XF
ND	1816 RP	250	300	325	375	—
ND	1817 RP	250	300	325	375	—

CM Date	Host Date	Good	VG	F	VF	XF
ND	1818 RP	250	300	325	375	—
ND	1819 RP	400	450	500	600	—
ND	1820 RP	450	500	550	650	—

KM# 264.3 8 REALES
Silver **Issuer:** Labor Vincit Semper, Some authorities believe
L.V.S. is for "La Villa de Sombrerete" **Countermark:** L.V.S.
Note: Countermark on Guadalajara KM#111.3.

CM Date	Host Date	Good	VG	F	VF	XF
ND	1817	185	220	250	310	—

KM# 264.4 8 REALES
Silver **Issuer:** Labor Vincit Semper, Some authorities believe
L.V.S. is for "La Villa de Sombrerete" **Countermark:** L.V.S.
Note: Countermark on Nueva Vizcaya KM#165.

CM Date	Host Date	Good	VG	F	VF	XF
ND	1811 RM	1,150	3,150	5,250	8,250	—

KM# 264.5 8 REALES
Silver **Issuer:** Labor Vincit Semper, Some authorities believe
L.V.S. is for "La Villa de Sombrerete" **Countermark:** L.V.S.
Note: Countermark on Sombrerete KM#177.

CM Date	Host Date	Good	VG	F	VF	XF
ND	1811	300	350	450	550	—
ND	1812	300	350	450	550	—

KM# 264.6 8 REALES
Silver **Issuer:** Labor Vincit Semper, Some authorities believe
L.V.S. is for "La Villa de Sombrerete" **Countermark:** L.V.S.
Note: Countermark on Zacatecas KM#190.

CM Date	Host Date	Good	VG	F	VF	XF
ND	1811	350	400	450	550	—

KM# 264.7 8 REALES
Silver **Issuer:** Labor Vincit Semper, Some authorities believe
L.V.S. is for "La Villa de Sombrerete" **Countermark:** L.V.S.
Note: Countermark on Zacatecas KM#192.

CM Date	Host Date	Good	VG	F	VF	XF
ND	1813	350	400	450	550	—

INSURGENT COUNTERMARKED COINAGE

Morelos

Morelos monogram

Type A: Stars above and below monogram in circle.

Type B: Dots above and below monogram in oval.

Type C: Monogram in rectangle.
Note: Many specimens of Type C available in todays
market are considered spurious.

KM# A265 2 REALES
Copper **Issuer:** Morelos **Countermark:** Type A stars above and below monogram in circle **Note:** Countermark on Oaxaca Sud, KM#226.1.

CM Date	Host Date	Good	VG	F	VF	XF
ND	1812	—	—	—	—	—

KM# 265.1 8 REALES
Silver **Issuer:** Morelos **Countermark:** Type A star above and below monogram in circle **Note:** Countermark on Mexico City KM#109.

CM Date	Host Date	Good	VG	F	VF	XF
ND	1797 FM	45.00	50.00	60.00	85.00	—
ND	1798 FM	45.00	50.00	60.00	85.00	—
ND	1800 FM	45.00	50.00	60.00	85.00	—
ND	1807 TH	45.00	50.00	60.00	85.00	—

KM# 265.2 8 REALES
Silver **Issuer:** Morelos **Countermark:** Type A stars above and below monogram in circle **Note:** Countermark on Mexico City KM#110.

CM Date	Host Date	Good	VG	F	VF	XF
ND	1809 TH	55.00	65.00	85.00	120	—
ND	1811 HJ	55.00	65.00	85.00	120	—

KM# 265.3 8 REALES
Silver **Issuer:** Morelos **Countermark:** Type A stars above and below monogram in circle **Note:** Countermark on Mexico City KM#111.

CM Date	Host Date	Good	VG	F	VF	XF
ND	1812 JJ	50.00	60.00	75.00	110	—

KM# 265.5 8 REALES
Cast Silver **Issuer:** Morelos **Countermark:** Type A stars above and below monogram in circle **Note:** Countermark on Supreme National Congress KM#206.

CM Date	Host Date	Good	VG	F	VF	XF
ND	1811	200	250	375	600	—

KM# 266.1 8 REALES
Silver **Issuer:** Morelos **Countermark:** Type B dots above and below monogram in oval **Note:** Countermark on Guatamala 8 Reales, C#67.

CM Date	Host Date	Good	VG	F	VF	XF
ND	1810 M Rare	—	—	—	—	—

KM# 266.2 8 REALES
Silver **Issuer:** Morelos **Countermark:** Type B dots above and below monogram in oval **Note:** Countermark on Mexico City KM#110.

CM Date	Host Date	Good	VG	F	VF	XF
ND	1809 TH	45.00	55.00	65.00	90.00	—

KM# 267.1 8 REALES
Silver **Issuer:** Morelos **Countermark:** Type C monogram in rectangle **Note:** Countermark on Zacatecas KM#189. Many specimens of Type C available in today's market are considered spurious.

CM Date	Host Date	Good	VG	F	VF	XF
ND	1811	300	350	425	650	—

KM# 265.4 8 REALES
Copper **Issuer:** Morelos **Countermark:** Type A stars above and below monogram in circle **Note:** Countermark on Oaxaca Sud KM#233.2.

CM Date	Host Date	Good	VG	F	VF	XF
ND	1812	12.50	17.50	25.00	40.00	—
ND	1813	12.50	17.50	25.00	40.00	—
ND	1814	12.50	17.50	25.00	40.00	—

KM# 265.6 8 REALES
Silver **Issuer:** Morelos **Countermark:** Type A stars above and below monogram in circle **Note:** Countermark on Zacatecas KM#190.

CM Date	Host Date	Good	VG	F	VF	XF
ND	1811	375	625	900	—	—

KM# 265.7 8 REALES
Silver **Issuer:** Morelos **Countermark:** Type A stars above and below monogram in circle **Note:** Countermark on Zacatecas KM#191.

CM Date	Host Date	Good	VG	F	VF	XF
ND	1811	200	250	375	600	—

KM# 267.2 8 REALES
Silver **Issuer:** Morelos **Countermark:** Type C: monogram in rectangle **Note:** Countermark Type C on Zacatecas KM#190. Many specimens of Type C available in today's market are considered spurious.

CM Date	Host Date	Good	VG	F	VF	XF
ND	1811	300	350	425	650	—

INSURGENT COUNTERMARKED COINAGE

Norte

Issued by the Supreme National Congress and the Army of the North.

Countermark: Eagle on cactus; star to left; NORTE below.

KM# 268 1/2 REAL
Silver **Issuer:** Supreme National Congress and the Army of the North **Countermark:** Eagle on cactus; star to left; NORTE below **Note:** Countermark on Zacatecas KM#180.

CM Date	Host Date	Good	VG	F	VF	XF
ND	1811	250	300	375	450	—

KM# 269 2 REALES
Silver **Issuer:** Supreme National Congress and the Army of the North **Countermark:** Eagle on cactus; star to left; NORTE below **Note:** Countermark on Zacatecas KM#187.

CM Date	Host Date	Good	VG	F	VF	XF
ND	1811	225	275	325	400	—

KM# A269 2 REALES
Silver **Issuer:** Supreme National Congress and the Army of the North **Countermark:** Eagle on cactus; star to left; NORTE below **Note:** Countermark on Zacatecas KM#188.

CM Date	Host Date	Good	VG	F	VF	XF
ND	1812	—	—	—	—	—

KM# B269 4 REALES
Silver **Issuer:** Supreme National Congress and the Army of the North **Countermark:** Eagle on cactus; star to left; NORTE below **Note:** Countermark on Sombrerete KM#175.

CM Date	Host Date	Good	VG	F	VF	XF
ND	1812	100	150	200	275	—

KM# 270.4 8 REALES
Silver **Issuer:** Supreme National Congress and the Army of the North **Countermark:** Eagle on cactus; star to left; NORTE below **Note:** Countermark on Zacatecas KM#191.

CM Date	Host Date	Good	VG	F	VF	XF
ND	1811	200	300	400	550	—
ND	1811	200	300	400	550	—
ND	1812	200	300	400	550	—

KM# 270.1 8 REALES
Silver **Issuer:** Supreme National Congress and the Army of the North **Countermark:** Eagle on cactus; star to left; NORTE below **Note:** Countermark on Chihuahua KM#111.1.

CM Date	Host Date	Good	VG	F	VF	XF
ND	1813 RP	250	350	450	550	—

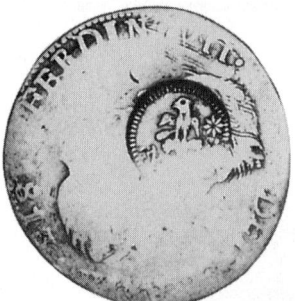

KM# 270.2 8 REALES
Silver **Issuer:** Supreme National Congress and the Army of the North **Countermark:** Eagle on cactus; star to left; NORTE below **Note:** Countermark on Guanajuato KM#111.4.

CM Date	Host Date	Good	VG	F	VF	XF
ND	1813 JM	400	550	700	800	—

KM# 270.3   8 REALES
Silver **Issuer:** Supreme National Congress and the Army of the North **Countermark:** Eagle on cactus; star to left; NORTE below **Note:** Countermark on Zacatecas KM#190.

CM Date	Host Date	Good	VG	F	VF	XF
ND	1811	300	400	500	650	—

INSURGENT COUNTERMARKED COINAGE

Osorno

Countermark: Osorno monogram.
(Jose Francisco Osorno)

KM# 271.1   1/2 REAL
Silver **Issuer:** Jose Francisco Osorno **Countermark:** Osorno monogram **Note:** Countermark on Mexico City KM#72.

CM Date	Host Date	Good	VG	F	VF	XF
ND	1798 FM	65.00	100	150	200	—
ND	1802 FT	65.00	100	150	200	—
ND	1806	65.00	100	150	200	—

KM# 271.2   1/2 REAL
Silver **Issuer:** Jose Francisco Osorno **Countermark:** Osorno monogram **Note:** Countermark on Mexico City KM#73.

CM Date	Host Date	Good	VG	F	VF	XF
ND	1809 TH	65.00	100	150	200	—

KM# 272.1   REAL
Silver **Issuer:** Jose Francisco Osorno **Countermark:** Osorno monogram **Note:** Countermark on Mexico City KM#81.

CM Date	Host Date	Good	VG	F	VF	XF
ND	1803 FT	65.00	100	150	200	—

 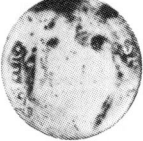

KM# 272.2   REAL
Silver **Issuer:** Jose Francisco Osorno **Countermark:** Osorno monogram **Note:** Countermark on Potosi KM#70.

CM Date	Host Date	Good	VG	F	VF	XF
ND	ND	75.00	115	175	250	—

KM# 272.3   REAL
Silver **Issuer:** Jose Francisco Osorno **Countermark:** Osorno monogram **Note:** Countermark on Guatemala KM#54.

CM Date	Host Date	Good	VG	F	VF	XF
ND	1804	75.00	115	175	250	—

KM# A272.1   2 REALES
Silver **Issuer:** Jose Francisco Osorno **Countermark:** Osorno monogram **Note:** Countermark on Mexico City KM#88.2.

CM Date	Host Date	Good	VG	F	VF	XF
ND	1788 FM	75.00	125	175	250	—

KM# A272.2   2 REALES
Silver **Issuer:** Jose Francisco Osorno **Countermark:** Osorno monogram **Note:** Countermark on Mexico City KM#91.

CM Date	Host Date	Good	VG	F	VF	XF
ND	1808 TH	75.00	125	175	250	—

KM# A272.3   2 REALES
Silver **Issuer:** Jose Francisco Osorno **Countermark:** Osorno monogram **Note:** Countermark on Mexico City KM#92.

CM Date	Host Date	Good	VG	F	VF	XF
ND	1809 TH	75.00	125	175	250	—

KM# A272.4   2 REALES
Silver **Issuer:** Jose Francisco Osorno **Countermark:** Osorno monogram **Note:** Countermark on Zacatlan KM#252.

CM Date	Host Date	Good	VG	F	VF	XF
ND	1813	150	200	300	400	—

KM# 273.1   4 REALES
Silver **Issuer:** Jose Francisco Osorno **Countermark:** Osorno monogram **Note:** Countermark on Mexico City KM#97.2.

CM Date	Host Date	Good	VG	F	VF	XF
ND	1782 FF	85.00	150	200	275	—

KM# 273.2   4 REALES
Silver **Issuer:** Jose Francisco Osorno **Countermark:** Osorno monogram **Note:** Countermark on Mexico City KM#100.

CM Date	Host Date	Good	VG	F	VF	XF
ND	1799 FM	85.00	150	200	275	—

KM# 274.1   8 REALES
Silver **Issuer:** Jose Francisco Osorno **Countermark:** Osorno monogram **Note:** Countermark on Lima 8 Reales, C#101.

CM Date	Host Date	Good	VG	F	VF	XF
ND	1811 JP	200	225	250	300	—

KM# 274.2   8 REALES
Silver **Issuer:** Jose Francisco Osorno **Countermark:** Osorno monogram **Note:** Countermark on Mexico City KM#110.

CM Date	Host Date	Good	VG	F	VF	XF
ND	1809 TH	125	150	225	300	—
ND	1810 HJ	125	150	225	300	—
ND	1811 HJ	125	150	225	300	—

INSURGENT COUNTERMARKED COINAGE
VILLA / GRAN

(Julian Villagran)

KM# 298   2 REALES
Cast Silver , Julian Villagran **Countermark:** VILLA/GRAN **Note:** Countermark on cast Mexico City KM#91.

CM Date	Host Date	Good	VG	F	VF	XF
ND	1799 FM	150	200	250	350	—
ND	1802 FT	150	200	250	350	—

KM# 275   8 REALES
Cast Silver **Issuer:** Julian Villagran **Countermark:** VILLA/GRAN **Note:** Countermark on cast Mexico City KM#109.

CM Date	Host Date	Good	VG	F	VF	XF
ND	1796 FM	200	250	300	400	—
ND	1806 TH	200	250	300	400	—

COUNTERMARKED COINAGE
Multiple Countermarks
Many combinations of Royalist and Insurgent countermarks are usually found on the cast copies produced by Chihuahua and Mexico City and on the other crude provisional issues of this period. Struck Mexico City coins were used to make molds for casting necessity issues and countermarked afterwards to show issuing authority. Some were marked again by either both or separate opposing friendly forces to authorize circulation in their areas of occupation. Some countermarks are only obtainable with companion markings.

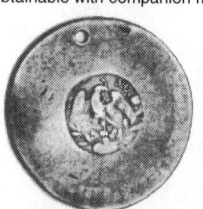

KM# 289   2 REALES
Silver **Issuer:** C.M.S. and S.C.M. **Countermark:** C.M.S. (Comandancia Militar Suriana) and eagle with S.C.M. (Soberano Congreso Mexicano) **Note:** Countermark on Mexico City KM#91.

CM Date	Host Date	Good	VG	F	VF	XF
ND	ND	—	—	—	—	—

KM# 295 2 REALES
Silver **Issuer:** Militar del Sur and Soberano Congreso
Mexicano **Countermark:** M.d.S. and eagle with S.C.M **Note:**
Countermark on Mexico City KM#91.

CM Date	Host Date	Good	VG	F	VF	XF
ND	ND	150	250	450	—	—

KM# 296 2 REALES
Silver **Issuer:** Jose Francisco Osorno and Julian Villagran
Countermark: Osorno monogram and VILLA/GRAN **Note:**
Countermark on cast Mexico City KM#110.

CM Date	Host Date	Good	VG	F	VF	XF
ND	1809 TH	—	—	—	—	—

KM# A286 2 REALES
Silver **Issuer:** Jose Maria Liceaga and VTIL **Countermark:**
J.M.L./D.S. AND VTIL **Note:** Countermark on Zacatecas
KM#186.

CM Date	Host Date	Good	VG	F	VF	XF
ND	1811	75.00	125	175	250	—

KM# B286 2 REALES
Silver **Issuer:** Jose Maria Liceaga and VTIL **Countermark:**
J.M.L./V.E. and VTIL **Note:** Countermark on Zacatecas
KM#186.

CM Date	Host Date	Good	VG	F	VF	XF
ND	1810	75.00	125	175	250	—
ND	1811	75.00	125	175	250	—

KM# 285.2 8 REALES
Silver **Issuer:** Chilpanzingo and Morelos **Countermark:**
Chilpanzingo Type A and Morelos monogram Type A **Note:**
Countermark on cast Mexico City KM#110.

CM Date	Host Date	Good	VG	F	VF	XF
ND	1810 HJ	35.00	45.00	60.00	140	—
ND	1811 HJ	35.00	45.00	60.00	140	—

KM# C286 8 REALES
Silver **Issuer:** Chilpanzingo and Morelos and LVS
Countermark: Chilpanzingo Type A, Morelos Type A and
LVS monogram on cast Mexico City KM#110

CM Date	Host Date	Good	VG	F	VF	XF
ND	1809 HJ	50.00	75.00	125	275	—

KM# A298 8 REALES
Silver **Issuer:** S.J.N.G. and VTIL **Countermark:** S.J.N.G
and VTIL on Zacatecas KM#191

CM Date	Host Date	Good	VG	F	VF	XF
ND	ND	35.00	50.00	75.00	200	—

KM# A297 8 REALES
Silver **Issuer:** Chilpanzingo and ENSAIE **Countermark:**
Chilpanzingo Type B and ENSAIE **Note:** Countermark on
Zacatecas KM#189.

CM Date	Host Date	Good	VG	F	VF	XF
ND	ND	175	250	350	—	—

KM# 297 8 REALES
Silver **Issuer:** Chilpanzingo and LVA **Countermark:**
Chilpanzingo Type A and LVA **Note:** Countermark on Mexico
City KM#109.

CM Date	Host Date	Good	VG	F	VF	XF
ND	1805 TH	45.00	75.00	145	250	—

KM# 281 8 REALES
Silver **Issuer:** Chilpanzingo and LVS **Countermark:**
Chilpanzingo Type A and script LVS **Note:** Countermark on
cast Mexico City KM#110.

CM Date	Host Date	Good	VG	F	VF	XF
ND	1809 HJ	45.00	65.00	135	250	—

KM# 283   8 REALES
Silver **Issuer:** Morelos and Morelos **Countermark:** Morelos
Type A and C **Note:** Countermark on cast Mexico City
KM#109.

CM Date	Host Date	Good	VG	F	VF	XF
ND	1806 TH	—	—	—	—	—

KM# 288.2   8 REALES
Silver **Issuer:** Chilpanzingo and Suprema Junta Nacional
Gubernativa **Countermark:** Chilpanzingo Type B **Note:**
Countermark on Zacatecas KM#190. Prev. KM#288.

CM Date	Host Date	Good	VG	F	VF	XF
ND	1811	—	—	—	—	—

KM# 290.2   8 REALES
Silver **Issuer:** ENSAIE and VTIL **Countermark:** ENSAIE
and VTIL **Note:** Countermark on Zacatecas KM#190. Prev.
KM#290.

CM Date	Host Date	Good	VG	F	VF	XF
ND	1811	100	175	275	350	—

KM# 284   8 REALES
Silver **Issuer:** Chilpanzingo and Morelos **Countermark:**
Chilpanzingo Type A and Morelos monogram Type A **Note:**
Countermark on cast Mexico City KM#109.

CM Date	Host Date	Good	VG	F	VF	XF
ND	1806 TH	35.00	50.00	100	200	—
ND	1807 TH	35.00	50.00	100	200	—

KM# 291   8 REALES
Silver **Issuer:** Jose Maria Liceaga and VTIL **Countermark:**
J.M.L./D.S. and VTIL **Note:** Countermark on Mexico City
KM#110.

CM Date	Host Date	Good	VG	F	VF	XF
ND	1810 HJ	85.00	150	250	400	—

KM# 285.1   8 REALES
Silver **Issuer:** Chilpanzingo and Morelos **Countermark:**
Chilpanzingo Type A and Morelos monogram Type A **Note:**
Countermark on struck Mexico City KM#110.

CM Date	Host Date	Good	VG	F	VF	XF
ND	1809 TH	45.00	65.00	135	250	—

KM# 282   8 REALES
Silver **Issuer:** La Comandancia Militar and Morelos
Countermark: L.C.M and Morelos monogram Type A **Note:**
Countermark on cast Mexico City KM#109.

CM Date	Host Date	Good	VG	F	VF	XF
ND	1792 FM	—	—	—	—	—

KM# 285.3   8 REALES
Silver **Issuer:** Chilpanzingo and Morelos **Countermark:**
Chilpanzingo Type A and Morelos monogram Type A **Note:**
Countermark on cast Mexico City KM#111.

CM Date	Host Date	Good	VG	F	VF	XF
ND	1811 HJ	75.00	120	175	275	—

KM# A290 8 REALES
Silver **Issuer:** ENSAIE and Jose Maria Liceaga
Countermark: ENSAIE and J.M.L. **Note:** Countermark on
Zacatecas KM#190.

CM Date	Host Date	Good	VG	F	VF	XF
ND	1811	100	175	275	350	—

KM# 294 8 REALES
Silver **Issuer:** L.V.A. and Morelos **Countermark:** Script LVA
and Morelos monogram Type A **Note:** Countermark on cast
Mexico City KM#110.

CM Date	Host Date	Good	VG	F	VF	XF
ND	ND HJ	45.00	75.00	135	250	—

KM# 288.1 8 REALES
Silver **Issuer:** Chilpanzingo and Suprema Junta Nacional
Gubernativa **Countermark:** Chilpanzingo Type B and
S.J.N.G **Note:** Countermark on Zacatecas KM#189.

CM Date	Host Date	Good	VG	F	VF	XF
ND	1811	—	—	—	—	—

KM# 280.1 8 REALES
Silver **Issuer:** Chilpanzingo and Crown and flag
Countermark: Chilpanzingo Type B and Crown and flag
Note: Countermark on Zacatecas KM#189.

CM Date	Host Date	Good	VG	F	VF	XF
ND	1811	—	—	—	—	—

KM# 290.1 8 REALES
Silver **Issuer:** ENSAIE and VTIL **Countermark:** ENSAIE
and VTIL **Note:** Countermark on Zacatecas KM#189.

CM Date	Host Date	Good	VG	F	VF	XF
ND	1811	100	175	275	350	—

KM# 280.2 8 REALES
Silver **Issuer:** Chilpanzingo and crown and flag
Countermark: Chilpanzingo Type B and crown and flag **Note:**
Countermark on Zacatecas KM#190.

CM Date	Host Date	Good	VG	F	VF	XF
ND	1811	—	—	—	—	—

KM# 287 8 REALES
Silver **Issuer:** Chilpanzingo - Provisional De Valladolid
Countermark: Chilpanzingo Type B and P.D.V **Note:**
Countermark on Valladolid KM#178.

CM Date	Host Date	Good	VG	F	VF	XF
ND	1813	—	—	—	—	—

ZACATECAS

The city of Zacatecas, in a rich mining region has provided silver for the world since mid-1500. On November 14,
1810 a mint began production for the Royalist cause. Zacatecas was the most prolific during the War of Independence.
Four of the 5 standard silver denominations were made here,
4 Reales were not. The first, a local type showing mountains
of silver on the coins were made only in 1810 and 1811. Some
1811 coins were made by the Insurgents who took the city on
April 15, 1811, later retaken by the Royalists on May 21, 1811.
Zacatecas struck the standard Ferdinand VII bust type until
1922.
Mint marks: Z, ZS, Zs.

WAR OF INDEPENDENCE

ROYALIST COINAGE

KM# 180 1/2 REAL
0.9030 Silver **Ruler:** Ferdinand VII **Obv:** Local arms with
flowers and castles **Rev:** Mountain **Note:** Mint marks: Z, ZS,
Zs.

Date	Mintage	Good	VG	F	VF	XF
1810	—	75.00	125	200	400	—
1811	—	30.00	50.00	90.00	175	—

Note: Date aligned with legend

KM# 181 1/2 REAL
0.9030 Silver **Ruler:** Ferdinand VII **Obv:** Royal arms **Rev:**
Mountain **Rev. Legend:** MONEDA PROVISIÓNAL DE
ZACATECAS **Note:** Mint marks: Z, ZS, Zs.

Date	Mintage	Good	VG	F	VF	XF
1811	—	30.00	50.00	90.00	175	—

KM# 182   1/2 REAL
0.9030 Silver **Ruler:** Ferdinand VII **Obv:** Provincial bust **Obv. Legend:** FERDIN. VII **Rev:** Mountain **Rev. Legend:** MONEDA PROVISIONAL DE ZACATECAS **Note:** Mint marks: Z, ZS, Zs.

Date	Mintage	Good	VG	F	VF	XF
1811	—	30.00	40.00	65.00	135	—
1812	—	25.00	35.00	60.00	120	—

KM# 73.1   1/2 REAL
1.6900 g., 0.9030 Silver .0491 oz. ASW **Ruler:** Ferdinand VII **Obv:** Armored bust of Ferdinand VII **Rev:** Crowned arms, pillars **Note:** Mint marks: Z, ZS, Zs.

Date	Mintage	Good	VG	F	VF	XF
1813 AG	—	20.00	40.00	60.00	100	—
1813 FP	—	25.00	45.00	85.00	175	—
1814 AG	—	15.00	30.00	60.00	100	—
1815 AG	—	12.50	25.00	40.00	60.00	—
1816 AG	—	10.00	15.00	25.00	50.00	—
1817 AG	—	10.00	15.00	25.00	50.00	—
1818 AG	—	10.00	15.00	25.00	50.00	—
1819 AG	—	10.00	15.00	25.00	50.00	—

KM# 74.3   1/2 REAL
1.6900 g., 0.9030 Silver .0491 oz. ASW **Ruler:** Ferdinand VII **Obv:** Draped bust Ferdinand VII **Rev:** Crowned arms, pillars **Note:** Mint marks: Z, ZS, Zs.

Date	Mintage	VG	F	VF	XF	Unc
1819 AG	—	8.00	12.00	25.00	50.00	—
1820 AG	—	8.00	12.00	25.00	50.00	—
1820 RG	—	5.00	10.00	20.00	45.00	—
1821 AG	—	150	250	450	850	—
1821 RG	—	5.00	10.00	20.00	45.00	—

KM# 183   REAL
0.9030 Silver **Ruler:** Ferdinand VII **Obv:** Local arms with flowers and castles **Rev:** Mountain **Note:** Mint marks: Z, ZS, Zs.

Date	Mintage	Good	VG	F	VF	XF
1810	—	100	150	300	500	—
1811	—	20.00	40.00	75.00	150	—

Note: Date aligned with legend

KM# 184   REAL
0.9030 Silver **Ruler:** Ferdinand VII **Obv:** Royal arms **Rev:** Mountain **Rev. Legend:** MONEDA PROVISIONAL DE ZACATECAS **Note:** Mint marks: Z, ZS, Zs.

Date	Mintage	Good	VG	F	VF	XF
1811	—	15.00	30.00	60.00	135	—

KM# 185   REAL
0.9030 Silver **Ruler:** Ferdinand VII **Obv:** Provincial bust **Obv. Legend:** FERDIN. VII. **Rev:** Crowned arms, pillars **Rev. Legend:** MONEDA PROVISIONAL DE ZACATECAS **Note:** Mint marks: Z, ZS, Zs.

Date	Mintage	Good	VG	F	VF	XF
1811	—	50.00	85.00	120	200	—
1812	—	40.00	70.00	100	175	—

KM# 82.1   REAL
3.3800 g., 0.9030 Silver .0981 oz. ASW **Ruler:** Ferdinand VII **Obv:** Armored bust of Ferdinand VII **Obv. Legend:** FERDIN. VII. **Rev:** Crowned arms, pillars **Note:** Mint marks: Z, ZS, Zs.

Date	Mintage	Good	VG	F	VF	XF
1813 FP	—	50.00	100	150	250	—
1814 FP	—	20.00	35.00	50.00	85.00	—
1814 AG	—	20.00	35.00	50.00	85.00	—
1815 AG	—	20.00	35.00	50.00	85.00	—
1816 AG	—	10.00	20.00	30.00	65.00	—
1817 AG	—	6.50	12.50	20.00	45.00	—
1818 AG	—	6.50	12.50	20.00	45.00	—
1819 AG	—	5.00	9.00	15.00	35.00	—

KM# 83.3   REAL
3.3800 g., 0.9030 Silver .0981 oz. ASW **Ruler:** Ferdinand VII **Obv:** Draped bust of Ferdinand VII **Obv. Legend:** FERDIN. VII. **Rev:** Crowned arms, pillars **Note:** Mint marks: Z, ZS, Zs.

Date	Mintage	VG	F	VF	XF	Unc
1820 AG	—	5.00	10.00	20.00	60.00	—
1820 RG	—	5.00	10.00	20.00	60.00	—
1821 AG	—	15.00	30.00	45.00	90.00	—
1821 AZ	—	10.00	20.00	40.00	85.00	—
1821 RG	—	6.00	12.00	25.00	65.00	—
1822 AZ	—	6.00	12.00	25.00	65.00	—
1822 RG	—	15.00	30.00	45.00	90.00	—

KM# 186   2 REALES
0.9030 Silver **Ruler:** Ferdinand VII **Obv:** Local arms with flowers and castles **Rev:** Mountain **Note:** Mint marks: Z, ZS, Zs.

Date	Mintage	Good	VG	F	VF	XF
1810 Rare	—	—	—	—	—	—
1811	—	25.00	40.00	70.00	120	—

Note: Date aligned with legend

KM# 187   2 REALES
0.9030 Silver **Ruler:** Ferdinand VII **Obv:** Royal arms **Rev:**

Mountain above L. V. O **Rev. Legend:** MONEDA
PROVISIONAL DE ZACATECAS **Note:** Mint marks: Z, ZS, Zs.

Date	Mintage	Good	VG	F	VF	XF
1811	—	15.00	30.00	60.00	100	—

KM# 188 2 REALES
0.9030 Silver **Ruler:** Ferdinand VII **Obv:** Armored bust **Obv.
Legend:** FERDIN. VII **Rev:** Crowned arms, pillars **Rev.
Legend:** MONEDA PROVISIONAL DE ZACATECAS **Note:**
Mint marks: Z, ZS, Zs.

Date	Mintage	Good	VG	F	VF	XF
1811	—	35.00	65.00	135	225	—
1812	—	30.00	60.00	125	200	—

KM# 92.1 2 REALES
6.7700 g., 0.9030 Silver .1966 oz. ASW **Ruler:** Ferdinand VII
Obv: Large armored bust of Ferdinand VII **Obv. Legend:**
FERDIN. VII **Rev:** Crowned arms, pillars **Note:** Mint marks:
Z, ZS, Zs.

Date	Mintage	Good	VG	F	VF	XF
1813 FP	—	35.00	50.00	75.00	125	—
1814 FP	—	35.00	50.00	75.00	125	—
1814 AG	—	35.00	50.00	75.00	125	—
1815 AG	—	6.50	12.50	25.00	55.00	—
1816 AG	—	6.50	12.50	25.00	55.00	—
1817 AG	—	6.50	12.50	25.00	55.00	—
1818 AG	—	6.50	12.50	25.00	55.00	—

KM# 93.4 2 REALES
6.7700 g., 0.9030 Silver .1966 oz. ASW **Ruler:** Ferdinand VII
Obv: Draped bust of Ferdinand VII **Obv. Legend:** FERDIN.
VII **Rev:** Crowned arms, pillars **Note:** Mint marks: Z, ZS, Zs.

Date	Mintage	VG	F	VF	XF	Unc
1818 AG	—	6.50	12.50	25.00	50.00	—
1819 AG	—	10.00	20.00	40.00	85.00	—
1819 AG Reversed 'S' in HISPAN	—	10.00	20.00	40.00	85.00	—
1820 AG	—	10.00	20.00	40.00	85.00	—
1820 RG	—	10.00	20.00	40.00	85.00	—
1821 AG	—	10.00	20.00	40.00	85.00	—
1821 AZ/RG	—	10.00	20.00	40.00	85.00	—
1821 AZ	—	10.00	20.00	40.00	85.00	—
1821 RG	—	10.00	20.00	40.00	85.00	—
1822 AG	—	10.00	20.00	40.00	85.00	—
1822 RG	—	10.00	20.00	40.00	85.00	—

KM# A92 2 REALES
6.7700 g., 0.9030 Silver .1966 oz. ASW **Ruler:** Ferdinand VII
Obv: Small armored bust of Ferdinand VII **Obv. Legend:**
FERDIN. VII **Rev:** Crowned arms, pillars **Note:** Mint marks:
Z, ZS, Zs.

Date	Mintage	Good	VG	F	VF	XF
1819 AG	—	45.00	100	200	400	—

KM# 189 8 REALES
0.9030 Silver **Ruler:** Ferdinand VII **Obv:** Local arm with
flowers and castles **Rev:** Mountain above L.V.O. **Note:** Mint
Zacatecas.

Date	Mintage	Good	VG	F	VF	XF
1810	—	300	500	750	1,250	—
1811	—	100	150	225	350	—

Note: Date aligned with legend. Also exists with incomplete
date

KM# 190   8 REALES
0.9030 Silver **Ruler:** Ferdinand VII **Obv:** Royal arms **Obv. Legend:** FERDIN. VII. DEI... **Rev:** Mountain above L. V. O **Rev. Legend:** MONEDA PROVISIONAL DE ZACATECAS

Date	Mintage	Good	VG	F	VF	XF
1811	—	65.00	100	135	220	—

Note: Date aligned with legend

KM# 191   8 REALES
0.9030 Silver **Ruler:** Ferdinand VII **Obv:** Armored bust of Ferdinand VII **Obv. Legend:** FERDIN. VII. 8.R. DEI... **Rev:** Crowned arms, pillars **Rev. Legend:** MONEDA PROVISIONAL DE ZACATECAS

Date	Mintage	Good	VG	F	VF	XF
1811	—	45.00	75.00	145	275	—
1812	—	50.00	85.00	160	300	—

KM# 192   8 REALES
0.9030 Silver **Ruler:** Ferdinand VII **Obv:** Draped bust of Ferdinand VII **Obv. Legend:** FERDIN. VII. DEI... **Rev:** Crowned arms, pillars **Rev. Legend:** MONEDA PROVISIONAL DE ZACATECAS

Date	Mintage	Good	VG	F	VF	XF
1812	—	75.00	150	275	450	—

KM# 111.5   8 REALES
27.0700 g., 0.9030 Silver .7860 oz. ASW **Ruler:** Ferdinand VII **Obv:** Draped bust of Ferdinand VII **Obv. Legend:** FERDIN. VII. DEI. GRATIA **Rev:** Crowned arms, pillars **Rev. Legend:** HISPAN. ET IND. REX **Note:** Mint mark: Zs. Several bust types exist for the 1821 issues.

Date	Mintage	VG	F	VF	XF	Unc
1813 FP	—	75.00	125	175	275	—
1814 FP	—	150	250	350	450	—
1814 AG	—	100	150	200	300	—
1814 AG D over horizontal D in IND	—	125	175	225	325	—
1814 AG/FP	—	100	150	200	300	—
1815 AG	—	50.00	100	150	250	—
1816 AG	—	35.00	50.00	65.00	125	—
1817 AG	—	35.00	50.00	65.00	125	—
1818 AG	—	30.00	40.00	50.00	100	—
1819 AG	—	30.00	40.00	50.00	100	—
1819 AG 'GRATIA' error	—	100	200	300	400	—
1820 AG 18/11 error	—	100	200	300	400	—
1820 AG	—	30.00	40.00	50.00	100	—
1820 RG	—	30.00	40.00	50.00	100	—
1821/81 RG	—	75.00	150	225	300	—
1821 RG	—	15.00	25.00	35.00	65.00	—
1821 AZ/RG	—	50.00	100	150	200	—
1821 AZ	—	50.00	100	150	200	—
1822 RG	—	40.00	60.00	100	175	—

KM# 111.6   8 REALES
27.0700 g., 0.9030 Silver .7860 oz. ASW **Ruler:** Ferdinand VII **Obv:** Draped bust of Ferdinand VII **Obv. Legend:** FERDIN. VII. DEI. GRATIA **Rev:** Crown with lower rear arc **Rev. Legend:** HISAV. ET IND. REX

Date	Mintage	VG	F	VF	XF	Unc
1821 Zs	—	160	320	550	750	—

ROYALIST COUNTERMARKED COINAGE
LCM - La Comandancia Militar

Crown and Flag

This countermark exists in 15 various sizes.

KM# 193.1   2 REALES
0.9030 Silver **Issuer:** La Comandancia Militar **Countermark:** LCM **Note:** Countermark on Mexico KM#92.

CM Date	Host Date	Good	VG	F	VF	XF
ND	1809 TH	85.00	165	250	400	—

KM# 193.2   2 REALES
0.9030 Silver **Issuer:** La Comandancia Militar, (The LCM countermark exists in 15 various sizes) **Countermark:** LCM **Note:** Countermark on Mexico KM#186.

CM Date	Host Date	Good	VG	F	VF	XF
ND	1811	85.00	165	250	400	—

KM# 194.1   8 REALES
Cast Silver   **Issuer:** La Comandancia Militar, (The LCM
countermark exists in 15 various sizes) **Countermark:** LCM
Note: Countermark on Chihuahua KM#123.

CM Date	Host Date	Good	VG	F	VF	XF
ND	1811 RP	100	200	300	450	—
ND	1812 RP	100	200	300	450	—

KM# 194.2   8 REALES
0.9030 Silver   **Issuer:** La Comandancia Militar, The LCM
countermark exists in 15 different sizes **Countermark:** LCM
Note: Countermark on Chihuahua KM#111.1 struck over
KM#123.

CM Date	Host Date	Good	VG	F	VF	XF
ND	1815 RP	200	275	400	550	—
ND	1817 RP	125	175	225	300	—
ND	1820 RP	125	175	225	300	—
ND	1821 RP	125	175	225	300	—

KM# 194.3   8 REALES
0.9030 Silver   **Issuer:** La Comandancia Militar, The LCM
countermark exists in 15 different sizes **Countermark:** LCM
Note: Countermark on Durango KM#111.2.

CM Date	Host Date	Good	VG	F	VF	XF
ND	1812 RM	70.00	125	190	250	—
ND	1821 CG	70.00	125	190	250	—

KM# 194.4   8 REALES
0.9030 Silver   **Issuer:** La Comandancia Militar, The LCM
countermark exists in 15 different sizes **Countermark:** LCM
Note: Countermark on Guadalajara KM#111.3.

CM Date	Host Date	Good	VG	F	VF	XF
ND	1813 MR	150	225	300	475	—

KM# 194.5   8 REALES
0.9030 Silver   **Issuer:** La Comandancia Militar, The LCM
countermark exists in 15 different sizes **Countermark:** LCM
Note: Countermark on Guanajuato KM#111.4.

CM Date	Host Date	Good	VG	F	VF	XF
ND	1813 JJ	225	350	475	650	—

KM# 194.6   8 REALES
0.9030 Silver   **Issuer:** La Comandancia Militar, The LCM
countermark exists in 15 different sizes **Countermark:** LCM
Note: Countermark on Nueva Viscaya KM#165.

CM Date	Host Date	Good	VG	F	VF	XF
ND	1811 RM Rare	—	—	—	—	—

KM# 194.7   8 REALES
0.9030 Silver   **Issuer:** La Comandancia Militar, The LCM
countermark exists in 15 different sizes **Countermark:** LCM
Note: Countermark on Mexico KM#111.

CM Date	Host Date	Good	VG	F	VF	XF
ND	1811 HJ	125	225	350	600	—
ND	1812 JJ	110	135	190	325	—
ND	1817 JJ	50.00	65.00	85.00	125	—
ND	1818 JJ	50.00	65.00	85.00	125	—
ND	1820 JJ	—	—	—	—	—

KM# 194.8   8 REALES
0.9030 Silver   **Issuer:** La Comandancia Militar, The LCM
countermark exists in 15 different sizes **Countermark:** LCM
Note: Countermark on Sombrerete KM#176.

CM Date	Host Date	Good	VG	F	VF	XF
ND	1811 Rare	—	—	—	—	—
ND	1812 Rare	—	—	—	—	—

KM# 194.9   8 REALES
0.9030 Silver   **Issuer:** La Comandancia Militar, The LCM
countermark exists in 15 different sizes **Countermark:** LCM
Note: Countermark on Zacatecas KM#190.

CM Date	Host Date	Good	VG	F	VF	XF
ND	1811	225	350	450	—	—

KM# 194.10   8 REALES
0.9030 Silver   **Issuer:** La Comandancia Militar, The LCM
countermark exists in 15 different sizes **Countermark:** LCM
Note: Countermark on Zacatecas KM#111.5.

CM Date	Host Date	Good	VG	F	VF	XF
ND	1813 FP	—	—	—	—	—
ND	1814 AG	—	—	—	—	—
ND	1822 RG	—	—	—	—	—

ROYALIST COUNTERMARKED COINAGE

LCV - Las Cajas de Veracruz

The Royal Treasury of the City of Veracruz

KM# 195   7 REALES
Silver   **Issuer:** Las Cajas de Veracruz, The Royal Treasury
of the City of Veracruz **Countermark:** LCV **Note:**
Countermark and 7 on underweight 8 Reales.

CM Date	Host Date	Good	VG	F	VF	XF
ND	ND Rare	—	—	—	—	—

Note: Most examples are counterfeit

KM# 196   7-1/4 REALES
Silver   **Issuer:** Las Cajas de Veracruz, The Royal Treasury
of the City of Veracruz **Countermark:** LCV **Note:**
Countermark and 7-1/4 on underweight 8 Reales.

CM Date	Host Date	Good	VG	F	VF	XF
ND	ND Rare	—	—	—	—	—

Note: Most examples are counterfeit

KM# 197   7-1/2 REALES
Silver   **Issuer:** Las Cajas de Veracruz, The Royal Treasury
of the City of Veracruz **Countermark:** LCV **Note:**
Countermark and 7-1/2 on underweight 8 Reales.

CM Date	Host Date	Good	VG	F	VF	XF
ND	ND Rare	—	—	—	—	—

Note: Most examples are counterfeit

KM# 198   7-3/4 REALES
Silver   **Issuer:** Las Cajas de Veracruz, The Royal Treasury
of the City of Veracruz **Countermark:** LCV **Note:**
Countermark and 7-3/4 on underweight 8 Reales.

CM Date	Host Date	Good	VG	F	VF	XF
ND	ND	300	375	450	600	—

Note: Many examples are counterfeit

KM# A198   8 REALES
Cast Silver   **Issuer:** Las Cajas de Veracruz, The Royal
Treasury of the City of Veracruz **Countermark:** LCV **Note:**
Countermark on Chihuahua KM#123.

CM Date	Host Date	Good	VG	F	VF	XF
ND	1811 RP	150	250	400	500	—

KM# 199   8 REALES
Silver   **Issuer:** Las Cajas de Veracruz, The Royal Treasury
of the City of Veracruz **Countermark:** LCV **Note:**
Countermark on Zacatecas KM#191.

CM Date	Host Date	Good	VG	F	VF	XF
ND	1811	175	225	275	350	—
ND	1812	175	225	275	350	—

ROYALIST COUNTERMARKED COINAGE
MS (Monogram) - Manuel Salcedo

KM# 200   8 REALES
Silver **Issuer:** Manuel Salcedo **Countermark:** MS monogram **Note:** Countermark on Mexico KM#110.

CM Date	Host Date	Good	VG	F	VF	XF
ND	1809 TH	150	250	400	500	—
ND	1810 HJ	150	250	400	500	—
ND	1811 HJ	150	250	400	500	—

ROYALIST COUNTERMARKED COINAGE
MVA - Monclova

KM# 202.3   8 REALES
Silver **Issuer:** Monclova, MVA **Countermark:** MVA/1812 **Note:** Countermark on cast Mexico KM#110.

CM Date	Host Date	Good	VG	F	VF	XF
1812	1809 HJ	100	150	250	350	—
1812	1809 TH	100	150	250	350	—
1812	1810 HJ	100	150	250	350	—

KM# 201   8 REALES
Silver **Issuer:** Monclova, MVA **Countermark:** MVA/1811 **Note:** Countermark on Chihuahua KM#111.1; struck over cast Mexico KM#110.

CM Date	Host Date	Good	VG	F	VF	XF
ND	1809	250	450	700	1,000	—
ND	1816 RP	250	450	700	1,000	—
ND	1821 RP	250	450	700	1,000	—

KM# 202.1   8 REALES
Silver **Issuer:** Monclova, MVA **Countermark:** MVA/1812 **Note:** Countermark on Chihuahua KM#111.1; struck over cast Mexico KM#109.

CM Date	Host Date	Good	VG	F	VF	XF
1812	1810	125	175	250	350	—

KM# 202.5   8 REALES
Silver **Issuer:** Monclova, MVA **Countermark:** MVA/1812 **Note:** Countermark on Zacatecas KM#189.

CM Date	Host Date	Good	VG	F	VF	XF
1812	1813	300	350	450	550	—

KM# 202.2   8 REALES
Silver **Issuer:** Monclova, MVA **Countermark:** MVA/1812 **Note:** Countermark on cast Mexico KM#109.

CM Date	Host Date	Good	VG	F	VF	XF
1812	1798 FM	100	150	250	350	—
1812	1802 FT	100	150	250	350	—

INSURGENT COINAGE
American Congress

KM# 216   REAL
0.9030 Silver   **Issuer:** American Congress **Obv:** Eagle on cactus **Obv. Legend:** CONGRESO AMERICANO **Rev:** F. 7 on spread mantle **Rev. Legend:** DEPOSIT D.L. AUCTORI J

Date	Mintage	Good	VG	F	VF	XF
ND(1813)	—	35.00	75.00	120	200	—

KM# 217   REAL
0.9030 Silver   **Issuer:** American Congress **Obv:** Eagle on cactus **Obv. Legend:** CONGR. AMER. **Rev:** F. 7 on spread mantle **Rev. Legend:** DEPOS. D. L. AUT. D.

Date	Mintage	Good	VG	F	VF	XF
ND(1813)	—	35.00	75.00	120	200	—

INSURGENT COINAGE
National Congress

KM# 209   1/2 REAL
Struck Copper   **Issuer:** National Congress **Obv:** Eagle on bridge **Obv. Legend:** VICE FERD. VII DEI GRATIA ET **Rev:** Value, bow quiver, etc **Rev. Legend:** S. P. CONG. NAT. IND.

Date	Mintage	Good	VG	F	VF	XF
1811	—	45.00	85.00	150	200	—
1812	—	27.50	60.00	100	150	—
1813	—	27.50	60.00	100	150	—
1814	—	45.00	85.00	150	200	—

KM# 210   1/2 REAL
0.9030 Silver   **Issuer:** National Congress **Obv:** Eagle on bridge **Obv. Legend:** VICE FERD. VII DEI GRATIA ET **Rev:** Value, bow quiver, etc **Rev. Legend:** S. P. CONG. NAT. IND.

Date	Mintage	Good	VG	F	VF	XF
1812	—	27.50	60.00	100	150	—
1813	—	45.00	90.00	175	275	—

Note: 1812 exists with the date reading inwards and outwards

KM# 211   REAL
0.9030 Silver   **Issuer:** National Congress **Obv:** Eagle on bridge **Obv. Legend:** VICE FERD. VII DEI GRATIA ET **Rev:** Value, bow quiver, etc **Rev. Legend:** S. P. CONG. NAT. IND.

Date	Mintage	Good	VG	F	VF	XF
1812	—	22.50	45.00	80.00	125	—
1813	—	22.50	45.00	80.00	125	—

Note: 1812 exists with the date reading either inward or outward

KM# 212   2 REALES
Struck Copper   **Issuer:** National Congress **Obv:** Eagle on bridge **Obv. Legend:** VICE FERD. VII DEI GRATIA ET **Rev:** Value, bow quiver, etc **Rev. Legend:** S. P. CONG. NAT. IND.

Date	Mintage	Good	VG	F	VF	XF
1812	—	100	150	200	275	—
1813	—	23.50	50.00	75.00	120	—
1814	—	32.50	75.00	110	165	—

KM# A213   2 REALES
Struck Silver   **Issuer:** National Congress **Obv:** Eagle on bridge **Obv. Legend:** VICE FERD. VII DEI GRATIA ET **Rev:** Value, bow, quiver, etc **Rev. Legend:** S. P. CONG. NAT. IND.

Date	Mintage	Good	VG	F	VF	XF
1813	—	950	1,750	3,000	4,850	—

KM# 213   2 REALES
0.9030 Silver   **Issuer:** National Congress **Obv:** Eagle on bridge in shield, denomination at sides **Obv. Legend:** VICE FERD. VII DEI GRATIA ET **Rev:** Canon, quiver, arm, etc

Date	Mintage	Good	VG	F	VF	XF
1813	—	75.00	155	265	375	—

Note: These dies were believed to be intended for the striking of 2 Escudos

KM# 214   4 REALES
0.9030 Silver   **Issuer:** National Congress **Obv:** Eagle on bridge **Obv. Legend:** VICE FERD. VII DEI GRATIA ET **Rev:** Value, bow, quiver, etc **Rev. Legend:** S. P. CONG. NAT. IND.

Date	Mintage	Good	VG	F	VF	XF
1813	—	600	1,200	2,450	4,400	—

KM# 215.1 8 REALES
0.9030 Silver **Issuer:** National Congress **Obv:** Small crowned eagle **Obv. Legend:** VICE FERD. VII DEI GRATIA ET **Rev:** Value, bow, quiver, etc **Rev. Legend:** S. P. CONG. NAT. IND.

Date	Mintage	Good	VG	F	VF	XF
1812Mo	—	600	1,150	2,350	4,250	—

KM# 215.2 8 REALES
0.9030 Silver **Issuer:** National Congress **Obv:** Large crowned eagle **Obv. Legend:** VICE FERD. VII DEI GRATIA ET **Rev:** Value, bow, quiver, etc **Rev. Legend:** S. P. CONG. NAT. IND.

Date	Mintage	Good	VG	F	VF	XF
1813Mo	—	600	1,150	2,350	4,250	—

INSURGENT COINAGE

Supreme National Congress of America

PDV - Provisional de Valladolid

VTIL - Util = useful

(Refer to Multiple countermarks)

KM# 203 1/2 REAL
Struck Copper **Issuer:** Supreme National Congress of America **Obv:** Eagle on bridge **Obv. Legend:** FERDIN. VII DEI GRATIA **Rev:** Value, bow, quiver, etc **Rev. Legend:** S. P. CONG. NAT. IND. GUV.T.

Date	Mintage	Good	VG	F	VF	XF
1811	—	27.50	45.00	60.00	100	—
1812	—	27.50	45.00	60.00	100	—
1813	—	27.50	45.00	60.00	100	—
1814	—	27.50	45.00	60.00	100	—

KM# 204 REAL
Struck Copper **Issuer:** Supreme National Congress of America **Obv:** Eagle on bridge **Obv. Legend:** FERDIN. VII DEI GRATIA **Rev:** Value, bow, quiver, etc **Rev. Legend:** S. P. CONG. NAT. IND. GUV.T.

Date	Mintage	Good	VG	F	VF	XF
1811	—	45.00	75.00	125	200	—

KM# 205 2 REALES
Struck Copper **Issuer:** Supreme National Congress of America **Obv:** Eagle on bridge **Obv. Legend:** FERDIN. VII DEI GRATIA **Rev:** Value, bow, quiver, etc

Date	Mintage	Good	VG	F	VF	XF
1812	—	225	325	475	750	—

KM# 206 8 REALES
Cast Silver **Issuer:** Supreme National Congress of America **Obv:** Eagle on bridge **Obv. Legend:** FERDIN. VII DEI GRATIA **Rev:** Value, bow, quiver, etc

Date	Mintage	Good	VG	F	VF	XF
1811	—	150	250	350	500	—
1812	—	150	250	350	500	—

KM# 207 8 REALES
Struck Silver **Issuer:** Supreme National Congress of America **Obv:** Eagle on bridge **Obv. Legend:** FERDIN. VII DEI GRATIA **Rev:** Value, bow, quiver, etc

Date	Mintage	Good	VG	F	VF	XF
1811	—	—	—	—	—	—
1812	—	300	600	1,000	1,500	—

KM# 208 8 REALES
Struck Copper **Issuer:** Supreme National Congress of America **Obv:** Eagle on bridge **Obv. Legend:** FERDIN. VII... **Rev:** Bow, sword and quiver **Rev. Legend:** PROVICIONAL POR LA SUPREMA JUNTA DE AMERICA

Date	Mintage	Good	VG	F	VF	XF
1811	—	100	150	225	450	—
1812	—	100	150	225	450	—

Bibliography

Boyd, Julian P. (Editor). The Papers of Thomas Jefferson. Vol. 7. New Jersey: Princeton University Press, 1953.

Bowers, Q. David. The History of United States Coinage as Illustrated by the Garrett Collection. Los Angeles: Bowers & Ruddy Galleries, 1979.

Breen, Walter. Walter Breen's Complete Encyclopedia of U.S. and Colonial Coins. New York: F.C.I. Press, Doubleday, 1988.

Bressett, Ken, and Kosoff, A. Official A.N.A. Grading Standard for United States Coins. Fourth Edition. Colorado Springs, Colo.: American Numismatic Association, 1991.

Brown, Martin R., and Dunn, John W. A Guide to the Grading of United States Coins. Fourth and Fifth Editions. Racine, Wis.: Whitman Publishing Co., 1964 and 1969.

Bullowa, David M. Numismatic Notes and Monographs No. 83: The Commemorative Coinage of the United States 1892-1938. New York, N.Y.: American Numismatic Society, 1938.

Evans, George G. Illustrated History of the United States Mint. Revised Edition. Philadelphia: George G. Evans, 1892.

Fitzpatrick, John E. (Editor). The Writings of George Washington. Vol. 28. Washington: U.S. Government Printing Office, 1938.

Heath, Dr. George. The Numismatist, September 1888 and February 1892.

Hepburn, A. Barton. A History of Currency in the United States. Revised Edition. New York: Sentry Press, 1967.

Krause, Chester L., and Mishler, Clifford. Colin R. Bruce II (Senior Editor). The Standard Catalog of World Gold Coins. Fourth Edition. Iola, Wis.: Krause Publications, 2000.

Krueger, Kurt R. "Grading: Bestial Pandemonium Unleashed." The Numismatist, January 1976. Colorado Springs, Colo.: American Numismatic Association, 1975.

Ruddy, James F. Photograde. Wolfeboro, N.H.: Bowers and Merena Galleries In., 1983.

Sheldon, William H. Early American Cents. New York: Harper & Row. 1949.

Syrett, Harold C. The Papers of Alexander Hamilton. Vol. 7. New York: Columbia University Press, 1963.

Taxay, Don. The U.S. Mint and Coinage: An Illustrated History From 1776 to the Present. Second Edition. New York: Arco Publishing Co., 1969.

U.S. Congress. Senate. International Monetary Conference. 1878. Senate Ex. Doc. 58. 45th Congress, Third Session. Washington, 1879.

U.S. Congress. Senate. Coinage Laws of the United States 1792 to 1894 with an Appendix of Statistics Relating to Coins and Currency. Fourth Edition. Washington, D.C.: Government Printing Office, 1894.

Van Allen, Leroy C., and Mallis, A. George. Comprehensive Catalog and Encyclopedia of U.S. Morgan and Peace Silver Dollars. New York: F.C.I. Press, 1976.

Willem, John M. The United States Trade Dollar: America's Only Unwanted, Unhonored Coin. New York: By the author, 1959; reprint edition, Racine, Wis.: Western Publishing Co., 1965.

Yeoman, R.S. A Guidebook of United States Coins. 45th Edition. Racine, Wis.: Western Publishing Co., 1991.